University Casebook Series

December, 1982

ACCOUNTING AND THE LAW, Fourth Edition (1978), with Problems Pamphlet (Successor to Dohr, Phillips, Thompson & Warren)

George C. Thompson, Professor, Columbia University Graduate School of Business.
Robert Whitman, Professor of Law, University of Connecticut.
Ellis L. Phillips, Jr., Member of the New York Bar.
William C. Warren, Professor of Law Emeritus, Columbia University.

ACCOUNTING FOR LAWYERS, MATERIALS ON (1980)

David R. Herwitz, Professor of Law, Harvard University.

ADMINISTRATIVE LAW, Seventh Edition (1979), with 1983 Problems Supplement (Supplement edited in association with Paul R. Verkuil, Dean and Professor of Law, Tulane University)

Walter Gellhorn, University Professor Emeritus, Columbia University.
Clark Byse, Professor of Law, Harvard University.
Peter L. Strauss, Professor of Law, Columbia University.

ADMIRALTY, Second Edition (1978), with Statute and Rule Supplement

Jo Desha Lucas, Professor of Law, University of Chicago.

ADVOCACY, see also Lawyering Process

AGENCY, see also Enterprise Organization

AGENCY—PARTNERSHIPS, Third Edition (1982)

Abridgement from Conard, Knauss & Siegel's Enterprise Organization, Third Edition.

ANTITRUST AND REGULATORY ALTERNATIVES (1977), Fifth Edition

Louis B. Schwartz, Professor of Law, University of Pennsylvania.
John J. Flynn, Professor of Law, University of Utah.

ANTITRUST SUPPLEMENT—SELECTED STATUTES AND RELATED MATERIALS (1977)

John J. Flynn, Professor of Law, University of Utah.

BUSINESS ORGANIZATION, see also Enterprise Organization

BUSINESS PLANNING (1966), with 1982 Supplement

David R. Herwitz, Professor of Law, Harvard University.

BUSINESS TORTS (1972)

Milton Handler, Professor of Law Emeritus, Columbia University.

CHILDREN IN THE LEGAL SYSTEM (1983)

Walter Wadlington, Professor of Law, University of Virginia.
Charles H. Whitebread, Professor of Law, University of Southern California.
Samuel Davis, Professor of Law, University of Georgia.

CIVIL PROCEDURE, see Procedure

CLINIC, see also Lawyering Process

COMMERCIAL AND CONSUMER TRANSACTIONS, Second Edition (1978)

William D. Warren, Dean of the School of Law, University of California, Los Angeles.
William E. Hogan, Professor of Law, Cornell University.
Robert L. Jordan, Professor of Law, University of California, Los Angeles.

COMMERCIAL LAW, CASES & MATERIALS ON, Third Edition (1976), with 1982 Supplement

E. Allan Farnsworth, Professor of Law, Columbia University.
John Honnold, Professor of Law, University of Pennsylvania.

COMMERCIAL PAPER, Second Edition (1976)

E. Allan Farnsworth, Professor of Law, Columbia University.

COMMERCIAL PAPER AND BANK DEPOSITS AND COLLECTIONS (1967), with Statutory Supplement

William D. Hawkland, Professor of Law, University of Illinois.

COMMERCIAL TRANSACTIONS—Principles and Policies (1982)

Alan Schwartz, Professor of Law, University of Southern California.
Robert E. Scott, Professor of Law, University of Virginia.

COMPARATIVE LAW, Fourth Edition (1980)

Rudolf B. Schlesinger, Professor of Law, Hastings College of the Law.

COMPETITIVE PROCESS, LEGAL REGULATION OF THE, Second Edition (1979), with Statutory Supplement and 1982 Case Supplement

Edmund W. Kitch, Professor of Law, University of Chicago.
Harvey S. Perlman, Professor of Law, University of Virginia.

CONFLICT OF LAWS, Seventh Edition (1978), with 1982 Supplement

Willis L. M. Reese, Professor of Law, Columbia University,
Maurice Rosenberg, Professor of Law, Columbia University.

CONSTITUTIONAL LAW, Sixth Edition (1981), with 1982 Supplement

Edward L. Barrett, Jr., Professor of Law, University of California, Davis.
William Cohen, Professor of Law, Stanford University.

CONSTITUTIONAL LAW: THE STRUCTURE OF GOVERNMENT (Reprinted from CONSTITUTIONAL LAW, Sixth Edition), with 1982 Supplement

Edward L. Barrett, Jr., Professor of Law, University of California, Davis.
William Cohen, Professor of Law, Stanford University.

CONSTITUTIONAL LAW, CIVIL LIBERTY AND INDIVIDUAL RIGHTS, Second Edition (1982)

William Cohen, Professor of Law, Stanford Law School.
John Kaplan, Professor of Law, Stanford Law School.

CONSTITUTIONAL LAW, Tenth Edition (1980), with 1982 Supplement

Gerald Gunther, Professor of Law, Stanford University.

CONSTITUTIONAL LAW, INDIVIDUAL RIGHTS IN, Third Edition (1981), with 1982 Supplement (Reprinted from CONSTITUTIONAL LAW, Tenth Edition)

Gerald Gunther, Professor of Law, Stanford University.

UNIVERSITY CASEBOOK SERIES—Continued

CONTRACT LAW AND ITS APPLICATION, Second Edition (1977)

The late Addison Mueller, Professor of Law, University of California, Los Angeles.
Arthur I. Rosett, Professor of Law, University of California, Los Angeles.

CONTRACT LAW, STUDIES IN, Second Edition (1977)

Edward J. Murphy, Professor of Law, University of Notre Dame.
Richard E. Speidel, Professor of Law, University of Virginia.

CONTRACTS, Fourth Edition (1982)

John P. Dawson, Professor of Law Emeritus, Harvard University.
William Burnett Harvey, Professor of Law and Political Science, Boston University.
Stanley D. Henderson, Professor of Law, University of Virginia.

CONTRACTS, Third Edition (1980), with Statutory Supplement

E. Allan Farnsworth, Professor of Law, Columbia University.
William F. Young, Professor of Law, Columbia University.

CONTRACTS, Second Edition (1978), with Statutory and Administrative Law Supplement (1978)

Ian R. Macneil, Professor of Law, Cornell University.

COPYRIGHT, PATENTS AND TRADEMARKS, see also Competitive Process

COPYRIGHT, PATENT, TRADEMARK AND RELATED STATE DOCTRINES, Second Edition (1981), with Problem Supplement and Statutory Supplement

Paul Goldstein, Professor of Law, Stanford University.

COPYRIGHT, Unfair Competition, and Other Topics Bearing on the Protection of Literary, Musical, and Artistic Works, Third Edition (1978)

Benjamin Kaplan, Professor of Law Emeritus, Harvard University,
Ralph S. Brown, Jr., Professor of Law, Yale University.

CORPORATE FINANCE, Second Edition (1979), with 1982 New Developments Supplement

Victor Brudney, Professor of Law, Harvard University.
Marvin A. Chirelstein, Professor of Law, Yale University.

CORPORATE READJUSTMENTS AND REORGANIZATIONS (1976)

Walter J. Blum, Professor of Law, University of Chicago.
Stanley A. Kaplan, Professor of Law, University of Chicago.

CORPORATION LAW, BASIC, Second Edition (1979), with Documentary Supplement

Detlev F. Vagts, Professor of Law, Harvard University.

CORPORATIONS, see also Enterprise Organization

CORPORATIONS, Fifth Edition—Unabridged (1980)

William L. Cary, Professor of Law, Columbia University.
Melvin Aron Eisenberg, Professor of Law, University of California, Berkeley.

CORPORATIONS, Fifth Edition—Abridged (1980)

William L. Cary, Professor of Law, Columbia University.
Melvin Aron Eisenberg, Professor of Law, University of California, Berkeley.

CORPORATIONS, Second Edition (1982)

Alfred F. Conard, Professor of Law, University of Michigan.
Robert N. Knauss, Dean of the Law School, University of Houston.
Stanley Siegel, Professor of Law, University of California, Los Angeles.

CORPORATIONS, THE LAW OF: WHAT CORPORATE LAWYERS DO (1976)

Jan G. Deutsch, Professor of Law, Yale University.
Joseph J. Bianco, Professor of Law, Yeshiva University.

CORPORATIONS COURSE GAME PLAN (1975)

David R. Herwitz, Professor of Law, Harvard University.

CORRECTIONS, SEE SENTENCING

CREDIT TRANSACTIONS AND CONSUMER PROTECTION (1976)

John Honnold, Professor of Law, University of Pennsylvania.

CREDITORS' RIGHTS, see also Debtor-Creditor Law

CRIMINAL JUSTICE, THE ADMINISTRATION OF, Second Edition (1969)

Francis C. Sullivan, Professor of Law, Louisiana State University.
Paul Hardin III, Professor of Law, Duke University.
John Huston, Professor of Law, University of Washington.
Frank R. Lacy, Professor of Law, University of Oregon.
Daniel E. Murray, Professor of Law, University of Miami.
George W. Pugh, Professor of Law, Louisiana State University.

CRIMINAL JUSTICE ADMINISTRATION, Second Edition (1982)

Frank W. Miller, Professor of Law, Washington University.
Robert O. Dawson, Professor of Law, University of Texas.
George E. Dix, Professor of Law, University of Texas.
Raymond I. Parnas, Professor of Law, University of California, Davis.

CRIMINAL LAW, Second Edition (1979)

Fred E. Inbau, Professor of Law Emeritus, Northwestern University.
James R. Thompson, Professor of Law Emeritus, Northwestern University.
Andre A. Moenssens, Professor of Law, University of Richmond.

CRIMINAL LAW (1982)

Peter W. Low, Professor of Law, University of Virginia.
John C. Jeffries, Jr., Professor of Law, University of Virginia.
Richard C. Bonnie, Professor of Law, University of Virginia.

CRIMINAL LAW, Third Edition (1980)

Lloyd L. Weinreb, Professor of Law, Harvard University.

CRIMINAL LAW AND PROCEDURE, Fifth Edition (1977)

Rollin M. Perkins, Professor of Law Emeritus, University of California, Hastings
College of the Law.
Ronald N. Boyce, Professor of Law, University of Utah.

CRIMINAL PROCEDURE, Second Edition (1980), with 1982 Supplement

Fred E. Inbau, Professor of Law Emeritus, Northwestern University.
James R. Thompson, Professor of Law Emeritus, Northwestern University.
James B. Haddad, Professor of Law, Northwestern University.
James B. Zagel, Chief, Criminal Justice Division, Office of Attorney General of
Illinois.
Gary L. Starkman, Assistant U. S. Attorney, Northern District of Illinois.

UNIVERSITY CASEBOOK SERIES—Continued

EQUITY, RESTITUTION AND DAMAGES, Second Edition (1974)

Robert Childres, late Professor of Law, Northwestern University.
William F. Johnson, Jr., Professor of Law, New York University.

ESTATE PLANNING, Second Edition (1982), with Documentary Supplement

David Westfall, Professor of Law, Harvard University.

ETHICS, see Legal Profession, and Professional Responsibility

ETHICS AND PROFESSIONAL RESPONSIBILITY (1981) (Reprinted from THE LAWYERING PROCESS)

Gary Bellow, Professor of Law, Harvard University.
Bea Moulton, Legal Services Corporation.

EVIDENCE, Fourth Edition (1981)

David W. Louisell, late Professor of Law, University of California, Berkeley.
John Kaplan, Professor of Law, Stanford University.
Jon R. Waltz, Professor of Law, Northwestern University.

EVIDENCE (1968)

Francis C. Sullivan, Professor of Law, Louisiana State University.
Paul Hardin, III, Professor of Law, Duke University.

EVIDENCE, Seventh Edition (1983) with Rules and Statute Supplement (1981)

Jack B. Weinstein, Chief Judge, United States District Court.
John H. Mansfield, Professor of Law, Harvard University.
Norman Abrams, Professor of Law, University of California, Los Angeles.
Margaret Berger, Professor of Law, Brooklyn Law School.

FAMILY LAW, see also Domestic Relations

FAMILY LAW (1978), with 1983 Supplement

Judith C. Areen, Professor of Law, Georgetown University.

FAMILY LAW AND CHILDREN IN THE LEGAL SYSTEM, STATUTORY MATERI- ALS (1981)

Walter Wadlington, Professor of Law, University of Virginia.

FEDERAL COURTS, Seventh Edition (1982)

Charles T. McCormick, late Professor of Law, University of Texas.
James H. Chadbourn, Professor of Law, Harvard University.
Charles Alan Wright, Professor of Law, University of Texas.

FEDERAL COURTS AND THE FEDERAL SYSTEM, Hart and Wechsler's Sec- ond Edition (1973), with 1981 Supplement

Paul M. Bator, Professor of Law, Harvard University.
Paul J. Mishkin, Professor of Law, University of California, Berkeley.
David L. Shapiro, Professor of Law, Harvard University.
Herbert Wechsler, Professor of Law, Columbia University.

FEDERAL PUBLIC LAND AND RESOURCES LAW (1981)

George C. Coggins, Professor of Law, University of Kansas.
Charles F. Wilkinson, Professor of Law, University of Oregon.

FEDERAL RULES OF CIVIL PROCEDURE, 1982 Edition

FEDERAL TAXATION, see Taxation

UNIVERSITY CASEBOOK SERIES—Continued

FOOD AND DRUG LAW (1980), with Statutory Supplement

Richard A. Merrill, Dean of the School of Law, University of Virginia.
Peter Barton Hutt, Esq.

FUTURE INTERESTS (1958)

Philip Mechem, late Professor of Law Emeritus, University of Pennsylvania.

FUTURE INTERESTS (1970)

Howard R. Williams, Professor of Law, Stanford University.

FUTURE INTERESTS AND ESTATE PLANNING (1961), with 1962 Supplement

W. Barton Leach, late Professor of Law, Harvard University.
James K. Logan, formerly Dean of the Law School, University of Kansas.

GOVERNMENT CONTRACTS, FEDERAL (1975), with 1980 Supplement

John W. Whelan, Professor of Law, Hastings College of the Law.
Robert S. Pasley, Professor of Law Emeritus, Cornell University.

INJUNCTIONS (1972)

Owen M. Fiss, Professor of Law, Yale University.

INSTITUTIONAL INVESTORS, 1978

David L. Ratner, Professor of Law, Cornell University.

INSURANCE (1971)

William F. Young, Professor of Law, Columbia University.

INTERNATIONAL LAW, see also Transnational Legal Problems and United Nations Law

INTERNATIONAL LAW IN CONTEMPORARY PERSPECTIVE (1981), with Essay Supplement

Myres S. McDougal, Professor of Law, Yale University.
W. Michael Reisman, Professor of Law, Yale University.

INTERNATIONAL LEGAL SYSTEM, Second Edition (1981), with Documentary Supplement

Joseph Modeste Sweeney, Professor of Law, Tulane University.
Covey T. Oliver, Professor of Law, University of Pennsylvania.
Noyes E. Leech, Professor of Law, University of Pennsylvania.

INTERNATIONAL TRADE AND INVESTMENT, REGULATION OF (1970)

Carl H. Fulda, late Professor of Law, University of Texas.
Warren F. Schwartz, Professor of Law, University of Virginia.

INTRODUCTION TO LAW, see also Legal Method, On Law in Courts, and Dynamics of American Law

INTRODUCTION TO THE STUDY OF LAW (1970)

E. Wayne Thode, late Professor of Law, University of Utah.
Leon Lebowitz, Professor of Law, University of Texas.
Lester J. Mazor, Professor of Law, University of Utah.

JUDICIAL CODE and Rules of Procedure in the Federal Courts with Excerpts from the Criminal Code, 1981 Edition

Henry M. Hart, Jr., late Professor of Law, Harvard University.
Herbert Wechsler, Professor of Law, Columbia University.

JURISPRUDENCE (Temporary Edition Hardbound) (1949)

Lon L. Fuller, Professor of Law Emeritus, Harvard University.

JUVENILE, see also Children

JUVENILE JUSTICE PROCESS, Second Edition (1976), with 1980 Supplement

Frank W. Miller, Professor of Law, Washington University.
Robert O. Dawson, Professor of Law, University of Texas.
George E. Dix, Professor of Law, University of Texas.
Raymond I. Parnas, Professor of Law, University of California, Davis.

LABOR LAW, Ninth Edition (1981), with Statutory Supplement

Archibald Cox, Professor of Law, Harvard University.
Derek C. Bok, President, Harvard University.
Robert A. Gorman, Professor of Law, University of Pennsylvania.

LABOR LAW, Second Edition (1982), with Statutory Supplement

Clyde W. Summers, Professor of Law, University of Pennsylvania.
Harry H. Wellington, Dean of the Law School, Yale University.
Alan Hyde, Professor of Law, Rutgers University.

LAND FINANCING, Second Edition (1977)

Norman Penney, Professor of Law, Cornell University.
Richard F. Broude, Member of the California Bar.

LAW AND MEDICINE (1980)

Walter Wadlington, Professor of Law and Professor of Legal Medicine, University
of Virginia.
Jon R. Waltz, Professor of Law, Northwestern University.
Roger B. Dworkin, Professor of Law, Indiana University, and Professor of Biomedical History, University of Washington.

LAW, LANGUAGE AND ETHICS (1972)

William R. Bishin, Professor of Law, University of Southern California.
Christopher D. Stone, Professor of Law, University of Southern California.

**LAWYERING PROCESS (1978), with Civil Problem Supplement and Criminal
Problem Supplement**

Gary Bellow, Professor of Law, Harvard University.
Bea Moulton, Professor of Law, Arizona State University.

LEGAL METHOD (1980)

Harry W. Jones, Professor of Law Emeritus, Columbia University.
John M. Kernochan, Professor of Law, Columbia University.
Arthur W. Murphy, Professor of Law, Columbia University.

LEGAL METHODS (1969)

Robert N. Covington, Professor of Law, Vanderbilt University.
E. Blythe Stason, late Professor of Law, Vanderbilt University.
John W. Wade, Professor of Law, Vanderbilt University.
Elliott E. Cheatham, late Professor of Law, Vanderbilt University.
Theodore A. Smedley, Professor of Law, Vanderbilt University.

LEGAL PROFESSION (1970)

Samuel D. Thurman, Dean of the College of Law, University of Utah.
Ellis L. Phillips, Jr., Professor of Law, Columbia University.
Elliott E. Cheatham, late Professor of Law, Vanderbilt University.

UNIVERSITY CASEBOOK SERIES—Continued

LEGISLATION, Fourth Edition (1982) (by Fordham)

Horace E. Read, late Vice President, Dalhousie University.
John W. MacDonald, Professor of Law Emeritus, Cornell Law School.
Jefferson B. Fordham, Professor of Law, University of Utah.
William J. Pierce, Professor of Law, University of Michigan.

LEGISLATIVE AND ADMINISTRATIVE PROCESSES, Second Edition (1981)

Hans A. Linde, Judge, Supreme Court of Oregon.
George Bunn, Professor of Law, University of Wisconsin.
Fredericka Paff, Professor of Law, University of Wisconsin.
W. Lawrence Church, Professor of Law, University of Wisconsin.

LOCAL GOVERNMENT LAW, Revised Edition (1975)

Jefferson B. Fordham, Professor of Law, University of Utah.

MASS MEDIA LAW, Second Edition (1982)

Marc A. Franklin, Professor of Law, Stanford University.

MENTAL HEALTH PROCESS, Second Edition (1976), with 1981 Supplement

Frank W. Miller, Professor of Law, Washington University.
Robert O. Dawson, Professor of Law, University of Texas.
George E. Dix, Professor of Law, University of Texas.
Raymond I. Parnas, Professor of Law, University of California, Davis.

MUNICIPAL CORPORATIONS, see Local Government Law

NEGOTIABLE INSTRUMENTS, see Commercial Paper

NEGOTIATION (1981) (Reprinted from THE LAWYERING PROCESS)

Gary Bellow, Professor of Law, Harvard Law School.
Bea Moulton, Legal Services Corporation.

NEW YORK PRACTICE, Fourth Edition (1978)

Herbert Peterfreund, Professor of Law, New York University.
Joseph M. McLaughlin, Dean of the Law School, Fordham University.

OIL AND GAS, Fourth Edition (1979)

Howard R. Williams, Professor of Law, Stanford University.
Richard C. Maxwell, Professor of Law, University of California, Los Angeles.
Charles J. Meyers, Dean of the Law School, Stanford University.

ON LAW IN COURTS (1965)

Paul J. Mishkin, Professor of Law, University of California, Berkeley.
Clarence Morris, Professor of Law Emeritus, University of Pennsylvania.

PERSPECTIVES ON THE LAWYER AS PLANNER (Reprint of Chapters One through Five of Planning by Lawyers) (1978)

Louis M. Brown, Professor of Law, University of Southern California.
Edward A. Dauer, Professor of Law, Yale University.

PLANNING BY LAWYERS, MATERIALS ON A NONADVERSARIAL LEGAL PROCESS (1978)

Louis M. Brown, Professor of Law, University of Southern California.
Edward A. Dauer, Professor of Law, Yale University.

PLEADING AND PROCEDURE, see Procedure, Civil

ix

UNIVERSITY CASEBOOK SERIES—Continued

POLICE FUNCTION, Third Edition (1982)

Reprint of Chapters 1–10 of Miller, Dawson, Dix and Parnas' Criminal Justice Administration, Second Edition.

PREPARING AND PRESENTING THE CASE (1981) (Reprinted from THE LAWYERING PROCESS)

Gary Bellow, Professor of Law, Harvard Law School.
Bea Moulton, Legal Services Corporation.

PREVENTIVE LAW, see also Planning by Lawyers

PROCEDURE—CIVIL PROCEDURE, Second Edition (1974), with 1979 Supplement

James H. Chadbourn, Professor of Law, Harvard University.
A. Leo Levin, Professor of Law, University of Pennsylvania.
Philip Shuchman, Professor of Law, University of Connecticut.

PROCEDURE—CIVIL PROCEDURE, Fourth Edition (1978), with 1982 Supplement

Richard H. Field, late Professor of Law, Harvard University.
Benjamin Kaplan, Professor of Law Emeritus, Harvard University.
Kevin M. Clermont, Professor of Law, Cornell University.

PROCEDURE—CIVIL PROCEDURE, Third Edition (1976), with 1982 Supplement

Maurice Rosenberg, Professor of Law, Columbia University.
Jack B. Weinstein, Professor of Law, Columbia University.
Hans Smit, Professor of Law, Columbia University.
Harold L. Korn, Professor of Law, Columbia University.

PROCEDURE—PLEADING AND PROCEDURE: State and Federal, Fourth Edition (1979), with 1982 Supplement

David W. Louisell, late Professor of Law, University of California, Berkeley.
Geoffrey C. Hazard, Jr., Professor of Law, Yale University.

PROCEDURE—FEDERAL RULES OF CIVIL PROCEDURE, 1982 Edition

PRODUCTS LIABILITY (1980)

Marshall S. Shapo, Professor of Law, Northwestern University.

PRODUCTS LIABILITY AND SAFETY (1980), with Statutory Supplement

W. Page Keeton, Professor of Law, University of Texas.
David G. Owen, Professor of Law, University of South Carolina.
John E. Montgomery, Professor of Law, University of South Carolina.

PROFESSIONAL RESPONSIBILITY, Second Edition (1981), with Selected National Standards Supplement

Thomas D. Morgan, Dean of the Law School, Emory University.
Ronald D. Rotunda, Professor of Law, University of Illinois.

PROPERTY, Fourth Edition (1978)

John E. Cribbet, Dean of the Law School, University of Illinois.
Corwin W. Johnson, Professor of Law, University of Texas.

PROPERTY—PERSONAL (1953)

S. Kenneth Skolfield, late Professor of Law Emeritus, Boston University.

PROPERTY—PERSONAL, Third Edition (1954)

Everett Fraser, late Dean of the Law School Emeritus, University of Minnesota. Third Edition by Charles W. Taintor, late Professor of Law, University of Pittsburgh.

PROPERTY—INTRODUCTION, TO REAL PROPERTY, Third Edition (1954)

Everett Fraser, late Dean of the Law School Emeritus, University of Minnesota.

PROPERTY—REAL AND PERSONAL, Combined Edition (1954)

Everett Fraser, late Dean of the Law School Emeritus, University of Minnesota. Third Edition of Personal Property by Charles W. Taintor, late Professor of Law, University of Pittsburgh.

PROPERTY—REAL PROPERTY AND CONVEYANCING (1954)

Edward E. Bade, late Professor of Law, University of Minnesota.

PROPERTY—FUNDAMENTALS OF MODERN REAL PROPERTY, Second Edition (1982)

Edward H. Rabin, Professor of Law, University of California, Davis.

PROPERTY—PROBLEMS IN REAL PROPERTY (Pamphlet) (1969)

Edward H. Rabin, Professor of Law, University of California, Davis.

PROSECUTION AND ADJUDICATION, Second Edition (1982)

Reprint of Chapters 11–26 of Miller, Dawson, Dix and Parnas' Criminal Justice Administration, Second Edition.

PUBLIC REGULATION OF DANGEROUS PRODUCTS (paperback) (1980)

Marshall S. Shapo, Professor of Law, Northwestern University.

PUBLIC UTILITY LAW, see Free Enterprise, also Regulated Industries

REAL ESTATE PLANNING (1980), with 1980 Problems, Statutes and New Materials Supplement

Norton L. Steuben, Professor of Law, University of Colorado.

REAL ESTATE TRANSACTIONS (1980), with Statute, Form and Problem Supplement

Paul Goldstein, Professor of Law, Stanford University.

RECEIVERSHIP AND CORPORATE REORGANIZATION, see Creditors' Rights

REGULATED INDUSTRIES, Second Edition, 1976

William K. Jones, Professor of Law, Columbia University.

REMEDIES (1982)

Edward D. Re, Chief Judge, U. S. Court of International Trade.

RESTITUTION, Second Edition (1966)

John W. Wade, Professor of Law, Vanderbilt University.

SALES (1980)

Marion W. Benfield, Jr., Professor of Law, University of Illinois.
William D. Hawkland, Chancellor, Louisiana State University Law Center.

SALES AND SALES FINANCING, Fourth Edition (1976), with 1982 Supplement

John Honnold, Professor of Law, University of Pennsylvania.

SALES LAW AND THE CONTRACTING PROCESS (1982)

Reprint of Chapters 1–10 of Schwartz and Scott's Commercial Transactions.

SECURITIES REGULATION, Fifth Edition (1982), with 1982 Selected Statutes, Rules and Forms Supplement

Richard W. Jennings, Professor of Law, University of California, Berkeley.
Harold Marsh, Jr., Member of the California Bar.

SECURITIES REGULATION (1982), with 1983 Supplement

Larry D. Soderquist, Professor of Law, Vanderbilt University.

SENTENCING AND THE CORRECTIONAL PROCESS, Second Edition (1976)

Frank W. Miller, Professor of Law, Washington University.
Robert O. Dawson, Professor of Law, University of Texas.
George E. Dix, Professor of Law, University of Texas.
Raymond I. Parnas, Professor of Law, University of California, Davis.

SOCIAL WELFARE AND THE INDIVIDUAL (1971)

Robert J. Levy, Professor of Law, University of Minnesota.
Thomas P. Lewis, Dean of the College of Law, University of Kentucky.
Peter W. Martin, Professor of Law, Cornell University.

TAX, POLICY ANALYSIS OF THE FEDERAL INCOME (1976)

William A. Klein, Professor of Law, University of California, Los Angeles.

TAXATION, FEDERAL INCOME (1976), with 1982 Supplement

Erwin N. Griswold, Dean Emeritus, Harvard Law School.
Michael J. Graetz, Professor of Law, University of Virginia.

TAXATION, FEDERAL INCOME, Fourth Edition (1982)

James J. Freeland, Professor of Law, University of Florida.
Stephen A. Lind, Professor of Law, University of Florida.
Richard B. Stephens, Professor of Law Emeritus, University of Florida.

TAXATION, FEDERAL INCOME, Volume I, Personal Income Taxation (1972), with 1982 Supplement; Volume II, Taxation of Partnerships and Corporations, Second Edition (1980)

Stanley S. Surrey, Professor of Law, Harvard University.
William C. Warren, Professor of Law Emeritus, Columbia University.
Paul R. McDaniel, Professor of Law, Boston College Law School.
Hugh J. Ault, Professor of Law, Boston College Law School.

TAXATION, FEDERAL WEALTH TRANSFER, Second Edition (1982)

Stanley S. Surrey, Professor of Law, Harvard University.
William C. Warren, Professor of Law Emeritus, Columbia University.
Paul R. McDaniel, Professor of Law, Boston College Law School.
Harry L. Gutman, Instructor, Harvard Law School and Boston College Law School.

TAXATION OF INDIVIDUALS, PARTNERSHIPS AND CORPORATIONS, PROBLEMS in the (1978)

Norton L. Steuben, Professor of Law, University of Colorado.
William J. Turnier, Professor of Law, University of North Carolina.

TAXES AND FINANCE—STATE AND LOCAL (1974)

Oliver Oldman, Professor of Law, Harvard University.
Ferdinand P. Schoettle, Professor of Law, University of Minnesota.

TORT LAW AND ALTERNATIVES: INJURIES AND REMEDIES, Second Edition (1979)

Marc A. Franklin, Professor of Law, Stanford University.

University Casebook Series

CASES AND MATERIALS

ON

CHILDREN

IN THE

LEGAL SYSTEM

By

WALTER WADLINGTON
James Madison Professor of Law
University of Virginia Law School

CHARLES H. WHITEBREAD
George T. Pfleger Professor of Law
University of Southern California Law Center

SAMUEL M. DAVIS
Professor of Law
University of Georgia School of Law

Mineola, New York
THE FOUNDATION PRESS, INC.
1983

Library of Congress Cataloging in Publication Data

Wadlington, Walter, 1931–
  Cases and materials on children in the legal system.

  (University casebook series)
  Includes index.
  1. Children—Legal status, laws, etc.—United States—
Cases. 2. Juvenile courts—United States—Cases.
I. Whitebread, Charles H. II. Davis, Samuel M.
III. Title. IV. Series.
KF479.A7W33   1983   346.7301'35   82-21114
                        347.306135

ISBN 0-88277-101-9

W., W. & D. Cs. Children Legal System UCB

W.W.

To my children, Claire, Charlotte, Susan
and Derek, and to the memory of Ian.

C.H.W.

To my mother, Mrs. Helen M. Whitebread.

S.M.D.

To my mother, and to the memory of my father.

*

FOREWORD

During the past two decades our courts have confronted an increasing number and variety of cases calling for expansion or delineation of the legal rights of children. Some were provoked by specific exercises of legislative paternalism, while others stemmed from legislative unwillingness to modify antiquarian common law rules. Some of the new judicial decisions, along with important but unresolved children's rights issues, may be examined in family law, constitutional law, criminal law or juvenile courts courses—if indeed they are included anywhere in the law school curriculum. Broader courses such as constitutional law, family law and criminal law already have so many other themes and issues to deal with that little room remains for careful treatment of the special problems that children face under our legal system. Established family law teaching materials particularly reflect the difficulties of producing a single volume that can be covered effectively in the typical three-hour offering. Important legal problems of children often are squeezed into a small part of such a course. At the same time, some juvenile courts courses limit their scope almost entirely to the procedure used in such tribunals.

This book stems from our perception of the need for a course (or courses) that will augment the typical family law course. We believe that such an offering should include adequate coverage of the juvenile justice system as well as a broader examination of how our legal system has dealt with children generally in the past. And there should be some exploration of alternatives for improving our handling of children's problems in the future. The underlying thesis is that we should examine the rights and duties of children from a substantially expanded perspective. How can we continue to rationalize virtually unlimited tort responsibility, for example, while refusing to let children make testamentary gifts at an age when many have entered college?

Crucial to an expanded approach is discussion of children's legal issues in the context of such jurisprudential concerns as the proper balance of judicial discretion and legislative standards, the use of state intervention to regulate intrafamily relations, and the goals of and justification for state sanctions that result in involuntary loss of liberty. These issues are not unique to cases involving children, as present popular and scholarly debates well illustrate. What is important to understand is that a course on children in the legal system should come to terms with the significant jurisprudential issues of our day. In this sense, the course for which these materials are designed should be viewed not simply as a specialty offering for students interested in family law, but rather as a vehicle for discussing the uses and limits of law in a free society.

Because there is no standardized course in the field we have tried to produce materials that will allow a teacher to follow an eclectic approach, varying the emphasis to be placed on private law, constitutional law, juvenile justice, adequate parenting, or abuse and neglect materials. Some may style the course "Family Law II"; others may prefer to perpetuate a "Juvenile Justice" or "Juvenile Courts" label. Our own choice of title reflects our strong view that such a course should include a wide range of legal problems confronted by children. Even the English language presented some difficulty in our settling on a name. The word "children", for example, can have a relational meaning (adults are "children" of their parents), though it is used more typically to refer to minors or young persons. On the other hand, "minor", "adolescent", "juvenile" and some other terms that might have been selected can take on "term of art" status that varies from one discipline to another.

Charles Whitebread gratefully acknowledges the research and editing help of his student assistants John Heilman and James Curtis.

Sam Davis wishes to acknowledge the invaluable research assistance provided by Ms. Sue Carey Lindholm.

Walter Wadlington expresses his thanks to Professor John Calvin Jeffries, Jr. for serving as a highly resonant sounding board for his off-the-wall ideas.

We thank John Hasko, research librarian of the University of Southern California Law Center, for preparation of bibliographic research materials.

WALTER WADLINGTON
CHARLES H. WHITEBREAD
SAMUEL M. DAVIS

November, 1982

NOTE ON EDITING

Citations and text have been selectively omitted from many of the judicial opinions which are reproduced. This was necessary in order to maintain manageable proportions for classroom use and still include relevant portions of many key, but often lengthy, decisions. Footnotes that are retained bear the official reporter numbering. Although some citations to cases and secondary authorities in opinions have been deleted without a note or symbol to indicate this, ellipses have been inserted to indicate where portions of text have been omitted.

A similar policy has been followed with regard to excerpts from books and law review articles.

SUMMARY OF CONTENTS

TABLE OF CONTENTS

*

TABLE OF CASES

Principal cases are in italic type. Nonprincipal cases are in roman type.
References are to Pages.

---

*

TABLE OF AUTHORS

Not including authors cited only in cases or excerpts from articles or books. References are to Pages

*

CASES AND MATERIALS

ON

CHILDREN

IN THE

LEGAL SYSTEM

*

I. PROTECTION OR AUTONOMY FOR MINORS: SOME PRIVATE LAW RESPONSES

The thought that children might go to court to seek protection of their constitutional rights regarding matters such as education, free speech, or privacy and personal autonomy even in conflicts with their parents is relatively new, as the series of judicial opinions in Chapter II will illustrate. However, courts long have dealt with the private law problems of children in such matters as contracting, gratuitously transferring property, suing and being sued, torts, and participation in the labor force. The often elaborate rules governing the rights, duties, and infirmities of children in such contexts developed with little or no influence from concern over actual or threatened litigation involving denial of constitutional liberties. The various rules regarding children typically grew up separately according to the legal category or pigeonhole, such as contracts or torts, in which the problem came up. Thus the treatment accorded a child in contract law might be distinctly protectionist in nature, while tort rules might reflect greater willingness to place full responsibility on the shoulders of children even at relatively early age. The contrasting treatment sometimes reflects varying approaches to resolution of questions of authority and responsibility of parents as well as perceptions about the capacities of children. Anachronisms still prevail in many sectors. The materials that follow have been designed to give an overview of the dimensions of the problem of conceptually inconsistent treatment in the private law sector today. It is suggested that the student attempt to reconcile the differing approaches as they unfold, while keeping in mind the question whether the various rules are responsive to the needs of today's society. After the cases in Chapter II have been considered, one also should ask the question whether a new round of constitutional litigation may be in the offing.

NOTE

Professor Robert Batey in Rights of Adolescents, 31 Wm. & Mary L.Rev. 363 (1982), questions the validity of the widely accepted judicial view exemplified by Chief Justice Burger's statement in Parham v. J. R., 442 U.S. 584, 603 (1979), infra at p. 169, that:

Most children, even in adolescence, simply are not able to make sound judgments concerning many decisions. . . . Parents can and must make those judgments.

Reviewing existing evidence of the capacity of adolescents for moral reasoning found in the works of major modern psychologists such as Piaget and Kohlberg, Professor Batey concludes that "the law should accord the considered choices of competent adolescents the same treatment it accords similar choices of adults", which should mean that "the state can refuse to defer to

1

the considered desires of an adolescent only upon a showing that the adolescent is not competent to make a decision."

In his sensitive and provocative book, The Changing World of Legal Adolescence (1982), Professor Franklin E. Zimring refers to growing up as a process. He argues against "using a single binary box, specifically age 18, as an all-purpose criterion for adulthood." Id. at 111. He asserts that in American law there are three different attributes of "adulthood" that are associated with the age of majority. These are "liberty, entitlement, and responsibility." The first involves the right to make choices just as other adults; decisions regarding medical care are an example. "Entitlements" are described as "those special opportunities the state might wish to provide only to those who have not yet reached adulthood." Responsibility would involve being responsible for one's own support and "paying the full price for misdeeds". Professor Zimring asks whether the age of majority should be 18 for liberty and 21 for responsibility and entitlement. Ibid.

In the preface to his book Professor Zimring makes the very important point that lawyers speak a different language from that found in the social science literature. Words such as "adolescent" and "adolescence", for example, rarely are found in law review and other legal literature. Lawyers have developed their own terms of art such as "mature minors", or "persons in need of supervision". For some current perceptions of psychologists about children's decisionmaking capacity see G. Melton, G. Koocher, and M. Saks (eds.), Developmental Factors in Competence to Consent (1983).

In reviewing the material which follows one should keep in mind the questions raised by Professors Batey and Zimring and try to determine whether extant legal doctrine and rules make sense in today's world.

A.   LIMITATIONS ON CONTRACTING

HALBMAN v. LEMKE

Supreme Court of Wisconsin, 1980.
99 Wis.2d 241, 298 N.W.2d 562.

CALLOW, JUSTICE.

. . . On or about July 13, 1973, James Halbman, Jr. (Halbman), a minor, entered into an agreement with Michael Lemke (Lemke) whereby Lemke agreed to sell Halbman a 1968 Oldsmobile for the sum of $1,250. Lemke was the manager of L & M Standard Station in Greenfield, Wisconsin, and Halbman was an employe at L & M. At the time the agreement was made Halbman paid Lemke $1,000 cash and took possession of the car. Arrangements were made for Halbman to pay $25 per week until the balance was paid, at which time title would be transferred. About five weeks after the purchase agreement, and after Halbman had paid a total of $1,100 of the purchase price, a connecting rod on the vehicle's engine broke. Lemke, while denying any obligation, offered to assist Halbman in installing a used engine in the vehicle if Halbman, at his expense, could secure one. Halbman declined the offer and in September took the vehicle to a garage where it was repaired at a cost of $637.40. Halbman did not pay the repair bill.

In October of 1973 Lemke endorsed the vehicle's title over to Halbman, although the full purchase price had not been paid by Halbman, in an effort to avoid any liability for the operation, maintenance, or use of the vehicle. On October 15, 1973, Halbman returned the title to Lemke by letter which disaffirmed the purchase contract and demanded the return of all money theretofore paid by Halbman. Lemke did not return the money paid by Halbman.

The repair bill remained unpaid, and the vehicle remained in the garage where the repairs had been made. In the spring of 1974, in satisfaction of a garageman's lien for the outstanding amount, the garage elected to remove the vehicle's engine and transmission and then towed the vehicle to the residence of James Halbman, Sr., the father of the plaintiff minor. Lemke was asked several times to remove the vehicle from the senior Halbman's home, but he declined to do so, claiming he was under no legal obligation to remove it. During the period when the vehicle was at the garage and then subsequently at the home of the plaintiff's father, it was subjected to vandalism, making it unsalvageable.

Halbman initiated this action seeking the return of the $1,100 he had paid toward the purchase of the vehicle, and Lemke counterclaimed for $150, the amount still owing on the contract. Based upon the uncontroverted facts, the trial court granted judgment in favor of Halbman, concluding that when a minor disaffirms a contract for the purchase of an item, he need only offer to return the property remaining in his hands without making restitution for any use or depreciation. . . .

. . . [The court of appeals] affirmed the trial court with respect to the question of restitution for depreciation. . . .

The sole issue before us is whether a minor, having disaffirmed a contract for the purchase of an item which is not a necessity and having tendered the property back to the vendor, must make restitution to the vendor for damage to the property prior to the disaffirmance. Lemke argues that he should be entitled to recover for the damage to the vehicle up to the time of disaffirmance, which he claims equals the amount of the repair bill.

Neither party challenges the absolute right of a minor to disaffirm a contract for the purchase of items which are not necessities. That right, variously known as the doctrine of incapacity or the "infancy doctrine," is one of the oldest and most venerable of our common law traditions. Although the origins of the doctrine are somewhat obscure, it is generally recognized that its purpose is the protection of minors from foolishly squandering their wealth through improvident contracts with crafty adults who would take advantage of them in the marketplace. Kiefer v. Fred Howe Motors, Inc., 39 Wis.2d 20, 24, 158 N.W.2d 288 (1968). Thus it is settled law in this state that a contract of a minor for items which are not necessities is void or voidable at the minor's option.

Once there has been a disaffirmance, however, as in this case between a minor vendee and an adult vendor, unresolved problems arise regarding the rights and responsibilities of the parties relative to the disposition of the consideration exchanged on the contract. As a general rule a minor who disaffirms a contract is entitled to recover all consideration he has conferred incident to the transaction. In return the minor is expected to restore as much of the consideration as, at the time of disaffirmance, remains in the minor's possession. The minor's right to disaffirm is not contingent upon the return of the property, however, as disaffirmance is permitted even where such return cannot be made. Olson v. Veum, 197 Wis. 342, 222 N.W. 233 (1928).

The return of property remaining in the hands of the minor is not the issue presented here. In this case we have a situation where the property cannot be returned to the vendor in its entirety because it has been damaged and therefore diminished in value, and the vendor seeks to recover the depreciation. . . .

The law regarding the rights and responsibilities of the parties relative to the consideration exchanged on a disaffirmed contract is characterized by confusion, inconsistency, and a general lack of uniformity as jurisdictions attempt to reach a fair application of the infancy doctrine in today's marketplace. See Robert G. Edge, Voidability of Minors' Contracts: A Feudal Doctrine in a Modern Economy, 1 Ga.L.Rev. 205 (1967); Walter D. Navin, Jr., The Contracts of Minors Viewed from the Perspective of Fair Exchange, 50 N.C.L.Rev. 517 (1972); Note, Restitution in Minors' Contracts in California, 19 Hastings L.Rev. 1199 (1968); 52 Marq.L.Rev. 437 (1969). See also: John D. McCamus, Restitution of Benefits Conferred Under Minors' Contracts, 28 U.N.B.L.J. 89 (1979); . . . That both parties rely on this court's decision in Olson v. Veum, supra, is symptomatic of the problem.

In *Olson* a minor, with his brother, an adult, purchased farm implements and materials, paying by signing notes payable at a future date. Prior to the maturity of the first note, the brothers ceased their joint farming business, and the minor abandoned his interest in the material purchased by leaving it with his brother. The vendor initiated an action against the minor to recover on the note, and the minor (who had by then reached majority) disaffirmed. The trial court ordered judgment for the plaintiff on the note, finding there had been insufficient disaffirmance to sustain the plea of infancy. This court reversed, holding that the contract of a minor for the purchase of items which are not necessities may be disaffirmed even when the minor cannot make restitution. Lemke calls our attention to the following language in that decision:

> "To sustain the judgment below is to overlook the substantial distinction between a mere denial by an infant of contract liability where the other party is seeking to enforce it and those cases

where he who was the minor not only disaffirms such contract but seeks the aid of the court to restore to him that with which he has parted at the making of the contract. In the one case he is using his infancy merely as a shield, in the other also as a sword." 197 Wis. at 344, 222 N.W. 233.

From this Lemke infers that when a minor, as a plaintiff, seeks to disaffirm a contract and recover his consideration, different rules should apply than if the minor is defending against an action on the contract by the other party. This theory is not without some support among scholars. See: Calamari and Perillo, The Law of Contracts, sec. 126, 207–09 (Hornbook Series 1970), treating separately the obligations of the infant as a plaintiff and the infant as a defendant.

Additionally, Lemke advances the thesis in the dissenting opinion by court of appeals Judge Cannon, arguing that a disaffirming minor's obligation to make restitution turns upon his ability to do so. For this proposition, the following language in Olson v. Veum, supra, 197 Wis. at 345, 222 N.W. 233, is cited:

"The authorities are clear that when it is shown, as it is here, that the infant cannot make restitution, then his absolute right to disaffirm is not to be questioned."

In this case Lemke argues that the *Olson* language excuses the minor only when restitution is not possible. Here Lemke holds Halbman's $1,100, and accordingly there is no question as to Halbman's ability to make restitution.

Halbman argues in response that, while the "sword-shield" dichotomy may apply where the minor has misrepresented his age to induce the contract, that did not occur here and he may avoid the contract without making restitution notwithstanding his ability to do so.

The principal problem is the use of the word "restitution" in *Olson*. A minor, as we have stated, is under an enforceable duty to return to the vendor, upon disaffirmance, as much of the consideration as remains in his possession. When the contract is disaffirmed, title to that part of the purchased property which is retained by the minor revests in the vendor; it no longer belongs to the minor. See, e.g., Restatement (Second) of Contracts, sec. 18B, comment c, (Tent. Draft No. 1, 1964). The rationale for the rule is plain: a minor who disaffirms a purchase and recovers his purchase price should not also be permitted to profit by retaining the property purchased. The infancy doctrine is designed to protect the minor, sometimes at the expense of an innocent vendor, but it is not to be used to bilk merchants out of property as well as proceeds of the sale. Consequently, it is clear that, when the minor no longer possesses the property which was the subject matter of the contract, the rule requiring the return of property does not apply.[1] The minor will not be required to give

---

1. Although we are not presented with the question here, we recognize there is considerable disagreement among the authorities on whether a minor who disposes of the property should be made to restore the vendor with some-

up what he does not have. We conclude that *Olson* does no more than set forth the foregoing rationale and that the word "restitution" as it is used in that opinion is limited to the return of the property to the vendor. We do not agree with Lemke and the court of appeals' dissent that *Olson* requires a minor to make restitution for loss or damage to the property if he is capable of doing so.

Here Lemke seeks restitution of the value of the depreciation by virtue of the damage to the vehicle prior to disaffirmance. Such a recovery would require Halbman to return more than that remaining in his possession. It seeks compensatory value for that which he cannot return. Where there is misrepresentation by a minor or willful destruction of property, the vendor may be able to recover damages in tort. See, e.g., Kiefer v. Fred Howe Motors, Inc., supra; . . . But absent these factors, as in the present case, we believe that to require a disaffirming minor to make restitution for diminished value is, in effect, to bind the minor to a part of the obligation which by law he is privileged to avoid.

The cases upon which the petitioner relies for the proposition that a disaffirming minor must make restitution for loss and depreciation serve to illustrate some of the ways other jurisdictions have approached this problem of balancing the needs of minors against the rights of innocent merchants. In Barber v. Gross, 74 S.D. 254, 51 N.W.2d 696 (1952), the South Dakota Supreme Court held that a minor could disaffirm a contract as a defense to an action by the merchant to enforce the contract but that the minor was obligated by a South Dakota statute, upon sufficient proof of loss by the plaintiff, to make restitution for depreciation. Cain v. Coleman, 396 S.W.2d 251 (Tex.Civ.App.1965), involved a minor seeking to disaffirm a contract for the purchase of a used car where the dealer claimed the minor had misrepresented his age. In reversing summary judgment granted in favor of the minor, the court recognized the minor's obligation to make restitution for the depreciation of the vehicle. The Texas court has also ruled, in a case where there was no issue of misrepresentation, that upon disaffirmance and tender by a minor the vendor is obligated to take the property "as is." Rutherford v. Hughes, 228 S.W.2d 909, 912 (Tex.Civ.App.1950). Scalone v. Talley Motors, Inc., 158 N.Y.S.2d 615, 3 App.Div.2d 674 (1957), and Rose v.

thing in its stead. The general rule appears to limit the minor's responsibility for restoration to specie only. Terrace Company v. Calhoun, 37 Ill.App.3d 757, 347 N.E.2d 315, 320 (1976); Adamowski v. Curtiss-Wright Flying Service, 300 Mass. 281, 15 N.E.2d 467 (1938); Quality Motors v. Hays, 216 Ark. 264, 225 S.W.2d 326, 328 (1949). But see: Boyce v. Doyle, 113 N.J.Super. 240, 273 A.2d 408 (1971), adopting a "status quo" theory which requires the minor to restore the precontract status quo, even if it means returning proceeds or other value; Fisher v. Taylor Motor Co., 249 N.C. 617, 107 S.E.2d 94 (1959), requiring the minor to restore only the property remaining in the hands of the minor, " 'or account for so much of its value as may have been invested in other property which he has in hand or owns and controls.' " Id. at 97. Finally, some attention is given to the "New Hampshire Rule" or benefits theory which requires the disaffirming minor to pay for the contract to the extent he benefited from it. Hall v. Butterfield, 59 N.H. 354 (1879); Porter v. Wilson, 106 N.H. 270, 209 A.2d 730 (1965).

Sheehan Buick, Inc., 204 So.2d 903 (Fla.App.1967), represent the proposition that a disaffirming minor must do equity in the form of restitution for loss or depreciation of the property returned. Because these cases would at some point force the minor to bear the cost of the very improvidence from which the infancy doctrine is supposed to protect him, we cannot follow them.

As we noted in *Kiefer*, modifications of the rules governing the capacity of infants to contract are best left to the legislature. Until such changes are forthcoming, however, we hold that, absent misrepresentation or tortious damage to the property, a minor who disaffirms a contract for the purchase of an item which is not a necessity may recover his purchase price without liability for use, depreciation, damage, or other diminution in value.

. . .

The decision of the court of appeals is affirmed.

NOTES

(1) Whether a minor has disaffirmed a contract or ratified or affirmed it in timely fashion after reaching majority often has been the subject of litigation. In Jones v. Dressel, ___ Colo. ___, 623 P.2d 370 (1981), a 17-year-old had signed a contract for use of defendant's recreational skydiving facilities, which included an airplane to ferry parachutists to the jumping site. The contract contained an exculpatory clause and a covenant not to sue defendant. Ten months after plaintiff turned 18 (the Colorado age of majority), he suffered serious injuries in the crash of an aircraft that defendant had furnished as part of the skydiving operation. Eleven months later he filed action against defendant, including an allegation that he had disaffirmed the contract within a reasonable time after reaching majority. Upholding the trial court's rejection of this argument by plaintiff, the Supreme Court of Colorado explained:

> Affirmance is not merely a matter of intent. It may be determined by the actions of a minor who accepts the benefits of a contract after reaching the age of majority, or who is silent or acquiesces in the contract for a considerable length of time. What act constitutes ratification or disaffirmance is ordinarily a question of law to be determined by the trial court. Sullivan v. Bennett, 261 Mich. 232, 246 N.W. 90 (1933). We agree that what constitutes a reasonable time for affirmance or disaffirmance is ordinarily a question of fact to be determined by the facts in a particular case. We conclude, however, that the trial court properly determined that Jones ratified the contract, as a matter of law, by accepting the benefits of the contract when he used Free Flight's facilities on [the date of the crash].

(2) Some states have adopted legislation altering the general common law rules governing minors' contracts. Such provisions often follow a pattern of lowering the age for entering contracts for certain items or transactions such as insurance or banking. There also may be special provisions for professional athletes or entertainers who are minors. The California Civil Code contains the following provision:

§ 36. Minors; contracts not disaffirmable

(a) Contracts not disaffirmable

(a) A contract, otherwise valid, entered into during minority, cannot be disaffirmed upon that ground either during the actual minority of the person entering into such contract, or at any time thereafter, in the following cases:

1. Necessaries.

(1) A contract to pay the reasonable value of things necessary for his support, or that of his family, entered into by him when not under the care of a parent or guardian able to provide for him or them; provided, that these things have been actually furnished to him or to his family.

2. Artistic or creative services; judicial approval.

(2)(A) A contract or agreement pursuant to which such person is employed or agrees to render artistic or creative services, or agrees to purchase, or otherwise secure, sell, lease, license, or otherwise dispose of literary, musical or dramatic properties (either tangible or intangible) or any rights therein for use in motion pictures, television, the production of phonograph records, the legitimate or living stage, or otherwise in the entertainment field, if the contract or agreement has been approved by the superior court in the county in which such minor resides or is employed or, if the minor neither resides in or is employed in this state, if any party to the contract or agreement has its principal office in this state for the transaction of business.

(B) As used in this paragraph, "artistic or creative services" shall include, but not be limited to, services as an actor, actress, dancer, musician, comedian, singer, or other performer or entertainer, or as a writer, director, producer, production executive, choreographer, composer, conductor, or designer.

3. Professional sports contracts; judicial approval.

(3) A contract or agreement pursuant to which such person is employed or agrees to render services as a participant or player in professional sports, including, but without being limited to, professional boxers, professional wrestlers, and professional jockeys, if the contract or agreement has been approved by the superior court in the county in which such minor resides or is employed or, if the minor neither resides in or is employed in this state, if any party to the contract or agreement has its principal office in this state for the transaction of business.

(b) Judicial approval; procedure; extent

(b) The approval of the superior court referred to in paragraphs (2) and (3) of subdivision (a) may be given upon the petition of either party to the contract or agreement after such reasonable notice to the other party thereto as may be fixed by said court, with opportunity to such other party to appear and be heard; and its approval when given shall extend to the whole of the contract or agreement, and all of the terms and provisions thereof, including, but without being limited to, any optional or conditional provisions contained therein for extension, prolongation, or termination of the term thereof.

For another example of a statute dealing with the special problem of the child athlete or performing artist by setting up a mechanism for judicial approval, see N.Y.Gen.Obligations Law § 3–105 (1976). A discussion of broader emancipation statutes now being adopted in some jurisdictions (including California) appears infra at p. 38.

One subject on which a great many states have adopted specific legislation permitting minors to contract, sometimes without any age floor, is that of medical services. The special peculiarities of these statutes and the rationale behind them is reviewed at pp. 951–960, infra.

(3) Is it realistic to maintain a strongly protective approach to minors' contracts in our present consumer-oriented society in which teenage markets often amount to very substantial segments of buying power? Should it be relevant that it is legally and socially acceptable for minors to engage in certain activities, such as driving a motor vehicle, for which state licensure often can be obtained years before a driver has reached majority? If a minor can be legally engaged in an "adult activity" such as driving, why should he or she not have the contractual capacity to buy a car? For a comparison of the tort approach to responsibility for such an activity see the discussion at p. 14 infra.

(4) The Juvenile Justice Standards Relating to Rights of Minors * proposes the following approach to dealing with minors' contracts. Does it provide a more realistic response to contemporary mores? Can you offer a better scheme?

6.1 Minors' contracts

The validity of contracts of minors, other than those governed by other standards of this volume, should be governed by the following principles:

A. The contract of a minor who is at least twelve years of age should be valid and enforceable by and against the minor, as long as such a contract of an adult would be valid and enforceable, if:

    1. the minor's parent or duly constituted guardian consented in writing to the contract; or

    2. the minor represented to the other party that he or she was at least eighteen years of age and a reasonable person under the circumstances would have believed the representation; or

    3. the minor was a purchaser and is unable to return the goods to the seller in substantially the condition they were in when purchased because the minor lost or caused them to be damaged, the minor consumed them, or the minor gave them away.

B. The contract of a minor who has not reached the age of twelve should be void.

. . .

B. TORTS: INDIVIDUAL RESPONSIBILITY
AND CAPACITY TO SUE

HUCHTING v. ENGEL, by his Guardian

Supreme Court of Wisconsin, 1863.
17 Wis. 237.

ERROR to the Circuit Court for *Dane* County.

Huchting brought an action before a justice of the peace against *Moirtz Engel*, for breaking and entering the plaintiff's premises, and breaking down and destroying his shrubbery and flowers therein standing and growing. The answer, after a general denial, stated that if the defendant ever committed the alleged trespass, "he did so through the want of judgment and discretion, being an infant of about six years of age." On the trial before the justice, the plaintiff proved the alleged trespass and damages; and on the part of the defense it was shown that the defendant, at the time of the trespass, was but little more than six years old. A motion to dismiss the action, on the ground that the defendant was "of such tender years that a suit at law could not be maintained against him, nor execution issued on a judgment against him," was overruled. The justice rendered judgment against the defendant for $3.00 damages, with costs. The circuit court, on appeal, reversed the judgment; and the plaintiff sued out his writ of error.

By the Court, DIXON, C. J. "Infants are liable in actions arising *ex delicto*, whether founded on positive wrongs, as trespass or assault, or constructive torts or frauds." 2 Kent's Com., 241.

"Where the minor has committed a tort with force, he is liable at any age; for in case of civil injuries with force, the intention is not regarded; for in such a case a lunatic is as liable to compensate in damages as a man in his right mind." Reeve's Dom.Rel. 258.

"The privilege of infancy is purely protective, and infants are liable to actions for wrong done by them; as to an action for slander, an action of trover for property embezzled, or an action grounded on fraud committed." Macpherson on Infants, 481 (41 Law Lib., 305).

"Infants are liable for torts and injuries of a private nature; as disseisins, trespass, slander, assault, &c." Bingham on Infancy, 110.

"All the cases agree that trespass lies against an infant." Hartfield v. Roper, 21 Wend., 620.

This is the language of a few of the many writers and courts who have spoken upon the subject. All agree, and all are supported by the authorities, with no single adjudged case to the contrary. In [Humphrey v. Douglass, 10 Vermont, 71] the minor was held answerable for a trespass committed by him, although he acted by command of his father.

The authorities cited by the counsel for the defendant in error have no bearing upon the question. They relate to the criminal responsibility of infants; to the question of negligence on their part, as whether it can be imputed to them so as to defeat actions brought by them to recover damages for personal injuries sustained in part in consequence of the negligence or unskilfulness of others; and to the liability of parents and guardians for wrongs committed by infants under their charge by reason of the neglect or want of proper care of such parents or guardians. The case at bar is none of these. The defendant is not prosecuted criminally; the action is not by him to recover damages for personal injury occasioned by the joint negligence of himself or his parents, and another; nor is the liability of the parents involved. The suit is brought to recover damages for a trespass committed by him; not vindictive or punitory damages, but compensation; and for that he is clearly liable. If damages by way of punishment were demanded, undoubtedly his extreme youth and consequent want of discretion would be a good answer.

Judgment of the circuit reversed, and that of the justice of the peace affirmed.

NOTES

(1) As the preceding case indicates, the rule that minors are liable for their torts is of long standing and has been pronounced emphatically by courts and commentators. Practical problems may arise when there is an attempt to recover against a minor in tort but the asserted wrong is in fact nonperformance of a contract—breach of warranty affords one such example. As a general rule, no such action will lie unless liability can be established without reliance on the contract's existence. See W. Prosser, Handbook of the Law of Torts 998 (4th ed. 1971). As the author there points out, however, the authorities disagree over whether an infant can be sued in tort, say for deceit, based on obtaining the contract through misrepresentation. Id. at 999.

Are there any sound policy reasons for applying a narrowly protectionist approach to minors' contracts while requiring compensation broadly against minors for their torts?

(2) Louisiana provides the broad exception in this country to the rule that minors alone are liable for their torts in the absence of special agency or parental conduct that would amount to negligence. La.Civil Code Art. 2318 long has provided that:

> The father, or after his decease, the mother, are responsible for the damage occasioned by their minor or unemancipated children, residing with them, or placed by them under the care of other persons, reserving to them recourse against those persons.

> The same responsibility attaches to the tutors of minors.

In 1934 the Louisiana Supreme Court held in Johnson v. Butterworth, 180 La. 586, 157 So. 121 (1934), that a parent was not responsible for damage caused by a minor of tender years who lacked the capacity for discernment; this decision was overruled in Turner v. Bucher, 308 So.2d 270 (La.1975), which contains an extensive history of the development of Art. 2318. The court held that a parent can escape liability for damages caused by a child's conduct that would be delictual except for the disability of tender years only by showing that "the harm was caused by the fault of the victim, by the fault of a third person, or by a fortuitous event". Id. at 277.

Many states in recent years have adopted more limited parental responsibility statutes designed largely to encourage parents to curb vandalism by their children. Mass.Gen.Laws Ann. ch. 231, § 85G (Supp.1981) contains this provision:

> Parents of an unemancipated child under the age of eighteen and over the age of seven years shall be liable in a civil action for any willful act committed by said child which results in injury or death to another person or damage to the property of another, damage to cemetery property, or damage to any state, county or municipal property. This section shall not apply to a parent who, as a result of a decree of any court of competent jurisdiction, does not have custody of such a child at the time of the commission of the tort. Recovery under this section shall not exceed one thousand dollars for any such cause of action.

Provisions of this type typically contain a low ceiling on the monetary amount of an award against a parent not otherwise liable for the child's actions; many of the statutes are limited to recovery for property damage. In 1971 Georgia's Supreme Court invalidated a state provision imposing liability on parents or persons in loco parentis for death, injury or damage to property caused by the "wilful and wanton acts" of a minor child in their "custody or control". The law was said to violate the due process clauses of both the Georgia and U.S. constitutions, as well as the equal protection clause of the latter. Of particular concern to the court was the fact that the statute based vicarious liability solely on the parent-child relationship. Statutes in other states, the court stated, were penal in nature because they involved only limited liability. Corley v. Lewless, 227 Ga. 745, 182 S.E.2d 766 (1971). The Georgia legislature in 1976 enacted a new parental responsibility law with a $500 limit on the amount of damages that can be imposed on a parent or person in loco parentis. Ga.Code Ann. § 51–2–3 (1982). The legislative purpose as described in Ga.Acts 1976, p. 511 is "to provide for the public welfare and aid in the control of juvenile delinquency, not to provide restorative compensation to victims of injurious or tortious conduct by children."

In Piscataway Township Board of Education v. Caffiero, 86 N.J. 308, 431 A.2d 799 (1981) the Supreme Court of New Jersey upheld the constitutionality of a state statute that imposed vicarious liability on parents or guardians of pupils who damage school property. N.J.Stat.Ann. 18A:37–3 (West 1968). The statute was independent of New Jersey's provisions for limited liability of parents for acts of vandalism by their children when they have failed to exercise reasonable supervision and control over them. N.J.Stat.Ann. 2A:53A–15 (Supp.1981–82). The court explained:

> The existence of the parent-child relationship provides a rational basis for imposing liability and is a reasonable means to accomplish the purposes of compensation and deterrence. The United States Supreme Court has recognized that "parents have an important 'guiding role' to play in the upbringing of their children." H. L. v. Matheson, 450 U.S. 398, 411, 101 S.Ct. 1164, 1172, 67 L.Ed.2d 388, 399 (1981); Bellotti v. Baird, 443 U.S. 622, 637–39, 99 S.Ct. 3035, 3045–46, 61 L.Ed.2d 797 (1979). The Leg-

islature could have reasonably believed that subjecting parents to vicarious liability for their children's willful and malicious acts of vandalism would encourage parents to exercise their "guiding role" in the upbringing of their children. Through better parental supervision and guidance, the Legislature hoped to deter delinquent conduct. Our concern is not whether that hope has been or will be fulfilled but whether there is a rational basis for it. Though we acknowledge the difficulties of being a parent, we cannot say that there is no rational basis for the statute.

431 A.2d 805.

In Lamb v. Peck, ___ Conn. ___, 441 A.2d 14 (1981), four minor defendants were found to have knocked to the ground and either punched, kicked at or pushed the minor plaintiff. All five parties were 16 years old. Finding that defendants had acted in concert (though it was conceded that only one threw the punch that caused plaintiff to lose three teeth), the court found each defendant vicariously liable for the whole of the injury caused by their concerted action. The court further held defendants' parents jointly and severally liable up to the maximum amount provided for in Conn.Gen.Stat. § 52–572 (Supp.1982).

RESTATEMENT (SECOND) OF TORTS (1977)

§ 283. A. Children

If the actor is a child, the standard of conduct to which he must conform to avoid being negligent is that of a reasonable person of like age, intelligence, and experience under like circumstances.

Comment

a. Children. A child is a person of such immature years as to be incapable of exercising the judgment, intelligence, knowledge, experience, and prudence demanded by the standard of the reasonable man applicable to adults. The rule stated in this Section is commonly applied to children of tender years. In practice, it has seldom been applied to anyone over the age of sixteen, although situations may possibly arise where the rule might be applicable to persons above that age, and no definite line can be drawn. . . .

Most of the cases which have applied the rule stated in this Section have involved the contributory negligence of children, where the reason for special protection of them is readily apparent; but the rule is equally applicable to child defendants.

b. Special standard for children. The special standard to be applied in the case of children arises out of the public interest in their welfare and protection, together with the fact that there is a wide basis of community experience upon which it is possible, as a practical matter, to determine what is to be expected of them.

A child of tender years is not required to conform to the standard of behavior which it is reasonable to expect of an adult. His conduct is to be judged by the standard of behavior to be expected of a child of like age, intelligence, and experience. A child may be so young as to be manifestly and utterly incapable of exercising any of those qualities of attention, perception, knowledge, experience, intelligence, and judgment which are necessary to enable him to perceive a risk and to realize its unreasonable character. On the other hand, it is obvious that a minor who has not yet attained his majority may be quite as capable as an adult of exercising such qualities. Some courts have endeavored to lay down fixed rules as to a minimum age below which the child is incapable of being negligent, and a maximum age above which he is to be treated like an adult. Usually these rules have been derived from the old rules of the criminal law, by which a child under the age of seven was considered incapable of crime, and one over fourteen was considered to be as capable as an adult. The prevailing view is that in tort cases no such arbitrary limits can be fixed. Undoubtedly there is a minimum age, probably somewhere in the vicinity of four years, below which negligence can never be found; but with the great variation in the capacities of children and the situations which may arise, it cannot be fixed definitely for all cases.

Between the two extremes there are children whose capacities are infinitely various. The standard of conduct required of the child is that which it is reasonable to expect of children of like age, intelligence, and experience. "Intelligence" includes other mental capacities, but does not include judgment, which is an exercise of capacity rather than the capacity itself. The fact that the child is mentally retarded, or that he is unusually bright for his years, is to be taken into account; but once such account is taken, the child is still required to exercise the judgment of a reasonable person of that intelligence. Likewise to be taken into account are the circumstances under which the child has lived, and his experience in encountering particular hazards, or the education he has received concerning them. If the child is of sufficient age, intelligence, and experience to understand the risks of a given situation, he is required to exercise such prudence in protecting himself, and such caution for the safety of others, as is common to children similarly qualified.

It is impossible to lay down definite rules as to whether any child, or any class of children, should be able to appreciate and cope with the dangers of many situations. A child of ten may in one situation have sufficient capacity to appreciate the risk involved in his conduct, and to realize its unreasonable character, but in another situation he may lack the necessary mental capacity or experience to do so; and in the case of another child of ten of different mental capacity or experience a different conclusion may be reached in the same situation.

  c. Child engaging in adult activity. An exception to the rule stated in this Section may arise where the child engages in an activity which is normally undertaken only by adults, and for which adult qualifications are required. As in the case of one entering upon a professional activity which requires special skill (see § 299A), he may be held to the standard of adult skill, knowledge, and competence, and no allowance may be made for his immaturity. Thus, for example, if a boy of fourteen were to attempt to fly an airplane, his age and inexperience would not excuse him from liability for flying it in a negligent manner. The same may be true where the child drives an automobile. In this connection licensing statutes, and the examinations given to drivers, may be important in determining the qualifications required; but even if the child succeeds in obtaining a license he may thereafter be required to meet the standard established primarily for adults.

NOTES

(1) It should be noted that although Louisiana imposes liability upon parents for the torts even of those children incapable of discerning the consequences of their acts (see Note (2), supra at 11), it nevertheless follows the rule that certain minor children are incapable of contributory negligence. See Turner v. Bucher, 308 So.2d 270, 277 (La.1975).

What conceivable policy basis is there for placing different weights on the factors of age and/or individual development of children according to whether they are being sued in negligence or for an intentional tort, or whether their contributory negligence is being raised as a defense in an action by a minor plaintiff?

(2) The role of age and maturity as mitigating factors in a criminal prosecution involving a 16-year-old who had been tried as an adult and sentenced to death, was the subject of an interesting colloquy in the United States Supreme Court in Eddings v. Oklahoma, ___ U.S. ___, 102 S.Ct. 869, 71 L.Ed.2d 1 (1982). The case was remanded because the trial judge refused, as a matter of law, to consider various aspects of the petitioner's background such as his unhappy upbringing and emotional disturbance, holding that age could be the only relevant mitigating circumstance and that it was insufficient to outweigh the aggravating circumstances in the particular case. Speaking for the Supreme Court in ordering the remand, Justice Powell stated, at 102 S.Ct. 876–77:

> The trial judge recognized that youth must be considered a relevant mitigating factor. But youth is more than a chronological fact. It is a time and condition of life when a person may be most susceptible to influence and to psychological damage. Our history is replete with laws and judicial recognition that minors, especially in their earlier years, generally are less mature and responsible than adults. Particularly "during the formative years of childhood and adolescence, minors often lack the experience, perspective, and judgment" expected of adults. Bellotti v. Baird, 443 U.S. 622, 635 (1979).

> Even the normal 16 year old customarily lacks the maturity of an adult. In this case, Eddings was not a normal 16 year old; he had been deprived of the care, concern and paternal attention that children deserve. On the contrary, it is not disputed that he was a juvenile with serious emotional problems, and had been raised in a neglectful, sometimes even violent, family background. In addition, there was testimony that Eddings' mental and emotional development were at a level several years below his chronological age. All of this does not suggest an absence of responsibility for the crime of murder, deliberately committed in this

case. Rather, it is to say that just as the chronological age of a minor is itself a relevant mitigating factor of great weight, so must the background and mental and emotional development of a youthful defendant be duly considered in sentencing.

We are not unaware of the extent to which minors engage increasingly in violent crime. Nor do we suggest an absence of legal responsibility where crime is committed by a minor. We are concerned here only with the manner of the imposition of the ultimate penalty: the death sentence imposed for the crime of murder upon an emotionally disturbed youth with a disturbed child's immaturity.

Chief Justice Burger, in a dissenting opinion in which Justices White, Blackmun, and Rehnquist joined, expressed a different view:

To be sure, neither the Court of Criminal Appeals nor the trial court labelled Eddings' family background and personality disturbance as "mitigating factors." It is plain to me, however, that this was purely a matter of semantics associated with the rational belief that "evidence in mitigation" must rise to a certain level of persuasiveness before it can be said to constitute a "mitigating circumstance." In contrast, the Court seems to require that any potentially mitigating evidence be described as a "mitigating factor"—regardless of its weight; the insubstantiality of the evidence is simply to be a factor in the process of weighing the evidence against aggravating circumstances. Yet if this is all the Court's opinion stands for, it provides scant support for the result reached. For it is clearly the choice of the Oklahoma courts to accord relatively little weight to Eddings' family background and emotional problems as balanced against the circumstances of his crime and his potential for future dangerousness.

It can never be less than the most painful of our duties to pass on capital cases, and the more so in a case such as this one. However, there comes a time in every case when a court must "bite the bullet."

102 S.Ct. 882–83.

ANDERSON v. STREAM

Supreme Court of Minnesota, 1980.
295 N.W.2d 595.

Scott, Justice.

These two appeals raise similar issues regarding the exceptions to the abrogation of parental immunity as adopted by this court in Silesky v. Kelman, 281 Minn. 431, 161 N.W.2d 631 (1968). . . .

The operative facts of these appeals have been stipulated to by the respective parties:

Anderson v. Stream v. Anderson

Edward and Ruth Anderson are the parents of Breeanna Anderson, who was born on June 16, 1975. Defendants Edna and Martin Stream live in a house next door to the Anderson home, and the two families share a common driveway. The line dividing the two properties runs generally down the center of the driveway. There is no fence between the two houses.

On Sunday morning, May 15, 1977, Breeanna, who was approximately 23 months of age, asked her parents if she could go outside and play. Breeanna was allowed to do so, but was told to "stay in the back." While Breeanna played outdoors, Mr. Anderson read the Sunday newspaper and Mrs. Anderson did housework. About 10 or 15 minutes after she began to play, Breeanna was injured when Edna Stream backed her automobile over the child's leg. After the accident occurred, Breeanna was found sitting partially on the Streams' lawn and partially on the portion of the driveway located closest to the Stream home.

Neither Mr. nor Mrs. Anderson saw the accident. However, during the 10–15 minute period Breeanna was playing, Mrs. Anderson saw her daughter twice; once, when Breeanna was playing by the back step, and later, when she was playing in the front yard of the Anderson home. Also, the parties agree that the Andersons had observed Breeanna playing on or about the common driveway on several occasions prior to May 15, 1977.

Edward Anderson, as guardian for his minor daughter, and in an individual capacity, brought an action against the Streams for the damages which resulted from the child's injuries. The Streams later impleaded Mr. Anderson and his wife for contribution and indemnity. Thereafter, the Andersons moved for summary judgment against the Streams on the third-party complaint, claiming no common liability existed because they could not be held liable to their child. The district court granted the motion and dismissed the third-party complaint on the ground that parental immunity was applicable. . . .

Nuessle v. Nuessle

On the afternoon of October 4, 1975, Michael Nuessle, who was about 3 years old at the time, accompanied his father, James Nuessle, on an errand to a drugstore located on the northwest corner of the intersection of Victoria Street and Grand Avenue in St. Paul. Defendant entered the drugstore, and after 10 to 15 seconds noticed that his son was not with him. It is unclear whether Michael actually entered the store. After looking briefly in the store for his son, defendant, through the glass door of the store, saw Michael crossing Grand Avenue. Michael was walking alongside an adult male, whom the child may have mistaken for his father. Defendant hurried outside, and without looking for traffic and in an act which defendant described as one of "panic," yelled Michael's nickname, "Micker." The child turned around, saw his father, and took a few steps to the north, recrossing the center line of Grand Avenue, while remaining in the crosswalk. Michael was then struck by the left front part of an automobile driven by a westbound driver who did not see the boy before hitting him. The child sustained serious injuries, including damage to his brain stem.

This action was commenced to recover damages against James Nuessle for Michael's injuries. Defendant subsequently moved for summary judgment on the ground that in this case the parental immunity doctrine operated to bar his son's claim. The trial court agreed, ruling that the first exception to the abolishment of parental immunity was applicable. . . .

The parties raise a number of issues in these appeals, including: whether the parents' conduct constitutes an "affirmative act of negligence" as recognized by this court in Romanik v. Toro Co., 277 N.W.2d 515 (Minn.1979); whether the parents' alleged wrongdoing involves parental supervision; whether parental supervision qualifies as an exercise of "parental authority" under the first *Silesky* exception, and, if so, whether the conduct in question is "reasonable" within the meaning of *Silesky*; and, solely in regard to the Anderson appeal, whether the parents' alleged negligent act involves an exercise of "parental discretion with respect to the provision . . . of housing" as contemplated by the second *Silesky* exception, and, if so, whether that exercise of parental discretion is "ordinary." An additional issue presented, and the one we find decisive in these cases, is whether the *Silesky* exceptions to the abrogation of parental immunity should be retained. After a careful and painstaking examination of this difficult and important question, we conclude, for the reasons discussed herein, that the exceptions should no longer be followed in this state.

The *Silesky* decision, rendered in 1968, abrogated the long-standing doctrine of parental immunity subject to the following exceptions: "(1) where the alleged negligent act involves an exercise of *reasonable parental authority* over the child; and (2) where the alleged negligent act involves an exercise of *ordinary parental discretion* with respect to the provision of food, clothing, housing, medical and dental services, and other care . . . ." 281 Minn. 442, 161 N.W.2d 638 (emphasis added). These exceptions were expressly adopted from the Wisconsin Supreme Court's decision in Goller v. White, 20 Wis.2d 404, 122 N.W.2d 193 (1963). The language used in *Silesky* is identical to that set out in *Goller* except for the addition by this court of the term "reasonable" to modify the phrase "parental authority," in the first exception.

While the *Silesky* court was well-intentioned in continuing the immunity doctrine in regard to certain parental conduct, application of the exceptions has proven to be very difficult because their precise scope is by no means clear. . . . The prospect of applying these vaguely worded, highly subjective standards to the ever-increasing number of parent-child liability cases coming before this court is reason to reflect upon the degree of difficulty in meaningful interpretation of the exceptions and alternative means of providing parents with some leeway in exercising their parental authority and discretion. We believe that since the problems inherent in construing the *Silesky* exceptions present a real danger of arbitrary line-drawing and in light of the fact that instructing the jury on a "reasonable parent" standard adequately protects functions which are parental in nature, the continued existence of the *Silesky* exceptions cannot be justified.

. . .

Difficulty in application would not, in and of itself, cause us to cast aside the *Silesky* exceptions. The determinative consideration upon which we rest our decision is that the areas of parental authority and discretion, for which the *Silesky* exceptions were designed to provide safeguards, can be effectively protected by use of a "reasonable parent" standard, as adopted by the court in Gibson v. Gibson, 3 Cal.3d 914, 92 Cal.Rptr. 288, 479 P.2d 648 (1971). In that case, the California Supreme Court completely abolished the doctrine of parental immunity. While recognizing that "traditional concepts of negligence cannot be blindly applied to" acts involving parental authority and discretion, the court refused to adopt the *Goller* exceptions by reasoning, in part, that "[t]he *Goller* view will inevitably result in the drawing of arbitrary distinctions about when particular parental conduct falls within or without the immunity guidelines." 3 Cal.3d 921, 92 Cal.Rptr. 293, 479 P.2d 653. Instead, the *Gibson* opinion held that the better approach is to have the jury take into consideration the parental function when determining whether the parent acted negligently. As stated by the *Gibson* court:

> The standard to be applied is the traditional one of reasonableness, but viewed in light of the parental role. Thus, we think the proper test of a parent's conduct is this: What would an ordinarily reasonable and prudent *parent* have done in similar circumstances?

3 Cal.3d 921, 92 Cal.Rptr. 293, 479 P.2d 653 (emphasis in original).

. . . [O]ur preference for the *Gibson* approach recognizes the practical advantages offered by utilization of a "reasonable parent" standard. It attains the *Silesky* goal of according parents some flexibility in their exercise of parental functions, but the interpretive pitfalls associated with the *Silesky* exceptions are avoided. In reaching this conclusion, we reject the contention that juries are incapable of rationally and equitably deciding whether a parent has acted negligently in exercising his parental control and discretion. Our system of justice places great faith in juries, and we see no compelling reason to distrust their effectiveness in the parent-child context. Nor do the arguments relating to family discord and collusion require a different result than that reached herein. These claims, which were found to be unpersuasive in the initial decision abrogating intrafamilial immunity, see Balts v. Balts, 273 Minn. 419, 142 N.W.2d 66 (1966) [4] (involving a child's liability to his parents), are no more convincing today.

It should also be observed that our decision to abolish the *Silesky* exceptions in favor of a "reasonable parent" standard is supported by basic principles of public policy.   A fundamental concept of our legal system and a right guaranteed by our state constitution, is that a remedy be afforded to those who have been injured due to the conduct of another.   Related thereto is the equitable doctrine of contribution, which requires that those who contribute to an injury bear liability in direct proportion to their relative culpability.   See, e.g., Tolbert v. Gerber Industries, 255 N.W.2d 362 (Minn.1977).   These considerations are promoted by today's holding.

Finally, the prevalence of liability insurance is a pertinent and important factor in subjecting parents to suit by their children.   After all, our paramount objective is to compensate the child for his or her injuries, and the widespread existence of homeowner's and renter's liability insurance will help effectuate this goal.   To deny the injured child this source of funds on the ground that prosecution of the claim would in some way disrupt the family unit is an anomaly this court will not tolerate.   Similar sentiments were expressed in the *Balts*, supra, opinion: "[W]here a child is protected by liability insurance there is more likelihood of friction, resentment, and discord by a parent's failure to assert a claim than by instituting suit."   273 Minn. 430, 142 N.W.2d 73.

In summary, by this decision we totally abolish the doctrine of parental immunity [9] and consequently overrule *Silesky* to the extent it retained parental immunity in the form of the aforementioned exceptions.   In so doing, we adopt the approach of the California Supreme Court in *Gibson*, supra, of charging the jury on a "reasonable parent" standard.

Reversed and remanded for trial.

---

4. In regard to the family disruption contention, the *Balts* decision reasoned that:

> The argument that litigation by a parent against a child promotes discord is difficult to follow. Where a wrong has been committed of a character sufficiently aggravated to justify recovery were the parties strangers, the harm has been done. We believe the prospect of reconciliation is enhanced as much by equitable reparation as by denying relief altogether, particularly where the defendant is insured.

273 Minn. 429, 142 N.W.2d 73; see, also, discussion of liability insurance, text, infra. With respect to collusion, the *Balts* court stated that a jury is capable of seeing through "colored testimony" and consequently our "judicial system is adequate to accommodate itself to threats of collusion . . . ." 273 Minn. 431, 142 N.W.2d 73.

9. We note that our complete abrogation of parental immunity will not subject parents to suit for negligent child rearing. Such claims of improper parenting are not actionable on public policy grounds. See, e.g., Burnette v. Wahl, 284 Or. 705, 588 P.2d 1105 (1978).

ROGOSHESKE, JUSTICE (dissenting).

I disagree with the majority's complete abrogation of parent-child tort immunity in negligence cases. I am not persuaded that the parent-child relationship, long preserved from legal interference on public policy grounds, has so declined in importance that considerations of insurance and simplified judicial administration under a jury standard warrant application of general tort principles to family interactions. In my view, the *Silesky* exceptions to abrogation of parental immunity should be retained and, on these facts, the first exception should be applied to immunize negligent parental supervision.

. . .

The parent-child relationship is legally unique in at least two principal respects. First, a parent is required to provide his child with such necessaries as food, clothing and shelter. Second, a parent has the authority to impose the supervision, discipline and control of his child that is essential to his exercise of the socially conferred responsibility and privilege of training the child. The *Silesky* exceptions, which embrace these two special aspects of the parent-child relationship, encourage performance of parental obligations by preserving the integrity of family decisionmaking and fostering a family atmosphere of respect and trust. The exceptions implicitly acknowledge that the varied economic, educational, cultural, religious and ethnic backgrounds of parents, and the individual personalities and development paces of children result in such a multitude of permutations of parent-child relationships that no objective standard of proper child rearing is possible. While the exceptions recognize that discharge of parental functions depends on natural instinct, love and morality rather than legal sanctions, they do not assume too much by permitting parents to act negligently toward their children with impunity. Each exception contains language of limitation, i.e., the exercise of parental authority must be "reasonable," the exercise of parental discretion "ordinary." Thus I remain convinced that the parent-child relationship is a special one which the law ought to protect so long as the protection is of conduct tending to fulfill the duties and objectives of the relationship.

In my view, the *Silesky* exceptions possess major advantages over the "reasonable parent" approach. First, the objective standard encourages parents to disparage the favored American principle of freedom of choice in family matters [3] by holding out the possibility of an insurance recovery if a parent is willing to expose his conduct and judgment to public scrutiny. Second, jury verdicts based on a reasonable parent standard in this value-laden area do not inspire public confidence, since they would necessarily substitute parental judgments based upon the individual juror's views of proper or ideal child-

---

3. See, e.g., Wisconsin v. Yoder, 406 U.S. 205, 92 S.Ct. 1526, 32 L.Ed.2d 15 (1972); Pierce v. Society of Sisters, 268 U.S. 510, 45 S.Ct. 571, 69 L.Ed. 1070 (1925).

rearing practices. The tendency toward arbitrary and intrusive standards of good parenting, which stems from the fact that most jurors have strong views in this area due to their personal experiences as parents and children, cannot be alleviated by precise instructions. The reasonable parent standard thus invites a recovery-oriented parent to gamble that a jury will find him negligent. Moreover, since the jury must consider the family context and the parent is the best, and perhaps only, witness capable of expressing the personal, cultural and socio-economic principles by which he raises his children, the danger of collusion is significant. These are not the types of claims our adversary system of factfinding is equipped to impartially resolve, and the parent's incentive for an opportunity to influence the result is so great as to further undermine the process.

Moreover, abolition of immunity is not restricted to parents who voluntarily put their conduct in issue. An estranged or divorced parent may sue on the child's behalf, thereby compelling the other parent to have his actions publicly aired and judged, adding to the acrimony normally incident to the breakup of the family unit. Such suits could be used as tools to manipulate the child's affections and to destroy loyalty to the sued parent. Also, parents who value family privacy may decline to sue negligent third parties because our third-party procedural rules invite, if not require, their being impleaded on claims that they negligently supervised their child. To the extent that parents cannot control when they will be sued, the reasonable parent standard discourages novel child-rearing practices. In addition, it creates potential for judgments discriminating against parents whose conduct does not conform to prevailing community standards.

. . .

. . . It is incontrovertible that the *Silesky* exceptions are in some respects difficult to apply. I believe, however, that the limited protection afforded the family relationship by the exceptions has social value. By abolishing the exceptions we would make available monetary recovery to injured children; by retaining them we foster a family atmosphere in which emotional and psychological reparation can be made. At the very least, so long as the parent alone rather than the parent and his insurer is named the defendant, there still exist, in my opinion, multiple valid reasons to retain the exceptions.*

[Chief Justice Sheran and Justices Otis and Peterson joined in agreement with Justice Rogosheske's dissent.]

NOTE

In Gibson v. Gibson, 3 Cal.3d 914, 92 Cal.Rptr. 288, 479 P.2d 648 (1971), the guide for the majority in *Anderson*, the California Supreme Court explained that the parental immunity doctrine is "an invention of the American

* Ed.—Earlier in the opinion it was pointed out that in Minnesota the jury is not informed that an insurance company is the real party in interest when a child sues his or her parent.

courts" that is regarded as dating from Hewlett v. George, 68 Miss. 703, 9 So. 885 (1891), in which Mississippi's Supreme Court barred a minor daughter from suing her mother for false imprisonment based on wrongfully committing her to an insane asylum. The doctrine has undergone considerable erosion in the courts during recent years and is now disappearing almost completely in some jurisdictions. This is likely to be of substantial importance in view of the increasing significance that tort actions generally are assuming as vehicles for the protection or vindication of minors' rights. Illustrations of contemporary uses and attempted or suggested uses of a tort action in this regard will be examined subsequently at a number of points in the book; they will deal with matters ranging from parental abandonment (p. 713, infra) and educational malpractice (p. 114, infra) to excessive or unjustified corporal punishment (p. 140, infra).

C. STATE CONTROL OF CHILD EMPLOYMENT

VINCENT v. RIGGI & SONS, INC.

Court of Appeals of New York, 1972.
30 N.Y.2d 406, 334 N.Y.S.2d 380, 285 N.E.2d 689.

BREITEL, JUDGE.

In an action for personal injuries, plaintiff appeals. The injuries occurred when a 13-year-old boy, hired by a building contractor to mow a lawn of a new house for sale, used his father's power lawnmower and accidentally amputated three toes. . . .

On May 25, 1963 Jerry Riggi, defendant building contractor's president, asked Howard Vincent, the injured boy, and another taller boy if they wanted to make some money. When they indicated they were "happy" about the opportunity, Mr. Riggi told them, "If you want to cut the lawn go right ahead." Mr. Riggi pointed out the lawn of a newly-constructed house that had not yet been sold. There was no discussion, however, as to how or when the job was to be done or as to the rate of pay.

Mr. Riggi and his firm had built all the houses in the area, over 200 in number. The mowing of this one lawn, however, was the only task Howard did for Mr. Riggi.

A few days after speaking to Mr. Riggi, Howard borrowed his father's rotary power lawnmower, which he had used on other occasions, and began to mow the lawn. The lawn sloped gently towards the street. One time when he reached the street and started to pull the lawnmower back away from the curb, his foot slipped under the mower amputating three toes.

. . .

The case was submitted to the jury, with exception, on a common-law negligence theory. Over plaintiffs' objections, moreover, the court refused to charge the provisions of section 130 of the Labor Law.

The jury returned a verdict for defendant. In response to special interrogatories submitted by the court, the jury found defendant free from negligence and Howard guilty of contributory negligence. The jury also found that Howard was an independent contractor and not an employee.

Plaintiff contends that the employment of Howard violated section 130 and that the jury should have been charged that the violation creates "absolute" liability without regard to negligence or contributory negligence.

At the time of the accident section 130 of the Labor Law provided: "Employment of minors under fourteen years of age. 1. No minor under fourteen years of age shall be employed in or in connection with any trade, business, or service, except as otherwise provided in this section. 2. Exceptions: Nothing in this section shall be construed to prohibit the employment of: a. A minor under fourteen years of age as a child performer in compliance with sections four hundred eighty-five and four hundred eighty-five-a of the penal law, and section thirty-two hundred sixteen-a of the education law. b. A boy twelve or thirteen years of age as a newspaper carrier boy in compliance with section thirty-two hundred nineteen-a of the education law. c. A minor twelve or thirteen years of age by his parents or guardians, either on the home farm or at other outdoor work not connected with or for any trade, business, or service, when attendance upon instruction is not required by the education law. d. A minor over twelve years of age who presents a farm work permit, in assisting in the hand work harvest of berries, fruits and vegetables, for a period of four hours in any work day between the hours of nine o'clock in the forenoon and four o'clock in the afternoon and at times when school is not in session and the minor is accompanied by a parent or has presented the written consent of a parent or party with whom he resides to the employer." "Employed" is elsewhere defined to include those "permitted or suffered to work" (Labor Law, § 2, subd. 7). The language has been construed to include independent contractors. . . .

The phrase "employed in or in connection with any trade, business, or service" includes the hiring by a building contractor of a boy to mow a lawn of a house for sale. . . .

The casual and even trivial nature of the employment makes no difference. In Warney v. Board of Educ., 290 N.Y. 329, 49 N.E.2d 466, the court held the prohibition applicable to the employment of a 12-year-old girl in a school lunchroom. Her tasks included shelving dishes in exchange for a 15-cent lunch each day. The school lunch program was required to be self-supporting. The court found the cafeteria was a " 'service' of some kind", and that the self-supporting requirement made it commercial, bringing it within the statutory prohibition.

Although Ludwig v. Lowe (29 A.D.2d 267, 287 N.Y.S.2d 202, affd. 25 N.Y.2d 853, 303 N.Y.S.2d 871, 250 N.E.2d 866) distinguished the rule in the *Warney* case it in effect emphasizes the applicability of the rule to the facts in this case. In *Ludwig* the prohibition was held not to apply where a child aided his half-brother in constructing a house for himself. The court stated that the "child labor legislation encompasses only those activities incidental to a business or commercial establishment and not those carried on by a relative out of a sense of family loyalty" (29 A.D.2d, at p. 271, 287 N.Y.S.2d at p. 206). Applying the test in the *Ludwig* case, Howard's employment was "incidental to a business or commercial establishment". The lawn mowing job was incidental to the business of building and selling houses. Although no general practice of hiring boys to mow lawns was proved, if this employment were allowed, hiring boys might well be inexpensive enough to become a regular business practice. It is in this sense that this employment, unlike the usual employment of boys by homeowners to mow lawns and to perform other odd chores, is prohibited by the statute.

The analysis thus far is supported by the statutory scheme which reveals a detailed rational classification of child employment in the context of hazards, and, independently of hazards, limiting the commercial exploitation of children. At the same time, a purpose in protecting children from their own negligence is revealed.

The statutory scheme contains three types of provisions. Section 130, set forth above, contains the blanket prohibition against the employment of minors under 14, followed by certain limited exceptions. Sections 131 and 132 provide for the employment of minors 14 to 17 in specified occupations, some requiring work permits. For example, 14- and 15-year-olds may do yard work not involving the use of power-driven machinery (Labor Law, § 131, subd. 3, par. a, cl. [3]). Children 16 and 17 years old may do the same work, but they are permitted to use power-driven machinery ordinarily used for yard work (Labor Law, § 132, subd. 3, par. a, cl. [4]). Finally, section 133 prohibits the employment of minors under 16, 18, or 21 from being employed in certain listed occupations, for the most part quite dangerous. The specific prohibitions of section 133 overlap the broader prohibitions for younger children in sections 130, 131, and 132. Not all dangerous occupations are listed in section 133. Moreover, the statutory scheme, as indicated by the example of power-driven yard equipment reflects the premise that some tasks are more dangerous for the younger age groups.

Child labor statutes concerned with particular activities have been construed as making the employer liable, regardless of contributory negligence, thus protecting the class of children from their own negligence (Karpeles v. Heine, 227 N.Y. 74, 78-84, 124 N.E. 101, 102-104; . . .) Where the question has arisen, child labor statutes broadly prohibiting, but for stated narrow exceptions, the employment of infants under 14 years of age have also been construed as eliminating the defense of contributory negligence . . ..

Although the availability of contributory negligence has not been determined in an action based on section 130, liability, regardless of contributory negligence, was imposed under former section 70, the predecessor to section 130. . . .

It is quite true that the original child labor statutes were passed at a time when children were often employed for long hours at low wages to the detriment of their health, education, and general upbringing. Circumstances have changed. Children nowadays may be handicapped instead by the lack of opportunity for work experience at an early age. The ends sought by the statute have necessarily shifted. But one purpose remains unchanged, that of preventing the injury and maiming of young children.

As stated in *Karpeles* (227 N.Y. 74, 80, 124 N.E. 101, 103, supra) involving the employment of a minor as an elevator operator: "In the case of an infant employed in violation of the direct unqualified prohibition of the statute, public policy requires that a recovery for injuries received by such a child in the course of his unlawful employment shall not be defeated by the very negligence, lack of care and caution that the statute was designed to prevent and make impossible, by prohibiting the employment of such a child in such a capacity [citations omitted]." Since the jury was charged that contributory negligence was a defense, there must be a new trial.

The jury found that defendant was not negligent, but this finding is irrelevant. In its charge to the jury the trial court defined negligence in terms of a defective condition of the premises known to the defendant. Nothing was said about the hiring of the boy in violation of the statute. At the very least, a violation of section 130 establishes fault, however stated, whether as negligence per se, liability per se, or negligence as a matter of law.

Upon a new trial the question may arise whether the issue of the employer's knowledge of the employee's age should be submitted to the jury. The leading case, Koester v. Rochester Candy Works, 194 N.Y. 92, 87 N.E. 77, states: "[I]f the employer, in the exercise of proper vigilance and due caution, is led to believe that the employee is above the statutory age, he cannot well be charged with negligence in employing an infant, whether such belief would be available as a defense in a criminal prosecution or not. The representation of the employee as to his age, even if accompanied by a similar statement by his parents, is not conclusive on the question. No principle of estoppel is applicable to the case. The question always is whether the employer is justified in believing that the employee is of sufficient age to authorize his employment. For this purpose he may not rest alone on the representation of the plaintiff, but is required to exercise proper vigilance to discover the fact. What such vigilance would dictate differs in different cases. There can readily be imagined a case where the employee is of such mature appearance that the employer may naturally and properly accept his statement as to age. In other cases the appearance of the employee might be the exact reverse. No definite rule can be laid down to relieve the employer from liability in violating the statute. The jury must be satisfied that under the circumstances of the particular case the employer believed, and was justified in the belief, that the employee was of the prescribed age to work." (id., at pp. 95–96). The *Koester* case was explained in Matter of Sackolwitz v. Hamburg & Co., 295 N.Y. 264, 67 N.E.2d 152, to mean that the employer "could be held liable for failing to exercise due care in ascertaining the facts as to the worker's age . . . [T]here was no negligence if the employer had made proper inquiries" (id., at p. 269, 67 N.E.2d at p. 154). In each of the cases in which the issue was raised, it was argued that the defendant should be excused of liability as a matter of law for lack of knowledge of the child's age, whether because of the child's misrepresentations or other circumstances, and, in each instance, the court held the question was at least one for the jury . . .. Consequently, in this State the issue is generally one of fact for the jury.[2]

Accordingly, the order of the Appellate Division should be reversed and a new trial granted, with costs.

NOTES

(1) Child labor laws in all the states regulate aspects of youth employment ranging from hours of employment to working conditions generally. The statutes, which often differ considerably, have seen little broad, critical reappraisal in the light of modern conditions. One issue that has been debated recently is whether employers should be permitted to pay a lower minimum wage to minors, now allowed in a number of jurisdictions. For a view of the various types of contemporary legislative restrictions, see Note, Child Labor Laws—Time to Grow Up, 59 Minn.L.Rev. 574 (1975) (which includes a table of current laws); Standards Relating to Rights of Minors 87 et seq. (1980); for a historical background, see G. Abbott, The Child and the State, Vol. I., Legal Status in the Family, Apprenticeship and Child Labor (1938).

(2) For examination of a state's child labor laws from a constitutional perspective, see Prince v. Massachusetts, infra at 55.

(3) The federal Fair Labor Standards Act of 1938, 29 U.S.C.A. § 201 et seq., attempts to improve the standard of living for workers by regulating the conditions of their employment. Included in the Act are several provisions that deal specifically with child labor. These prohibit, among other things, any employer involved in interstate commerce or in the production of goods for such commerce from engaging in "oppressive child labor" practices, § 212(c), and subject any violator to threat of criminal sanction. § 215(a)(4). Oppressive child labor is defined by the Act as the employment of children under the minimum legal age for a particular type of occupation or industry. § 203(1). In general, the minimum age for employment is eigh-

---

2. Outside New York, the uniform rule appears to be that in case of violation of a child labor statute, the employer must ascertain the age of the child at his peril, diligence in questioning the child being no defense . . ..

teen years for non-agricultural occupations that the Secretary of Labor has declared to be particularly hazardous or detrimental to the health and wellbeing of minors. Hazardous occupations currently include mining; logging; slaughtering or meatpacking; brick, tile and explosives manufacturing; and those occupations involving exposure to various types of machinery or radioactive materials. See 29 C.F.R. §§ 570.51–570.68. Employment in any other occupations, including hazardous agricultural occupations, § 213(c), is generally permissible for minors who have reached the age of sixteen. Under specified conditions designed to protect their welfare, children also may be employed in some occupations at fourteen; this does not include mining or manufacturing, however.

(4) During early 1981 there was considerable public discussion of proposals to lower the federal minimum wage with regard to teenagers, possibly as a trade-off for raising it for adults. Speaking in opposition, the president of the A.F.L.–C.I.O. complained that it would foster discrimination based on age. Another union leader suggested that the proposal might be labeled the "McDonald's windfall amendment" because of the enormous savings it would effect for the fast-food chain, a large employer of teenagers. The proposal was not adopted by the Congress. See N.Y. Times, Mar. 26, 1981, at Sec. II, p.15, col. 5.

D. GRATUITOUS TRANSFERS

DEANE v. LITTLEFIELD

Supreme Judicial Court of Massachusetts, 1822.
18 Mass. (1 Pick.) 239.

PARKER, C.J. . . .

That an infant of fourteen years and upwards, is capable of disposing of his personal estate by will, seems to be a well settled doctrine at common law. Being then of legal discretion so as to be liable to punishment for crimes, and according to our statute having a right to choose his own guardian over his person and property, he is also of discretion in point of law to dispose of by will his personal estate. Our statute which requires the testator to be twenty-one years and upwards relates only to the devising of lands, tenements and hereditaments, and the common law is left in full force in relation to personal estate, except when both real and personal shall be disposed of in one will which is not properly attested and subscribed to pass the real estate. If there should be objections on the ground of want of discretion in point of fact, which might appear from the disposition actually made, as well as from other circumstances, the court of probate will exercise its discretion in approving or rejecting the will. In the case before us the objection rests altogether on the want of age, and we are to presume there was no evidence of want of discretion in fact; certainly such defect cannot be inferred from the gift to the minor's mother of all his property, it not appearing that there was enough to make a division of it among brothers and sisters. The cases and authorities cited by the counsel for the appellant fully support the doctrine we contend for; and not a single decision or dictum to the contrary has been produced by the counsel for the appellees. It is only said that it is not according to the usage of the country to support wills so made. No doubt the instances are rare of wills made by minors, because it rarely happens that they have property to dispose of, and when they have, they are generally willing that the wise disposal of the law should have its course; but a common law right cannot be taken away from one individual, merely because others have not chosen to exercise it. Neither the legislature of the colony, province or commonwealth have seen fit to abolish this right, and certainly a court of law cannot do it. Although cases may arise which would seem to require that the law should be altered, yet guarded as the privilege is by the right to inquire into the *actual discretion* of the testator, it is questionable whether any legislative interference is necessary.

The right of a minor to give his property to a mother in straitened circumstances, or to sisters unprovided for, instead of allowing it to be divided among brothers who may have the means of subsistence without his aid, is a valuable right in minors, which, when exercised discreetly, ought not to be complained of; and especially as his real estate, if he have any, cannot be diverted from the channels which the law has established.

The decree of the judge of probate was reversed, and the will allowed and proved so far as respects the *personal property only*, of which the testator died possessed.

UNIFORM PROBATE CODE, § 2–501, 8 U.L.A. 348 (1969)

Any person 18 or more years of age who is of sound mind may make a will.

INHERITANCE RIGHTS OF CHILDREN

Although the American system of inheritance presumes freedom of testation, states bar decedents from disinheriting surviving spouses. Community property, elective or forced share schemes and the common law doctrine of dower guarantee a share of the decedent's estate to his, or perhaps his or her, surviving spouse.[1]

Except in Louisiana there is no similar blanket protection against disinheritance of children.[2] There are three kinds of limited protections that apply directly to children: the protections for pretermitted

1. Common law dower is sexist and runs only to the benefit of surviving wives. Community property and elective shares are sex neutral and protect surviving spouses of either sex.

2. Louisiana, a civil law state, has adopted the French concept of legitime which limits the decedent's power to exclude children. The testator may dispose of only one-third of his estate to others if

children, afterborn child statutes, and statutes in some states limiting the amount of the parent's estate that may be left to charity when there are surviving children.

Statutory protections for pretermitted and afterborn children apply only when the testator fails to mention the child in the will. Typical is California Probate Code § 90:

> When a testator omits to provide in his will for any of his children, or for the issue of any deceased child, whether born before or after the making of the will or before or after the death of the testator, and such child or issue are unprovided for by any settlement, and have not had an equal proportion of the testator's property bestowed on them by way of advancement, unless it appears from the will that such omission was intentional, such child or such issue succeeds to the same share in the estate of the testator as if he had died intestate.

How may the executor show "such omission was intentional?" May evidence extrinsic of the language of the will be used to show the decedent knew of his children and meant to leave them out? In almost all states children are aided by a long standing presumption that omission of the child was by accident or mistake.[3]

The Uniform Probate Code protects only children born after or adopted after the execution of the will and those children omitted in a mistaken belief that they were dead. The section will not apply if it appears from the will that the omission was intentional or that substantially all the estate was left to a surviving spouse when other children of the marriage were living or the omitted child has received outside the will transfers intended by the decedent to be in lieu of a will provision.[4]

If a testator wants to avoid his children taking from the estate, all he or she need do is mention them and explicitly disinherit them. Do either the afterborn child or pretermitted heir provisions offer any real protections for children? Do you think most unmentioned children are forgotten? How will these statutes really work in the administration of estates?[5] Don't we usually include the names of the people we want to take legacies in wills, not the names of those to be excluded?[6]

Some states such as New York restrict the size of charitable gifts when there are surviving children. Section 5–3.3 of New York's Estates, Powers and Trusts Law limits a charitable disposition to one-

---

he leaves three or more children, one-half if he leaves two children and two-thirds if he is survived by a single child. The testator cannot bar his children except for just cause recognized in the Civil Code and these reasons must be set out explicitly in his will. See La.Civil Code art. 1493.

3. See e.g., Thomas v. Black, 113 Mo. 66, 20 S.W. 657 (1892) and Draper v.

Draper, 267 Mass. 528, 166 N.E. 874 (1929).

4. Uniform Probate Code, § 2–302.

5. See Goff v. Goff, 352 Mo. 809, 179 S.W.2d 707 (1944).

6. See Rees, American Wills Statutes, 46 Va.L.Rev. 856, 892–94 (1960).

half of the testator's estate if he is survived by children. Perhaps the most publicized recent use of this provision was in the estate of abstract expressionist painter Mark Rothko, who died in 1970 leaving two surviving children. Rothko's will made no provision for the children and left nearly his entire estate (consisting of some 798 of his paintings) to a charitable foundation. The children elected a share of the painter's estate pursuant to the New York statute.[7]

The inheritance rights of adopted children have undergone significant change. Historically adopted children could inherit from both their natural and adoptive parents. Today, in an effort fully to integrate the adopted child in his or her adopted family, most states limit adopted children to inheritance from the adoptive family only.[8] Unless the testator expresses a contrary intention, adopted children are included in any testamentary reference to the classes "children," "issue," or "heirs." [9] Typical of the modern trend with regard to inheritance rights is § 257 of the California Probate Code:

> An adopted child shall be deemed a descendant of one who has adopted him, the same as a natural child, for all purposes of succession by, from or through the adopting parent the same as a natural parent. An adopted child does not succeed to the estate of a natural parent when the relationship between them has been severed by adoption, nor does such natural parent succeed to the estate of such adopted child, nor does such adopted child succeed to the estate of a relative of the natural parent, nor does any relative of the natural parent succeed to the estate of an adopted child.

For a discussion of the difficult constitutional questions concerning the inheritance rights of illegitimate children see p. 117 infra.

NOTE

State laws today typically provide that one over age 18, the most popular point for fixing the basic age for majority, can dispose of property by will. For older adults, including those verging on (or perhaps having reached) senility, there is a presumption in favor of testamentary capacity. See, e.g., Matter of Estate of Thomas, 290 N.W.2d 223 (N.D.1980). Also, mental capacity may be considerably diminished but still remain sufficient to make valid gratuitous transfers.

Why should the limitation on testamentary capacity be wholly age specific in today's society? Should the teen-age performer who has been specially accommodated by laws like those discussed at p. 7, supra with regard to contracting be unable to dispose of his or her fortune by testamentary gift?

7. For a detailed account of the Rothko case, see L. Seldes, The Legacy of Mark Rothko (1979), and Estate of Rothko, 98 Misc.2d 718, 414 N.Y.S.2d 444 (Sur.1979).

8. See, e.g., Alaska Stat. § 20.15.130 (1975) (unless decree specifically provides for continuance of inheritance rights); Mass.Gen.Laws Ann. ch. 210, § 7 (West 1977); N.Y.Dom.Rel.Law § 117 (McKinney 1977); Ohio Rev.Code Ann. § 3107.15 (1976); Wisc.Stat.Ann. § 851.51 (1977).

9. See e.g., N.Y.E.P.T.L.Law § 2–1.3.

Could there be some flexible test for testamentary capacity, just as we have developed some "floating standards" in the context of contributory negligence, as noted at p. 15, supra?

E. THE SLOWLY TOLLING STATUTES
OF LIMITATION

CODE OF VIRGINIA (1950, as amended)

§ 8.01–229

A. *Disabilities which toll the statute of limitations.*—Except as otherwise specifically provided in . . . other provisions of this Code,

1. If a person entitled to bring any action is at the time the cause of action accrues an infant . . ., such person may bring it within the prescribed limitation period after such disability is removed; or

2. After a cause of action accrues,

a. If an infant becomes entitled to bring such action, the time during which he is within the age of minority shall not be counted as any part of the period during which the action must be brought. . . .

NOTES

(1) Even with the widespread lowering of majority age to 18, the potential for lengthy postponement of a minor's action remains high under a statute like Virginia's, which is by no means atypical. Recently there has been specific legislative focus on the statute of limitations in the context of minors' actions for medical malpractice. Ohio, for example, now provides that in medical malpractice cases the actions of minors who are 10 years of age or older will be governed by the same limitation period applicable to adults, notwithstanding the provision for suspension of the running of the limitation period until majority in other types of actions. A minor less than age 10 has until age 14 to bring such a suit. Ohio Rev.Code Ann. § 2305.11(B) (Supp. 1981); Vance v. St. Vincent Hospital and Medical Center, 64 Ohio St.2d 36, 414 N.E.2d 406 (1980). Similarly, Texas Rev.Civ.Stat.Ann. Art. 45901i, § 10.01 (Supp.1982) provides:

> Notwithstanding any other law, no health care liability claim may be commenced unless the action is filed within two years from the occurrence of the breach or tort or from the date of the medical or health care treatment that is the subject of the claim or the hospitalization for which the claim is made is completed; provided that, minors under the age of 12 years shall have until their 14th birthday in which to file, or have filed on their behalf, the claim. Except as herein provided, this subchapter applies to all persons regardless of minority or other legal disability.

Is there good reason why there should be a shorter limitation period for medical malpractice than for other actions by minors?

Would it be inappropriate to shorten the statute of limitations generally and simply put the duty of commencing timely action on the parent or guardian of a child? In one sense that might lengthen the period in which a child could recover, at least against the parent, in the event that parental immunity has been eliminated and the parent's failure to act is deemed to constitute negligence. Would such a duty be inconsistent with the basic concept of parental rights and authority?

(2) A special, but related, problem arises concerning the settlement or compromise of tort claims or suits for injuries to minors. Many states require appointment of a guardian to execute such a release, which also must be judicially approved. The obvious concern is to prove a method of assuring that any settlement will be binding on the child rather than subject to disaffirmance after majority has been reached. Some concern has been raised as to whether such a guardianship proceeding is in fact administered in too perfunctory a fashion, to the potential detriment of the child plaintiff. Section 6.1 of the Standards Relating to Rights of Minors includes the following language:

C. Release of a tort claim by a minor should be valid, if an adult's release would be valid under the same circumstances:

1. if the minor is at least twelve years of age, if the release is approved by the minor, the minor's parent, and, if suit is pending, by the court; or

2. if the minor has not reached the age of twelve, if the release is approved by the minor's parent, and, if suit is pending, by the court.

For further discussion of this problem, see H. Clark, Law of Domestic Relations 238–240 (1968).

(3) Other statutes may specifically govern such matters as the time in which actions to determine heirship can be brought; a shorter period may be applied in such instances. An interesting statute of limitations in an otherwise modern statutory model, the Uniform Parentage Act, provides:

Section 7. An action to determine the existence of the father and child relationship as to a child who has no presumed father under Section 4 may not be brought later than [3] years after the birth of the child, or later than [3] years after the effective date of this Act, whichever is later. However, an action brought by or on behalf of a child whose paternity has not been determined is not barred until [3] years after the child reaches the age of majority. Sections 6 and 7 do not extend the time within which a right of inheritance or a right to a succession may be asserted beyond the time provided by law relating to the distribution and closing of decedents' estates or to the determination of heirship, or otherwise.

As the Comment to the statute acknowledges, although the opening sentence serves as an admonition to bring a paternity action promptly the section nevertheless provides for a period much longer than three years because the statute is in fact suspended during minority except for the actions described in the closing sentence.

In Mills v. Habluetzel, ___ U.S. ___, 102 S.Ct. 1549, 71 L.Ed.2d 770 (1982), the Supreme Court of the United States invalidated a Texas statute requiring that:

> A suit to establish the parent-child relationship between a child who is not the legitimate child of a man and the child's natural father by proof of paternity must be brought before the child is one year old, or the suit is barred.

The opinion for the Court, written by Justice Rehnquist, described the one year period as "unrealistically short". In a separate concurring opinion Justice O'Connor, joined by the Chief Justice and two other Justices, and in part by Justice Powell, explained:

> It is also significant to the result today that a paternity suit is one of the few Texas causes of action not tolled during the minority of the plaintiff. Of all the difficult proof problems that may arise in civil actions generally, paternity, an issue unique to illegitimate children, is singled out for special treatment. When this observation is coupled with the Texas legislature's efforts to deny illegitimate children any significant opportunity to prove paternity and thus obtain child support, it is fair to question whether the burden placed on illegitimates is designed to advance permissible state interests.

(4) In Bradford v. Davis, 290 Or. 855, 626 P.2d 1376 (1981), plaintiff sued the state's Children's Services Division and various of its officials, along with the director of the Department of Human Resources, to recover damages for injuries he allegedly suffered while a minor in the division's custody. The general statute of limitations for personal injuries provided an extension for filing tort actions up to a maximum of five years from a child's eighteenth birthday. The state's Tort Claims Act contained a two year limitation period and was silent about the effect of minority. The Oregon Supreme Court held that plaintiff was entitled to the extension of time based on his minority when the action ostensibly accrued. The court explained that "Actions under the Tort Claims Act are tort actions, not special statutory causes of action . . ." As to the fact that the Tort Claims Act did contain a special provision for minority in its notice requirement, the court added:

> It is consistent with the remedial policy of the Tort Claims Act to assume that the legislature meant to assure local governments of an early opportunity to investigate claims even by minors, but that thereafter the extension of time to commence an action generally provided to minors and incapacitated persons . . . would apply to the same kinds of actions when brought against a public defendant.

F.   EMANCIPATION: CLARIFYING AND
REMODELING AN OBSCURITY

ACCENT SERVICE CO., INC. v. EBSEN

Supreme Court of Nebraska, 1981.
209 Neb. 94, 306 N.W.2d 575.

VAN PELT, DISTRICT JUDGE.

This is an appeal from a $2,555.01 judgment of the District Court of Knox County, Nebraska, entered in favor of the plaintiff appellee, as assignee, against the defendant-appellant for hospital expenses incurred by defendant's son.   The District Court, in affirming the judgment of the county court, found that the evidence was insufficient to establish emancipation by the minor, and that the evidence did establish a contractual liability on the part of the defendant to pay for her son's medical services.

Appellant's first assignment of error is that the trial court erred in finding that there was insufficient evidence of a complete emancipation.   Violet Ebsen, a widow, and her 18-year-old son, Dwaine, lived together until approximately December 1976.   Dwaine then began associating and staying overnight with people his mother did not like and of whom she did not approve.   Arguments over his associations and conduct took place in December of 1976 and in January of 1977.   As a result of one such argument, on February 1, 1977, Dwaine took his personal belongings and moved from his mother's home in Verdigre, Nebraska, to Orchard, Nebraska.   Both the mother and son agreed that he should move out and support himself.   After moving out, Dwaine received no further support from his mother.   On February 24, 1977, while still living in Orchard, Dwaine was shot and taken to a hospital in Norfolk, Nebraska.   There, the hospital expenses were incurred that are the subject of this litigation.   After being hospitalized for 2 weeks, Dwaine returned to his mother's home for 3 days and then left.   He has been self-supporting and has not returned to his mother's home since leaving.

Whether Dwaine Ebsen was emancipated at the time of his hospitalization is relevant, since the complete emancipation of a child relieves the parent from liability to those who furnish necessaries of life to that child.   Brosius v. Barker, 154 Mo.App. 657, 136 S.W. 18 (1911); Poudre Valley Hospital District v. Heckart, 491 P.2d 984 (Colo.App.1971).

The emancipation of a child by a parent may be proved by circumstantial evidence or by an express agreement, or implied from the conduct of the parties.   Although this court has not had an occasion to discuss the factors to be considered in determining whether a minor has become emancipated, they were recently analyzed in Annot., 98 A.L.R. 3rd 334, 335–36 (1980): "In general, even in the absence of statute, parents are under a legal as well as a moral obligation to support, maintain, and care for their children, the basis of such a duty resting not only upon the fact of the parent-child relationship, but also upon the interest of the state as parens patriae of children and of the community at large in preventing them from becoming a public burden. However, various voluntary acts of a child, such as marriage or enlistment in military service, have been held to terminate the parent's obligation of support, the issue generally being considered by the courts in terms of whether an emancipation of the child has been effectuated. In those cases involving the issue of whether a parent is obligated to support an unmarried minor child who has voluntarily left home without the consent of the parent, the courts, in actions to compel support from the parent, have uniformly held that such conduct on the part of the child terminated the support obligation.

"Correlative to a parent's obligation of support and maintenance of a minor child is the liability of a parent to others who have performed the support obligation for the parent by furnishing the child with necessaries. Generally, a parent's liability for necessaries furnished a minor child will depend on a variety of circumstances, but it appears clear that no liability exists where the parent has been ready and willing at all times to supply necessaries himself and to otherwise fulfill his obligation to support the child. Thus, it has been held that a parent was not liable to a third person furnishing necessaries to an unmarried minor child while voluntarily living apart from the parent with consent, the courts concluding that in such a case the parent was under no obligation to support the child and that the child carried with him no authority to bind the parent for the necessaries furnished. However, a parent has been held liable for necessaries furnished his unmarried minor child by a third person while the child was living apart from the parent without consent, where there was evidence that the parent authorized the sale of the goods to the child."

Where a child departed from the family home and the parent consented to the departure, the child was found to be emancipated in Holland v. Hartley, 171 N.C. 376, 88 S.E. 507 (1916); in Poudre Valley Hospital District v. Heckart, supra; and in Timmerman v. Brown, 268 S.C. 303, 233 S.E.2d 106 (1977).

In the instant case, after several months of arguing and the defendant in effect telling her son to either change his behavior or move out, he left his mother's home with her consent. From that time until the hospital expense was incurred, he furnished his own support and received nothing from his mother. Under these facts, Dwaine Ebsen became emancipated, and his mother became relieved of liability to those furnishing him necessaries.

Appellant's second assignment of error is that the trial court erred in finding that there was evidence of a contractual agreement by the defendant to pay her son's hospital expenses. If such an agreement existed, defendant would be liable, regardless of her son's emancipation, under general principles of contract law.

The county court was unable to make a finding that there was or was not a contractual agreement, but entered judgment for the plaintiff on the basis that Dwaine Ebsen was not emancipated. The District Court affirmed the judgment of the county court, with the following additional finding: "3. That Defendant authorized Plaintiff's assignor to furnish medical services of an emergency nature to her minor son, Dwaine Ebsen, orally and by the execution of Exhibit '3' in writing, immediately prior to the furnishing of the first of said services."

Exhibit 3, referred to, is a consent to operation, anesthetics, and other medical services. This document contains no language of a promise, express or implied, to pay for the services. Lucille Loberg, the hospital employee who was present when the defendant signed exhibit 3, testified that normally the hospital uses another document which specifies how the bill is to be paid. However, no such document signed by the defendant was ever produced or received in evidence.

Nor does the record reveal any oral promise to pay the hospital expenses. The closest testimony to such a promise was in the county court, where the defendant, under examination by the plaintiff's attorney, stated that by signing exhibit 3 she wanted her son attended to and wanted him to stay alive. Under examination by her own attorney, she testified that at no time did she say anything to anyone at the hospital that she could or would pay the bill. Plaintiff has the burden of proving any oral or written agreement by a preponderance of the evidence. There is no such evidence in the record. . . .

Reversed and remanded with directions to dismiss.

NOTE

Common law emancipation has been described as "a legal doctrine primarily designed for parents." See Gottesfeld, The Uncertain Status of the Emancipated Minor: Why We Need A Uniform Statutory Emancipation of Minors Act (USEMA), 15 U.S.F.L.Rev. 473, 476 (1981). Emancipation in this form is said to be accomplished at least in part by some act or omission of the parent; even the widely recognized exceptions of emancipation by marriage or entry into military service may in fact be contingent on parental consent.

In some jurisdictions emancipation through this mode can be either partial or complete. Whether emancipation has been effected is a question of fact, but guidelines laid down by the courts to assist in the determination often are sparse. See, e.g., Lawson v. Brown, 349 F.Supp. 203 (W.D.Va. 1972); Brumfield v. Brumfield, 192 Va. 577, 74 S.E.2d 170 (1953).

While some contend that widespread lowering of majority age to 18 has diminished the importance of emancipation considerably, others strongly reject this argument and today there is substantial legislative sentiment for adoption of comprehensive statutes on the subject, as illustrated by the material that follows. For further discussion of the history of common law emancipation see Cady, Emancipation of Minors, 12 Conn.L.Rev. 62 (1979); H. Clark, Law of Domestic Relations 240 (1968); Standards Relating to Rights of Minors 21 (1980); and Katz, Schroeder and Sidman, Emancipating Our Children—Coming of Legal Age in America, 7 Fam.L.Q. 211 (1973).

CALIFORNIA CIVIL CODE. Emancipation of Minors Act (1978, as amended 1979)

§ 61. Legislative findings and declaration

The Legislature finds and declares that the case law of this state is unclear as to the definition and consequences of emancipation of minors; that a legislative statement is required; and that a process should be provided so that emancipated minors can obtain an official declaration of their status. It is the purpose of this part to provide a clear statement defining emancipation and its consequences and to permit an emancipated minor to obtain a court declaration of his status. This part is not intended to affect the status of minors who are now or may become emancipated under present decisional case law.

§ 62. Emancipated minor; description

Any person under the age of 18 years who comes within the following description is an emancipated minor:

(a) Who has entered into a valid marriage, whether or not such marriage was terminated by dissolution; or

(b) Who is on active duty with any of the armed forces of the United States of America; or

(c) Who has received a declaration of emancipation pursuant to Section 64.

§ 63. Over the age of majority; purposes

An emancipated minor shall be considered as being over the age of majority for the following purposes:

(a) For the purpose of consenting to medical, dental, or psychiatric care, without parental consent, knowledge, or liability.

(b) For the purpose of his capacity to enter into a binding contract.

(c) For the purpose of his capacity to sue and be sued in his own name.

(d) For the purpose of his right to support by his parents.

(e) For purposes of the rights of his parents to his earnings, and to control him.

(f) For the purpose of establishing his own residence.

(g) For the purpose of buying or selling real property.

(h) For purposes of the application of Sections 300 and 601 * of the Welfare and Institutions Code.

(i) For purposes of applying for a work permit pursuant to Section 49110 of the Education Code without the request of parents or guardian.

(j) For the purpose of ending all vicarious liability of the minor's parents or guardian for the minor's torts; provided, that nothing in this section shall affect any liability of a parent, guardian, spouse, or employer imposed by the Vehicle Code, or any vicarious liability which arises from an agency relationship.

(k) For the purpose of enrolling in any school or college.

§ 64. Declaration of emancipation; petition; contents; notice; mandate

(a) A minor may petition the superior court of the county in which he or she resides or is temporarily domiciled, for a declaration of emancipation. The petition shall be verified and shall set forth with specificity all of the following facts:

(1) That he or she is at least 14 years of age.

(2) That he or she willingly lives separate and apart from his or her parents or legal guardian with the consent or acquiescence of his or her parents or legal guardian.

(3) That he or she is managing his or her own financial affairs.

(4) That the source of his or her income is not derived from any activity declared to be a crime by the laws of the State of California or the laws of the United States.

(b) Before the petition is heard, such notice as the court deems reasonable must be given to the minor's parents, guardian, or other person entitled to the custody of the minor, or proof made to the court that their addresses are unknown, or that for other reasons such notice cannot be given. When a minor is a ward or dependent child of the court, notice shall be given to the probation department.

(c) The court shall sustain the petition if it finds that the minor is a person described by subdivision (a) and that emancipation would not be contrary to his or her best interests.

(d) If the petition is sustained, the court shall forthwith issue a declaration of emancipation, which shall be filed by the county clerk. Upon application of the emancipated minor, the Department of Motor Vehicles shall enter identifying information in its law enforcement computer network, and the fact of emancipation shall be stated on the department's identification cards issued to emancipated minors.

(e) If the petition is denied, the minor shall have a right to file a petition for a writ of mandate.

* Ed.—Welfare and Institutions Code § 300 deals with a person under age 18 who may be adjudged "a dependent child of the court". § 601 deals with habitually disobedient or truant minors.

(f) If the petition is sustained, the parents or guardian shall have a right to file a petition for a writ of mandate if they have appeared in the proceeding and opposed the granting of the petition.

(g) A declaration shall be conclusive evidence that the minor is emancipated.

§ 65. Rescission of declaration; petition; notice; findings; order; effect upon contractual and property obligations, rights and interests

(a) A minor declared emancipated under . . . Section 64 or his conservator may petition the superior court of the county in which he resides, to rescind the declaration issued under Section 64.

(b) Before the petition is heard, such notice as the court deems reasonable must be given to the minor's parents or guardian or proof made to the court that their addresses are unknown, or that for other reasons such notice cannot be given, however, no liability shall accrue to any parent or guardian not given actual notice, as a result of rescission of the declaration of emancipation, until such parent or guardian is given actual notice.

(c) The court shall sustain the petition and rescind the declaration of emancipation if it finds that the minor is indigent and has no means of support.

(d) If the petition is sustained, the court shall forthwith issue a court order rescinding the declaration of emancipation granted under Section 64, which shall be filed by the county clerk. Notice shall be sent immediately to the Department of Motor Vehicles which shall remove the information relating to emancipation in its law enforcement computer network entered pursuant to subdivision (d) of Section 64. Any identification card issued stating emancipation shall be invalidated.

(e) Rescission of the declaration of emancipation shall not alter any contractual obligations or rights or any property rights or interests which arose during the period that the declaration was in effect.

§ 66. Reliance on representation of emancipation; effect

A person who, in good faith, has examined a minor's identification card and relies upon a minor's representation that he is emancipated, shall have the same rights and obligations as if the minor were in fact emancipated at the time of the representation.

§ 67. Issuance of declaration of emancipation; effect on public social service benefits

The issuance of a declaration of emancipation shall not entitle the minor to any benefits under Division 9 (commencing with Section

10000) ** of the Welfare and Institutions Code which would not otherwise accrue to an emancipated minor.

§ 68. Liability for false or inaccurate information in Department of Motor Vehicles record system or identification cards

No public entity or employee shall be liable for any loss or injury resulting directly or indirectly from false or inaccurate information contained in the Department of Motor Vehicles records system or identification cards as provided in this part.

§ 69. Declaration of emancipation obtained by fraud or withholding material information; voidability; effect on rights and obligations; commencement of proceeding

A declaration of emancipation obtained by fraud or by the withholding of material information shall be voidable. The voiding of any such declaration pursuant to this section shall not alter any contractual obligations or rights or any property rights or interests which arose during the period that the declaration was in effect.

A proceeding under this section may be commenced by any person or by any public or private agency. Notice of the commencement of such a proceeding and of any order declaring the declaration of emancipation to be void shall be consistent with the requirements of subdivisions (b) and (d) of Section 65.

§ 70. Legislative intent; minimum expense; forms

It is the intent of the Legislature that proceedings under Sections 64 and 65 shall be as simple and inexpensive as possible, and to that end, the Judicial Council is requested to prepare and distribute to the clerks of the superior courts appropriate forms for such proceedings which are suitable for use by minors acting as their own counsel.

** Ed.—Welfare and Institutions Code Division 9 deals with public social services (including protective services) and guardianships, along with other matters.

OFFICIAL FORMS

ATTORNEY OR MINOR WITHOUT ATTORNEY (NAME AND ADDRESS):	TELEPHONE NO.:	FOR COURT USE ONLY

SUPERIOR COURT OF CALIFORNIA, COUNTY OF

IN THE MATTER OF (NAME):

Petitioner, a minor

PETITION FOR DECLARATION OF EMANCIPATION OF MINOR ☐ **CONSENT AND WAIVER OF NOTICE** ☐ **ORDER PRESCRIBING NOTICE** ☐ **DECLARATION OF EMANCIPATION**	CASE NUMBER:

1. Becoming an emancipated minor would not be contrary to my best interests and I request that the court issue a declaration of my emancipation.
2. I am a resident of or temporarily domiciled in this county and
   a. I have lived in this county since (date):
   b. My current address is (specify):

3. I am at least 14 years of age and was born on (date):
4. I am willingly living separate and apart from my parents or legal guardian, with their consent or acquiescence, and have been living apart from them since (date):
5. I am managing my own financial affairs.
6. No part of my income comes from any activity declared to be a crime by the laws of the State of California or of the United States.
7. Persons entitled to notice of this proceeding are
   a. My father (name):
      (1) ☐ He has consented to a declaration of my emancipation and waived notice of hearing.
      (2) ☐ Notice cannot be given because (give reason):
      (3) ☐ His address is:

   b. My mother (name):
      (1) ☐ She has consented to a declaration of my emancipation and waived notice of hearing.
      (2) ☐ Notice cannot be given because (give reason):
      (3) ☐ Her address is:

   c. ☐ My legal guardian (name):
      (1) ☐ My legal guardian has consented to a declaration of my emancipation and waived notice of hearing.
      (2) ☐ Notice cannot be given because (give reason):
      (3) ☐ Address:

   d. ☐ Other person entitled to my legal custody (name):
      (1) ☐ This person has consented to a declaration of my emancipation and waived notice of hearing.
      (2) ☐ Notice cannot be given because (give reason):
      (3) ☐ Address:

   e. ☐ I am a ward or dependent child of the Juvenile Court of (county):

I declare under penalty of perjury that the foregoing is true and correct and that this declaration is executed on (date):. . . . . at (place): . . . . , California.

_____
(Continued on reverse)   (Signature of petitioner)

Form Approved by the
Judicial Council of California
Effective July 1, 1980

**PETITION FOR DECLARATION OF EMANCIPATION OF MINOR,
CONSENT AND WAIVER OF NOTICE, ORDER PRESCRIBING NOTICE
AND DECLARATION OF EMANCIPATION**

Civil Code
section 64
[C1773]

NAME OF MINOR	CASE NUMBER:

CONSENT AND WAIVER OF NOTICE

8. The undersigned, who are entitled to notice of hearing, give up the right to notice and give their consent to a declaration of emancipation without a hearing.
   a. ☐ Father . . . . Signature: _____ Dated: . . . . . .
      Telephone number:
   b. ☐ Mother . . . . Signature: _____ Dated: . . . . . .
      Telephone number:
   c. ☐ Legal guardian . . . . . . Signature: _____ Dated: . . . . . .
      Telephone number:
   d. ☐ Other person with legal custody . Signature: _____ Dated: . . . . . .
      Telephone number:
   e. ☐ Probation Officer-Social Worker . Signature: _____ Dated: . . . . . .
      Telephone number:

ORDER PRESCRIBING NOTICE

9. The court finds that
   a. ☐ All persons entitled to notice of this proceeding have consented to a declaration of emancipation and waived notice of a hearing.
   b. ☐ The addresses of the following persons entitled to notice, as named in item 7, are unknown
      (1) ☐ Father   (3) ☐ Legal guardian
      (2) ☐ Mother   (4) ☐ Other person with legal custody
   c. ☐ Notice cannot be given to the following persons entitled to notice, as set forth in item 7
      (1) ☐ Father   (3) ☐ Legal guardian
      (2) ☐ Mother   (4) ☐ Other person with legal custody
   d. ☐ Other (specify):
10. **IT IS ORDERED** that notice of this proceeding
   a. ☐ Is not required and a declaration of emancipation may issue forthwith.
   b. ☐ Is required. A copy of this petition shall be served personally or by mail on persons set forth in item 7 as follows:
      (1) ☐ Father   (4) ☐ Other person with legal custody
      (2) ☐ Mother   (5) ☐ Juvenile Court for service on Probation Officer
      (3) ☐ Legal guardian   or Social Worker
   c. ☐ and this matter is set for hearing on (date):   at (time):   in (dept.):

Dated: . . . . _____
                                   Judge of the Superior Court

DECLARATION OF EMANCIPATION
(To be used ONLY if item 10a has been ordered by court)

11. The court finds that the minor is a person described by Civil Code section 64(a) and that
   a. All persons entitled to notice have consented to a declaration of emancipation and waived notice.
   b. Emancipation would not be contrary to the best interests of the minor.
   c. The allegations of the petition are true.
12. ☐ IT IS ORDERED that the petition is granted and the minor is declared to be emancipated.

Dated: . . . . _____
                                   Judge of the Superior Court

CLERK'S CERTIFICATION

[Seal]   I certify that the foregoing is a true and correct copy of the original on file in my office.

      Date: . . . .   Clerk, By _____
                                                        Deputy

EMANCIPATED MINOR'S APPLICATION

I apply to the California Department of Motor Vehicles for entry of identifying information in its law enforcement computer network and for inclusion of the fact of my emancipation on any identification card issued to me by the Department.

Dated: . . . . _____
                                   (Signature of emancipated minor)   [C1774]

ATTORNEY OR MINOR WITHOUT ATTORNEY (NAME AND ADDRESS):	TELEPHONE NO.:	FOR COURT USE ONLY

SUPERIOR COURT OF CALIFORNIA, COUNTY OF

IN THE MATTER OF (NAME):

Petitioner, a minor

DECLARATION OF EMANCIPATION OF MINOR AFTER HEARING	CASE NUMBER:

1. This proceeding came on for hearing as follows:

   a. Date: Time: ☐ Dept.:   ☐ Div.:   ☐ Room:

   b. Judge (name):

   c. ☐ Petitioner present in court   ☐ Attorney present in court (name):
   d. ☐ Minor's father present in court   ☐ Attorney present in court (name):
   e. ☐ Minor's mother present in court   ☐ Attorney present in court (name):
   f. ☐ Minor's legal guardian present in court ☐ Attorney present in court (name):
   g. ☐ Other person with legal custody present
      in court (name):   ☐ Attorney present in court (name):

   h. ☐ Probation Officer-Social Worker present
      in court (name):   Attorney present in court (name):

2. ☐ Evidence was presented   ☐ the parties entered into a stipulation, and the matter was submitted.

3. The court finds that
   a. ☐ Notice of hearing was given as prescribed by this court.
   b. The minor is a person described by Civil Code section 64(a) and was born on (date):
   c. Emancipation would not be contrary to the best interests of the minor.
   d. The allegations of the petition are true.
   e. Other *(specify)*:

4. IT IS ORDERED that the petition is granted and the minor is declared to be emancipated.

Dated: . . . .

_____
Judge of the Superior Court

CLERK'S CERTIFICATION

[Seal]   I certify that the foregoing is a true and correct copy of the original on file in my office.

Date: . . . .   Clerk, by _____ , Deputy

EMANCIPATED MINOR'S APPLICATION

I apply to the California Department of Motor Vehicles for entry of identifying information in its law enforcement computer network and for inclusion of the fact of my emancipation on any identification card issued to me by the Department.

Dated: . . . .

_____
(Signature of emancipated minor)

Form Approved by the   **DECLARATION OF EMANCIPATION OF MINOR**   Civil Code
Judicial Council of California   **AFTER HEARING**   section 64
Effective July 1, 1980   [C1775]

NOTES

(1) Statutes dealing with emancipation are by no means new; some even date from the beginning of this century. Described as "first generation" statutes by one commentator, they offered little in the way of satisfactory guidelines for courts to apply. Nor could the minor file his or her own petition under the typical statute. California's comprehensive law is an example of the newer, or "second generation" approach. For a listing of statutes in the two groups see Gottesfeld, The Uncertain Status of the Emancipated Minor: Why We Need A Uniform Statutory Emancipation of Minors Act (USEMA), 15 U.S.F.L.Rev. 473, 477–479 (1981).

(2) In 1979 Connecticut adopted a statute that permits a minor who has reached age sixteen to petition for emancipation. As originally enacted, this law seemed to provide a means for emancipation based on irretrievable breakdown. However the provision was changed substantially by a 1980 amendment. The relevant section of the statute before and after amendment is printed below, with additions to the text by the 1980 legislation shown by CAPITALS and deletions shown by ~~strikeouts~~.

EMANCIPATION OF MINORS. CONNECTICUT PUBLIC ACT

NO. 79–397, as amended by PUBLIC ACT NO. 80–283

. . .

Sec. 3.

If the court, after hearing, finds that: (1) The minor has entered into a valid marrriage, whether or not that marriage has been terminated by dissolution; or (2) the minor is on active duty with any of the armed forces of the United States of America; or (3) the minor willingly lives separate and apart from his parents or guardian, with or without the consent of the parents or guardian, and that the minor is managing his own financial affairs, regardless of the source of any lawful income; or (4) [~~other facts exist which demonstrate that the parent-child relationship has irretrievably broken down~~] FOR GOOD CAUSE SHOWN, IT IS IN THE BEST INTEREST OF EITHER OR BOTH PARTIES, the court [~~shall~~] MAY enter an order declaring that the minor is emancipated.

(3) The Juvenile Justice Standards Relating to Rights of Minors incorporate in § 2.1 what is described as "A new approach to emancipation." The section first states that narrowly drawn legislation obviating the need for reliance on "the vague criteria of the traditional emancipation doctrine" should include the principles that (1) a parent should not be permitted to recover wages due or paid to the child from the child's employer, and (2) tort suits between parent and child should be permitted so long as the behavior that forms the basis for the action "is not related to the exercise of family functions." It is then asserted that the legislature should enact "an emancipation doctrine of general applicability," though it should not allow emancipation "by judicial decree." Further, the doctrine should be limited explicitly to issues not addressed elsewhere in the Standards, and it should authorize a finding of emancipation where a minor child has established a residence separate from his or her family.

This somewhat confusing and questionably modern, if indeed "new", approach is discussed and criticized in Cady, Emancipation of Minors, 12 Conn. L.Rev. 62, 81–85 (1979).

(4) What would you consider to be the needs for and purposes of an emancipation statute today? Is the California statute overly broad in scope? Would it be preferable to have a series of limited functions for which application for legal authority might be requested separately?

To what extent would it be desirable to provide a mechanism by which a "divorce" between parent and child could be obtained at the instance of either of them? If such a mechanism is appropriate, what should be the criteria or "grounds" for invoking it?

In In re Welfare of Snyder, 85 Wn.2d 182, 532 P.2d 278 (1975), the Supreme Court of Washington upheld a juvenile court judge's decision granting a 16-year-old girl's request that she be declared "incorrigible" and placed in a foster home because of friction with her parents concerning matters such as dating, smoking, and participation in extracurricular activities. As the court stated: "These hostilities culminated in a total collapse of the parent-child relationship." Professor Bruce Hafen has written the following perceptive commentary:

> The *Snyder* result seems to imply that, even when a family problem does not reach the level of traditional juvenile court jurisdictional requirements, a dissatisfied child should be permitted to leave the family at her own request when her discontent is serious enough to indicate that jurisdictional levels may soon be reached and when some stress can be avoided if the court simply moves in. This theory is essentially an argument for the proposition that a child should be able to "divorce" (or at least achieve separation from) his or her parents on grounds of incompatibility.

Professor Hafen adds that resolving the effects of a collision between such significant American traditions as individualism and the family may be "one of the critical problems of our time." Hafen, Children's Liberation and the New Egalitarianism: Some Reservations About Abandoning Youth to Their "Rights", 1976 B.Y.U.L.Rev. 605, 608–9.*

(5) The special problems of termination of parental rights will be discussed at p. 851, infra.

II. CHILDREN'S RIGHTS: THE CON-
STITUTIONAL GUIDELINES

AN EQUIVOCAL LABEL

The phrase "children's rights" has received increasing use and prominence during recent years. Unfortunately this has not sharpened its definition. Some who speak of a "children's rights movement" assert that its goal should be the extension of broad freedom of personal action and decision making to children at a much lower age than this is done today; for them, the term is synonymous with "children's autonomy". Others marching under a similarly labeled banner equate children's rights with protection—one might say increased protection—from governmental intrusion in matters of parental (and thus family) decision making about children. A popular rationale for this view is that parents are presumed to act in the best interests of their children and thus if families are left to govern themselves this will accomplish the best result for minor children within them in the largest number of cases.

Another approach to defining children's rights is by formulating (and perhaps promulgating) statements of fundamental principles to be used judicially as guidelines for interpreting or applying various laws or procedures, or politically to focus legislative policy. Adopters of the term in this sense would tend to speak broadly of a child's right to health care, or to basic education, or to adequate parenting.

There are other definitions, but one can recognize from just these three approaches that there is considerable potential for conflict between different persons who describe themselves through use of the same label. One also can project that in today's climate of litigiousness and near obsessiveness about defining and vindicating rights, a number of recurring issues are likely to emerge. For example, when (if at all) should the state intervene to overrule parental decisions, or to protect children from unreasonable or undesirable parental conduct? Should children be accorded the same due process and other constitutional protections as adults in all cases? Should state laws be vulnerable to challenge because they create age categories arbitrarily in some areas under the guise of protecting children from themselves or of protecting others from children's acts? To what extent should state sponsored or regulated entities such as schools be permitted to assume a parental role in matters such as discipline or value inculcation?

One could continue to raise more, and equally serious questions, many of which by now are reaching or have reached the courts in a variety of contexts. To those who might be surprised that they were not presented to the courts with frequency much earlier, it is important to recognize that historically the federal judiciary has long followed a policy of abstention in family law matters,[1] and state courts have been reluctant to intervene in cases dealing with day-to-day operations of the family outside of divorce. Despite frequent generalizations over the past fifty years that matters of marriage and family life were subject to the protection of the fourteenth amendment, the meaningful use of constitutional jurisprudence to regulate children and families began just a decade or two ago. This trend has escalated in the past five years at the United States Supreme Court. In a series of cases which regularly cite and quote their predecessors, the Court has promulgated a body of law on children's rights. Some critics regard these cases as lacking in clarity, consistency and conceptualization; others look at them as reflecting the personal values of the judges rather than contemporary norms. That we question whether the cases are subject to reasonable division from a conceptual standpoint may seem obvious from our decision to present them chronologically, for the most part.

BIBLIOGRAPHICAL NOTE

There are today a number of significant articles on the subject of the rights of children. Among these are M. Wald, Children's Rights: A Framework for Analysis, 12 U.C.D.L.Rev. 255 (1979); P. Wald, Making Sense Out of the Rights of Youth, 4 Human Rights 13 (1974); Garvey, Child, Parent, State and the Due Process Clause: An Essay on the Supreme Court's Recent Work, 51 So.Cal.L.Rev. 769 (1978); Foster and Freed, A Bill of Rights for Children, 6 Fam.L.Q. 343 (1972); Kaufman, Protecting the Rights of Minors: On Juvenile Autonomy and the Limits of Law, 52 N.Y.U.L.Rev. 1015(1977): Hafen, Children's Liberation and the New Egalitarianism: Some Reservations About Abandoning Children to Their "Rights", 1976 B.Y.U.L.Rev. 605; Teitelbaum and Ellis, The Liberty Interest of Children: Due Process Rights and Their Application, 12 Fam.L.Q. 153 (1978); Developments in the Law— The Constitution and the Family, 93 Harv.L.Rev. 1156 (1980); Keiter, Privacy, Children, and Their Parents: Reflections On and Beyond the Supreme Court's Approach, 66 Minn.L.Rev. 459 (1982); Batey, The Rights of Adolescents, 23 Wm. & Mary L.Rev. 363 (1982).

A special two issue symposium on The Rights of Children was published by the Harvard Educational Review in Volume 43 (1973). An issue of Law and Contemporary Problems on Children and the Law, Vol. 39, No. 3 (Summer 1975), contains several especially important works, including Burt, Developing Constitutional Rights Of, In, and For Children, 39 Law & Contemp. Prob. 118 (1975); Tribe, Childhood, Suspect Classifications, and Conclusive

1. That such a belief in the desirability of abstention still is viable is reflected in the dissenting opinion of Justice Rehnquist during the 1982 term of the Supreme Court in Santosky v. Kramer, __ U.S. __, __, 102 S.Ct. 1388, 1403, 71 L.Ed.2d 599, 617 (1982):

If ever there were an area in which federal courts should heed the admoni-

tion of Justice Holmes that "a page of history is worth a volume of logic," it is in the area of domestic relations. This area has been left to the States from time immemorial, and not without good reason.

Presumptions: Three Linked Riddles, 39 Law & Contemp.Prob. 8 (1975); and Mnookin, Child-Custody Adjudication: Judicial Functions in the Face of Indeterminacy, 39 Law & Contemp.Prob. 226 (1975).

A number of books also provide helpful insights and resources in the area of children's rights. Worthy of special mention are Professor Robert Mnookin's collection of materials, Child, Family and State (1978) and Professor Laurence Houlgate's The Child and the State: A Normative Theory of Juvenile Rights (1980). The latter is the work of a philosopher who has written and worked extensively in the children's rights area.

Finally the student should consider the Standards for Juvenile Justice Relating to Rights of Minors.

MEYER v. NEBRASKA

Supreme Court of the United States, 1923.
262 U.S. 390, 43 S.Ct. 625, 67 L.Ed. 1042.

MR. JUSTICE MCREYNOLDS delivered the opinion of the Court:

[Plaintiff in error was convicted of violating the following Nebraska statute enacted in 1919:]

"Section 1. No person, individually or as a teacher, shall, in any private, denominational, parochial or public school, teach any subject to any person in any language other than the English language.

"Sec. 2. Languages, other than the English language, may be taught as languages only after a pupil shall have attained and successfully passed the eighth grade as evidenced by a certificate of graduation issued by the county superintendent of the county in which the child resides.

"Sec. 3. Any person who violates any of the provisions of this act shall be deemed guilty of a misdemeanor and upon conviction, shall be subject to a fine of not less than twenty-five ($25) dollars, nor more than one hundred ($100) dollars or be confined in the county jail for any period not exceeding thirty days for each offense.

"Sec. 4. Whereas, an emergency exists, this act shall be in force from and after its passage and approval." [Laws 1919, chap. 249.]

The supreme court of the state affirmed the judgment of conviction. It declared the offense charged and established was "the direct and intentional teaching of the German language as a distinct subject to a child who had not passed the eighth grade," in the parochial school maintained by Zion Evangelical Lutheran Congregation, a collection of Biblical stories being used therefor. . . .

. . .

The problem for our determination is whether the statute, as construed and applied, unreasonably infringes the liberty guaranteed to the plaintiff in error by the 14th Amendment. "No state . . . shall deprive any person of life, liberty, or property without due process of law."

While this court has not attempted to define with exactness the liberty thus guaranteed, the term has received much consideration, and some of the included things have been definitely stated. Without doubt, it denotes not merely freedom from bodily restraint, but also the right of the individual to contract, to engage in any of the common occupations of life, to acquire useful knowledge, to marry, establish a home and bring up children, to worship God according to the dictates of his own conscience, and, generally, to enjoy those privileges long recognized at common law as essential to the orderly pursuit of happiness by free men. The established doctrine is that this liberty may not be interfered with, under the guise of protecting the public interest, by legislative action which is arbitrary or without reasonable relation to some purpose within the competency of the state to effect. Determination by the legislature of what constitutes proper exercise of police power is not final or conclusive, but is subject to supervision by the courts.

The American people have always regarded education and acquisition of knowledge as matters of supreme importance, which should be diligently promoted. The Ordinance of 1787 declares: "Religion, morality and knowledge being necessary to good government and the happiness of mankind, schools and the means of education shall forever be encouraged." Corresponding to the right of control, it is the natural duty of the parent to give his children education suitable to their station in life; and nearly all the states, including Nebraska, enforce this obligation by compulsory laws.

Practically, education of the young is only possible in schools conducted by especially qualified persons who devote themselves thereto. The calling always has been regarded as useful and honorable,—essential, indeed, to the public welfare. Mere knowledge of the German language cannot reasonably be regarded as harmful. Heretofore it has been commonly looked upon as helpful and desirable. Plaintiff in error taught this language in school as part of his occupation. His right thus to teach and the right of parents to engage him so to instruct their children, we think, are within the liberty of the Amendment.

. . . The supreme court of the state has held that "the so-called ancient or dead languages" are not "within the spirit or the purpose of the act." Nebraska District of Evangelical Lutheran Synod, etc., v. McKelvie, et al (Neb.) 187 N.W. 927 (April 19, 1922). Latin, Greek, Hebrew are not proscribed; but German, French, Spanish, Italian, and every other alien speech are within the ban. Evidently the legislature has attempted materially to interfere with the calling of modern language teachers, with the opportunities of pupils to acquire knowledge, and with the power of parents to control the education of their own.

It is said the purpose of the legislation was to promote civic development by inhibiting training and education of the immature in foreign tongues and ideals before they could learn English and acquire American ideals; and "that the English language should be and become the mother tongue of all children reared in this state." It is also affirmed that the foreign-born population is very large, that certain communities commonly use foreign words, follow foreign leaders, move in a foreign atmosphere, and that the children are thereby hindered from becoming citizens of the most useful type, and the public safety is imperiled.

That the state may do much, go very far, indeed, in order to improve the quality of its citizens, physically, mentally, and morally, is clear; but the individual has certain fundamental rights which must be respected. The protection of the Constitution extends to all,—to those who speak other languages as well as to those born with English on the tongue. Perhaps it would be highly advantageous if all had ready understanding of our ordinary speech, but this cannot be coerced by methods which conflict with the Constitution,—a desirable end cannot be promoted by prohibited means.

For the welfare of his Ideal Commonwealth, Plato suggested a law which should provide: "That the wives of our guardians are to be common, and their children are to be common, and no parent is to know his own child nor any child his parent. . . . The proper officers will take the offspring of the good parents to the pen or fold, and there they will deposit them with certain nurses who dwell in a separate quarter; but the offspring of the inferior, or of the better when they chance to be deformed, will be put away in some mysterious, unknown place, as they should be." In order to submerge the individual and develop ideal citizens, Sparta assembled the males at seven into barracks and intrusted their subsequent education and training to official guardians. Although such measures have been deliberately approved by men of great genius, their ideas touching the relation between individual and state were wholly different from those upon which our institutions rest; and it hardly will be affirmed that any legislature could impose such restrictions upon the people of a state without doing violence to both letter and spirit of the Constitution.

The desire of the legislature to foster a homogeneous people with American ideals, prepared readily to understand current discussions of civic matters, is easy to appreciate. Unfortunate experiences during the late war, and aversion toward every characteristic of truculent adversaries, were certainly enough to quicken that aspiration. But the means adopted, we think, exceed the limitations upon the power of the state, and conflict with rights assured to plaintiff in error. The interference is plain enough, and no adequate reason therefor in time of peace and domestic tranquillity has been shown.

The power of the state to compel attendance at some school and to make reasonable regulations for all schools, including a requirement that they shall give instructions in English, is not questioned. Nor has challenge been made of the state's power to prescribe a curriculum for institutions which it supports. Those matters are not within the present controversy. Our concern is with the prohibition approved by the supreme court. Adams v. Tanner, 244 U.S. 594, 61 L.Ed. 1342 pointed out that mere abuse incident to an occupation ordinarily useful is not enough to justify its abolition, although regulation may be entirely proper. No emergency has arisen which renders knowledge by a child of some language other than English so clearly harmful as to justify its inhibition, with the consequent infringement of rights long freely enjoyed. We are constrained to conclude that the statute as applied is arbitrary, and without reasonable relation to any end within the competency of the state.

As the statute undertakes to interfere only with teaching which involves a modern language, leaving complete freedom as to other matters, there seems no adequate foundation for the suggestion that the purpose was to protect the child's health by limiting his mental activities. It is well known that proficiency in a foreign language seldom comes to one not instructed at an early age, and experience shows that this is not injurious to the health, morals, or understanding of the ordinary child.

. . .

Reversed.

[The dissenting opinion of Justice Holmes, concurred in by Justice Sutherland, is omitted. It appears at 262 U.S. 412, after Bartels v. Iowa.]

NOTE

Prior to the U.S. Supreme Court's decision in Loving v. Virginia, 388 U.S. 1, 87 S.Ct. 1817, 18 L.Ed. 1010 (1967), which struck down state proscriptions against miscegenation, Meyer v. Nebraska was widely cited for the proposition that the fourteenth amendment defines the outer boundaries for state regulation of marriage and family life in general.

PIERCE v. SOCIETY OF SISTERS OF THE HOLY NAMES OF JESUS AND MARY

Supreme Court of the United States, 1925.
268 U.S. 510, 45 S.Ct. 571, 69 L.Ed. 1070.

MR. JUSTICE MCREYNOLDS delivered the opinion of the Court.

These appeals are from decrees, based upon undenied allegations, which granted preliminary orders restraining appellants from threatening or attempting to enforce the Compulsory Education Act
. . . ..

The challenged act, effective September 1, 1926, requires every parent, guardian, or other person having control or charge or custody of a child between 8 and 16 years to send him "to a public school for the period of time a public school shall be held during the current year" in the district where the child resides; and failure so to do is declared a misdemeanor. There are exemptions—not specially important here—for children who are not normal, or who have completed the eighth grade, or whose parents or private teachers reside at considerable distances from any public school, or who hold special permits from the county superintendent. The manifest purpose is to compel general attendance at public schools by normal children, between 8 and 16, who have not completed the eighth grade. . . .

Appellee the Society of Sisters is an Oregon corporation, organized in 1880, with power to care for orphans, educate and instruct the youth, establish and maintain academies or schools, and acquire necessary real and personal property. It has long devoted its property and effort to the secular and religious education and care of children, and has acquired the valuable good will of many parents and guardians. It conducts interdependent primary and high schools and junior colleges, and maintains orphanages for the custody and control of children between 8 and 16. In its primary schools many children between those ages are taught the subjects usually pursued in Oregon public schools during the first eight years. Systematic religious instruction and moral training according to the tenets of the Roman Catholic Church are also regularly provided. All courses of study, both temporal and religious, contemplate continuity of training under appellee's charge; the primary schools are essential to the system and the most profitable. . . . The Compulsory Education Act of 1922 has already caused the withdrawal from its schools of children who would otherwise continue, and their income has steadily declined. The appellants, public officers, have proclaimed their purpose strictly to enforce the statute.

. . . [T]he Society's bill alleges that the enactment conflicts with the right of parents to choose schools where their children will receive appropriate mental and religious training, the right of the child to influence the parents' choice of a school, the right of schools and teachers therein to engage in a useful business or profession, and is accordingly repugnant to the Constitution and void. And, further, that unless enforcement of the measure is enjoined the corporation's business and property will suffer irreparable injury.

Appellee Hill Military Academy is a private corporation organized in 1908 under the laws of Oregon, engaged in owning, operating, and conducting for profit an elementary, college preparatory, and military training school for boys between the ages of 5 and 21 years. The average attendance is 100, and the annual fees received for each student amount to some $800. The elementary department is divided into eight grades, as in the public schools; the college preparatory department has four grades, similar to those of the public high schools; the courses of study conform to the requirements of the state board of education. Military instruction and training are also given, under the supervision of an army officer. . . . By reason of the statute and threat of enforcement appellee's business is being destroyed and its property depreciated; parents and guardians are refusing to make contracts for the future instruction of their sons, and some are being withdrawn.

The Academy's bill . . . alleges that the challenged act contravenes the corporation's rights guaranteed by the Fourteenth Amendment and that unless appellants are restrained from proclaiming its validity and threatening to enforce it irreparable injury will result. The prayer is for an appropriate injunction.

No answer was interposed in either cause, and after proper notices they were heard by three judges on motions for preliminary injunctions . . . .. The court ruled that the Fourteenth Amendment guaranteed appellees against the deprivation of their property without due process of law consequent upon the unlawful interference by appellants with the free choice of patrons, present and prospective. It declared the right to conduct schools was property and that parents and guardians, as a part of their liberty, might direct the education of children by selecting reputable teachers and places. . . .

No question is raised concerning the power of the state reasonably to regulate all schools, to inspect, supervise and examine them, their teachers and pupils; to require that all children of proper age attend some school, that teachers shall be of good moral character and patriotic disposition, that certain studies plainly essential to good citizenship must be taught, and that nothing be taught which is manifestly inimical to the public welfare.

The inevitable practical result of enforcing the act under consideration would be destruction of appellees' primary schools, and perhaps all other private primary schools for normal children within the state of Oregon. Appellees are engaged in a kind of undertaking not inherently harmful, but long regarded as useful and meritorious. Certainly there is nothing in the present records to indicate that they have failed to discharge their obligations to patrons, students, or the state. And there are no peculiar circumstances or present emergencies which demand extraordinary measures relative to primary education.

Under the doctrine of Meyer v. Nebraska, 262 U.S. 390, 43 S.Ct. 625, 67 L.Ed. 1042, we think it entirely plain that the Act of 1922 unreasonably interferes with the liberty of parents and guardians to direct the upbringing and education of children under their control. As often heretofore pointed out, rights guaranteed by the Constitution may not be abridged by legislation which has no reasonable relation to some purpose within the competency of the state. The fundamental theory of liberty upon which all governments in this Union repose excludes any general power of the state to standardize its children by forcing them to accept instruction from public teachers only. The child is not the mere creature of the state; those who nurture him and direct his destiny have the right, coupled with the high duty, to recognize and prepare him for additional obligations.

. . .

The decrees below are affirmed.

NOTE

For a discussion of compulsory education requirements in America generally, see p. 108, infra.

PRINCE v. MASSACHUSETTS

Supreme Court of the United States, 1944.
321 U.S. 158, 64 S.Ct. 438, 88 L.Ed. 645.

MR. JUSTICE RUTLEDGE delivered the opinion of the Court.

The case brings for review another episode in the conflict between Jehovah's Witnesses and state authority. This time Sarah Prince appeals from convictions for violating Massachusetts' child labor laws, by acts said to be a rightful exercise of her religious convictions.

When the offenses were committed she was the aunt and custodian of Betty M. Simmons, a girl nine years of age. Originally there were three separate complaints. They were, shortly, for (1) refusal to disclose Betty's identity and age to a public officer whose duty was to enforce the statutes; (2) furnishing her with magazines, knowing she was to sell them unlawfully, that is, on the street; and (3) as Betty's custodian, permitting her to work contrary to law. The complaints were made, respectively, pursuant to Sections 79, 80 and 81 of Chapter 149, Gen.Laws of Mass. (Ter.Ed.). The Supreme Judicial Court reversed the conviction under the first complaint on state grounds;[1] but sustained the judgments founded on the other two. 313 Mass. 223, 46 N.E.2d 755. They present the only questions for our decision. These are whether Sections 80 and 81, as applied, contravene the Fourteenth Amendment by denying or abridging appellant's freedom of religion and by denying to her the equal protection of the laws.

Sections 80 and 81 form parts of Massachusetts' comprehensive child labor law. They provide methods for enforcing the prohibitions of Section 69, which is as follows:

"No boy under twelve and no girl under eighteen shall sell, expose or offer for sale any newspapers, magazines, periodicals or any other articles of merchandise of any description, or exercise the trade of

---

1. The court found there was no evidence that appellant was asked Betty's age. It then held that conviction for refusal to disclose the child's name, based on the charge under Section 79, would violate Article 12 of the Declaration of Rights of the Commonwealth, which provides in part: "No subject shall be held to answer for any crimes or offence, until the same is fully and plainly, substantially and formally, described to him; or be compelled to accuse, or furnish evidence against himself."

bootblack or scavenger, or any other trade, in any street or public place."

Sections 80 and 81, so far as pertinent, read:

"Whoever furnishes or sells to any minor any article of any description with the knowledge that the minor intends to sell such article in violation of any provision of sections sixty-nine to seventy-three, inclusive, or after having received written notice to this effect from any officer charged with the enforcement thereof, or knowingly procures or encourages any minor to violate any provisions of said sections, shall be punished by a fine of not less than ten nor more than two hundred dollars or by imprisonment for not more than two months, or both." [Section 80]

"Any parent, guardian or custodian having a minor under his control who compels or permits such minor to work in violation of any provision of sections sixty to seventy-four, inclusive, . . . shall for a first offence be punished by a fine of not less than two nor more than ten dollars or by imprisonment for not more than five days, or both; . . ." [Section 81]

The story told by the evidence has become familiar. It hardly needs repeating, except to give setting to the variations introduced through the part played by a child of tender years. Mrs. Prince, living in Brockton, is the mother of two young sons. She also has legal custody of Betty Simmons who lives with them. The children too are Jehovah's Witnesses and both Mrs. Prince and Betty testified they were ordained ministers. The former was accustomed to go each week on the streets of Brockton to distribute "Watchtower" and "Consolation," according to the usual plan. She had permitted the children to engage in this activity previously, and had been warned against doing so by the school attendance officer, Mr. Perkins. But, until December 18, 1941, she generally did not take them with her at night.

That evening, as Mrs. Prince was preparing to leave her home, the children asked to go. She at first refused. Childlike, they resorted to tears and, motherlike, she yielded. Arriving downtown, Mrs. Prince permitted the children "to engage in the preaching work with her upon the sidewalks." That is, with specific reference to Betty, she and Mrs. Prince took positions about twenty feet apart near a street intersection. Betty held up in her hand, for passersby to see, copies of "Watch Tower" and "Consolation." From her shoulder hung the usual canvas magazine bag, on which was printed "Watchtower and Consolation 5¢ per copy." No one accepted a copy from Betty that evening and she received no money. Nor did her aunt. But on other occasions, Betty had received funds and given out copies.

Mrs. Prince and Betty remained until 8:45 p. m. A few minutes before this Mr. Perkins approached Mrs. Prince. A discussion ensued. He inquired and she refused to give Betty's name. However, she stated the child attended the Shaw School. Mr. Perkins referred to his previous warnings and said he would allow five minutes for them to get off the street. Mrs. Prince admitted she supplied Betty with the magazines and said, "[N]either you nor anybody else can stop me . . . . This child is exercising her God-given right and her constitutional right to preach the gospel, and no creature has a right to interfere with God's commands." However, Mrs. Prince and Betty departed. She remarked as she went, "I'm not going through this any more. We've been through it time and time again. I'm going home and put the little girl to bed." It may be added that testimony, by Betty, her aunt and others, was offered at the trials, and was excluded, to show that Betty believed it was her religious duty to perform this work and failure would bring condemnation "to everlasting destruction at Armageddon."

As the case reaches us, the questions are no longer open whether what the child did was a "sale" or an "offer to sell" within Section 69 [5] or was "work" within Section 81. The state court's decision has foreclosed them adversely to appellant as a matter of state law. The only question remaining therefore is whether, as construed and applied, the statute is valid. Upon this the court said: "We think that freedom of the press and of religion is subject to incidental regulation to the slight degree involved in the prohibition of the selling of religious literature in streets and public places by boys under twelve and girls under eighteen and in the further statutory provisions herein considered, which have been adopted as a means of enforcing that prohibition." 313 Mass. 223, 229, 46 N.E.2d 755, 758.

Appellant does not stand on freedom of the press. . . . [S]he rests squarely on freedom of religion under the First Amendment, applied by the Fourteenth to the states. She buttresses this foundation, however, with a claim of parental right as secured by the due process clause of the latter Amendment. Cf. Meyer v. Nebraska, 262 U.S. 390, 43 S.Ct. 625, 67 L.Ed. 1042. These guaranties, she thinks, guard alike herself and the child in what they have done. Thus, two claimed liberties are at stake. One is the parent's, to bring up the child in the way he should go, which for appellant means to teach him the tenets and the practices of their faith. The other freedom is the child's, to observe these; and among them is "to preach the gospel . . . by public distribution" of "Watchtower" and "Consolation," in conformity with the scripture: "A little child shall lead them."

. . .

To make accommodation between these freedoms and an exercise of state authority always is delicate. It hardly could be more so than in such a clash as this case presents. On one side is the obviously earnest claim for freedom of conscience and religious practice. With

5. In this respect the Massachusetts decision is contrary to the trend in other states. . . .

it is allied the parent's claim to authority in her own household and in the rearing of her children. The parent's conflict with the state over control of the child and his training is serious enough when only secular matters are concerned. It becomes the more so when an element of religious conviction enters. Against these sacred private interests, basic in a democracy, stand the interests of society to protect the welfare of children, and the state's assertion of authority to that end, made here in a manner conceded valid if only secular things were involved. The last is no mere corporate concern of official authority. It is the interest of youth itself, and of the whole community, that children be both safeguarded from abuses and given opportunities for growth into free and independent well-developed men and citizens. Between contrary pulls of such weight, the safest and most objective recourse is to the lines already marked out, not precisely but for guides, in narrowing the no man's land where this battle has gone on.

The rights of children to exercise their religion, and of parents to give them religious training and to encourage them in the practice of religious belief, as against preponderant sentiment and assertion of state power voicing it, have had recognition here, most recently in West Virginia State Board of Education v. Barnette, 319 U.S. 624, 63 S.Ct. 1178. Previously in Pierce v. Society of Sisters, 268 U.S. 510, 45 S.Ct. 571, 69 L.Ed. 1070, this Court had sustained the parent's authority to provide religious with secular schooling, and the child's right to receive it, as against the state's requirement of attendance at public schools. And in Meyer v. Nebraska, 262 U.S. 390, 43 S.Ct. 625, 67 L.Ed. 1042, children's rights to receive teaching in languages other than the nation's common tongue were guarded against the state's encroachment. It is cardinal with us that the custody, care and nurture of the child reside first in the parents, whose primary function and freedom include preparation for obligations the state can neither supply nor hinder. Pierce v. Society of Sisters, supra. And it is in recognition of this that these decisions have respected the private realm of family life which the state cannot enter.

But the family itself is not beyond regulation in the public interest, as against a claim of religious liberty. Reynolds v. United States, 98 U.S. 145, 25 L.Ed. 244; Davis v. Beason, 133 U.S. 333, 10 S.Ct. 299, 33 L.Ed. 637. And neither rights of religion nor rights of parenthood are beyond limitation. Acting to guard the general interest in youth's well being, the state as parens patriae may restrict the parent's control by requiring school attendance, regulating or prohibiting the child's labor, and in many other ways. Its authority is not nullified merely because the parent grounds his claim to control the child's course of conduct on religion or conscience. Thus, he cannot claim freedom from compulsory vaccination for the child more than for himself on religious grounds. The right to practice religion freely does not include liberty to expose the community or the child to communicable disease or the latter to ill health or death. People v. Pierson, 176 N.Y. 201, 68 N.E. 243. The catalogue need not be lengthened. It is sufficient to show what indeed appellant hardly disputes, that the state has a wide range of power for limiting parental freedom and authority in things affecting the child's welfare; and that this includes, to some extent, matters of conscience and religious conviction.

But it is said the state cannot do so here. This, first, because when state action impinges upon a claimed religious freedom, it must fall unless shown to be necessary for or conducive to the child's protection against some clear and present danger, cf. Schenck v. United States, 249 U.S. 47, 39 S.Ct. 247, 63 L.Ed. 470; and, it is added, there was no such showing here. The child's presence on the street, with her guardian, distributing or offering to distribute the magazines, it is urged, was in no way harmful to her, nor in any event more so than the presence of many other children at the same time and place, engaged in shopping and other activities not prohibited. Accordingly, in view of the preferred position the freedoms of the First Article occupy, the statute in its present application must fall. It cannot be sustained by any presumption of validity. And, finally, it is said, the statute is, as to children, an absolute prohibition, not merely a reasonable regulation, of the denounced activity.

Concededly a statute or ordinance identical in terms with Section 69, except that it is applicable to adults or all persons generally, would be invalid. But the mere fact a state could not wholly prohibit this form of adult activity, whether characterized locally as a "sale" or otherwise, does not mean it cannot do so for children. Such a conclusion granted would mean that a state could impose no greater limitation upon child labor than upon adult labor. Or, if an adult were free to enter dance halls, saloons, and disreputable places generally, in order to discharge his conceived religious duty to admonish or dissuade persons from frequenting such places, so would be a child with similar convictions and objectives, if not alone then in the parent's company, against the state's command.

The state's authority over children's activities is broader than over like actions of adults. This is peculiarly true of public activities and in matters of employment. A democratic society rests, for its continuance, upon the healthy, well-rounded growth of young people into full maturity as citizens, with all that implies. It may secure this against impeding restraints and dangers, within a broad range of selection. Among evils most appropriate for such action are the crippling effects of child employment, more especially in public places, and the possible harms arising from other activities subject to all the diverse influences of the street. It is too late now to doubt that legislation appropriately designed to reach such evils is within the state's police power, whether against the parent's claim to control of the child or one that religious scruples dictate contrary action.

It is true children have rights, in common with older people, in the primary use of highways. But even in such use streets afford dangers for them not affecting adults. And in other uses, whether in work or in other things, this difference may be magnified. This is so not only when children are unaccompanied but certainly to some extent when they are with their parents. What may be wholly permissible for adults therefore may not be so for children, either with or without their parents' presence.

Street preaching, whether oral or by handing out literature, is not the primary use of the highway, even for adults. While for them it cannot be wholly prohibited, it can be regulated within reasonable limits in accommodation to the primary and other incidental uses. But, for obvious reasons, notwithstanding appellant's contrary view, the validity of such a prohibition applied to children not accompanied by an older person hardly would seem open to question. The case reduces itself therefore to the question whether the presence of the child's guardian puts a limit to the state's power. That fact may lessen the likelihood that some evils the legislation seeks to avert will occur. But it cannot forestall all of them. The zealous though lawful exercise of the right to engage in propagandizing the community, whether in religious, political or other matters, may and at times does create situations difficult enough for adults to cope with and wholly inappropriate for children, especially of tender years, to face. Other harmful possibilities could be stated, of emotional excitement and psychological or physical injury. Parents may be free to become martyrs themselves. But it does not follow they are free, in identical circumstances, to make martyrs of their children before they have reached the age of full and legal discretion when they can make that choice for themselves. Massachusetts has determined that an absolute prohibition, though one limited to streets and public places and to the incidental uses proscribed, is necessary to accomplish its legitimate objectives. Its power to attain them is broad enough to reach these peripheral instances in which the parent's supervision may reduce but cannot eliminate entirely the ill effects of the prohibited conduct. We think that with reference to the public proclaiming of religion, upon the streets and in other similar public places, the power of the state to control the conduct of children reaches beyond the scope of its authority over adults, as is true in the case of other freedoms, and the rightful boundary of its power has not been crossed in this case.

. . .

Our ruling does not extend beyond the facts the case presents. We neither lay the foundation "for any [that is, every] state intervention in the indoctrination and participation of children in religion" which may be done "in the name of their health and welfare" nor give warrant for "every limitation on their religious training and activities." The religious training and indoctrination of children may be accomplished in many ways, some of which, as we have noted, have received constitutional protection through decisions of this Court. These and all others except the public proclaiming of religion on the streets, if this may be taken as either training or indoctrination of the proclaimer, remain unaffected by the decision.

The judgment is affirmed.

[Mr. Justice Jackson, in a separate opinion in which Mr. Justice Roberts and Mr. Justice Frankfurter, joined, dissented from the grounds for affirmance, stating the view that the judgment "was rightly decided, and upon right grounds, by the Supreme Judicial Court of Massachusetts. 313 Mass. 223, 46 N.E.2d 755."]

MR. JUSTICE MURPHY, dissenting.

This attempt by the state of Massachusetts to prohibit a child from exercising her constitutional right to practice her religion on the public streets cannot, in my opinion, be sustained.

The record makes clear the basic fact that Betty Simmons, the nine-year-old child in question, was engaged in a genuine religious, rather than commercial, activity.

. . . [T]he human freedoms enumerated in the First Amendment and carried over into the Fourteenth Amendment are to be presumed to be invulnerable and any attempt to sweep away those freedoms is prima facie invalid. It follows that any restriction or prohibition must be justified by those who deny that the freedoms have been unlawfully invaded. The burden was therefore on the state of Massachusetts to prove the reasonableness and necessity of prohibiting children from engaging in religious activity of the type involved in this case.

The burden in this instance, however, is not met by vague references to the reasonableness underlying child labor legislation in general. The great interest of the state in shielding minors from the evil vicissitudes of early life does not warrant every limitation on their religious training and activities. The reasonableness that justifies the prohibition of the ordinary distribution of literature in the public streets by children is not necessarily the reasonableness that justifies such a drastic restriction when the distribution is part of their religious faith. Murdock v. Pennsylvania, supra, 319 U.S. 111, 63 S.Ct. 874, 87 L.Ed. 1292. If the right of a child to practice its religion in that manner is to be forbidden by constitutional means, there must be convincing proof that such a practice constitutes a grave and immediate danger to the state or to the health, morals or welfare of the child. West Virginia State Board of Education v. Barnette, 319 U.S. 624, 639, 63 S.Ct. 1178, 1186. The vital freedom of religion, which is "of the very essence of a scheme of ordered liberty," Palko v. Connecticut, 302 U.S. 319, 325, 58 S.Ct. 149, 152, 82 L.Ed. 288, cannot be erased by slender references to the state's power to restrict the more secular activities of children.

The state, in my opinion, has completely failed to sustain its burden of proving the existence of any grave or immediate danger to any interest which it may lawfully protect. . . .

. . .

NOTE.

For materials on child labor laws outside the context of constitutional issues, see p. 23, supra. For discussion of the problems of state intervention in the face of parental religious objections to medical care for children, see p. 894 infra.

GINSBERG v. STATE OF NEW YORK

Supreme Court of the United States, 1968.
390 U.S. 629, 88 S.Ct. 1274, 20 L.Ed.2d 195.

MR. JUSTICE BRENNAN delivered the opinion of the Court.

This case presents the question of the constitutionality on its face of a New York criminal obscenity statute which prohibits the sale to minors under 17 years of age of material defined to be obscene on the basis of its appeal to them whether or not it would be obscene to adults.

Appellant and his wife operate "Sam's Stationery and Luncheonette" in Bellmore, Long Island. They have a lunch counter, and, among other things, also sell magazines including some so-called "girlie" magazines. Appellant was prosecuted under two informations, each in two counts, which charged that he personally sold a 16-year-old boy two "girlie" magazines on each of two dates in October, 1965, in violation of § 484–h of the New York Penal Law, McKinney's Consol.Laws, c. 40. He was tried before a judge without a jury in Nassau County District Court and was found guilty on both counts. The judge found (1) that the magazines contained pictures which depicted female "nudity" in a manner defined in subsection 1(b), that is "the showing of . . . female . . . buttocks with less than a full opaque covering, or the showing of the female breast with less than a fully opaque covering of any portion thereof below the top of the nipple . . .," and (2) that the pictures were "harmful to minors" in that they had, within the meaning of subsection 1(f) "that quality of . . . representation . . . of nudity . . . [which] . . . . (i) predominantly appeals to the prurient, shameful or morbid interest of minors, and (ii) is patently offensive to prevailing standards in the adult community as a whole with respect to what is suitable material for minors, and (iii) is utterly without redeeming social importance for minors." He held that both sales to the 16-year-old boy therefore constituted the violation under § 484–h of "knowingly to sell . . . to a minor" under 17 of "(a) any picture . . . which depicts nudity . . . and which is harmful to minors," and "(b) any . . . magazine . . . which contains . . . [such

pictures] . . . and which, taken as a whole, is harmful to minors."
. . . We affirm.

I.

The "girlie" picture magazines involved in the sales here are not obscene for adults . . .. § 484–h does not bar the appellant from stocking the magazines and selling them to persons 17 years of age or older, and therefore the conviction is not invalid under our decision in Butler v. State of Michigan, 352 U.S. 380, 77 S.Ct. 524, 1 L.Ed.2d 412.

Obscenity is not within the area of protected speech or press. Roth v. United States, 354 U.S. 476, 485, 77 S.Ct. 1304, 1309, 1 L.Ed. 2d 1498. The three-pronged test of subsection 1(f) for judging the obscenity of material sold to minors under 17 is a variable from the formulation for determining obscenity under *Roth* stated in the plurality opinion in A Book Named "John Cleland's Memoirs of a Woman of Pleasure" v. Attorney General of Com. of Massachusetts, 383 U.S. 413, 418, 86 S.Ct. 975, 977, 16 L.Ed.2d 1. Appellant's primary attack upon § 484–h is leveled at the power of the State to adapt this *Memoirs* formulation to define the material's obscenity on the basis of its appeal to minors, and thus exclude material so defined from the area of protected expression. He makes no argument that the magazines are not "harmful to minors" within the definition in subsection 1(f). Thus "[n]o issue is presented . . . concerning the obscenity of the material involved." Roth, 354 U.S., at 481, 77 S.Ct., at 1307, n. 8.

The New York Court of Appeals "upheld the Legislature's power to employ variable concepts of obscenity"[4] in a case in which the same challenge to state power to enact such a law was also addressed to § 484–h. Bookcase, Inc. v. Broderick, 18 N.Y.2d 71, 271 N.Y.S.2d 947, 218 N.E.2d 668, appeal dismissed for want of a properly presented federal question, sub nom. Bookcase, Inc. v. Leary, 385 U.S. 12. In sustaining state power to enact the law, the Court of Appeals said:

> "[M]aterial which is protected for distribution to adults is not necessarily constitutionally protected from restriction upon its dissemination to children. In other words, the concept of obscenity or of unprotected matter may vary according to the group to whom the questionable material is directed or from whom it is

4. People v. Tannenbaum, 18 N.Y.2d 268, 270, 274 N.Y.S.2d 131, 133, 220 N.E.2d 783, 785, dismissed as moot, 388 U.S. 439, 87 S.Ct. 2107, 18 L.Ed.2d 1300. The concept of variable obscenity is developed in Lockhart & McClure, Censorship of Obscenity: The Developing Constitutional Standards, 45 Minn.L.Rev. 5 (1960). At 85 the authors state:

"Variable obscenity . . . furnishes a useful analytical tool for dealing with the problem of denying adolescents access to material aimed at a primary audience of sexually mature adults. For variable obscenity focuses attention upon the make-up of primary and peripheral audiences in varying circumstances, and provides a reasonably satisfactory means for delineating the obscene in each circumstance."

quarantined. Because of the State's exigent interest in preventing distribution to children of objectionable material, it can exercise its power to protect the health, safety, welfare and morals of its community by barring the distribution to children of books recognized to be suitable for adults."

Appellant's attack is not that New York was without power to draw the line at age 17. Rather, his contention is the broad proposition that the scope of the constitutional freedom of expression secured to a citizen to read or see material concerned with sex cannot be made to depend upon whether the citizen is an adult or a minor. He accordingly insists that the denial to minors under 17 of access to material condemned by § 484–h, insofar as that material is not obscene for persons 17 years of age or older, constitutes an unconstitutional deprivation of protected liberty.

We have no occasion in this case to consider the impact of the guarantees of freedom of expression upon the totality of the relationship of the minor and the State. . . . It is enough for the purposes of this case that we inquire whether it was constitutionally impermissible for New York, insofar as § 484–h does so, to accord minors under 17 a more restricted right than that assured to adults to judge and determine for themselves what sex material they may read or see. We conclude that we cannot say that the statute invades the area of freedom of expression constitutionally secured to minors.

Appellant argues that there is an invasion of protected rights under § 484–h constitutionally indistinguishable from the invasions under the Nebraska statute forbidding children to study German, which was struck down in Meyer v. State of Nebraska, 262 U.S. 390, 43 S.Ct. 625, 67 L.Ed. 1042; the Oregon statute interfering with children's attendance at private and parochial schools, which was struck down in Pierce v. Society of Sisters of the Holy Names of Jesus and Mary, 268 U.S. 510, 45 S.Ct. 571, 69 L.Ed. 1070; and the statute compelling children against their religious scruples to give the flag salute, which was struck down in West Virginia State Board of Education v. Barnette, 319 U.S. 624, 63 S.Ct. 1178, 87 L.Ed. 1628. We reject that argument. We do not regard New York's regulation in defining obscenity on the basis of its appeal to minors under 17 as involving an invasion of such minors' constitutionally protected freedoms. Rather § 484–h simply adjusts the definition of obscenity "to social realities by permitting the appeal of this type of material to be assessed in term of the sexual interests . . ." of such minors. Mishkin v. State of New York, 383 U.S. 502, 509, 86 S.Ct. 958, 16 L.Ed.2d 56; Bookcase, Inc. v. Broderick, supra. That the State has power to make that adjustment seems clear, for we have recognized that even where there is an invasion of protected freedoms "the power of the state to control the conduct of children reaches beyond the scope of its authority over adults . . . ." Prince v. Commonwealth of Massachusetts, 321 U.S. 158, 170, 64 S.Ct. 438, 444, 88 L.Ed. 645.[6] . . .

The well-being of its children is of course a subject within the State's constitutional power to regulate, and, in our view, two interests justify the limitations in § 484–h upon the availability of sex material to minors under 17, at least if it was rational for the legislature to find that the minors' exposure to such material might be harmful. First of all, constitutional interpretation has consistently recognized that the parents' claim to authority in their own household to direct the rearing of their children is basic in the structure of our society. "It is cardinal with us that the custody, care and nurture of the child reside first in the parents, whose primary function and freedom include preparation for obligations the state can neither supply nor hinder." Prince v. Commonwealth of Massachusetts, supra, at 166, 64 S.Ct., at 442. The legislature could properly conclude that parents and others, teachers for example, who have this primary responsibility for children's well-being are entitled to the support of laws designed to aid discharge of that responsibility. Indeed, subsection 1(f)(ii) of § 484–h expressly recognizes the parental role in assessing sex-related material harmful to minors according "to prevailing standards in the adult community as a whole with respect to what is suitable material for minors." Moreover, the prohibition against sales to minors does not bar parents who so desire from purchasing the magazines for their children.[7]

6. Many commentators, including many committed to the proposition that "[n]o general restriction on expression in terms of 'obscenity' can . . . be reconciled with the first amendment," recognize that "the power of the state to control the conduct of children reaches beyond the scope of its authority over adults," and accordingly acknowledge a supervening state interest in the regulation of literature sold to children, Emerson, Toward a General Theory of the First Amendment, 72 Yale L.J. 877, 938, 939 (1963):

"Different factors come into play, also, where the interest at stake is the effect of erotic expression upon children. The world of children is not strictly part of the adult realm of free expression. The factor of immaturity, and perhaps other considerations, impose different rules. Without attempting here to formulate the principles relevant to freedom of expression for children, it suffices to say that regulations of communication addressed to them need not conform to the requirements of the first amendment in the same way as those applicable to adults."

. . .

7. One commentator who argues that obscenity legislation might be constitutionally defective as an imposition of a single standard of public morality would give effect to the parental role and accept laws relating only to minors. Henkin, Morals and the Constitution: The Sin of Obscenity, 63 Col.L.Rev. 391, 413, n. 68 (1963):

"One must consider also how much difference it makes if laws are designed to protect only the morals of a child. While many of the constitutional arguments against morals legislation apply equally to legislation protecting the morals of children, one can well distinguish laws which do not impose a morality on children, but which support the right of parents to deal with the morals of their children as they see fit."

See also Elias, Sex Publications and Moral Corruption: The Supreme Court Dilemma, 9 Wm. & Mary L.Rev. 302, 320–321 (1967).

The State also has an independent interest in the well-being of its youth. The New York Court of Appeals squarely bottomed its decision on that interest in Bookcase, Inc. v. Broderick, supra. Judge Fuld, now Chief Judge Fuld, also emphasized its significance in the earlier case of People v. Kahan, 15 N.Y.2d 311, 258 N.Y.S.2d 391, 206 N.E.2d 333, which had struck down the first version of § 484–h on grounds of vagueness. In his concurring opinion, 15 N.Y.2d, at 312, 258 N.Y.S.2d at 392, 206 N.E.2d, at 334, he said:

> "While the supervision of children's reading may best be left to their parents, the knowledge that parental control or guidance cannot always be provided and society's transcendent interest in protecting the welfare of children justify reasonable regulation of the sale of material to them. It is, therefore, altogether fitting and proper for a state to include in a statute designed to regulate the sale of pornography to children special standards, broader then those embodied in legislation aimed at controlling dissemination of such material to adults."

In Prince v. Commonwealth of Massachusetts, supra, 321 U.S., at 165, this Court, too, recognized that the State has an interest "to protect the welfare of children" and to see that they are "safeguarded from abuses" which might prevent their "growth into free and independent well-developed men and citizens." The only question remaining, therefore, is whether the New York Legislature might rationally conclude, as it has, that exposure to the materials proscribed by § 484–h constitutes such an "abuse."

Section 484–e of the law states a legislative finding that the material condemned by § 484–h is "a basic factor in impairing the ethical and moral development of our youth and a clear and present danger to the people of the state." It is very doubtful that this finding expresses an accepted scientific fact. But obscenity is not protected expression and may be suppressed without a showing of the circumstances which lie behind the phrase "clear and present danger" in its application to protected speech. Roth v. United States, supra.[9] To sustain state power to exclude material defined as obscenity by § 484–h requires only that we be able to say that it was not irrational for the legislature to find that exposure to material condemned by the statute is harmful to minors. In Meyer v. State of Nebraska, supra, we were able to say that children's knowledge of the German language "cannot reasonably be regarded as harmful." That cannot be said by us of minors' reading and seeing sex material. To be sure, there is no lack of "studies" which purport to demonstrate that obscenity is or is not "a basic factor in impairing the ethical and moral development of . . . youth and a clear and present danger to the people of the state." But the growing consensus of commentators is

9. Our conclusion in Roth, 354 U.S., at 486–487, 77 S.Ct., that the clear and present danger test was irrelevant to the determination of obscenity made it un-necessary in that case to consider the debate among the authorities whether exposure to pornography caused antisocial consequences. . . .

that "while these studies all agree that a causal link has not been demonstrated, they are equally agreed that a causal link has not been disproved either." [10] We do not demand of legislatures "scientifically certain criteria of legislation." Noble State Bank v. Haskell, 219 U.S. 104, 110, 31 S.Ct. 186, 187, 55 L.Ed. 112. We therefore cannot say that § 484–h, in defining the obscenity of material on the basis of its appeal to minors under 17, has no rational relation to the objective of safeguarding such minors from harm.

[Appellant's arguments that the statute in question was void for vagueness and that it failed to meet the requirement of *scienter* also were rejected by the Court.]

Affirmed.

APPENDIX A TO OPINION OF THE COURT

New York Penal Law § 484–h as enacted by L.1965, c. 327, provides:

§ 484–h. Exposing minors to harmful materials

1. Definitions. As used in this section:

(a) "Minor" means any person under the age of seventeen years.

(b) "Nudity" means the showing of the human male or female genitals, pubic area or buttocks with less than a full opaque covering, or the showing of the female breast with less than a fully opaque covering of any portion thereof below the top of the nipple, or the depiction of covered male genitals in a discernibly turgid state.

(c) "Sexual conduct" means acts of masturbation, homosexuality, sexual intercourse, or physical contact with a person's clothed or unclothed genitals, pubic area, buttocks or, if such person be a female, breast.

10. . . . [D]espite the vigor of the ongoing controversy whether obscene material will perceptibly create a danger of antisocial conduct, or will probably induce its recipients to such conduct, a medical practitioner recently suggested that the possibility of harmful effects to youth cannot be dismissed as frivolous. Dr. Gaylin of the Columbia University Psychoanalytic Clinic, reporting on the views of some psychiatrists in 77 Yale L.J., at 592–593, said:

"It is in the period of growth [of youth] when these patterns of behavior are laid down, when environmental stimuli of all sorts must be integrated into a workable sense of self, when sensuality is being defined and fears elaborated, when pleasure confronts security and impulse encounters control—it is in this period, undramatically and with time, that legalized pornography may conceivably be damaging."

Dr. Gaylin emphasizes that a child might not be as well prepared as an adult to make an intelligent choice as to the material he chooses to read:

"[P]sychiatrists . . . made a distinction between the reading of pornography, as unlikely to be per se harmful, and the permitting of the reading of pornography, which was conceived as potentially destructive. The child is protected in his reading of pornography by the knowledge that it is pornographic, i.e., disapproved. It is outside of parental standards and not a part of his identification processes. To openly permit implies parental approval and even suggests seductive encouragement. If this is so of parental approval, it is equally so of societal approval—another potent influence on the developing ego." Id., at 594.

(d) "Sexual excitement" means the condition of human male or female genitals when in a state of sexual stimulation or arousal.

(e) "Sado-masochistic abuse" means flagellation or torture by or upon a person clad in undergarments, a mask or bizarre costume, or the condition of being fettered, bound or otherwise physically restrained on the part of one so clothed.

(f) "Harmful to minors" means that quality of any description or representation, in whatever form, of nudity, sexual conduct, sexual excitement, or sadomasochistic abuse, when it:

(i) predominantly appeals to the prurient, shameful or morbid interest of minors, and

(ii) is patently offensive to prevailing standards in the adult community as a whole with respect to what is suitable material for minors, and

(iii) is utterly without redeeming social importance for minors.

(g) "Knowingly" means having general knowledge of, or reason to know, or a belief or ground for belief which warrants further inspection or inquiry of both:

(i) the character and content of any material described herein which is reasonably susceptible of examination by the defendant, and

(ii) the age of the minor, provided however, that an honest mistake shall constitute an excuse from liability hereunder if the defendant made a reasonable bona fide attempt to ascertain the true age of such minor.

2. It shall be unlawful for any person knowingly to sell or loan for monetary consideration to a minor:

(a) any picture, photograph, drawing, sculpture, motion picture film, or similar visual representation or image of a person or portion of the human body which depicts nudity, sexual conduct or sado-masochistic abuse and which is harmful to minors, or

(b) any book, pamphlet, magazine, printed matter however reproduced, or sound recording which contains any matter enumerated in paragraph (a) of subdivision two hereof, or explicit and detailed verbal descriptions or narrative accounts of sexual excitement, sexual conduct or sado-masochistic abuse and which, taken as a whole is harmful to minors.

3. It shall be unlawful for any person knowingly to exhibit for a monetary consideration to a minor or knowingly to sell to a minor an admission ticket or pass or knowingly to admit a minor for a monetary consideration to premises whereon there is exhibited, a motion picture, show or other presentation which, in whole or in part, depicts nudity, sexual conduct or sado-masochistic abuse and which is harmful to minors.

4. A violation of any provision hereof shall constitute a misdemeanor.

MR. JUSTICE STEWART, concurring in the result.

A doctrinaire, knee-jerk application of the First Amendment would, of course, dictate the nullification of this New York statute. But that result is not required, I think, if we bear in mind what it is that the First Amendment protects.

The First Amendment guarantees liberty of human expression in order to preserve in our Nation what Mr. Justice Holmes called a "free trade in ideas." To that end, the Constitution protects more than just a man's freedom to say or write or publish what he wants. It secures as well the liberty of each man to decide for himself what he will read and to what he will listen. The Constitution guarantees, in short, a society of free choice. Such a society presupposes the capacity of its members to choose.

When expression occurs in a setting where the capacity to make a choice is absent, government regulation of that expression may coexist with and even implement First Amendment guarantees. . . .

I think a State may permissibly determine that, at least in some precisely delineated areas, a child—like someone in a captive audience—is not possessed of that full capacity for individual choice which is the presupposition of First Amendment guarantees. It is only upon such a premise, I should suppose, that a State may deprive children of other rights—the right to marry, for example, or the right to vote—deprivations that would be constitutionally intolerable for adults.

I cannot hold that this state law, on its face, violates the First and Fourteenth Amendments.

[The dissenting opinion of MR. JUSTICE DOUGLAS, with whom MR. JUSTICE BLACK concurs, is omitted.]

MR. JUSTICE FORTAS, dissenting.

. . .

The Court avoids facing the problem whether the magazines in the present case are "obscene" when viewed by a 16-year-old boy, although not "obscene" when viewed by someone 17 years of age or older. It says that Ginsberg's lawyer did not choose to challenge the conviction on the ground that the magazines are not "obscene." He chose only to attack the statute on its face. Therefore, the Court reasons, we need not look at the magazines and determine whether they may be excluded from the ambit of the First Amendment as "obscene" for purposes of this case. . . .

In my judgment, the Court cannot properly avoid its fundamental duty to define "obscenity" for purposes of censorship of material sold to youths, merely because of counsel's position. By so doing the Court avoids the essence of the problem; for if the State's power to censor freed from the prohibitions of the First Amendment depends upon obscenity, and if obscenity turns on the specific content of the publication, how can we sustain the conviction here without deciding whether the particular magazines in question are obscene?

The Court certainly cannot mean that the States and cities and counties and villages have unlimited power to withhold anything and everything that is written or pictorial from younger people. But it here justifies the conviction of Sam Ginsberg because the impact of the Constitution, it says, is variable, and what is not obscene for an adult may be obscene for a child. This it calls "variable obscenity." I do not disagree with this, but I insist that to assess the principle— certainly to apply it—the Court must define it. . . .

I agree that the State in the exercise of its police power—even in the First Amendment domain—may make proper and careful differ- entiation between adults and children. But I do not agree that this power may be used on an arbitrary, free-wheeling basis. This is not a case where, on any standard enunciated by the Court, the magazines are obscene, nor one where the seller is at fault. Petition- er is being prosecuted for the sale of magazines which he had a right under the decisions of this Court to offer for sale, and he is being prosecuted without proof of "fault"—without even a claim that he deliberately, calculatedly sought to induce children to buy "obscene" material. Bookselling should not be a hazardous profession.

The conviction of Ginsberg on the present facts is a serious inva- sion of freedom. To sustain the conviction without inquiry as to whether the material is "obscene" and without any evidence of push- ing or pandering, in face of this Court's asserted solicitude for First Amendment values, is to give the State a role in the rearing of chil- dren which is contrary to our traditions and to our conception of fami- ly responsibility. Cf. In re Gault, 387 U.S. 1, 87 S.Ct. 1428, 18 L.Ed. 2d 527 (1967). It begs the question to present this undefined, unlimit- ed censorship as an aid to parents in the rearing of their children. This decision does not merely protect children from activities which all sensible parents would condemn. Rather, its undefined and unlim- ited approval of state censorship in this area denies to children free access to books and works of art to which many parents may wish their children to have uninhibited access. For denial of access to these magazines, without any standard or definition of their allegedly distinguishing characteristics, is also denial of access to great works of art and literature.

. . .

NOTES

(1) Recently much attention has been focused on the problems of ex- ploitation of children for sexually explicit or obscene theatrical, cinematic or other performances. The provision of the Illinois Criminal Code that follows provides an illustration of one approach to this issue.

§ 11-20a. Child Pornography

(a) Definitions.

(1) Matter or a performance, whether live, cinematic or over broadcast media, of whatever nature, is "child pornography" for purposes of this section if:

(A) it has as one of its participants or portrayed observers a child under the age of 16 or who appears as pre-pubescent; and

(B) it contains depictions or descriptions of sexual conduct which are patently offensive; and

(C) taken as a whole, the average person, applying contemporary standards of this State, would find it has as its dominant theme an appeal to prurient interest; and

(D) taken as a whole, it lacks serious literary, artistic, educational, political or scientific purpose or value.

(2) "Sexual conduct" includes any of the following:

(A) sexual intercourse, which for purposes of this Section includes any intercourse which is normal or perverted, actual or simulated;

(B) deviate sexual conduct as defined in Section 11-2 of this Act;

(C) acts of masturbation;

(D) acts of sadomasochistic abuse, which includes but is not limited to (1) flagellation or torture by or upon any person who is nude or clad in undergarments or in a costume which is of a revealing nature or (2) the condition of being fettered, bound or otherwise physically restrained on the part of one who is nude or so clothed;

(E) acts of excretion in a sexual context; or

(F) exhibition of post-pubertal human genitals or pubic areas.

The above types of sexual conduct in subsections (a)(2)(A) through (F) are intended to include situations where, when appropriate to the type of conduct, the conduct is performed alone or between members of the same or opposite sex or between humans and animals in an act of apparent sexual stimulation or gratification. A thing is child pornography even though the pornographic element is latent, as in the case of undeveloped photographs.

(3) "Matter", for the purposes of this Section, means and includes any photographic product depicting actual human models or actors, whether in the form of still photographs, motion pictures, or videotape. A thing is included under this definition of matter, whether it is a purely photographic product or a reproduction of such a product in any book, pamphlet, magazine or other publication.

(b) Offense. (1) Any person, who with knowledge of the nature or content thereof, or recklessly failing to exercise reasonable inspection which would have disclosed such nature or content, commits a Class 4 felony to which a fine of up to $25,000 may be added when he or she:

(A) Sells, delivers, exhibits or otherwise makes available, or offers or agrees to sell, deliver, exhibit, or otherwise make available, any child pornography; or

(B) Buys, procures or possesses child pornography with intent to disseminate it.

(2) Any person who photographs, films, videotapes, produces, publishes or otherwise creates child pornography, or knowingly causes another to do so, commits a Class 1 felony to which a fine of up to $50,000 may be added.

(3) Any person who solicits any minor under the age of 16 to appear in child pornography or, as the parent, legal guardian, or person having care or custody of the minor, knowingly permits or arranges for the child to so appear, commits a Class 1 felony.

(c) Interpretation of Evidence.

Child pornography shall be judged with reference to ordinary adults, except that it shall be judged with reference to children or other specially susceptible audiences if it appears from the character of the material or the circumstances of its dissemination to be specially designed for or directed to such an audience.

Where circumstances of production, presentation, sale, dissemination, distribution, or publicity indicate that material is being commercially exploited for the sake of its prurient appeal, such evidence is probative with respect to the nature of the matter and can justify the conclusion that the matter is without serious literary, artistic, educational, political, or scientific purpose or value.

In any prosecution for an offense under this Section evidence shall be admissible to show:

(1) The character of the audience for which the material was designed or to which it was directed;

(2) What the predominant appeal of the material would be for ordinary adults or a special audience, and what effect, if any, it would probably have on the behavior of such people;

(3) The artistic, literary, scientific, educational or other merits of the material, or absence thereof;

(4) The degree, if any, of public acceptance of the material in this State;

(5) Appeal to prurient interest, or absence thereof, in advertising or other promotion of the material;

(6) Purpose of the author, creator, publisher or disseminator.

(d) Prima Facie Evidence.

The creation, purchase, procurement or possession of a mold, engraved plate or other embodiment of obscenity specially adapted for reproducing multiple copies, or the possession of more than 3 copies of obscene material shall be prima facie evidence of an intent to disseminate.

(e) Affirmative Defenses.

It shall be an affirmative defense to obscenity that the dissemination was to institutions or individuals having scientific or other special justification for possession of such material.

(2) In New York v. Ferber, ___ U.S. ___, 102 S.Ct. 3348, 73 L.Ed.2d 1113 (1982), the United States Supreme Court upheld the constitutionality of a New York statute prohibiting anyone from knowingly promoting a sexual

performance by a child under 16 by distributing material that depicts such a performance. The New York Court of Appeals had held that the statute violated the first amendment because it was both underinclusive and over-broad; the Supreme Court disagreed, holding that it is not necessary that the depicting material be legally obscene in cases involving children.

TINKER v. DES MOINES INDEPENDENT COMMUNITY SCHOOL DISTRICT

Supreme Court of the United States, 1969.
393 U.S. 503, 89 S.Ct. 733, 21 L.Ed.2d 731.

MR. JUSTICE FORTAS delivered the opinion of the Court.

Petitioner John F. Tinker, 15 years old, and petitioner Christopher Eckhardt, 16 years old, attended high schools in Des Moines, Iowa. Petitioner Mary Beth Tinker, John's sister, was a 13-year-old student in junior high school.

In December 1965, a group of adults and students in Des Moines held a meeting at the Eckhardt home. The group determined to pub-licize their objections to the hostilities in Vietnam and their support for a truce by wearing black armbands during the holiday season and by fasting on December 16 and New Year's Eve. Petitioners and their parents had previously engaged in similar activities, and they decided to participate in the program.

The principals of the Des Moines schools became aware of the plan to wear armbands. On December 14, 1965, they met and adopt-ed a policy that any student wearing an armband to school would be asked to remove it, and if he refused he would be suspended until he returned without the armband. Petitioners were aware of the regu-lation that the school authorities adopted.

On December 16, Mary Beth and Christopher wore black arm-bands to their schools. John Tinker wore his armband the next day. They were all sent home and suspended from school until they would come back without their armbands. They did not return to school until after the planned period for wearing armbands had expired—that is, until after New Year's Day.

This complaint was filed in the United States District Court by petitioners, through their fathers, under § 1983 of Title 42 of the United States Code. It prayed for an injunction restraining the re-spondent school officials and the respondent members of the board of directors of the school district from disciplining the petitioners, and it sought nominal damages. After an evidentiary hearing the District Court dismissed the complaint. It upheld the constitutionality of the school authorities' action on the ground that it was reasonable in or-der to prevent disturbance of school discipline. 258 F.Supp. 971 (1966). The court referred to but expressly declined to follow the Fifth Circuit's holding in a similar case that the wearing of symbols like the armbands cannot be prohibited unless it "materially and sub-stantially interfere[s] with the requirements of appropriate discipline in the operation of the school." Burnside v. Byars, 363 F.2d 744, 749 (1966).[1]

On appeal, the Court of Appeals for the Eighth Circuit considered the case *en banc*. The court was equally divided, and the District Court's decision was accordingly affirmed. . . .

The District Court recognized that the wearing of an armband for the purpose of expressing certain views is the type of symbolic act that is within the Free Speech Clause of the First Amendment. As we shall discuss, the wearing of armbands in the circumstances of this case was entirely divorced from actually or potentially disruptive conduct by those participating in it. It was closely akin to "pure speech" which, we have repeatedly held, is entitled to comprehensive protection under the First Amendment.

First Amendment rights, applied in light of the special characteristics of the school environment, are available to teachers and students. It can hardly be argued that either students or teachers shed their constitutional rights to freedom of speech or expression at the schoolhouse gate. This has been the unmistakable holding of this Court for almost 50 years.

In West Virginia State Board of Education v. Barnette, 319 U.S. 624, 63 S.Ct. 1178, 87 L.Ed. 1628 (1943), this Court held that under the First Amendment, the student in public school may not be compelled to salute the flag. Speaking through Mr. Justice Jackson, the Court said:

> "The Fourteenth Amendment, as now applied to the States, protects the citizen against the State itself and all of its creatures—Boards of Education not excepted. These have, of course, important, delicate, and highly discretionary functions, but none that they may not perform within the limits of the Bill of Rights. That they are educating the young for citizenship is reason for scrupulous protection of Constitutional freedoms of the individual, if we are not to strangle the free mind at its source and teach youth to discount important principles of our government as mere platitudes." 319 U.S., at 637, 63 S.Ct. at 1185.

On the other hand, the Court has repeatedly emphasized the need for affirming the comprehensive authority of the States and of school officials, consistent with fundamental constitutional safeguards, to prescribe and control conduct in the schools. Our problem lies in the area where students in the exercise of First Amendment rights collide with the rules of the school authorities.

1. In *Burnside*, the Fifth Circuit ordered that high school authorities be enjoined from enforcing a regulation forbidding students to wear "freedom buttons." It is instructive that in Blackwell v. Issaquena County Board of Education, 363 F.2d 749 (1966), the same panel on the same day reached the opposite result on different facts. It declined to enjoin enforcement of such a regulation in another high school where the students wearing freedom buttons harassed students who did not wear them and created much disturbance.

The problem posed by the present case does not relate to regulation of the length of skirts or the type of clothing, to hair style, or deportment. It does not concern aggressive, disruptive action or even group demonstrations. Our problem involves direct, primary First Amendment rights akin to "pure speech."

The school officials banned and sought to punish petitioners for a silent, passive expression of opinion, unaccompanied by any disorder or disturbance on the part of petitioners. There is here no evidence whatever of petitioners' interference, actual or nascent, with the schools' work or of collision with the rights of other students to be secure and to be let alone. Accordingly, this case does not concern speech or action that intrudes upon the work of the schools or the rights of other students.

Only a few of the 18,000 students in the school system wore the black armbands. Only five students were suspended for wearing them. There is no indication that the work of the schools or any class was disrupted. Outside the classrooms, a few students made hostile remarks to the children wearing armbands, but there were no threats or acts of violence on school premises.

The District Court concluded that the action of the school authorities was reasonable because it was based upon their fear of a disturbance from the wearing of the armbands. But, in our system, undifferentiated fear or apprehension of disturbance is not enough to overcome the right to freedom of expression. Any departure from absolute regimentation may cause trouble. Any variation from the majority's opinion may inspire fear. Any word spoken, in class, in the lunchroom, or on the campus, that deviates from the views of another person may start an argument or cause a disturbance. But our Constitution says we must take this risk . . . .

In order for the State in the person of school officials to justify prohibition of a particular expression of opinion, it must be able to show that its action was caused by something more than a mere desire to avoid the discomfort and unpleasantness that always accompany an unpopular viewpoint. Certainly where there is no finding and no showing that engaging in the forbidden conduct would "materially and substantially interfere with the requirements of appropriate discipline in the operation of the school," the prohibition cannot be sustained. Burnside v. Byars, supra, 363 F.2d at 749.

In the present case, the District Court made no such finding, and our independent examination of the record fails to yield evidence that the school authorities had reason to anticipate that the wearing of the armbands would substantially interfere with the work of the school or impinge upon the rights of other students. Even an official memorandum prepared after the suspension that listed the reasons for the ban on wearing the armbands made no reference to the anticipation of such disruption.[3]

On the contrary, the action of the school authorities appears to have been based upon an urgent wish to avoid the controversy which might result from the expression, even by the silent symbol of armbands, of opposition to this Nation's part in the conflagration in Vietnam. It is revealing, in this respect, that the meeting at which the school principals decided to issue the contested regulation was called in response to a student's statement to the journalism teacher in one of the schools that he wanted to write an article on Vietnam and have it published in the school paper. (The student was dissuaded.)

It is also relevant that the school authorities did not purport to prohibit the wearing of all symbols of political or controversial significance. The record shows that students in some of the schools wore buttons relating to national political campaigns, and some even wore the Iron Cross, traditionally a symbol of Nazism. The order prohibiting the wearing of armbands did not extend to these. Instead, a particular symbol—black armbands worn to exhibit opposition to this Nation's involvement in Vietnam—was singled out for prohibition. Clearly, the prohibition of expression of one particular opinion, at least without evidence that it is necessary to avoid material and substantial interference with schoolwork or discipline, is not constitutionally permissible.

In our system, state-operated schools may not be enclaves of totalitarianism. School officials do not possess absolute authority over their students. Students in school as well as out of school are "persons" under our Constitution. They are possessed of fundamental rights which the State must respect, just as they themselves must respect their obligations to the State. In our system, students may not be regarded as closed-circuit recipients of only that which the State chooses to communicate. They may not be confined to the expression of those sentiments that are officially approved. In the absence of a specific showing of constitutionally valid reasons to regulate their speech, students are entitled to freedom of expression of their views. . . .

. . . In Keyishian v. Board of Regents, 385 U.S. 589, 603, 87 S.Ct. 675, 683, 17 L.Ed.2d 629, Mr. Justice Brennan, speaking for the Court, said:

" 'The vigilant protection of constitutional freedoms is nowhere more vital than in the community of American schools.' Shelton v. Tucker, [364 U.S. 479], at 487 [81 S.Ct. 247, 5 L.Ed.2d 231]. The

3. . . . [T]he testimony of school authorities at trial indicates that it was not fear of disruption that motivated the regulation prohibiting the armbands; the regulation was directed against "the principle of the demonstration" itself. School authorities simply felt that "the schools are no place for demonstrations," and if the students "didn't like the way our elected officials were handling things, it should be handled with the ballot box and not in the halls of our public schools."

classroom is peculiarly the 'marketplace of ideas.' The Nation's future depends upon leaders trained through wide exposure to that robust exchange of ideas which discovers truth 'out of a multitude of tongues, [rather] than through any kind of authoritative selection.' "

The principle of these cases is not confined to the supervised and ordained discussion which takes place in the classroom. The principal use to which the schools are dedicated is to accommodate students during prescribed hours for the purpose of certain types of activities. Among those activities is personal intercommunication among the students.[6] This is not only an inevitable part of the process of attending school; it is also an important part of the educational process. A student's rights, therefore, do not embrace merely the classroom hours. When he is in the cafeteria, or on the playing field, or on the campus during the authorized hours, he may express his opinions, even on controversial subjects like the conflict in Vietnam, if he does so without "materially and substantially interfer[ing] with the requirements of appropriate discipline in the operation of the school" and without colliding with the rights of others. Burnside v. Byars, supra, 363 F.2d at 749. But conduct by the student, in class or out of it, which for any reason—whether it stems from time, place, or type of behavior—materially disrupts classwork or involves substantial disorder or invasion of the rights of others is, of course, not immunized by the constitutional guarantee of freedom of speech.

. . .

As we have discussed, the record does not demonstrate any facts which might reasonably have led school authorities to forecast substantial disruption of or material interference with school activities, and no disturbances or disorders on the school premises in fact occurred. These petitioners merely went about their ordained rounds in school. Their deviation consisted only in wearing on their sleeve a band of black cloth, not more than two inches wide. They wore it to exhibit their disapproval of the Vietnam hostilities and their advocacy of a truce, to make their views known, and, by their example, to influence others to adopt them. They neither interrupted school activities nor sought to intrude in the school affairs or the lives of others. They caused discussion outside of the classrooms, but no interference with work and no disorder. In the circumstances, our Constitution does not permit officials of the State to deny their form of expression.

6. In Hammond v. South Carolina State College, 272 F.Supp. 947 (D.C.S.C. 1967), District Judge Hemphill had before him a case involving a meeting on campus of 300 students to express their views on school practices. He pointed out that a school is not like a hospital or a jail enclosure. It is a public place, and its dedication to specific uses does not imply that the constitutional rights of persons entitled to be there are to be gauged as if the premises were purely private property.

We express no opinion as to the form of relief which should be granted, this being a matter for the lower courts to determine. . . .

Reversed and remanded.

MR. JUSTICE STEWART, concurring.

Although I agree with much of what is said in the Court's opinion, and with its judgment in this case, I cannot share the Court's uncritical assumption that, school discipline aside, the First Amendment rights of children are co-extensive with those of adults. Indeed, I had thought the Court decided otherwise just last Term in Ginsberg v. New York, 390 U.S. 629, 88 S.Ct. 1274, 20 L.Ed.2d 195. I continue to hold the view I expressed in that case: "[A] State may permissibly determine that, at least in some precisely delineated areas, a child— like someone in a captive audience—is not possessed of that full capacity for individual choice which is the presupposition of First Amendment guarantees." Id., at 649–650, 88 S.Ct. at 1285–1286 (concurring in result). Cf. Prince v. Massachusetts, 321 U.S. 158, 64 S.Ct. 438, 88 L.Ed. 645.

[The concurring opinion of MR. JUSTICE WHITE is omitted.]

MR. JUSTICE BLACK, dissenting.

The Court's holding in this case ushers in what I deem to be an entirely new era in which the power to control pupils by the elected "officials of state supported public schools . . ." in the United States is in ultimate effect transferred to the Supreme Court. The Court brought this particular case here on a petition for certiorari urging that the First and Fourteenth Amendments protect the right of school pupils to express their political views all the way "from kindergarten through high school." Here the constitutional right to "political expression" asserted was a right to wear black armbands during school hours and at classes in order to demonstrate to the other students that the petitioners were mourning because of the death of United States soldiers in Vietnam and to protest that war which they were against. Ordered to refrain from wearing the armbands in school by the elected school officials and the teachers vested with state authority to do so, apparently only seven out of the school system's 18,000 pupils deliberately refused to obey the order. One defying pupil was Paul Tinker, 8 years old, who was in the second grade; another, Hope Tinker, was 11 years old and in the fifth grade; a third member of the Tinker family was 13, in the eighth grade; and a fourth member of the same family was John Tinker, 15 years old, an 11th grade high school pupil. Their father, a Methodist minister without a church, is paid a salary by the American Friends Service Committee. Another student who defied the school order and insisted on wearing an armband in school was Christopher Eckhardt, an

11th grade pupil and a petitioner in this case. His mother is an official in the Women's International League for Peace and Freedom.

. . .

Assuming that the Court is correct in holding that the conduct of wearing armbands for the purpose of conveying political ideas is protected by the First Amendment, the crucial remaining questions are whether students and teachers may use the schools at their whim as a platform for the exercise of free speech—"symbolic" or "pure"—and whether the courts will allocate to themselves the function of deciding how the pupils' school day will be spent. . . .

While the record does not show that any of these armband students shouted, used profane language, or were violent in any manner, detailed testimony by some of them shows their armbands caused comments, warnings by other students, the poking of fun at them, and a warning by an older football player that other, nonprotesting students had better let them alone. There is also evidence that a teacher of mathematics had his lesson period practically "wrecked" chiefly by disputes with Mary Beth Tinker, who wore her armband for her "demonstration." Even a casual reading of the record shows that this armband did divert students' minds from their regular lessons, and that talk, comments, etc., made John Tinker "self-conscious" in attending school with his armband. While the absence of obscene remarks or boisterous and loud disorder perhaps justifies the Court's statement that the few armband students did not actually "disrupt" the classwork, I think the record overwhelmingly shows that the armbands did exactly what the elected school officials and principals foresaw they would, that is, took the students' minds off their classwork and diverted them to thoughts about the highly emotional subject of the Vietnam war. And I repeat that if the time has come when pupils of state-supported schools, kindergartens, grammar schools, or high schools, can defy and flout orders of school officials to keep their minds on their own schoolwork, it is the beginning of a new revolutionary era of permissiveness in this country fostered by the judiciary. The next logical step, it appears to me, would be to hold unconstitutional laws that bar pupils under 21 or 18 from voting, or from being elected members of the boards of education.[2]

. . .

I deny . . . that it has been the "unmistakable holding of this Court for almost 50 years" that "students" and "teachers" take with them into the "schoolhouse gate" constitutional rights to "freedom of

2. The following Associated Press article appeared in the Washington Evening Star, January 11, 1969, p. A–2, col. 1: "Bellingham, Mass. (AP)—Todd R. Hennessy, 16, has filed nominating papers to run for town park commissioner in the March election.

" 'I can see nothing illegal in the youth's seeking the elective office,' said Lee Ambler, the town counsel. 'But I can't overlook the possibility that if he is elected any legal contract entered into by the park commissioner would be void because he is a juvenile.'

"Todd is a junior in Mount St. Charles Academy, where he has a top scholastic record."

speech or expression." Even *Meyer* did not hold that. It makes no reference to "symbolic speech" at all; . . .

. . .

In my view, teachers in state-controlled public schools are hired to teach there. Although Mr. Justice McReynolds may have intimated to the contrary in Meyer v. Nebraska, supra, certainly a teacher is not paid to go into school and teach subjects the State does not hire him to teach as a part of its selected curriculum. Nor are public school students sent to the schools at public expense to broadcast political or any other views to educate and inform the public. The original idea of schools, which I do not believe is yet abandoned as worthless or out of date, was that children had not yet reached the point of experience and wisdom which enabled them to teach all of their elders. It may be that the Nation has outworn the old-fashioned slogan that "children are to be seen not heard," but one may, I hope, be permitted to harbor the thought that taxpayers send children to school on the premise that at their age they need to learn, not teach.

. . .

Change has been said to be truly the law of life but sometimes the old and the tried and true are worth holding. The schools of this Nation have undoubtedly contributed to giving us tranquility and to making us a more law-abiding people. Uncontrolled and uncontrollable liberty is an enemy to domestic peace. We cannot close our eyes to the fact that some of the country's greatest problems are crimes committed by the youth, too many of school age. School discipline, like parental discipline, is an integral and important part of training our children to be good citizens—to be better citizens. Here a very small number of students have crisply and summarily refused to obey a school order designed to give pupils who want to learn the opportunity to do so. One does not need to be a prophet or the son of a prophet to know that after the Court's holding today some students in Iowa schools and indeed in all schools will be ready, able, and willing to defy their teachers on practically all orders. This is the more unfortunate for the schools since groups of students all over the land are already running loose, conducting break-ins, sit-ins, lie-ins, and smash-ins. . . . Students engaged in such activities are apparently confident that they know far more about how to operate public school systems than do their parents, teachers, and elected school officials. It is no answer to say that the particular students here have not yet reached such high points in their demands to attend classes in order to exercise their political pressures. Turned loose with lawsuits for damages and injunctions against their teachers as they are here, it is nothing but wishful thinking to imagine that young, immature students will not soon believe it is their right to control the schools rather than the right of the States that collect the taxes to hire the teachers for the benefit of the pupils. This case, therefore, wholly without constitutional reasons in my judgment, subjects all the public schools in the country to the whims and caprices of their loudest-mouthed, but maybe not their brightest, students. I, for one, am not fully persuaded that school pupils are wise enough, even with this Court's expert held from Washington, to run the 23,390 public school systems in our 50 States. I wish, therefore, wholly to disclaim any purpose on my part to hold that the Federal Constitution compels the teachers, parents, and elected school officials to surrender control of the American public school system to public school students. I dissent.

MR. JUSTICE HARLAN, dissenting.

I certainly agree that state public school authorities in the discharge of their responsibilities are not wholly exempt from the requirements of the Fourteenth Amendment respecting the freedoms of expression and association. At the same time I am reluctant to believe that there is any disagreement between the majority and myself on the proposition that school officials should be accorded the widest authority in maintaining discipline and good order in their institutions. To translate that proposition into a workable constitutional rule, I would, in cases like this, cast upon those complaining the burden of showing that a particular school measure was motivated by other than legitimate school concerns—for example, a desire to prohibit the expression of an unpopular point of view, while permitting expression of the dominant opinion.

Finding nothing in this record which impugns the good faith of respondents in promulgating the armband regulation, I would affirm the judgment below.

NOTES

(1) Was *Tinker* really a case about children's rights, or was it more a case upholding family expression or parental inculcation of values? If it is the first, can it be said that children are accorded greater freedom to express themselves in political matters than to learn about sex, in view of the Court's holding in the *Ginsberg* case?

Note that Justice Black's dissent points out that two other defiant pupils were Paul Tinker, age 8, and Hope Tinker, age 11, who were not plaintiffs in the action. How would their presence as participants in the litigation have affected your answers to the previous questions? Should it have had effect on the Supreme Court's decision? For a discussion, see Garvey, Child, Parent, State, and the Due Process Clause: An Essay on the Supreme Court's Recent Work, 51 So.Cal.L.Rev. 769, 785 (1978), in which the author asserts that *Tinker* was really about "family rights". Not inconsistent, it would seem, is Professor Hafen's statement that *"Tinker* is not an obstacle to the assertion that none of the Supreme Court's children's rights cases provide authority for upholding the exercise of minors' choice rights—particularly against contrary parental claims." Hafen, Children's Liberation and the New Egalitarianism: Some Reservations about Abandoning Youth to Their "Rights", 1976 B.Y.U.L. Rev. 605, 646.

Professor Robert Burt has written this sensitive appraisal:

Even if *Tinker* is—as *Yoder* and *Prince* may be—a symbolic battle between adults, each using children as sacrificial pawns, the Constitution clearly constrains the state more than parents in this matter. If the Des Moines school officials, that is, insist on one brand of ideological conformity, the traditions of the first amendment amply justify a court ruling that this is impermissible state action in itself.

The *Tinker* Court erred not in its result, but in its failure to acknowledge the potential educational and constitutional relevance of the facts in the case suggesting that the children's armbands reflected more their parents' convictions than theirs. The Court ignored the possibility that school officials might exclude parental political views from school in order to free children to think through these questions for themselves. As noted, that motivation was implausible on the face of the *Tinker* record, but it is not an implausible educational goal, nor should that goal be prohibited by the Constitution. The *Tinker* Court should have acknowledged that the constitutional question would have changed complexion if the school officials had convincingly argued that they were acting not to impose their political views on students, but rather on behalf of the root values of the first amendment—tolerance, diversity of thought, individual autonomy—against parental impositions on children.

Burt, Developing Constitutional Rights Of, In, and For Children, 39 Law & Contemp. Probs. 118, 123–24 (1975).*

(2) The confusion about whether the child's or the adult's rights are at issue is reflected in Marina Point v. Wolfson, 30 Cal.3d 721, 180 Cal.Rptr. 496, 640 P.2d 115 (1982) in which the California Supreme Court held that renting only to adults violated the state statutory prohibition on housing discrimination. The court hedged as to who was being protected and given rights under the anti-discrimination statute: children themselves or families with children.

In *Wolfson*, the court rejected the landlord's argument that children as a class "generally cause more wear and tear on property than adults do, and that as a consequence, landlords who rent to families with children generally have higher maintenance costs than landlords who exclude children." The court held that a landlord could establish rules that prohibited tenants from damaging property or being noisy. However, California's anti-discrimination law does not permit a business "to exclude an *entire class* of individuals on the basis of a generalized prediction that the class 'as a whole' is more likely to commit misconduct than some other class of the public." (Emphasis in original).

In *Wolfson*, the landlord argued that the presence of children was inconsistent with its "adults only" apartment complex. The landlord analogized to adult bookstores, adult theaters, taverns and senior citizen homes which are permitted to exclude children. The court noted that taverns, and certain bookstores and theaters must exclude children because of statutorily sanctioned restrictions on the rights of children. Housing for the elderly was also distinguished as a means of meeting the special housing needs of old people.

THE SCHOOL NEWSPAPER CASES

Tinker involved symbolic speech. More frequently the first amendment issues raised by schoolchildren involve newspapers—either an in-school paper or an alternative, underground paper. Different issues are raised by the different kinds of papers. In-school newspapers are less frequently involved in litigation than underground newspapers produced off-campus and often designed as an alternative to the official school newspaper with the express purpose of challenging school policy.

Many issues of school censorship of in-house newspapers have been resolved. For example, school boards frequently have sought to justify censorship by asserting that the school newspaper is part of the curriculum and that the board has complete authority to determine the content of the curriculum. This argument has generally been rejected. First, requiring schools to comply with the first amendment does not interfere with the school board's choice of what courses to offer. Second, schools need not offer journalism or publish newspapers, but once they do, they cannot censor or otherwise restrict the first amendment rights of students who publish the paper. In addition, public schools do not have absolute control over their curricula; like other government functions they are limited by the Constitution. For example, it is well-settled that public schools could not constitutionally require religious instruction.

Schools have also argued that they provide the funds for school papers and can therefore determine what the student editors print. This argument also has been unsuccessful, mainly because the government generally provides the funds for parks, streets, and auditoria that have full first amendment protection notwithstanding their government funding.

What motivates school officials to censor or impose limitations on school newspapers? Protection of students? Fear of parental reactions? Suppression of student criticism? Does censorship further the goals of school officials? Consider the following excerpts from Gambino v. Fairfax County School Board, 429 F.Supp. 731 (E.D.Va. 1977), affirmed 564 F.2d 157 (4th Cir.), especially footnote one.

This action was brought pursuant to 42 U.S.C.A. 1983 and 28 U.S.C.A. 1343 to enjoin the defendant from prohibiting the publication of an article entitled "Sexually Active Students Fail to Use Contraception" in "The Farm News," a newspaper published in the Hayfield Secondary School (Hayfield). Pursuant to a prior agreement regarding potentially controversial material, this article was submitted to the principal, Doris Torrice, for review. Perceiving that portions of the submission containing information on contraceptives [violated a School Board prohibition of sex education instruction], she ordered plaintiffs not to publish it as written. Although plaintiffs were given the option of publishing the article with the objectionable passages excised, they chose to insist on printing all or none of the piece. . . .

As noted above, the Farm News is a student activity. Some staff members are enrolled in Journalism and receive academic credit for their work on the paper. Other staff members work on the paper as an extracurricular activity. The paper is written and edited in the school during school hours and at the homes of the participants. Revenues are generated from advertising, allocations from the School Board, sales of individual issues, and student subscriptions. . . . Copies of the newspaper usually are distributed to student subscribers in homeroom.

As the Court views it, this case turns upon one issue—whether the Farm News is a publication protected by the First Amendment. The authority of the School Board to determine course content in the school curriculum is not questioned. Nor is there any contention that the content of the article would fall outside the limits of First Amendment freedom if the newspaper otherwise is protected. In fact, upon an actual reading of the article, the Court is surprised at its innocuousness and that it could spawn the controversy at hand.[1] Nevertheless, the defendants have perceived sufficient danger in the publication to warrant judicial resolution of the problem. Defendants also recognize that if the newspaper is found to be a First Amendment forum the regulations pursuant to which this suppression was undertaken are open to serious question. . . .

The defendants rely on the contention that the Farm News is not a public forum entitled to First Amendment protection. They argue that the newspaper is essentially an "in-house" organ of the school system, or alternatively that the students in Hayfield are a "captive audience," rendering the publication subject to reasonable regulation.

While the state may have a particular proprietary interest in a publication that legitimately precludes it from being a vehicle for First Amendment expression, it may not foreclose constitutional scrutiny by mere labelling. . . . Once a publication is determined to be in substance a free speech forum, constitutional protections attach and the state may restrict the content of that instrument only in accordance with First Amendment dictates. . . .

The defendants urge that this principle is inapposite because (prior) decisions have arisen out of the college environment. They point out, and the Court does not dispute, that the "First Amendment rights of children are not co-extensive with those of adults." Tinker v. Des Moines Independent Community School District, 393

1. A controversy which, given the normal curiosity and ingenuity of youth, had assured that copies of the offending article now have been secured by many if not most of the students sought to be protected.

U.S. 503, 515, 89 S.Ct. 733, 741, 21 L.Ed.2d 731 (1969) (Stewart, J., concurring). . . . Further, the defendants assert the illogic of applying the First Amendment to a high school newspaper, conjuring up visions of irresponsible and uncontrollable publication.

There are, however, two distinctions that invalidate these objections. While the scope of constitutional freedom may vary with the nature of the environment and the maturity of the individuals affected, the considerations governing the applicability of First Amendment analysis in the first instance do not change. Either the First Amendment is operative, or it is not. And if it is applicable, only then does the distinction between the extent to which speech is protected in colleges and in high schools become significant.

The youth of the audience is not determinative of the existence *vel non* of First Amendment protection, however. The immaturity of readers may necessitate limiting constitutional freedom, but any such limitation would require an examination of the content of the matter to be published and a balancing of the impact of that content against the state's interest measured by reference to constitutionally valid standards. As the defendants here stake their position on the inapplicability of the First Amendment, the Court does not need to define the boundaries of its protection in terms of the content of this article except insofar as the regulatory scheme may or may not be adequate to support the defendants' action. Consistent with their contention, the defendants introduced no evidence that the information in the article would be harmful to students in any of the age groups at Hayfield.

Defendants' fears of irresponsible journalism are met first by the fact that no evidence of it has surfaced in the past or in the article here in question, nor has there been any demonstrated likelihood of it in the future. . . . Irresponsible journalism may occur at some point in the future, but speculation is not a proper consideration in the decision of the case presently before the Court. . . .

The defendants have suggested, however, that the circumstances under which the newspaper is produced require an application of the "captive audience" principle most recently employed by the Supreme Court in Lehman v. City of Shaker Heights, 418 U.S. 298, 94 S.Ct. 2714, 41 L.Ed.2d 770 (1974). There the Court focused upon the lack of free choice which effectively compelled the users of the city transit system to receive the messages displayed on the system's vehicles, and determined that no public forum existed. Reliance was placed upon Packer Corp. v. Utah, 285 U.S. 105, 52 S.Ct. 273, 76 L.Ed. 643 (1932), where Justice Brandeis observed that communication of this sort is "constantly before the eyes of observers on the streets and in street cars to be seen without the exercise of choice or volition on their part." Id. at 110.

But Justice Brandeis also distinguished "the case of newspapers and magazines (where) there must be some seeking by the one who is to see and read the advertisement." Id. From that standpoint, defendants' application of the "captive audience" concept appears untenable. . . .

Finally defendants argue that to allow the students to publish this article would permit them to override the decision of the School Board not to include birth control in the sex education curriculum. As noted above, the Court does not question the authority of the School Board to prescribe course content. Further, while even under principles of liberal construction a considerable effort is required to find the questioned portions of the article instructional, the Court assumes that the article does contain information which, if it appeared in material used in a sex education course, would contravene the School Board's policy.

. . . (T)he newspaper cannot be construed objectively as an integral part of the curriculum offered at Hayfield. . . . Rather, it occupies a position more akin to the school library where more extensive and explicit information on birth control philosophy and methodology is available. In either place, the material is not suppressible by reason of its objectionability to the sensibilities of the School Board or its constituents. . . . Therefore, because the newspaper is not in reality a part of the curriculum of the school, and because it is entitled to First Amendment protection, the power of the School Board to regulate course content will not support its action in this case. . . .

Accordingly the plaintiffs are entitled to an injunction prohibiting the defendants, or those acting in concert with them, from banning the publication in the Farm News of those portions of the article which were found objectionable. . . .

As noted previously, somewhat different issues are raised by underground rather than in-school newspapers. By their very nature underground newspapers typically are more critical of school officials and therefore more at risk to suppression. One recurring issue is whether school officials can require submission of underground papers before they are distributed. Another is whether school officials can prevent students from distributing underground papers away from school grounds during non-school hours. Compare Nitzberg v. Parks, 525 F.2d 378 (4th Cir. 1975) (*Tinker* permits school authorities to use prior restraints for material that is libelous, obscene or would disrupt school activities) with Fujishima v. Board of Education, 460 F.2d 1355 (7th Cir. 1972) (*Tinker* permits punishment after publication but no prior restraints). See also Eisner v. Stamford Board of Education, 440 F.2d 803, 810–11 (2d Cir. 1971).

BRIGHT v. LOS ANGELES UNIFIED SCHOOL DISTRICT

Supreme Court of California, 1976.
18 Cal.3d 450, 134 Cal.Rptr. 639, 556 P.2d 1090.

SULLIVAN, J.—In this case we inquire into the right of California public school students to speak and write freely (see U.S.Const., First Amend.; Cal.Const., art. I, § 2) in the school environment and examine the scope and extent of such right in relation to the authority and supervision of school officials. Specifically, we are called upon to determine whether and to what extent, in the light of section 10611 of the Education Code [1] dealing with the students' "right to exercise free expression," school authorities may require the submission, for approval prior to distribution on school premises, of so called "alternative" or "underground" newspapers produced by the students off campus. As will appear, we conclude that the pertinent statute does not authorize any such prior restraint by school officials and that rules and regulations adopted by a school district insofar as they purport to effectuate it are void.

Plaintiff Susannah Bright, in May 1974 a 10th grade student at University High School (school) in Los Angeles, was a writer for the Red Tide, a newspaper intended for distribution to high school students, but produced independently of the public school system. On Friday, May 31, 1974, plaintiff and two other students of the school, desiring to distribute the then current edition of the paper, in accordance with the rules of defendant Los Angeles Unified School District [2] (District) submitted a copy of the paper to defendant Homer

1. Section 10611 of the Education Code provides: "Students of the public schools have the right to exercise free expression including, but not limited to, the use of bulletin boards, the distribution of printed materials or petitions, and the wearing of buttons, badges, and other insignia, except that expression which is obscene, libelous, or slanderous according to current legal standards, or which so incites students as to create a clear and present danger of the commission of unlawful acts on school premises or the violation of lawful school regulations, or the substantial disruption of the orderly operation of the school, shall be prohibited.

"Each governing board of a school district and each county superintendent of schools shall adopt rules and regulations relating to the exercise of free expression by students upon the premises of each school within their respective jurisdictions, which shall include reasonable provisions for the time, place, and manner of conducting such activities."

Hereafter, unless otherwise indicated, all section references are to the Education Code.

2. Los Angeles School Board Administrative Regulation 1276–1 provides in pertinent part:

"The procedures to be followed in the implementation of guidelines relating to student expression on campus are as follows:

"a. Circulation of Petitions, Circulars, Newspapers, and Other Printed Matter. Students should be allowed to distribute petitions, circulars, leaflets, newspapers, and other printed matter subject to the following limitations:

". . .

"d. Prohibited Material.

"1. Material which is obscene to minors according to current legal definitions.

"2. Material which is libelous according to current legal definitions.

"3. Material which incites students so as to create a clear and pre-

Gansz, the assistant principal. Gansz noticed on the front page of the Red Tide an article entitled "Students Fight Rules at Locke," concerning a dress code at Locke High School which prohibited male students from wearing hats in class. A portion of the article also on the front page, under a subheading "Principal Lies" [3] raised a question in Gansz' mind as to whether the article was libelous. Accordingly, he informed the three students that he could not immediately approve distribution of the paper but would have to consult with defendant John Welch, the school principal.

Having no personal knowledge of the events described in the Red Tide article, Welch and Gansz undertook an investigation to determine the truth of the assertion that Hobbs, the Locke principal, had lied. Upon advice of the county counsel, Welch attempted to contact Hobbs, but without success, and therefore spoke with Caras, the assistant principal. Caras stated that the charges in the article were

sent danger of the imminent commission of unlawful acts or of the substantial disruption of the orderly operation of the school.

"4. Material which expresses or advocates racial, ethnic, or religious prejudice so as to create a clear and present danger of imminent commission of unlawful acts or of the substantial disruption of the orderly operation of the school.

"5. Material which is distributed in violation of the time, place, and manner requirements.

"e. Disciplinary Action.

"Any student who wilfully and knowingly:

"1. distributes any petitions, circulars, newspapers, and other printed matter;

"2. wears any buttons, badges, or other insignia;

"3. posts on a bulletin board any item in violation of the aforementioned prohibitions should be suspended, expelled or otherwise penalized depending on the severity of the violation, and in accordance with established disciplinary procedures."

The students at University High School were apprised of the Board regulations and the procedures to be followed thereunder on that campus by circulars, such as the following:

"UNIVERSITY HIGH SCHOOL

"TO: STUDENTS

"FROM: John Welch, Principal

"SUBJECT: DISTRIBUTION OF 'NON SCHOOL LITERATURE'

"The rules at University High School regarding distribution of 'Non-School Literature' are based on the STUDENT RIGHTS AND RESPONSIBILITIES HANDBOOK' (1972) page 6.

"A student wishing to distribute 'Non-School Literature' must attach an informational copy of the literature to this form and give them to the principal or his secretary 24 hours in advance of desired distribution time. Within 24 hours the principal will respond to your request, and return this sheet to you. It is necessary to have this signed sheet before distribution is made. Permission to distribute this material does not imply approval of contents by either the Board of Education or the administration of University High School. . . ."

The circular further stated that the distribution of the printed material, if permitted, was subject to limitations in respect to time, place and manner of distribution.

3. "Also during the course of this meeting, Hobbs stated a number of lies (1) that the no hats in class rule was made both by students and teachers, and not by him, (2) that the hats question is neither a frequent or heated subject of debate in faculty meetings and in fact the faculty is generally in support of the no hats rule, (3) that the student council has never made any attempt to change this rule, and (4) that the faculty and students are generally in support of this rule."

inaccurate. Welch thereupon informed plaintiff and her companions that he would have to postpone until the following Monday, June 3, any decision as to the distribution of the Red Tide.

On Monday, Welch reached Hobbs by telephone. The latter, who in the meantime had read the article in question, acknowledged that he had made the statements attributed to him but denied that they were untrue. Eventually on the advice of both the county counsel's office and the legal adviser's office, and on the basis of his discussions with Caras and Hobbs, Welch decided not to allow distribution of the Red Tide on the campus. Nevertheless he later permitted the distribution of a flyer protesting his decision and a noon protest meeting.

Plaintiff commenced the instant action on June 5, 1974. Her first amended complaint (hereafter complaint), in two counts, sought injunctive and declarative relief on the ground that the rules and regulations of defendant district, on their face and as applied, constitute an illegal prior censorship scheme, are violative of section 10611, and alternatively are violative of the First Amendment to the United States Constitution and article I, section 2 of the California Constitution, and are also violative of the equal protection and due process clauses of the federal and state Constitutions. The first count sought relief for the banning of distribution of the newspaper for the alleged reason that it contained libelous material; the second count sought relief for the flat ban on the sale of underground newspapers.

. . .

Tinker in boldly proclaiming students' freedom of speech in the school environment introduced a significant change in the control of students by school authorities and in a real sense gave voice to a different theory of education. The older and, until *Tinker*, the prevailing view regarded the school administration's authority as nearly absolute. For example, in 1913, a California high school student, during school hours, delivered an address to the student body in which he denounced the board of education for maintaining the school buildings as firetraps and belittled it for doing nothing to improve the safety of the school. He was expelled from school. The court in upholding the expulsion declared: "The admitted purpose of the plaintiff's address was to belittle the defendants in their official capacity; and the whole tenor of the address was well calculated to produce not only that result, but to engender as well in the minds of the students a feeling of disrespect for the defendants, and a secret if not an open hostility to their control of the student body and management of school affairs. Such being the natural tenor and tendency of the plaintiff's address, his conduct in making the same cannot be classed as anything but a species of insubordination to constituted authority, which required correction at the hands of the defendants in order that the discipline of the school might be maintained unimpaired by anything that was said and done by the plaintiff." (Wooster v. Sunderland (1915) 27 Cal.App. 51, 55–56, 148 P. 959, 961.)

By way of contrast, the court in *Tinker* specifically recognized that "personal intercommunication among the students . . . is not only an inevitable part of the process of attending school; it is also an important part of the educational process." (393 U.S. at p. 512, 89 S.Ct. at p. 739.) Moreover, this student communication, especially the expression of an unpopular view, may cause trouble and lead to disturbance, but "our history says that it is this sort of hazardous freedom—this kind of openness—that is the basis of our national strength and of the independence and vigor of Americans who grow up and live in this relatively permissive, often disputatious, society." (Id. at pp. 508–509, 89 S.Ct. at p. 738.)

In today's world, student criticism of government, society and the school system itself constantly seeks expression in a variety of ways. One medium of this expression is the so-called "underground newspaper" produced by students off campus without the authorization of school officials, but distributed on the school premises. Newspapers of this genre typically contain material which criticizes the school administration, challenges the principles and policies of public school education and covers controversial topics outside the curriculum—all frequently couched in strident and blunt, even earthy language. (See Letwin, Regulation of Underground Newspapers on Public School Campuses in California (1974–1975) 22 U.C.L.A.L.Rev. 141, 142–143.) The attempted distribution of these newspapers on high school campuses and the restriction of their distribution by school authorities have spawned a substantial amount of litigation in the federal courts. (See, for example, Jacobs v. Board of School Commissioners (7th Cir. 1973) 490 F.2d 601, vac. and dism. (1975) 420 U.S. 128, 95 S.Ct. 848, 43 L.Ed.2d 74; Baughman v. Freienmuth (4th Cir. 1973) 478 F.2d 1345; Fujishima v. Board of Education (7th Cir. 1972) 460 F.2d 1355; Eisner v. Stamford Board of Education (2d Cir. 1971) 440 F.2d 803; Quarterman v. Byrd (4th Cir. 1971) 453 F.2d 54.) [4]

Plaintiff contends that the prior restraint inherent in [the] regulations is contrary to the requirements of section 10611 and that therefore the regulations are void as being violative of an act of the Legislature. . . . Plaintiff argues that when section 10611 is examined in the light of its legislative history, it may be fairly and reasonably construed as not authorizing prior restraint so that the section of its

---

4. In the case at bench, the issue of the "Red Tide" here in dispute appears to conform to this pattern. In addition to the column attacking the principal of Locke High School, it contains articles discussing the right of pregnant minors to obtain abortions without prior consent, describing as a myth the portrayal in textbooks of Abraham Lincoln as a hero, and examining the relationship between the family of Patricia Hearst and the Symbionese Liberation Army. We of course intimate no views on any of these articles.

own force invalidates defendants' scheme of prior censorship. We think that the argument has merit.

. . .

. . . [W]e are of the view that the section when considered in the light of the legislative history detailed above, can be more reasonably construed as not authorizing prior restraint but rather as authorizing the stopping of such distribution once begun and the imposition of sanctions against those students responsible for such distribution. . . .

. . .

While the federal circuits which have considered the problem appear to have indicated that some system of prior restraint may be constitutional (Jacobs v. Board of School Commissioners, supra, 490 F.2d 601; Baughman v. Freienmuth, supra, 478 F.2d 1345; Sullivan v. Houston Independent School District (5th Cir. 1973) 475 F.2d 1071; Shanley v. Northeast Ind. Sch. Dist., Bexar County, Tex. (5th Cir. 1972) 462 F.2d 960; Quarterman v. Byrd, supra, 453 F.2d 54; Eisner v. Stamford Board of Education, supra, 440 F.2d 80; but see Fujishima v. Board of Education, supra, 460 F.2d 1355) none of them actually upheld a system of prior restraint. Some courts have focused upon the need for clear, precise standards of review and have found the standards proposed unacceptable (e.g., *Jacobs, Baughman,* and *Shanley*) while other courts have focused upon the need for procedural safeguards, such as prompt review within a definite time limit, as well as provision for appeal, either judicial or administrative (e.g., *Eisner, Quarterman* and *Baughman*). Since the case at bench involves the prior censorship of libelous material, we think that *Baughman* is the case most in point and most illustrative of the constitutional problems in this area.

Baughman dealt with a challenge to a regulation requiring students to submit any "underground" newspaper to the principal for review and authorizing the principal to bar distribution of the paper if in his opinion it contained libelous language. The court held the regulation unconstitutional on three bases: (1) that it was procedurally defective in that it failed to specify a reasonably short time for the principal's action and to provide for an expeditious review of his decision; (2) that the term "distribution" was unconstitutionally vague, stating that "there may be no prior restraint unless there is 'a *substantial* distribution'" (*Baughman,* supra, at p. 1349); and (3) that "[t]he use of terms of art such as 'libelous' and 'obscene' are not sufficiently precise and understandable by high school students and administrators untutored in the law to be acceptable criteria [in the context of prior restraint]. . . . Thus, while school authorities may ban obscenity and unprivileged libelous material there is an intolerable danger, in the context of prior restraint, that under the guise of such vague labels they may unconstitutionally choke off criticism, ei-

ther of themselves, or of school policies, which they find disrespect-
ful, tasteless, or offensive." (Id. at pp. 1350–1351.)

. . .

For the foregoing reasons, we hold that section 10611 does not
authorize school districts to establish systems of prior restraint in respect to the distribution of the prohibited categories of expression delineated in the statute. We do not say that the Legislature could not
constitutionally establish such a system in the public school environment. We say only that it has not done so. Therefore, under the
settled principle that regulations which are violative of an act of the
Legislature are void (Morris v. Williams (1967) 67 Cal.2d 733, 737,
748–749, 63 Cal.Rptr. 689, 433 P.2d 697) we hold that the regulations
of defendant Los Angeles Unified School District here under review
(see fn. 2, ante) insofar as they purport to authorize prior censorship
of the contents of student publications, are invalid. We emphasize,
however, that our holding does not leave school authorities without
adequate sanctions, since of course they retain their power to discipline students who attempt to distribute prohibited material.

In the second count of her complaint, plaintiff attacks the constitutionality and the legislative authority for the flat ban on the *sale* of
newspapers on her high school campus, even if their distribution
without charge should be permitted. Administrative Regulation
1276–1 of the Los Angeles School Board purports to ban the sale of
publications as a regulation governing the manner of distribution:
"1276–1. . . . a. Circulation of Petitions, Circulars, Newspapers,
and Other Printed Matter. Students should be allowed to distribute
petitions, circulars, leaflets, newspapers, and other printed matter
subject to the following limitations: . . . 3. Manner. The manner
of distribution be such that: . . . (b) Funds or donations are not
collected for the material distributed," [8] apparently invoking the power conferred by section 10611 on school districts to make "reasonable
provisions for the time, place, and manner of conducting such activities." However, section 10611, which grants students the right to
exercise free expression on school premises, with the exception of
certain unprotected speech does not in itself prohibit the *sale* of
printed materials. Indeed the section expressly confers the right of
"distribution of printed materials." There is nothing in the statute
which suggests that the word "distribution" is to be limited to distribution without charge or without seeking donations for the distribution.

While it may be possible to construe the Legislature's grant of
power to school districts to regulate the manner of the distribution of
printed materials on school premises as including the right to ban distribution by sale, it is at best a strained reading. . . .

8. This language appears among certain "time, place and manner" limitations
prescribed for the circulation of petitions
and other printed matter. It therefore
follows the second paragraph of Regulation 1276–1 quoted in footnote 2, ante.

Finally to construe section 10611 as empowering school districts to flatly ban the sale of printed materials on school premises would again raise serious constitutional questions. Those courts which have considered regulations flatly banning the sale of underground newspapers, have uniformly held them to be unconstitutionally overbroad restrictions on the freedom of speech of the students. . . . The right to publish a newspaper would be meaningless indeed if it did not include the right to sell it. We are of the view that . . . the school's legitimate interest in maintaining good order and an educational atmosphere can be adequately promoted by reasonable time, place and manner regulations, but that a flat ban on sale is unconstitutionally overbroad. Given reasonable time, place and manner regulations as to distribution of printed matter, we fail to see how the *sale* of newspapers on the school premises will necessarily disrupt the work and discipline of the school, whereas their distribution free of charge will not.

. . .

NOTES

(1) See also Sullivan v. Houston Independent School District, 475 F.2d 1071 (5th Cir. 1973), cert. denied 414 U.S. 1032 (1974) (discipline can be imposed for violation of school regulations; regulations requiring students to submit written material to school authorities prior to distribution are not per se unconstitutional); Graham v. Houston Independent School District, 335 F.Supp. 1164 (S.D.Tex.1970) (discipline can be imposed for disobeying school principal's order to stop on-campus distribution of off-campus publication); Schwartz v. Schuker, 298 F.Supp. 238 (E.D.N.Y.1969) (student can be suspended for defying principal in connection with attempts to distribute off-campus newspaper on and near school grounds).

For a sample of an off-campus newspaper that caused problems see Baker v. Downey City Board of Education, 307 F.Supp. 517, 528-33 (C.D.Cal. 1969) (reproduction of off-campus paper called Oink). For a more thorough examination of first amendment rights of children in schools see A. Levine & E. Cary, The Rights of Students: An American Civil Liberties Union Handbook 23-47 (1977); Note, Public Forum Theory in the Educational Setting: The First Amendment and the Student Press, 1979 U.Ill.L.F. 879; and Note, Due Process, Due Politics and Due Respect: Three Models of Legitimate School Governance, 94 Harv.L.Rev. 1106 (1981).

(2) For an argument that *Tinker's* "substantial disruption" standard is inconsistent with the nature and mission of schools and that courts should refrain from interfering with school officials' decisions that demonstrate minimum rationality, see Diamond, The First Amendment and Public Schools: The Case Against Judicial Intervention, 59 Tex.L.Rev. 477 (1981).

WISCONSIN v. YODER

Supreme Court of the United States, 1972.
406 U.S. 205, 92 S.Ct. 1526, 32 L.Ed.2d 15.

MR. CHIEF JUSTICE BURGER delivered the opinion of the Court.

[We granted certiorari to review a] Wisconsin Supreme Court holding that respondents' convictions for violating the State's compulsory school-attendance law were invalid under the Free Exercise Clause of the First Amendment to the United States Constitution made applicable to the States by the Fourteenth Amendment. . . . [W]e affirm the judgment of the Supreme Court of Wisconsin.

[Respondents were Wisconsin residents and members of either the Old Order Amish religion or the Conservative Amish Mennonite Church. Their children, ages 14 and 15 were not enrolled in any public or private school, although Wisconsin's compulsory school-attendance law requires parents to cause their children to attend school until they reach age .16. Respondents were convicted of violating the law and fined $5 each.]

. .' . The trial testimony showed that respondents believed, in accordance with the tenets of Old Order Amish communities generally, that their children's attendance at high school, public or private, was contrary to the Amish religion and way of life. They believed that by sending their children to high school, they would not only expose themselves to the danger of the censure of the church community, but, as found by the county court, also endanger their own salvation and that of their children. The State stipulated that respondents' religious beliefs were sincere.

In support of their position, respondents presented as expert witnesses scholars on religion and education whose testimony is uncontradicted. They expressed their opinions on the relationship of the Amish belief concerning school attendance to the more general tenets of their religion, and described the impact that compulsory high school attendance could have on the continued survival of Amish communities as they exist in the United States today. . . . .

Formal high school education beyond the eighth grade is contrary to Amish beliefs, not only because it places Amish children in an environment hostile to Amish beliefs with increasing emphasis on competition in class work and sports and with pressure to conform to the styles, manners, and ways of the peer group, but also because it takes them away from their community, physically and emotionally, during the crucial and formative adolescent period of life. During this period, the children must acquire Amish attitudes favoring manual work and self-reliance and the specific skills needed to perform the adult role of an Amish farmer or housewife. They must learn to enjoy physical labor. Once a child has learned basic reading, writing, and elementary mathematics, these traits, skills, and attitudes admittedly fall within the category of those best learned through example and "doing" rather than in a classroom. And, at this time in life, the Amish child must also grow in his faith and his relationship to the Amish community if he is to be prepared to accept the heavy obligations imposed by adult baptism. In short, high school attendance with teachers who are not of the Amish faith—and may even be hostile to it—interposes a serious barrier to the integration of the Amish child into the Amish religious community. Dr. John Hostetler, one of the experts on Amish society, testified that the modern high school is not equipped, in curriculum or social environment, to impart the values promoted by Amish society.

The Amish do not object to elementary education through the first eight grades as a general proposition because they agree that their children must have basic skills in the "three R's" in order to read the Bible, to be good farmers and citizens, and to be able to deal with non-Amish people when necessary in the course of daily affairs. They view such a basic education as acceptable because it does not significantly expose their children to worldly values or interfere with their development in the Amish community during the crucial adolescent period. While Amish accept compulsory elementary education generally, wherever possible they have established their own elementary schools in many respects like the small local schools of the past. In the Amish belief higher learning tends to develop values they reject as influences that alienate man from God.

On the basis of such considerations, Dr. Hostetler testified that compulsory high school attendance could not only result in great psychological harm to Amish children, because of the conflicts it would produce, but would also, in his opinion, ultimately result in the destruction of the Old Order Amish church community as it exists in the United States. . . .

I

. . . [A] State's interest in universal education, however highly we rank it, is not totally free from a balancing process when it impinges on fundamental rights and interests, such as those specifically protected by the Free Exercise Clause of the First Amendment, and the traditional interest of parents with respect to the religious upbringing of their children so long as they, in the words of Pierce [v. Society of Sisters], "prepare [them] for additional obligations." 268 U.S., at 535, 45 S.Ct., at 573.

It follows that in order for Wisconsin to compel school attendance beyond the eighth grade against a claim that such attendance interferes with the practice of a legitimate religious belief, it must appear either that the State does not deny the free exercise of religious belief by its requirement, or that there is a state interest of sufficient magnitude to override the interest claiming protection under the Free Exercise Clause. Long before there was general acknowledgment of the need for universal formal education, the Religion Clauses had specifically and firmly fixed the right to free exercise of religious beliefs, and buttressing this fundamental right was an equally firm, even if less explicit, prohibition against the establishment of any religion by government. The values underlying these two provisions relating to religion have been zealously protected, sometimes even at the expense of other interests of admittedly high social importance. The invalidation of financial aid to parochial schools by government grants for a salary subsidy for teachers is but one example of the extent to which courts have gone in this regard, notwithstanding that such aid programs were legislatively determined to be in the public interest and the service of sound educational policy by States and by Congress. Lemon v. Kurtzman, 403 U.S. 602, 91 S.Ct. 2105, 29 L.Ed. 2d 745 (1971); . . .

The essence of all that has been said and written on the subject is that only those interests of the highest order and those not otherwise served can overbalance legitimate claims to the free exercise of religion. We can accept it as settled, therefore, that, however strong the State's interest in universal compulsory education, it is by no means absolute to the exclusion or subordination of all other interests.

II

We come then to the quality of the claims of the respondents concerning the alleged encroachment of Wisconsin's compulsory school-attendance statute on their rights and the rights of their children to the free exercise of the religious beliefs they and their forbears have adhered to for almost three centuries. In evaluating those claims we must be careful to determine whether the Amish religious faith and their mode of life are, as they claim, inseparable and interdependent. . . .

. . . [T]he record in this case abundantly supports the claim that the traditional way of life of the Amish is not merely a matter of personal preference, but one of deep religious conviction, shared by an organized group, and intimately related to daily living. . . .

. . . [T]he unchallenged testimony of acknowledged experts in education and religious history, almost 300 years of consistent practice, and strong evidence of a sustained faith pervading and regulating respondents' entire mode of life support the claim that enforcement of the State's requirement of compulsory formal education after the eighth grade would gravely endanger if not destroy the free exercise of respondents' religious beliefs.

III

. . .

We turn . . . to the State's broader contention that its interest in its system of compulsory education is so compelling that even the established religious practices of the Amish must give away.

. . .

The State advances two primary arguments in support of its system of compulsory education. It notes, as Thomas Jefferson pointed out early in our history, that some degree of education is necessary to prepare citizens to participate effectively and intelligently in our open political system if we are to preserve freedom and independence. Further, education prepares individuals to be self-reliant and self-sufficient participants in society. We accept these propositions.

However, the evidence adduced by the Amish in this case is persuasively to the effect that an additional one or two years of formal high school for Amish children in place of their long-established program of informal vocational education would do little to serve those interests. Respondents' experts testified at trial, without challenge, that the value of all education must be assessed in terms of its capacity to prepare the child for life. It is one thing to say that compulsory education for a year or two beyond the eighth grade may be necessary when its goal is the preparation of the child for life in modern society as the majority live, but it is quite another if the goal of education be viewed as the preparation of the child for life in the separated agrarian community that is the keystone of the Amish faith. See Meyer v. Nebraska, 262 U.S., at 400, 43 S.Ct., at 627, 67 L.Ed. 1042.

The State attacks respondents' position as one fostering "ignorance" from which the child must be protected by the State. No one can question the State's duty to protect children from ignorance but this argument does not square with the facts disclosed in the record. Whatever their idiosyncrasies as seen by the majority, this record strongly shows that the Amish community has been a highly successful social unit within our society, even if apart from the conventional "mainstream." Its members are productive and very law-abiding members of society; they reject public welfare in any of its usual modern forms. The Congress itself recognized their self-sufficiency by authorizing exemption of such groups as the Amish from the obligation to pay social security taxes.[11]

11. Title 26 U.S.C. § 1402(h) authorizes the Secretary of Health, Education, and Welfare to exempt members of "a recognized religious sect" existing at all times since December 31, 1950, from the obligation to pay social security taxes if they are, by reason of the tenets of their sect, opposed to receipt of such benefits and agree to waive them, provided the Secretary finds that the sect makes reasonable provision for its dependent members. The history of the exemption shows it was enacted with the situation of the Old Order Amish specifically in view. H.R.Rep.No.213, 89th Cong., 1st Sess., 101–102 (1965).

The record in this case establishes without contradiction that the Green County Amish had never been known to

It is neither fair nor correct to suggest that the Amish are opposed to education beyond the eighth grade level. What this record shows is that they are opposed to conventional formal education of the type provided by a certified high school because it comes at the child's crucial adolescent period of religious development. Dr. Donald Erickson, for example, testified that their system of learning-by-doing was an "ideal system" of education in terms of preparing Amish children for life as adults in the Amish community, ...

We must not forget that in the Middle Ages important values of the civilization of the Western World were preserved by members of religious orders who isolated themselves from all worldly influences against great obstacles. There can be no assumption that today's majority is "right" and the Amish and others like them are "wrong." A way of life that is odd or even erratic but interferes with no rights or interests of others is not to be condemned because it is different.

The State, however, supports its interest in providing an additional one or two years of compulsory high school education to Amish children because of the possibility that some such children will choose to leave the Amish community, and that if this occurs they will be ill-equipped for life. The State argues that if Amish children leave their church they should not be in the position of making their way in the world without the education available in the one or two additional years the State requires. However, on this record, that argument is highly speculative. There is no specific evidence of the loss of Amish adherents by attrition, nor is there any showing that upon leaving the Amish community Amish children, with their practical agricultural training and habits of industry and self-reliance, would become burdens on society because of educational shortcomings. Indeed, this argument of the State appears to rest primarily on the State's mistaken assumption, already noted, that the Amish do not provide any education for their children beyond the eighth grade, but allow them to grow in "ignorance." To the contrary, not only do the Amish accept the necessity for formal schooling through the eighth grade level, but continue to provide what has been characterized by the undisputed testimony of expert educators as an "ideal" vocational education for their children in the adolescent years.

There is nothing in this record to suggest that the Amish qualities of reliability, self-reliance, and dedication to work would fail to find ready markets in today's society. Absent some contrary evidence supporting the State's position, we are unwilling to assume that persons possessing such valuable vocational skills and habits are doomed to become burdens on society should they determine to leave the Amish faith, nor is there any basis in the record to warrant a finding that an additional one or two years of formal school education beyond

commit crimes, that none had been
known to receive public assistance, and
that none were unemployed.

the eighth grade would serve to eliminate any such problem that might exist.

. . .

The requirement for compulsory education beyond the eighth grade is a relatively recent development in our history. Less than 60 years ago, the educational requirements of almost all of the States were satisfied by completion of the elementary grades, at least where the child was regularly and lawfully employed. The independence and successful social functioning of the Amish community for a period approaching almost three centuries and more than 200 years in this country are strong evidence that there is at best a speculative gain, in terms of meeting the duties of citizenship, from an additional one or two years of compulsory formal education. Against this background it would require a more particularized showing from the State on this point to justify the severe interference with religious freedom such additional compulsory attendance would entail.

We should also note that compulsory education and child labor laws find their historical origin in common humanitarian instincts, and that the age limits of both laws have been coordinated to achieve their related objectives. In the context of this case, such considerations, if anything, support rather than detract from respondents' position. The origins of the requirement for school attendance to age 16, an age falling after the completion of elementary school but before completion of high school, are not entirely clear. But to some extent such laws reflected the movement to prohibit most child labor under age 16 that culminated in the provisions of the Federal Fair Labor Standards Act of 1938. It is true, then, that the 16-year child labor age limit may to some degree derive from a contemporary impression that children should be in school until that age. But at the same time, it cannot be denied that, conversely, the 16-year education limit reflects, in substantial measure, the concern that children under that age not be employed under conditions hazardous to their health, or in work that should be performed by adults.

The requirement of compulsory schooling to age 16 must therefore be viewed as aimed not merely at providing educational opportunities for children, but as an alternative to the equally undesirable consequence of unhealthful child labor displacing adult workers, or, on the other hand, forced idleness. The two kinds of statutes—compulsory school attendance and child labor laws—tend to keep children of certain ages off the labor market and in school; this regimen in turn provides opportunity to prepare for a livelihood of a higher order than that which children could pursue without education and protects their health in adolescence.

In these terms, Wisconsin's interest in compelling the school attendance of Amish children to age 16 emerges as somewhat less substantial than requiring such attendance for children generally. For, while agricultural employment is not totally outside the legitimate concerns of the child labor laws, employment of children under parental guidance and on the family farm from age 14 to age 16 is an ancient tradition that lies at the periphery of the objectives of such laws. There is no intimation that the Amish employment of their children on family farms is in any way deleterious to their health or that Amish parents exploit children at tender years. Any such inference would be contrary to the record before us. Moreover, employment of Amish children on the family farm does not present the undesirable economic aspects of eliminating jobs that might otherwise be held by adults.

IV

Finally, the State, on authority of Prince v. Massachusetts, argues that a decision exempting Amish children from the State's requirement fails to recognize the substantive right of the Amish child to a secondary education, and fails to give due regard to the power of the State as *parens patriae* to extend the benefit of secondary education to children regardless of the wishes of their parents. Taken at its broadest sweep, the Court's language in *Prince*, might be read to give support to the State's position. However, the Court was not confronted in *Prince* with a situation comparable to that of the Amish as revealed in this record; this is shown by the Court's severe characterization of the evils that it thought the legislature could legitimately associate with child labor, even when performed in the company of an adult. 321 U.S., at 169–170, 64 S.Ct., at 443–444. The Court later took great care to confine *Prince* to a narrow scope in Sherbert v. Verner, when it stated:

"On the other hand, the Court has rejected challenges under the Free Exercise Clause to governmental regulation of certain overt acts prompted by religious beliefs or principles, for 'even when the action is in accord with one's religious convictions, [it] is not totally free from legislative restrictions.' Braunfeld v. Brown, 366 U.S. 599, 603, 81 S.Ct. 1144, 1146, 6 L.Ed.2d 563. The conduct or actions so regulated have invariably posed some substantial threat to public safety, peace or order. See, e.g., Reynolds v. United States, 98 U.S. 145, 25 L.Ed. 244; Jacobson v. Massachusetts, 197 U.S. 11, 25 S.Ct. 358, 49 L.Ed. 643; Prince v. Massachusetts, 321 U.S. 158, 64 S.Ct. 438, 88 L.Ed. 645 . . . ." 374 U.S., at 402–403, 83 S.Ct., at 1793.

This case, of course, is not one in which any harm to the physical or mental health of the child or to the public safety, peace, order, or welfare has been demonstrated or may be properly inferred. The record is to the contrary, and any reliance on that theory would find no support in the evidence.

Contrary to the suggestion of the dissenting opinion of Mr. Justice Douglas, our holding today in no degree depends on the assertion of the religious interest of the child as contrasted with that of the parents. It is the parents who are subject to prosecution here for failing to cause their children to attend school, and it is their right of free exercise, not that of their children, that must determine Wisconsin's power to impose criminal penalties on the parent. The dissent argues that a child who expresses a desire to attend public high school in conflict with the wishes of his parents should not be prevented from doing so. There is no reason for the Court to consider that point since it is not an issue in the case. The children are not parties to this litigation. The State has at no point tried this case on the theory that respondents were preventing their children from attending school against their expressed desires, and indeed the record is to the contrary. The State's position from the outset has been that it is empowered to apply its compulsory-attendance law to Amish parents in the same manner as to other parents—that is, without regard to the wishes of the child. That is the claim we reject today.

Our holding in no way determines the proper resolution of possible competing interests of parents, children, and the State in an appropriate state court proceeding in which the power of the State is asserted on the theory that Amish parents are preventing their minor children from attending high school despite their expressed desires to the contrary. Recognition of the claim of the State in such a proceeding would, of course, call into question traditional concepts of parental control over the religious upbringing and education of their minor children recognized in this Court's past decisions. It is clear that such an intrusion by a State into family decisions in the area of religious training would give rise to grave questions of religious freedom comparable to those raised here and those presented in Pierce v. Society of Sisters, 268 U.S. 510, 45 S.Ct. 571, 69 L.Ed. 1070 (1925). On this record we neither reach nor decide those issues.

The State's argument proceeds without reliance on any actual conflict between the wishes of parents and children. It appears to rest on the potential that exemption of Amish parents from the requirements of the compulsory-education law might allow some parents to act contrary to the best interests of their children by foreclosing their opportunity to make an intelligent choice between the Amish way of life and that of the outside world. The same argument could, of course, be made with respect to all church schools short of college. There is nothing in the record or in the ordinary course of human experience to suggest that non-Amish parents generally consult with children of ages 14–16 if they are placed in a church school of the parents' faith.

Indeed it seems clear that if the State is empowered, as *parens patriae*, to "save" a child from himself or his Amish parents by requiring an additional two years of compulsory formal high school education, the State will in large measure influence, if not determine, the religious future of the child. Even more markedly than in *Prince*, therefore, this case involves the fundamental interest of parents, as contrasted with that of the State, to guide the religious future and education of their children. The history and culture of Western civilization reflect a strong tradition of parental concern for the nurture and upbringing of their children. This primary role of the parents in the upbringing of their children is now established beyond debate as an enduring American tradition. If not the first, perhaps the most significant statements of the Court in this area are found in Pierce v. Society of Sisters, in which the Court observed:

"Under the doctrine of Meyer v. Nebraska, 262 U.S. 390, 43 S.Ct. 625, 67 L.Ed. 1042, we think it entirely plain that the Act of 1922 unreasonably interferes with the liberty of parents and guardians to direct the upbringing and education of children under their control. As often heretofore pointed out, rights guaranteed by the Constitution may not be abridged by legislation which has no reasonable relation to some purpose within the competency of the State. The fundamental theory of liberty upon which all governments in this Union repose excludes any general power of the State to standardize its children by forcing them to accept instruction from public teachers only. The child is not the mere creature of the State; those who nurture him and direct his destiny have the right, coupled with the high duty, to recognize and prepare him for additional obligations." 268 U.S., at 534–535, 45 S.Ct., at 573.

The duty to prepare the child for "additional obligations," referred to by the Court, must be read to include the inculcation of moral standards, religious beliefs, and elements of good citizenship. *Pierce*, of course, recognized that where nothing more than the general interest of the parent in the nurture and education of his children is involved, it is beyond dispute that the State acts "reasonably" and constitutionally in requiring education to age 16 in some public or private school meeting the standards prescribed by the State.

However read, the Court's holding in *Pierce* stands as a charter of the rights of parents to direct the religious upbringing of their children. And, when the interests of parenthood are combined with a free exercise claim of the nature revealed by this record, more than merely a "reasonable relation to some purpose within the competency of the State" is required to sustain the validity of the State's requirement under the First Amendment. To be sure, the power of the parent, even when linked to a free exercise claim, may be subject to limitation under *Prince* if it appears that parental decisions will jeopardize the health or safety of the child, or have a potential for significant social burdens. But in this case, the Amish have introduced persuasive evidence undermining the arguments the State has advanced to support its claims in terms of the welfare of the child and society as a whole. The record strongly indicates that accommodating the religious objections of the Amish by forgoing one, or at most two, additional years of compulsory education will not impair the physical or mental health of the child, or result in an inability to be self-supporting or to discharge the duties and responsibilities of citizenship, or in any other way materially detract from the welfare of society.

In the fact of our consistent emphasis on the central values underlying the Religion Clauses in our constitutional scheme of government, we cannot accept a *parens patriae* claim of such all-encompassing scope and with such sweeping potential for broad and unforeseeable application as that urged by the State.

V

For the reasons stated we hold, with the Supreme Court of Wisconsin, that the First and Fourteenth Amendments prevent the State from compelling respondents to cause their children to attend formal high school to age 16. Our disposition of this case, however, in no way alters our recognition of the obvious fact that courts are not school boards or legislatures, and are ill-equipped to determine the "necessity" of discrete aspects of a State's program of compulsory education. This should suggest that courts must move with great circumspection in performing the sensitive and delicate task of weighing a State's legitimate social concern when faced with religious claims for exemption from generally applicable educational requirements. It cannot be overemphasized that we are not dealing with a way of life and mode of education by a group claiming to have recently discovered some "progressive" or more enlightened process for rearing children for modern life.

Aided by a history of three centuries as an identifiable religious sect and a long history as a successful and self-sufficient segment of American society, the Amish in this case have convincingly demonstrated the sincerity of their religious beliefs, the interrelationship of belief with their mode of life, the vital role that belief and daily conduct play in the continued survival of Old Order Amish communities and their religious organization, and the hazards presented by the State's enforcement of a statute generally valid as to others. Beyond this, they have carried the even more difficult burden of demonstrating the adequacy of their alternative mode of continuing informal vocational education in terms of precisely those overall interests that the State advances in support of its program of compulsory high school education. In light of this convincing showing, one that probably few other religious groups or sects could make, and weighing the minimal difference between what the State would require and what the Amish already accept, it was incumbent on the State to show with more particularity how its admittedly strong interest in compulsory education would be adversely affected by granting an exemption to the Amish. Sherbert v. Verner, supra.

Nothing we hold is intended to undermine the general applicability of the State's compulsory school-attendance statutes or to limit the power of the State to promulgate reasonable standards that, while not impairing the free exercise of religion, provide for continuing agricultural vocational education under parental and church guidance by the Old Order Amish or others similarly situated. The States have had a long history of amicable and effective relationships with church-sponsored schools, and there is no basis for assuming that, in this related context, reasonable standards cannot be established concerning the content of the continuing vocational education of Amish children under parental guidance, provided always that state regulations are not inconsistent with what we have said in this opinion.

Affirmed.

Mr. Justice Powell and Mr. Justice Rehnquist took no part in the consideration or decision of this case.

Mr. Justice Stewart, with whom Mr. Justice Brennan joins, concurring.

This case involves the constitutionality of imposing criminal punishment upon Amish parents for their religiously based refusal to compel their children to attend public high schools. Wisconsin has sought to brand these parents as criminals for following *their* religious beliefs, and the Court today rightly holds that Wisconsin cannot constitutionally do so.

This case in no way involves any questions regarding the right of the children of Amish parents to attend public high schools, or any other institutions of learning, if they wish to do so. As the Court points out, there is no suggestion whatever in the record that the religious beliefs of the children here concerned differ in any way from those of their parents. Only one of the children testified. The last two questions and answers on her cross-examination accurately sum up her testimony:

"Q. So I take it then, Frieda, the only reason you are not going to school, and did not go to school since last September, is because of *your* religion?

"A. Yes.

"Q. That is the only reason?

"A. Yes." (Emphasis supplied.)

It is clear to me, therefore, that this record simply does not present the interesting and important issue discussed in Part II of the dissenting opinion of Mr. Justice Douglas. With this observation, I join the opinion and the judgment of the Court.

Mr. Justice White, with whom Mr. Justice Brennan and Mr. Justice Stewart join, concurring.

. . .

. . . In the present case, the State is not concerned with the maintenance of an educational system as an end in itself, it is rather attempting to nurture and develop the human potential of its children, whether Amish or non-Amish: to expand their knowledge, broaden their sensibilities, kindle their imagination, foster a spirit of free inquiry, and increase their human understanding and tolerance. It is possible that most Amish children will wish to continue living the rural life of their parents, in which case their training at home will adequately equip them for their future role. Others, however, may wish to become nuclear physicists, ballet dancers, computer programmers, or historians, and for these occupations, formal training will be necessary. . . . [A]lthough the question is close, I am unable to say that the State has demonstrated that Amish children who leave school in the eighth grade will be intellectually stultified or unable to acquire new academic skills later. . . .

. . . I join the Court because the sincerity of the Amish religious policy here is uncontested, because the potentially adverse impact of the state requirement is great, and because the State's valid interest in education has already been largely satisfied by the eight years the children have already spent in school.

MR. JUSTICE DOUGLAS, dissenting in part.

. . . The Court's analysis assumes that the only interests at stake in the case are those of the Amish parents on the one hand, and those of the State on the other. The difficulty with this approach is that, despite the Court's claim, the parents are seeking to vindicate not only their own free exercise claims, but also those of their high-school-age children.

It is argued that the right of the Amish children to religious freedom is not presented by the facts of the case, as the issue before the Court involves only the Amish parents' religious freedom to defy a state criminal statute imposing upon them an affirmative duty to cause their children to attend high school.

First, respondents' motion to dismiss in the trial court expressly asserts, not only the religious liberty of the adults, but also that of the children, as a defense to the prosecutions. It is, of course, beyond question that the parents have standing as defendants in a criminal prosecution to assert the religious interests of their children as a defense.[1] Although the lower courts and a majority of this Court assume an identity of interest between parent and child, it is clear

1. Thus, in Prince v. Massachusetts, 321 U.S. 158, 64 S.Ct. 438, 88 L.Ed. 645, a Jehovah's Witness was convicted for having violated a state child labor law by allowing her nine-year-old niece and ward to circulate religious literature on the public streets. There, as here, the narrow question was the religious liberty of the adult. There, as here, the Court analyzed the problem from the point of view of the State's conflicting interest in the welfare of the child. But, as Mr. Justice Brennan, speaking for the Court, has so recently pointed out, "The Court [in *Prince*] implicitly held that the custodian had standing to assert alleged freedom of religion . . . rights of the child that were threatened in the very litigation before the Court and that the child had no effective way of asserting herself." Eisenstadt v. Baird, 405 U.S. 438, 446 n. 6, 92 S.Ct. 1029, 1034, 31 L.Ed.2d 349. Here, as in *Prince*, the children have no effective alternate means to vindicate their rights. The question, therefore, is squarely before us.

that they have treated the religious interest of the child as a factor in the analysis.

Second, it is essential to reach the question to decide the case, not only because the question was squarely raised in the motion to dismiss, but also because no analysis of religious-liberty claims can take place in a vacuum. If the parents in this case are allowed a religious exemption, the inevitable effect is to impose the parents' notions of religious duty upon their children. Where the child is mature enough to express potentially conflicting desires, it would be an invasion of the child's rights to permit such an imposition without canvassing his views. As in Prince v. Massachusetts, 321 U.S. 158, 64 S.Ct. 438, 88 L.Ed. 645, it is an imposition resulting from this very litigation. As the child has no other effective forum, it is in this litigation that his rights should be considered. And, if an Amish child desires to attend high school, and is mature enough to have that desire respected, the State may well be able to override the parents' religiously motivated objections. Religion is an individual experience. It is not necessary, nor even appropriate, for every Amish child to express his views on the subject in a prosecution of a single adult. Crucial, however, are the views of the child whose parent is the subject of the suit. Frieda Yoder has in fact testified that her own religious views are opposed to high-school education. I therefore join the judgment of the Court as to respondent Jonas Yoder. But Frieda Yoder's views may not be those of Vernon Yutzy or Barbara Miller. I must dissent, therefore, as to respondents Adin Yutzy and Wallace Miller as their motion to dismiss also raised the question of their children's religious liberty.

II

This issue has never been squarely presented before today. Our opinions are full of talk about the power of the parents over the child's education. See Pierce v. Society of Sisters, 268 U.S. 510, 45 S.Ct. 571, 69 L.Ed. 1070; Meyer v. Nebraska, 262 U.S. 390, 43 S.Ct. 625, 67 L.Ed. 1042. And we have in the past analyzed similar conflicts between parent and State with little regard for the views of the child. See Prince v. Massachusetts, supra. Recent cases, however, have clearly held that the children themselves have constitutionally protectible interests.

These children are "persons" within the meaning of the Bill of Rights. We have so held over and over again. . . .

. . .

On this important and vital matter of education, I think the children should be entitled to be heard. While the parents, absent dissent, normally speak for the entire family, the education of the child is a matter on which the child will often have decided views. He may want to be a pianist or an astronaut or an oceanographer. To do so he will have to break from the Amish tradition.

It is the future of the student, not the future of the parents, that is imperiled by today's decision. If a parent keeps his child out of school beyond the grade school, then the child will be forever barred from entry into the new and amazing world of diversity that we have today. The child may decide that that is the preferred course, or he may rebel. It is the student's judgment, not his parents', that is essential if we are to give full meaning to what we have said about the Bill of Rights and of the right of students to be masters of their own destiny.[3] If he is harnessed to the Amish way of life by those in authority over him and if his education is truncated, his entire life may be stunted and deformed. The child, therefore, should be given an opportunity to be heard before the State gives the exemption which we honor today.

The views of the two children in question were not canvassed by the Wisconsin courts. The matter should be explicitly reserved so that new hearings can be held on remand of the case.[4]

NOTE

How do you regard Justice Douglas's proposal for canvassing the Amish schoolchildren? Should the courts be open after *Yoder* to petitions from Amish children who disagree with their parents about whether education until age 16 is a good thing? If so, should the courts' decisions necessarily turn on the perceived strength of the religious commitment of the children?

For discussion of the conflicts between parent and child with regard to medical decisions in the face of religious beliefs see p. 894, infra.

3. The court below brushed aside the students' interests with the offhand comment that "[w]hen a child reaches the age of judgment, he can choose for himself his religion." 49 Wis.2d 430, 440, 182 N.W.2d 539, 543. But there is nothing in this record to indicate that the moral and intellectual judgment demanded of the student by the question in this case is beyond his capacity. Children far younger than the 14- and 15-year-olds involved here are regularly permitted to testify in custody and other proceedings. Indeed, the failure to call the affected child in a custody hearing is often reversible error. See, e.g., Callicott v. Callicott, 364 S.W.2d 455 (Tex.Civ.App.) (reversible error for trial judge to refuse to hear testimony of eight-year-old in custody battle). Moreover, there is substantial agreement among child psychologists and sociologists that the moral and intellectual maturity of the 14-year-old approaches that of the adult. See, e.g., J.

Piaget, The Moral Judgment of the Child (1948); D. Elkind, Children and Adolescents 75–80 (1970); Kohlberg, Moral Education in the Schools: A Development View, in R. Muuss, Adolescent Behavior and Society 193, 199–200 (1971); W. Kay, Moral Development 172–183 (1968); A. Gesell & F. Ilg, Youth: The Years From Ten to Sixteen 175–182 (1956). The maturity of Amish youth, who identify with and assume adult roles from early childhood, see M. Goodman, The Culture of Childhood 92–94 (1970), is certainly not less than that of children in the general population.

4. Canvassing the views of all school-age Amish children in the State of Wisconsin would not present insurmountable difficulties. A 1968 survey indicated that there were at that time only 256 such children in the entire State. Comment, 1971 Wis.L.Rev. 832, 852 n. 132.

COMPULSORY SCHOOL ATTENDANCE LAWS

Although the New England colonies, and particularly Massachusetts, regarded education in the basics as essential, the movement toward universal education and comprehensive compulsory attendance laws came after the Civil War.[1] As the Supreme Court points out in *Yoder*, it was especially strong shortly after the turn of this century. School attendance laws thus should not be viewed as an isolated phenomenon but rather as one of many elements in a period of social, cultural, and economic upheaval and adjustment. For example, as the *Yoder* Court further points out, one can discern a definite parallel between the growth of school attendance laws and child labor laws, evidenced both by their timing and the fact that they commonly shared an age level, 16, below which children should be in school rather than at work. Although opposition to child labor was in part motivated by humanitarian concerns about exploitation of children, it was not entirely altruistic. Support for both child labor and compulsory school attendance laws came from organized labor at least partly because cheap child labor might depress wages generally or even displace adult workers. Compulsory school attendance requirements carried with them a ready means of enforcement that worked equally well to enforce the child labor laws.[2]

All states and the District of Columbia now have compulsory attendance laws.[3] Implicit in decisions such as *Yoder* and Pierce v. Society of Sisters is the conclusion that a state has the authority to compel children to attend school, absent infringement of a protected constitutional right. Indeed, the Court in *Yoder* referred to the "paramount responsibility" of states to educate its citizens, an obligation that permits states "to impose reasonable regulations for the control and duration of basic education." However equal emphasis was given to the fact that a state's interest in universal education "is not totally free from a balancing process when it impinges on fundamental rights and interests."

In its recitation of the factual background in the *Yoder* case, the Court pointed out that the Amish children were not enrolled in a private school nor did they fit within any recognized exception to Wisconsin's compulsory attendance law. Some exceptions traditionally have been recognized, e.g., where the child is attending a private school that meets the minimal education requirements applicable to public schools or where the child is unable to attend school because of

1. For a detailed and thoughtful history of the development of education in America generally as well as the development of compulsory school attendance provisions, see F. Butts and L. Cremin, A History of Education in American Culture (1953), and N. Edwards and H. Richey, The School in the American Social Order (2d ed. 1963).

2. See M. Carroll, Labor and Politics 81–84 (1923); N. Edwards and H. Richey, supra n. 1, at 489; R. Fuller, The Meaning of Child Labor 62–64 (1922).

3. Mississippi, after repealing its compulsory school attendance statute in 1956, rejoined the rest of the country by enacting a new statute in 1977.

a physical or mental disability.[4] In *Yoder*, of course, the Court seemingly created a new exception, albeit perhaps a narrow one, for school attendance that interferes unduly with a genuinely held religious belief.

Although the private school exception now often is specifically allowed by statute, it also was implicit in Pierce v. Society of Sisters that parents who chose to send their children to an approved private school were in compliance with compulsory school attendance laws. "Approved" is perhaps the key word here. In State v. Shaver,[5] a case involving elements of both the religious and private school exceptions, the North Dakota Supreme Court upheld convictions of parents for failure to send their children to either a public school or an approved private school. In that case fundamentalist Baptist parents, in lieu of enrolling their children in public school, sent them to a fundamentalist religious school based on their belief in a Biblical duty to educate them according to Christian principles. The private school was not "approved" within the meaning of the statutes, nor did it plan to seek such approval. Teachers in the school were not certified by the state.

Applying the three-pronged analysis of *Yoder*, the court first determined that the parents' religious beliefs were legitimately and sincerely held. On the second point of analysis, however, the court found that the state's requirements for approval did not impose an undue burden on the parents' right of free exercise of religion. Unlike in *Yoder* the tenets of the fundamentalist Baptist church did not forbid a public education. And contrary to the threat posed to the Amish community in *Yoder*, no evidence was presented in this case to demonstrate that compliance with state regulations for approval of private schools—namely, that teachers be certified by the state, that courses mandated by statute be taught, and that state health, fire, and safety laws be observed—would adversely affect the practice of religion by parents or children. Finally, on the third point of analysis the court found that the state had a compelling interest in educating its children, as recognized in *Yoder*, and that the state's interest far outweighed the minimal burden on the parents' free exercise of religion. Concluding that the parents had not met the burden of showing that the state had imposed an undue burden on their free exercise of religion, the convictions were affirmed.[6]

An exception to compulsory school attendance also can be allowed for a child who is receiving adequate instruction at home. Some statutes require that the instruction be performed by a certified teacher,[7]

4. See, e.g., Ill.Ann.Stat. ch. 122, § 26–1 (Smith-Hurd Supp.1982).

5. State v. Shaver, 294 N.W.2d 883 (N.D.1980).

6. Compare, on similar facts, the decision of the Ohio Supreme Court in State ex rel. Nagle v. Olin, 64 Ohio St.2d 341, 415 N.E.2d 279 (1980), reversing convictions of parents because the state's requirements exceeded the bounds of reasonable regulation as applied to the particular school in that case.

7. See, e.g., Colo.Rev.Stat.Ann. § 22–33–104(2)(i) (1973).

while others require only that instruction be performed by a "competent" or "qualified" person or tutor.[8]   More commonly, statutes simply require that the home instruction be equivalent to what would be obtained in public school.[9]   Case law has dealt mostly with the adequacy of parental instruction at home as an alternative to regular school attendance.   In In re Falk,[10] a case in which parents were charged with educational neglect of their child arising from their failure to send him to school in compliance with the compulsory attendance law, a New York court dismissed the petition on a finding that the parents were giving the child instruction at home equivalent to what he would have received in public school.   The child, a boy of first grade age, engaged in studies for the periods required by law and covered the same subjects as children of his grade level in public schools, including writing, spelling, language, and math.   His mother used lesson plans and kept records of his progress.   The family had a library of some 200 volumes, many of which the child had read.   His instruction also included field trips, education in practical life skills, music, and hygiene.

Another New York court, however, earlier found three children ranging from 10 to 13 years of age to be neglected because of the inadequacy of parental home instruction.[11]   As the court pointed out in *Falk*, parents have the burden of demonstrating that home instruction furnishes the equivalent of public school programs, which they failed to meet.   Doesn't the exemption for home tutoring defeat a major social goal of compulsory education—that is, removing children from their homes and exposing them to new values and experiences?   Reconsider Professor Burt's observations, supra at p. 82.

Another exception to the requirement of school attendance—actually an exemption since no alternative to public education is required—sometimes is allowed in the case of a child emancipated by marriage.   In In re Rogers,[12] a New York court dismissed a petition against a 15-year-old girl alleged to be in need of supervision because of her failure to attend school.   She had been lawfully married since the age of 14, but marriage was not one of the exceptions to required school attendance until age 16.   The court expressed concern not only for the child's well-being (she did not want to go to school and preferred to stay home and assume domestic responsibilities) but for the well-being of unmarried children of her age at the school she would attend.   Drawing an analogy to the vaccination cases, the court found it "ludicrous" that children who had not been vaccinated could be excluded but that attendance of a married 15-year-old with other, nonmarried 15-year-old children could be compelled.

8. See, e.g., S.D.Comp.Laws Ann. § 13–27–3 (Supp.1981).

9. See, e.g., N.Y.Educ.Law § 3204(2) (McKinney 1981).

10.   110 Misc.2d 104, 441 N.Y.S.2d 785 (Fam.Ct., Lewis County 1981).

11. In re Thomas H., 78 Misc.2d 412, 357 N.Y.S.2d 384 (Fam.Ct., Yates County 1974).

12.   36 Misc.2d 680, 234 N.Y.S.2d 172 (Fam.Ct., Schuyler County 1962).

In *Yoder* the Supreme Court emphasized that in order for a parent's claim to have the protection of the free exercise clause, it must be firmly rooted in religious belief rather than being simply philosophical or social. What if the claim arises out of cultural belief? In In re McMillan,[13] a North Carolina appeals court upheld a decision that American Indian children were neglected for the reason that their parents had failed to send them to the public schools. The court so held over the parental argument that their decision was based on the failure of the public schools to present adequate instruction in American Indian heritage and culture, and that their deeply rooted cultural convictions, like religious beliefs, were entitled to constitutional protection. In rejecting this argument the court distinguished *Yoder*: "There is no showing that Shelby and Abe McMillan receive any mode of educational programs alternative to those in the public school. There is also no showing that the Indian heritage or culture of these children will be endangered or threatened in any way by their attending school." [14]

Yoder involved use of the criminal sanction against parents for failure to send their children to public school. Other cases, such as In re McMillan, often involved neglect or similar proceedings as a means of enforcing compulsory attendance requirements. Suppose the child is proceeded against as a delinquent for failure to attend school. In In re Peters,[15] the North Carolina Court of Appeals reversed an adjudication of delinquency and institutional commitment of a 15-year-old boy based on his truancy. In so holding the court observed: "Eddie obviously is a child who should be afforded some technical training where he can use his hands and develop his aptitudes along that line and have some motivation. He obviously does not take to book learning. Forcing him into a classical schoolroom introduces a disruptive element which is not good for the school, the teachers, the other students and likewise is not good for Eddie." [16] A number of states now permit vocational training as an alternative to the regular classroom for children who are so inclined.[17]

Two basic threads seem to run through the cases dealing with application of compulsory school attendance laws. First, regardless of whether objections to instruction in public schools are based on religious beliefs, cultural beliefs, sociological or philosophical differences of opinion, or personal or other preferences, courts are concerned with asserting the state's interest in educating its children and this

13. 30 N.C.App. 235, 226 S.E.2d 693 (1976).

14. 30 N.C. at 238, 226 S.E.2d at 695. In a similar case, although no constitutional question was presented, a New York Court reached the same result based on a finding that no alternative instruction was being provided. See In re Baum, 61 A.D.2d 123, 401 N.Y.S.2d 514 (1978).

15. 14 N.C.App. 426, 188 S.E.2d 619 (1972).

16. 14 N.C.App. at 430, 188 S.E.2d at 621.

17. See, e.g., 24 Pa.Cons.Stat.Ann. § 13–1327 (Purdon Supp.1982).

interest generally prevails absent some superior right of parents entitled to protection. Second, courts as well as legislatures are concerned with whether there are adequate alternatives to public education. The universality and to some degree the rigidity of compulsory
school attendance requirements would seem to suggest a need for
maximum flexibility, in terms of both available alternatives and sanctions for noncompliance. Foster and Freed, in A Bill of Rights for
Children,[18] have directed this criticism: *

> Perhaps the most obvious example of currently questionable
> regulation and restriction is to be found in compulsory school at-
> tendance and child labor laws. With some exceptions, minors be-
> tween 6 and 16 in New York must attend school for full time in-
> struction. There is no need to comment here upon drop-out rates
> or the traditional orientation of secondary schools towards prepa-
> ration for college entrance. It is sufficient to note that we are
> doing an inadequate job of providing a bridge between school and
> life work for many of our young people. Whatever the cause or
> the blame, the fact remains that the primary function of some
> schools is a warehousing or custodial one to keep kids off the
> streets. Many of these teen-agers might be better off on job
> training or apprenticeship work, but due to compulsory attendance
> and child labor laws are frozen into a meaningless routine.
>
>   . . .
>
> It is no exaggeration to say that for many minors in New York
> the combination of compulsory school attendance and child labor
> laws is an intolerable burden that forces them into becoming
> "drop outs" and bars access to meaningful work. The human and
> social cost of the system is exorbitant. Unless flexibility is
> achieved, the system itself is bound to fail.

Perhaps in response to such arguments, the Juvenile Justice Standards Relating to Schools and Education (Tentative Draft 1977),
adopted a three-fold approach. First, the school experience ought to
be made interesting, meaningful, imaginative, varied, and "relevant"
to meet the educational needs of as many students as possible to encourage attendance. Second, no matter how varied and interesting
the school experience, some students will remain for whom the regular classroom setting is unsuitable or unacceptable, and for these children, "[t]he problem . . . is not to make school appealing but to
find alternative useful, or at least harmless, things for these children
to do with their lives outside the school—or at least outside the entity
or concept that is conventionally thought to be embraced by the term
'school.' " Finally, if the child does not attend school or participate in
an alternative learning experience, the Standards provide for a graduated approach to resolving the problem including conferences with

18. 6 Fam.L.Q. 343, 369–70 (1972).   * Copyright 1972, The Family Law
                                            Quarterly. Reprinted with permission.

parents, counseling, and if necessary, resort to the court, but only for the purpose of soliciting the court's aid in developing a supervised plan for the student's attendance. Truancy is not a basis for exercise of the court's coercive powers, and the Standards provide that failure to attend school is not a basis for the child to be taken into custody, nor is failure to send children to school a basis for imposition of criminal sanctions against parents or for finding that parents have neglected a child.[19]

In the Introduction to the volume on Standards Relating to Schools and Education the draftsmen observed:

. . . The standards of this volume generally reflect what is probably a paradoxical truth of both American law and American education: all are treated equal because assumed to be equal, yet the individual differences of each must be recognized and protected. A crowning achievement of American education has been its universality. But its very inclusiveness has created many of its problems. In addition to vast numbers, public schools in the United States attempt to educate vastly different types of children. They have different backgrounds, interests, and needs and develop at different rates of speed. The educational challenge that has never been met is to adapt schools to these variations without resorting to an unstimulating blandness or a lowest common denominator. . . .[20]

Again, flexibility in alternatives and responses seems best calculated to assure achievement of the state's interest in educating its citizens while at the same time preserving to the greatest degree possible the integrity and autonomy of the family unit. Perhaps the New York court was sensitive to achieving this delicate balance when it observed in In re Falk that "The ideal college is Mark Hopkins (1802–1887) on one end of a log and a student on the other, so said President James A. Garfield, his former student."[21]

NOTES

(1) In San Antonio Independent School District v. Rodriguez, 411 U.S. 1, 93 S.Ct. 1278, 36 L.Ed.2d 16 (1973), the Supreme Court rejected the contention that there is a constitutional right to education. In Texas the financing of public elementary and secondary schools had been based to a large extent on local property taxes. Appellees brought a class action in the name of members of poor families who reside in school districts having a low property tax base, claiming that the reliance on local property taxation favors the more affluent and violates equal protection requirements because of substantial interdistrict disparities in the value of assessable property among the districts. Finding that wealth is a "suspect" classification and that education is a "fundamental" right, the District Court struck down the system

19. See, generally, Commentary to Standard 1.11 at 51–53.

20. Standards Relating to Schools and Education (Tentative Draft 1977), at 5.

21. 110 Misc.2d at 108, 441 N.Y.S.2d at 788.

for lack of a compelling state interest. In reversing, Justice Powell wrote for the Court:

> It is not the province of this Court to create substantive constitutional rights in the name of guaranteeing equal protection of the laws. Thus, the key to discovering whether education is "fundamental" is not to be found in comparisons of the relative societal significance of education as opposed to subsistence or housing. Nor is it to be found by weighing whether education is as important as the right to travel. Rather, the answer lies in assessing whether there is a right to education explicitly or implicitly guaranteed by the Constitution.
>
> Education, of course, is not among the rights afforded explicit protection under our Federal Constitution. Nor do we find any basis for saying it is implicitly so protected. As we have said, the undisputed importance of education will not alone cause this Court to depart from the usual standard for reviewing a State's social and economic legislation. It is appellees' contention, however, that education is distinguishable from other services and benefits provided by the State because it bears a peculiarly close relationship to other rights and liberties accorded protection under the Constitution. Specifically, they insist that education is itself a fundamental personal right because it is essential to the effective exercise of First Amendment freedoms and to intelligent utilization of the right to vote. In asserting a nexus between speech and education, appellees urge that the right to speak is meaningless unless the speaker is capable of articulating his thoughts intelligently and persuasively. The "marketplace of ideas" is an empty forum for those lacking basic communicative tools. Likewise, they argue that the corollary right to receive information becomes little more than a hollow privilege when the recipient has not been taught to read, assimilate, and utilize available knowledge.
>
> A similar line of reasoning is pursued with respect to the right to vote. Exercise of the franchise, it is contended, cannot be divorced from the educational foundation of the voter. The electoral process, if reality is to conform to the democratic ideal, depends on an informed electorate: a voter cannot cast his ballot intelligently unless his reading skills and thought processes have been adequately developed.
>
> We need not dispute any of these propositions. The Court has long afforded zealous protection against unjustifiable governmental interference with the individual's rights to speak and to vote. Yet we have never presumed to possess either the ability or the authority to guarantee to the citizenry the most *effective* speech or the most *informed* electoral choice. That these may be desirable goals of a system of freedom of expression and of a representative form of government is not to be doubted. These are indeed goals to be pursued by a people whose thoughts and beliefs are freed from governmental interference. But they are not values to be implemented by judicial intrusion into otherwise legitimate state activities.

411 U.S. at 33–36.

(2) In recent years some students have sought to establish a tort action for what is frequently dubbed "educational malpractice." Thus far such suits have met with little or no success, though the facts alleged in some of the cases would seem to present appealing situations for some sort of recovery.

In Peter W. v. San Francisco Unified School District, 60 Cal.App.3d 814, 131 Cal.Rptr. 854 (1976), the plaintiff was an 18-year-old who had a history of "social promotion." He alleged the schools had "negligently and carelessly" failed to provide him with adequate instruction "in basic academic skills such as reading and writing" and had promoted him knowing that he had not achieved the skills necessary to succeed or benefit from the next level of course work. He sought damages for inability to gain meaningful employment and for the cost of compensatory tutoring. The claim was dismissed because the court was unable to identify the basis for a teacher's duty to educate students successfully, and it pointed out that many other factors from outside the teaching process influence the achievement of literacy in the schools.

The New York Court of Appeals faced somewhat similar facts in Donohue v. Copiague Union Free School District, 47 N.Y.2d 440, 418 N.Y.S.2d 375, 391 N.E.2d 1352 (1979). According to the court, the thrust of the claim was "that notwithstanding his receipt of a certificate of graduation [appellant] lacks even the rudimentary ability to comprehend written English on a level sufficient to enable him to complete applications for employment." In rejecting the claim, the court explained that:

> The heart of the matter is whether, assuming that such a cause of action may be stated, the courts should, as a matter of public policy, entertain such claims. We believe they should not.

The court added:

> To entertain a cause of action for "educational malpractice" would require the courts not merely to make judgments as to the validity of broad educational policies—a course we have unalteringly eschewed in the past—but, more imporantly, to sit in review of the day-to-day implementation of these policies. Recognition . . . of this cause of action would constitute blatant interference with the responsibility for the administration of the public school system lodged by Constitution and statute in school administrative agencies.

In Helm v. Professional Children's School, 103 Misc.2d 1053, 431 N.Y.S.2d 246 (App.Term 1980), another New York court applied the *Donohue* rationale to a private school. The Maryland Court of Special Appeals also has followed *Donohue* in a case that discusses in some detail the practical difficulties of proving negligence in the educational process. Hunter v. Board of Education, 47 Md.App. 709, 425 A.2d 681 (1981).

Should the policy decision differ in cases involving children with definable learning disabilities that go undetected or are improperly evaluated? The Education of the All Handicapped Act of 1975, 20 U.S.C.A. §§ 1401–1461, known in educational circles as Public Law 94–142, places a number of specific requirements regarding placement alternatives and special schools or instruction on those states that decide to adhere to the act in order to qualify for certain federal funding. In Loughran v. Flanders, 470 F.Supp. 110 (D.Conn.1970), the court decided that a private right of action could not be implied from Public Law 94–142. But see Boxall v. Sequoia Union High School District, 464 F.Supp. 1104 (N.D.Cal.1979).

In Hoffman v. Board of Education of City of New York, 49 N.Y.2d 121, 424 N.Y.S.2d 396, 400 N.E.2d 317 (1979), not involving Public Law 94–142, a child at kindergarten level had been placed in a class for Children with Retarded Mental Development (CRMD), based on the examination and recommendation of a psychologist in the school system. This occurred in 1956. In 1969, a year after the child had been transferred to a manual and shop training center for retarded youths, his mother requested, for the first time, that his intelligence be retested. It was determined then that he was not retarded, and thus he was not allowed to return to the special program the following term. In a suit against the Board of Education based on the initial assessment and failure to retest (as had been recommended by the original testing psychologist, who had indicated uncertainty about his findings, evidently because of the child's speech defect), the plaintiff was awarded damages of $750,000. *Donohue* was distinguished as involving nonfeasance, while it was asserted in the present case there had been active misfeasance. The decision was reversed by the New York Court of Appeals, which explained:

> The court below distinguished *Donohue* upon the ground that the negligence alleged in that case was a failure to educate properly or nonfeasance, whereas, in that court's view, the present case involves an affirmative act of misfeasance. At the outset, we would note that both *Donohue* and the present case involved allegations of various negligent acts and omissions. Furthermore, even if we were to accept the distinction drawn by the court below, and argued by plaintiff on appeal, we would not reach a contrary result. The policy considerations which prompted our decision in *Donohue* apply with equal force to "educational malpractice" actions based upon allegations of educational misfeasance and nonfeasance.

> Our decision in *Donohue* was grounded upon the principle that courts ought not interfere with the professional judgment of those charged by the Constitution and by statute with the responsibility for the administration of the schools of this State. In the present case, the decision of the school officials and educators who classified plaintiff as retarded and continued his enrollment in CRMD classes was based upon the results of a recognized intelligence test administered by a qualified psychologist and the daily observation of plaintiff's teachers. In order to affirm a finding of liability in these circumstances, this court would be required to allow the finder of fact to substitute its judgment for the professional judgment of the board of education as to the type of psychometric devices to be used and the frequency with which such tests are to be given. Such a decision would also allow a court or a jury to second-guess the determinations of each of plaintiff's teachers. To do so would open the door to an examination of the propriety of each of the procedures used in the education of every student in our school system. Clearly, each and every time a student fails to progress academically, it can be argued that he or she would have done better and received a greater benefit if another educational approach or diagnostic tool had been utilized. Similarly, whenever there was a failure to implement a recommendation made by any person in the school system with respect to the evaluation of a pupil or his or her educational program, it could be said, as here, that liability could be predicated on misfeasance. However, the court system is not the proper forum to test the validity of the educational decision to place a particular student in one of the many educational programs offered by the schools of this State. In our view, any dispute concerning the proper placement of a child in a particular educational program can best be resolved by seeking review of such professional educational judgment through the ad-

ministrative processes provided by statute. (See Education Law, § 310, subd. 7.)

400 N.E.2d 317, 320 (1979).

In Board of Education v. Rowley, ___ U.S. ___, 102 S.Ct. 3034, 73 L.Ed.2d 690 (1982), the United States Supreme Court rejected the claim of parents of a deaf child that the All Handicapped Children Act of 1975 required the state to provide a qualified sign-language interpreter for all of the child's academic classes. Writing for the Court, Justice Rehnquist explained that the standard imposed by the Act on the states was not "to maximize the potential of each handicapped child commensurate with the opportunity provided non-handicapped children." Instead, according to the opinion, "Congress sought primarily to identify and evaluate handicapped children, and to provide them with access to a free public education."

ILLEGITIMACY AND THE EQUAL PROTECTION CLAUSE

A considerable body of private law has built up around the legal status of illegitimacy during the past 150 years. This can be illustrated most dramatically for lawyers by pointing to the 106 Key Numbers under the heading "Bastards" in the Eighth Decennial Digest.[1]

During the 1968 term the Supreme Court surprised many observers by deciding in Levy v. Louisiana [2] that it was unconstitutional for a state to create a right of action in favor of children for the wrongful death of a parent and exclude illegitimate children from its benefits. Describing illegitimate children as "clearly 'persons' within the meaning of the Equal Protection Clause", the Court concluded that it "is invidious to discriminate against them when no action, conduct, or demeanor of theirs is possibly relevant to the harm that was done to the mother." In a companion case, Glona v. American Guarantee & Liability Insurance Company,[3] the Court invalidated another Louisiana law that provided that a mother had no right of action for the death of her illegitimate son even though such an action would have been available had the child been legitimate.

Since Levy and Glona the Supreme Court has produced a flow of decisions dealing with the application of the Equal Protection Clause in cases involving inheritance, support and workmen's compensation benefits for illegitimate children. In Labine v. Vincent,[4] an illegitimate child attacked the constitutionality of a Louisiana statute that disqualified her from sharing in the intestate distribution of her father's estate. Justice Black, writing for the Court, found illegitimacy

1. 5 Am.Dig. System 1966–1976 (Eighth Decennial Digest) 939–40 (West 1978). Although the concluding Key Number is 105, a number 17.5, dealing with "Neglect to Support" was slipped in at some point. Key numbers, of course, are the categories used to retrieve digests of cases published in the National Reporter System.

2. 391 U.S. 68, 88 S.Ct. 1509, 20 L.Ed. 2d 436 (1968).

3. 391 U.S. 73, 88 S.Ct. 1515, 20 L.Ed. 2d 441 (1968).

4. 401 U.S. 532, 91 S.Ct. 1017, 28 L.Ed.2d 288 (1971).

not to be a suspect classification; thus, the state needed only a rational basis to sustain the succession provision. He also found the exclusion of acknowledged illegitimate children to be rationally related to the state's desire to promote family life and the need to supervise the distribution of estates without onerous problems of proof regarding paternity.

Some thought that the scope of *Levy* and *Glona* had been severely limited by *Labine* in definite contrast to developments that were taking place on the legislative front. The Uniform Parentage Act (1973), for example, was based on the premise that

> The parent and child relationship extends equally to every child and to every parent, regardless of the marital status of the parents.[5]

Others regarded *Labine* as peculiar to the problems of Louisiana's inheritance law, which differs from that in other states. Such doubts were justified. In Weber v. Aetna Casualty and Surety Co.,[6] the Court held that a blanket exclusion of illegitimate children from bringing a workman's compensation claim on behalf of their deceased father was an unconstitutional denial of both due process and equal protection. Nothing about the child's illegitimate status was seen to justify such a bar. The court found that condemning a child to show disapproval of the parent's relationship "is illogical and unjust. Moreover, imposing disabilities on the illegitimate child is contrary to the basic concept of our system that legal burdens should bear some relationship to individual responsibility or wrongdoing. Obviously, no child is responsible for his birth and penalizing the illegitimate child is an ineffectual—as well as an unjust—way of deterring the parent."

In the following year, 1973, the Supreme Court in a short per curiam decision [7] held that a state could not constitutionally grant legitimate children a right of support from their natural fathers and at the same time deny such a right to illegitimate children.

By contrast, the Supreme Court in Mathews v. Lucas [8] upheld a requirement of the Federal Social Security Act that unacknowledged, illegitimate children make a special proof of dependency on the father as a prerequisite to receiving his death benefits under the Act. Legitimate children and even acknowledged illegitimate children were given the benefit of a statutory presumption of dependency and were, therefore, exempted from proving the dependent relationship. The Court in upholding the differential treatment found the classification rationally related to problems of proof.

---

5. § 2, 9A U.L.A. 588 (West 1979).

6. 406 U.S. 164, 92 S.Ct. 1400, 31 L.Ed.2d 768 (1972).

7. Gomez v. Perez, 409 U.S. 535, 93 S.Ct. 872, 35 L.Ed.2d 56 (1973).

8. 427 U.S. 495, 96 S.Ct. 2755, 49 L.Ed.2d 651 (1976).

The Court in *Mathews* again determined that illegitimacy is not entitled to strict scrutiny because:

[W]hile the law has long placed the illegitimate child in an inferior position relative to the legitimate in certain circumstances, particularly in regard to obligations of support or other aspects of family law, perhaps in part because the roots of the discrimination rest in the conduct of the parents rather than the child, and perhaps in part because illegitimacy does not carry an obvious badge, as race or sex do, this discrimination against illegitimates has never approached the severity or pervasiveness of the historic legal and political discrimination against women and Negroes.

We therefore adhere to our earlier view, see Labine v. Vincent, 401 U.S. 532, 91 S.Ct. 1017, 28 L.Ed.2d 288 (1971) that the Act's discrimination between individuals on the basis of their legitimacy does not command extraordinary protection from the majoritarian political process . . . which our most exacting scrutiny would entail.[9]

Applying the rational basis standard, the majority found the challenged statutory requirement reasonably related to the likelihood of dependency at death. Since the purpose of the Act is to pay death benefits to dependent children, Congress was free to put the burden of case by case proof on unacknowledged illegitimates while exempting all children whose relationship to the decedent was more clearly established during his life.

One year later in Trimble v. Gordon [10] Mr. Justice Powell delivered an opinion of the court which stated again that illegitimacy is not a suspect classification but nevertheless (in something of an upset given the overwhelming evidence that whoever bears the burden of proof usually loses in such challenges) struck down § 12 of the Illinois Probate Act, which barred illegitimates from sharing in the distribution of intestate property. In an opinion that some have read as according illegitimacy "quasi-suspect" status entitled to an intermediate level of scrutiny,[11] Justice Powell rejected all the government's purported bases for the statutory bar. As to the promotion of family life by penalizing the status of illegitimacy, which had been persuasive to Justice Black in *Labine*, Justice Powell followed *Weber*'s analysis and stated:

In subsequent decisions [after *Labine*] we have expressly considered and rejected the argument that a State may attempt to influ-

9. 427 U.S. at 505–06, 96 S.Ct. at 2762.

10. 430 U.S. 762, 97 S.Ct. 1459, 52 L.Ed.2d 31 (1977).

11. Justice Rehnquist's dissent in *Trimble* noted for example that the Court's opinion gave illegitimacy classification greater scrutiny than mere rationality, but they have never held those classifications to be "suspect". 430 U.S. at 781, 97 S.Ct. at 1470–71.

ence the actions of men and women by imposing sanctions on the children born of their illegitimate relationships.

. . .

The parents have the ability to conform their conduct to societal norms, but their illegitimate children can affect neither their parents' conduct nor their own status.[12]

The Court, echoing Mathews v. Lucas, acknowledged the appropriateness of upholding statutory distinctions closely related to the problem of proof and the need for orderly administration of decedents' estates, but nevertheless struck down Illinois' blanket disinheritance of illegitimates.

Finally the Court addressed the state's argument that the intestate succession statutes should be written to reflect what most people would do if they were to write a will; according to the state, most people would not include illegitimate children in their wills and the Illinois Probate Act merely reflected this presumed intent. However, Justice Powell found it unnecessary to resolve the issue of "presumed intent" because the court did not think that the provision of the Illinois statute had been adopted for such a purpose. In a footnote, however, he pointed out that:

> The issue . . . becomes one of where the burden of inertia in writing a will is to fall. At least when the disadvantaged group has been a frequent target of discrimination, as illegitimates have, we doubt that a State constitutionally may place the burden on that group by invoking the theory of "presumed intent." [13]

It seemed almost inevitable that a case like Lalli v. Lalli [14] would appear before the Court after *Trimble*. In *Lalli* illegitimate children of a decedent attacked a New York statute [15] that required a filiation order declaring paternity during the father's lifetime before an illegitimate could share in the intestate distribution of his father's estate. The Court upheld the New York statute as specifically related to the state's legitimate concern—the problems of proving the relationship of putative illegitimates to the decedent and the difficulty of exposing spurious claims. The Court next analyzed the legislative means the state had chosen to further these legitimate legislative goals:

> As the State's interests are substantial, we now consider the means adopted by New York to further these interests. . . .
> [T]he Commission recommended a requirement designed to ensure the accurate resolution of claims of paternity and to minimize the potential for disruption of estate administration. Accuracy is enhanced by placing paternity disputes in a judicial forum during the

12. 430 U.S. 769, 770.

13. Id. at 775, n. 16.

14. 439 U.S. 259, 99 S.Ct. 518, 58 L.Ed.2d 503 (1978).

15. N.Y. Decedent's Estates Law § 4-1.2.

lifetime of the father. As the New York Court of Appeals observed in its first opinion in this case, the "availability [of the putative father] should be a substantial factor contributing to the reliability of the fact-finding process." In re Lalli, 38 N.Y.2d at 82, 340 N.E.2d at 724. In addition, requiring that the order be issued during the father's lifetime permits a man to defend his reputation against "unjust accusations in paternity claims," which was a secondary purpose of § 4–1.2.

The administration of an estate will be facilitated, and the possibility of delay and uncertainty minimized, where the entitlement of an illegitimate child to notice and participation is a matter of judicial record before the administration commences. Fraudulent assertions of paternity will be much less likely to succeed, or even to arise, where the proof is put before a court of law at a time when the putative father is available to respond, rather than first brought to light when the distribution of the assets of an estate is in the offing.

Appellant contends that § 4–1.2, like the statute at issue in Trimble, excludes "significant categories of illegitimate children" who could be allowed to inherit, "without jeopardizing the orderly settlement" of their intestate fathers' estates. He urges that those in his position—"known" illegitimate children who, despite the absence of an order of filiation obtained during their fathers' lifetimes, can present convincing proof of paternity—cannot rationally be denied inheritance as they pose none of the risks § 4–1.2 was intended to minimize.

We do not question that there will be some illegitimate children who would be able to establish their relationship to their deceased fathers without serious disruption of the administration of estates and that, as applied to such individuals § 4–1.2 appears to operate unfairly. But few statutory classifications are entirely free from the criticism that they sometimes produce inequitable results. Our inquiry under the Equal Protection Clause does not focus on the abstract "fairness" of a state law, but on whether the statute's relation to the state interests it is intended to promote is so tenuous that it lacks the rationality contemplated by the Fourteenth Amendment.

The Illinois statute in Trimble was constitutionally unacceptable because it effected a total statutory disinheritance of children born out of wedlock who were not legitimated by the subsequent marriage of their parents. The reach of the statute was far in excess of its justifiable purposes. Section 4–1.2 does not share this defect. Inheritance is barred only where there has been a failure to secure evidence of paternity during the father's lifetime in the manner prescribed by the State. This is not a requirement that inevitably disqualifies an unnecessarily large number of children born out of wedlock.[16]

After this series of cases the following principles emerge: (1) The Court does not regard illegitimacy as a suspect classification for equal protection analysis but does suggest illegitimacy is entitled to the heightened scrutiny accorded a "quasi-suspect" classification; [17] (2) statutes making distinctions between legitimate and illegitimate children must be narrowly drawn and closely related to real problems of proof in order to be on sound constitutional footing.[18]

NOTE

For further background on the law of illegitimacy in this country and the contemporary directions toward change, see H. Krause, Illegitimacy: Law and Social Policy (1971); and H. Krause, Child Support in America, 103–162 (1981).

STANLEY v. ILLINOIS

Supreme Court of the United States, 1972.
405 U.S. 645, 92 S.Ct. 1208, 31 L.Ed.2d 551.

MR. JUSTICE WHITE delivered the opinion of the Court.

Joan Stanley lived with Peter Stanley intermittently for 18 years, during which time they had three children. When Joan Stanley died, Peter Stanley lost not only her but also his children. Under Illinois law, the children of unwed fathers become wards of the State upon the death of the mother. Accordingly, upon Joan Stanley's death, in a dependency proceeding instituted by the State of Illinois, Stanley's children [2] were declared wards of the State and placed with court-appointed guardians. Stanley appealed, claiming that he had never been shown to be an unfit parent and that since married fathers and unwed mothers could not be deprived of their children without such a showing, he had been deprived of the equal protection of the laws guaranteed him by the Fourteenth Amendment. The Illinois Supreme Court accepted the fact that Stanley's own unfitness had not been established but rejected the equal protection claim, holding that Stanley could properly be separated from his children upon proof of the single fact that he and the dead mother had not been married. Stanley's actual fitness as a father was irrelevant. In re Stanley, 45 Ill.2d 132, 256 N.E.2d 814 (1970).

Stanley presses his equal protection claim here. The State continues to respond that unwed fathers are presumed unfit to raise their

16. 439 U.S. at 271–73, 99 S.Ct. at 526–527.

17. See L.Tribe, American Constitutional Law § 16–23, at 1057, 1090 (1978) (while illegitimacy has not been declared a suspect classification, the Court's scrutiny is significantly closer than the "mini-mum rationality" standard would demand).

18. See Mills v. Habluetzel, —— U.S. ——, 102 S.Ct. 1549, 1554 (1982), discussed supra at 34.

2. Only two children are involved in this litigation.

children and that it is unnecessary to hold individualized hearings to determine whether particular fathers are in fact unfit parents before they are separated from their children. . . .

I

At the outset we reject any suggestion that we need not consider the propriety of the dependency proceeding that separated the Stanleys because Stanley might be able to regain custody of his children as a guardian or through adoption proceedings. The suggestion is that if Stanley has been treated differently from other parents, the difference is immaterial and not legally cognizable for the purposes of the Fourteenth Amendment. This Court has not, however, embraced the general proposition that a wrong may be done if it can be undone. Surely, in the case before us, if there is delay between the doing and the undoing petitioner suffers from the deprivation of his children, and the children suffer from uncertainty and dislocation.

It is clear, moreover, that Stanley does not have the means at hand promptly to erase the adverse consequences of the proceeding in the course of which his children were declared wards of the State. It is first urged that Stanley could act to adopt his children. . . . Insofar as we are informed, Illinois law affords him no priority in adoption proceedings. It would be his burden to establish not only that he would be a suitable parent but also that he would be the most suitable of all who might want custody of the children. Neither can we ignore that in the proceedings from which this action developed, the "probation officer," the assistant state's attorney, and the judge charged with the case, made it apparent that Stanley, unmarried and impecunious as he is, could not now expect to profit from adoption proceedings. . . .

Before us, the State focuses on Stanley's failure to petition for "custody and control"—the second route by which, it is urged, he might regain authority for his children. Passing the obvious issue whether it would be futile or burdensome for an unmarried father— without funds and already once presumed unfit—to petition for custody, this suggestion overlooks the fact that legal custody is not parenthood or adoption. A person appointed guardian in an action for custody and control is subject to removal at any time without such cause as must be shown in a neglect proceeding against a parent. He may not take the children out of the jurisdiction without the court's approval. He may be required to report to the court as to his disposition of the children's affairs. Obviously then, even if Stanley were a mere step away from "custody and control," to give an unwed father only "custody and control" would still be to leave him seriously prejudiced by reason of his status.

We must therefore examine the question that Illinois would have us avoid: Is a presumption that distinguishes and burdens all unwed fathers constitutionally repugnant? We conclude that, as a matter of due process of law, Stanley was entitled to a hearing on his fitness as a parent before his children were taken from him and that, by denying him a hearing and extending it to all other parents whose custody of their children is challenged, the State denied Stanley the equal protection of the laws guaranteed by the Fourteenth Amendment.

II

Illinois has two principal methods of removing nondelinquent children from the homes of their parents. In a dependency proceeding it may demonstrate that the children are wards of the State because they have no surviving parent or guardian. In a neglect proceeding it may show that children should be wards of the State because the present parent(s) or guardian does not provide suitable care.

The State's right—indeed, duty—to protect minor children through a judicial determination of their interests in a neglect proceeding is not challenged here. Rather, we are faced with a dependency statute that empowers state officials to circumvent neglect proceedings on the theory that an unwed father is not a "parent" whose existing relationship with his children must be considered. "Parents," says the State, "means the father and mother of a legitimate child, or the survivor of them, or the natural mother of an illegitimate child, and includes any adoptive parent," Ill.Rev.Stat., c. 37, § 701–14, but the term does not include unwed fathers.

. . .

The private interest here, that of a man in the children he has sired and raised, undeniably warrants deference and, absent a powerful countervailing interest, protection. It is plain that the interest of a parent in the companionship, care, custody, and management of his or her children "come[s] to this Court with a momentum for respect lacking when appeal is made to liberties which derive merely from shifting economic arrangements." Kovacs v. Cooper, 336 U.S. 77, 95, (1949) (Frankfurter, J., concurring).

The Court has frequently emphasized the importance of the family. The rights to conceive and to raise one's children have been deemed "essential," Meyer v. Nebraska, 262 U.S. 390, 399 (1923), "basic civil rights of man," Skinner v. Oklahoma, 316 U.S. 535, 541 (1942), and "[r]ights far more precious . . . than property rights," May v. Anderson, 345 U.S. 528, 533 (1953). "It is cardinal with us that the custody, care and nurture of the child reside first in the parents, whose primary function and freedom include preparation for obligations the state can neither supply nor hinder." Prince v. Massachusetts, 321 U.S. 158, 166 (1944). The integrity of the family unit has found protection in the Due Process Clause of the Fourteenth Amendment, Meyer v. Nebraska, supra, 262 U.S. at 399, the Equal Protection Clause of the Fourteenth Amendment, Skinner v. Oklahoma, supra, 316 U.S., at 541, and the Ninth Amendment, Griswold v. Connecticut, 381 U.S. 479, 496 (1965) (Goldberg, J., concurring).

Nor has the law refused to recognize those family relationships unlegitimized by a marriage ceremony. The Court has declared unconstitutional a state statute denying natural, but illegitimate, children a wrongful-death action for the death of their mother, emphasizing that such children cannot be denied the right of other children because familial bonds in such cases were often as warm, enduring, and important as those arising within a more formally organized family unit. Levy v. Louisiana, 391 U.S. 68, 71–72 (1968). "To say that the test of equal protection should be the 'legal' rather than the biological relationship is to avoid the issue. For the Equal Protection Clause necessarily limits the authority of a State to draw such 'legal' lines as it chooses." Glona v. American Guarantee & Liability Ins. Co., 391 U.S. 73, 75–76 (1968).

. . .

For its part, the State has made its interest quite plain: Illinois has declared that the aim of the Juvenile Court Act is to protect "the moral, emotional, mental, and physical welfare of the minor and the best interests of the community" and to "strengthen the minor's family ties whenever possible, removing him from the custody of his parents only when his welfare or safety or the protection of the public cannot be adequately safeguarded without removal . . ." Ill.Rev. Stat., c. 37, § 701-2. These are legitimate interests, well within the power of the State to implement. We do not question the assertion that neglectful parents may be separated from their children.

But we are here not asked to evaluate the legitimacy of the state ends, rather, to determine whether the means used to achieve these ends are constitutionally defensible. What is the state interest in separating children from fathers without a hearing designed to determine whether the father is unfit in a particular disputed case? We observe that the State registers no gain towards its declared goals when it separates children from the custody of fit parents. Indeed, if Stanley is a fit father, the State spites its own articulated goals when it needlessly separates him from his family.

In Bell v. Burson, 402 U.S. 535, 91 S.Ct. 1586, 29 L.Ed.2d 90 (1971), we found a scheme repugnant to the Due Process Clause because it deprived a driver of his license without reference to the very factor (there fault in driving, here fitness as a parent) that the State itself deemed fundamental to its statutory scheme. Illinois would avoid the self-contradiction that rendered the Georgia license suspension system invalid by arguing that Stanley and all other unmarried fathers can reasonably be presumed to be unqualified to raise their children.[5]

5. Illinois says in its brief, at 21–23, "[T]he only relevant consideration in determining the propriety of governmental intervention in the raising of children is whether the best interests of the child are served by such intervention.

It may be, as the State insists, that most unmarried fathers are unsuitable and neglectful parents. It may also be that Stanley is such a parent and that his children should be placed in other hands. But all unmarried fathers are not in this category; some are wholly suited to have custody of their children. This much the State readily concedes, and nothing in this record indicates that Stanley is or has been a neglectful father who has not cared for his children. Given the opportunity to make his case, Stanley may have been seen to be deserving of custody of his offspring. Had this been so, the State's statutory policy would have been furthered by leaving custody in him.

. . . [I]t may be argued that unmarried fathers are so seldom fit that Illinois need not undergo the administrative inconvenience of inquiry in any case, including Stanley's. The establishment of prompt efficacious procedures to achieve legitimate state ends is a proper state interest worthy of cognizance in constitutional adjudication. But the Constitution recognizes higher values than speed and efficiency. Indeed, one might fairly say of the Bill of Rights in general, and the Due Process Clause in particular, that they were designed to protect the fragile values of a vulnerable citizenry from the overbearing concern for efficiency and efficacy that may characterize praiseworthy government officials no less, and perhaps more, than mediocre ones.

Procedure by presumption is always cheaper and easier than individualized determination. But when, as here, the procedure forecloses the determinative issues of competence and care, when it explicitly disdains present realities in deference to past formalities, it needlessly risks running roughshod over the important interests of both parent and child. It therefore cannot stand.[9]

"In effect, Illinois has imposed a statutory presumption that the best interests of a particular group of children necessitates some governmental supervision in certain clearly defined situations. The group of children who are illegitimate are distinguishable from legitimate children not so much by their status at birth as by the factual differences in their upbringing. While a legitimate child usually is raised by both parents with the attendant familial relationships and a firm concept of home and identity, the illegitimate child normally knows only one parent— the mother. . . .

". . . The petitioner has premised his argument upon particular factual circumstances—a lengthy relationship with the mother . . . a familial relationship with the two children, and a general assumption that this relationship approximates that in which the natural parents are married to each other.

". . . Even if this characterization were accurate (the record is insufficient to support it) it would not affect the validity of the statutory definition of parent. . . . The petitioner does not deny that the children are illegitimate. The record reflects their natural mother's death. Given these two factors, grounds exist for the State's intervention to ensure adequate care and protection for these children. This is true whether or not this particular petitioner assimilates all or none of the normal characteristics common to the classification of fathers who are not married to the mothers of their children."

. . .

9. We note in passing that the incremental cost of offering unwed fathers an opportunity for individualized hearings on fitness appears to be minimal. If unwed fathers, in the main, do not care about the disposition of their children,

Bell v. Burson held that the State could not, while purporting to be concerned with fault in suspending a driver's license, deprive a citizen of his license without a hearing that would assess fault. Absent fault, the State's declared interest was so attenuated that administrative convenience was insufficient to excuse a hearing where evidence of fault could be considered. That drivers involved in accidents, as a statistical matter, might be very likely to have been wholly or partially at fault did not foreclose hearing and proof in specific cases before licenses were suspended.

We think the Due Process Clause mandates a similar result here. The State's interest in caring for Stanley's children is *de minimis* if Stanley is shown to be a fit father. It insists on presuming rather than proving Stanley's unfitness solely because it is more convenient to presume than to prove. Under the Due Process Clause that advantage is insufficient to justify refusing a father a hearing when the issue at stake is the dismemberment of his family.

III

The State of Illinois assumes custody of the children of married parents, divorced parents, and unmarried mothers only after a hearing and proof of neglect. The children of unmarried fathers, however, are declared dependent children without a hearing on parental fitness and without proof of neglect. Stanley's claim in the state courts and here is that failure to afford him a hearing on his parental qualifications while extending it to other parents denied him equal protection of the laws. We have concluded that all Illinois parents are constitutionally entitled to a hearing on their fitness before their children are removed from their custody. It follows that denying such a hearing to Stanley and those like him while granting it to other Illinois parents, is inescapably contrary to the Equal Protection Clause.

. . .

Reversed and remanded.

MR. CHIEF JUSTICE BURGER, with whom MR. JUSTICE BLACKMUN concurs, dissenting.

. . .

they will not appear to demand hearings. If they do care, under the scheme here held invalid, Illinois would admittedly at some later time have to afford them a properly focused hearing in a custody or adoption proceeding.

Extending opportunity for hearing to unwed fathers who desire and claim competence to care for their children creates no constitutional or procedural obstacle to foreclosing those unwed fathers who are not so inclined. The Illinois law governing procedure in juvenile cases, Ill. Rev.Stat., c. 37, § 704–1 et seq., provides for personal service, notice by certified mail, or for notice by publication when personal or certified mail service cannot be had or when notice is directed to unknown respondents under the style of "All whom it may Concern." Unwed fathers who do not promptly respond cannot complain if their children are declared wards of the State. Those who do respond retain the burden of proving their fatherhood.

No due process issue was raised in the state courts; and no due process issue was decided by any state court.

. . .

All of those persons in Illinois who may have followed the progress of this case will, I expect, experience no little surprise at the Court's opinion handed down today. Stanley will undoubtedly be surprised to find that he has prevailed on an issue never advanced by him. The judges who dealt with this case in the state courts will be surprised to find their decisions overturned on a ground they never considered. . . .

Stanley argued before the Supreme Court of Illinois that the definition of "parents," set out in Ill.Rev.Stat., c. 37, § 701–14, as including "the father and mother of a legitimate child, or the survivor of them, or the natural mother of an illegitimate child, [or] . . . any adoptive parent," violates the Equal Protection Clause in that it treats unwed mothers and unwed fathers differently. Stanley then enlarged upon his equal protection argument when he brought the case here; he argued before this Court that Illinois is not permitted by the Equal Protection Clause to distinguish between unwed fathers and any of the other biological parents included in the statutory definition of legal "parents."

The Illinois Supreme Court correctly held that the State may constitutionally distinguish between unwed fathers and unwed mothers. Here, Illinois' different treatment of the two is part of that State's statutory scheme for protecting the welfare of illegitimate children. In almost all cases, the unwed mother is readily identifiable, generally from hospital records, and alternatively by physicians or others attending the child's birth. Unwed fathers, as a class, are not traditionally quite so easy to identify and locate. Many of them either deny all responsibility or exhibit no interest in the child or its welfare; and, of course, many unwed fathers are simply not aware of their parenthood.

Furthermore, I believe that a State is fully justified in concluding, on the basis of common human experience, that the biological role of the mother in carrying and nursing an infant creates stronger bonds between her and the child than the bonds resulting from the male's often casual encounter. This view is reinforced by the observable fact that most unwed mothers exhibit a concern for their offspring either permanently or at least until they are safely placed for adoption, while unwed fathers rarely burden either the mother or the child with their attentions or loyalties. Centuries of human experience buttress this view of the realities of human conditions and suggest that unwed mothers of illegitimate children are generally more dependable protectors of their children than are unwed fathers. While these, like most generalizations, are not without exceptions, they nevertheless provide a sufficient basis to sustain a statutory classification whose objective is not to penalize unwed parents but to further the welfare of illegitimate children in fulfillment of the State's obligations as *parens patriae.*

Stanley depicts himself as a somewhat unusual unwed father, namely, as one who has always acknowledged and never doubted his fatherhood of these children. He alleges that he loved, cared for, and supported these children from the time of their birth until the death of their mother. He contends that he consequently must be treated the same as a married father of legitimate children. Even assuming the truth of Stanley's allegations, I am unable to construe the Equal Protection Clause as requiring Illinois to tailor its statutory definition of "parents" so meticulously as to include such unusual unwed fathers, while at the same time excluding those unwed, and generally unidentified, biological fathers who in no way share Stanley's professed desires.

Indeed, the nature of Stanley's own desires is less than absolutely clear from the record in this case. Shortly after the death of the mother, Stanley turned these two children over to the care of a Mr. and Mrs. Ness; he took no action to gain recognition of himself as a father, through adoption, or as a legal custodian, through a guardianship proceeding. Eventually it came to the attention of the State that there was no living adult who had any legally enforceable obligation for the care and support of the children; it was only then that the dependency proceeding here under review took place and that Stanley made himself known to the juvenile court in connection with these two children.[5] Even then, however, Stanley did not ask to be charged with the legal responsibility for the children. He asked only that such legal responsibility be given to no one else. He seemed, in particular, to be concerned with the loss of the welfare payments he would suffer as a result of the designation of others as guardians of the children.

Not only, then, do I see no ground for holding that Illinois' statutory definition of "parents" on its face violates the Equal Protection Clause; I see no ground for holding that any constitutional right of Stanley has been denied in the application of that statutory definition in the case at bar.

. . .

NOTES

(1) Do you think that the Court viewed the principal issue presented in *Stanley* as discrimination based on sex, defining parental rights based on blood kinship, or protecting the rights of children? If you perceive that the

5. As the majority notes, Joan Stanley gave birth to three children during the 18 years Peter Stanley was living "intermittently" with her. At oral argument, we were told by Stanley's counsel that the oldest of these three children had previously been declared a ward of the court pursuant to a neglect proceeding that was "proven against" Stanley at a time, apparently, when the juvenile court officials were under the erroneous impression that Peter and Joan Stanley had been married.

court sought to accommodate several possibly conflicting interests, how would you identify them and what relative weights do you believe that the court attached to each one?

(2) The greatest immediate impact of the *Stanley* decision came from interpretation and attempts at application of the Court's remarks in footnote 9. It was common for states at that time to permit the natural mother of a child born out of wedlock to relinquish the child for adoption without consent from or notice to the natural father if he had neither legitimated nor formally acknowledged the child. *Stanley* was construed by many state legal officials as requiring notice to an unwed father regardless of his contacts with the child, in order to satisfy due process. Lawyers are quick to equate "notice" with publication in cases in which the whereabouts of a party is unknown, and not surprisingly it was urged that this would be the way to accomplish the goal. This argument was reinforced by the Supreme Court's mention of publication in footnote 9.

Because a large number of the children then being placed for adoption by licensed placement agencies were illegitimate and had been relinquished only by their mothers, the adoption process was thrown into turmoil in many states. Agencies were reluctant to advertise for fathers to come forward for fear that this would discourage mothers from relinquishing their children, perhaps even diverting babies to the illicit market for them which flourishes from time to time.

State legislative responses to *Stanley* have varied from establishment of a system in Michigan whereby a possible putative father could register his claim to fatherhood in advance of a child's birth (now refined somewhat from its original version), Mich.Comp.Laws Ann., § 710.33–.39 (Supp.1981–82), to methods for effecting notice through certified mail or avoiding attempts at notice by mail or publication if there is evidence to show that the father's identity cannot be ascertained. Illustrative of the latter group of statutes, Va.Code § 63.1–225 requires consent to adoption by both living parents of an illegitimate as well as a legitimate child. However subsection B(2) of the statute states:

> The consent of the father of a child born to an unmarried woman shall not be required (i) if the identity of the father is not reasonably ascertainable, or (ii) if the identity of such father is ascertainable and his whereabouts are known, such father is given notice of the adoption proceeding by registered or certified mail to his last known address and such father fails to object to the adoption proceeding within twenty-one days of the mailing of such notice. . . .

Subsection C of the statute permits a court to grant an adoption petition in instances in which the identity of the party is unobtainable and this is certified on the record. The statute provides:

> . . . an affidavit of the mother that the identity of the father is not reasonably ascertainable shall be sufficient evidence of this fact, provided there is no other evidence before the court which would refute such an affidavit. For purposes of determining whether the identity of the father is reasonably ascertainable, the standard of what is reasonable under the circumstances shall control, taking into account the relative interests of the child, the mother and the father.

Section 25 of the Uniform Parentage Act (1974) also provides a somewhat elaborate method for trying to cope with the problems for adoption left in the wake of *Stanley*. See, also, Note, The Strange Boundaries of Stanley: Providing Notice of Adoption to the Unknown Putative Father, 59 Va.L.Rev. 517 (1973).

Was footnote 9 necessary to the decision by the Court in *Stanley*?

(3) One also can view *Stanley* as a case in which the rights of children— particularly those children affected by its impact on adoption generally— were never briefed or presented to the Court. If you had been called on to file an *amicus curiae* brief with the Supreme Court as attorney for an orga- nization dedicated to the protection of children's rights, what would you have urged the Court to do or not to do in reaching its decision? Should there be some mechanism through which the interests of children in general can be raised in cases of such potential magnitude?

GOSS v. LOPEZ

Supreme Court of the United States, 1975.
419 U.S. 565, 95 S.Ct. 729, 42 L.Ed.2d 725.

MR. JUSTICE WHITE delivered the opinion of the Court.

[Public school students in Ohio who had been suspended for mis- conduct for up to 10 days without a hearing brought this class action against appellant school officials. They sought a declaration that Ohio's statute allowing such suspensions was unconstitutional and an order enjoining school officials to remove references to the suspen- sions from the students' records. A three-judge District Court de- clared that the statute and its implementing regulations were uncon- stitutional, found that appellant students had been denied due process of law, and granted the injunction.]

. . .

At the outset, appellants contend that because there is no consti- tutional right to an education at public expense, the Due Process Clause does not protect against expulsions from the public school sys- tem. This position misconceives the nature of the issue and is refut- ed by prior decisions. The Fourteenth Amendment forbids the State to deprive any person of life, liberty, or property without due process of law. Protected interests in property are normally "not created by the Constitution. Rather, they are created and their dimensions are defined" by an independent source such as state statutes or rules en- titling the citizen to certain benefits.

. . .

Here, on the basis of state law, appellees plainly had legitimate claims of entitlement to a public education. Ohio Rev.Code Ann. §§ 3313.48 and 3313.64 (1972 and Supp.1973) direct local authorities to provide a free education to all residents between five and 21 years of age, and a compulsory-attendance law requires attendance for a school year of not less than 32 weeks. It is true that § 3313.66 of the Code permits school principals to suspend students for up to 10 days; but suspensions may not be imposed without any grounds whatsoev- er. All of the schools had their own rules specifying the grounds for expulsion or suspension. Having chosen to extend the right to an education to people of appellees' class generally, Ohio may not withdraw that right on grounds of misconduct, absent fundamentally fair procedures to determine whether the misconduct has occurred.

Although Ohio may not be constitutionally obligated to establish and maintain a public school system, it has nevertheless done so and has required its children to attend. Those young people do not "shed their constitutional rights" at the schoolhouse door. Tinker v. Des Moines School Dist., 393 U.S. 503, 506, 89 S.Ct. 733, 736, 21 L.Ed.2d 731 (1969). "The Fourteenth Amendment, as now applied to the States, protects the citizen against the State itself and all of its creatures—Boards of Education not excepted." West Virginia Board of Education v. Barnette, 319 U.S. 624, 637, 63 S.Ct. 1178, 1185, 87 L.Ed. 1628 (1943). The authority possessed by the State to prescribe and enforce standards of conduct in its schools, although concededly very broad, must be exercised consistently with constitutional safeguards. Among other things, the State is constrained to recognize a student's legitimate entitlement to a public education as a property interest which is protected by the Due Process Clause and which may not be taken away for misconduct without adherence to the minimum procedures required by that Clause.

The Due Process Clause also forbids arbitrary deprivations of liberty. "Where a person's good name, reputation, honor, or integrity is at stake because of what the government is doing to him," the minimal requirements of the Clause must be satisfied. Wisconsin v. Constantineau, 400 U.S. 433, 437, 91 S.Ct. 507, 510, 27 L.Ed.2d 515 (1971); . . . School authorities here suspended appellees from school for periods of up to 10 days based on charges of misconduct. If sustained and recorded, those charges could seriously damage the students' standing with their fellow pupils and their teachers as well as interfere with later opportunities for higher education and employment. It is apparent that the claimed right of the State to determine unilaterally and without process whether that misconduct has occurred immediately collides with the requirements of the Constitution.

Appellants proceed to argue that even if there is a right to a public education protected by the Due Process Clause generally, the Clause comes into play only when the State subjects a student to a "severe detriment or grievous loss." The loss of 10 days, it is said, is neither severe nor grievous and the Due Process Clause is therefore of no relevance. Appellants' argument is again refuted by our prior decisions; for in determining "whether due process requirements apply in the first place, we must look not to the 'weight' but to the *nature* of the interest at stake." Board of Regents v. Roth, supra [408 U.S. 564 (1972)] at 570–571, 92 S.Ct. at 2705–2706. Appellees were excluded from school only temporarily, it is true, but the length and consequent severity of a deprivation, while another factor to weigh in determining the appropriate form of hearing, "is not decisive of the basic right" to a hearing of some kind. Fuentes v. Shevin, 407 U.S. 67, 86, 92 S.Ct. 1983, 1997, 32 L.Ed.2d 556 (1972). The Court's view has been that as long as a property deprivation is not *de minimis*, its gravity is irrelevant to the question whether account must be taken of the Due Process Clause. A 10-day suspension from school is not *de minimis* in our view and may not be imposed in complete disregard of the Due Process Clause.

A short suspension is, of course, a far milder deprivation than expulsion. But, "education is perhaps the most important function of state and local governments," Brown v. Board of Education, 347 U.S. 483, 493, 74 S.Ct. 686, 691, 98 L.Ed. 873 (1954), and the total exclusion from the educational process for more than a trivial period, and certainly if the suspension is for 10 days, is a serious event in the life of the suspended child. Neither the property interest in educational benefits temporarily denied nor the liberty interest in reputation, which is also implicated, is so insubstantial that suspensions may constitutionally be imposed by any procedure the school chooses, no matter how arbitrary.

III

"Once it is determined that due process applies, the question remains what process is due." Morrissey v. Brewer, 408 U.S., at 481, 92 S.Ct. at 2600. We turn to that question, fully realizing as our cases regularly do that the interpretation and application of the Due Process Clause are intensely practical matters and that "[t]he very nature of due process negates any concept of inflexible procedures universally applicable to every imaginable situation." Cafeteria Workers v. McElroy, 367 U.S. 886, 895, 81 S.Ct. 1743, 1748, 6 L.Ed.2d 1230 (1961).

. . .

. . . At the very minimum . . . students facing suspension and the consequent interference with a protected property interest must be given *some* kind of notice and afforded *some* kind of hearing. "Parties whose rights are to be affected are entitled to be heard; and in order that they may enjoy that right they must first be notified." Baldwin v. Hale, 1 Wall. 223, 233, 17 L.Ed. 531 (1864).

. . . [T]he timing and content of the notice and the nature of the hearing will depend on appropriate accommodation of the competing interests involved. Cafeteria Workers v. McElroy, supra, at 895; Morrissey v. Brewer, supra at 481. The student's interest is to avoid unfair or mistaken exclusion from the educational process, with all of its unfortunate consequences. The Due Process Clause will not shield him from suspensions properly imposed, but it disserves both his interest and the interest of the State if his suspension is in fact unwarranted. The concern would be mostly academic if the disciplinary process were a totally accurate, unerring process, never mistaken and never unfair. Unfortunately, that is not the case, and no one suggests that it is. Disciplinarians, although proceeding in utmost good faith, frequently act on the reports and advice of others; and the controlling facts and the nature of the conduct under challenge are often disputed. The risk of error is not at all trivial, and it should be guarded against if that may be done without prohibitive cost or interference with the educational process.

The difficulty is that our schools are vast and complex. Some modicum of discipline and order is essential if the educational function is to be performed. Events calling for discipline are frequent occurrences and sometimes require immediate, effective action. Suspension is considered not only to be a necessary tool to maintain order but a valuable educational device. The prospect of imposing elaborate hearing requirements in every suspension case is viewed with great concern, and many school authorities may well prefer the untrammeled power to act unilaterally, unhampered by rules about notice and hearing. But it would be a strange disciplinary system in an educational institution if no communication was sought by the disciplinarian with the student in an effort to inform him of his dereliction and to let him tell his side of the story in order to make sure that an injustice is not done. . . .

We do not believe that school authorities must be totally free from notice and hearing requirements if their schools are to operate with acceptable efficiency. Students facing temporary suspension have interests qualifying for protection of the Due Process Clause, and due process requires, in connection with a suspension of 10 days or less, that the student be given oral or written notice of the charges against him and, if he denies them, an explanation of the evidence the authorities have and an opportunity to present his side of the story. The Clause requires at least these rudimentary precautions against unfair or mistaken findings of misconduct and arbitrary exclusion from school.

There need be no delay between the time "notice" is given and the time of the hearing. In the great majority of cases the disciplinarian may informally discuss the alleged misconduct with the student minutes after it has occurred. We hold only that, in being given an opportunity to explain his version of the facts at this discussion, the student first be told what he is accused of doing and what the basis of the accusation is. Lower courts which have addressed the question of the *nature* of the procedures required in short suspension cases have reached the same conclusion. Since the hearing may occur almost immediately following the misconduct, it follows that as a general rule notice and hearing should precede removal of the student from school. We agree with the District Court, however, that there are recurring situations in which prior notice and hearing cannot be insisted upon. Students whose presence poses a continuing danger to persons or property or an ongoing threat of disrupting the academic process may be immediately removed from school. In such cases, the necessary notice and rudimentary hearing should follow as soon as practicable, as the District Court indicated.

. . .

We stop short of construing the Due Process Clause to require, countrywide, that hearings in connection with short suspensions must afford the student the opportunity to secure counsel, to confront and cross-examine witnesses supporting the charge, or to call his own witnesses to verify his version of the incident. Brief disciplinary suspensions are almost countless. To impose in each such case even truncated trial-type procedures might well overwhelm administrative facilities in many places and, by diverting resources, cost more than it would save in educational effectiveness. Moreover, further formalizing the suspension process and escalating its formality and adversary nature may not only make it too costly as a regular disciplinary tool but also destroy its effectiveness as part of the teaching process.

On the other hand, requiring effective notice and informal hearing permitting the student to give his version of the events will provide a meaningful hedge against erroneous action. At least the disciplinarian will be alerted to the existence of disputes about facts and arguments about cause and effect. He may then determine himself to summon the accuser, permit cross-examination, and allow the student to present his own witnesses. In more difficult cases, he may permit counsel. In any event, his discretion will be more informed and we think the risk of error substantially reduced.

. . .

We should also make it clear that we have addressed ourselves solely to the short suspension, not exceeding 10 days. Longer suspensions or expulsions for the remainder of the school term, or permanently, may require more formal procedures. Nor do we put aside the possibility that in unusual situations, although involving only a short suspension, something more than the rudimentary procedures will be required.

. . .

Affirmed.

MR. JUSTICE POWELL, with whom THE CHIEF JUSTICE, MR. JUSTICE BLACKMUN, and MR. JUSTICE REHNQUIST join, dissenting.

The Court today invalidates an Ohio statute that permits student suspensions from school without a hearing "for not more than ten days." The decision unnecessarily opens avenues for judicial intervention in the operation of our public schools that may affect adversely the quality of education. The Court holds for the first time that the federal courts, rather than educational officials and state legislatures, have the authority to determine the rules applicable to routine classroom discipline of children and teenagers in the public schools. It justifies this unprecedented intrusion into the process of elementary and secondary education by identifying a new constitutional right: the right of a student not to be suspended for as much as a single day without notice and a due process hearing either before or promptly following the suspension.

. . .

One of the more disturbing aspects of today's decision is its indiscriminate reliance upon the judiciary, and the adversary process, as the means of resolving many of the most routine problems arising in the classroom. In mandating due process procedures the Court misapprehends the reality of the normal teacher-pupil relationship. There is an ongoing relationship, one in which the teacher must occupy many roles—educator, adviser, friend, and, at times, parent-substitute. It is rarely adversary in nature except with respect to the chronically disruptive or insubordinate pupil whom the teacher must be free to discipline without frustrating formalities.

The Ohio statute, providing as it does for due notice both to parents and the Board, is compatible with the teacher-pupil relationship and the informal resolution of mistaken disciplinary action. We have relied for generations upon the experience, good faith and dedication of those who staff our public schools, and the nonadversary means of airing grievances that always have been available to pupils and their parents. One would have thought before today's opinion that this informal method of resolving differences was more compatible with the interests of all concerned than resort to any constitutionalized procedure, however blandly it may be defined by the Court.

In my view, the constitutionalizing of routine classroom decisions not only represents a significant and unwise extension of the Due Process Clause, but it also was quite unnecessary in view of the safeguards prescribed by the Ohio statute. This is demonstrable from a comparison of what the Court mandates as required by due process with the protective procedures it finds constitutionally insufficient.

The Ohio statute, limiting suspensions to not more than eight school days, requires *written* notice including the "reasons therefor" to the student's parents and to the Board of Education within 24 hours of any suspension. The Court only requires oral *or* written notice to the pupil, with no notice being required to the parents or the Board of Education. The mere fact of the statutory requirement is a deterrent against arbitrary action by the principal. The Board, usually elected by the people and sensitive to constituent relations, may be expected to identify a principal whose record of suspensions merits inquiry. In any event, parents placed on written notice may exercise their rights as constituents by going directly to the Board or a member thereof if dissatisfied with the principal's decision.

Nor does the Court's due process "hearing" appear to provide significantly more protection than that already available. The Court holds only that the principal must listen to the student's "version of the events," either before suspension or thereafter—depending upon the circumstances. Such a truncated "hearing" is likely to be considerably less meaningful than the opportunities for correcting mistakes already available to students and parents. Indeed, in this case all of the students and parents were offered an opportunity to attend a conference with school officials.

In its rush to mandate a constitutional rule, the Court appears to give no weight to the practical manner in which suspension problems normally would be worked out under Ohio law. One must doubt, then, whether the constitutionalization of the student-teacher relationship, with all of its attendant doctrinal and practical difficulties, will assure in any meaningful sense greater protection than that already afforded under Ohio law.

No one can foresee the ultimate frontiers of the new "thicket" the Court now enters. Today's ruling appears to sweep within the protected interest in education a multitude of discretionary decisions in the educational process. Teachers and other school authorities are required to make many decisions that may have serious consequences for the pupil. They must decide, for example, how to grade the student's work, whether a student passes or fails a course, whether he is to be promoted, whether he is required to take certain subjects, whether he may be excluded from interscholastic athletics or other extracurricular activities, whether he may be removed from one school and sent to another, whether he may be bused long distances when available schools are nearby, and whether he should be placed in a "general," "vocational," or "college-preparatory" track.

In these and many similar situations claims of impairment of one's educational entitlement identical in principle to those before the Court today can be asserted with equal or greater justification. . . .

. . .

Not so long ago, state deprivations of the most significant forms of state largesse were not thought to require due process protection on the ground that the deprivation resulted only in the loss of a state-provided "benefit." E.g., Bailey v. Richardson, 86 U.S.App.D.C. 248, 182 F.2d 46 (1950), aff'd by an equally divided Court, 341 U.S. 918, 71 S.Ct. 669, 95 L.Ed. 1352 (1951). In recent years the Court, wisely in my view, has rejected the "wooden distinction between 'rights' and 'privileges,' " Board of Regents v. Roth, 408 U.S., at 571, 92 S.Ct., at 2706, and looked instead to the significance of the state-created or state-enforced right and to the substantiality of the alleged deprivation. Today's opinion appears to abandon this reasonable approach by holding in effect that government infringement of any interest to which a person is entitled, no matter what the interest or how inconsequential the infringement, requires *constitutional* protection. As it is difficult to think of any less consequential infringement than suspension of a junior high school student for a single day, it is equally difficult to perceive any principled limit to the new reach of procedural due process.[22]

. . .

NOTES

(1) In Wood v. Strickland, 420 U.S. 308, 95 S.Ct. 992, 43 L.Ed.2d 214 (1975), the Supreme Court determined that while school officials are entitled to a qualified good-faith immunity from damages pursuant to 42 U.S.C.A. § 1983, they are not immune from liability if they knew or reasonably should have known that their official action would violate the constitutional rights of the students involved, or if the action was taken with the malicious intention of causing a deprivation of rights or injury to the student. Thus, students have been provided with a means of enforcing the rights they were granted through *Goss.* However the scope of review of the federal courts is quite limited with respect to such disciplinary decisions of high school officials as are likely to spawn dispute:

> Given the fact that there was evidence supporting the charge against respondents, the contrary judgment of the Court of Appeals is improvident. It is not the role of the federal courts to set aside decisions of school administrators which the court may view as lacking a basis in wisdom or compassion. Public high school students do have substantive and procedural rights while at school. . . . But § 1983 does not extend the right to relitigate in federal court evidentiary questions arising in school disciplinary proceedings or the proper construction of school regulations. The system of public education that has evolved in this Nation relies necessarily upon the discretion and judgment of school administrators and school board members, and § 1983 was not intended to be a vehicle for federal court correction of errors in the exercise of that discretion which do not rise to the level of violations of specific constitutional guarantees.

420 U.S. at 326.

(2) The limitations of *Goss* were illustrated in Alex v. Allen, 409 F.Supp. 379 (W.D.Pa.1976) where a high school student, Henry Alex, brought an action under 42 U.S.C.A. § 1983 challenging the grounds of his 30-day disciplinary suspension. The District Court held that high school regulations are subject to less stringent scrutiny for specificity than college regulations be-

---

22. Some half dozen years ago, the Court extended First Amendment rights under limited circumstances to public school pupils. Mr. Justice Black, dissenting, viewed the decision as ushering in "an entirely new era in which the power to control pupils by the elected 'officials of state supported public schools' . . . is in ultimate effect transferred to the Supreme Court." Tinker v. Des Moines School Dist., 393 U.S. 503, 515, 89 S.Ct. 733, 741, 21 L.Ed.2d 731 (1969). There were some who thought Mr. Justice Black was unduly concerned. But his prophecy is now being fulfilled. In the few years since *Tinker* there have been literally hundreds of cases by schoolchildren alleging violation of their constitutional rights. This flood of litigation, between pupils and school authorities, was triggered by a narrowly written First Amendment opinion which I could well have joined on its facts. One can only speculate as to the extent to which public education will be disrupted by giving every schoolchild the power to contest in *court* any decision made by his teacher which arguably infringes the state-conferred right to education.

cause of greater flexibility possessed by the state to regulate conduct of children as opposed to adults:

> Conduct such as "flagrant disregard of teachers", "loitering in areas of heavy traffic", and "rowdy behavior in the areas of heavy traffic" clearly disrupts the educational process. The Cranberry High School regulations are directed at the patterns of behavior which may legitimately be proscribed by public school authorities and in light of the minimal constitutional standards of specificity for high school regulations, the plaintiffs void for vagueness and overbreadth arguments will be dismissed. Id. at 385.

The only procedural safeguards in reference to the charges found by the court to be constitutionally mandated were notice of the charges and an opportunity to be heard.

(3) In Board of Curators of University of Missouri v. Horowitz, 435 U.S. 78, 98 S.Ct. 948, 55 L.Ed.2d 124 (1978), the question of applying due process standards to review academic grading reached the U.S. Supreme Court in the context of an adult medical student who had been dismissed. Although the special problems of the case, including the fact that decisions about clinical performance were involved, may make the case seem far afield from the situation of a middle or high school student, some of the language from the opinion of the Court by Justice Rehnquist no doubt will resurface in the literature and the jurisprudence for years to come. Upholding the District Court's finding that due process requirements had been satisfied in the case, the opinion by Justice Rehnquist states:

> Since the issue first arose 50 years ago, state and lower federal courts have recognized that there are distinct differences between decisions to suspend or dismiss a student for disciplinary purposes and similar actions taken for academic reasons which may call for hearings in connection with the former but not the latter.
>
> . . .
>
> Academic evaluations of a student, in contrast to disciplinary determinations, bear little resemblance to the judicial and administrative fact-finding proceedings to which we have traditionally attached a full hearing requirement. In *Goss*, the school's decision to suspend the students rested on factual conclusions that the individual students had participated in demonstrations that had disrupted classes, attacked a police officer, or caused physical damage to school property. The requirement of a hearing, where the student could present his side of the factual issue, could under such circumstances "provide a meaningful hedge against erroneous action." The decision to dismiss respondent, by comparison, rested on the academic judgment of school officials that she did not have the necessary clinical ability to perform adequately as a medical doctor and was making insufficient progress toward that goal. Such a judgment is by its nature more subjective and evaluative than the typical factual questions presented in the average disciplinary decision. Like the decision of an individual professor as to the proper grade for a student in his course, the determination whether to dismiss a student for academic reasons requires an expert evaluation of cumulative information and is not readily adapted to the procedural tools of judicial or administrative decisionmaking.
>
> Under such circumstances, we decline to ignore the historic judgment of educators and thereby formalize the academic dismissal process by re-

quiring a hearing. The educational process is not by nature adversarial; instead it centers around a continuing relationship between faculty and students, "one in which the teacher must occupy many roles—educator, adviser, friend, and at times, parent-substitute." Goss v. Lopez, 419 U.S. 565, 594, 95 S.Ct. 729, 746, 42 L.Ed.2d 725 (1975) (Powell, J., dissenting). This is especially true as one advances through the varying regimes of the educational system, and the instruction becomes both more individualized and more specialized. In *Goss*, this Court concluded that the value of some form of hearing in a disciplinary context outweighs any resulting harm to the academic environment. Influencing this conclusion was clearly the belief that disciplinary proceedings, in which the teacher must decide whether to punish a student for disruptive or insubordinate behavior, may automatically bring an adversarial flavor to the normal student-teacher relationship. The same conclusion does not follow in the academic context. We decline to further enlarge the judicial presence in the academic community and thereby risk deterioration of many beneficial aspects of the faculty-student relationship. . . .

435 U.S. 87, 89–90.

INGRAHAM v. WRIGHT

Supreme Court of the United States, 1977.
430 U.S. 651, 97 S.Ct. 1401, 51 L.Ed.2d 711.

MR. JUSTICE POWELL delivered the opinion of the Court.

This case presents questions concerning the use of corporal punishment in public schools: First, whether the paddling of students as a means of maintaining school discipline constitutes cruel and unusual punishment in violation of the Eighth Amendment; and, second, to the extent that paddling is constitutionally permissible, whether the Due Process Clause of the Fourteenth Amendment requires prior notice and an opportunity to be heard.

I

Petitioners James Ingraham and Roosevelt Andrews filed the complaint in this case on January 7, 1971, in the United States District Court for the Southern District of Florida.[1] At the time both were enrolled in the Charles R. Drew Junior High School in Dade County, Fla., Ingraham in the eighth grade and Andrews in the ninth. The complaint contained three counts, each alleging a separate cause of action for deprivation of constitutional rights, under 42 U.S.C. §§ 1981–1988. Counts one and two were individual actions for damages by Ingraham and Andrews based on paddling incidents that allegedly occurred in October 1970 at Drew Junior High School. Count three was a class action for declaratory and injunctive relief filed on behalf of all students in the Dade County schools.[2] Named as de-

---

1. As Ingraham and Andrews were minors, the complaint was filed in the names of Eloise Ingraham, James' mother, and Willie Everett, Roosevelt's father.

2. The District Court certified the class, under Fed.Rules Civ.Proc. 23(b)(2) and (c)(1), as follows: " 'All students of the Dade County School system who are

fendants in all counts were respondents Willie J. Wright (principal at Drew Junior High School), Lemmie Deliford (an assistant principal), Solomon Barnes (an assistant to the principal), and Edward L. Whigham (superintendent of the Dade County School System).

Petitioners presented their evidence at a week-long trial before the District Court. At the close of petitioners' case, respondents moved for dismissal of count three "on the ground that upon the facts and the law the plaintiff has shown no right to relief," Fed.Rule Civ.Proc. 41(b), and for a ruling that the evidence would be insufficient to go to a jury on counts one and two. The District Court granted the motion as to all three counts, and dismissed the complaint without hearing evidence on behalf of the school authorities.

Petitioners' evidence may be summarized briefly. In the 1970–1971 school year many of the 237 schools in Dade County used corporal punishment as a means of maintaining discipline pursuant to Florida legislation and a local School Board regulation. The statute then in effect authorized limited corporal punishment by negative inference, proscribing punishment which was "degrading or unduly severe" or which was inflicted without prior consultation with the principal or the teacher in charge of the school. Fla.Stat.Ann. § 232.27 (1961).[6] The regulation, Dade County School Board Policy 5144, con-

subject to the corporal punishment policies issued by the Defendant, Dade County School Board . . . .'" App. 17. One student was specifically excepted from the class by request.

6. In the 1970–1971 school year, § 232.27 provided:

"Each teacher or other member of the staff of any school shall assume such authority for the control of pupils as may be assigned to him by the principal and shall keep good order in the classroom and in other places in which he is assigned to be in charge of pupils, but he shall not inflict corporal punishment before consulting the principal or teacher in charge of the school, and in no case shall such punishment be degrading or unduly severe in its nature. . . ."

Effective July 1, 1976, the Florida Legislature amended the law governing corporal punishment. Section 232.27 now reads:

"Subject to law and to the rules of the district school board, each teacher or other member of the staff of any school shall have such authority for the control and discipline of students as may be assigned to him by the principal or his designated representative and shall keep good order in the classroom and in other places in which he is assigned to be in charge of students.

If a teacher feels that corporal punishment is necessary, at least the following procedures shall be followed:

"(1) The use of corporal punishment shall be approved in principle by the principal before it is used, but approval is not necessary for each specific instance in which it is used.

"(2) A teacher or principal may administer corporal punishment only in the presence of another adult who is informed beforehand, and in the student's presence, of the reason for the punishment.

"(3) A teacher or principal who has administered punishment shall, upon request, provide the pupil's parent or guardian with a written explanation of the reason for the punishment and the name of the other [adult] who was present." Fla.Stat.Ann. § 232.27 (1977) (codifier's notation omitted).

Corporal punishment is now defined as "the moderate use of physical force or physical contact by a teacher or principal as may be necessary to maintain discipline or to enforce school rules." § 228.041(28). The local school boards are expressly authorized to adopt rules governing student conduct and discipline and are directed to make available codes of student conduct, § 230.23(6). Teachers and principals are given immunity from civil and criminal liability for en-tained explicit directions and limitations.[7] The authorized punishment consisted of paddling the recalcitrant student on the buttocks with a flat wooden paddle measuring less than two feet long, three to four inches wide, and about one-half inch thick. The normal punishment was limited to one to five "licks" or blows with the paddle and resulted in no apparent physical injury to the student. School authorities viewed corporal punishment as a less drastic means of discipline than suspension or expulsion. Contrary to the procedural requirements of the statute and regulation, teachers often paddled students on their own authority without first consulting the principal.

Petitioners focused on Drew Junior High School, . . . The evidence . . . suggests that the regime at Drew was exceptionally harsh. The testimony of Ingraham and Andrews, in support of their individual claims for damages, is illustrative. Because he was slow to respond to his teacher's instructions, Ingraham was subjected to more than 20 licks with a paddle while being held over a table in the principal's office. The paddling was so severe that he suffered a hematoma requiring medical attention and keeping him out of school for several days. Andrews was paddled several times for minor infractions. On two occasions he was struck on his arms, once depriving him of the full use of his arm for a week.

The District Court made no findings on the credibility of the students' testimony. Rather, assuming their testimony to be credible, the court found no constitutional basis for relief. With respect to count three, the class action, the court concluded that the punishment authorized and practiced generally in the county schools violated no constitutional right. . . .

A panel of the Court of Appeals voted to reverse. The panel concluded that the punishment was so severe and oppressive as to violate the Eighth and Fourteenth Amendments, and that the procedures outlined in Policy 5144 failed to satisfy the requirements of the Due Process Clause. Upon rehearing, the en banc court rejected these

forcing disciplinary rules, "[e]xcept in the case of excessive force or cruel and unusual punishment . . . ." § 232.275.

7. In the 1970–1971 school year, Policy 5144 authorized corporal punishment where the failure of other means of seeking cooperation from the student made its use necessary. The regulation specified that the principal should determine the necessity for corporal punishment, that the student should understand the seriousness of the offense and the reason for the punishment, and that the punishment should be administered in the presence of another adult in circumstances not calculated to hold the student up to shame or ridicule. The regulation cautioned against using corporal punishment against a student under psychological or

medical treatment, and warned that the person administering the punishment "must realize his own personal liabilities" in any case of physical injury.

While this litigation was pending in the District Court, the Dade County School Board amended Policy 5144 to standardize the size of the paddles used in accordance with the description in the text, to proscribe striking a child with a paddle elsewhere than on the buttocks, to limit the permissible number of "licks" (five for elementary and intermediate grades and seven for junior and senior grades), and to require a contemporaneous explanation of the need for the punishment to the student and a subsequent notification to the parents.

conclusions and affirmed the judgment of the District Court. 525 F.2d 909 (1976). The full court held that the Due Process Clause did not require notice or an opportunity to be heard. . . .

The court also rejected the petitioners' substantive contentions. The Eighth Amendment, in the court's view, was simply inapplicable to corporal punishment in public schools. . . .

. . .

We granted certiorari, limited to the questions of cruel and unusual punishment and procedural due process.

II

In addressing the scope of the Eighth Amendment's prohibition on cruel and unusual punishment this Court has found it useful to refer to "[t]raditional common-law concepts," Powell v. Texas, 392 U.S. 514, 535, 88 S.Ct. 2145, 2155, 20 L.Ed.2d 1254 (1968) (plurality opinion), and to the "attitude[s] which our society has traditionally taken." Id., at 531, 88 S.Ct., at 2153. So, too, in defining the requirements of procedural due process under the Fifth and Fourteenth Amendments, the Court has been attuned to what "has always been the law of the land," United States v. Barnett, 376 U.S. 681, 692, 84 S.Ct. 984, 990, 12 L.Ed.2d 23 (1964), and to "traditional ideas of fair procedure." Greene v. McElroy, 360 U.S. 474, 508, 79 S.Ct. 1400, 1419, 3 L.Ed.2d 1377 (1959). We therefore begin by examining the way in which our traditions and our laws have responded to the use of corporal punishment in public schools.

The use of corporal punishment in this country as a means of disciplining school children dates back to the colonial period. It has survived the transformation of primary and secondary education from the colonials' reliance on optional private arrangements to our present system of compulsory education and dependence on public schools. Despite the general abandonment of corporal punishment as a means of punishing criminal offenders, the practice continues to play a role in the public education of school children in most parts of the country. Professional and public opinion is sharply divided on the practice, and has been for more than a century. Yet we can discern no trend toward its elimination.

At common law a single principle has governed the use of corporal punishment since before the American Revolution: Teachers may impose reasonable but not excessive force to discipline a child. Blackstone catalogued among the "absolute rights of individuals" the right "to security from the corporal insults of menaces, assaults, beating, and wounding," 1 W. Blackstone, Commentaries * 134, but he did not regard it a "corporal insult" for a teacher to inflict "moderate correction" on a child in his care. To the extent that force was "necessary to answer the purposes for which [the teacher] is employed," Blackstone viewed it as "justifiable or lawful." Id., at * 453; 3 id., at

* 120. The basic doctrine has not changed. The prevalent rule in this country today privileges such force as a teacher or administrator "reasonably believes to be necessary for [the child's] proper control, training, or education." Restatement (Second) of Torts § 147(2) (1965); see id., § 153(2). To the extent that the force is excessive or unreasonable, the educator in virtually all States is subject to possible civil and criminal liability.

Although the early cases viewed the authority of the teacher as deriving from the parents, the concept of parental delegation has been replaced by the view—more consonant with compulsory education laws—that the State itself may impose such corporal punishment as is reasonably necessary "for the proper education of the child and for the maintenance of group discipline." 1 F. Harper & F. James, Law of Torts § 3.20, p. 292 (1956). All of the circumstances are to be taken into account in determining whether the punishment is reasonable in a particular case. Among the most important considerations are the seriousness of the offense, the attitude and past behavior of the child, the nature and severity of the punishment, the age and strength of the child, and the availability of less severe but equally effective means of discipline. Id., at 290–291; Restatement (Second) of Torts § 150, Comments *c–e*, p. 268 (1965).

Of the 23 States that have addressed the problem through legislation, 21 have authorized the moderate use of corporal punishment in public schools. Of these States only a few have elaborated on the common-law test of reasonableness, typically providing for approval or notification of the child's parents, or for infliction of punishment only by the principal or in the presence of an adult witness. Only two States, Massachusetts and New Jersey, have prohibited all corporal punishment in their public schools. Where the legislatures have not acted, the state courts have uniformly preserved the common-law rule permitting teachers to use reasonable force in disciplining children in their charge.

Against this background of historical and contemporary approval of reasonable corporal punishment, we turn to the constitutional questions before us.

III

The Eighth Amendment provides: "Excessive bail shall not be required, nor excessive fines imposed, nor cruel and unusual punishments inflicted." Bail, fines, and punishment traditionally have been associated with the criminal process, and by subjecting the three to parallel limitations the text of the Amendment suggests an intention to limit the power of those entrusted with the criminal-law function of government. An examination of the history of the Amendment and the decisions of this Court construing the proscription against cruel and unusual punishment confirms that it was designed to protect those convicted of crimes. . . .

. . .

Petitioners acknowledge that the original design of the Cruel and Unusual Punishments Clause was to limit criminal punishments, but urge nonetheless that the prohibition should be extended to ban the paddling of schoolchildren. Observing that the Framers of the Eighth Amendment could not have envisioned our present system of public and compulsory education, with its opportunities for noncriminal punishments, petitioners contend that extension of the prohibition against cruel punishments is necessary lest we afford greater protection to criminals than to schoolchildren. It would be anomalous, they say, if schoolchildren could be beaten without constitutional redress, while hardened criminals suffering the same beatings at the hands of their jailers might have a valid claim under the Eighth Amendment. Whatever force this logic may have in other settings,[37] we find it an inadequate basis for wrenching the Eighth Amendment from its historical context and extending it to traditional disciplinary practices in the public schools.

The prisoner and the schoolchild stand in wholly different circumstances, separated by the harsh facts of criminal conviction and incarceration. The prisoner's conviction entitles the State to classify him as a "criminal," and his incarceration deprives him of the freedom "to be with family and friends and to form the other enduring attachments of normal life." Morrissey v. Brewer, 408 U.S. 471, 482, 92 S.Ct. 2593, 2600, 33 L.Ed.2d 484 (1972); . . .

The schoolchild has little need for the protection of the Eighth Amendment. Though attendance may not always be voluntary, the public school remains an open institution. Except perhaps when very young, the child is not physically restrained from leaving school during school hours; and at the end of the school day, the child is invariably free to return home. Even while at school, the child brings with him the support of family and friends and is rarely apart from teachers and other pupils who may witness and protest any instances of mistreatment.

The openness of the public school and its supervision by the community afford significant safeguards against the kinds of abuses from which the Eighth Amendment protects the prisoner. In virtually every community where corporal punishment is permitted in the schools, these safeguards are reinforced by the legal constraints of the common law. Public school teachers and administrators are privi-

---

37. Some punishments, though not labeled "criminal" by the State, may be sufficiently analogous to criminal punishments in the circumstances in which they are administered to justify application of the Eighth Amendment. Cf. In re Gault, 387 U.S. 1, 87 S.Ct. 1428, 18 L.Ed.2d 527 (1967). We have no occasion in this case, for example, to consider whether or under what circumstances persons involuntarily confined in mental or juvenile institutions can claim the protection of the Eighth Amendment.

leged at common law to inflict only such corporal punishment as is reasonably necessary for the proper education and discipline of the child; any punishment going beyond the privilege may result in both civil and criminal liability. See Part II, supra. As long as the schools are open to public scrutiny, there is no reason to believe that the common-law constraints will not effectively remedy and deter excesses such as those alleged in this case.[39]

We conclude that when public school teachers or administrators impose disciplinary corporal punishment, the Eighth Amendment is inapplicable. The pertinent constitutional question is whether the imposition is consonant with the requirements of due process.

IV

The Fourteenth Amendment prohibits any state deprivation of life, liberty, or property without due process of law. Application of this prohibition requires the familiar two-stage analysis: We must first ask whether the asserted individual interests are encompassed within the Fourteenth Amendment's protection of "life, liberty or property"; if protected interests are implicated, we then must decide what procedures constitute "due process of law." Morrissey v. Brewer, 408 U.S. at 481, 92 S.Ct., at 2600; . . . Following that analysis here, we find that corporal punishment in public schools implicates a constitutionally protected liberty interest, but we hold that the traditional common-law remedies are fully adequate to afford due process.

39. Putting history aside as irrelevant, the dissenting opinion of Mr. Justice White argues that a "purposive analysis" should control the reach of the Eighth Amendment. There is no support whatever for this approach in the decisions of this Court. Although an imposition must be "punishment" for the Cruel and Unusual Punishments Clause to apply, the Court has never held that *all* punishments are subject to Eighth Amendment scrutiny. The applicability of the Eighth Amendment always has turned on its original meaning, as demonstrated by its historical derivation.

The dissenting opinion warns that as a consequence of our decision today, teachers may "cut off a child's ear for being late to class". This rhetoric bears no relation to reality or to the issues presented in this case. The laws of virtually every State forbid the excessive physical punishment of schoolchildren. Yet the logic of the dissent would make the judgment of which disciplinary punishments are reasonable and which are excessive a matter of constitutional principle in every case, to be decided ultimately by this Court. The hazards of such a broad reading of the Eighth Amendment are clear. "It is always time to say that this Nation is too large, too complex and composed of too great a diversity of peoples for any one of us to have the wisdom to establish the rules by which local Americans must govern their local affairs. The constitutional rule we are urged to adopt is not merely revolutionary—it departs from the ancient faith based on the premise that experience in making local laws by local people themselves is by far the safest guide for a nation like ours to follow." Powell v. Texas, 392 U.S. 514, 547–548, 88 S.Ct. 2145, 2161, 20 L.Ed.2d 1254 (1968) (opinion of Black, J.).

A

. . .

The Due Process Clause of the Fifth Amendment, later incorporated into the Fourteenth, was intended to give Americans at least the protection against governmental power that they had enjoyed as Englishmen against the power of the Crown. The liberty preserved from deprivation without due process included the right "generally to enjoy those privileges long recognized at common law as essential to the orderly pursuit of happiness by free men." Meyer v. Nebraska, 262 U.S. 390, 399, 43 S.Ct. 625, 626, 67 L.Ed. 1042 (1923); . . . Among the historic liberties so protected was a right to be free from and to obtain judicial relief, for unjustified intrusions on personal security.

While the contours of this historic liberty interest in the context of our federal system of government have not been defined precisely, they always have been thought to encompass freedom from bodily restraint and punishment. It is fundamental that the state cannot hold and physically punish an individual except in accordance with due process of law.

This constitutionally protected liberty interest is at stake in this case. There is, of course a *de minimis* level of imposition with which the Constitution is not concerned. But at least where school authorities, acting under color of state law, deliberately decide to punish a child for misconduct by restraining the child and inflicting appreciable physical pain, we hold that Fourteenth Amendment liberty interests are implicated.[43]

B

"[T]he question remains what process is due." Morrissey v. Brewer, supra, at 481, 92 S.Ct., at 2600. Were it not for the common-law privilege permitting teachers to inflict reasonable corporal punishment on children in their care, and the availability of the traditional remedies for abuse, the case for requiring advance procedural safeguards would be strong indeed.[44] But here we deal with a punishment—paddling—within that tradition, and the question is

43. Unlike Goss v. Lopez, 419 U.S. 565, 95 S.Ct. 729, 42 L.Ed.2d 725 (1975), this case does not involve the state-created property interest in public education. The purpose of corporal punishment is to correct a child's behavior without interrupting his education. That corporal punishment may, in a rare case, have the unintended effect of temporarily removing a child from school affords no basis for concluding that the practice itself deprives students of property protected by the Fourteenth Amendment. . . .

44. If the common-law privilege to inflict reasonable corporal punishment in school were inapplicable, it is doubtful whether any procedure short of a trial in a criminal or juvenile court could satisfy the requirements of procedural due process for the imposition of such punishment. See United States v. Lovett, 328 U.S., at 317–318, 66 S.Ct. 1073, 1079–1080, 90 L.Ed. 1252; cf. Breed v. Jones, 421 U.S. 519, 528, 529, 95 S.Ct. 1779, 1785–1786, 44 L.Ed.2d 346 (1975).

whether the common-law remedies are adequate to afford due process.

> " '[D]ue process,' unlike some legal rules, is not a technical conception with a fixed content unrelated to time, place and circumstances. . . . Representing a profound attitude of fairness . . . 'due process' is compounded of history, reason, the past course of decisions, and stout confidence in the strength of the democratic faith which we profess. . . ." Anti-Fascist Comm. v. McGrath, 341 U.S. 123, 162–163, 71 S.Ct. 624, 643, 95 L.Ed. 817 (1951) (Frankfurter, J., concurring).

Whether in this case the common-law remedies for excessive corporal punishment constitute due process of law must turn on an analysis of the competing interests at stake, viewed against the background of "history, reason, [and] the past course of decisions." The analysis requires consideration of three distinct factors: "First, the private interest that will be affected . . . ; second, the risk of an erroneous deprivation of such interest . . . and the probable value, if any, of additional or substitute procedural safeguards; and, finally, the [state] interest, including the function involved and the fiscal and administrative burdens that the additional or substitute procedural requirement would entail." Mathews v. Eldridge, 424 U.S. 319, 335, 96 S.Ct. 893, 903, 47 L.Ed.2d 18 (1976).

1

Because it is rooted in history, the child's liberty interest in avoiding corporal punishment while in the care of public school authorities is subject to historical limitations. Under the common law, an invasion of personal security gave rise to a right to recover damages in a subsequent judicial proceeding. 3 W. Blackstone, Commentaries * 120–121. But the right of recovery was qualified by the concept of justification. Thus, there could be no recovery against a teacher who gave only "moderate correction" to a child. Id., at * 120. To the extent that the force used was reasonable in light of its purpose, it was not wrongful, but rather "justifiable or lawful." Ibid.

The concept that reasonable corporal punishment in school is justifiable continues to be recognized in the laws of most States. It represents "the balance struck by this country," Poe v. Ullman, 367 U.S. 497, 542, 81 S.Ct. 1752, 1776, 6 L.Ed.2d 989 (1961) (Harlan, J., dissenting), between the child's interest in personal security and the traditional view that some limited corporal punishment may be necessary in the course of a child's education. Under that longstanding accommodation of interests, there can be no deprivation of substantive rights as long as disciplinary corporal punishment is within the limits of the common-law privilege.

This is not to say that the child's interest in procedural safeguards is insubstantial. The school disciplinary process is not "a totally accurate, unerring process, never mistaken and never unfair. . . ."

Goss v. Lopez, 419 U.S. 565, 579–580, 95 S.Ct. 729, 739, 42 L.Ed.2d 725 (1975). In any deliberate infliction of corporal punishment on a child who is restrained for that purpose, there is some risk that the intrusion on the child's liberty will be unjustified and therefore unlawful. In these circumstances the child has a strong interest in procedural safeguards that minimize the risk of wrongful punishment and provide for the resolution of disputed questions of justification.

We turn now to a consideration of the safeguards that are available under applicable Florida law.

2

Florida has continued to recognize, and indeed has strengthened by statute, the common-law right of a child not to be subjected to excessive corporal punishment in school. Under Florida law the teacher and principal of the school decide in the first instance whether corporal punishment is reasonably necessary under the circumstances in order to discipline a child who has misbehaved. But they must exercise prudence and restraint. For Florida has preserved the traditional judicial proceedings for determining whether the punishment was justified. If the punishment inflicted is later found to have been excessive—not reasonably believed at the time to be necessary for the child's discipline or training—the school authorities inflicting it may be held liable in damages to the child and, if malice is shown, they may be subject to criminal penalties.

Although students have testified in this case to specific instances of abuse, there is every reason to believe that such mistreatment is an aberration. . . . [B]ecause paddlings are usually inflicted in response to conduct directly observed by teachers in their presence, the risk that a child will be paddled without cause is typically insignificant. . . .

In those cases where severe punishment is contemplated, the available civil and criminal sanctions for abuse—considered in light of the openness of the school environment—afford significant protection against unjustified corporal punishment. Teachers and school authorities are unlikely to inflict corporal punishment unnecessarily or excessively when a possible consequence of doing so is the institution of civil or criminal proceedings against them.[46]

46. The low incidence of abuse, and the availability of established judicial remedies in the event of abuse, distinguish this case from Goss v. Lopez, 419 U.S. 565, 95 S.Ct. 729, 42 L.Ed.2d 725 (1975). The Ohio law struck down in Goss provided for suspensions from public school of up to 10 days without "any written procedure applicable to suspensions." Id., at 567, 95 S.Ct., at 733. Although Ohio law provided generally for administrative review, Ohio Rev.Code Ann. § 2506.01 (Supp.1973), the Court assumed that the short suspensions would not be stayed pending review, with the result that the review proceeding could serve neither a deterrent nor a remedial function. 419 U.S., at 581 n. 10, 95 S.Ct., at 740. In these circumstances, the Court held the law authorizing suspensions unconstitutional for failure to require "that there be at least an informal give-and-take between student and disciplinarian, preferably prior to the suspen-

It still may be argued, of course, that the child's liberty interest would be better protected if the common-law remedies were supplemented by the administrative safeguards of prior notice and a hearing. We have found frequently that some kind of prior hearing is necessary to guard against arbitrary impositions on interests protected by the Fourteenth Amendment. But where the State has preserved what "has always been the law of the land," United States v. Barnett, 376 U.S. 681, 84 S.Ct. 984, 12 L.Ed.2d 23 (1964), the case for administrative safeguards is significantly less compelling.

There is a relevant analogy in the criminal law. Although the Fourth Amendment specifically proscribes "seizure" of a person without probable cause, the risk that police will act unreasonably in arresting a suspect is not thought to require an advance determination of the facts. In United States v. Watson, 423 U.S. 411, 96 S.Ct. 820, 46 L.Ed.2d 598 (1976), we reaffirmed the traditional common-law rule that police officers may make warrantless public arrests on probable cause. Although we observed that an advance determination of probable cause by a magistrate would be desirable, we declined "to transform this judicial preference into a constitutional rule when the judgment of the Nation and Congress has for so long been to authorize warrantless public arrests on probable cause . . . ." Id., at 423, 96 S.Ct., at 828; see id., at 429, 96 S.Ct., at 830 (Powell, J., concurring). Despite the distinct possibility that a police officer may improperly assess the facts and thus unconstitutionally deprive an individual of liberty, we declined to depart from the traditional rule by which the officer's perception is subjected to judicial scrutiny only after the fact. There is no more reason to depart from tradition and require advance procedural safeguards for intrusions on personal security to which the Fourth Amendment does not apply.

3

But even if the need for advance procedural safeguards were clear, the question would remain whether the incremental benefit could justify the cost. Acceptance of petitioners' claims would work a transformation in the law governing corporal punishment in Florida and most other States. Given the impracticability of formulating a rule of procedural due process that varies with the severity of the particular imposition, the prior hearing petitioners seek would have to precede *any* paddling, however moderate or trivial.

Such a universal constitutional requirement would significantly burden the use of corporal punishment as a disciplinary measure. Hearings—even informal hearings—require time, personnel, and a diversion of attention from normal school pursuits. School authorities may well choose to abandon corporal punishment rather than incur

sion . . . ." Id., at 584, 95 S.Ct., at 741. The subsequent civil and criminal proceedings available in this case may be viewed as affording substantially greater protection to the child than the informal conference mandated by *Goss*.

the burdens of complying with the procedural requirements. Teachers, properly concerned with maintaining authority in the classroom, may well prefer to rely on other disciplinary measures—which they may view as less effective—rather than confront the possible disruption that prior notice and a hearing may entail.[50] Paradoxically, such an alteration of disciplinary policy is most likely to occur in the ordinary case where the contemplated punishment is well within the common-law privilege.[51]

Elimination or curtailment of corporal punishment would be welcomed by many as a societal advance. But when such a policy choice may result from this Court's determination of an asserted right to due process, rather than from the normal processes of community debate and legislative action, the societal costs cannot be dismissed as insubstantial.[52] We are reviewing here a legislative judgment, rooted in history and reaffirmed in the laws of many States, that corporal punishment serves important educational interests. This judgment must be viewed in light of the disciplinary problems common-place in the schools. As noted in Goss v. Lopez, 419 U.S., at 580, 95 S.Ct., at 739: "Events calling for discipline are frequent occurrences and sometimes require immediate, effective action." Assessment of the need for, and the appropriate means of maintaining, school discipline is committed generally to the discretion of school authorities subject to state law. "[T]he Court has repeatedly emphasized the need for affirming the comprehensive authority of the States and of school officials, consistent with fundamental constitutional safeguards, to prescribe and control conduct in the schools." Tinker v. Des Moines School Dist., 393 U.S. 503, 507, 89 S.Ct. 733, 737, 21 L.Ed.2d 731 (1969).

"At some point the benefit of an additional safeguard to the individual affected . . . and to society in terms of increased assurance that the action is just, may be outweighed by the cost." Mathews v. Eldridge, 424 U.S., at 348, 96 S.Ct., at 909. We think that point has been reached in this case. In view of the low incidence of abuse, the openness of our schools, and the common-law safeguards that already exist, the risk of error that may result in violation of a schoolchild's substantive rights can only be regarded as minimal.

50. If a prior hearing, with the inevitable attendant publicity within the school, resulted in rejection of the teacher's recommendation, the consequent impairment of the teacher's ability to maintain discipline in the classroom would not be insubstantial.

51. The effect of interposing prior procedural safeguards may well be to make the punishment more severe by increasing the anxiety of the child. For this reason, the school authorities in Dade County found it desirable that the punishment be inflicted as soon as possible after the infraction.

52. "It may be true that procedural regularity in disciplinary proceedings promotes a sense of institutional rapport and open communication, a perception of fair treatment, and provides the offender and his fellow students a showcase of democracy at work. But . . . [r]espect for democratic institutions will equally dissipate if they are thought too ineffectual to provide their students an environment of order in which the educational process may go forward. . . ." Wilkinson, Goss v. Lopez: The Supreme Court as School Superintendent, 1975 Sup.Ct.Rev. 25, 71–72.

Imposing additional administrative safeguards as a constitutional requirement might reduce that risk marginally, but would also entail a significant intrusion into an area of primary educational responsibility. We conclude that the Due Process Clause does not require notice and a hearing prior to the imposition of corporal punishment in the public schools, as that practice is authorized and limited by the common law.

. . .

Affirmed.

MR. JUSTICE WHITE, with whom MR. JUSTICE BRENNAN, MR. JUSTICE MARSHALL, and MR. JUSTICE STEVENS join, dissenting.

. . .

The Eighth Amendment places a flat prohibition against the infliction of "cruel and unusual punishments." This reflects a societal judgment that there are some punishments that are so barbaric and inhumane that we will not permit them to be imposed on anyone, no matter how opprobrious the offense. See Robinson v. California, 370 U.S. 660, 676, 82 S.Ct. 1417, 1425, 8 L.Ed.2d 758 (1962) (Douglas, J., concurring). If there are some punishments that are so barbaric that they may not be imposed for the commission of crimes, designated by out social system as the most thoroughly reprehensible acts an individual can commit, then, *a fortiori,* similar punishments may not be imposed on persons for less culpable acts, such as breaches of school discipline. Thus, if it is constitutionally impermissible to cut off someone's ear for the commission of murder, it must be unconstitutional to cut off a child's ear for being late to class.[1] Although there were no ears cut off in this case, the record reveals beatings so se-

---

1. There is little reason to fear that if the Eighth Amendment is held to apply *at all* to corporal punishment of school children, *all* paddlings, however moderate, would be prohibited. Jackson v. Bishop, 404 F.2d 571 (CA8 1968), held that *any* paddling or flogging of prisoners, convicted of crime and serving prison terms, violated the cruel and unusual punishment ban of the Eighth Amendment. But aside from the fact that *Bishop* has never been embraced by this Court, the theory of that case was not that bodily punishments are intrinsically barbaric or excessively severe but that paddling of prisoners is "degrading to the punisher and to the punished alike." Id., at 580. That approach may be acceptable in the criminal justice system, but it has little if any relevance to corporal punishment in the schools, for it can hardly be said that the use of moderate paddlings in the discipline of children is inconsistent with the country's evolving standards of decency.

On the other hand, when punishment involves a cruel, severe beating or chopping off an ear, something more than merely the dignity of the individual is involved. Whenever a given criminal punishment is "cruel and unusual" because it is inhumane or barbaric, I can think of no reason why it would be any less inhumane or barbaric when inflicted on a schoolchild, as punishment for classroom misconduct.

The issue in this case is whether spankings inflicted on public schoolchildren for breaking school rules is "punishment," not whether such punishment is "cruel and unusual." If the Eighth Amendment does not bar moderate spanking in public schools, it is because moderate spanking is not "cruel and unusual," not because it is not "punishment" as the majority suggests.

vere that if they were inflicted on a hardened criminal for the commission of a serious crime, they might not pass constitutional muster.

Nevertheless, the majority holds that the Eighth Amendment "was designed to protect [only] those convicted of crimes," relying on a vague and inconclusive recitation of the history of the Amendment. Yet the constitutional prohibition is against cruel and unusual *punishments*; nowhere is that prohibition limited or modified by the language of the Constitution. Certainly the fact that the Framers did not choose to insert the word "criminal" into the language of the Eighth Amendment is strong evidence that the Amendment was designed to prohibit all inhumane or barbaric punishments, no matter what the nature of the offense for which the punishment is imposed.

No one can deny that spanking of schoolchildren is "punishment" under any reasonable reading of the word, for the similarities between spanking in public schools and other forms of punishment are too obvious to ignore. Like other forms of punishment, spanking of schoolchildren involves an institutionalized response to the violation of some official rule or regulation proscribing certain conduct and is imposed for the purpose of rehabilitating the offender, deterring the offender and others like him from committing the violation in the future, and inflicting some measure of social retribution for the harm that has been done.

B

We are fortunate that in our society punishments that are severe enough to raise a doubt as to their constitutional validity are ordinarily not imposed without first affording the accused the full panoply of procedural safeguards provided by the criminal process.[2] The effect has been that "every decision of this Court considering whether a punishment is 'cruel and unusual' within the meaning of the Eighth and Fourteenth Amendments has dealt with a criminal punishment." The Court would have us believe from this fact that there is a recognized distinction between criminal and noncriminal punishment for purposes of the Eighth Amendment. This is plainly wrong. "[E]ven a clear legislative classification of a statute as 'non-penal' would not alter the fundamental nature of a plainly penal statute." Trop v. Dulles, 356 U.S. 86, 95, 78 S.Ct. 590, 595, 2 L.Ed.2d 630 (1958) (plurality opinion). The relevant inquiry is not whether the offense for which a punishment is inflicted has been labeled as criminal, but whether the purpose of the deprivation is among those ordinarily associated with punishment, such as retribution, rehabilitation, or deterrence.[3] Id., at 96, 78 S.Ct., at 595.

2. By no means is it suggested that just because spanking of schoolchildren is "punishment" within the meaning of the Cruel and Unusual Punishments Clause, the school disciplinary process is in any way "criminal" and therefore subject to the full panoply of criminal procedural guarantees. . . .

3. The majority cites *Trop* as one of the cases that "dealt with a criminal punishment" but neglects to follow the analysis mandated by that decision. In *Trop*

If this purposive approach were followed in the present case, it would be clear that spanking in the Florida public schools is punishment within the meaning of the Eighth Amendment. The District Court found that "[c]orporal punishment is one of a variety of measures employed in the school system for the correction of pupil behavior and the preservation of order." App., at 146. Behavior correction and preservation of order are purposes ordinarily associated with punishment.

Without even mentioning the purposive analysis applied in the prior decisions of this Court, the majority adopts a rule that turns on the label given to the offense for which the punishment is inflicted. Thus, the record in this case reveals that one student at Drew Junior High School received 50 licks with a paddle for allegedly making an obscene telephone call. Brief for Petitioners 13. The majority holds that the Eighth Amendment does not prohibit such punishment since it was only inflicted for a breach of school discipline. However, that same conduct is punishable as a misdemeanor under Florida law, Fla. Stat.Ann. § 365.16 (Supp.1977) and there can be little doubt that if that same "punishment" had been inflicted by an officer of the state courts for violation of § 365.16, it would have had to satisfy the requirements of the Eighth Amendment.

C

. . .

The essence of the majority's argument is that school children do not need Eighth Amendment protection because corporal punishment is less subject to abuse in the public schools than it is in the prison

the petitioner was convicted of desertion by a military court-martial and sentenced to three years at hard labor, forfeiture of all pay and allowances, and a dishonorable discharge. After he was punished for the offense he committed, petitioner's application for a passport was turned down. Petitioner was told that he had been deprived of the "rights of citizenship" under § 401(g) of the Nationality Act of 1940 because he had been dishonorably discharged from the Armed Forces. The plurality took the view that denationalization in this context was cruel and unusual punishment prohibited by the Eighth Amendment.

The majority would have us believe that the determinative factor in *Trop* was that the petitioner had been convicted of desertion, yet there is no suggestion in *Trop* that the disposition of the military court-martial had anything to do with the decision in that case. Instead, while recognizing that the Eighth Amendment extends only to punishments that are penal

in nature, the plurality adopted a purposive approach for determining when punishment is penal.

"In deciding whether or not a law is penal, this Court has generally based its determination upon the purpose of the statute. If the statute imposes a disability for the purposes of punishment—that is, to reprimand the wrongdoer, to deter others, etc.—it has been considered penal. But a statute has been considered nonpenal if it imposes a disability, not to punish, but to accomplish some other legitimate governmental purpose." 356 U.S., at 96, 78 S.Ct., at 595 (footnotes omitted).

Although the quoted passage is taken from the plurality opinion of Mr. Chief Justice Warren, joined by three other Justices, Mr. Justice Brennan, in a concurring opinion, adopted a similar approach in concluding that § 401(g) was beyond the power of Congress to enact.

system. However, it cannot be reasonably suggested that just because cruel and unusual punishments may occur less frequently under public scrutiny, they will not occur at all. The mere fact that a public flogging or a public execution would be available for all to see would not render the punishment constitutional if it were otherwise impermissible. Similarly, the majority would not suggest that a prisoner who is placed in a minimum-security prison and permitted to go home to his family on the weekends should be any less entitled to Eighth Amendment protections than his counterpart in a maximum-security prison. In short, if a punishment is so barbaric and inhumane that it goes beyond the tolerance of a civilized society, its openness to public scrutiny should have nothing to do with its constitutional validity.

Nor is it an adequate answer that schoolchildren may have other state and constitutional remedies available to them. Even assuming that the remedies available to public school students are adequate under Florida law, the availability of state remedies has never been determinative of the coverage or of the protections afforded by the Eighth Amendment. The reason is obvious. The fact that a person may have a state-law cause of action against a public official who tortures him with a thumbscrew for the commission of an antisocial act has nothing to do with the fact that such official conduct is cruel and unusual punishment prohibited by the Eighth Amendment. Indeed, the majority's view was implicitly rejected this Term in Estelle v. Gamble, 429 U.S. 97, 97 S.Ct. 285, 50 L.Ed.2d 251 (1976), when the Court held that failure to provide for the medical needs of prisoners could constitute cruel and unusual punishment even though a medical malpractice remedy in tort was available to prisoners under state law.

D

By holding that the Eighth Amendment protects only criminals, the majority adopts the view that one is entitled to the protections afforded by the Eighth Amendment only if he is punished for acts that are sufficiently opprobrious for society to make them "criminal." This is a curious holding in view of the fact that the more culpable the offender the more likely it is that the punishment will not be disproportionate to the offense, and consequently, the less likely it is that the punishment will be cruel and unusual. Conversely, a public school student who is spanked for a mere breach of discipline may sometimes have a strong argument that the punishment does not fit the offense, depending upon the severity of the beating, and therefore that it is cruel and unusual. Yet the majority would afford the student no protection no matter how inhumane and barbaric the punishment inflicted on him might be.

The issue presented in this phase of the case is limited to whether corporal punishment in public schools can *ever* be prohibited by the Eighth Amendment. I am therefore not suggesting that spanking in the public schools is in every instance prohibited by the Eighth Amendment. My own view is that it is not. I only take issue with the extreme view of the majority that corporal punishment in public schools, no matter how barbaric, inhumane, or severe, is never limited by the Eighth Amendment. Where corporal punishment becomes so severe as to be unacceptable in a civilized society, I can see no reason that it should become any more acceptable just because it is inflicted on children in the public schools.

II

. . .

. . . Although the respondent school authorities provide absolutely *no* process to the student before the punishment is finally inflicted, the majority concludes that the student is nonetheless given due process because he can later sue the teacher and recover damages if the punishment was "excessive."

This tort action is utterly inadequate to protect against erroneous infliction of punishment for two reasons. First, under Florida law, a student punished for an act he did not commit cannot recover damages from a teacher "proceeding in utmost good faith . . . on the reports and advice of others,"; the student has no remedy at all for punishment imposed on the basis of mistaken facts, at least as long as the punishment was reasonable from the point of view of the disciplinarian, uninformed by any prior hearing.[11] The "traditional com-

11. The majority's assurances to the contrary, it is unclear to me whether and to what extent Florida law provides a damages action against school officials for excessive corporal punishment. Giving the majority the benefit of every doubt, I think it is fair to say that the most a student punished on the basis of mistaken allegations of misconduct can hope for in Florida is a recovery for unreasonable or bad-faith error. But I strongly suspect that even this remedy is not available.

Although the majority does not cite a single case decided under Florida law that recognizes a student's right to sue a school official to recover damages for excessive punishment, I am willing to assume that such a tort action does exist in Florida. I nevertheless have serious doubts about whether it would ever provide a recovery to a student simply because he was punished for an offense he did not commit. All the cases in other jurisdictions cited by the majority, . . . involved allegations of punishment disproportionate to the misconduct with which the student was charged; none of the decisions even suggest that a student could recover by showing that the teach-

er incorrectly imposed punishment for something the student had not done. . . .

Even if the common-law remedy for excessive punishment extends to punishment that is "excessive" only in the sense that it is imposed on the basis of mistaken facts, the school authorities are still protected from personal liability by common-law immunity. (They are protected by statutory immunity for liability for enforcing disciplinary rules "[e]xcept in the case of excessive force or cruel and unusual punishment." Fla.Stat.Ann. § 232.275 (1976).) At a minimum, this immunity would protect school officials from damages liability for reasonable mistakes made in good faith. . . .

A final limitation on the student's damages remedy under Florida law is that the student can recover only from the personal assets of the official; the school board's treasury is absolutely protected by sovereign immunity from damages for the torts of its agents. Buck v. McLean, 115 So.2d 764 (Fla.Dist.Ct.App.1959). A teacher's limited resources may deter the jury from awarding, or prevent the student from collecting, the full amount of damages to which he is entitled. . . .

mon-law remedies" on which the majority relies, thus do nothing to protect the student from the danger that concerned the Court in *Goss*—the risk of reasonable, good-faith mistake in the school disciplinary process.

. . . [E]ven if the student could sue for good-faith error in the infliction of punishment, the lawsuit occurs after the punishment has been finally imposed. The infliction of physical pain is final and irreparable; it cannot be undone in a subsequent proceeding. There is every reason to require, as the Court did in *Goss*, a few minutes of "informal give-and-take between student and disciplinarian" as a "meaningful hedge" against the erroneous infliction of irreparable injury. 419 U.S., at 583–584, 95 S.Ct., at 741.

. . .

[A separate dissenting opinion of Mr. Justice Stevens has been omitted.]

NOTES

(1) Is it realistic to expect that a tort remedy will provide a viable safeguard in many cases of overly hasty or ill founded punishment? In this regard, compare the cases dealing with educational malpractice, supra at 114.

(2) Nelson v. Heyne, 491 F.2d 352 (7th Cir. 1974), cert. denied 417 U.S. 976, infra at 573, involved the issue of corporal punishment in a medium security correctional institution for boys aged 12 to 18. The court, while noting that the law seemed to be well settled that "reasonable and moderate" corporal punishment was not barred by the Eighth Amendment in academic institutions, pointed out that the school in this instance was correctional as well as academic. In that setting the disciplinary beatings were held to violate plaintiffs' fourteenth amendment rights protecting them from cruel and unusual punishment.

(3) The Supreme Court affirmed in summary opinion the decision of a three-judge District Court that corporal punishment of a sixth-grader against his mother's express wishes denied neither the mother nor the child federally protected constitutional rights. Baker v. Owen, 395 F.Supp. 294 (M.D.N.C. 1975), affirmed 423 U.S. 907. The mother asserted that administering such punishment after her specific objections was violative of her right to determine the appropriate disciplinary methods for her child. She urged that her right as a parent to make such choices was of a fundamental character. Although agreeing that "the fourteenth amendment concept of liberty embraces the right of a parent to determine and choose between means of discipline of children", the District Court denied that the mother's right was "fundamental" in the sense that the state would be required to show a "compelling interest" that outweighed her parental right, explaining that "We do not read *Meyer* and *Pierce* to enshrine parental rights so high in the hierarchy of constitutional values. In each case the parental right prevailed not because the Court termed it fundamental and the State's interest uncompelling, but because the Court considered the action to be arbitrary, without

reasonable relation to an end legitimately within its power." 395 F.Supp. 299.

With regard to the child's claim, the District Court stated, in rejecting the eighth amendment claim:

> . . . [T]his record does not begin to present a picture of punishment comparable to that in *Ingraham,* [498 F.2d 248,] at 255–59 [5th Cir. 1974] or in Nelson v. Heyne, 491 F.2d 352 (7th Cir. 1974), which we believe indicate the kinds of beatings that could constitute cruel and unusual punishment if the eighth amendment is indeed applicable.

Id. at 303.

The District Court did indicate that the child had a liberty interest in avoiding corporal punishment, protectible under the fourteenth amendment. The net result of this finding was that certain procedural safeguards would be required:

> First, except for those acts of misconduct which are so anti-social or disruptive in nature as to shock the conscience, corporal punishment may never be used unless the student was informed beforehand that specific misbehavior could occasion its use, and, subject to this exception, it should never be employed as a first line of punishment for misbehavior. The requirements of an announced possibility of corporal punishment and an attempt to modify behavior by some other means—keeping after school, assigning extra work, or some other punishment—will insure that the child has clear notice that certain behavior subjects him to physical punishment. Second, a teacher or principal must punish corporally in the presence of a second school official (teacher or principal), who must be informed beforehand and in the student's presence of the reason for the punishment. The student need not be afforded a formal opportunity to present his side to the second official; the requirement is intended only to allow a student to protest, spontaneously, an egregiously arbitrary or contrived application of punishment. And finally, an official who has administered such punishment must provide the child's parent, upon request, a written explanation of his reasons and the name of the second official who was present.

Id. at 302.

Which approach do you prefer, the guidelines of *Baker* or the rule in *Ingraham?*

(4) Commenting on *Ingraham* not long after the decision had been announced, Professor Edward Zigler and Ms. Susan Hunsinger stated that "It is difficult to imagine a more sweeping setback for child abuse prevention efforts because the decision makes a mockery of the entire prevention campaign." Zigler and Hunsinger, Supreme Court on Spanking: Upholding Discipline or Abuse?, Young Children, Sept. 1977, at 14. The authors point out that although it is assumed that corporal punishment is exercised for the sake of discipline rather than to vent teacher frustrations, most corporal punishment takes place in elementary and junior high schools rather than high schools, where the physical threat to school personnel presumably would be greatest.

For further discussion of excessive discipline in the context of child abuse reporting, see p. 770 infra.

For an interesting evaluation of the Supreme Court's decision in the context of contemporary American thought, see Piele, Neither Corporal Punishment Cruel nor Due Process Due: The United States Supreme Court's Decision in Ingraham v. Wright, 7 J. of Law and Ed. 1 (1978).

(5) Is the Court's attachment of such significance to the historical use and acceptance of corporal punishment for children from Puritan times consistent with the trend toward according children greater individual rights and trying to uphold and maintain an educational system that will prepare them to enter our modern technological society effectively?

(6) Through the efforts of a number of groups interested in school discipline problems, The National Center for the Study of Corporal Punishment and Alternatives in the Schools has been established. Based at the Department of Psychology, Temple University, Philadelphia, it maintains an extensive library on school discipline. For a book of readings on the general subject, see I. Hyman and J. Wise (Eds.), Corporal Punishment in American Education: Readings in History, Practice, and Alternatives (1979).

PEOPLE v. CHAMBERS

Supreme Court of Illinois, 1977.
66 Ill.2d 36, 4 Ill.Dec. 308, 360 N.E.2d 55.

SCHAEFER, JUSTICE: [Defendants were convicted in a jury trial of violating Ill.Rev.Stat.1973, ch. 23, par. 2371. Each was fined $10 and costs. This appeal was granted the State from the intermediate Appellate Court's reversal on the ground that the statute is unconstitutional.]

. . .

In 1973, when this offense was committed, section 1 of the statute provided:

"(a) It is unlawful for a person less than 18 years of age to be present at or upon any public assembly, building, place, street or highway at the following times unless accompanied and supervised by a parent, legal guardian or other responsible companion at least 21 years of age approved by a parent or legal guardian or unless engaged in a business or occupation which the laws of this State authorize a person less than 18 years of age to perform:

1. Between 12:01 a.m. and 6:00 a.m. Saturday;

2. Between 12:01 a.m. and 6:00 a.m. Sunday; and

3. Between 11:00 p.m. on Sunday to Thursday, inclusive, and 6:00 a.m. on the following day.

(b) It is unlawful for a parent, legal guardian or other person to knowingly permit a person in his custody or control to violate subparagraph (a) of this Section.

(c) A person convicted of a violation of any provision of this Section shall be guilty of a petty offense and shall be fined not less than $10 nor more than $100."

In 1975 the Act was amended by substituting "17" for "18" and "18" for "21". Ill.Rev.Stat.1975, ch. 23, par. 2371.

The facts are summarized in the opinion of the appellate court (32 Ill.App.3d 444, 335 N.E.2d 612):

". . . In the early morning hours of March 25, 1973, Cynthia Chambers, 17 years of age, her sister, Patricia Chambers, 15 years of age, and a friend who is not involved in this appeal were in a car driven by Cynthia in the rural area of Ogle County. At approximately 1 a.m. their car was parked on a one lane bridge with its lights out. An Ogle County deputy sheriff saw the darkened vehicle as he drove by on patrol. As he approached the bridge, the car's lights came on and it proceeded across the bridge. When the deputy followed her car, Cynthia stopped and got out to speak to him. After several questions he determined that the girls were of 'curfew age' and that no adult accompanied them. He arrested them both for curfew violation."

Basically, the defendants and the *amici curiae* contend that the statute unconstitutionally restricts the rights of minors to move about and to exercise their first amendment rights of freedom of speech, assembly and association. They also argue that the statute is invalid since there is no governmental interest which justifies the broad prohibition of the statute, and they urge that the statute contains an inherent potential for arbitrary enforcement. While it is by no means clear that these defendants have standing to raise all of these constitutional issues (see Broadrick v. Oklahoma (1973), 413 U.S. 601, 93 S.Ct. 2908, 37 L.Ed.2d 830; People v. Raby (1968), 40 Ill. 2d 392, 240 N.E.2d 595, cert. denied (1969), 393 U.S. 1083, 89 S.Ct. 867, 21 L.Ed.2d 776), the State has not raised that question, and we have decided to consider the merits of the contentions that have been raised.

In holding the statute invalid, the appellate court said:

". . . The right of individuals to move about in public, whenever they choose to do so, is of the utmost importance. This right involves not so much the freedom to travel to a certain place (which was held protected by the United States Constitution in Aptheker v. Secretary of State, 378 U.S. 500, 84 S.Ct. 1659, 12 L.Ed.2d 992 (1964), and Kent v. Dulles, 357 U.S. 116, 78 S.Ct. 1113, 2 L.Ed.2d 1204 (1958)) as it does the freedom to enter into an invaluable social relationship. When a person walks out into public he removes the barriers that inhibit ready association and communication by him and his fellow citizens. Only when he is in public may he enjoy the most meaningful exercise of his freedom of speech, his freedom of association, his freedom peaceably to assemble with others, and his freedom of religion. These are freedoms secured by the First Amendment to the United States Constitution and by Article I of the Constitution of Illinois, 1970. In order to safeguard them, the right of an individual to go into public, to travel in public places, at any hour of any day, must also be considered as protected by the First Amendment. . . .

. . .

The importance of the right to move about in public has been discussed. That it is a right possessed by juveniles equally with adults, has been asserted. And other specific constitutional guarantees necessarily affected by the enforcement of a curfew have been noted. However, it is not necessary to point out with particularity constitutional infirmities inherent in a curfew statute such as the one here at issue. Suffice it to say that the overall attitude of our constitutions and our democratic society mandate freedom and notions of liberty which our legislature may not override. Something more than police convenience or a mere hope that juveniles or society will be benefited by a curfew should be necessary to justify a state-wide curfew law for juveniles." 32 Ill.App. 3d 444, 448–49, 335 N.E.2d 612, 617.

We do not find the problem presented by this case so simple as these broadly stated arguments and positions would suggest. In evaluating them it is essential to keep in mind exactly what is involved. The statute is concerned with the conduct of children under the age of 18, and it affects their conduct only between the specified hours, and then only if they are not accompanied by an adult. The exception for minors engaged in a business or occupation necessarily includes getting to and from the job.

The statute is not aimed at any of the fundamental values of speech, association or expression protected by the first amendment, and indeed the suggestion that those values are impaired by the restriction here involved seems to trivialize them. Insofar as the right to travel is concerned, the restrictions of the present statute are hardly comparable to those involved in Kent v. Dulles (1958), 357 U.S. 116, 78 S.Ct. 1113, 2 L.Ed.2d 1204, and Aptheker v. Secretary of State (1964), 378 U.S. 500, 84 S.Ct. 1659, 12 L.Ed.2d 992, which involved restrictions upon the issuance of passports to certain persons because of their political beliefs or associations. Nor do we see any reason to anticipate that this statute will give rise to problems under the commerce clause of the Federal Constitution.

The primary interest advanced by the State to justify the restrictions of the statute as to time, place and circumstance is the traditional right of the State to protect its children. The statute proceeds upon the basic assumption that when a child is at home during the late night and early morning hours, it is protected from physical as well as moral dangers. Although there are instances, unfortunately, in which this assumption is untrue, we are satisfied that the State is justified in acting upon it.

In legislating for the welfare of its children, the State is not required, in our opinion, to proceed upon the assumption that minor children have an absolutely unlimited right not only to choose their own associates, but also to decide when and where they will associate with them. Recognition of such a right would require wholesale revision of the large body of law that relates to guardian and ward, parent and child, and minors generally. Compulsory school attendance would be prohibited. A child is carefully safeguarded against errors of choice and judgment in most of the ordinary affairs of life, and we see no constitutional impairment in the limited restriction upon the child's judgment that is involved in this statute. It is only during the very late night and early morning hours that the State has interfered, and then only by requiring that the child be accompanied by an adult.

By providing a sanction against the parent who knowingly permits a child to violate the statute, the cooperation of the parent is commanded. That sanction may also operate indirectly to enlist cooperation from the child, who may be willing to risk getting into trouble himself, but unwilling to involve his parents in a violation of the law. Parental control is thereby strengthened.

In addition to the concern of the State with the moral and physical welfare of its children, there are other considerations which bear upon the validity of the statute. The phenomenon of increased juvenile crime has been frequently noted. In 1958 a note in the Pennsylvania Law Review pointed out:

"The number of persons arrested in the United States under eighteen years of age increased from 31,750 in 1948 to 234,474 in 1956. During the same period the percentage of arrests of persons under eighteen years of age as compared to total arrests increased from 4.2% to 11.3%. Changes in some of the more serious crimes are:

	1948		1956	
	No. of persons arrested under 18	Percentage of total arrests	No. of persons arrested under 18	Percentage of total arrests
Criminal Homicide	208	3.1	213	6.2
Robbery	1,121	5.4	2,692	24.7
Assault	1,157	2.0	7,531	7.3
Rape	773	8.1	840	18.3
Larceny	6,093	8.9	46,477	50.4
Auto Theft	3,030	17.1	18,622	66.4

FBI, 19 Uniform Crime Reports 117 (1948); FBI, 27 Uniform Crime Reports 110 (1956)." 107 Pa.L.Rev. 66 n. 1.

The trend thus noted in 1958 has continued:

"In recent years the number of delinquency arrests has increased sharply in the United States, as it has in several European countries studied by the Commission. Between 1960 and 1965, arrests of persons under 18 years of age jumped 52 percent for willful homicide, rape, robbery, aggravated assault, larceny, burglary and motor vehicle theft. During the same period, arrests of persons 18 and over for these offenses rose only 20 percent. This is explained in large part by the disproportionate increase in the population under 18 and, in particular, the crime-prone part of that population—the 11- to 17-year-old age group." President's Commission on Law Enforcement and Administration of Justice, The Challenge of Crime in a Free Society, at 56 (1967).

That the continuing increase was not wholly attributable to the post-World War II "baby boom" has become clear, however, because between 1970 and 1975 the total number of arrests of males under 18 for property crimes (burglary, larceny and motor vehicle theft) increased by 20.8% and the number of females under 18 arrested for those crimes increased 38.6%. During the same period, in the case of violent crimes (murder, manslaughter, forcible rape, robbery and aggravated assault) the number of arrests of males under 18 increased by 51.9% and the number of arrests of females under 18 increased by 74.2%. 1975 Uniform Crime Reports (Table 33).

We have engaged in this somewhat tedious statistical demonstration of what is actually common knowledge to show that the General Assembly was not acting upon whim or caprice in adopting this statute, but rather was engaged in an essential—indeed vital—effort to deal with what is certainly one of the most serious problems of our time. Far more is involved than "police convenience." Of course this statute can not effect a complete cure. The causes of the shocking increase in juvenile crime lie too deep. Even so, however, it does not follow that this legislative effort infringes constitutional rights.

The appellate court was also of the opinion that the statute in this case swept too broadly since it was not confined with particularity to geographical areas of the State in which the crime rate is extraordinarily high. In our opinion this conclusion was erroneous. The question of geographical scope is a matter for legislative, rather than judicial, determination. And in any case the current increase in crime in rural and suburban areas would justify statewide action. The 1975 Uniform Crime Reports (Tables 40, 46, 51) show an increase between 1974 and 1975 of 0.9% in arrests of persons under 18 in cities; the comparable increase in suburbs was 4.4%, and in rural areas 4.3%.

The judgment of the appellate court is reversed.

GOLDENHERSH, JUSTICE, dissenting:

I dissent. Although I agree with the appellate court that the statute unreasonably restricted the rights of persons under 18, I am of the opinion that it was invalid for reasons not mentioned either by the appellate court or the majority. The statute proscribed the presence of persons less than 18 years of age at enumerated places and times "unless accompanied and supervised by a parent, legal guardian or other responsible companion at least 21 years of age approved by a parent or legal guardian or unless engaged in a business or occupation which the laws of this State authorize a person less than 18 years of age to perform: . . . ." In Connally v. General Construction Co., 269 U.S. 385, 391, 46 S.Ct. 126, 127, 70 L.Ed. 322, 328, in holding an Oklahoma statute invalid the Supreme Court said: "That the terms of a penal statute creating a new offense must be sufficiently explicit to inform those who are subject to it what conduct on their part will render them liable to its penalties, is a well-recognized requirement, consonant alike with ordinary notions of fair play and the settled rules of law; and a statute which either forbids or requires the doing of an act in terms so vague that men of common intelligence must necessarily guess at its meaning and differ as to its application, violates the first essential of due process of law." The vice of this statute is that "men of common intelligence must necessarily guess at its meaning" and that it left to the subjective determination of the arresting officer the questions whether the minor was being "supervised" and whether the companion over 21 was "responsible." Furthermore, the police officer was left free to determine whether the "responsible companion" was responsible in the sense that he was trustworthy or that he must answer to the parent or legal guardian. Had there been two young men 21 years of age in the car at the time of the incident, the arresting officer, without any standards, would have been free to determine whether they were "responsible companions" and whether the defendants were being "supervised."

The statistics cited by the majority are, of course, interesting but are utterly without value insofar as the crucial question presented is concerned, i.e., how many of these offenses are committed between 12:01 a.m. and 6 a.m. on Saturday and Sunday and between 11 p.m. and 6 a.m. the remainder of the week.

The majority's construction of the exception for minors engaged in a business or occupation is that it "necessarily includes getting to and from the job." (66 Ill.2d at 41, 4 Ill.Dec. at 310, 360 N.E.2d at 57.) Once again the arresting officer, without statutory standards, must subjectively determine whether this construction required the minor to travel by the shortest and most direct route and whether a stop for food or refreshment was permissible. Furthermore, no provision was made for minors emancipated by marriage or other means, and unquestionably the junior class of almost every high school in the State, *en masse*, violated this statute at least once each year.

I am aware that the welfare of minors is of concern to the General Assembly, but enactment of a statute so vague as to violate due process is not the method of achieving its goals. I would affirm the judgment of the appellate court.

WARD, C. J., joins in this dissent.

NOTES

(1) Curfew laws often have been viewed more skeptically than in People v. Chambers. As early as 1898 such an ordinance was held unconstitutional

by the Texas Court of Criminal Appeals in Ex parte McCarver, 39 Tex.Cr.R. 448, 46 S.W. 936 (1898). The court said:

> The rule laid down here is as rigid as under military law, and makes the tolling of the curfew bell equivalent to the drum taps of the camp. In our opinion, it is an undue invasion of the personal liberty of the citizen, as the boy or girl (for it applies equally to both) have the same rights of ingress and egress that citizens of mature years enjoy. We regard this character of legislation as an attempt to usurp the parental functions, and as unreasonable, and we therefore hold the ordinance in question as illegal and void. Id. at 937.

A City of Honolulu ordinance prohibiting any person under 18 from loitering about public streets, parks or other places between 10 p.m. and sunrise was invalidated by the Supreme Court of Hawaii in 1973 because it was "so vague and overbroad as to violate due process standards." In re Doe, 54 Hawaii 647, 513 P.2d 1385, 1388 (1973). In the same year, the Supreme Court of Washington struck down a somewhat similar ordinance also on vagueness grounds. City of Seattle v. Pullman, 82 Wn.2d 794, 514 P.2d 1059 (1973). However the Washington court pointed out that:

> General curfew ordinances have been found valid when imposed in emergency circumstances to restore public order. Similarly, minor curfew ordinances may be permissible where they are specific in their prohibition and necessary in curing a demonstrable social evil.

Id. at 1065.

In Illinois, an intermediate appellate court subsequently extended the *Chambers* rationale by finding that a curfew statute could be applied to minors on private as well as public property. People v. Coleman, 50 Ill.App.3d 1053, 7 Ill.Dec. 581, 364 N.E.2d 742 (1977). The court proclaimed:

> It would be a gross distortion of the intent of the curfew statute to hold that it permitted the protection of the children of this state only if they were on public property such as a highway, but that such protection would not be afforded to them if they were on privately owned property.

Id. at 746.

For a view of the legal problems of curfew ordinances generally, see Note, Curfew Ordinances and the Control of Nocturnal Juvenile Crime, 107 U.Pa.L.Rev. 66 (1958). For a specific discussion of *Chambers*, see Grossman, Juvenile Curfews in Illinois: A Step Backward, 13 Urban L.Ann. 193 (1977).

(2) Aladdin's Castle, Inc. v. City of Mesquite placed before the courts a related problem in the form not of a curfew statute but a city ordinance prohibiting certain amusement center operators from allowing children under age 17 to play coin-operated games unless accompanied by a parent or guardian. An amusement center operator challenged the limitation along with the city's licensure provision directing investigation of the license applicant's character and conduct as a law abiding person and considering "connection with criminal elements. . . ." The United States Court of Appeals for the Fifth Circuit upheld a District Court's finding that the latter restriction (§ 6) was void for vagueness, and also held that the constitutionality of the age restriction (§ 5) had been improperly sustained. Aladdin's Castle, Inc. v. City of Mesquite, 630 F.2d 1029 (5th Cir. 1980). As to § 5, the

court first responded with regard to the argument that the ordinance was designed to prevent truancy:

> The decision to bar all people under seventeen years of age, whether or not they are required to be in a school, from all coin-operated amusement centers at all times is patently irrational. See, e.g., Stanley v. Illinois, 405 U.S. at 652–59, 92 S.Ct. at 1213–1216. Barring young people from using coin-operated amusement devices at times and on days when school is closed simply bears no relation whatever to the city's alleged interest in eliminating truancy. See Eisenstadt v. Baird, 405 U.S. at 447–52, 92 S.Ct. at 1035–1037 (contrived purpose evidenced by irrationality). The regulation instead evidences the city's disapproval of such centers in general or of Aladdin's owners in particular. See Orr v. Orr, 440 U.S. 268, 280 n.10, 99 S.Ct. 1102, 1112 n.10, 59 L.Ed.2d 306 (1979). Such disapproval may justify private action, such as the withholding of patronage, but mere disapproval is not enough constitutionally to justify bringing the full weight of the municipality's regulatory apparatus into play.
>
> By the same token, the regulation denies Aladdin's equal protection of the laws. Just as the "all hours" restriction is grossly overinclusive, the limitation of that restriction to coin-operated amusement centers is equally underinclusive. Before such centers existed, children found places and opportunities for truancy, and they would find places were such centers to become extinct. Singling out coin-operated amusement centers from all other establishments is an act of discrimination, not policy.

Id. at 1039–40.

As to the regulation of minors generally, the Fifth Circuit stated:

> We do not doubt that the state may have a legitimate interest in protecting young people from certain unhealthy influences. Yet "a governmental purpose to control or prevent activities constitutionally subject to state regulation may not be achieved by means which sweep unnecessarily broadly and thereby invade the area of protected freedoms." NAACP v. Alabama, 377 U.S. 288, 307, 84 S.Ct. 1302, 1313, 12 L.Ed.2d 325 (1964); Sawyer v. Sandstrom, 615 F.2d at 316 (association as one such protected freedom).
>
> Mesquite's interest in shielding young people from undesirable influences may be achieved in other ways. Activities such as gambling with children or selling them drugs can be criminalized and vigorously prosecuted.[17] The ordinance before us, however, sweeps too broadly and cannot be justified under our Constitution. "[T]he deterrents ordinarily to be applied to prevent crime or education and punishment for violations of the law, not abridgement of the rights of free speech and assembly." Whitney v. California, 274 U.S. 357, 378, 47 S.Ct. 641, 649, 71 L.Ed. 1095 (1927) (Brandeis, J., concurring).
>
> The standard that the ordinance must meet is not reduced because minors are involved. "A child, merely on account of his minority, is not beyond the protection of the Constitution." Bellotti v. Baird, 443 U.S. 622, 633, 99 S.Ct. 3035, 3043, 61 L.Ed.2d 797 (1979) (Powell, J., joined by

---

17. We do not intimate by our holding that Mesquite cannot appropriately restrict minors in connection with establish-ments which dispense alcoholic beverages or illicit drugs.

Burger, C. J. & Stewart & Rehnquist, JJ.). Minors "are possessed of fundamental rights which the State must respect." Tinker v. Des Moines Independent Community School District, 393 U.S. 503, 511, 89 S.Ct. 733, 739, 21 L.Ed.2d 731 (1969). "[N]either the Fourteenth Amendment nor the Bill of Rights is for adults alone." In re Gault, 387 U.S. 1, 13, 87 S.Ct. 1428, 1436, 18 L.Ed.2d 527 (1967). Accord, Planned Parenthood v. Danforth, 428 U.S. 52, 74, 96 S.Ct. 2831, 2843, 49 L.Ed.2d 788 (1976).

In some cases to be sure, the state may have greater power to regulate conduct that is otherwise constitutionally protected if the regulation applies only to children. This "somewhat broader authority to regulate the activities of children than adults," Planned Parenthood v. Danforth, 428 U.S. at 74, 96 S.Ct. at 2843, is warranted only if a special circumstance of youth creates a unique danger to minors which presents the state with an interest in regulating their activities that does not exist in the case of adults. Ginsberg v. New York, 390 U.S. 629, 638–41, 88 S.Ct. 1274, 1279–81, 20 L.Ed.2d 195 (1968); Prince v. Massachusetts, 321 U.S. 158, 169–70, 64 S.Ct. 438, 443–444, 88 L.Ed. 645 (1944). Control and restraint by the state, which would otherwise be intolerable under our Constitution, may be justified if the regulation serves a " 'significant state interest . . . that is not present in the case of an adult,' " which arises from the fact of youthful vulnerability to harm. Carey v. Population Services International, 431 U.S. 678, 693, 97 S.Ct. 2010, 2020, 52 L.Ed.2d 675 (1977) (citing Planned Parenthood v. Danforth, 428 U.S. at 75, 96 S.Ct. at 2843).

In Bellotti v. Baird, 443 U.S. at 633–39, 99 S.Ct. at 3035–46, Justice Powell set out for himself and three other Justices three reasons which in some circumstances might permit the state to restrain minors in a way which would be unconstitutional if applied to adults:

the peculiar vulnerability of children; their inability to make critical decisions in an informed, mature manner; and the importance of the parental role in child-rearing.

Id. at 634, 99 S.Ct. at 3043. These reasons may be viewed as threshold criteria. If Mesquite's ordinance were based on any of them, we would be required to determine the strength of the support provided, its relation to the ordinance as a whole, and the extent, if any, to which it might serve to justify any special restraints on the associational rights of minors. Neither the Supreme Court nor this circuit has set forth the appropriate standards under which such an inquiry would be conducted. We need not undertake to resolve this matter here, since none of Justice Powell's factors even remotely apply to the present ordinance.

There is no issue of special vulnerability presented in this case. Justice Powell limited his discussion of this factor to juvenile criminal proceedings, where the special needs of children have served as a basis for distinguishing certain aspects of procedural due process from adult cases. Compare In re Gault, 387 U.S. 1, 87 S.Ct. 1428, 18 L.Ed.2d 527 (1967) with McKeiver v. Pennsylvania, 403 U.S. 528, 91 S.Ct. 1976, 29 L.Ed.2d 647 (1971). Even extending the vulnerability rationale to its broadest extent, it is impossible to conclude that a coin-operated amusement device presents a physical, mental, or moral threat under which "the State is entitled to adjust its legal system to account for children's vulnerability and their needs for 'concern, . . . sympathy, and . . . paternal attention.'" Bellotti v. Baird, 443 U.S. at 635, 99 S.Ct. at 3044, citing McKeiver v. Pennsylvania, 403 U.S. at 550, 91 S.Ct. at 1988 (plurality opinion). That Mesquite may disapprove of Aladdin's Castle is hardly a sufficient justification for invoking "the peculiar vulnerability of children." Associations "cannot be suppressed solely to protect the young from ideas or images that a legislative body thinks unsuitable for them." Erznoznik v. City of Jacksonville, 422 U.S. 205, 213–14, 95 S.Ct. 2268, 2274–75, 45 L.Ed.2d 125 (1975).

The irrelevance of the "critical decision" rationale is manifest on its face. To suggest that minors be permitted to express their views on divisive public issues, Tinker v. Des Moines Independent School District, and to secure abortions without parental consent, Bellotti v. Baird, Planned Parenthood v. Danforth, but that they can be barred from making the "critical decision" of whether or not to deposit a quarter in a coin-operated amusement device is not a proposition that deserves serious consideration.

As for Justice Powell's third element, the role of parents, clearly this concern militates against the ordinance, not for it. Even if youthfulness is relevant in the case before us, parents, not the state, should decide whether their children are to enter coin-operated amusement centers. The state may not burden parents who decide to allow their children to enter the centers by requiring these parents to accompany their children. If a parent would rather shop or work and decides to trust Aladdin's personnel or the child, that is the parent's prerogative.

> The history and culture of Western civilization reflect a strong tradition of parental concern for the nurture and upbringing of their children. This primary role of the parents in the upbringing of their children is now established beyond debate as an enduring American tradition.

Wisconsin v. Yoder, 406 U.S. 205, 232, 92 S.Ct. 1526, 1541, 32 L.Ed.2d 15 (1972). Accord, Parham v. J. R., 442 U.S. 584, 602, 99 S.Ct. 2493, 2504, 61 L.Ed.2d 101 (1979). Thus for minors as for adults, the ordinance impermissibly and unconstitutionally infringes on freedom of association.

Id. at 1042–44.

On appeal, the U.S. Supreme Court held that the ordinance was not unconstitutionally vague, reversing the finding as to § 6. However the court declined to decide on the validity of § 5, remanding the case for clarification as to whether the issue had been decided under a Texas constitutional question possibly based on language in that document differing from and broader than that of corresponding federal provisions. Ostensibly, the purpose of the remand was to avoid the Court's unnecessary adjudication of federal questions.

Subsequent to the *Aladdin's Castle* decision, the Court of Appeals for the Fifth Circuit used its rationale in part to strike down a nocturnal juvenile curfew law in Johnson v. City of Opelousas, 658 F.2d 1065 (5th Cir. 1981).

PARHAM v. J. R.

Supreme Court of the United States, 1979.
442 U.S. 584, 99 S.Ct. 2493, 61 L.Ed.2d 101.

MR. CHIEF JUSTICE BURGER delivered the opinion of the Court.

The question presented in this appeal is what process is constitutionally due a minor child whose parents or guardian seek state administered institutional mental health care for the child and specifically whether an adversary proceeding is required prior to or after the commitment.

I

(a) Appellee, J. R., a child being treated in a Georgia state mental hospital, was a plaintiff in this class-action [2] suit based on 42 U.S.C. § 1983, in the District Court for the Middle District of Georgia. . . . Appellee sought a declaratory judgment that Georgia's voluntary commitment procedures for children under the age of 18, Ga. Code, §§ 88–503.1, 88–503.2,[3] violated the Due Process Clause of the Fourteenth Amendment and requested an injunction against its future enforcement.

. . . [A three-judge District Court] held that Georgia's statutory scheme was unconstitutional because it failed to protect adequately the appellees' due process rights.

To remedy this violation the court enjoined future commitments based on the procedures in the Georgia statute. It also commanded Georgia to appropriate and expend whatever amount was "reasonably necessary" to provide nonhospital facilities deemed by the appellant state officials to be the most appropriate for the treatment of those members of plaintiffs' class, n. 2, supra, who could be treated in a less drastic, nonhospital environment.

. . .

2. The class certified by the District Court, without objection by appellants, consisted "of all persons younger than 18 years of age now or hereafter received by any defendant for observation and diagnosis and/or detained for care and treatment at any 'facility' within the State of Georgia pursuant to" Ga.Code § 88–503.1. Although one witness testified that on any given day there may be 200 children in the class, in December 1975 there were only 140.

3. Section 88–503.1 provides:

"The superintendent of any facility may receive for observation and diagnosis . . . any individual under 18 years of age for whom such application is made by his parent or guardian . . . . If found to show evidence of mental illness and to be suitable for treatment, such person may be given care and treatment at such facility and such person may be detained by such facility for such period and under such conditions as may be authorized by law."

Section 88–503.2 provides:

"The superintendent of the facility shall discharge any voluntary patient who has recovered from his mental illness or who has sufficiently improved that the superintendent determines that hospitalization of the patient is no longer desirable."

(b) J. L., a plaintiff before the District Court who is now deceased, was admitted in 1970 at the age of six years to Central State Regional Hospital in Milledgeville, Ga. Prior to his admission, J. L. had received outpatient treatment at the hospital for over two months. J. L.'s mother then requested the hospital to admit him indefinitely.

The admitting physician interviewed J. L. and his parents. He learned that J. L.'s natural parents had divorced and his mother had remarried. He also learned that J. L. had been expelled from school because he was uncontrollable. He accepted the parents' representation that the boy had been extremely aggressive and diagnosed the child as having a "hyperkinetic reaction to childhood."

J. L.'s mother and stepfather agreed to participate in family therapy during the time their son was hospitalized. Under this program J. L. was permitted to go home for short stays. Apparently his behavior during these visits was erratic. After several months the parents requested discontinuance of the program.

In 1972, the child was returned to his mother and stepfather on a furlough basis, i.e., he would live at home but go to school at the hospital. The parents found they were unable to control J. L. to their satisfaction which created family stress. Within two months they requested his readmission to Central State. J. L.'s parents relinquished their parental rights to the county in 1974.

Although several hospital employees recommended that J. L. should be placed in a special foster home with "a warm, supported, truly involved couple," the Department of Family and Children Services was unable to place him in such a setting. On October 24, 1975, J. L. filed this suit requesting an order of the court placing him in a less drastic environment suitable to his needs.

(c) Appellee, J. R., was declared a neglected child by the county and removed from his natural parents when he was three months old. He was placed in seven different foster homes in succession prior to his admission to Central State Hospital at the age of seven.

Immediately preceding his hospitalization, J. R. received out-patient treatment at a county mental health center for several months. He then began attending school where he was so disruptive and incorrigible that he could not conform to normal behavior patterns. Because of his abnormal behavior J. R.'s seventh set of foster parents requested his removal from their home. The Department of Family and Children Services then sought his admission at Central State. The agency provided the hospital with a complete sociomedical history at the time of his admission. In addition, three separate interviews were conducted with J. R. by the admission team of the hospital.

It was determined that he was borderline retarded, and suffered an "unsocialized, aggressive reaction to childhood." It was recommended unanimously that he would "benefit from the structured environment" of the hospital and would "enjoy living and playing with boys of the same age."

J. R.'s progress was re-examined periodically. In addition, unsuccessful efforts were made by the Department of Family and Children Services during his stay at the hospital to place J. R. in various foster homes. On October 24, 1975, J. R. filed this suit requesting an order of the court placing him in a less drastic environment suitable to his needs.

(d) Georgia Code, § 88–503.1 provides for the voluntary admission to a state regional hospital of children such as J. L. and J. R. Under that provision admission begins with an application for hospitalization signed by a "parent or guardian." Upon application the superintendent of each hospital is given the power to admit temporarily any child for "observation and diagnosis." If, after observation, the superintendent finds "evidence of mental illness" and that the child is "suitable for treatment" in the hospital, then the child may be admitted "for such period and under such conditions as may be authorized by law."

Georgia's mental health statute also provides for the discharge of voluntary patients. Any child who has been hospitalized for more than five days may be discharged at the request of a parent or guardian. § 88–503.3(a). Even without a request for discharge, however, the superintendent of each regional hospital has an affirmative duty to release any child "who has recovered from his mental illness or who has sufficiently improved that the superintendent determines that hospitalization of the patient is no longer desirable." § 88–503.2.

Georgia's Mental Health Director has not published any statewide regulations defining what specific procedures each superintendent must employ when admitting a child under 18. Instead, each regional hospital's superintendent is responsible for the procedures in his or her facility. [Acknowledging that "substantial variation" exists between them, the court describes the procedures of different hospitals. It also notes that Georgia funds over 50 community mental health clinics and 13 specialized foster care homes. . . . Georgia ranks 22d nationally in per capita expenditures for mental health.]

The District Court nonetheless rejected the State's entire system of providing mental health care on both procedural and substantive grounds. The District Court found that 46 children could be "optimally cared for in another, less restrictive, non-hospital setting if it were available." These "optimal" settings included group homes, therapeutic camps and home care services. [State officials testified that Georgia] could not justify enlarging its budget during fiscal year 1977 to provide the specialized treatment settings urged by appellees in addition to those then available.

. . .

II

In holding unconstitutional Georgia's statutory procedure for voluntary commitment of juveniles, the District Court first determined that commitment to any of the eight regional hospitals constitutes a severe deprivation of a child's liberty. The court defined this liberty interest both in terms of a freedom from bodily restraint and freedom from the "emotional and psychic harm" caused by the institutionalization.[7] Having determined that a liberty interest is implicated by a child's admission to a mental hospital, the court considered what process is required to protect that interest. It held that the process due "includes at least the right after notice to be heard before an impartial tribunal."

In requiring the prescribed hearing, the court rejected Georgia's argument that no adversary-type hearing was required since the State was merely assisting parents who could not afford private care by making available treatment similar to that offered in private hospitals and by private physicians. The court acknowledged that most parents who seek to have their children admitted to a state mental hospital do so in good faith. It, however, relied on one of appellees' witnesses who expressed an opinion that "some still look upon mental hospitals as a 'dumping ground.'" Id., at 138.[8] No specific evidence of such "dumping," however, can be found in the record.

The District Court also rejected the argument that review by the superintendents of the hospitals and their staffs was sufficient to protect the child's liberty interest. The court held that the inexactness of psychiatry, coupled with the possibility that the sources of information used to make the commitment decision may not always be reliable, made the superintendent's decision too arbitrary to satisfy due process.

. . .

III

In an earlier day, the problems inherent in coping with children afflicted with mental or emotional abnormalities were dealt with largely within the family. See S. Brakel & R. Rock, The Mentally Disabled and the Law 4 (1971). Sometimes parents were aided by

7. In both respects the District Court found strong support for its holding in this Court's decision in In re Gault, 387 U.S. 1, 87 S.Ct. 1428, 18 L.Ed.2d 527 (1967). In that decision we held that a state cannot institutionalize a juvenile delinquent without first providing certain due process protections.

8. In light of the District Court's holding that a judicial or quasi-judicial body should review voluntary commitment decisions, it is at least interesting to note that the witness who made the statement quoted in the text was not referring to parents as the people who "dump" children into hospitals. This witness opined that some juvenile court judges and child welfare agencies misused the hospitals. App. to Juris. Statement 768. See also Rolfe & MacClintock, The Due Process Rights of Minors "Voluntarily Admitted" to Mental Institutions, 4 J. Psych. & L. 333, 351 (1976) (hereinafter Rolfe & MacClintock).

teachers or a family doctor. While some parents no doubt were able to deal with their disturbed children without specialized assistance, others especially those of limited means and education, were not. Increasingly, they turned for assistance to local, public sources or private charities. Until recently most of the states did little more than provide custodial institutions for the confinement of persons who were considered dangerous. Id., at 5–6; Slovenko, Criminal Justice Procedures in Civil Commitment, 24 Wayne L.Rev. 1, 3 (1977) (hereinafter Slovenko).

. . . Ironically, as most states have expanded their efforts to assist the mentally ill, their actions have been subjected to increasing litigation and heightened constitutional scrutiny. . . .

The parties agree that our prior holdings have set out a general approach for testing challenged state procedures under a due process claim. Assuming the existence of a protectible property or liberty interest, the Court has required a balancing of a number of factors:

> "First, the private interest that will be affected by the official action; second, the risk of an erroneous deprivation of such interest through the procedures used, and the probable value, if any, of additional or substitute procedural safeguards; and finally, the Government's interest, including the function involved and the fiscal and administrative burdens that the additional or substitute procedural requirement would entail." Mathews v. Eldridge, 424 U.S. 319, 335, 96 S.Ct. 893, 903, 47 L.Ed.2d 18 (1976), quoted in Smith v. Organization of Foster Families, 431 U.S. 816, 847–848, 97 S.Ct. 2094, 2111–2112, 53 L.Ed.2d 14 (1977).

In applying these criteria, we must consider first the child's interest in not being committed. Normally, however, since this interest is inextricably linked with the parents' interest in and obligation for the welfare and health of the child, the private interest at stake is a combination of the child's and parents' concerns. Next we must examine the State's interest in the procedures it has adopted for commitment and treatment of children. Finally, we must consider how well Georgia's procedures protect against arbitrariness in the decision to commit a child to a state mental hospital.

(a) It is not disputed that a child, in common with adults, has a substantial liberty interest in not being confined unnecessarily for medical treatment and that the State's involvement in the commitment decision constitutes state action under the Fourteenth Amendment. See Addington v. Texas, 441 U.S. 418, 425, 99 S.Ct. 1804, 1809, 60 L.Ed.2d 323 (1979); In re Gault, 387 U.S. 1, 27, 87 S.Ct. 1428, 1443, 18 L.Ed.2d 527 (1967). We also recognize that commitment sometimes produces adverse social consequences for the child because of the reaction of some to the discovery that the child has received psychiatric care.

This reaction, however, need not be equated with the community response resulting from being labeled by the state as delinquent, criminal, or mentally ill and possibly dangerous. The state through its voluntary commitment procedures does not "label" the child; it provides a diagnosis and treatment that medical specialists conclude the child requires. In terms of public reaction, the child who exhibits abnormal behavior may be seriously injured by an erroneous decision not to commit. Appellees overlook a significant source of the public reaction to the mentally ill, for what is truly "stigmatizing" is the symptomatology of a mental or emotional illness. The pattern of untreated, abnormal behavior—even if nondangerous—arouses at least as much negative reaction as treatment that becomes public knowledge. A person needing, but not receiving, appropriate medical care may well face even greater social ostracism resulting from the observable symptoms of an untreated disorder.

However, we need not decide what effect these factors might have in a different case. For purposes of this decision, we assume that a child has a protectible interest not only in being free of unnecessary bodily restraints but also in not being labeled erroneously by some because of an improper decision by the state hospital superintendent.

(b) We next deal with the interests of the parents who have decided, on the basis of their observations and independent professional recommendations, that their child needs institutional care. Appellees argue that the constitutional rights of the child are of such magnitude and the likelihood of parental abuse is so great that the parents' traditional interests in and responsibility for the upbringing of their child must be subordinated at least to the extent of providing a formal adversary hearing prior to a voluntary commitment.

Our jurisprudence historically has reflected Western Civilization concepts of the family as a unit with broad parental authority over minor children. Our cases have consistently followed that course; our constitutional system long ago rejected any notion that a child is "the mere creature of the State" and, on the contrary, asserted that parents generally "have the right, coupled with the high duty, to recognize and prepare [their children] for additional obligations." Pierce v. Society of Sisters, 268 U.S. 510, 535, 45 S.Ct. 571, 573, 69 L.Ed. 1070 (1924). See also Wisconsin v. Yoder, 406 U.S. 205, 213, 92 S.Ct. 1526, 1532, 32 L.Ed.2d 15 (1972); Prince v. Massachusetts, 321 U.S. 158, 166, 64 S.Ct. 438, 442, 88 L.Ed. 645 (1944); Meyer v. Nebraska, 262 U.S. 390, 400, 43 S.Ct. 625, 627, 67 L.Ed. 1042 (1923). Surely, this includes a "high duty" to recognize symptoms of illness and to seek and follow medical advice. The law's concept of the family rests on a presumption that parents possess what a child lacks in maturity, experience, and capacity for judgment required for making life's difficult decisions. More important, historically it has recognized that natural bonds of affection lead parents to act in the best interests of their children. 1 W. Blackstone, Commentaries * 447; 2 Kent, Commentaries on American Law * 190.

As with so many other legal presumptions, experience and reality may rebut what the law accepts as a starting point; the incidence of child neglect and abuse cases attests to this. That some parents "may at times be acting against the interests of their child" as was stated in Bartley v. Kremens, 402 F.Supp. 1039, 1047–1048 (ED Pa. 1975), vacated, 431 U.S. 119, 97 S.Ct. 1709, 52 L.Ed.2d 184 (1977), creates a basis for caution, but is hardly a reason to discard wholesale those pages of human experience that teach that parents generally do act in the child's best interests. See Rolfe & MacClintock 348–349. The statist notion that governmental power should supersede parental authority in *all* cases because *some* parents abuse and neglect children is repugnant to American tradition.

Nonetheless, we have recognized that a state is not without constitutional control over parental discretion in dealing with children when their physical or mental health is jeopardized. See Wisconsin v. Yoder, supra, 406 U.S., at 230, 92 S.Ct., at 1540; Prince v. Massachusetts, supra, 321 U.S., at 166, 64 S.Ct., at 442. Moreover, the Court recently declared unconstitutional a state statute that granted parents an absolute veto over a minor child's decision to have an abortion. Planned Parenthood of Missouri v. Danforth, 428 U.S. 52, 96 S.Ct. 2831, 49 L.Ed.2d 788 (1976). Appellees urge that these precedents limiting the traditional rights of parents, if viewed in the context of the liberty interest of the child and the likelihood of parental abuse, require us to hold that the parents' decision to have a child admitted to a mental hospital must be subjected to an exacting constitutional scrutiny, including a formal, adversary, preadmission hearing.

Appellees' argument, however, sweeps too broadly. Simply because the decision of a parent is not agreeable to a child or because it involves risks does not automatically transfer the power to make that decision from the parents to some agency or officer of the state. The same characterizations can be made for a tonsillectomy, appendectomy or other medical procedure. Most children, even in adolescence, simply are not able to make sound judgments concerning many decisions, including their need for medical care or treatment. Parents can and must make those judgments. Here there is no finding by the District Court of even a single instance of bad faith by any parent of any member of appellees' class. We cannot assume that the result of Meyer v. Nebraska, supra, and Pierce v. Society of Sisters, supra, would have been different if the children there had announced a preference to learn only English or a preference to go to a public, rather than a church, school. The fact that a child may balk at hospitalization or complain about a parental refusal to provide cosmetic surgery does not diminish the parents' authority to decide what is best for the child. See generally Goldstein, Medical Case for the Child at Risk: On State Supervention of Parental Autonomy, 86 Yale L.J. 645, 664–668 (1977). Bennett, Allocation of Child Medical Care Decisionmaking Authority: A Suggested Interest Analysis, 62 Va.L.Rev. 285,

308 (1976).   Neither state officials nor federal courts are equipped to review such parental decisions.

Appellees place particular reliance on *Planned Parenthood*, arguing that its holding indicates how little deference to parents is appropriate when the child is exercising a constitutional right.   The basic situation in that case, however, was very different;   *Planned Parenthood* involved an absolute parental veto over the child's ability to obtain an abortion.   Parents in Georgia in no sense have an absolute right to commit their children to state mental hospitals;   the statute requires the superintendent of each regional hospital to exercise independent judgment as to the child's need for confinement.

In defining the respective rights and prerogatives of the child and parent in the voluntary commitment setting, we conclude that our precedents permit the parents to retain a substantial, if not the dominant, role in the decision, absent a finding of neglect or abuse, and that the traditional presumption that the parents act in the best interests of their child should apply.   We also conclude, however, that the child's rights and the nature of the commitment decision are such that parents cannot always have absolute and unreviewable discretion to decide whether to have a child institutionalized.   They, of course, retain plenary authority to seek such care for their children, subject to a physician's independent examination and medical judgment.

(c) The State obviously has a significant interest in confining the use of its costly mental health facilities to cases of genuine need. . . .

The State . . .   also has a significant interest in not imposing unnecessary procedural obstacles that may discourage the mentally ill or their families from seeking needed psychiatric assistance.   The *parens patriae* interest in helping parents care for the mental health of their children cannot be fulfilled if the parents are unwilling to take advantage of the opportunities because the admission process is too onerous, too embarrassing or too contentious. . . .

The State also has a genuine interest in allocating priority to the diagnosis and treatment of patients as soon as they are admitted to a hospital rather than to time-consuming procedural minuets before the admission.   One factor that must be considered is the utilization of the time of psychiatrists, psychologists and other behavioral specialists in preparing for and participating in hearings rather than performing the task for which their special training has fitted them.   Behavioral experts in courtrooms and hearings are of little help to patients.

The *amicus* brief of the American Psychiatric Association points out at page 20 that the average staff psychiatrist in a hospital presently is able to devote only 47% of his time to direct patient care. One consequence of increasing the procedures the state must provide prior to a child's voluntary admission will be that mental health professionals will be diverted even more from the treatment of patients in order to travel to and participate in—and wait for—what could be hundreds—or even thousands—of hearings each year. . . .

(d) We now turn to consideration of what process protects adequately the child's constitutional rights by reducing risks of error without unduly trenching on traditional parental authority and without undercutting "efforts to further the legitimate interests of both the state and the patient that are served by" voluntary commitments. Addington v. Texas, 441 U.S., at 430, 99 S.Ct., at 1811. We conclude that the risk of error inherent in the parental decision to have a child institutionalized for mental health care is sufficiently great that some kind of inquiry should be made by a "neutral factfinder" to determine whether the statutory requirements for admission are satisfied. That inquiry must carefully probe the child's background using all available sources, including, but not limited to, parents, schools and other social agencies. Of course, the review must also include an interview with the child. It is necessary that the decisionmaker have the authority to refuse to admit any child who does not satisfy the medical standards for admission. Finally, it is necessary that the child's continuing need for commitment be reviewed periodically by a similarly independent procedure.

We are satisfied that such procedures will protect the child from an erroneous admission decision in a way that neither unduly burdens the states nor inhibits parental decisions to seek state help.

Due process has never been thought to require that the neutral and detached trier of fact be law-trained or a judicial or administrative officer. Surely, this is the case as to medical decisions for "neither judges nor administrative hearing officers are better qualified than psychiatrists to render psychiatric judgments." In re Roger S., 19 Cal.3d 921, 942, 141 Cal.Rptr. 298, 311, 569 P.2d 1286, 1299 (1977) (Clark, J., dissenting). Thus, a staff physician will suffice, so long as he or she is free to evalutate independently the child's mental and emotional condition and need for treatment.

It is not necessary that the deciding physician conduct a formal or quasi-formal hearing. A state is free to require such a hearing, but due process is not violated by use of informal traditional medical investigative techniques. Since well-established medical procedures already exist, we do not undertake to outline with specificity precisely what this investigation must involve. The mode and procedure of medical diagnostic procedures is not the business of judges. What is best for a child is an individual medical decision that must be left to the judgment of physicians in each case. We do no more than emphasize that the decision should represent an independent judgment of what the child requires and that all sources of information that are traditionally relied on by physicians and behavioral specialists should be consulted.

What process is constitutionally due cannot be divorced from the nature of the ultimate decision that is being made. Not every determination by state officers can be made most effectively by use of "the procedural tools of judicial or administrative decisionmaking." Board of Curators of Univ. of Missouri v. Horowitz, 435 U.S. 78, 90, 98 S.Ct. 948, 955, 55 L.Ed.2d 124 (1978).

Here the questions are essentially medical in character: whether the child is mentally or emotionally ill and whether he can benefit from the treatment that is provided by the state. While facts are plainly necessary for a proper resolution of those questions, they are only a first step in the process. In an opinion for a unanimous Court, we recently stated in Addington v. Texas, supra, 441 U.S., at 429, 99 S.Ct., at 1811, "whether [a person] is mentally ill . . . turns on the *meaning* of the facts which must be interpreted by expert psychiatrists and psychologists."

Although we acknowledge the fallibility of medical and psychiatric diagnosis, we do not accept the notion that the shortcomings of specialists can always be avoided by shifting the decision from a trained specialist using the traditional tools of medical science to an untrained judge or administrative hearing officer after a judicial-type hearing. Even after a hearing, the nonspecialist decisionmaker must make a medical-psychiatric decision. Common human experience and scholarly opinions suggest that the supposed protections of an adversary proceeding to determine the appropriateness of medical decisions for the commitment and treatment of mental and emotional illness may well be more illusory than real.

Another problem with requiring a formalized, factfinding hearing lies in the danger it poses for significant intrusion into the parent-child relationship. Pitting the parents and child as adversaries often will be at odds with the presumption that parents act in the best interests of their child. It is one thing to require a neutral physician to make a careful review of the parents' decision in order to make sure it is proper from a medical standpoint; it is a wholly different matter to employ an adversary contest to ascertain whether the parents' motivation is consistent with the child's interests.

Moreover, it is appropriate to inquire into how such a hearing would contribute to the long range successful treatment of the patient. Surely, there is a risk that it would exacerbate whatever tensions already existed between the child and the parents. Since the parents can and usually do play a significant role in the treatment while the child is hospitalized and even more so after release, there is a serious risk that an adversary confrontation will adversely affect the ability of the parents to assist the child while in the hospital. Moreover, it will make his subsequent return home more difficult. These unfortunate results are especially critical with an emotionally disturbed child; they seem likely to occur in the context of an adversary hearing in which the parents testify. A confrontation over such intimate family relationships would distress the normal adult parents and the impact on a disturbed child almost certainly would be significantly greater.[18]

It has been suggested that a hearing conducted by someone other than the admitting physician is necessary in order to detect instances where parents are "guilty of railroading their children into asylums" or are using "voluntary commitment procedures in order to sanction behavior of which they disapprove." Ellis, Volunteering Children: Parental Commitment of Minors to Mental Institutions, 62 Calif.L. Rev. 840, 850–851 (1974). Curiously it seems to be taken for granted that parents who seek to "dump" their children on the state will inevitably be able to conceal their motives and thus deceive the admitting psychiatrists and the other mental health professionals who make and review the admission decision. It is elementary that one early diagnostic inquiry into the cause of an emotional disturbance of a child is an examination into the environment of the child. It is unlikely if not inconceivable that a decision to abandon an emotionally normal, healthy child and thrust him into an institution will be a discrete act leaving no trail of circumstances. Evidence of such conflicts will emerge either in the interviews or from secondary sources. It is unrealistic to believe that trained psychiatrists, skilled in eliciting responses, sorting medically relevant facts and sensitive to motivational nuances will often be deceived about the family situation surrounding a child's emotional disturbance.[19] . . .

By expressing some confidence in the medical decisionmaking process, we are by no means suggesting it is error free. . . . That there may be risks of error in the process affords no rational predicate for holding unconstitutional an entire statutory and administrative scheme that is generally followed in more than 30 states. "[P]rocedural due process rules are shaped by the risk of error inher-

18. While not altogether clear, the District Court opinion apparently contemplated a hearing preceded by a written notice of the proposed commitment. At the hearing the child presumably would be given an opportunity to be heard and present evidence, and the right to cross-examine witnesses, including, of course, the parents. The court also required an impartial trier of fact who would render a written decision reciting the reasons for accepting or rejecting the parental application.

Since the parents in this situation are seeking the child's admission to the state institution, the procedure contemplated by the District Court presumably would call for some other person to be designated as a guardian *ad litem* to act for the child. The guardian, in turn, if not a lawyer, would be empowered to retain counsel to act as an advocate of the child's interest.

Of course, a state may elect to provide such adversary hearings in situations where it perceives that parents and a child may be at odds, but nothing in the Constitution compels such procedures.

19. In evaluating the problem of detecting "dumping" by parents, it is important to keep in mind that each of the regional hospitals has a continuing relationship with the Department of Family and Children Services. The staffs at those hospitals refer cases to the Department when they suspect a child is being mistreated and thus are sensitive to this problem. In fact, J. L.'s situation is in point. The family conflicts and problems were well documented in the hospital records. Equally well documented, however, were the child's severe emotional disturbances and his need for treatment.

ent in the truthfinding process as applied to the generality of cases, not the rare exceptions." Mathews v. Eldridge, 424 U.S. at 344, 96 S.Ct, at 907, 47 L.Ed.2d 18 (1976). In general, we are satisfied that an independent medical decisionmaking process, which includes the thorough psychiatric investigation described earlier followed by additional periodic review of a child's condition, will protect children who should not be admitted; we do not believe the risks of error in that process would be significantly reduced by a more formal, judicial-type hearing. The issue remains whether the Georgia practices . . . comport with these minimum due process requirements.

[In subpart (e) the opinion reviews Georgia's statutory procedure, which "envisions a careful diagnostic medical inquiry . . . by the admitting physician at each regional hospital." The Court rejects the District Court's view that the medical decision constitutes "an exercise of 'unbridled discretion.' " The Court notes again that the superintendent of each hospital is charged statutorily "to discharge any child who is no longer mentally ill or in need of therapy." The Court also expressed its satisfaction with the conclusion that hospital admissions staffs "have acted in a neutral and detached fashion in making medical judgments in the best interests of the children." It notes that on remand, the District Court "is free to and should consider any individual claims that initial admissions did not meet the standards . . . described in this opinion."]

IV

. . . Some members of appellees' class, including J. R., were wards of the state of Georgia at the time of their admission. . . . While the determination of what process is due varies somewhat when the state, rather than a natural parent, makes the request for commitment, we conclude that the differences in the two situations do not justify requiring different procedures at the time of the child's initial admission to the hospital.

For a ward of the State, there may well be no adult who knows him thoroughly and who cares for him deeply. Unlike with natural parents where there is a presumed natural affection to guide their action, Blackstone * 447; Kent * 190, the presumption that the state will protect a child's general welfare stems from a specific state statute. Ga.Code Ann. § 24A 101. Contrary to the suggestion of the dissent, however, we cannot assume that when the State of Georgia has custody of a child it acts so differently from a natural parent in seeking medical assistance for the child. . . . Nor could such a challenge be mounted on the record before us. There is no evidence that the State, acting as guardian, attempted to admit any child for reasons unrelated to the child's need for treatment. . . .

Once we accept that the State's application of a child for admission to a hospital is made in good faith, then the question is whether the medical decisionmaking approach of the admitting physician is adequate to satisfy due process. We have already recognized that an independent medical judgment made from the perspective of the best interests of the child after a careful investigation is an acceptable means of justifying a voluntary commitment. We do not believe that the soundness of this decisionmaking is any the less reasonable in this setting. . . .

It is possible that the procedures required in reviewing a ward's need for continuing care should be different from those used to review a child with natural parents.

. . .

The absence of an adult who cares deeply for a child has little effect on the reliability of the initial admission decision, but it may have some effect on how long a child will remain in the hospital. We noted in Addington v. Texas, supra, 441 U.S., at 428, 99 S.Ct., at 1811, "the concern of family and friends generally will provide continuous opportunities for an erroneous commitment to be corrected." For a child without natural parents, we must acknowledge the risk of being "lost in the shuffle." Moreover, there is at least some indication that J. R.'s commitment was prolonged because the Department of Family and Children Services had difficulty finding a foster home for him. Whether wards of the State generally have received less protection than children with natural parents, and, if so, what should be done about it, however, are matters that must be decided in the first instance by the District Court on remand, if the Court concludes the issue is still alive.

V

It is important that we remember the purpose of Georgia's comprehensive mental health program. It seeks substantively and at great cost to provide care for those who cannot afford to obtain private treatment and procedurally to screen carefully all applicants to assure that institutional care is suited to the particular patient. The State resists the complex of procedures ordered by the District Court because in its view they are unnecessary to protect the child's rights, they divert public resources from the central objective of administering health care, they risk aggravating the tensions inherent in the family situation and they erect barriers that may discourage parents from seeking medical aid for a disturbed child.

On this record we are satisfied that Georgia's medical factfinding processes are reasonable and consistent with constitutional guarantees. Accordingly, it was error to hold unconstitutional the State's procedures for admitting a child for treatment to a state mental hospital. . . .

Reversed and remanded.

[The concurring opinion of MR. JUSTICE STEWART is omitted.]

[In a separate opinion MR. JUSTICE BRENNAN, joined by MR. JUSTICE MARSHALL and MR. JUSTICE STEVENS concurred in part and dissented in part.

While finding the present Georgia admission procedures "reasonably consistent" with the constitutional principles outlined in detail at the outset of the dissenting opinion, the dissenters regard the postadmission procedures as "simply not enough to qualify as hearings—let alone reasonably prompt hearings. The procedures lack all the traditional due process safeguards." As to juvenile wards of the State, the dissenters suggest that "the special considerations that justify postponement of formal commitment proceedings whenever parents seek to hospitalize their children are absent when the children are wards of the State and are being committed upon recommendations of their social workers." In the absence of "exigent circumstances" they would require preadmission commitment hearings for such juveniles.]

NOTES

(1) An unfortunate characteristic of the subsequent usage of the decisions in this chapter is that courts tend to extract pithy quotations that become more important than the holdings of the cases. Almost inevitably destined for such treatment is the language in the majority opinion to the effect that our law "historically . . . has recognized that natural bonds of affection lead parents to act in the best interests of their children." Ironically, the authorities cited for the proposition are Blackstone and Kent. The particular citation to Blackstone's Commentaries refers to the treatment of bastards, who seemed to have had more disabilities than rights in English law at the time and were questionably within the "natural bonds of affection" of their fathers, at least. The citation might refer to a later edition of Blackstone, but even so we must recognize that English law in the time of the Commentaries was often quite harsh, focusing on such issues as the rights of parents to the wages and services of their offspring. Similarly, the passage referred to in Kent's Commentaries deals largely with the disabilities of infants in such matters as contract.

Should the Court have ignored the underlying policy behind the adoption of provisions such as child abuse reporting statutes that are designed specifically to protect children from harmful acts by their parents and other family members at the expense of a considerable sacrifice in family privacy?

(2) Would an action of the sort brought in *Parham* have had greater chance of success had it been instituted not as a class action but on behalf of a child who had sustained some demonstrable harm?

(3) In 1977, the California Supreme Court in In re Roger S., 19 Cal.3d 921, 141 Cal.Rptr. 298, 569 P.2d 1286 (1977) held that minors 14 and above who object to being institutionalized for mental illness or psychiatric problems are constitutionally entitled to an administrative hearing on whether commitment is appropriate under the circumstances. For a discussion of the effect that this decision has had, see Dillon, Roisman, Sanders & Adler, In re Roger S.: The Impact of a Child's Due Process Victory on the California Mental Health System, 70 Calif.L.Rev. 373 (1982).

H. L. v. MATHESON

Supreme Court of the United States, 1981.
450 U.S. 398, 101 S.Ct. 1164, 67 L.Ed.2d 388.

CHIEF JUSTICE BURGER delivered the opinion of the Court.

The question presented in this case is whether a state statute which requires a physician to "notify, if possible" the parents of a dependent, unmarried minor girl prior to performing an abortion on the girl violates federal constitutional guarantees.

In the spring of 1978, appellant was an unmarried 15-year-old girl living with her parents in Utah and dependent on them for her support. She discovered she was pregnant. She consulted with a social worker and a physician. The physician advised appellant that an abortion would be in her best medical interest. However, because of Utah Code Ann. (1953) § 76–7–304, he refused to perform the abortion without first notifying appellant's parents.

Section 76–7–304, enacted in 1974, provides:

"To enable a physician to exercise his best medical judgment [in considering a possible abortion], he shall:

"(1) Consider all factors relevant to the well-being of the woman upon whom the abortion is to be performed including, but not limited to,

"(a) Her physical, emotional and psychological health and safety,

"(b) Her age,

"(c) Her familial situation.

"(2) *Notify, if possible, the parents or guardian of the woman upon whom the abortion is to be performed, if she is a minor* or the husband of the woman, if she is married." (Emphasis supplied.)

Violation of this section is a misdemeanor punishable by imprisonment for not more than one year or a fine of not more than $1,000.

Appellant believed "for [her] own reasons" that she should proceed with the abortion without notifying her parents. According to appellant, the social worker concurred in this decision. While still in the first trimester of her pregnancy, appellant instituted this action in the Third Judicial District Court of Utah. She sought a declaration that § 76–7–304(2) is unconstitutional and an injunction prohibiting appellees, the Governor and the Attorney General of Utah, from enforcing the statute. Appellant sought to represent a class consisting of unmarried "minor women who are suffering unwanted pregnancies and desire to terminate the pregnancies but may not do so" because of their physicians' insistence on complying with § 76–7–304(2).

. . .

. . . [The trial judge] concluded that appellant "is an appropriate representative to represent the class she purports to represent." He construed the statute to require notice to appellant's parents "if it is physically possible." He concluded that § 76–7–304(2) "do[es] not unconstitutionally restrict the right of privacy of a minor to obtain an abortion or to enter into a doctor-patient relationship." Accordingly, he dismissed the complaint.

On appeal, the Supreme Court of Utah unanimously upheld the statute. . . .

. . .

Appellant challenges the statute as unconstitutional on its face. She contends it is overbroad in that it can be construed to apply to all unmarried minor girls, including those who are mature and emancipated. We need not reach that question since she did not allege or proffer any evidence that either she or any member of her class is mature or emancipated. The trial court found that appellant "is unmarried, fifteen years of age, resides at home and is a dependent of her parents." That affords an insufficient basis for a finding that she is either mature or emancipated. . . . [S]he therefore lacks "the personal stake in the controversy needed to confer standing" to advance the overbreadth argument.

. . .

The only issue before us, then, is the facial constitutionality of a statute requiring a physician to give notice to parents "if possible," prior to performing an abortion on their minor daughter, (a) when the girl is living with and dependent upon her parents, (b) when she is not emancipated by marriage or otherwise, and (c) when she has made no claim or showing as to her maturity or as to her relations with her parents.

Appellant contends the statute violates the right to privacy recognized in our prior cases with respect to abortions. She places primary reliance on *Bellotti II*, [443 U.S. 622, 99 S.Ct. 3035, 61 L.Ed.2d 797 (1979)]. In [Planned Parenthood of Central Missouri v.] *Danforth*, [428 U.S. 52, 96 S.Ct. 2831, 49 L.Ed.2d 788 (1976)], we struck down state statutes that imposed a requirement of prior written *consent* of the patient's spouse and of a minor patient's parents as a prerequisite for an abortion. We held that a state

> "does not have the constitutional authority to give a third party an absolute, and possibly arbitrary, veto over the decision of the physician and his patient to terminate the patient's pregnancy, regardless of the reason for withholding the consent." Id., 428 U.S., at 74, 96 S.Ct., at 2843.

We emphasized, however, "that our holding . . . does not suggest that every minor, regardless of age or maturity, may give effective consent for termination of her pregnancy." Id., at 75, 96 S.Ct., at 2844, citing *Bellotti I*, [428 U.S. 132, 96 S.Ct. 2857, 49 L.Ed.2d 844 (1976)]. There is no logical relationship between the capacity to become pregnant and the capacity for mature judgment concerning the wisdom of an abortion.

In *Bellotti II*, dealing with a class of concededly mature pregnant minors, we struck down a Massachusetts statute requiring parental or judicial consent before an abortion could be performed on any unmarried minor. There the State's highest court had construed the statute to allow a court to overrule the minor's decision even if the court found that the minor was capable of making, and in fact had made, an informed and reasonable decision to have an abortion. We held, among other things, that the statute was unconstitutional for failure to allow mature minors to decide to undergo abortions without parental consent. Four Justices concluded that the flaws in the statute were that, as construed by the state court, (a) it permitted overruling of a mature minor's decision to abort her pregnancy; and (b) "it requires parental consultation or notification in every instance, without affording the pregnant minor an opportunity to receive an independent judicial determination that she is mature enough to consent or that an abortion would be in her best interest." Id., 433 U.S., at 651, 99 S.Ct., at 3052–3053. Four other Justices concluded that the defect was in making the abortion decision of a minor subject to veto by a third party, whether parent or judge, "no matter how mature and capable of informed decisionmaking" the minor might be. Id., at 653–656, 99 S.Ct., at 3053–3055.

Although we have held that a state may not constitutionally legislate a blanket, unreviewable power of parents to veto their daughter's abortion, a statute setting out a "mere requirement of parental notice" does not violate the constitutional rights of an immature, dependent minor. Four Justices in *Bellotti II* joined in stating:

"[Plaintiffs] suggest . . . that the mere requirement of parental notice [unduly burdens the right to seek an abortion]. As stated in Part II above, however, parental notice and consent are qualifications that typically may be imposed by the State on a minor's right to make important decisions. As immature minors often lack the ability to make fully informed choices that take account of both immediate and long-range consequences, a State reasonably may determine that parental consultation often is desirable and in the best interest of the minor.

It may further determine, as a general proposition, that such consultation is particularly desirable with respect to the abortion decision—one that for some people raises profound moral and religious concerns.

. . . .

" 'There can be little doubt that the State furthers a constitutionally permissible end by encouraging an unmarried pregnant minor to seek the help and advice of her parents in making the very important decision whether or not to bear a child. That is a grave decision, and a girl of tender years, under emotional stress,

may be ill-equipped to make it without mature advice and emotional support. It seems unlikely that she will obtain adequate counsel and support from the attending physician at an abortion clinic,
where abortions for pregnant minors frequently take place.' "
Id., at 640–641, 99 S.Ct., at 3046–3047, quoting *Danforth*, supra,
428 U.S., at 91, 96 S.Ct., at 2851 (concurring opinion), (footnotes
omitted).

Accord, 443 U.S., at 657, 99 S.Ct., at 3055 (dissenting opinion).

In addition, "constitutional interpretation has consistently recognized that the parents' claim to authority in their own household to
direct the rearing of their children is basic in the structure of our
society." Ginsberg v. New York, 390 U.S. 629, 639, 88 S.Ct. 1274,
1280, 20 L.Ed.2d 195 (1968) (plurality opinion). In Quilloin v. Walcott,
434 U.S. 246, 98 S.Ct. 549, 54 L.Ed.2d 511 (1978), the Court expanded
on this theme:

> "We have recognized on numerous occasions that the relation-
> ship between parent and child is constitutionally protected. See,
> e.g., Wisconsin v. Yoder, 406 U.S. 205, 231–233 [92 S.Ct. 1526,
> 1541–1542, 32 L.Ed.2d 15] (1972); Stanley v. Illinois [405 U.S. 645,
> 92 S.Ct. 1208, 31 L.Ed.2d 551 (1972)]; Meyer v. Nebraska, 262
> U.S. 390, 399–401 [43 S.Ct. 625, 626–627, 67 L.Ed. 1042] (1923). 'It
> is cardinal with us that the custody, care and nurture of the child
> reside first in the parents, whose primary function and freedom
> include preparation for obligations the state can neither supply
> nor hinder.' "

Id., at 255, 98 S.Ct. at 554–555, quoting Prince v. Massachusetts,
321 U.S. 158, 166, 64 S.Ct. 438, 442, 88 L.Ed. 645 (1944).

See also Parham v. J. R., 442 U.S. 584, 602, 99 S.Ct. 2493, 2504, 61
L.Ed.2d 101 (1979); Pierce v. Society of Sisters, 268 U.S. 510, 535, 45
S.Ct. 571, 573–574, 69 L.Ed. 1070 (1925). . . .

. . .

The Utah statute gives neither parents nor judges a veto power
over the minor's abortion decision. . . . As applied to immature
and dependent minors, the statute plainly serves the important considerations of family integrity and protecting adolescents which we
identified in *Bellotti II*. In addition, as applied to that class, the statute serves a significant state interest by providing an opportunity for
parents to supply essential medical and other information to a physician. . . .

. . .

Appellant intimates that the statute's failure to declare, in terms,
a detailed description of what information parents may provide to
physicians, or to provide for a mandatory period of delay after the
physician notifies the parents, renders the statute unconstitutional.
The notion that the statute must itemize information to be supplied
by parents finds no support in logic, experience, or our decisions.

And as the Utah Supreme Court recognized, time is likely to be of the essence in an abortion decision. The Utah statute is reasonably calculated to protect minors in appellant's class by enhancing the potential for parental consultation concerning a decision that has potentially traumatic and permanent consequences.[22]

Appellant also contends that the constitutionality of the statute is undermined because Utah allows a pregnant minor to consent to other medical procedures without formal notice to her parents if she carries the child to term. But a State's interests in full-term pregnancies are sufficiently different to justify the line drawn by the statutes. Cf. Maher v. Roe, 432 U.S. 464, 473–474, 97 S.Ct. 2376, 2382, 53 L.Ed.2d 484 (1977). If the pregnant girl elects to carry her child to term, the *medical* decisions to be made entail few—perhaps none—of the potentially grave emotional and psychological consequences of the decision to abort.

That the requirement of notice to parents may inhibit some minors from seeking abortions is not a valid basis to void the statute as applied to appellant and the class properly before us. The Constitution does not compel a State to fine-tune its statutes so as to encourage or facilitate abortions. To the contrary, state action "encouraging childbirth except in the most urgent circumstances" is "rationally related to the legitimate governmental objective of protecting potential life." Harris v. McRae, [448 U.S. 297, 100 S.Ct. 2671, 65 L.Ed.2d 784 (1980)].

As applied to the class properly before us, the statute plainly serves important state interests, is narrowly drawn to protect only those interests, and does not violate any guarantees of the Constitution. The judgment of the Supreme Court of Utah is

Affirmed.

[The concurring opinion of Justice Powell, in which Justice Stewart joined, and the concurring opinion of Justice Stevens, have been omitted.]

JUSTICE MARSHALL, with whom JUSTICE BRENNAN and JUSTICE BLACKMUN join, dissenting.

· · ·

Our cases have established that a pregnant woman has a fundamental right to choose whether to obtain an abortion or carry the pregnancy to term. Roe v. Wade, 410 U.S. 113, 93 S.Ct. 705, 35 L.Ed. 2d 147 (1973); Doe v. Bolton, supra. Her choice, like the deeply intimate decisions to marry, to procreate, and to use contraceptives, is guarded from unwarranted state intervention by the right to privacy.

· · ·

22. Members of the particular class now before us in this case have no constitutional right to notify a court in lieu of notifying their parents. See *Bellotti II*, supra, 443 U.S., at 647, 99 S.Ct., at 2590. This case does not require us to decide in what circumstances a State must provide alternatives to parental notification.

It is also settled that the right to privacy, like many constitutional rights, extends to minors. Planned Parenthood of Central Missouri v. Danforth, 428 U.S. 52, 96 S.Ct. 2831, 49 L.Ed.2d 788 (1976); Bellotti v. Baird, 443, U.S. 622, 639, 99 S.Ct. 3035, 3046, 61 L.Ed.2d 797 (1979) (Powell, J.) (*Bellotti II*); id., at 653, 99 S.Ct., at 3053 (Stevens, J.); . . . Indeed, because an unwanted pregnancy is probably more of a crisis for a minor than for an adult, because the abortion decision cannot be postponed until her majority, "there are few situations in which denying a minor the right to make an important decision will have consequences so grave and indelible." *Bellotti II*, 443 U.S., at 646, 99 S.Ct., at 3048 (Powell, J.). Thus, for both the adult and the minor woman, state-imposed burdens on the abortion decision can be justified only upon a showing that the restrictions advance "important state interests." Roe v. Wade, 410 U.S., at 154, 93 S.Ct., at 727, accord, Planned Parenthood of Central Missouri v. Danforth, 428 U.S., at 61, 96 S.Ct., at 2837. Before examining the state interests asserted here, it is necessary first to consider Utah's claim that its statute does not "imping[e] on a woman's decision to have an abortion" or "plac[e] obstacles in the path of effectuating such a decision." Brief for Appellee 9. This requires an examination of whether the parental notice requirement of the Utah statute imposes any burdens in the abortion decision.

The ideal of a supportive family so pervades our culture that it may seem incongruous to examine "burdens" imposed by a statute requiring parental notice of a minor daughter's decision to terminate her pregnancy. This Court has long deferred to the bonds which join family members for mutual sustenance. See Pierce v. Society of Sisters, 268 U.S. 510, 534–535, 45 S.Ct. 571, 573, 69 L.Ed. 1070 (1925); . . . Stanley v. Illinois, 405 U.S. 645, 651, 92 S.Ct. 1208, 1212, 31 L.Ed.2d 551 (1972); . . . Especially in times of adversity, the relationships within a family can offer the security of constant caring and aid. Ideally, a minor facing an important decision will naturally seek advice and support from her parents, and they in turn will respond with comfort and wisdom. If the pregnant minor herself confides in her family, she plainly relinquishes her right to avoid telling or involving them. For a minor in that circumstance, the statutory requirement of parental notice hardly imposes a burden.

Realistically, however, many families do not conform to this ideal. Many minors, like appellant, oppose parental notice and seek instead to preserve the fundamental, personal right to privacy. It is for these minors that the parental notification requirement creates a problem. In this context, involving the minor's parents against her wishes effectively cancels her right to avoid disclosure of her personal choice. Moreover, the absolute notice requirement publicizes her private consultation with her doctor and interjects additional parties in the very conference held confidential in Roe v. Wade, supra, 410 U.S., at 164, 93 S.Ct., at 732. Besides revealing a confidential decision, the parental notice requirement may limit "access to the means of effectuating that decision." Carey v. Population Services International, 431 U.S. 678, 688, 97 S.Ct. 2010, 2017, 52 L.Ed.2d 675 (1977). Many minor women will encounter interference from their parents after the state-imposed notification. In addition to parental disappointment and disapproval, the minor may confront physical or emotional abuse, withdrawal of financial support, or actual obstruction of the abortion decision. Furthermore, the threat of parental notice may cause some minor women to delay past the first trimester of pregnancy, after which the health risks increase significantly. Other pregnant minors may attempt to self-abort or to obtain an illegal abortion rather than risk parental notification. Still others may foresake an abortion and bear an unwanted child, which, given the minor's "probable education, employment skills, financial resources and emotional resources, . . . may be exceptionally burdensome." Bellotti II, 443 U.S., at 642, 99 S.Ct., at 3048 (Powell, J.). The possibility that such problems may not occur in particular cases does not alter the hardship created by the notice requirement on its face. And that hardship is not a mere disincentive created by the State, but is instead an actual state-imposed obstacle to the exercise of the minor woman's free choice. For the class of pregnant minors represented by appellant, this obstacle is so onerous as to bar the desired abortions. Significantly, the interference sanctioned by the statute does not operate in a neutral fashion. No notice is required for any pregnancy-related medical care, so only the minor women who wish to abort encounter the burden imposed by the notification statute. Because the Utah requirement of mandatory parental notice unquestionably burdens the minor's privacy right, the proper analysis turns next to the State's proffered justifications for the infringements posed by the statute.

As established by this Court in Planned Parenthood of Central Missouri v. Danforth, supra, the statute cannot survive appellant's challenge unless it is justified by a "significant state interest." Further, the State must demonstrate that the means it selected are closely tailored to serve that interest. Where regulations burden the rights of pregnant adults, we have held that the state legitimately may be concerned with "protection of health, medical standards, and pre-natal life." Roe v. Wade, 410 U.S., at 155, 93 S.Ct., at 728. We concluded, however, that during the first trimester of pregnancy none of these interests sufficiently justifies state interference with the decision reached by the pregnant woman and her physician. Id., at 162–163, 93 S.Ct., at 731. Nonetheless, Utah asserts here that the parental notice requirement advances additional state interests not implicated by a pregnant adult's decision to abort. Specifically, Utah contends that the notice requirement improves the physician's medical judgment about a pregnant minor in two ways: it permits the parents to provide additional information to the physician, and it encourages consultation between the parents and the minor woman. Utah also advances an independent state interest in preserving parental rights and family autonomy. I consider each of these asserted interests in turn.

A

In upholding the statute, the Utah Supreme Court concluded that the notification provision might encourage parental transmission of "additional information, which might prove invaluable to the physician in exercising his 'best medical judgment.'" Yet neither the Utah courts nor the statute itself specifies the kind of information contemplated for this purpose, nor why it is available to the parents but not to the minor woman herself. Most parents lack the medical expertise necessary to supplement the physician's medical judgment, and at best could provide facts about the patient's medical history. It seems doubtful that a minor mature enough to become pregnant and to seek medical advice on her own initiative would be unable or unwilling to provide her physician with information crucial to the abortion decision. In addition, by law the physician already is obligated to obtain all information necessary to form his best medical judgment, and nothing bars consultation with the parents should the physician find it necessary.

Even if mandatory parental notice serves a substantial state purpose in this regard, the Utah statute fails to implement it. Simply put, the statute on its face does not require or even encourage the transfer of information; it does not even call for a conversation between the physician and the parents. A letter from the physician to the parents would satisfy the statute, as would a brief telephone call made moments before the abortion. Moreover, the statute is patently underinclusive if its aim is the transfer of information known to the parents but unavailable from the minor woman herself. The statute specifically excludes married minors from the parental notice requirement; only her husband need be told of the planned abortion, Utah Code Ann. § 76–7–304(2), and Utah makes no claim that he possesses any information valuable to the physician's judgment but unavailable from the pregnant woman. Furthermore, no notice is required for other pregnancy-related care sought by the minor. See Utah Code Ann. § 78–14–5(4)(f) (authorizing women of any age to consent to pregnancy-related medical care). The minor woman may consent to surgical removal and analysis of amniotic fluid, caesarian delivery, and other medical care related to pregnancy. The physician's decisions concerning such procedures would be enhanced by parental information as much as would the abortion decision, yet only the abortion decision triggers the parental notice requirement. This result is especially anomalous given the comparatively lesser health risks associated with abortion as contrasted with other pregnancy-related medical care.[38] Thus, the statute not only fails to promote the

38. I am baffled by the majority's statement today that "[i]f the pregnant girl elects to carry her child to term, the *medical* decisions to be made entail

transfer of information as is claimed, it does not apply to other closely related contexts in which such exchange of information would be no less important. The goal of promoting consultation between the physician and the parents of the pregnant minor cannot sustain a statute that is so ill-fitted to serve it.[39]

Appellees also claim the statute serves the legitimate purpose of improving the minor's decision by encouraging consultation between the minor woman and her parents. The State does not dispute that it cannot legally or practically require such consultation. Nor does the State contest the fact that the decision is ultimately the minor's to make. Nonetheless, the State seeks through the notice requirement to give parents the opportunity to contribute to the minor woman's abortion decision.

Ideally, facilitation of supportive conversation would assist the pregnant minor during an undoubtedly difficult experience. Again, however, when measured against the rationality of the means employed, the Utah statute simply fails to advance this asserted goal. The statute imposes no requirement that the notice be sufficiently timely to permit any discussion between the pregnant minor and the parents. Moreover, appellant's claims require us to examine the statute's purpose in relation to the parents who the minor believes are likely to respond with hostility or opposition. In this light, the statute is plainly overbroad. Parental consultation hardly seems a legitimate state purpose where the minor's pregnancy resulted from incest, where a hostile or abusive parental response is assured, or where the minor's fears of such a response deter her from the abortion she desires. The absolute nature of the statutory requirement,

few—perhaps none—of the potentially grave and emotional and psychological consequences of the decision to abort," ante, at 1173 (opinion of Burger, C.J.). Choosing to participate in diagnostic tests involves risks to both mother and child, and also may burden the pregnant woman with knowledge that the child will be handicapped. See Prevention of Embryonic, Fetal, and Perinatal Disease 347–352 (R. Brent & M. Harris, eds. 1076); Risks in the Practice of Modern Obstetrics 59–81, 369–370 (S. Aladjem, ed. 1975). The decision to undergo surgery to save the child's life certainly carries as serious "emotional and psychological consequences" for the pregnant adolescent as does the decision to abort; in both instances, the minor confronts the task of calculating not only medical risks, but also all the issues involved in giving birth to a child. See Risks in the Practice of Modern Obstetrics, supra, at 59–81. For an unwed adolescent, these issues include her future educational and job opportunities, as well as the more immediate problems of finding financial and emotional support for offspring dependent entirely on her. Michael M. v. Sonoma County Superior Court, 450 U.S. 464, 470, 101 S.Ct. 1200, 1205, 66 L.Ed.2d 437 (1981) (Rehnquist, J.) (plurality). When surgery to save the child's life poses greater risks to the mother's life, the emotional and ethical dimensions of the medical care decision assume crisis proportion. Of course, for minors, the mere fact of pregnancy and the experience of child-birth can produce psychological upheaval.

39. More flexible regulations which defer to the physician's judgment but provide for parental notice in emergencies have been proposed. E.g., IJA–ABA, Juvenile Justice Standards Project, Standards Relating to Rights of Minors §§ 4.2, 4.6, 4.8 (1980) (minor can consent to pregnancy-related medical care; physician should seek to obtain minor's permission to notify parent, and notify parent over minor's objection only if failure to inform "could seriously jeopardize the health of the minor").

with exception permitted only if the parents are physically unavailable, violates the requirement that regulations in this fundamentally personal area be carefully tailored to serve a significant state interest.[42] "The need to preserve the constitutional right and the unique nature of the abortion decision, especially when made by a minor, require a State to act with particular sensitivity when it legislates to foster parental involvement in this matter." *Bellotti II*, 443 U.S., at 642, 99 S.Ct., at 3047 (Powell, J.). Because Utah's absolute notice requirement demonstrates no such sensitivity, I cannot approve its interference with the minor's private consultation with the physician during the first trimester of her pregnancy.

Finally, the state asserts an interest in protecting parental authority and family integrity.[43] This Court, of course, has recognized that the "primary role of the parents in the upbringing of their children is now established beyond debate as an enduring American tradition." Wisconsin v. Yoder, 406 U.S. 205, 232, 92 S.Ct. 1526, 1541, 32 L.Ed.2d 15 (1972). See Prince v. Massachusetts, 321 U.S. 158, 64 S.Ct. 438, 88 L.Ed. 645 (1944); Meyer v. Nebraska, 262 U.S. 390, 43 S.Ct. 625, 67 L.Ed. 1042 (1923). Indeed, "those who nurture [the child] and direct his destiny have the right, coupled with the high duty, to recognize and prepare him for additional obligations." Pierce v. Society of Sisters, 268 U.S., at 535, 45 S.Ct., at 573 (1924). Similarly, our decisions "have respected the private realm of family life which the state cannot enter." Prince v. Massachusetts, 321 U.S., at 166, 64 S.Ct., at 442.

The critical thrust of these decisions has been to protect the privacy of individual families from unwarranted state intrusion. Ironically, Utah invokes these decisions in seeking to justify state interference in the normal functioning of the family. Through its notice requirement, the State in fact enters the private realm of the family rather than leaving unaltered the pattern of interactions chosen by the family. Whatever its motive, state intervention is hardly likely to resurrect parental authority that the parents themselves are unable to preserve.[45] In rejecting a statute permitting parental veto of the

42. State sponsored counseling services, in contrast, could promote family dialogue and also improve the minor's decisionmaking process. Appellant H. L., for example, consulted with a counsel who supported her decision. The role of counselors can be significant in facilitating the pregnant woman's adjustment to decisions related to her pregnancy. See Smith, A Follow-Up Study of Women who Request Abortion, 43 Am.J. Orthopsychiatry 574, 583–585 (1973).

43. This interest, although not discussed by the state courts below, was the subject of the State's most vigorous argument before this Court. The challenged provision does fall within the "Of-

fenses Against the Family" chapter of the Utah Criminal Code, ante, at 1166 (opinion of Burger, C. J.), which also provides criminal sanctions for bigamy, Utah Code Ann. § 76-7-101, incest, § 76-7-102, adultery, § 76-7-103, fornication, § 76-7-104, and nonsupport and sale of children, §§ 76-7-201 to 76-7-203.

45. "The fact that the minor became pregnant and sought an abortion contrary to the parents' wishes indicates that whatever control the parent once had over the minor has diminished, if not evaporated entirely. And we believe that enforcing a single, albeit important, parental decision—at a time when the minor is near to majority status—by an in-

minor woman's abortion decision in Planned Parenthood of Central Missouri v. Danforth, 428 U.S., at 75, 96 S.Ct., at 2844, we found it difficult to conclude that

"providing a parent with absolute power to overrule a determination, made by the physician and his minor patient, to terminate the patient's pregnancy will serve to strengthen the family unit. Neither is it likely that such veto power will enhance parental authority or control where the minor and the nonconsenting parent are so fundamentally in conflict and the very existence of the pregnancy already has fractured the family structure."

More recently, in Bellotti v. Baird II, 443 U.S., at 638, 99 S.Ct., at 3045. Justice Powell observed that efforts to guide the social and moral development of young people are "in large part . . . beyond the competence of impersonal political institutions."

Appellees maintain, however, that Utah's statute "merely safeguards a reserved right which parents have to know of the important activities of their children by attempting to prevent a denial of the parental rights through deception." Brief for Appellees 3. Casting its purpose this way does not salvage the statute. For when the threat to parental authority originates not from the State but from the minor child, invocation of "reserved" rights of parents cannot sustain blanket state intrusion into family life such as that mandated by the Utah statute. Such a result not only runs counter to the private domain of the family which the State may not breach; it also conflicts with the limits traditionally placed on parental authority. Parental authority is never absolute, and has been denied legal protection when its exercise threatens the health or safety of the minor children. E.g., Prince v. Massachusetts, 321 U.S., at 169–170, 64 S.Ct., at 443–444. Indeed, legal protection for parental rights is frequently tempered if not replaced by concern for the child's interest. Whatever its importance elsewhere, parental authority deserves de minimus legal reinforcement where the minor's exercise of a fundamental right is burdened.

To decide this case, there is no need to determine whether parental rights never deserve legal protection when their assertion conflicts with the minor's rights and interests.[47] I conclude that this

strument as blunt as a state statute is extremely unlikely to restore parental control." Poe v. Gerstein, 517 F.2d 787, 794–795 (CA7 1975), summarily aff'd. 428 U.S. 901, 96 S.Ct. 3202, 49 L.Ed.2d 1205 (1976).

47. The contexts in which this issue may arise are too varied to support any general rule. Appellee cites our recent decision in Parham v. J. R., 442 U.S. 584, 99 S.Ct. 2493, 61 L.Ed.2d 101 (1979), to support its claim that parents should be presumed competent to be involved in their minor daughter's abortion decision.

That decision is inapposite to this case in several respects. First, the minor child in *Parham* who was committed to a mental hospital was presumed incompetent to make the commitment decision himself. Id., at 623, 99 S.Ct., at 2154 (Steward, J., concurring). In contrast, appellant by statute is presumed competent to make the decision about whether to complete or abort her pregnancy. Furthermore, in *Parham*, the Court placed critical reliance on the ultimately determinative, independent review of the commitment decision by medical experts.

statute cannot be defended as a mere reinforcement of existing parental rights, for the statute reaches beyond the legal limits of those rights. The statute applies, without exception, to emancipated minors, mature minors, and minors with emergency health care needs, all of whom, as Utah recognizes, by law have long been entitled to medical care unencumbered by parental involvement. Most relevant to appellant's own claim, the statutory restriction applies even where the minor's best interests—as evaluated by her physician—call for an abortion. . . .

In this area, I believe this Court must join the state courts and legislatures which have acknowledged the undoubted social reality: some minors, in some circumstances, have the capacity and need to determine their health care needs without involving their parents. As we recognized in Planned Parenthood of Central Missouri v. Danforth, supra, 428 U.S., at 75, 96 S.Ct., at 2844, "[a]ny independent interest the parent may have in the termination of the minor daughter's pregnancy is no more weighty than the right of privacy of the competent minor mature enough to have become pregnant." Utah itself has allocated pregnancy-related health care decisions entirely to the pregnant minor. Where the physician has cause to doubt the minor's actual ability to understand and consent, by law he must pursue the requisites of the State's informed consent procedures. The State cannot have a legitimate interest in adding to this scheme mandatory parental notice of the minor's abortion decision. This conclusion does not affect parents' traditional responsibility to guide their children's development, especially in personal and moral concerns. I am persuaded that the Utah notice requirement is not necessary to assure parents this traditional child-rearing role, and that it burdens the minor's fundamental right to choose with her physician whether to terminate her pregnancy.

.   .   .

NOTES

(1) The Supreme Court in Roe v. Wade, 410 U.S. 113, 93 S.Ct. 705, 35 L.Ed.2d 147 (1973), sketched limits that state legislatures could impose on abortion practice. During the first trimester of pregnancy abortion is a matter between a woman and her physician. During a second stage following that, abortion procedure can be regulated by the state "in ways that are reasonably related to maternal health." During a third stage, said to be after "viability", the state may regulate and even proscribe abortion "except where it is necessary, in appropriate medical judgment, for the preservation of the life or health of the mother."

Here, the physician's independent medical judgment—that an abortion was in appellant's best medical interest—not only was not ultimate, it was defeated by the notice requirement. Finally, as Justice Steward emphasized in his concurring opinion in *Parham*, the pregnant minor has a "personal substantive right" to decide on an abortion. Id., at 623–624, n. 6, 99 S.Ct., at 2514–2515, n. 6.

Since *Roe*, the Supreme Court has faced a series of cases dealing with statutes that tried to restrict abortion to the limits legally permitted. Several have dealt with minors and whether their privacy rights should be the same as those of adults with regard to the decision whether to carry a fetus to term. In Planned Parenthood v. Danforth, 428 U.S. 52, 96 S.Ct. 2831, 49 L.Ed.2d 788 (1976), the Supreme Court invalidated a provision of Missouri's statute requiring permission from a parent or one *in loco parentis* for a non-lifesaving abortion on an unmarried woman less than 18 years old during the first 12 weeks of her pregnancy. The Court held that the state lacked power to give a third party "absolute, and possibly arbitrary, veto over the decision of the physician and his patient to terminate the patient's pregnancy"; the possibility of upholding some less invasive requirement of communication or consultation was not resolved.

On the same day when *Danforth* was decided, Bellotti v. Baird (Bellotti I), 428 U.S. 132, 96 S.Ct. 2857, 49 L.Ed.2d 844 (1976) sent back to a federal District Court for certification of certain questions regarding interpretation of a Massachusetts statute on parental involvement in children's abortion decisions. The case eventually returned to the Supreme Court as Bellotti II, which is outlined and explained in the *Matheson* opinion. Still unclear after *Matheson* is the definition of a "mature" minor and the scope of the limitations that can be imposed on such a person. For a discussion of the mature minor rule in the context of medical treatment generally, see 951, infra.

(2) In Matter of Mary P., 111 Misc.2d 532, 444 N.Y.S.2d 545 (Fam.Ct., Queens County 1981), a mother sought to have her 15½-year-old daughter declared a person in need of supervision because of her refusal to have an abortion. Instead of granting the mother's petition, the court issued an order of protection to the daughter, directing the mother not to interfere with the daughter's determination to deliver her child. The court explained:

> The court is well aware that parents may and should play a meaningful role in counseling their children on all matters involving their well-being. Moreover, a minor's decision on whether or not to abort is of such far reaching consequence and sensitivity as to cry out for the understanding counsel of parents who care. And yet, such counsel must originate from the premise that it is the child who has the ultimate right to decide. Children are not the chattel of their parents. Rather, they are citizens in their own right, endowed with certain fundamental freedoms of which they may not be divested by parental fiat. The right to give birth is among those freedoms.

> Inevitably, there comes a point in time when the child's decision making process reaches fruition, with or without parental input, and a firm choice is made. Mary has made her choice and it is, indeed, her choice to make. In deciding to give birth, she has exercised a personal liberty guaranteed to her by the fourteenth amendment. Her decision now requires parental forbearance. There is a very thin line between counsel and coercion, expecially when they originate from a relationship as special as that of parent-child. A child's right to decide for herself whether or not to give birth, is particularly susceptible to subversion by a parent. Thus the free exercise of her will may be overcome by feelings of guilt, disloyalty, and even fear. Surely not every parental reaction to a child's pregnancy is as overt as that of the petitioner's herein. To the extent that parents, either directly or indirectly, fail to respect their child's right

to make the ultimate decision on whether to give birth, their conduct may indeed be labelled "offensive" to the child within the meaning of section 759(a) of the Family Court Act.

Id. at 548. For an earlier case reversing a juvenile court's order that a minor submit to medical procedures to terminate her pregnancy see In re Smith, 16 Md.App. 209, 295 A.2d 238 (1972). Consent by minors to health care is discussed generally infra at 893.

(3) In Carey v. Population Services International, 431 U.S. 678, 97 S.Ct. 2010, 52 L.Ed.2d 675 (1977), the Supreme Court invalidated a provision in a New York statute proscribing distribution of contraceptives to persons below age 16. Writing for a plurality of four, Justice Brennan found that the restriction inhibited minors' privacy rights without serving any significant state interest not present in the case of an adult. Justice Stevens, who regarded the prohibition as irrational, likened it to a decision "to dramatize . . . disapproval of motorcycles by forbidding the use of safety helmets."

III. RESHAPING THE JUVENILE JUSTICE SYSTEM: BEFORE AND AFTER *IN RE GAULT*

THE POST-*GAULT* WORLD IN HISTORICAL PERSPECTIVE

The subject matter jurisdiction of juvenile and family courts traditionally has included delinquency (conduct by a child that would be a crime if he were an adult); noncriminal misbehavior (the so-called status offenses unique to children such as truancy, running away from home or engaging in other conduct injurious to the child's health, welfare or morals); and abuse and neglect (failure of parents to provide the minimum tolerable level of care for their children). More recently, some states have structured their juvenile justice systems around full-service family courts which have been given significantly increased jurisdiction, including adoption, child custody, intrafamily assaults, juvenile traffic offenses, or even divorce.

While most observers of the juvenile justice system would point to child custody and neglect adjudications with the possible remedy of permanent termination of parental rights as the most agonizing decisions a juvenile or family court judge must make, it is ironic that until very recently the greatest scrutiny of the system by the United States Supreme Court has focused on delinquency cases. This chapter discusses those decisions as a prelude to and catalyst for modern proposals for juvenile court reform and also provides an introduction to delinquency jurisdiction.

Beginning in the middle of the nineteenth century, progressives called for the creation of special courts to deal with delinquent minors. Although the "delinquent" label covered both vagrant and neglected children, the principal focus of the Illinois Juvenile Court Act of 1899 was criminal conduct by children. The Illinois Act, America's first juvenile code, was a direct product of the reformers' sense of outrage at the handling of children in the criminal courts. It enshrined the major ideas of what came to be called the Juvenile Court Philosophy:

(1) A special court was created for neglected, dependent or delinquent children under age sixteen.

(2) The purpose of that court was to rehabilitate children rather than punish them.

(3) Ostensibly, no stigma would attach to a child from a court appearance; all records and proceedings were to be confidential.

(4) The Act required that juveniles be separated from adults when incarcerated or placed in the same institution in order to avoid the corrupting influence of adult criminals on juveniles. All detention of children under twelve in police stations or jails was barred.

197

(5) Juvenile court proceedings were to be informal. Indeed, these new tribunals were not to operate on a legal model at all; the analogy from the start was medical, reflecting proposals by early reformers utilizing techniques of the then newly-developed social and behavioral sciences to diagnose, treat and cure socially sick children.

Between 1899 and 1917, all but three states created special courts for children. Fueled by the Progressive movement in the decade around World War I, the Juvenile Court Philosophy swept the country. Although modern scholars disagree about the origins of the reform impulses that led to the creation of juvenile courts, by 1925 the Juvenile Court Philosophy had triumphed almost everywhere.[1]

From 1925 until Justice Fortas's decision in *Kent*[2] in 1966, juvenile courts operated without legal oversight or monitoring. Many would say that juvenile courts in this period were not really courts at all. There was little or no place for law, lawyers, reporters and the usual paraphernalia of courts; this is not at all surprising because the proponents of the Juvenile Court movement had specifically rejected legal institutions as appropriate to the rehabilitation of children.

Beginning with *Kent* and continuing immediately in *Gault*[3] the Supreme Court examined the operation of the juvenile justice system and found, in Justice Fortas's words in *Kent*, that:

> While there can be no doubt of the original laudable purpose of juvenile courts, studies and critiques in recent years raise serious questions as to whether actual performance measures well enough against theoretical purpose to make tolerable the immunity of the process from the reach of constitutional guaranties applicable to adults. There is much evidence that some juvenile courts . . . lack the personnel, facilities and techniques to perform adequately as representatives of the State in a *parens patriae* capacity, at least with respect to children charged with law violation. There is evidence, in fact, that there may be grounds for concern that the child receives the worst of both worlds: that he gets neither the protections accorded to adults nor the solicitous care and regenerative treatment postulated for children.[4]

Kent, Gault and the other cases in this chapter present the most significant judicial response to this perceived malfunction of juvenile courts. By the 1970s, however, the major arena of reform shifted from judicial decisions to legislation. In the period from 1970 to the present, nearly every state has radically revised its juvenile code—

1. For conflicting views about the motivation of the proponents of the Juvenile Court movement between 1899 and 1925 compare, A. M. Platt, The Child Savers: The Invention of Delinquency (2d ed. 1972) and Fox, Juvenile Justice Reform: An Historical Perspective, 22 Stan.L.Rev. 1187 (1970) with Schulz, The Cycle of Juvenile Court History, 19 Crime and Delinq. 457 (1973). For a contemporary statement of the goals of juvenile courts see, Mack, The Juvenile Court, 23 Harv. L.Rev. 104 (1909).

2. Kent v. United States, 383 U.S. 541, 86 S.Ct. 1045, 16 L.Ed.2d 84 (1966).

3. In re Gault, 387 U.S. 1, 87 S.Ct. 1428, 18 L.Ed.2d 527 (1967).

4. 383 U.S. at 555, 86 S.Ct. at 1054.

usually to provide more exacting and precise guidelines for the exercise of discretion by juvenile judges, expecially in delinquency cases.

Probably the most complete reform proposals of recent years are found in the twenty-three volumes of Juvenile Justice Standards prepared under the auspices of the Institute of Judicial Administration and the American Bar Association. Twenty of the twenty-three volumes of standards have been approved by the A.B.A. House of Delegates. Revised versions of the Standards Relating to Abuse and Neglect, Noncriminal Misbehavior, and Schools and Education, all recommended by the IJA–ABA Commission on Juvenile Justice Standards, and a 2nd edition of Standards for Juvenile Justice: A Summary and Analysis, by Barbara Danziger Flicker, were released as this book went to press.

Many of the ideas from the Juvenile Justice Standards Project will be presented throughout this book. These proposals are not intended for enactment as model statutes but rather to serve as a broad compendium of current thought about juvenile courts and children's rights. The primary conceptual bases of the Standards almost undoubtedly will provide building blocks for legislative reform in the decades to come.

In the materials we have excerpted or discussed from the Juvenile Justice Standards Project, we relied especially on the following:

Volume	Reporters
Abuse and Neglect (Tentative Draft)	Robert Burt and Michael Wald
Adjudication	Robert D. Dawson
Disposition Procedures	Fred Cohen
Dispositions	Linda Singer
Interim Status	Daniel J. Freed and Timothy P. Terrell
The Juvenile Probation Function: Intake and Predisposition Investigative Service	Josephine Gittler
Juvenile Records and Information Systems	Michael L. Altman
Noncriminal Misbehavior (Tentative Draft)	Aidan Gough
Police Handling of Juvenile Problems	Egon Bittner and Sheldon Krantz
Pretrial Court Proceedings	Stanley Z. Fisher
Rights of Minors	Barry Feld and Robert J. Levy
Schools and Education (Tentative Draft)	William Buss and Stephen Goldstein
Transfers Between Courts	Charles H. Whitebread
Youth Service Agencies	Judith Areen

Certain basic principles that underlie the entire set of standards were capsulized as follows in the summary volume to the 1977 Drafts:

1. Proportionality in sanctions for juvenile offenders based on the seriousness of the offense committed, and not merely the court's view of the juvenile's needs, should replace vague and subjective criteria.

2. Sentences or dispositions should be determinate. The practice of indeterminate sentencing, allowing correctional authorities to act arbitrarily to release or confine juveniles as the convenience of their programs dictates, should be abolished. Such sentences permit wide disparity in the punishment received for the same misconduct and create a potential for abuse that the public is helpless to prevent.

3. The least restrictive alternative should be the choice of decision makers for intervention in the lives of juveniles and their families. If a decision maker, such as a judge or an intake officer, imposes a restrictive disposition, he or she must state in writing the reasons for finding less drastic remedies inappropriate or inadequate to further the purposes of the juvenile justice system.

4. Noncriminal misbehavior (status offenses, PINS) and private offenses (victimless crimes) should be removed from juvenile court jurisdiction. Possession of narcotic drugs, however, has been retained as a basis for court jurisdiction. Juvenile court intervention in these areas have proven ineffective, if not socially harmful, damaging a significant number of children and frequently turning unruly juveniles into criminals. Voluntary community services to deal with these problems, such as crisis intervention programs, mediation for parent-child disputes, and alternative residences or "crash-pads" for runaways, are proposed as more suitable responses to noncriminal misconduct. School disciplinary proceedings, alternate programs, peer counseling, and other remedies within the educational system are suggested for truants. Neglect or abuse petitions would be filed where children are found living in dangerous conditions.

5. Visibility and accountability of decision making should replace closed proceedings and unrestrained official discretion.

6. There should be a right to counsel for all affected interests at all crucial stages of the proceeding.

7. Juveniles should have the right to decide on actions affecting their lives and freedom, unless they are found incapable of making reasoned decisions.

8. The role of parents in juvenile proceedings should be redefined with particular attention to possible conflicts between the interests of parent and child.

9. Limitations should be imposed on detention, treatment, or other intervention prior to adjudication and disposition.

10. Strict criteria should be established for waiver of juvenile court jurisdiction to regulate transfer of juveniles to adult criminal court.*

The cases in this chapter are the prerequisite to the work of the Standards Project and all modern reform proposals. For that reason we have chosen to present them as a unit before undertaking a detailed analysis of the delinquency jurisdiction.

NOTE

The Federal Juvenile Justice and Delinquency Prevention Act of 1974 as amended in 1977 and again in 1981 reflects congressional concern over the extent of youth crime. The Act (1) creates the Office of Juvenile Justice and Delinquency Prevention to administer and monitor grants to fund state experimental programs for delinquency prevention; (2) conditions receipt of federal monies under the Act on removing juveniles from adult jails and deinstitutionalizing the so-called status offenders and (3) contains a juvenile code to be applied to conduct by children that would be crimes in the federal jurisdiction.

By conditioning and monitoring the dispersal of federal money, the Act serves as a major engine of law reform in the states. Much of the recent pressure to remove juveniles from adult correctional facilities is a direct result of the desire of states to qualify for funding under the federal program.

Although the substantive provisions of the Act only come into play when the child cannot be deferred to state juvenile courts, the Act contains the most recent, complete statement from Congress of its model for appropriate handling of juveniles who have engaged in conduct that would be crimes if they were adults. The provisions of the Federal Delinquency Act differ substantially from the proposals of the Juvenile Justice Standards Project and some other recent legislative reforms.

Finally, the 1977 and 1981 amendments to the Act show Congress responding to growing public concern for protection from the serious youthful offender. The change in focus from 1974 to 1981 in the Federal Act is parallel to a similar redirection in state juvenile codes.

KENT v. UNITED STATES

Supreme Court of the United States, 1966.
383 U.S. 541, 86 S.Ct. 1045, 16 L.Ed.2d 84.

MR. JUSTICE FORTAS delivered the opinion of the Court.

[Morris Kent, age 16, was accused of committing a number of robberies and housebreakings in the District of Columbia. One robbery victim was raped. The principal evidence against Kent was a latent fingerprint left at the scene of the robbery and rape. Kent was on

* Reprinted with permission from STANDARDS FOR JUVENILE JUS-TICE: A SUMMARY AND ANALYSIS (First Edition), Copyright 1977, Ballinger Publishing Company.

probation from the Juvenile Court at the time of his apprehension. He was interrogated over a seven hour period and confessed to several housebreakings. Kent and his mother met with the Social Service Director of the Juvenile Court who informed them Kent might be transferred for trial in adult court. Kent's attorney sought a court order to provide for psychiatric evaluation and for access to any social reports on Kent in the court's possession. Without a hearing, the juvenile judge transferred Kent's case to the criminal court; after a denial of his motion to dismiss Kent was tried there. He presented an insanity defense in the criminal proceeding. The jury found Kent guilty of robbery and housebreaking but not guilty by reason of insanity on the rape charge. Sentenced to serve 90 years in prison on the charges as to which he was found guilty, Kent first was sent to a mental hospital for the treatment mandated in the District of Columbia when a defendant is found not guilty by reason of insanity. Time in the mental hospital was to be credited against his prison sentence. Kent appealed his conviction and the Court of Appeals affirmed.]

It is to petitioner's arguments as to the infirmity of the proceedings by which the Juvenile Court waived its otherwise exclusive jurisdiction that we address our attention. Petitioner attacks the waiver of jurisdiction on a number of statutory and constitutional grounds. He contends that the waiver is defective because no hearing was held; because no findings were made by the Juvenile Court; because the Juvenile Court stated no reasons for waiver; and because counsel was denied access to the Social Service file which presumably was considered by the Juvenile Court in determining to waive jurisdiction.

We agree that the order of the Juvenile Court waiving its jurisdiction and transferring petitioner for trial in the United States District Court for the District of Columbia was invalid. . . .

We agree with the Court of Appeals that the statute contemplates that the Juvenile Court should have considerable latitude within which to determine whether it should retain jurisdiction over a child or—subject to the statutory delimitation—should waive jurisdiction. But this latitude is not complete. At the outset, it assumes procedural regularity sufficient in the particular circumstances to satisfy the basic requirements of due process and fairness, as well as compliance with the statutory requirement of a "full investigation." The statute gives the Juvenile Court a substantial degree of discretion as to the factual considerations to be evaluated, the weight to be given them and the conclusion to be reached. It does not confer upon the Juvenile Court a license for arbitrary procedure. The statute does not permit the Juvenile Court to determine in isolation and without the participation or any representation of the child the "critically important" question whether a child will be deprived of the special protections and provisions of the Juvenile Court Act. It does not authorize the Juvenile Court, in total disregard of a motion for hearing filed by counsel, and without any hearing or statement or reasons, to decide— as in this case—that the child will be taken from the Receiving Home for Children and transferred to jail along with adults, and that he will be exposed to the possibility of a death sentence instead of treatment for a maximum, in Kent's case, of five years, until he is 21.

We do not consider whether, on the merits, Kent should have been transferred; but there is no place in our system of law for reaching a result of such tremendous consequences without ceremony—without hearing, without effective assistance of counsel, without a statement of reasons. It is inconceivable that a court of justice dealing with adults, with respect to a similar issue, would proceed in this manner. It would be extraordinary if society's special concern for children, as reflected in the District of Columbia's Juvenile Court Act, permitted this procedure. We hold that it does not.

(1.) The theory of the District's Juvenile Court Act, like that of other jurisdictions, is rooted in social welfare philosophy rather than in the *corpus juris*. Its proceedings are designated as civil rather than criminal. The Juvenile Court is theoretically engaged in determining the needs of the child and of society rather than adjudicating criminal conduct. The objectives are to provide measures of guidance and rehabilitation for the child and protection for society, not to fix criminal responsibility, guilt and punishment. The State is *parens patriae* rather than prosecuting attorney and judge. But the admonition to function in a "parental" relationship is not an invitation to procedural arbitrariness.

(2.) Because the State is supposed to proceed in respect of the child as *parens patriae* and not as adversary, courts have relied on the premise that the proceedings are "civil" in nature and not criminal, and have asserted that the child cannot complain of the deprivation of important rights available in criminal cases. It has been asserted that he can claim only the fundamental due process right to fair treatment. For example, it has been held that he is not entitled to bail; to indictment by grand jury; to a speedy and public trial; to trial by jury; to immunity against self-incrimination; to confrontation of his accusers; and in some jurisdictions . . . that he is not entitled to counsel.

While there can be no doubt of the original laudable purpose of juvenile courts, studies and critiques in recent years raise serious questions as to whether actual performance measures well enough against theoretical purpose to make tolerable the immunity of the process from the reach of constitutional guaranties applicable to adults. There is much evidence that some juvenile courts, including that of the District of Columbia, lack the personnel, facilities and techniques to perform adequately as representatives of the State in a *parens patriae* capacity, at least with respect to children charged with law violation. There is evidence, in fact, that there may be grounds for concern that the child receives the worst of both worlds: that he gets neither the protections accorded to adults nor the solicitous care and regenerative treatment postulated for children.

[handwritten margin note: "are not necessarily given adult court guaranties"]

This concern, however, does not induce us in this case to accept the invitation to rule that constitutional guaranties which would be applicable to adults charged with the serious offenses for which Kent was tried must be applied in juvenile court proceedings concerned with allegations of law violation. The Juvenile Court Act and the decisions of the United States Court of Appeals for the District of Columbia Circuit provide an adequate basis for decision of this case, and we go no further.

3. It is clear beyond dispute that the waiver of jurisdiction is a "critically important" action determining vitally important statutory rights of the juvenile. . . . The statutory scheme makes this plain. The Juvenile Court is vested with "original and exclusive jurisdiction" of the child. This jurisdiction confers special rights and immunities. He is as specified by the statute, shielded from publicity. He may be confined, but with rare exceptions he may not be jailed along with adults. He may be detained, but only until he is 21 years of age. The court is admonished by the statute to give preference to retaining the child in the custody of his parents "unless his welfare and the safety and protection of the public can not be adequately safeguarded without . . . removal." The child is protected against consequences of adult conviction such as the loss of civil rights, the use of adjudication against him in subsequent proceedings, and disqualification for public employment.

[handwritten margin note: "entitled to hearing"]

The net, therefore, is that petitioner—then a boy of 16—was by statute entitled to certain procedures and benefits as a consequence of his statutory right to the "exclusive" jurisdiction of the Juvenile Court. In these circumstances, considering particularly that decision as to waiver of jurisdiction and transfer of the matter to the District Court was potentially as important to petitioner as the difference between five years' confinement and a death sentence, we conclude that, as a condition to a valid waiver order, petitioner was entitled to a hearing, including access by his counsel to the social records and probation or similar reports which presumably are considered by the court, and to a statement of reasons for the Juvenile Court's decision. We believe that this result is required by the statute read in the context of constitutional principles relating to due process and the assistance of counsel.

. . .

We are of the opinion that the Court of Appeals misconceived the basic issue and the underlying values in this case. It did note, as another panel of the same court did a few months later in *Black* and *Watkins*, that the determination of whether to transfer a child from the statutory structure of the Juvenile Court to the criminal processes of the District Court is "critically important." We hold that it is, indeed, a "critically important" proceeding. The Juvenile Court Act confers upon the child a right to avail himself of that court's "exclusive" jurisdiction. As the Court of Appeals has said, "[I]t is implicit

Basis

in [the Juvenile Court] scheme that non-criminal treatment is to be the rule—and the adult criminal treatment, the exception which must be governed by the particular factors of individual cases."

. . .

. . . [W]e hold that it is incumbent upon the Juvenile Court to accompany its waiver order with a statement of the reasons or considerations therefor. We do not read the statute as requiring that this statement must be formal or that it should necessarily include conventional findings of fact. But the statement should be sufficient to demonstrate that the statutory requirement of "full investigation" has been met; and that the question has received the careful consideration of the Juvenile Court; and it must set forth the basis for the order with sufficient specificity to permit meaningful review.

requirements waiver

Correspondingly, we conclude that an opportunity for a hearing which may be informal, must be given the child prior to entry of a waiver order. . . .

The right to representation by counsel is not a formality. It is not a grudging gesture to a ritualistic requirement. It is of the essence of justice. Appointment of counsel without affording an opportunity for hearing on a "critically important" decision is tantamount to denial of counsel. There is no justification for the failure of the Juvenile Court to rule on the motion for hearing filed by petitioner's counsel, and it was error to fail to grant a hearing.

counsel

We do not mean by this to indicate that the hearing to be held must conform with all of the requirements of a criminal trial or even of the usual administrative hearing; but we do hold that the hearing must measure up to the essentials of due process and fair treatment.

With respect to access by the child's counsel to the social records of the child, we deem it obvious that since these are to be considered by the Juvenile Court in making its decision to waive they must be made available to the child's counsel. . . . [C]ounsel must be afforded to the child in waiver proceedings. Counsel, therefore, have a "legitimate interest" in the protection of the child, and must be afforded access to these records.

records

We do not agree with the Court of Appeals' statement attempting to justify denial of access to these records, that counsel's role is limited to presenting "to the court anything on behalf of the child which might help the court in arriving at a decision; it is not to denigrate the staff's submissions and recommendations." On the contrary, if the staff's submissions include materials which are susceptible to challenge or impeachment, it is precisely the role of counsel to "denigrate" such matter. There is no irrebuttable presumption of accuracy attached to staff reports. If a decision on waiver is "critically important" it is equally of "critical importance" that the material submitted to the judge—which is protected by the statute only against "indiscriminate" inspection—be subjected, within reasonable limits having regard to the theory of the Juvenile Court Act, to examination, criticism and refutation. While the Juvenile Court judge may, of course, receive *ex parte* analyses and recommendations from his staff, he may not, for purposes of a decision on waiver, receive and rely upon secret information, whether emanating from his staff or otherwise. The Juvenile Court is governed in this respect by the established principles which control courts and quasi-judicial agencies of the Government.

For the reasons stated, we conclude that the Court of Appeals and the District Court erred in sustaining the validity of the waiver by the Juvenile Court. . . .

Ordinarily we would reverse the Court of Appeals and direct the District Court to remand the case to the Juvenile Court for a new determination of waiver. If on remand the decision were against waiver, the indictment in the District Court would be dismissed. However, petitioner has now passed the age of 21 and the Juvenile Court can no longer exercise jurisdiction over him. In view of the unavailability of a redetermination of the waiver question by the Juvenile Court, it is urged by petitioner that the conviction should be vacated and the indictment dismissed. . . . [We] do not consider it appropriate to grant this drastic relief.[33] Accordingly, we vacate the order of the Court of Appeals and the judgment of the District Court and remand the case to the District Court for a hearing *de novo* on waiver, consistent with this opinion. If that court finds that waiver was inappropriate, petitioner's conviction must be vacated. If, however, it finds that the waiver order was proper when originally made, the District Court may proceed, after consideration of such motions as counsel may make and such further proceedings, if any, as may be warranted to enter an appropriate judgment.

APPENDIX TO OPINION OF THE COURT

Policy Memorandum No. 7, November 30, 1959.

The authority of the Judge of the Juvenile Court of the District of Columbia to waive or transfer jurisdiction to the U. S. District Court for the District of Columbia is contained in the Juvenile Court Act (§ 11–914 D.C.Code, 1951 Ed.). This section permits the Judge to waive jurisdiction "after full investigation" in the case of any child "sixteen years of age or older [who is] charged with an offense which would amount to a felony in the case of an adult, or any child charged with an offense which if committed by an adult is punishable by death or life imprisonment."

The statute sets forth no specific standards for the exercise of this important discretionary act, but leaves the formulation of such criteria to the Judge. A knowledge of the Judge's criteria is impor-

---

33. Petitioner is in St. Elizabeth's Hospital for psychiatric treatment as a result of the jury verdict on the rape charges.

tant to the child, his parents, his attorney, to the judges of the U. S. District Court for the District of Columbia, to the United States Attorney and his assistants and to the Metropolitan Police Department, as well as to the staff of this court, expecially the Juvenile Intake Section.

Therefore, the Judge has consulted with the Chief Judge and other judges of the U. S. District Court for the District of Columbia, with the United States Attorney, with representatives of the Bar, and with other groups concerned and has formulated the following criteria and principles concerning waiver of jurisdiction which are consistent with the basic aims and purposes of the Juvenile Court Act.

An offense falling within the statutory limitations (set forth above) will be waived if it has prosecutive merit and if it is heinous or of an aggravated character, or—even though less serious—if it represents a pattern of repeated offenses which indicate that the juvenile may be beyond rehabilitation under Juvenile Court procedures, or if the public needs the protection afforded by such action.

The determinative factors which will be considered by the Judge in deciding whether the Juvenile Court's jurisdiction over such offenses will be waived are the following:

1. The seriousness of the alleged offense to the community and whether the protection of the community requires waiver.

2. Whether the alleged offense was committed in an aggressive, violent, premeditated or willful manner.

3. Whether the alleged offense was against persons or against property, greater weight being given to offenses against persons especially if personal injury resulted.

4. The prosecutive merit of the complaint, i.e., whether there is evidence upon which a Grand Jury may be expected to return an indictment (to be determined by consultation with the United States Attorney).

5. The desirability of trial and disposition of the entire offense in one court when the juvenile's associates in the alleged offense are adults who will be charged with a crime in the U. S. District Court for the District of Columbia.

6. The sophistication and maturity of the juvenile as determined by consideration of his home, environmental situation, emotional attitude and pattern of living.

7. The record and previous history of the juvenile, including previous contacts with the Youth Aid Division, other law enforcement agencies, juvenile courts and the other jurisdictions, prior periods of probation to this Court, or prior commitments to juvenile institutions.

8. The prospects for adequate protection of the public and the likelihood of reasonable rehabilitation of the juvenile (if he is found to have committed the alleged offense) by the use of procedures, services and facilities currently available to the Juvenile Court.

It will be the responsibility of any officer of the Court's staff assigned to make the investigation of any complaint in which waiver of jurisdiction is being considered to develop fully all available information which may bear upon the criteria and factors set forth above. Although not all such factors will be involved in an individual case, the Judge will consider the relevant factors in a specific case before reaching a conclusion to waive juvenile jurisdiction and transfer the case to the U. S. District Court for the District of Columbia for trial under the adult procedures of that Court.

MR. JUSTICE STEWART, with whom MR. JUSTICE BLACK, MR. JUSTICE HARLAN and MR. JUSTICE WHITE join, dissenting.

This case involves the construction of a statute applicable only to the District of Columbia. Our general practice is to leave undisturbed decisions of the Court of Appeals for the District of Columbia Circuit concerning the import of legislation governing the affairs of the District. It appears, however, that two cases decided by the Court of Appeals subsequent to its decision in the present case may have considerably modified the court's construction of the statute. Therefore, I would vacate this judgment and remand the case to the Court of Appeals for reconsideration in the light of its subsequent decisions, Watkins v. United States, 119 U.S.App.D.C. 409, 343 F.2d 278, and Black v. United States, 122 U.S.App.D.C. 393, 355 F.2d 104.

NOTES

(1) For a full discussion of the transfer of juveniles to be tried in adult court, see Chapter VII, infra.

(2) What is the constitutional basis for the *Kent* holding? Does *Kent* apply in jurisdictions other than the District of Columbia? Immediately after the decision, some states read *Kent* broadly while others limited it to an exercise of the United States Supreme Court's supervisory power over the administration of justice in the District of Columbia.

(3) On remand the United States District Court, after a full hearing with access by Kent's counsel to all social reports, concluded that the waiver by the juvenile court had been proper in the first place and affirmed the convictions. This conclusion was reversed by the Court of Appeals as being inappropriate under the circumstances. 401 F.2d 408 (D.C.Cir. 1968).

(4) The Court of Appeals in *Kent* had held the D.C. statute "ambiguous" as to the right of the juvenile's counsel to access to social reports. It said that Kent's attorney wanted the opportunity to challenge the social records "presumably in a manner akin to cross-examination". 343 F.2d at 258. The Court of Appeals went on to decry "the kind of adversarial tactics the system is designed to avoid." Counsel may bring forward affirmative information that could help the court but should not "denigrate the staff's submissions and recommendations." The United States Supreme Court strongly disagreed.

What is the proper role of counsel with regard to social reports? Will sources be less willing to speak to probation staff if they know that their opinions will be subject to inspection and cross-examination? What kinds of "submissions" should defense counsel challenge? See J. Areen, Representing Juveniles in Neglect, PINS and Delinquency Cases in the District of Columbia (1975).

(5) Kent's attorney also challenged certain post-arrest police practices. The Court did not rule on these claims because it grounded its decision in the impropriety of the waiver of juvenile court jurisdiction. In what might be considered a prelude to *Gault*, which would follow in the next term, Justice Fortas remarked in passing:

> These contentions raise problems of substantial concern as to the construction of and compliance with the Juvenile Court Act. They also suggest basic issues as to the justifiability of affording a juvenile less protection than is accorded to adults suspected of criminal offenses, particularly where, as here, there is an absence of any indication that the denial of rights available to adults was offset, mitigated or explained by action of the Government, as *parens patriae*, evidencing the special solicitude for juveniles commanded by the Juvenile Court Act. However, because we remand the case on account of the procedural error with respect to waiver of jurisdiction, we do not pass upon these questions.

387 U.S. 551.

IN RE GAULT

Supreme Court of the United States, 1967.
387 U.S. 1, 87 S.Ct. 1428, 18 L.Ed.2d 527.

MR. JUSTICE FORTAS delivered the opinion of the Court.

This is an appeal under 28 U.S.C. § 1257(2) from a judgment of the Supreme Court of Arizona affirming the dismissal of a petition for a writ of habeas corpus. 99 Ariz. 181, 407 P.2d 760 (1965). The petition sought the release of Gerald Francis Gault, appellants' 15-year-old son, who had been committed as a juvenile delinquent to the State Industrial School by the Juvenile Court of Gila County, Arizona. The Supreme Court of Arizona affirmed dismissal of the writ against various arguments which included an attack upon the constitutionality of the Arizona Juvenile Code because of its alleged denial of procedural due process rights to juveniles charged with being "delinquents." The court agreed that the constitutional guarantee of due process of law is applicable in such proceedings. It held that Arizona's Juvenile Code is to be read as "impliedly" implementing the "due process concept." It then proceeded to identify and describe "the particular elements which constitute due process in a juvenile hearing." It concluded that the proceedings ending in commitment of Gerald Gault did not offend those requirements. We do not agree, and we reverse. We begin with a statement of the facts.

I.

On Monday, June 8, 1964, at about 10 a.m., Gerald Francis Gault and a friend, Ronald Lewis, were taken into custody by the Sheriff of Gila County. Gerald was then still subject to a six months' probation

FACTS

V

order which had been entered on February 25, 1964, as a result of his having been in the company of another boy who had stolen a wallet from a lady's purse. The police action on June 8 was taken as the result of a verbal complaint by a neighbor of the boys, Mrs. Cook, about a telephone call made to her in which the caller or callers made lewd or indecent remarks. It will suffice for purposes of this opinion to say that the remarks or questions put to her were of the irritatingly offensive, adolescent, sex variety.

At the time Gerald was picked up, his mother and father were both at work. No notice that Gerald was being taken into custody was left at the home. No other steps were taken to advise them that their son had, in effect, been arrested. Gerald was taken to the Children's Detention Home. When his mother arrived home at about 6 o'clock, Gerald was not there. Gerald's older brother was sent to look for him at the trailer home of the Lewis family. He apparently learned then that Gerald was in custody. He so informed his mother. The two of them went to the Detention Home. The deputy probation officer, Flagg, who was also superintendent of the Detention Home, told Mrs. Gault "why Jerry was there" and said that a hearing would be held in Juvenile Court at 3 o'clock the following day, June 9.

Officer Flagg filed a petition with the court on the hearing day, June 9, 1964. It was not served on the Gaults. Indeed, none of them saw this petition until the habeas corpus hearing on August 17, 1964. The petition was entirely formal. It made no reference to any factual basis for the judicial action which it initiated. It recited only that "said minor is under the age of eighteen years, and is in need of the protection of this Honorable Court; [and that] said minor is a delinquent minor." It prayed for a hearing and an order regarding "the care and custody of said minor." Officer Flagg executed a formal affidavit in support of the petition.

On June 9, Gerald, his mother, his older brother, and Probation Officers Flagg and Henderson appeared before the Juvenile Judge in chambers. Gerald's father was not there. He was at work out of the city. Mrs. Cook, the complainant, was not there. No one was sworn at this hearing. No transcript or recording was made. No memorandum or record of the substance of the proceedings was prepared. Our information about the proceedings and the subsequent hearing on June 15, derives entirely from the testimony of the Juvenile Court Judge, Mr. and Mrs. Gault and Officer Flagg at the habeas corpus proceeding conducted two months later. From this, it appears that at the June 9 hearing Gerald was questioned by the judge about the telephone call. There was conflict as to what he said. His mother recalled that Gerald said he only dialed Mrs. Cook's number and handed the telephone to his friend, Ronald. Officer Flagg recalled that Gerald had admitted making the lewd remarks. Judge McGhee testified that Gerald "admitted making one of these [lewd] statements." At the conclusion of the hearing, the judge said he would "think about it." Gerald was taken back to the Detention Home. He was not sent to his own home with his parents. On June 11 or 12, after having been detained since June 8, Gerald was released and driven home.[2] There is no explanation in the record as to why he was kept in the Detention Home or why he was released. At 5 p.m. on the day of Gerald's release, Mrs. Gault received a note signed by Officer Flagg. It was on plain paper, not letterhead. Its entire text was as follows:

"Mrs. Gault:

"Judge McGhee has set Monday June 15, 1964 at 11:00 A.M. as the date and time for further Hearings on Gerald's delinquency

"/s/Flagg"

At the appointed time on Monday, June 15, Gerald, his father and mother, Ronald Lewis and his father, and Officers Flagg and Henderson were present before Judge McGhee. Witnesses at the habeas corpus proceeding differed in their recollections of Gerald's testimony at the June 15 hearing. Mr. and Mrs. Gault recalled that Gerald again testified that he had only dialed the number and that the other boy had made the remarks. Officer Flagg agreed that at this hearing Gerald did not admit making the lewd remarks. But Judge McGhee recalled that "there was some admission again of some of the lewd statements. He—he didn't admit any of the more serious lewd statements." Again, the complainant, Mrs. Cook, was not present. Mrs. Gault asked that Mrs. Cook be present "so she could see which boy that done the talking, the dirty talking over the phone." The Juvenile Judge said "she didn't have to be present at that hearing." The judge did not speak to Mrs. Cook or communicate with her at any time. Probation Officer Flagg had talked to her once—over the telephone on June 9.

At this June 15 hearing a "referral report" made by the probation officers was filed with the court, although not disclosed to Gerald or his parents. This listed the charge as "Lewd Phone Calls." At the conclusion of the hearing, the judge committed Gerald as a juvenile delinquent to the State Industrial School "for the period of his minority [that is, until 21], unless sooner discharged by due process of law." An order to that effect was entered. It recites that "after a full hearing and due deliberation the Court finds that said minor is a delinquent child, and that said minor is of the age of 15 years."

No appeal is permitted by Arizona law in juvenile cases. On August 3, 1964, a petition for a writ of habeas corpus was filed with the Supreme Court of Arizona and referred by it to the Superior Court for hearing.

At the habeas corpus hearing on August 17, Judge McGhee was vigorously cross-examined as to the basis for his actions. He testi-

2. There is a conflict between the recollection of Mrs. Gault and that of Officer Flagg. Mrs. Gault testified that Gerald was released on Friday, June 12, Officer Flagg that it had been on Thursday, June 11. This was from memory; he had no record, and the note hereafter referred to was undated.

fied that he had taken into account the fact that Gerald was on probation. He was asked "under what section of . . . the code you
found the boy delinquent?"

His answer is set forth in the margin.[5] In substance, he concluded that Gerald came within ARS § 8–201–6(a), which specifies that a
"delinquent child" includes one "who has violated a law of the state
or an ordinance or regulation of a political subdivision thereof." The
law which Gerald was found to have violated is ARS § 13–377. This
section of the Arizona Criminal Code provides that a person who "in
the presence or hearing of any woman or child . . . uses vulgar,
abusive or obscene language, is guilty of a misdemeanor. . . ."
The penalty specified in the Criminal Code, which would apply to an
adult, is $5 to $50, or imprisonment for not more than two months.
. . .

. . .

The Superior Court dismissed the writ, and appellants sought review in the Arizona Supreme Court. That court stated that it considered appellants' assignments of error as urging (1) that the Juvenile
Code, ARS § 8–201 to § 8–239, is unconstitutional because it does not
require that parents and children be apprised of the specific charges,
does not require proper notice of a hearing, and does not provide for
an appeal; and (2) that the proceedings and order relating to Gerald
constituted a denial of due process of law because of the absence of
adequate notice of the charge and the hearing; failure to notify appellants of certain constitutional rights including the rights to counsel
and to confrontation, and the privilege against self-incrimination; the
use of unsworn hearsay testimony; and the failure to make a record
of the proceedings. Appellants further asserted that it was error for
the Juvenile Court to remove Gerald from the custody of his parents
without a showing and finding of their unsuitability, and alleged a
miscellany of other errors under state law.

The Supreme Court handed down an elaborate and wide-ranging
opinion affirming dismissal of the writ and stating the court's conclusions as to the issues raised by appellants and other aspects of the
juvenile process. In their jurisdictional statement and brief in this
Court, appellants do not urge upon us all of the points passed upon
by the Supreme Court of Arizona. They urge that we hold the Juvenile Code of Arizona invalid on its face or as applied in this case because, contrary to the Due Process Clause of the Fourteenth Amendment, the juvenile is taken from the custody of his parents and

5. "Q. All right. Now, Judge,
would you tell me under what section of
the law or tell me under what section
of—of the code you found the boy delinquent?

"A. Well, there is a—I think it
amounts to disturbing the peace. I can't
give you the section, but I can tell you
the law, that when one person uses lewd
language in the presence of another person, that it can amount to—and I consider that when a person makes it over the
phone, that it is considered in the presence, I might be wrong, that is one section. The other section upon which I consider the boy delinquent is Section 8–201,
Subsection (d), habitually involved in immoral matters."

committed to a state institution pursuant to proceedings in which the Juvenile Court has virtually unlimited discretion, and in which the following basic rights are denied:

1. Notice of the charges;

2. Right to counsel;

3. Right to confrontation and cross-examination;

4. Privilege against self-incrimination;

5. Right to a transcript of the proceedings; and

6. Right to appellate review.

. . .

II.

The Supreme Court of Arizona held that due process of law is requisite to the constitutional validity of proceedings in which a court reaches the conclusion that a juvenile has been at fault, has engaged in conduct prohibited by law, or has otherwise misbehaved with the consequence that he is committed to an institution in which his freedom is curtailed. This conclusion is in accord with the decisions of a number of courts under both federal and state constitutions.

This Court has not heretofore decided the precise question. In Kent v. United States, 383 U.S. 541, 86 S.Ct. 1045, 16 L.Ed.2d 84 (1966), we considered the requirements for a valid waiver of the "exclusive" jurisdiction of the Juvenile Court of the District of Columbia so that a juvenile could be tried in the adult criminal court of the District. Although our decision turned upon the language of the statute, we emphasized the necessity that "the basic requirements of due process and fairness" be satisfied in such proceedings. . . . [N]either the Fourteenth Amendment nor the Bill of Rights is for adults alone.

We do not in this opinion consider the impact of these constitutional provisions upon the totality of the relationship of the juvenile and the state. We do not even consider the entire process relating to juvenile "delinquents." For example, we are not here concerned with the procedures or constitutional rights applicable to the pre-judicial stages of the juvenile process, nor do we direct our attention to the post-adjudicative or dispositional process. We consider only the problems presented to us by this case. These relate to the proceedings by which a determination is made as to whether a juvenile is a "delinquent" as a result of alleged misconduct on his part, with the consequence that he may be committed to a state institution. As to these proceedings, there appears to be little current dissent from the proposition that the Due Process Clause has a role to play.[11] The problem

11. See Report by the President's Commission on Law Enforcement and Administration of Justice, "The Challenge of Crime in a Free Society" (1967) (hereinafter cited as Nat'l Crime Comm'n Report), pp. 81, 85–86; Standards, p. 71;

is to ascertain the precise impact of the due process requirement upon such proceedings.

From the inception of the juvenile court system, wide differences have been tolerated—indeed insisted upon—between the procedural rights accorded to adults and those of juveniles. In practically all jurisdictions, there are rights granted to adults which are withheld from juveniles. In addition to the specific problems involved in the present case, for example, it has been held that the juvenile is not entitled to bail, to indictment by grand jury, to a public trial or to trial by jury. It is frequent practice that rules governing the arrest and interrogation of adults by the police are not observed in the case of juveniles.

The history and theory underlying this development are well-known, but a recapitulation is necessary for purposes of this opinion. The juvenile court movement began in this country at the end of the last century. From the Juvenile Court statute adopted in Illinois in 1899, the system has spread to every State in the Union, the District of Columbia, and Puerto Rico.[14] The constitutionality of Juvenile Court laws has been sustained in over 40 jurisdictions against a variety of attacks.

The early reformers were appalled by adult procedures and penalties, and by the fact that children could be given long prison sentences and mixed in jails with hardened criminals. They were profoundly convinced that society's duty to the child could not be confined by the concept of justice alone. They believed that society's role was not to ascertain whether the child was "guilty" or "innocent," but "What is he, how has he become what he is, and what had

---

Gardner, The Kent Case and the Juvenile Court: A Challenge to Lawyers, 52 A.B.A.J. 923 (1966); Paulsen, Fairness to the Juvenile Offender, 41 Minn.L.Rev. 547 (1957); Ketcham, The Legal Renaissance in the Juvenile Court, 60 Nw.U.L.Rev. 585 (1965); Allen, The Borderland of Criminal Justice (1964), pp. 19–23; Harvard Law Review Note, p. 791; Note, Rights and Rehabilitation in the Juvenile Courts, 67 Col.L.Rev. 281 (1967); Comment, Criminal Offenders in the Juvenile Court: More Brickbats and Another Proposal, 114 U.Pa.L.Rev. 1171 (1966).

14. See National Counsel of Juvenile Court Judges, Directory and Manual (1964), p. 1. The number of Juvenile Judges as of 1964 is listed as 2,987, of whom 213 are full-time Juvenile Court Judges. Id., at 305. The Nat'l Crime Comm'n Report indicates that half of these judges have no undergraduate degree, a fifth have no college education at all, a fifth are not members of the bar, and three-quarters devote less than one-quarter of their time to juvenile matters.

See also McCune, Profile of the Nation's Juvenile Court Judges (monograph, George Washington University, Center for the Behavioral Sciences, 1965), which is a detailed statistical study of Juvenile Court Judges, and indicates additionally that about a quarter of these judges have no law school training at all. About one-third of all judges have no probation and social work staff available to them; between eighty and ninety percent have no available psychologist or psychiatrist. Ibid. It has been observed that while "good will, compassion, and similar virtues are . . . admirably prevalent throughout the system . . . expertise, the keystone of the whole venture, is lacking." Harvard Law Review Note, p. 809. In 1965, over 697,000 delinquency cases (excluding traffic) were disposed of in these courts, involving some 601,000 children, or 2% of all children between 10 and 17. Juvenile Court Statistics—1965, Children's Bureau Statistical Series No. 85 (1966), p. 2.

best be done in his interest and in the interest of the state to save him from a downward career."[16] The child—essentially good, as they saw it—was to be made "to feel that he is the object of [the state's] care and solicitude,"[17] not that he was under arrest or on trial. The rules of criminal procedure were therefore altogether inapplicable. The apparent rigidities, technicalities, and harshness which they observed in both substantive and procedural criminal law were therefore to be discarded. The idea of crime and punishment was to be abandoned. The child was to be "treated" and "rehabilitated" and the procedures, from apprehension through institutionalization, were to be "clinical" rather than punitive.

These results were to be achieved, without coming to conceptual and constitutional grief, by insisting that the proceedings were not adversary, but that the state was proceeding as parens patriae.[18] The Latin phrase proved to be a great help to those who sought to rationalize the exclusion of juveniles from the constitutional scheme; but its meaning is murky and its historic credentials are of dubious relevance. The phrase was taken from chancery practice, where, however, it was used to describe the power of the state to act in loco parentis for the purpose of protecting the property interests and the person of the child. But there is no trace of the doctrine in the history of criminal jurisprudence. At common law, children under seven were considered incapable of possessing criminal intent. Beyond that age, they were subjected to arrest, trial, and in theory to punishment like adult offenders. In these old days, the state was not deemed to have authority to accord them fewer procedural rights than adults.

The right of the state, as parens patriae, to deny to the child procedural rights available to his elders was elaborated by the assertion that a child, unlike an adult, has a right "not to liberty but to custody." He can be made to attorn to his parents, to go to school, etc. If his parents default in effectively performing their custodial functions—that is, if the child is "delinquent"—the state may intervene. In doing so, it does not deprive the child of any rights, because he has none. It merely provides the "custody" to which the child is entitled. On this basis, proceedings involving juveniles were described as "civil" not "criminal" and therefore not subject to the requirements which restrict the state when it seeks to deprive a person of his liberty.

---

16. Julian Mack, The Juvenile Court, 23 Harv.L.Rev. 104, 119–120 (1909).

17. Id., at 120.

18. Id., at 109; Paulsen, [Kent v. United States: The Constitutional Context of Juvenile Cases, 1967 Sup.Ct.Review 167], at 173–174. There seems to have been little early constitutional objection to the special procedures of juvenile courts. But see Waite, How Far Can Court Procedure Be Socialized Without Impairing Individual Rights, 12 J.Crim.L. & Criminology 339, 340 (1922): "The Court which must direct its procedure even apparently to do something *to* a child because of what he *has done*, is parted from the court which is avowedly concerned only with doing something *for* a child because of what he *is* and *needs*, by a gulf too wide to be bridged by any humanity which the judge may introduce into his hearings, or by the habitual use of corrective rather than punitive methods after conviction."

no med model theory has resulted in unfairness

Accordingly, the highest motives and most enlightened impulses led to a peculiar system for juveniles, unknown to our law in any comparable context. The constitutional and theoretical basis for this peculiar system is—to say the least—debatable. And in practice, as we remarked in the Kent case, supra, the results have not been entirely satisfactory.[23] Juvenile Court history has again demonstrated that unbridled discretion, however benevolently motivated, is frequently a poor substitute for principle and procedure. In 1937, Dean Pound wrote: "The powers of the Star Chamber were a trifle in comparison with those of our juvenile courts . . . ."[24] The absence of substantive standards has not necessarily meant that children receive careful, compassionate, individualized treatment. The absence of procedural rules based upon constitutional principle has not always produced fair, efficient, and effective procedures. Departures from established principles of due process have frequently resulted not in enlightened procedure, but in arbitrariness. The Chairman of the Pennsylvania Council of Juvenile Court Judges has recently observed: "Unfortunately, loose procedures, high-handed methods and crowded court calendars, either singly or in combination, all too often, have resulted in depriving some juveniles of fundamental rights that have resulted in a denial of due process."

Failure to observe the fundamental requirements of due process has resulted in instances, which might have been avoided, of unfairness to individuals and inadequate or inaccurate findings of fact and unfortunate prescriptions of remedy. Due process of law is the primary and indispensable foundation of individual freedom. It is the basic and essential term in the social compact which defines the rights of the individual and delimits the powers which the state may exercise. As Mr. Justice Frankfurter has said: "The history of

23. "There is evidence . . . that there may be grounds for concern that the child receives the worst of both worlds: that he gets neither the protections accorded to adults nor the solicitous care and regenerative treatment postulated for children." 383 U.S. at 556, 86 S.Ct. at 1054, citing Handler, The Juvenile Court and the Adversary System: Problems of Function and Form, 1965 Wis.L.Rev. 7; Harvard Law Review Note; and various congressional materials set forth in 383 U.S. at 546, note 5, 86 S.Ct. at 1050 n. 5.

On the other hand, while this opinion and much recent writing concentrate upon the failures of the Juvenile Court system to live up to the expectations of its founders, the observation of the Nat'l Crime Comm'n Report should be kept in mind:

"Although its shortcomings are many and its results too often disap-

pointing, the juvenile justice system in many cities is operated by people who are better educated and more highly skilled, can call on more and better facilities and services, and has more ancillary agencies to which to refer its clientele than its adult counterpart." Id., at 78.

24. Foreword to Young, Social Treatment in Probation and Delinquency (1937), p. xxvii. The 1965 Report of the United States Commission on Civil Rights, "Law Enforcement—A Report on Equal Protection in the South," pp. 80–83, documents numerous instances in which "local authorities used the broad discretion afforded them by the absence of safeguards [in the juvenile process]" to punish, intimidate, and obstruct youthful participants in civil rights demonstrations. See also Paulsen, Juvenile Courts, Family Courts, and the Poor Man, 54 Calif.L.Rev. 694, 707–709 (1966).

American freedom is, in no small measure, the history of procedure." But in addition, the procedural rules which have been fashioned from the generality of due process are our best instruments for the distillation and evaluation of essential facts from the conflicting welter of data that life and our adversary methods present. It is these instruments of due process which enhance the possibility that truth will emerge from the confrontation of opposing versions and conflicting data. "Procedure is to law what 'scientific method' is to science."

It is claimed that juveniles obtain benefits from the special procedures applicable to them which more than offset the disadvantages of denial of the substance of normal due process. As we shall discuss, the observance of due process standards, intelligently and not ruthlessly administered, will not compel the States to abandon or displace any of the substantive benefits of the juvenile process. But it is important, we think, that the claimed benefits of the juvenile process should be candidly appraised. Neither sentiment nor folklore should cause us to shut our eyes, for example, to such startling findings as that reported in an exceptionally reliable study of repeaters or recidivism conducted by the Stanford Research Institute for the President's Commission on Crime in the District of Columbia. This Commission's Report states:

> "In fiscal 1966 approximately 66 percent of the 16- and 17-year-old juveniles referred to the court by the Youth Aid Division had been before the court previously. In 1965, 56 percent of those in the Receiving Home were repeaters. The SRI study revealed that 61 percent of the sample Juvenile Court referrals in 1965 had been previously referred at least once and that 42 percent had been referred at least twice before." Id., at 773.

Certainly, these figures and the high crime rates among juveniles . . . could not lead us to conclude that the absence of constitutional protections reduces crime, or that the juvenile system, functioning free of constitutional inhibitions as it has largely done, is effective to reduce crime or rehabilitate offenders. We do not mean by this to denigrate the juvenile court process or to suggest that there are not aspects of the juvenile system relating to offenders which are valuable. But the features of the juvenile system which its proponents have asserted are of unique benefit will not be impaired by constitutional domestication. For example, the commendable principles relating to the processing and treatment of juveniles separately from adults are in no way involved or affected by the procedural issues under discussion.[30] Further, we are told that one of the important

---

30. Here again, however, there is substantial question as to whether fact and pretension, with respect to the separate handling and treatment of children, coincide.

While we are concerned only with procedure before the juvenile court in this case, it should be noted that to the extent that the special procedures for juveniles are thought to be justified by the special consideration and treatment afforded them, there is reason to doubt that juveniles always receive the benefits of such a *quid pro quo*.

In fact, some courts have recently indicated that appropriate treatment is es-

benefits of the special juvenile court procedures is that they avoid classifying the juvenile as a "criminal." The juvenile offender is now classed as a "delinquent." There is, of course, no reason why this should not continue. It is disconcerting, however, that this term has come to involve only slightly less stigma than the term "criminal" applied to adults.[31] It is also emphasized that in practically all jurisdictions, statutes provide that an adjudication of the child as a delinquent shall not operate as a civil disability or disqualify him for civil service appointment. There is no reason why the application of due process requirements should interfere with such provisions.

Beyond this, it is frequently said that juveniles are protected by the process from disclosure of their deviational behavior. As the Supreme Court of Arizona phrased it in the present case, the summary procedures of Juvenile Courts are sometimes defended by a statement that it is the law's policy "to hide youthful errors from the full gaze of the public and bury them in the graveyard of the forgotten past." This claim of secrecy, however, is more rhetoric than reality. Disclosure of court records is discretionary with the judge in most jurisdictions. Statutory restrictions almost invariably apply only to the court records, and even as to those the evidence is that many courts routinely furnish information to the FBI and the military, and on request to government agencies and even to private employers. Of more importance are police records. In most States the police keep a complete file of juvenile "police contacts" and have complete discretion as to disclosure of juvenile records. Police departments receive requests for information from the FBI and other law-enforcement agencies, the Armed Forces, and social service agencies, and most of them generally comply. Private employers word their application forms to produce information concerning juvenile arrests and court proceedings, and in some jurisdictions information concerning juvenile police contacts is furnished private employers as well as government agencies.

In any event, there is no reason why, consistently with due process, a State cannot continue, if it deem appropriate, to provide and to improve provision for the confidentiality of records of police contacts and court action relating to juveniles. . . . .

Further, it is urged that the juvenile benefits from informal proceedings in the court. The early conception of the Juvenile Court proceeding was one in which a fatherly judge touched the heart and conscience of the erring youth by talking over his problems, by paternal advice and admonition, and in which, in extreme situations, benev

---

sential to the validity of juvenile custody, and therefore that a juvenile may challenge the validity of his custody on the ground that he is not in fact receiving any special treatment.

31. "[T]he word 'delinquent' has today developed such invidious connotations that the terminology is in the pro

cess of being altered; the new descriptive phrase is 'persons in need of supervision,' usually shortened to 'pins.'" Harvard Law Review Note, p. 799, n. 140. The N.Y. Family Court Act § 712 distinguishes between "delinquents" and "persons in need of supervision."

olent and wise institutions of the State provided guidance and help "to save him from a downward career." Then, as now, goodwill and compassion were admirably prevalent. But recent studies have, with surprising unanimity, entered sharp dissent as to the validity of this gentle conception. They suggest that the appearance as well as the actuality of fairness, impartiality and orderliness—in short, the essentials of due process—may be a more impressive and more therapeutic attitude so far as the juvenile is concerned. . . . While due process requirements will, in some instances, introduce a degree of order and regularity to Juvenile Court proceedings to determine delinquency, and in contested cases will introduce some elements of the adversary system, nothing will require that the conception of the kindly juvenile judge be replaced by its opposite, nor do we here rule upon the question whether ordinary due process requirements must be observed with respect to hearings to determine the disposition of the delinquent child.

Ultimately, however, we confront the reality of that portion of the Juvenile Court process with which we deal in this case. A boy is charged with misconduct. The boy is committed to an institution where he may be restrained of liberty for years. It is of no constitutional consequence—and of limited practical meaning—that the institution to which he is committed is called an Industrial School. The fact of the matter is that, however euphemistic the title, a "receiving home" or an "industrial school" for juveniles is an institution of confinement in which the child is incarcerated for a greater or lesser time. His world becomes "a building with whitewashed walls, regimented routine and institutional hours . . . ." Instead of mother and father and sisters and brothers and friends and classmates, his world is peopled by guards, custodians, state employees, and "delinquents" confined with him for anything from waywardness to rape and homicide.

In view of this, it would be extraordinary if our Constitution did not require the procedural regularity and the exercise of care implied in the phrase "due process." Under our Constitution, the condition of being a boy does not justify a kangaroo court. The traditional ideas of Juvenile Court procedure, indeed, contemplated that time would be available and care would be used to establish precisely what the juvenile did and why he did it—was it a prank of adolescence or a brutal act threatening serious consequences to himself or society unless corrected? Under traditional notions, one would assume that in a case like that of Gerald Gault, where the juvenile appears to have a home, a working mother and father, and an older brother, the Juvenile Judge would have made a careful inquiry and judgment as to the possibility that the boy could be disciplined and dealt with at home, despite his previous transgressions. Indeed, so far as appears in the record before us, except for some conversation with Gerald about his school work and his "wanting to go to . . . Grand Canyon with his father," the points to which the judge directed his attention were

220   *RESHAPING THE JUVENILE JUSTICE SYSTEM*

little different from those that would be involved in determining any charge of violation of a penal statute. The essential difference between Gerald's case and a normal criminal case is that safeguards available to adults were discarded in Gerald's case. The summary procedure as well as the long commitment was possible because Gerald was 15 years of age instead of over 18.

If Gerald had been over 18, he would not have been subject to Juvenile Court proceedings. For the particular offense immediately involved, the maximum punishment would have been a fine of $5 to $50, or imprisonment in jail for not more than two months. Instead, he was committed to custody for a maximum of six years. If he had been over 18 and had committed an offense to which such a sentence might apply, he would have been entitled to substantial rights under the Constitution of the United States as well as under Arizona's laws and constitution. The United States Constitution would guarantee him rights and protections with respect to arrest, search and seizure, and pretrial interrogation. It would assure him of specific notice of the charges and adequate time to decide his course of action and to prepare his defense. He would be entitled to clear advice that he could be represented by counsel, and, at least if a felony were involved, the State would be required to provide counsel if his parents were unable to afford it. If the court acted on the basis of his confession, careful procedures would be required to assure its voluntariness. If the case went to trial, confrontation and opportunity for cross-examination would be guaranteed. So wide a gulf between the State's treatment of the adult and of the child requires a bridge sturdier than mere verbiage, and reasons more persuasive than cliché can provide. . . .

. . . .

We now turn to the specific issues which are presented to us in the present case.

III.

NOTICE OF CHARGES

. . .

We cannot agree with the court's conclusion that adequate notice was given in this case. Notice, to comply with due process requirements, must be given sufficiently in advance of scheduled court proceedings so that reasonable opportunity to prepare will be afforded, and it must "set forth the alleged misconduct with particularity." It is obvious, as we have discussed above, that no purpose of shielding the child from the public stigma of knowledge of his having been taken into custody and scheduled for hearing is served by the procedure approved by the court below. The "initial hearing" in the present case was a hearing on the merits. Notice at that time is not timely;

and even if there were a conceivable purpose served by the deferral proposed by the court below, it would have to yield to the requirements that the child and his parents or guardian be notified, in writing, of the specific charge or factual allegations to be considered at the hearing, and that such written notice be given at the earliest practicable time, and in any event sufficiently in advance of the hearing to permit preparation. Due process of law requires notice of the sort we have described—that is, notice which would be deemed constitutionally adequate in a civil or criminal proceeding.

. . .

IV.

RIGHT TO COUNSEL

Appellants charge that the Juvenile Court proceedings were fatally defective because the court did not advise Gerald or his parents of their right to counsel, and proceeded with the hearing, the adjudication of delinquency and the order of commitment in the absence of counsel for the child and his parents or an express waiver of the right thereto. The Supreme Court of Arizona pointed out that "[t]here is disagreement [among the various jurisdictions] as to whether the court must advise the infant that he has a right to counsel." It noted its own decision . . . to the effect "that *the parents* of an infant in a juvenile proceeding cannot be denied representation by counsel of their choosing." (Emphasis added.) It referred to a provision of the Juvenile Code which it characterized as requiring "that the probation officer shall look after the interests of neglected, delinquent and dependent children," including representing their interests in court. The court argued that "The parent and the probation officer may be relied upon to protect the infant's interests." Accordingly it rejected the proposition that "due process requires that an infant have a right to counsel." It said that juvenile courts have the discretion, but not the duty, to allow such representation; it referred specifically to the situation in which the Juvenile Court discerns conflict between the child and his parents as an instance in which this discretion might be exercised. We do not agree. Probation officers, in the Arizona scheme, are also arresting officers. They initiate proceedings and file petitions which they verify, as here, alleging the delinquency of the child; and they testify, as here, against the child. And here the probation officer was also superintendent of the Detention Home. The probation officer cannot act as counsel for the child. His role in the adjudicatory hearing, by statute and in fact, is as arresting officer and witness against the child. Nor can the judge represent the child. There is no material difference in this respect between adult and juvenile proceedings of the sort here involved. In adult proceedings, this contention has been foreclosed by decisions of this Court. A proceeding where the issue is whether the child will be found to be "delinquent" and subjected to the loss of his liberty for years is comparable in seriousness to a felony prosecution. The juvenile needs the assistance of counsel to cope with problems of law, to make skilled inquiry into the facts, to insist upon regularity of the proceedings, and to ascertain whether he has a defense and to prepare and submit it. The child "requires the guiding hand of counsel at every step in the proceedings against him." . . .

During the last decade, court decisions, experts, and legislatures have demonstrated increasing recognition of this view. In at least one-third of the States, statutes now provide for the right of representation by retained counsel in juvenile delinquency proceedings, notice of the right, or assignment of counsel, or a combination of these. In other States, court rules have similar provisions.

The President's Crime Commission has recently recommended that in order to assure "procedural justice for the child," it is necessary that "Counsel . . . be appointed as a matter of course wherever coercive action is a possibility, without requiring any affirmative choice by child or parent." . . .

We conclude that the Due Process Clause of the Fourteenth Amendment requires that in respect of proceedings to determine delinquency which may result in commitment to an institution in which the juvenile's freedom is curtailed, the child and his parents must be notified to the child's right to be represented by counsel retained by them, or if they are unable to afford counsel, that counsel will be appointed to represent the child.

. . .

V.

CONFRONTATION, SELF-INCRIMINATION,
CROSS-EXAMINATION

Appellants urge that the writ of habeas corpus should have been granted because of the denial of the rights of confrontation and cross-examination in the Juvenile Court hearings, and because the privilege against self-incrimination was not observed. The Juvenile Court Judge testified at the habeas corpus hearing that he had proceeded on the basis of Gerald's admissions at the two hearings. Appellants attack this on the ground that the admissions were obtained in disregard of the privilege against self-incrimination.

. . .

We shall assume that Gerald made admissions of the sort described by the Juvenile Court Judge, as quoted above. Neither Gerald nor his parents were advised that he did not have to testify or make a statement, or that an incriminating statement might result in his commitment as a "delinquent."

The Arizona Supreme Court rejected appellants' contention that Gerald had a right to be advised that he need not incriminate himself.

It said: "We think the necessary flexibility for individualized treatment will be enhanced by a rule which does not require the judge to advise the infant of a privilege against self-incrimination."

In reviewing this conclusion of Arizona's Supreme Court, we emphasize again that we are here concerned only with a proceeding to determine whether a minor is a "delinquent" and which may result in commitment to a state institution. Specifically, the question is whether, in such a proceeding, an admission by the juvenile may be used against him in the absence of clear and unequivocal evidence that the admission was made with knowledge that he was not obliged to speak and would not be penalized for remaining silent. In light of Miranda v. Arizona, 384 U.S. 436, 86 S.Ct. 1602, 16 L.Ed.2d 694 (1966), we must also consider whether, if the privilege against self-incrimination is available, it can effectively be waived unless counsel is present or the right to counsel has been waived.

. . .

The privilege against self-incrimination is, of course, related to the question of the safeguards necessary to assure that admissions or confessions are reasonably trustworthy, that they are not the mere fruits of fear or coercion, but are reliable expressions of the truth. The roots of the privilege are, however, far deeper. They tap the basic stream of religious and political principle because the privilege reflects the limits of the individual's attornment to the state and—in a philosophical sense—insists upon the equality of the individual and the state. In other words, the privilege has a broader and deeper thrust than the rule which prevents the use of confessions which are the product of coercion because coercion is thought to carry with it the danger of unreliability. One of its purposes is to prevent the state, whether by force or by psychological domination, from overcoming the mind and will of the person under investigation and depriving him of the freedom to decide whether to assist the state in securing his conviction.

It would indeed be surprising if the privilege against self-incrimination were available to hardened criminals but not to children. The language of the Fifth Amendment, applicable to the States by operation of the Fourteenth Amendment, is unequivocal and without exception. . . .

. . .

Against the application to juveniles of the right to silence, it is argued that juvenile proceedings are "civil" and not "criminal," and therefore the privilege should not apply. It is true that the statement of the privilege in the Fifth Amendment, which is applicable to the States by reason of the Fourteenth Amendment, is that no person "shall be compelled in any *criminal case* to be a witness against himself." However, it is also clear that the availability of the privilege does not turn upon the type of proceeding in which its protection is invoked, but upon the nature of the statement or admission and the exposure which it invites. The privilege may, for example, be claimed in a civil or administrative proceeding, if the statement is or may be inculpatory.

It would be entirely unrealistic to carve out of the Fifth Amendment all statements by juveniles on the ground that these cannot lead to "criminal" involvement. In the first place, juvenile proceedings to determine "delinquency," which may lead to commitment to a state institution, must be regarded as "criminal" for purposes of the privilege against self-incrimination. To hold otherwise would be to disregard substance because of the feeble enticement of the "civil" label-of-convenience which has been attached to juvenile proceedings. Indeed, in over half of the States, there is not even assurance that the juvenile will be kept in separate institutions, apart from adult "criminals." In those States juveniles may be placed in or transferred to adult penal institutions after having been found "delinquent" by a juvenile court. For this purpose, at least, commitment is a deprivation of liberty. It is incarceration against one's will, whether it is called "criminal" or "civil." And our Constitution guarantees that no person shall be "compelled" to be a witness against himself when he is threatened with deprivation of his liberty—a command which this Court has broadly applied and generously implemented in accordance with the teaching of the history of the privilege and its great office in mankind's battle for freedom.

In addition, apart from the equivalence for this purpose of exposure to commitment as a juvenile delinquent and exposure to imprisonment as an adult offender, the fact of the matter is that there is little or no assurance in Arizona, as in most if not all of the States, that a juvenile apprehended and interrogated by the police or even by the Juvenile Court itself will remain outside of the reach of adult courts as a consequence of the offense for which he has been taken into custody. In Arizona, as in other States, provision is made for Juvenile Courts to relinquish or waive jurisdiction to the ordinary criminal courts. In the present case, when Gerald Gault was interrogated concerning violation of a section of the Arizona Criminal Code, it could not be certain that the Juvenile Court Judge would decide to "suspend" criminal prosecution in court for adults by proceeding to an adjudication in Juvenile Court.

It is also urged, as the Supreme Court of Arizona here asserted, that the juvenile and presumably his parents should not be advised of the juvenile's right to silence because confession is good for the child as the commencement of the assumed therapy of the juvenile court process, and he should be encouraged to assume an attitude of trust and confidence toward the officials of the juvenile process. This proposition has been subjected to widespread challenge on the basis of current reappraisals of the rhetoric and realities of the handling of juvenile offenders.

In fact, evidence is accumulating that confessions by juveniles do not aid in "individualized treatment," as the court below put it, and that compelling the child to answer questions, without warning or advice as to his right to remain silent, does not serve this or any other good purpose. In light of the observations of Wheeler and Cottrell, and others, it seems probable that where children are induced to confess by "paternal" urgings on the part of officials and the confession is then followed by disciplinary action, the child's reaction is likely to be hostile and adverse—the child may well feel that he has been led or tricked into confession and that despite his confession, he is being punished.

Further, authoritative opinion has cast formidable doubt upon the reliability and trustworthiness of "confessions" by children. . . .

The "confession" of Gerald Gault was first obtained by Officer Flagg, out of the presence of Gerald's parents, without counsel and without advising him of his right to silence, as far as appears. The judgment of the Juvenile Court was stated by the judge to be based on Gerald's admissions in court. Neither "admission" was reduced to writing, and, to say the least, the process by which the "admissions" were obtained and received must be characterized as lacking the certainty and order which are required of proceedings of such formidable consequences. Apart from the "admissions," there was nothing upon which a judgment or finding might be based. There was no sworn testimony. Mrs. Cook, the complainant, was not present. The Arizona Supreme Court held that "sworn testimony must be required of all witnesses including police officers, probation officers and others who are part of or officially related to the juvenile court structure." We hold that this is not enough. No reason is suggested or appears for a different rule in respect of sworn testimony in juvenile courts than in adult tribunals. Absent a valid confession adequate to support the determination of the Juvenile Court, confrontation and sworn testimony by witnesses available for cross-examination were essential for a finding of "delinquency" and an order committing Gerald to a state institution for a maximum of six years.

. . .

As we said in Kent v. United States, 383 U.S. 541, 554, 86 S.Ct. 1045, 1053, 16 L.Ed.2d 84 (1966), with respect to waiver proceedings, "there is no place in our system of law for reaching a result of such tremendous consequences without ceremony . . . ." We now hold that, absent a valid confession, a determination of delinquency and an order of commitment to a state institution cannot be sustained in the absence of sworn testimony subjected to the opportunity for cross-examination in accordance with our law and constitutional requirements.

VI.

APPELLATE REVIEW AND TRANSCRIPT OF PROCEEDINGS

Appellants urge that the Arizona statute is unconstitutional under the Due Process Clause because, as construed by its Supreme Court, "there is no right of appeal from a juvenile court order . . . ." The court held that there is no right to a transcript because there is no right to appeal and because the proceedings are confidential and any record must be destroyed after a prescribed period of time. Whether a transcript or other recording is made, it held, is a matter for the discretion of the juvenile court.

This Court has not held that a State is required by the Federal Constitution "to provide appellate courts or a right to appellate review at all." In view of the fact that we must reverse the Supreme Court of Arizona's affirmance of the dismissal of the writ of habeas corpus for other reasons, we need not rule on this question in the present case or upon the failure to provide a transcript or recording of the hearings—or, indeed, the failure of the Juvenile Judge to state the grounds for his conclusion. Cf. Kent v. United States, supra, 383 U.S., at 561, 86 S.Ct., at 1057, where we said, in the context of a decision of the juvenile court waiving jurisdiction to the adult court, which by local law, was permissible: ". . . it is incumbent upon the Juvenile Court to accompany its waiver order with a statement of the reasons or considerations therefor." As the present case illustrates, the consequences of failure to provide an appeal, to record the proceedings, or to make findings or state the grounds for the juvenile court's conclusion may be to throw a burden upon the machinery for habeas corpus, to saddle the reviewing process with the burden of attempting to reconstruct a record, and to impose upon the Juvenile Judge the unseemly duty of testifying under cross-examination as to the events that transpired in the hearings before him.

For the reasons stated, the judgment of the Supreme Court of Arizona is reversed and the cause remanded for further proceedings not inconsistent with this opinion.

[The separate concurring opinions of Mr. Justice Black and Mr. Justice White have been omitted because of space limitations.]

MR. JUSTICE HARLAN, concurring in part and dissenting in part.

. . .

No more evidence of the importance of the public interests at stake here is required than that furnished by the opinion of the Court; it indicates that "some 601,000 children under 18, or 2% of all children between 10 and 17, came before juvenile courts" in 1965, and that "about one-fifth of all arrests for serious crimes" in 1965 were of juveniles. The Court adds that the rate of juvenile crime is steadily rising. All this, as the Court suggests, indicates the importance of these due process issues, but it mirrors no less vividly that state authorities are confronted by formidable and immediate problems involving the most fundamental social values. The state legislatures have determined that the most hopeful solution for these problems is to be found in specialized courts, organized under their own rules and imposing distinctive consequences. The terms and limitations of these systems are not identical, nor are the procedural arrangements which they include, but the States are uniform in their insistence that the ordinary processes of criminal justice are inappropriate, and that relatively informal proceedings, dedicated to premises and purposes only imperfectly reflected in the criminal law, are instead necessary.

It is well settled that the Court must give the widest deference to legislative judgments that concern the character and urgency of the problems with which the State is confronted. Legislatures are, as this Court has often acknowledged, the "main guardian" of the public interest, and, within their constitutional competence, their understanding of that interest must be accepted as "well-nigh" conclusive. Berman v. Parker, 348 U.S. 26, 32, 75 S.Ct. 98, 102, 99 L.Ed. 27. This principle does not, however, reach all the questions essential to the resolution of this case. The legislative judgments at issue here embrace assessments of the necessity and wisdom of procedural guarantees; these are questions which the Constitution has entrusted at least in part to courts, and upon which courts have been understood to possess particular competence. The fundamental issue here is, therefore, in what measure and fashion the Court must defer to legislative determinations which encompass constitutional issues of procedural protection.

It suffices for present purposes to summarize the factors which I believe to be pertinent. It must first be emphasized that the deference given to legislators upon substantive issues must realistically extend in part to ancillary procedural questions. Procedure at once reflects and creates substantive rights, and every effort of courts since the beginnings of the common law to separate the two has proved essentially futile. The distinction between them is particularly inadequate here, where the legislature's substantive preferences directly and unavoidably require judgments about procedural issues. The procedural framework is here a principal element of the substantive legislative system; meaningful deference to the latter must include a portion of deference to the former. The substantive-procedural dichotomy is, nonetheless, an indispensable tool of analysis, for it stems from fundamental limitations upon judicial authority under the Constitution. Its premise is ultimately that courts may not substitute for the judgments of legislators their own understanding of the public welfare, but must instead concern themselves with the validity under the Constitution of the methods which the legislature has selected. The Constitution has in this manner created for courts and legislators areas of primary responsibility which are essentially congruent to their areas of special competence. Courts are thus obliged both by constitutional command and by their distinctive functions to bear particular responsibility for the measurement of procedural due process. These factors in combination suggest that legislatures may properly expect only a cautious deference for their procedural judgments, but that, conversely, courts must exercise their special responsibility for procedural guarantees with care to permit ample scope for achieving the purposes of legislative programs. Plainly, courts can exercise such care only if they have in each case first studied thoroughly the objectives and implementation of the program at stake; if, upon completion of those studies, the effect of extensive procedural restrictions upon valid legislative purposes cannot be assessed with reasonable certainty, the court should necessarily proceed with restraint.

The foregoing considerations, which I believe to be fair distillations of relevant judicial history, suggest three criteria by which the procedural requirements of due process should be measured here: first, no more restrictions should be imposed than are imperative to assure the proceedings' fundamental fairness; second, the restrictions which are imposed should be those which preserve, so far as possible, the essential elements of the State's purpose; and finally, restrictions should be chosen which will later permit the orderly selection of any additional protections which may ultimately prove necessary. In this way, the Court may guarantee the fundamental fairness of the proceeding, and yet permit the State to continue development of an effective response to the problems of juvenile crime. . . .

Measured by these criteria, only three procedural requirements should, in my opinion, now be deemed required of state juvenile courts by the Due Process Clause of the Fourteenth Amendment: first, timely notice must be provided to parents and children of the nature and terms of any juvenile court proceeding in which a determination affecting their rights or interests may be made; second, unequivocal and timely notice must be given that counsel may appear in any such proceeding in behalf of the child and its parents, and that in cases in which the child may be confined in an institution, counsel may, in circumstances of indigency, be appointed for them; and third, the court must maintain a written record, or its equivalent, adequate to permit effective review on appeal or in collateral proceedings. These requirements would guarantee to juveniles the tools with which their rights could be fully vindicated, and yet permit the States to pursue without unnecessary hindrance the purposes which they believe imperative in this field. Further, their imposition now would later permit more intelligent assessment of the necessity under the Fourteenth Amendment of additional requirements, by creating suitable records from which the character and deficiencies of juvenile proceedings could be accurately judged. . . .

NOTES

(1) *Gault* by its own terms is limited to delinquency proceedings "which may result in commitment to an institution in which the juvenile's freedom is curtailed." Today many states would require at least as much process for adjudication under the status offense jurisdiction for noncriminal misbehavior if such an adjudication can result in an involuntary loss of liberty. See p. 629, infra.

(2) The *Gault* decision is concerned primarily with the adjudicatory hearing at which the crucial question is: are the facts alleged in the petition true? Justice Fortas suggests that there is nothing about the status of being a child that justifies sloppiness or lack of due process in fact-finding on the ultimate issue of guilt. What impact should the *Gault* reasoning have on the kinds of evidence that should properly be admissible at such adjudicatory hearings? What is the logical impact of *Gault* on disposition decisionmaking? These questions will be considered in greater detail in Chapters VIII and IX.

(3) Most state courts had rejected the application of due process rights to juvenile courts on the ground that delinquency adjudications were not criminal but rather civil proceedings at which such rights as counsel, notice, the fifth amendment right and the right to confront and cross-examine were inappropriate. See e.g., Moquin v. State, 216 Md. 524, 140 A.2d 914 (1958) or the Arizona Supreme Court's decision in *Gault*, 99 Ariz. 181, 407 P.2d 760 (1965). See also, R. M. Emerson, Judging Delinquents: Context and Process in Juvenile Court (1969). What is the jurisprudential problem with determining the rights accorded litigants based on the civil or criminal label? Should it make any difference that the state's motivation for Gerald Gault's commitment to the State Industrial School was therapeutic—to rehabilitate rather than punish him? Justice Fortas asserts that involuntary loss of liberty is the appropriate dividing line to determine the applicability of due process requirements. Do you find this functional division constitutionally persuasive?

(4) In 1965 more than one-quarter of all juvenile judges were not legally trained, and most were not full-time judges. The decision to provide attorneys for juveniles meant that for the first time juvenile courts would become law courts. It is not surprising that juvenile judges of the time, some of whom were hostile to the *Gault* decision, were especially unhappy with the prospect of attorneys in delinquency proceedings. At first many attorneys had no idea how adversary their role should be and how it should differ if at all from representation in an adult criminal case. See e.g., the language of Matter of Samuel W. v. Family Court, 24 N.Y.2d 196, 199, 202, 299 N.Y.S.2d 414, 417, 419, 247 N.E.2d 253, 255, 257, reversed on other grounds sub nom. In re Winship, 397 U.S. 358, 90 S.Ct. 1068, 25 L.Ed.2d 368 (1970):

> A lawyer's traditional professional duty in an adversary proceeding is to do what he can and fight as hard as he can, to see his client wins. In the criminal case this is to see his client acquitted, the charge reduced, or the punishment minimized. But a child's best interest is not necessarily, or even probably, promoted if he wins in the particular inquiry which may bring him to the juvenile court. 247 N.E.2d 255.

. . .

It seems probable we cannot have the best of two worlds. If the emphasis is on constitutional rights something of the essential freedom of method and choice which the sound juvenile court Judge ought to have is lost; if range be given to that freedom, rights which the law gives to criminal offenders will not be respected. But the danger is that we may lose the child and his potential for good while giving him his constitutional rights. 247 N.E.2d 257.

Even before *Gault*, many urged that attorneys should serve as vigorous advocates in juvenile delinquency adjudicatory hearings. A defense of the vigorous advocate in juvenile court comes from the President's Commission on Law Enforcement and Administration of Justice:

> The case against counsel in juvenile proceedings rests in part on the fear that lawyers will inject into juvenile court proceedings the worst features of criminal trials: Emphasis on technical and legalistic points without regard to the larger interests at stake; use of dilatory devices such as needless requests for adjournments; preoccupation with "getting the client off" rather than concern for furthering the interests of child and state.

> First, even to the extent those fears are well-grounded, the pervasive and fundamental commitment to fairness and the unfortunate experience with departure from procedural regularity in the juvenile courts require provision of counsel. But some of the consequences of introducing lawyers are not at all undesirable. Effective representation of the rights and interests of the offender inevitably appears to those accustomed to complete freedom of decision making as needless obstreperousness and dilatoriness. Of course law is an irksome restraint upon the free exercise of discretion. But its virtue resides precisely in the restraints it imposes on the freedom of the probation officer and the judge to follow their own course without having to demonstrate its legitimacy or even the legitimacy of their intervention.

Task Force on Juvenile Delinquency, Juvenile Delinquency and Youth Crime 33 (1967). Further, a study by sociologists Wheeler and Cottrell urged:

> Unless appropriate due process of law is followed, even the juvenile who has violated the law may not feel that he is being fairly treated and may therefore resist the rehabilitative efforts of court personnel.

S. S. Wheeler & L. Cottrell, Juvenile Delinquency:—Its Prevention and Control (1966). See also, W. Stapleton and L. Teitelbaum, In Defense of Youth: A Study of the Role of Counsel in American Juvenile Courts (1972).

By the early 1970s despite lamentation from Chief Justice Burger and others (see dissenting opinion of Burger, C.J. in In re Winship, 397 U.S. 358, 376, 90 S.Ct. 1068, 1079, 25 L.Ed.2d 368 (1970) advocacy was the rule rather than the exception in post-*Gault* courts.

In order to accommodate the rule of law, the juvenile or family court required a full-time legally trained judge. Between 1968 and 1972 about 40% of all juvenile and family court judgeships changed hands usually from laymen to lawyers. In order to attract attorneys as full-time juvenile court judges, many jurisdictions had to upgrade both the staff and prestige of the courts. See K. Smith, A Profile of Juvenile Court Judges, (National Council of Juvenile Judges 1972). In rural areas where no one county could support a full-time juvenile judge and an adequate probation staff, regionalization was used to create one full-time court to serve several counties on a circuit riding model. See, e.g., Model Rules for Virginia Regional Juvenile and Domestic Relations Courts, 1968–75.

(5) For a contemporary analysis of *Gault*, see Paulsen, The Constitutional Domestication of the Juvenile Court, 1967 Supreme Court Review 233.

IN RE WINSHIP

Supreme Court of the United States, 1970.
397 U.S. 358, 90 S.Ct. 1068, 25 L.Ed.2d 368.

MR. JUSTICE BRENNAN delivered the opinion of the Court.

. . . This case presents the single, narrow question whether proof beyond a reasonable doubt is among the "essentials of due process and fair treatment" required during the adjudicatory stage when a juvenile is charged with an act which would constitute a crime if committed by an adult.

Section 712 of the New York Family Court Act defines a juvenile delinquent as "a person over seven and less than sixteen years of age who does any act which, if done by an adult, would constitute a crime." During a 1967 adjudicatory hearing, conducted pursuant to § 742 of the Act, a judge in New York Family Court found that appellant, then a 12-year-old boy, had entered a locker and stolen $112 from a woman's pocketbook. The petition which charged appellant with delinquency alleged that his act, "if done by an adult, would constitute the crime or crimes of Larceny." The judge acknowledged that the proof might not establish guilt beyond a reasonable doubt, but rejected appellant's contention that such proof was required by the Fourteenth Amendment. The judge relied instead on § 744(b) of the New York Family Court Act which provides that "[a]ny determination at the conclusion of [an adjudicatory] hearing that a [juvenile] did an act or acts must be based on a preponderance of the evidence."[2] During a subsequent dispositional hearing, appellant was ordered placed in a training school for an initial period of 18 months, subject to annual extensions of his commitment until his 18th birthday—six years in appellant's case. The Appellate Division of the New York Supreme Court, First Judicial Department, affirmed without opinion. . . . The New York Court of Appeals then affirmed by a four-to-three vote, expressly sustaining the constitutionality of § 744(b), 24 N.Y.2d 196, 299 N.Y.S.2d 414, 247 N.E.2d 253 (1969). . . .

2. The ruling appears in the following portion of the hearing transcript:

    Counsel: "Your Honor is making a finding by the preponderance of the evidence."

    Court: "Well, it convinces me."

    Counsel: "It's not beyond a reasonable doubt, Your Honor."

    Court: "That is true . . . Our statute says a preponderance and a preponderance it is."

I

. . .

Expressions in many opinions of this Court indicate that it has long been assumed that proof of a criminal charge beyond a reasonable doubt is constitutionally required. . . .

. . .

The reasonable-doubt standard plays a vital role in the American scheme of criminal procedure. It is a prime instrument for reducing the risk of convictions resting on factual error. The standard provides concrete substance for the presumption of innocence—that bedrock "axiomatic and elementary" principle whose "enforcement lies at the foundation of the administration of our criminal law." . . .

. . .

The requirement of proof beyond a reasonable doubt has this vital role in our criminal procedure for cogent reasons. The accused during a criminal prosecution has at stake interest of immense importance, both because of the possibility that he may lose his liberty upon conviction and because of the certainty that he would be stigmatized by the conviction. Accordingly, a society that values the good name and freedom of every individual should not condemn a man for commission of a crime when there is reasonable doubt about his guilt. . . .

Moreover, use of the reasonable-doubt standard is indispensable to command the respect and confidence of the community in applications of the criminal law. It is critical that the moral force of the criminal law not be diluted by a standard of proof that leaves people in doubt whether innocent men are being condemned. It is also important in our free society that every individual going about his ordinary affairs have confidence that his government cannot adjudge him guilty of a criminal offense without convincing a proper factfinder of his guilt with utmost certainty.

Lest there remain any doubt about the constitutional stature of the reasonable-doubt standard, we explicitly hold that the Due Process Clause protects the accused against conviction except upon proof beyond a reasonable doubt of every fact necessary to constitute the crime with which he is charged.

II

We turn to the question whether juveniles, like adults, are constitutionally entitled to proof beyond a reasonable doubt when they are charged with violation of a criminal law. The same considerations that demand extreme caution in factfinding to protect the innocent adult apply as well to the innocent child. We do not find convincing the contrary arguments of the New York Court of Appeals. *Gault* rendered untenable much of the reasoning relied upon by that court to sustain the constitutionality of § 744(b). The Court of Appeals indicated that a delinquency adjudication "is not a 'conviction' (§ 781); that it affects no right or privilege, including the right to hold public office or to obtain a license (§ 782); and a cloak of protective confidentiality is thrown around all the proceedings (§§ 783–784)." The court said further: "The delinquency status is not made a crime; and the proceedings are not criminal. There is, hence, no deprivation of due process in the statutory provision [challenged by appellant] * * *." In effect the Court of Appeals distinguished the proceedings in question here from a criminal prosecution by use of what *Gault* called the " 'civil' label-of-convenience which has been attached to juvenile proceedings." But *Gault* expressly rejected that distinction as a reason for holding the Due Process Clause inapplicable to a juvenile proceeding. The Court of Appeals also attempted to justify the preponderance standard on the related ground that juvenile proceedings are designed "not to punish, but to save the child." Again, however, *Gault* expressly rejected this justification. We made clear in that decision that civil labels and good intentions do not themselves obviate the need for criminal due process safeguards in juvenile courts, for "[a] proceeding where the issue is whether the child will be found to be 'delinquent' and subjected to the loss of his liberty for years is comparable in seriousness to a felony prosecution."

Nor do we perceive any merit in the argument that to afford juveniles the protection of proof beyond a reasonable doubt would risk destruction of beneficial aspects of the juvenile process.[4] Use of the reasonable-doubt standard during the adjudicatory hearing will not disturb New York's policies that a finding that a child has violated a criminal law does not constitute a criminal conviction, that such a finding does not deprive the child of his civil rights, and that juvenile proceedings are confidential. Nor will there be any effect on the informality, flexibility, or speed of the hearing at which the factfinding takes place. And the opportunity during the post-adjudicatory or dispositional hearing for a wide-ranging review of the child's social history and for his individualized treatment will remain unimpaired. Similarly, there will be no effect on the procedures distinctive to juvenile proceedings that are employed prior to the adjudicatory hearing.

---

4. Appellee, New York City, apparently concedes as much in its Brief, page 8, where it states:

"A determination that the New York law unconstitutionally denies due process because it does not provide for use of the reasonable doubt standard probably would not have a serious impact if all that resulted would be a change in the quantum of proof."

And Dorsen & Rezneck, [In Re Gault and the Future of Juvenile Law, 1 Fam. L.Q., Vol. 1(4):1 (1967)] at 27, have observed:

"[T]he reasonable doubt test is superior to all others in protecting against an unjust adjudication of guilt, and that is as much a concern of the juvenile court as of the criminal court. It is difficult to see how the distinctive objectives of the juvenile court give rise to a legitimate institutional interest in finding a juvenile to have committed a violation of the criminal law on less evidence than if he were an adult."

The Court of Appeals observed that "a child's best interest is not necessarily, or even probably, promoted if he wins in the particular inquiry which may bring him to the juvenile court." It is true, of course, that the juvenile may be engaging in a general course of conduct inimical to his welfare that calls for judicial intervention. But that intervention cannot take the form of subjecting the child to the stigma of a finding that he violated a criminal law [5] and to the possibility of institutional confinement on proof insufficient to convict him were he an adult.

We conclude, as we concluded regarding the essential due process safeguards applied in *Gault*, that the observance of the standard of proof beyond a reasonable doubt "will not compel the States to abandon or displace any of the substantive benefits of the juvenile process."

Reversed.

MR. JUSTICE HARLAN, concurring.

. . .

I wish to emphasize, as I did in my separate opinion in *Gault*, that there is no automatic congruence between the procedural requirements imposed by due process in a criminal case, and those imposed by due process in juvenile cases. It is of great importance, in my view, that procedural strictures not be constitutionally imposed that jeopardize "the essential elements of the State's purpose" in creating juvenile courts, . . . In this regard, I think it worth emphasizing that the requirement of proof beyond a reasonable doubt that a juvenile committed a criminal act before he is found to be a delinquent does not (1) interfere with the worthy goal of rehabilitating the juvenile, (2) make any significant difference in the extent to which a youth is stigmatized as a "criminal" because he has been found to be a delinquent, or (3) burden the juvenile courts with a procedural requirement that will make juvenile adjudications significantly more time consuming, or rigid. Today's decision simply requires a juvenile court judge to be more confident in his belief that the youth did the act with which he has been charged.

With these observations, I join the Court's opinion, subject only to the constitutional reservations expressed in my opinion in *Gault*.

MR. CHIEF JUSTICE BURGER, with whom MR. JUSTICE STEWART joins, dissenting.

The Court's opinion today rests entirely on the assumption that all juvenile proceedings are "criminal presecutions," hence subject to constitutional limitations. This derives from earlier holdings, which,

5. The more comprehensive and effective the procedures used to prevent public disclosure of the finding, the less the danger of stigma. As we indicated in *Gault*, however, often the "claim of secrecy . . . is more rhetoric than reality."

like today's holding, were steps eroding the differences between juvenile courts and traditional criminal courts. The original concept of the juvenile court system was to provide a benevolent and less formal means than criminal courts could provide for dealing with the special and often sensitive problems of youthful offenders. Since I see no constitutional requirement of due process sufficient to overcome the legislative judgment of the States in this area, I dissent from further strait-jacketing of an already overly restricted system. What the juvenile court system needs is not more but less of the trappings of legal procedure and judicial formalism; the juvenile court system requires breathing room and flexibility in order to survive, if it can survive the repeated assaults from this Court.

Much of the judicial attitude manifested by the Court's opinion today and earlier holdings in this field is really a protest against inadequate juvenile court staffs and facilities; we "burn down the stable to get rid of the mice." The lack of support and the distressing growth of juvenile crime have combined to make for a literal breakdown in many if not most juvenile courts. Constitutional problems were not seen while those courts functioned in an atmosphere where juvenile judges were not crushed with an avalanche of cases.

My hope is that today's decision will not spell the end of a generously conceived program of compassionate treatment intended to mitigate the rigors and trauma of exposing youthful offenders to a traditional criminal court; each step we take turns the clock back to the pre-juvenile-court era. I cannot regard it as a manifestation of progress to transform juvenile courts into criminal courts, which is what we are well on the way to accomplishing. We can only hope the legislative response will not reflect our own by having these courts abolished.

[The dissenting opinion of MR. JUSTICE BLACK is omitted.]

NOTES

(1) It is very difficult to make an adequate record in standard of proof cases because of the problem of establishing what standard was employed. In *Winship* the trial judge helped to set up the litigation by stating for the record his use of the preponderance standard set out in N.Y. Family Court Act § 744(b). The clear implication of the comments, set forth in fn. 2 of the Supreme Court's opinion, is that he would not have held Winship guilty beyond a reasonable doubt.

(2) For discussion of the rejection of the reasonable doubt standard in most adjudications of noncriminal misbehavior, see p. 629, infra.

(3) The *Winship* holding has had greatest impact in criminal procedure. When may a state require a criminal defendant to raise and prove a particular defense? Are presumptions—whether mandatory or permissive—unconstitutional as shifting the burden of proof to the defendant? See Mullaney v. Wilbur, 421 U.S. 684, 95 S.Ct. 1881, 44 L.Ed.2d 508 (1975); Patterson v. New York, 432 U.S. 197, 97 S.Ct. 2319, 53 L.Ed.2d 281 (1977); Underwood, The Thumb on the Scales of Justice: Burdens of Persuasion in Criminal

Cases, 86 Yale L.J. 1299 (1977); Jeffries and Stephan, Defenses, Presumptions, and Burden of Proof in the Criminal Law, 88 Yale L.J. 1325 (1979); and Allen, More on Constitutional Process-of-Proof Problems in Criminal Cases, 94 Harv.L.Rev. 1795 (1981).

(4) Picking up on the sentiments expressed in Chief Justice Burger's dissenting opinion, some commentators have suggested the abolition of juvenile court jurisdiction over conduct by children that would be criminal if they were adults. See, e.g., McCarthy, Delinquency Dispositions Under the Juvenile Justice Standards: The Consequences of a Change of Rationale, 52 N.Y. U.L.Rev. 1093 (1977).

McKEIVER v. PENNSYLVANIA

Supreme Court of the United States, 1971.
403 U.S. 528, 91 S.Ct. 1976, 29 L.Ed.2d 647.

MR. JUSTICE BLACKMUN announced the judgments of the Court and an opinion in which THE CHIEF JUSTICE, MR. JUSTICE STEWART, and MR. JUSTICE WHITE join.

These cases present the narrow but precise issue whether the Due Process Clause of the Fourteenth Amendment assures the right to trial by jury in the adjudicative phase of a state juvenile court delinquency proceeding.

. . .

The details of the McKeiver and Terry offenses are set forth in Justice Roberts' opinion for the Pennsylvania court, 438 Pa., at 341–342, nn. 1 and 2, 265 A.2d, at 351 nn. 1 and 2, and need not be repeated at any length here. It suffices to say that McKeiver's offense was his participating with 20 or 30 youths who pursued three young teenagers and took 25 cents from them; that McKeiver never before had been arrested and had a record of gainful employment; that the testimony of two of the victims was described by the court as somewhat inconsistent and as "weak"; and that Terry's offense consisted of hitting a police officer with his fists and with a stick when the officer broke up a boys' fight Terry and others were watching.

No. 128. Barbara Burrus and approximately 45 other black children, ranging in age from 11 to 15 years,[3] were the subjects of juvenile court summonses issued in Hyde County, North Carolina, in January 1969.

The charges arose out of a series of demonstrations in the county in late 1968 by black adults and children protesting school assignments and a school consolidation plan. Petitions were filed by North Carolina state highway patrolmen. Except for one relating to James Lambert Howard, the petitions charged the respective juveniles with wilfully impeding traffic. The charge against Howard was that he

3. In North Carolina juvenile court procedures are provided only for persons under the age of 16.

wilfully made riotous noise and was disorderly in the O. A. Peay School in Swan Quarter; interrupted and disturbed the school during its regular sessions; and defaced school furniture. The acts so charged are misdemeanors under North Carolina law.

The several cases were consolidated into groups for hearing before District Judge Hallett S. Ward, sitting as a juvenile court. The same lawyer appeared for all the juveniles. Over counsel's objection, made in all except two of the cases, the general public was excluded. A request for a jury trial in each case was denied.

The evidence as to the juveniles other than Howard consisted solely of testimony of highway patrolmen. No juvenile took the stand or offered any witness. The testimony was to the effect that on various occasions the juveniles and adults were observed walking along Highway 64 singing, shouting, clapping, and playing basketball. As a result, there was interference with traffic. The marchers were asked to leave the paved portion of the highway and they were warned that they were committing a statutory offense. They either refused or left the roadway and immediately returned. The juveniles and participating adults were taken into custody. Juvenile petitions were then filed with respect to those under the age of 16.

The evidence as to Howard was that on the morning of December 5, he was in the office of the principal of the O. A. Peay School with 15 other persons while school was in session and was moving furniture around; that the office was in disarray; that as a result the school closed before noon; and that neither he nor any of the others was a student at the school or authorized to enter the principal's office.

In each case the court found that the juvenile had committed "an act for which an adult may be punished by law." A custody order was entered declaring the juvenile a delinquent "in need of more suitable guardianship" and committing him to the custody of the County Department of Public Welfare for placement in a suitable institution "until such time as the Board of Juvenile Correction or the Superintendent of said institution may determine, not inconsistent with the laws of this State." The court, however, suspended these commitments and placed each juvenile on probation for either one or two years conditioned upon his violating none of the State's laws, upon his reporting monthly to the County Department of Welfare, upon his being home by 11 p. m. each evening, and upon his attending a school approved by the Welfare Director. None of the juveniles has been confined on these charges.

On appeal, the cases were consolidated into two groups. The North Carolina Court of Appeals affirmed. In re Burrus, 4 N.C.App. 523, 167 S.E.2d 454 (1969); In re Shelton, 5 N.C.App. 487, 168 S.E.2d 695 (1969). In its turn the Supreme Court of North Carolina deleted that portion of the order in each case relating to commitment, but otherwise affirmed. In re Burrus, 275 N.C. 517, 169 S.E.2d 879 (1969). We granted certiorari.

III

It is instructive to review, as an illustration, the substance of Justice Roberts' opinion for the Pennsylvania court. He observes that "[f]or over sixty-five years the Supreme Court gave no consideration at all to the constitutional problems involved in the juvenile court area"; that *Gault* "is somewhat of a paradox, being both broad and narrow at the same time"; that it "is broad in that it evidences a fundamental and far-reaching disillusionment with the anticipated benefits of the juvenile court system"; that it is narrow because the court enumerated four due process rights which it held applicable in juvenile proceedings, but declined to rule on two other claimed rights; that as a consequence the Pennsylvania court was "confronted with a sweeping rationale and a carefully tailored holding,"; that the procedural safeguards "*Gault* specifically made applicable to juvenile courts have already caused a significant 'constitutional domestication' of juvenile court proceedings," that those safeguards and other rights, including the reasonable-doubt standard established by *Winship*, "insure that the juvenile court will operate in an atmosphere which is orderly enough to impress the juvenile with the gravity of the situation and the impartiality of the tribunal and at the same time informal enough to permit the benefits of the juvenile system to operate"; that the "proper inquiry, then, is whether the right to a trial by jury is 'fundamental' within the meaning of *Duncan*, in the context of a juvenile court which operates with *all* of the above constitutional safeguards," and that his court's inquiry turned "upon whether there are elements in the juvenile process which render the right to a trial by jury less essential to the protection of an accused's rights in the juvenile system than in the normal criminal process."

Justice Roberts then concluded that such factors do inhere in the Pennsylvania juvenile system: (1) Although realizing that "faith in the quality of the juvenile bench is not an entirely satisfactory substitute for due process," the judges in the juvenile courts "to take a different view of their role than that taken by their counterparts in the criminal courts." (2) While one regrets its inadequacies, "the juvenile system has available and utilizes much more fully various diagnostic and rehabilitative services" that are "far superior to those available in the regular criminal process." (3) Although conceding that the post-adjudication process "has in many respects fallen far short of its goals, and its reality is far harsher than its theory," the end result of a declaration of delinquency "*is* significantly different from and less onerous than a finding of criminal guilt" and "we are not yet convinced that the current practices do not contain the seeds from which a truly appropriate system can be brought forth." (4) Finally, "of all the possible due process rights which could be applied in the juvenile courts, the right to trial by jury is the one which would most likely be disruptive of the unique nature of the juvenile process." It is the jury trial that "would probably require substantial alteration of the traditional practices." The other procedural rights held applicable to the juvenile process "will give the juveniles sufficient protection" and the addition of the trial by jury "might well destroy the traditional character of juvenile proceedings."

The court concluded that it was confident "that a properly structured and fairly administered juvenile court system can serve our present societal needs without infringing on individual freedoms."

IV

The right to an impartial jury "[i]n all criminal prosecutions" under federal law is guaranteed by the Sixth Amendment. Through the Fourteenth Amendment that requirement has now been imposed upon the States "in all criminal cases which—were they to be tried in a federal court—would come within the Sixth Amendment's guarantee." This is because the Court has said it believes "that trial by jury in criminal cases is fundamental to the American scheme of justice."

This, of course, does not automatically provide the answer to the present jury trial issue, if for no other reason than that the juvenile court proceeding has not yet been held to be a "criminal prosecution," within the meaning and reach of the Sixth Amendment, and also has not yet been regarded as devoid of criminal aspects merely because it usually has been given the civil label. *Kent*, 383 U.S., at 554, 86 S.Ct., at 1054; *Gault*, 387 U.S., at 17, 49–50, 87 S.Ct., at 1438, 1455–1456; *Winship*, 397 U.S., at 365–366, 90 S.Ct., at 1073–1074.

Little, indeed, is to be gained by any attempt simplistically to call the juvenile court proceeding either "civil" or "criminal." The Court carefully has avoided this wooden approach. Before *Gault* was decided in 1967, the Fifth Amendment's guarantee against self-incrimination had been imposed upon the state criminal trial. So, too, had the Sixth Amendment's rights of confrontation and cross-examination. Yet the Court did not automatically and peremptorily apply those rights to the juvenile proceeding. A reading of *Gault* reveals the opposite. And the same separate approach to the standard-of-proof issue is evident from the carefully separated application of the standard, first to the criminal trial, and then to the juvenile proceeding, displayed in *Winship*. 397 U.S., at 361 and 365, 90 S.Ct., at 1071 and 1073.

Thus, accepting "the proposition that the Due Process Clause has a role to play," *Gault*, 387 U.S., at 13, 87 S.Ct., at 1436, our task here with respect to trial by jury, as it was in *Gault* with respect to other claimed rights, "is to ascertain the precise impact of the due process requirement." Id. at 13–14, 87 S.Ct., at 1436.

V

The Pennsylvania juveniles' basic argument is that they were tried in proceedings "substantially similar to a criminal trial." They say that a delinquency proceeding in their State is initiated by a petition charging a penal code violation in the conclusory language of an indictment; that a juvenile detained prior to trial is held in a building substantially similar to an adult prison; that in Philadelphia juveniles over 16 are, in fact, held in the cells of a prison; that counsel and the prosecution engage in plea bargaining; that motions to suppress are routinely heard and decided; that the usual rules of evidence are applied; that the customary common-law defenses are available; that the press is generally admitted in the Philadelphia juvenile courtrooms; that members of the public enter the room; that arrest and prior record may be reported by the press (from police sources, however, rather than from the juvenile court records); that, once adjudged delinquent, a juvenile may be confined until his majority in what amounts to a prison describing the state correctional institution at Camp Hill as a "maximum security prison for adjudged delinquents and youthful criminal offenders"); and that the stigma attached upon delinquency adjudication approximates that resulting from conviction in an adult criminal proceeding.

. . . .

VI

All the litigants here agree that the applicable due process standard in juvenile proceedings, as developed by *Gault* and *Winship*, is fundamental fairness. As that standard was applied in those two cases, we have an emphasis on factfinding procedures. The requirements of notice, counsel, confrontation, cross-examination, and standard of proof naturally flowed from this emphasis. But one cannot say that in our legal system the jury is a necessary component of accurate factfinding. There is much to be said for it, to be sure, but we have been content to pursue other ways for determining facts. Juries are not required, and have not been, for example, in equity cases, in workmen's compensation, in probate, or in deportation cases. Neither have they been generally used in military trials. . . .

We must recognize, as the Court has recognized before, that the fond and idealistic hopes of the juvenile court proponents and early reformers of three generations ago have not been realized. The devastating commentary upon the system's failures as a whole, contained in the President's Commission on Law Enforcement and Administration of Justice, Task Force Report: Juvenile Delinquency and Youth Crime 7–9 (1967), reveals the depth of disappointment in what has been accomplished. Too often the juvenile court judge falls far short of that stalwart, protective, and communicating figure the system envisaged.[4] The community's unwillingness to provide people and facilities and to be concerned, the insufficiency of time devoted, the scarcity of professional help, the inadequacy of dispositional alternatives, and our general lack of knowledge all contribute to dissatisfaction with the experiment.[5]

Despite all these disappointments, all these failures, and all these shortcomings, we conclude that trial by jury in the juvenile court's adjudicative stage is not a constitutional requirement. We so conclude for a number of reasons:

1. The Court has refrained, in the cases heretofore decided, from taking the easy way with a flat holding that all rights constitutionally assured for the adult accused are to be imposed upon the state juvenile proceeding. . . .

2. There is a possibility, at least, that the jury trial, if required as a matter of constitutional precept, will remake the juvenile proceeding into a fully adversary process and will put an effective end to what has been the idealistic prospect of an intimate, informal protective proceeding.

. . .

5. The imposition of the jury trial on the juvenile court system would not strengthen greatly, if at all, the factfinding function, and would, contrarily, provide an attrition of the juvenile court's assumed ability to function in a unique manner. It would not remedy the defects of the system. Meager as has been the hoped-for advance in the juvenile field, the alternative would be regressive, would lose what has been gained, and would tend once again to place the juvenile squarely in the routine of the criminal process.

4. "A recent study of juvenile court judges . . . revealed that half had not received undergraduate degrees; a fifth had received no college education at all; a fifth were not members of the bar." Task Force Report 7.

5. "What emerges, then, is this: In theory the juvenile court was to be helpful and rehabilitative rather than punitive. In fact the distinction often disappears, not only because of the absence of facilities and personnel but also because of the limits of knowledge and technique. In theory the court's action was to affix no stigmatizing label. In fact a delinquent is generally viewed by employers, schools, the armed services—by society generally—as a criminal. In theory the court was to treat children guilty of criminal acts in noncriminal ways. In fact it labels truants and runaways as junior criminals.

"In theory the court's operations could justifiably be informal, its findings and decisions made without observing ordinary procedural safeguards, because it would act only in the best interest of the child. In fact it frequently does nothing more nor less than deprive a child of liberty without due process of law—knowing not what else to do and needing, whether admittedly or not, to act in the community's interest even more imperatively than the child's. In theory it was to exercise its protective powers to bring an errant child back into the fold. In fact there is increasing reason to believe that its intervention reinforces the juvenile's unlawful impulses. In theory it was to concentrate on each case the best of current social science learning. In fact it has often become a vested interest in its turn, loathe to cooperate with innovative programs or avail itself of forward-looking methods." Task Force Report 9.

6. The juvenile concept held high promise. We are reluctant to say that, despite disappointments of grave dimensions, it still does not hold promise, and we are particularly reluctant to say, as do the Pennsylvania appellants here, that the system cannot accomplish its rehabilitative goals. So much depends on the availability of resources, on the interest and commitment of the public, on willingness to learn, and on understanding as to cause and effect and cure. In this field, as in so many others, one perhaps learns best by doing. We are reluctant to disallow the States to experiment further and to seek in new and different ways the elusive answers to the problems of the young, and we feel that we would be impeding that experimentation by imposing the jury trial. The States, indeed, must go forward. If, in its wisdom, any State feels the jury trial is desirable in all cases, or in certain kinds, there appears to be no impediment to its installing a system embracing that feature. That, however, is the State's privilege and not its obligation.

7. Of course there have been abuses. . . . We refrain from saying at this point that those abuses are of constitutional dimension. They relate to the lack of resources and of dedication rather than to inherent unfairness.

8. There is, of course, nothing to prevent a juvenile court judge, in a particular case where he feels the need, or when the need is demonstrated, from using an advisory jury.

9. "The fact that a practice is followed by a large number of states is not conclusive in a decision as to whether that practice accords with due process, but it is plainly worth considering . . . .. It therefore is of more than passing interest that at least 28 States and the District of Columbia by statute deny the juvenile a right to a jury trial in cases such as these. The same result is achieved in other States by judicial decision. In 10 States statutes provide for a jury trial under certain circumstances.

10. Since *Gault* . . . the great majority of States, in addition to Pennsylvania and North Carolina, that have faced the issue have concluded that the considerations that led to the result in those two cases do not compel trial by jury in the juvenile court.

. . . .

12. If the jury trial were to be injected into the juvenile court system as a matter of right, it would bring with it into that system the traditional delay, the formality, and the clamor of the adversary system and, possibly, the public trial. It is of interest that these very factors were stressed by the District Committee of the Senate when, through Senator Tydings, it recommended, and Congress then approved, as a provision in the District of Columbia Crime Bill, the abolition of the jury trial in the juvenile court. S.Rep.No.91–620, pp. 13–14 (1969).

13. Finally, the arguments advanced by the juveniles here are, of course, the identical arguments that underlie the demand for the jury trial for criminal proceedings. The arguments necessarily equate the juvenile proceeding—or at least the adjudicative phase of it—with the criminal trial. Whether they should be so equated is our issue. Concern about the inapplicability of exclusionary and other rules of evidence, about the juvenile court judge's possible awareness of the juvenile's prior record and of the contents of the social file; about repeated appearances of the same familiar witnesses in the persons of juvenile and probation officers and social workers—all to the effect that this will create the likelihood of pre-judgment—chooses to ignore it seems to us, every aspect of fairness, of concern, of sympathy, and of paternal attention that the juvenile court system contemplates.

If the formalities of the criminal adjudicative process are to be superimposed upon the juvenile court system, there is little need for its separate existence. Perhaps that ultimate disillusionment will come one day, but for the moment we are disinclined to give impetus to it.

Affirmed.

[The concurring opinion of Mr. Justice White, the opinion of Mr. Justice Brennan concurring in the judgment in No. 322 and dissenting in No. 128, the opinion of Mr. Justice Harlan concurring in the judgments, and the dissenting opinion of Mr. Justice Douglas, with whom Mr. Justice Black and Mr. Justice Marshall concur, have been omitted.]

NOTES

(1) As the Court points out, some states accord children a right to jury trial either by statute or judicial decision. However a clear majority of jurisdictions have declined to require jury trials in delinquency proceedings.

As Justice Blackmun suggests, judges may elect to use advisory juries. The California Supreme Court has permitted judges to empanel advisory juries to assist in fact-finding. People v. Superior Court of Santa Clara County, 15 Cal.3d 271, 124 Cal.Rptr. 47, 539 P.2d 807 (1975). For a contrary view, see People ex rel. Carey v. White, 65 Ill.2d 193, 2 Ill.Dec. 345, 357 N.E.2d 512 (1976).

(2) If juries are utilized, are juveniles entitled to teenage juries under the concept of trial by jury of one's peers? Judge De Ciantis of the Family Court of Providence, Rhode Island, addressed this issue in In the Matter of McCloud, a 1971 opinion appended to Mr. Justice Douglas's dissent in *McKeiver*, at 570–571:

One of the most interesting questions raised is that concerning the right of a juvenile to a trial by his peers. Counsel has suggested that a jury of a juvenile's peers would be composed of other juveniles, that is, a "teenage jury." Webster's Dictionary, Second Edition, 1966, defines a peer as an equal, one of the same rank, quality, value. The word "peers" means nothing more than citizens. In re Grilli, 110 Misc. 45, 179 N.Y.S. 795, 797. The phrase "judgment of his peers" means at common law, a trial by a jury of twelve men, State v. Simons, 61 Kan. 752, 60 P. 1052. "Judgment of his peers" is a term expressly borrowed from the Magna Charta, and it means a trial by jury, Ex parte Wagner, 58 Okl.Cr. 161, 50 P.2d 1135. The Declaration of Independence also speaks of the equality of *all* men. Are we now to say that a juvenile is a second-class citizen, not equal to an adult? The Constitution has never been construed to say women must be tried by their peers, to wit, by all-female juries, or Negroes by all-Negro juries.

The only restriction on the makeup of the jury is that there can be no systematic exclusion of those who meet local and federal requirements, in particular, voting qualifications.

The Court notes that presently in some states 18-year-olds can vote. Presumably, if they can vote, they may also serve on juries. Our own legislature has given first passage to an amendment to the Constitution to permit 18-year-olds to vote. Thus, it is quite possible that we will have teenage jurors sitting in judgment of their so-called "peers."

(3) One pillar of Justice Blackmun's opinion in *McKeiver* is that extension of the right to jury trial would materially disrupt the nature and purpose of the juvenile court. A study of states using juries suggests that the request for jury trial is rare. This was explained in the *McKeiver* decision in a footnote at p. 561. The Public Defender Service for the District of Columbia filed a brief *amicus curiae* in which they presented:

. . . the results of a survey of jury trials in delinquency cases in the 10 States requiring jury trials plus the District of Columbia are set forth. The cities selected were mostly large metropolitan areas. Thirty juvenile courts processing about 75,000 juvenile cases a year were canvassed:

"[W]e discovered that during the past five and a half years, in 22 out of 26 courts surveyed, cumulative requests for jury trials totaled 15 or less. In the remaining five courts in our sample, statistics were unavailable. During the same period, in 26 out of 29 courts the cumulative number of jury trials actually held numbered 15 or less, with statistics unavailable for two courts in our sample. For example, in Tulsa, Oklahoma, counsel is present in 100% of delinquency cases, but only one jury trial has been requested and held during the past five and one-half years. In the Juvenile Court of Fort Worth, Texas, counsel is also present in 100% of the cases, and only two jury trials have been requested since 1967. The Juvenile Court in Detroit, Michigan, reports that counsel is appointed in 70–80% of its delinquency cases, but thus far in 1970, it has had only four requests for a jury. Between 1965 and 1969 requests for juries were reported as 'very few.'

"In only four juvenile courts in our sample has there clearly been a total during the past five and one-half years of more than 15 jury trial requests and/or more than 15 such trials held."

The four courts showing more than 15 requests for jury trials were Denver, Houston, Milwaukee, and Washington, D.C.

BREED v. JONES

Supreme Court of the United States, 1975.
421 U.S. 519, 95 S.Ct. 1779, 44 L.Ed.2d 346.

Mr. Chief Justice Burger delivered the opinion of the Court.

We granted certiorari to decide whether the prosecution of respondent as an adult, after juvenile court proceedings which resulted in a finding that respondent had violated a criminal statute and a subsequent finding that he was unfit for treatment as a juvenile, violated the Fifth and Fourteenth Amendments to the United States Constitution.

Issue

. . . . .

Jeopardy denotes risk. In the constitutional sense, jeopardy describes the risk that is traditionally associated with a criminal prosecution. Although the constitutional language, "jeopardy of life or limb," suggests proceedings in which only the most serious penalties can be imposed, the Clause has long been construed to mean something far broader than its literal language. At the same time, however, we have held that the risk to which the Clause refers is not present in proceedings that are not "essentially criminal."

Although the juvenile court system had its genesis in the desire to provide a distinctive procedure and setting to deal with the problems of youth, including those manifested by antisocial conduct, our decisions in recent years have recognized that there is a gap between the originally benign conception of the system and its realities. With the exception of McKeiver v. Pennsylvania, 403 U.S. 528, 91 S.Ct. 1976, 29 L.Ed.2d 647 (1971), the Court's response to that perception has been to make applicable in juvenile proceedings constitutional guarantees associated with traditional criminal prosecutions. In re Gault, 387 U.S. 1, 87 S.Ct. 1428, 18 L.Ed.2d 527 (1967); In re Winship, 397 U.S. 358, 90 S.Ct. 1068, 25 L.Ed.2d 368 (1970). In so doing the Court has evinced awareness of the threat which such a process represents to the efforts of the juvenile court system, functioning in a unique manner, to ameliorate the harshness of criminal justice when applied to youthful offenders. That the system has fallen short of the high expectations of its sponsors in no way detracts from the broad social benefits sought or from those benefits that can survive constitutional scrutiny.

We believe it is simply too late in the day to conclude, as did the District Court in this case, that a juvenile is not put in jeopardy at a proceeding whose object is to determine whether he has committed acts that violate a criminal law and whose potential consequences include both the stigma inherent in such a determination and the deprivation of liberty for many years.[11] For it is clear under our cases

jeopardy when stigma + loss liberty faced

---

11. At the time of respondent's dispositional hearing, permissible dispositions included commitment to the California Youth Authority until he reached the age of 21 years. See Cal.Welf. & Inst'ns Code §§ 607, 731 (West 1966). Petitioner

that determining the relevance of constitutional policies, like determining the applicability of constitutional rights, in juvenile proceedings, requires that courts eschew "the 'civil' label-of-convenience which has been attached to juvenile proceedings," In re Gault, supra, 387 U.S. at 50, 87 S.Ct. at 1455, and that "the juvenile process . . . be candidly appraised." 387 U.S. at 21, 87 S.Ct. at 1440. See In re Winship, supra, 397 U.S. at 365–366, 90 S.Ct. at 1073.

As we have observed the risk to which the term jeopardy refers is that traditionally associated with "actions intended to authorize criminal punishment to vindicate public justice." United States ex rel. Marcus v. Hess, supra, 317 U.S. at 548–549, 63 S.Ct. at 388. Because of its purpose and potential consequences, and the nature and resources of the State, such a proceeding imposes heavy pressures and burdens—psychological, physical, and financial—on a person charged. The purpose of the Double Jeopardy Clause is to require that he be subject to the experience only once "for the same offence." See Green v. United States, 355 U.S. 184, 187, 78 S.Ct. 221, 223, 2 L.Ed.2d 199 (1957); Price v. Georgia, 398 U.S., at 331, 90 S.Ct. at 1762; United States v. Jorn, 400 U.S. 470, 479, 91 S.Ct. 547, 554, 27 L.Ed.2d 543 (1971).

In In re Gault, supra, 387 U.S. at 36, 87 S.Ct. at 1448, this Court concluded that, for purposes of the right to counsel, a "proceeding where the issue is whether the child will be found to be 'delinquent' and subject to the loss of his liberty for years is comparable in seriousness to a felony prosecution." See In re Winship, supra, 397 U.S. at 366, 90 S.Ct. at 1073. The Court stated that the term "delinquent" had "come to involve only slightly less stigma than the term 'criminal' applied to adults," In re Gault, supra, 387 U.S. at 24, 87 S.Ct. at 1441; see In re Winship, supra, 397 U.S. at 367, 90 S.Ct. at 1074, and that for purposes of the privilege against self-incrimination, "commitment is a deprivation of liberty. It is incarceration against one's will, whether it is called 'criminal' or 'civil.'" In re Gault, supra, 387 U.S. at 50, 87 S.Ct. at 1455. See 387 U.S., at 27, 87 S.Ct. at 1443; In re Winship, supra, 397 U.S. at 367,[12] 90 S.Ct. at 1074.

Thus, in terms of potential consequences, there is little to distinguish an adjudicatory hearing such as was held in this case from a traditional criminal prosecution. For that reason, it engenders elements of "anxiety and insecurity" in a juvenile, and imposes a "heavy personal strain." See Green v. United States, supra, 355 U.S. at 187,

has conceded that the "adjudicatory hearing is, in every sense, a court trial." Tr. of Oral Arg. 4.

12. Nor does the fact "that the purpose of the commitment is rehabilitative and not punitive . . . change its nature. . . . Regardless of the purposes for which incarceration is imposed, the fact remains that it is incarceration. The rehabilitative goals of the system are admirable, but they do not change the drastic nature of the action taken. Incarceration of adults is also intended to produce rehabilitation." Fain v. Duff, 488 F.2d, at 225. See President's Commission on Law Enforcement and Administration of Justice, Task Force Report: Juvenile Delinquency and Youth Crime 8–9 (1967).

78 S.Ct. at 223; United States v. Jorn, supra, 400 U.S. at 479, 91 S.Ct. at 554; Snyder, The Impact of the Juvenile Court Hearing on the Child, 17 Crime & Delinquency 180 (1971). And we can expect that, since our decisions implementing fundamental fairness in the juvenile court system, hearings have been prolonged, and some of the burdens incident to a juvenile's defense increased as the system has assimulated the process thereby imposed.

We deal here, not with "the formalities of the criminal adjudicative process," McKeiver v. Pennsylvania, 403 U.S., at 551, 91 S.Ct. at 1989, but with an analysis of an aspect of the juvenile court system in terms of the kind of risk to which jeopardy refers. Under our decisions we can find no persuasive distinction in that regard between the proceeding conducted in this case pursuant to Cal.Welf. & Inst'ns Code § 701 and a criminal prosecution, each of which is designed "to vindicate [the] very vital interest in enforcement of criminal laws." United States v. Jorn, supra, 400 U.S. at 479, 91 S.Ct. at 554. We therefore conclude that respondent was put in jeopardy at the adjudicatory hearing. Jeopardy attached when respondent was "put to trial before the trier of the facts," ibid., that is, when the Juvenile Court, as the trier of the facts, began to hear evidence. See Serfass v. United States, 420 U.S. at 388, 95 S.Ct. 1055.

III

Petitioner argues that, even assuming jeopardy attached to respondent's adjudicatory hearing, the procedure by which he was transferred from Juvenile Court and tried on a felony information in Superior Court did not violate the Double Jeopardy Clause. The argument is supported by two distinct, but in this case overlapping, lines of analysis. First, petitioner reasons that the procedure violated none of the policies of the Double Jeopardy Clause or that, alternatively, it should be upheld by analogy to those cases which permit retrial of an accused who has obtained reversal of a conviction on appeal. Second, pointing to this Court's concern for "the juvenile court's assumed ability to function in a unique manner," McKeiver v. Pennsylvania, supra, 403 U.S. at 547, 91 S.Ct. at 1987, petitioner urges that, should we conclude traditional principles "would otherwise bar a transfer to adult court after a delinquency adjudication," we should avoid that result here because it "would diminish the flexibility and informality of juvenile court proceedings without conferring any additional due process benefits upon juveniles charged with delinquent acts."

A

We cannot agree with petitioner that the trial of respondent in Superior Court on an information charging the same offense as that for which he had been tried in Juvenile Court violated none of the policies of the Double Jeopardy Clause. For, even accepting petitioner's premise that respondent "never faced the risk of more than one punishment," we have pointed out that "the Double Jeopardy Clause . . . is written in terms of potential or risk of *trial* and conviction not punishment."

. . .

Respondent was subjected to the burden of two trials for the same offense; he was twice put to the task of marshaling his resources against those of the State, twice subjected to the "heavy personal strain" which such an experience represents. . . .

B

In denying respondent's petitions for writs of habeas corpus, the California Court of Appeal first, and the United States District Court later, concluded that no new jeopardy arose as a result of his transfer from Juvenile Court and trial in Superior Court. See In re Gary Steven J., 17 Cal.App.3d, at 710, 95 Cal.Rptr. at 189; 343 F.Supp., at 692. In the view of those courts, the jeopardy that attaches at an adjudicatory hearing continues until there is a final disposition of the case under the adult charge.

The phrase "continuing jeopardy" describes both a concept and a conclusion. As originally articulated by Mr. Justice Holmes in his dissent in Kepner v. United States, 195 U.S. 100, 134–137, 24 S.Ct. 797, 806, 49 L.Ed. 114 (1904), the concept has proved an interesting model for comparison with the system of constitutional protection which the Court has in fact derived from the rather ambiguous language and history of the Double Jeopardy Clause. See United States v. Wilson, supra, at 351–352, 95 S.Ct. 1013. Holmes' view has "never been adopted by a majority of this Court." United States v. Jenkins, 420 U.S. 358, 369, 95 S.Ct. 1006, 1013, 43 L.Ed.2d 250 (1975).

The conclusion, "continuing jeopardy," as distinguished from the concept, has occasionally been used to explain why an accused who has secured the reversal of a conviction on appeal may be retried for the same offense. Probably a more satisfactory explanation lies in analysis of the respective interests involved. Similarly, the fact that the proceedings against respondent had not "run their full course," Price v. Georgia, 398 U.S. at 326, 90 S.Ct. at 1759, within the contemplation of the California Welfare and Institutions Code, at the time of transfer, does not satisfactorily explain why respondent should be deprived of the constitutional protection against a second trial. If there is to be an exception to that protection in the context of the juvenile court system, it must be justified by interests of society, reflected in that unique institution, or of juveniles themselves, of sufficient substance to render tolerable the costs and burdens, noted earlier, which the exception will entail in individual cases.

C

The possibility of transfer from Juvenile Court to a court of general criminal jurisdiction is a matter of great significance to the juvenile. At the same time, there appears to be widely shared agreement that not all juveniles can benefit from the special features and programs of the juvenile court system and that a procedure for transfer to an adult court should be available. This general agreement is reflected in the fact that an overwhelming majority of jurisdictions permits transfer in certain circumstances. As might be expected, the statutory provisions differ in numerous details. Whatever their differences, however, such transfer provisions represent an attempt to impart to the juvenile court system the flexibility needed to deal with youthful offenders who cannot benefit from the specialized guidance and treatment contemplated by the system.

We do not agree with petitioner that giving respondent the constitutional protection against multiple trials in this context will diminish flexibility and informality to the extent that those qualities relate uniquely to the goals of the juvenile court system.[15] We agree that such a holding will require, in most cases, that the transfer decision be made prior to an adjudicatory hearing. To the extent that evidence concerning the alleged offense is considered relevant,[16] it may be that, in those cases where transfer is considered and rejected, some added burden will be imposed on the juvenile courts by reason of duplicative proceedings. Finally, the nature of the evidence considered at a transfer hearing may in some States require that, if transfer is rejected, a different judge preside at the adjudicatory hearing.

15. That the flexibility and informality of juvenile proceedings are diminished by the application of due process standards is not open to doubt. Due process standards inevitably produce such an effect, but that tells us no more than that the Constitution imposes burdens on the functioning of government and especially of law enforcement institutions.

16. Under Cal.Welf. & Inst'ns Code § 707 (West 1972), the governing criterion with respect to transfer, assuming the juvenile is 16 years of age is charged with a violation of a criminal statute or ordinance, is amenability "to the care, treatment and training program available through the facilities of the juvenile court." The section further provides that neither "the offense, in itself" nor the denial by the juvenile of the facts or conclusions set forth in the petition shall be "sufficient to support a finding that [he] is not a fit and proper subject to be dealt with under the provisions of the Juvenile Court Law." See n. 5, supra. The California Supreme Court has held that the only factor a juvenile court must consider is the juvenile's "behavior pattern as described in the probation officer's report," Jimmy H. v. Superior Court, 3 Cal. 3d 709, 714, 478 P.2d 32, 35 (1970), but that it may also consider, *inter alia*, the nature and circumstances of the alleged offense. See id., at 716, 478 P.2d, at 36.

In contrast to California, which does not require any evidentiary showing with respect to the commission of the offense, a number of jurisdictions require a finding of probable cause to believe the juvenile committed the offense before transfer is permitted. See Rudstein, supra, n. 14, at 298–299; Carr, supra, n. 14, at 21–22. In addition, two jurisdictions appear presently to require a finding of delinquency before the transfer of a juvenile to adult court. Ala.Code, Tit. 13, § 364 (1958) [see Rudolph v. State, 286 Ala. 189, 238 So.2d 542 (1970)]; W.Va. Code Ann. § 49–5–14 (1966).

We recognize that juvenile courts, perhaps even more than most courts, suffer from the problems created by spiraling caseloads unaccompanied by enlarged resources and manpower. See President's Commission of Law Enforcement and Administration of Justice, Task Force Report: Juvenile Delinquency and Youth Crime 7–8 (1967). And courts should be reluctant to impose on the juvenile court system any additional requirements which could so strain its resources as to endanger its unique functions. However, the burdens that petitioner envisions appear to us neither qualitatively nor quantitatively sufficient to justify a departure in this context from the fundamental prohibition against double jeopardy.

A requirement that transfer hearings be held prior to adjudicatory hearings affects not all the nature of the latter proceedings. More significant, such a requirement need not affect the quality of decisionmaking at transfer hearings themselves. In Kent v. United States, 383 U.S., at 562, 86 S.Ct. at 1057, the Court held that hearings under the statute there involved "must measure up to the essentials of due process and fair treatment." However, the Court has never attempted to prescribe criteria for, or the nature and quantum of evidence that must support, a decision to transfer a juvenile for trial in adult court. We require only that, whatever the relevant criteria, and whatever the evidence demanded, a State determine whether it wants to treat a juvenile within the juvenile court system before entering upon a proceeding that may result in an adjudication that he has violated a criminal law and in a substantial deprivation of liberty, rather than subject him to the expense, delay, strain and embarrassment of two such proceedings.[18]

Moreover, we are not persuaded that the burdens petitioner envisions would pose a significant problem for the administration of the juvenile court system. The large number of jurisdictions that presently require that the transfer decision be made prior to an adjudicatory hearing, and the absence of any indication that the juvenile courts in those jurisdictions have not been able to perform their task within that framework, suggest the contrary. The likelihood that in many cases the lack of need or basis for a transfer hearing can be recognized promptly reduces the number of cases in which a commitment of resources is necessary. In addition, we have no reason to believe that the resources available to those who recommend transfer or participate in the process leading to transfer decisions are inade-

---

18. We note that nothing decided today forecloses States from requiring, as a prerequisite to the transfer of a juvenile, substantial evidence that he committed the offense charged, so long as the showing required is not made in an adjudicatory proceeding. See Collins v. Loisel, 262 U.S. 426, 429, 43 S.Ct. 618, 625, 67 L.Ed. 1062 (1923); Serfass v. United States, 420 U.S. 377, 391–392, 95 S.Ct. 1055, 43 L.Ed.2d 265 (1975). The instant case is not one in which the judicial determination was simply a finding of e.g., probable cause. Rather, it was an adjudication that respondent had violated a criminal statute.

quate to enable them to gather the information relevant to informed decision prior to an adjudicatory hearing.[20]

To the extent that transfer hearings held prior to adjudication result in some duplication of evidence if transfer is rejected, the burden on juvenile courts will tend to be offset somewhat by the cases in which, because of transfer, no further proceedings in Juvenile Court are required. Moreover, when transfer has previously been rejected, juveniles may well be more likely to admit the commission of the offense charged, thereby obviating the need for adjudicatory hearings, then if transfer remains a possibility. Finally, we note that those States which presently require a different judge to preside at an adjudicatory hearing if transfer is rejected also permit waiver of that requirement. Where the requirement is not waived, it is difficult to see a substantial strain on judicial resources.

Quite apart from our conclusions with respect to the burdens on the juvenile court system envisioned by petitioner, we are persuaded that transfer hearings prior to adjudication will aid the objectives of that system. What concerns us here is the dilemma that the possibility of transfer after an adjudicatory hearing presents for a juvenile, a dilemma to which the Court of Appeals alluded. See supra, at 1784. Because of that possibility, a juvenile, thought to be the beneficiary of special consideration, may in fact suffer substantial disadvantages. If he appears uncooperative, he runs the risk of an adverse adjudication, as well as of an unfavorable dispositional recommendation. If, on the other hand, he is cooperative, he runs the risk of prejudicing his chances in adult court if transfer is ordered. We regard a procedure that results in such a dilemma as at odds with the goal that to the extent fundamental fairness permits, adjudicatory hearings be informal and nonadversary. See In re Gault, 387 U.S., at 25–27, 87 S.Ct. at 1442; In re Winship, 397 U.S., at 366–367, 90 S.Ct. at 1074; McKeiver v. Pennsylvania, 403 U.S., at 534, 550, 91 S.Ct. at 1981. Knowledge of the risk of transfer after an adjudicatory hearing can only undermine the potential for informality and cooperation which was intended to be the hallmark of the juvenile court system. Rather than concerning themselves with the matter at hand, establishing innocence or seeking a disposition best suited to individual correctional needs, the juvenile and his attorney are pressed into a posture of adversary wariness that is conducive to neither.

IV

We hold that the prosecution of respondent in Superior Court, after an adjudicatory proceeding in Juvenile Court, violated the Double Jeopardy Clause of the Fifth Amendment, as applied to the States

---

20. We intimate no views concerning the constitutional validity of transfer following the attachment of jeopardy at an adjudicatory hearing where the information which forms the predicate for the transfer decision could not, by the exercise of due diligence, reasonably have been obtained previously. Cf., e.g., Illinois v. Somerville, 410 U.S. 458, 93 S.Ct. 1066, 35 L.Ed.2d 425 (1973).

through the Fourteenth Amendment. The mandate of the Court of Appeals, which was stayed by that court pending our decision, directs the District Court "to issue a writ of habeas corpus directing the state court, within 60 days, to vacate the adult conviction of Jones and either set him free or remand him to the juvenile court for disposition." Since respondent is no longer subject to the jurisdiction of the California Juvenile Court, we vacate the judgment and remand the case to the Court of Appeals for such further proceedings consistent with this opinion as may be appropriate in the circumstances.

NOTES

(1) Cases decided prior to *Gault* held that the double jeopardy prohibition did not prevent a subsequent conviction in criminal court for an offense for which the juvenile had already committed prior to his being adjudicated delinquent. See, e.g., Moquin v. State, 216 Md. 524, 140 A.2d 914 (1958); Dearing v. State, 151 Tex.Cr.App. 6, 204 S.W.2d 983 (1947); but see Garza v. State, 369 S.W.2d 36 (Tex.Cr.App.1963). Courts also generally held that successive delinquency proceedings arising out of the same conduct did not violate the double jeopardy ban. See, e.g., In re McDonald, 153 A.2d 651 (D.C. Mun.App.1959); State v. Smith, 75 N.D. 29, 25 N.W.2d 270 (1946). In either case the usual explanation for this result was that because juvenile proceedings were civil and not criminal and were protective rather than punitive in nature, a juvenile was not placed in jeopardy in proceedings in juvenile court. See, e.g., Moquin v. State, 216 Md. at 527–30, 140 A.2d at 916–17.

Following *Gault*, most courts held that the double jeopardy prohibition was applicable to juvenile proceedings and thus barred institution of criminal proceedings subsequent to proceedings in juvenile court arising out of the same conduct. See, e.g., Fain v. Duff, 488 F.2d 218 (5th Cir. 1973) cert. denied 421 U.S. 999 (1975); Commonwealth ex rel. Freeman v. Superintendent of State Correctional Institution at Camp Hill, 212 Pa.Super. 422, 242 A.2d 903 (1968). Contra, State v. R.E.F., 251 So.2d 672 (Fla.App.1971), affirmed, 265 So.2d 701 (1972) (per curiam). Post-*Gault* decisions also concluded that successive delinquency proceedings for the same offense were barred by the double jeopardy clause. See, e.g., Richard M. v. Superior Court, 4 Cal.3d 370, 93 Cal.Rptr. 752, 482 P.2d 644 (1971); District of Columbia v. I.P., 335 A.2d 224 (D.C.App.1975); Fonseca v. Judges of Family Court, 59 Misc.2d 492, 299 N.Y.S.2d 493 (S.Ct., Kings Co. 1969); Collins v. State, 429 S.W.2d 650 (Tex.Civ.App.1968).

(2) Breed v. Jones raised the double jeopardy issue in the typical context of a criminal trial following an adjudicatory hearing in juvenile court. There are many other possibilities. Whitebread and Batey, Juvenile Double Jeopardy, 63 Geo.L.J. 857 (1975), explain that there are five basic situations in which the juvenile double jeopardy issue might arise. These are: (1) successive juvenile adjudications, (2) criminal proceedings that follow juvenile proceedings without a waiver hearing, (3) a juvenile adjudication that follows a criminal trial without a certification hearing, (4) criminal proceedings linked to a previous juvenile adjudication by waiver, and (5) juvenile proceedings linked to a previous criminal trial by waiver. The authors recommend legislative action to prohibit original criminal jurisdiction over acts committed by juveniles; thus, waiver would be required. Such waiver should be barred

after juvenile jeopardy has attached. Finally, they recommend that legislatures should also add a bar to jeopardy from successive juvenile adjudications. There are indications that legislatures have already begun to take some of these steps. See note (3) infra.

Without such legislative help, the authors explain, the courts have only rather sketchy case law in some of these situations to carry out the dictates of Breed v. Jones. They demonstrate that each of the five situations will require of judges a different analytical framework to implement protection against double jeopardy. Armed, however, with the Supreme Court's decision in Breed v. Jones that a juvenile court adjudication is a jeopardizing situation, the full protection against double jeopardy in the juvenile court now seems a reality. For example, in subsequent cases in which a juvenile already subjected to a delinquency adjudication was subsequently criminally prosecuted for the same offense, courts have found a violation of double jeopardy in reliance on Breed. See, e.g., Smith v. State, 316 So.2d 552 (Fla. 1975); Lincoln v. State, 138 Ga.App. 234, 225 S.E.2d 708 (1976); Parojinog v. State, 282 Md. 256, 384 A.2d 86 (1978); In re Farney, 91 Wn.2d 72, 583 P.2d 1210 (1978). Courts have also found successive delinquency proceedings based on the same conduct to be prohibitd by *Breed*. See, e.g., In re Drakeford, 32 N.C.App. 113, 230 S.E.2d 779 (1977).

(3) In the context of juvenile proceedings, when does jeopardy attach? Prior to Breed v. Jones some courts had suggested that transfer was possible after the juvenile court started hearing evidence but prior to adjudication. See, e.g., In re a Juvenile, 364 Mass. 531, 306 N.E.2d 822 (1974). One commentator had urged that transfer was possible even after an adjudication but prior to disposition. Carr, The Effect of the Double Jeopardy Clause on Juvenile Proceedings, 6 U.Toledo L.Rev. 1, 23–24 (1974). Moreover, the practice in some states was to *require* an adjudication of delinquency before transfer to criminal court. See, e.g., In re Jackson, 21 Ohio St.2d 215, 257 N.E.2d 74 (1970). The Court in Breed v. Jones rejected all of these positions, stating that jeopardy attaches when the juvenile court starts hearing evidence. For implementation of this approach see Sims v. Engle, 619 F.2d 598 (6th Cir. 1980) (prohibition against double jeopardy violated where, under state law existing at time of transfer hearing, juvenile court after investigation of charges and hearing evidence, adjudicated juvenile delinquent before transferring case for criminal prosecution).

A number of states now provide by statute that a subsequent criminal prosecution is barred if the juvenile court has started taking evidence in the case. See, e.g., Ill.Ann.Stat. ch. 37, § 702–7(3)(b) (1972). One state makes similar provision but adds that if the case is heard before a jury, jeopardy attaches when the jury selection is completed and the jury sworn. Wis.Stat. Ann. § 48.317 (1979). The latter expression, of course, is in keeping with the Supreme Court's decision in Crist v. Bretz, 437 U.S. 28, 98 S.Ct. 2156, 57 L.Ed.2d 24 (1978). Still another state provides that jeopardy attaches even earlier with the filing of a delinquency petition. Utah Code Ann. § 78–3a–44(4) (1977). A statute that provides double jeopardy protection in terms of barring a subsequent criminal prosecution if an adjudication has been entered based on the same offense would appear to be in violation of Breed v. Jones. See, e.g., Ark.Stat.Ann. § 45–429 (1977).

(4) As a part of waiver proceedings, evidence tending to show commission of the offense is often heard on the issue of waiver, particularly where there

is a requirement to establish probable cause to believe the offense was committed by the juvenile. As the Court indicated in its opinion, the decision in Breed v. Jones was not intended to affect waiver hearings; it only requires that the waiver hearing be held prior to an adjudicatory hearing. Jeopardy does not attach when the court hears evidence in a waiver hearing that can not result in an adjudication and whose only purpose is to determine whether the case should be retained by the juvenile court or transferred for criminal prosecution. Subsequent lower court decisions have borne out this conclusion. See, e.g., Stokes v. Commonwealth, 368 Mass. 754, 336 N.E.2d 735 (1975); In re L.V.A., 248 N.W.2d 864 (S.D.1976).

(5) The double jeopardy clause forbids two successive prosecutions for the same offense. When are the offenses in separate proceedings "the same" for double jeopardy purposes? In the context of successive criminal proceedings the Supreme Court in Brown v. Ohio, 432 U.S. 161, 97 S.Ct. 2221, 53 L.Ed.2d 187 (1977), relying on an even earlier decision, Blockburger v. United States, 284 U.S. 299, 52 S.Ct. 180, 76 L.Ed. 306 (1932), stated that where the same conduct is a violation of two separate criminal statutes, the test for determining whether the offenses are the same for double jeopardy purposes is whether each statutory provision requires proof of an element that the other does not.

In Illinois v. Vitale, 447 U.S. 410, 100 S.Ct. 2660, 65 L.Ed.2d 228 (1980), the Supreme Court adopted this same test for application in situations involving separate juvenile and criminal proceedings arising out of the same conduct. There the juvenile was first convicted in criminal court for failure to reduce speed to avoid an accident. Subsequently, a delinquency petition arising out of the same incident was filed in juvenile court alleging involuntary manslaughter by reckless operation of a motor vehicle. The juvenile's motion to dismiss, claiming prior jeopardy as a bar, was successful, and the state appealed. The Supreme Court of Illinois ruled in Vitale's favor on the double jeopardy issue, holding that a lesser offense necessarily includes the same elements as a greater offense and that prosecution for both offenses constitutes a violation of the double jeopardy prohibition. In re Vitale, 71 Ill. 2d 229, 375 N.E.2d 87 (1978).

Following remand by the Supreme Court for determination of whether the Illinois court's decision was based on federal or state law, 439 U.S. 974 (1978), and a decision by the Illinois court that its decision was based on federal constitutional law, the case went before the Supreme Court a second time. After stating the test as set forth above the Court expressed uncertainty as to the relationship between the two offenses under Illinois law and remanded the case a second time for further clarification. 447 U.S. 410 (1980).

The test as stated by the Supreme Court seems simple enough—whether *each* offense requires proof of an element that the other does not. In holding that double jeopardy was violated because a lesser offense necessarily includes all elements of a greater offense, did the Illinois court correctly apply the proper test?

In a Missouri case a juvenile was first adjudicated delinquent in juvenile court based on a petition alleging assault. The victim subsequently died, and a second petition containing an allegation of murder was filed. The case was transferred to criminal court where the juvenile was convicted of murder. On appeal the Missouri Court of Appeals held that the prohibition against double jeopardy had not been violated. Durant v. State, 523 S.W.2d 837 (Mo.App.1975). Did the Missouri court correctly apply the proper test?

In a North Carolina case the juvenile court dismissed a delinquency petition based on an assault charge on grounds of insufficient evidence. A subsequent petition was filed charging an affray (common law definition: a fight between two or more persons in a public place causing terror to other persons). The second petition resulted in an adjudication of delinquency. On appeal the court held that the prohibition against double jeopardy had been violated because both offenses arose out of the same conduct and the assault was a lesser included offense to the affray; proof of the affray necessarily included proof of all elements of assault. In re Drakeford, 32 N.C. App. 113, 230 S.E.2d 779 (1977). Was the reverse true, i.e., did proof of the assault include all elements of the affray? Did the North Carolina court correctly apply the proper test?

In a case involving facts almost identical to those in *Vitale* the California Supreme Court held that the ban against double jeopardy was not violated, that one can violate the Vehicular Code provision (making an unsafe lane change) without violating the vehicular manslaughter statute, and one can commit vehicular manslaughter without violating the unsafe lane change provision; therefore, the offenses are not the same. In re Dennis B., 18 Cal. 3d 687, 135 Cal.Rptr. 82, 557 P.2d 514 (1976). Did the California court correctly apply the proper test?

Compare the constitutional test as stated in *Vitale* with the following language from § 12–15–66(c) of the Alabama Code: "Criminal proceedings and other juvenile proceedings based upon the offense alleged in the petition *or an offense based upon the same conduct* are barred where the court has begun taking evidence or where the court has accepted a child's plea of guilty to the petition." (Emphasis added.) Are the two tests the same? Since the Alabama statute is an expression of state law, must they be the same?

(6) Would successive juvenile proceedings concerning the same conduct but invoking the separate delinquency and status jurisdictions of the juvenile court run afoul of the double jeopardy bar? Consider In re R.L.K., 67 Ill. App.3d 451, 23 Ill.Dec. 737, 384 N.E.2d 531 (1978), in which the court held that the double jeopardy prohibition barred delinquency proceedings against a juvenile based on the same conduct that was the subject of an earlier MINS hearing that resulted in a dismissal. Also, consider the similar issue in Garrision v. Jennings, 529 P.2d 536 (Okl.Cr.App.1974), in which the court held that jeopardy attached in a juvenile proceeding to adjudicate the juvenile a CINS where the CINS petition was based on commission of a criminal act; therefore, criminal prosecution following the CINS adjudication was barred.

(7) The Juvenile Justice Standards Relating to Transfer Between Courts provide:

2.1 Time Requirements

. . .

F. No waiver notice should be given, no waiver motion should be accepted for filing, no waiver hearing should be initiated, and no waiver decision should be issued relating to any juvenile court petition after commencement of any adjudicatory hearing relating to any transaction or episode alleged in that petition.

The Commentary explains that since the threat of a juvenile court adjudication constitutes jeopardy, the juvenile judge should not consider waiver of jurisdiction after an adjudicatory hearing has begun: "Since the only purpose which waiver can have is to facilitate the commencement of a second jeopardizing proceeding, it ought not be available."

Does 2.1(F) do any more than restate the holding in Breed v. Jones?

(8) Many commentators and Court analysts suggested that *McKeiver* signaled the end of the extension of adult constitutional protections in children's cases. The unanimous decision in Breed v. Jones may indicate that those earlier predictions do not adequately reflect the Court's direction. A better set of conclusions would seem to be that (1) use of the civil label to bar extension of due process rights in juvenile cases is finally over ("[I]t is simply too late in the day . . .", as the Court puts it); and (2) the Court is especially likely to extend adult protections where there will be little disruption to state practice in doing so. Here only Alabama, California, Massachusetts and West Virginia were required to amend their procedures for transfer to comply with the Court's vindication of the juvenile's right to be free from double jeopardy. Compare this with the major disruption the majority projects in *McKeiver* from granting a right to jury trial.

SWISHER v. BRADY

Supreme Court of the United States, 1978.
438 U.S. 204, 98 S.Ct. 2699, 57 L.Ed.2d 705.

MR. CHIEF JUSTICE BURGER delivered the opinion of the Court.

. . .

In order to understand the present Maryland scheme for the use of masters in juvenile court proceedings, it is necessary to trace briefly the history both of antecedent schemes and of this and related litigation.

Prior to July 1975, the use of masters in Maryland juvenile proceedings was governed by Rule 908(e), Maryland Rules of Procedure. It provided that a master "shall hear such cases as may be assigned to him by the court." The Rule further directed that, at the conclusion of the hearing, the master transmit the case file and his "findings and recommendations" to the Juvenile Court. If no party filed exceptions to these findings and recommendations, they were to be "promptly . . . confirmed, modified or remanded by the judge." If, however, a party filed exceptions—and in delinquency hearings, only the State had the authority to do so—then, after notice, the Juvenile Court judge would "hear the entire matter or such specific matters as set forth in the exceptions *de novo.*"

In the city of Baltimore, after the State filed a petition alleging that a minor had committed a delinquent act, the clerk of the Juvenile Court generally would assign the case to one of seven masters. In the ensuing unrecorded hearing, the State would call its witnesses and present its evidence in accordance with the rules of evidence applicable in criminal cases. The minor could offer evidence in defense. At the conclusion of the presentation of evidence, the master usually would announce his findings and contemplated recommendations. In a minority of those cases where the recommendations favored the minor's position, the State would file exceptions, whereupon the Juvenile Court judge would try the case *de novo*.

. . . .

In November 1974, . . . nine juveniles sought federal habeas corpus relief, contending that by taking exceptions to masters' recommendations favorable to them the State was violating their rights under the Double Jeopardy Clause. These same nine minors also initiated a class action under 42 U.S.C. § 1983 in which they sought a declaratory judgment and injunctive relief against the future operation of Rule 908(e). The sole constitutional basis for their complaint was, again, the Double Jeopardy Clause. A three-judge court was convened to hear this matter, and it is the judgment of that court we now review.

Before either the three-judge District Court or the single judge reviewing the habeas corpus petitions could act, the Maryland Legislature enacted legislation which, for the first time, provided a statutory basis for the use of masters in juvenile court proceedings. In doing so, it modified slightly the scheme previously operative under Rule 908(e). The new legislation required that hearings before a master be recorded and that, at their conclusion, the master submit to the Juvenile Court judge written findings of fact, conclusions of law, and recommendations. Either party was authorized to file exceptions and could elect a hearing on the record or a *de novo* hearing before the judge. The legislature specified that the master's "proposals and recommendations . . . for juvenile causes do not constitute orders or final action of the court." Accordingly, the judge could, even in the absence of exceptions, reject a master's recommendations and conduct a *de novo* hearing or, if the parties agreed, a hearing on the record. Md.Cts. & Jud.Proc.Code Ann. § 3–813 (Supp.1977).

In June, 1975, within two months of the enactment of § 3–813 and before its July 1, 1975, effective date, the single-judge United States District Court held that the Rule 908(e) provision for a *de novo* hearing on the State's exceptions violated the Double Jeopardy Clause. Aldridge v. Dean, 395 F.Supp. 1161 (Md.1975). In that court's view, a juvenile was placed in jeopardy as soon as the State offered evidence in the hearing before a master. The court also concluded that to subject a juvenile to a *de novo* hearing before the Juvenile Court judge was to place him in jeopardy a second time. Accordingly, it granted habeas corpus relief to the six petitioners already subjected by the State to a *de novo* hearing. The petitions of the remaining three, who had not yet been brought before the Juvenile Court judge, were dismissed without prejudice as being premature.

In response to both the enactment of § 3–813 and the decision in Aldridge v. Dean, supra, the Maryland Court of Appeals, in the exercise of its rulemaking power, promulgated a new rule, and the one currently in force, Rule 911, to govern the use of masters in juvenile proceedings. Rule 911 differs from the statute in significant aspects. First, in order to emphasize the nonfinal nature of a master's conclusions, it stresses that all of his "findings, conclusions, recommendations or . . . orders" are only *proposed.* Second, the State no longer has power to secure a *de novo* hearing before the Juvenile Court judge after unfavorable proposals by the master. The State still may file exceptions, but the judge can act on them only on the basis of the record made before the master and "such additional [relevant] evidence . . . to which the parties raise no objection." The judge retains his power to accept, reject, or modify the master's proposals, to remand to the master for further hearings, and to supplement the record for his own review with additional evidence to which the parties do not object.

. . .

After the effective date of Rule 911, July 1, 1975, the plaintiffs in the § 1983 action amended their complaint to bring Rule 911 within its scope. They continued to challenge the state procedure, however, only on the basis of the Double Jeopardy Clause. Other juveniles intervened as the ongoing work of the juvenile court brought them within the definition of the proposed class. Their complaints in intervention likewise rested only on the Double Jeopardy Clause.

The three-judge District Court certified the proposed class under Fed.Rule Civ.Proc. 23(b)(2) to consist of all juveniles involved in proceedings where the State had filed exceptions to a master's proposed findings of nondelinquency. That court then held that a juvenile subjected to a hearing before a master is placed in jeopardy, even though the master has no power to enter a final order. It also held that the Juvenile Court judge's review of the record constitutes a "second proceeding at which [the juvenile] must once again marshal whatever resources he can against the State's and at which the State is given a second opportunity to obtain a conviction." 436 F.Supp. 1361, 1369 (Md.1977). Accordingly, the three-judge District Court enjoined the defendant state officials from taking exceptions to either a master's proposed finding of nondelinquency or his proposed disposition.

. . .

II

The general principles governing this case are well established.

"A State may not put a defendant in jeopardy twice for the same offense. Benton v. Maryland, 395 U.S. 784. The constitutional protection against double jeopardy unequivocally prohibits a second trial following an acquittal. The public interest in the finality of criminal judgments is so strong that an acquitted defendant may not be retried even though 'the acquittal was based upon an egregiously erroneous foundation.' . . . If the innocence of the accused has been confirmed by a final judgment, the Constitution conclusively presumes that a second trial would be unfair.

"Because jeopardy attaches before the judgment becomes final, the constitutional protection also embraces the defendant's 'valued right to have his trial completed by a particular tribunal.' . . . Consequently, as a general rule, the prosecutor is entitled to one, and only one, opportunity to require an accused to stand trial." Arizona v. Washington, 434 U.S. 497, 503–505 (1978) (footnotes omitted).

In the application of these general principles, the narrow question here [12] is whether the State in filing exceptions to a master's proposals, pursuant to Rule 911, thereby "require[s] an accused to stand trial" a second time. We hold that it does not. Maryland has created a system with Rule 911 in which an accused juvenile is subjected to a single proceeding which begins with a master's hearing and culminates with an adjudication by a judge.

Importantly, a Rule 911 proceeding does not impinge on the purposes of the Double Jeopardy Clause. A central purpose "of the prohibition against successive trials" is to bar "the prosecution [from] another opportunity to supply evidence which it failed to muster in the first proceeding." Burks v. United States, 437 U.S. 1, 11, 98 S.Ct. 2141, 2147, 57 L.Ed.2d 1 (1978). A Rule 911 proceeding does not provide the prosecution that forbidden "second crack." The State presents its evidence once before the master. The record is then closed, and additional evidence can be received by the Juvenile Court judge only with the consent of the minor.

The Double Jeopardy Clause also precludes the prosecutor from "enhanc[ing] the risk that an innocent defendant may be convicted," . . . by taking the question of guilt to a series of persons or groups empowered to make binding determinations. Appellees contend that in its operation Rule 911 gives the State the chance to persuade two such factfinders: first the master, then the Juvenile Court judge. In support of this contention they point to evidence that

---

12. The State contends that jeopardy does not attach at the hearing before the master. Our decision in Breed v. Jones, 421 U.S. 519, 95 S.Ct. 1779, 44 L.Ed.2d 346 (1975), however, suggests the contrary conclusion. "We believe it is simply too late in the day to conclude . . . that a juvenile is not put in jeopardy at a proceeding whose object is to determine whether he has committed acts that violate a criminal law and whose potential consequences include both the stigma inherent in such a determination and the deprivation of liberty for many years."

Id., at 529. The California juvenile proceeding reviewed in *Breed* involved the use of a referee, or master, and was not materially different—for purposes of analysis of attachment of jeopardy—from a Rule 911 proceeding. See generally In re Edgar M., 14 Cal.3d 727, 537 P.2d 406 (1975); cf. Jesse W. v. Superior Court, 20 Cal.3d 893, 576 P.2d 963 (1978).

It is not essential to decision in this case, however, to fix the precise time when jeopardy attaches.

juveniles and their parents sometimes consider the master "the judge" and his recommendations "the verdict." Within the limits of jury trial rights, see McKeiver v. Pennsylvania, 403 U.S. 528, 91 S.Ct. 1976, 29 L.Ed.2d 647 (1971), and other constitutional constraints, it is for the State, not the parties, to designate and empower the factfinder and adjudicator. And here Maryland has conferred those roles only on the Juvenile Court judge. Thus, regardless of which party is initially favored by the master's proposals, and regardless of the presence or absence of exceptions, the judge is empowered to accept, modify, or reject those proposals.

Finally, there is nothing in the record to indicate that the procedure authorized under Rule 911 unfairly subjects the defendant to the embarrassment, expense, and ordeal of a second trial proscribed in Green v. United States, 355 U.S. 184, 78 S.Ct. 221, 2 L.Ed.2d 199 (1957). Indeed, there is nothing to indicate that the juvenile is even brought before the judge while he conducts the "hearing on the record," or that the juvenile's attorney appears at the "hearing" and presents oral argument or written briefs. But even if there were such participation or appearance, the burdens are more akin to those resulting from a judge's permissible request for post-trial briefing or argument following a bench trial than to the "expense" of a full–blown second trial contemplated by the Court in *Green.*

In their effort to characterize a Rule 911 proceeding as two trials for double jeopardy purposes, appellees rely on two decisions of this Court, Breed v. Jones, 421 U.S. 519, 95 S.Ct. 1779, 44 L.Ed.2d 346 (1975), and United States v. Jenkins, 420 U.S. 358, 95 S.Ct. 1006, 43 L.Ed.2d 250 (1975).

In *Breed,* we held that a juvenile was placed twice in jeopardy when, after an adjudicatory hearing in Juvenile Court on a charge of delinquent conduct, he was transferred to adult criminal court, tried, and convicted for the same conduct. All parties conceded that jeopardy attached at the second proceeding in criminal court. The State contended, however, that jeopardy did not attach in the Juvenile Court proceeding, although that proceeding could have culminated in a deprivation of the juvenile's liberty. We rejected this contention and also the contention that somehow jeopardy "continued" from the first to the second trial. *Breed* is therefore inapplicable to the Maryland scheme, where juveniles are subjected to only one proceeding, or "trial."

Appellees also stress this language from *Jenkins*:

"[I]t is enough for purposes of the Double Jeopardy Clause . . . that further proceedings of some sort, devoted to the resolution of factual issues going to the elements of the offense charged, would have been required upon reversal and remand. *Even if the District Court were to receive no additional evidence, it would still be necessary for it to make supplemental findings* . . .. [To do so] would violate the Double Jeopardy Clause." 420 U.S., at 370 (emphasis added).

Although we doubt that the Court's decision in a case can be correctly identified by reference to three isolated sentences, any language in *Jenkins* must now be read in light of our subsequent decision in United States v. Scott, 437 U.S. 82, 98 S.Ct. 2187, 57 L.Ed.2d 65 (1978). In *Scott* we held that it is not all proceedings requiring the making of supplemental findings that are barred by the Double Jeopardy Clause, but only those that follow a previous trial ending in an acquittal; in a conviction either not reversed on appeal or reversed because of insufficient evidence, see Burks v. United States, supra; or in a mistrial ruling not prompted by "manifest necessity," see Arizona v. Washington, 434 U.S. 497, 98 S.Ct. 824, 54 L.Ed.2d 717 (1978). A Juvenile Court judge's decision terminating a Rule 911 proceeding follows none of those occurrences. Furthermore, *Jenkins* involved appellate review of the final judgment of a trial court fully empowered to enter that judgment. Nothing comparable occurs in a Rule 911 proceeding. . . .

To the extent the Juvenile Court judge makes supplemental findings in a manner permitted by Rule 911—either *sua sponte*, in response to the State's exceptions, or in response to the juvenile's exceptions, and either on the record or on a record supplemented by evidence to which the parties raise no objection—he does so without violating the constraints of the Double Jeopardy Clause.

Accordingly, we reverse and remand for further proceedings consistent with this opinion.

NOTES

(1) A number of states provide for hearings before referees or masters. What characteristic of the Maryland procedure was critical to the Court's conclusion that there was one continuous hearing and thus no second exposure to jeopardy? Was it significant that the master's findings were advisory, or that the juvenile court judge could only review the record and not conduct a *de novo* hearing? In California a similar case was first heard by a referee, who dismissed the petition for insufficiency of evidence. The juvenile court judge ordered a rehearing, and the juvenile sought a writ of prohibition raising prior jeopardy as a bar. The California Supreme Court, while acknowledging that under the California procedure a referee's findings are only advisory, held that where the juvenile court acts not just to review the referee's findings but rather to conduct a *de novo* hearing, this constitutes a second exposure to jeopardy and violates the prohibition against double jeopardy. Jesse W. v. Superior Court, 20 Cal.3d 893, 145 Cal.Rptr. 1, 576 P.2d 963 (1978).

In California v. Jesse W., 439 U.S. 922, 99 S.Ct. 304, 58 L.Ed.2d 315 (1978), the Supreme Court granted certiorari, vacated the judgment, and remanded the case for reconsideration in light of Swisher v. Brady. On remand, however, the California Supreme Court distinguished *Swisher* and re-affirmed its earlier decision:

It is now undisputed that jeopardy attaches in juvenile proceedings when "entered upon" whether before a juvenile court judge or referee, notwithstanding that a referee's findings and orders may be advisory only. We held in our earlier opinion that the advisory nature of a referee's findings and orders were such that no second exposure to jeopardy occurred when such findings and orders were merely reviewed and acted upon by the court: "In such instance there is but one continuing proceeding leading to but a single adjudication." We approved such "review" proceedings by a juvenile court judge, and held they did not infringe any constitutional prohibition.

Our statutory proceedings were held deficient when—in place of juvenile court review and action on a referee's recommended findings and orders—the juvenile court abandons those findings and recommendations and embarks upon a rehearing de novo. "A rehearing de novo 'is in no sense a review of the hearing previously held, but is a complete trial of the controversy, the same as if no previous hearing had ever been held.' . . . The question thus becomes whether there is a second exposure to jeopardy *after* an initial exposure in proceedings before the referee, the referee's determinations are abandoned rather than reviewed, and another, independent proceeding is commenced before a juvenile court judge."

Jesse W. v. Superior Court, 26 Cal.3d 41, 44, 160 Cal.Rptr. 700, 701, 603 P.2d 1296, 1297 (1979).

(2) The Juvenile Justice Standards Relating to Court Organization and Administration oppose the continued use of referees. Section 2.2 of the standards asserts that "only judges should perform judicial case decision-making functions." Id. at 22. In the Commentary to the section it is stated that the utilization of referees in the juvenile court "seems to symbolize the lowered status of that court." Id. at 23.

IV. POLICE INVESTIGATION

A. TAKING INTO CUSTODY

STATE IN INTEREST OF J.B.

Juvenile and Domestic Relations Court, Union County, New Jersey, 1974.
131 N.J.Super. 6, 328 A.2d 46.

BRODY, J. J. D. R. C.

The juvenile, charged with delinquency for possessing more than 25 grams of marijuana, moves to suppress the fruits of a warrantless search of his person.

Plainfield police officers Peter Cochin and Robert Robinson were on radio car patrol early December 9, 1973 when at approximately 1:30 a. m. they received a dispatch from headquarters followed shortly by a dispatch from an officer at the scene of an accident. The substance of these dispatches was that a car had struck a parked car, that witnesses had observed a white male with long hair alight from the errant vehicle and flee on foot toward nearby railroad tracks, and that the ignition key was missing from the vehicle which caused the accident.

As the officers drove toward where the fleeing driver was reported heading, they saw a 15-year-old white boy with long hair walking on the sidewalk in a black neighborhood several blocks from the accident site. His lip was bleeding, his right arm appeared to be hurt and his clothes were wet. At the time, bushes along the railroad tracks were wet from an earlier rain.

The officers stopped the boy, the juvenile in this case, and asked him to account for himself. He offered a succession of three inconsistent stories. Initially he claimed to have been beaten by a "black dude" but could not give details. He then claimed he got hurt in a tavern fight but was unable to give any corroborating detail. Finally, after being advised where he was, he described being beaten up somewhere on Richmond Street in Plainfield but was unable to give details.

Officer Cochin then conducted a full search of the juvenile. He testified that he was looking for the ignition key to the car involved in the accident. In a right jacket pocket he uncovered two plastic bags allegedly containing marijuana, whereupon he told the juvenile that he was under arrest. The officers took the boy to a hospital where they conducted a more extensive search, uncovering in one of his socks a third bag allegedly containing marijuana.

After the searches the officers learned that the vehicle causing the accident had been reported stolen. They both testified that at the

263

time of the searches they believed the juvenile guilty only of "hit and run." It did not then occur to them that the car he was driving might have been stolen.

On the State's motion before hearing the judge dismissed for lack of evidence all complaints against the juvenile predicated on his use of the car at the time of the accident.

. . .

While the term "arrest" is not to be used to describe taking a juvenile into custody, it will be so used in this opinion for the purpose of evaluating the lawfulness of the search.

New Jersey adheres to the common-law rule that a warrantless arrest for a felony is lawful if the arresting officer has probable cause, but unlawful for a misdemeanor unless the offense was committed in the presence of the officer. . . .

. . .

New Jersey does not classify its offenses as common-law misdemeanors and felonies. As to the application of the in-presence requirement, the distinction depends upon the maximum punishment attached to the offense: an offense carrying a punishment of imprisonment up to one year is the equivalent of a common-law misdemeanor, and an offense carrying a maximum imprisonment in excess of one year is the equivalent of a common-law felony. Thus, the in-presence requirement applies to disorderly persons and motor vehicle offenses.

A lawful custodial arrest itself justifies a full search of the person arrested. . . .

The criteria for the lawful arrest of a juvenile are those applicable to arrest for an adult offense (II hereafter) supplemented by criteria contained in rules of court pertaining to juvenile offenses.

. . .

[The court concludes the boy could not have been lawfully arrested on these facts had he been an adult.]

The Juvenile Act and implementing rules of court, both effective March 1, 1974, address themselves to searches and arrests of juveniles. N.J.S.A. 2A:4–60 guarantees juveniles "the right to be secure from unreasonable searches and seizures." N.J.S.A. 2A:4–54(a) (2) delegates to the Supreme Court the authority to establish appropriate standards for making a warrantless arrest for delinquency.

R. 5:8–2, implementing the new statute, provides in part:

A law enforcement officer may take into custody without process any juvenile who he has probable cause to believe is delinquent or in need of supervision.

Since delinquency is now a violation of any penal statute, had the events in this case occurred on or after March 1, 1974, the search would have been lawful because the officers had probable cause to believe that the juvenile violated N.J.S.A. 39:4–129 by failing to attach notice of his identity to the parked car. Lacking an in-presence requirement, the new rule thus renders admissible against a juvenile evidence which would be excluded from the trial of an adult.

This disparity is not constitutionally offensive. The in-presence requirement being nonconstitutional, it may be legislatively abolished as to particular offenses or circumstances. Because the applicability of the requirement depends upon the severity of the punishment attached to an offense, the requirement is alien to juvenile cases, where there is no punishment. State in the Interest of M. L., 64 N.J. 438, 317 A.2d 65 (1974). This is not just a matter of semantics. Juvenile offenses are not classified in terms of the severity of possible judicial dispositions. Under the new act, juveniles coming within the jurisdiction of the court are classified either as delinquent or in need of supervision. The disposition of a case turns less on what the juvenile has done or failed to do, than on what needs to be done for the juvenile. The absence of the in-presence requirement does not, therefore, deny juveniles due process, the constitutional standard established for juvenile cases in In re Gault, 387 U.S. 1 (1967).

The search and arrest in the present case, however, occurred before the effective date of the Juvenile Act and its implementing rules of court. Because the purpose of the exclusionary rule is to curb police excesses, the standards of a lawful arrest and search are those in effect at the time of the police action. Linkletter v. Walker, 381 U.S. 618, 85 S.Ct. 1731, 14 L.Ed.2d 601 (1965).

R. 5:8–2 then in effect provided in part:

> A law enforcement officer may take into custody without process any juvenile who in his opinion *is engaging* in conduct defined by law as juvenile delinquency. [Emphasis supplied]

Unlike the new rule which has no in-presence requirement, the former rule required it in all cases. The Supreme Court avoided this aspect of the former rule in a juvenile homicide case by holding that the arrest criteria for adult offenses are also applicable to juveniles. State v. Smith, 32 N.J. 501, 531, 161 A.2d 520 (1960). As discussed in II above, however, the search in this case cannot be sustained under those criteria.

The conduct which the arresting officer must have witnessed under the former rule is "juvenile delinquency" as then defined by law. That definition, found in the former Juvenile Act, includes "idly roaming the streets at night" and any "deportment endangering the morals, health or general welfare of [a child under 18 years of age]." N.J.S.A. 2A:4–14(2)(k), (m). The constitutionality of these definitions has been sustained.

The words of the former rule, "in his opinion," do not permit the officer to arrest at whim. He must be held to the constitutional standard of probable cause which is implicit in the language of the rule.

I have no difficulty finding that the arresting officers had probable cause to believe that the juvenile was at the time of the search engaging in conduct then defined by law as juvenile delinquency. Indeed, if "idly roaming" the streets at night is inaccurate, it is so only because there was probable cause to believe that the juvenile was purposefully escaping from the scene of an accident he had just caused which together with his apparent injuries was deportment endangering his morals, health and general welfare.

The initial search was lawful. The later search was also lawful either as a continuation of the first search or as an incident to the formal lawful arrest. United States v. Robinson, supra.

The juvenile's motion to suppress is denied.

NOTES

(1) Juvenile codes typically provide law enforcement officials with a broad grant of jurisdiction to take juveniles into custody. Situations involving noncriminal conduct, e.g., truancy, running away from home, disobedience to parents, may also be included within the scope of jurisdiction. See e.g., Wis.Stat.Ann. § 48.19(1)(d) (1979); Ohio Rev.Code Ann. § 2151.31(C), (E) (1981); Ga.Code Ann. § 15–11–17(a) (1982). These statutes indicate that the decision to take a youth into custody is regarded primarily as a police decision. A serious question arises as to whether a police officer should be allowed such unchecked discretion in deciding whether to take into custody a youth not charged with a criminal violation. New York's juvenile jurisdiction statute, N.Y.Fam.Ct.Act § 721 (McKinney, 1975), furnishes a progressive alternative in providing that a person under the age of sixteen may be taken into custody without a warrant only when he is committing an act that if performed by an adult would justify an arrest. Thus, the statute does not authorize taking a juvenile into custody on the ground that he is in need of supervision, because in such situations there is no such urgency that the matter may not be dealt with by summons.

Under this statutory scheme if a juvenile violates a criminal law he can be taken into custody on the same basis that an adult can be arrested. If the juvenile's conduct or surroundings indicate something less than criminal behavior, New York law does not authorize taking him into custody; rather, one may make application to a judicial officer for issuance of a summons, presumably upon presenting the magistrate with facts supporting the belief that the minor requires supervision.

As the Committee Comment following Section 721 explains, no situation in which a youth requires supervision is so compelling that it cannot be handled through use of a summons. See S. Davis, Rights of Juveniles, 3–10 (1981).

(2) Cases may arise, of course, in which the child's immediate safety is in peril, and in such cases the officer may need to act immediately to prevent harm to the child. In State v. Hunt, 2 Ariz.App. 6, 406 P.2d 208 (1965), an officer responded to the call of a babysitter who had discovered a five-year-old child lying on the floor of a furnace room, her hands tied behind her back, her head under the hot water heater, and blood on her face from what appeared to be strap marks. The court held the police officer had not only a right but a duty to enter Dr. and Mrs. Hunt's home immediately to protect the child and that he would have been remiss to have sought a warrant or

delayed in any way in the face of such exigent circumstances. The police officer acted properly to remove the child quickly from immediate risk of substantial harm.

The New York Family Court Act provides express statutory authority for emergency warrantless removal of the child in such a case:

§ 1024. Emergency removal without court order

(a) A peace officer, a law enforcement official, or an agent of a duly incorporated society for the prevention of cruelty to children or a designated employee of a city of county department of social services may take a child into protective custody of any such person or any physician treating such child may keep a child in his custody without an order under section one thousand twenty-two and without the consent of the parent or other person legally responsible for the child's care, regardless of whether the parent or other person legally responsible for the child's care is absent, if (i) the child is in such circumstances or condition that his continuing in said place of residence or in the care and custody of the parent or person legally responsible for the child's care presents an imminent danger to the child's life or health; and

(ii) there is not time enough to apply for an order under section one thousand twenty-two.

(3) As the principal case illustrates, the trend is that the law of arrest applies to juveniles in the same manner in which it is applicable to adults. The Juvenile Justice Standards Relating to Police Handling of Juvenile Problems support the court's view in the principal case. The Standards provide:

3.2   Police investigation into criminal matters should be similar whether the suspect is an adult or a juvenile. Juveniles, therefore, should receive at least the same safeguards available to adults in the criminal justice system. This should apply to:

A. preliminary investigations (e.g., stop and frisk);

B. the arrest process;

C. search and seizure;

D. questioning;

E. pretrial identification; and

F. prehearing detention and release.

For some investigative procedures, greater constitutional safeguards are needed because of the vulnerability of juveniles. Juveniles should not be permitted to waive constitutional rights on their own. In certain investigative areas not governed by constitutional guidelines, guidance to police officers should be provided either legislatively or administratively by court rules or through police agency policies.

See also the Commentary to Standard 3.2 contained in the Standards Relating to Police Handling of Juvenile Problems volume at pages 54–65.

(4) Following the decision to take the child into custody, the police officer must then decide whether to invoke the formal juvenile justice process. While most police officers are well aware of the inevitable stigmatizing effect of this second decision, they often lack the resources and opportunities to conduct extensive inquiries into individual cases. As a result, stereotypes

may exert inordinate influence. Young people whose backgrounds indicate that they have bright futures may be treated differently from those whose situation indicates that their prospects are not so auspicious. To minimize this undesirable result, the Juvenile Justice Standards Relating to Police Handling of Juvenile Problems propose the following:

2.3 Since other volumes in the Juvenile Justice Standards Project conclude that serious harm can be done to juveniles simply by their being referred into the formal juvenile justice process, police should not make such referrals unless:

A. serious or repeated criminal conduct is involved; or

B. less serious criminal conduct is involved and lesser restrictive alternatives such as those described in Standard 2.4 are not appropriate under the circumstances.

(5) State statutes typically require police officers to handle arrested juveniles in special ways. The following are examples of some of the special duties imposed upon the police. Consider how and why these duties differ from those imposed when the arrestee is an adult. Do you feel in each instance that the difference in treatment is justified as a matter of legislative policy?

(a) *Notification of Parents, the Court, and Others*

Alaska Stat. § 47.10.140:

Temporary detention and detention hearing. (a) A peace officer may arrest a minor who violates a law or ordinance in his presence, or who he reasonably believes is a fugitive from justice. A peace officer may continue a lawful arrest made by a citizen. He may have the minor detained in a juvenile detention facility if in his opinion it is necessary to do so to protect the minor or the community.

(b) A peace officer who has a minor detained under (a) of this section shall immediately, and in no event more than 12 hours later, notify the court, the minor's parents or guardian, and the Department of Health and Social Services of the officer's action. . . .

. . .

California Welf. and Inst.Code § 308:

Notice to parent or guardian; right to make telephone calls

(a) When an officer takes a minor before a probation officer pursuant to this article, he shall take immediate steps to notify the minor's parent, guardian, or a responsible relative that such minor is in custody and the place where he is being held.

(b) Immediately after being taken to a place of confinement pursuant to this article and, except where physically impossible, no later than one hour after he has been taken into custody, the minor shall be advised and has the right to make at least two telephone calls from the place where he is being held, one call completed to his parent or guardian, a responsible relative, or his employer, and another call completed to an attorney. The calls shall be at public expense, if the calls are completed to telephone numbers within the local calling area, and in the presence of a public officer or employee. Any public officer or employee who willfully deprives a minor taken into custody of his right to make such telephone calls is guilty of a misdemeanor.

(b) *Duties of peace officer after taking into custody or on delivery by private person*

New York Fam.Ct.Act § 724:

(a) If a peace officer or a police officer takes into custody under section seven hundred twenty-one or if a person is delivered to him under section seven hundred twenty-three, the officer shall immediately notify the parent or other person legally responsible for his care, or the person with whom he is domiciled, that he has been taken into custody.

(b) After making every reasonable effort to give notice under paragraph (a), the officer shall:

(i) release the child to the custody of his parent or other person legally responsible for his care upon the written promise, without security, of the person to whose custody the child is released that he will produce the child before the family court in that county at a time and place specified in writing; or

(ii) forthwith and with all reasonable speed take the child directly, and without his first being taken to the police station house, to the family court located in the county in which the act occasioning the taking into custody allegedly was done, unless the officer determines that it is necessary to question the child, in which case he may take the child to a facility designated by the appropriate appellate division of the supreme court as a suitable place for the questioning of children and there question him for a reasonable period of time; or

(iii) take the child to a place certified by the state division for youth as a juvenile detention facility for the reception of children.

(c) In the absence of special circumstances, the peace officer shall release the child in accord with paragraph (b)(i)

(d) In determining what is a "reasonable period of time" for questioning a child, the child's age and the presence or absence of his parents or other person legally responsible for his care shall be included among the relevant considerations.

(c) *Separate Detention and Incarceration*

Alaska Stat. § 47.10.130:

Detention. No minor under 18 years of age who is detained pending hearing may be incarcerated in a jail unless assigned to separate quarters so that the minor cannot communicate with or view adult prisoners convicted of, under arrest for, or charged with a crime. When a minor is detained pending hearing, his parent, guardian, or custodian shall be notified immediately. . . .

California Welf. and Inst.Code § 207:

Place of detention

(a) No court, judge, referee, or peace officer shall knowingly detain in any jail or lockup any person under the age of 18 years, unless a judge of the juvenile court shall determine that there are no other proper and adequate facilities for the care and detention of such person, or unless such person has been transferred by the juvenile court to another court for proceedings not under the Juvenile Court Law and has been charged with or convicted of a felony. . . .

(b) Notwithstanding the provisions of subdivision (a), no minor shall be detained in any jail, lockup, juvenile hall, or other secure facility who is taken into custody solely upon the ground that he is a person described by Section 601 or adjudged to be such or made a ward of the juvenile court solely upon that ground, except as provided in subdivision (c). If any such minor, other than a minor described in subdivision (c), is detained, he shall be detained in a sheltered-care facility or crisis resolution home as provided for in Section 654, or in a nonsecure facility provided for in subdivision (a), (b), (c), or (d) of Section 727.

(d) *Limitations on the taking and the distribution of Fingerprints and Photographs as a means of identification.*

Kan.Stat.Ann. § 38–805c(a):

(a) No fingerprints or photograph shall be taken of any child less than 18 years of age who is taken into custody for any purposes except that: (1) Fingerprints and photographs of such child may be taken if authorized by the judge of the district court having jurisdiction; or (2) fingerprints of such child may be taken if the child is taken into custody for an offense which, if committed by a person 18 or more years of age, would make such person liable to be arrested and prosecuted for the commission of a felony . . . . When fingerprints or photographs are taken, they shall be taken as a civil record and not as a criminal record.

(e) *In the interest of confidentiality, limitations may be placed on distribution to other law enforcement agencies.*

Ill.Ann.Stat. ch. 37, § 702–8(2):

(2) No law enforcement officer or other person or agency may knowingly transmit to the Department of Corrections, Adult Division or the Department of Law Enforcement or to the Federal Bureau of Investigation any fingerprint or photograph relating to a minor who has been arrested or taken into custody before his 17th birthday, unless the court in proceedings under this Act authorizes the transmission or enters an order under Section 2–7 permitting the institution of criminal proceedings.

(f) *Separate and Confidential Police Records (sometimes including the possibility of expungement).*

Kan.Stat.Ann. § 38–805c(b)–(d):

(b) All records of law enforcement officers or agencies, municipal courts and other governmental entities in this state concerning a public offense committed or alleged to have been committed by a child less than 18 years of age, shall be kept separate from criminal or other records, and shall not be disclosed to anyone, except:

(1) The judge, and members of the court staff designated by the judge, of a district court having the child before it in any proceeding;

(2) the parties to the proceeding and their counsel;

(3) the officers of public institutions or agencies to whom the child is committed;

(4) law enforcement officers of other jurisdictions when necessary for the discharge of their official duties;

(5) to any other person, when ordered by a judge of a district court in this state, under such conditions as the judge may prescribe; or

(6) as provided in subsection (c) of K.S.A. 38–805 and amendments thereto.

(c) Subsections (b) and (d) shall not apply to records and files:

(1) Made in conjunction with prosecutions pursuant to the code of criminal procedure;

(2) concerning an offense for which a district court has directed prosecution pursuant to K.S.A. 38–808;

(3) concerning a traffic offense described in subsection (e) of K.S.A. 38–802, which was committed or alleged to have been committed by a child 14 years of age or more; or

(4) specified in K.S.A. 38–805 and amendments thereto.

(d) It shall be the duty of any law enforcement officer, judge or other public officer, making or causing to be made any record or file concerning an offense committed or alleged to have been committed by a person less than 18 years of age, to promptly report to the judge of the district court of the district of such officer or judge the fact that such record or file has been made and the substance thereof together with all of the information in the possession of the officer or judge pertaining to the making of such record or file.

B.   SEARCHES AND SEIZURES

IN RE RONALD B.

Supreme Court, Appellate Division, Second Department, 1978.
61 A.D.2d 204, 401 N.Y.S.2d 544.

LATHAM, JUSTICE.

The incident giving rise to the finding of juvenile delinquency occurred on January 27, 1976, when Ronald B., a 14-year-old boy, was enrolled in a Public School in Queens. Sometime during that day, Gary Simmons, a school official was conversing with Ronald in the hallway of the school. Another school official, Richard Salter, came over to Ronald and told him that he had been informed that Ronald had a gun. Ronald denied it and refused to allow Salter to search him. While Ronald was talking to him, Salter noticed that Ronald's right hand was in his pocket. He asked him to withdraw it. At first Ronald ignored the request, then made a sudden movement to take his hand out of his pocket. Both Salter and Simmons grabbed his arm and withdrew it slowly from the pocket. Ronald was holding a .32 caliber pistol. Salter called the police and the gun was confiscated. A ballistics test showed that the gun was operable.

A hearing was held in the Family Court to determine whether Ronald was a juvenile delinquent. At the hearing, Ronald's attorney raised two points which are now before this court. The first raises the issue whether the seizure of the gun should be suppressed because it was allegedly based on an unconstitutional search. The second questions the admissibility into evidence of the ballistics report without requiring the testimony of the police officer who conducted the test. The Family Court resolved both issues contrary to the position of the appellant. We agree and therefore affirm.

The Court of Appeals, in People v. Scott D., 34 N.Y.2d 483, 358 N.Y.S.2d 403, 315 N.E.2d 466, held that students are protected from unreasonable searches and seizures by agents of the State, whether they are school officials or police officers. Appellant erroneously contends that *Scott D.* holds that a search in a school by a teacher should be equated to a search by a policeman in the street, and that it must be based on probable cause. Appellant's interpretation indicates his misunderstanding of the holding in the *Scott D.* case. That case does not require that a search by a school official be based on the same standard applicable to a police officer i.e., probable cause.

The Fourth Amendment of the United States Constitution requires only that searches be "reasonable" (see People v. Peters, 18 N.Y.2d 238, 273 N.Y.S.2d 217, 219 N.E.2d 595). A school official may have a reasonable suspicion that a dangerous situation exists, and may act on that suspicion. "A school is a special kind of place in which serious and dangerous wrongdoing is intolerable. Youngsters in a school, for their own sake, as well as that of their age peers in the school, may not be treated with the same circumspection required outside the school or to which self-sufficient adults are entitled" (People v. Scott D., 34 N.Y.2d 483, 486–487, 358 N.Y.S.2d 403, 406, 315 N.E.2d 466, 468, supra).

Officials in a school act *in loco parentis.* Although this concept is limited, it does allow school personnel to exercise such powers of control, restraint and correction over pupils as is reasonably necessary to facilitate the educational functions of a school. The doctrine is embedded in common law and has recently been enunciated by the decision of the Supreme Court of the United States in Ingraham v. Wright, 430 U.S. 651, which upheld a teacher's right to discipline children by use of corporal punishment. The Supreme Court held (p. 1418):

> " '[T]he court has repeatedly emphasized the need for affirming the comprehensive authority of the States and of school officials, consistent with fundamental constitutional safeguards, to prescribe and control conduct in the schools.' Tinker v. Des Moines School District, 393 U.S. 503, 89 S.Ct. 733, 21 L.Ed.2d 731".

A balance must always be reached between protecting personal rights and safeguarding the security of all of the students. *Scott D.* sets forth some factors to consider in determining the reasonableness of a school search. These factors include "the child's age, history and record in the school, the prevalence and seriousness of the problem in the school to which the search was directed, and, of course, the exigency to make the search without delay." (34 N.Y.2d at p. 489, 358 N.Y.S.2d at p. 408, 315 N.E.2d at p. 470.)

In the case now before us, we are dealing with a 14-year-old boy, in a school, with a loaded weapon in his pocket. There is no doubt in our minds that a school official has the right to "frisk" a child based on a reasonble suspicion that he has a gun. Police officers are given that same standard when searching adults for guns (see CPL 140.50). It would be absurd to have a higher standard for those with a quasi-parental obligation than for police officers who approach an adult on the street. The mere fact that a child may have a loaded gun in a school creates exigencies affecting the security of all of the children in the school (cf. People v. Taggart, 20 N.Y.2d 335, 283 N.Y.S.2d 1, 229 N.E.2d 581).

Furthermore, the officials in this case did not in fact search Ronald. When he made a suspicious movement, they merely grabbed his hand and found a gun in it. If, however, they had frisked him, their action would still have been reasonable under the circumstances. The primary purpose of school searches is to protect the school environment. What is not allowed are unjustified random searches that may psychologically harm a child. However, a "school official, standing *in loco parentis* to the children entrusted to his care, has, *inter alia*, the long-honored obligation to protect them while in his charge, so far as possible, from harmful and dangerous influences" (People v. Jackson, 65 Misc.2d 909, 910, 319 N.Y.S.2d 731, 733, affd. 30 N.Y.2d 734, 333 N.Y.S.2d 167, 284 N.E.2d 153). Salter and Simmons, without regard to their own safety, fulfilled this obligation when they questioned Ronald, found the gun and confiscated it. The Law Guardian, apparently, believes that the hands of school officials should be tied when dealing with unfortunate children caught in criminal activity at young ages. We cannot sanction such a legal doctrine.

. . .

Thus, Family Court was correct in its rulings involving the admissibility of the gun and the ballistics report, and properly found that appellant was a juvenile delinquent.

Order of the Family Court, Queens County, dated September 1, 1977, affirmed . . . .

NOTES

(1) The leading case holding the fourth amendment applicable to juvenile proceedings is State v. Lowry, 95 N.J.Super. 307, 230 A.2d 907 (1967). Relying heavily upon the rationale enunciated in Mapp v. Ohio, 367 U.S. 643, 81 S.Ct. 1684, 6 L.Ed.2d 1081 (1961), the *Lowry* court emphasized that:

> The historical development clearly indicates that the rule is not only a basic right to *all* persons to privacy, security and liberty, whether accused of a crime or not, but is fundamental to the concept of due process, a principle precluding adjudications based on methods that offend a sense of justice and one that must endure if our society is to remain free. To insure a fact-finding process which at least measures up to the essentials of fair treatment, State v. Carlo, 48 N.J. 224, 236, 225 A.2d 110 (1966), the constitutional safeguard enunciated in the Fourth Amendment must be applicable to juveniles. 230 A.2d 910–11.

(2) Most state courts that have dealt with the fourth amendment in the juvenile context have employed instead the traditional due process and fair treatment analysis that marks inquiries into the constitutionality of state conduct under the fourteenth amendment. Other courts have interpreted *Gault* to require that juveniles in delinquency proceedings be accorded the same protections as adults in criminal trials, including the right to the exclusion of illegally seized evidence. Can you explain why such a broad interpretation of *Gault* is incorrect? Although the reasoning may differ, with few exceptions the decisions are uniform nationwide. See In re Morris, 29 Ohio Misc. 71, 278 N.E.2d 701 (Com.Pleas, Juv.Div., Columbiana County 1971); In re Harvey, 222 Pa.Super. 222, 295 A.2d 93 (1972); Ciulla v. State, 434 S.W.2d 948 (Tex. 1968).

A number of other state courts hold the fourth amendment applicable to juvenile proceedings without stating the basis or rationale for so doing. See e.g. In re Robert T., 8 Cal.App.3d 990, 88 Cal.Rptr. 37 (1970); In re Marsh, 40 Ill.2d 53, 237 N.E.2d 529 (1960); In re Urbasek, 76 Ill.App.2d 375, 222 N.E.2d 233 (1966), reversed on other grounds, 38 Ill.2d 535, 232 N.E.2d 716 (1968); In re J.R.M., 487 S.W.2d 502 (Mo.1972); In re Robert P., 40 A.D.2d 638, 336 N.Y.S.2d 212 (1972) (per curiam). This often occurs when the court resolves the merits of the juvenile's search and seizure claim against him assuming but not discussing the applicability of the fourth amendment.

(3) Once the threshold question of the fourth amendment's applicability is answered in the affirmative, courts tend to resolve basic search and seizure issues in juvenile cases in precisely the same manner in which they are resolved in criminal cases. As in criminal proceedings, a warrantless search made incident to an arrest is lawful only if the arrest itself is lawful. See, e.g., In re Marsh, 40 Ill.2d 53, 237 N.E.2d 529 (1968). Stop and frisk procedures apply to juveniles as well as adults. See, e.g., In re Tony C., 21 Cal.3d 888, 148 Cal.Rptr. 366, 582 P.2d 957 (1978); In re "Lang," 44 Misc.2d 900, 255 N.Y.S.2d 887 (Fam.Ct., New York, County 1965); see also In re Herman S., 79 Misc.2d 519, 359 N.Y.S.2d 645 (Fam.Ct., New York County 1974). The *Lang* decision actually preceded Terry v. Ohio, 392 U.S. 1, 88 S.Ct. 1868, 20 L.Ed.2d 889 (1968), which gave police officers limited authority to stop persons and conduct a limited search for weapons. The same is true of the automobile search exception to the warrant requirement. See, e.g., In re J.R.M., 487 S.W.2d 502 (Mo.1972), which contains an excellent fourth amendment analysis in a case involving a juvenile, just as if the case were a criminal case. Also as in the criminal process, absent exigent circumstances justifying an immediate warrantless intrusion, a house or apartment may not be searched without a warrant. See, e.g., In re Kwok T. v. Mouriello, 43 N.Y.2d 213, 401 N.Y.S.2d 52, 371 N.E.2d 814 (1977). All of the cases suggest in the strongest terms that the fourth amendment is equally applicable to all persons regardless of age, and is fully applicable in juvenile proceedings regardless of the civil nature of the proceedings. See especially State v. Lowry, 95 N.J.Super. 307, 313, 230 A.2d 907, 909–10 (1967). For a complete treatment of the warrant requirement and the recognized exceptions in the adult context, see C. Whitebread, Criminal Procedure: An Analysis of Constitutional Cases and Concepts 85–226 (1980).

(4) In addition to judicial decisions that have held the fourth amendment applicable to juvenile proceedings, several states have incorporated the exclusionary rule safeguard into their juvenile codes in the form of a provision stating that evidence illegally seized shall be inadmissible in any hearing in

the juvenile court. See, e.g., Ga.Code Ann. § 15–11–31(b) (1982); N.D.Cent. Code § 27–20–27(2) (1974); 42 Pa.Cons.Stat.Ann. § 6338(b) (1982); Tex.Fam. Code Ann. § 54.03(e) (1975); Vt.Stat.Ann. tit. 33, § 652 (Supp.1979); see also Cal.Welf. & Inst. Code § 701 (1972) (evidence is admissible that would be "legally admissible in the trial of criminal cases"); Ill.Ann.Stat. ch. 37, § 704–6 (1972) (applicable rules of evidence in juvenile proceedings are those prescribed for criminal cases); Miss.Code Ann. §§ 43–21–203(4), 43–21–559(1) (1981) (adjudicatory hearing conducted in accordance with such rules of evidence "as may comply with applicable constitutional standards"; evidence is admissible "that would be admissible in a criminal proceeding"). If the fourth amendment and its remedy of exclusion is generally applicable in juvenile proceedings the first analytical questions in any search and seizure claim are whether the defendant (a) had a reasonable expectation of privacy that entitled him to standing to raise an objection to a search and (b) whether the conduct complained of was governmental conduct. Since the fourth amendment protection extends only to searches by the government, private party searches do not implicate fourth amendment values. Both of these issues have been addressed in the context of personal and locker searches in schools.

1. ARE SCHOOL ADMINISTRATORS GOVERNMENTAL AGENTS?

STATE v. WALKER

Court of Appeals of Oregon, 1974.
19 Or.App. 420, 528 P.2d 113.

FOLEY, JUDGE.

Defendant seeks reversal of his conviction for criminal activity in drugs, assigning as error the denial of his motion to suppress evidence. Two questions are presented: (1) Is an assistant school principal who searches a student a governmental agent subject to the limitations of the Fourth Amendment or, instead, a private citizen not subject to such limitations; (2) if applicable, what are the governing Fourth Amendment standards in the context of a search of a student at school? For the reasons that follow, our answer to the first question is that he is a governmental agent, and we find that the present record is insufficient to reach the second question.

On the morning of February 15, 1974, Mr. Alfred Meunier, the assistant principal at Hermiston High School, was given a tip by a student that defendant had "hard drugs" in his possession and was selling them. Mr. Meunier telephoned the Hermiston Police Department and informed Lt. Grant Asher of the situation. During the conversation Lt. Asher said he felt Mr. Meunier had the right to search defendant; Meunier replied that he knew he did.

Mr. Meunier went to defendant's classroom and invited him to the school office. Upon arrival at the office, Mr. Meunier related his suspicion to defendant and then ordered him to empty his pockets. Defendant emptied his trouser pockets, revealing some $40 in cash. After questioning defendant about the cash, Mr. Meunier told him to take his sweater-vest off. Defendant took his sweater-vest partially off and started to put it on again. Just as he did so, Mr. Meunier observed a slight bulge in defendant's shirt pocket. Mr. Meunier then reached in the shirt pocket and removed three bags of amphetamines. Mr. Meunier then called the police department and reported the results of his search. Lt. Asher arrived and took defendant into custody.

The exclusionary rules arising from the Fourth Amendment apply only to searches and seizures by federal, state and municipal officers and not to those by private citizens unless they are acting at the direction of or under sovereign authority. In State v. Bryan, 1 Or.App. 15, 457 P.2d 661 (1969), we quoted Burdeau v. McDowell, 256 U.S. 465, 41 S.Ct. 574, 65 L.Ed. 1048, 13 A.L.R. 1159 (1921):

" 'The Fourth Amendment gives protection against unlawful searches and seizures, and as shown in the previous cases, its protection applies to governmental action. Its origin and history clearly show that it was intended as a restraint upon the activities of sovereign authority, and was not intended to be a limitation upon other than governmental agencies. . . . .' 256 U.S. at 475, 41 S.Ct. at 576." 1 Or.App. at 17, 457 P.2d at 662.

A number of courts have taken the position that school officials, acting alone, are private persons for the purposes of the exclusionary rule. In re Christopher W., 29 Cal.App.3d 777, 105 Cal.Rptr. 775 (1973); In re Donaldson, 269 Cal.App.2d 509, 75 Cal.Rptr. 220 (1969); People v. Stewart, 63 Misc.2d 601, 313 N.Y.S.2d 253 (N.Y.C.Crim.Ct. 1970). These courts generally reason that the Fourth Amendment prohibition against unreasonable searches and seizures requires the exclusion of evidence only where the unreasonable search is made by a law enforcement officer.

Other courts have held that a school official acting alone in conducting a search is a governmental agent for purposes of the exclusionary rule. State v. Baccino, 282 A.2d 869, 49 A.L.R.3d 973 (Del. Super.1971); State in the Interest of G. C., 121 N.J.Super. 108, 296 A.2d 102 (1972).

So far as we can determine, Oregon has not previously passed upon the question of whether public school administrators are public officials whose acts lie within the scope of the Fourth Amendment and its exclusionary rule.

School districts are governmental agencies. Hermiston High School is organized under the laws of Oregon and is part of School District 8–R. Assistant principal Meunier is employed by that district and takes his orders through two superiors from the school district. When Mr. Meunier brought defendant to his office and searched him he was acting in his capacity as assistant principal on school property during school hours. It would be incongruous for us to conclude the assistant principal was acting in the capacity of a private person. We thus find that Mr. Meunier was acting as a public official and it follows that the Fourth Amendment right of the defendant to be free from unreasonable searches and seizures has application here.

. . .

Reversed and remanded for further proceedings consistent with this opinion.

NOTES

(1) *Private citizen-state agent distinction.* In Burdeau v. McDowell, 256 U.S. 465, 41 S.Ct. 574, 65 L.Ed. 1048 (1921), the Supreme Court established the proposition that the fourth amendment does not protect persons from searches and seizures conducted by private citizens not acting as agents of the government. Accordingly, many courts have disposed of the school search issue on the threshold ground that school officials and teachers conducting searches of students act as private citizens and not as agents of the state, and, therefore, their actions are not controlled by the fourth amendment. See, e.g., In re Donaldson, 269 Cal.App.2d 509, 75 Cal.Rptr. 220 (1969); People v. Stewart, 63 Misc.2d 601, 313 N.Y.S.2d 253 (Cr.Ct., New York, County 1970); Commonwealth v. Dingfelt, 227 Pa.Super. 380, 323 A.2d 145 (1974); Mercer v. State, 450 S.W.2d 715 (Tex.Civ.App.1970). Characterization of the search as private may change, however, depending on a number of factors. One such factor is the function of the person conducting the search. In People v. Bowers, 77 Misc.2d 697, 356 N.Y.S.2d 432 (Sup.Ct., App.Term 1974), e.g., the court held that a school security officer who had no teaching responsibilities and who was placed in the school solely for security purposes was functioning as a state agent when he conducted the search in question. Accord, People v. Jackson, 65 Misc.2d 909, 319 N.Y.S.2d 731 (Sup. Ct., App.Term 1971), affirmed 30 N.Y.2d 734, 333 N.Y.S.2d 167, 284 N.E.2d 153 (1972).

It is often unclear whether such decisions as *Donaldson*, *Stewart*, and *Mercer* are grounded on analogy to parents—that is, school administrators standing in loco parentis have the same legal status as parents—or are based more on the noncriminal, non-law enforcement purpose for conducting the search, that is, to maintain school discipline.

What if the police accompany the school administrators at the time of the search? Does that make the conduct "governmental" for fourth amendment analysis? Another way of stating the same qualification is to inquire into the purpose of the search, i.e., whether it was related to a legitimate educational purpose, such as maintaining order and discipline or promoting safety of other students, or whether it was conducted for the purpose of gathering evidence for a criminal prosecution.

If school officials act in cooperation with police to the extent that they become agents of the police, or if the search is conducted for a noneducation-related purpose, the search may lose its private character and become a search conducted under state authority, subject to the limitations of the fourth amendment. See, e.g., Piazzola v. Watkins, 316 F.Supp. 624, 626–27 (M.D.Ala.1970), affirmed 442 F.2d 284 (5th Cir. 1971); Picha v. Wielgos, 410 F.Supp. 1214, 1219–21 (N.D.Ill.1976). See also In re Donaldson, supra, 269 Cal.App.2d at 510–12, 75 Cal.Rptr. at 222, citing Stapleton v. Superior Court,

70 Cal.2d 97, 73 Cal.Rptr. 575, 447 P.2d 967 (1969); People v. Stewart, supra, 63 Misc.2d at 603–04, 313 N.Y.S.2d at 256–57.

In Picha v. Wielgos, 410 F.Supp. 1214 (N.D.Ill.1976), Judge Flaum would require full probable cause where police are involved while school officials acting alone would be given the benefit of a lesser standard.

Should there be a difference in legal rights and duties under the fourth amendment depending upon the age of the school child?

In Smyth v. Lubbers, 398 F.Supp. 777 (W.D.Mich.1975), while acknowledging that a different rule might apply in the case of elementary and secondary school students who require a great deal more supervision, the court held that a search of a college student's room could not be characterized as administrative where its purpose was to gather evidence of criminal conduct. 398 F.Supp. at 786–87.

2. A REASONABLE EXPECTATION OF PRIVACY? THE SCHOOL LOCKER CASES

PEOPLE v. OVERTON

Court of Appeals of New York, 1967.
20 N.Y.2d 360, 283 N.Y.S.2d 22, 229 N.E.2d 596.

KEATING, JUDGE.

Three detectives of the Mount Vernon Police Department having obtained a search warrant went to the Mount Vernon High School. The warrant directed a search of the persons of two students and, also, of their lockers.

The detectives presented the warrant to the vice-principal, Dr. Panitz, who sent for the two students, one of whom was the defendant, Carlos Overton. The detectives searched them and found nothing. A subsequent search of Overton's locker, however, revealed four marijuana cigarettes.

The defendant moved to invalidate that portion of the search warrant which directed a search of his locker, on the ground that the papers were defective upon which it was based. This motion was granted. The court denied the motion to suppress, however, on the grounds that the vice-principal had consented to the search and that he had a right to do so. The Appellate Term reversed and dismissed the information, holding that the consent of the vice-principal could not justify an otherwise illegal search. The People have appealed from this order of the Appellate Term.

It is axiomatic that the protection of the Fourth Amendment is not restricted to dwellings (Go-Bart Importing Co. v. United States, 282 U.S. 344, 51 S.Ct. 153, 75 L.Ed. 374). A depository such as a locker or even a desk is safeguarded from unreasonable searches for evidence of a crime (United States v. Blok, 88 U.S.App.D.C. 326, 188 F.2d 1019).

There are situations, however, where someone other than the defendant in possession of a depository may consent to what otherwise would have been an illegal search. Such a case was United States v. Botsch, 364 F.2d 542 [2d Cir., 1966], cert. den. 386 U.S. 937. In that case, the defendant had rented a shed from one Stein. Stein retained a key to the shed and accepted deliveries on behalf of the defendant. When the police approached Stein and informed him of their suspicion that the defendant was receiving goods obtained through fraud, Stein consented to a search of the shed.

In upholding the search, the court noted two significant factors. First Stein had a key to the shed and, second, more than a mere landlord-tenant relationship existed, since Stein was empowered to take deliveries on behalf of the defendant. The court also noted that Stein had a right to exculpate himself from implication in the defendant's scheme.

Considering all these factors cumulatively, the court concluded that, in this situation, Stein could give consent to the search. Thus, the search was not unreasonable in contravention of the Fourth Amendment.

Dr. Panitz, in this case, gave his consent to the search of Overton's locker. The dissenting opinion suggests, however, that Dr. Panitz' consent was not freely given, because he acted under compulsion of the invalid search warrant. If this were the case, his consent might be rendered somewhat questionable. However, Dr. Panitz testified that: "Being responsible for the order, assignment, and maintenance of the physical facilities, if *any* report were given to me by *anyone* of an article or item of the nature that does not belong there, or of an illegal nature, I would inspect the locker." (Italics supplied.)

This testimony demonstrates beyond doubt that Dr. Panitz would have consented as he did regardless of the presence of the invalid search warrant.

The power of Dr. Panitz to give his consent to this search arises out of the distinct relationship between school authorities and students.

The school authorities have an obligation to maintain discipline over the students. It is recognized that, when large numbers of teenagers are gathered together in such an environment, their inexperience and lack of mature judgment can often create hazards to each other. Parents, who surrender their children to this type of environment, in order that they may continue developing both intellectually and socially, have a right to expect certain safeguards.

It is in the high school years particularly that parents are justifiably concerned that their children not become accustomed to antisocial behavior, such as the use of illegal drugs. The susceptibility to suggestion of students of high school age increases the danger. Thus, it is the affirmative obligation of the school authorities to investigate any charge that a student is using or possessing narcotics and to take appropriate steps, if the charge is substantiated.

When Overton was assigned his locker, he, like all the other students at Mount Vernon High School, gave the combination to his home room teacher who, in turn, returned it to an office where it was kept on file. The students at Mount Vernon are well aware that the school authorities possess the combinations of their lockers. It appears understood that the lock and the combination are provided in order that each student may have exclusive possession of the locker vis-à-vis other students, but the student does not have such exclusivity over the locker as against the school authorities. In fact, the school issues regulations regarding what may and may not be kept in the lockers and presumably can spot check to insure compliance. The vice-principal testified that he had, on occasion, inspected the lockers of students.

Indeed, it is doubtful if a school would be properly discharging its duty of supervision over the students, if it failed to retain control over the lockers. Not only have the school authorities a right to inspect but this right becomes a duty when suspicion arises that something of an illegal nature may be secreted there. When Dr. Panitz learned of the detectives' suspicion, he was obligated to inspect the locker. This interest, together with the nonexclusive nature of the locker, empowered him to consent to the search by the officers.

Accordingly, the order of the Appellate Term should be reversed and the matter remitted to that court for consideration of the other points raised by the defendant which were not decided on the prior appeal.

NOTES

(1) The proprietary interest theory is a rationale that some courts have employed in upholding searches of school lockers. According to the theory, although students may have exclusive possessory rights as against other students, they do not retain a reasonable expectation of privacy as against school officials because school officials normally exercise substantial control over lockers, including right of access. Recall that fourth amendment rights do not obtain if the person asserting the right did not have a reasonable expectation of privacy in the place searched or item seized. People v. Overton is the leading, as well as the most dramatic case upholding a warrantless search of a school locker. Note the particularly strong language of the court: "Not only have the school authorities a right to inspect but this right becomes a *duty* when suspicion arises that something of an illegal nature may be secreted there." (Emphasis supplied.)

(2) Among the circumstances that courts emphasize in the determination of whether a school enjoys the kind of joint control over a school locker to warrant a search of a locker without cause or the permission of the student are the following: (1) the presence or absence of school practice or regulations allowing inspections by school officials; (2) whether the school furnishes the locks for the lockers and maintains a list of combinations; and (3)

whether the school promulgates rules and regulations concerning the use of lockers and what may or may not be kept in them. Might you argue that, even when all three conditions are satisfied, the student still retains a reasonable expectation of privacy as against searches by law enforcement officials, and hence, while evidence obtained in locker searches by school officials might be admissible in a school disciplinary hearing in accordance with school regulations, such evidence can not be used to ground a juvenile or criminal proceeding?

3. SCHOOL SEARCHES: EVOLUTION OF A REASONABLE SUSPICION STANDARD

STATE v. YOUNG

Supreme Court of Georgia, 1975.
234 Ga. 488, 216 S.E.2d 586.

HALL, JUSTICE.

We granted certiorari in this case to determine the extent to which the Fourth Amendment right against unreasonable searches and seizures and the associated exclusionary rule could be invoked by a minor student of a public high school to secure the suppression in a pending criminal prosecution of marijuana found upon his person by an assistant principal conducting a personal search not without cause but with less than probable cause for a search by a law enforcement officer.

The Court of Appeals ruled that the assistant principal was a government agent, and concluded that his search of the student violated the Fourth Amendment and that the student's motion to suppress the marijuana should therefore have been granted. Young v. State, 132 Ga.App. 790, 209 S.E.2d 96. The Court of Appeals wrote that ". . . we cannot in view of the Fourth Amendment, grant a school official, when acting as a governmental agent, greater rights than an ordinary policeman would have with reference to searching a student in his charge." Upon consideration of the knotty issue presented by this appeal, we reverse, holding that the exclusionary rule would not apply even if the Fourth Amendment had been violated, but that in any event no Fourth Amendment violation occurred here.

The search in question was made after the assistant principal observed Young, a seventeen year old student, on the premises of the public school he attended. Young was with two other students during school hours and as the principal approached "one of the fellows jumped up and put something down, ran his hand in his pants." The three students were than directed to empty their pockets and Young produced marijuana. Young's motion to suppress this evidence was denied, and he was convicted in Fulton Criminal Court of a misdemeanor. He argues here that his Fourth Amendment rights were violated, and that he was entitled to suppression of the marijuana.

. . .

The first step in any analysis is to recognize the separation between the Fourth Amendment and the associated exclusionary rule: They are not coextensive. The Fourth Amendment requires only state action; the latter requires state law enforcement action. Moreover, with respect to both the scope of the Fourth Amendment protections and the sweep of the exclusionary rule, the proper test is a balancing test. In the Fourth Amendment area, in determining the reasonableness of a search, the social utility of the search must be balanced against the individual's reasonable expectation of privacy.
. . . This balance sometimes is struck in favor of allowing searches which could not be justified under more typical circumstances. Such searches are approved as reasonable, and therefore as comporting with the Fourth Amendment, because the necessity for the kind of search made is weighed heavily in the balance against the expectation of privacy. . . .

After application of the foregoing standards to determine whether a Fourth Amendment violation has occurred, if such a violation is found, the expected benefits and the expected detriments of applying the exclusionary rule must be weighed to determine whether that rule may be invoked to suppress the fruits of the search. . . . There is nothing sacrosanct about the exclusionary rule; it is not embedded in the constitution and it is not a personal constitutional right: "In sum, the rule is a judicially-created remedy designed to safeguard Fourth Amendment rights generally through its deterrent effect, rather than a personal constitutional right of the party aggrieved." The Supreme Court has as much as suggested that the rule might be abandoned altogether if statistics should bear out the suspicion that in its primary, and perhaps sole, purpose of deterring future police misconduct, it is ineffective.

"The Robinson, Gustafson, and Calandra cases indicate a distinct shift in the attitude of the majority of the Supreme Court in evaluating whether the exclusionary rule should be extended to additional contexts involving illegal searches and seizures. The majority's failure to extend the rule in these cases, as well as the implication discussed previously of making the deterrent effect of the rule the sole justification for its application, suggest that the majority agree with the findings of the rule's critics. Furthermore, the Court's actions imply that presented with the proper case and statistical backing to prove the rule's ineffectiveness, it might analyze the deterrent benefit of the rule in criminal trials and find that the costs of the rule outweigh its benefits." . . .

. . . "It is well to remember that when incriminating evidence is found on a suspect and that evidence is then suppressed, 'the pain of suppression is felt, not by the inanimate State or by some penitent policeman, but by the offender's next victims.' " In re State in the Interest of G. C., 121 N.J.Super. 108, 296 A.2d 102 (1972).

Against this background we turn to a consideration of the issues of student searches now before us. From jurisdictions all over the country have come cases delineating the rights of public school students against their school officials in a search context. Almost all these cases have decided that evidence seized by such officials is admissible; however, the theories have varied. Many courts have concluded that public school officials are not "government agents" within the meaning of the Fourth Amendment, thus avoiding entirely any possibility of a constitutional violation and any possibility of the exclusion of evidence. Several other courts have concluded that school officials are government agents, but that their actions were reasonable in the light of the lowered standard, sometimes called the "reasonable suspicion" standard, which the amendment required of them; and thus the standard was not violated and the exclusionary rule was not applicable. Still others have admitted the evidence upon an unclear theory. . . .

We find that these cases in the main have failed to separate the issues with sufficient sensitivity to delineate comprehensively the rights we are considering. They have tended to divide those making searches, for purposes of the Fourth Amendment, into two groups: private persons, and government agents. We conclude that there are really three groups: private persons; governmental agents whose conduct is state action invoking the Fourth Amendment; and governmental *law enforcement* agents for whose violations of the Fourth Amendment the exclusionary rule will be applied.

With reference to searches by private persons, there is no Fourth Amendment prohibition and therefore no occasion for applying the exclusionary rule. The third group, law enforcement officers, of course, are bound by the full panoply of Fourth Amendment rights and are subject to the application of the exclusionary rule. But the intermediate group, including public school officials, plainly are state officers whose action is state action bringing the Fourth Amendment into play; but they are not state law enforcement officials, with respect to whom the exclusionary rule is applied.

. . . The tide is turning, we think properly, away from the exclusionary rule; and we decline to extend it to apply to searches by non-law enforcement persons. There can be no serious contention that public school officials are law enforcement personnel. Therefore, it follows that although school officials are governmental officers subject to some Fourth Amendment limitations in searching their students, should they violate those limitations the exclusionary rule would not be available to the students to exclude from evidence items illegally seized. Instead, for the violation of their constitutional rights the students would be relegated to such other remedies as the law affords them, whether by actions based upon a claimed violation of their civil rights by state officers, or by some tort claim seeking damages.

Though what we have written is sufficient to decide that the marijuana found on Young was not subject to suppression at his trial regardless of whether the search violated his constitutional rights, this case raises additionally a sensitive issue concerning the allowable scope under the Fourth Amendment of a schoolhouse search of a student conducted by a public primary or secondary school official, entirely without the participation of law enforcement officers. We rule that on the facts before us no Fourth Amendment violation occurred in the search by the assistant principal.

As we have seen, the allowable scope of a search is not absolute, but varies with varying circumstances as we balance fundamentally competing interests. In determining the reasonableness of a search, we must "first . . . focus upon the governmental interest which allegedly justifies official intrusion upon the constitutionally protected interests of the private citizen." There are governmental interests of discipline, security, and enablement of the education function, to be served by allowing searches of students by the officials charged with their education and control. Primarily, these searches are not undertaken in any law enforcement capacity but are designed to allow enforcement of multiple rules, regulations and prohibitions which are imposed to maintain an atmosphere of security and calm necessary to allow education to take place. This may and does involve controlling students' behavior, and it may and does involve controlling the deleterious items they are allowed to possess on the premises. Such a deleterious item may be as relatively innocuous as a secreted noise-maker; it may be as dangerous as heroin or a handgun. In both examples the administrators are functioning within their legitimate area of concern in seeking to root out such disturbances and evils; and they must be allowed the latitude to make effective searches to that end.

The law recognizes that students through the secondary school grades do not have the maturity of the adult citizen. To the end that they may be formed and educated, they are subject to the control of others in various circumstances. The citizen on the street is subject only to the restraints of the criminal law; but the student in school is subject additionally to all reasonable school rules and regulations. The administrators to whom we afford the right to make such rules and regulations must be allowed to enforce them.

. . .

. . . The state owes those students a safe and secure environment. Searches of students directed to that end are reasonable under the Fourth Amendment on considerably less than probable cause. We conclude that in the good faith exercise of their public trust teachers and administrators must be allowed to search without hindrance or delay subject only to the most minimal restraints necessary to insure that students are not whimsically stripped of personal priva-

cy and subjected to petty tyranny. The search we consider here met
this minimal standard.

. . .

We do not anticipate that our ruling will encourage school officials
to make of themselves largely unfettered searching agents of law enforcement officers. We emphasize that the standards announced
here for action by school officials will pass constitutional muster only
if those officials are acting in their proper capacity and the search is
free of involvement by law enforcement personnel.

In conclusion, to reiterate our ruling today, granting that public
primary and secondary school students have minimal Fourth Amendment rights to be free from searches and seizures by school officials,
nonetheless the exclusionary rule is not applicable to enforce those
rights, and students aggrieved by the action of their officials must
fall back upon such other legal remedies as applicable law may allow
them.

The trial court properly denied Young's motion to suppress the
marijuana, and the Court of Appeals erred in reversing that court's
judgment.

The judgment of the Court of Appeals is reversed.

. . .

GUNTER, JUSTICE (dissenting).

The Court today denies a public school student his right to suppress evidence obtained by the government through an unconstitutional search and seizure. This is a right accorded to all Georgia citizens, and I therefore think this right cannot be denied to a student in
Georgia's public school system. I agree with the decision of the
Georgia Court of Appeals when it decided this case and said: "Therefore, we hold that when a student is searched by a school official
which results in criminal prosecution the student must have been afforded the Fourth Amendment rights accorded to every other citizen." Young v. The State, 132 Ga.App. 790 at p. 791, 209 S.E.2d 96
at p. 98.

I dissent and would affirm the judgment of the Court of Appeals.

The Fourth Amendment stands as a bulwark between the government and a citizen. It means that the government, federal or state or
local, which can act only through its agents-employees, cannot invade
the person of a citizen by conducting an "unreasonable search and
seizure." The Fourth Amendment, as well as its equivalent in the
Georgia Constitution, reads: "The right of the people to be secure in
their persons, houses, papers, and effects, against unreasonable
searches and seizures, shall not be violated, . . ."

. . .

School administrators are considered government officials for purposes of the First Amendment and procedural due process requirements. See Tinker v. Des Moines School District, 393 U.S. 503 (1969);

Goss v. Lopez, 419 U.S. 565 (1975). And it is now clearly established that a minor, whether a public school student or not, is a person under our Constitution and entitled to its protections. See *Tinker* and *Goss*, supra, and In Re Gault, 387 U.S. 1 (1967).

In Georgia, an assistant school principal is clearly an agent-employee of the state or local government. He is therefore subject to the proscriptions of the Fourth Amendment, and a public school student is a person entitled to the benefits of the Fourth Amendment.

. . .

The Standard of Reasonableness to be Applied in the Public School System

The majority concedes that "probable cause", the standard applicable in searches of citizens by law enforcement officers, did not exist for the search of the student in this case. The analysis of the majority also suggests that the search of a student in a public school by a law enforcement officer without "probable cause" would result in suppression of the evidence even under an evidentiary rule of exclusion. The "probable cause" standard is applicable to the police search but not to the search by the school official.

The majority asserts that searches of students in public schools by school officials "are reasonable under the Fourth Amendment on considerably less than probable cause. We conclude that in the good faith exercise of their public trust teachers and administrators must be allowed to search without hindrance or delay subject only to the most minimal restraints necessary to insure that students are not whimsically stripped of personal privacy and subjected to petty tyranny."

My view, of course, is that there must be "probable cause" for the search of a student in a public school by a school official, and such a search without "probable cause" violates the Fourth Amendment rights of a student as a citizen. A student, in my view, cannot be stripped of his Fourth Amendment rights at the entrance to the public school. Nor do I think that the Fourth Amendment rights of a high school student are a diluted version of the Fourth Amendment rights of an adult.

There can be no doubt that the need for order and discipline in a public school is a valid concern; but it must be conceded that the maintenance of order and discipline in a public school is one thing, and the acknowledgement and enforcement of constitutional rights in a criminal prosecution is an entirely different thing. This case has nothing to do with the maintenance of school discipline; the State is prosecuting a student for having committed an alleged crime; the student is entitled to a "fair prosecution" which is an integral part of a "fair trial"; if an adult had been searched by a government official in the manner that this student was searched, the adult would have, as the majority concedes, a right to suppress any item seized; the adult is entitled to a fair prosecution as an integral part of a fair trial, but a student is not; and all of this adds up to making a public school student a second-class citizen not entitled to a fair prosecution by the State in a fair trial conducted by the State.

In the context of criminal prosecutions where Fourth Amendment rights must be acknowledged and enforced, I would hold that the standard of reasonableness for the search of a public school student is the same standard that must be applied to searches of adults, "probable cause."

I do not think that students have mere "minimal Fourth Amendment rights." And I certainly do not subscribe to the "adequate reason for the searches" enunciated by the majority in this case. As quoted from the majority opinion, the acts of the students in this case involved at most "a furtive gesture and an obvious consciousness of guilt by these students at the approach of the assistant principal." In fact, the record shows only that one of three students jumped up and put his hand down his pants. All three were searched. The record does not show whether the student in the present case was the one who jumped up. The majority's standard, subjectively applied by a school official, will justify the search of the person of any student in a public school. Such a standard is really no standard at all.

The majority has arrived at its standard by a general balancing test. The majority has placed upon the scales the age of the student, the status of the student, the status of the administrator, the fact that the search occurred in the schoolhouse, and the "governmental interests of discipline, security, and enablement of the education function." But why each of these considerations is relevant for purposes of the Fourth Amendment and what weight each brings to the scales remain unclear.

. . .

What then are the relevant considerations? As the majority states, it is necessary first to focus upon the governmental interest which allegedly justifies official intrusion upon the constitutionally protected interest of the private citizen. Most searches are made in vindication of the State's interest in enforcing the criminal law, which includes of course, an interest in protecting law abiding citizens from lawless ones. Ordinarily, a lower standard than probable cause is justified only when some additional interest is involved. Even then, the nature and extent of the governmental intrusion must be considered as well as the necessity for the particular form of intrusion. If the governmental interests can be served by a limited intrusion, then the Fourth Amendment permits only the limited intrusion. . . .

The reasoning of the majority places no limits on the nature and extent of the search a school official may make, as long as the search is justified in the first instance under the majority's "minimal standard." Furthermore, the facts of the case do not show a limited intrusion of the kind associated with the relaxed standards of reasonableness in *Camara* and *Terry*. The search here was personal in nature and aimed at the discovery of evidence of specific misconduct. . . .

The governmental considerations said to be in issue are not very convincing in the context of this case. The facts give not the slightest hint of any threat to "the enablement of the education function" in the conduct of the students before the search. If we are to restrict a student's privacy in his own person in the name of education, let us do so on a record which provides evidence of potential disruption or disorder. There is none here. . . .

. . . Furthermore, in the context of the present case, the government's interest in discipline and security is indistinguishable from the general law enforcement interest. See Buss, "The Fourth Amendment and Searches of Students in Public Schools," 59 Iowa L.Rev. 739 (1974).

What of the special status of the school official? Most courts ruling on schoolhouse searches have stressed this factor, noting that at common law school officials are said to stand *in loco parentis*. The majority here correctly avoids reliance on common law maxims, although much of the reasoning has the same familiar ring. It cannot be doubted that a school official occupies a status different from a police officer for many purposes. But the school official also has essentially law enforcement responsibilities. When he acts upon a suspicion of specific misconduct and conducts an investigation he is performing a law enforcement function. "What so many of the courts persist in talking about as a parental relationship between school and the student is really a law enforcement relationship in which the general student society is protected from the harms of anti-social conduct. As such, it should be subjected to law enforcement rules. Besides presenting a false picture of a person acting in a parental fashion, casting the school administrator in the parental role diverts attention from the relevant considerations that might argue for or against permitting the search." Buss, supra, at p. 768.

The schoolhouse search presents a unique situation. The question is whether its unique aspects reduce high school students to second-class citizens under the Fourth Amendment. I have examined what the case law establishes as the primary considerations under the Fourth Amendment and have tried to examine the facts of this particular case in the light of those considerations. I conclude that a school official performing a law enforcement function conducted a search of the person. I find no basis on this record for relieving the official of the probable cause requirement. Furthermore, I conclude that a search of three students after one of them jumps up and puts his hand down his pants is unreasonable.

. . .

Conclusion.

The public school student in this case was, in my opinion, the victim of an unconstitutional search and seizure. I think that he had a constitutional right to suppress any item seized, and I further think that he had a statutory right, conferred by the Georgia Legislature, to suppress any item seized.

STATE v. MORA

Supreme Court of Louisiana, 1975.
307 So.2d 317.

BARHAM, JUSTICE.

Relator was convicted of possession of marijuana, a violation of La.R.S. 40–966C, and was sentenced to six months' imprisonment in the parish jail. We granted certiorari upon relator's application to review the trial court's denial of a motion to suppress the marijuana which formed the basis of the prosecution and a motion to suppress a confession. We find merit in relator's arguments alleging error in the trial court's ruling on his motion to suppress the marijuana and we therefore pretermit consideration of relator's other complaint.

At the time that the marijuana was seized, relator was a seventeen-year-old high school senior who was participating in a physical education class at the school he attended. Each participant changed from street clothes to gym clothes before joining in the class activities and, in accordance with a customary practice, placed his wallet and other valuables in an individual small canvas bag provided for that purpose. Once the small valuables bags were filled, they were all placed in a large duffel bag which was locked for safekeeping in the instructor's office for the duration of the class.

On the day of the search and seizure, relator obtained his small valuables bag from the instructor. The instructor testified at the hearing on the motion to suppress that the relator turned his back while filling the canvas bag, that his actions were furtive, and that he experienced some difficulty in placing his wallet, which appeared to be bulky, into the small canvas bag. Once the small valuables bag had been placed in the duffel bag, the instructor locked the duffel bag in his office. The instructor further testified that after reflecting on relator's furtive actions and considering them in light of his knowledge that some of relator's companions were narcotics users and that there was talk of the use of drugs by different student groups, he decided to inspect the contents of relator's wallet. When he opened the wallet, he found a plastic bag which contained a leafy green substance. Believing the substance to be marijuana, he summoned the school principal. The principal concurred in the instructor's belief and notified the juvenile authorities, to whom the marijuana was ultimately released. Relator's prosecution ensued and the motion to suppress the marijuana was heard and denied.

The Fourth Amendment to the United States Constitution and Article I, § 7 of the Louisiana Constitution of 1921 (in effect at the time of the search in question) safeguard persons from unreasonable searches conducted without a warrant. However, the applicability of these constitutional prohibitions against unreasonable searches and the exclusionary rule of Mapp v. Ohio, 367 U.S. 643, 81 S.Ct. 1684, 6 L.Ed.2d 1081 (1961) is limited to cases where the seizure is effected by governmental agencies. Concomitantly, the fruits of searches and seizures conducted by private persons are not subject to exclusion. See e.g., Barnes v. United States, 373 F.2d 517 (5th Cir. 1967). See also Burdeau v. McDowell, 256 U.S. 465, 41 S.Ct. 574, 65 L.Ed. 1048 (1921). Therefore, before we can decide the constitutionality of the search itself, we must initially determine whether the instructor and the school principal who effected the search and seizure were functioning as private persons, exempt from the stricture of the constitutional provisions, or as governmental agents, subject to those provisions.

Principals and instructors, like others employed by the State through its school boards, are responsible for public education in this State and are charged with the responsibility of implementing the policies of the State in this respect. By state law a teacher is authorized to hold each pupil strictly accountable for disorderly conduct at school. A principal may suspend from school any pupil who is guilty of willful disobedience or who uses tobacco or alcoholic beverages in any form in school buildings or on school grounds or whom commits any other serious offense. Because of the function of these school officials and their strict accountability to the State, we must conclude that these school officials, insofar as they are discharging their duties by enforcing State policies and regulations, are within the purview of the Fourth Amendment's prohibition; therefore, their students must be accorded their constitutional right to be free from warrantless searches and seizures.

We must now consider whether the search and seizure effected by these State officials violated the constitutional stricture against unreasonable searches and seizures and whether suppression of the seized marijuana was consequently mandated under *Mapp*.

"The general rule is that a search conducted without a warrant is per se unconstitutional. Schneckloth v. Bustamonte, 412 U.S. 218, 93 S.Ct. 2041, 36 L.Ed.2d 854 (1973) . . ." State v. Tant, 287 So.2d 458, 459 (La.1973). However, it is possible for a search without a warrant to be constitutional, if and only if it falls within one of those categories recognized as "specifically established and well-delineated exceptions" to the warrant requirement. See Coolidge v. New Hampshire, 403 U.S. 443, 91 S.Ct. 2022, 29 L.Ed.2d 564 (1971), citing Katz v. United States, 389 U.S. 347, 88 S.Ct. 507, 19 L.Ed.2d 576 (1967). Two examples of such exceptions are searches incident to a lawful arrest and certain automobile searches.

We hold that a search on school grounds of a student's personal effects by a school official who suspects the presence or possession of some unlawful substance is not a "specifically established and well-delineated" exception to the warrant requirement and that the fruits of such a search may not be used by the State prosecutorial agency as the basis for criminal proceedings.

For the reasons assigned, the relator's motion to suppress is maintained and his conviction and sentence are reversed.

NOTE

The United States Supreme Court vacated *Mora*, remanding it for a determination whether the judgment had been based on federal or state constitutional grounds, or both. The Louisiana Supreme Court then held that the decision on inadmissibility had been based on both federal and state constitutional grounds, and also on state statutory law. State v. Mora, 330 So.2d 900 (1976), cert. denied 429 U.S. 1004.

STATE EX REL. T.L.O.

Juvenile and Dom.Rel.Ct., Middlesex County, New Jersey 1980.
178 N.J.Super. 329, 428 A.2d 1327.

NICOLA, P.J.J. & D.R.

. . .

This complaint arises from an occurrence on March 7, 1980. A Piscataway High School teacher observed the juvenile and another girl smoking cigarettes while in the girls' lavatory. The teacher escorted the girls to the assistant vice-principal's office and accused them of violating the school's no-smoking restriction. When asked by the vice-principal whether she had, in fact, been smoking in the girls' room, T.L.O. replied that "she didn't smoke at all." With this conflicting response the vice-principal requested the student's purse and upon inspection found a package of cigarettes plainly visible. While removing the cigarettes, marijuana and marijuana paraphernalia became visible. Further inspection revealed $40.98 in single dollar bills and change, as well as a handwritten letter by T.L.O. to a friend asking her to sell marijuana in school.

The assistant vice-principal summoned the police and turned over the marijuana and paraphernalia to them. The juvenile's parents were also notified. In the presence of her mother at police headquarters, T.L.O. admitted to selling marijuana in school, after being advised of her rights. She stated that on the day in question, she had sold approximately 18 to 20 marijuana cigarettes for a price of one dollar each.

T.L.O. was suspended from school for three days for smoking cigarettes and seven days for possession of marijuana. As previously indicated, the juvenile obtained an order to show cause why she should not be reinstated in school. At the hearing on that matter the judge found that the search conducted by the vice-principal violated the Fourth Amendment guarantees. Any consent to the search of the purse by the juvenile was ruled ineffective due to a failure to advise her that she had a right to withhold such consent.

. . .

This court will first address the constitutionality of the search and seizure; more specifically, the issue is whether or not a school official is subject to the Fourth Amendment and the standard of probable cause which must exist before said official may engage in a search of a student on school grounds in order to enforce a disciplinary rule.

. . .

A number of courts have already addressed the issue of searches of students in school by school officials. Their approaches to the applicability of the Fourth Amendment and the exclusionary rule have varied and may be placed in the following categories:

(1) The Fourth Amendment does not apply because the school official acted *in loco parentis*, that is, he stands in the place of the parents; In re G, 11 Cal.App.3d 1193, 90 Cal.Rptr. 361 (D.Ct.App. 1970); In re Donaldson, 269 Cal.App.2d 509, 75 Cal.Rptr. 220 (D.Ct. App.1969); People v. Stewart, 63 Misc.2d 601, 313 N.Y.S.2d 253 (1970); Commonwealth v. Dingfelt, 227 Pa.Super. 380, 323 A.2d 145 (Super.Ct.1974); Mercer v. State, 450 S.W.2d 715 (Tex.Civ.App.1970);

(2) The Fourth Amendment applies, but the exclusionary rule does not; Doe v. Renfrow, 475 F.Supp. 1012 (N.D.Ind.1979); United States v. Coles, 302 F.Supp. 99 (D.Me., N.D.1969); State v. Young, 234 Ga. 488, 216 S.E.2d 586 (Sup.Ct.1975); State v.Wingerd, 40 Ohio App.2d 236, 318 N.E.2d 866 (Ct.App.1974);

(3) The Fourth Amendment applies but the doctrine of *in loco parentis* lowers the standard to be applied in determining the reasonableness of the search; Bilbrey v. Brown, 481 F.Supp. 26 (D.C.Or., 1979); In re W., 29 Cal.App.3d 777, 105 Cal.Rptr. 775 (D.Ct.App.1973); In re C., 26 Cal.App.3d 320, 102 Cal.Rptr. 682 (D.Ct.App.1972); State v. Baccino, 282 A.2d 869 (Del.Super.1971); State v. F.W.E., 360 So.2d 148 (Fla.D.Ct.App.1978); People v. Ward, 62 Mich.App. 46, 233 N.W.2d 180 (App.Ct.1975); In re G.C., 121 N.J.Super. 108, 296 A.2d 102 (J.Dr.Ct.1972); Doe v. State, 88 N.M. 347, 540 P.2d 827 (Sup.Ct. 1975); People v. Singletary, 37 N.Y.2d 310, 372 N.Y.S.2d 68, 333 N.E.2d 369 (Ct.App.1975); People v. D., 34 N.Y.2d 483, 358 N.Y.S.2d 403, 315 N.E.2d 466 (Ct.App.1974); People v. Jackson, 65 Misc.2d 909, 319 N.Y.S.2d 731 (App.Term, 1st Dept. 1971), aff'd, 30 N.Y.2d 734, 333 N.Y.S.2d 167, 284 N.E.2d 153 (Ct.App.1972); State v. McKinnon, 88 Wash.2d 75, 558 P.2d 781 (Sup.Ct.1977); In re L.L., 90 Wis.2d 585, 280 N.W.2d 343 (Sup.Ct.1979);

(4) The Fourth Amendment applies and requires a finding of probable cause in order for the search to be reasonable; Picha v. Wielgos,

410 F.Supp. 1214 (W.D.Ill.1976); State v. Mora, 307 So.2d 317 (La. 1975), vacated 423 U.S. 809, 96 S.Ct. 20, 46 L.Ed.2d 29; 330 So.2d 900 (La.1976).

This court, in accordance with the New Jersey case of In re G.C., decided by a court of comparable jurisdiction, finds that public school officials are to be considered governmental officers, and therefore the approach taken by the preceding category of cases, which holds the Fourth Amendment applicable to school searches but lowers the reasonableness standard as a result of the application of the *in loco parentis* doctrine, to be the most persuasive.

The court in the recent case of In re L.L., in a review of the authorities on this issue, analyzed the interests involved which allowed the lower standard sufficient to satisfy the Fourth Amendment requirement of reasonableness. These interests may be summarized as: (1) the State's strong interest in providing an education in an "orderly atmosphere which is free from danger and disruption"; (2) the student's reasonable expectation of privacy while in school, which is lower than in other places because of the expected restraint exercised over students for security or discipline; (3) "the realities of the classroom present few less intrusive alternatives to an immediate search for suspected dangerous or illegal items or substances." 90 Wis.2d at 600–601, 280 N.W.2d at 350–51.

The Federal District Court in Doe v. Renfrow considered the factor of an absence of any normal or justifiable expectation of privacy on behalf of the students. The court stated that students cannot be said to enjoy any absolute expectation of privacy while in the classroom setting because of the constant interaction among students, faculty and school administrators. A reasonable right to inspection is necessary for the school's performance of its duty to protect all students and the educational process. The court went on to state:

> There is no question as to the right, and indeed, the duty of school officials to maintain an educationally sound environment within the school. It is the responsibility of the school administrator to insure the proper functioning of the educational process . . . . Maintaining an educationally productive atmosphere within the school rests upon the school administration certain heavy responsibilities. One of these is that of providing an environment free from activities harmful to the educational function and to the individual student. [475 F.Supp. at 1020]

In accordance with the foregoing standards, the United States District Court, in Bilbrey v. Brown, 481 F.Supp. 26 (D.Or.1979), a case in which plaintiffs challenged the constitutionality of a school district's search and seizure policies as set forth in the district's "Minimum Standards for Student Conduct and Discipline," held that such searches may properly be conducted when a school official has reasonable cause to believe a student has violated school policy.

Therefore, this court finds that a school official may properly conduct a search of a student's person if the official has a reasonable suspicion that a crime has been or is in the process of being committed, *or* reasonable cause to believe that the search is necessary to maintain school discipline or enforce school policies.

The present case deals with a school standard of discipline and not criminal activity. The standard of reasonableness must be applied, whether we are dealing with noncriminal activity or a school standard of discipline. A reasonable standard is defined as one designed to protect the health, safety and welfare of the child involved, as well as the student population. School officials, therefore, have the right to deliberately restrict smoking to certain areas within the school. Such designations are not arbitrary, but rather based on the school official's experience and knowledge of fire codes and standards. When a school drafts its smoking regulations it considers the following factors: the structure of the building with respect to fire resistance (e.g., fire walls); the ability to control smoking in the area where it is permitted (e.g., by teacher supervision) in order to insure that the privilege is not abused and to reduce the threat of hostile fires; the availability of fire escapes. A further consideration, of increasing importance, is the right of the nonsmoking student to be free from exposure to the detrimental effects of cigarette smoke. Certainly the potential harm and detrimental effect that can be caused by the abuse of smoking privileges are as serious as those which may result from criminal activity committed within the schools. School officials, therefore, must have the same rights to investigate and control the abuse of noncriminal activities as they do in instances involving weapons and drugs. Thus, this court finds that the school's nonsmoking regulation has satisfied the reasonableness standard.

While accepting a lower standard in determining the reasonableness of a search, this court is aware of the other factors which the courts have stated would be considered in determining the sufficiency of cause to search. The factors to be judged are: (1) the child's age, history and school record; (2) the prevalence and seriousness of the problem in the school to which the search was directed; (3) the exigency of the situation requiring an immediate warrantless search; (4) the probative value and reliability of the information used as a justification for the search; (5) the teacher's prior experience with the student. In re L.L., State v. McKinnon, Bellnier v. Lund, Doe v. State, all supra. These factors should serve as a guideline in determining whether some reasonable suspicion of a crime or violation of school regulation has occurred.

Applying the foregoing to the facts of this case, it is apparent that the vice-principal had a right to conduct a search of the student. A teacher had observed the student smoking in an area where such was prohibited. Although the student denied smoking, the school official had a duty to investigate and determine whether a violation of the school's code had occurred. The nature of this situation dictated the actions taken by the vice-principal.

. . .

NOTES

(1) The reasonable suspicion standard has been extensively applied to uphold the propriety of school searches. See, e.g., In re J.A., 40 Ill.Dec. 755, 85 Ill.App.3d 567, 406 N.E.2d 958 (1980), where the court writes:

The proper standard by which searches by school officials should be measured is not the probable cause standard of criminal law, but whether or not the officials have a reasonable suspicion that a student is in possession of contraband which might endanger that student or other students. This "reasonable suspicion" standard should give a proper balance between the student's Fourth Amendment rights to be free from arbitrary searches and the school officials' duty to discipline and protect the students for whom they stand *in loco parentis.*

Applying this "reasonable suspicion" standard to the facts of the instant case, we cannot say that the search conducted by [Dean of Students] Brasher was an unreasonable one under the circumstances. School officials had been informed by an apparently credible authority that the student was in possession of marijuana and intended to sell it to other students. It then became the duty of the school officials to investigate the truth of this information; indeed, they would have been derelict in their duty if they had failed to do so. Although this information, without more, would not have given a police officer probable cause to search an adult, we think that the school authorities were justified under all the circumstances here in conducting the search of the student's person. 406 N.E.2d at 962, 963 (1980) [parenthesis added]

To the same effect, see M v. Board of Education, 429 F.Supp. 288 (S.D.Ill. 1977) (reasonable suspicion standard used to uphold search of high school student required to empty his pockets based on information from another student he was carrying drugs and had a large amount of money in his possession); State v. McKinnon, 88 Wn.2d 75, 558 P.2d 781 (1977) (see especially, Justice Rosellini's dissent from the use of the reasonable suspicion standard to uphold a search by school officials based on a telephone call from the local police chief—Rosellini would require full probable cause to justify a school search); Nelson v. State, 319 So.2d 154 (Fla.App.1975) (student found smoking required to empty pockets revealing marijuana—search upheld as school official had reasonable suspicion); People v. Ward, 62 Mich.App. 46, 233 N.W.2d 180 (1975) (high school principal had reasonable suspicion to compel student to empty pockets where student's guidance counselor told principal that a teacher had seen the student selling pills). Is the use of double hearsay in *Ward* proper even under the lesser standard reasonable suspicion? In Doe v. State, 88 N.M. 347, 540 P.2d 827 (Ct.App.1975), the court set out relevant factors to be considered in assessing the reasonableness of the school official's suspicion:

Thus, we adopt the standard that school officials may conduct a search of a student's person if they have a reasonable suspicion that a crime is being or has been committed or they have reasonable cause to believe that the search is necessary in the aid of maintaining school discipline. We believe that this standard, arrived at by balancing the privacy rights of the students against the unique administrative responsibilities of the school officials, should adequately protect the students from arbitrary searches and give the school officials enough leeway to fulfill their duties. Among the factors to be considered in determining the sufficiency to cause to search a student are the child's age, history and record in school, the prevalence and seriousness of the problem in the school to which the search was directed, the exigency to make the search without delay and the probative value and reliability of the information used as a justification for the search.

Judged by the above enunciated standards, it cannot be doubted that the instant search was reasonable. The subject of the search was a thirteen year old boy who was actually seen by the school official smoking a pipe on school property against school regulations. We hold that the search of Respondent X was based upon reasonable cause to believe that the search was necessary in the aid of maintaining school discipline. The trial court was accordingly correct in admitting into evidence the fruits of that search. . . .

540 P.2d 832–33.

(2) For extensive discussion of school searches see Buss, The Fourth Amendment and Searches of Students in Public Schools, 59 Iowa L.Rev. 739 (1974).

(3) The reasonable suspicion standard is analogous to the standard for a police stop and frisk. See C. Whitebread, Criminal Procedure: An Analysis of Constitutional Cases and Concepts 171–196 (1980) for a full treatment of other reasonable suspicion cases.

(4) The lesser standard for school official searches of students rests in the first instance on the courts' notion that public school officials stand in the place of the students' parents with regard to the education and protection of children while they are at school. See Mercer v. State, 450 S.W.2d 715, 717 (Tex.Civ.App.1970).

Occasionally, however, school officials seem to possess powers and duties greater than those of parents. For example, if a parent conducts a search of his or her child and discovers evidence implying criminal guilt, the parent can choose to remain silent and not report the child to the police. Indeed, would not virtually every parent choose silence in such a situation? School officials, on the other hand, are often under a statutory duty to report evidence of potential criminal liability. Doesn't this difference make the *in loco parentis* rationale for warrantless school searches harder to justify?

(5) A careful reading of all the school search cases, plus consideration of the principles announced in In re Gault, 387 U.S. 1, 87 S.Ct. 1428, 18 L.Ed.2d 527 (1967), reveals a tendency of courts to treat these cases differently from other search and seizure cases not because of a distinction between safeguards available to juveniles and those available to adults or between applicable standards in juvenile proceedings and those applicable in criminal proceedings but rather because of a perceived difference between students and nonstudents, i.e., between the school environment and the outside world. Thus, as pointed out in the preceding note, some courts have adopted a "reasonable suspicion" or similar standard in criminal cases as well as in juvenile proceedings and regardless of whether the student was a juvenile as defined by state law or an adult. The determining factors in all of these cases are

that the subject of the search and seizure was a student and the search and seizure occurred during school or on school property.

JUVENILE JUSTICE STANDARDS, STANDARDS RELATING TO SCHOOLS AND EDUCATION (Tentative Draft 1977) *

8.1 The limits imposed by the fourth amendment upon searches and seizures conducted by police officers are not qualified or alleviated in any way by reason of the fact that a student is the object of the search or that the search is conducted in a school building or on school grounds.

8.2 A search by a police officer of a student, or a protected student area, is unreasonable unless it is made:

A. 1. Under the authority and pursuant to the terms of a valid search warrant,

2. on the basis of exigent circumstances such as those that have been authoritatively recognized as justifying warrantless searches,

3. incident to a lawful arrest,

4. incident to a lawful "stop", or

5. with the consent of the student whose person or protected student area is searched; and

B. in a manner entailing no greater invasion of privacy than the conditions justifying the search make necessary.

8.3 As used in these standards, a protected student area includes (but is not limited to):

A. 1. a school desk assigned to a student if

a. the student sits at that desk on a daily, weekly, or other regular basis,

b. by custom, practice, or express authorization the student does in fact store or is expressly permitted to store, in the desk, papers, equipment, supplies, or other items that belong to the student, and

c. the student does in fact lock or is permitted to lock the desk whether or not

(1) any school official or a small number of other students have the key or combination to the lock,

(2) school officials have informed the student or issued regulations calculated to inform the student either that only certain specified items may be kept in the desk or that the desk may be inspected or searched under specified conditions,

---

* Reprinted with permission from Standards Relating to Schools and Education (Tentative Draft), Copyright 1977, Ballinger Publishing Company.

(3) the student has consented to or entered into an agreement acknowledging the restrictions described in Standard 8.3A. 1. c. (1) and (2) above, or

(4) the student has paid the school for the use of the desk;

B. 1.   a school locker assigned to a student if

a.   the student has either exclusive use of the locker or jointly uses the locker with one or two other students and

b.   the student does in fact lock or is permitted to lock the locker whether or not

(1) school officials or a small number of other students have the key or combination to the lock,

(2) school officials have informed the student or issued regulations calculated to inform the student either that only certain specified items may be kept in the locker or that the locker may be inspected or searched under specified conditions,

(3) the student has consented to or entered into an agreement acknowledging the restrictions described in Standard 8.3 B. 1. b. (1) and (2) or

(4) the student has paid the school for the use of the locker;

C. 1.   a motor vehicle located on or near school premises if

a.   it is owned by a student, or

b.   has been driven to school by a student with the owner's permission.

8.4   As used in these standards, a search "of a student" includes search of the student's

A.   body,

B.   clothes being worn or carried by the student, or

C.   pocketbook, briefcase, duffel bag, bookbag, backpack, or any other container used by the student for holding or carrying personal belongings of any kind and in the possession or immediate proximity of the student.

8.5   The validity of a search of a student, or protected student area, conducted by a police officer in school buildings or on school grounds may not be based in whole or in part upon the fact that the search is conducted with the consent of:

A.   a school official, or

B.   the student's parent except insofar as the parent's approval is necessary to validate a student consent.

8.6 A.   If a school official searches a student or a student protected area:

1.   at the invitation or direction of a police officer,

2.   in cooperation with a police officer, or

3. for the purpose of discovering and turning over to the police evidence that might be used against the student in a criminal proceeding,

the school official should be governed by the requirements made applicable to a police search under Standard 8.2.

B. In connection with any search of a student or student protected area that leads directly or indirectly to information that results in criminal charges against the student, it will be presumed in the absence of affirmative proof to the contrary that each of the characteristics identified in Standard 8.6 A. 1.–3. applies to the school official's search.

8.7 A. If a search of a student or protected student area is conducted by a school official for the purpose of obtaining evidence of student misconduct that might result in a serious disciplinary sanction, the search is unreasonable unless it is made:

1. under the authority and pursuant to the terms of a valid search warrant, or

2. with the consent of the student whose person or protected student area is searched, or

3. after a reasonable determination by the school official that

a. it was not possible to detain the student and/or guard the protected student area until police officers could arrive and take responsibility for the search and

b. failure to make the search would be likely to result in danger to any person (including the student), destruction of evidence, or flight of the student, and

4. in a manner entailing no greater invasion of privacy than the conditions justifying the search make necessary.

B. If, under Standard 8.7 A., the sanction that might result from the suspected misconduct includes expulsion, long-term suspension, or transfer to a school used or designated as a school for problem students of any kind, the search should be subject to all of the requirements of a police search under Standard 8.2.

8.8 Any evidence obtained directly or indirectly as a result of a search conducted in violation of these standards should be inadmissible (without the student's express consent) in any proceeding that might result in either criminal or disciplinary sanctions against the student.

8.9 If a search of a student by a school official is conducted without providing the student the safeguards specified in Standard 8.7 A., evidence obtained directly or indirectly as a result of that search should be inadmissible (without the student's express consent) in any proceeding that might result in the imposition of either a criminal or a serious disciplinary sanction against the student searched.

4. DISCUSSION PROBLEMS

GIRARD SCHOOL

Students at Girard Elementary School attend each of six daily classes in a different room. Students sit at assigned desks in every class and traditionally leave their textbooks and other school supplies inside their desks. When $50 belonging to one of the teachers is reported missing, a surprise desk check reveals the money hidden between the pages of little Kerry Smith's geography book.

Refer to the standards in considering the following questions:

1. Assume that teachers performed the search. Is such a wide-ranging search valid? Would it matter whether or not the desk was locked? What if the desk was locked and the student who happened to be occupying it during the period of the search consented? Assume that the Standards are not intended to change the law of consent. Does the third-party consent validate the search? Can the evidence be used to suspend Kerry for two weeks?

2. Assume that the search of the desks did not turn up the money. The police, operating on the knowledge that Kerry is the school "troublemaker," came to the school and searched Kerry's person without a warrant and over her objection. Would this be a valid search? Could school officials have performed such a search under the Standards? What if the police had obtained prior consent from Kerry's mother, who did not believe her little angel would do anything wrong? Do you believe that parental consent should bind a minor? Should the minor be informed of his or her right to refuse a search?

3. Do you think the case law would support Kerry's claim that she had a reasonable expectation of privacy in an unlocked desk that she shared with five other students? Assuming that the proposed Standards would provide the basis for such a claim, how should school officials handle such a situation?

BOMB THREAT

An anonymous phone call informs the high school principal that a bomb has been placed in one of the student lockers. The police are called in and along with school officials conduct a search of every locker. They do not find a bomb, but during the investigation seize a pound of marijuana from one of the lockers.

Do the Standards say anything about whether the marijuana is admissible in a subsequent delinquency proceeding? A subsequent disciplinary proceeding? Note that the same conduct by a student may result in both a delinquency disposition and a disciplinary action. As attorney for the student, can you think of any basis to argue for suppression? How will the ruling in *Overton* affect your case?

JIM SMITH'S CAR

A group of students are gathered in the school parking lot sitting on the hood of Jim Smith's car. They appear to be drinking from a bottle being passed from one to the other. As the school vice-principal approaches, the bottle is tossed into a nearby patch of bushes. A search of Jim's car reveals several partially consumed bottles of liquor.

1. Assuming that the car is owned by Jim's parents, does Jim have standing to assert a fourth amendment right? What do the Standards say?

2. Assuming that the vice-principal conducted the search with the knowledge that the penalty for alcohol consumption on school grounds is suspension for one week, may the bottles be admitted in a subsequent disciplinary hearing?

5. THIRD PARTY CONSENT TO SEARCHES OF JUVENILE'S PERSON OR BELONGINGS

AMERICAN LAW INSTITUTE, MODEL CODE OF PRE–ARRAIGNMENT PROCEDURE (1975)

§ 240.2 Requirements of Effective Consent

(1) *Persons from Whom Effective Consent May Be Obtained.* The consent justifying a search and seizure . . . must be given, in the case of

(a) Search of an individual's person, by the individual in question or, if the person be under the age of 16, by such individual's parent or guardian;

. . .

(2) *Required Warning to Persons Not in Custody or Under Arrest.* Before undertaking a search, . . . an officer present shall inform the individual whose consent is sought that he is under no obligation to give such consent and that anything found may be taken and used in evidence.

(3) *Required Warning to Persons in Custody or Under Arrest.* If the individual whose consent is sought . . . is in custody or under arrest at the time such consent is offered or invited, such consent shall not justify a search and seizure . . . unless in addition to the warning required by Subsection (2), such individual has been informed that he has the right to consult an attorney, either retained or appointed, and to communicate with relatives or friends, before deciding whether to grant or withhold consent.

NOTES

(1) Can school searches be upheld on the ground that school officials have the power to consent for the child? See People v. Overton, 20 N.Y.2d 360, 283 N.Y.S.2d 22, 229 N.E.2d 596 (1967), remanded per curiam 393 U.S. 85 (1968), for reconsideration of the consent issue.

(2) May school officials extending the *in loco parentis* concept claim that because parents could consent to a search of the child they should enjoy that power by analogy as well? For a case holding parents may not lawfully consent to warrantless search of a seventeen year old's toolbox where he was present and objected to the police conduct, see In re Scott K., 24 Cal.3d 395, 155 Cal.Rptr. 671, 595 P.2d 105 (1979) where the California Supreme Court said in part:

NEWMAN, JUSTICE.

A 17-year-old defendant appeals from an order declaring him a juvenile court ward and placing him on probation. The order was based on the court's finding that defendant unlawfully possessed marijuana for purpose of sale in violation of section 11359 of the Health and Safety Code. The question is whether a warrantless, parent-approved, police search of defendant's personal property was permissible.

Defendant's mother found marijuana in his desk drawer. She gave it to an off-duty police officer who lived in the neighborhood and told him that conversations with other parents led her to believe that her son might be selling marijuana. A week later that officer's report was given to Narcotics Officer Schian for follow-up. He telephoned the father to advise that he was about to arrest defendant. The conversation was as follows: "In substance, I advised the father that I was in charge of the follow-up investigation of the marijuana that his wife had turned over to the police officer; that an arrest would result from this situation, arrest of the son; that I intended to come out and arrest his son if his son was home, and then I received the information that he was working on his motorcycle in the garage.

"And I asked him, 'Is it all right with you then that I go to the garage and arrest your boy there and do you wish to join us out there then, or what shall we do to make easy on maybe the rest of the family?'

"And he indicated, 'Why don't you just come on inside after you have arrested him?'"

Without warrant, Schian and other officers went to the garage. Schian arrested defendant and took him to the house, where the father gave permission to search defendant's bedroom. The search disclosed a locked toolbox. The father told Schian that he had no key and that it was defendant's box. When asked about the key, defendant replied he had lost it. Schian said, "Your father already told me I could break the toolbox open if I couldn't find a key, but it's not in my interest to destroy the lock. Let me see the keys you have in your pocket." Defendant gave Schian his keys, one of which opened the box. Inside were nine baggies of marijuana.

. . .

The People argue that, because a parent is responsible for minor children and may himself inspect their property, police search of that property when pursuant to parental consent is reasonable and accordingly constitutional. Implicit is the notion that the father here could effectively waive his son's right to be secure in the son's effects. We reject that view.

. . .

The trial court here held that the father's authority was based on the combined circumstance of his ownership of the home and his duty to control his son. Yet neither fact shows the requisite link between the father's interest and the property inspected. Common authority over personal property may not be implied from the father's proprietary interest in the premises. (United States v. Matlock, supra, 415 U.S. 164, 171, fn. 7, 94 S.Ct. 988.) Neither may it be premised on the nature of the parent-child relation.[10]

Juveniles are entitled "to acquire and hold property, real and personal (Estate of Yano (1922) 188 Cal. 645, 649, 206 P. 995, 997); and a "minor child's property is his own . . . not that of his parents." (Emery v. Emery (1955) 45 Cal.2d 421, 432, 289 P.2d 218, 225; see also Civ.Code § 202) Parents may have a protectible interest in property belonging to children, but that fact may not be assumed. When a warrantless search is challenged the People must show that it was reasonable. Here the People did not establish that the consenting parent had a sufficient interest under search and seizure law. The father claimed no interest in the box or its contents. He acknowledged that the son was owner, and the son did not consent to the search. Because those facts were known to the police there was not justification for their relying on the father's consent to conduct the search. . . .

(3) May children consent to warrantless police searches of their parents' homes? See generally, C. Whitebread, Criminal Procedure: An Analysis of Constitutional Cases and Concepts 206–210 (1980). For a recent case upholding consent to entry into parent's home by a young son (estimated age 11–14 by police testimony), see Doyle v. State, 633 P.2d 306 (Alaska Ct.App.1981).

10. Courts have not previously embraced the notion that the government can use the relationship between parties to impute "common authority" to the consenting party when one in fact existed. (Cf. People v. Daniels, 16 Cal.App.3d 36, 93 Cal.Rptr. 628 (1971); People v. Murillo, 241 Cal.App.2d 173, 50 Cal.Rptr. 290 (1966); also see dictum in People v. Terry 2 Cal.3d 362, 392, 85 Cal.Rptr. 409, 428, 466 P.2d 961, 980 (1970), where this court held the wife could give valid consent to police search of her husband's property because "[t]here is no evidence that the murder weapon was in a sealed box or other container belonging to Terry [the husband], which Mrs. Terry might not have had authority to permit to be searched."

6. A SPECIAL ISSUE: DOG SNIFFING AT SCHOOL

DOE v. RENFROW

United States District Court, N. D. Indiana, 1979.
475 F.Supp. 1012.

ALLEN SHARP, DISTRICT JUDGE.

. . .

At issue in this law suit is the constitutional propriety of an investigation conducted by administrators of the Highland school system assisted by local police officers at the Junior and Senior High Schools in Highland, Indiana.

Highland, Indiana is a community consisting of approximately 30,000 residents located in the northwest corner of the state in Lake County, Indiana. The school community of Highland has, among several elementary schools, a Junior and Senior High School. Both these campuses are located on the same site. The school buildings are adjacent to one another and the approximately 2,780 students of both schools share common facilities located in the buildings.

Although the problem of illicit drug use within the schools was not a novel one in Highland before 1978, it became progressively more acute and more visible within the Senior and Junior High Schools during the 1978 academic year. Beginning in the fall of that year, concern over drug use within the school intensified as school officials recorded instances of drug use by students. From September 1978 to March 22, 1979, twenty-one instances were recorded when students were found in possession of drugs, drug paraphernalia or alcohol or under the influence of drugs. More alarming to school officials was the fact that of those twenty-one instances, thirteen occurred within a twenty school day span just prior to the complained of activities. Also, during this four week period, school administrators received daily reports from faculty, students and parents concerning the use of drugs within the Junior and Senior High Schools. Out of these general reports, two students were identified as drug users, however, after investigation by school officials, no evidence of any drug use was found concerning the named students.

Throughout the year, and especially during this four week period, school officials, teachers and even members of the student body became concerned about the negative impact the use of drugs within the school was having on the educational environment. Classroom disruptions and the concomitant loss of learning time occurred as a result of disciplining those students found to have been using drugs in the school during the regular school hours. Moreover, there was a feeling, at least by some students including the plaintiff, that peer pressure existed in favor of using drugs while on campus. Not to use drugs was considered not to be "cool" by members of the student body who did use drugs. Because of the increasing use of drugs within the school, students, faculty and administrators suffered a loss of morale at both the Senior and Junior High School.

To combat what was perceived as an increasingly alarming drug problem within the school system, members of the Highland Town School District Board suggested the use of properly trained dogs to search for drugs within the school building. The use of drug detecting canine units was discussed at the March 6, 1979 meeting of the Board of the Highland Community School District and Superintendent of Schools, Omer Renfrow. Renfrow decided to use the trained dogs in a drug investigation and he arranged a second meeting for March 14, 1979. This meeting was attended by school administrators of the Senior and Junior High Schools and by members of the Highland Police Department. Also present at this meeting was Patricia Little, a trainer of drug detecting canines. Little was asked to attend because she had had experience in the field of canine searches in schools.

At this meeting, the school administrators informed the police officers that they intended to conduct an investigation within the school buildings using canine units to detect and remove any narcotics or narcotic paraphernalia. To carry out this procedure, they requested the assistance of the Highland Police Department and of volunteer canine units experienced in drug detection. The objective was to rid the Junior and Senior High Schools of illicit drugs and discourage further drug use on the campuses. The school officials insisted, and the police agreed, that no criminal investigations would occur as a result of any evidence recovered during the school investigation. The school officials did intend, however, to bring any necessary disciplinary actions against students found in possession of contraband.

A. *Activities Inside The School*

On March 23, 1979, a school wide drug inspection was conducted by the administrators of the Highland School System with the assistance of the Highland Police Department and volunteer canine units trained in marijuana detection. The inspection occurred in both the Junior and Senior High School campuses and began during the first period class. Teachers were informed of the inspection that morning by means of a sealed note upon their classroom desks. Each classroom teacher was instructed to keep their students in the first period class and to have them perform their customary work. A canine team visited each classroom in both the Junior and Senior High School buildings. Each team consisted of a school administrator or teacher, a dog and its handler and a uniformed police officer. Four such teams were used in the Senior High School building and two were operating in the Junior High School rooms. Students were instructed to sit quietly in their seats with their hands and any purses to be placed upon their desk tops while the dog handler introduced the dog and led it up and down the desk aisles. The canine teams spent approximately five minutes in each room. No incidents of disruption occurred in the classrooms because of the presence of the dogs or the teams. The entire investigation lasted approximately two and one-half hours during which time students wishing to use the washrooms were allowed to leave the classroom with an escort of the same sex to the washroom door. The administrative purpose of the escort was to prevent the disposal of any drugs on the way to the washroom. No students were observed while in the washrooms. In order to keep disruptions to a minimum, late arrivals at the school were directed to a room other than their regular first period classroom. Uniformed police officers and school administrators were present in the halls during the entire investigation. Custodians were present near all locked doors to provide immediate exit if necessary. During the inspection, a dog alerted [5] to a particular student on approximately fifty occasions. After each alert, the student was asked to empty his or her pockets or purse. A body search was conducted with respect to eleven students because the dog continued to alert after the student had emptied pockets or purse. Plaintiff Doe was one of those students to which a dog continued to alert after she emptied her pockets. She was quietly escorted to a nurse's station in the Junior High School and was asked to remain in the waiting room. Upon being asked to enter the inner office, two women introduced themselves to the plaintiff. One was a friend of the plaintiff's mother. Plaintiff was asked if she had ever used marijuana to which she answered she had not. She was then asked to remove her clothing. She was permitted to turn her back to the two women while she was disrobing. Upon removal, her clothing was briefly examined, her hair was lifted to determine if any substances were hidden in it, and she was immediately permitted to dress. No marijuana or other drugs were found in plaintiff's possession, although it was later discovered that plaintiff had been playing with one of her dogs that morning of the search and that dog was in heat.

As a result of the investigation seventeen students were found in possession of drugs; twelve of those students withdrew voluntarily from school and three students were expelled pursuant to the due process statutes of the State of Indiana. I.C. 20–8.1–5–5 et seq. Additionally, two students were suspended by the administration because they were found to be in possession of drug paraphernalia.

. . .

III. *The Fourth Amendment*

This Court is specifically confronted with the following issues: (1) whether the investigative procedure used by the school officials with the assistance of law enforcement officers, for the sole and exclusive

---

5. An alert is an indication of a trained canine that the odor of the drug, in this case marijuana, is present in the air or upon the individual.

purpose of furthering a valid educational goal of eliminating drug use within the school, was a seizure and search under the Fourth Amendment; (2) whether the use of dogs to detect marijuana and marijuana paraphernalia in the classroom was, standing alone, a search under the Fourth Amendment; (3) whether the admitted search of a student's clothing upon the continued alert of a trained drug detecting canine was violative of rights protected by the Fourth Amendment; and (4) whether the nude body search conducted solely upon the basis of a trained drug detecting canine's alert violated the plaintiff's right to be free from unreasonable search and seizure.

. . .

A. *The General Inspection*

Considering first plaintiff's contention that the investigation of March 23, 1979 constituted a mass detention and deprivation of freedom in violation of the Fourth Amendment, this Court finds the assertion to be without merit. Plaintiff, as well as other students, is subject to the daily routine of class attendance in an educational environment. During an eight hour day, students must move from room to room, attending classes designated by the administration and taught by teachers hired by the school system. Students are made to change this routine every year, if not every semester. Movement from class to class entails intrusions upon the students' freedoms. Times allocated for each class period are determined by the school officials, not the students. Plaintiff must attend the scheduled classes for the times designated. It was not unusual for students to be kept in their classrooms longer than the normal periods.

Such a regulation of a student's movement in no way denies that person any constitutionally guaranteed right. On the morning in question all students were given an opportunity to perform their usual classroom schedule for an extra 1 and ½ periods. Except for the five minute interval when the canine unit entered the room, plaintiff and all other students were exposed only to a longer than normal first period class. Such an extended period had been experienced at other times during convocations and school assemblies.

School officials maintain the discretion and authority for scheduling all student activities each school day. Plaintiff will not be heard to say that because she was made to stay in her classroom an extra 1½ hours, she was denied a constitutionally protected freedom from unreasonable seizure. No evidence was presented at trial that shows plaintiff was in any way discomforted by the mere fact of being made to continue her class work for an extra 95 minutes. Although the students were requested to remain in their first period classes, those wishing to use the washroom facilities were accommodated by an escort to the washroom door. Care was taken by the school officials to provide custodians at each exit in case an emergency arose. Although unknown by the students, those uniformed officers in the halls that morning were under orders not to pursue any students outside the building. Although it can be argued that the spectre of a uniformed officer may chill some vague right to movement within the school, such contention fails in light of the fact that student movement is constantly restricted for other legitimate educational purposes. Moreover, uniformed police officers are, unfortunately, not an uncommon sight in today's public schools. Therefore, this Court finds no seizure of the plaintiff or other students within the Senior and Junior High School prior to any alert by the trained dogs.

Turning next to the search aspect of the Fourth Amendment, the issue becomes whether the activity of the defendants on the morning in question prior to any alert by the trained dogs was a search and, if so, whether the search, although warrantless, was reasonable. This Court finds for the reasons stated below that entry by the school officials into each classroom for five minutes was not a search contemplated by the Fourth Amendment but, rather, was a justified action taken in accordance with the *in loco parentis* doctrine. Furthermore, the presence of the uniformed police officer in the room, at the request of the school official and with the agreement that no arrests would occur as a result of finding any drugs upon students, did not alter the basic function of the school official's activities. Moreover, the presence of the dog and its trainer within the classroom, also at the request and supervision of the school officials, was only an aide to that official's observation of students. Finally, for purposes of this section, the sniffing of a trained narcotic detecting canine is not a search. Since no search was performed up until the time the dogs alerted, no warrant was necessary for the initial observation by the school officials.

There is no question as to the right and, indeed, the duty of school officials to maintain an educationally sound environment within the school.[10] It is the responsibility of the school corporation personnel to supervise students while they attend classes.[11] It is also the responsibility of the school administrator to insure the proper functioning of the educational process. M. v. Bd. of Ed. Ball-Chatham C.U. S.D. No. 5, 429 F.Supp. 288 (S.D.Ill.1977). Maintaining an educationally productive atmosphere within the school rests upon the school administrator certain heavy responsibilities. One of these is that of providing an environment free from activities harmful to the educational function and to the individual students. Drug use within the school became an activity the school administrator wished to eliminate. It cannot be denied that each of the school administrators possessed the authority to enter a classroom on the day in question in order to prevent the use of illicit drugs. People v. Overton, 20 N.Y.2d 360, 283 N.Y.S.2d 22, 229 N.E.2d 596 (1967); M. v. Bd., supra; Bellnier v. Lund, 438 F.Supp. 47 (N.D.N.Y.1977). Acting alone, each school administrator could have unquestionably surveyed a classroom

10. Ind.Code, § 20–8.1–5–2.   11. Ind.Code, § 20–8.1–5–1.

to prevent drug use. Because those administrators now acted with assistance from a uniformed officer does not change their function. The officers were merely aiding in the inspection, at the request of the school administrators. Their presence does not change the actions of the school official from that of supervision *in loco parentis* to that of an unwarranted search. Although they were obviously clothed with their state authority, they had previously agreed that no arrests would be made as a result of any drugs found that morning. No police investigations took place on that day nor have any arrests or prosecutions been initiated as a result of the March 23, 1979 inspection.

B. *The Dogs Within The Classroom*

Nor does this court believe the presence of the dog unit within the classroom changes the nature of the observation. Again, the trainer and dog were in the rooms at the request and with the permission of the school administrators. The dog acted merely as an aide to the school administrator in detecting the scent of marijuana. The dog handler interpreted the actions of the dog for the benefit of the school administrator. Bringing these nonschool personnel into the classroom to aid the school administrators in their observation for drug abuse is, of itself, not a search. Students are exposed to various intrusions into their classroom environment. The presence of the canine team for several minutes was a minimal intrusion at best and not so serious as to invoke the protections of the Fourth Amendment.

Plaintiff, however, contends that the walking up the aisles and the sniffing of the dog constituted a search within the meaning of the Fourth Amendment and, as such, it was not based upon probable cause and was therefore in violation of her constitutionally protected rights. Plaintiff's assertion misreads the present state of the law concerning the use of drug detecting canines.

The use of the dogs in this case occurred in the public school environment, an area where courts have not granted full application of the Fourth Amendment's protections. . . .

. . .

Turning to this case, the evidence shows the school administrators had compiled an extensive list of previous incidents of drug use within the school. In twenty school days before the investigation, thirteen incidents were reported where students were found either to be in possession of drugs or drug paraphernalia or under the influence of drugs or alcohol. The atmosphere within the Highland Junior and Senior High Schools was one of frustration on the part of school administrators and faculty brought about by their inability to control or arrest the drug use problem. Additionally, there was evidence from some students of refusal to speak out against those students using drugs for fear of reprisals. The use of the canine units was decided upon only after the upsurge in drug use at the schools. The school officials, therefore, had outside independent evidence indicating drug abuse within the school. Use of the dogs to detect where those drugs were located was not unreasonable under the circumstances. Nor does the fact that the officials had no information about specific students and drug possession invalidate the use of the dogs. This Court now finds that in a public school setting, school officials clothed with the responsibilities of caring for the health and welfare of the entire student population, may rely on such general information to justify the use of the canines to detect narcotics. What level of information is necessary must be determined on a case by case basis, however, this Court holds the lesser standard of a "reasonable cause to believe" applicable in such a determination. See, M. v. Bd., supra. School officials fulfilling their state empowered duties will not be held to the same standards as law enforcement officials when determining if the use of canines is necessary to detect drugs within the schools. This lesser standard applies only when the purpose of the dog's use is to fulfill the school's duty to provide a safe, ordered and healthy educational environment.

. . .

. . . . A reasonable right to inspection is necessary to the school's performance of its duty to provide an educational environment.

The health and safety of all students at the two schools was threatened by an increase in drug use. The schools' administrators delegated by the state with the duty and responsibility to maintain order, discipline, safety and education within the school system supervised the investigation which was designed with the single purpose of eliminating drug use inside the school buildings. The operation was carried out in an unintrusive manner in each classroom.

Moreover, the procedure of bringing the trained dogs into each classroom was planned so as to cause only a few minutes interruption. All students were treated similarly up until an alert by one of the dogs. No student was treated with any malice nor was the operation planned in a way so as to embarrass any particular student. Weighing the minimal intrusion against the school's need to rid itself of the drug problem, the actions of the school officials leading up to an alert by one of the dogs was reasonable and not a search for purposes of the Fourth Amendment. Up until the trained dogs indicated the presence of marijuana, no violation of any basic Fourth Amendment rights occurred.

The Pocket Search

When a dog alerted to the plaintiff, she was ordered by a police officer to empty her pockets onto the desk under the supervision of a school administrator. She contends that this violated her constitutional right to be secure against unreasonable search and seizure.

Pl arg

. . .

In conducting the pocket search, as well as the other searches in question, the school officials clearly were not concerned with the discovery of evidence to be used in criminal prosecutions, but rather were concerned solely with the elimination of drug trafficking within the schools. It cannot be disputed that the school's interest in maintaining the safety, health and education of its students justified its grappling with the grave, even lethal, threat of drug abuse. The pocket search was conducted in furtherance of the school's legitimate interest in eliminating drug trafficking within the school.

reason

It should be noted at this point that had the role of the police been different, this court's reasoning and conclusion may well have been different. If the search had been conducted for the purpose of discovering evidence to be used in a criminal prosecution, the school may well have had to satisfy a standard of probable cause rather than reasonable cause to believe. Picha v. Wielgos, supra. Furthermore, this court is not here ruling whether any evidence obtained in the search could have been used in a criminal prosecution. This court is ruling that so long as a school is pursuing those legitimate interests which are the source of its *in loco parentis* status, "maintaining the order, discipline, safety, supervision, and education of the students within the school" (Picha v. Wielgos, supra, 410 F.Supp. at 1221), it is the general rule that the Fourth Amendment allows a warrantless intrusion into the student's sphere of privacy, if and only if the school has reasonable cause to believe that the student has violated or is violating school policies.

If wanted to prosecute them diff standard for search

gen rule

The pocket search was an invasion of the sphere of privacy which the Fourth Amendment protects; it was a search. But the alert of the dog constituted reasonable cause to believe that the plaintiff was concealing narcotics. Having that requisite reasonable cause to believe that the plaintiff was concealing narcotics, the defendants did not violate the plaintiff's Fourth Amendment rights by ordering her to empty her pockets onto the desk. By conducting the pocket search, the school officials did not violate the plaintiff's right to be secure against *unreasonable* search and seizure.

Conclude pocket search not unreas.

D. *The Nude Search*

Plaintiff further alleges that being subjected to the nude search that morning violated her right against unreasonable search and seizure. It was only upon a continued alert of the trained canine that the school officials based their decision to search the plaintiff. This Court must focus upon the reasonableness of the search to determine its constitutionality. Upon doing so, this Court holds that conducting a nude search of a student solely upon the continued alert of a

Pl arg

Nude search unreas

trained drug-detecting canine is unreasonable even under the lesser "reasonable cause to believe" standard.

Subjecting a student to a nude search is more than just the mild inconvenience of a pocket search, rather, it is an intrusion into an individual's basic justifiable expectation of privacy. Before such a search can be performed, the school administrators must articulate some facts that provide a reasonable cause to believe the student possesses the contraband sought. The continued alert by the trained canine alone is insufficient to justify such a search because the animal reacts only to the scent or odor of the marijuana plant, not the substance itself. There is always the possibility that one's clothing may have been inadvertently exposed to the pungent odor of the drug. Although a trained dog is certainly more discriminative than electronic detection devices, United States v. Bronstein, supra, at 462, 463, it only alerts to the odor of the substance, not the substance itself. Therefore, the alert of the dog alone does not provide the necessary reasonable cause to believe the student actually *possesses* the drug.

factors

Factors considered important when determining the reasonableness of a student search are: (1) the student's age; (2) the student's history and record in school; (3) the seriousness and prevalence of the problem to which the search is directed; and (4) the exigency requiring an immediate warrantless search.

Hold

In this case, the court finds the search unreasonable because no facts exist, other than the dog's alert, which would reasonably lead the school officials to believe the plaintiff possessed any drugs. Therefore, the nude search of plaintiff was unlawful because it did violate her Fourth Amendment right against an unreasonable search and seizure.

. . .

NOTE

The Seventh Circuit Court of Appeals affirmed, 631 F.2d 91 (1980), and denied rehearing and rehearing en banc 635 F.2d 582. There were four dissents from the denial of rehearing en banc. The United States Supreme Court denied certiorari, 451 U.S. 1022 (1981), but a dissent by Justice Brennan echoed the concern of several of the judges of the Seventh Circuit:

. . . I cannot agree that the Fourth Amendment authorizes local school and police officials to detain every junior and senior high school student present in a town's public schools and then, using drug-detecting, police-trained German shepherds, to conduct a warrantless, student-by student dragnet inspection "to see if there were any drugs present." While school officials acting in loco parentis may take reasonable steps to maintain a safe and healthful educational environment, their actions must nonetheless be consistent with the Fourth Amendment. The problem of drug abuse in the schools is not to be solved by conducting school-house raids on unsuspecting students absent particularized information regarding drug users or suppliers.

. . .

I cannot agree that the Highland school officials' use of the trained police dogs did not constitute a search. The dogs were led from student to student for the express purpose of sniffing their clothing and their bodies to obtain information that the school authorities and police officers, with their less-developed sense of smell, were incapable of obtaining. In the case of petitioner, the dog repeatedly jabbed its nose into her legs. Petitioner testified that the experience of being sniffed and prodded by trained police dogs in the presence of the police and representatives of the press was degrading and embarrassing. I am astonished that the court did not find that the school's use of the dogs constituted an invasion of petitioner's reasonable expectation of privacy. See *Katz v. United States*, 389 U.S. 347, 88 S.Ct. 507, 19 L.Ed.2d 576 (1967); *Wolf v. Colorado*, 338 U.S. 25, 69 S.Ct. 1359, 93 L.Ed.2d 1782 (1949).[4]

Moreover, even if the Fourth Amendment permits school authorities, acting in loco parentis, to conduct exploratory inspections if they have "reasonable cause to believe" contraband will be found, that standard could not apply where, as here, the school officials planned and conducted the search with the full participation of local police officials.[5] Once school authorities enlist the aid of police officers to help maintain control over the school's drug problem, they step outside the bounds of any quasi-parental relationship, and their conduct must be judged according to the traditional probable cause standard.[6]

Although a number of incidents involving alcohol, drugs, and related paraphernalia had been reported to school authorities in the seven months preceding the raid on the Highland schools, those incidents involved only 21 students, 13 of whom had been "withdrawn" from the school system by March 1979. 475 F.Supp. at 1015, and n. 1. At the time of the raid, school authorities possessed no particularized information as to drugs or contraband, suppliers or users. Furthermore, they had made no effort to focus the search on particular individuals who might have been engaged in drug activity at school. The authorities had no more than a generalized hope that their sweeping investigative techniques would lead to the discovery of contraband.

4. Although the court below relied on a number of cases holding that the use of trained dogs to sniff out contraband does not constitute a search, see, e.g., United States v. Solis, 536 F.2d 880 (9th Cir. 1976); United States v. Bronstein, 521 F.2d 459 (2d Cir. 1975), cert. denied 424 U.S. 918 (1976); United States v. Fulero, 162 U.S.App.D.C. 206, 498 F.2d 748 (1974), those cases involved the sniffing of inanimate and unattended objects rather than persons. Thus, even if those cases correctly state the law, they are inapposite.

5. For that same reason, I would disagree with the Court of Appeals' conclusion that the mass detention of students by school authorities and police officers did not constitute an unreasonable seizure. See Terry v. Ohio, 392 U.S. 1, 88 S.Ct. 1868, 20 L.Ed.2d 889 (1968).

6. The Court of Appeals found it significant that the police officials agreed not to seek prosecution of students found to possess drugs. However, I agree with the dissenting opinion of Judge Swygert that the Fourth Amendment's protection against unreasonable searches is based on "the right of the people to be secure in their persons," and that it is constitutionally irrelevant that the police officers may have agreed not to arrest students found to be in possession of contraband. 635 F.2d at 584.

This Court has long expressed its abhorrence of unfocused general- ized, information-seeking searches. . . .

But that is precisely the type of search the Highland officials conducted. They certainly had far less than probable cause—or in my view even rea- sonable suspicion—to believe that each student searched would possess drugs or other contraband. Accordingly, I believe the search was uncon- stitutional.

We do not know what class petitioner was attending when the police and dogs burst in, but the lesson the school authorities taught her that day will undoubtedly make a greater impression than the one her teacher had hoped to convey. I would grant certiorari to teach petitioner another lesson; that the Fourth Amendment protects "the right of the people to be secure in their persons, houses, papers, and effects, against unreason- able searches and seizures," and that before police and local officers are permitted to conduct dog-assisted dragnet inspections of public school students, they must obtain a warrant based on sufficient particularized evidence to establish probable cause to believe a crime has been or is be- ing committed. Schools cannot expect their students to learn the lessons of good citizenship when the school authorities themselves disregard the fundamental principles underpinning our constitutional freedoms.

451 U.S. at 1022, 1025–27.

JONES v. LATEXO INDEPENDENT SCHOOL DISTRICT

United States District Court, E.D. Texas, 1980.
499 F.Supp. 223.

JUSTICE, CHIEF JUDGE.

On April 11, 1980, the student body at the school operated by the Latexo Independent School District was subjected to the supersensi- tive nose of "Merko", a dog trained to detect the odor of marijuana and other narcotics, as well as various other substances. Those stu- dents designated by Merko to be emanating such odors were subse- quently searched by school authorities. Merko also sniffed the stu- dents' automobiles, which were parked in the school parking lot, in an effort to detect the odor of contraband. Vehicles singled out by the dog were thoroughly searched. As a result of this procedure, six stu- dents were suspended from school for possession of "drug parapher- nalia" on campus in violation of school regulations.

Plaintiffs in this action are three of the suspended students, all siblings, and their parent. They challenge the school's actions, de- manding injunctive and declaratory relief, and likewise damages un- der 42 U.S.C. § 1983. . . .

. . .

In deciding whether the inspection by Merko, the "sniffer dog", violated the fourth amendment rights of plaintiffs, a twofold test is required. First, it must be determined whether a search of constitu-

tional dimension actually occurred. If it is found that a search occurred, the (second) issue is whether or not the search was reasonable.

. . .

The dog's inspection was virtually equivalent to a physical entry
into the students' pockets and personal possessions. In effect, he
perceived what the students had secreted and communicated that information to his handler. By way of analogy, if the police approached citizens on the street with a portable x-ray machine to discern what they were carrying in their pockets, purses, and briefcases,
surely such a procedure would be a search under the fourth amendment. Yet that was precisely the way in which Merko was employed.
Like an x-ray machine, his superhuman sense of smell invaded the
students' outer garments and detected the presence of items they
were expecting to keep private. All citizens have a reasonable expectation that their privacy will not be intruded upon by electronic surveillance, x-ray machines, or sniffing dogs at the whim of the state.
The use of the "sniffer dog" in the Latexo school was thus a search
under the fourth amendment.

The designation of the sniffing conducted by Merko as a search
does not end the constitutional inquiry, for the fourth amendment
prohibits only those searches which are "unreasonable". . . .

. . .

The degree of intrusion committed by Merko's sniffing the students and their property was somewhat less extensive than that
stemming from a physical search. No laying on of hands was contemplated during the procedure until the dog had completed his tour
of each classroom. In that respect, the intrusion more closely resembled electronic bugging or x-rays, which convey private information
without a discernible physical intrusion. Moreover, since Merko only
signalled his trainer if contraband was detected, this type of search
was more limited in nature than other surveillance methods which
pick up private information, both incriminating and non-incriminating,
in an indiscriminate manner.

On the other hand, the use of an animal such as Merko to conduct
a search may offend the sensibilities of those targeted for inspection
more seriously than would an electronic gadget. Merko, a German
Shepherd, is a large animal who had been trained as an attack dog.
Testimony by the school's principal, Mr. Emmons, indicated that the
dog "slobbered" on one child in the course of a search. The dog's
trainer acknowledged that Merko might physically touch a child during a search if the dog became overly excited. Such a tool of surveillance could prove both intimidating and frightening, particularly to
the children, some as young as kindergarten age, enrolled at Latexo.
Hence, the degree of intrusion caused by the search was significant,
far greater than that which the Fifth Circuit has found unacceptable
in the "beeper" cases.

Defendants particularly emphasize that the student body was warned by Superintendent Acker that Merko would be conducting surprise inspections of the school prior to the search conducted on April 11th. They suggest that such a disclosure greatly diminished any expectation of privacy plaintiffs might have held prior to that time. But the mere announcement by officials that individual rights are about to be infringed upon cannot justify the subsequent infringement. Again through the medium of comparison, if the Government announced that all telephone lines would henceforth be tapped, it is apparent that, nevertheless, the public would not lose its expectation of privacy in using the telephone.

The search at the Latexo school cannot be analogized to passenger searches at airports, where citizens are warned that they will be subject to search should they choose to board a plane. In such circumstances, the individual is free to avoid the search by refraining from air travel. But the students at the Latexo school had no means of avoiding the impending searches, after they were announced, had they wished to do so. School attendance is compelled by law, and no students were permitted to leave their classrooms before Merko commenced sniffing. The search was mandatory for all. Thus, the reasonable expectation of students to be free from such an intrusion survived all warnings by school officials that such searches were to take place.

. . .

. . . [T]he state must have a basis for subjecting a particular person to search before intruding upon his privacy. Neither the police nor any other official may stop and search all persons present at a particular location simply because of a generalized suspicion that somebody in attendance might possess contraband. The blanket search or dragnet is, except in the most unusual and compelling circumstances, anathema to the protection accorded citizens under the fourth amendment.

The defendants in this case ignored the need to ascertain individualized suspicion prior to intruding upon the privacy rights of the students at Latexo. There was not a shred of evidence at the time of the sniff-search on April 11th that any of the student-plaintiffs were in possession of drugs or any other contraband on school grounds. It was, instead, the purpose of the search itself to ferret out such evidence in order to justify a more extensive search of selected students and property. But the ultimate fruits of a search, however bountiful, cannot justify the intrusion after the fact. United States v. Di Re, 332 U.S. 581, 595, 68 S.Ct. 222, 228, 90 L.Ed. 210 (1948); State of Texas v. Gonzales, 388 F.2d 145, 148 (5th Cir. 1968). Just as the police could not lawfully bring Merko into a restaurant, football stadium, or shopping center to sniff-search citizens indiscriminately for hidden drugs, the school officials exceeded the bounds of reasonableness in using Merko to inspect virtually the entire Latexo student body without any facts to raise a reasonable suspicion regarding specific individuals.

The sniff-search of plaintiffs' vehicles, isolated from the search of the plaintiffs themselves, also exceeded the bounds of reasonableness. Under school regulations, students had no access to their vehicles while school was in session. Thus, the school's legitimate interest in what students had left in their vehicles was minimal at best. The search was conducted in a blanket, indiscriminate manner without individualized suspicion of any kind. The capabilities of the dog, in penetrating the closed doors of the vehicles in a manner far beyond the range of human senses, resembled those of an x-ray machine or bugging device. While the extent of personal intrusion was somewhat less serious than in the dog's sniffing each individual student, the combination of other factors place the vehicle searches on the wrong side of the constitutional line.

As mentioned above, the determination of reasonableness in each case must be made on an *ad hoc* basis. To date, five courts of appeals have approved searches by "sniffer dogs" in circumstances which contrast sharply with those presented by the case at bar. None of those cases support the reasonableness of defendant's indiscriminate search of the students at Latexo.[11]

11. The five cases are: United States v. Venema, 563 F.2d 1003 (10th Cir. 1977); United States v. Solis, 536 F.2d 880, (9th Cir. 1976); United States v. Bronstein, 521 F.2d 459 (2nd Cir. 1975) cert. denied, 424 U.S. 918, 96 S.Ct. 1121, 47 L.Ed.2d 324 (1976); United States v. Race, 529 F.2d 12 (1st Cir. 1976); and United States v. Fulero, 498 F.2d 748 (D.C.Cir.1974) (*per curiam*). In *Venema*, the police had individualized suspicion before conducting a sniff-search of a storage locker. The target trailer in *Solis* also exhibited suspicious characteristics before being singled out for sniff-search. Talcum powder, frequently used to mask the scent of marijuana, was visible on the trailer frame. The court, which found that the "sniffer dog" was employed merely to corroborate other evidence of crime, stressed that the sniff-search was not indiscriminate in scope. Id. at 882. *Bronstein*, the Second Circuit case, involved the sniff-search of airline baggage after individualized suspicion had developed. The court found no reasonable expectation of privacy in baggage shipped by plane and emphasized that "Meisha [the "sniffer dog"] was not employed in a dragnet operation against all flight passengers . . ." Id. at 463. The court also stressed the difference in degree of intrusion between a baggage search and a sniff-search of persons themselves. Id. at 462, n. 5. Judge

Mansfield, concurring, asserted that wholesale sniff-searches of all baggage without individualized suspicion would violate the fourth amendment. Id. at 465.

The two remaining court of appeals cases also differ markedly in their facts from the case at bar. *Race* involved the sniff-search of freight, both domestic and foreign, arriving at a major airport from all over the world. While the search was indiscriminate in nature, it was, in effect, a border or customs search since it encompassed items from abroad. Those choosing to utilize such channels of transportation for their property voluntarily assume a diminished expectation of privacy. In *Fulero*, the police had individualized suspicion before ordering a sniff-search of a footlocker ticketed for cross-country shipment. The smell of mothballs, another substance commonly used to mask the odor of marijuana, was readily discernible when the truck was brought into the bus terminal to be shipped.

None of these five cases involved a sniff-search carried out upon individual citizens. All but one concerned items in the stream of interstate commerce, manifesting a greatly reduced expectation of privacy. In four of the cases, the officials who ordered the sniff-search had particularized suspicion directed against specific individuals beforehand. None of

The only case decided to date on facts even remotely resembling those now before the court is Doe v. Renfrow, 475 F.Supp. 1012 (N.D. Ind.1979) *(appeal pending)*. The court's approval of a blanket high school sniff-search in that case stemmed from an erroneous view that the dog merely augmented or enhanced school officials in their own inspection of the school. Id. at 1022. As noted above, however, a "sniffer dog" actually perceives odors undetectable to humans, much as an electronic listening device picks up sounds inaudible to the human ear. Doe v. Renfrow has been justifiably criticized by legal writers on this and other grounds. See "The Constitutionality of Canine Searches in the Classroom", 71 Journal of Criminal Law & Criminology 1 (1980); Helfer, "Search and Seizure in Public Schools: Are Our Children's Rights Going to the Dogs?", 24 St. Louis U.L.J. 119 (1979).[12]

Despite the apparent unreasonableness of defendants' blanket sniff-search at the Latexo school, defendants make an additional argument which merits attention. Under the *in loco parentis* doctrine, school teachers and administrators have specific responsibility for the health, safety, and conduct of students during school hours which gives them authority to impose discipline and maintain order. See Picha v. Wielgos, 410 F.Supp. 1214, 1217–1221 (N.D.Ill.1976). Defendants suggest that the sniff-search was necessarily reasonable since it was carried out in the exercise of that power and in furtherance of valid school regulations.

It is certainly true that the standards for a search in the public school context are considerably more lax than they are in the community at large. Courts have generally approved searches conducted in schools on the basis of "reasonable cause to believe" that contraband would be found, rather than requiring that the stricter standard of probable cause be met. See, e.g., M. v. Bd. of Ed. Ball-Chatham C.U. S.D., 429 F.Supp. 288, 292 (S.D.Ill.1977). Moreover, a warrant may not be required for such a search in many cases when the school is pursuing its legitimate interest in maintaining a safe environment conducive to the learning process. Bilbrey v. Brown, 481 F.Supp. 26, 28 (D.Or.1979).

But the doctrine of *in loco parentis* does not render the fourth amendment completely inapplicable to school searches, nor does it strip students attending school of their constitutional rights. Picha v. Wielgos, 410 F.Supp. 1214, 1218 (N.D.Ill.1976). State-operated schools may not operate as enclaves of totalitarianism where students are searched at the caprice of school officials. Thus, while the

these cases support the blanket search of individual students during class which was carried out at Latexo.

12. It should be noted that the strong evidence of widespread drug abuse at the high school inspected in Doe v. Renfrow far exceeded any evidence that Latexo students were using drugs. While this distinction is not, in itself, dispositive, it would necessarily alter the *ad hoc* balancing required to be carried out in assessing reasonableness on the facts of each case.

unique role of education in our society is a factor to be taken into account in assessing the reasonableness of this search, it does not necessarily outweigh all other factors. Some articulable facts which focus suspicion on specific students must be demonstrated before any school search can be carried out. Bellnier v. Lund, 438 F.Supp. 47, 53 (N.D.N.Y.1977). That requirement was not met prior to the sniff-search conducted at Latexo.

Defendants' indiscriminate search of plaintiffs and other students was not rendered constitutionally permissible because it took place on the campus of a public school. The sniff-search conducted on April 11th was unreasonable under the fourth amendment, and since the search was carried out under color of state law, the constitutional rights of plaintiffs have been violated under the fourth amendment. Unless some other justification can be found to validate the subsequent searches of plaintiffs and their vehicles, those searches violated the fourth amendment as well.

. . .

Defendants shall further be enjoined from using "sniffer dogs" to search the person or property of plaintiffs Michele or Michael Jones in the absence of reasonable cause to believe that those particular individuals are in possession of contraband in violation of school rules.

NOTE

For a full discussion of dog sniffing in the schools see Gardner, Sniffing for Drugs in the Classroom—Perspectives on Fourth Amendment Scope, 74 Nw.U.L.Rev. 803 (1980).

C. INTERROGATION

IN RE THOMPSON

Supreme Court of Iowa, 1976.
241 N.W.2d 2.

REYNOLDSON, JUSTICE.

Seventeen-year old Thompson was adjudicated a delinquent under § 232.2(12)(a), The Code, for breaking and entering a business establishment in Iowa City. Upon this appeal which raises issues concerning the validity of Thompson's oral confessions and the permissible scope of his cross-examination under § 781.13, The Code, we affirm.

At 2:30 A.M. September 3, 1975, Iowa City police received a telephone report from an individual who heard breaking glass or metal indicating a breakin at Blackstone Beauty Shop. Several officers hurried to the scene in police cars. Officer Saylor observed Thompson and two other juveniles emerging from an alley. Located in the alley was the beauty shop back door which had been broken.

At some later point in the investigation a police search of the alley disclosed in a recessed doorway of a nearby building a television stolen from the beauty shop, and the tools apparently used to force the beauty shop door.

The officers took the juveniles to the police station and began questioning them together about why they were out so late. According to officer Saylor, the police thought the boys could have been involved in the breakin but had asked no questions concerning it when one of the three, Ambrisco, said "We did it." The officers responded: "Did what?" to which he replied "We broke into it." Saylor ambiguously testified Thompson agreed by gestures, and words he could not recall, but he did recollect Thompson volunteering, following Ambrisco's admission, that the three of them were together.

The juveniles were then read their constitutional rights from the standard form. Thompson signed a waiver of his rights. Sometime between 4:00 and 5:00 A.M. officer Saylor brought Thompson from his cell to the interrogation room and again advised him of his rights. Thompson then related the "whole story" of the breakin.

Shortly after 8:00 A.M. detective Burns, who was fingerprinting and photographing the juveniles, again advised Thompson of his rights. The latter verbally waived these rights and again confessed his involvement in the crime.

Upon cross-examination officer Saylor was asked if Thompson made a request for someone to represent him. Saylor responded, "I don't know if he was—they were asked if they had attorneys and Mr. Thompson said you [attorney Robinson] were his attorney and I believe detective Kidwell said that, who had evidently been involved with him before, said he knew you were his attorney and that is how you came into play, that is the extent of the mention of legal counsel."

Thompson testified the officers refused his request to call attorney Robinson, who had represented him in a prior proceeding. Cross-examined concerning his written waiver of statutory § 755.17 communication rights, Thompson replied, "Well, I believe he—okay, that paper—he [Kidwell] said I could call my lawyer so I asked if I could call him and he said 'Well, you can call him in the morning, I sure as hell'—excuse that—'I'm not going to wake him up at three in the morning just to come down here and talk to you about this.'"

Other evidence bearing on Thompson's background, mental ability, education and personal characteristics will be discussed, infra.

. . . .

[Section 1 of the opinion, discussing scope of review has been omitted.]

Thompson launches a two-pronged attack on the validity of his confession. He first argues for adoption of a rule that a minor should be held incapable of voluntarily and knowingly waiving his right to remain silent in absence of a parent, adult friend, or lawyer.

As a second argument he insists the totality of the circumstances surrounding the confession demonstrates it was involuntarily obtained.

The *per se* exclusionary rule Thompson first contends for has a logical appeal. The legal safeguards the law provides minors in most civil matters, see Shearer v. Perry Community Sch. Dist., 236 N.W.2d 688, 697, 699 (Iowa 1975) (Reynoldson, J., dissenting), have no counterparts in the criminal law surrounding confessions, where liberty is at stake. It is anomalous that a minor who is civilly *non sui juris* may nonetheless be held to have waived his constitutional rights in a proceeding affecting his personal freedom.

Two closely related but distinct arguments have been made by those seeking to impose a *per se* exclusion of juvenile confessions. One argument is that a juvenile's confession should be inadmissible if the police did not obtain the *consent* of a parent or guardian to the juvenile's waiver of rights. . . .

Another argument, made here, is that a juvenile's confession given without presence of or opportunity to *consult with* a parent, adult friend or lawyer should be inadmissible *per se*. This theory, too, has been almost unanimously rejected. . . .

Although the *per se* rule has received almost unanimous support from commentators, . . . it has been adopted in only two decisions and a few statutes. See In re K.W.B., 500 S.W.2d 275, 283 (Mo. Ct.App.1973); Lewis v. State, 259 Ind. 431, 439, 288 N.E.2d 138, 142 (1972); General Statutes of Connecticut § 17–66d (1975); 10 Oklahoma Statutes Annot. § 1109 (Supp.1975–1976).

It is apparent most courts, required to deal pragmatically with an ever-mounting crime wave in which minors play a disproportionate role, have considered society's self-preservation interest in rejecting a blanket exclusion for juvenile confessions. . . .

We find almost all decisions apply to both adults and minors the same "totality of surrounding circumstances" test for determining a confession's voluntariness, but weigh heavily in the balance the facts of minority and failure to provide consultation with a parent, guardian, custodian, adult friend or lawyer. See, e.g., Gallegos v. Colorado, 370 U.S. 49 (1962); Haley v. Ohio, 332 U.S. 596 (1948); Commonwealth v. Cain, 361 Mass. 224, 279 N.E.2d 706, 709 (1972).

. . .

. . . [W]e again decline to adopt the concept every minor is incompetent as a matter of law to waive his rights to remain silent and to an attorney. At the same time, we emphasize the importance of securing for the minor under interrogation the advice and consultation of a parent, guardian, custodian, adult friend, or lawyer. See § 232.16, The Code. Failure to provide such support will throw a deep shadow of judicial distrust over the resulting confession. . . .

Turning to the question whether Thompson's confession was voluntary, we consider two distinct factors. The first is the effect of his request for counsel and its denial. The second is Thompson's person-

al characteristics and their cumulative effect on his ability to waive
constitutional rights.

We start from the premise that courts indulge every reasonable
presumption against waiver of constitutional rights. Johnson v.
Zerbst, 304 U.S. 458 (1938). We then consider applicability of two
principles laid down in Miranda v. Arizona, 384 U.S. 436, 474–475
(1966):

"If the individual states that he wants an attorney, the interrogation must cease until an attorney is present. . . .

. . .

    If the interrogation continues without the presence of an attor-
ney and a statement is taken, a heavy burden rests on the government to demonstrate that the defendant knowingly and intelligently waived his privilege against self-incrimination and his right to
retained or appointed counsel."

Factors which ordinarily play a role in determining the issue of
the voluntariness of a confession, in addition to the youth of the accused and his opportunity to consult with a parent, guardian, custodian, adult friend or lawyer (see West v. United States, 399 F.2d 467,
469 [5 Cir. 1968], cert. denied, 393 U.S. 1102 [1969]) are summarized
in Schneckloth v. Bustamonte, 412 U.S. 218, 226 (1973):

". . . his lack of education, e.g., Payne v. Arkansas, 356 U.S.
560 or his low intelligence, e.g., Fikes v. Alabama, 352 U.S. 191,
the lack of any advice to the accused of his constitutional rights,
e.g., Davis v. North Carolina, 384 U.S. 737 the length of detention,
e.g., Chambers v. Florida, supra [309 U.S. 277 . . .]. The repeated and prolonged nature of the questioning, e.g., Ashcraft v.
Tennessee, 322 U.S. 143 and the use of physical punishment such
as the deprivation of food or sleep, e.g., Rock v. Pate, 367 U.S.
433."

With these standards in mind, we have already noted Thompson
was only seventeen. The record reflects he was virtually abandoned
by his parents at an early age. Most of the four prior years were
spent at the Mount Pleasant Mental Health Center. Before that he
was in various institutions and placement situations.

In the spring of 1975 Thompson was, according to an April 1975
social investigation work-up, "sleeping occasionally at the Lutheran
Social Services' Boys' Group Home, camping out occasionally, and
has been calling attention to himself in the community with misbehavior . . . ."

Accompanying psychological and psychiatric reports from 1973
show him to have a full scale I.Q. of only 71. It was observed
Thompson's "practical judgment is *very* low." He has an abnormal
electroencephalogram with "two highly significant signs of brain
damage and six significant signs." He was able to read at a fourth-
grade level. Tests indicated he was frightened, insecure and frus-

trated. In addition to the abnormal electroencephalogram the diagnosis included "passive aggressive behavior" and borderline mental retardation.

While a confession will not be excluded on the sole ground of mental weakness unless the abnormality deprives the accused of the capacity to understand the meaning and effect of the confession, State v. Winfrey, 221 N.W.2d 269, 273 (Iowa 1974); State v. Conner, 241 N.W.2d 447 (Iowa, filed April 14, 1976), this combination of *factors* mental weakness, emotional instability and judgmental incapacity bears heavily on the ultimate decision.

It is true Thompson was advised of his constitutional rights. This, as we have above observed, does not terminate the State's burden to prove the confession was voluntary. It is also true Thompson testified in cross-examination he knew he had a right to talk to a lawyer before he answered any questions. But on this record we find he was denied that right. Thompson's testimony detective Kidwell refused to call attorney Robinson rings true. The State did not call Kidwell as a witness, nor was there any showing he was unavailable. A juvenile with Thompson's characteristics should not be expected to persistently, repeatedly and articulately invoke his constitutional rights before they will be recognized.

The importance of counsel reaches beyond merely advising a client he is not required to answer questions. The requirement of "knowing and intelligent waiver" implies a rational choice based upon some appreciation of the consequences of the decision. Cooper v. Griffin, 455 F.2d 1142, 1146 (5 Cir. 1972). The lawyer whom Thompson wanted to call could have advised him concerning probable consequences of confessing.

The record does not reflect Thompson was provided any food. He was obviously without sleep. These factors are also to be weighed in the balance.

Finally, and crucially important, we observe this juvenile's verbal confessions were secured absent any consultation with a parent, guardian, custodian, adult friend or lawyer.

Thompson's interrogation should have ceased when he requested his lawyer be called. Viewing the evidence in the light most favorable to the prosecution, the State did not carry its subsequent *conclusion* heavy burden of proof to show Thompson subsequently waived either his privilege against self-incrimination or his right to counsel. *Miranda*, supra.

Considering the totality of the surrounding circumstances, including failure to provide him requested counsel, we hold Thompson's verbal confessions are involuntary. They should not have been considered below and will not be considered here.

This does not apply, however, to Thompson's spontaneous statement made prior to any direct interrogation by the officers concern-

ing the breakin. Such statements are not within the *Miranda*
prohibitions, even though the accused is in custody.

. . .

Affirmed.

NOTES

(1) Certainly prior to Miranda v. Arizona, 384 U.S. 436, 86 S.Ct. 1602, 16
L.Ed.2d 694 (1966), and In re Gault, 387 U.S. 1, 87 S.Ct. 1428, 18 L.Ed.2d 527
(1967), the test of admissibility of statements by juveniles and adults was
voluntariness. In Haley v. Ohio, 332 U.S. 596, 68 S.Ct. 302, 92 L.Ed.2d 224
(1948), and Gallegos v. Colorado, 370 U.S. 49, 82 S.Ct. 1209, 8 L.Ed.2d 325
(1962), both of which involved juveniles convicted of crimes in criminal court,
the Supreme Court held statements inadmissible that were obtained in violation of fourteenth amendment due process standards.

In *Haley*, which concerned a 15-year-old defendant, Justice Douglas acknowledged that the circumstances "would make us pause for careful inquiry if a mature man were involved," and went on to add: "And when, as
here, a mere child—an easy victim of the law—is before us, special care in
scrutinizing the record must be used." 332 U.S. at 599. Justice Douglas
also wrote the opinion for the Court in *Gallegos*, which involved a 14-year-old
defendant. Describing the test to be employed in such cases, he observed:
"There is no guide to the decision of cases such as this, except the totality of
circumstances that bear on the . . . factors we have mentioned. The
youth of the petitioner, the long detention, the failure to send for his parents, the failure immediately to bring him before the judge of the Juvenile
Court, the failure to see to it that he had the advice of a lawyer or a friend—
all these combine to make us conclude that the formal confession on which
this conviction may have rested was obtained in violation of due process."
370 U.S. at 55.

(2) In *Miranda*, the Supreme Court shifted away from its totality of circumstances approach and focused on the fifth amendment privilege against
self-incrimination and the sixth amendment right to counsel. The Court set
forth certain requirements that must be met before any statement made by a
defendant while in police custody can be used at a criminal trial:

> To summarize, we hold that when an individual is taken into custody
> or otherwise deprived of his freedom by the authorities in any significant
> way and is subjected to questioning, the privilege against self-incrimina-
> tion is jeopardized. Procedural safeguards must be employed to protect
> the privilege, and unless other fully effective means are adopted to notify
> the person of his right of silence and to assure that the exercise of the
> right will be scrupulously honored, the following measures are required.
> He must be warned prior to any questioning that he has the right to re-
> main silent, that anything he says can be used against him in a court of
> law, that he has the right to the presence of an attorney, and that if he
> cannot afford an attorney one will be appointed for him prior to any ques-
> tioning if he so desires. Opportunity to exercise these rights must be
> afforded to him throughout the interrogation. After such warnings have
> been given, and such opportunity afforded him, the individual may know-
> ingly and intelligently waive these rights and agree to answer questions
> or make a statement. But unless and until such warnings and waiver are

Miranda safeguards

demonstrated by the prosecution at trial, no evidence obtained as a result of interrogation can be used against him. 384 U.S. at 478–79.

Subsequently, in *Gault*, the Court held the fifth amendment privilege against self-incrimination applicable to juveniles during a fact-finding hearing to determine delinquency, where the juvenile was exposed to the possibility of commitment to an institution. The Court specifically refrained, however, from passing on the question of applicability of its holding to the pre-hearing, investigatory phase of proceedings. 387 U.S. at 13. Perhaps significantly, however, the Court in *Gault*, in holding the fifth amendment privilege against self-incrimination applicable to juveniles, quoted from its earlier decision in *Haley*: "No friend stood at the side of this 15-year old boy as the police, working in relays, questioned him hour after hour, from midnight until dawn. No lawyer stood guard to make sure that the police went so far and no further, to see to it that they stopped short of the point where he became the victim of coercion. No counsel or friend was called during the critical hours of questioning." 387 U.S. at 45–46.

In any event, subsequent to *Gault*, courts uniformly held the *Miranda* requirements to be applicable to juvenile proceedings. In addition to the principal case see In re William L., 29 A.D.2d 182, 287 N.Y.S.2d 218 (1968); Leach v. State, 428 S.W.2d 817 (Tex.Civ.App.1968). In some instances the *Miranda* requirements were held applicable to juveniles even prior to the *Gault* decision. In re Knox, 53 Misc.2d 889, 280 N.Y.S.2d 65 (Fam.Ct., Monroe County 1967); In re Rust, 53 Misc.2d 51, 278 N.Y.S.2d 333 (Fam.Ct., Kings County 1967). The real issue has been to define when a child may waive the right to counsel and the right to silence.

(3) The state bears the burden of proving that an alleged waiver of *Miranda* rights was voluntary. The Supreme Court has declared that the appropriate standard of proof governing the issue of voluntariness is preponderance of the evidence. Lego v. Twomey, 404 U.S. 477, 92 S.Ct. 619, 30 L.Ed.2d 618 (1972).

As a practical matter, the trial court's determination on the question of voluntariness is generally viewed as a factual finding that will not be disturbed on appeal unless it is contrary to the manifest weight of the evidence. As attorney for the juvenile, one must therefore make the strongest arguments at the time of the first motion to suppress the confession.

(4) If the state's evidence consists solely of an extra-judicial (i.e. out of court) confession, and at the delinquency proceeding the state presents no other evidence that a crime was actually committed, a motion for a directed verdict of acquittal should succeed under the general doctrine applicable to criminal law that an extra-judicial confession alone is insufficient to convict. There must be independent evidence that a crime was committed. This required evidence of the crime is called the *corpus delicti*, or body of the crime. See In re Way, 319 So.2d 651 (Miss.1975). See also W. LaFave and A. Scott, Criminal Law 16–17 (1972).

FARE v. MICHAEL C.

Supreme Court of the United States, 1979.
442 U.S. 707, 99 S.Ct. 2560, 61 L.Ed.2d 197.

MR. JUSTICE BLACKMUN delivered the opinion of the Court.

In Miranda v. Arizona, 384 U.S. 436, 86 S.Ct. 1602, 16 L.Ed.2d 694 (1966), this Court established certain procedural safeguards designed to protect the rights of an accused, under the Fifth and Fourteenth Amendments, to be free from compelled self-incrimination during custodial interrogation. The Court specified, among other things, that if the accused indicates in any manner that he wishes to remain silent or to consult an attorney, interrogation must cease, and any statement obtained from him during interrogation thereafter may not be admitted against him at his trial. Id., at 444–445, 473–474, 86 S.Ct., at 1612–1613, 1627–1628.

In this case, the State of California, in the person of its acting chief probation officer, attacks the conclusion of the Supreme Court of California that a juvenile's request, made while undergoing custodial interrogation, to see his *probation officer* is *per se* an invocation of the juvenile's Fifth Amendment rights as pronounced in *Miranda*.

Claim

I

Respondent Michael C. was implicated in the murder of Robert Yeager. The murder occurred during a robbery of the victim's home on January 19, 1976. A small truck registered in the name of respondent's mother was identified as having been near the Yeager home at the time of the killing, and a young man answering respondent's description was seen by witnesses near the truck and near the home shortly before Yeager was murdered.

On the basis of this information, Van Nuys, Cal., police took respondent into custody at approximately 6:30 p. m. on February 4. Respondent then was 16½ years old and on probation to the Juvenile Court. He had been on probation since the age of 12. Approximately one year earlier he had served a term in a youth corrections camp under the supervision of the Juvenile Court. He had a record of several previous offenses, including burglary of guns and purse snatching, stretching back over several years.

Upon respondent's arrival at the Van Nuys station house two police officers began to interrogate him. The officers and respondent were the only persons in the room during the interrogation. The conversation was tape recorded. One of the officers initiated the interview by informing respondent that he had been brought in for questioning in relation to a murder. The officer fully advised respondent of his *Miranda* rights. The following exchange then occurred, as set out in the opinion of the California Supreme Court, In re Michael C.,

21 Cal.3d 471, 473–474, 146 Cal.Rptr. 358, 359–360, 579 P.2d 7, 8 (1978) (emphasis added by that court):

"Q. . . . Do you understand all of these rights as I have explained them to you?

"A. Yeah.

"Q. Okay, do you wish to give up your right to remain silent and talk to us about this murder?

"A. What murder? I don't know about no murder.

"Q. I'll explain to you which one it is if you want to talk to us about it.

"A. Yeah, I might talk to you.

"Q. Do you want to give up your right to have an attorney present here while we talk about it?

"A. *Can I have my probation officer here?* ✕

"Q. Well I can't get a hold of your probation officer right now. You have the right to an attorney.

"A. How I know you guys won't pull no police officer in and tell me he's an attorney?

"Q. Huh?

"A. [How I know you guys won't pull no police officer in and tell me he's an attorney?]

"Q. Your probation officer is Mr. Christiansen.

"A. Yeah.

"Q. Well I'm not going to call Mr. Christiansen tonight. There's a good chance we can talk to him later, but I'm not going to call him right now. If you want to talk to us without an attorney present, you can. If you don't want to, you don't have to. But if you want to say something you can, and if you don't want to say something you don't have to. That's your right. You understand that right?

"A. Yeah.

"Q. Okay, will you talk to us without an attorney present?

"A. Yeah I want to talk to you."

Respondent thereupon proceeded to answer questions put to him by the officers. He made statements and drew sketches that incriminated him in the Yeager murder.

Largely on the basis of respondent's incriminating statements, probation authorities filed a petition in Juvenile Court alleging that respondent had murdered Robert Yeager, in violation of Cal. Penal Code Ann. § 187 (West Supp. 1979), and that respondent therefore should be adjudged a ward of the Juvenile Court, pursuant to Cal.

Welf. & Inst. Code Ann. § 602 (West Supp. 1979).[1] App. 4–5. Respondent thereupon moved to suppress the statements and sketches he gave the police during the interrogation. He alleged that the statements had been obtained in violation of *Miranda* in that his request to see his probation officer at the outset of the questioning constituted an invocation of his Fifth Amendment right to remain silent, just as if he had requested the assistance of an attorney. Accordingly, respondent argued that since the interrogation did not cease until he had a chance to confer with his probation officer, the statements and sketches could not be admitted against him in the Juvenile Court proceedings. . . .

. . .

On appeal, the Supreme Court of California took the case by transfer from the California Court of Appeal and, by a divided vote, reversed. In re Michael C., 21 Cal.3d 471, 146 Cal.Rptr. 358, 579 P.2d 7 (1978). The court held that respondent's "request to see his probation officer at the commencement of interrogation negated any possible willingness on his part to discuss his case with the police [and] thereby invoked his Fifth Amendment privilege." Id., at 474, 579 P.2d, at 8. The court based this conclusion on its view that, because of the juvenile court system's emphasis on the relationship between a probation officer and the probationer, the officer was "a trusted guardian figure who exercises the authority of the state as *parens patriae* and whose duty it is to implement the protective and rehabilitative powers of the juvenile court." Id., at 476, 579 P.2d, at 10. As a consequence, the court found that a minor's request for his probation officer was the same as a request to see his parents during interrogation, and thus under the rule of *Burton* constituted an invocation of the minor's Fifth Amendment rights.

The court accordingly held that the probation officer would act to protect the minor's Fifth Amendment rights in precisely the way an attorney would act if called for by the accused. . . .

We . . . believe it clear that the probation officer is not in a position to offer the type of legal assistance necessary to protect the Fifth Amendment rights of an accused undergoing custodial interrogation that a lawyer can offer. The Court in *Miranda* recognized that "the attorney plays a vital role in the administration of criminal justice under our Constitution." 384 U.S., at 481. It is this pivotal role of legal counsel that justifies the *per se* rule established in *Miranda*, and that distinguishes the request for counsel from the request for a probation officer, a clergyman, or a close friend. A probation officer simply is not necessary, in the way an attorney is, for

---

1. The petition also alleged that respondent had participated in an attempted armed robbery earlier on the same evening Yeager was murdered. The Juvenile Court, however, held that the evidence was insufficient to support this charge and it was dismissed. No issue relating to this second charge is before the Court.

the protection of the legal rights of the accused, juvenile or adult. He is significantly handicapped by the position he occupies in the juvenile system from serving as an effective protector of the rights of a juvenile suspected of a crime.

The California Supreme Court, however, found that the close relationship between juveniles and their probation officers compelled the conclusion that a probation officer, for purposes of *Miranda*, was sufficiently like a lawyer to justify extension of the *per se* rule. 21 Cal.3d, at 476, 146 Cal.Rptr. at 361, 579 P.2d, at 10. The fact that a relationship of trust and cooperation between a probation officer and a juvenile might exist, however, does not indicate that the probation officer is capable of rendering effective legal advice sufficient to protect the juvenile's rights during interrogation by the police, or of providing the other services rendered by a lawyer. To find otherwise would be "an extension of the *Miranda* requirements [that] would cut this Court's holding in that case completely loose from its own explicitly stated rationale." Beckwith v. United States, 425 U.S. 341, 345, 96 S.Ct. 1612, 1615, 48 L.Ed.2d 1 (1976). Such an extension would impose the burdens associated with the rule of *Miranda* on the juvenile justice system and the police without serving the interests that rule was designed simultaneously to protect. If it were otherwise, a juvenile's request for almost anyone he considered trustworthy enough to give him reliable advice would trigger the rigid rule of *Miranda*.

Similarly, the fact that the State has created a statutory duty on the part of the probation officer to protect the interests of the juvenile does not render the probation officer any more capable of rendering legal assistance to the juvenile or of protecting his legal rights, especially in light of the fact that the State has also legislated a duty on the part of the officer to report wrongdoing by the juvenile and serve the ends of the juvenile court system. The State cannot transmute the relationship between probation officer and juvenile offender into the type of relationship between attorney and client that was essential to the holding of *Miranda* simply by legislating an amorphous "duty to advise and care for the juvenile defendant." 21 Cal.3d, at 477, 146 Cal.Rptr. at 361, 579 P.2d, at 10. Though such a statutory duty might serve to distinguish to some degree the probation officer from the coach and the clergyman, it does not justify the extension of *Miranda* to requests to see probation officers. If it did, the State could expand the class of persons covered by the *Miranda per se* rule simply by creating a duty to care for the juvenile on the part of other persons, regardless of whether the logic of *Miranda* would justify that extension.

Nor do we believe that a request by a juvenile to speak with his probation officer constitutes a *per se* request to remain silent. As indicated, since a probation officer does not fulfill the important role in protecting the rights of the accused juvenile that an attorney plays, we decline to find that the request for the probation officer is tantamount to the request for an attorney. And there is nothing inherent in the request for a probation officer that requires us to find that a juvenile's request to see one necessarily constitutes an expression of the juvenile's right to remain silent. As discussed below, courts may take into account such a request in evaluating whether a juvenile in fact had waived his Fifth Amendment rights before confessing. But in other circumstances such a request might well be consistent with a desire to speak with the police. In the absence of further evidence that the minor intended in the circumstances to invoke his Fifth Amendment rights by such a request, we decline to attach such overwhelming significance to this request.

We hold, therefore, that it was error to find that the request by respondent to speak with his probation officer *per se* constituted an invocation of respondent's Fifth Amendment right to be free from compelled self-incrimination. It therefore was also error to hold that because the police did not then cease interrogating respondent the statements he made during interrogation should have been suppressed.

.   .   .

MR. JUSTICE MARSHALL, with whom MR. JUSTICE BRENNAN and MR. JUSTICE STEVENS join, dissenting.

.   .   .

It is therefore critical in the present context that we construe *Miranda*'s prophylactic requirements broadly to accomplish their intended purpose—"dispel[ling] the compulsion inherent in custodial surroundings." 384 U.S., at 458, 86 S.Ct., at 1619. To effectuate this purpose, the Court must ensure that the "protective device" of legal counsel, id., at 465–466, 469, 86 S.Ct. at 1623–1624, 1625, be readily available, and that any intimation of a desire to preclude questioning be scrupulously honored. Thus, I believe *Miranda* requires that interrogation cease whenever a juvenile requests an adult who is obligated to represent his interests. Such a request, in my judgment, constitutes both an attempt to obtain advice and a general invocation of the right to silence. For, as the California Supreme Court recognized, " '[i]t is fatuous to assume that a minor in custody will be in a position to call an attorney for assistance,' " 21 Cal.3d 471, 475–476, 146 Cal.Rptr. 358, 360, 579 P.2d 7, 9 (1978), quoting People v. Burton, 6 Cal.3d 375, 382, 491 P.2d 793, 797 (1971), or that he will trust the police to obtain a lawyer for him.[1] A juvenile in these circumstances will likely turn to his parents, or another adult responsible for his welfare, as the only means of securing legal counsel. Moreover, a request for such adult assistance is surely inconsistent with a present desire to speak freely. Requiring a strict verbal formula to invoke

---

1. The facts of the instant case are illustrative. When the police offered to obtain an attorney for respondent, he replied: "How I know you guys won't pull no police officer in and tell me he's an attorney?" Significantly, the police made no attempt to allay that concern.

the protections of *Miranda* would "protect the knowledgeable accused from stationhouse coercion while abandoning the young person who knows no more than to ask for the . . . person he trusts." Chaney v. Wainwright, 561 F.2d 1129, 1134 (CA5 1977) (Goldberg, J., dissenting).

On my reading of *Miranda*, a California juvenile's request for his probation officer should be treated as a *per se* assertion of Fifth Amendment rights. The California Supreme Court determined that probation officers have a statutory duty to represent minors' interests and, indeed, are "trusted guardian figure[s]" to whom a juvenile would likely turn for assistance. 21 Cal.3d, at 476, 146 Cal.Rptr., at 361, 579 P.2d, at 10. In addition, the court found, probation officers are particularly well suited to assist a juvenile "on such matters as to whether or not he should obtain an attorney" and "how to conduct himself with police." Id., at 476, 477, 146 Cal.Rptr., at 361, 579 P.2d, at 10. Hence, a juvenile's request for a probation officer may frequently be an attempt to secure protection from the coercive aspects of custodial questioning.

This Court concludes, however, that because a probation officer has law enforcement duties, juveniles generally would not call upon him to represent their interests, and if they did, would not be well served. But that conclusion ignores the California Supreme Court's express determination that the officer's responsibility to initiate juvenile proceedings did not negate his function as personal adviser to his wards. I decline to second-guess that court's assessment of state law. Further, although the majority here speculates that probation officers have a duty to advise cooperation with the police—a proposition suggested only in the concurring opinion of two justices below, 21 Cal.3d, at 479, 146 Cal.Rptr., at 363, 579 P.2d, at 11–12 (Mosk, J., concurring)—respondent's probation officer instructed all his charges "not to go and admit openly to an offense, [but rather] to get some type of advice from . . . parents or a lawyer." App. 30. Absent an explicit statutory provision or judicial holding, the officer's assessment of the obligations imposed by state law is entitled to deference by this Court.

Thus, given the role of probation officers under California law, a juvenile's request to see his officer may reflect a desire for precisely the kind of assistance *Miranda* guarantees an accused before he waives his Fifth Amendment rights. At the very least, such a request signals a desire to remain silent until contact with the officer is made. Because the Court's contrary determination withdraws the safeguards of *Miranda* from those most in need of protection, I respectfully dissent.

[The separate dissenting opinion of Justice Powell has been omitted.]

NOTES

(1) For the immediate reaction of the state courts in California to the *Fare* decision, consider the following opinion by Kingsley, Acting Presiding Justice, in In re Patrick W., 104 Cal.App.3d 615, 163 Cal.Rptr. 848 (1980):

> The minor was found by the juvenile court to be a person coming under section 602 of the Welfare & Institutions Code in that he had committed murder in violation of section 187 of the Penal Code. He was committed to the Youth Authority; he has appealed; we reverse.

> The case for the People is that, angry at his father, a police officer, the minor had intentionally shot and killed him. Alerted by school authorities and other persons, deputy sheriffs arrested the minor and took him to the station for interrogation. Admittedly they gave him the formal *Miranda* rights and also asked if he desired to talk to the "parents." Quite understandably the minor declined to face his mother, whom he had just widowed. It is the contention of the minor here that, since his grandparents were available and had sought to speak to the minor, the deputies were under an obligation to ask him if he desired to talk to them and that the deputies had not done so.

> This is the second time that this case has been before this court. On September 1, 1978, we held that the order of commitment must be reversed because of that failure. (In re Patrick W. (1978) 84 Cal.App.3d 520, 148 Cal.Rptr. 735.) On October 23, 1978, our Supreme Court denied hearing. The People then sought certiorari and, on June 25, 1979, the United States Supreme Court remanded the case to us "for further consideration in the light of Fare v. Michael C. (1979) 442 U.S. 707, 99 S.Ct. 2560, 61 L.Ed.2d 197."

> In In re Michael C. (1978) 21 Cal.3d 471, 146 Cal.Rptr. 358, 579 P.2d 7, our Supreme Court had held that a confession obtained from a minor after his request to see his probation officer had been denied, was obtained in violation of the minor's *Miranda* rights. It was that holding which the United States Supreme Court reversed, primarily on the ground that a probation officer, by virtue of his dual allegiance, was not the kind of person on whom a minor was entitled, within the purpose of *Miranda*, to rely.

> It is clear that the United States Supreme Court's decision in *Michael C.* rests on facts distinguishable from those before us on this appeal. The grandparents here did not have the official ambivalence that the Supreme Court saw in the *Michael C.* case. They fall more in the group of which our Supreme Court said, in People v. Burton (1971) 6 Cal.3d 375, at page 382, 99 Cal.Rptr. 1, at page 5, 491 P.2d 793, at page 797, "person to whom he [a minor] normally looks" for help. Admittedly there is *language* in the Supreme Court opinion that might be interpreted as indicating that that court would take a similar view of a right to see grandparents. However, in its action in the case before us, the United States Supreme Court did not reverse our judgment on the authority of *Michael C.* but merely directed us to reconsider our opinion "in the light of" that opinion. We have obeyed that direction.

In a footnote the court stated:

> It is here immaterial to speculate over whether the minor would have exhibited the same reluctance to facing his grandparents as he had to facing his mother. The choice was his; he was never given that choice.

(2) Should a child be incapable of waiving his rights as a matter of law by analogy to other legal disabilities of childhood? *Thompson* is representative of the majority view that age alone is no bar to knowing and intelligent waiver of constitutional rights. See People v. Lara, 67 Cal.2d 365, 62 Cal.Rptr. 586, 432 P.2d 202 (1967), cert. denied 392 U.S. 945 (1968). For a more recent statement to the same effect see Quick v. State, 599 P.2d 712 (Alaska 1979) where the court wrote:

> The mere fact that a person is under the age of majority does not automatically render him incapable of making a knowing and voluntary waiver. The surrounding circumstances must be considered in each case to determine whether a particular juvenile had sufficient knowledge and maturity to make a reasoned decision. Among the factors to be considered are age, intelligence, length of the questioning, education, prior experience with law enforcement officers, mental state at the time of the waiver, and whether there has been any prior opportunity to consult with a parent, guardian, or attorney.[9]
>
> It is unquestionably a better practice to see to it that a juvenile consults with an adult before he waives his *Miranda* rights, but, at least in those cases where it has not been requested, we decline to adopt a rule requiring such consultation. The state has always had the burden of proof to show that a waiver was knowing and voluntary. Where a juvenile is concerned, the burden on the state is even heavier than it would be with an adult. We believe that the careful scrutiny to be afforded an unsupervised waiver is sufficient to ensure that the rights of a juvenile suspect will be safeguarded.

Other applications of the totality of circumstances test in which the age of the defendant is an important but not dispositive factor include State v. Jackson, 118 Ariz. 270, 576 P.2d 129, 131 (1978); Riley v. State, 237 Ga. 124, 226 S.E.2d 922, 926 (1977); State v. Young, 220 Kan. 541, 552 P.2d 905 (1976); State v. Gullings, 244 Or. 173, 416 P.2d 311, 315 (1966); State v. Luoma, 88 Wash.2d 28, 558 P.2d 756, 761 (1977). See also, ALI Model Code of Pre-Arraignment Procedure, Commentary to § 140.6, at 361–63 n. 4 (1975).

In West v. United States, 399 F.2d 467 (5th Cir. 1968), the court set forth the circumstances to be considered in resolving the waiver issue:

> (1) age of the accused; (2) education of the accused; (3) knowledge of the accused as to both the substance of the charge, if any has been filed, and the nature of his rights to consult with an attorney and remain silent; (4) whether the accused is held incommunicado or allowed to consult with relatives, friends or an attorney; (5) whether the accused was interrogated before or after formal charges had been filed; (6) methods used in interrogation; (7) length of interrogations; (8) whether vel non the ac-

9. Fare v. Michael C., 442 U.S. 707, 724, 99 S.Ct. 2560, 2571, 61 L.Ed.2d 197, 211 (1979). See Peterson v. State, 562 P.2d 1350, 1363 (Alaska 1977); cf. Gregory v. State, 550 P.2d 374, 380 (Alaska 1976) (court can be certain that defendant's waiver of counsel at guilty plea hearing is voluntary only after examining circumstances under which the plea is made, including mental condition, age, education, experience, complexity of the case, and other factors).

cused refused to voluntarily give statements on prior occasions; and (9) whether the accused had repudiated an extra judicial statement at a later date.

399 F.2d at 469.

Age is clearly the most critical factor considered by courts. Virtually without exception the cases that have held that age alone is not determinative of the effectiveness of the waiver have involved children 14 years of age or older, most often 16 or 17. The younger the child the more important the age factor becomes. See, for example, In re Peter T.G., 110 Cal.App.3d 576, 168 Cal.Rptr. 3 (1980), where the California Court of Appeals held involuntary a purported waiver after hearing the *Miranda* warnings by a 100 pound, thirteen year old boy who had been drinking before the interrogation.

A juvenile's mental age, as opposed to his chronological age, is occasionally taken into account in determining the effectiveness of a waiver. Thus, some courts applying the totality of circumstances test have determined that juveniles who are mentally deficient lack the capacity to understand and waive their rights alone, without advice of counsel or a parent. State ex rel. Holifield, 319 So.2d 471 (La.Ct.App.1975) (14-year-old boy with I.Q. of 67 who attended school for mentally retarded children, functioned on a third grade level, and exhibited the behavior of an 8-year-old child, held incompetent to make a knowing, understanding waiver); In re Appeal No. 245 from the Circuit Court of Kent County, 29 Md.App. 131, 349 A.2d 434 (1975) (confession of 17-year-old boy whose I.Q. had tested 73 on one occasion and 81 on a later occasion, held invalid); but see People v. Morris, 49 Ill.App.3d 284, 7 Ill.Dec. 667, 364 N.E.2d 958 (1977) (confession by ninth grader who had I.Q. of 52 and mental level "below age 5" held admissible because he did understand the meaning of "silent" and was streetwise enough to understand his right not to speak).

(3) Lewis v. State, 259 Ind. 431, 288 N.E.2d 138 (1972):

We hold . . . that a juvenile's statement or confession cannot be used against him at a subsequent trial or hearing unless both he and his parents or guardian were informed of his rights to an attorney, and to remain silent. Furthermore, the child must be given an opportunity to consult with his parents, guardian or an attorney representing the juvenile as to whether or not he wishes to waive those rights. After such consultation the child may waive his rights if he so chooses provided of course that there are no elements of coercion, force or inducement present. This approach has been advocated by several commissions who have studied this area and we believe it represents the best solution to a difficult and reoccurring problem. Model Rules for Juvenile Courts, Rule 25, Evidence (1969), proposed by the Council of Judges of the National Council on Crime and Delinquency; Proposed Indiana Rules of Juvenile Procedure, Rule 9. Having a familiar and friendly influence present at the time the juvenile is required to waive or assert his fundamental rights assures at least some equalization of the pressures borne by a juvenile and an adult in the same situation.

The rule adopted here does not mean that a minor's confession is per se inadmissible but merely holds that, as a result of the age of the accused, the law requires certain specific and concrete safeguards to insure the voluntariness of a confession. The long standing tradition, that juveniles can waive their right to silence or to an attorney is continued, but at the same time another long termed tradition, that such waivers require special precautions to insure it be done knowingly and intelligently, is recognized.

We believe that this rule goes far in protecting the juvenile from waiving his rights simply because of the unfamiliarity or hostility of his surroundings. At the same time it lays down a concrete and specific procedure for the authorities to follow in order to dispel some of the confusion and doubt which confronts them in the area of juvenile interrogation and waiver of rights.

259 Ind. at 439–440, 288 N.E.2d at 142–143.

Since the *Lewis* court's decision requiring parental presence was based on an interpretation of federal constitutional requirements, does it represent valid law following Fare v. Michael C.? Compare Commonwealth v. Henderson, 496 Pa. 349, 437 A.2d 387 (1981), in which the Pennsylvania Supreme Court held that its "interested adult" requirement * survived Fare v. Michael C. because the rule is based on state law; therefore, the independent state ground for the rule makes it immune from review by the United States Supreme Court. Accord, State ex rel. Dino, 359 So.2d 586 (La.1978), cert. den. 439 U.S. 1047 (1979).

In contrast to the trend of other state judicial decisions extending the requirement of parental notification prior to taking an admissible statement from a juvenile, the Missouri Supreme Court has refused to follow an earlier decision of the intermediate appellate court requiring access to parents. In re A.D.R., 603 S.W.2d 575 (Mo.1980). Footnote 7 of the opinion states:

In whatever respect State v. White, 494 S.W.2d 687 (Mo.App.1973) and In re K.W.B., 500 S.W.2d 275 (Mo.App.1973), cited by movant, suggest a test for the admissibility of juvenile confessions other than "the totality of the circumstances standard" reenunciated herein, those cases are not to be followed.

(4) Some states have made a parent's presence mandatory through legislation. Colo.Rev.Stat.Ann. § 19–2–102(3)(c)(I) provides in pertinent part:

No statements or admissions of a child made as a result of interrogation of the child by a law enforcement official concerning acts alleged to have been committed by the child which would constitute a crime if committed by an adult shall be admissible in evidence against the child unless a parent, guardian, or legal custodian of the child was present at such interrogation and the child and his parent, guardian, or legal custodian were advised [of certain specified rights] . . . .

For application of the Colorado statute, see People v. L.A., 609 P.2d 116 (Colo.1980) holding the statute applies only to custodial police interrogation, not to volunteered statements. See also Conn.Gen.Stat.Ann. § 46b–137(a) (Supp.1982); Okla.Stat.Ann. tit. 10, § 1109(a) (Supp.1982) (requires that warnings be given both to parent and child).

(5) Will the presence of parents insulate children from police pressure or simply add another impetus to confess? One study has found that only 10 percent of Israeli children under police investigation told their parents and

---

* In a long line of cases culminating in Commonwealth v. Barnes, 482 Pa. 555, 394 A.2d 461 (1978), the rule has evolved in Pennsylvania that a child's confession given in the absence of a parent or other interested adult is inadmissible. These cases are discussed in S. Davis, Rights of Juveniles 3–58 — 3–59 (1981).

that nearly half of parents expressed anger as their first reaction on hearing of the child's involvement with the police. Nevertheless, about three-quarters of parents expressed a clear desire to be present during police interrogation of their children. For the complete results of this study, which argues in favor of requiring the presence of parents, see Hassin, Presence of Parents During Interrogation of Their Children, 32 Juv. & Fam. Ct.J. 33 (August 1981).

(6) Recent empirical research questions juveniles' (especially those under fifteen) capacity to understand and meaningfully waive *Miranda* rights. Thomas Grisso reports the following results from his extensive testing of juveniles and adults as to their understanding of *Miranda* warnings:

> The results of Study I and Study II support the following conclusions regarding juveniles' abilities to waive the rights to remain silent and to legal counsel conveyed by standard *Miranda* warning statements and hypothetical interrogation situations.
>
> (1) As a class, juveniles younger than fifteen years of age failed to meet both the absolute and relative (adult norm) standards for comprehension measured in Study I and in Study II. The vast majority of these juveniles misunderstood at least one of the four standard *Miranda* statements, and compared with adults, demonstrated significantly poorer comprehension of the nature and significance of the *Miranda* rights.
>
> (2) As a class, fifteen- and sixteen-year-old juveniles with IQ scores below 80 also failed to meet both the absolute and relative standards.
>
> (3) As a class, sixteen-year-olds (and, more equivocally, fifteen-year-olds) understood their rights as well as seventeen- to twenty-two-year-old adults. It should be noted that between one-third to one-half of fifteen- to sixteen-year-olds with IQ scores above 80 exhibited inadequate comprehension using the absolute criterion, however.
>
> (4) Juveniles' sex and socioeconomic status were not significantly related to comprehension of the *Miranda* rights. Race was related only among juveniles with low IQ scores, black juveniles having poorer *Miranda* comprehension.
>
> (5) Prior court experience bore no direct relation to understanding the words and phrases in the *Miranda* warning. However, it was related to increased understanding of the function and significance of the rights to remain silent and to counsel.

Grisso, Juveniles' Capacities to Waive Miranda Rights: An Empirical Analysis, 68 Calif.L.Rev. 1134, 1160 (1980).*

From these test results, Grisso argues for the adoption of a requirement that counsel be present during interrogation. He rejects other palliatives such as the use of simplified *Miranda* warnings, pre–interrogation screening of the child's comprehension level and requiring the presence of parent or other non-legally trained adult at the interrogation.

See also T. Grisso, Juveniles' Waiver of Rights (1981) and Ferguson and Douglas, A Study of Juvenile Waiver, 7 San Diego L.Rev. 39 (1970) (a California study conducted among a random sampling of fourteen year old delinquent and nondelinquent children showing a vast majority of them failed to understand the *Miranda* warnings although they voluntarily waived their rights.) For a discussion of the limitations of the Ferguson and Douglas study, see Grisso, op. cit., 68 Calif.L.Rev. at 1143, fn. 50.

V. INTAKE AND DIVERSION

A. INTRODUCTION

After a juvenile is apprehended but before formal court proceedings, some member of the probation staff must decide whether to file a petition that will lead to adjudication by the court or to divert the juvenile from the court system entirely by informal adjustment or referral to a non-court social service agency. At this stage—often called intake—the probation officer will usually meet with the child, his parents, perhaps the police officer or complaining witness, and sometimes an attorney for the child. In this meeting, the intake officer may decide the matter can be settled without a court appearance, in which case several options are available including dismissal of the case, informal probation or referral to some other social service agency or youth service bureau.

Intake and diversion present an early opportunity to exercise discretion in the juvenile justice system. The decision whether to proceed to adjudication or divert has a profound effect on the juvenile and his family. In fact, the study of juvenile law is to some extent misleading in focusing so heavily on adjudication and disposition because some research indicates petitions are filed in less than half the cases. See Juvenile Justice Standards Relating to the Juvenile Probation Function: Intake and Predisposition Investigative Services (hereinafter "Standards Relating to the Juvenile Probation Function"), Commentary to Standard 2.2 at page 32. Thus, the decisions made at intake may be the most significant ones in the whole process for an allegedly delinquent youth.[1]

JUVENILE JUSTICE STANDARDS PROJECT, STANDARDS RELATING TO THE JUVENILE PROBATION FUNCTION (1980), Introduction at 2–3 *

Intake is one of the most critical points in the juvenile justice system for it is then that a decision is made as to what action to take regarding a juvenile who is allegedly delinquent and who has been brought to the attention of the juvenile court. It may be decided at intake that the juvenile should be judicially processed.

1. This chapter is not concerned with abused and neglected children. For a discussion of what happens to these children after juvenile officials become cognizant of abuse or neglect see Chapter XIII. Similarly, status offenders will only be considered tangentially in this chap-ter. For a more thorough discussion of status offenders see Chapter XI.

* Reprinted with permission from Standards Relating to the Juvenile Probation Function, Copyright 1980, Ballinger Publishing Company.

As a result a petition will be filed against the juvenile initiating formal judicial proceedings, and such proceedings may lead to the juvenile being adjudicated delinquent by the court. Another alternative is for no further action to be taken against the juvenile. Still another alternative is for the juvenile to be handled nonjudicially, which involves the taking of some action with respect to the juvenile without the filing of a petition or a formal delinquency adjudication. One of the more common forms of nonjudicial handling is placement of the juvenile on nonjudicial probation, under which the juvenile is supervised for a period of time generally by personnel of a juvenile probation agency, without specific judicial authorization for such supervision. Nonjudicial handling may also often take such forms as the referral of a juvenile to a community agency for services. The importance of intake screening can be seen from the fact that nationwide approximately half of the total number of juveniles brought to the attention of juvenile and family courts are handled at intake without the filing of a petition.

A central premise of the standards relating to the intake function is that intake screening and certain forms of nonjudicial handling of juveniles should be encouraged. Nonjudicial handling has the following briefly stated benefits. It allows the exercise of some control over and the provision of services to a delinquent juvenile without the detrimental consequences of judicial processing, which labels the juvenile as a delinquent and by so doing stigmatizes the juvenile. Primarily for this reason, nonjudicial handling is more effective than judicial processing in "rehabilitating" the juvenile. In addition, nonjudicial handling keeps court dockets at a manageable level in relation to the limited resources available for the judicial processing of juveniles.

Underlying the intake standards, however, is also the recognition that there are dangers in encouraging the nonjudicial handling of juveniles because of its potential for misuse. Some forms of nonjudicial dispositions, such as nonjudicial probation, may result in substantial intervention in the juvenile's life for a substantial period of time without the truly intelligent and voluntary consent of a juvenile and his or her parents. Moreover, intake officers generally have virtually unlimited discretion in making intake dispositional decisions. Such discretion can be exercised in an arbitrary or discriminatory manner; it also leads to the unequal treatment of juveniles because different intake officers handle similarly situated juveniles differently; and it may simply be exercised in an imprudent or ill-advised manner with the result that juveniles who should be judicially processed are handled nonjudicially and vice-versa. The aforementioned problems are compounded by the informality of the intake process, and the fact that almost no procedural due process protections are afforded juveniles at intake.

The intake standards reflect the view that intake screening and nonjudicial handling are highly beneficial provided they are properly used, and the objective of these standards is to minimize the dangers that they will be misused. In accordance with this objective, these standards call for the narrowing of the range of intake dispositional alternatives by eliminating those forms of nonjudicial dispositions that are most susceptible to abuse and by surrounding the other forms of nonjudicial dispositions with safeguards aimed at preventing such abuse. For example, one standard provides that nonjudicial probation is not a permissible intake dispositional alternative. These standards also call for the promulgation of administrative guidelines and rules that enunciate clearly defined criteria for intake dispositional decisionmaking. Finally, the standards call for the introduction of procedural due process protections to juveniles during this process. For example, one standard provides that juveniles should have the right to the assistance of counsel at intake.

At intake, (1) the juvenile's case can be referred for formal judicial proceedings by filing a petition; (2) the complaint can be dismissed; or, (3) the complaint can be handled through "nonjudicial disposition."

The Standards delineate the existing types of nonjudicial dispositions:

2.4   Nonjudicial disposition of a complaint.

. . .

B.   The existing types of nonjudicial dispositions are as follows:

1.   "Nonjudicial probation" is a nonjudicial disposition involving the supervision by juvenile intake or probation personnel of a juvenile who is the subject of a complaint, for a period of time during which the juvenile may be required to comply with certain restrictive conditions with respect to his or her conduct and activities.

2.   The "provision of intake services" is the direct provision of services by juvenile intake and probation personnel on a continuing basis to a juvenile who is the subject of a complaint.

3.   A "conditional dismissal of a complaint" is the termination of all proceedings against a juvenile subject to certain conditions not involving the acceptance of nonjudicial supervision or intake services. It includes a "community agency referral," which is the referral of a juvenile who is the subject of a complaint to a community agency or agencies for services.

The Standards would limit non-judicial disposition solely to referral to youth service bureaus or other community agencies:

2.4 Nonjudicial disposition of a complaint.

. . .

C. A "community agency referral" is the only permissible
nonjudicial disposition, subject to the conditions set forth in Standard 2.4E. Intake personnel should refer juveniles in need of services whenever possible to youth service bureaus and other public
and private community agencies. Juvenile probation agencies and
other agencies responsible for the administration and provision of
intake services and intake personnel should actively promote and
encourage the establishment and the development of a wide range
of community-based services and programs for delinquent and
nondelinquent juveniles.

D. Nonjudicial probation, provision of intake services, and
conditional dismissal other than community agency referral are
not permissible intake dispositions.

. . .

Why do the Standards disapprove nonjudicial probation, the provision of intake services and conditional dismissal of a complaint?
What do you think of the use of these options?

NOTE

In one sense, labelling a single phase of the juvenile system Intake and
Diversion is misleading. Diversion can actually occur when the police first
have contact with the juvenile. Police may decide at the scene not to intervene if they are convinced that the juvenile is not in serious danger of engaging in further anti-social behavior. In making this decision, police usually
consider the juvenile's demeanor and his past contacts with police in addition,
of course, to the juvenile's observed behavior.

The police may merely warn a juvenile and release him to his parents or
take him to the police station and then release him without further formal
action. In addition, the police may resolve a minor dispute involving a juvenile by requiring immediate restitution from the juvenile to the complainant.
These examples of "police diversion" are really examples of police discretion.
Police discretion involves such legal issues as whether it is appropriate to
vest such power in the police, where the discretion should be exercised (on
the street or at the station) and how to avoid the discriminatory impact of
discretion on minorities and the poor. A thorough discussion of police discretion, however, is outside the scope of this book. For complete development
of these issues, see A.B.A. Project on Standards for Criminal Justice, Standards Relating to the Urban Police Function (1973); K. Davis, Police Discretion (1975); H. Goldstein, Policing a Free Society (1977); A. Reiss, The Police
and the Public (1971); C. Silberman, Criminal Violence, Criminal Justice
(1978) (esp. ch. 7); J. Skolnick, Justice Without Trial (1966); Symposium, Police Practices, 36 Law & Contemp. Prob. 445–588 (1971).

B.   WHO GETS DIVERTED?

Juvenile intake officers generally consider a variety of factors in deciding whether a juvenile should be diverted including:

1. The child's attitude toward the offense: has the child admitted the misbehavior or does he deny involvement?
2. Parental control over the youth.
3. The child's school and/or employment status.
4. The psychiatric history of the child.
5. The willingness of the child and his parents to participate in a diversion program.
6. The age of the juvenile.
7. The nature of the offense.

Under the traditional rehabilitative model of juvenile justice, the seventh factor theoretically was not a major consideration. In reality, however, the nature of the misbehavior was always part of the diversion calculus. A child who has raped or killed is less likely to be diverted to a youth service bureau than a child who violated a curfew. The public clamor over juvenile crime has put even more pressure on probation officers to ensure that juveniles who engage in violent behavior go to court.

In recent years, intake staff have published specific guidelines for the exercise of discretion. California probation officers, in accord with this modern trend, have developed the following guidelines for the processing of both alleged delinquents and status offenders.

H. THOMPSON, CALIFORNIA JUVENILE COURT DESKBOOK (2d ed. 1981), CHAPTER FOUR: GUIDELINES FOR PETITIONING MINORS *

I.   RESPONSIBILITY FOR PETITIONING AND NEED FOR GUIDELINES

. . .

B. [§ 4.2]   Need for Petitioning Guidelines

The decision regarding whether to petition has been a ready source of conflict between the court and the probation department. The court may feel that the probation officer has not been petitioning those cases that should have been petitioned, or has been petitioning minors or offenses that should not have been petitioned. This situation indicates the need to establish a set of general guidelines to petitioning for use by the probation officer.

. . .

C. [§ 4.3] Intake Program

Every intake program should be designed to provide swift and objective evaluation of the circumstances of the referral and initiation of whatever course of action appears necessary. In essence, the intake program is a screening process during which the probation officer obtains all available information regarding the minor and the circumstances of referral, and makes a decision as to the action to be taken.

. . .

II. POLICY GUIDELINE FOR PETITIONING

A. [§ 4.4] Delinquent and Predelinquent Cases

The courses of action available in delinquent and predelinquent cases are: (1) settlement at intake, (2) informal supervision pursuant to § 654, or (3) filing of a petition. See Rule 1307(b).

1. [§ 4.5] Settled at Intake

The matter may be settled at intake when (a) the problem appears to be a temporary one within the family . . ., (b) the violation is minor but the referral was not by citation, (c) the child has previously presented no serious social problem in school or community and the violation is minor, (d) there is insufficient evidence of an offense, or (e) an agency or other resource within the community is better suited to serve the needs of the minor, the parents, or both. Certain other factors may influence a decision to settle at intake or to take more restrictive action: (f) attitude of the parents, (g) attitude of the child, (h) age, maturity, and mentality of the minor, (i) family history, (j) future planning, (k) the assessment of the referring agency (school, parent, or law enforcement officer) as to the seriousness of the child's involvement, and (*l*) any other circumstances that indicate that settling the matter at intake would be inconsistent with the welfare of the minor and the safety and protection of the public. . . .

If the probation officer decides that the case may be settled at intake, he may reprimand and release the child, or refer the case to another agency better suited to serve the needs of the child, his parents, or both.

2. [§ 4.6] Informal Supervision

Pursuant to § 654, the minor may be placed on informal supervision for a period not to exceed six months when (a) the child and his parents seem able to resolve the matter without official juvenile court action, (b) the offense is minor, but some type of supervision is required, or (c) there is a need for further observation before a decision can be reached. A petition may be filed on the original offense at any time during the six-month period. If the probation officer determines that the minor has not involved himself in the specific programs of supervision within 60 days, the probation officer must immediately file a petition or request that a petition be filed by the prosecuting attorney. . . .

Additional factors referred to above, such as attitudes of parents and child, age, maturity, and mentality of the minor, family history, future planning, and the position of the referring agency are also applicable here. . . .

. . .

3. [§ 4.7] When To Petition

In determining whether to file a petition under § 300 or § 601 or to request the prosecuting attorney to file a petition under § 602, the probation officer, pursuant to Rule 1307(g), shall consider:

(1) Whether any of the statutory criteria listed under rule 1348(b)(2) relating to the fitness of the minor are present:

(A) The degree of criminal sophistication exhibited by the minor;

(B) Whether the minor can be rehabilitated prior to the expiration of the juvenile court's jurisdiction;

(C) The minor's previous delinquent history;

(D) Success of previous attempts by the juvenile court to rehabilitate the minor;

(E) The circumstances and gravity of the offense alleged to have been committed by the minor.

(2) Whether the alleged conduct would be a felony if committed by an adult;

(3) Whether the alleged conduct involved physical harm or the threat of physical harm to person or property;

(4) Whether the alleged condition or conduct is not itself serious, but the minor has had serious problems in the home, school or community which indicate that formal juvenile court action would be desirable;

(5) Where the alleged condition or conduct is not itself serious, whether the minor is already a ward or dependent child of the juvenile court;

(6) Whether the alleged condition or conduct involves a threat to the physical or mental condition of the minor;

(7) Whether a chronic serious family problem continues to exist after other efforts to improve the problem have failed;

(8) Whether the alleged condition or conduct is in dispute and, if proven, court ordered disposition appears desirable;

(9) The attitude of the minor and the parent or guardian;

(10) The age, maturity and mentality of the minor;

(11) The status of the minor as a probationer or parolee;

(12) The recommendation, if any, of the referring party or agency;

(13) The attitude of any affected persons;

(14) Whether any other referrals or petitions are pending;

(15) Any other circumstances which indicate the filing of a petition is necessary to promote the welfare of the minor or the safety and protection of the public.

factors

NOTES

(1) Will the California guidelines really remove discretion from the intake and diversion process? Consider the following:

> Even in probation departments with official diversion policies, diversion is likely to occur only if the intake officers want it to occur. Although these men surely are influenced by the policies, programs, and philosophies favored by their superiors—especially their immediate supervisors—they still have great latitude to decide who shall be diverted and who shall not. The degree and direction in which juvenile offenders are diverted is influenced by the individual intake officer's conception of justice and his philosophy and theory of correction, as well as by his knowledge of community resources, by his relationships with other professional welfare workers both within and without his department, by his personal assumptions, attitudes, biases, and prejudices, by the size of his case load and the work load of his department, and by many other subtle conditions. He cannot easily be ordered to make his decisions in a specified way. Ultimately, then, decisions to divert or not divert are his to make. Pressuring him to make his decisions in a certain way, overruling his decisions, and even hesitant questioning of his decisions are usually viewed as unwarranted interference by both intake officers and their superiors.

D. Cressey & R. McDermott, Diversion from the Juvenile Justice System 12–13 (1973).*

(2) California permits informal probation. Recall that the Standards indicate that informal probation is "impermissible." What are the benefits of informal probation? What are the dangers inherent in informal probation? Should there be any time limits on an informal probation period? See Colo. Rev.Stat.Ann. § 19–3–101(3) (1978).

(3) In recent years, intake officers have begun to focus not just on the social history and psychological make-up of the juvenile, but also on the "legal facts" involved. In determining whether to file a petition it is now considered important to view the seriousness of the offense, prior offense records, prior dispositions, and the possibility of obtaining a favorable adjudication from the prosecutor's standpoint. See Juveniles in Justice: A Book of Readings 226–27 (H. Rubin ed. 1980). In fact, in some states there is criticism that prosecutors have begun to dominate the decisionmaking process. Id. at 227. Nevertheless, the trend is to eliminate the prosecutor's ability to

file a complaint over the objection of the intake staff. Similarly, most states do not permit the complainant to force a juvenile to court if the intake staff decides to divert. But see Ill.Ann.Stat. ch. 37, § 703–8 (1972); N.Y. Fam.Ct. Act § 734 (McKinney Supp.1981). The juvenile, however, can almost always go to court if he desires. Can you think of any cases in which a juvenile would want to go to court when the intake staff has proposed diversion?

(4) The Standards require that the intake officer should "make an initial determination of whether the complaint is legally sufficient for the filing of a petition." Juvenile Justice Standards Relating to the Juvenile Probation Function, Standard 2.7. If the intake officer is unsure about such legal sufficiency, the officer should ask the appropriate prosecuting official. Is it sensible to require non–lawyers to determine the legal sufficiency of a complaint, including whether the court has jurisdiction and whether there is enough evidence to support the charges against the juvenile?

(5) Must the juvenile admit his behavior in order to be diverted? Some jurisdictions require an admission before diversion on the rationale that admission is essential to rehabilitation. Some states, however, permit diversion so long as the juvenile agrees that he does not want to contest the allegations. The issue of admission is rarely raised, however, because juveniles often confess and admit their conduct and want to avoid an adjudication of delinquency. In other words, they cooperate to qualify for diversion. This common occurrence raises the issue of whether the state is conditioning a benefit upon a "compelled" confession, thereby violating the juvenile's fifth amendment privilege against self-incrimination.

A related issue is whether a juvenile's statements during intake are admissible against him at a later court proceeding. Some states permit statements during intake to be used against the juvenile, but the Juvenile Justice Standards disagree:

2.12 Juvenile's privilege against self-incrimination at intake.

A. A juvenile should have a privilege against self-incrimination in connection with questioning by intake personnel during the intake process.

B. Any statement made by a juvenile to an intake officer or other information derived directly or indirectly from such a statement is inadmissible in evidence in any judicial proceeding prior to a formal finding of delinquency unless the statement was made after consultation with and in the presence of counsel.

C. RIGHTS AT INTAKE

IN RE ANTHONY S., 73 Misc.2d 187, 341 N.Y.S.2d 11 (Fam.Ct., Richmond County 1973). STANLEY GARTENSTEIN, Judge:

. . .

Respondent . . . moves for an order of dismissal based upon the undisputed contention that he was not represented by counsel in the informal pre-court intake conference at which time he had the opportunity to have this matter adjusted before a petition was drawn. He argues that this deprived him of his constitutional right to counsel.

. . .

RIGHT TO COUNSEL AT INTAKE CONFERENCE

The informal conference prior to judicial proceedings is unique to the system of juvenile justice in the United States. It is a clearing house in which solutions are worked out under the protective eye of court sanctioned social workers which insures the fact that lessons will be learned and the prospective respondent put back into the community with all possible assurance that, having had his brush with the law, he will not return either to this or the Criminal Court. This "preventive medicine" stage, unique to the juvenile courts, insures that no one will come to the "fail safe" point in contact with the Court and not be able to turn back. Sometimes a simple apology will soothe ruffled feelings; often restitution can be worked out to everyone's satisfaction buttressed by voluntary probation and supervision. Even novel solutions such as cleaning subway graffiti are utilized. In point of fact, with everyone satisfied and the youthful perpetrator having permanently learned his lesson, in this county alone, for a period between January and November, 1972, statistics show that of 515 delinquency matters handled at Intake, 360 were adjusted while 155 were referred to Court, a ratio in excess of two-thirds disposed of informally.

Should an aggrieved party insist on his right to be heard in court after informal Intake has been exhausted, that party may not be prevented from filing a petition and bringing the matter on for adjudication (Family Court Rules, rule 7.3; 22 NYCRR 2502.4). Moreover, whether or not a case is adjusted at Intake, Section 735 of the Family Court Act provides:

> "No statement made during a preliminary conference may be admitted into evidence at a factfinding hearing. . . ."

Does the constitutional right to counsel attach to the Intake conference?

PRIOR HOLDINGS OF THE SUPREME COURT

The convulsions now being felt throughout the juvenile justice system are the result of a chain of holdings by the United States Supreme Court and the problem of ascertaining what areas were or were not affected.

. . .

From these decisions, the Court in *McKeiver* stressed that although the *hearing* (added emphasis) must measure up to essentials of due process, not all rights in connection therewith guaranteed to adults were guaranteed to juveniles, lest this destroy the very fabric of the unique nature of the juvenile court, and in the words of the Court, (p. 534, 91 S.Ct. p. 1981) "deprive it of its 'informality, flexibility or speed.'"

It is significant that the *McKeiver* Court quotes with approval the opinion of Justice Roberts of the Pennsylvania Supreme Court in that matter that " 'of all the possible due process rights which could be applied in the juvenile courts, the right to trial by jury is the one which would most likely be disruptive of the unique nature of the juvenile process.' " Thus, the criteria of "disruptive of the unique nature of the juvenile process" must, by mandate of the Supreme Court, temper and further define the impact of the *Kent-Gault-Winship* emphasis on "fundamental fairness" with particular reference to fact-finding procedures.

At all times, the courts must heed the warning of the *McKeiver* Court that (supra, p. 545, 91 S.Ct. p. 1986) we are not to "remake the juvenile proceeding into a fully adversary process and . . . put an effective end to what has been the idealistic prospect of an intimate, informal protective proceeding."

.   .   .

This Court recognizes that the presence of counsel at informal Intake would in effect convert that conference to a formal rigid adversary proceeding, halting the free exchange of ideas which is buttressed by statutory absolute privilege, and relegating this conference to the redundancy of a minor trial prior to trial, thereby emasculating the innovative techniques of Probation services.

The Court holds that the informal Intake conference is not part of the adjudication process, therefore not subject in the first instance to *Kent-Gault-Winship*. However, should future holding deem it to be part of the hearing procedure, thereby subject to the admonitions of *Kent-Gault-Winship*, the court holds that *McKeiver's* criteria of "disruptive of the juvenile process" would form sufficient basis for excluding the right to counsel at the Intake conference, especially in view of the absolute statutory privilege of Section 735.

It is always in order to recall the admonition of the *McKeiver* Court, 403 U.S. on page 551, 91 S.Ct. on page 1989:

"If the formalities of the criminal adjudicative process are to be super-imposed upon the juvenile court system, there is little need for its separate existence."

The motion is accordingly denied.

.   .   .

NOTES

(1) In re Anthony S. represents the majority view that juveniles are not constitutionally entitled to counsel at intake. However, in most jurisdictions, if the juvenile has retained an attorney, the attorney is permitted to participate in the intake process.

Considering the impact an attorney can have at intake, should all juveniles be entitled to representation at this stage? For arguments supporting the right to counsel at intake, see Maron, Constitutional Problems of Diversion of Juvenile Delinquents, 51 Notre Dame L.Rev. 22, 38–41 (1975).

(2) Do you agree that the provision of attorneys at the intake conference will convert it into "a formal rigid adversary proceeding"? What is the appropriate role of counsel at intake? Aren't there grave dangers in the attorney's becoming overbearing and counterproductive? If an attorney persistently raises legal points with intake staff, they may very well let the attorney obtain a more receptive audience: the juvenile court judge. Isn't it possible that intake staff might prefer attorneys present at these conferences?

Consider the following roles of the attorney in representing his or her client at intake:

1. To assess and make recommendations as to available non-court programs for which the juvenile qualifies.

2. To arrange restitution.

3. To interpret the proceeding to the child and his family and to present the family's preferred course of action to the intake officer.

4. To collect and present relevant school, medical and social records.

For a general discussion of the role of attorneys at intake, see M. Paulsen & C. Whitebread, Juvenile Law and Procedure 23–31 (1974).

D.   WHY ARE WE DIVERTING?

Commentators and juvenile authorities have long extolled the benefits of diverting youths from the juvenile court to increase the likelihood of rehabilitation. Several aspects of diversion make rehabilitation more likely. First diversion is nonstigmatizing or at least less stigmatizing than formal adjudication. Second diversion programs often begin soon after the juvenile has engaged in the delinquent behavior. Utilizing social services for the juvenile at this crisis point increases the possibility that the juvenile may modify his antisocial behavior. Finally diversion programs usually involve intervention by agencies that are not associated with law enforcement. Rehabilitation becomes more likely because troubled youths generally react more favorably toward probation officers and mental health professionals than toward police officers. See E. Schur, Radical Non-Intervention: Rethinking the Delinquency Problem (1973); E. Lemert, Instead of Court: Diversion in Juvenile Justice (1971).

Whatever its impact on the likelihood of rehabilitation, diversion serves the additional function of reducing court backlog and congestion. Is that result really beneficial?

One of the most well-known commentators on diversion, Paul Nejelski, has argued that reduced case loads have drawn attention away from the need for more fundamental reform of juvenile justice, and that diversion programs often reduce the visibility of "coercive state intervention" in the lives of juveniles, which permits administrators to act discriminatorily. Nejelski explains:

> In the adult system, society is coming to realize the impracticability of processing drunks or alcoholics as criminals. In contrast, where there is case by case diversion of minor cases, especially in the so-called status offenses, there is little pressure for radical change; sentiment for the repeal of the statutes which form the basis for state intervention does not develop. Instead, an administrator is deciding privately that some "juvenile offenders" are better treated in noncourt systems. Such a scheme currently calls for ad hoc decisions in individual cases by someone in the large system which deals with children in trouble. This discretion has low visibility and may be exercised in a discriminatory or arbitrary fashion.

> Discretionary screening of cases, which has the most serious impact on the poor and minorities, may have the unfortunate result of postponing more basic reform. . . . Outright abolition, and not passing the buck to anonymous administrators, may be a more appropriate solution in dealing with status offenses.

Nejelski, Diversion: Unleashing the Hounds of Heaven?, in Pursuing Justice for the Child 94, 115 (M. Rosenheim ed. 1976).*

Furthermore, Nejelski contends diversion presents a more basic problem in that it may increase "coercive intervention in the lives of children and families without proper concern for their rights." Despite his criticism of diversion programs, Nejelski concludes that when properly monitored, such programs have "considerable promise." See also Nejelski, Diversion: The Promise and the Danger, 22 Crime & Delinq. 393 (1976).

Some commentators have been more critical of diversion programs. For example, Margo Andriessen studied American diversion programs because she planned to establish similar programs in Holland. She concluded that the majority of programs were not diversion at all, but rather extensions of the criminal justice system. Current programs, according to Andriessen, are designed not for diversion but to appease critics of the juvenile system. Andriessen, A Foreigner's View of American Diversion, 26 Crime & Delinq. 70 (1980).

NOTES

(1) For a discussion of the history of diversion, see Maron, Constitutional Problems of Diversion of Juvenile Delinquents, 51 Notre Dame L.Rev. 22, 26–28 (1975). Maron notes that diversion was "well established" by 1926 and chronicles the growth of diversion programs during the late 1960s and 1970s as a result of a recommendation from a Presidential Task Force extolling the benefits of diversion.

(2) For one proposal for establishing a beneficial diversion program based on the idea that some deviant behavior is essentially "normal" and need not be viewed as portending future pathology, see Rosenheim, Notes on Helping Juvenile Nuisances, in Pursuing Justice for the Child 43, 60 (M. Rosenheim ed. 1976).

E. DIVERSION TO WHAT?

One of the most striking features of juveniles in trouble may be their sense that no one cares about them or their problems. Psychologists and child development experts have long indicated that misbehavior often reflects the juvenile's need for some type of love and care. What implications does this have for diversion programs? Consider the following example of a diversion program from Ingham County, Michigan, that used student volunteers to work intensively with diverted youths.

INTERVENTION

Students were assigned to referred youth on a one-to-one basis by their supervisors. In other words, students worked with one and only one youth during their involvement with the project. Students and youth were matched on the basis of sex, race, and mutual interests. Each student spent six to eight hours (by report of the youth and parents, the actual time is closer to eight hours) per week with his/her youth. The time and location of these meetings were usually a matter of mutual convenience, but the youth's home was the most common meeting place. The student's work with youth was based on an individualized goal attainment model of intervention. Namely, the student might get involved in a variety of areas of the youth's life depending on the changes which seemed indicated in the particular case. Common areas included family relationship, school performance, employment, and recreational activities. All youth received eighteen weeks of intervention.

While the program adhered to an individualized model of intervention, there was a good deal of similarity in the pattern followed in all cases. Initially, the volunteer concentrated on establishing a positive relationship with the youth, while assessing areas which both represented strength and weaknesses (areas of unmet need) or problems. Some common areas scrutinized included family relationships, school situations, employment possibilities, and recreational activities. The volunteer then began to initiate change in areas which he/she and the youth deemed important to alter. For example, the volunteer, youth, and parents might enter into a behavioral contract concerning allowance and chores; or the volunteer and youth might have a discussion with the principal and a school counselor concerning class schedules or cooperative education availability. Next, the volunteer would carefully monitor changes which he/she had helped initiate. This was viewed as critical to the intervention process since many times initial intervention efforts did not produce desired changes and had to be altered. For example, at the end of three weeks of a behavioral contract, all members involved in the contract might have met to assess how the intervention was working. Or a school principal might have been consulted regarding the youth's improved attendance as a result of a schedule change. The cycle of assessment, intervention, and monitoring was repeated during the eighteen week intervention as often as necessary. As the end of the assigned time period approached, the volunteer planned for the termination of the case by insuring changes would be maintained after his/her case involvement ended. Such techniques as instruction of those involved, the chance to practice specific skills or to roleplay potential difficult situations which were utilized to accomplish this purpose. Of particular importance was seeing that the youth and/or significant others had gained the required skills to handle difficult situations on their own.

Bauer, Bordeaux, Cole, Davidson, Martinez, Mitchell & Singleton, A Diversion Program for Juvenile Offenders: The Experience of Ingham County, Michigan, 31 Juv. & Fam.Ct.J. 53, 59 (August 1980).*

Another innovative approach, the Bronx Neighborhood Youth Diversion Program, is described in Nejelski, Diversion: Unleashing the Hounds of Heaven?, in Pursuing Justice for the Child 94, 103–04 (M. Rosenheim ed. 1976). The focus is on juveniles charged with delinquency. A juvenile diverted to the project is assigned an advocate, generally someone below age 30 who lives in the neighborhood of the youth. There also is a panel of community residents known as the "forum". Its members are nonprofessionals from the community who have received mediation and conciliation training. They address problems stemming from minor offenses by neighborhood juveniles and help in the resolution of problems between children and parents.

NOTES

(1) Diversion programs are as varied as the juveniles who enter them. In many jurisdictions there is simply a youth service bureau designed to handle all diversions. In larger cities, however, diversion programs become quite

specialized and often include drug and alcohol rehabilitation, vocational training and remedial education. In addition, some jurisdictions have Outward Bound programs or some type of wilderness appreciation program. Finally, in some instances the only necessary intervention may be referral to a physician for medical treatment. Sometimes frustrating physical disorders contribute to a youth's inability to perform in school and to resultant antisocial behavior.

(2) Many churches sponsor programs for their young people. Should intake officers utilize these programs when diverting juveniles? Are there constitutional questions raised by such referrals?

(3) The Standards and a few jurisdictions permit intake personnel, the juvenile and the juvenile's family to enter into a consent decree that has the force of a court order but is not a formal adjudication. The use of decrees may hold a great deal of rehabilitative promise because they allow a juvenile to help fashion his own diversion program. See Juvenile Justice Standards Relating to the Juvenile Probation Function, 2.5 at 53–57.

VI.   PRETRIAL DETENTION

A.   INTRODUCTION

P. M. WALD, PRETRIAL DETENTION FOR JUVENILES

In M. ROSENHEIM (Ed.) PURSUING JUSTICE
FOR THE CHILD 119–120 (1976).*

For years, critics of our juvenile court system have deplored the
horrors of juvenile detention before trial. The statistics are dreary:
over half a million juveniles annually detained in "junior jails," another several hundred thousand.held in adult jails, penned like cattle,
demoralized by lack of activities and trained staff, often brutalized.
Over half the facilities in which juveniles are held have no psychiatric
or social work staff. A fourth have no school program. The median
age of detainees is fourteen; the novice may be sodomized within a
matter of hours. Many have not been charged with a crime at all.
From New York to California, the field reports repeat themselves de-
pressingly.

Generally critics agree about where the fault lies and what ought
to be done. They have scored the police, intake officers at the juvenile court, and the courts themselves. They have shown that too little money is spent on recruiting and training good staff and on
mounting constructive programs in detention facilities. They have
called for alternatives to detention for juveniles who "can't go home
again" but are not really dangerous to anyone. Still, progress is
painfully slow. While several of our larger cities report that fewer
juveniles are being detained before trial than in previous years, in
other cities overall estimates continue to grow. When a situation as
unsavory as juvenile detention persists as long as it has, reappraisal
is essential. Any new look at the problem requires an assessment of
what has been done or attempted in the past.

OPENING STATEMENT OF SENATOR BIRCH BAYH, HEAR-
INGS BEFORE THE SENATE SUBCOMMITTEE TO IN-
VESTIGATE JUVENILE DELINQUENCY: THE
DETENTION AND JAILING OF
JUVENILES (1973)

The period of detention for juveniles is critical because it is frequently the juvenile's first contact with the juvenile justice system.
Detention generally refers to the incarceration of a juvenile in a secure facility prior to adjudication or disposition of his case. The insti-

tutions involved may range from ultra-modern detention facilities to ancient city and county jails. Youth locked up in these institutions may frequently spend long periods of enforced idleness without educational, recreational or counselling facilities. Worse still, some juveniles in detention are brutalized, beaten and exposed to vicious sexual attacks. Neglect, abuse, isolation and punishment in detention facilities or jail often destroy any possibility of subsequent rehabilitation. This is doubly tragic when we consider that many of the detained children have committed no crime but are locked up because they are runaways, truants or not wanted at home, or have no other place to go.

The enormity of the problems of juvenile detention is staggering. On any given day, there are close to 8,000 juveniles held in jails in the United States. It is estimated that more than 100,000 youths spend one or more days each year in adult jails or police lock-ups. In addition, the average daily population in juvenile detention facilities is over 12,000, with close to 500,000 held annually in such facilities. We intend to consider in these hearings not only the conditions of such jailing and detention but whether this amount of incarceration is necessary.

JUVENILE JUSTICE STANDARDS PROJECT, STANDARDS RELATING TO INTERIM STATUS: THE RELEASE, CONTROL, AND DETENTION OF ACCUSED JUVENILE OFFENDERS BETWEEN ARREST AND DISPOSITION, 1–3 (1980) *

General Introduction

The detention of juveniles prior to adjudication or disposition of their cases represents one of the most serious problems in the administration of juvenile justice. The problem is characterized by the very large number of juveniles incarcerated during this stage annually, the harsh conditions under which they are held, the high costs of such detention, and the harmful after-effects detention produces. These difficulties are caused or compounded by profound defects in the system of juvenile justice itself: in the inadequacy of the information and the decision-making process that leads to detention; in the delays between arrest and ultimate disposition; and in the lack of visibility and accountability that pervades the process.

In contrast to the pretrial stage, much greater care and sensitivity is usually devoted to the postadjudicative disposition, its facilities, and its alternatives to incarceration. The result, paradoxically, is considerably less detention under better conditions once the juvenile justice system ceases to presume that the juvenile is innocent.

The basis of reform in this area should be a new focus on the importance and integrity of pretrial decision making, and on the development of an informed, speedy, and responsible process. Standards must be formulated and rules imposed to limit the process, to the extent possible, to performing the historic function of bail in the criminal process—ensuring the presence of the accused at future court proceedings. The standards also need to recognize and regulate candidly the function that bail in the adult criminal process plays in fact, but declines to acknowledge in law—that some arrested persons are too obviously guilty and apparently too dangerous to others to be released by any reasonable judicial officer.

B.   STATUTORY LIMITATIONS

UNITED STATES EX REL. MARTIN v. STRASBURG

United States District Court, Southern District of New York, 1981.
513 F.Supp. 691.

ROBERT L. CARTER, DISTRICT JUDGE.

This habeas corpus class action proceeding is being brought on behalf of all juveniles who are being held or who will be held . . . in pretrial detention under N.Y. Family Court Act § 739(a)(ii) (McKinney) ("the Act"). Petitioners seek a declaratory judgment that § 739(a)(ii) violates the due process and equal protection clauses of the 14th Amendment. . . .

In New York persons between the ages of 7 and 16 accused of various acts which would be a crime if committed by an adult are subject to the exclusive jurisdiction of the family court to be prosecuted as juvenile delinquents.[1]   In the exercise of its exclusive jurisdiction over juvenile delinquents, the family court is authorized under the Act to subject an alleged delinquent to pretrial detention prior to a probable cause or fact finding determination if it determines that "there is a serious risk that he may before the return date do an act which if committed by an adult would constitute a crime." § 739(ii). The youth may also be detained because of the substantial probability that he will not appear on the return date 739(a)(i), but this provision is not involved or challenged in this litigation.[2]

. . .

1. For most serious crimes such as murder and arson, members of this group 13 years old and older may be prosecuted as juvenile offenders in the criminal court. N.Y.Penal Law § 10.00(18) (McKinney). This subclass, however, does not concern us.

2. N.Y.Family Court Act § 739 (McKinney) provides:

(a) After the filing of a petition under section seven hundred thirty-one or seven hundred thirty-two, the court in its discretion may release the respon-

The Parties' Contentions

Petitioners contend that the statute is unconstitutional on its face and as applied in that it offends the due process and equal protection guaranties of the 14th Amendment. Petitioners argue that the subjective prediction or prognosis of the imminence of future misconduct which § 739(a)(ii) authorizes as the basis for the pretrial detention of juveniles is a vague, arbitrary and capricious standard and that no rationally based prediction or reasoned determination is possible under the statutory scheme. They insist that the statute is overbroad and violates equal protection constraints in authorizing pretrial detention of juveniles, since they are thereby treated differently from adults, and there is neither a rational basis pertinent to the differentiation between the two groups, nor any compelling state justification to warrant imposition of the restrictions imposed on juveniles under the statutory scheme. . . .

The attorney general argues *pro se* that the statutory scheme is constitutionally and legislatively permissible; that all judicial and administrative decision making in the criminal justice system has the same potential for inaccuracy in predicting future acts, as does the statute involved here, but nonetheless the judge's subjective determinations as to bail, parole, and length of sentence have been accepted as appropriate exercises of judicial discretion free of constitutional infirmities; that the statute does not result in random detention; that pretrial detention does not constitute punishment without trial and does not deny juveniles any due process or equal protection rights, and in any event, the compelling interest of the state in reducing the risk of pretrial crimes by juveniles justifies the difference in the treatment of juveniles and adults and validates the statute.

Determination

A

The issues raised in this litigation are difficult and complex. Petitioners contend that the statutory scheme is at war with the guaran-

dent or direct his detention. In exercising its discretion under this section, the court shall not direct detention unless it finds that unless the respondent is detained:

(i) there is a substantial probability that he will not appear in court on the return date; or

(ii) there is a serious risk that he may before the return date do an act which if committed by an adult would constitute a crime.

(b) Unless the respondent waives a determination that probable cause exists to believe that he is a juvenile delinquent or a person in need of supervision, no detention under this section may last more than three days (i) unless the court finds, pursuant to the evidentiary standards applicable to a hearing on a felony complaint in a criminal court, that such probable cause exists, or (ii) unless special circumstances exist, in which cases such detention may be extended not more than an additional three days exclusive of Saturdays, Sundays and public holidays.

tee of equal protection since juveniles are subjected to pretrial detention while adults are not. Both parties argue that the appropriate test to measure the constitutional validity of § 739(a)(ii) under the equal protection clause is whether the state has demonstrated a compelling, overriding state interest justifying the legislation, and no feasible, less drastic measures are appropriate to accomplish the state's objective.

In People ex rel. Wayburn v. Schupf, 39 N.Y.2d 682, 385 N.Y.S.2d 518, 350 N.E.2d 906 (1976), the New York Court of Appeals upheld the Act against an equal protection challenge on the ground that the statute served a compelling state interest. That interest as articulated by the court was the juveniles' emotional and intellectual immaturity, necessitating that they not be held to the more onerous adult standards of responsibility for their conduct. Moreover, the court reasoned that immaturity and lack of comprehension caused juveniles to view criminal conduct less seriously than adults. Accordingly, procedures designed to prevent further criminal acts by juveniles accused of delinquency were held to be justified to protect the public.

If the parties are, and the state court was, correct that compelling justification and unavailability of any feasible less drastic alternatives are the criteria to measure the statute's validity under the equal protection clause, my task would be considerably eased. § 739 clearly cannot withstand a constitutional challenge when the equal protection test of strict scrutiny is applied.

The record made at trial reveals that roughly 3,546 juvenile delinquents were subjected to pretrial detention in 1977. The figures on final disposition of all juvenile delinquencies show that 667 were placed in training schools of the Division for Youth and 47 others were accorded some other form of restricted placement. Assuming that the above 714 juveniles were all among those subjected to pretrial detention (an assumption not necessarily correct), the remaining 2,832 cases resulted in probation to the custody of the parent, guardian or placement in a foster home, or placement in a youth camp.

The 1979 figures paint the same picture. . . . Under any yardstick when at final disposition the overwhelming majority of juveniles are paroled and sent home, the claim that there is a compelling need to subject them to pretrial detention becomes hard to credit.

. . .

Remand has been deemed warranted in this case because of the seriousness of the crime, because of prior court contact, because the court always orders detention in certain cases, because such is warranted to punish the juvenile or, as Judge Quinones testified, to protect the public. . . .

. . .

This provision seems to lack the high minded purpose of protecting the juvenile which is the objective generally cited to justify deviations from adult standards in the juvenile justice system. Rather, the purpose seems to be to protect society from the juvenile. No articulated rationale has been set forth on this record which would warrant disadvantaging the young on this ground. Nonetheless, I regard the equal protection challenge to the statute as insubstantial.

The right of a state to differentiate between adults and minors is too ingrained in the fabric of the law for such classifications at this late date to be held to the test of strict scrutiny. Even though pretrial detention interferes with the juveniles' personal liberty, that alone would not seem to warrant application of the strict scrutiny test. The more appropriate inquiry is whether § 739(a)(ii) can be justified on grounds of rationality, and under this less rigorous yardstick, the statutory scheme would qualify as meeting the constitutional requirements of equal protection. . . .

B

The statutory scheme curtails the freedom of one presumptively innocent, albeit a juvenile, on the prediction or hunch of a judge that unless held in custody he will commit another crime within 3 to 6 days. The more fundamental consideration, therefore, is whether on its face or as applied, § 739(a)(ii) meets due process standards. There is little doubt that due process is a requisite to the constitutional validity of proceedings which may result in the curtailment of a juvenile's freedom, since all "individuals possess a liberty interest in being free from physical restraint." Greenholtz v. Inmates of Nebraska Penal & Correctional Complex, 442 U.S. 1, 33, 99 S.Ct. 2100, 2117, 60 L.Ed.2d 668 (1979) (Marshall, J. dissenting). While the limits of the liberty interest protected from deprivation without due process have never been precisely defined, it has "always been thought to encompass freedom from bodily harm and punishment. It is fundamental that a state cannot hold and physically punish an individual except in accordance with due process of law." Ingraham v. Wright, 430 U.S. 651, 673–74, 97 S.Ct. 1401, 1413–14, 51 L.Ed.2d 711 (1977).

Juvenile proceedings which may result in confinement to state institutions because of alleged misconduct must have the essential ingredients of fair treatment. . . . Application of due process standards may not be defeated because of the labels attached by the state to the pertinent proceedings, and a "claim that the traditional requirements of due process are applicable in the context of pretrial detention" has not been foreclosed. Gerstein v. Pugh, 420 U.S. 103, 127, 95 S.Ct. 854, 870, 43 L.Ed.2d 54 (1975) (Stewart, J. concurring).

The predictive § 739 determination is made before any proceeding, either adversarial or neutral, has found probable cause or rendered a determination on the merits that the juvenile committed the delinquent act charged. The Act violates due process requirements because: (1) it gives the judge a license to act arbitrarily and capriciously in a § 739 prediction of the likelihood of future criminal conduct which cannot result from a reasoned determination, (2) pretrial detention without a prior adjudication of probable cause is, itself, a per se violation of due process, and (3) in addition, constitutes punishment that is constitutionally impermissible under the due process clause.

1.   The first defect is perhaps the most pernicious.   The judge is empowered to make a prediction about the probability of an individual committing a crime if released.   No guidelines for making that determination are set out in the statute, and none has been adopted by the court.   The judge's determination is moored to no concrete or reasonably determinable yardsticks.   We were advised at trial that each judge utilizes his own personal standards.   Accordingly, there can be no uniform application of § 739, since each judge's subjective views and biases must necessarily govern.   The whole process is riddled with subjectivity and caprice and confers upon the judge "a license for arbitrary procedure."   Kent v. United States, supra, 383 U.S. at 553, 86 S.Ct. at 1053.

. . .

2.   A juvenile subjected to pretrial detention has not as yet had a "judicial determination of probable cause which the Fourth Amendment requires as a prerequisite to extended restraint of liberty following arrest."   Gerstein v. Pugh, 420 U.S. 103, 114, 95 S.Ct. 854, 863, 43 L.Ed.2d 54 (1975).   When a juvenile is arrested and held in custody he must be taken before a family court judge within 24 hours for a § 739 hearing.   The judges may postpone the hearing for another 24 hours.   No probable cause determination is made before the § 739 hearing.   The juvenile at this stage is without counsel until he appears for the § 739 hearing.   In some instances he is before the court on a delinquency petition filed on information and belief.   That is, the charges in the petition are not verified by someone with direct knowledge of what took place.   If ordered remanded, a fact finding hearing must occur 3–6 days thereafter.   That hearing may be delayed for as long as 14 days after the § 739 hearing but in such a case a probable cause hearing must be held within 72 hours of the § 739 hearing.   Accordingly a juvenile may be held in pretrial detention under a § 739 determination for as long as 5 days prior to any proceedings being held, neutral or adversary, pursuant to which a judicial determination of probable cause is made.

The burdens of pretrial detention are substantial to impose on a presumptively innocent man, even when there is probable cause to believe he has committed a crime.   Baker v. McCollan, 443 U.S. 137, 153, 99 S.Ct. 2689, 2699, 61 L.Ed.2d 433 (1979) (Stevens, J., dissenting).   To allow a state to impose these burdens on a juvenile before the state has taken the initial validating step of establishing its right to restrict the individual's liberty, in order to insure his presence at trial, would seem to be at war with accepted concepts of due process of law.

. . .

3. When a court pronounces the judgment that a youth must be incarcerated under § 739 because he or she is likely to commit additional crimes if released, the act of incarceration constitutes punishment which cannot constitutionally be imposed prior to an adjudication of guilt. Such a decision to incarcerate offends the due process clause of the 14th Amendment because it is imbued with what have long been recognized as the three essential attributes of punishment: it inflicts a deprivation of a constitutionally protected liberty or property interest; it is officially imposed rather than being the spontaneous act of an errant official, see Hernandez v. Lattimore, 612 F.2d 61 (2d Cir. 1979); and it stigmatizes the youthful detainee in a way that associates him with criminal behavior.

. . . .

For these reasons I find § 739(a)(ii), both on its face and as applied, contravenes the rights of petitioners and the class they represent to due process of law as guaranteed by the 14th Amendment to the Constitution of the United States.

MARTIN v. STRASBURG

United States Court of Appeals 2d Circuit, 1982.
689 F.2d 365.

RALPH K. WINTER, CIRCUIT JUDGE:

[Appeal from United States ex rel. Martin v. Strasburg.]

. . .

The presumption of innocence and the requirement that guilt be proven beyond a reasonable doubt are important elements of Due Process itself, which would be gravely diminished in the protection they afford if individuals can be routinely incarcerated pending trial. Even the most persuasive demonstration of innocence cannot prevent the deprivation of liberty if incarceration precedes, rather than follows, the adjudication of criminal liability.

The only exceptions presently recognized to this general rule appear to be brief detentions pending bail hearings, detention for failure to post bail subject to the Eighth Amendment's prohibition on "excessive" bail, or in limited classes of cases, denial or revocation of bail. See generally C. Whitebread, Criminal Procedure §§ 17.01–17.03 (1980).

The extent to which exceptions other than those relating to bail may be carved out is not clear. We believe all would agree, however, that any exception to the general rule that incarceration follow, rather than precede, adjudications of guilt can be justified, if at all, by a compelling governmental interest. Cf. Gerstein v. Pugh, 420 U.S. 103, 95 S.Ct. 854, 43 L.Ed.2d 54 (1975). The defendants argue, in the case of 739(a)(ii), that crime prevention is such an interest. That statute ostensibly responds to calls for preventive detention to protect the community from criminally inclined individuals. As conceived by its proponents, preventive detention is a method of confining inherently dangerous individuals accused of crimes pending trial and sentence of confinement. See Note, Preventive Detention Before Trial, 79 Harv.L.Rev. 1489, 1496–98 (1966). The underlying theory is not that propensity alone justifies confinement but that the expectation of an adjudication of guilt and subsequent sentence of confinement, along with a finding of propensity, justifies protecting the community from the individual in the interim period. Such a scheme raises serious constitutional questions which the parties have asked us to address. We decline, however, to reach those issues because 739(a)(ii) is utilized principally, not for preventive purposes, but to impose punishment for unadjudicated criminal acts.

Crime prevention simply does not provide a justification for the detention of the vast majority of juveniles actually held under 739(a)(ii). Family Court Judges, we are told, release large numbers of detainees at disposition because much more information pertaining to the particular juvenile is available there than at the detention stage and because the Judges tend to find that the time already served is punishment enough. While the record is silent as to explanations for the similarly large number of prosecutorial dismissals before adjudication, it can be inferred that such cases as a class involve facts even less compelling as to guilt or appropriateness of further incarceration.

Accepting the defendants' view, the vast majority, in all likelihood over two-thirds, of the 739(a)(ii) detainees fall into one or more of the following categories: (1) those against whom the evidence of guilt is weak or insufficient; (2) those who are not so dangerous that they cannot be released after a short period of detention; and (3) those who are regarded as having served enough time in confinement. Crime prevention is not a sufficiently compelling governmental interest as to any of these detainees to justify shortcutting the fundamental procedural requirement that imprisonment follow, rather than precede, adjudication. Category (1) involves detainees ultimately released by prosecutorial dismissal or on a judicial finding of insufficient evidence. As to them, incarceration is imposed but guilt is never adjudicated. Category (2) involves detainees about whom a mistaken judgment was made in the course of the summary hearing held under 739(a)(ii). As to them, no constitutional purpose justifies their detention. Category (3) involves adjudicated delinquents considered to have been punished enough by the time served. No compelling governmental interest justifies the imposition of sanctions on members of this group before, rather than after, adjudication. As to them, detention serves the purpose of punishment rather than crime prevention, since early release—within days or at most a few weeks—by a Family Court Judge contradicts any asserted need for pre-trial confinement to protect the community.

In practice, therefore, the vast majority of the pre-trial detentions involve either mistakes in judgment fostered by 739(a)(ii)'s procedurally and substantively unlimited terms or the imposition of incarceration solely as punishment for unadjudicated crimes. To the degree that the goal of crime prevention is implicated at all in the actual operation of 739(a)(ii), it is only as to the minority, perhaps less than one-third, of the juveniles actually detained under its provisions. As to this group, moreover, only the risk that some might commit crimes is eliminated.

In re Winship directly ruled that an adjudication of delinquency which entails the possibility of institutional confinement must rest on proof beyond a reasonable doubt, because such confinement is constitutionally analogous to punishment for criminal acts. The provision invalidated in *Winship* under the Due Process Clause was in fact a provision of the New York Family Court Act which applied a preponderance of the evidence test in delinquency adjudications. The practice under 739(a)(ii) is, if anything, more offensive since confinement is imposed initially only upon a verified petition and later at best upon a finding of probable cause. The Family Court Judge ordering detention is well aware that most detainees will either not go to fact-finding or, if they do, will be released on probation. Section 739(a)(ii) thus incarcerates—punishes—large numbers of persons upon a standard of proof which is constitutionally invalid and which cannot be justified in the name of crime prevention.

Section 739(a)(ii) thus has an unconstitutional impact as to the vast majority of the juveniles detained under it. We must now determine whether the statute is invalid as to all juveniles or whether individual detainees must litigate the particular circumstances of their confinement.

We hold 739(a)(ii) unconstitutional as to all juveniles. The preponderant number of persons affected by its terms suffer punishment without adjudication of guilt beyond a reasonable doubt and absent a compelling governmental interest. Individual litigation, however, is a practical impossibility because the periods of detention are so short that the litigation is mooted before the merits are determined. Moreover, the record clearly demonstrates that the unconstitutional impact of the statute results directly from its substantively and procedurally unlimited terms which cause Family Court Judges to incarcerate juveniles they know will be released before or at disposition. Whether we view the statutory scheme as commanding the results it in fact attains or as simply failing "to provide sufficiently clear guidance for police, prosecutors and the courts to enforce [it] in a manner . . . consistent with [the Due Process Clause]," United States ex rel. Newsome v. Malcolm, 492 F.2d 1166 (2d Cir. 1974) aff'd sub nom. Lefkowitz v. Newsome, 420 U.S. 283, 95 S.Ct. 886, 43 L.Ed.2d 196 (1975), matters not, for under either view it violates constitutional guarantees.[35]

. . . .

Affirmed.

[The concurring opinion of NEUMAN, C. J., is omitted.]

35. Our view conflicts with that of New York's Court of Appeals, which has upheld 739(a)(ii) against constitutional attack. People ex rel. Wayburn v. Schupf,

NOTES

(1) In People ex rel. Wayburn v. Schupf, 39 N.Y.2d 682, 385 N.Y.S.2d 518, 350 N.E.2d 906 (1976), the state court decision mentioned in *Strasburg*, the New York Court of Appeals rejected both due process and equal protection challenges to the pretrial detention provision of § 739. Although the court applied a test of strict scrutiny, it upheld the statute because it served a compelling state interest. The opinion explained:

> Subdivision (b) of section 739 authorizes pretrial detention to prevent another crime from being committed by the juvenile. This statute reflects the merger of two fundamental concerns of the State—to protect the community prospectively from the perpetration of serious crimes and to protect and shelter children who in consequence of grave antisocial behavior are demonstrably in need of special treatment and care. . . .

Our society recognizes that juveniles in general are in the earlier stages of their emotional growth, that their intellectual development is incomplete, that they have had only limited practical experience, and that their value systems have not yet been clearly identified or firmly adopted. In consequence of what might be characterized as this immaturity, juveniles are not held to the same standard of individual responsibility for their conduct as are adult members of our society. . . .

For the same reasons that our society does not hold juveniles to an adult standard of responsibility for their conduct, our society may also conclude that there is a greater likelihood that a juvenile charged with delinquency, if released, will commit another criminal act than that an adult charged with crime will do so. To the extent that self-restraint may be expected to constrain adults, it may not be expected to operate with equal force as to juveniles. Because of the possibility of juvenile delinquency treatment and the absence of second-offender sentencing, there will not be the deterrent for the juvenile which confronts the adult. Perhaps more significant is the fact that in consequence of lack of experience and comprehension the juvenile does not view the commission of what are criminal acts in the same perspective as an adult. It serves to refer to the common recognition of the high school "lark", or to the relative indifference which the young attach, for instance, to shoplifting or to "borrowing" an automobile and the unconcern with which they view the possibility of being apprehended. There is the element of gamesmanship and the excitement of "getting away" with something and the powerful inducement of peer pressures. All of these commonly acknowledged factors make the commission of criminal conduct on the part of juveniles in general more likely than in the case of adults. Antisocial behavior of the young may be dismissed, or even be expected, as a "prank", a characterization never applied to similar conduct of an adult. In consequence of these and other like considerations, protection of the public peace and general welfare justifies resort to special procedures designed to prevent

39 N.Y.2d 682, 385 N.Y.S.2d 518, 350 N. E.2d 906 (1976). Although the burden of the Court's opinion was directed to a claim that differential treatment of juveniles and adults violated the Equal Protection Clause, it recognized that preventive detention under 739(a)(ii) is imposed upon large numbers of juveniles who are in fact released after the dispositional hearing. This was attributed to the superior information available at that stage to inform the Family Court Judge as to the proper disposition. The Court held this constitutionally insignificant. We disagree for the reasons stated.

the commission of further criminal acts on the part of juveniles as differentiated from adults.

. . .

Nor can we accept the assertion, advanced under a due process heading . . . that because the degree of probability of repetition of criminal behavior cannot be predicted with scientific precision, there is ineluctably involved an unconstitutional element of vagueness or speculation. Such an element is necessarily present in the administration of any bail system, in the imposition of alternatively available sentences, in the administration of a parole system, or in any other procedure in which discretionary authority for differing criminal dispositions is vested in a court or an administrative body.

There is another aspect. The children who come before Family Court fall largely into two categories—those who are no longer subject to the guidance or effective control of their parents or guardians, and those who have no custodians at all. Indeed this is what has contributed to their difficulties. In this circumstance to a very real extent Family Court must exercise a substitute parental control for which there can be no particularized criteria.

. . .

This case draws attention to what appears to be a growing tragedy—the thus far elusive and largely unmanageable problem of the neglected and delinquent child in our society. Most important—intelligent, effective and compassionate means must be found to assist children that are not subject to parental guidance or control, or whose custodians are ineffectual, through the temptations and turbulence of adolescence. In this aspect the children are the victims. On the other hand, if they are victims it must also be acknowledged that they are the perpetrators—of homicides, robberies, burglaries and rapes which threaten to make the modern city an imprisoning fortress for the old, the weak and the timid. Probable cause was found here, for instance, to conclude that this youth had engaged in a mugging which led to the death by strangulation of a pedestrian on the streets of New York.

How would you have decided the issues raised in *Strasburg* and *Wayburn*?

(2) Would your views be different with regard to detention of adults as potentially dangerous?

In United States v. Edwards, 430 A.2d 1321 (D.C.App.1981), an adult defendant challenged the District of Columbia pretrial detention statute, asserting that it violated his constitutional rights to bail and to due process. In rejecting the defendant's claims, the D.C. Court of Appeals held that the eighth amendment's prohibition against excessive bail does not guarantee a right to bail in criminal cases. As to the due process claim that pretrial detention is punishment that cannot be imposed prior to an adjudication of guilt, the court concluded that pretrial detention is "regulatory rather than penal" in nature. It noted that:

The statutory history makes clear that pretrial detention was intended to protect the safety of the community until it can be determined whether society may properly punish the defendant . . . . [P]retrial detention is closely circumscribed so as not to go beyond the need to protect the safety of the community pending the detainee's trial.

(3) As in New York, most states have enacted statutory criteria for determining whether a juvenile shall be released or detained pending trial. For example, California's Welfare and Institutions Code, § 635, provides that:

> [U]nless it appears that such minor has violated an order of the juvenile court or has escaped from the commitment of the juvenile court or that it is a matter of immediate and urgent necessity for the protection of such minor or reasonably necessary for the protection of the person or property of another that he be detained or that such minor is likely to flee to avoid the jurisdiction of the court, the court shall make its order releasing such minor from custody.
>
> The circumstances and gravity of the alleged offense may be considered, in conjunction with other factors, to determine whether it is a matter of immediate and urgent necessity for the protection of the minor or reasonably necessary for the protection of the person or property of another that the minor be detained.

Similarly, Texas Family Code Tit. 3, § 53.02 requires that:

> (b) A child taken into custody may be detained prior to hearing on the petition only if:
>
> (1) he is likely to abscond or be removed from the jurisdiction of the court;
>
> (2) suitable supervision, care, or protection for him is not being provided by a parent, guardian, custodian, or other person;
>
> (3) he has no parent, guardian, custodian, or other person able to return him to the court when required;
>
> (4) he is accused of committing a felony offense and may be dangerous to himself or others if released; or
>
> (5) he has previously been found to be a delinquent child or has previously been convicted of a penal offense punishable by a term in jail or prison and is likely to commit an offense if released.

(4) Although the wording of pretrial detention provisions generally would seem to extend wide discretion to judicial officers, certain limitations have been imposed by courts to assure fairness and consistency. For example, in In re William M., 3 Cal.3d 16, 89 Cal.Rptr. 33, 473 P.2d 737 (1970), a juvenile court judge had followed a policy of detaining all children charged with illegal sale of drugs. The Supreme Court of California declared that practice a violation of the statutorily formulated policy of the state (see § 635, Calif. Welf. & Inst.Code, note (3) above), because the judge was not actually considering the particularized relevant facts with respect to each individual case. And in In re G. M. B., 483 P.2d 1006 (Alaska 1971), the Supreme Court of Alaska held that a family court master's temporary detention order stating that "[the] child should be detained for his own protection in view of present offense and past violations" was insufficiently specific to show that incarceration was necessary for the protection of the juvenile and therefore was void.

In Commonwealth ex rel. Sprowal v. Hendrick, 438 Pa. 435, 265 A.2d 348 (1970), a juvenile was detained, apparently to ensure his appearance at subsequent judicial proceedings. Although the court stated that this could be a valid reason for detention, it cautioned that "[s]uch measures should be utilized . . . only when the hearing court determines that there is *no other less coercive method whereby future attendance can be reasonably assured and places the reasons for this finding on the record.*" 265 A.2d at 349 [Emphasis added].

(5) The divergence of factors that a detention officer must be prepared to take into consideration is illustrated by Kinney v. Lenon, 425 F.2d 209 (9th Cir. 1970), even though it is a case that is factually restrictive as to application. Appellant, a black youth of 17, was being detained on charges arising out of a schoolyard fight. He claimed that there were many witnesses to the fight who he did not know by name but could recognize on sight, and that because his potential witnesses were all black his white attorneys would have great difficulty in preparing his defense unless he were free to aid them. The Court of Appeals, in ordering his release, stated:

> This is not a case where release from detention is sought simply for the convenience of the appellant. There is here a strong showing that the appellant is the only person who can effectively prepare his own defense. We may take notice, as judges and lawyers, of the difficulties often encountered, even by able and conscientious counsel, in overcoming the apathy and reluctance of potential witnesses to testify. It would require blindness to social reality not to understand that these difficulties may be exacerbated by the barriers of age and race. Yet the alternative to some sort of release for appellant is to cast the entire burden of assembling witnesses onto his attorneys, with almost certain prejudice to appellant's case.

Id. at 210.

JUVENILE JUSTICE STANDARDS PROJECT, STANDARDS RELATING TO INTERIM STATUS: THE RELEASE, CONTROL, AND DETENTION OF ACCUSED JUVENILE OFFENDERS BETWEEN ARREST AND DISPOSITION (1980) *

3.1 Policy favoring release

Restraints on the freedom of accused juveniles pending trial and disposition are generally contrary to public policy. The preferred course in each case should be unconditional release.

3.2 Permissible control or detention

The imposition of interim control or detention on an accused juvenile may be considered for the purposes of:

A. protecting the jurisdiction and process of the court;

B. reducing the likelihood that the juvenile may inflict serious bodily harm on others during the interim period; or

C. protecting the accused juvenile from imminent bodily harm upon his or her request.

However, these purposes should be exercised only under the circumstances and to the extent authorized by the procedures, requirements, and limitations detailed in Parts IV through X of these standards.

3.3 Prohibited control or detention

Interim control or detention should not be imposed on an accused juvenile:

    A.   to punish, treat, or rehabilitate the juvenile;

    B.   to allow parents to avoid their legal responsibilities;

    C.   to satisfy demands by a victim, the police, or the community;

    D.   to permit more convenient administrative access to the juvenile;

    E.   to facilitate further interrogation or investigation; or

    F.   due to a lack of a more appropriate facility or status alternative.

3.4 Least intrusive alternative

Whenever an accused juvenile cannot be unconditionally released, conditional or supervised release that results in the least necessary interference with the liberty of the juvenile should be favored over more intrusive alternatives.

3.5 Values

Whenever the interim curtailment of an accused juvenile's freedom is permitted under these standards, the exercise of authority should reflect the following values:

    A.   respect for the privacy, dignity, and individuality of the accused juvenile and his or her family;

    B.   protection of the psychological and physical health of the juvenile;

    C.   tolerance of the diverse values and preferences among different groups and individuals;

    D.   ensurance of equality of treatment by race, class, ethnicity, and sex;

    E.   avoidance of regimentation and depersonalization of the juvenile;

    F.   avoidance of stigmatization of the juvenile; and

    G.   ensurance that the juvenile receives adequate legal assistance.

. . .

4.2 Burden of proof

The state should bear the burden at every stage of the proceedings of persuading the relevant decision maker with clear and convincing evidence that restraints on an accused juvenile's liberty are necessary, and that no less intrusive alternative will suffice.

. . .

5.1 Policy favoring release

Each police department should adopt policies and issue written rules and regulations requiring release of all accused juveniles at the arrest stage pursuant to Standard 5.6 A., and adherence to the guidelines specified in Standard 5.6 B. in discretionary situations. Citations should be employed to the greatest degree consistent with the policies of public safety and ensuring appearance in court to release a juvenile on his or her own recognizance, or to a parent.

. . .

5.6 Guidelines for status decision

A. Mandatory release. Whenever the juvenile has been arrested for a crime which in the case of an adult would be punishable by a sentence of [less than one year], the arresting officer should, if charges are to be pressed, release the juvenile with a citation or to a parent, unless the juvenile is in need of emergency medical treatment (Standard 4.5 A. 1. b.), requests protective custody (Standard 5.7), or is known to be in a fugitive status.

B. Discretionary release. In all other situations, the arresting officer should release the juvenile unless the evidence as defined below demonstrates that continued custody is necessary. The seriousness of the alleged offense should not, except in cases of a class one juvenile offense involving a crime of violence, be sufficient grounds for continued custody. Such evidence should only consist of one or more of the following factors as to which reliable information is available to the arresting officer:

1. that the arrest was made while the juvenile was in a fugitive status;

2. that the juvenile has a recent record of willful failure to appear at juvenile proceedings.

. . .

9.2 Policy of encouraging release

It should be the policy of prosecutors to encourage the police and other interim decision makers to release accused juveniles with a citation or without forms of control. Special efforts should be made to enter into stipulations to this effect in order to avoid unnecessary detention inquiries and to promote efficiency in the administration of justice.

NOTES

(1) For a critique of the preventive detention of allegedly dangerous juveniles, see M. Guggenhem, Paternalism, Prevention, and Punishment: Pretrial Detention of Juveniles, 52 N.Y.U.L.Rev. 1064 (1977). For a dissenting view about the approach taken in the Juvenile Justice Standards on Interim Status, see the Statement of Commissioner Wilfred W. Nuernberger at p. 107 of the Standards.

(2) Should a juvenile who is later adjudicated delinquent and sent to an incarcerative facility be entitled to credit against his "sentence" for the time he spent detained prior to disposition? See In re Ricky H., 30 Cal.3d 176, 178 Cal.Rptr. 324 at 329–333, 636 P.2d 13 at 18–22 (1981).

C. CONSTITUTIONAL ISSUES

1. PROBABLE CAUSE TO DETAIN

BELL v. SUPERIOR COURT IN & FOR COUNTY OF PIMA

Court of Appeals of Arizona, Division 2, 1977.
117 Ariz. 551, 574 P.2d 39.

RICHMOND, JUDGE.

Is a juvenile detained while awaiting adjudication of a delinquency charge entitled to bail and a probable cause hearing? Although we deny relief because the question has become moot as to petitioner, . . . we assume jurisdiction to answer it as one of statewide concern that is likely to recur.

Petitioner was arrested by Tucson police officers on September 30, 1977, and immediately transported to the Pima County Juvenile Court Center. . . . On October 3, 1977, while he was still in detention, the state filed a formal petition alleging that petitioner was a delinquent child in that he had violated the law as follows:

"(RECEIVING STOLEN PROPERTY)"

"On or about the 30 day of September 1977, DENNIS BELL bought, sold, possessed, concealed, or received stolen personal property, valued at $100, or more, to wit: four Mag wheels and tires; one car seat, all in violation of A.R.S. § 13–621, as amended, 13–1645, and 13–1647, as amended."

The following day petitioner, his mother, and his attorney appeared before a juvenile court referee at a detention hearing. No evidence was presented as to the alleged delinquent act. Petitioner requested a probable cause hearing and that bail be fixed in a reasonable amount. The requests were denied and the referee recommended that petitioner be detained because he lacked custodial supervision, would be a danger to himself or others if released, and might not be present for trial. The recommendation was appealed to the juvenile court judge and the matter was heard the same day. Petitioner, by counsel, requested the court to order the state to produce forthwith evidence of the alleged crime, receiving stolen property, so as to establish probable cause for detaining him, and that bond be set in a reasonable amount. The court ruled adversely to petitioner and found that it was not required to hold a probable cause hearing or set bond in a reasonable amount.

The Rules of Procedure for Juvenile Court, A.R.S. 17A, contain no provision for release on bail. Rule 3(b), however, sets forth the only conditions for detention:

"A child shall be detained only if there are reasonable grounds to believe:

"(1) That otherwise he will not be present at any hearing; or

"(2) That he is likely to commit an offense injurious to himself or others; or

"(3) That he must be held for another jurisdiction; or

"(4) That the interests of the child or the public require custodial protection."

Unless the situation falls within one of these specified categories, release from custody is mandated. It is unnecessary to reach the question of whether there is a constitutional right to bail in juvenile proceedings. When Rule 3(b) is applied consistent with the requirements of due process, an adequate substitute for bail is provided. . . .

We agree with petitioner, however, that pre-trial detention of juveniles without determination of probable cause violates the Fourth Amendment. Several courts have held that a probable cause determination is required if the juvenile is at the risk of being incarcerated before trial. . . .

In Gerstein v. Pugh, 420 U.S. 103, 95 S.Ct. 854, 43 L.Ed.2d 54 (1975), the United States Supreme Court held that arrest and detention under a prosecutor's information violated the Fourth Amendment because of failure to afford a probable cause determination by a magistrate. The court noted:

". . . [A] policeman's on-the-scene assessment of probable cause provides legal justification for arresting a person suspected of crime, and for a brief period of detention to take the administrative steps incident to arrest. Once the suspect is in custody, however, the reasons that justify dispensing with the magistrate's neutral judgment evaporate. There no longer is any danger that the suspect will escape or commit further crimes while the police submit their evidence to a magistrate. And, while the State's reasons for taking summary action subside, the suspect's need for a neutral determination of probable cause increases significantly. . . . Accordingly, we hold that the Fourth Amendment requires a judicial determination of probable cause as a prerequisite to extended restraint of liberty following arrest."

The state relies on the requirement in Rule V, Local Rules of Procedure for the Pima County Juvenile Court, that an adjudicatory hearing be held no later than 15 days from the filing of the petition when a juvenile is detained. We do not believe this 15-day requirement obviates the need for a probable cause determination as a prerequisite to detention in addition to the other grounds enumerated in Rule 3(b), Rules of Procedure for Juvenile Court, supra.

We are of the opinion, and so hold, that a finding of probable cause—i.e., of "facts and circumstances, 'sufficient to warrant a prudent man in believing that the [suspect] had committed or was committing an offense,'" *Gerstein*, supra, 95 S.Ct. at 862—is required to justify pre-trial detention of a juvenile. As stated in Moss v. Weaver, [525 F.2d 1258, 1260 (5th Cir. 1976)]:

> "A finding of probable cause . . . is central to the [Fourth] Amendment's protections against official abuse of power. Pre-trial detention is an onerous experience, especially for juveniles, and the Constitution is affronted when this burden is imposed without adequate assurance that the accused has in fact committed the alleged crime."

The state argues that the philosophy of the juvenile court system to expedite juvenile matters and to afford juveniles special treatment would be subverted by requiring a probable cause hearing. We agree with the state that the Fourth Amendment itself does not require adversary safeguards. We cannot agree, however, that detained juveniles have less Fourth Amendment protection than detained adults in adult felony criminal proceedings. In Gerstein v. Pugh, supra, the court indicated that the standard to be applied in determining whether there is probable cause for detention is the same as that for arrest. The court also observed in *Gerstein* that the question of probable cause has for many years been resolved "in a nonadversary proceeding on hearsay and written testimony," 95 S.Ct. at 866, usually in the context of a magistrate's decision whether or not to issue an arrest warrant.

In holding that judicial determination of probable cause to believe that an alleged juvenile delinquent has committed an offense is constitutionally required before a juvenile may be detained pending the adjudicatory hearing, we do not believe that a hearing is required in every instance. The record, whether in the form of affidavit or a description of the circumstances of the offense in the delinquency petition, may suffice to satisfy a detached judicial officer that probable cause does exist. However, the mere filing of a petition in juvenile court charging an act which if committed by an adult would constitute a crime is not a sufficient showing of probable cause for issuance of an arrest warrant, and is not sufficient to support an independent judicial determination.

Because no factual materials sufficient to warrant a prudent man in believing that petitioner had committed an offense were presented by sworn statement or otherwise, the state failed to establish a prima facie case of probable cause to detain and petitioner's request for a probable cause hearing should have been granted.

Relief denied solely on the grounds of mootness.

2. DURATION AND TIMING

NATIONAL ADVISORY COMMISSION ON CRIMINAL JUSTICE STANDARDS AND GOALS: TASK FORCE ON CORRECTIONS, CHAPTER 8, JUVENILE INTAKE AND DETENTION, at 260 (1973)

Although there is considerable variation among States, there is consensus regarding the detrimental effects on children of undue delays in hearing. The Standard Juvenile and Family Court Act proposed by the National Council on Crime and Delinquency provides that children may not be held in a shelter or detention facility without a court order for more than 48 hours, excluding Sundays and holidays. California requires that a child admitted to detention must receive a hearing on the next judicial day after filing of a petition. Illinois has reduced this requirement to 36 hours.

In view of the consensus of most jurisdictions on the gravity of detention and the well-documented proof that long detention periods are unnecessary, detention hearings ordinarily should be afforded within 24 hours after a child is detained. The period should not exceed 48 hours without a court order. Every effort should be made to dispose of these hearings during the day of admission. This recommendation should pose no particular problems in jurisdictions where the court is in operation regularly throughout the work week. However, small rural counties, where hearings tend to be held on an "as needed" or other irregular basis, will need to realign judicial officers so that detention hearings can be held at any time during the work week, even though other juvenile cases are not heard. Current discriminatory practices resulting from the happenstance of geographical location should be discontinued.

Whenever court is not in session within the 24-hour period, the child ordinarily should be released from detention.

The need for speedy hearing makes it all the more essential that intake personnel notify court personnel promptly whenever children are being detained. According to the Model Rules of Juvenile Courts, they should also obtain scheduling of the detention hearing and notify the parents and the child.

JUVENILE JUSTICE STANDARDS PROJECT, STANDARDS RELATING TO INTERIM STATUS: THE RELEASE, CONTROL, AND DETENTION OF ACCUSED JUVENILE OFFENDERS BETWEEN ARREST AND DISPOSITION (1980) *

7.6   Release hearing

A.   Timing.   An accused juvenile taken into custody should, unless sooner released, be accorded a hearing in court within [twenty-four hours] of the filing of the petition for a release hearing required by Standard 6.5 D. 2.

B.   Notice.   Actual notice of the detention review hearing should be given to the accused juvenile, the parents, and their attorneys, immediately upon an intake official's decision that the juvenile will not be released prior to the hearing.

. . .

F.   Probable cause.   At the time of the initial detention hearing, the burden should be on the state to demonstrate that there is probable cause to believe that the juvenile committed the offense charged.

NOTE

In Cox v. Turley, 506 F.2d 1347 (6th Cir. 1974), a 16 year old youth was arrested and detained for a curfew violation.   After his confinement from Saturday evening until the following Wednesday, he was told by the judge to have his hair cut and then was released to his father.   On appeal from dismissal of his suit for injunctive and declaratory relief, it was held that the youth's due process rights had been violated "by reason of his confinement . . . without being taken before any judicial officer 'at the earliest possible time' . . . ."   The court found that "both the Fourth Amendment and the Fifth Amendment were violated because there was no prompt determination of probable cause—a constitutional mandate that protects juveniles as well as adults."   Id. at 1352, 1353.

3.   PRESENCE OF COUNSEL

In recent years there has been general recognition of the importance of counsel at detention hearings.   A good explanation was given by the National Advisory Commission on Criminal Justice Standards:

> Because a child's liberty is at stake, a child and his parents should have the right to counsel at each phase of the formal juvenile justice process, detention, adjudication, and disposition hearing.   The right to counsel should be a non-waiverable right.   In the interest of an equitable and more uniform process, a juvenile taken into

custody should be referred immediately to court intake services. Professionally trained personnel must again inform him of his rights in a version of *Miranda* that, it is hoped, he can understand. His parents, if not already present, should be notified immediately and informed of their child's rights. At this point, the intake worker would gather the information necessary to decide whether or not an informal disposition is desirable.[1]

Section 7.6 of the Juvenile Justice Standards Relating to Interim Status, dealing with release hearings, recognizes that an attorney for the accused juvenile should be present and adds that "no waiver should be valid unless made in writing by the juvenile and his or her counsel."

In Doe v. State, 487 P.2d 47 (Alaska 1971), the Supreme Court of Alaska stated that

[D]ue process standards must be observed at a detention inquiry since it may result in the deprivation of the child's liberty. Due process requires at the very least that detention orders be based on competent, sworn testimony, that the child have the right to be represented by counsel at the detention inquiry, and that the detention order state with particularity the facts supporting it.

In T. K. v. State, 126 Ga.App. 269, 190 S.E.2d 588 (1972), the court described a juvenile detention hearing as serving a function analogous to a commitment hearing in the criminal process and thus a proceeding in which it is intended that procedural due process requirements be observed. The court further explained that the statutory and constitutional right to be represented by counsel at a juvenile detention hearing includes the right to a reasonable opportunity to secure counsel.

4. BAIL

DOE v. STATE

Supreme Court of Alaska, 1971.
487 P.2d 47.

CONNOR, JUSTICE.

On January 8, 1970, a petition was filed in the superior court asking that John Doe be declared a delinquent child. The petition, signed by a probation-parole officer, charged John Doe, then a child of sixteen, with having sold, on December 23, 1969, one-half a tablet of lysergic acid diethylamide (LSD) to one Fred Lee Williams for three dollars. . . . A summons was issued on January 8, 1970, directing John Doe to appear before the juvenile judge the following

1. National Advisory Commission on Criminal Justice Standards and Goals: Task Force on Corrections, Ch. 8, Juvenile Intake and Detention 257 (1973).

day at 2:30 p. m., to "assist the Court in rendering a final determination in the above-entitled action."

John Doe appeared with his parents at the 2:30 p. m. hearing on January 9, 1970. Mr. Irwin Ravin was appointed as counsel for John Doe at that time. The child denied the petition, and the superior court prepared to commence immediately with the adjudication of the merits of the petition. John Doe's counsel indicated that he was not ready and asked for a continuance so that he could prepare the defense. January 9, 1970, was a Friday. The court continued the hearing until the following Monday morning. With the hearing on the merits now set for Monday, the court inquired of the district attorney whether he wished to be heard on the subject of John Doe's detention over the weekend. The district attorney stated:

"This defendant has threatened one of our witnesses and our witnesses have been subject of threats generally and there are threats out in the community and threats against life and I—I would ask for that reason that he be detained."

John Doe's attorney denied knowledge of any threats and objected to the district attorney's hearsay statement. He further stated that John Doe had never previously been before the children's court; that there had been no showing under the rules that the child should be detained; that detention would hamper the preparation of the defense; and that the state had had knowledge of John Doe's alleged conduct since December 23, 1969, but had not asked until January 9, 1970, that the boy be placed in custody. The court ordered that "this defendant be committed to the detention home over this weekend so that he'll be present at 9:00 or shortly thereafter for the hearing in this case." A commitment order was issued.[2]

. . .

1. *Right to Release Pending the Adjudication Hearing*

Appellant John Doe asks this court to hold that children have a constitutional right to bail under the Alaska Constitution,[4] or in the alternative, that the Alaska Rules of Children's Procedure contravene the bail provision of the Alaska Constitution to the extent that they allow detention of children for reasons other than availability for trial.

Children's Rule 7(b) provides:

"No juvenile shall be detained nor may any detention be continued prior to a first hearing of the case unless the court finds at a detention inquiry, which must be held not more than 48 hours after

2. The order itself stated that the grounds for detention were that the boy would harm himself or harm others.

4. Alas.Const. art. I, § 11, states in part: "Section 11. *Rights of Accused.*

In all criminal prosecutions, the accused . . . is entitled to be . . . released on bail, except for capital offenses when the proof is evident or the presumption great . . . ."

the juvenile has been taken into custody, not excluding weekends and holidays, that:

(1) Detention is necessary to protect the juvenile from others; or

(2) The juvenile will not be available for subsequent court proceedings; or

(3) The juvenile will cause harm to himself or to others if he is not detained."

. . .

Under the Alaska Constitution, all persons accused of a criminal offense are entitled to be released on bail except for capital offenses where the proof is evident or the presumption great. In Reeves v. State, 411 P.2d 212, 215 (Alaska 1966), we stated:

"The purpose of bail in the administration of criminal justice is to insure the defendant's appearance at trial."

We held in that case that while an adult criminal defendant has a constitutional right to be released on bail (except in certain capital cases), he does not have an absolute right to be released on his own recognizance, without bail, if he is financially unable to post the bond. We cited with approval and emphasis, however, the following language from Bandy v. United States, 81 S.Ct. 197, 198, 5 L.Ed.2d 218, 219–220 (1960):

". . . the right to release is heavily favored and . . . the requirement of security for the bond may, in a proper case, be dispensed with. . . . For there may be other deterrents to jumping bail: long residence in a locality, the ties of friends and family, the efficiency of modern police. All these in a given case may offer a deterrent at least equal to that of the threat of forfeiture."

Therefore, in adult criminal prosecutions, the central consideration with respect to pretrial release is whether the defendant will appear for trial. This is true for setting the amount of bail and for ruling on applications to be released on one's own recognizance. Society's interest in pretrial freedom for persons accused of crimes is strong. Under both the United States and Alaska Constitutions, excessive bail may not be imposed. Excessive bail has been held to be that which goes beyond the amount reasonably necessary to assure the defendant's presence at trial. Stack v. Boyle, 342 U.S. 1, 5, 72 S.Ct. 1, 96 L.Ed. 3 (1951). The presumption of innocence, central to our system of criminal justice, also dictates in favor of pretrial release. As the United States Supreme Court stated in Stack v. Boyle, supra:

"Unless this right to bail before trial is preserved, the presumption of innocence, secured only after centuries of struggle, would lose its meaning." 342 U.S., at 4, 72 S.Ct. at 3.

Certain problems peculiar to children are encountered in children's proceedings, however, which make a blanket application of the right to pre-adjudication release upon adequate assurance of future court appearance unworkable and undesirable from the child's viewpoint. In some cases, a parent whose child has become involved in delinquency proceedings may be unwilling to take the child back into the home pending an adjudication hearing. In other cases, a child may not wish to return to his home, or facts adduced at a detention inquiry may show that he should not return home, because the child fears he will be in danger of abuse at the hands of his parents. But the existence of these problems does not mean that the right to remain free pending an adjudication proceeding should be denied to children. Other courts have found that the children's rules can be construed and applied so that children are provided with an adequate substitute for bail.

. . . We believe, . . . because of the pecularities of children's proceedings, that the present adult bail system would be practically unsuitable as a device for securing the child's future appearance before the court, and would not necessarily result in the child's release. Because contracts entered into by minors have been held to be voidable, a bail bondsman surely would be unwilling to deal directly with a child in providing a bail bond. Unless the child's parents are willing and financially able to secure the bond, the child's right to bail will not result in release. Where the child's parents are not able to assure the bail bondsman of their financial security, the often criticized injustices of the adult bail system as applied to indigents would be visited upon the child.

Thus we are faced with conflicting interests. A child who is charged under the children's rules with an act which would be a crime, if committed by an adult, should have no less right to pre-adjudication freedom than an adult criminal defendant has pending trial. On the other hand, a child is in need of some care and supervision. If his parents are not willing to care for the child or if harm will come to the child in his present home situation, the children's court should not allow the child to return or remain at home; yet the child cannot be released entirely on his own responsibility. While these are serious conflicts, we believe they can be reconciled.

We hold that a child has the right to remain free pending an adjudication that the child is delinquent, dependent, or in need of supervision, where the facts supporting the petition involve an act which, if committed by an adult, would be a crime, and where the court has been given reasonable assurance that the child will appear at future court proceedings. If the facts produced at the inquiry show that the child cannot return or remain at home, every effort must be made to place the child in a situation where his freedom will not be curtailed. Only if there is clearly no alternative available may the child be committed to a detention facility and deprived of his freedom.

. . .

We hold, therefore, that the superior court's detention order in this case was invalid . . . .

. . .

Reversed and remanded.

NOTES

(1) Most courts, as in Doe v. State, have focused on the existence of "adequate alternatives" as a reason for not holding bail constitutionally required in the juvenile justice system. See, e.g., In re William M., 3 Cal.3d 16, 89 Cal.Rptr. 33, 473 P.2d 737 (1970); Fulwood v. Stone, 394 F.2d 939 (D.C.Cir. 1967); Baldwin v. Lewis, 300 F.Supp. 1220 (E.D.Wis.1969), reversed on other grounds 442 F.2d 29 (7th Cir. 1971). See also Pauley v. Gross, 1 Kan.App.2d 736, 574 P.2d 234 (1977), Baker v. Smith, 477 S.W.2d 149 (Ky.1971) and Morris v. D'Amario, ___ R.I. ___, 416 A.2d 137 (1980). Contra, State in the Interest of Banks, 402 So.2d 690 (La.1981).

In Baldwin v. Lewis, 300 F.Supp. 1220 (E.D.Wis.1969), reversed on other grounds 442 F.2d 29 (7th Cir. 1971), Judge Reynolds more clearly explained the "adequate alternatives" rationale:

Petitioner contends that the refusal of the State courts to admit him to bail is a violation of his rights under the Eighth Amendment to the United States Constitution. I find it unnecessary to reach the question of whether there is a "constitutional right to bail" in juvenile proceedings, because I believe that the Wisconsin Children's Code, when applied consistent with the . . . requirements of due process, provides an adequate substitute for bail.

The Wisconsin Children's Code, specifically § 48.29, requires that a juvenile *shall* be released to the custody of his parents unless there is a finding that because of the circumstances, including the gravity of the alleged crime, the nature of the juvenile's home life, and the juvenile's previous contacts with the court, the parents or guardian of the juvenile are incapable under the circumstances to care for him. Only if such a finding is made may the juvenile be detained pending trial of the accusations against him. As I have already held, the hearing at which the question of detention of the juvenile is determined must satisfy the requirements of due process of law. When this is done, the interest of the juvenile is protected, and he is not subjected to the arbitrary confinement which the Eighth Amendment is designed to prohibit.

In an earlier case, Trimble v. Stone, 187 F.Supp. 483, 488 (D.D.C.1960), the court found otherwise:

It was the beneficent purpose of the progressive legislation creating juvenile courts to ameliorate some of the rigidity and formality of the criminal law in cases in which the accused is a juvenile. The objective was to introduce more leniency, humanity, and informality in dealing with juvenile offenders. . . .

The Court recognizes that it may be desirable in the interest of the public, or even in the interest of the individual, in some instances to confine the accused while awaiting final disposition of his case, instead of permitting him to be liberated on bail. These considerations are as applicable to some adult offenders as to juveniles. Yet the Constitution forbids this result. It is far more important to preserve the basic safe-guards of the Bill of Rights, which were developed as a result of centuries of experience, than it is to sacrifice any one of them in order to achieve a desirable result in an individual case no matter how beneficial it may seem to be for the moment. . . .

The Court concludes that the right to bail exists in cases pending in the Juvenile Court and that hence the petitioner should be admitted to bail until the outcome of the proceeding against him in the Juvenile Court.

(2) Judicial inquiry may be precluded when state statutes speak specifically to the issue of whether or not bail is required. However only 13 states have clearly delineated this issue through legislation. Four states (Hawaii, Kentucky, Oregon and Utah) deny juveniles the right to bail. Nine states (Arkansas, Colorado, Connecticut, Georgia, Massachusetts, Nebraska, Oklahoma, South Dakota and West Virginia) have enacted laws expressly granting juveniles the right to bail. (Some of the latter statutes use the word "bond".)

In the remaining jurisdictions the granting of bail either is made a matter of discretion or is not mentioned at all. It is expressly left to the hearing officer's discretion in 9 states (Delaware, Louisiana, Michigan, Minnesota, Nebraska, South Carolina, Tennessee, Vermont and Virginia). Two states (Maryland and Texas) impliedly provide for such discretionary use of bail. The remaining 26 states and the District of Columbia have no statutory provision with regard to a juvenile's right to bail; it is in this group that the "adequate alternative" jurisprudence has flourished. Section 4.7 of The Juvenile Justice Standards Relating to Interim Status prohibits "use of bail bonds in any form as an alternate interim status . . . ."

(3) The issue of whether bail must be extended to juveniles reached the court through an imaginative argument in Aubry v. Gadbois, 50 Cal.App.3d 470, 123 Cal.Rptr. 365 (1975). A taxpayer sought to enjoin an asserted illegal expenditure of funds by a judge with juvenile jurisdiction. Plaintiff theorized that since a juvenile could be detained without bail pursuant to Calif. Welf. & Inst.Code §§ 635 and 636 for 15 judicial days before a hearing on the offense, while an adult charged with a similar offense would be entitled to bail pending trial, this was a denial of the juvenile's due process rights, equal protection rights, or both. Therefore, because such pretrial detention of juveniles is illegal, it was asserted to involve unlawful expenditure of public funds. Relying on the jurisprudence differentiating between treatment of juvenile and adult offenders, however, the court held that bail was not required by either the California or United States Constitution.

5. PLACE OF DETENTION

OSORIO v. RIOS

United States District Court, District of Puerto Rico, 1976.
429 F.Supp. 570.

LEVIN H. CAMPBELL, CIRCUIT JUDGE.

This class action is brought by certain juvenile offenders in Puerto Rico who were placed in adult jails by judicial order. Plaintiffs contend that 34 L.P.R.A. § 2007(c), a statute allowing courts to put juvenile offenders in adult jails or prisons, violates the Constitution of the United States, and is therefore invalid. The challenged portion of the statute reads as follows:

"No child shall be held in a police station, lockup, jail, or prison, except that, by order of the Judge, setting forth the reasons therefor, a child over 16 years of age whose behavior or condition is such as to endanger his safety or welfare or that of other inmates in the custody center for children, may be put in jail or other place of detention for adults, provided it is a room or apartment entirely separated from the adults confined therein."

. . .

Plaintiffs' equal protection argument is that as they are being punished like adults, they should receive the benefit of the same procedures Puerto Rico gives adults. Under the Puerto Rican Constitution, a person is entitled to a jury trial; and before conviction "every accused shall be entitled to be admitted to bail". Art. II § 11. Incarceration prior to trial is limited to six months. Persons charged with felonies are entitled to trial-type preliminary hearings.

As we have stated above, we are unimpressed with the suggestion that merely by placing a child briefly in an adult lockup the state loses all right to classify him in other ways separately from adult offenders. One can envision many circumstances where the short-term use of an adult detention facility is not incompatible with the separate purposes of the juvenile law. The aim of such short-term utilization of adult facilities is only to restrain the child pending a settled disposition of his case, not punishment, and juveniles no less than adults may require restraint of this nature.

On the other hand, if a child is placed in an adult jail and left there indefinitely—without even the pretense of rehabilitative programs, as in the case at the two adult institutions mentioned herein—it becomes impossible to distinguish meaningfully between his position and that of an adult inmate. True, the child does not receive an adult "record" but, standing alone, we do not think that that is enough to justify depriving the child of the procedural protections afforded an adult where the child, in all other respects, is jailed like a common criminal in an adult jail.

We think that if a juvenile is to be jailed like an adult under the conditions revealed in this proceeding for a substantial, as opposed to a relatively brief, period, the juvenile is denied equal protection of the law unless afforded, prior to incarceration, the same basic procedures granted to adults.

. . .

[In dealing with the plaintiffs' cruel and inhuman punishment arguments, the court further held that "custody under minimally humane conditions in adult jails is not in and of itself violative of the eighth amendment."]

NOTE

Perhaps the primary premise underlying our juvenile justice system to-day is that it should be separate and distinct from the adult criminal justice system. Consonant with this, it has long been recognized that juveniles should not be detained in jails with adults. Section 10.2 of the Juvenile Justice Standards Relating to Interim Status states a prohibition against "interim detention of accused juveniles in any facility or part thereof also used to detain adults . . . ." Even so, cases continue to arise in which such detention practices exist, perhaps through lack of proper training and disciplining of intake personnel or, more likely, through lack of proper facilities for juveniles. Swansey v. Elrod, 386 F.Supp. 1138 (N.D.Ill.1975), is not atypical in this regard.

In *Swansey*, juveniles between ages 13 and 17 were detained an Cook County Jail, an adult facility, pending criminal prosecution. Several of them commenced a civil rights action alleging that confinement in such a location constituted cruel and unusual punishment and violated the equal protection clause. Granting the motion of the juveniles for a preliminary injunction against transferring any more youths to the Cook County jail and denying the defendants' motion to dismiss, the court ruled that there was "sufficient likelihood of success" on both of plaintiffs' claims. As to the eighth amendment argument, it held that though the juveniles had been transferred to adult authority and would thereby receive the "full panoply of criminal constitutional rights" to which an adult would be entitled, this did not mean that juveniles were entitled to no higher degree of care than any other detainee in the criminal justice system. Rather, juveniles still warrant fundamentally different treatment from adults, and a showing by the plaintiffs of possible devastating psychological harm and reprehensible physical results from detention with adults was sufficient to establish a likelihood of success as to their claim.

As to the assertion of a violation of equal protection, the court stated that since juveniles convicted as adults are incarcerated in separate facilities from adults where they can receive adequate rehabilitative services, "incarcerated juveniles under adult jurisdiction who are unconvicted can receive no less." Id. at 1143. Such differential treatment was not justified upon any rational reason by the defendants, and thus the court ruled that plaintiffs had demonstrated a likelihood of success on this claim also.

For other cases containing admonitions against detaining juveniles in adult jails, see Schaffer v. Green, 496 P.2d 375 (Okl.Cr.App.1972); Cox v. Turley, 506 F.2d 1347 (6th Cir. 1974); and Miller v. Carson, 392 F.Supp. 515 (M.D.Fla.1975), modified and remanded 563 F.2d 741 (5th Cir. 1977).

One recent study found that only Arizona, Maryland, Mississippi, Pennsylvania and Rhode Island absolutely prohibit the detention of juveniles in adult jails. Many more states would prohibit jail detention of children under a certain age. Most states require the separation of juveniles from adults in adult facilities. J. L. King, A Comparative Analysis of Juvenile Codes 39–40 (Washington: Office of Juvenile Justice and Delinquency Prevention, 1980).

6. LENGTH OF DETENTION AND RIGHT TO SPEEDY TRIAL

MATTER OF ANTHONY P.

Family Court, New York County, 1980.
104 Misc.2d 1024, 430 N.Y.S.2d 479.

ELRICH A. EASTMAN, J.

Before the court in this juvenile delinquency proceeding is a motion to dismiss the petition on the ground that respondent's right to a speedy trial has been denied. . . .

The facts are undisputed. On July 5, 1978, respondent was arrested as an assault suspect and held overnight by the police. On September 11, 1978 and again on November 3, 1978, respondent participated in lineups relative to the assault incident of July 5, 1978. On January 24, 1980 a petition was filed in the Family Court alleging respondent committed a designated felony act pursuant to section 712 of the Family Court Act.

A SPEEDY TRIAL

Speedy justice has been part of the Anglo-American common-law tradition since the Magna Carta. It became part of our earliest State Constitutions and was subsequently incorporated into the Sixth Amendment to the United States Constitution. . . .

The New York Court of Appeals has held that the Criminal Procedure Law does not govern Family Court procedure. Hence, the speedy trial provisions embodied in CPL 30.30 are not applicable in juvenile delinquency proceedings. Notwithstanding the fact that juveniles are not entitled to all of the procedures set forth in the CPL, "fundamental fairness" dictates that constitutional guarantees be applied to juvenile proceedings where no adverse impact is realized thereby. Thus, the constitutional right to a speedy trial deemed so important by our legal forebears applies equally to juveniles in delinquency proceedings. Accordingly, this respondent is entitled to full protection of his constitutional right to a speedy trial.

. . .

In considering this juvenile's right to a prompt trial, four factors are of primary importance: (1) the length of the delay, (2) the reason for the delay, (3) the degree of actual prejudice to the defendant, and (4) the seriousness of the offense.

Furthermore, because New York's rule is broader than the Federally recognized right to due process, a lengthy and unjustified delay in instituting proceedings may require dismissal even though no actual prejudice to the defendant is shown. The reason for this is clear since both the accused and the public have a right to expect prompt prosecution of acts which, if committed by an adult, would constitute crimes. . . .

. . .

Here, no reason whatever is set forth to constitute good cause for the 18-month delay in bringing the instant petition and thereby depriving the respondent of his constitutional right to a speedy trial. Thus, the matter must be set down for a hearing to determine whether the delay was justified. . . .

NOTES

(1) Appellant, a 13 year old charged with bank robbery, asserted that his right to speedy trial under 18 U.S.C. § 5036 had been violated. United States v. Cuomo, 525 F.2d 1285 (5th Cir. 1976). The court responded:

Section 5036 of Title 18 provides:

If an alleged delinquent who is in detention pending trial is not brought to trial within thirty days from the date upon which such detention was begun, the information shall be dismissed on motion of the alleged delinquent or at the direction of the court, unless the Attorney General shows that additional delay was caused by the juvenile or his counsel, or consented to by the juvenile and his counsel, or would be in the interest of justice in the particular case. Delays attributable solely to court calendar congestion may not be considered in the interest of justice. Except in extraordinary circumstances, an information dismissed under this section may not be reinstituted.

The appellant vigorously contends that he was "detained", within the ambit of § 5036, from the time he was arrested and throughout the time he was released from custody on restrictive bail conditions. Since there were seventy days between the time of his arrest and the time of his trial, he asserts that the information against him must be dismissed. The government, on the other hand, argues that Cuomo was "in detention" only while he was in the El Paso County Jail.

After a discussion as to the meaning of the word "detention", drawing on such sources as the legislative history of the statute, language in other statutes, the "understanding of juvenile court specialists", and judicial opinions, the court stated:

Our conclusion is that the phrase "in detention" in § 5036 means "in physically restrictive detention amounting to institutionalization". Section 5036 was not transgressed by Cuomo's prosecution.

(2) In United States v. Calloway, 505 F.2d 311 (D.C.Cir. 1974), appellant, a 17 year old youth, had been charged with rape and tried and convicted as an adult. On appeal he claimed that he had been denied a speedy trial by the 15 month delay between arrest and trial, during which time he was incarcerated in the D.C. jail. The court reversed appellant's convictions and ordered dismissal of the indictment "for lack of a speedy trial", noting:

The personal prejudice resulting from pre-trial incarceration was exacerbated in the present case by two factors. First, the defendant was a youth being confined in an adult jail. As Judge Wright warned in his dissent in United States v. Bland, 153 U.S.App.D.C. 254, 472 F.2d 1329,

1349–1350 (1972)—in which this court upheld the D.C. statute permitting youths aged 16 and 17 to be tried as adults solely on the basis of the charge filed by the prosecutor—"*I am confident that a child is unlikely to succeed in the long, difficult process of rehabilitation when his teachers during his confinement are adult criminals.*" Subsequent events have shown that this confidence was well placed. Speaking of the D.C. Jail—the institution in which Calloway was confined for almost two years—Judge Wright later wrote:

> The recent prisoners' riot . . . tragically demonstrates the inhumanity as well as the danger of treating children as adults for the purposes of correction and rehabilitation. Apparently one of the causes of the prison riot was the homosexual assaults by the adult prisoners on the 16- and 17-year old children being held in the jail as "adult" prisoners.

The record in this case, too, lends heavy support to the view that confining young offenders with hardened criminals is equivalent to simply abandoning them. In Calloway's jail records there are several entries in which he claims he was homosexually assaulted by other inmates. Moreover, Calloway (and apparently others) were able to secure enough drugs to induce a seizure. As a result he became so hostile and uncommunicative that his lawyers requested permission to withdraw from the case. Finally, when, after serving two years in the D.C. Jail, Calloway was sentenced under the Youth Corrections Act, he immediately "tr[ied] to be a leader of his peers . . . [by] impress[ing] the other inmates with his belligerent attitude." From the date of his arrival at the Youth Center the authorities noted that he "will probably be a problem in the future."

JUVENILE JUSTICE STANDARDS PROJECT, STANDARDS RELATING TO INTERIM STATUS: THE RELEASE, CONTROL, AND DETENTION OF ACCUSED JUVENILE OFFENDERS BETWEEN ARREST AND DISPOSITION, 89–90 (1980) *

7.10 Speedy trial

To curtail detention and reduce the risks of release and control, all juvenile offense cases should be governed by the following timetable:

A. Each case should proceed to trial:

1. within [fifteen days] of arrest or the filing of charges, whichever occurs first, if the accused juvenile has been held in detention by order of a court for more than [twenty-four hours]; or

2. within [thirty days] in all other cases.

B. In any case in which the juvenile is convicted of a criminal offense, a disposition should be carried out:

1. within [fifteen days] of conviction if the juvenile is held in detention by order of a court following conviction; or

---

* Reprinted with permission from Standards Relating to Interim Status, copyright 1980, Ballinger Publishing Company.

  2. within [thirty days] of conviction in all other cases.

  The time prescribed for carrying out the disposition may be extended at the request of the juvenile, if necessary in order to secure a better placement.

  C. The limits stated in A. and B. may be extended not more than [sixty days] if the juvenile is released, and not more than [thirty days] if the juvenile is in detention, when:

    1. the prosecution certifies that a witness or other evidence necessary to the state's case will not be available, despite the prosecution's best efforts, during the original time limits;

    2. any proceeding concerning waiver of the juvenile court's jurisdiction is pending;

    3. a motion for change of venue made by either the prosecutor or the juvenile is pending; or

    4. a request for extradition is pending.

  D. The limits stated in A. and B. may also be extended for specified periods authorized by the court when:

    1. the juvenile is a fugitive from court proceedings; or

    2. deferred adjudication or disposition for a specific period has been agreed to in writing by the juvenile and his or her attorney.

  E. The limits in A. and B. may be phased in during a period not to exceed [twelve months] from the effective date of adoption of these standards, in order to enable a court to obtain the necessary resources to adjudicate cases on the merits. During such period, the maximum limit for detention cases should be [thirty days] from arrest to trial and [thirty days] from trial to final disposition.

  F. In any case in which trial or disposition fails to meet these standards, the charges should be dismissed with prejudice.

NOTE

  Most states have statutory provisions dealing with when a petition must be filed and when an adjudicatory hearing must be held. In Doe v. State of New Mexico, 88 N.M. 644, 545 P.2d 1022 (App.1976), the Court of Appeals of New Mexico held that failure to comply with the state's statutory time limit was grounds for dismissing the petition with prejudice.

  Other cases dealing with a juvenile's right to a speedy trial are Sanchez v. Walker County Department of Family and Children Services, 237 Ga. 406, 229 S.E.2d 66 (1976); J. B. H. v. State, 139 Ga.App. 199, 228 S.E.2d 189 (1976); In re Russell C., 120 N.H. 260, 414 A.2d 934 (1980); State in the Interest of C. B., 173 N.J.Super. 424, 414 A.2d 572 (1980); In re F. E. B., 133 Vt. 463, 346 A.2d 191 (1975).

VII. TRANSFER BETWEEN COURTS

A. THE CONSTITUTIONAL IMPLICATIONS

KENT v. UNITED STATES

Supreme Court of the United States, 1966.
383 U.S. 541, 86 S.Ct. 1045, 16 L.Ed.2d 84.

(The opinion of the Court appears at page 201, supra.)

B. THE NATURE OF A TRANSFER HEARING

KEMPLEN v. MARYLAND

United States Court of Appeals, Fourth Circuit, 1970.
428 F.2d 169.

CRAVEN, CIRCUIT JUDGE:

The primary question presented by this appeal is whether a state may, in enforcing its criminal laws, elect to proceed against a juvenile as if he were an adult without his having counsel at the "waiver hearing" in the juvenile court. We think not, and reverse the decision of the district court denying habeas corpus relief to John Wayne Kemplen.

According to the petition, the petitioner was 17 years old at the time of his arrest on February 17, 1965. The next day he appeared, without counsel, before the Juvenile Court of Harford County, Maryland, for a determination of whether he should be tried as a juvenile or as an adult. Kemplen and his parents were present at this "waiver hearing." Kemplen was not, however, informed of any right to retain counsel for the hearing, nor was counsel appointed for him by the court. The juvenile court ordered its jurisdiction waived without making any specific findings of fact. Petitioner was tried as an adult by the Circuit Court of Harford County on August 13, 1965, and was sentenced to two years' imprisonment in the Maryland Correctional Institution for larceny, and malicious damage to property. . . . .

387

WAIVER OF JUVENILE JURISDICTION: RIGHT
TO COUNSEL AND TO NOTICE

. . .

The Supreme Court stated in *Gault* that "neither the Fourteenth Amendment nor the Bill of Rights is for adults alone."

. . .

. . . We must consider Kemplen's claims in this context.

. . .

There is no proceeding for adults comparable directly to the juvenile jurisdiction waiver hearing. . . . By deciding the waiver issue, the juvenile court determines whether the accused, if found guilty, will receive nonpunitive rehabilitation as a juvenile from the state's social service agencies or will be sentenced as an adult. The state argues that this is not a critical stage in the guilt determining process. But, it seems to us nothing can be more critical to the accused than determining *whether there will be a guilt determining process in an adult-type criminal trial.* The waiver proceeding can result in dire consequences indeed for the guilty accused. If the juvenile court decides to keep jurisdiction, he can be detained only until he reaches majority. But, if jurisdiction is waived to the adult court, the accused may be incarcerated for much longer, depending upon the gravity of the offense, and, if the offense be a felony, lose certain of his rights of citizenship.

For Kemplen, waiver proved to be a very critical stage in the proceedings against him. He received a two year active prison sentence rather than commitment to a training school for rehabilitation.

. . .

The Supreme Court has been careful to require that sentencing of convicted adult defendants be carried out in strictest compliance with Fourteenth Amendment due process requirements. In holding that the Sixth Amendment right to counsel extends to the sentencing in state court of a convicted adult offender and that sentencing is a critical stage in the criminal proceeding, the Court quoted from its decision in Townsend v. Burke, 334 U.S. 736, 68 S.Ct. 1252, 92 L.Ed. 1690 (1948): "In this case, counsel might not have changed the sentence, but he could have taken steps to see that the conviction and sentence were not predicated on misinformation or misreading of court records, a requirement of fair play which absence of counsel withheld from this prisoner. 334 U.S. at 741, 68 S.Ct. at 1255." This rationale applies no less to a waiver of juvenile jurisdiction that renders the juvenile susceptible to adult sentencing and which is more likely to be based on misinformation without counsel's presence. Counsel is of special importance at waiver proceedings because he can provide the juvenile judge with information about the child's background and prior record which may be otherwise unavailable in practice due to the tremendous load now carried by understaffed juvenile courts and social service agencies. The statutory framework for dealing with juvenile offenders contemplates that those under the age of eighteen are to be treated as juveniles and that juvenile jurisdiction is to be waived only where the offender is found, by an exercise of sound judicial discretion based upon a thorough investigation, to be an unfit subject for juvenile rehabilitative measures. Counsel for the accused presumably can marshal information favorable to his client and suggest to the court alternative schemes for rehabilitative disposition. "The child's advocate should search for a plan, or perhaps a range of plans, which may persuade the court that the welfare of the child and the safety of the community can be served without waiver." Haziel v. United States, 404 F.2d 1275 (D.C. Cir. 1968) (interpreting *Kent* and the District of Columbia juvenile statute). "[I]n all cases children need advocates to speak for them and guard their interests, particularly when disposition decisions are made. It is the disposition stage at which the opportunity arises to offer individualized treatment plans and in which the danger inheres that the court's coercive power will be applied without adequate knowledge of the circumstances." *Gault*, 387 U.S. at 38, 87 S.Ct. at 1450, n. 65, quoting from the National Crime Commission Report.

The juvenile jurisdiction waiver proceeding may also be viewed as the only point in Kemplen's criminal proceeding where he could assert the "defense" that he was a juvenile when the offense was committed and that he was a proper subject for juvenile rehabilitative treatment. Juvenile status is, in effect, a basis upon which a youthful offender can plead diminished responsibility for his unlawful act. If he can show that juvenile jurisdiction should not be waived by the court, he is not subject to the usual adult penal sanctions. A criminal accused is entitled to counsel at any point in a criminal action at which he must assert a defense or lose its benefit. A juvenile facing possible waiver of juvenile jurisdiction is no less entitled to advice of counsel.

For the reasons stated, we hold that the Sixth Amendment, as applied to the states by the Fourteenth Amendment, requires that an accused be allowed to retain counsel to represent and advise him at a hearing concerning the waiver of juvenile jurisdiction over the accused or, if the accused be indigent, that counsel be appointed to there represent and advise him.

In order that child, parents, and counsel may have a reasonable opportunity to prepare the child's case as to waiver, due process demands that they be given adequate notice of the nature of the proceeding, its date, and the charges to be considered. Arrest on one day and waiver on the next, as in Kemplen's case, does not comport with this requirement. Under such circumstances, justice can be unconstitutionally swift. If the right to counsel insured by our holding above is to be of value, adequate notice must likewise be guaranteed. We so hold.

. . .

Reversed and remanded.

ON PETITION FOR REHEARING

Although we think Maryland's petition for rehearing should be denied, we are not unsympathetic with the expressed perplexity of her attorney general regarding the proper remedy on remand. We adhere to our decision that the right to counsel in a juvenile waiver proceeding must be accorded retroactivity. Without delimiting the range of remedies left open by *Kent*, we think the proper remedy for this petitioner, on the facts of this case, will be the reconstruction in the Maryland courts, or failing that in the United States District Court, of the circumstances bearing on the waiver question and a determination *nunc pro tunc* or what the juvenile court judge would probably have done in light of all the information then available that might reasonably have been proffered by competent counsel.

If Kemplen was not represented by counsel at his waiver hearing, or if notice of that hearing was inadequate, or both, these factors alone will not entitle him to relief from his conviction. But either one will entitle him to a de novo determination of whether, "waiver was appropriate." If the court finds that waiver was inappropriate, Kemplen's conviction must be vacated. He may not be tried again because he has served his full adult sentence and is over 21. If it finds that the waiver order was appropriate when made, despite lack of counsel and/or lack of proper notice his adult conviction will stand and relief will be denied.

. . .

COUNCIL OF JUDGES, NATIONAL COUNCIL ON CRIME AND DELINQUENCY: MODEL RULES FOR JUVENILE COURTS (1969)

Rule 9. Initiation of Proceeding

If at any time after the filing of a petition and before the commencement of the adjudicatory hearing the court is informed that the child is legally subject to transfer to criminal court and that there is reason to believe that retention of jurisdiction in the juvenile court is contrary to the best interests of the child or the public, a transfer hearing may be scheduled, and the probation department shall conduct a transfer investigation.

Rule 10. Notice of Transfer Hearing

Upon the scheduling of a hearing under Rule 9, the summons provisions of Rules 20 and 21 shall apply. The summons shall also contain a statement that the child may be transferred to the jurisdiction of the criminal court if the court finds at the hearing that retention of jurisdiction is contrary to the best interests of the child or the public. After the hearing is scheduled, the court shall serve a copy of the petition and notice of the transfer hearing on the [appropriate prosecutor's office].

Rule 11. Transfer Hearing

The transfer hearing shall not commence until the transfer investigation has been completed and is embodied in a written report. This report shall include all social records that are to be made available to the court at the hearing. If the report has not been completed, or if the court wishes additional information not contained in the report, the hearing may be continued.

Unless privately obtained, counsel shall be appointed to represent the child at the transfer hearing.

The report of the transfer investigation shall be made available to counsel for all parties before or at the commencement of the hearing.

If, after the transfer hearing, the court orders the case to be transferred to criminal court, it shall make and enter specific findings supporting its decision, separate from the order of transfer. Such written findings shall be available to any court in which the transfer is challenged.

JUVENILE JUSTICE STANDARDS PROJECT, STANDARDS RELATING TO TRANSFER BETWEEN COURTS *

2.1 Time requirements

A. Within two court days of the filing of any petition alleging conduct which constitutes a Class One Juvenile Offense against a person who was sixteen or seventeen years of age when the alleged offense occurred, the clerk of the juvenile court should give the prosecuting attorney written notice of the possibility of waiver.

B. Within three court days of the filing of any petition alleging conduct which constitutes a Class One Juvenile Offense against a person who was sixteen or seventeen years of age when the alleged offense occurred, the prosecuting attorney should give such person written notice, multilingual if appropriate, of the possibility of waiver.

C. Within seven court days of the filing of any petition alleging conduct which constitutes a Class One Juvenile Offense against a person who was sixteen or seventeen years of age when the alleged offense occurred, the prosecuting attorney may request by written motion that the juvenile court waive its jurisdiction over the juvenile.

* Reprinted with permission from Standards Relating to Transfer Between Courts, Copyright 1980, Ballinger Publishing Company.

The prosecuting attorney should deliver a signed, acknowledged copy of the waiver motion to the juvenile and counsel for the juvenile within twenty-four hours after the filing of such motion in the juvenile court.

D.   The juvenile court should initiate a hearing on waiver within ten court days of the filing of the waiver motion or, if the juvenile seeks to suspend this requirement, within a reasonable time thereafter.

E.   The juvenile court should issue a written decision setting forth its findings and the reasons therefor, including a statement of the evidence relied on in reaching the decision, within ten court days after conclusion of the waiver hearing.

F.   No waiver notice should be given, no waiver motion should be accepted for filing, no waiver hearing should be initiated, and no waiver decision should be issued relating to any juvenile court petition after commencement of any adjudicatory hearing relating to any transaction or episode alleged in that petition.

.   .   .

2.3   The hearing

A.   The juvenile should be represented by counsel at the waiver hearing. The clerk of the juvenile court should give written notice to the juvenile, multilingual if appropriate, of this requirement at least five court days before commencement of the waiver hearing.

B.   The juvenile court should appoint counsel to represent any juvenile unable to afford representation by counsel at the waiver hearing. The clerk of the juvenile court should give written notice to the juvenile, multilingual if appropriate, of this right at least five court days before commencement of the waiver hearing.

C.   The juvenile court should pay the reasonable fees and expenses of an expert witness for the juvenile if the juvenile desires, but is unable to afford, the services of such an expert witness at the waiver hearing.

D.   The juvenile should have access to all evidence available to the juvenile court which could be used either to support or contest the waiver motion.

E.   The prosecuting attorney should bear the burden of proving that probable cause exists to believe that the juvenile has committed a Class One Juvenile Offense and that the juvenile is not a proper person for handling by the juvenile court.

F.   The juvenile may contest the waiver motion by challenging, or producing evidence tending to challenge, the evidence of the prosecuting attorney.

G. The juvenile may examine any person who prepared any report concerning the juvenile which is presented at the waiver hearing.

H. All evidence presented at the waiver hearing should be under oath and subject to cross-examination.

I. The juvenile may remain silent at the waiver hearing. No admission by the juvenile during the waiver hearing should be admissible to establish guilt or to impeach testimony in any subsequent criminal proceeding.

J. The juvenile may disqualify the presiding officer at the waiver hearing from presiding at any subsequent criminal trial or juvenile court adjudicatory hearing relating to any transaction or episode alleged in the petition initiating juvenile court proceedings.

2.4 Appeal

A. The juvenile or the prosecuting attorney may file an appeal of the waiver decision with the court authorized to hear appeals from final judgments of the juvenile court within seven court days of the decision of the juvenile court.

B. The appellate court should render its decision expeditiously, according the findings of the juvenile court the same weight given the findings of the highest court of general trial jurisdiction.

C. No criminal court should have jurisdiction in any proceeding, relating to any transaction or episode alleged in the juvenile court petition as to which a waiver motion was made, against any person over whom the juvenile court has waived jurisdiction, until the time for filing an appeal from that determination has passed or, if such an appeal has been filed, until the final decision of the appellate court has been issued.

SOME RECURRING ISSUES

RIGHT TO COUNSEL

Kent did not finally decide the issue of right to counsel at the waiver hearing, since the Court was not faced with that issue. Morris Kent had retained counsel. Yet the Court did state that "there is no place in our system of law for reaching a result of such tremendous consequences without ceremony—without hearing, without effective assistance of counsel." 383 U.S. at 554, 86 S.Ct. at 1053. *Kemplen,* using a "critical stage" analysis, makes clear that under *Kent* and *Gault* a juvenile is constitutionally entitled to counsel at a waiver hearing.

Counsel has a critical role to play at juvenile waiver hearings. The child's counsel can gather information favorable to his client, scrutinize the reports of the social staff, and suggest alternatives for handling the child within the juvenile process. "The child's advocate should search for a plan, or perhaps a range of plans, which may persuade the court that the welfare of the child and the safety of the community can be served without waiver." Haziel v. United States, 404 F.2d 1275 (D.C.Cir. 1968).

Providing the child with a right to counsel implies a right to effective or competent counsel. The combined effect of a failure to appoint counsel until a waiver hearing was about to begin and "counsel's notable lack of zeal" in attempting to present the court alternatives to waiver of the child, led the Seventh Circuit to conclude the juvenile had been denied the effective assistance of counsel, rendering his transfer to adult court invalid. Geboy v. Gray, 471 F.2d 575 (7th Cir. 1973). Mere lateness of appointment of counsel does not establish ineffective assistance. In People v. Banks, 29 Ill.App.3d 923, 331 N.E.2d 561 (1975), the court held that an attorney appointed to represent the child was not denied adequate time to prepare when the transfer hearing was held on the day of counsel's appointment, especially in light of counsel's prior representation of the child in other recent delinquency proceedings. Should lateness of appointment create a presumption of ineffective assistance? What if counsel in *Banks* had objected to going forward with the transfer hearing?

A difficult issue is that of waiver of the right to counsel at a transfer hearing. The Juvenile Justice Standards Relating to Transfer Between Courts and the Model Rules for Juvenile Courts of the National Council on Crime and Delinquency do not permit waiver of the right to counsel at a transfer hearing. The Commentary to Section 2.3(a) of the Standards and Rule 11 of the Model Rules stresses the critical importance of the presence of counsel at the transfer hearing, concluding that the absolute prohibition of waiver of counsel at that stage is the better rule.

The issue usually arises when the juvenile pleads guilty or goes to trial in the criminal court without having objected to the failure to appoint counsel at the waiver hearing. The general rule is that a guilty plea operates to waive any nonjurisdictional defects. Courts disagree, however, over whether procedural irregularities constitute jurisdictional defects. Acuna v. Baker, 418 F.2d 639 (10th Cir. 1969) held that a guilty plea by a juvenile in the criminal court waives denial of the right to counsel at the waiver hearing. Powell v. Hocker, 453 F.2d 652 (9th Cir. 1971), reached the opposite conclusion, holding that a guilty plea in the subsequent adult case does not waive a defect in the transfer proceedings. Crumley v. State, 3 Tenn.Cr.App. 835, 462 S.W.2d 252 (1970) and Neller v. State, 79 N.M. 528, 445 P.2d 949 (1968), are cases in accord with the Tenth Circuit's decision in *Acuna.* On the other hand, in State v. Grenz, 243 N.W.2d 375 (N.D.1976), the court held that denial of the right to counsel at the waiver hearing is a jurisdictional defect not waived by the guilty plea in criminal court, and James v. Cox, 323 F.Supp. 15 (E.D.Va.1971), held that a juvenile's failure to request counsel at the transfer proceeding did not amount to a waiver. Of course, if the juvenile is represented by competent counsel and fails to raise any claim of irregularities during the transfer proceedings, the guilty plea operates as a waiver of the irregularities. State v. LePage, 536 S.W.2d 834 (Mo. App.1976).

In Texas the juvenile court must conduct a diagnostic study of the child as a mandatory precondition to transfer to adult court. Where the child's attorney refused to permit him to answer any questions concerning the homicide he was alleged to have committed it was error for the juvenile court judge to hold such refusal a waiver of the right to the diagnostic study. Further the appellate court held the attorney alone could not make an effective waiver of any substantial right of the child without the presence and concurrence of the subject child. R.E.M. v. State, 532 S.W.2d 645 (Tex.Civ.App. 1975).

NOTICE

Notice of the waiver hearing to the child, his parents and counsel is a constitutional requirement. Reasonable notice of the waiver hearing and the charge to be considered and a reasonable opportunity to prepare a defense must be given. See State v. McArdle, 156 W.Va. 409, 194 S.E.2d 174 (1973), where the waiver was held invalid for lack of prior notice and opportunity to prepare a defense even though the child's parents and counsel were present at the waiver hearing. See also State v. Grenz, 243 N.W.2d 375 (N.D.1976), in which the court held adequate notice constitutionally required.

Model Rule 10 expressly requires adequate notice of the transfer hearing, including a statement of the purpose of the hearing. Reed v. State, 125 Ga.App. 568, 188 S.E.2d 392 (1972), held that the failure to meet statutory notice requirements was not waived by the appearance of the parents at the hearing since they may not have known the purpose of the hearing. Ferguson v. Slayton, 340 F.Supp. 276 (W.D. Va.1972), is another case where the failure to notify parents of a transfer hearing rendered a subsequent conviction void. In L.C.L. v. State, 319 So.2d 133 (Fla.App.1975) the court held it reversible error to proceed with a waiver hearing where defendant's mother had not been sent a summons even though the child's sister with whom he was living was present and he was represented by counsel. Similarly, in In re D.W.M., 562 S.W.2d 851 (Tex.1978), the court held that failure to give notice to the *juvenile* as required by statute invalidated the waiver and transfer.

There are, however, cases to the contrary on the issue of waiver of the right to notice. A Colorado notice requirement that parents be served with a summons prior to the beginning of a transfer proceeding was found to be waived in In re People In Interest of G.A.T., 183 Colo. 111, 515 P.2d 104 (1973), when the mother voluntarily appeared at the hearing. In Turner v. Commonwealth, 216 Va. 666, 222 S.E.2d 517 (1976), the court held that failure to give notice is a procedural rather than jurisdictional defect, and the defect was cured in this case because all necessary parties actually appeared at the waiver hearing. Failure to notify the natural father and adoptive mother of the transfer hearing was not error where the child's natural mother acted as guardian ad litem and he was represented by counsel. Matter of Honsaker, 539 S.W.2d 198 (Tex.Civ.App. 1976). In that case the court stated: "The natural father and adoptive mother are not parties to the lawsuit, and no contention is advanced that they have parental rights which might be affected by the [transfer] hearing." See also In re Juvenile, 364 Mass. 531, 306 N.E.2d 822 (1974).

PRESENTATION OF EVIDENCE

A juvenile has a right to the production of witnesses and records that are needed to resist a petition for waiver to an adult court. In re Brown, 183 N.W.2d 731 (Iowa 1971).

The Juvenile Justice Standards Relating to Transfer Between Courts Section 2.3(C), provide for the services of expert witnesses to resist the motion for transfer at court expense for indigents.

Some state statutes guarantee the child and his attorney access to social reports prepared by the court or its probation staff. See, e.g., Mo.Ann.Stat. § 211.401 (1969); Okla.Stat.Ann. Tit. 10, § 1112(b) (Supp.1982); Tex. Family Code Ann. § 54.02 (1975). See note 4, p. 208, Chapter III for discussion of access to social reports.

RULES OF EVIDENCE

The rules of evidence are not always strictly followed at a waiver hearing, largely because courts tend to view the waiver hearing as dispositional in nature. Representative cases to that effect are Vincent v. State, 349 So.2d 1145 (Ala.1977); People v. Taylor, 76 Ill.2d 289, 29 Ill.Dec. 103, 391 N.E.2d 366 (1979); and In re M.W.N., 590 P.2d 692 (Okl.Cr.App.1979). Thus, social reports, though hearsay in character, are admissible. See, e.g., People v. Taylor, supra; In re Murphy, 15 Md.App. 434, 291 A.2d 867. Of course, this is tempered by the *Kent* mandate that the juvenile's counsel must have access to social reports to be used at a waiver proceeding and an opportunity to challenge or impeach the findings. Hazell v. State, 12 Md.App. 144, 277 A.2d 639 (1971). Probation officers' reports, law enforcement officers' reports and arrest records are other items that may be admitted though in the nature of hearsay. In re T.D.S., 289 N.W.2d 137 (Minn.1980); Sheppard v. Rhay, 73 Wn.2d 734, 440 P.2d 422 (1968). Even illegally seized evidence, where it was found to be reliable, has been held admissible in a waiver hearing. Marvin v. State, 95 Nev. 836, 603 P.2d 1056 (1979).

Is a waiver hearing dispositional if in addition to a finding of nonamenability a state requires a finding of probable cause to believe the juvenile committed the alleged delinquent act? At least one state provides by statute that hearsay or other incompetent evidence is not admissible to support a probable cause finding. N.C.Gen.Stat.Ann.

§ 7A–609(c) (1981). The Juvenile Justice Standards recognize the distinction between the two required findings. Standard 2.2(B) of the Standards Relating to Transfer Between Courts provides that only evidence that would be admissible in an adjudicatory hearing is admissible to support a finding of probable cause in a waiver hearing, whereas Standard 2.2(C) provides that on the issue of nonamenability evidence is admissible that would be admissible in a dispositional hearing. The rationale for this view is set forth in the Commentary to Standard 2.2(B) at pp. 35–36: to encourage reliable fact finding and judicial economy. Use of evidence that would not be admissible in a subsequent adjudicatory hearing or criminal trial would be a waste of time and effort.

Even if hearsay or other incompetent evidence is admissible in support of a transfer decision there may be some point at which the sole ground of the state's case for transfer is hearsay. When this occurs, it may be argued the juvenile's constitutional rights to confront and cross-examine the witnesses against him has been denied. See In re Harris, 218 Kan. 625, 544 P.2d 1403 (1976) (all state's evidence of nonamenability to juvenile treatment based on written reports admitted over hearsay objection of juvenile's attorney—held transfer order error); People ex rel. Guggenheim v. Mucci, 77 Misc. 2d 41, 352 N.Y.S.2d 561 (Sup.Ct., Kings County), affirmed 46 A.D.2d 683, 360 N.Y.S.2d 71 (1974) (due process requires that probable cause determination not be based solely on hearsay).

One might think that occasionally a juvenile might benefit from relaxed application of the rules of evidence. In People v. Reese, 90 Ill.App.3d 284, 45 Ill.Dec. 597, 412 N.E.2d 1179 (1980), however, the court, while holding hearsay admissible to sustain a nonamenability finding, emphasized the differences between a waiver hearing and an adjudicatory hearing or criminal trial and held that the trial court did not abuse its discretion in refusing to admit the juvenile's offer of polygraph evidence to refute the hearsay offered by the state.

STANDARD OF PROOF

The standard of proof applied at the waiver hearing varies from jurisdiction to jurisdiction, from substantial evidence, In re G.L.W., 580 P.2d 998 (Okl.Cr.App. 1978), to clear and convincing evidence, Mass.Gen. Laws Ann. ch. 119, § 61 (Supp.1981), to perhaps the most common standard, preponderance of the evidence, In re F.S., 586 P.2d 607 (Alaska 1978); Hazell v. State, 12 Md.App. 144, 277 A.2d 639 (1971). In re Winship, 397 U.S. 358, 90 S.Ct. 1068, 25 L.Ed.2d 368 (1970), which held that the applicable standard of proof in delinquency cases is proof beyond a reasonable doubt, was expressly limited to the adjudicatory hearing.

The Juvenile Justice Standards reject the preponderance standard for the requirement of a finding by clear and convincing evidence in 2.2(C). "The finding that a juvenile is not a proper person to be handled by the juvenile court must include determinations, *by clear and convincing evidence,* . . . " (emphasis added). <u>Will the choice of standard of proof really make a functional difference at transfer hearings?</u>

<u>Can the burden of proof ever constitutionally be placed on the ju-</u>venile to show amenability to juvenile treatment? Section 707(c) of California's Welfare and Institutions Code provides:

> With regard to a minor alleged to be [delinquent] by reason of the violation, when he or she was 16 years of age or older, of any of the offenses listed in subdivision (b) [murder, arson, armed robbery, forcible rape, forcible sodomy, kidnapping, aggravated assault, and other serious crimes], upon motion of the petitioner made prior to the attachment of jeopardy the court shall cause the probation officer to investigate and submit a report on the behavioral patterns and social history of the minor being considered for a determination of unfitness. Following submission and consideration of the report, and of any other relevant evidence which the petitioner or the minor may wish to submit the minor shall be presumed to be not a fit and proper subject to be dealt with under the juvenile court law unless the juvenile court concludes, based upon evidence, which evidence may be of extenuating or mitigating circumstances, that the minor would be amenable to the care, treatment, and training program available through the facilities of the juvenile court . . . .

In Sheila O. v. Superior Court of City and County of San Francisco, 125 Cal.App.3d 812, 178 Cal.Rptr. 418 (1981) the court upheld as constitutional the § 707 presumption of unfitness for juvenile court treatment, saying:

> Petitioner . . . contends that the presumed fact of unfitness cannot reasonably be said . . . to flow from the proved fact of age and the charge of a serious crime. But the tangible effect of the new language in Section 707 was to lower the age of adult criminal responsibility for specified crimes unless the minor could show reasons why he should be treated as a juvenile. That change in juvenile court law was well within the power of the Legislature.

178 Cal.Rptr. at 421.

For operation of the California statute, see People v. Superior Court of Yuba County, 122 Cal.App.3d 263, 175 Cal.Rptr. 733 (1981). See also Commonwealth v. Wallace, 495 Pa. 295, 433 A.2d 856 (1981) upholding a similar Pennsylvania statute requiring the juvenile seeking return to juvenile court to bear the burden of showing his or her need of and amenability to juvenile court treatment.

<u>Statistics from Los Angeles County strongly indicate that the shift in the burden of proof to 16 and 17 year olds charged with certain offenses pursuant to § 707(c) has resulted in far more transfers</u> from juvenile to adult court. In 1979, 602 transfer hearings were

held resulting in 250 (42%) transfers. In 1980, under the new section 707, 814 hearings were held producing 507 (62%) transfers. Juvenile Court Coordinators Yearly Judicial Workload Report (Delinquency) Los Angeles County, California 1979 and 1980.

SELF INCRIMINATION

Commonwealth v. Ransom, 446 Pa. 457, 288 A.2d 762 (1972), held that evidence given at a waiver hearing shall not be admissible as evidence against the child in any case or proceeding in any other court. See also State v. Ross, 516 S.W.2d 311 (Mo.App.1974) and Mo. Ann.Stat. § 211.271 (1969).

Section 2.3(I) of the Juvenile Justice Standards reads: "The juvenile may remain silent at the waiver hearing. No admission by the juvenile during the waiver hearing should be admissible to establish guilt or to impeach testimony in any subsequent criminal proceeding." Should the juvenile's refusal to confess be used as an index of nonamenability and uncooperative attitude to justify a transfer? See R.E.M. v. State, 532 S.W.2d 645 (Tex.Civ.App. 1975). Should the protection of § 2.3(I) of the Transfer Standards be extended to bar the admissibility of the child's statements made at the transfer hearing at a subsequent adjudicatory hearing if juvenile court jurisdiction is retained?

In Sheila O. v. Superior Court, 125 Cal.App.3d 812, 178 Cal.Rptr. 418 (1981) the court held that statements made by a juvenile at his or her transfer hearing are inadmissible at the subsequent adjudicatory hearing except for the purpose of impeaching the juvenile's testimony.

APPEAL

Most states today do not permit immediate appeal of the order of the juvenile court transferring the child to adult court. The prevailing rule requires a final judgment on the merits in adult court prior to obtaining appellate review of the transfer decision. See, e.g., People v. Browning, 45 Cal.App.3d 125, 119 Cal.Rptr. 420 (1975); D.H. v. People, 192 Colo. 542, 561 P.2d 5 (1977); In re Clay, 246 N.W.2d 263 (Iowa 1976); In re T.J.H., 479 S.W.2d 433 (Mo.1972); W.C.H. v. Matthews, 536 S.W.2d 679 (Tex.Civ.App. 1976). In a subsequent review of the *T.J.H.* case the Missouri Court of Appeals issued a writ of prohibition against the juvenile court judge who transferred the case. State ex rel. T.J.H. v. Bills, 495 S.W.2d 722 (Mo.App.1973). For a contrary view on the use of the writ of prohibition to sidestep the final judgment rule with regard to a juvenile transfer order see W.C.H. v. Matthews, supra.

On the other hand, some states allow immediate appeal of a waiver order on the ground that it is a final order in the sense that it terminates the jurisdiction of the juvenile court. See, e.g., In re Doe

I, 50 Hawaii 537, 444 P.2d 459 (1968); In re I.Q.S., 309 Minn. 78, 244 N.W.2d 30 (1976); State ex rel. Atcheson, 575 P.2d 181 (Utah 1978).

In still other states appealability of a waiver order depends on which party seeks to appeal. Illinois does not permit the juvenile to appeal because the waiver order is reviewable on appeal of the conviction in criminal court, People v. Jiles, 43 Ill.2d 145, 251 N.E.2d 529 (1969), but does permit the state to appeal a denial of motion to transfer because such an order is not reviewable at the conclusion of the proceedings in juvenile court, People v. Martin, 67 Ill.2d 462, 367 N.E.2d 1329 (1977). But in Oregon the juvenile is allowed to appeal because the effect of an order transferring jurisdiction to the criminal court is to terminate the jurisdiction of the juvenile court, In re Little, 241 Or. 557, 407 P.2d 627 (1965), whereas the state can not appeal because the effect of an order denying the state's motion to transfer is that the status quo is maintained and jurisdiction continues in the juvenile court, In re Brown, 33 Or.App. 423, 576 P.2d 830 (1978).

Sometimes it is not clear whether the appropriate procedure is appeal of the waiver order or motion to dismiss the indictment on the adult prosecution. See, e.g., Murphy v. State 403 So.2d 314 (Ala.Civ. App. 1981).

For the problems caused by the subject of the waiver order outgrowing the maximum age for juvenile court jurisdiction while awaiting appeal of the waiver order, see Brown v. Cox, 319 F.Supp. 999 (E.D.Va.1970), reversed and remanded, 467 F.2d 1255 (4th Cir. 1972). In light of this problem, Standard 2.4 provides that transfer decisions are appealable and stays criminal court jurisdiction until the appeal is decided or the time to file an appeal has elapsed.

See M. Paulsen and C. Whitebread, Juvenile Law and Procedure 150 n. 24 (1974), for additional cases on both sides of the issue of immediate appeal of the waiver order. See also Note, Review of Improper Transfer Hearings, 60 Va.L.Rev. 818 (1974), in which the author recommends the direct appeal of waiver orders because of the difficulties of reviewing improper transfer hearings at a later date.

STATEMENT OF REASONS

The requirement set forth in *Kent* of a statement of reasons by the juvenile court judge justifying the decision to transfer the child to adult court lessens the chance that the judge will consider the waiver decision lightly, and make a hasty and unreasoned decision. See Whitebread and Batey, Transfer Between Courts: Proposals of the Juvenile Justice Standards Project, 63 Va.L.Rev. 221, 240–41 (1977). The written statement of reasons also enhances meaningful review by the appellate court. In the words of the Supreme Court of Indiana, the waiver order is to be such that a reviewing court is not "remitted to assumptions" about the reasons for the order. Atkins v. State, 259 Ind. 596, 600, 290 N.E.2d 441, 444 (1972).

If a juvenile court's order is not accompanied by a sufficient statement of reasons, the waiver order is invalid. See C.L.A. v. State, 137 Ga.App. 511, 224 S.E.2d 491 (1976); Hopkins v. State, 209 So.2d 841 (Miss.1968); State v. Kemper, 535 S.W.2d 241 (Mo.App.1975); and J.T.P. v. State, 544 P.2d 1270 (Okl.Cr.App. 1975). Contra, State v. Jiminez, 109 Ariz. 305, 509 P.2d 198 (1973) (the failure of the juvenile court to provide a written statement of reasons for the transfer was harmless error.) How formal should the required statement be? See In re Honsaker, 539 S.W.2d 198 (Tex.Civ.App. 1976); O.A.H. v. State, 332 So.2d 641 (Fla.App.1976); and especially In re B., 619 S.W.2d 584 (Tex.Civ.App. 1981), where the transferring juvenile court judge merely parroted the statutory language in his statement of reasons for transfer. The Texas Court of Civil Appeals found that, so long as those reasons have evidentiary support in the record, no more detailed statement is required.

C. WHO SHOULD BE WAIVED? ASSESSING STATUTORY CRITERIA

MATTER OF JOHNSON

Court of Special Appeals of Maryland, 1973.
17 Md.App. 705, 304 A.2d 859.

GILBERT, JUSTICE.

. . .

The Legislature has mandated that five factors are to be considered by the juvenile judge in any waiver proceeding. Md.Ann.Code art. 26, § 70–16(b). Those factors are:

"(1) Age of child.

(2) Mental and physical condition of child.

(3) The child's amenability to treatment in any institution, facility, or programs available to delinquents.

(4) The nature of the offense.

(5) The safety of the public."

Not all of the five factors need be resolved against the juvenile in order for the waiver to be justifiable.

. . .

In the instant case, the appellant, Diane Connie Johnson, was charged in a "Petition" filed in the Juvenile Court on August 16, 1972, with being a delinquent child, "For the reason that on May 21, 1972, Hrs. 5:30 p.m. . . . [she] unlawfully in a grossly negligent manner did kill and slay Lawrence Brittingham, [age 2 years]." Miss Johnson was 16 years of age at the time of the occurrence.

On September 14, 1972, the State's Attorney for Baltimore City sought a waiver of jurisdiction. The waiver hearing was held on

November 1, 1972, at which time the appellant was 17 years of age. At the hearing, the judge stated that the "ground rules" were to be "an examination of the five criteria set forth in the statute to determine whether or not to waive jurisdiction." The Assistant State's Attorney then told the juvenile court judge:

> ". . . [T]he basis for the State's request for waiver is that this charge is too serious to be tried in juvenile court."

The State then stated to the judge that:

> "[Miss Johnson], who is an unlicensed driver, asked the boy friend, who was twenty-one years old and is a licensed driver, if she could drive the car. He gave her permission. A short while later as she was turning the corner, she made a wide turn . . . and instead of putting her foot on the brake she put her foot on the accelerator and she went up on the sidewalk and struck three children. One of them was pronounced dead upon arrival at the hospital."

After the incident, Miss Johnson was sent home by her boy friend, and he told the police upon their arrival at the scene that he was the driver of the car at the time of the accident. Information supplied to the police by witnesses led the investigating officers to conclude that the "boy friend" had not told them the truth. When confronted with the statements of witnesses, the boy friend recanted and implicated Miss Johnson.

The Assistant State's Attorney concluded his presentation of facts with the remark that, "We also feel . . . that the safety of the public would dictate that this case be tried in criminal court rather than [in] juvenile court."

A "Waiver Summary" dated September 20, 1972, was prepared by the Department of Juvenile Services and submitted to the judge. The "Summary" stated that Miss Johnson was in the eleventh grade at Dunbar High School and was an above-average student. She was described by her tenth grade counselor as "very responsible and reliable and has presented no conduct problem." According to the "Summary" the appellant has been an active participant in "extracurricular activities," and in the opinion of the counselor had the "potential to be a productive citizen." Miss Johnson attends church on a regular basis and is a member of her church choir.

The appellant offered the testimony of Rev. Leroy Gill, Sr. who informed the court that Miss Johnson was active in civic affairs, and that from his association with her it was apparent to him that she was "very concerned about what has happened," and that there were times when "she has been crying because of the death of the two year old." Rev. Gill expressed the opinion that if Miss Johnson were tried in the juvenile court "it would be [a] greater help [to her] rather than being tried in a criminal court type environment."

The hearing judge opined:

"Well, I am going to grant the State's request and waive jurisdiction in this petition. It is a very difficult step for me to take because we have a young lady who has had a very credible record for herself. She has not been in any difficulty and she has done well in school and has been active in school activities, has been active in community activities, but I base my decision on her age, almost seventeen when this occurred, *but essentially on the very grievous nature of the offense*; the fact that there was this very tragic killing, the fact that the respondent used subterfuge, the responsibility for it, all of this is a tragedy of immense proportions as we all recognize. It is essentially because of this that I feel that this is not the appropriate tribunal for this matter." (Emphasis supplied).

When asked whether the State had any recommendation to make relative to bail for Miss Johnson, the Assistant State's Attorney, who had professed the belief that waiver should be granted because of the involvement of the "safety to the public," stated: ". . . .[T]he State would recommend that [Miss Johnson] be released on her own recognizance. . . . ."

On appeal to this Court, Miss Johnson avers that the judge abused his discretion by granting waiver. The State's answer is somewhat unique. They urge upon us that the juvenile court "had before it testimony relating to all of the five factors. . . . While the court made its decision primarily on Appellant's age, the nature of the offense and her subterfuge in attempting to avoid responsibility . . . such was proper. . . . All that is necessary is that the court consider all five factors. That the court so considered is evident from the record." After conceding on oral argument before this Court that this was not "the strongest case" for waiver of jurisdiction, the State suggested that Miss Johnson was not in need of the rehabilitative measures afforded by the Department of Juvenile Services and that because she did not need rehabilitation she should be tried in the Criminal Court.

We think it apparent that the hearing judge was unduly influenced by the "nature of the offense" to the extent that the amenability of the appellant to rehabilitation was cast aside and not considered, or, if considered, was not afforded its proper weight. The mere statement that the five legislative factors were considered by the hearing judge does not divest this Court of its right to determine whether *vel non* those factors were actually considered and properly weighed in relation to each other and relative to the legislative purpose embodied in § 70.

It is specious to argue that because Miss Johnson is not in need of rehabilitative measures that she should be charged as an adult. Such an argument is the inverse of the legislative will, § 70, and injects into waiver hearings the anomalistic proposition that waiver should be granted because the juvenile is too good for rehabilitation, and, as such, should be subjected to the regular criminal procedures. It creates a penalty for good conduct.

We think it apparent from the "Waiver Summary" and the testimony of Rev. Gill that the juvenile appellant is, if adjudged a delinquent child, an ideal subject for the rehabilitative measures available from the Department of Juvenile Services.

. . .

Waiver of jurisdiction reversed and case remanded for further proceedings in the juvenile court.

IN THE MATTER OF PIMA COUNTY

Court of Appeals of Arizona, Division 2, 1973.
20 Ariz.App. 10, 509 P.2d 1047.

KRUCKER, JUDGE.

This appeal questions the correctness of a juvenile court order refusing to suspend criminal prosecution of a minor and ordering him transferred for prosecution as an adult. Appellant claims that there were no reasonable grounds to believe (1) he was not amenable to treatment or rehabilitation and (2) that he was not commitable to an institution for mentally deficient or mentally ill persons.

Pursuant to Rule 14, Rules of Juvenile Court, [17 A.R.S.] the court made the requisite finding of probable cause (not challenged on appeal) and also found that the minor was not amenable to treatment or rehabilitation as a delinquent child through available facilities, that he was not commitable to an institution for mentally deficient, mentally defective or mentally ill persons, and that the safety or interests of the public required that he be transferred for criminal prosecution. Also in accordance with said Rule, the court stated its reasons:

"1. The minor will reach his 18th birthday on the 12 day of April 1973, approximately 45 days from the date of transfer. At that time the jurisdiction of the juvenile court or juvenile division of the Department of Corrections would cease.

2. The minor is charged with an extremely violent offense that would indicate a need for court services in an excess of the 45 days available if he were found guilty.

3. That by transferring the minor to adult jurisdiction the child would receive the extended court services that a violation of this type would indicate.

4. That there are no rehabilitative services available to the juvenile court or juvenile division of the Department of Corrections that could be effective within the available time frame.

5. That [minor] has been a member of the United States Marine Corps since June of 1972 and by virtue of this has received

training and has been treated in the same manner as an adult, therefore treatment as a juvenile would be inappropriate.

6. That because of his enlistment in the Marine Corps the minor has attained the status of an emancipated minor and is solely responsible for his own actions.

7. That rehabilitation of juveniles is generally attempted through use of the family unit and this is impractical in this case because of the minor's emancipated state and because his family resides out of the jurisdiction.

8. That no evidence has been presented that would indicate any physical or mental disorders."

. . .

. . . In Kent v. United States, 383 U.S. 541, 86 S.Ct. 1045, 16 L.Ed.2d 84 (1966), the landmark decision on waiver of juvenile court jurisdiction, the United States Supreme Court set forth the following determinative factors to be considered on a transfer hearing:

1. The seriousness of the alleged offense to the community and whether protection of the community requires waiver.

2. Whether the alleged offense was committed in an aggressive, violent, premeditated or wilful manner.

3. Whether the alleged offense was against persons or against property, greater weight being given to offenses against persons especially if personal injury resulted.

4. The prosecutive merit of the complaint. . . .

5. The desirability of trial and disposition of the entire offense in one court when the juvenile's associates in the alleged offense are adults. . . .

6. The sophistication and maturity of the juvenile as determined by consideration of his home, environmental situation, emotional attitude and pattern of living.

7. The record and previous history of the juvenile. . . .

8. The prospect for adequate protection of the public and the likelihood of reasonable rehabilitation of the juvenile (if he is found to have committed the alleged offense) by the use of procedures, services and facilities currently available to the Juvenile Court.

Applying these criteria to the facts of this case, we are unable to agree with appellant's position. At the time of the hearing he was 17 years and 10 and ½ months old. He had been serving in the Marine Corps for approximately eight months, had completed his basic training and was assigned to an artillery unit at Camp Pendleton, California. In January, 1972, he went AWOL and hitchhiked to Tucson with three other persons, all adults. In the early morning hours of January 19 they were picked up by Patrick Corrales on South Sixth Avenue, Tucson, who offered to help them in finding a place to spend the night. While thus engaged, the appellant, who was seated in the back of the car, proceeded to choke the driver with a chain and a companion beat the driver with a tire iron. The victim received blows to the head that required hospitalization.

After the assault the victim was dumped on the ground and the four hitchhikers drove off in his car. The appellant's mother resided in Oklahoma City and his father in Henderson, Kentucky. For the previous five years appellant had resided in California with his grandparents. He had no history of prior offenses but there was some evidence that he had become involved with drugs after completion of his basic training and continued to be so involved.

A Pima County Juvenile Court investigator to whom this case had been assigned for investigation testified at the hearing. He had spoken with appellant approximately twenty times and concluded that he would not be amenable to treatment as a juvenile. He gave as his reasons the fact that there was such a brief time to work with him since he would soon be 18, there would be no opportunity to work with his family since they resided out of state, and the lack of facilities at the juvenile level to cope with appellant's drug problem. He also indicated that he had observed no health problems. In his written report he stated that appellant had quit school in the ninth grade (October, 1970) and had been pretty much on his own since then; that he had not been observed either by himself or other members of the detention staff to have any strange behavior patterns which would give any indication that psychiatric treatment was necessary; that on June 9, 1972, appellant had been admitted to the Marine Corps, given a "clean bill of health," and that the Marine Corps at that time felt that he was mentally healthy. He had had conversations with appellant's mother who gave him no reason to believe that her son had "ever needed any mental help."

There is no question that the alleged offense was serious, was committed in an aggressive and violent manner and was entitled to greater weight since it was against a person and resulted in personal injury. There was clearly sufficient evidence upon which a grand jury might be expected to return an indictment and appellant's associates in the alleged offense were adults so that the entire offense could be disposed of by trial in one court. Appellant's entire background reflects a sophistication and maturity—in fact, when he was taken to the juvenile detention facility he refused to make a statement and asked for a lawyer. Although he had no previous juvenile court record, we are disinclined to give undue emphasis to such a factor.

We are unable to say that it was error to find that there was no likelihood of reasonable rehabilitation of appellant by the use of procedures, services and facilities available to the juvenile court. Under

A.R.S. § 8–241, subsec. A(2), as amended, the juvenile court can "award" a delinquent child:

"(a) To the care of his parents, subject to supervision of a probation department.

(b) To a probation department, subject to such conditions as the court may impose.

(c) To a reputable citizen of good moral character, subject to the supervision of a probation department.

(d) To a private agency or institution, subject to the supervision of a probation officer.

(e) To the department of corrections without further directions as to placement by that department."

However, A.R.S. § 8–246, subsec. B provides:

"The awarding of a child *shall not extend beyond the minority* of the child, and commitments to the department of corrections shall be for the term of *the child's minority* unless sooner discharged by the department of corrections." (Emphasis added.)

The legislative definition of the term "minority" was altered by Ch. 146, Laws of 1972. A "minor" now means a person under the age of 18 years. A.R.S. § 1–215, subsec. 17. Thus we see that any disposition available to the juvenile court under the existing juvenile code could not extend beyond April 12, 1973, when appellant would become 18 years of age.

A juvenile court judge in waiver proceedings must consider the alternatives to criminal prosecution and decide whether the *parens patriae* plan of procedure is desirable and proper in the particular case. It is proper for him to consider the short time span available to ensure success in any rehabilitative endeavor. Appellant was so close to the age of 18 years there was no disposition reasonably calculated to effect rehabilitation since commitment to the department of corrections or to any of the persons enumerated in the statute would terminate when he reached 18.

. . . .

In allowing juvenile courts to waive jurisdiction as to minors under 18, the legislature has removed the protective shield against criminal responsibility for those individuals who, in the court's opinion, would more appropriately be dealt with as an adult. In the instant case, after a proper examination of relevant criteria, the juvenile court found it would be contrary to the best interests of appellant and the public to hear the matter in juvenile court. We find no error in the transfer order and therefore affirm.

JUVENILE JUSTICE STANDARDS PROJECT, STANDARDS RELATING TO TRANSFER BETWEEN COURTS *

2.2 Necessary findings

A. The juvenile court should waive its jurisdiction only upon finding:

1. that probable cause exists to believe that the juvenile has committed the Class One Juvenile Offense alleged in the petition; and

2. that by clear and convincing evidence the juvenile is not a proper person to be handled by the juvenile court.

B. A finding of probable cause to believe that a juvenile has committed a Class One Juvenile Offense should be based solely on evidence admissible in an adjudicatory hearing of the Juvenile Court.

C. A finding that a juvenile is not a proper person to be handled by the juvenile court must include determinations, by clear and convincing evidence, of:

1. the seriousness of the alleged Class One Juvenile Offense;

2. a prior record of adjudicated delinquency involving the infliction or threat of significant bodily injury;

3. the likely inefficacy of the dispositions available to the juvenile court as demonstrated by previous dispositions of the juvenile; and

4. the appropriateness of the services and dispositional alternatives available in the criminal justice system for dealing with the juvenile's problems and whether they are, in fact, available.

Expert opinion should be considered in assessing the likely efficacy of the dispositions available to the juvenile court. A finding that a juvenile is not a proper person to be handled by the juvenile court should be based solely on evidence admissible in a disposition hearing of the juvenile court.

D. A finding of probable cause to believe that a juvenile has committed a Class One Juvenile Offense may be substituted for a probable cause determination relating to that offense (or a lesser included offense) required in any subsequent juvenile court proceeding. Such a finding should not be substituted for any finding of probable cause required in any subsequent criminal proceeding.

NOTES

(1) Both of the preceding cases demonstrate some of the factors that will be considered by the juvenile judge in making a waiver determination, whether provided for by the legislature, as in Maryland, or left to the discre-

tion of the judge, as in Arizona. Would all Arizona youth over seventeen likely be waived? Why? See Jimmy H. v. Superior Court, 3 Cal.3d 709, 91 Cal.Rptr. 600, 478 P.2d 32 (1970).

(2) See State v. Gibbs, 94 Idaho 908, 500 P.2d 209, 217 n.35 (1972) for a listing of law review articles that discuss the most significant factors considered by juvenile court judges in making a waiver decision.

(3) Few states have waiver statutes that formulate precise criteria to govern the judge when making the transfer decision. More often the statutes contain only general phrases, such as "the best interest of the child or public," which leave a great deal to the discretion of the juvenile court judge. The Juvenile Justice Standards Project reports that 36 of the states have statutes which elaborate conditions sufficient to justify waiver: Of these, 27 states cite the public interest in treating the juvenile as a factor, while 24 states list the nonamenability of the juvenile to rehabilitation through juvenile facilities.

With increased enactment of new juvenile court codes or amendment of existing ones, the trend is toward setting forth specific waiver criteria in the statutes. Representative statutes are: Ala.Code § 12–15–34(d) (1975); Alaska Stat. § 47.10.060(d) (1979); D.C.Code § 16–2307(e) (1981); Fla.Stat.Ann. § 39.09(2)(c) (Supp.1981); Ill.Ann.Stat. ch. 37, § 702–7(3)(a) (1972); Md.Cts. & Jud.Proc.Code Ann. § 3–817(d) (1980); Mass.Gen.Laws Ann. ch. 119, § 61 (Supp.1981); Mich.Comp.Laws Ann. § 712A.4(4) (Supp.1982); Mont.Code Ann. § 41–5–206(1)(d), (2) (1981); Okla.Stat.Ann. tit. 10, § 1112(b) (Supp. 1982); Tex.Fam.Code Ann. § 54.02(f) (1975).

Is a waiver statute unconstitutional for lack of sufficient standards? The Louisiana Supreme Court so held in State ex rel. Hunter, 387 So.2d 1086 (La. 1980). The statute, which lacked even a general nonamenability standard, allowed waiver of juveniles who were 15 or older at the time of the alleged offense and charged with one of certain enumerated serious offenses. The waiver hearing was, in effect, a probable cause hearing. The court held the statute unconstitutional on due process grounds as well as on state constitutional grounds. The waiver statute was subsequently amended to include a general nonamenability standard and to furnish specific criteria as well. La. Rev.Stat.Ann. § 13:1571.1(A) (Supp.1981).

The Supreme Court of California, on the other hand, rejected such an attack on § 707 of the California Welfare and Institutions Code. In Donald L. v. Superior Court, 7 Cal.3d 592, 102 Cal.Rptr. 850, 498 P.2d 1098 (1972), the court concluded that the statutory phrases "not amenable" and "not a fit and proper subject" were not unconstitutionally vague. The great majority of courts that have considered constitutional challenges to statutes employing a general nonamenability standard have held them valid. In addition to the California decision see Davis v. State, 297 So.2d 289 (Fla.1974); State v. Gibbs, 94 Idaho 908, 500 P.2d 209 (1972); Summers v. State, 248 Ind. 551, 230 N.E.2d 320 (1967); State v. Smagula, 117 N.H. 663, 377 A.2d 608 (1977); In re Bullard, 22 N.C.App. 245, 206 S.E.2d 305 (1974), appeal dismissed 285 N.C. 758, 209 S.E.2d 279. In most of these cases the courts held the general standard sufficient, leaving the courts free to fashion specific criteria to be applied by judges in making waiver decisions. Such judicial criteria are, in effect, incorporated into the waiver statute. See, e.g., Speck v. Auger, 558 F.2d 394 (8th Cir. 1977) (Iowa waiver statute not unconstitutionally vague as interpreted by Iowa Supreme Court, which, in State v. Halverson, 192 N.W. 2d 765 (Iowa 1971), set forth criteria to be considered).

(4) How do the Standards differ from the Arizona and Maryland statutes in the principal cases?

Seriousness of the offense alone gives rise to no presumption that the child should be transferred to adult court. It is a permissible factor to be considered in the overall calculus of the transfer decision. See, e.g., State v. Kemper, 535 S.W.2d 241 (Mo.App.1975). Indeed, cases abound in which courts have held that waiver can not be based on a single factor alone, at least where the judge simply cites the factor without elaboration of *why* the juvenile for that reason is not amenable to juvenile treatment. See, e.g., Commonwealth v. Greiner, 479 Pa. 364, 388 A.2d 698 (1978) (nature of the crime); J.G.B. v. State, 136 Ga.App. 75, 220 S.E.2d 79 (1975) (number and severity of the alleged offenses); Duvall v. State, 170 Ind.App. 473, 353 N.E.2d 478 (1976) (seriousness of the offense and consent of the juvenile); In re Dahl, 278 N.W.2d 316 (Minn.1979) (age of the juvenile and seriousness of the offense); S.H. v. State, 555 P.2d 1050 (Okl.Cr.App.1976) (a finding that the juvenile knows the difference between right and wrong).

Similarly, suppose the nonamenability determination is based solely on the court's conclusion that no facilities are available to the court for treatment of the juvenile. For a decision upholding such a waiver determination, see In re Pima County, Juvenile Action No. J–218–1, 22 Ariz.App. 327, 527 P.2d 104 (1974). Contra, In re J.E.C., 302 Minn. 387, 225 N.W.2d 245 (1975). In People v. Joe T., 48 Cal.App.3d 114, 121 Cal.Rptr. 329 (1975), where "the finding of unfitness was based solely on the referee's belief that the sentencing alternatives in the adult court would be better suited for appellant than the local treatment programs available through the juvenile court," the waiver order was held invalid. In the latter case the court pointed out that where the standard for waiver is nonamenability to juvenile treatment (or unfitness), absence of the required finding of unfitness is a jurisdictional defect and the waiver order is a nullity.

In assessing nonamenability to juvenile court treatment, should the state's mistakes on the child's prior court contacts give rise to a concept of contributory negligence by the state barring transfer? In People v. Browning, 45 Cal.App.2d 125, 119 Cal.Rptr. 420 (1975) the child's attorney argued that the California Youth Authority had been grossly negligent in letting his client run away from a foster home placement and live in another less constructive environment. This negligence by the state although characterized by the juvenile judge as "grossly stupid" and "incomprehensible" was no bar to a non-amenability finding.

Of what value is so-called expert opinion on the determination of non-amenability? One source of considerable disillusionment about the conduct of juvenile courts has been disappointment with the inability of the social and behavioral sciences to live up to their early promise. See S. J. Morse and C. H. Whitebread, The Implications of the Juvenile Justice Standards for Mental Health Professionals in G. Melton (ed.) Child and Youth Services and the Law 6 (Haworth 1982). What should we expect experts to say and who will those experts be? The use of psychiatrists and psychologists in criminal cases has been the subject of extensive scholarly debate. See S. J. Morse, Crazy Behavior, Morals, and Science: An Analysis of Mental Health Law, 51 So.Cal.L.Rev. 527 (1978); R. Bonnie and C. Slobogin, The Role of the Mental

Health Professional in the Criminal Process: The Case for Informed Speculation, 66 Va.L.Rev. 427 (1980); and S. Morse, Failed Expectations and Criminal Responsibility: Experts and the Unconscious, 68 Va.L.Rev. 971 (1982).

(5) The Juvenile Justice Standards' required finding of probable cause before a youth may be waived is typical. In most states a finding of probable
cause is a prerequisite to a transfer decision. See, e.g. Va. Code
§ 16.1–269(A)(3)(a) (Supp.1981). Some states permit the juvenile judge to assume the existence of probable cause at the waiver hearing. Md. Cts. & Jud.
Proc. Code Ann. § 3–817(c) (1980). How does this square with the time
honored presumption of innocence? Should the juvenile court's finding of
probable cause at the waiver hearing be a sufficient substitute for the usual
preliminary hearing in adult proceedings if the child is transferred? See Davis, The Efficacy of a Probable Cause Requirement in Juvenile Proceedings,
59 N.C.L.Rev. 723, 735–37 (1981) for a discussion of the problem.

D. ALLOCATING JURISDICTION BETWEEN COURTS

There are at least five ways in which statutes have dealt with the
problem of allocation of jurisdiction between juvenile and criminal
courts. The first is to leave the decision to the discretion of the prosecutor, an example being the Wyoming statute. A second way is to
exclude certain offenses from the jurisdiction of the juvenile court.
The District of Columbia follows this technique. Another method is
to provide for concurrent jurisdiction between the juvenile and criminal courts over certain offenses or classes of offenses. The Georgia
statute is representative of this approach. The most common method
is to leave the decision to the discretion of the juvenile court judge, of
which the California statute is an example. Finally some or all
transfer decisions may be made by the criminal court judge in a system of reverse certification. Of course, in a particular state one may
find a combination of these various methods. The following statutes
are illustrative of the alternatives.

1. PROSECUTORIAL DISCRETION

WYOMING STATUTES

**§ 14–6–203. Jurisdiction generally; not deemed exclusive; when
district court not deprived of jurisdiction**

. . .

(c) The jurisdiction of the juvenile court is not exclusive. If a minor is alleged to have violated a municipal ordinance, a complaint may
be processed in the municipal court in the manner provided by general law or the complaint may be referred to the county and prosecuting attorney for disposition as provided in this subsection. All complaints alleging misconduct of a minor other than violation of a

municipal ordinance, of W.S. 12–6–101 or a misdemeanor violation of the Uniform Act Regulating Traffic on Highways, must be referred to the county and prosecuting attorney who shall determine the appropriate action to be taken and the appropriate court in which to prosecute the action. . . .

. . .

§ 14–6–211. Complaints child delinquent, etc.; determination; assistance; petition

Complaints alleging a child is delinquent, in need of supervision or neglected shall be referred to the office of the county and prosecuting attorney. The county attorney shall determine whether the best interest of the child or of the public require that judicial action be taken. The county department of health and social services, the county sheriff and the county and state probation departments shall provide the county attorney with any assistance he may require in making an investigation. The county attorney shall prepare and file a petition with the court if he believes action is necessary to protect the interest of the public or child.

2. LEGISLATIVE ALLOCATION

DISTRICT OF COLUMBIA CODE

SUBCHAPTER I.—PROCEEDINGS REGARDING DELINQUENCY, NEGLECT, OR NEED OF SUPERVISION

§ 16–2301. Definitions

As used in this subchapter—

. . .

(3) The term "child" means an individual who is under 18 years of age, except that the term "child" does not include an individual who is sixteen years of age or older and—

(A) charged by the United States attorney with (i) murder, forcible rape, burglary in the first degree, robbery while armed, or assault with intent to commit any such offense, or (ii) an offense listed in clause (i) and any other offense properly joinable with such an offense;

(B) charged with an offense referred to in subparagraph (A)(i) and convicted by plea or verdict of a lesser included offense; or

(C) charged with a traffic offense.

For purposes of this subchapter the term "child" also includes a person under the age of twenty-one who is charged with an offense referred to in subparagraph (A)(i) or (C) committed before he attained the age of sixteen, or a delinquent act committed before he attained the age of eighteen.

UNITED STATES v. BLAND

United States Court of Appeals, District of Columbia Circuit, 1972.
472 F.2d 1329.

WILKEY, CIRCUIT JUDGE:

[Bland had been transferred to adult court pursuant to § 2301(3) of the Code of the District of Columbia. He challenged the constitutionality of that provision.]

. . .

II. *The Due Process and Equal Protection of the Law Issue*

The District Court found Section 2301(3)(A) invalid as violative of due process of law:

> The determination that a child should be tried as an adult cannot be made without the safeguard of basic due process. Without a provision in the new statute that would require some determination, reached after a fair hearing, that an individual is beyond the help of the Family Division, that statute must fall as violative of due process.

. . .

A.

In relation to this holding of the District Court, we note in the first place that legislative classifications are entitled to a strong presumption of validity and may be "set aside only if no grounds can be conceived to justify them."

. . .

Secondly, legislative exclusion of individuals charged with certain specified crimes from the jurisdiction of the juvenile justice system is not unusual. The Federal Juvenile Delinquency Act excludes offenses which are punishable by death or life imprisonment. Several states have similarly excluded certain crimes in defining the jurisdiction of their respective systems of juvenile justice,[19] while others vest concurrent jurisdiction over enumerated crimes in both their adult

---

19. Colo.Rev.Stat., §§ 22–1–3(17)(b), 22–1–4(4)(b); 10 Del. Code Ann. § 957, 11 Del. Code Ann. §§ 360(b), 363(d), 468A; Burns' Ind. Stat. §§ 9–3204(1), 9–3213; Iowa Code Ann. § 232.64; La.Const., art. 7, § 52; Md. Code Ann., art. 26, § 70–2(d)(1); Miss. Code Ann. § 7185–15; Nev. Rev.Stat. § 62.050; S.C.Const., art. 5, § 1; and Tenn. Code Ann. § 37–265.

Challenges to these provisions as violative of due process and equal protection of the law have not prevailed. See State v. Ayers, 260 A.2d 162 (Del.1969), in which the court rejected a Fourteenth Amendment challenge to 11 Del. Code Ann. § 363(d) (an anti-riot statute), which provided that those over sixteen years of age and charged with violating this statute were to be tried as adults. See also, to the same effect, Prevatte v. Director, 5 Md.App. 406, 248 A.2d 170 (1968), and Davis v. State, Miss., 204 So.2d 270, rev'd on other grounds, 397 U.S. 721, 89 S.Ct. 1394, 22 L.Ed.2d 676 (1969).

and juvenile courts.[20] (Finally, the United States District Court for the District of Maryland, upheld by the Fourth Circuit, while it did find a geographic age distinction in the jurisdiction of the Maryland Juvenile Court violative of due process, found no difficulties with the exclusion of those 14 years of age and over charged with capital crimes from juvenile jurisdiction.[21]

B.

The disagreement of our dissenting colleague arises almost solely from his fundamental unwillingness to accept Congress' power to define what is a "child." The words "child," "infant," and "minor" from early times in various legal systems have been susceptible to definition by statute; the critical "age" for specified purposes has varied, and differed between male and female. See Bouvier's Law Dictionary; Black's Law Dictionary. Before 1970 the District of Columbia Code (16 D.C. Code § 2301 (1967), defined "child" as "a person under 18 years of age." Our dissenting colleague seems to consider this statute and its definition immutable, apparently because it was involved in Kent v. United States; we accept the fact that Congress has abolished this statutory definition and by statute substituted another, to which we simply give full effect.

. . .

. . . Until it is determined whether a person is a "child" within the statutory definition, there is no jurisdiction; therefore, *a fortiori* there can be no waiver of jurisdiction.

Nor is it true "a suspected juvenile remains a child until he is charged with an enumerated offense by the United States Attorney." There is just no classification of the person as a child or an adult until (1) his age is accurately ascertained, and (2) the decision on prosecution is made. Congress has incorporated more than one element in the definition of a "child." Until all the elements of the definition are ascertained, the status of the person is simply uncertain, just as under the 1967 definition the status of a person would be uncertain until his true age was established.

C.

The District Court's finding in the case at bar, and appellee's assertion to the same effect—that the exercise of the discretion vested by Section 2301(3)(A) in the United States Attorney to charge a person 16 years of age or older with certain enumerated offenses, there-

20. 37 Ill.Ann.Stat. § 702–7(3), upheld in People v. Carlson, 108 Ill.App.2d 463, 247 N.E.2d 919 (1969). See also DeBacker v. Sigler, 185 Neb. 352, 175 N.W.2d 912 (1970), and Mayne v. Turner, 24 Utah 2d 195, 468 P.2d 369 (1970), sustaining concurrent jurisdiction in their respective adult and juvenile courts over certain enumerated offenses.

21. Long v. Robinson, 316 F.Supp. 22 (D.Md.), aff'd 436 F.2d 1116 (4th Cir. 1971).

by initiating that person's prosecution as an adult, violates due process—ignores the long and widely accepted concept of prosecutorial discretion, which derives from the constitutional principle of separation of powers. . . .

. . .

The District Court and appellee in the case at bar point to the acknowledged significant effect of the United States Attorney's decision whether to charge an individual 16 years of age or older with certain enumerated offenses, and conclude that, in the absence of a hearing, due process is violated when such a decision is made. This, however, overlooks the significance of a variety of other common prosecutorial decisions, e.g., whether to charge one person but not another possible codefendant; whether to charge an individual with a misdemeanor or a felony; etc. Furthermore, the decision whether to charge an individual with a misdemeanor or a felony has long determined the court in which that person will be tried. We cannot accept the hitherto unaccepted argument that due process requires an adversary hearing before the prosecutor can exercise his age-old function of deciding what charge to bring against whom. Grave consequences have always flowed from this, but never has a hearing been required.

. . .

. . . [J]udicial consideration of the legitimate scope of prosecutorial discretion clearly encompasses the exercise of such discretion where it has the effect of determining whether a person will be charged as a juvenile or as an adult. In the absence of such "suspect" factors as "race, religion, or other arbitrary classification," the exercise of discretion by the United States Attorney in the case at bar involves no violation of due process or equal protection of the law.

III. *The Presumption of Innocence Issue*

The District Court and appellee assert that the exercise of discretion by the United States Attorney under Section 2301(3)(A) violates due process in that it denies the individual charged the presumption of innocence.

This, however, mistakes the nature of the United States Attorney's decision in the case at bar to charge appellee with an offense enumerated in Section 2301(3)(A). While the decision does have the effect of determining whether appellee is to be tried as an adult or a juvenile, it is not a judgment of guilt or an imposition of penalty. On the contrary, it is simply the result of a determination by the United States Attorney that there is sufficient evidence to warrant prosecution of the appellee for the offense charged and that adult prosecution is appropriate. It in no manner relieves the Government of its obligation to prove appellee's guilt beyond a reasonable doubt. Nor does it remove appellee's right to a jury trial. . . .

The presumption of innocence, as the Supreme Court has long held, applies to the prosecution at trial and ". . . . is a conclusion drawn by the law in favor of the citizen, by virtue whereof, *when brought to trial* upon a criminal charge, he must be acquitted, unless he is proven [beyond a reasonable doubt] to be guilty." . . . [T]he United States Attorney's decision in the case at bar marks only the beginning of the process of adjudication of appellee's guilt, a process marked by the presence of all the traditional protections or procedural due process . . ..

IV. *Conclusion*

For these reasons, the order of the District Court dismissing appellee's indictment, on the basis of its opinion holding 16 D.C. Code § 2301(3)(A) unconstitutional as an arbitrary legislative classification and as a negation of the presumption of innocence, is accordingly reversed and the case remanded for trial.

Reversed and Remanded.

WRIGHT, CIRCUIT JUDGE, dissenting: As a matter of abstract legal analysis, the opinion of my brethren might appear to some degree persuasive. But we do not sit to decide questions in the abstract, and we are not writing on a clean slate. In 1966 the Supreme Court spoke clearly and specifically about this area. . . . Kent v. United States. It held, in unmistakable terms, that before a child under 18 can be tried in adult court the Constitution requires a hearing "sufficient in the particular circumstances to satisfy the basic requirements of due process and fairness . . . ." I had not supposed that it was within our power as a lower federal court to change this mandate. Nor had I imagined that congress could "overrule" this constitutional decision by a simple statutory enactment. Yet the majority holds that whereas before passage of the Court Reform Act of 1970 the Constitution required a hearing, after its passage the Constitution requires no such thing. While I must confess that this display of judicial legerdemain leaves me properly dazzled and mystified, I cannot quite persuade myself that the rabbit has really emerged from the hat. I would therefore hold that appellee is entitled to a hearing with counsel and a statement of reasons before he can be charged and tried as an adult.

. . . .

As a moment's reflection makes clear, this so-called "definition" in fact establishes a second, parallel waiver procedure whereby a juvenile can be transferred from the Family Division to adult court. If the Government chooses, it may institute waiver proceedings in Family Court and attempt to convince the judge that under the standards enunciated in the Act the child could more appropriately be tried in adult court. It would be surprising if this procedure were much utilized in cases covered by 16 D.C. Code § 2301(3)(A), however, since under it the Government must observe the procedural rules mandated by *Kent.* Moreover, there is always the possibility that the Government will not carry its burden before the Family Court judge, in which case the waiver attempt would fail.

These risks and inconveniences can be avoided by following the second alternative. If the prosecutor simply charges the juvenile with one of the enumerated offenses, the juvenile ceases to be a "child" under 16 D.C. Code 2301(3)(A) and, hence, the Family Court is automatically divested of jurisdiction. Thus if the prosecutor follows the second alternative the waiver decision becomes his alone, and he is permitted to make it without the encumbrance of a hearing, the requirement that he state reasons, the inconvenience of bearing the burden of proof, or the necessity of appointing counsel for the accused.

I think it obvious that this second procedure was written into the Act in order to countermand the Supreme Court's decision in *Kent* . . . . Indeed, the House Committee primarily responsible for drafting the provision virtually admitted as much. The Committee Report explains 16 D.C. Code § 2301(3)(A) as follows:

> "Because of the great increase in the number of serious felonies committed by juveniles *and because of the substantial difficulties in transferring juvenile offenders charged with serious felonies to the jurisdiction of the adult court under present law*, provisions are made in this subchapter for a better mechanism for separation of the violent youthful offender and recidivist from the rest of the juvenile community."

H. Rep. 91–907, 91st Cong., 2d Sess., at 50 (1970). (Emphasis added.) While the surface veneer of legalese which encrusts this explanation need fool no one, a simultaneous translation into ordinary English might, perhaps, prove helpful. The "substantial difficulties . . . under present law" to which the Committee coyly refers are, of course, none other than the constitutional rights explicated in the *Kent* decision. And the "better mechanism" which the Committee proposes is a system for running roughshod over those rights in a manner which is unlikely to encourage those of us still committed to constitutionalism and the rule of law.

This blatant attempt to evade the force of the *Kent* decision should not be permitted to succeed. The result in *Kent* did not turn on the particular wording of the statute involved or on the particular waiver mechanism there employed. Rather, as the Court itself made clear, the rights expounded in *Kent* are fundamental and immutable. "The right to representation by counsel is not a formality. It is not a grudging gesture to a ritualistic requirement. It is of the essence of justice." 383 U.S. at 561, 86 S.Ct. at 1057. I must confess, therefore, that I find myself unable to approach the majority's elaborate argumentation with an entirely open mind. As one who has long believed that our Constitution prohibits abrogations of due process "whether accomplished ingeniously or ingenuously," I react with a good deal of skepticism to an argument which supposes that "the essence of justice" can be defeated by a juggling of the definition of juvenile or a minor modification of Family Court jurisdiction. Nonetheless, I am willing to meet the majority on its own ground, since I am convinced that when its arguments are closely examined they must inevitably fall of their own weight.

. . .

. . . [M]y brethren adopt two . . . arguments which, to me at least, seem . . . unconvincing. First, the majority seems to contend that *Kent* is inapposite because it applied to a judicial decision, whereas 16 D.C.Code § 2301 contemplates a prosecutorial decision. Thus the majority apparently concedes, as it must, that *Kent* continues to guarantee procedural rights when the waiver is effected by a judge. . . . But these rights do not attach when the same decision is made by a prosecutor, apparently because "the United States Attorney's decision . . . marks only the beginning of the process of adjudication of appellee's guilt, a process marked by the presence of all the traditional protections of procedural due process, followed by the extraordinarily liberal rehabilitation provisions of the Federal Youth Corrections Act." . . . This argument will not stand analysis. The decision by a juvenile judge or by the United States Attorney to treat the child as an adult for prosecution purposes marks the beginning of precisely the same process of adjudication. And it cannot be doubted that the United States Attorney is certainly a less disinterested decision maker than the Juvenile Court judge. It would seem then that, in order to compensate for lack of neutrality, . . . procedural niceties should be *more* rather than less carefully observed when the prosecutor is the decision maker.

. . .

It should be clear, then, that the test for when the Constitution demands a bearing depends not on which government official makes the decision, but rather on the importance of that decision to the individual affected. . . . .

. . .

The majority's opinion suggests reliance on a broad appeal to prosecutorial discretion, but ultimately comes to rest on the more specialized argument that the prosecutor has unreviewable discretion as to whether or not to grant a hearing. As should be readily apparent, this formulation merely assumes the answer to the very question before us for decision. The assumption is made, moreover, on the basis of flimsy evidence and a fallacious analogy.

My brothers point to "the significance of a variety of other common prosecutorial decisions, e.g., whether to charge one person but not another possible codefendant; whether to charge an individual with a misdemeanor or a felony; etc. . . . Grave consequences have always flowed from this, but never has a hearing been required." . . . With all respect, one could just as easily infer from the lack of authority provided to support this proposition that never has a hearing been *requested*. But even if one assumes, *arguendo*, that a hearing is not necessary in these situations, it hardly follows that a child may be summarily deprived of his right to juvenile treatment without being heard. As the majority itself indicates, there are dramatically real differences between run-of-the-mill charging decisions and prosecutorial waiver of Family Court jurisdiction. A normal charging decision is "only the beginning of the process of adjudication of [defendant's] guilt, a process marked by the presence of all the traditional protections of procedural due process . . . ." . . . A defendant has the opportunity to show that he was improperly charged—that is, that he is not guilty—at the preliminary hearing, at the trial itself, and, if necessary, on appeal.

In contrast, the waiver decision marks not only the beginning but also the end of adjudication as to the child's suitability for juvenile treatment. . . . The question of juvenile treatment turns not on the issue of guilt, but on such factors as the maturity of the child and his susceptibility to rehabilitation. These factors, unlike the question of guilt, drop out of the case once the initial waiver decision is made. Hence it is especially vital that the procedures be fair at the one point in the criminal process where these matters are considered. The very fact that the prosecutor's decision is largely unreviewable and therefore final argues for, rather than against, making certain that he has all the facts before him when he exercises his great responsibility.

Nor is the majority on firm ground when it compares prosecutorial waiver to the decision "whether to charge an individual with a misdemeanor or a felony [which] has long determined the court in which that person will be tried." . . . It trivializes the juvenile court system to suggest that it represents merely an alternative forum for the trial of criminal offenses. The Family Court is more than just another judicial body; it is another system of justice with different procedures, a different penalty structure, and a different philosophy of rehabilitation. We play a cruel joke on our children by arguing that the juvenile system is a nonadversary, noncriminal, beneficent instrument of rehabilitation when determining whether criminal procedures are to be required at trial, while at the same time maintaining that it is just another criminal court when determining the procedures which must accompany waiver.

. . .

Thus I do not think we can escape the fact that after our decision today there will be many impressionable 16- and 17-year-olds who will be packed off to adult prisons where they will serve their time with hardened criminals. These children will be sentenced, moreover, without any meaningful inquiry into the possibility of rehabilitation through humane juvenile disposition. Sometimes I think our treatment of these hapless "criminals" is dictated by the age-old principle "out of sight—out of mind." Yet there is no denying the fact that we cannot write these children off forever. Some day they will grow up and at some point they will have to be freed from incarceration. We will inevitably hear from the Blands and Kents again, and the kind of society we have in the years to come will in no small measure depend upon our treatment of them now.

Perhaps I should add that I harbor no illusions as to the efficacy of our juvenile court system. I share Mr. Justice Fortas' view that "the highest motives and most enlightened impulses [have] led to a peculiar system for juveniles, unknown to our law in any comparable context. The constitutional and theoretical basis for this peculiar system is—to say the least—debatable. And in practice . . . the results have not been entirely satisfactory." In re Gault, 387 U.S. 1, 17–18, 87 S.Ct. 1428, 1438, 18 L.Ed.2d 527 (1967). Nor do I believe that a fair and constitutional waiver system would rescue from the clutches of adult punishment every juvenile capable of rehabilitation in a more beneficent environment. As Chief Judge Bazelon has pointed out, "The job of saving the boy who has compiled a long juvenile record and then committed a serious offense after his sixteenth birthday may be so costly, or so difficult even if no cost were spared, that the [waiver procedures] required by statute cannot but be a pious charade in many cases."

I must admit, then, to considerable uncertainty as to the ultimately proper disposition of a case such as Bland's, given our scarce societal resources, our limited knowledge of juvenile corrections, and the intractable nature of the root problems of poverty and social disintegration. I am certain of a few propositions, however. I am confident that a child is unlikely to succeed in the long, difficult process of rehabilitation when his teachers during his confinement are adult criminals. I am sure that playing fast and loose with fundamental rights will never buy us "law and order": constitutional rights for children won in *Kent*, like other constitutional rights, are protected from "sophisticated as well as simple-minded" modes of revision or repeal. And I am convinced that the beginning of wisdom in this area, as in so many others, is a respect and concern for the individual—the kind of respect and concern which the due process clause guarantees. I would therefore hold that Congress may not abrogate a child's constitutional rights to a hearing, representation by counsel and a statement of reasons before he is charged and tried as an adult.

I must respectfully dissent.

3. CONCURRENT JURISDICTION

GEORGIA CODE ANNOTATED

15–11–5. Jurisdiction of juvenile court

. . .

(b) The court shall have concurrent jurisdiction with the superior court over a child who is alleged to have committed a delinquent act which would be considered a crime if tried in a superior court and for which the child may be punished by loss of life or confinement for life in a penal institution.

. . .

NOTES

(1) The Wyoming statutory scheme, supra p. 411, is not an example of the pure prosecutorial discretion model because Wyoming also employs traditional waiver by the juvenile court as well as discretionary transfer to the juvenile court from the criminal court. Wyo.Stat. § 14–6–237 (1978). It is used as an example here for two reasons: (1) no state currently uses a pure prosecutorial discretion model, and (2) in Wyoming every case is initiated by the prosecutor and only at a later stage is any sort of transfer between courts a possibility.

Illinois formerly employed a pure prosecutorial discretion model. For its operation see State v. Hawkins, 53 Ill.2d 181, 290 N.E.2d 231 (1972). The Illinois statute has been changed to place responsibility for transfer decisions solely in the juvenile court judge. Ill.Ann.Stat. ch. 37, § 702–7(3), (5) (1972). See People v. Rahn, 59 Ill.2d 302, 319 N.E.2d 787 (1974); People v. Sprinkle, 56 Ill.2d 257, 307 N.E.2d 161 (1974).

At least three other states explicitly grant prosecutors the power to make some allocation decisions. In Nebraska the juvenile and criminal courts have concurrent jurisdiction over all felony cases and over any case in which the juvenile is 16 or older, and the prosecutor is empowered to decide the court in which such cases will be handled. Neb.Rev.Stat. §§ 43–247, 276 (Supp. 1981). If the case originates in criminal court, the criminal court has discretion to transfer appropriate cases to juvenile court. Id. § 43–261. In Arkansas, a juvenile arrested without a warrant is taken before the juvenile court, and the prosecutor is notified and must decide the appropriate court in which to commence the action. Ark.Stat.Ann. § 45–418 (Supp.1981). The statutes also provide for judicial transfer between courts. Id. § 45–417, 420. In Vermont the jurisdictional age for juveniles alleged to be delinquent is 16. Vt. Stat.Ann. tit. 33, § 632(a)(1) (Spec.Supp.1981). In addition to allowing transfer by both the juvenile court, id. § 635a(a), and the criminal court, id. §§ 635(b), 644(c), the statutes allow the prosecutor to make the jurisdictional decision in cases of juveniles who were over 16 but under 18 at the time of the alleged act and the alleged act is not one of the serious offenses enumerated in the statutes. Id. § 635(c).

(2) Some states, while employing other allocation models, have created the functional equivalent of the prosecutorial model, thus allowing the prosecutor to make some allocation decisions. For example, Georgia provides for traditional judicial waiver, but as the statutory example illustrates, Georgia also provides for concurrent jurisdiction between the juvenile and criminal courts over certain offenses. The prosecutor, by charging one of these offenses, causes the case to be handled in criminal court. See also Fla.Stat. Ann. § 39.02(5)(c) (Supp.1981); S.D.Comp. Laws Ann. § 26–11–3 (1976). In New York (statutory example is at p. 426, infra) certain enumerated offenses are initially excluded from the juvenile court's jurisdiction, although the criminal court has discretion to transfer appropriate cases to the juvenile court. Even if the evidence will only support a lesser offense the prosecutor, by charging a juvenile with a more serious offense, assures that the case will at least originate in criminal court. Similar statutory schemes are noted following the New York statutory model.

The D.C. statute, supra at 412, is only slightly different. There certain statutorily designated offenses are excluded altogether from the jurisdiction of the juvenile court. By deciding what offense to charge the prosecutor, in effect, determines the court in which the juvenile shall be tried. See Whitebread and Batey, Transfer Between Courts: Proposals of the Juvenile Justice Standards Project, 63 Va.L.Rev. 221, 233–35 (1977). For a discussion of the problem of prosecutorial abuse and a suggested solution see Davis, The Efficacy of a Probable Cause Requirement in Juvenile Proceedings, 59 N.C.L.Rev. 723, 740–44 (1981).

(3) The issue immediately raised by such statutes is whether the exercise of the discretion vested by statute in a prosecutor to charge a person with certain enumerated offenses, thereby initiating that person's prosecution as an adult, is violative of due process. These statutes have been upheld time and again against attacks on due process or equal protection grounds, and against the argument in *Bland*, supra p. 413, that the statute negates the presumption of innocence. See also Woodard v. Wainwright, 556 F.2d 781 (5th Cir. 1977); Russell v. Parratt, 543 F.2d 1214 (8th Cir. 1976); Cox v. United States, 473 F.2d 334 (4th Cir. 1973); Myers v. District Court, 184 Colo. 81, 518 P.2d 836 (1974); State v. Cain, 381 So.2d 1361 (Fla.1980); People v. Sprinkle, 56 Ill.2d 257, 307 N.E.2d 161 (1974); State v. Grayer, 191 Neb. 523, 215 N.W.2d 859 (1974); Sherfield v. State, 511 P.2d 598 (Okl.Cr.App.1973).

(4) What if a child who is transferred to adult court, having been charged with one of the serious offenses enumerated in the transfer statute is then convicted of or pleads guilty to a less serious offense for which he could not have been automatically waived? Take, for example, a youth in the District of Columbia charged with murder who pleads guilty in the criminal court to battery—should the child be returned to the jurisdiction of the juvenile court? How will your answer affect plea bargaining in the adult proceeding?

A Louisiana statute provides that if a charge originates in criminal court (because the offense charged is excluded from the juvenile court's jurisdiction), the criminal court may retain jurisdiction over the case even if the juvenile pleads guilty to or is convicted of a lesser offense over which the juvenile court would have had original jurisdiction. La.Rev.Stat.Ann. § 13:1570(A)(5) (Supp.1981). See Miller v. Quatsoe, 348 F.Supp. 764 (E.D. Wis.1972) holding waiver of a juvenile is effective only with regard to the charge alleged. If the trial is to be on another charge, waiver must be sought again because a juvenile court can only waive its jurisdiction with respect to the allegations of delinquency actually before it. People v. Smith, 35 Mich.App. 597, 192 N.W.2d 666 (1971), on the other hand, held that a juvenile charged with armed robbery could, after waiver of jurisdiction by the juvenile court, enter a guilty plea in the adult court to a lesser included felony. The court rejected the contention that a juvenile could not plead guilty to a lesser offense not specifically waived by the juvenile court.

Vesting the prosecutor with even limited discretion raises the spectre of prosecutorial abuse. While the traditional waiver process is replete with due process safeguards as a result of *Kent*, what safeguards assure fair decisionmaking by the prosecutor? What is to prevent the prosecutor from charging an offense over which the criminal court has concurrent jurisdiction, when the evidence will support at best commission of a lesser offense over which the juvenile court has original jurisdiction? Or charging an offense that is excluded from the juvenile court's jurisdiction, even though the evidence will only support commission of a lesser offense? Or, in a jurisdiction in which certain offenses must originate in the criminal court, from charging such an offense even though the evidence will not support an offense of that grade? In all of these examples overcharging could be used, in effect, as a means of prosecutorial allocation of jurisdiction between courts while avoiding the necessity of a waiver hearing in juvenile court.

In Vermont, the statutes provide for waiver and transfer to criminal court of a juvenile who was over 10 but under 14 at the time of the alleged commission of any one of certain enumerated serious offenses, Vt.Stat.Ann. tit. 33, § 635a(a) (Spec.Supp.1981). The statutes further provide, however, that if the juvenile is not convicted of one of the enumerated offenses but is only convicted of a lesser offense, the case shall be remanded to juvenile court for disposition, the conviction shall be treated as a delinquency adjudication, and the case shall be treated as though it had remained in juvenile court at all times. Id. § 635a(h). Should a similar safeguard exist for juveniles whose cases originate in criminal court as a result of prosecutorial discretion rather than judicial decisionmaking?

For a discussion of the problem and a proposed solution see Davis, The Efficacy of a Probable Cause Requirement in Juvenile Proceedings, 59 N.C.L.Rev. 723, 737–44 (1981).

4. JUDICIAL TRANSFER BY THE JUVENILE COURT

CALIFORNIA WELFARE AND INSTITUTIONS CODE

§ 606. Subjecting minor to criminal prosecution

When a petition has been filed in a juvenile court, the minor who is the subject of the petition shall not thereafter be subject to criminal prosecution based on the facts giving rise to the petition unless the juvenile court finds that the minor is not a fit and proper subject to be dealt with under this chapter and orders that criminal proceedings be resumed or instituted against him.

§ 707. Fitness hearing

(a) In any case in which a minor is alleged to be a person described in Section 602 by reason of the violation, when he or she was 16 years of age or older, of any criminal statute or ordinance except those listed in subdivision (b), upon motion of the petitioner made prior to the attachment of jeopardy the court shall cause the probation officer to investigate and submit a report on the behavioral patterns and social history of the minor being considered for a determination of unfitness. Following submission and consideration of the report, and of any other relevant evidence which the petitioner or the minor may wish to submit, the juvenile court may find that the minor is not a fit and proper subject to be dealt with under the juvenile court law if it concludes that the minor would not be amenable to the care, treatment, and training program available through the facilities of the juvenile court, based upon an evaluation of the following criteria:

(1) The degree of criminal sophistication exhibited by the minor.

(2) Whether the minor can be rehabilitated prior to the expiration of the juvenile court's jurisdiction.

(3) The minor's previous delinquent history.

(4) Success of previous attempts by the juvenile court to rehabilitate the minor.

(5) The circumstances and gravity of the offense alleged to have been committed by the minor.

A determination that the minor is not a fit and proper subject to be dealt with under the juvenile court law may be based on any one or a combination of the factors set forth above, which shall be recited in the order of unfitness. In any case in which a hearing has been noticed pursuant to this section, the court shall postpone the taking of a plea to the petition until the conclusion of the fitness hearing, and no plea which may already have been entered shall constitute evidence at such hearing.

(b) The provisions of subdivision (c) shall be applicable in any case in which a minor is alleged to be a person described in Section 602 by reason of the violation, when he or she was 16 years of age or older, of one of the following offenses:

(1) Murder;

(2) Arson of an inhabited building;

(3) Robbery while armed with a dangerous or deadly weapon;

(4) Rape with force or violence or threat of great bodily harm;

(5) Sodomy by force, violence, duress, menace, or threat of great bodily harm;

(6) Lewd or lascivious act as provided in subdivision (b) of Section 288 of the Penal Code;

(7) Oral copulation by force, violence, duress, menace, or threat of great bodily harm;

(8) Any offense specified in Section 289 of the Penal Code;

(9) Kidnapping for ransom;

(10) Kidnapping for purpose of robbery;

(11) Kidnapping with bodily harm;

(12) Assault with intent to murder or attempted murder;

(13) Assault with a firearm or destructive device;

(14) Assault by any means of force likely to produce great bodily injury;

(15) Discharge of a firearm into an inhabited or occupied building;

(16) Any offense described in Section 1203.09 of the Penal Code.

(c) With regard to a minor alleged to be a person described in Section 602 by reason of the violation, when he or she was 16 years of age or older, of any of the offenses listed in subdivision (b), upon motion of the petitioner made prior to the attachment of jeopardy the court shall cause the probation officer to investigate and submit a report on the behavioral patterns and social history of the minor being considered for a determination of unfitness. Following submission and consideration of the report, and of any other relevant evidence which the petitioner or the minor may wish to submit the minor shall be presumed to be not a fit and proper subject to be dealt with under the juvenile court law unless the juvenile court concludes, based upon evidence, which evidence may be of extenuating or mitigating circumstances, that the minor would be amenable to the care, treatment, and training program available through the facilities of the juvenile court based upon an evaluation of each of the following criteria:

(1) The degree of criminal sophistication exhibited by the minor.

(2) Whether the minor can be rehabilitated prior to the expiration of the juvenile court's jurisdiction.

(3) The minor's previous delinquent history.

(4) Success of previous attempts by the juvenile court to rehabilitate the minor.

(5) The circumstances and gravity of the offenses alleged to have been committed by the minor.

A determination that the minor is a fit and proper subject to be dealt with under the juvenile court law shall be based on a finding of amenability after consideration of the criteria set forth above, and findings therefor recited in the order as to each of the above criteria that the minor is fit and proper under each and every one of the above criteria. In making a finding of fitness, the court may consider extenuating or mitigating circumstances in evaluating each of the above criteria. In any case in which a hearing has been noticed pursuant to this section, the court shall postpone the taking of a plea to the petition until the conclusion of the fitness hearing and no plea which may already have been entered shall constitute evidence at such hearing.

NOTES

(1) The most common way that the waiver decision is made is to leave that determination to the discretion of the juvenile court.. As was seen above, standards of varying specificity are sometimes provided to guide or limit that discretion. It is here that the procedural rights provided by *Kent* and its progeny become significant. See Donald L. v. Superior Court, 7 Cal. 3d 592, 102 Cal.Rptr. 850, 498 P.2d 1098 (1972).

(2) The Juvenile Justice Standards adopt traditional judicial waiver by the juvenile court as the exclusive means of allocating jurisdiction between courts. Standard 1.1 of the Standards Relating to Transfer Between Courts posits original jurisdiction over all juveniles (persons under 17 years of age) in the juvenile court and provides that the criminal court can exercise jurisdiction in appropriate cases only upon transfer from the juvenile court following a waiver hearing. Standards 2.1 through 2.4 deal with waiver procedures, including the requirement of a hearing.

(3) In some states in connection with waiver proceedings the child may ask to be tried as an adult. See, e.g., Fla.Stat.Ann. § 39.02(5)(b) (1976); Ill. Ann.Stat. ch. 37, § 702–7(5) (1972); Sumner v. Williams, 304 So.2d 472 (Fla. App.1974) (court rule in Florida that child may be waived on demand is mandatory, not discretionary, with juvenile court judge); accord, People v. Thomas, 34 Ill.App.3d 1002, 341 N.E.2d 178 (1976). See also United States v. Hill, 538 F.2d 1072 (4th Cir. 1976) (18 U.S.C.A. § 5032 permits the child on advice of counsel to be waived on demand to be tried as an adult).

5. JUDICIAL TRANSFER BY THE CRIMINAL COURT

NEW YORK FAMILY COURT ACT (McKINNEY)

§ 712. Definitions

As used in this article, the following terms shall have the following meanings:

(a) "Juvenile delinquent". A person over seven and less than sixteen years of age who, having done an act that would constitute a crime, (i) is not criminally responsible for such conduct by reason of infancy, or (ii) is the defendant in an action ordered removed from a criminal court to the family court . . . .

NEW YORK PENAL LAW (McKINNEY)

§ 10.00   Definitions of terms of general use in this chapter

. . .

18. "Juvenile offender" means (1) a person thirteen years old who is criminally responsible for acts constituting murder in the second degree . . .; and (2) a person fourteen or fifteen years old who is criminally responsible for acts constituting [murder in the second degree]; [felony murder], provided that the underlying crime for

the murder charge is one for which such person is criminally responsible; [kidnapping in the first degree]; [arson in the first or second degree]; [assault in the first degree]; [manslaughter in the first degree]; [rape in the first degree]; [sodomy in the first degree]; [burglary in the first or second degree]; [robbery in the first or second degree]; or . . . attempt to commit murder in the second degree or kidnapping in the first degree.

§ 30.00 Infancy

1. Except as provided in subdivision two of this section, <u>a person less than sixteen years old is not criminally responsible for conduct.</u>

2. <u>A person thirteen, fourteen, or fifteen years of age is criminally responsible for acts constituting murder in the second degree</u> . . . and [felony murder] provided that the underlying crime for the murder charge is one for which such person is criminally responsible; and a person fourteen or fifteen years of age is criminally responsible for acts constituting [kidnapping in the first degree]; [arson in the first or second degree]; [assault in the first degree]; [manslaughter in the first degree]; [rape in the first degree]; [sodomy in the first degree]; [burglary in the first or second degree]; [robbery in the first or second degree]; or . . . attempt to commit murder in the second degree or kidnapping in the first degree.

3. In any prosecution for an offense, lack of criminal responsibility by reason of infancy, as defined in this section, is a defense.

NEW YORK CRIMINAL PROCEDURE LAW (McKINNEY)

§ 180.75 Proceedings upon felony complaint; juvenile offender

1. When a juvenile offender is arraigned before a local criminal court, the provisions of this section shall apply in lieu of the provisions of sections 180.30, 180.50 and 180.70 of this article.

2. If the defendant waives a hearing upon the felony complaint, the court must order that the defendant be held for the action of the grand jury of the appropriate superior court with respect to the charge or charges contained in the felony complaint. . . .

3. If there be a hearing, then at the conclusion of the hearing, the court must dispose of the felony complaint as follows:

(a) If there is reasonable cause to believe that the defendant committed a crime for which a person under the age of sixteen is criminally responsible, the court must order that the defendant be held for the action of a grand jury of the appropriate superior court . . .; or

(b) If there is not reasonable cause to believe that the defendant committed a crime for which a person under the age of sixteen is criminally responsible but there is reasonable cause to believe that the defendant is a "juvenile delinquent" as defined in subdivision (a) of section seven hundred twelve of the family court act, the court must specify the act or acts it found reasonable cause to believe the defendant did and direct that the action be removed to the family court . . .; or

(c) If there is not reasonable cause to believe that the defendant committed any criminal act, the court must dismiss the felony complaint and discharge the defendant from custody if he is in custody, or if he is at liberty on bail, it must exonerate the bail.

4. Notwithstanding the provisions of subdivision two and three of this section, a local criminal court shall, at the request of the district attorney, order removal of an action against a juvenile offender to the family court . . . if, upon consideration of the criteria specified in subdivision two of section 210.43 of this chapter, it is determined that to do so would be in the interests of justice. Where, however, the felony complaint charges the juvenile offender with murder in the second degree . . ., rape in the first degree . . . ., sodomy in the first degree . . . ., or an armed felony . . . ., a determination that such action be removed to the family court shall, in addition, be based upon a finding of one or more of the following factors: (i) mitigating circumstances that bear directly upon the manner in which the crime was committed; or (ii) where the defendant was not the sole participant in the crime, the defendant's participation was relatively minor although not so minor as to constitute a defense to the prosecution; or (iii) possible deficiencies in proof of the crime.

5. Notwithstanding the provisions of subdivision two, three, or four, if a currently undetermined felony complaint against a juvenile offender is pending in a local criminal court, and the defendant has not waived a hearing pursuant to subdivision two and a hearing pursuant to subdivision three has not commenced, the defendant may move in the superior court which would exercise the trial jurisdiction of the offense or offenses charged were an indictment therefor to result, to remove the action to family court. . . . Upon such motion, the superior court shall be authorized to sit as a local criminal court to exercise the preliminary jurisdiction specified in subdivisions two and three of this section, and shall proceed and determine the motion as provided in section 210.43 of this chapter; provided, however, that the exception provisions of paragraph (b) of subdivision one of such section 210.43 shall not apply when there is not reasonable cause to believe that the juvenile offender committed one or more of the crimes enumerated therein, and in such event the provisions of paragraph (a) thereof shall apply.

. . .

§ 210.43 Motion to remove juvenile offender to family court

1. After a motion by a juvenile offender, pursuant to subdivision five of section 180.75 of this chapter, or after arraignment of a juve-

nile offender upon an indictment, the superior court may, on motion of any party or on its own motion:

(a) except as otherwise provided by paragraph (b), order removal of the action to the family court . . . ., if, after consideration of the factors set forth in subdivision two of this section, the court determines that to do so would be in the interests of justice; or

(b) with the consent of the district attorney, order removal of an action involving an indictment charging a juvenile offender with murder in the second degree . . . .; rape in the first degree . . . .; sodomy in the first degree . . . .; or an armed felony . . . ., to the family court . . . if the court finds one or more of the following factors: (i) mitigating circumstances that bear directly upon the manner in which the crime was committed; (ii) where the defendant was not the sole participant in the crime, the defendant's participation was relatively minor although not so minor as to constitute a defense to the prosecution; or (iii) possible deficiencies in the proof of the crime, and, after consideration of the factors set forth in subdivision two of this section, the court determined that removal of the action to the family court would be in the interests of justice.

2. In making its determination pursuant to subdivision one of this section the court shall, to the extent applicable, examine individually and collectively, the following:

(a) the seriousness and circumstances of the offense;

(b) the extent of harm caused by the offense;

(c) the evidence of guilt, whether admissible or inadmissible at trial;

(d) the history, character and condition of the defendant;

(e) the purpose and effect of imposing upon the defendant a sentence authorized for the offense;

(f) the impact of a removal of the case to the family court on the safety or welfare of the community;

(g) the impact of a removal of the case to the family court upon the confidence of the public in the criminal justice system;

(h) where the court deems it appropriate, the attitude of the complainant or victim with respect to the motion; and

(i) any other relevant fact indicating that a judgment of conviction in the criminal court would serve no useful purpose.

. . . .

4. For the purpose of making a determination pursuant to this section, any evidence which is not legally privileged may be introduced. If the defendant testifies, his testimony may not be introduced against him in any future proceeding, except to impeach his testimony at such future proceeding as inconsistent prior testimony.

5. a. If the court orders removal of the action to family court, it shall state on the record the factor or factors upon which its determi-

nation is based, and, the court shall give its reasons for removal in detail and not in conclusory terms.

b. The district attorney shall state upon the record the reasons for his consent to removal of the action to the family court. The reasons shall be stated in detail and not in conclusory terms.

VEGA v. BELL

Court of Appeals of New York, 1979.
47 N.Y.2d 543, 419 N.Y.S.2d 454, 393 N.E.2d 450.

OPINION OF THE COURT

GABRIELLI, JUDGE.

We are called upon in this article 78 proceeding to determine whether a juvenile offender may be indicted by a Grand Jury and be brought to trial without first being afforded a hearing in a local criminal court on the issue whether the interests of justice require removal of the action to Family Court for treatment as a juvenile delinquency proceeding. We conclude that a local criminal court hearing is not a jurisdictional prerequisite to indictment by a Grand Jury, and thus there exists no bar to continuation of criminal proceedings commenced by Grand Jury indictment despite the failure to hold a removal hearing in a local criminal court.

Petitioner, then 15 years of age, was arrested on October 4, 1978 and arraigned the following day in the Criminal Court of the City of New York, Bronx County, upon a felony complaint charging him with one count of sodomy in the first degree. The complaint alleged that petitioner had engaged in deviate sexual intercourse with a minor by forcible compulsion. On October 11, petitioner requested both a felony hearing and removal of the case to the Family Court. The prosecutor informed the court that on the previous day a Grand Jury had voted to indict petitioner on four counts of sodomy in the first degree based on four incidents, one of which formed the basis for the felony complaint. Reasoning that it lacked the power to continue the proceeding before it after the Grand Jury had acted, the court denied petitioner's applications for a felony hearing and for removal to Family Court, and instead transferred the action to the appropriate superior criminal court, Supreme Court, Bronx County.

Petitioner subsequently moved in Supreme Court, Bronx County, to transfer the action back to Criminal Court for resolution of his removal motion on the merits. Following the denial of the transfer motion, petitioner commenced the instant article 78 proceeding seeking to prohibit his prosecution on the ground that the Grand Jury lacked the power to indict him unless the local criminal court first provided him a hearing on his removal motion. The Appellate Division granted the petition, over a dissent by two Justices, and respondents now appeal to this court as of right pursuant to CPLR 5601 (subd. [a], par. [i]).

. . .

Prior to September 1, 1978, children under the age of 16 were not subject to criminal sanctions in New York State in any circumstances. Instead, juveniles who performed acts which would have been crimes had they been committed by adults, were all dealt with through a separate juvenile delinquency system . . . . This method of attempting to deal with the problem of criminal actions performed by juveniles was deemed somewhat less than completely successful by many, especially as public attention in recent years focused on what has been perceived to be an increase in the rate of acts of violence by minors. Responding to this troublesome state of affairs, the Legislature last year made certain substantial modifications in the traditional mechanisms for resolving the problem of juvenile crime . . . . Among other drastic changes in the law, juveniles between the ages of 13 and 15 who are charged with certain enumerated, serious crimes of violence are not classified as "juvenile offenders" and are prosecuted within the adult criminal justice system (CPL 1.20, subd. 42; Penal Law, § 10.00, subd. 18; § 30.00, subd. 2).

While deciding that such harsh measures were necessary to control violent juvenile crime in the face of what was considered to be the failure of the traditional means of treating that problem, the Legislature nonetheless remained sensitive to the fact that special considerations are sometimes appropriate when dealing with juveniles, who are more easily influenced by their companions and their environment than are adults. Hence, rather than simply applying every feature of the adult criminal justice system to juvenile offenders, the Legislature carefully created several modifications in normal procedure so as to displace "the ones applicable to adults insofar as they would be inappropriate or incongruous to the handling of such 'juveniles' charged with very serious crimes". Of special significance in the instant case are several provisions whereby, at various stages in a criminal proceeding, a juvenile offender may be removed to Family Court if it becomes apparent in a particular case that such treatment would be more appropriate than continuation of criminal prosecution . . . .

Most of these provisions provide for removal to Family Court only with the approval of the District Attorney. CPL 180.75 (subd. 4), however, provides that where a juvenile offender is arraigned before a local criminal court upon a felony complaint, that court may order, even over the objection of the District Attorney, that the defendant be removed to Family Court in the interests of justice unless the defendant is accused of either murder in the second degree or an armed felony . . . . Petitioner contends that this is the only stage in a criminal proceeding against a juvenile offender at which a court may order removal of the accused to Family Court despite the objections of the District Attorney. Petitioner suggests that since the Legislature deemed it necessary to provide such a safety valve, it must have intended that mechanism to be applicable to every alleged juvenile offender. Hence, petitioner would have us interpret the statutory scheme governing the prosecution of juvenile offenders as requiring that each juvenile defendant must be granted a hearing before a local criminal court to decide whether the interests of justice mandate removal to Family Court, before he or she may be indicted by a Grand Jury. In addition to his statutory arguments, petitioner contends that due process mandates a full hearing to determine whether a juvenile may be prosecuted in the adult criminal justice system or whether he or she should be removed to Family Court. Finally, it is also suggested that a scheme whereby only those juvenile offenders who are arraigned before a local criminal court are afforded an opportunity for removal without the consent of the District Attorney would itself be so inherently arbitrary as to violate due process.

Our examination of the statutes, however, persuades us that a juvenile offender may indeed be indicted by a Grand Jury without first being afforded a removal hearing before a local criminal court. Petitioner's arguments are based on a misunderstanding of the nature and function of CPL 180.75. That section deals only with those accused juvenile offenders who have been arrested and are arraigned on a felony complaint prior to Grand Jury action. The primary function of the section is to provide a prompt felony hearing, similar to that granted to an accused adult defendant . . .. In both situations, the primary purpose of such a hearing and such a procedure is to determine whether there exists reasonable cause to hold a defendant in custody pending action by a Grand Jury. It is a preliminary proceeding at which a preliminary determination is made pending a decision by the Grand Jury as to whether there exists probable cause to indict. Once the Grand Jury does act, the determination whether there exist [sic] reasonable cause to hold and prosecute a defendant has been made by the Grand Jury itself, the body constitutionally authorized to make that decision, and hence the need for a felony hearing is obviated. The power of the Grand Jury to indict felons is in no way dependent upon the existence of a prior felony hearing, for the purpose of the felony hearing is simply to temporarily determine the fate of the accused pending Grand Jury consideration. Thus, an otherwise valid indictment is not tainted by any error at the felony hearing, since "the Grand Jury [has] power to investigate and indict regardless of what [has] occurred before the magistrate and regardless of whether the magistrate had held or discharged the prisoner or still had the matter pending, or of whether there had ever been such a preliminary hearing".

Defendant would have us hold that simply because the Legislature has seen fit to provide the local criminal court with additional dispositional powers at the felony complaint arraignment state, it has in some way made arraignment before a local criminal court a neces-

sary jurisdictional predicate for indictment by a grand jury. Were
this so, it would mean that no juvenile offender could be indicted
without first being arrested upon a felony complaint and arraigned
before a local criminal court, since that is the way in which a juvenile
is brought before a local criminal court pursuant to CPL 180.75.
Such a result would be unthinkable, for the Grand Jury certainly has
the power to indict a person not yet arrested or arraigned. Indeed, to
require arrest and arraignment as a prerequisite to Grand Jury consideration would be to mandate unnecessary preindictment incarceration and to place a totally unneeded burden upon the judicial system.

The Legislature's decision to provide a local criminal court with
power to remove an accused juvenile offender to Family Court was
plainly intended to serve as a means of removing from the criminal
system as quickly as possible those juveniles who, because of exceptional circumstances, can be dealt with more effectively within the
juvenile system. It was not intended to mandate local criminal court
consideration of every alleged juvenile offender as a prerequisite to
Grand Jury consideration. We decline petitioner's invitation to interpret the statutory scheme as creating such a novel and cumbersome
mechanism without a much clearer indication of legislative intent to
so elevate local criminal court arraignment proceedings.

Nor are we persuaded by petitioner's contention that due process
requires that an accused juvenile offender be provided with a hearing
at the local criminal court, or elsewhere, to determine whether the
interests of justice require removal to Family Court before that defendant may be prosecuted within the adult criminal justice system.
This argument is based in large part on the decision of the United
States Supreme Court in Kent v. United States, 383 U.S. 541, 86 S.Ct.
1045, 16 L.Ed.2d 84. We consider that reliance to be misplaced. In
Kent, the Supreme Court held that due process mandates a hearing
before a juvenile can be transferred from the "exclusive jurisdiction"
of a juvenile court into the adult criminal justice system. The statutory plan underlying that decision established a juvenile justice system whereby all juveniles were initially and presumptively subject to
the exclusive jurisdiction of the juvenile court unless the juvenile
court deemed it proper to waive its jurisdiction and transfer a particular minor to the jurisdiction of the criminal courts (Kent v. United
states, supra, at pp. 547–548, 86 S.Ct. 1045). Obviously, under that
system the great majority of minor offenders were to be treated
within the framework of the juvenile system, and transferral to the
adult criminal justice system was envisioned only in certain rare instances in which it was determined that treatment as a juvenile would
be ineffectual. Because of the significant effects of such a transfer,
and the potentially severe results, the Supreme Court ruled that due
process mandated a hearing lest the decision to transfer be an arbitrary one by which randomly selected juveniles were subjected to the
adult system while most of their peers continued to reap the benefits
of their status as juveniles.

The current New York statutory scheme, on the other hand, is significantly different. All youngsters over a certain age who are accused of certain criminal activities are now automatically prosecuted within the adult criminal justice system unless there exist certain special circumstances warranting more lenient treatment and transfer to the Family Court. Hence there exists no opportunity for that which the Supreme Court found to be abhorrent in *Kent*: namely, the possibility that some juveniles would be arbitrarily transferred to the adult criminal system, thereby subjecting them to significantly harsher potential penalties than could be imposed upon the majority of juveniles who engaged in similar antisocial behavior. Under the New York plan, in contradistinction, all juveniles accused of certain designated crimes are subject to the adult criminal system, except in those unusual cases in which treatment as a juvenile is deemed appropriate.

This is not to suggest, of course, that the decision whether to remove a particular juvenile to Family Court in the interests of justice may be a completely arbitrary one. Hence, were we to interpret the statutory scheme as affording the opportunity for possible removal over the opposition of the District Attorney only to those juveniles who are arraigned in a local criminal court, there might well be some doubt as to the validity of such a plan. It would seem somewhat unreasonable to provide such a potential benefit only to those juveniles whose behavior is such that immediate arrest is deemed necessary, while denying it to those youths left at liberty pending consideration by a Grand Jury.

As it is, however, we need not reach this question, for we view the statutory scheme as providing the power to remove an accused juvenile offender to Family Court in the interests of justice and over the objections of the prosecutor to superior criminal courts following Grand Jury indictment, as well as to local criminal courts at arraignment. We are cognizant of the fact that no such power was explicitly given superior criminal courts when the Legislature revised the traditional juvenile justice system in 1978. Indeed, the Legislature did specifically provide several opportunities for removal with the consent of the District Attorney. This does not lead us to conclude, however, that this was because the Legislature wished only the local criminal courts to have the power to remove over the objection of the District Attorney, for such a result would be unreasonable, and it is the duty of the courts to interpret statutes so as to reach a reasonable result whenever possible. Hence, we conclude that the Legislature's failure to explicitly grant such powers to the superior criminal courts was based on the belief of the Legislature that such a grant was unnecessary because such a power was impliedly founded in the superior criminal courts' authority to dismiss an indictment in the interests of justice . . . . Surely the power to remove in the interests of justice, which is a much lesser relief than outright dismissal in the interests of justice, must be deemed to be included within the power to dismiss. Hence, although CPL 210.40 does not expressly provide superior criminal courts with the power to remove an accused juvenile offender to Family Court in the interests of justice and over the objections of the District Attorney, it is certainly reasonable to conclude that the statute impliedly provides such power, especially since such an interpretation is necessary to avoid doubts as to the validity of the statutory scheme. Although it might be suggested that the existence of this power is at odds with the explicit provision of several opportunities to remove with the consent of the prosecutor, we would interpret the latter sections as indicative of a legislative intent that removal over the District Attorney's objections only be ordered in the exceptional case. At the same time, the Legislature deemed it necessary to provide some authority to remove without the District Attorney's approval because of its realization that in certain rare instances a prosecutor may be too closely involved in the prosecution to appreciate the benefits of juvenile treatment.

Finally, we reject petitioner's suggestion that a hearing will in all cases be necessary to determine whether the interests of justice mandate removal to Family Court. This is a matter best left to the sound discretion of the court in which the removal motion is made. We note that the Legislature has already decided that in most cases juveniles accused of certain serious crimes are to be prosecuted within the criminal justice system. It is not for the courts to question the wisdom of this legislative decision, nor to seek to undermine its operation by removal to Family Court in the "typical" case, if indeed any case involving juveniles can ever be deemed typical. At any rate, under the present scheme it will only be in the unusual or exceptional case that removal will be proper, and thus a hearing will be necessary only if it appears for some special reason that removal would be appropriate in the particular case.

In sum, we conclude that the failure to provide petitioner with a removal hearing at the local criminal court did not deprive the Grand Jury of the power to indict him. Hence, there exists no jurisdictional bar to the continuation of his prosecution, and no basis for issuance of a writ of prohibition.

Accordingly, the judgment appealed from should be reserved, without costs, and the petition seeking writ of prohibition should be dismissed.

NOTES

(1) As the court in the principal case notes, prior to the current legislation no provision was made for transfer of juveniles from juvenile court to criminal court or vice versa. Under the present statutory scheme discretionary transfer of some cases from criminal court to juvenile court is the exclusive means of allocating jurisdiction between the two courts.

Only two states—New York and Nebraska—authorize the criminal court to make all judicial transfer decisions. The Nebraska procedure differs from the New York statutory scheme in that the juvenile and criminal courts have concurrent jurisdiction over juveniles charged with a felony and juveniles 16 or older charged with any offense. Neb.Rev.Stat. § 43–247 (Supp.1981). No provision is made for waiver of jurisdiction by the juvenile court. The prosecutor decides the court in which any such case shall be handled, Id. § 43–276, and the criminal court is given discretionary authority to transfer appropriate cases to the juvenile court, Id. § 43–261. Thus, in Nebraska the prosecutor and the criminal court share in the decision to allocate jurisdiction between the juvenile and criminal courts, although only the criminal court may make a *transfer* decision.

At least 10 other states authorize the criminal court to make some transfer decisions. South Carolina provides for waiver by the juvenile court but also provides that if a juvenile appears before the criminal court initially, that court has discretion to bind over appropriate cases, based on age and other factors, for criminal prosecution. S.C. Code §§ 20–7–400(C), 20–7–430(4)–(6) (Supp.1981). Wyoming, in addition to permitting waiver by the juvenile court, authorizes the prosecutor to make the initial decision in all delinquency cases to proceed in either the juvenile or criminal court and vests the criminal court with discretion to transfer some cases to juvenile court. Wyo.Stat.Ann. §§ 14–6–203(c), 14–6–211, 14–6–237 (1977). Vermont also provides for prosecutorial decisionmaking in certain cases. Vt.Stat.Ann. tit. 33, §§ 635(c), 635a (Spec.Supp.1981). In addition, the criminal court may transfer to juvenile court cases that for reasons of age or seriousness of the offense (or both) originate in criminal court. Id. §§ 635(b), 644(c). Arkansas does not provide for traditional waiver at all, but in a case in which a juvenile is arrested pursuant to a warrant and is brought before the court issuing the warrant, the court may retain jurisdiction over the case or transfer it to the appropriate court. Ark.Stat.Ann. §§ 45–417, 45–420 (Supp.1981). Presumably, in such cases transfer could be from the juvenile court to the criminal court as well as vice versa, depending on which court first takes jurisdiction.

(2) Pennsylvania is one of those states that employ, in part, a reverse certification model for allocating jurisdiction between courts. In Pennsylvania murder is initially excluded from the juvenile court's jurisdiction, and the criminal court has discretion to transfer appropriate cases to the juvenile court. 42 Pa.Cons.Stat.Ann. §§ 6302, 6322(a) (Purdon 1981).

In Commonwealth v. Wade, 485 Pa. 453, 402 A.2d 1360 (1979), the Pennsylvania Supreme Court upheld the constitutionality of this statutory scheme against both equal protection and due process claims. In denying the equal protection claim the court held that the classification scheme bore a rational relationship to the legitimate state objective of protection of the public interest and public safety.

The court also rejected the due process argument that the reverse transfer statute lacked adequate standards by which a court could determine a juvenile's transfer status. The court had held earlier in Commonwealth v. Pyle, 462 Pa. 613, 342 A.2d 101 (1975), that the same standards that provide for transfer from juvenile court to criminal court were also applicable to transfers from criminal court to juvenile court. The only difference is that in the latter cases the burden of proof is reversed, i.e., the burden is on the juvenile to show amenability to treatment as a juvenile. In any event, since the statute had been construed to embrace the same standards as the regular waiver statute, the court held that the due process claim was without merit.

The court also held that the trial court had adequately expressed its reasons for denying transfer, in compliance with *Kent*'s requirement of a statement of reasons in order to permit meaningful review. Significantly, then, the court in *Wade* implicitly concluded that the safeguards imposed in *Kent* are applicable as well to reverse certification procedures in criminal court, with the sole exception of reversing the burden of proof.

(3) When Oklahoma's reverse certification procedures were added in 1978, no corresponding revisions were made to the existing jurisdictional and waiver provisions of the juvenile court code. In holding the reverse certification and waiver statutes unconstitutionally vague, the Oklahoma Court of Criminal Appeals observed:

> . . . Since it became effective . . . Oklahoma's reverse certification statutes have been interpreted at various times to create concurrent juvenile and felony division jurisdiction, to vest initial exclusive jurisdiction in the felony division, to confer discretion on the prosecutor to determine where to file, and to create exclusive initial juvenile division jurisdiction. There is some justification for each of the four interpretations.
>
> . . .
>
> We cannot glean from the statutes what procedures are required if a 16 or 17-year-old is accused of one of the 11 enumerated crimes; nor can we determine what are the rights and responsibilities of either the State or of accused juveniles. For this Court to determine what it thinks would be an acceptable procedure, would not be a matter of interpretation of the statute but would rather be an exercise in judicial legislation. We cannot rewrite the statute on the pretext of construction. Therefore, we hold that [the reverse certification and waiver statutes] are void and without effect.

State ex rel. Coats v. Johnson, 597 P.2d 328, 329–330 (Okl.Cr.App. 1979). The statutes subsequently were revised to provide a coherent scheme for allocating jurisdiction between courts, see Okla.Stat.Ann. tit. 10, §§ 1104.2, 1112(b) (Supp.1982), and as revised were held constitutionally valid in State ex rel. Coats v. Rakestraw, 610 P.2d 256 (Okl.Cr.App. 1980).

(4) Many statutes give adult courts that are properly exercising jurisdiction over a juvenile the power to try the juvenile as a juvenile court would, or to sit as a criminal court but to make a juvenile disposition. See, e.g., Va. Code Ann. § 16.1–272 (Supp.1981).

E. THE RELATION OF TRANSFER TO THE FUTURE OF THE JUVENILE COURT

In the past several years legislatures have reacted to concern for the level of juvenile crime and to skepticism about the ability of the juvenile justice system to rehabilitate youthful offenders by enacting statutes that result in more transfers of 16 and 17 year olds to adult criminal court. Typical is the shift in the burden of proof in California Welf. and Inst. Code § 707, supra, at 424. Minnesota now provides that if the state can show that the juvenile is sixteen or older and is charged with certain serious offenses or has a certain prior record, a prima facie case for transfer is established. Minn.Stat.Ann.

§ 260.125(3). In Matter of Welfare of Givens, 307 N.W.2d 489 (Minn. 1981) the state established a prima facie case for transfer of a sixteen year old to adult court by showing that he was charged with first degree murder. No other independent showing of non-amenability or dangerousness was required to support the transfer.

Compare the new transfer decisionmaking to the proposals for change in the rationale for juvenile delinquency dispositions discussed at length in Chapter Nine. As juvenile court proceedings become more like adult criminal prosecutions, does any reason remain for a separate juvenile court system? One commentator recently has suggested that a possible solution to the transfer problem might be to try all offenders regardless of age in the same courts with the same full set of procedural rights. Dispositions could then vary based on age, prior record, and the availability of appropriate programs and facilities. See Feld, Juvenile Court Legislative Reform and the Serious Young Offender: Dismantling the "Rehabilitative Ideal", 65 Minn.L.Rev. 167 (1981). As you study delinquency adjudication and disposition in the next two chapters, consider this possible convergence of the adult and juvenile systems. Does recent scholarship and legislative reform inexorably press in the direction of a unified court system or abolition of separate juvenile court jurisdiction over conduct by children that would be criminal if they were adults?

VIII. ADJUDICATORY HEARING

A. ADEQUATE AND TIMELY NOTICE

IN RE GAULT

Supreme Court of the United States, 1967.
387 U.S. 1, 87 S.Ct. 1428, 18 L.Ed.2d 527.

(For the opinion in this case, see page 209, supra.)

THE TIMELINESS OF NOTICE

The Supreme Court in *Gault* in setting forth notice requirements spoke of notice that is both (1) timely and (2) adequate to advise the juvenile and his parents of the allegations of misconduct. Most juvenile court statutes provide for time limitations within which persons must be notified, depending upon whether they are served personally or by mail. If personal service is effected, the statutes typically provide that service must be made at least 24 hours in advance of the scheduled hearing. See, e.g., Ga.Code Ann. § 15–11–27(a) (1982); Minn.Stat.Ann. § 260.141(1)(a) (Supp.1982) (five days if notice is personally served outside the state); N.D.Cent.Code § 27–20–23(1) (1974). If service is to be by mail, the statutes typically require that notice be mailed at least five days before the scheduled date of the hearing. See, e.g., Ga.Code Ann. § 15–11–27(a) (1982); Minn.Stat. Ann. § 260.141(1)(b) (Supp.1982) (14 days if notice is mailed out of state); N.D.Cent.Code § 27–20–23(1) (1974).

Some states require more advance notice. Tennessee, for example, requires notice at least three days in advance of the scheduled date of the hearing where the summons is personally served in the state. Tenn.Code Ann. § 37–223(a) (1977). Texas requires notice two days in advance. Tex.Fam.Code Ann. § 53.07(a) (1975). In both states if the summons is personally served outside the state or if it is served by mail in or outside the state, the more typical five-day requirement applies.

There are other variances as well. In California if the juvenile is detained, notice must be given at least five days before the scheduled hearing date, but if the hearing has been scheduled for a date less than five days after the date of filing of the petition, notice must be served no later than 24 hours prior to the hearing. If the juvenile is not in detention, a 10-day time limitation applies, whether service is made personally or by mail. Cal.Welf. & Inst. Code § 660(a)–(b) (Supp.1982).

Most of the codes also provide for service by publication to a party who, after reasonable efforts, can not be found or whose address can not be ascertained. See, e.g., Ga.Code Ann. § 15–11–27(b) (1982); Minn.Stat.Ann. § 260.141(1)(b) (Supp.1982); N.D.Cent.Code § 27–20–23(2) (1974); Tenn.Code Ann. § 37–223(b) (1977). Texas simply provides that the court shall have jurisdiction if, after reasonable efforts, any person required to be notified, other than the juvenile, can not be found nor his address determined. Tex.Fam.Code Ann. § 53.07(b) (1975).

The 24-hour notice requirement seems to be the barest minimum allowable under due process standards. In Doe v. State, 487 P.2d 47 (Alaska 1971), in which the petition was filed on one day and the juvenile was notified to appear in court the next day, a Friday, the court held that one day's notice was insufficient under the due process standards established in *Gault*. The defect was not cured by the granting of a continuance until Monday morning, because the juvenile's attorney had the same day been appointed to another major juvenile case and did not have adequate time to prepare both cases over the weekend. Normally this problem is alleviated by requiring a sufficient interval between the filing of the petition and the scheduling of the hearing. Texas, for example, while requiring only two days notice prior to a scheduled hearing, Tex.Fam.Code Ann. § 53.07(a) (1975), also provides: "Any attorney representing a child in proceedings under this title is entitled to 10 days to prepare for any adjudication or transfer hearing under this title." Id. § 51.10(h).

IN RE DENNIS

Supreme Court of Mississippi, 1974.
291 So.2d 731.

SUGG, JUSTICE:

This is an appeal from an order of the Youth Court Division of the Chancery Court of Rankin County by Terry Wayne Dennis. The court found that Dennis was a delinquent minor and committed him to the custody of a state supported training school until he reached the age of 18 years.

Dennis' first contention is that the petition filed against him was insufficient because the facts which would bring him within the purview of the "Youth Court Law" were stated in the petition as "grand larceny and breaking and entering." Miss.Code Ann. § 43–21–11 (1972) as amended by Chapter 469, Laws of 1973 sets forth the requirements of a petition filed thereunder, one of the requirements being "The facts which bring the child within the purview of the chapter." . . .

. . .

We reaffirm our position that a petition which institutes a youth court proceeding must recite factual allegations specific and definite enough to fairly apprise the juvenile, his parents, custodians or guardians of the particular act or acts of misconduct or the particular circumstances which will be inquired into at the adjudicatory proceedings.

We further hold that in those cases where a charge of delinquency is based upon the violation of a criminal law, the petition must charge the offense with the same particularity required in a criminal indictment. The petition in this case fails to meet these standards and is therefore insufficient to support the committal of Dennis to a training school.

. . .

It naturally follows that a child may not be committed to an institution without a petition and an adjudicatory hearing. Neither can the custody of a child be changed from its parents, guardian or custodian except by consent of the parents, guardian or custodian, or by order of the court after an adjudicatory hearing based on a petition. The Youth Court Law authorizes a temporary change of custody in urgent and necessitous circumstances, but the courts should exercise care to limit temporary changes of custody to urgent and necessitous cases, and see that a petition is filed and a hearing held within the time limits prescribed by statute.

We recognize that the Youth Court Law was enacted by the legislature for the care, protection and rehabilitation of children, but the law provides that any hearing shall be conducted under such rules of evidence as may comply with applicable constitutional standards. It also authorizes the court to make an informal adjustment for the best interest of a child without a petition. We recognize that battered and delinquent children are protected and delinquent children are rehabilitated without the necessity of a petition in a majority of cases arising under the law.

We do not intend to do away with the beneficial aspects of the law; however, when a petition is filed the child, his parents, guardians, or custodians, as the case may be, must be afforded due process in any adjudicatory hearing.

Reversed and remanded.

NOTES

(1) In accord with the principal case is Davies v. State, 171 Ind.App. 487, 357 N.E.2d 914 (1976) (bare charge that juvenile was "involved in first degree burglary," without reference to a specific time, place, or set of circumstances, insufficient to give adequate notice); see also In re Bryant, 18 Ill. App.3d 887, 310 N.E.2d 713 (1974).

In passing on the identical issue, the Georgia Court of Appeals, while holding the petition in question to be sufficient to furnish adequate notice, explained the test to be applied: "Although the petition does not have to be drafted with the exactitude of a criminal accusation, it must satisfy 'due process.' To meet this constitutional requirement the language must pass two tests: (1) it must contain sufficient factual details to inform the juvenile of the nature of the offense; and (2) it must provide data adequate to enable the accused to prepare his defense." T.L.T. v. State, 133 Ga.App. 895, 897, 212 S.E.2d 650, 653 (1975). The approved petition stated that "On October 4, 1973, at approximately 5:30 p.m., said youth was an accessory to the delinquent acts of breaking and entering and theft by taking [at a specified residence and] said youth had full knowledge that the delinquent acts were taking place, and, although said youth did not take part in the actual breaking and entering and theft by taking, he did, with full knowledge, assist in the attempts to sell the property." The petition also contained an itemized list of the stolen property.

Compare Neb.Rev.Stat. § 43–274 (Supp.1981), which provides that the petition must be drawn with the same specificity required in a criminal complaint.

(2) Normally the petition rather than the summons is the document that sets forth the alleged misconduct, but juvenile court statutes usually require that a copy of the petition be attached to the summons. See, e.g., Cal.Welf. & Inst.Code § 658 (Supp.1982); Minn.Stat.Ann. § 260.135(1) (Supp.1982); Tex.Fam.Code Ann. § 53.06(b) (1975).

(3) Most statutes provide for notice to both the juvenile and the parents or custodian of the juvenile and occasionally to other parties as well. The Texas statute, for example, provides:

> (a) The juvenile court shall direct issuance of a summons to:
>
>   (1) the child named in the petition;
>
>   (2) the child's parent, guardian, or custodian;
>
>   (3) the child's guardian ad litem; and
>
>   (4) any other person who appears to the court to be a proper or necessary party to the proceeding.
>
>   . . .

Tex.Fam.Code Ann. § 53.06(a) (1975). See also Cal.Welf. & Inst.Code § 658 (Supp.1982); Minn.Stat.Ann. § 260.135(2) (Supp.1982); Or.Rev.Stat. § 419.486(4) (1979). The Juvenile Justice Standards provide:

> . . .
>
> D. The summons should be served upon the following persons:
>
>   1. the juvenile;
>
>   2. the juvenile's parents and/or guardian, and, if the juvenile is in custody of some other person whose knowledge or participation in the proceedings would be appropriate, such custodian;
>
>   3. the attorney[s] for the juvenile and parents, if the identity of the attorney[s] is known; and
>
>   4. any other persons who appear to the court to be necessary or proper parties to the proceedings.
>
>   . . .

Juvenile Justice Standards Project, Standards Relating to Pretrial Court Proceedings, Standard 1.5(D) (1980).

(4) Is there any reason for a requirement that a very young child should receive notice of charges and a pending hearing if a parent or custodian has

been properly notified? Section 15–11–26(b) of the Georgia Code Annotated, which is based on the Uniform Juvenile Court Act, after requiring notice to parents or other custodian, provides: "The summons shall also be directed to the child if he is 14 or more years of age or is alleged to be a delinquent or unruly child." Thus, if the child is alleged to be delinquent he must receive notice regardless of age. The California provision, on the other hand, provides that notice, together with a copy of the petition, shall be "served upon the minor, if the minor is eight or more years of age." Cal.Welf. & Inst. Code § 658 (Supp.1982).

In RLR v. State, 487 P.2d 27, 40–41 (Alaska 1971), the Alaska Supreme Court, after concluding that process must be delivered to the child himself, commented:

> This requirement is not only constitutionally required but is desirable as a matter of policy. Parents may fail to give the petition and summons to the child because they do not understand its seriousness or, especially in the large proportion of cases in which parents are the complainants, because they are hostile or indifferent to the child's interests. Concerned parents might, as a disciplinary measure, refuse to show children the summons and petition and instead tell them an exaggerated, more frightening version of their contents. Even if the children learned of their court dates, they would not have a fair chance to retain counsel and prepare to meet the charges. Of course, personal service of process on extremely young children will be an empty form, but pointless service on a few children does little harm compared to absence of service on many children to whom it would be meaningful.

(5) Service of summons can be waived in certain instances. The Texas statute is typical of many that provide for waiver by any party other than the juvenile, e.g., a parent: "A party, other than the child, may waive service of summons by written stipulation or by voluntary appearance at the hearing." Tex.Fam.Code Ann. § 53.06(e) (1975); see also Ga.Code Ann. § 15–11–26(f) (1982); Tenn.Code Ann. § 37–221(d) (1977); Juvenile Justice Standards Project, Standards Relating to Pretrial Court Proceedings, Standard 1.7(B) (1980).

Normally, these same statutes do not allow waiver by the juvenile, probably as a result of the common law rule that a child lacked legal capacity to waive service of process. See, e.g., In re W.L.C., 562 S.W.2d 454 (Tex.1978). A juvenile may waive the right to service of summons under some circumstances, however, usually following the advice of counsel. See, e.g., Ga.Code Ann. § 15–11–26(f) (1982). The Juvenile Justice Standards provide a rather elaborate means by which a juvenile may waive any right other than the right to counsel. A "mature" juvenile may waive a right on his or her own behalf, whereas an "immature" juvenile may waive a right only upon advice of counsel. The estimate of whether a juvenile is mature or immature is made primarily by counsel. Juvenile Justice Standards Project, Standards Relating to Pretrial Court Proceedings, Standards 1.7(A), 6.1–6.4 (1980).

(6) Cal.Welf. & Inst.Code § 660(c) (Supp.1982): "For purposes of this section, service on the minor's attorney shall constitute service on the minor's parent or guardian."

(7) Many statutes provide for inclusion of notice of the right to counsel in the notice of the charges and the scheduled court appearance. See, e.g.,

Cal.Welf. & Inst.Code § 659 (1972); Ga.Code Ann. § 15–11–26(e) (1982); Minn.Stat.Ann. § 260.135(1) (Supp.1982).

B.   DISCOVERY

KENT v. UNITED STATES

Supreme Court of the United States, 1966.
383 U.S. 541, 86 S.Ct. 1045, 16 L.Ed.2d 84.

(For the opinion in this case, see p. 201, supra.)

NOTE

Although it dealt with the waiver stage rather than the adjudicatory stage of delinquency proceedings, the *Kent* decision represents the logical beginning point of any study of judicial treatment of discovery in juvenile proceedings. In *Kent* the Supreme Court held that counsel was entitled to access to certain social service records on which the court had relied in making its waiver determination. Access to the records was viewed by the Court as an essential element of effective assistance of counsel.

Despite the fact that *Kent* had certain constitutional underpinnings lower courts have not held that juveniles are entitled to discovery as a matter of constitutional right.

For the most part, however, the availability of discovery in juvenile proceedings has not turned on the constitutional question but rather has depended on judicial and legislative rule-making with respect to discovery in juvenile court, as the cases and statutory examples that follow illustrate. As a practical matter many states, even if they do not provide for discovery in general in juvenile cases, provide by statute for access of counsel to social service and other court records. See, e.g., D.C.Code §§ 16–2331, 16–2332 (1981); Minn.Stat.Ann. § 260.161(2) (1971); N.D.Cent.Code § 27–20–51 (1974); Tenn.Code Ann. § 37–251 (1977); Tex.Fam.Code Ann. § 51.14(a) (1975); Wyo.Stat.Ann. § 14–6–221 (1977). Access to law enforcement records is sometimes allowed as well. See, e.g., D.C.Code § 16–2333 (1981); N.D.Cent.Code § 27–20–52 (1974); Tenn.Code Ann. § 37–252 (1977); Tex. Fam.Code Ann. § 51.14(d) (1975).

JOE Z. v. SUPERIOR COURT

Supreme Court of California, In Bank, 1970.
3 Cal.3d 797, 91 Cal.Rptr. 594, 478 P.2d 26.

BURKE, JUSTICE.

In this case we discuss the extent to which juveniles in delinquency proceedings are entitled to the benefit of pretrial discovery. We have concluded that the juvenile courts have the inherent and discretionary power to permit pretrial discovery upon a showing of good cause, that in the instant case the court exceeded its discretion in denying petitioner inspection of his own statements and admissions to the police and the recordings of his conversations with them, but that petitioner has failed to establish good cause for inspection of the statements, admissions and recorded conversations of his former co-defendants.

Petitioner, a 15-year-old juvenile, was arrested on May 16, 1970, for allegedly violating Penal Code sections 187 (murder) and 217 (assault with intent to commit murder—two counts). . . . On June 3, petitioner's counsel filed a motion for pretrial discovery, together with a declaration of counsel and memorandum of points and authorities, seeking inspection of material falling principally in these two categories: (1) All oral and written statements and admissions of petitioner and the recorded or transcribed conversations with him, together with all notes or memoranda regarding such conversations, and (2) all statements, admissions and conversations of petitioner's "codefendants," the minors Joe S. and Robert A. Counsel's declaration in support of the motion alleged that the foregoing information was necessary in order to prepare for the adjudication hearing, was relevant and material to the case, was solely under the control of the police or district attorney, and was "not known to the minor or his counsel."

The court, proceeding upon the assumption that it had the inherent power to order discovery, nevertheless denied without prejudice petitioner's request to inspect his own statements, admissions and conversations. The court indicated, however, that it would grant a renewed motion to inspect such material if supported by an affidavit of petitioner averring that he could not recall the contents of his statements or conversations and therefore sought inspection to refresh his recollection. The court denied with prejudice petitioner's request to inspect the statements, admissions and conversations of Joe S. and Robert A. Petitioner now seeks mandate to compel respondent court to grant pretrial inspection as to both categories of material. . . .

As a preliminary matter, we must determine to what extent, if any, a juvenile is entitled to invoke pretrial discovery in delinquency proceedings in juvenile court. The provisions of the Welfare and Institutions Code which establish and define the scope of these proceedings are silent regarding this question, and there appear to be no reported decisions in California which have considered it.

Initially, we do not believe that the extensive discovery procedures generally applicable to "civil" proceedings are or should be available to minors in juvenile court. Section 2035 of the Code of Civil Procedure in effect makes civil discovery applicable to special proceedings of a civil nature "whenever it is necessary so to do." Since proceedings in juvenile court are not criminal proceedings presumably they are "civil" or "essentially civil," as they have been previously described. However, the " 'civil' label-of-convenience" (In re Gault, 387 U.S. 1, 50, 87 S.Ct. 1428, 18 L.Ed.2d 527) cannot obscure the quasi-criminal nature of juvenile proceedings, involving as they often do the possibility of a substantial loss of personal freedom. Moreover, the need for expeditious and informal adjudications in juvenile court belies the wisdom or necessity of any indiscriminate application of civil discovery procedures.

Nevertheless, the quasi-criminal character of delinquency proceedings does lead us to conclude that the juvenile courts should have the same degree of discretion as a court in an ordinary criminal case to permit, upon a proper showing, discovery between the parties. Authority for such discovery derives not from statute but from the inherent power of every court to develop rules of procedure aimed at facilitating the administration of criminal justice and promoting the orderly ascertainment of the truth. To assist us in determining whether the juvenile court exceeded the bounds of its discretion in denying petitioner's motion herein, we turn to the cases which have passed upon similar motions in the context of a criminal proceeding.

1.   Statements, Admissions and Conversations of Defendant

This court has on several occasions sanctioned the inspection of statements, admissions or recorded conversations of the defendant in a criminal case. . . .

In each . . . [case], defendant or his attorney had supported the request for inspection with an affidavit which stated, among other things, that defendant was unable to recall the substance of his statement or conversation and that pretrial inspection thereof was necessary to refresh his recollection. The People herein urge that such an affidavit is a prerequisite to discovery, or at least that the trial court should have discretion to require it as a condition to discovery. Indeed, some cases and authorities appear to make that assumption. However, such a requirement would necessarily be founded upon the false premise that the only good cause for pretrial inspection of such material is to refresh defendant's memory. On the contrary, inspection is ordinarily vital for the intelligent and efficient preparation of one's defense, quite apart from assisting the defendant in remembering what he said to police officers.

First of all, due to the obvious incriminatory effect of a confession or admission, it becomes "uniquely important" that defense counsel be permitted to inspect and copy the statement to assist him in determining its voluntary character and its admissibility. In addition, counsel will need to know the precise words used by defendant in his statement in order to determine its probable impact upon the trier of fact, its relevance to the penalty or sentencing phase of the proceedings, its completeness and accuracy, and its possible prejudicial effect.

Pretrial inspection affords the defendant an opportunity to clarify and correct ambiguities or errors in transcription, and provides his counsel with information which might lead to the discovery of other evidence important to the defense. Moreover, pretrial inspection of taped or transcribed conversations between defendant and police officers may furnish valuable opportunities for impeachment at trial. . . .

The foregoing considerations would apply with equal force to delinquency proceedings in juvenile court. Indeed, the minority of the accused furnishes an additional compelling reason for permitting pretrial inspection of his statements and admissions. . . . Pretrial inspection of the statement would be essential to enable counsel to assess its voluntary character. We conclude that a minor's statements, admissions, recorded conversations, and the notes and memoranda concerning those conversations are discoverable even though the minor fails to allege nonrecollection thereof.

Of course, we do not suggest that the minor is entitled to inspect his statements, or any other material, as a matter of right without regard to the adverse effects of disclosure and without a prior showing of good cause. In criminal cases, the court retains wide discretion to protect against the disclosure of information which might unduly hamper the prosecution or violate some other legitimate governmental interest. . . .

The juvenile courts should possess a like degree of discretion in determining the extent to which they will permit pretrial discovery in delinquency proceedings. However, in the instant case, real parties have not contended that disclosure of petitioner's statements would adversely affect their case or violate some other governmental interest, and petitioner has shown good cause for inspection. As set forth above, petitioner alleged, through counsel, that the information sought was necessary for the preparation of the defense, was relevant and material to the case, was solely in the control of real parties, and was unknown to petitioner or his counsel. Although these allegations could have been more precise and factual, they are adequate in view of the gravity of the charges brought against petitioner, and the general necessity for pretrial inspection of a minor's statement or confession. Accordingly, we have concluded that the juvenile court exceeded its discretion in denying discovery of this material merely because petitioner failed to allege his nonrecollection thereof.

2. Statements, Admissions and Conversations of Former Codefendants

As noted above, petitioner also moved to inspect the statements, admissions and conversations of two other juveniles, whom petitioner then characterized as his "codefendants." As a general rule, a defendant in a criminal case may, for purposes of impeachment, inspect the statements or recorded conversations of any witness whom the prosecution intends to call at trial. This rule has been extended to include the statements of one's codefendants in a joint trial. Therefore, the juvenile court may have exceeded its discretion in denying inspection of the statements of petitioner's codefendants, at least upon the basis of the facts then before the court.

However, real parties have pointed out that following the court's denial of petitioner's motion, the proceedings against these minors were severed from petitioner's case and were terminated following their pleas of guilty to lesser offenses. Moreover, real parties state that "the District Attorney plans to call neither of them [the minors] at the Juvenile Court hearing in this matter," and offer to furnish the statements to petitioner in the event the district attorney decides to call the minors as witnesses. In each of the cases cited above, the declarants were to be called at trial, thereby justifying pretrial disclosure of their statements or conversations. None of these cases suggests that such material must be made available to defendant simply because it might assist in the preparation of the defense. To the contrary, in People v. Cooper, supra, this court upheld the trial court's discretionary denial of a defense motion to inspect all statements gathered by the prosecution, whether or not the declarants were to testify at trial. We pointed out that the prosecution can be compelled to disclose the names and addresses of all such witnesses or declarants, and that defendant may subpoena and question them without interference by the prosecution. We concluded that although defendant need not establish the admissibility of the information sought, he must show more than a "mere desire" to inspect it. These principles would be equally applicable to delinquency proceedings.[5]

Petitioner makes no showing that pretrial discovery of the statements and conversations of his former codefendants are in fact necessary for the preparation of his case, and he offers no explanation why he could not obtain the factual information contained therein directly from the juveniles themselves. Accordingly, petitioner has not established his present right to a writ of mandate with respect to this material.

In the event the district attorney does decide to call Joe S. or Robert A. as witnesses at petitioner's adjudication hearing, petitioner may renew his application for inspection and, if appropriate, may request a reasonable continuance in order to examine the information furnished.[6]

Let a peremptory writ of mandate issue with respect to that portion of petitioner's motion which sought pretrial inspection of his own

---

5. Of course, just as the prosecution in a criminal case may have an affirmative duty to disclose, upon request, evidence which exculpates defendant (see Brady v. Maryland, 373 U.S. 83, 87, 83 S.Ct. 1194, 10 L.Ed.2d 215), real parties should disclose to petitioner any exculpatory evidence contained in the statements or conversations of his former codefendants. (District of Columbia v. Jackson, supra, 261 A.2d 511, 513.)

6. Similarly, if petitioner in good faith asserts that he intends to call these juveniles as *defense* witnesses, he may have a legitimate need to examine the contents of their statements in order to assess the probable credibility of their testimony and the extent to which they may be impeached.

statements, admissions, conversations, and notes or memoranda pertaining thereto.

Subsequent to the decision in *Joe Z*, the following court rules were adopted. How do they differ from the requirements set forth in that case?

CALIFORNIA RULES OF COURT, JUVENILE COURT RULES

Rule 1341. Prehearing discovery

(a) **[General purpose]** The purpose of this rule is to encourage in any juvenile court proceeding the timely and informal disclosure of materials and information within the possession or control of the petitioner to the minor, parent, guardian or their counsel so as to avoid the continuance or delay of any scheduled hearing and to minimize the necessity for court involvement. . . . To that end, this rule shall be liberally construed in favor of maximizing informal disclosures, subject to the right of a party to show privilege or other good cause why specific material or information should not be disclosed.

(b) **[Duty to disclose police reports]** Upon filing the petition, petitioner shall forthwith deliver to or make accessible for inspection and copying by the minor and the parent or guardian, or their counsel, copies of the police, arrest, and crime reports relating to the pending matter. Privileged information in such reports may be omitted if notice of the ommission is given simultaneously.

(c) **[Affirmative duty to disclose]** In every case, the petitioner shall disclose any substantial material evidence or information within the possession or control of the petitioner favorable to the minor, parent, or guardian.

(d) **[Material and information to be disclosed on request]** Except as provided in subdivisions (g) and (h), the petitioner shall, upon timely request in any juvenile court proceeding, disclose to the minor, parent, guardian, or their counsel, the following material and information within the petitioner's possession or control:

(1) Any probation report prepared in connection with the pending matter relating to the minor, parent or guardian;

(2) Any records of statements, admissions, or conversations by the minor, parent or guardian;

(3) Any records of statements, admissions, or conversations by any alleged coparticipant;

(4) The name and address of any witness interviewed by any investigating authority in connection with the pending matter;

(5) Any records of statements or conversations of any witness or other person interviewed by any investigating authority in connection with the pending matter;

(6) Any reports or statements of experts made regarding the pending matter, including results of physical or mental examinations and of scientific tests, experiments, or comparisons;

(7) Any photographs or physical evidence relating to the pending matter;

(8) Any record of a prior felony conviction of any witness that any party intends to call.

(e) [Disclosure in section 300(a), (b), or (c)* proceedings] Except as provided in subdivisions (g) and (h), in proceedings under section 300(a), (b), or (c) the parent or guardian shall, upon timely request, disclose to the petitioner material and information within the possession or control of the parent or guardian which is relevant and material to the pending proceedings. If the parent or guardian is represented by counsel, any disclosure request shall be made through counsel.

(f) [Motion for prehearing discovery] On refusal of a party to permit disclosure of information or inspection of materials, the requesting party or counsel may move the court for an order requiring timely disclosure prior to the jurisdiction hearing of the information or materials. The motion shall specifically and clearly designate the items sought, the relevancy and materiality of the items to the pending proceeding, and state that a timely request has been made for the items and the other party has refused to provide them to the moving party. Each court may by local rule establish the manner and time limitation within which a motion under this subdivision shall be made.

(g) [Limits on duty to disclose—protective orders] Upon a showing of privilege or other good cause by a party or other persons with possession or control of the material or information, the court may at any time order that specified disclosures be restricted, deferred or denied, or make any other order as is appropriate, provided that all material and information to which a party is entitled must be disclosed in time to permit counsel to make beneficial use thereof.

(h) [—Excision] When some parts of certain materials are discoverable under subdivision (d) and (e) and other parts are not discoverable, the nondiscoverable material may be excised and need not be disclosed if the requesting party or counsel has been notified that privileged material has not been disclosed. Material excised pursuant to judicial order shall be sealed and preserved in the records of the court for review in the event of an appeal.

(i) [Conditions of discovery] An order of the court granting discovery under this rule may specify the time, place, and manner of

* These subparts of § 300 of the California Welfare and Institutions Code relate to children in need of supervision.

making the discovery and inspection permitted and may prescribe terms and conditions. Discovery shall be completed in a timely manner so as to avoid the delay or continuance of any scheduled hearing.

(j) [Failure to comply; sanctions] If at any time during the course of the proceedings it is brought to the attention of the court that a person has failed to comply with this rule or with an order issued pursuant to this rule, the court may order the person to permit the discovery or inspection of materials not previously disclosed, grant a continuance, prohibit a party from introducing in evidence the material not disclosed, dismiss the proceedings, or enter any other order the court deems just under the circumstances.

(k) [Continuing duty to disclose] If, subsequent to compliance with these rules or orders pursuant thereto, a party discovers additional material or information which is subject to disclosure, that party shall promptly notify the minor and parent or guardian, or their counsel, of the existence of the additional material.

NOTES

(1) Juvenile Justice Standards Project, Standards Relating to Pretrial Court Proceedings, Commentary to Standard 3.1 at 55–56 (1980)* provides:

In civil proceedings there has been growing acceptance of the philosophy that "prior to every trial every party . . . is entitled to the disclosure of all relevant information in the possession of any person, unless the information is privileged." Wright, Law of the Federal Courts § 81 (1970). Following the promulgation in 1938 of new rules of civil procedure, most states abandoned the old "sporting theory of justice," Tiedman v. American Pigment Corp., 253 F.2d 803, 808 (4th Cir. 1958), with its emphasis on surprise as a trial tactic.

However, in criminal proceedings,

[d]espite the applicability to criminal cases of the reasons for a change in traditional adversary notions on the civil side, the resistance to the expansion of formal disclosure to the accused has been formidable. ABA Standards for Criminal Justice, *Discovery and Procedure Before Trial* (Approved Draft, 1970) (hereafter ABA Standards, *Discovery*), commentary at 36.

Pretrial discovery in criminal cases has generally remained more restrictive than in civil cases in several respects. Although both parties in civil proceedings have access to discovery, in criminal cases, the existence of the privilege against self-incrimination has inhibited the development of discovery by the prosecution, and criminal discovery has tended to be unilateral for the defendant.

In civil proceedings, counsel for the parties may generally conduct discovery without resort to judicial intervention. However, in criminal proceedings, the defendant's discovery rights have tended to require resort to the judge's discretion in each instance. Finally, in civil proceedings, the available discovery devices typically include oral and written deposi-

* Reprinted with permission from Standards Relating to Pretrial Court Proceedings, Copyright 1980, Ballinger Publishing Company.

tions, which, may not be used for discovery purposes in criminal proceedings. Compare, e.g., Fed.R.Civ.P. 30(a) with Fed.R.Crim.P. 15.

(2) Texas Family Code Annotated (1975) states:

§ 51.17. Procedure

Except when in conflict with a provision of this title, the Texas Rules of Civil Procedure govern proceedings under this title. . . .

In construing the above provision, which seems rather clear on its face, the Texas Court of Civil Appeals concluded that the statute does not mean literally what it says:

> . . . [a]ppellant complains that the juvenile court acted arbitrarily in quashing his notice to take the deposition of Sergeant Gus Rose, an investigating officer who later became a witness for the State at the transfer hearing. Counsel contends that if he had been permitted to take this deposition, new evidentiary leads might have been developed that would have assisted him in preparing for the transfer hearing and might have resulted in a different judgment. Counsel also argues that a deposition would have allowed for more effective cross-examination of Sergeant Rose.
>
> Although section 51.17 of the Code provides that the Texas Rules of Civil Procedure govern proceedings involving delinquent children and children in need of supervision, it is doubtful whether all the discovery procedures available under the Rules are applicable. Although we find no Texas authority on this question, courts in other jurisdictions have held that the trial judge may restrict the scope of discovery more in a juvenile case than in other civil cases. Joe Z. v. The Superior Court of Los Angeles County, 3 Cal.3d 797, 91 Cal.Rptr. 594, 478 P.2d 26 (1970); Hanrahan v. Felt, 48 Ill.2d 171, 269 N.E.2d 1 (1971). In the present case, Sergeant Rose testified fully at the transfer hearing, and appellant has not undertaken to demonstrate any particular in which he was surprised by the testimony or otherwise prejudiced by lack of opportunity to take the deposition. Consequently, we hold that appellant has failed to show reversible error in this respect.

T.P.S. v. State, 590 S.W.2d 946, 954 (Tex.Civ.App.1979).

Compare Louisiana Code of Juvenile Procedure Annotated (1981):

Art. 59. Discovery in delinquency proceedings

In delinquency proceedings, discovery shall be as provided in the Louisiana Code of Criminal Procedure.

Art. 71. Evidence

The adjudication hearing shall be conducted according to the rules of evidence applicable to civil proceedings.

(3) Virtually all courts considering the issue have concluded, as did the California Supreme Court in the principal case, that civil discovery rules are inappropriate in juvenile cases. Most courts, in the absence of formal rules or statutory guidance, have held that the rules of discovery in juvenile cases should approximate those applicable in criminal cases. A few courts have held that the appropriate range of discovery in juvenile cases lies somewhere

between civil and criminal discovery. The conflict was discussed in People ex rel. Hanrahan v. Felt, 48 Ill.2d 171, 269 N.E.2d 1 (1971):

> In issuing these [discovery] orders the trial judge held that a proceeding under the Juvenile Court Act is a civil proceeding and that he was therefore required to follow the discovery procedures applicable in civil cases. The State's principal contention is that a juvenile delinquency proceeding is criminal in nature and that the order was beyond the jurisdiction of the trial court. It is also argued that "civil practice discovery in criminal cases would be detrimental to the administration of justice" because broadened discovery would lead to harassment and intimidation of witnesses, suppression of evidence and an increase of perjury, "and that the question is governed by amendments to the Juvenile Court Act which provide that the standard of proof in criminal cases and the rules of evidence applicable to those cases are also applicable to juvenile delinquency proceedings."
>
> The answer asserts that juvenile proceedings are basically civil, although certain procedural safeguards employed in criminal proceedings are required, and that the underlying purpose of a delinquency proceeding would best be served by allowing broad pretrial discovery. It notes that the juvenile proceeding is specifically intended not to be an adversary proceeding, and that broad discovery can insure that all relevant factual information is brought before the court. The answer denies the State's contention that broadened discovery will lead to harassment and intimidation of witnesses, suppression of evidence and increased perjury.
>
> . . .
>
> . . . Although the paramount concern of the Juvenile Court Act is the welfare of the juvenile, the legitimate interests of the community in being safeguarded from such activity must also be considered. We can foresee situations in which the danger inherent in a particular attempt at discovery might outweigh any benefit that could be received, and we hold, therefore, that although a delinquency proceeding is civil in nature, it is sufficiently distinct from other civil actions to make inappropriate the automatic application of discovery provisions applicable to civil cases.
>
> This is not to say that the juvenile court may never allow a broader discovery than is allowed in criminal cases. It may be that the purposes behind the delinquency proceeding would be furthered by doing so. If, in the case before us, it appeared that the judge had considered any possible adverse effects and had then exercised his discretion and entered the challenged orders, we would not interfere.
>
> It appears, however, that he did not view the power to allow the discovery requested as a matter within his discretion but, rather as compelled by the civil nature of the action. There was no showing, for example, as to the wisdom of directing that the deposition of the prosecuting witness be taken. We hold that the civil discovery provisions do not routinely apply to juvenile delinquency proceedings but that their applicability should be left to the discretion of the court. . . .

Id. at 173, 175–76, 269 N.E.2d at 2–4.

The development of case law on juvenile discovery, as well as more recent attempts to establish discovery procedures through rules and statutes, is covered in Geraghty, Juvenile Discovery: A Developing Trend and a Word of

Caution, 7 Pepperdine L.Rev. 897 (1980); see also Juvenile Justice Standards Project, Standards Relating to Pretrial Court Proceedings, Commentary to Standard 3.1 at 59–64.

C. RIGHT TO COUNSEL

IN RE GAULT

Supreme Court of the United States, 1967.
387 U.S. 1, 87 S.Ct. 1428, 18 L.Ed.2d 527.

(For the opinion in this case, see page 299, supra.)

————

PENNSYLVANIA CONSOLIDATED STATUTES ANNOTATED, TITLE 42

§ 6337. Right to counsel

Except as otherwise provided under this chapter a party is entitled to representation by legal counsel at all stages of any proceedings under this chapter and if he is without financial resources or otherwise unable to employ counsel, to have the court provide counsel for him. If a party appears without counsel the court shall ascertain whether he knows of his right thereto and to be provided with counsel by the court if applicable. The court may continue the proceeding to enable a party to obtain counsel. Counsel must be provided for a child unless his parent, guardian, or custodian is present in court and affirmatively waive it. However, the parent, guardian, or custodian may not waive counsel for a child when their interest may be in conflict with the interest or interests of the child. If the interests of two or more parties may conflict, separate counsel shall be provided for each of them.

————

ILLINOIS ANNOTATED STATUTES, CHAPTER 37

701–20. Rights of parties to proceedings

§ 1–20. Rights of parties to proceedings. (1) Except as [otherwise provided] the minor who is the subject of the proceeding and his parents, guardian, legal custodian or responsible relative who are parties respondent have the right to be present, to be heard, to present evidence material to the proceedings, to cross-examine witnesses, to examine pertinent court files and records and also, although proceedings under this Act are not intended to be adversary in character, the right to be represented by counsel. At the request of any party financially unable to employ counsel, the court shall appoint the Public Defender or such other counsel as the case may require.

No hearing on any petition filed under this Act may be commenced unless the minor who is the subject of the proceeding is represented by counsel.

. . .

———

NEVADA REVISED STATUTES

62.085 Appointment of attorney; fees and expenses

1. The judge may appoint an attorney to represent any child in any proceeding in which the court has jurisdiction under the provisions of this chapter if it appears that such person is unable to employ counsel.

2. Each attorney appointed under the provisions of this section is entitled to the same compensation and expenses from the county as provided in NRS 7.125 for attorneys appointed to represent persons charged with crimes.

———

VIRGINIA CODE

§ 16.1–266. **Appointment of counsel.**—A. Prior to the hearing by the court of any case involving a child who is alleged to be abused or neglected or who is the subject of an entrustment agreement or a petition terminating residual parental rights or is otherwise before the court pursuant to subsection A 4 of § 16.1–241, the court shall appoint a discreet and competent attorney-at-law as guardian ad litem to represent the child.

B. Prior to the adjudicatory or transfer hearing by the court of any case involving a child who is alleged to be in need of services or delinquent, such child and his or her parent, guardian, legal custodian or other person standing in loco parentis shall be informed by a judge, clerk or probation officer of the child's right to counsel and of the liability of the parent, guardian, legal custodian or other person standing in loco parentis for the costs of such legal services pursuant to § 16.1–267 and be given an opportunity to:

1. Obtain and employ counsel of the child's own choice; or

2. If the court determines that the child is indigent within the contemplation of the law and his or her parent, guardian, legal custodian or other person standing in loco parentis does not retain an attorney for the child, a statement shall be executed substantially in the form provided by § 19.2–159 by such child, and the court shall appoint an attorney-at-law to represent him; or

3.   Waive the right to representation by an attorney, if the court finds the child and the parent, guardian, legal custodian or other person standing in loco parentis of the child consent, in writing, to such waiver and that the interests of the child and the parent, guardian, legal custodian or other person standing in loco parentis in the proceeding are not adverse. Such written waiver shall be in accordance with law and shall be filed with the court records of the case.

C.   Prior to the hearing by the court of any case involving a parent, guardian or other adult charged with abuse or neglect of a child or a parent or guardian who could be subjected to the loss of residual parental rights and responsibilities, such parent, guardian or other adult shall be informed by a judge, clerk or probation officer of his right to counsel and be given an opportunity to:

1.   Obtain and employ counsel of the parent's, guardian's or other adult's own choice; or

2.   If the court determines that the parent, guardian or other adult is indigent within the contemplation of the law, a statement shall be executed substantially in the form provided by § 19.2–159 by such parent, guardian or other adult and the court shall appoint an attorney-at-law to represent him; or

3.   Waive the right to representation by an attorney in accordance with the provisions of § 19.2–160.

D.   In all other cases which in the discretion of the court require counsel or a guardian ad litem to represent the interests of the child or children or the parent or guardian, a discreet and competent attorney-at-law may be appointed by the court. However, in cases where the custody of a child or children is the subject of controversy or requires determination and each of the parents or other persons claiming a right to custody is represented by counsel, the court shall not appoint counsel or a guardian ad litem to represent the interests of the child or children unless the court finds, at any stage in the proceedings in a specific case, that the interests of the child or children are not otherwise adequately represented.

THE SCOPE OF THE RIGHT TO COUNSEL

The key language in *Gault* relating to the right to representation by counsel is:

. . . A proceeding where the issue is whether the child will be found to be "delinquent" and subjected to the loss of his liberty for years is comparable in seriousness to a felony prosecution. The juvenile needs the assistance of counsel to cope with problems of law, to make skilled inquiry into the facts, to insist upon regularity of the proceedings, and to ascertain whether he has a defense and to prepare and submit it. The child "requires the guid-

ing hand of counsel at every step in the proceedings against him."
. . .

387 U.S. at 36.

Basing its decision on this realization the Court held:

We conclude that the Due Process Clause of the Fourteenth Amendment requires that in respect of proceedings to determine delinquency which may result in commitment to an institution in which the juvenile's freedom is curtailed, the child and his parents must be notified of the child's right to be represented by counsel retained by them, or if they are unable to afford counsel, that counsel will be appointed to represent the child.

387 U.S. at 41.

Early in its opinion, however, the Court limited the scope of its holding:

We do not in this opinion consider the impact of these constitutional provisions upon the totality of the relationship of the juvenile and the state. We do not even consider the entire process relating to juvenile "delinquents." For example, we are not here concerned with the procedures or constitutional rights applicable to the pre-judicial stages of the juvenile process, nor do we direct our attention to the post-adjudicative or dispositional process. We consider only the problems presented to us by this case. These relate to the proceedings by which a determination is made as to whether a juvenile is a "delinquent" as a result of alleged misconduct on his part, with the consequence that he may be committed to a state institution. . . .

387 U.S. at 13.

One can clearly see, then, that the specific mandate of *Gault* was that a juvenile is entitled to representation by counsel at the (1) adjudicatory stage of a (2) delinquency proceeding (3) in which the juvenile may be committed to a juvenile institution. The Court did not address whether the right to counsel attaches at other stages of the proceedings, whether it applies in cases alleging noncriminal misbehavior wherein the same risk of commitment is present, or whether parents under some circumstances might have a right to counsel. In light of the limited nature of the Court's decision, it is interesting to note how the states have expanded the right to counsel beyond the literal mandate of *Gault*. This expansion has been covered to some degree earlier in the material dealing with police investigation. See pp. 274, 325, supra.

The statutory examples typify the variety one finds in juvenile codes. A large number of statutes, of which the Pennsylvania statute is an example, simply state that "a party" or "the child" or "the child and his parent, custodian, or guardian" is entitled to representation by counsel "at all stages of the proceedings." If parents are not specifically mentioned, "party" presumably would include persons other than the juvenile, e.g., parents in a termination of parental rights proceeding. Since no limitation appears, the right to counsel would seem to extend to cases other than those nominally labeled "delinquency" cases, e.g., cases of noncriminal misbehavior and even those alleging neglect and abuse. Other statutes conferring a broad right to counsel are Md.Cts. & Jud.Proc.Code Ann. § 3–821 (1980); N.D.Cent.Code § 27–20–26 (1974); Ohio Rev.Code Ann. § 2151.352 (1980); S.D.Comp.Laws Ann. §§ 26–8–22.1, 26–8–22.2 (1976); Tex.Fam.Code Ann. § 51.10(a)–(b) (1975); Utah Code Ann. § 78–3a–35 (Supp.1981); W.Va.Code Ann. § 49–5–1(c) (Supp.1981); Wyo.Stat. Ann. § 14–6–222 (1977).

Another group of statutes, of which the Illinois statute is an example, simply state that the juvenile (and sometimes parents, as in the Illinois example) has the right to representation by counsel without specifying whether this right extends to all stages of the proceedings or applies to cases other than delinquency cases. Other statutes that make similar provision are: Minn.Stat.Ann. § 260.155(2) (Supp. 1982); Neb.Rev.Stat. § 43–272(a) (Supp.1981).

A few statutes suggest a more limited right to counsel. While appearing broad in their application to all kinds of cases, they leave the question of appointment of counsel in individual cases to the discretion of the court. The Nevada statute is an example of this group. See also Mich.Comp.Laws Ann. § 712A.17(3) (Supp.1982).

Finally, a number of statutes clearly state that the right to counsel is applicable not only in delinquency cases, i.e., cases alleging a violation of law, but noncriminal misbehavior cases and even neglect and dependency cases. The Virginia statute is an example. Others include: Colo.Rev.Stat.Ann. § 19–1–106(1) (1978) (references to other sections indicate that right to counsel applies to children in need of supervision and neglect and dependency cases where termination of parental rights is a possibility); Ga.Code Ann. § 15–11–30(b) (1982). A few statutes specifically extend the child's right to counsel to noncriminal misbehavior cases but do not extend it to neglect and dependency cases. See, e.g., D.C.Code § 16–2304(a) (1981); N.M.Stat.Ann. § 32–1–27(H) (1981). Legislative extension of the right to counsel to neglect and dependency cases is particularly significant in that it clearly goes beyond the mandate of *Gault* since delinquency, in the sense of a violation of law, is not involved and since, unless the petition also alleges delinquent conduct, no risk of commitment is generally present.

Courts on occasion have been called upon to resolve the issue of applicability of the right to counsel in nondelinquency cases, with somewhat interesting results. In State ex rel. Juvenile Department of Multnomah County v. Wade, 19 Or.App. 314, 527 P.2d 753 (1974), for example, the court held that a child is entitled to counsel in juvenile court proceedings to terminate parental rights. Two years later, in a case involving the right to counsel of a child in an adoption proceeding also involving termination of parental rights, the court agreed that there was no distinction between the two kinds of cases, but rather than extend the child's right to counsel to adoption proceedings it rescinded its earlier rule and held that a child has no right to counsel in either proceeding. In re D., 24 Or.App. 601, 547 P.2d 175 (1976). In somewhat similar fashion the Pennsylvania Supreme Court held that although a child has a statutory right to counsel in a dependency proceeding in juvenile court (see the Pennsylvania statute supra), a child does not have a statutory or constitutional right to counsel in an adoption proceeding. In re Kapcsos, 468 Pa. 50, 360 A.2d 174 (1976).

The child dependency cases involving possible termination of parental rights raise the issue of a parent's right to counsel in such proceedings. Some statutes specifically provide that parents in neglect or dependency proceedings have a right to counsel, including the right to court-appointed counsel if they are indigent. The Virginia statute is an example. Others include: Conn.Gen.Stat.Ann. § 46b–135(b) (Supp.1981); D.C.Code § 16–2304(b) (1981); N.M.Stat. Ann. § 32–1–27(J) (1981); N.Y.Fam.Ct.Act § 262(a)(i) (McKinney Supp.1981).

Recently the United States Supreme Court held that due process does not require a court to appoint counsel for an indigent parent in all termination proceedings. In Lassiter v. Department of Social Services, 452 U.S. 18, 101 S.Ct. 2153, 68 L.Ed.2d 640 (1981), the Court held that the issue of appointment of counsel in these proceedings is to be decided on a case-by-case basis in the first instance by the trial court, subject to appellate review. The Court stated that a presumption exists that an indigent person only has a right to appointed counsel when he faces a risk of loss of liberty, although other factors must be weighed against this presumption, namely the private interest at stake, the government's interest, and the risk that the procedures employed may lead to erroneous decisions. The Court did acknowledge:

> In its Fourteenth Amendment, our Constitution imposes on the States the standards necessary to ensure that judicial proceedings are fundamentally fair. A wise public policy, however, may require that higher standards be adopted than those minimally tolerable under the Constitution. Informed opinion has clearly come to hold that an indigent parent is entitled to the assistance of appointed counsel not only in parental termination proceedings, but in dependency and neglect proceedings as well. Most significantly, 33 States and the District of Columbia provide statutorily for the appointment of counsel in termination cases. The Court's opinion today in no way implies that the standards increasingly urged by informed public opinion and now widely followed by the States are other than enlightened and wise.

452 U.S. at 33–34.

In those states already providing a statutory right to counsel for indigent parents in termination proceedings the *Lassiter* decision will have no impact. Moreover, it will have no impact in those states that have found such a right based in whole or in part on state constitutional law, e.g., Department of Public Welfare v. J.K.B., 379 Mass. 1, 393 N.E.2d 406 (1979). Where it will have an impact is in those states whose courts have held, on the basis of federal constitutional law, that indigent parents have a right to appointed counsel, e.g., In re Ella R.B., 30 N.Y.2d 352, 334 N.Y.S.2d 133, 285 N.E.2d 288 (1972), unless, of course, the legislatures in those states choose to provide a statutory right or the courts in future cases base their decisions on state law.

STATE EX REL. J. M. v. TAYLOR

Supreme Court of Appeals of West Virginia, 1981.
___ W.Va. ___, 276 S.E.2d 199.

HARSHBARGER, CHIEF JUSTICE:

We have consolidated these three juvenile cases because they present common issues.

G. E. was a few days shy of eighteen when he had a probation revocation hearing for participating in an interstate automobile theft ring. The judge asked him if he wanted counsel and told him that if he were indigent, the court would appoint an attorney; but he and his father waived this right. After the hearing, his probation was revoked and he was committed to the Department of Corrections for examination at Pruntytown (our "industrial school" for boys), then to forestry camp for an indeterminate term until he was twenty-one. He got a lawyer who presented a habeas corpus petition to us, and we ordered the circuit court to determine whether G. E. voluntarily waived counsel; and the learned trial judge decided that he did.

J. M., then sixteen, was accused of breaking and entering a market with intent to steal. He did not have counsel at preliminary, adjudicatory or dispositional hearings, pled guilty, and was committed to the Department of Corrections until he became twenty-one years old.

The third juvenile, A. H., was sixteen when his father and mother filed multiple petitions against him for assault, forging checks, and possession of marijuana with intent to deliver. A. H., with his father present, waived counsel. We have no record of the preliminary hearing, but relevant colloquy from his adjudicatory hearing transcript is:

> COURT: At that [preliminary] hearing the Court, I think, in some detail explained to the infant and his parents that he had the right to be represented by counsel. I don't see counsel here today.

. . .

[A. H.], are you ready to proceed with this hearing without being represented by an attorney?

JUVENILE: Yes, sir.

After he pled guilty and was adjudicated delinquent:

COURT: . . . Again, at that dispositional hearing you have the right to be represented by an attorney.

Do you want to be represented by an attorney?

JUVENILE: Should I?

COURT: Well, that's not for me to say. I just want to inform you that you definitely have that right if you want to be represented by an attorney.

JUVENILE: No, sir.

. . .

COURT: All right. I realize, of course, that being an infant that you are without funds, and if that's the only drawback, then if the parents would not furnish counsel for you, this court would appoint an attorney to serve you in this case, and his expenses would be paid by the State of West Virginia. Do you understand that?

JUVENILE: Yes, sir.

I.

A juvenile's constitutional right to counsel was recognized by the Supreme Court in 1967 in In re Gault, 387 U.S. 1, 87 S.Ct. 1428, 18 L.Ed.2d 527. That right is in W.Va.Const. art. 3, § 14, codified at W.Va.Code, 49–5–1(c) and is recognized in many state cases, . . .

Any defendant may relinquish constitutional rights by knowing and intelligent waiver. Johnson v. Zerbst, 304 U.S. 458, 58 S.Ct. 1019, 82 L.Ed. 1461 (1938); State v. Rissler, W.Va., 270 S.E.2d 778 (1980). In Von Moltke v. Gillies, 332 U.S. 708, 723–24, 68 S.Ct. 316, 92 L.Ed. 309 (1947), the Supreme Court discussed adult waiver of counsel:

To discharge this duty [of determining whether there is an intelligent and competent waiver] properly in light of the strong presumption against waiver of the constitutional right to counsel, a judge must investigate as long and as thoroughly as the circumstances of the case before him demand. The fact that an accused may tell him that he is informed of his right to counsel and desires to waive this right does not automatically end the judge's responsibility. To be valid such waiver must be made with an apprehension of the nature of the charges, the statutory offenses include within them, the range of allowable punishments thereunder, possible defenses to the charges and circumstances in mitigation thereof, and all other facts essential to a broad understanding of the whole matter. A judge can make certain that an accused's professed waiver of counsel is understandingly and wisely made only from a penetrating and comprehensive examination of all the circumstances under which such a plea is tendered. (Footnotes omitted.)

We have written about waivers of constitutional rights generally:

But waiver of a constitutional right is not to be lightly regarded, and if such a waiver is to be implied at all, it can only be in situations in which it is clear that the accused has not only a full knowledge of all facts and of his rights, but a full appreciation of the effects of his voluntary relinquishment. Holland v. Boles, 225 F.Supp. 863 (N.D.W.Va.1963). This Court has held that courts indulge every reasonable presumption against waiver of a constitutional right and will not presume acquiescence in the loss of such fundamental right. State ex rel. Calloway v. Boles, 149 W.Va. 297, 140 S.E.2d 624 (1965); syl. pt. 2, State ex rel. May v. Boles, 149 W.Va. 155, 139 S.E.2d 177 (1964). An accused may, by declaration and conduct, waive a fundamental right protected by the Constitution, but it must be demonstrated that the waiver was made knowingly and intelligently. State ex rel. Grob v. Blair [214 S.E.2d 330], supra. State v. Eden, W.Va., 256 S.E.2d 868, 873 (1979).

Courts, scholars, and legislatures have developed two juvenile waiver tests. One weighs the "totality of circumstances"; the other keys on whether there was an interested adult present when the waiver occurred.*

The "totality of circumstances" analysis was made in Haley v. Ohio, 332 U.S. 596, 68 S.Ct. 302, 92 L.Ed. 224 (1948), and Gallegos v. Colorado, 370 U.S. 49, 82 S.Ct. 1209, 8 L.Ed.2d 325 (1962), wherein juvenile waivers of counsel and privileges against self-incrimination were not accepted because circumstances indicated that they were not knowingly and intelligently made.

Most cases about juvenile waiver involve custodial interrogations and confessions, and factors such as age, mental age, previous police or court experience, advice of parent or counsel, physical condition, whether held incommunicado, methods of interrogation, education, knowledge of the substance of a charge, and the nature of rights waived, must also be evaluated.

A more objective and workable standard simply invalidates juvenile waivers not secured with counsel, guardian, parent or interested adult present. An interested, friendly adult is supposed to protect an infant from governmental coercion or pressure and to allow someone capable of understanding the nature and consequences of the waiver to help in the decision and to protect the child from inaccurate ac-

---

* Waiver of constitutional rights, including the right to counsel, in connection with police interrogation is discussed at 325, 333–37 supra.

counts of his statements at proceedings in which waiver is made.
. . . .

Some states have legislatively mandated that an adult be present when a juvenile waives. Our code prevents interrogation of juveniles without the presence of a parent or counsel, W.Va.Code, 49–5–8(d), reflecting a legislative judgment that a juvenile is not capable of knowingly waiving his Fifth Amendment privilege against self-incrimination.

But a parent or other adult, even one intensely involved in and interested in a child's welfare, may not be sufficiently knowledgeable, educated or informed about constitutional law to competently waive protections. Commonwealth v. Webster, 466 Pa. 314, 353 A.2d 372 (1976). Sometimes parents' interests may even be opposite a child's, as A. H.'s record here illustrates.

Courts have had difficulty defining an "interested adult". Is a probation officer an interested adult? Is a grandparent? Is a parent who initiated the complaint? or is drunk? or is apathetic? See generally Fare v. Michael C., 442 U.S. 707, 99 S.Ct. 2560, 61 L.Ed.2d 197 (1979), reh. denied, 444 U.S. 887, 100 S.Ct. 186, 62 L.Ed.2d 121.

In its *Standards Relating to Adjudication*, the Juvenile Justice Standards Project has drafted Rule 1.2:

1.2 Attorneys for respondent and the government.

The juvenile court should not begin adjudication proceedings unless the respondent is represented by an attorney who is present in court and the government is represented by an attorney who is present in court.

A commentary teaches that the juvenile right to counsel should be non-waivable, citing a 1967 recommendation by the President's Commission on Law Enforcement and Administration of Justice, IJA/ABA Juvenile Justice Standards Project, Standards Relating to Adjudication, § 1.2 (1977).

We admire this rule, but are confronted with a suggestion that our Legislature intended that there could be knowing waiver of counsel. Our statute about the preliminary hearing stage of juvenile proceedings provides that a court or juvenile referee shall:

(2) Appoint counsel by order entered of record, if counsel has not already been retained, appointed *or knowingly waived*. (Emphasis added.) Code, 49–5–9(a)(2).

Juvenile waiver of constitutional rights obviously must be more carefully proscribed than adult waiver because of the unrebuttable presumption, long memorialized by courts and legislatures, that juveniles lack the capacity to make legally binding decisions. No juvenile legal status is treated the same as that of an adult, to our knowledge. Examples of legislative recognition of juvenile incapacity are statutes requiring guardians ad litem for infants: in civil actions when a minor is a defendant, Code, 56–4–10; if a minor is plaintiff in a lawsuit (next friend or guardian) § 56–4–9; in eminent domain proceedings involving land in which a minor has an interest, § 54–2–4; for will probate in solemn form, § 41–5–5; for the sale, lease or mortgage of real property owned by a minor, §§ 37–1–3, 37–1–4 and 37–1–12; for sale or lease of real or personal property subject to a future interest, § 36–2–5; for depositions to preserve testimony in which an infant is affected, § 57–4–7; and for actions proving the contents of lost records or papers, § 39–3–7. A child is also given the right to his own counsel in civil neglect proceedings, Code, 49–6–2. There is no statutory authority that counsel can be waived in any of these instances that require a lawyer or a counselor for infants.

We therefore recognize that juvenile waiver has been contemplated by our Legislature; but must also observe that it seems to be a contradiction that an infant might waive his constitutional right to counsel in proceedings wherein his very liberty is threatened, but not do so if someone is about to force sale of a piece of land in which he owns even a $1.00 interest.

We will, therefore, accommodate the statutory implication that he can waive his right to counsel, by requiring that he can do so, but only upon advice of counsel. Only then can there be knowing waiver.

. . .

Writs granted.

NOTES

(1) Texas Family Code Annotated (1975 & Supp.1981):

§ 51.09. Waiver of Rights

(a) Unless a contrary intent clearly appears elsewhere in this title, any right granted to a child by this title or by the constitution or laws of this state or the United States may be waived in proceedings under this title if:

(1) the waiver is made by the child and the attorney for the child;

(2) the child and the attorney waiving the right are informed of and understand the right and the possible consequences of waiving it;

(3) the waiver is voluntary; and

(4) the waiver is made in writing or in court proceedings that are recorded.

. . .

§ 51.10. Right to Assistance of Attorney; Compensation

(a) A child may be represented by an attorney at every stage of proceedings under this title, including:

(1) the detention hearing required by Section 54.01 of this code;

(2) the hearing to consider transfer to criminal court required by Section 54.02 of this code;

(3) the adjudication hearing required by Section 54.03 of this code;

(4) the disposition hearing required by Section 54.04 of this code;

(5) the hearing to modify disposition required by Section 54.05 of this code;

(6) hearings required by Chapter 55 of this code; *

(7) habeas corpus proceedings challenging the legality of detention resulting from action under this title; and

(8) proceedings in a court of civil appeals or the Texas Supreme Court reviewing proceedings under this title.

(b) The child's right to representation by an attorney shall not be waived in:

(1) a hearing to consider transfer to criminal court as required by Section 54.02 of this code;

(2) an adjudication hearing as required by Section 54.03 of this code;

(3) a disposition hearing as required by Section 54.04 of this code;

(4) a hearing prior to commitment to the Texas Youth Council as a modified disposition in accordance with Section 54.05(f) of this code; or

(5) hearings required by Chapter 55 of this code.*

. . . .

(f) The court shall appoint an attorney to represent the interest of a child entitled to representation by an attorney, if:

(1) the child is not represented by an attorney;

(2) the court determines that the child's parent or other person responsible for support of the child is financially unable to employ an attorney to represent the child; and

(3) the child's right to representation by an attorney:

(A) has not been waived under Section 51.09 of this code; or

(B) may not be waived under Subsection (b) of this section.

(g) The juvenile court may appoint an attorney in any case in which it deems representation necessary to protect the interests of the child.

. . . .

(2) Juvenile Justice Standards Project, Standards Relating to Pretrial Court Proceedings, Standards 5.1–5.3 and Commentary, pp. 88–89, 91–95 (1980): †

5.1 Scope of the juvenile's right to counsel

A. In delinquency cases, the juvenile should have the effective assistance of counsel at all stages of the proceeding.

---

* Chapter 55 concerns children with mental illness, retardation, disease, or defect.—Ed.

† Reprinted with permission from Standards Relating to Pretrial Court Proceedings, Copyright 1980, Ballinger Publishing Company.

B.   The right to counsel should attach as soon as the juvenile is taken into custody by an agent of the state, when a petition is filed against the juvenile, or when the juvenile appears personally at an intake conference, whichever occurs first.   The police and other detention authorities should have the duty to ascertain whether a juvenile in custody has counsel and, if not, to facilitate the retention or provision of counsel without delay.

C.   Unless advised by counsel, the statements of a juvenile or other information or evidence derived directly or indirectly from such statements made while in custody to police or law enforcement officers, or made to the prosecutor, intake officer, or social service worker during the process of the case, including statements made during intake, a predisposition study, or consent decree, should not be admissible in evidence prior to a determination of the petition's allegations in a delinquency case, or prior to conviction in a criminal proceeding.

Commentary

Introduction.   This standard provides that respondents in delinquency cases should have "the effective assistance of counsel at all stages of the proceeding."   As implemented by Standard 5.2, this means that the juvenile's right to counsel should not be defeasible for any reason, including willingness to waive the right, parental refusal to employ counsel, or financial ineligibility for appointed counsel.   This proposal for mandatory defense counsel departs from the law and practice of most jurisdictions.

The reasons for recommending that the juvenile's right to counsel not be waivable are discussed immediately below.   Financial eligibility is discussed in the commentary to Standard 5.3.

. . .

This standard adopts the view that counsel is necessary in delinquency proceedings to protect the interests of the juvenile, and the right should therefore be nonwaivable.   This is now the federal rule, 18 U.S.C. §§ 5032, 5034 (1974) and it has also been adopted in the several other jurisdictions cited above.   As stated by the 1967 Task Force Report:

> . . . providing counsel only when the child is sophisticated enough to be aware of his need and to ask for one or when he fails to waive his announced right is not enough, as experience in numerous jurisdictions reveals.   Counsel should be appointed as a matter of course wherever coercive action is a possibility, without requiring any affirmative choice by the child or parent.   President's Commission on Law Enforcement and Administration of Justice, "Task Force Report: Juvenile Delinquency and Youth Crime" 34 (1967).

Mandatory representation not only protects the juvenile, but assists the court in handling cases efficiently.   Also, the presence of defense counsel facilitates obtaining effective waivers of other rights by the juvenile.   (See Part VI.)   The "totality" test by which most courts judge the validity of waivers is difficult to administer, and invites uncertainty at all stages of the proceedings.   It has been criticized by many commentators. See, e.g., Comment, "Waiver of Counsel by Minor Defendants," 3 Tulsa L.J. 193 (1966); Fox, Juvenile Courts in a Nutshell 165 (1971); Handler, "The Juvenile Court and the Adversary System: Problems of Function and Form," 1965 Wis. L.Rev. 7, 34 (1965); Isaacs, "The Lawyer in the

Juvenile Court," 10 Crim.L.Q. 222, 231 (1968); Lefstein, Stapleton, and Teitelbaum, "In Search of Juvenile Justice: Gault, and Its Implementation," 3 L. and Soc.Rev. 491, 561–62 (1968–69); Note, "Juvenile Case Law After Gault," 8 J.Fam.L. 416, 428 (1968); Note, "Pre-Interrogation Waiver of Constitutional Rights by Juveniles," 14 Ariz.L.Rev. 487 (1972); "Position Statement for National Conference on the Role of the Lawyer in Juvenile Court" (Chi.Ill. Feb. 27–29, 1964) in National Council of Juvenile Court Judges, Counsel for the Child, 2 (1964); Skoler, "The Right to Counsel and the Role of Counsel in Juvenile Court Proceedings," 43 Ind. L.J. 558, 572 (1967–68). Few juveniles have the experience and understanding to decide meaningfully that the assistance of counsel would not be helpful. One study indicates that in waiving *Miranda* rights, 86 of 90 minors waived without a thorough understanding of their action. Ferguson and Douglas, "A Study of Juvenile Waiver," 7 San Diego L.Rev. 39, 53–54 (1970).

Nor does the requirement that the juvenile's parent advise the juvenile and/or concur in the waiver cure these difficulties. Studies indicate that, for several reasons, parents may be of little aid to their children in deciding whether to waive counsel. The parents may themselves not be able to adequately understand the consequences of waiver, and may be equally swayed by official pressures to waive. Lefstein, Stapleton, and Teitelbaum, "In Search of Juvenile Justice," supra; Schlam, "Police Interrogation and 'Self'-Incrimination of Children by Parents; A Problem Not Yet Solved," 6 Clearinghouse Rev. 618 (1973). In order to appear "cooperative," parents may in fact increase the pressure on their children to waive their rights. McMillian and McMurtry, "The Role of Defense Counsel in the Juvenile Court—Advocate or Social Worker?" 14 St. Louis U.L.J. 561 (1970).

In recommending that the respondent's right to counsel in delinquency proceedings should be nonwaivable, this standard is not intended to foreclose absolutely the possibility of *pro se* representation by a juvenile. A number of courts have recognized the right of a criminal defendant to waive counsel and conduct his or her own defense. United States v. Plattner, 330 F.2d 371 (2d Cir. 1964); United States ex rel. McCann, 317 U.S. 269 (1942).* The right is recognized by state constitutions and statutes in some jurisdictions. But the majority view is that the right to appear *pro se* in criminal cases is qualified by the public interest in maintaining a fair trial process. See, e.g., People v. Sharp, 7 Cal.2d 448, 103 Cal.Rptr. 233, 499 P.2d 489 (1972), United States v. Dougherty, 473 F.2d 1113 (D.C.Cir. 1972). In delinquency proceedingss, it would be rare for a respondent to possess sufficient maturity to persuade the court that *pro se* representation would result in a fair trial. Comment, "In re Gault and the Persistent Questions of Procedural Due Process and Legal Ethics in Juvenile Court," 47 Neb.L.Rev. 558, 570 (1968). It would seem, also, that any "right" to appear *pro se* should apply only if the juvenile indicated a wish to contest the proceedings, not to admit the allegations of the petition.

* In Faretta v. California, 422 U.S. 806, 95 S.Ct. 2525, 45 L.Ed.2d 562 (1975), the Supreme Court held that a defendant in a state criminal trial has a constitutional right to represent himself when he voluntarily and intelligently chooses to do so.—Ed.

Subject to those cautions, the court should have discretion, in exceptional cases, to respond affirmatively to a juvenile's positive insistence on appearing *pro se*. In such cases, the court should nevertheless appoint standby counsel to "assist the [respondent] when called upon and to call the judge's attention to matters favorable to the [youth] upon which the judge should rule on his own motion." ABA, Standards Relating to Function of the Trial Judge § 6.7 (Tent.Draft 1972); Faretta v. California, 422 U.S. 806, 95 S.Ct. 2525, 45 L.Ed.2d 562 (1975).

. . .

5.2 Notification of the juvenile's right to counsel

As soon as a juvenile's right to counsel attaches under Standard 5.1 B., the authorities should advise the juvenile that representation by counsel is mandatory, that there is a right to employ private counsel, and that if private counsel is not retained counsel will be provided without cost.

5.3 Juvenile's eligibility for court-appointed counsel; parent-juvenile conflicts

A. In any delinquency proceeding, if counsel has not been retained for the juvenile, and if it does not appear that counsel will be retained, the court should appoint counsel. No reimbursement should be sought from the parent or the juvenile for the cost of court-appointed counsel for the juvenile, regardless of the parent's or juvenile's financial resources.

B. At the earliest feasible stage of a delinquency proceeding the intake department should determine whether a conflict of interest exists between the juvenile and the parent, and should notify the court and the parties of any finding that a conflict exists.

C. If a parent has retained counsel for a juvenile and it appears to the court that the parent's interest in the case conflicts with the juvenile's interest, the court should caution both the parent and counsel as to counsel's duty of loyalty to the juvenile's interests. If the parent's dominant language is not English, the court's caution should be communicated in a language understood by the parent.

Should the juvenile court appoint an attorney for the child over parental objection? This long has been the practice since *Gault*, as the *Taylor* case indicates (see quotes from the record). Should children have an independent right to counsel? For an argument that courts invade family autonomy unduly when they appoint counsel for children against the wishes of their parents, see J. Goldstein, A. Freud, and A. Solnit, Before the Best Interests of the Child, Ch. 7 (1980).

D. CONDUCT OF THE HEARING

1. RULES OF EVIDENCE

ILLINOIS ANNOTATED STATUTES, CHAPTER 37

§ 704–6. Evidence at Adjudicatory Hearing

. . . The standard of proof and the rules of evidence in the nature of criminal proceedings in this State are applicable to Section 2–2.* The standard of proof and the rules of evidence in the nature of civil proceedings in this State are applicable to Sections 2–3, 2–4 and 2–5.**

LOUISIANA CODE OF JUVENILE PROCEDURE

Art. 71. Evidence

The adjudication hearing shall be conducted according to the rules of evidence applicable to civil proceedings.

. . .

NEW YORK FAMILY COURT ACT

§ 744. Evidence in fact-finding hearings; required quantum

(a) Only evidence that is competent, material and relevant may be admitted in a fact-finding hearing.

. . .

JUVENILE JUSTICE STANDARDS PROJECT, STANDARDS RELATING TO ADJUDICATION (1980)

4.2 Rules of Evidence

The rules of evidence employed in the trial of criminal cases should be used in delinquency adjudication proceedings when the respondent has denied the allegations of the petition.

---

* This section relates to children alleged to be delinquent.

** These sections relate to children alleged to be in need of supervision, neglected children, and dependent children, respectively.

IN RE M.L.H.

District of Columbia Court of Appeals, 1979.
399 A.2d 556.

KELLY, ASSOCIATE JUDGE:

Appellant challenges his adjudication as a delinquent, following a nonjury trial, for receiving stolen property. His principal contention on appeal is that the trial judge committed reversible error by admitting and relying upon hearsay testimony as the primary basis for conviction. We agree, and accordingly reverse and remand.

The government presented two witnesses to prove its case. The first, the complainant, testified that his home was broken into and that a tape deck, a watch, and some imitation pearl necklaces were stolen. A few days later, he identified these items when they were shown to him by a police officer. The stolen items were not introduced at the trial.

The government's other witness, a police detective, testified that while he was executing a search warrant at 4296 Southern Avenue, S.E., the home of appellant, he discovered and seized three imitation pearl necklaces, a watch, a watchband, and a stereo. The stereo was secreted behind the furnace in the basement, but the jewelry was found in a dresser drawer in a bedroom alleged to be appellant's.

The only evidence which linked appellant to the bedroom and the dresser where the stolen items were recovered was the detective's response to a question put to him by the trial judge after defense counsel objected that there was no testimony to support the officer's assertion that the items were found in appellant's room:

THE COURT: Do you know whose bedroom it was, that you went in, Officer?

THE WITNESS: Yes, sir. The respondent's mother directed me to the bedroom and stated that was her son's bedroom.

The objection to this testimony on hearsay grounds was overruled.

No other evidence was offered by the government to clarify how many people used the bedroom in question, how many sons the woman the officer spoke to had, or to whom the dresser actually belonged.

After the government rested its case, appellant moved for judgment of acquittal but the motion was denied. A post-trial motion for reconsideration of judgment complaining of the admission of the hearsay testimony on evidentiary and constitutional grounds, as well as the insufficiency of the evidence, was also denied.

. . .

On appeal, the government argues that the hearsay was admissible because it was reliable and probative. Its theory is that since the detective had a valid search warrant presumably inplicating appellant in a crime, it can be assumed that appellant's mother would respond truthfully to the officer's inquiry. Appellant argues, on the other hand, that she may have sought to confuse and mislead the officer in order to protect her husband, another son, or even herself. These arguments highlight the classic purpose of the hearsay rule. There was no showing that appellant's mother was unavailable and therefore could not participate in the trial, yet the government attempts to justify her absence as necessary to maintain positive family relations and thus not to frustrate appellant's rehabilitation. It is true that rehabilitation is a primary goal of the juvenile justice system, but so is the reliable determination of guilt. To attempt to cut corners with justice is to sacrifice a juvenile's right to a fair trial for the convenience of the prosecutor. See In re Winship, 397 U.S. 358, 90 S.Ct. 1068, 25 L.Ed.2d 368 (1970).

All agree that this essential testimony was hearsay. It fell within no recognized exception to the hearsay rule and therefore the trial court erred in allowing it in evidence. Accordingly, since the challenged hearsay was the only evidence linking appellant with the stolen property, the case is remanded with instructions that the adjudication of delinquency be vacated and that the petition be dismissed.
. . .

NOTES

(1) The statutory examples illustrate the various views of what rules of evidence are applicable generally in juvenile cases. The Illinois statute is an example of those that provide that the rules of evidence applicable in criminal cases apply in delinquency proceedings, whereas the rules applicable in civil cases apply in other kinds of juvenile proceedings. Other statutes are: Cal.Welf. & Inst.Code § 701 (Supp.1982); Fla.Stat.Ann. §§ 39.09(1)(b), 39.408(1)(b) (Supp.1981); Hawaii Rev.Stat. § 571–41 (1976); Iowa Code Ann. §§ 232.47(5), 232.96(3) (Supp.1982).

Some jurisdictions—Louisiana, for example—provide that the rules applicable in civil cases apply in all types of juvenile proceedings without regard to the nature of the conduct or status alleged. See also Mo.Ann.Stat. § 211.171(6) (1962); Tex.Fam.Code Ann. § 54.03(d) (1975). Still other jurisdictions simply provide that to be admissible evidence must be competent, relevant, and material. In addition to the New York statute see D.C.Code § 16–2316(b) (1981); Wyo.Stat.Ann. § 14–6–226(b) (1977).

As a practical matter, does it make any difference which rules apply, except in a few narrow circumstances peculiar to criminal cases, e.g., the requirement of corroboration of a confession or an accomplice's testimony?* See Juvenile Justice Standards Project, Standards Relating to Adjudication, Commentary to Standard 4.2 at 57–58 (1980).

(2) While there may be little practical difference between rules of evidence applicable in criminal cases and those applicable in civil cases, there is a great deal of difference between having rules of evidence apply, whether they are civil or criminal, and having no rules of evidence apply. Some early,

---

* These and other issues are covered separately at pages 480–482, infra.

i.e., pre-*Gault*, cases held that because of the nonadversary, protective nature of juvenile proceedings, the rules of evidence did not apply. See, e.g., In re Holmes, 379 Pa. 599, 109 A.2d 523 (1954). Contra, In re Contreras, 109 Cal.App.2d 787, 241 P.2d 631 (1952); Garner v. Wood, 188 Ga. 463, 4 S.E.2d 137 (1939); In re Ross, 45 Wn.2d 654, 277 P.2d 335 (1954). Most courts have concluded that the rules of evidence do apply to juvenile proceedings, particularly the rules relating to hearsay, as the principal case illustrates. See, e.g., In re Johnson, 214 Kan. 780, 522 P.2d 330 (1974); In re Kevin G., 80 Misc.2d 517, 363 N.Y.S.2d 999 (Fam.Ct.N.Y.County 1975).

2. STANDARD OF PROOF

IN RE WINSHIP

Supreme Court of the United States, 1970.
397 U.S. 358, 90 S.Ct. 1068, 25 L.Ed.2d 368.

(For the opinion in this case, see page 231, supra.)

MARYLAND COURTS AND JUDICIAL PROCEEDINGS CODE ANNOTATED

§ 3–819. Adjudication

.   .   .

(b) Before a child is adjudicated delinquent, the allegations in the petition that the child has committed a delinquent act must be proved beyond a reasonable doubt.

.   .   .

(d) In all other cases the allegations must be proved by a preponderance of the evidence.

TENNESSEE CODE ANNOTATED

37–230. Dependent or neglected child—Disposition.

.   .   .

(b) If the court finds on proof beyond a reasonable doubt that the child committed the acts by reason of which he is alleged to be delinquent, it shall proceed immediately or at a postponed hearing to hear evidence as to whether the child is in need of treatment or rehabilitation and to make and file its findings thereon.   .   .   .

(c) If the court finds from clear and convincing evidence that the child is dependent or neglected or unruly, the court shall proceed immediately or at a postponed hearing to make a proper disposition of the case.

. . .

NEW MEXICO STATUTES ANNOTATED

32–1–31. Conduct of hearings; findings; dismissal; dispositional matters

. . .

E. If the court finds on the basis of a valid admission of the allegations of the petition, or on the basis of proof beyond a reasonable doubt based upon competent, material and relevant evidence, that the child committed the acts by reason of which he is alleged to be delinquent or in need of supervision, it may, in the absence of objection, proceed immediately to hear evidence on whether or not the child is in need of care or rehabilitation and file its finding thereon. . . .

F. If the court finds on the basis of a valid admission of the allegations of the petition, or on the basis of clear and convincing evidence, competent, material and relevant in nature, that the child is neglected, abused or is in need of care or rehabilitation as a delinquent child or child in need of supervision, the court may proceed immediately or at a postponed hearing to make disposition of the case.

. . .

WYOMING STATUTES ANNOTATED

§ 14–6–225. Burden of proof required; verdict of jury; effect thereof

(a) Allegations that a child has committed a delinquent act or is in need of supervision must be proved beyond a reasonable doubt. Allegations of conduct showing a child to be neglected must be proved by a preponderance of the evidence.

. . .

NOTE

The narrow constitutional principle that emerges from *Winship* is that proof beyond a reasonable doubt is constitutionally required only in delinquency cases, i.e., in cases in which criminal misconduct is alleged. Many states, as exemplified by the Maryland and Tennessee statutes, apply this mandate literally and require proof beyond a reasonable doubt only in delinquency cases. Other statutes are: Cal.Welf. & Inst.Code § 701 (Supp.1982); Ill.Ann.Stat. ch. 37, § 704–6 (1972); Iowa Code Ann. § 232.47(10) (Supp.

1982); La.Code Juv.Proc. art. 73 (1981). These states provide that in other kinds of cases the applicable standard of proof is either clear and convincing evidence (e.g., Iowa, Iowa Code Ann. § 232.96(2) (Supp.1982), and Tennessee) or a preponderance of the evidence (e.g., California, Illinois, Louisiana, and Maryland).

A number of states, however, go beyond the literal mandate of *Winship* and require proof beyond a reasonable doubt in cases of noncriminal misbehavior as well as delinquency. The New Mexico and Wyoming statutes are examples. Others are: Ga.Code Ann. § 15–11–33(c) (1982); N.Y.Fam.Ct. Act § 744(b) (McKinney Supp.1981); N.D.Cent.Code § 27–20–29(2) (1974)); S.D. Comp.Laws Ann. §§ 26–8–22.9, 26–8–22.10 (1976); Tex.Fam.Code Ann. § 54.03(f) (1975). In neglect and dependency cases these states provide that proof must be by clear and convincing evidence (e.g., Georgia, Ga.Code Ann. § 15–11–33(b) (1982), New Mexico, and North Dakota, N.D.Cent.Code § 27–20–29(3) (1974)) or a preponderance of the evidence (e.g., New York, N.Y.Fam.Ct. Act § 1046(b)(i) (McKinney 1975), South Dakota, and Wyoming).

In Santosky v. Kramer, ____ U.S. ____, 102 S.Ct. 1388, 71 L.Ed.2d 599 (1982), infra at p. 851, the United States Supreme Court held that in proceedings to terminate parental rights due process requires that the state's allegations be supported by at least clear and convincing evidence.

3. PRIVILEGE AGAINST SELF INCRIMINATION; GUILTY PLEAS IN JUVENILE COURTS

IN RE GAULT

Supreme Court of the United States, 1967.
387 U.S. 1, 87 S.Ct. 1428, 18 L.Ed.2d 527.

(For the opinion in this case, see page 209, supra).

NOTES

(1) The requirement of *Gault* that a juvenile is entitled to the privilege against self-incrimination in an adjudicatory hearing for the most part has been codified. See, e.g., Ga.Code Ann. § 15–11–31(b) (1982); N.D.Cent.Code § 27–20–27(2) (1974); 42 Pa.Cons.Stat.Ann. § 6338(b) (Purdon 1981); Tenn. Code Ann. § 37–227(b) (1977); Tex.Fam.Code Ann. § 54.03(e) (Supp.1982); Vt.Stat.Ann. tit. 33, § 652 (Supp.1980); Wyo.Stat.Ann. § 14–6–223(a) (1977). In addition, many states require that the juvenile and his parents or guardian be advised of the right against self-incrimination at the hearing. See, e.g., N.Y.Fam.Ct.Act § 741(a) (McKinney 1975); Tex.Fam.Code Ann. § 54.03(b) (1975); Wyo.Stat.Ann. § 14–6–226(a) (1977).

(2) As in adult cases, it is constitutional error for the juvenile court to consider the juvenile's failure to testify at the adjudication hearing as evidence of guilt. In State ex rel. D.A.M., 132 N.J.Super. 192, 333 A.2d 270 (1975), the appellate court reversed a delinquency adjudication on self-incrimination grounds because the juvenile judge said:

I also must take note of the fact that the juvenile has not taken the stand to deny any of the allegations in this matter and even though we cannot mention to a jury, I am sure the jury would have that in mind as to why an individual doesn't deny any of the allegations made in a particular case.

IN RE CHAVIS

Court of Appeals of North Carolina, 1976.
31 N.C.App. 579, 230 S.E.2d 198.

ARNOLD, JUDGE.

These appeals were consolidated because they present a single question: where the record does not affirmatively show that the juvenile respondent voluntarily and knowingly admitted the allegations in the juvenile petition, did the court err in adjudicating the juvenile delinquent upon a finding, based on the admission, that the respondent committed the acts alleged in the petition.

Respondents correctly argue that juvenile delinquency hearings, pursuant to G.S. Chap. 7A, Article 23, place them in danger of confinement, and, therefore, the proceedings are to be treated as criminal proceedings, conducted with due process in accord with constitutional safeguards of the Fifth Amendment. In re Gault, 387 U.S. 1, 87 S.Ct. 1428, 18 L.Ed.2d 527 (1967); In re Burrus, 275 N.C. 517, 169 S.E.2d 879 (1969); In re Arthur, 27 N.C.App. 227, 218 S.E.2d 869 (1975). Among the rights of the Fifth Amendment is that "No person . . . shall be compelled in any criminal case to be a witness against himself." This is commonly known as the privilege against self-incrimination, and it may be waived if done so knowingly and voluntarily.

A plea of guilty in a criminal case amounts to a waiver of the privilege against self-incrimination if the guilty plea is made knowingly and voluntarily. The requirement that the plea knowing and voluntary is so important that the record must affirmatively show on its face that the guilty plea was knowing and voluntary. If the record does not affirmatively show on its face that the plea was knowing and voluntary, the defendant must be allowed to replead.

Respondents' position is that an "admission" in a juvenile hearing is equivalent to a guilty plea in a criminal case, and that the record must therefore affirmatively show on its face that the admission was entered knowingly and voluntarily. We agree.

There are some significant differences between criminal trials and juvenile proceedings. In the juvenile proceeding there is no jury and the district judge rules on the admissibility of the evidence as well as on the weight and credibility of the evidence. However, if we are to require an affirmative showing from the face of the record that a guilty plea was understandingly and voluntarily entered, and we are so required then we see no less reason to require the same affirmative showing in juvenile proceedings. . . .

At a juvenile hearing an admission by a juvenile must be made knowingly and voluntarily, and this fact must affirmatively appear on the face of the record, or the juvenile will be allowed to replead. . . .

. . .

All three of these cases are reversed and remanded for proceedings not inconsistent with this opinion.

Reversed and remanded.

NOTES

(1) Subsequent to the decision in the principal case the legislature adopted a new juvenile court code. North Carolina General Statutes now provide:

§ 7A–633. When admissions by juvenile may be accepted

(a) A judge may accept an admission from a juvenile only after first addressing him personally and

(1) Informing him that he has a right to remain silent and that any statement he makes may be used against him;

(2) Determining that he understands the nature of the charge;

(3) Informing him that he has a right to deny the allegations;

(4) Informing him that by his admissions he waives his right to be confronted by the witnesses against him;

(5) Determining that the juvenile is satisfied with his representation; and

(6) Informing him of the most restrictive disposition on the charge.

(b) By inquiring of the prosecutor, the juvenile's attorney, and the juvenile personally, the judge shall determine whether there were any prior discussions involving admissions, whether the parties have entered into any arrangement with respect to the admissions and the terms thereof, and whether any improper pressure was exerted. The judge may accept an admission from a juvenile only after determining that the admission is a product of informed choice.

(c) The judge may accept an admission only after determining that there is a factual basis for the admission. This determination may be based upon any of the following information: a statement of the facts by the prosecutor; a written statement of the juvenile; sworn testimony which may include reliable hearsay; or a statement of facts by the juvenile's attorney.

(2) Juvenile Justice Standards Project, Standards Relating to Adjudication (1980) states:

3.2 Admonitions before accepting a plea admitting an allegation of the petition

The judge of the juvenile court should not accept a plea admitting an allegation of the petition without first addressing the respondent personally, in language calculated to communicate effectively with the respondent, and:

A. determining that the respondent understands the nature of the allegations;

B. informing the respondent of the right to a hearing at which the government must confront respondent with witnesses and prove the allegations beyond a reasonable doubt and at which respondent's attorney will be permitted to cross-examine the witnesses called by the government and to call witnesses on the respondent's behalf;

C. informing the respondent of the right to remain silent with respect to the allegations of the petition as well as of the right to testify if desired;

D. informing the respondent of the right to appeal from the decision reached in the trial;

E. informing the respondent of the right to a trial by jury;

F. informing the respondent that one gives up those rights by a plea admitting an allegation of the petition; and

G. informing the respondent that if the court accepts the plea, the court can place respondent on conditional freedom for (_____) years or commit respondent to (the appropriate correctional agency) for (_____) years.

4. CONFRONTATION AND CROSS EXAMINATION

IN RE GAULT

Supreme Court of the United States, 1967.
387 U.S. 1, 87 S.Ct. 1428, 18 L.Ed.2d 527.

(For the opinion in this case, see page 209, supra).

NOTES

(1) In *Gault* the Supreme Court held that "absent a valid confession, a determination of delinquency and an order of commitment to a state institution cannot be sustained in the absence of sworn testimony subjected to the opportunity for cross examination in accordance with our law and constitutional requirements." 387 U.S. at 57. The rights to confrontation and cross examination were violated in *Gault* because a police officer was allowed to give hearsay testimony to establish the acts committed by Gerald Gault.

Courts frequently have allowed the use of hearsay in juvenile adjudicatory hearings where the evidence fell within a recognized exception to the hearsay rule, see, e.g., C.A.J. v. State, 127 Ga.App. 813, 195 S.E.2d 225 (1973); In re Kevin G., 80 Misc.2d 517, 363 N.Y.S.2d 999 (Fam.Ct., N.Y.County 1975), or where admission of the hearsay was harmless error or otherwise not prejudical, see, e.g., P. H. v. State, 504 P.2d 837 (Alaska 1972); In re Johnson, 214 Kan. 780, 522 P.2d 330 (1974).

On the other hand, courts have held that the rights to confrontation and cross examination were violated where hearsay evidence was received and did not fall within any recognized exception to the hearsay rule. See, e.g., In re Dennis H., 19 Cal.App.3d 350, 96 Cal.Rptr. 791 (1971); In re Baum, 8 Wn. App. 337, 506 P.2d 323 (1973).

(2) The rights to confrontation and cross examination recognized in *Gault* have been codified in a number of states. See, e.g., Conn.Gen.Stat. Ann. § 46b–136(a) (Supp.1981); Ill.Ann.Stat. ch. 37, § 701–20(1) (1972); Tenn. Code Ann. § 37–227(a) (1977); Wyo.Stat.Ann. § 14–6–223(b)(i) (1977).

(3) Juvenile Justice Standards Project, Standards Relating to Adjudication, Standard 4.4 (1980):

4.4 Social information

A. Except in preadjudication hearings in which social history information concerning the respondent is relevant and admissible, such as a detention hearing or a hearing to consider transfer to criminal court for prosecution as an adult, the judge of the juvenile court should not view a social history report or receive social history information concerning a respondent who has not been adjudicated delinquent.

B. Each jurisdiction should provide by law that when a jury is the trier of fact it should not view a social history report or receive social history information concerning the respondent.

Standard 4.4 codifies the position taken by some courts, see, e.g., In re Gladys R., 1 Cal.3d 855, 83 Cal.Rptr. 671, 464 P.2d 127 (1970) that social records, histories, and other such information are not proper evidence to be considered during the adjudicatory stage of the proceedings. Such information consists largely of hearsay, and, in addition to violating the juvenile's rights to confrontation and cross examination, it is unfairly prejudicial to the juvenile and is irrelevant to the issue of whether the alleged acts were committed. This information is relevant to the question of disposition and normally is received at the dispositional hearing.

RLR v. STATE

Supreme Court of Alaska, 1971.
487 P.2d 27.

RABINOWITZ, JUSTICE.

This appeal raises significant issues regarding the constitutional rights of a child to a public jury trial, ...

A probation officer for the Division of Corrections, Department of Health and Welfare, filed a petition alleging that RLR, a person under 18 years old, had unlawfully sold lysergic acid diethylamide (LSD) to Joseph Want on or about December 11, 1968, and praying that RLR be adjudicated a delinquent. RLR denied the allegations. Initially, a hearing was held to perpetuate the testimony of one William J. Gowans, a chemist employed by the United States Department of Justice. RLR was not present at this proceeding, although his attorney was present. Gowans testified that a substance he had received from the Fairbanks police department was, in his opinion, LSD. At a full adjudicative hearing with RLR present, Joseph W. Want, apparently a part-time secret informer for the Fairbanks police department, testified that he had purchased "a hit" from RLR at a pool hall on December 11 or 12, 1968, and had given the tablet to a police officer. Paul W. Tannenbaum, a Fairbanks police officer, testified that he had given Want money to buy drugs and several hours later Want had given him the tablet Gowans identified as LSD. RLR testified that he had been in school at the time the alleged sale was made, and did not sell LSD to Want. The court found that the allegations of the petition had been proved and adjudicated RLR a delinquent. At the disposition hearing, which was presided over by a judge other than the one who presided at the adjudicative hearing, the court decided to continue custody in the Division of Corrections, Department of Health and Welfare, for an indefinite time up to RLR's 21st birthday, on the understanding that he was to be boarded at a ranch south of Fairbanks on a trial basis. One week later a formal disposition order was entered in which it was ordered that the Department of Health and Welfare have custody of RLR and authority to place him in a foster home, detention home, or other facility without further application to the court. This appeal followed.

. . .

RLR'S ABSENCE AT THE GOWANS HEARING

Children's Rule 12(c)(1)[88] requires that the child be present at both the adjudicative and dispositive phases of his hearing. On April 18, 1969, at 9 a.m. the court held a hearing in which William J. Gowans, a chemist, testified that a tablet sent to him for analysis contained LSD. Counsel for RLR participated, but RLR was absent. RLR's attorney said that he did not know whether or not RLR wished to waive his right to be present, apparently because RLR had not been informed that the hearing was to take place. The prosecuting attorney said that he thought a written waiver of his right to be present by RLR was needed, though he doubted that RLR would actually be prejudiced by his absence. The court nevertheless proceeded to take Gowans' testimony. The record indicates that a summons to appear on April 18 at 10 a.m., an hour after the hearing began, without an attached copy of the petition, was served on RLR on April 9.

. . . .

. . . We see no difference in principle between the child's right to be present at his hearing and a criminal defendant's right to be present at his trial. . . .

. . .

---

88. Rules of Children's Procedure 12(c)(1) provides:

Parties Whose Presence is Required

The presence of the following parties is required at the child hearing:

(1) The child.

(2) All persons to whom summons are required to be directed under these rules unless the court in its discretion determines that a continuance for the purpose of securing the attendance of such persons will not be productive of their attendance.

(3) The guardian ad litem, if one was appointed.

(4) Counsel for the child or other parties, if counsel was retained or was appointed.

Proof that the tablet allegedly sold by RLR contained LSD was an essential and contested element in the state's case. The taking of Gowans' testimony was not an anteroom conference on a point of law, but a full-scale factual hearing. RLR's absence was not momentary and inadvertent, but extended throughout a lengthy hearing after explicit refusal by his attorney to waive it. Such a blatant violation of Children's Rule 12(c)(1) requires reversal. In a case of this sort, we will not weigh the possibility of prejudice . . ., but will presume it . . .. We need not conjure up possibilities of prejudice. Preservation of the fundamental right to be present against clear denials of it should not depend on the imaginative abilities of appellate judges. Children's Rule 12(c)(1) was broken in a clear and substantial manner despite counsel's explicit stated refusal to waive his client's right. That is enough to require reversal.

. . .

The superior court's adjudicative and dispositive orders are vacated and reversed, and the matter remanded for appropriate proceedings.

NOTE

The right of a juvenile to be present during adjudicatory proceedings is sometimes secured by statute. See, e.g., Cal.Welf. & Inst.Code § 679 (1972); Mont.Code Ann. § 41–5–521(4) (1981). Some states provide that the right to be present can be waived generally, but an exception is made in the case of a juvenile alleged to be delinquent, apparently out of regard for the juvenile's rights to confrontation and cross examination in such cases. See, e.g., Ala. Code § 12–15–65(a) (1975); Minn.Stat.Ann. § 260.155(5) (1971).

5. CORROBORATION OF CONFESSIONS AND ACCOMPLICE TESTIMONY

An uncorroborated extrajudicial confession cannot sustain a conviction for crime. To sustain a conviction based upon a confession, the state must show the confession is trustworthy by proof of facts and circumstances that the crime confessed did in fact occur. This rule has been applied to juvenile delinquency proceedings by case law, e.g., State ex rel. W. J., 116 N.J.Super. 462, 282 A.2d 770 (1970), or statute. See, e.g., Ga.Code Ann. § 15–11–31(b) (1982); N.M.Stat. Ann. § 32–1–27(G) (1981); N.Y.Fam.Ct.Act § 744(b) (McKinney Supp. 1981); N.D.Cent.Code § 27–20–27(2) (1974); 42 Pa.Cons.Stat.Ann. § 6338(b) (1981); Tenn.Code Ann. § 37–227(b) (1977); Tex.Fam.Code Ann. § 54.03(e) (Supp.1982); Vt.Stat.Ann. tit. 33, § 652 (Supp.1980). These provisions are based on § 27(b) of the Uniform Juvenile Court Act (1968).

Whether adopted judicially or by statute the rule no doubt is based on serious concern for the lack of reliability and trustworthiness of children's confessions (see, e.g., the expression of this concern in *Gault* at page 225, supra). As in so many other areas the tremendous influence of *Gault* is seen in the present requirement of corroboration of a juvenile's confession despite earlier cases to the contrary. See, e.g., In re Tillotson, 225 La. 573, 73 So.2d 466 (1954); People v. Lewis, 260 N.Y. 171, 183 N.E. 353 (1932). Moreover, the requirement of In re Winship that delinquency allegations be proved beyond a reasonable doubt has influenced courts and legislatures to require corroboration of confessions in delinquency cases.

With regard to corroboration of accomplice testimony, the court in State ex rel. Williams, 325 So.2d 854, 855–56 (La.App.1976) stated:

> In its attempt to prove the participation of Williams in the burglary, the State relies on the testimony of an alleged accomplice, Joseph McTear, Jr., another juvenile who had previously confessed to the burglary and who had been committed to the Louisiana Training Institute. At the time of his testimony, McTear was also under a pending charge of attempted rape.

> The weight to be accorded the testimony of an accomplice is stated in State v. Lewis, 236 La. 473, 108 So.2d 93 (1959) as follows:

>> "Although the testimony of an accomplice, even though uncorroborated, is competent evidence, it is well settled that such evidence is subject to suspicion and should be received and acted upon with extreme or at least grave caution. State v. Feroci, 167 La. 78, 118 So. 699; State v. Matassa, 222 La. 363, 62 So.2d 609."

> The testimony of McTear reflects that the idea to commit the burglary was his alone, and that he allegedly approached Williams to accompany him only a few minutes prior to the commission of the act. He admits they were not friends and had not discussed this matter previously at school. It was further established, the two boys had once had an altercation during and after football practice the preceding fall season.

> It appears that McTear did not implicate Williams during his initial interrogation nor at the time of his adjudication as a delinquent. As we understand the record, this accusation against Williams occurred at about the time McTear was subsequently charged with attempted rape.

> The only other evidence of a substantive nature presented by the State was the testimony of the owner of the station, Louis Testa, who described the method of entry and the amount of money believed to be in the cash register.

> The father, grandfather and grandmother of the juvenile testified he was at home at all times on the night of the occurrence of the alleged burglary. Testimony of two of Williams' teachers was offered to show his good school record and general good character.

We conclude that the testimony of McTear when judged in the light of his record and all other surrounding circumstances shown by the record is not sufficient without other corroborating evidence to constitute proof "beyond a reasonable doubt" of the participation of Williams in the burglary and that the trial court erred in its adjudication based on the evidence before it.

For these reasons, the adjudication of the delinquency of Rowan Williams is annulled and vacated, and the petition of the State in the interest of the juvenile is dismissed.

Prior to In re Winship courts did not feel any need for corroboration of accomplice testimony in delinquency cases because the preponderance standard of proof was so easy to meet. See, e.g., In re Collins, 20 Ohio App.2d 319, 253 N.E.2d 824 (1969). The requirement of *Winship* that delinquency be proved beyond a reasonable doubt has since influenced courts considering the issue. See, e.g., In re Arthur M., 34 A.D.2d 761, 310 N.Y.S.2d 399 (1970).

Typically courts have applied in juvenile cases the same rule applicable in criminal cases, whether that meant that uncorroborated accomplice testimony was insufficient by itself, T.L.T. v. State, 133 Ga. App. 895, 212 S.E.2d 650 (1975), or sufficient under certain circumstances, as in State ex rel. Williams. In In re S.J.C., 533 S.W.2d 746 (Tex.1976), however, the Texas Supreme Court held that uncorroborated accomplice testimony was sufficient to support an adjudication of delinquency, even though the same evidence would not be sufficient to sustain a criminal conviction. Subsequently the Texas Family Code was amended to provide as follows: "An adjudication of delinquent conduct or conduct indicating a need for supervision cannot be had upon the testimony of an accomplice unless corroborated by other evidence tending to connect the child with the alleged delinquent conduct or conduct indicating a need for supervision; and the corroboration is not sufficient if it merely shows the commission of the alleged conduct." Tex.Fam.Code Ann. § 54.03(e) (Supp.1982). The same statute provides that in both delinquency cases and cases indicating a need for supervision the required standard of proof is proof beyond a reasonable doubt. Id. § 54.03(f).

E. JURY TRIAL

McKEIVER v. PENNSYLVANIA

Supreme Court of the United States, 1971.
403 U.S. 528, 91 S.Ct. 1976, 29 L.Ed.2d 647.

(For the opinion in this case, see page 236, supra.)

NOTES

(1) The Supreme Court in *McKeiver* simply held that due process does not require states to afford jury trials in juvenile proceedings. The Court's decision does not prevent states from choosing to do so. Speaking for a four-member plurality, Justice Blackmun stated: "If in its wisdom, any State feels the jury trial is desirable in all cases, or in certain kinds, there appears to be no impediment to its installing a system embracing that feature. That, however, is the State's privilege and not its obligation." 403 U.S. at 547.

Indeed, a number of states provide for jury trial in juvenile proceedings, either by statute or judicial decision. Colo.Rev.Stat.Ann. § 19–1–106(4) (1978); Kan.Stat.Ann. § 38–808(a) (Supp.1980) (in discretion of court in case of juvenile charged with felony); Mass.Gen.Laws Ann. ch. 119, § 55A (Supp. 1981); Mich.Comp.Laws Ann. § 712A.17(2) (Supp.1982); Mont.Code Ann. § 41–5–521(1) (1981); N.M.Stat.Ann. § 32–1–31(A) (1981); Okla.Stat.Ann. tit. 10, § 1110 (Supp.1982); S.D.Comp.Laws Ann. § 26–8–31 (1976) (in discretion of court); Tex.Fam.Code Ann. § 54.03(c) (Supp.1982); W.Va.Code Ann. § 49–5–6 (1980); Wis.Stat.Ann. § 48.31(2) (1979); Wyo.Stat.Ann. § 14–6–223(c) (1977); RLR v. State, 487 P.2d 27 (Alaska 1971).† The great majority of states, however, have elected not to afford jury trials in adjudicatory hearings, or have decided that jury trials are not constitutionally required. The numerous statutes and cases are cited in S. Davis, Rights of Juveniles: The Juvenile Justice System at 5–13 n.55 (1980).

(2) Juvenile Justice Standards Project, Standards Relating to Adjudication,* Standard 4.1 (1980), and Commentary at 53–54:

4.1 Trial by jury

A. Each jurisdiction should provide by law that the respondent may demand trial by jury in adjudication proceedings when respondent has denied the allegations of the petition.

B. Each jurisdiction should provide by law that the jury may consist of as few as six persons and that the verdict of the jury must be unanimous.

Commentary

. . . The importance of the availability of jury trials in juvenile cases goes beyond neutralizing the biased juvenile court judge. A jury trial gives enhanced visibility to the adjudicative process. A jury trial requires the trial court judge to articulate his or her views of the applicable law in the case through jury instructions, thereby facilitating appellate court review of the legal issues involved. Without the focus on legal issues that such an exercise entails, the danger is great that the applicable law may be misperceived or misapplied and that the error will go uncorrected on appeal. In addition, many significant evidentiary protections in the adjudicative process are based on the assumption that preliminary rulings on admissibility will be made by the trial judge and that a jury will receive the evidence only if it has been ruled admissible. When a

---

† The Alaska Supreme Court's decision in RLR v. State actually postdated *McKeiver,* but the court based its decision on state constitutional law.

* Reprinted with permission from Standards Relating to Adjudication, Copyright 1980, Ballinger Publishing Company.

jury is not present, the evidentiary questions tend to become blurred and appellate review of evidentiary questions is made extremely difficult by the universal presumption that the trial judge disregarded inadmissible evidence and relied only upon competent evidence in arriving at his or her decision. . . . Of course, these same evidentiary problems may arise in a criminal trial when the jury has been waived, but at least the criminal defendant has had the option of demanding a jury in order to obtain meaningful rulings on what may be outcome-determining questions.

There may be special needs for having jury trials available in juvenile court. Although the position is taken in other volumes of standards that juvenile court intake should be an executive function, not subject to administrative control of the juvenile court judge, historically the juvenile court judge was the chief administrator of the juvenile process in his or her locality. Such a judge is likely to have had a substantial involvement in the structuring and operation of the court intake process and may have played a substantial part in persuading local officials of the importance of the juvenile process in local funding priorities. The judge may be committed to the juvenile court concept as a "social movement" and thus may find it difficult to view dispassionately the evidence produced by the operatives in that system. Further, such a judge is more likely than his or her counterpart in the criminal justice process to have had contact with a case prior to an adjudication hearing, in a detention hearing or perhaps even a hearing to consider transfer for prosecution in criminal court, in which background information that would be unfairly prejudicial to the respondent at adjudication was properly presented.

(3) Tennessee is one of the states that does not provide for jury trials in adjudicatory hearings. Tenn.Code Ann. § 37–224(a) (1977). In Tennessee a juvenile who has been adjudicated delinquent for commission of a felony has an appeal to the circuit court for trial de novo. Id. § 37–258(a). In such cases the courts have held that the juvenile is entitled to have the trial de novo heard by a jury. Arwood v. State, 62 Tenn.App. 453, 463 S.W.2d 943 (1970). Moreover, the juvenile does not have to make a timely demand for a jury trial as in civil cases, but rather is entitled to jury trial as a matter of right unless waived. State v. Johnson, 574 S.W.2d 739 (Tenn.1978).

(4) In recent years several states have revised their juvenile court codes as part of a general "reform" effort to deal more severely with juveniles, particularly those accused of serious offenses and those with prior records of criminal misbehavior. Claims have been raised that these changes are punitive in nature and have the effect of transforming juvenile proceedings into criminal proceedings, and, therefore, juveniles now have a right to jury trial.

In Washington, for example, the juvenile court code was revised to provide for accountability of juveniles for their acts and for proportional punishment for some juveniles, based on age, prior record, and seriousness of the offense. Wash.Rev.Code Ann. §§ 13.40.010(2)(c)–(d), 13.40.030 (Supp.1981). In rejecting a claim that under the revised code juveniles were entitled to jury trial, the Washington Supreme Court held that although "the philosophy and methodology of addressing the personal and societal problems of juvenile offenders" had changed, the fundamentally rehabilitative purpose of the court remained, and viewed in light of *McKeiver* the code's provision for hearings without juries measured up to the essentials of due process. State v. Lawley, 91 Wn.2d 654, 591 P.2d 772 (1979).

Lower courts in New York have split over the identical issue. In New York, as a result of the Juvenile Justice Reform Act of 1976, a juvenile may be committed to a secure facility for a definite period of time for commission of one of certain designated felonies. N.Y.Fam.Ct.Act § 753–a (McKinney Supp.1981). One court held that since the effect of this enactment was to transform juvenile proceedings into essentially criminal proceedings, juveniles are entitled to a jury trial in adjudicatory hearings. However, since New York law is very clear that a court may not order a jury trial without statutory authorization, the court held that in a designated felony proceeding tried without a jury, restrictive placement can not be ordered. In re Felder, 93 Misc.2d 369, 402 N.Y.S.2d 528 (Fam.Ct., Onondaga County 1978). Other courts have held that despite the punitive nature of the restrictive placement allowed under the new enactment, juveniles do not have a right to jury trial. People v. Young, 99 Misc.2d 328, 416 N.Y.S.2d 171 (Fam. Ct., Monroe County 1979); In re William M., 90 Misc.2d 173, 393 N.Y.S.2d 535 (Fam.Ct., Kings County 1977).

This issue is discussed in a broader context in Feld, Juvenile Court Legislative Reform and the Serious Young Offender: Dismantling the "Rehabilitative Ideal," 65 Minn.L.Rev. 167, 197–203 (1980).

(5) Texas permits jury trials in juvenile hearings. The Texas Court of Civil Appeals, however, held that since juvenile proceedings are civil in nature, the rule in civil cases allowing less than unanimous verdicts (10 out of 12) was applicable in juvenile cases as well. In re V.R.S., 512 S.W.2d 350 (Tex.Civ.App.1974). Unanimous verdicts are constitutionally required in felony cases, and the delinquent act alleged in this case was a felony. Subsequent to the court's decision the statute allowing jury trials in juvenile hearings was amended to require unanimous jury verdicts. Tex.Fam.Code Ann. § 54.03(c) (Supp.1982).

(6) People ex rel. R.A.D., 196 Colo. 430, 586 P.2d 46 (1978):

A juvenile, like an adult, is entitled to the essentials of due process before his freedom may be curtailed. Fundamental fairness mandates that the charges against a juvenile be evaluated by a fair and impartial jury. Thus we hold that the rule allowing one charged in an adult criminal prosecution to challenge for cause a prospective juror who is employed by a law enforcement agency, must also be applied in juvenile delinquency proceedings.

Logically the same likelihood of bias affects the law enforcement employee whether an adult or a child is charged with an offense. Logically the same rule should govern both situations. Due process, in the sense of obvious, fundamental fairness, should have prompted the trial judge here to sustain the appellant's challenge for cause.

The appellant was deprived of his statutorily guaranteed number of peremptory challenges, for he was forced to employ one of them to excuse a juror who should have been excused for cause. Had the challenge been sustained, the composition of the jury would have been different. No one can tell what effect this might have had upon the trial's outcome and it is not for us to speculate.

(7) Illinois makes no provision for jury trials in juvenile proceedings. Nevertheless, in In re Staley, 67 Ill.2d 33, 7 Ill.Dec. 85, 364 N.E.2d 72 (1977),

the Illinois Supreme Court held that requiring a juvenile to appear at the adjudicatory hearing while handcuffed constituted reversible error:

> The State points out that there was no trial by jury here. The possibility of prejudicing a jury, however, is not the only reason why courts should not allow the shackling of an accused in the absence of a strong necessity for doing so. The presumption of innocence is central to our administration of criminal justice. In the absence of exceptional circumstances, an accused has the right to stand trial "with the appearance, dignity, and self-respect of a free and innocent man." It jeopardizes the presumption's value and protection and demeans our justice for an accused without clear cause to be required to stand in a courtroom in manacles or other restraints while he is being judged. Also, . . . shackling restricts the ability of an accused to cooperate with his attorney and to assist in his defense. The reasons for forbidding shackling are not limited to trials by jury. Section 4.1(c) of the ABA Standards relating to trial by jury, . . . while it does concern the conduct of jury trials, does not limit its disapproval of physical restraint of a defendant to such trials. The commentary to section 4.1 provides:
>
> > ". . . [T]he matter of custody and restraint of defendants and witnesses at trial is not of concern solely in those cases in which there is a jury. Obviously, a defendant should be able to consult effectively with counsel in all cases. Prison attire and unnecessary physical restraint are offensive even when there is no jury. . . .
> >
> >   . . .
> >
> > (c) . . . Because the rule rests only in part upon the possibility of jury prejudice, it should not be limited to jury trials." ABA Standards, Trial by Jury sec. 4.1, Commentary 92–94 (1968).

F.   SPEEDY AND PUBLIC TRIAL

1.   RIGHT TO SPEEDY TRIAL

(See the cases and materials on speedy trial in Chapter VI, at page 383 supra.)

2.   PUBLIC TRIAL AND CONFIDENTIALITY

IN RE J.S.

Supreme Court of Vermont, 1981.
___ Vt. ___, 438 A.2d 1125.

UNDERWOOD, JUSTICE.

A juvenile, J.S., appeals from an order of the juvenile court allowing the public to attend proceedings to adjudge him a delinquent child for his alleged participation in the murder of one girl and the sexual assault of another.

In an attempt to comply with the confidentiality provisions of our juvenile shield law, 33 V.S.A. § 651, one trial judge issued an order of closure which barred the public from the proceedings. The Burlington Free Press was granted permission to intervene for the sole purpose of being heard on its petition for access to any and all of the proceedings involving J.S. A second trial judge granted the petition, holding that 33 V.S.A. § 651(c) violated the First Amendment. He ordered that J.S.'s juvenile proceedings be held in open court and that the public and the news media be permitted to attend.

J.S. sought relief from this order by two means. He was granted this interlocutory appeal . . . from the order opening the proceedings, and at the same time he filed a petition for extraordinary relief, . . . seeking to vacate the order and to exclude the public.

. . .

The principal question before us is whether the limited holding of Richmond Newspapers, Inc. v. Virginia, 448 U.S. 555, 100 S.Ct. 2814, 65 L.Ed.2d 973 (1980), that the First Amendment contains a right of access to criminal trials extends to a juvenile proceeding to determine delinquency and treatment. We must also consider additional arguments put forward by the Free Press in support of public proceedings.

Only a brief recital of the facts is necessary to enable us to grapple with the legal issues raised in this appeal. Two 12-year-old Essex Junction girls were brutally assaulted by two persons in or near an area park. One was killed. The other, left for dead, managed to survive. J.S. and a 16-year-old are the alleged assailants. J.S., who is 15, has been charged as a juvenile delinquent and will have his proceedings heard in juvenile court. The 16-year-old is awaiting trial as an adult in superior court on charges of first-degree murder and sexual assault.*

---

* The jurisdictional age in Vermont for juveniles alleged to be delinquent is 16, and until recently no provision was made for waiver of jurisdiction. The criminal court was given discretion to transfer to the juvenile court a person who was over 16 but under 18 at the time of the alleged offense; the juvenile court then had jurisdiction over these older youths. Following recent amendments, the criminal court still has original jurisdiction over these older youths with discretion to transfer some of them to the juvenile court and, in addition, has original jurisdiction over juveniles who were over 14 but under 16 at the time of commission of any one of certain enumerated serious offenses, with discretion to transfer some cases to juvenile court. Vt.Stat. Ann. tit. 33, §§ 635(b), 644(c) (Spec.Supp. 1981). Moreover, the juvenile court is now authorized to waive jurisdiction and transfer for criminal prosecution a juvenile who was over 10 but under 14 at the time of commission of one of the serious offenses enumerated in the statute. Id. § 635a(a).

Under either the former provisions or the current law, the case of the 16-year-old accomplice would have originated in criminal court, which, perhaps because of the seriousness of the offenses (murder and sexual assault), would not have been disposed to transfer the case to juvenile court. Had the current law been applicable to J.S., his case would have originated in criminal court since the offenses charged are among those set forth in the statute. Had the current law been applicable to J.S., his case would have originated in criminal court because of his age and because the offenses charged are among those set forth in the statute. Id. §§ 635(b), 635a(a), 644(c).

Our juvenile shield law requires that juvenile court proceedings be confidential. The relevant portions of that law provide:

(c) Except in hearings to declare a person in contempt of court, the general public shall be excluded from hearings under this chapter and only the parties, their counsel, witnesses and other persons accompanying a party for his assistance and such other person as the court finds to have a proper interest in the case or in the work of the court, may be admitted by the court. If the court finds that it is to the best interest and welfare of the child, his presence may be temporarily excluded, except while a charge of his delinquency is being heard at the hearing on the petition.

(d) There shall be no publicity given by any person to any proceedings under the authority of this chapter except with the consent of the child and his parent or guardian.

33 V.S.A. § 651.

On appeal, J.S. contends that 33 V.S.A. § 651(c) mandates that the juvenile proceedings be closed to the public and the news media, and that closed proceedings are perfectly consistent with the United States and Vermont Constitutions. The State, in effect, concurs. Both J.S. and the State ask us to reverse the court below and close the proceedings.

The Free Press makes three arguments in support of public proceedings: (1) The court below was correct in holding that 33 V.S.A. § 651(c) was unconstitutional. (2) Even if the statute is constitutional, the proceedings should be public because the court below erroneously found itself without discretion under § 651(c) to admit reporters, and in the proper exercise of that discretion, they should be admitted. (3) Even if we disagree with the first two arguments, the publicity involving J.S. has been and will be so pervasive that the reasons for confidentiality no longer exist, so a special exception from the general requirement of confidentiality should be made in this case to allow public access. We disagree with all three arguments and therefore reverse.

I.

The Free Press claims that *Richmond Newspapers*, supra, dictates that the general public and the news media have a First Amendment right to attend juvenile delinquency proceedings and to publicly report what they see and hear in the juvenile court during those proceedings.

The question facing the Supreme Court in the *Richmond Newspapers* case, however, was whether the public and press possess a constitutional right of access to criminal trials. *Richmond Newspapers*, supra, 448 U.S. at 558, 100 S.Ct. at 2818. The Supreme Court concluded that such a right existed. The plurality held that the combination of the unbroken tradition of open criminal trials at common law and the fact that openness of criminal trials serves important First Amendment goals requires public access, absent overriding interests. That limited holding, however, does not extend to the case at hand.

Far from a tradition of openness, juvenile proceedings are almost invariably closed. All 50 states, in fact, have some sort of juvenile shield law to limit public access. Smith v. Daily Mail Publishing Co., 443 U.S. 97, 105, 99 S.Ct. 2667, 2672, 61 L.Ed.2d 399 (1979). Further, juvenile proceedings are not criminal prosecutions, a fact which makes at least some of the First Amendment purposes served by open criminal trials inapplicable. Finally, inherent in the very nature of juvenile proceedings are compelling interests in confidentiality which the Supreme Court itself has endorsed in cases cited below, and which we hold override any remaining First Amendment goals which access might serve.

A.

The holding in *Richmond Newspapers* applies only to criminal trials. Our juvenile law expressly provides that juvenile proceedings are not criminal. The very purpose of the juvenile delinquency law is to provide an alternative to criminal prosecutions of children. Thus, the Legislature has stated:

(a) The purposes of this chapter are:

. . .

(2) to remove from children committing delinquent acts the taint of criminality and the consequences of criminal behavior.

. . .

(b) The provisions of this chapter shall be construed as superseding the provisions of the criminal law of this state to the extent the same are inconsistent herewith.

33 V.S.A. § 631.

An order of the juvenile court in proceedings under this chapter shall not be deemed a conviction of crime . . ..

33 V.S.A. § 662(a).

We underscored the fundamental characteristic of a juvenile proceeding in In re Rich, 125 Vt. 373, 375, 216 A.2d 266, 267–68 (1966):

It is a protective proceeding entirely concerned with the welfare of the child, and is not punitive. The procedures supersede the provisions of the criminal law and laws affecting minors in conflict with the authorizations of the juvenile court statutes. The inquiry relates to proper custody for the child, not his guilt or innocence as a criminal offender.

The only issue in a juvenile proceeding is "the care, needs and protection of the minor and his rehabilitation and restoration to useful citizenship." In re Delinquency Proceedings, 129 Vt. 185, 191, 274 A.2d 506, 510 (1970).

B.

The court below compared the similarities and differences of juvenile proceedings and criminal trials, cited the United States Supreme Court decisions in Breed v. Jones, 421 U.S. 519, 95 S.Ct. 1779, 44 L.Ed.2d 346 (1975); In re Winship, 397 U.S. 358, 90 S.Ct. 1068, 25 L.Ed.2d 368 (1970); and In re Gault, 387 U.S. 1, 87 S.Ct. 1428, 18 L.Ed.2d 527 (1967), and concluded that a juvenile proceeding was a juvenile prosecution for the purposes of the First Amendment. The differences and similarities it discussed were irrelevant in light of the fundamental distinction between the punitive purpose of a criminal prosecution and the rehabilitative purpose of a juvenile proceeding.

The cases cited by the court below do not support the proposition for which they were cited. Each merely extended certain procedural protections to the juvenile. Nothing in any one of them suggests that the Legislature may not further protect the juvenile by closing the proceedings. If anything, the great concern for the welfare of the child that they demonstrate suggests that the child's interests should prevail when in conflict with public access. To the extent that they are relevant at all, the precedents cited by the court below indicate that confidentiality is appropriate.

Thus it appears to us that a juvenile proceeding is so unlike a criminal prosecution that the limited right of access described in *Richmond Newspapers* does not govern. Certainly, neither the United States nor Vermont Constitutions expressly mandate a right of access. Nor do our opinions or those of the United States Supreme Court hint that such a right exists. The court below was in error when it held otherwise.

C.

Even if there were some constitutional right of access which presumptively reached juvenile proceedings, public access would not automatically follow. Rather, the First Amendment interests would first have to be weighed against the countervailing interests in confidentiality. See Richmond Newspapers, supra, 448 U.S. at 581, 100 S.Ct. at 2830 (plurality opinion), 585–86, 598, 100 S.Ct. 2832–2833, 2839 (Brennan, J., concurring).

The punitive purpose of criminal proceedings raises First Amendment issues which are not present here. There, public access serves as a check against unjust conviction, excessive punishment and the undeserved taint of criminality. See id. at 564–74, 100 S.Ct. at 2821–2826 (plurality opinion), 589–98, 100 S.Ct. 2834–2839 (Brennan, J., concurring). The juvenile proceeding, by contrast, involves no criminal conviction, no punishment, and, when confidential, no taint of

<u>criminality</u>. Thus fewer First Amendment interests are at stake here than was the case in *Richmond Newspapers*.

The other side of the balance, however, is more heavily weighted here than in *Richmond Newspapers*. The compelling interests in confidential juvenile proceedings have been recognized and implicitly endorsed by the United States Supreme Court. See, e.g., Smith v. Daily Mail Publishing Co., supra, 443 U.S. at 104–05, 99 S.Ct. at 2671–2672; In re Gault, supra; In re Winship, supra.

Justice Rehnquist has reiterated the Supreme Court's concern for maintaining the confidentiality of juvenile proceedings:

> It is a hallmark of our juvenile justice system in the United States that virtually from its inception at the end of the last century its proceedings have been conducted outside of the public's full gaze and the youths brought before our juvenile courts have been shielded from publicity. This insistence on confidentiality is born of a tender concern for the welfare of the child, to hide his youthful errors and 'bury them in the graveyard of the forgotten past.' The prohibition of publication of a juvenile's name is designed to protect the young person from the stigma of his misconduct and is rooted in the principle that a court concerned with juvenile affairs serves as a rehabilitative and protective agency of the State.

Smith v. Daily Mail Publishing Co., supra, 443 U.S. at 107, 99 S.Ct. at 2673 (Rehnquist, J., concurring) (citations omitted).

Even Davis v. Alaska, cited by the Free Press for the proposition that the State's interest in keeping juvenile matters confidential must yield to an overwhelming First Amendment right, supports the opposite conclusion. The Court there assumed the propriety of confidentiality in juvenile proceedings when it said, "We do not and need not challenge the State's interest as a matter of its own policy in the administration of criminal justice to seek to preserve the anonymity of a juvenile offender." Davis v. Alaska, 415 U.S. 308, 319, 94 S.Ct. 1105, 1112, 39 L.Ed.2d 347 (1974). If a right of access existed, there certainly could be no anonymity.

The holding in the <u>Davis</u> case only went so far as to protect the defendant's Sixth Amendment right to cross-examination in the context of the factual situation confronting that court. Id. The Court concluded that the State's witness, a juvenile called to identify the defendant, must submit to cross-examination about his juvenile delinquency record, because the defendant's right outweighed the state interest. Id.

Any right of the Free Press to report what takes place in juvenile court is hardly equivalent to the defendant's right to cross-examine the witness who fingered him as the prime suspect in a breaking and entering case, especially where a possible motive of the juvenile for turning State's witness was to take the heat off himself as a suspect in the same crime.

There are, however, many reasons why the State's compelling interests in the confidential juvenile proceedings prescribed by 33 V.S.A. § 651(c) and 33 V.S.A. § 651(d) override the countervailing interests of the public and the news media in access to those proceedings and the news media's interest in publicly disseminating what its reporters learn while attending.

Publication of the youth's name could impair the rehabilitative goals of the juvenile justice system. Confidential proceedings protect the delinquent from the stigma of conduct which may be outgrown and avoids the possibility that the adult is penalized for what he used to be, or worse yet, the possibility that the stigma becomes self-perpetuating, thereby making change and growth impossible. Publication of a delinquent's name may handicap his prospects for adjustment into society, for acceptance by the public, or it may cause him to lose employment opportunities. Public proceedings could so embarrass the youth's family members that they withhold their support in rehabilitative efforts. See Note, Freedom of the Press vs. Juvenile Anonymity: A Conflict Between Constitutional Priorities and Rehabilitation, 65 Iowa L.Rev. 1471, 1484–85 (1980).

The argument of the Free Press that its pervasive newspaper publicity has already compromised these goals and so it ought to be allowed to attend and publicize the proceedings concerning J.S., ignores still another purpose served by confidentiality. Publicity sometimes serves as a reward for the hardcore juvenile delinquent, thereby encouraging him to commit further antisocial acts to attract attention. Id. Further, the legislative goals of expunging the juvenile's delinquency record are vitiated if the same information could at any subsequent time be obtained freely from newspaper morgues.

Neither the Vermont nor the United States Constitution, as interpreted by the United States Supreme Court or our Court, provides a right of public access which overrides the compelling interests served by our juvenile confidentiality shield statutes. The trial court erred in holding otherwise and must be reversed.

II.

The Free Press insists, however, that its reporters are among those persons contemplated by the Legislature as having "a proper interest in the case or in the work of the court," 33 V.S.A. § 651(c), and that the second judge erred when he intimated in his order that the statute gave him no discretion to grant news reporters access to juvenile proceedings.

This argument collides with 33 V.S.A. § 651(d), which specifically prohibits any of those persons admitted under § 651(c) from publicly disseminating information gained from a juvenile hearing "except with the consent of the child and his parent or guardian." No provision is made in either § 651(c) or § 651(d) to give the judge discretion to permit public dissemination of these proceedings.

The Free Press, however, would have us hold that § 651(c) gives the judge discretion to admit their reporters and that § 651(d) forbids them from publishing what they learn once admitted. So construed, they say, § 651(d) is unenforceable as an unconstitutional prior restraint of the press in violation of the First Amendment. Oklahoma Publishing Co. v. District Court, 430 U.S. 308, 97 S.Ct. 1045, 51 L.Ed. 2d 355 (1977); Nebraska Press Ass'n v. Stuart, 427 U.S. 539, 96 S.Ct. 2791, 49 L.Ed.2d 683 (1976).

This statutory interpretation runs afoul of common sense and the canons of construction which we observe to keep ourselves within the bounds of judicial authority. Our function is not to pass upon the validity of a legislative concern or the wisdom of the means the Legislature chooses to address that concern, but merely to make sure that no constitutional bounds are exceeded.

When faced with a choice, we assume that the Legislature intended a constitutional result and construe statutes accordingly. Further, we avoid a construction which leads to absurd or irrational results. Reading § 651(c) and § 651(d) together, to give effect to each, leads to the inescapable result that a desire to publicly disseminate the facts of a juvenile proceeding is not "a proper interest in the case or in the work of the court."

These two sections of the juvenile shield law are clear and unambiguous. The Legislature did not intend that either the news media or the general public should attend juvenile hearings or report what transpired there. We do not base this conclusion on a single sentence or word or phrase in a sentence, but we have looked at the provisions of the whole juvenile law, 33 V.S.A. Chapter 12, and to its objects and its policy.

III.

The Free Press and other members of the news media apparently obtained the name of J.S. and his involvement in the murder and sexual assault of the two young girls in Essex Junction after examining the affidavits of probable cause in the two cases pending against the 16-year-old adult in superior court. Information about the juvenile will inevitably be disclosed at the adult's trial. Because this legally obtained information has been flagrantly publicized by the news media, and because more is to come, the Free Press next argues there is no longer any reason for the confidentiality imposed by 33 V.S.A. § 651(c) and § 651(d) and the Court should drop the barriers for this case as a special exception.

This argument also has several flaws. First, as we have already noted, publicity sometimes serves as a reward for incorrigible delinquents, encouraging the very behavior sought to be deterred. Secondly, this approach calls for a case by case analysis to determine if, when, and to what extent access to juvenile proceedings should be limited. Third, such a case by case analysis lets the news media determine which juvenile proceedings will be open to the public simply by turning up the volume of publicity concerning any case that strikes their fancy. Fourth, decisions to open proceedings will then be based, not on the child's needs, but on chance circumstances. Finally, it is not just the name of delinquents which are protected by the juvenile shield law. Other matters which surface in a juvenile proceeding are just as worthy of anonymity as the juvenile's name. They include the very fact of the adjudication of delinquency and the taint of criminality emanating therefrom; the specific program of treatment, training and rehabilitation ordered and the locale in which it takes place; the name of the individual or organization to whom custody of the juvenile may be entrusted; the fact and conditions of probation; disposition reports and recommendations made by the commissioner of social and rehabilitation services or the commissioner of corrections to the juvenile court; the disposition order of the juvenile court; law enforcement reports and files concerning the minor, as well as fingerprints and photographs, and the files and records of the juvenile court itself, including dismissal of the petition. These are all part and parcel of the record of a young person's life which the Legislature shielded from public access.

IV.

To summarize, the Free Press has failed to establish that any right of access to J.S.'s juvenile proceeding is contained in the United States or Vermont Constitutions. The juvenile shield law does not give the court below discretion to make the proceedings public. The fact that J.S.'s name is already a household word in Essex Junction, and that the nature of the offense and his alleged participation with a named adult defendant in certain crimes will be disclosed in the trial of the adult, is no reason to dismantle our juvenile court system. Confidential proceedings continue to serve overriding interests.

Any limitations in the juvenile justice system will not be cured by a public trial of J.S. If the Free Press feels that the underlying purposes of our juvenile laws are outmoded and no longer valid, it should not look to this Court, but to the Legislature to change the law. Only the Legislature has the power to relax the limitations imposed by 33 V.S.A. § 651(c) and § 651(d) upon the general public and the news media if it believes that would be more desirable than the present law. As of the commencement of these juvenile proceedings against J.S., however, the legislative intent is clear. Juveniles, as a class, are shielded from public exposure of any proceedings conducted in juvenile court to determine delinquency.

The order of the District Court of Vermont, Unit No. 2, Chittenden Circuit, granting the public and the press the right to attend any and all proceedings in juvenile court concerning J.S. is reversed.

NOTES

(1) In Smith v. Daily Mail Publishing Co., 443 U.S. 97, 99 S.Ct. 2667, 61 L.Ed.2d 399 (1979), to which reference is made in the principal case, the Supreme Court held unconstitutional a West Virginia statute subjecting newspapers to a criminal penalty for publishing the name of a juvenile offender without written authorization of the juvenile court. There, the name of the juvenile had been obtained by interviewing witnesses at the scene of the crime. The Court held that the state's interest in protecting the anonymity of the juvenile offender, which in turn would aid in his rehabilitation, did not outweigh the significant first amendment rights involved. The Court, however, took a narrow view of the scope of its decision:

> Our holding in this case is narrow. There is no issue before us of unlawful press access to confidential judicial proceedings; there is no issue here of privacy or prejudicial pretrial publicity. At issue is simply the power of a state to punish the truthful publication of an alleged juvenile delinquent's name lawfully obtained by a newspaper. The asserted state interest cannot justify the statute's imposition of criminal sanctions on this type of publication.

443 U.S. at 105–06.

The Court pointed out that all 50 states have statutes that, like West Virginia's, seek to protect the confidentiality of juvenile proceedings, but that only five states, including West Virginia, provided for a criminal penalty for publication of a juvenile offender's name. The Court listed the others as Colorado, Georgia, New Hampshire, and South Carolina. The Colorado provision was repealed in 1979, and the South Carolina statute was held unconstitutional, in reliance on Smith v. Daily Mail, in State ex rel. The Times and Democrat, 276 S.C. 26, 274 S.E.2d 910 (1981). The statutes remaining are: Ga.Code Ann. § 15–11–60(g)(1) (1982); N.H.Rev.Stat.Ann. §§ 169–B:37, 169–B:38 (Supp.1979).

In pointing out that most states have found means other than the criminal sanction of accomplishing the objective of protecting the confidentiality of a juvenile offender, the Supreme Court noted:

> The approach advocated by the National Council of Juvenile Court Judges is based on cooperation between juvenile court personnel and newspaper editors. It is suggested that if the courts make clear their purpose and methods then the press will exercise discretion and generally decline to publish the juvenile's name without some prior consultation with the juvenile court judge. See Conway, Publicizing the Juvenile Court: A Public Responsibility, 16 Juv.Ct. Judges J. 21, 21–22 (1965); Riederer, Secrecy or Privacy? Communications Problems in the Juvenile Court Field, 17 J.Mo.Bar 66, 69–70 (1961).

443 U.S. at 105 n.3.

The issue is explored generally in McNulty, First Amendment Versus Sixth Amendment: A Constitutional Battle in the Juvenile Courts, 10 N.M.L. Rev. 311 (1980).

(2) In In re J.S. the court also cited and discussed Davis v. Alaska, 415 U.S. 308, 94 S.Ct. 1105, 39 L.Ed.2d 347 (1974), where the Supreme Court was confronted with the issue of whether a defendant in a criminal prosecution may impeach a prosecution witness by using evidence of a prior delinquency

adjudication of the witness. Typical of most states, Alaska statutes and rules provided for the confidentiality of juvenile records and prohibited their use as evidence in subsequent proceedings, except for use in presentencing procedures in a criminal case. The Court held that the state's interest in protecting the confidentiality of juvenile records must yield to a criminal defendant's sixth amendment right to confrontation, which includes the right to effective cross examination of an adverse witness.

Should the prosecution be allowed to use a delinquency adjudication to impeach a defense witness? Is the balancing of interests the same as in Davis v. Alaska? Results have varied. In State v. Wilkins, 215 Kan. 145, 523 P.2d 728 (1974), impeachment of a defense witness was allowed, the court reasoning that the rule operates the same whether the witness is called by the prosecution or by the defendant. On the other hand, in State v. Thomas, 536 S.W.2d 529 (Mo.App.1976), the court held that permitting a defense witness to be cross examined about his prior juvenile record was improper because the state in a criminal prosecution has no sixth amendment right to confrontation to offset the state's interest in protecting the confidentiality of juvenile proceedings.

In People v. Puente, 98 Ill.App.3d 936, 54 Ill.Dec. 25, 424 N.E.2d 775 (1981), the court adopted the approach contained in Federal Rules of Evidence 609(d), which generally favors exclusion of evidence of juvenile adjudications but grants the court discretion to allow such evidence in the case of a witness other than the accused if (1) the adjudication is for an offense that, were it the subject of a conviction, would be useable to impeach, and (2) the court finds that use of the evidence is "necessary for a fair determination of the issue of guilt or innocence." In making the latter determination, the court stated, the trial court should weigh the value of the witness's testimony against the interest in protecting the confidentiality of the juvenile offender.

May a juvenile who is the subject of a delinquency proceeding be asked about his prior juvenile record? In State ex rel. K.P., 167 N.J.Super. 290, 400 A.2d 840 (1979), the court held that the prosecutor's cross examination of the juvenile about his prior juvenile record was improper. The court observed that such cross examination would have been improper even had the juvenile been an adult in a criminal trial because the applicable statute allows cross examination only with respect to prior convictions of crime. The court also concluded that the inquiry violated the statutory prohibition against consideration of the juvenile's background by the juvenile court prior to adjudication. On the latter point, see In re Gladys R., 1 Cal.3d 855, 83 Cal.Rptr. 671, 464 P.2d 127 (1970) (improper for juvenile court judge to consider social study report during adjudicative phase of proceedings).

Use of juvenile adjudications for impeachment purposes is described in Annot., 63 A.L.R.3d 1112 (1975).

(3) A number of states allow delinquency adjudications to be used in the sentencing stage of a criminal proceeding. See, e.g., Ariz.Rev.Stat. § 8–207(C) (Supp.1982); Mass.Gen.Laws Ann. ch. 119, § 60 (Supp.1981); S.D. Comp.Laws Ann. § 26–8–57 (Supp.1981); Vt.Stat.Ann. tit. 33, § 662(f) (Supp. 1980); Bell v. State, 365 So.2d 463 (Fla.App.1978); Bingham v. State, 285 Md. 59, 400 A.2d 765 (1979). The Juvenile Justice Standards Project, Standards Relating to Juvenile Records and Information Systems 18.4(A) (1980) also takes the position that delinquency adjudications may be used in a subse-

quent dispositional or sentencing hearing. The commentary explains that when an adjudication is used for this purpose, relevancy of the prior misconduct outweighs the reasons for preserving confidentiality.

(4) Use of juvenile records for any of the preceding purposes may be limited by other considerations. For example, most states provide for the eventual sealing or expungement of juvenile records after passage of a certain period of time. See, e.g., Ga.Code Ann. § 15–11–61 (1982); N.J.Stat.Ann. § 2A:4–67 (Supp.1982); Tex.Fam.Code Ann. § 51.16 (1975 and Supp.1982); Va.Code Ann. § 16.1–306 (Supp.1981). As a practical matter, if the records have been sealed or expunged, they will be unavailable for use for any purpose.

In addition, suppose the prior adjudication is constitutionally infirm. May it be used, for example, for impeachment or dispositional purposes? In Loper v. Beto, 405 U.S. 473, 92 S.Ct. 1014, 31 L.Ed.2d 374 (1972), the Supreme Court held that a prior conviction in a prosecution in which the accused was not represented by counsel is not useable for impeachment because the right to counsel goes to the integrity of the fact-finding process, and a conviction obtained without representation by counsel therefore lacks reliability. Further, in Majchszak v. Ralston, 454 F.Supp. 1137 (W.D.Wis.1978), the court held that in considering whether a prisoner should be released on parole, the parole board improperly considered prior delinquency adjudications resulting from proceedings in which the prisoner was not represented by counsel.

(5) As the Supreme Court observed in Smith v. Daily Mail, supra, all states have provisions protecting the confidentiality of juvenile records. Access to records typically is limited to court personnel; the juvenile, his or her parents, and counsel; law enforcement personnel under certain circumstances; and other courts and agencies for purposes of preparing presentence reports, parole recommendations, and the like. In addition, as mentioned in the preceding note, provision is usually made for sealing or expungement of records. Representative statutes are; Ga.Code Ann. § 15–11–58 through –60 (1982); N.J.Stat.Ann. §§ 2A:4–65 and –66 (Supp. 1982); Tex.Fam.Code Ann. §§ 51.14 (1975) and 51.15 (1975 and Supp.1982); Va.Code Ann. §§ 16.1–299 through –305 (Supp.1981).

The Juvenile Justice Standards Relating to Juvenile Records and Information Systems (1980) * provide for extensive regulations to protect the confidentiality of juvenile court records. In addition to furnishing general standards on dissemination of information, Standards 5.1–5.8, the Standards provide for specific standards on access to juvenile court records:

15.1 General policy on access

A. Juvenile records should not be public records.

B. Access to and the use of juvenile records should be strictly controlled to limit the risk that disclosure will result in the misuse or misinterpretation of information, the unnecessary denial of opportunities and benefits to juveniles, or an interference with the purposes of official intervention.

15.2 Access to case files

A.   Each juvenile court should provide access to a "case file" to the following persons:

1.   the juvenile who is the subject of the file, his or her parents, and his or her attorney;

2.   the prosecutor who has entered his or her appearance in the case;

3.   a party, and if he or she has an attorney who has entered an appearance on his or her behalf, the attorney;

4.   a judge, probation officer, or other professional person to whom the case has been assigned or before whom a proceeding with respect to the juvenile is pending or scheduled; and

5.   a person who is granted access for research purposes in accordance with Standard 5.6.

B.   A person who is a member of the clerical or administrative staff of a juvenile court, who has been previously designated in writing by the court, may be given direct access to a "case file" if such access is needed for authorized internal administrative purposes.

C.   A juvenile court should not provide access to nor permit the disclosure of information from a "case file" except in accordance with this standard.

15.3 Access to summary records

A.   Each juvenile court should provide access to "summary records" to the following persons:

1.   those persons enumerated in Standard 15.2 A.;

2.   the state juvenile correctional agency, if the juvenile is detained by or is otherwise subject to the custody or control of the agency;

3.   the state department of motor vehicles, provided that the information given to the department is limited to information relating to traffic offenses that is specifically required by statute to be given to the department for the purpose of regulating automobile licensing;

4.   a law enforcement agency for the purpose of executing an arrest warrant or other compulsory process or for the purpose of a current investigation.

B.   A juvenile court should notify the law enforcement agency that arrested the juvenile or that initiated the filing of the complaint or petition of the final disposition of the case after such information is entered in the "summary record."

C.   A juvenile court may provide direct access to a "summary record" to those persons enumerated in Standard 15.2 B.

D.   A juvenile court should not provide access to nor permit the disclosure of information from a "summary record" except in accordance with subsections A. and B. of this standard.

E.   A probation officer or other professional person may provide indirect access to a "summary record" with the written consent of the juvenile and his or her parents if the disclosure of summary information pertaining to the juvenile's record is necessary for the purpose of securing services or a benefit for the juvenile.

15.4 Access to probation records

A. Each juvenile court should provide access to a "temporary probation file," in accordance with Standard 9.1, to the juvenile who is the subject of the file, his or her parents, and his or her attorney and may permit the disclosure of information from a "temporary probation file" to other persons but only if such disclosure is necessary and for the sole purpose of verifying the information.

B. Each juvenile court should provide access to a "permanent probation file," in accordance with Standard 9.1, to the juvenile who is the subject of the file, his or her parents, and his or her attorney.

C. Each juvenile court should provide access to a "permanent probation file" to those persons enumerated in Standard 15.2 A., subsections 2., 4., and 5., and Standard 15.3 A. 2.

D. A person who is a member of the clerical, administrative, or professional staff of the probation office of a juvenile court, who has been previously designated in writing by the court, may be given direct access to a probation file if such access is needed for authorized internal administrative purposes.

E. A juvenile court may permit the disclosure of information from a "permanent probation file" to:

1. a person, agency, or department, with respect to a juvenile who has been committed to the care of the person, agency, or department;

2. a person, agency, or department that is providing or may provide services to the juvenile, upon obtaining the written consent of the juvenile or his or her parents after informing the juvenile and his or her parents of the information to be disclosed and the purposes of disclosure and provided further that the information that is disclosed is limited to the information necessary to provide or secure the services involved.

F. A juvenile court should not provide access to nor permit the disclosure of information from a probation file except in accordance with this standard.

15.5 Access for research and evaluation

Each juvenile court should accord access to its juvenile records for the purpose of research and monitoring in accordance with Standard 5.6.

15.6 Secondary disclosure limited

A person, other than the juvenile, his or her parents, and his or her attorney, who is accorded access to information, pursuant to Section III of these standards, should not disclose that information to any other person unless that person is also authorized to receive that information pursuant to this Section.

15.7 Waiver prohibited

The consent of a juvenile, his or her parents, or his or her attorney should not be sufficient to authorize the dissemination of a juvenile record to a person who is not specifically accorded the right to receive such information, pursuant to this Part, except as provided in Standard 15.4 E. 2.

15.8 Nondisclosure agreement

Any person, other than the juvenile who is the subject of a juvenile record, his or her parents, and his or her attorney, to whom a juvenile record or information from a juvenile record is to be disclosed, should be required to execute a nondisclosure agreement in which the person should certify that he or she is familiar with the applicable disclosure provisions and promise not to disclose any information to an unauthorized person.

The Standards also restrict access to social histories and provide for their eventual destruction, Standards 9.1 and 10.1; provide for eventual destruction of juvenile court records, Standards 17.1–17.7; and regulate the use of, limit access to, and provide for the destruction of law enforcement records, Standards 19.1–22.1. In a more general fashion the Standards also provide for establishment of a privacy committee with investigatory powers and authority to recommend policies and practices with respect to record-keeping operations, provide for civil, criminal, and administrative penalties for improper record-keeping or dissemination of information contained in records, and furnish procedures for correction and periodic audit of records. Standards 2.1–2.8.

RLR v. STATE

Supreme Court of Alaska, 1971.
487 P.2d 27.

(The statement of facts in this case appears at page 478 supra.)

RABINOWITZ, JUSTICE.

. . .

PUBLIC TRIAL

The Federal and Alaska's Constitutions provide that "[i]n all criminal prosecutions, the accused shall enjoy ["have" in Alaska's Constitution] the right to a . . . public trial . . . ." The sentence guaranteeing the right also guarantees the rights to speedy trial and an impartial jury. The leading case on public trial, Re Oliver,[51] holds that the Due Process Clause of the Fourteenth Amendment prohibits secret trials in criminal proceedings. *Oliver* says that the traditional Anglo-American distrust for secret trials has been attributed to the despotism of the Spanish Inquisition, the English Court of Star Chamber, and the French lettre de cachet, and quotes Bentham's charge that secret proceedings produce "indolent and arbitrary" judges, unchecked no matter how "corrupt" by recordation and ap-

51. 333 U.S. 257, 68 S.Ct. 499, 92 L.Ed. 682 (1948).

peal. The court cites as values of a public trial that it safeguards against attempts to employ the courts as instruments of persecution, restrains abuse of judicial power, brings the proceedings to the attention of key witnesses not known to the parties, and teaches the spectators about their government and gives them confidence in their judicial remedies. In a concurring opinion in Estes v. Texas,[54] Justice Harlan says that

> [e]ssentially, the public-trial guarantee embodies a view of human nature, true as a general rule, that judges, lawyers, witnesses, and jurors will perform their respective functions more responsibly in an open court than in secret proceedings. . . . A fair trial is the objective, and 'public trial' is an institutional safeguard for attaining it.

> Thus the right of 'public trial' is not one belonging to the public, but one belonging to the accused, and inhering in the institutional process by which justice is administered.

Appellant argues that he was denied his constitutional right to a public trial by AS 47.10.070. That statute provides in relevant part that

> [t]he public shall be excluded from the hearing, but the court, in its discretion, may permit individuals to attend a hearing, if their attendance is compatible with the best interest of the minor.

Rules of Children's Procedure 12(d)(2) provides that

> [c]hild hearings shall not be open to the general public. The court may, however, in its discretion after due consideration for the welfare of the child and of the public interest, admit particular individuals to the hearing.

The federal constitutional guarantee has not been construed to mean that all judicial proceedings must be open to any interested member of the public at any time. Some authorities hold that the right to public trial belongs to the public as well as the defendant so public trial is not subject to defendant's waiver, while others hold that the guarantee is for the benefit of the accused, and may be asserted or waived only by him. In both the federal and Alaska's constitutions, the right to public trial is part of a list of rights explicitly stated to be rights of the accused. Some jurisdictions hold that the general public may be excluded consistently with the public trial guarantee so long as the defendant has an opportunity to designate those whom he desires to have present. Others take the view that the general public cannot be excluded in this way. Where the right has been denied, no prejudice need be shown, since such a showing would be almost impossible to make. The right may be waived. We held in Flores v. State [62] that unintentional brief exclusion of a newspaper reporter from part of the reading back to the jury of a section

---

54. 381 U.S. 532, 85 S.Ct. 1628, 14 L.Ed.2d 543 (1965).

62. 475 P.2d 37, 39 (Alaska 1970).

of testimony previously given, when at least one other spectator was present, did not deny the right to public trial.

In re Burrus [63] holds that despite *Gault,* juveniles are not constitutionally entitled to public trial. It is weak authority, however, since it so concludes merely by labeling delinquency proceedings non-criminal, rather than by analyzing the purposes of the public trial requirement to see whether they would be served by applying the right to delinquency proceedings. Many authorities favor a policy in delinquency proceedings of avoiding total secrecy by admitting persons with a special interest in the case or the work of the court, including perhaps the press, but prohibiting disclosure of juveniles' names and excluding the general public.[64] Various reasons are given for this policy. It is said that permitting an audience to attend the hearing would interfere with the "case work relationship" between the judge and the child. Publicity is condemned on the grounds that it is an additional and excessive punishment to that prescribed by the court, or in the alternative that it encourages delinquency by permitting a youngster to "flaunt his unregeneracy." [65] Publication of names of juvenile delinquents is condemned on the ground that it confirms the child in his delinquent identity and impedes his integration into law-abiding society by reducing his ability to obtain legitimate employment, qualify for licenses and bonds, and join the armed services.[66] An important commentator on this subject recommends that the general public be excluded from juvenile hearings, but that the press should be admitted, though prohibited from publishing data which would identify particular juveniles; if he so desires, however, the juvenile should have a public hearing.[67] These social policy considerations are based on empirical propositions which may be false and have not been tested.[68] Some commentary favors open court proceedings for juveniles on the grounds that secrecy and the informality engendered thereby hinders rehabilitation partly by misleading juveniles and their parents into underestimating the seriousness of delinquency.[69] Recent commentary tends to be critical of secrecy be-

63. 275 N.C. 517, 169 S.E.2d 879 (1969).

64. Children's Bureau, Standards of Juvenile and Family Courts 76–77 (1966); Children's Bureau, Legislative Guide for Drafting Family and Juvenile Court Acts sec. 29(c), at 30 (1969); New Jersey Juv. & Dom.Rel.Ct. Rule 5:9–1(a) (1969).

65. President's Commission on Law Enforcement and Administration of Justice, Task Force Report: Juvenile Delinquency and Youth Crime 38 (1967).

66. Id. at 38–39.

67. Geis, Publicity and Juvenile Court Proceedings, 30 Rocky Mt.L.Rev. 101, 125–26 (1958); see also Geis, In Re: Juvenile Court Publicity, 16 Juv.Ct.Judges J. 12 (1965), reprinted in O. Ketcham &

M. Paulsen, Cases and Materials Relating to Juvenile Courts 407 (1967).

68. Geis, Publicity and Juvenile Court Proceedings, 30 Rocky Mt.L.Rev. 101, 124 (1958).

69. Parker, Instant Maturation for the Post-Gault "Hood", 4 Fam.L.Q. 113 (1970). See also Handler, The Juvenile Court and the Adversary System: Problems of Function and Form, 1965 Wisc.L. Rev. 7, 19–21 (1965). Handler argues that the high degree of informality in juvenile court interferes with rehabilitation by producing in the juvenile frustration, distrust, contempt, fear, and cynicism. "The word 'help,' coming from such a person in a position of power, is, in the

cause it screens from public view arbitrariness and lawlessness by juvenile courts.[70]

Just as alleged, bad motives of the legislature cannot be considered in determining constitutionality and construction of statutes, so we cannot withhold application of federal and state constitutional provisions on the grounds that those who created various systems of governmental activity such as the juvenile court acted from benevolent motives. Nor will constitutional problems be ignored in deference to untested empirical propositions about what sorts of judicial proceedings succeed in rehabilitating persons charged with misconduct; as between these sorts of prescriptions for what is good for society and constitutional prescriptions, the latter are authoritative. The reasons for the constitutional guarantees of public trial apply as much to juvenile delinquency proceedings as to adult criminal proceedings.[71] Delinquency proceedings as much as adult criminal prosecutions can be used as instruments of persecution, and may be subject to judicial abuse. The appellate process is not a sufficient check on juvenile courts, for problems of mootness and the cost of prosecuting an appeal screen most of what goes on from appellate court scrutiny. We cannot help but notice that the children's cases appealed to this court have often shown much more extensive and fundamental error than is generally found in adult criminal cases, and wonder whether secrecy is not fostering a judicial attitude of casualness toward the law in children's proceedings. In any event,

> civil labels and good intentions do not themselves obviate the need for criminal due process safeguards in juvenile courts, for '[a] proceeding where the issue is whether the child will be found to be "delinquent" and subjected to the loss of his liberty for years is comparable in seriousness to a felony prosecution.[73]

Therefore, we hold that children are guaranteed the right to a public trial by the Alaska Constitution.

One additional facet of the child's right to a public trial remains to be considered. AS 47.10.070,[74] and the similar Children's Rule 12(d)

---

mind of the adolescent, a familiar signal of danger." Handler at 21.

70. Note, Minnesota Juvenile Court Rules: Brightening One World for Juveniles, 54 Minn.L.Rev. 303, 324–325 (1969); Note, Criminal Offenders in the Juvenile Court: More Brickbats and Another Proposal, 114 U.Pa.L.Rev. 1171, 1185–1186 (1966).

71. Some of these reasons parallel those underlying the constitutional guarantees of jury trial. In one commentator's view, the jury provides the citizenry, in their capacity as jurors, with a vehicle to directly participate in government; that the jury system induces public confidence in the administration of justice; and that the jury system helps to

insure the independence and the quality of the judges. Foley, Juveniles and Their Right to a Jury Trial, 15 Villanova L.Rev. 972 (1970).

73. In re Winship, 397 U.S. 358, 365–366, 90 S.Ct. 1068, 1073, 25 L.Ed.2d 368, 376 (1970).

74. AS 47.10.070 provides in part that:

The public shall be excluded from the hearing, but the court, in its discretion, may permit individuals to attend a hearing, if their attendance is compatible with the best interests of the minor.

The statute providing for exclusion of the public from juvenile hearings is procedural, so is outside the scope of legisla-

(2), provide for the exclusion of the public from children's hearings. Rules of Children's Procedure 12(d)(2), which governs, provides that,

> Child hearings shall not be open to the general public. The court may, however, in its discretion after due consideration for the welfare of the child and of the public interest, admit particular individuals to the hearing.

This flexible rule must be interpreted and applied in a manner consistent with the child's constitutional right to public trial. The evils of secrecy may be avoided by permitting the child to open the adjudicative and dispositive hearings to any individuals. Where the child's choice may be adverse to his own interests, a guardian ad litem may be appointed under the principles discussed in the preceding section dealing with the right to trial by jury. It is an abuse of discretion for the court to refuse admittance to individuals whose presence is favored by the child, except in special circumstances such as the unavailability of a courtroom sufficiently large to hold all the individuals whose presence is sought. If the child or his guardian ad litem wants the press, friends, or others to be free to attend, then the hearing must be open to them. The area of discretion in the rule, where the court may refuse to open the hearing, involves persons whose presence is not desired by the child. Since we have determined that the case must be reversed on other grounds, we find it unnecessary to decide whether the denial of a public trial in the adjudicative stage in the case at bar was plain error.

. . .

The superior court's adjudicative and dispositive orders are vacated and reversed, and the matter remanded for appropriate proceedings.

NOTES

(1) Most states provide by statute that the general public shall be excluded from hearings in juvenile court, although the court usually has discretion to admit persons who are interested in the proceedings. See, e.g., Ga.Code Ann. § 15-11-28(c) (1982). Compare N.M.Stat.Ann. § 32-1-31(B), (C) (1981):

> B. All hearings to declare a person in contempt of court and all hearings on petitions alleging delinquency of a child shall be open to the general public except where the court in its discretion after a finding of exceptional circumstances deems it appropriate to conduct a closed delinquency hearing. All abuse and neglect and child in need of supervi-

tive authority unless two-thirds of each house of the legislature votes to change the rule promulgated by the supreme court in this matter. Alaska Const. art. IV, sec. 15. Children's proceedings are among the "civil and criminal cases in all courts" over which this constitutional provision gives this court rule-making authority which is intended to be plenary and not capable of reduction by re-label-

ling of proceedings. Cf. Silverton v. Marler, 389 P.2d 3 (Alaska 1964).

The statute making criminal the publication by newspapers, radio stations, and television stations of juvenile delinquents' names, AS 47.10.090(b), and the similar rule, Rules of Children's Procedure 26, are not challenged in this appeal.

sion hearings shall be closed to the general public. Only the parties, their counsel, witnesses and other persons requested by a party and approved by the court may be present at a closed hearing. Those other persons the court finds to have a proper interest in the case or in the work of the court, including members of the bar, may be admitted by the court to closed hearings on the condition that they refrain from divulging any information which would identify the child or family involved in the proceedings. Accredited representatives of the news media shall be allowed to be present at closed hearings subject to the conditions that they refrain from divulging information that would identify any child involved in the proceedings or the parent or guardian of that child, and subject to such enabling regulations as the court finds necessary for the maintenance of order, decorum and for the furtherance of the purposes of the Children's Code. If the court finds that it is in the best interest of the child, the child may be temporarily excluded from a neglect or an abuse hearing and during the taking of evidence on the issues of need for treatment and rehabilitation in delinquency and need of supervision hearings. Under the same conditions a child may be temporarily excluded by the court during a hearing on dispositional issues.

C. Those persons or parties granted admission to a closed hearing and who intentionally divulge information in violation of Subsection B of this section are guilty of a petty misdemeanor.

(2) Juvenile Justice Standards Project, Standards Relating to Adjudication (1980) *:

6.1 Right to a public trial

Each jurisdiction should provide by law that a respondent in a juvenile court adjudication proceeding has a right to a public trial.

6.2 Implementing the right to a public trial

A. Each jurisdiction should provide by law that the respondent, after consulting with counsel, may waive the right to a public trial.

B. Each jurisdiction should provide by law that the judge of the juvenile court has discretion to permit members of the public who have a legitimate interest in the proceedings or in the work of the court, including representatives of the news media, to view adjudication proceedings when the respondent has waived the right to a public trial.

C. The judge of the juvenile court should honor any request by the respondent, respondent's attorney, or family that specified members of the public be permitted to observe the respondent's adjudication proceeding when the respondent has waived the right to a public trial.

D. The judge of the juvenile court should use judicial power to prevent distractions from and disruptions of adjudication proceedings and should use that power to order removed from the courtroom any member of the public causing a distraction or disruption.

6.3 Prohibiting disclosure of respondent's identity

A. Each jurisdiction should provide by law that members of the public permitted by the judge of the juvenile court to observe adjudication proceedings may not disclose to others the identity of the respondent when the respondent has waived the right to a public trial.

B. Each jurisdiction should provide by law that the judge of the juvenile court should announce to members of the public present to view an adjudication proceeding when the respondent has waived the right to a public trial that they may not disclose to others the identity of the respondent.

The Commentary to Standard 6.1 gives the following explanation at pp. 71–72:

> . . . [B]ecause both model legislation and many state statutes allow for the presence of "interested persons" at the judge's discretion, juvenile hearings cannot truly be described as confidential. Frequent attendance by students, social workers, lawyers, and observers of the court system indicates that one need not be "interested" in the child in order to qualify as an "interested person." This practice vitiates the promise of confidentiality, without giving the benefits of a truly open hearing.

The benefits of public trial have been acknowledged by the Supreme Court in In re Oliver, 333 U.S. 257, 68 S.Ct. 499, 92 L.Ed. 682 (1948). According to *Oliver*, "[t]he knowledge that every criminal trial is subject to contemporaneous review in the forum of public opinion is an effective restraint on the possible abuse of judicial power." Id. at 270. In Estes v. Texas, 381 U.S. 532, 85 S.Ct. 1628, 14 L.Ed.2d 543 (1965), the Court observed that the constitutional guarantee of public trial is to ensure that "the accused is justly dealt with. . . ." Id. at 538.

Justice Brennan's concurring and dissenting opinion in McKeiver v. Pennsylvania, 403 U.S. 528, 91 S.Ct. 1976, 29 L.Ed.2d 647 (1971), stressed that openness of proceeding works analogously to jury trial to protect the accused from possible oppression by exposing improper judicial behavior to the indignation of the community at large. Id. at 554–55.

At least one juvenile court case that has dealt with the issue of open hearing has held that the respondent has a right to the presence and participation of his or her mother at the hearing. In the Interest of Bobby Hopkins, 227 So.2d 282 (Miss.1969). This is in congruence with In re Oliver, 333 U.S. 257, 272, 68 S.Ct. 499, 92 L.Ed. 682 (1948), which held that the accused at the least is entitled to the presence of his or her friends, relatives, and counsel.

R L R v. State, 487 P.2d 27 (Alaska 1971), granted juvenile respondents the right to a public hearing, noting that the appeal process is not a sufficient check on juvenile courts. In *R L R*, the Alaska Supreme Court observed that children's cases, when appealed, frequently show more extensive and fundamental errors than may be found in adult cases. This raised for the court a question whether the secrecy usually found in juvenile proceedings fosters a casual attitude toward legal safeguards. Id. at 38. *R L R*, while ruling that a juvenile does have the right to a public hearing, did not address itself to the question of the procedures to be used in implementing this right. If the child must bear the burden of asking for a public hearing, the request may be construed as an implicit criticism of the judge's impartiality. Comment, "Criminal Offenders in the Juvenile Court: More Brickbats and Another Proposal," 114 U.Pa.L. Rev. 1171, 1186 (1966). It would appear that the best solution is to assure the respondent a right to a public trial. This requires that the respondent be informed prior to the hearing of the right to an open adjudication proceeding. With advice of counsel, he or she may waive this right (see Standard 6.2 A.). This does not guarantee that the judge will exclude all persons not connected with the child's case (see commentary to Standard 6.2 B.), but rather allows a reversion to the current practice of permitting interested observers to view the hearing at the discretion of the judge.

(3) Juvenile Justice Standards Project, Standards Relating to Adjudication (1980),* Dissenting View (Statement by Commissioner Justine Wise Polier) at pp. 77–78:

I concur in the majority of the proposed standards in this volume directed to ensure due process to children charged with what would constitute criminal offenses if committed by an adult. However, I disagree with the position that the adjudication process for children ought not to differ significantly from that in criminal courts and that the unique features of juvenile justice should be postponed to the dispositional phase.

I find it necessary to dissent strongly to two of the proposed standards, which would transform the juvenile courts into criminal courts, regardless of the age of children charged with delinquent acts.

First, Standard 4.1 would require a jury trial at the option of the child, on the assumption it would rarely be used. In effect, its use would result in a public trial, with an end of the protection of privacy for the child, and with consequences that a child could not anticipate. The child would be subjected to being treated as an adult defendant at the center of a criminal trial.

Second, Standard 6.1 would establish the "right" of a child to a public trial regardless of age. The supportive arguments are largely taken from the benefits of public trials for adult offenders. No evidence is submitted in the commentary to establish the alleged benefits to children of opening adjudicatory hearings to the media. There is a presumption in favor of the right to trial and the requirement that the child may waive it only after advice of counsel, based on expressed distrust of how courts would regard the request of a child for a public trial (Standard 6.2). There are no provisions to inform a child of possible consequences, such as are set forth in regard to waiver of counsel or plea bargaining.

It is proposed that the juvenile court shall have discretion in each case to admit members of the public, including the media, to "view" adjudicatory proceedings, even when a child waives the right to a public trial. This procedure would place a heavy administrative burden on the court; it would subject judges to the risk of becoming targets for press attacks when they denied admission. Most important, since judges are not entitled to information about a child or family prior to an adjudicatory hearing, they have no crystal ball through which to foresee the need for protecting the privacy of a child at an adjudicatory hearing.

Finally, the protections proposed in Standard 6.3 to safeguard the identity of the child by those who "view" the trial are inadequate. To require that a judge "announce" to those present that they may not disclose the identity includes no remedy for noncompliance and appears to be largely hortatory. Even if followed, questions of the constitutionality of prior restraints would throw doubt on this safeguard.

G.   MENTAL CAPACITY: THE INSANITY DEFENSE AND COMPETENCY TO STAND TRIAL

STATE EX REL. CAUSEY

Supreme Court of Louisiana, 1978.
363 So.2d 472.

TATE, JUSTICE.

At the instance of a juvenile made defendant in juvenile proceedings, we granted certiorari to determine whether a juvenile has a right to plead not guilty by reason of insanity and a right to a hearing to determine his mental capacity to assist in his defense.

Facts

Pate Causey, age 16, was petitioned into the Orleans Parish juvenile court, charged with armed robbery. His attorney filed a motion, the substance of which was that defendant be allowed to plead not guilty and not guilty by reason of insanity, and that the judge appoint a panel of psychiatrists to perform comprehensive tests to determine whether defendant was legally insane at the time the act was committed, and also whether defendant was legally competent to aid in his own defense.

Several psychological tests had been performed upon the defendant, and the report of the testing psychologists had recommended psychiatric evaluation. A psychiatrist had interviewed the defendant, without access to the psychological test results. Defense counsel wished to subpoena the psychiatrist, whose report he had been given by the judge at the time of the hearing on the motion. After indicating his inclination to deny the motion, the judge asked the defense attorney if he would "submit it [the question whether defendant was competent to assist in his defense] on that [the psychiatrist's report]." Defense counsel responded, "I submit on the report," and the court denied the motion.

The Right of a Juvenile to Plead Insanity

There is no statutory right to plead not guilty by reason of insanity in a Louisiana juvenile proceeding, since such proceedings are conducted as civil proceedings, with certain enumerated differences. We hold, however, that the due process guaranties of the Fourteenth Amendment to the United States Constitution, and of Article I, Section 2 of the Louisiana Constitution, require that a juvenile be granted this right.

The only courts ever squarely confronted with the issue have held that, at least in adult proceedings, the denial of the right to plead insanity, with no alternative means of exculpation or special treatment for an insane person unable to understand the nature of his act, violates the concept of fundamental fairness implicit in the due process guaranties. Sinclair v. State, 161 Miss. 142, 132 So. 581 (1931); State v. Strasburg, 60 Wash. 106, 110 P. 1020 (1910). Some recent federal cases have also spoken of the insanity plea in terms indicating that the right to assert it has constitutional dimensions of a due process (fundamental fairness) nature.

The insanity defense, and the underlying notion that an accused must understand the nature of his acts in order to be criminally responsible (the *mens rea* concept), are deeply rooted in our legal tradition and philosophy, . . .

However, not every constitutional right guaranteed to adults by the concept of fundamental fairness is automatically guaranteed to juveniles.

The United States Supreme Court has undertaken a case-by-case analysis of juvenile proceedings, making not only the historical inquiry into whether the rights asserted were part of fundamental fairness, but also a functional analysis of whether giving the particular right in question to the juvenile defendant would interfere with any of the beneficial aspects of a juvenile proceeding. Only those rights that are both "fundamental" and "essential," in that they perform a function too important to sacrifice in favor of the benefits theoretically afforded by a civil-style juvenile proceeding, have been held to be required in such proceedings. McKeiver v. Pennsylvania, 403 U.S. 528, 91 S.Ct. 1976, 29 L.Ed.2d 647 (1970); In re Winship, 397 U.S. 358, 90 S.Ct. 1068, 25 L.Ed.2d 368 (1970); In re Gault, 387 U.S. 1, 87 S.Ct. 1428, 18 L.Ed.2d 527 (1967).

The same approach was adopted by a majority of this court in determining which due process rights are guaranteed to juveniles by the Louisiana Constitution, in State in Interest of Dino, 359 So.2d 586 (La.1978). (Since we ultimately find this defendant's right to plead insanity to be guaranteed by the state and federal due process clauses, we need not reach the additional equal protection argument advanced, by which juveniles would be denied the equal protection of the laws if they were not permitted as are adults to be exculpated by insanity from criminal responsibility.)

McKeiver, Winship, and *Gault* imposed on juvenile proceedings a host of traditional criminal trial safeguards—the right to appropriate notice, to counsel, to confrontation and cross-examination, and the privilege against self-incrimination—and declined to impose only one safeguard, the right to a jury trial.

While the due process right to a jury trial has been held to be an element of "fundamental fairness," at least in non-petty adult proceedings, Duncan v. Louisiana, 391 U.S. 145, 88 S.Ct. 1444, 20 L.Ed.2d

491 (1968), the court's emphasis in *McKeiver* was not on the degree of "fundamentality," but on the *function* served by the jury trial. The plurality saw the jury as a component in the factfinding process, and as such, *not* "a necessary component of accurate factfinding." Only after finding that the jury trial—although "fundamental" for adults—was not really "essential" to a fair trial proceeding, i.e., did not perform a function that could not be adequately performed by some other procedure, did the court examine the impact of a jury trial upon the beneficial effects of the juvenile system, and conclude that it would "bring with it into that system the traditional delay, the formality, and the clamor of the adversary system and, possibly, the public trial."

In *Winship*, the court held that a juvenile could not be adjudged to have violated a criminal statute by a mere preponderance of the evidence. The standard of proof "beyond a reasonable doubt" was held to play "a vital role in the American scheme of criminal procedure. It is a prime instrument for reducing the risk of convictions resting on factual error. . . . '[A] person accused of a crime . . . would be at a severe disadvantage . . . if he could be adjudged guilty and imprisoned for years on the strength of the same evidence as would suffice in a civil case."

Underlying the functional analysis of the two procedures examined in *McKeiver* and *Winship*, was not only the consideration of whether equally effective safeguards existed to the rights sought to be imported into juvenile proceedings, but also a consideration of the realistic role played by these two rights in safeguarding juvenile rights at actual trials: the "beyond a reasonable doubt standard" actually kept the juvenile in *Winship* out of jail, whereas there was no evidence that a jury trial in *McKeiver* would have done so.

The availability of some procedure for differentiating between those who are culpably responsible for their act and those who are merely ill is, as we have seen, a part of "fundamental fairness." Moreover, it is hard to see that any important aim of the juvenile system is thwarted by affording such a distinction to the mentally ill juvenile.

The function of the insanity plea is much more akin to that of the burden of proof imposed on juvenile proceedings in *Winship*, than of the jury trial involved in *McKeiver* and *Dino*. An insanity defense, like a high burden of proof, will generically spell the difference between conviction and acquittal. That there is perhaps a lesser stigma associated with an adjudication of juvenile delinquency than with an adult criminal conviction, and that juvenile incarceration is theoretically calculated to rehabilitate rather than to punish, were deemed constitutionally insignificant in *Winship*.

In the present case, further, the state expressly does not contest the issue whether this juvenile should be allowed to plead not guilty and not guilty by reason of insanity when charged with a serious crime.

. . .

[The court reaches the same conclusion as to competency to stand trial.]

The state does not suggest any special reason that a juvenile should be denied this right due an adult. The only reason that comes to mind is the argument that *many* juveniles, "sane" as well as "insane," "normal" as well as "retarded," are incompetent to assist in their own defenses, at least by normal adult standards. This, indeed, is a large part of the rationale for the special juvenile system. Where a juvenile is "incompetent" primarily because of his tender years, it might be unnecessary and perhaps unwise to substitute the full-dress examinations and hearings designed for adult incompetents, in place of procedures designed especially to deal with youth and inexperience.

But that is not the case here. Pate Causey was reported, by the psychologists who examined him for the court, to vary "from the upper end of the range of moderate mental retardation with regard to non-verbal intelligence . . . to the range of mild mental retardation with regard to verbal intelligence. . . ." He was reported to have "poor fine motor control, spatial disorientation, and problems in angling . . . suggestive of neuropsychological dysfunction," with "memory problems and the possibility of episodic 'blanking out'" as "further evidence of possible neuropathy." Psychiatric evaluation was recommended.

A psychiatrist did meet with the boy, without access to test results; the gist of his conclusions was that the boy was dull and a liar rather than retarded and psychotic.

The reports were given by the judge to the defense attorney at the trial, to read for five minutes before arguing the motion relating to incompetence. This data, inconclusive and perhaps contradictory but suggestive of possible problems, is much like that which, in *Bennett*, this court held to require further testing.

Conclusion

The right not to be tried while incompetent to assist in one's own defense is a fundamental due process right. The right to plead insanity, absent some other effective means of distinguishing mental illness from moral culpability, is also fundamental. There is no compelling reason to deny either of these constitutional rights to juveniles charged with conduct that would be serious crimes if committed by adults.

Here, there were facts in the record to put the trial court on notice that the defendant might be mentally retarded or insane. A defendant in a juvenile proceeding has the right to plead not guilty and not guilty by reason of insanity. Under the showing made, this defendant also had the right to a more thorough mental (psychiatric) examination, followed by a contradictory hearing.

. . .

REVERSED AND REMANDED.

[The dissenting opinion of Sanders, C.J., is omitted.]

NOTES

(1) As the principal case illustrates, the question of mental capacity can arise in two different ways in juvenile and adult proceedings. First, if the defendant is unable to understand the nature of the proceeding or assist in the defense he or she is incompetent to be tried or sentenced. This aspect is usually called competence. Second, defendant's insanity at the time of the offense is a defense to liability. Mental state at the time of the offense is usually styled the insanity defense. See, e.g., In re S.W.T., 277 N.W.2d 507 (Minn.1979).

Few statutes address the issue of incompetence. One exception is Maine Revised Statutes Annotated, Title 15:

§ 3318. Mentally ill or incapacitated juveniles

1. Suspension of proceedings. If it appears that a juvenile may be mentally ill or incapacitated . . . the court shall suspend the proceedings on the petition and shall either:

A. Initiate proceedings for voluntary or involuntary commitments . . . or

B. Order that the juvenile be examined by a physician or psychologist and refer the juvenile to a suitable facility or program for the purpose of examination, the costs of such examination to be paid by the court. If the report of such an examination is that the juvenile is mentally ill or incapacitated to the extent that short-term or long-term hospitalization or institutional confinement is required, the juvenile court shall initiate proceedings for voluntary or involuntary commitment . . . . The court shall continue the proceedings when a juvenile is voluntarily or involuntarily committed.

2. Resumption of proceedings. The court shall set a time for resuming the proceeding when:

A. The report of the examination made pursuant to subsection 1, paragraph B states that the child is not mentally ill or incapacitated to the extent that short-term or long-term hospitalization or institutional confinement is required; or

B. The child is not found by the appropriate court to be mentally ill or incapacitated as defined in section 101 and in Title 34, section 2616, subsection 1.

See also D.C.Code § 16–2315(a), (c) (1981).

(2) New Jersey's experience in addressing the applicability of the insanity defense in juvenile proceedings furnishes an interesting study. When the issue was first considered the courts took the position that insanity could not be raised as a defense during the adjudicatory hearing but that mental competency of the juvenile was a relevant consideration during dispositional pro-

ceedings. In re State ex rel. H.C., 106 N.J.Super. 583, 256 A.2d 322 (1969). Subsequently the juvenile court code was substantially revised, and one of the additions was a provision entitling juveniles to all defenses available to an adult in a criminal proceeding. N.J.Stat.Ann. § 2A:4–60 (Supp.1982). Interpreting this statute as overriding the earlier decision in *H.C.*, the New Jersey appellate courts held that a juvenile is entitled to raise an insanity defense in an adjudicatory hearing and is entitled to a separate hearing on the question of mental competency. State ex rel. R.G.W., 135 N.J.Super. 125, 342 A.2d 869 (1975), affirmed 70 N.J. 185, 358 A.2d 473 (1976).

(3) The Louisiana Supreme Court in the principal case seems to equate sanity with mens rea. Is it correct in this view? As a result of *Winship* due process requires the state to prove each element of an offense beyond a reasonable doubt in both criminal and juvenile proceedings. However, in Leland v. Oregon, 343 U.S. 790, 72 S.Ct. 1002, 96 L.Ed. 1302 (1952), the Supreme Court upheld the constitutionality of a statute requiring a defendant in a criminal case to prove his or her insanity beyond a reasonable doubt. One might argue that *Winship* has superceded *Leland*; however, in Rivera v. Delaware, 429 U.S. 877, 97 S.Ct. 226, 50 L.Ed.2d 160 (1976), the Court dismissed an appeal challenging a state statute placing the burden on a defendant to prove his or her insanity by a preponderance of the evidence, on the ground that no substantial federal question was presented.

What conclusions should be drawn from these cases? While they do not necessarily mean that a state could deprive a criminal defendant or an alleged delinquent of the insanity defense altogether, they certainly raise doubts whether the defense is guaranteed by due process of law. Furthermore, the cases indicate that responsibility for one's conduct is not to be equated with mens rea, nor is responsibility, unlike mens rea, an element of the offense that the state must prove beyond a reasonable doubt. Viewed in this light, was the Louisiana court's decision correct, at least on the basis of the reasons given? Consider the arguments presented by the Court of Appeals of the District of Columbia in the case discussed in the note following.

(4) The District of Columbia Code provides as follows:

§ 16–2315. Physical and mental examinations

(a) At any time following the filing of a petition, on motion of the Corporation Counsel or counsel for the child, or on its own motion, the Division may order a child to be examined to aid in determining his physical or mental condition.

. . .

(d) The results of an examination under this section shall be admissible in a transfer hearing pursuant to section 16–2307, in a dispositional hearing under this subchapter, or in a commitment proceeding under chapter 5 or 11 of title 21. The results of examination may be admitted into evidence at a factfinding hearing to aid the Division in determining a material allegation of the petition relating to the child's mental or physical condition, but not for the purpose of establishing a defense of insanity.

. . .

In upholding the constitutionality of this statute against claims that prohibiting an insanity defense during an adjudicatory hearing was a denial of due process and equal protection, the Court of Appeals of the District of Columbia stated:

> Appellant urges that because of the statutory prohibition, he was deprived of the opportunity, available to any adult criminal defendant, to obtain acquittal by showing that he did not at the time of the commission of the offense possess the requisite intent. . . .
>
> By this argument, appellant demonstrates a misconception of the nature and purpose of the insanity defense, for there is a fundamental difference between the concept of *mens rea* and the insanity defense.
>
> Moreover, it is well settled in this jurisdiction that proof of insanity at the time of the commission of an offense does not negate intent nor, without more, does it require an outright acquittal, since the trier of fact may not even consider the issue of insanity until after the government has established the essential elements of the offense, including intent.
>
> Consequently, even if the defense of insanity had been permitted and appellant had been successful in obtaining an acquittal by reason of insanity, it would not have established his innocence of the charged offense because "[a]n acquittal by reason of insanity, which . . . includes mental defects, is a determintion of guilt beyond a reasonable doubt of the acts charged."
>
> Thus, the function of the insanity defense is not to establish the innocence of the accused, but rather to absolve him of the moral and penal consequences of his criminal act.
>
> Insisting, however, that D.C.Code 1973, § 16–2315(d) violates the Fifth Amendment guarantees of due process and equal protection, appellant urges that because the statute precludes a child from raising the insanity defense at the factfinding hearing, he or she is afforded less protection than that afforded an adult offender who is found to have been insane at the time of the commission of the offense. . . .
>
> . . .
>
> That there are substantial differences between the criminal and juvenile justice systems is of course apparent from an examination of the controlling statutes. However, the relevant differences come into focus only after completion of the first phase of the bifurcated proceedings conducted in this jurisdiction when a criminal defendant interposes the defense of insanity.
>
> In a criminal case, the trier of fact may not even consider the issue of insanity until the government has established the essential elements of the offense, including intent in the first phase of that proceeding. The second phase is held only if the government is successful in proving guilt beyond a reasonable doubt and, only then, may the trier of fact reach the question of insanity. At this point, a criminal defendant may raise an insanity defense, which serves to permit the jury to decide whether the criminal defendant should be absolved of the criminal responsibility and penal consequences of his acts.
>
> The first phase of a bifurcated criminal proceeding is analogous to the factfinding proceeding of the juvenile process during which the Division is permitted to determine only whether the juvenile committed the act charged. Accordingly, contrary to appellant's argument, precluding a ju-

venile from raising an insanity defense at a factfinding hearing denies him no right that is otherwise accorded an adult.

A juvenile delinquency proceeding concededly does not incorporate the second step. Nevertheless, it is well settled now that unlike a criminal trial a juvenile factfinding hearing does not result in a determination of criminal responsibility. Nor is the succeeding dispositional hearing intended to result in the imposition of any penal sanction on the child. Rather, the purpose is to determine the treatment required to rehabilitate him. Accordingly, the insanity defense would be superfluous in a juvenile delinquency proceeding.

This conclusion, however, does not end our analysis. Appellant contends that the insanity defense in a criminal proceeding serves the secondary, but equally important purpose of providing a criminal defendant with procedural safeguards not otherwise available to a child. He concedes however that an adult offender found not guilty by reason of insanity must be committed to a hospital for the mentally ill until such time as he is able to establish his eligibility for release . . . . In contrast, appellant maintains that D.C.Code 1973, § 16–2315(d) does not require the Family Division to consider the result of any mental examination or make specific findings respecting a child's mental illness. Because of the broad discretion vested in the Division for dispositional purposes, appellant contends, as a possibility, that a child who was mentally ill at the time of the offense, but not at the time of disposition, could be "incarcerated for a lengthy period as an adjudicated delinquent," and that a child who was still mentally ill at the time of disposition could be institutionalized in a setting where psychiatric care is not available. We have found no support in the statute for these contentions.

We recognize that although the juvenile justice system is not intended to impose penal sanctions, the Family Division frequently orders forms of rehabilitation that a child might regard as punishment. We also recognized that an insanity acquittee, because morally blameless, may not be subject to any form of punishment. Of course, as pointed out above, an adjudication of delinquency does not result in the imposition of any penal sanction. Consequently it cannot be said with rationality that a disposition of a child offender deemed, by the Division, to serve his best interests, is punishment. Nevertheless we deem it to be an indispensable element of fundamental fairness that a mentally ill child offender be accorded the same opportunity for psychiatric treatment and ultimate release as a similarly situated adult. For these reasons, we have examined closely the statutory scheme governing the treatment of mentally ill child offenders in order to determine whether they are being denied any required procedural protections to ensure fundamental fairness. We conclude that the statutes and rules regulating juvenile delinquency proceedings in the District of Columbia presently provide adequate means of ensuring that any mentally ill child offender receives care and treatment similar to that provided for mentally ill criminal defendants.

In re C.W.M., 407 A.2d 617, 619–23 (D.C.App.1979).

IX. DISPOSITIONS

A. THEORETICAL JUSTIFICATION FOR COERCIVE DISPOSITIONS

The dispositional phase in delinquency cases presents theoretical problems that pervade not only juvenile courts but the criminal justice system as well. In order to determine what to do with a child who has been adjudicated delinquent, one must first decide the purpose of the court's use of coercive sanctions. No consistent theory of disposition is possible without first deciding the goals of delinquency dispositions.

Historically, the rehabilitative ideal supplied the requisite answer to questions about the goals of the juvenile justice system and its control over children. Rehabilitation required a focus on the particular needs of the offender and the programs of reform available to meet those needs. In the case of rehabilitation, juvenile court delinquency dispositions (a) were not tied to the child's antisocial conduct (any adjudicated conduct could support any disposition); (b) usually were not subject to any determinate period other than the child's attaining majority and (c) necessarily varied depending on the family's resources (well-to-do homes are usually more conducive rehabilitative settings than poor ones). The most important concomitant of the rehabilitative ideal is immense, largely unreviewable, discretion in decisionmakers to treat juveniles differently based on an assessment of what is needed to reform their behavior.

In the 1970s the rehabilitative ideal came under strident attack. As Professor Francis Allen has suggested, the rehabilitative ideal will flourish only when the society has faith in the malleability of human beings (which makes them responsive to efforts at reform) and a workable consensus on the goals of treatment. The society must believe in the perfectability of human nature and be quite clear about its social definition of perfection.

Allen concludes: "Such attributes are not descriptive of the United States in the 1970s. In contrast, modern America reveals a radical loss of confidence in its political and social institutions and a significant diminishment in its sense of public purpose." F. Allen, The Decline of the Rehabilitative Ideal 18 (1981). Even if some consensus could be achieved as to the ends of treatment, the considerable scientific data casting doubt on the ability of behavioral and social sciences to produce the hoped-for reformation in human conduct has added considerable ammunition to the attack. See, e.g., E. Schur, Radical Non-Intervention: Rethinking the Delinquency Problem 29–78 (1973) (and sources collected and cited in that chapter).

Finally, by the 1970s most observers of and participants in the juvenile justice system would agree with Judge Irving Kaufman, Chief Judge of the Second Circuit Court of Appeals and Chairman of the Joint Commission on Juvenile Justice Standards, in his recent assessment of the inadequacy of the juvenile justice system:

. . . Although social workers and judges have labored earnestly to improve the juvenile's lot and to protect society, it has become painfully clear that they are incapable of doing so within the existing system. Adolescent crime is on the rise. Today, more than half of all serious crimes in the United States are committed by youths aged ten to seventeen. Each day, newspapers and magazines graphically describe the costs of juvenile crime.

Youthful criminals prey on the most defenseless victims. The very young, the old, the lame, sick and blind are slugged, slashed and shot. They have retreated with broken limbs and emotional scars behind triple-locked doors. Many never venture out at night, some do not even risk the streets during the day. In confinement, their anguish is not heard.[7]

Nor do juveniles fare better than the society they victimize. The delusive simplicity of the rehabilitative model, which concentrates on the so-called "needs" of the juvenile, has prevented inquiry into the very acts that supposedly warrant sanction, and this curious perspective has led, not infrequently, to the "treatment" of juveniles who have committed no crime at all. In this same spirit of individualized "justice," the juvenile court judge has exercised broad discretion in determining dispositions leading to substantial disparities in dealing with identical conduct. And these problems of discretion have been compounded by the absence of procedural protections that adults accused of crime have long taken for granted.

Kaufman, Protecting the Rights of Minors: On Juvenile Autonomy and the Limits of Law, 52 N.Y.U.L.Rev. 1015, 1016–17 (1977).* See also Gilman, IJA/ABA Juvenile Justice Standards Project: An Introduction, 57 B.U.L.Rev. 617 (1977). Judge Kaufman's statement indicates yet another reason for the recent reevaluation of the juvenile justice system—the significant increase in violent crime committed by juveniles.

Most reassessment proposals would substitute general and specific deterrence and punishment for rehabilitation as the theoretical justifications for juvenile court use of coercive sanctions. Deterrence and punishment require the court to focus on the nature of the child's conduct and not on his or her perceived rehabilitative needs—disposition should be proportional to conduct. Further, children who have engaged in the same or similar conduct should under this "just des-

7. TIME, July 11, 1977, at 18.　　　* Copyright 1977, New York University Law Review. Reprinted with permission.

serts" model receive essentially similar treatment at disposition. Since the purpose of any disposition is to deter this juvenile from future anti-social conduct and to deter other teenagers from crime by example, the offender-related data so heavily relied upon today will take a back seat to the nature of the conduct that has brought the person before the court. Thus, if the goal of the system is punishment or deterrence, the decisionmaking calculus at disposition will be fundamentally different.

Many who argue for abandoning the rehabilitative ideal would limit in important ways the exercises of discretion by juvenile judges at all stages of delinquency cases but especially at disposition. The rehabilitative goal demanded a great deal of discretion in juvenile judges to decide on the proper disposition in light of an assessment of the child's past and future needs. Abuses of discretion were rampant. Reflecting, in part, the skepticism about our legal institutions to which Allen refers, modern reformers are nearly unanimous in abhoring the results of unbridled judicial discretion throughout the legal system as a whole, singling out the conduct of juvenile courts only as a peculiarly garish example.

The theoretical assault on the rehabilitative ideal has sparked vociferous and lively debate in scholarly literature, state legislative hearings and the popular press. Nowhere has that battle been more heated than in the debates over the proposal of the IJA–ABA Juvenile Justice Standards Project to substitute proportionality as the theoretical basis of juvenile delinquency dispositions.

JUVENILE JUSTICE STANDARDS PROJECT, STANDARDS RELATING TO DISPOSITIONS *

PART I: GENERAL PURPOSES AND LIMITATIONS

1.1 Purpose

The purpose of the juvenile correctional system is to reduce juvenile crime by maintaining the integrity of the substantive law proscribing certain behavior and by developing individual responsibility for lawful behavior. This purpose should be pursued through means that are fair and just, that recognize the unique characteristics and needs of juveniles, and that give juveniles access to opportunities for personal and social growth.

Commentary

This standard is based on the premise that we know little about the specific causes of crime and delinquency. The past fifty years have seen the flowering—and the waning—of the conviction that, giv-

---

en adequate research, behavioral and social scientists eventually might pinpoint the causes of delinquency and shape public policy to remove them. Instead, the efforts of science to date have served to illuminate the complexity and virtual insolubility of the problems of the causation and prevention of delinquent behavior. Indeed, if—as social scientists long have maintained—the root causes of delinquency lie in poverty, racial discrimination, and the breakdown of family structure and values, there may be little that a correctional system can do to reduce crime. According to a recent essay by James Q. Wilson:

> If a child is delinquent because his family made him so or his friends encourage him to be so, it is hard to conceive what society might do about this. No one knows how a government might restore affection, stability, and fair discipline to a family that rejects these characteristics; still less can one imagine how even a family once restored could affect a child who by now has left the formative years and in any event has developed an aversion to one or both of his parents. "Crime and the Criminologists," Commentary, July 1974, at 47, 48.

. . .

Of the recognized purposes of corrections, none recently has been subject to such relentless attack as rehabilitation. Mounting evidence indicates that the juvenile correctional system does not help young people and may even harm them. Beginning with Professor Allen's critique in the early 1960s, a steadily growing number of social and behavioral scientists have questioned the effectiveness and, indeed, the appropriateness of the "rehabilitative ideal." . . .

. . .

In the face of critical research findings, supporters of rehabilitation have argued that the failure to date does not compel abandonment of the ideal, but rather the development of new and better attempts. The standard does not disagree with this position. The route of future accommodation may well lie in the direction suggested recently by Norval Morris, in considering the future of the adult prison system:

> "Rehabilitation," whatever it means and whatever the programs that allegedly give it meaning, must cease to be a purpose of the prison sanction. This does not mean that the various developed treatment programs within prisons need to be abandoned; quite the contrary, they need expansion. But it does mean that they must not be seen as purposive in the sense that criminals are to be sent to prison for treatment. There is a sharp distinction between the purposes of incarceration and the opportunities for the training and assistance of prisoners that may be pursued within those purposes. The system is corrupted when we fail to preserve this distinction and this failure pervades the world's prison programs. The Future of Imprisonment 14–15 (1974).

The standards are intended to encourage the development of more meaningful ways of providing rehabilitative programs. The standards do reflect, however, the fact that we currently do not possess sufficient knowledge to make rehabilitation the exclusive—or even the fundamental—purpose of corrections. Thus, the standard is intended to serve as a limiting principle designed to narrow the aims of the correctional system to a more modest perspective.

Sufficient knowledge to base a correctional system on a theory of general deterrence also is lacking. While there is some evidence indicating that capital punishment has little effect on the murder rate, there is scarcely any empirical evidence on the impact of deterrence on other criminal activity. Our instincts and experience tell us that we are deterred from illegal behavior by the fear of apprehension and punishment, but to date the social scientists have found it difficult to provide the quantitative evidence to support our intuition. See N. Walker, Sentencing in a Rational Society 61 (1969). Here again, the standards do not deny the potential impact of deterrence, nor do they discourage further study of its value. They do, however, reject deterrence as the sole or fundamental purpose of a correctional system for juveniles.

In searching for the limiting principle made necessary by the failure of empirical science to provide the data on which to base a unitary, coherent approach to correctional policy, the standard returns to some of the basic elements of Anglo-American law. One important function of the sanctions provided for in the juvenile criminal code and the correctional system that implements it is to ensure that the code's substantive provisions are observed by making the strictures of the code credible. Thus, according to H.L.A. Hart, certain actions are forbidden by law and designated as offenses "to announce to society that these actions are not to be done and to secure that fewer of them are done."

More important in the framing of a limiting principle is the fundamental legal concept that confines the application of criminal law to past misconduct. . . .

This does not mean that the correctional system must look only to the past. The standard, which recognizes that a correctional system for juveniles also should contain prospective elements, attempts to promote the development of individual responsibility for lawful behavior on the part of offenders by providing opportunities for personal and social growth. The importance of this prospective element reflects the traditional legal perception of the physical dependence of the very young and the slow process of intellectual and emotional maturation during adolescence.[5]

5. "Juveniles may be viewed as incomplete adults, lacking in full moral and experiential development, extended unique jural status in other contexts, and deserving of the social moratorium extended by this and all other societies of which I am aware. Thus, removal of the treatment rationale does not destroy the rationale for a separate system or for the utilization of an ameliorative approach; it

In this view of corrections as one component in a broader system of preventing antisocial behavior, the role of the juvenile correctional system is modest. The system represents one way—and one way only—of dealing with juvenile crime. This attempt to limit the goals, as well as the claims, of corrections does not preclude either the obligation of the state to provide a full range of services for juveniles subject to the correctional system (see Part IV of these standards) or broader efforts outside of the correctional system to provide services aimed at improving their social and economic situation to all juveniles. Especially in view of the large number of juveniles who commit delinquent acts but entirely escape the juvenile justice system, no persuasive reason exists for making the correctional system the primary provider of services to juveniles who have broken the law. . . .

A final aspect of the standard emphasizes the effort to create a system that operates fairly and equitably and that is perceived by the young people affected by it to be fair and equitable. . . .

DISSENTING VIEWS

Statement of Hon. Justine Wise Polier

. . . The proposed standards invite an abandonment of the goals and raison d'être of the juvenile court system: the recognition that children should be treated differently from adults and are entitled to receive care and treatment in accordance with their individual needs. They fail to establish or support entitlements for children directed to providing unique benefits under law.

Statement of Commissioner Patricia M. Wald

. . . My views of what should and should not be changed in our juvenile justice system are, at points, sharply divergent.

I would, first of all, reaffirm the bedrock objective of juvenile justice to provide individualized attention to the needs of the juvenile—medical, educational, social, and psychological—insofar as they can reasonably be ascertained and satisfied. Yet the volume nowhere acknowledges the legitimacy of rehabilitation as a goal of the system (cf. Standard 1.1). Abandonment of this rationale could seriously undermine the constitutional basis for a separate system of juvenile justice. See J. White in McKeiver v. Pennsylvania, 403 U.S. 528, 91 S.Ct. 1976, 29 L.Ed.2d 647 (1971); and J. Harlan in In re Gault, 387 U.S. 1, 87 S.Ct. 1428, 18 L.Ed.2d 527 (1967).

. . . .

In short, I am not yet willing to give up on the concept of rehabilitating juveniles—however unfashionable that idea may currently seem. We are not yet omniscient enough to be sure such attempts

does, however, require a different rationale." Cohen, Position Paper (Juvenile Justice Standards Project, no. 18, 1974); see also Lasswell and Donnelly, "The Continuing Debate over Responsibility: An Introduction to Isolating the Condemnation Sanction," 68 Yale L.J. 869, 884–85 (1959).

will fail, and I hope we are not so cynical as to build a juvenile justice system on the tarnished "just deserts" model of the adult penal system. I agree with the volume that efforts at rehabilitation so far do not justify indefinite sentences or compulsory treatment, but I would continue the legal obligation of judges and correctional personnel to make bona fide attempts at meeting individual juvenile needs in the sentencing and correctional processes.

NOTES

(1) In the shift from rehabilitation to the just deserts criminal justice model of dispositions, what is left for a separate juvenile court to do in delinquency cases? Should juvenile courts surrender all jurisdiction over conduct by children that comes within the criminal code? If the only difference between adult criminal sentences and juvenile dispositions is the length and harshness of the sanction, do we need a parallel and separate court structure at all? For an argument that we do not, see McCarthy, Delinquency Dispositions Under the Juvenile Justice Standards: The Consequences of a Change of Rationale, 52 N.Y.U.L.Rev. 1093, 1115–19 (1977). For a further discussion of the Standards, see Fisher, The Disposition Process Under the Juvenile Justice Standards Project, 57 B.U.L.Rev. 732 (1977).

(2) Another possible reason for the recent reexamination of juvenile justice theory may be more profound. Perhaps the role of children in society and indeed children themselves have changed dramatically since the Progressive Era and the creation of juvenile courts. Parents have always told their children that, "in the good old days," children were well behaved, unlike today's children. Nevertheless, parents have recognized that "kids will be kids" and that rebellious behavior is part of the process of growth.

In recent years, however, there is growing sentiment that today's children are radically different from children in the past. This may stem, in part, from the "youth culture" that was generated by the post-war "baby boom." In addition, it certainly cannot be disputed that technological innovations, including television and automobiles, have dramatically affected the development of today's children. Through television, today's children are exposed to a whole spectrum of cultures, viewpoints and people that could previously be experienced only in a lifetime. In some respects, children are more sophisticated than ever before. In other respects, however, television and other technological changes may limit children's development and negatively affect their character. Some critics of television claim that it stunts the growth of interpersonal skills in children, destroys their idealism and imagination and, most importantly, increases the likelihood that children will engage in violent behavior. See Zamora v. State, 361 So.2d 776 (Fla.App. 1978) (attempted insanity defense to murder charge based upon "subliminal television intoxication"). Some commentators have argued that the possibility of sudden global destruction by nuclear weaponry has led to increased fatalism, apathy and self-destructive behavior among today's youth.

Whether modern technological growth is a step forward or a step backward for civilization is a question that must wait until the future for an answer. However, we cannot ignore the fact that the technological revolution of this century has had some impact on today's children. When reading this chapter, especially the theoretical sections, keep in mind that the juvenile justice system does not and cannot exist in a vacuum. Try to decide what you think should be the goals of the juvenile justice system and how those goals can best be implemented at the dispositional phase.

(3) The decline of the rehabilitative theory is not limited to the juvenile arena. Professor Francis Allen has asserted that the rehabilitative ideal has declined substantially and precipitously in recent years in all of American jurisprudence. F. Allen, The Decline of the Rehabilitative Ideal 10 (1981). He chronicles the erosion of support for rehabilitation by legislatures, the public and intellectuals, and criticizes the "war theory of criminal justice" that he fears is replacing the rehabilitative ideal. Id. at 62–63.

(4) Reread footnote 5 and the accompanying text in the Commentary to the Disposition Standards. This is the only section in which the Commentary clearly addresses the differences between juveniles and adults. Does the Commentary adequately analyze the complex differences between juveniles and adults? Do the Standards respond to the differences? For a lively debate over whether children are "incomplete adults" between a family court judge and the Reporter of the Dispositions volume, see The Standards' Recommendations on Dispositions: A Panel Discussion, 57 B.U.L.Rev. 754, 759–64 (1977).

(5) The move away from rehabilitation may merely indicate a recognition by the drafters of the Standards that punishment has always been a major feature of the juvenile justice system, notwithstanding the articulation of rehabilitative purposes. A delinquent child "placed" in the custody of a youth authority certainly views the restrictive placement as punishment.

One law review article has criticized the parens patriae rehabilitative approach as being a pretense for punishment:

There is no meaningful similarity between a state's acting to protect society and enforce morality through prosecution and sentencing of offenders, and parents' acting to nurture and socialize children through love, care, discipline, and education. The coercive nature of court-imposed "therapy" inevitably renders it punitive from the child's viewpoint. However benevolently it is intended, involuntary restriction of an individual's liberty because he has engaged in conduct deemed unacceptable is punishment. Similarly, the traditional pretense that the problems of juvenile delinquency can be cured with love and understanding is naive and simplistic. The causes of youth crime are so deeply rooted in the poverty and the social disorganization of urban communities, in the family, and in the individual personality, that even the best-intentioned efforts of kindly judges, friendly probation officers, and humane correctional personnel are unavailing in many cases.

Wizner & Keller, The Penal Model of Juvenile Justice: Is Juvenile Court Delinquency Jurisdiction Obsolete?, 52 N.Y.U.L.Rev. 1120, 1122 (1977).*

Similarly, sociologists have criticized the juvenile justice system's focus on individualized assessments. These critics argue that even assuming that the juvenile system is trying to rehabilitate delinquents, the emphasis on the individual child is misguided because it ignores the fact that most habitual offenders are "active members of a delinquent social system." Empey &

Rabow, The Provo Experiment in Delinquency Rehabilitation, 26 Am.Soc.
Rev. 679 (1961).

IN RE S.J.

Supreme Court of North Dakota, 1981.
304 N.W.2d 685.

PAULSON, JUSTICE.

S.J. appeals from an order issued by the Juvenile Court of Stutsman County on March 31, 1981, denying her motion for a stay of disposition. S.J. has submitted to this court a motion to stay the order
of disposition entered by the juvenile court. We deny the motion for
a stay of the juvenile court's order of disposition.

On January 19, 1981, a petition was filed in the Juvenile Court of
Stutsman County which alleged that S.J. was a delinquent child because S.J. and another juvenile had committed the offense of robbery.
At a hearing held on February 3, 1981, the juvenile court determined
that S.J. was a delinquent child. On March 31, 1981, a dispositional
hearing was held and the juvenile court ordered that S.J. be placed in
the care, custody, and control of the Superintendent of the State Industrial School until she attained the age of eighteen, which will occur on August 20, 1981.

. . .

. . . The issue presented for our consideration concerns whether or not the juvenile court's denial of the motion to stay the order of
disposition was proper. After a careful examination of the facts in
the instant case, we conclude that the order of disposition of the juvenile court was proper and that S.J.'s motion for a stay of the order of
disposition is denied.

The juvenile court considered in detail all of the categories for disposition of a delinquent child included in § 27–20–31, N.D.C.C., which
provides:

> "*27–20–31. Disposition of delinquent child.*—If the child is
> found to be a delinquent child the court may make any of the fol-
> lowing orders of disposition best suited to his treatment, rehabili-
> tation, and welfare:
>
> "1. Any order authorized by section 27–20–30 for the disposi-
> tion of a deprived child;
>
> "2. Placing the child on probation under the supervision of
> the juvenile supervisor, probation officer, or other appropriate
> officer of the court or of the court of another state as provided
> in section 27–20–41 or the director of the county welfare board
> under conditions and limitations the court prescribes;
>
> "3. Placing the child in an institution, camp, or other facility
> for delinquent children operated under the direction of the
> court or other local public authority; or

"4. Committing the child to the state industrial school or to a state department to which commitment of delinquent or unruly children may be made."

In arriving at an order of disposition of a delinquent child, the best interests of the child and the State of North Dakota must be considered. In re Walter, 172 N.W.2d 603 (N.D.1969); In Interest of K.B., 244 N.W.2d 297 (N.D.1976). S.J. asserts that a stay of the order of disposition would be proper because the delinquent child who accompanied her in the robbery received a stay despite the fact that such child was sixteen years of age. S.J. argues that the denial of the motion for a stay results in a form of retribution or punishment contrary to one of the purposes of the Uniform Juvenile Court Act, Chapter 27–20, N.D.C.C., which purpose is to remove from children committing delinquent acts the taint of criminality and the consequences of criminal behavior and to substitute a program of treatment, training, and rehabilitation.

In support of her contention, S.J. relies upon the affidavit of Doctor Awad A. Ismir, who determined that S.J. presented little danger to society if she were released and that she could return to the family home as long as she was placed in the custody of the State Youth Authority. The juvenile court considered and rejected this proposal as an ineffective method of disposition because S.J.'s past history indicated that she had difficulty adjusting to restrictions imposed at her family home. S.J. had lived by herself and with relatives and, in each case, her living arrangements were unsuccessful. In addition, S.J. had not attended school for some time. These facts lead us to conclude that the district court's order of disposition was proper because the structured environment of the State Industrial School accounts for S.J.'s best interests in view of her past behavior. By placing her in the care, custody, and control of the Superintendent of the State Industrial School, the juvenile court has provided the means by which S.J. may receive the necessary treatment, rehabilitation, and correction.

For reasons stated in this opinion, the motion for a stay of the order of disposition is denied.

IN RE JOSE P.

California Court of Appeal, 4th District, 1980.
101 Cal.App.3d 52, 161 Cal.Rptr. 400.

WORK, ASSOCIATE JUSTICE.

Jose P., a minor nonresident alien, appeals his commitment to California Youth Authority (CYA) following a contested hearing resulting in a true finding to the charge of unlawful use of a motor vehicle, a felony . . . .

Appellant does not challenge the true finding on this appeal, but attacks his commitment to CYA, . . .

. . .

Factual background.

Jose is a 15-year-old Mexican national whose legal residence is in Mexico. He first came to the attention of local juvenile authorities following an attempted auto theft, August 28, 1978. He admitted the offense as a misdemeanor, was made a ward of the court and placed on probation. Jose spent 26 days in custody and then was turned over to the immigration authorities.

Less than two months later, October 21, 1978, Jose again was apprehended illegally in this country stealing a car. This time he remained detained in juvenile hall until confinement in CYA.

Neither offense involved violence during the crime or apprehension. There is no indication of any misconduct by the minor during either period of custody.

The probation officer mentions the prior disposition and the present case and concludes "[t]his behavior indicates that the minor *probably* makes a living by committing thefts in the United States and then returning to Mexico to sell them." (Italics added.)

This speculation is the foundation for an opinion ". . . this indicates a certain degree of sophistication and causes him to be a danger to the community." The only facts from which this sophistication can be attributed to Jose is that he is a 15-year-old Mexican alien who bungled two car thefts.

The probation officer recommended CYA placement because of "his past and present offenses." Even though Jose had never been placed in any rehabilitation program, except being "floated" out of the country on his first contact, alternative treatments were expressly rejected, the officer reasoning:

". . . that in the past the Probation Officer has committed several Mexican aliens to the Juvenile Ranch Facilities, all of whom have escaped. The majority of these have returned and committed additional offenses. Consequently, in order to protect the community from further criminal behavior, the Probation Officer feels that a CYA commitment is appropriate."

Although Jose's widowed mother allegedly resides in Tijuana, the current record shows no actual notice to her of any of the proceedings. She did not appear, nor was she represented at any of them. It is apparent she was not contacted by the probation officer during this social study, nor does his report indicate any familiarity with Jose's home environment, or any attempt to make any evaluation of it.

The social study suggests only two factors to justify the CYA recommendation:

1. This 15-year-old bungling auto thief is a sophisticated criminal and, therefore, a danger to the community;

a. He is sophisticated because he "probably" makes a living by stealing in the U.S. and selling in Mexico;

(i)(a) is indicated to be true because Jose is a Mexican alien; and/or

2. Jose is a Mexican alien;

a. Several Mexican aliens have been committed to Juvenile Ranch Facilities, all of whom have escaped, and some of whom have committed more crimes. This compels the conclusion;

(i) Jose will escape from the Juvenile Ranch Facilities, and any other facility in which he is placed (except CYA) and will commit more crimes, therefore,

(ii) He is a danger to the community.

The referee found Jose had proved unamenable to the previous orders of the court evidenced by his single illegal reentry and criminal act. No express reasons were given by the court as to why existing less punitive alternatives for placement were rejected. We assume, therefore, it relied on the probation officer's reasoning. The minor's custody was removed from his parent pursuant to section 726, subdivision (b), of Welfare and Institutions Code.[1]

It is an abuse of discretion not to consider lesser restrictive placements before commitment to CYA even though the minor is a nonresident alien.

If there is any theme which has been consistently and clearly expressed by the Legislature and the courts, it is that " '[j]uvenile commitment proceedings are designed for the purposes of rehabilitation and treatment, not punishment.' " (In re Aline D., 14 Cal.3d 557, 567, 121 Cal.Rptr. 816, 536 P.2d 65, quoted in In re Eric J., supra, 25 Cal. 3d 522, 531, 159 Cal.Rptr. 317, 322, 601 P.2d 549, 554.)

The difference between the punitive intent of criminal adult sentencing statutes and the nonpunitive design of the juvenile law sometimes results in the anomaly of longer custodial commitments for minors than for adults who commit the same crime. Such may be

---

1. In an effort to gain some insight into the nature of the prior admitted offense, we augmented the record on appeal by bringing up the entire lower court file. We find the probation officer erred in his description of the prior charged offenses as "attempted auto theft" and "auto theft." In fact, they were count one—attempted auto theft—and count two—*tampering with a vehicle, a misdemeanor.*

The current social study shows a true finding as to "auto theft." In fact, the finding was to *"attempted* auto theft," a misdemeanor. The record reveals no probation report was prepared in the previous case and it was handled in summary fashion.

No contact was ever made with any parent, and all letters were returned showing there was no such street in Tijuana as that to which they were mailed.

justified where the disparity meaningfully relates to rehabilitation of the juvenile.

Confinement in CYA is the most restrictive and most punitive of all dispositional options available to the court. It thrusts this 15-year-old minor into custody, with adult offenders, and those having lengthy involvements in violent and illegal activity.[2]

. . .

The legislative treatment plan designed for minors "contemplates a progressively restrictive and punitive series of disposition orders in cases . . ."

Youth Authority placement should be deferred until lesser remedies of probation or other placements have failed or are clearly inappropriate. This is so even though the offenses committed are serious and violent.

When a minor is adjudged a ward, the court may make a disposition consistent with any alternative specified in sections 727, 730 and 731 of Welfare and Institutions Code.

In ascending order of severity, there are:

(1) Any reasonable order;[3]

(2) Supervision of the probation officer;

(3) Commitment of the minor to the custody of a reputable person consenting thereto;

(4) Award of custody to a public or private entity designed to care for minors, with the consent of the agency;

(5) Custody, to the probation officer, to be placed in a foster home facility (Welf. & Inst.Code, § 727);

(6) Commitment to a juvenile home, ranch camp or forestry camp;

(7) Juvenile hall confinement (Welf. & Inst.Code, § 730);

(8) All of the above plus orders for restitution and/or participation in uncompensated work programs;

(9) Commitment to a sheltered care facility;

(10) Commitment to CYA (Welf. & Inst.Code, § 731).

. . .

. . . Alternatives in ascending order of restrictiveness are

. . .

(1) Placement in the home of the person having physical custody;

(2) Placement in the home of a relative or friend;

2. In 1978, 41.8 per cent of all *first commitments* to CYA were from adult courts; 42 per cent were for violent offenses; 4.2 per cent for sex offenses; 1 per cent for arson; 1.5 per cent for kidnapping; and 2.4 per cent for narcotics and drugs. The average age of all first commitments was 17.4 years; 32 per cent had five or more convictions or sustained petitions before first commitment. (Dept. of Youth Authority Annual Report, 1978.)

3. With such conditions for the parent to engage in joint counseling under the supervision of the probation officer as the court deems appropriate (Welf. & Inst.Code, § 727, subd. (1)(d)).

(3) Placement in a foster home;

(4) Commitment to a private institution;

(5) Commitment to a county institution;

(6) CYA.

Although we are required to uphold the discretionary decision of the juvenile court if we can glean substantial evidence from the record to support it, we find none here. A single failure of prior probation where no supervision is afforded the minor as part of the probationary plan cannot justify disregard of less restrictive alternatives than CYA. The previous disposition was in the nature of a "floater." It was not designed to provide meaningful rehabilitative direction to Jose.

We can conceive of no reason for Jose being ordered to CYA on his first apprehension for the nonviolent offense without a social study except as an effort to deter him from reentering this country. Nor can we perceive, from the present record, any factors which would justify the court in not finding Jose suitable for a less punitive disposition than an aggregated four-year commitment to CYA other than his classification as a nonresident.

The social study candidly relies on Jose's alien status in making its recommendation. The referee decries such motivation but justifies his disposition on Jose's juvenile delinquency history.

The possibility Jose may escape from the ranch facility, based on an unsupported statement in the social study other Mexican aliens have done so, is not a rational basis to select the most punitive disposition. If the rehabilitation and treatment goals mean anything to juvenile placement, they must be tailored to the needs of the individual minor. Jose had never escaped. He was, in fact, detained in juvenile hall without apparent incident. No reason was given for rejecting a continued term in that facility.

Moreover, failure on a particular program, even on several, is not a ground for commitment to CYA.

. . .

The record does not reveal the unavailability of suitable alternative dispositions. The court has great flexibility in making an order appropriate for the individual. None has ever been attempted for Jose.

Where a wardship is established for a minor whose residence is in a foreign country, the minor, if placed on probation, may be sent to an official of a juvenile court of such foreign country or an agency of such country authorized to accept the minor. (Welf. & Inst.Code, § 738.) [4]

4. For instance, the Mexican state of Jose's residence, Baja, California, operates "La Granja," a facility for juveniles roughly equivalent to a combination juvenile hall and ranch. This is operated under the court system by El Tribunal para Menores. Imperial County, which like San Diego is proximate to the Mexican border, has a reciprocal relationship with the juvenile authorities in Baja, Califor-

No reason appears on the record why these provisions relating to nonresident wards were not available in this case. If in fact there are no facilities in Mexico to which the minor may be referred, this should be made clear. If there are available facilities but they are inappropriate, the reasons should be stated.

Section 738 does not distinguish between those nonresident wards who are in this country legally and those illegally.

The attempt to portray Jose as a sophisticate in the world of crime is pure bootstrapping. The facts of the present offense show the minor spent one and a half to two hours unsuccessfully attempting to start the car until residents called the police to give him assistance. When the police arrived, he was hiding in the back seat. As a car thief, Jose appears as criminally sophisticated as a member of the "Apple Dumpling Gang."

There is no psychological or social evaluation of Jose or his family environment. Jose is young in relation to the average CYA committee, unsophisticated in the criminal sphere and has never been tried in any meaningful alternative program. No psychological study has been made.

.   .   .

The commitment order is reversed. The case is remanded for a new disposition hearing at which the suitability of Jose as an individual for less restrictive alternative placement shall be considered.

.   .   .

JUVENILE JUSTICE STANDARDS PROJECT, STANDARDS RELATING TO DISPOSITIONS *

1.2   F.   Judicially determined dispositions

The nature and duration of all coercive dispositions should be determined by the court at the time of sentencing, within the limitations established by the legislature.

Commentary

The standard envisions that the nature and duration of all coercive dispositions will be determined by the judge at the time of sentencing. Thereafter, neither correctional authorities nor administrative agencies, such as parole boards, may independently alter the nature or duration of a juvenile's disposition without a judicial order. The two exceptions are the good time allowance provided pursuant to Standard 5.3 and the ability of administrators to petition the sentencing court (or an appellate court) for reduction of dispositions they consider inequitable, pursuant to Standard 5.1.

nia, to allow supervision over nonresident minors in appropriate cases.

* Reprinted with permission from Standards Relating to Dispositions, Copyright 1980, Ballinger Publishing Company.

The prohibition against administrators' changing the nature of a juvenile's disposition without returning to court applies only to changes from one category or subcategory of disposition to another, not to changes among placements within a dispositional category. For example, the correctional agency may move a juvenile from one foster home to another, but it may not, without a court order, move the juvenile from a foster home to a secure facility or to community supervision.

The standard is predicated on the adoption of much shorter maximum sentences than currently exist, so that administrative discretion will not be necessary as an escape from lengthy maxima imposed by legislatures or courts. The standard also presumes the abandonment of the automatic continuation of jurisdiction over juveniles adjudicated delinquent until they reach the age of majority. Preventing administrators from making determinations regarding juvenile dispositions is intended to reduce, not to lengthen, sentences.

The use of the indeterminate sentence is even more prevalent in juvenile court statutes than it is for adults. Forty-one states grant the juvenile court jurisdiction over juveniles found delinquent until they reach the age of twenty-one. Generally this dispositional pattern enables a juvenile court to commit a person to the custody of a private or public agency, which then makes the administrative decision of when to release the youth. . . .

The predominant statutory pattern is that the juvenile court retains jurisdiction over the youth until he or she reaches the age of majority. As the age of majority in many states has been lowered to eighteen, the jurisdiction of the court over a large segment of the young population has been reduced. . . .

. . .

The standard rejects the use of indeterminacy as a governing principle of juvenile sentencing. Indeterminacy can affect two aspects of an offender's sentence: the total length of jurisdiction over the juvenile; and the length of time he or she will have to spend at various levels of custody—e.g., an institution versus community supervision. Systems embracing indeterminacy all involve some sort of discretionary release, generally through parole. Proponents of such systems suggest several advantages: (A) indeterminacy allows maximum implementation of the rehabilitative ideal in corrections; (B) the chance for early release under an indeterminate sentence motivates the offender to work for rehabilitation; (C) indeterminacy best protects society from hard core recidivists and mentally defective offenders; (D) indeterminacy prevents warehousing by eliminating unnecessary incarceration; (E) indeterminacy removes the judgment concerning the duration of sentences from the hands of the judge and places it in the hands of more qualified professionals; (F) the decision as to the length of incarceration reflects the needs of the offender and his or her readiness for release, not just the offense; and (G) indeterminate sentences deter.

The arguments against indeterminacy and discretionary release on parole seem more persuasive. First, allowing administrators or correctional authorities to alter judicially imposed sentences would increase the disparate treatment of similar conduct that other standards aim to reduce. All information relevant to disposition according to these principles—seriousness of offense, age and prior record, and the culpability of the juvenile's conduct in the particular case (Standard 2.1)—is available to the judge at the time of disposition and remains unchanged during the term of the juvenile's commitment.

Sentencing juveniles to periods of indeterminate duration, with the concomitant authority of parole boards or institutional administrators to determine release dates, reflects adherence to the concept of individualized sentencing, which posits that offenders are "sick" and in need of "treatment" that can be successfully provided by the correctional system. These premises recently have been challenged, however, and the promises of individualized sentencing have remained largely unfulfilled.

. . . In fact, where the duration or the nature of the disposition is determined by administrators or correctional authorities, true treatment may be made more difficult by the juvenile's motivation to dissemble in order to procure early release. . . .

A second consideration is the anxiety experienced by offenders when the exact nature and duration of their dispositions are unknown. The "inmate experiences as cruel and degrading the command that he remain in custody for some uncertain period, while his keepers study him, grade him in secret, and decide if and when he may be let go." . . . For further discussion of the psychological impact of indeterminacy, see American Assembly, "Prisoners in America" 93 (1973). In addition, offenders frequently are convinced that no valid or consistent criteria are employed in the release determination. This leads to distrust and the belief that decisions are made arbitrarily and unjustly. Committee, supra at 93.

Third, indeterminacy introduces unregulated discretion into the system, which recently has been subject to extensive criticism and litigation. According to K.C. Davis, Discretionary Justice 170 (1969), "[t]he discretionary power to be lenient is an impossibility without a concomitant power not to be lenient, and injustice from the discretionary power not to be lenient is especially frequent; the power to be lenient is the power to discriminate" (original in italics). . . .

Mandating due process protections for offenders at parole release decision-making hearings may structure the administrative discretion of parole board members to some extent. The discretion of correctional staff members, who also play an immeasurably important role in recommending release for certain offenders and not for others, however, cannot be cured by instituting such safeguards. This discretion may be misused so that release denials can be used to punish offenders for their nonconforming beliefs and unpopular views.

. . .

Analysis of available data provides the most cogent reasons for rejecting indeterminacy. It appears that in systems employing indeterminate sentencing, release does not vary with those factors that proponents of individualized sentencing say should be taken into account; rather, considerations not related to offender needs or characteristics are most influential in lengths of stay.

Statistics compiled by the research division of the Ohio Youth Commission demonstrate that, while the indeterminate sentence is designed to "individualize" sentences, individualization in fact does not occur. Institutional lengths of stay vary more with institutional size, classification systems, and offender characteristics than with any measure of rehabilitative progress. In Ohio's institutions, for example, it is reported that

> the only offender-related variables linked to length of stay were age and sex. Controlling on institution, younger residents invariably stayed longer, as well as females. More important, when controlling on committing offense, the least serious status offenders were associated with longer institutional stay.

. . .

DISSENTING VIEWS

Statement of Hon. Justine Wise Polier

. . .

Stemming from disillusionment with the work of juvenile courts, these standards would shift significant power from both juvenile courts and from public agencies entrusted with the care of children, to state legislative bodies. In order to correct sentencing inequalities in dispositional orders by the juvenile courts, the standards propose "proportional punishment," based primarily on the child's offense. The nature and duration of dispositions would be determined by the court at the time of sentencing within maximum limitations set by the legislatures. Public agencies responsible for care and rehabilitation are allowed only minimal authority to reduce the duration of custodial care (5 percent for good behavior) without regard to a child's responses, attitude, or other changes in circumstances. Such restrictions would impose on juvenile court judges unrealistic requirements for prediction and run counter to the verbal recognition of the unique characteristics of juveniles, their malleability, and their capacity for change, although acknowledged in other sections of this volume.

The right of a child to treatment and to the least drastic treatment required to protect the community under the juvenile justice system, is subordinated to the concept of "proportional punishment." Consideration of the child's individual needs is postponed until after the category and the length of penalty are determined. The standards thus postpone consideration of the individual child's needs so late as to make it all but meaningless.

. . .

Statement of Commissioner Patricia M. Wald

. . .

I would also preserve the discretion of juvenile correctional authorities to adjust the duration and nature of the confinement originally imposed by the judge where the juvenile exhibits definite signs of improvement or constructive change in attitudes and behavior. Apart from a maximum 5 percent good time allowance, Standard 1.2 F. in this volume freezes the sentence imposed by the judge, regardless of how the juvenile responds or changes after sentence begins. I do not think we can attract creative, energetic, dedicated personnel into a correctional system that rejects the possibility of character change in juveniles. I am not against the concept of finite maximum sentences, but I firmly believe that some element of post-sentence discretion must be retained to permit positive interrelationships between confined juveniles and their custodians.

Nor would I disallow the juvenile's needs as an element to be taken into account by the sentencing judge as Standard 2.1 presently does. I acknowledge that the juvenile's needs should not necessarily be the dominant criteria for sentencing; the protection of others from youthful violence is a legitimate goal of any justice system. But I would let the judge consider *all* relevant individual and societal factors in imposing sentence.

NOTES

(1) Consider the adult criminal justice system in which the sentences imposed are generally proportional to the crime committed. Some commentators have argued that introducing proportionality into the juvenile justice system creates two problems. First, it creates an overwhelming temptation for the delinquent to plea bargain. Wizner & Keller, The Penal Model of Juvenile Justice: Is Juvenile Court Delinquency Jurisdiction Obsolete? 52 N.Y.U.L.Rev. 1120, 1127–28 (1977). Second, using determinate, proportional sentences for juveniles can result in extremely disparate treatment for two individuals whose behavior was the same. For example, a juvenile who commits a murder could be sentenced to two years in prison; an adult (or a juvenile tried as an adult) can be sentenced to life in prison or even death. This result is questionable considering the purposes of both the juvenile and adult systems. Because the Standards would make the goals of the juvenile system similar to the goals of the adult system, it is inconsistent to impose greatly disparate sentences on two similarly situated people whose only difference is age.

(2) The debate over discretion and proportionality has seen some strange bedfellows supporting proportionality. People who believe that the government should "get tough on crime" support proportionality because it is con-

sistent with their punishment-oriented philosophy; they believe that it will take away discretion from liberal judges who are "soft on crime."

On the other hand, liberals and minorities often support proportionality because it takes away the discretion of judges to impose sanctions upon youths under the guise of rehabilitation. Some supporters of proportionality argue that under the current system, white, upper-class children are placed in the custody of their parents while minority lower-class children are placed in institutions even though the children have engaged in identical behavior.

Although worlds apart on other issues, both sides have coalesced in support of proportionality in an interesting manner. As noted before, the "crime control" group supports proportionality as a logical corollary of its punishment-oriented philosophy. Liberals and minorities, on the other hand, have traditionally supported the rehabilitative goal but argue that in the current system rehabilitation is a sham and what is really occurring is punishment. And, if juveniles are going to be punished, the argument continues, they should be punished in accordance with what they did, not on the basis of their family background, socio-economic status, or race. See Commentary to Standard 1.2 F at 29–30.

B. THE CALIFORNIA EXPERIENCE

California presents a particularly interesting example of the changing philosophy of juvenile justice because the legislature and the courts both initially adopted the rehabilitative ideal wholeheartedly. However, the ideal became tarnished in the 1970s as the state felt the impact of rising juvenile crime. In 1974, a California Assembly committee on juvenile violence reported that the number of juveniles arrested in California for crimes against persons rose 46.8 percent between 1968 and 1973. Dixon, Juvenile Justice in Transition, 4 Pepperdine L.Rev. 469 (1977).

The materials that follow set out the originally articulated statutory purpose of the California juvenile justice system and the early judicial response. Against the backdrop of the dramatic rise in youth crime comes new legislation and finally judicial interpretation and implementation of the new statute.

IN RE ALINE D.

Supreme Court of California, 1975.
14 Cal.3d 557, 121 Cal.Rptr. 817, 536 P.2d 65.

RICHARDSON, JUSTICE.

We consider the question whether a minor who has previously been adjudicated a ward of the juvenile court and then placed, with unsuccessful results, in various local treatment facilities, may thereafter be committed to the California Youth Authority ("CYA") despite the expressed doubt of the court, acting through its referee, that she would benefit from such a commitment. The record before us reflects that the referee ordered the CYA commitment solely be-

cause there appeared to be no other available placement facility.
. . .

We recite pertinent portions of the troubled history of the minor,
Aline D. At the time of her commitment to CYA, she was 16, her
father was absent from the family home and her mother had rejected
her. She had an I.Q. of 67 and a behavioral history of assaultive
conduct and association with juvenile gangs. She was originally
placed in a family treatment program at juvenile hall, for reasons not
specified in the record. This placement continued from February 23,
1972, to May 1, 1972, and, according to a probation report, was "singularly unsuccessful." Thereafter, she was released to the care of
her mother but, one week later, ran away from home. An attempt
was made to place her in a probation department community day-care
program, but her limited intellectual potential disqualified her. On
September 25, 1972, Aline was placed at the McKinnon Girls Home in
Los Angeles, but soon thereafter the Home reported that she was
having "problems with stealing, shoplifting, . . . refusal to attend school," and was participating in a juvenile gang. Her placement with the Home terminated a few weeks later when she was arrested following an incident at a high school campus. Aline was
returned to juvenile court on allegations that she had violated Education Code section 13560 (wilful insult and abuse of teacher) and Penal
Code section 653g (unlawful loitering about a school). Following a
hearing, the first charge was sustained and, on November 10, 1972,
Aline's wardship was continued and "suitable placement" ordered for
her.

Thereafter, on November 20, 1972, Aline was placed at the Penny
Lane residential school in Los Angeles where she remained for ten
days after which time her placement was terminated for various reasons, including her use of marijuana, bullying of associates, and
membership in a juvenile gang.

On December 14, 1972, Aline was placed at the Detroit Arms
Home, where she remained until January 10, 1973. Her placement
there was terminated as a result of her "active association" with the
gang. A probation report, describing the circumstances of her association with the gang, reported that Aline let in eight or nine boy
members of the gang who thereafter took three or four girls and left
for two days, causing considerable difficulties.

Aline was returned to juvenile hall, pending further efforts to
place her. A report of the foregoing placement efforts summarizes
as follows: "Since this current detention on January 10, 1973 all efforts to place minor have met with defeat. Placements are not willing to handle the kinds of behavior minor has displayed in former
placements." The responsible placement coordinator indicated that
Los Angeles County has had no facilities capable of coping with the
minor other than the Las Palmas Girls School.

On February 13, 1973, Las Palmas rejected Aline as unsuitable, because of her record of "assaultive behavior." The Las Palmas officials by letter recommended a commitment to CYA "where she would have the structure she obviously needs and also vacational training." On March 1, 1973, the probation officer filed a supplemental petition in juvenile court, alleging that Aline is not acceptable for placement in Los Angeles County institutions or facilities.

On May 21, 1973, a hearing was held before a juvenile court referee. The referee heard testimony from Mrs. Holt, a probation officer, and considered the contents of her placement report as well as letters and evaluations from psychiatrists regarding Aline's situation. The officer described her investigation of all conceivable placements available to Aline, including her mother and potential foster parents. The investigation included seven different facilities. Each placement was found unsuitable for Aline, although Mrs. Holt learned that Penny Lane eventually planned to establish a "closed setting for girls." According to Mrs. Holt, Aline, as a "severely delinquent young girl," requires a "closed facility" (by which is meant one with locked doors and limited visitation privileges), similar to county camps available for the placement of delinquent boys. If Aline were male, rather than female, Mrs. Holt would have recommended a camp community placement rather than CYA.

. . . Near the conclusion of the hearing, the referee noted his lack of options. He observed that Aline could not simply be left in juvenile hall, as that facility serves only as a temporary detention facility. He explained his reluctance to order the proceedings dismissed, for Aline's mother had refused to accept her, and Aline would be back "on the streets." He agreed with Aline's counsel that it would be "very unwise to commit this minor to the California Youth Authority for the sole reason that it does not seem that there is anything else." Moreover, the referee acknowledged that "The fact remains, nevertheless, that all agree, including two psychiatrists, a clinical psychologist, Mrs. Holt, *all agree that she's not an appropriate subject for commitment to the youth authority, but that it is being done only because that seems to be the only recourse.*" (Italics added.)

. . . [T]he referee concluded that he must order Aline committed to CYA, since ". . . the only other alternative that seems available to me now would be to dismiss this case and turn this lady out in the street, and I'm not going to do that." . . . Aline appeals.

Although the referee, following the hearing, signed a written form which contained a printed "finding" to the effect that the ward probably would benefit from the CYA commitment, our review of the record, summarized above, leads us to conclude that the referee ordered Aline committed to CYA solely because there appeared to be no other suitable placement for her. The motivation of the referee appears in his conclusion that "it seems that we are powerless" to avoid a CYA commitment. As we will develop below the provisions of the Juvenile Court Law do not permit a CYA commitment under such circumstances.

Preliminarily, we note the provisions of Welfare and Institutions Code section 502, which express in broad terms the general purposes of the Juvenile Court Law. These are to "secure for each minor . . . such care and guidance, preferably in his own home, as will serve the . . . welfare of the minor and the best interests of the State; . . . and, when the minor is removed from his own family, to secure for him custody, care, and discipline as nearly as possible equivalent to that which should have been given by his parents." The Juvenile Court Law is to be liberally construed to carry out the foregoing purposes.

In specific amplification of the foregoing purposes and with particular reference to the matter before us, section 734 of the Welfare and Institutions Code provides that "No ward of the juvenile court shall be committed to the Youth Authority unless the judge of the court is *fully satisfied* that the mental and physical condition and qualifications of the ward are such as to render it *probable that he will be benefited* by the reformatory educational discipline or other treatment provided by the Youth Authority." (Italics added.)

The foregoing language makes it clear that a CYA commitment may not be made for the sole reason that suitable alternatives do not exist. Instead, the court must be "fully satisfied" that a CYA commitment probably will benefit the minor. In the instant case, the referee's in-court statements, far from indicating that he was "fully satisfied," disclosed instead a substantial *dissatisfaction* with a CYA commitment. The requirements of section 734 not having been met, the commitment order must be reversed.

. . .

As is evident from the applicable statutes, "Commitments to the California Youth Authority are made only in the most serious cases and only after all else has failed." This concept is well established and has been expressed by the CYA itself. In light of the general purposes of juvenile commitments expressed in Welfare and Institutions Code section 502, discussed above, ". . . commitment to the Youth Authority is generally viewed as *the final treatment resource* available to the juvenile court and which least meets the description in the above provision [§ 502]. Within the Youth Authority system, there is gathered from throughout the State the most severely delinquent youths which have exhausted local programs."

. . .

Furthermore, statistics compiled by CYA indicate that at Ventura School for Girls (the only suitable CYA institution for Aline), Aline would be placed in the company of girls who had committed serious criminal offenses, including 16 homicides, 31 robberies and 38 assaults. According to the CYA's 1973 annual report, 85 percent of all youths committed to CYA had three or more delinquency "contacts," and 35 percent had eight or more such contacts.

. . .

In order to assist the juvenile court in its reconsideration of the cause, we note a few possible alternative dispositions. Our suggestions should not be considered exhaustive of the possibilities, and the court should explore, of course, any other placement opportunities which the parties or the probation officer may suggest.

If the report indicates that Aline would not benefit from the treatment, she would receive at CYA, and if no appropriate alternative placement exists at that time, then the proceedings should be dismissed. (Welf. & Inst.Code, § 782.) Section 888 of the Welfare and Institutions Code provides in pertinent part that, "Any county establishing such juvenile home, ranch, or camp under the provisions of this article [to place §§ 601 or 602 wards] may, by mutual agreement, accept children committed to such home, ranch, or camp by the juvenile court of another county in the State and the State shall reimburse the county maintaining the home, ranch, or camp to the amount of one-half the administrative cost of maintaining each child so committed. . . ."

Second, reference was made at the May 1973 hearing to the anticipated establishment of closed facilities at the Penny Lane school where Aline had once been placed. Mrs. Holt seemed to believe that such closed facilities might be a suitable placement for Aline.

Third, testimony at Aline's hearing described facilities in Los Angeles County for *boys* of the type appropriate for minors such as Aline. Although appearing to be the least promising alternative, conceivably some arrangement could be made to provide care and treatment for Aline at these facilities under some segregated arrangement.

Fourth, the record indicates that Aline may be a "borderline" mentally retarded child. Under Welfare and Institutions Code sections 6550 et seq. provision is made for the commitment to state hospital of juvenile court wards found (following evaluation and report) to be mentally retarded or mentally disordered. (See also § 6512.)

Finally, if on reconsideration the court determines that no appropriate alternative placement exists, but also finds that Aline probably would benefit from a CYA commitment under present circumstances, the court could consider the possibility of a temporary 90-day CYA commitment for purposes of observation and diagnosis, with provision for a report by the director of CYA concerning Aline's amenability to treatment. (See Welf. & Inst.Code, § 704.) If the report indicates that Aline is not benefiting from the treatment she is receiving at CYA, and if no appropriate alternative placement exists at that time, then the proceedings should be dismissed. (Welf. & Inst.Code, § 782.)

Juvenile commitment proceedings are designed for the purposes of rehabilitation and treatment, not punishment. We fully recognize that in some cases, as in that before us, the question of appropriate placement poses to the appropriate officials seemingly insurmountable difficulties. Budgetary limitations, varying from county to county, may well preclude the maintenance of those specialized facilities otherwise necessary to provide the minor with optimum care and treatment. Even if such facilities exist, the minor's past conduct may itself require his or her exclusion therefrom. Nevertheless, under the present statutory scheme, supported by sound policy considerations, a commitment to CYA must be supported by a determination, based upon substantial evidence in the record, of probable benefit to the minor. The unavailability of suitable alternatives, standing alone, does not justify the commitment of a nondelinquent or marginally delinquent child to an institution primarily designed for the incarceration and discipline of serious offenders.

The order of commitment is reversed and the cause remanded for further proceedings consistent with this opinion.

WRIGHT, C.J., and TOBRINER, MOSK and SULLIVAN, JJ., concur.

CLARK, JUSTICE (dissenting).

I dissent.

Welfare and Institutions Code section 734 precludes neither a judge's expression of sorrow when required to commit a juvenile ward to the California Youth Authority, nor his expression of regret when less restrictive alternatives are unobtainable. Instead, section 734 only requires that the juvenile court find CYA commitment to be the most beneficial disposition available. The record reveals this statutory requirement has been more than satisfied.

Aline's history of delinquency includes shoplifting, theft, smoking marijuana and assaulting a grandmother. Her behavior has frequently been characterized as "assaultive," leading her probation officer to describe her as "a severely delinquent young girl . . . in terms of being a public menace."

Exhaustive efforts—all unsuccessful—were made to place Aline within the community. The first placement, in a family treatment program, was regarded as "singularly unsuccessful" and terminated after two months. Admission in a community day care program was then denied the ward due to her low intelligence. McKinnon Girls Home released Aline in two weeks because of "problems with stealing, shoplifting, bedwetting, refusal to attend school" and the claim she was a leader of a local street gang, the Cripts.

Aline's fourth placement, at Penny Lane School, lasted only 10 days because she "[s]moked grass at a concert—is muscle of the resistive kids—threatens weaker girls—girls are terrified as she leans on being a member of the Cript gang. About five Cript boys came to Penny Lane to see her—'freaked out' staff as one got into the house." Her fifth disposition, at the Detroit Arms, was terminated when Aline "let in eight or nine Cripts in the placement who took three or four girls and split for two days."

At this point the Los Angeles County placement coordinator concluded the county had no facility capable of coping with Aline, "other than possibly Las Palmas Girls School." However, Las Palmas declined to enroll the ward, concluding her assaultive behavior, low intelligent level and nonacceptance of responsibility revealed Aline "could not benefit from either our school or group therapy[,] the two main aspects of our program." Las Palmas recommended she be committed to the CYA "where she could have the structure she obviously needs and also vocational training."

Before Aline's commitment to the Youth Authority *seven* additional placement alternatives were investigated, all proving unsatisfactory. The commitment hearing itself was recessed to give the probation officer time to explore placement with the Department of Public Social Services. However, like previous efforts, this proved fruitless.

The record clearly reveals that all parties at the hearing—including Aline's counsel—agreed that every conceivable placement alternative had been exhausted, the only remaining disposition being to either completely dismiss Aline's wardship or to commit her to the CYA. Since Aline's mother has refused to accept her back into the home, dismissal would place this child in the streets and under the influence of her gang. In these circumstances, release would provide Aline nothing but the opportunity to qualify more fully for CYA commitment—hardly a course of action to be recommended to the juvenile court system.

In contrast, CYA commitment offers Aline foreseeable benefit through treatment and training. The authority is empowered "to make use of law enforcement, detention, probation, parole, medical, educational, correctional, segregative and other facilities, institutions and agencies, whether public or private, within the State." (Welf. & Ins.Code, § 1753.) Its director is authorized to "enter into agreements with the appropriate public officials for separate care and special treatment in existing institutions for persons subject to the control of the Authority." (Welf. & Inst.Code, § 1753.) Finally it can even train its own specialists. (Welf. & Inst.Code, § 1752.6.) Far from being a single "placement facility," the CYA is an *administration* comprised of *many* facilities, capable of providing individualized treatment where necessary.

The propriety of a CYA commitment under these circumstances cannot be negated by a juvenile court judge's expression of concern and regret. Such expression is not uncommon and should be commended—not masked by judicial indifference.

. . .

In conclusion, Aline must be characterized as an aggressive, assaultive delinquent who may benefit from CYA training and discipline. Disposition of her case should not rest on a judge's expression of sorrow or dismay. If it does, we fail both Aline and the juvenile justice system.

I would affirm the judgment of the juvenile court.

NOTE

In re Aline D. raises the issue of sexual discrimination in delinquency dispositions. If Aline was committed to the Youth Authority because no less-restrictive placement was available for girls, could she challenge the commitment as unconstitutional sex discrimination if a less restrictive placement was available for a similarly situated boy? Generally there are a wider variety of institutional placements available for boys for a number of reasons. First, male youths, like male adults, are more likely than females to engage in conduct that results in arrest. For example, in 1973 in California juvenile males comprised 75.3 percent and females 24.7 percent of all juveniles arrested. Dixon, Juvenile Justice in Transition, 4 Pepperdine L.Rev. 469, 470 (1977).

In addition, female juveniles are often taken into custody for status offenses. Girls are therefore more likely than boys to be placed in an institutional setting for reasons relating to morality. The Supreme Court in Michael M. v. Superior Court, 450 U.S. 464, 101 S.Ct. 1200, 67 L.Ed.2d 437 (1981), gave implicit approval to this disparate treatment when it upheld California's statutory rape law. The Court held that punishing only men for statutory rape did not violate equal protection because states have a substantial interest in preventing illegitimate teenage pregnancies. The Court emphasized that "[b]ecause virtually all of the significant harmful and inescapably identifiable consequences of teenage pregnancy fall on the young female, a legislature acts well within its authority when it elects to punish only the participant who, by nature, suffers few of the consequences of his conduct." 450 U.S. at 473. For more complete discussion of *Michael M.* and the question of sexism in the status offense jurisdiction of the juvenile court, see note 3, p. 627 infra.

California Welfare and Institutions Code § 202 (enacted in 1976, underlined language added by amendment in 1977) replaces former § 502:

§ 202. Purpose; liberal construction

(a) The purpose of this chapter is to secure for each minor under the jurisdiction of the juvenile court such care and guidance, preferably in his own home, as will serve the spiritual, emotional, mental, and physical welfare of the minor and the best interests of the state; *to protect the public from criminal conduct by minors; to impose on the minor a sense of responsibility for his own acts*; to preserve and strengthen the minor's family ties whenever possible, removing him from the custody of his parents only when necessary for his welfare or for the safety and protection of the public . . .   and, when the minor is removed from his own family, to secure for him custody, care, and discipline as nearly as possible equivalent to that which should have been given by his parents. This chapter shall be liberally construed to carry out these purposes.

(b) The purpose of this chapter also includes the protection of the public from the consequences of criminal activity, and to such purpose prob-tion officers, peace officers, and juvenile courts shall take into account such protection of the public in their determinations under this chapter.

IN RE ERIC J.

Supreme Court of California, 1979.
25 Cal.3d 522, 159 Cal.Rptr. 317, 601 P.2d 549.

CLARK, JUSTICE

Eric J., a minor, appeals from an order continuing his juvenile court wardship and committing him to the Youth Authority (Welf. & Inst.Code, §§ 602, 731) after findings he committed burglary and was in contempt of court for violating conditions of an earlier order granting probation. The maximum term for which he might be confined was determined to be three and one-half years—three years for the burglary and six months for the misdemeanor contempt. . . .

Facts

A month after 10 pairs of roller skates were taken in a burglary of the Sweetwater Roller Rink, Midge Rhoda, a professional skating instructor, informed the owner that appellant was at the Palisades Gardens Skating Rink attempting to sell roller skates which might be the ones stolen. In response to a call from the owner, Officer Merrell Davis went to the Sweetwater rink and was advised by the manager, Buddy Morris, of appellant's identity and his employment at the rink. Officer Davis had a copy of the burglary report.

The uniformed officer drove Morris to the Palisades Gardens where they met Rhoda. She suggested they talk to appellant in her office and summoned him. During questioning by Morris for 45 minutes to an hour, appellant confessed to the burglary, implicated his brother as his accomplice, and stated that he had sold some of the skates to individuals still at the Palisades Gardens, and that the remaining skates were at his house. . . .

. . .

Equal Protection

Relying on People v. Olivas, 17 Cal.3d 236 (1976), appellant contends Welfare and Institutions Code section 726 denies him equal protection of the laws by providing that the maximum term of confinement for a juvenile is the longest term imposable upon an adult for the same offense, without the necessity of finding circumstances in aggravation of the crime justifying imposition of the upper term as is required in adult criminal procedure by Penal Code section 1170, subdivision (b).

Section 726, subdivision (c), of the Welfare and Institutions Code provides in relevant part: "In any case in which the minor is removed from the physical custody of his parent or guardian as the result of

an order of wardship made pursuant to Section 602, the order shall
specify that the minor may not be held in physical confinement for a
period in excess of the maximum term of imprisonment which could
be imposed upon an adult convicted of the offense or offenses which
brought or continued the minor under the jurisdiction of the juvenile
court. [¶] As used in this section and in Section 731, 'maximum term
of imprisonment' means the longest of the three time periods set
forth in paragraph (2) of subdivision (a) of Section 1170 of the Penal
Code, but without the need to follow the provisions of subdivision (b)
of Section 1170 of the Penal Code or to consider time for good behavior or participation pursuant to Sections 2930, 2931, and 2932 of the
Penal Code, plus enhancements which must be proven if pled."

Section 1170, subdivision (b), of the Penal Code provides: "When a
judgment of imprisonment is to be imposed and the statute specifies
three possible terms, the court shall order imposition of the middle
term, unless there are circumstances in aggravation or mitigation of
the crime. At least four days prior to the time set for imposition of
judgment either party may submit a statement in aggravation or mitigation to dispute facts in the record or the probation officer's report,
or to present additional facts. In determining whether there are circumstances that justify imposition of the upper or lower term, the
court may consider the record in the case, the probation officer's report, other reports including reports received pursuant to Section
1203.03 and statements in aggravation or mitigation submitted by the
prosecution or the defendant, and any further evidence introduced at
the sentencing hearing. The court shall set forth on the record the
facts and reasons for imposing the upper or lower term . . . ."

Appellant was found to have committed [second degree] burglary.
. . . Second degree burglary is punishable "by imprisonment in
the county jail not exceeding one year or in the state prison." Where
it is not otherwise specified, the term for an offense punishable by
imprisonment in a state prison is "16 months, or two or three years."
Pursuant to Welfare and Institutions Code section 726, subdivision
(c), the maximum term for which appellant might be confined for the
burglary was determined to be three years. He contends that, in the
absence of any finding of aggravation, it is a denial of equal protection of the law not to set the maximum at two years.

In People v. Olivas this court held that section 1770 of the Welfare
and Institutions Code violated the equal protection clauses of the California and United States Constitutions insofar as it permitted misdemeanants between the ages of 16 and 21 to be committed to the
Youth Authority for a term potentially longer than the maximum jail
term which might have been imposed for the same offense if committed by a person over the age of 21 years. We emphasized that youthful misdemeanants committed pursuant to section 1731.5 "have been
prosecuted *as adults*, adjudged by the same standards which apply to
any competent adult, and convicted *as adults in adult courts*."
"We are not confronted," we stressed, "by a situation in which a ju-

venile adjudged *under the Juvenile Court Law as a juvenile* contends that his term of involuntary confinement may exceed that which might have been imposed on an adult or juvenile who committed the identical unlawful act and was thereafter convicted *in the criminal courts*. Since that situation is not before us, we reserve consideration of the issue should it arise in some future case and we express no opinion on the merits of such a contention."

The situation not before us in *Olivas* is presented here. Appellant was adjudged under Juvenile Court Law as a juvenile. Pursuant to Welfare and Institutions Code section 726, subdivision (c), the maximum term for which he might be confined for the burglary was automatically set at three years. An adult or juvenile convicted in the criminal courts of committing the identical unlawful act could not, without a finding of aggravating circumstances, be imprisoned more than two years.

Despite this disparity, appellant has not been denied equal protection of the laws. The first prerequisite to a meritorious claim under the equal protection clause is a showing that the state has adopted a classification that affects two or more *similarly situated* groups in an unequal manner. Adults convicted in the criminal courts and sentenced to prison and youths adjudged wards of the juvenile courts and committed to the Youth Authority are not "similarly situated."

For purposes of this discussion, the most significant difference between minors and adults is that "[t]he liberty interest of a minor is qualitatively different than that of an adult, being subject both to reasonable regulation by the state to an extent not permissible with adults (Planned Parenthood of Cent. Mo. v. Danforth, supra [1976] 428 U.S. 52, [74], 96 S.Ct. 2831, 2843, 49 L.Ed.2d 788, [808]; Ginsberg v. New York [1968] 390 U.S. 629, 638 [20 L.Ed.2d 195, 203, 88 S.Ct. 1274]; Prince v. Massachusetts, supra [1944] 321 U.S. 158, 170, 64 S.Ct. 438, 88 L.Ed. 645, [654–655]), and to an even greater extent to the control of the minor's parents unless 'it appears that the parental decisions will jeopardize the health or safety of the child or have a potential for significant social burdens.' (Wisconsin v. Yoder [supra, 1972] 406 U.S. 205, 234, 92 S.Ct. 1526, 1542, 32 L.Ed.2d 15, [35].)" When the minor must be removed from the custody of his parents for his own welfare or for the safety and protection of the public, the state assuming the parents' role, the state also assumes the parents' authority to limit the minor's freedom of action.

" 'The concept of the equal protection of the laws compels recognition of the proposition that persons similarly situated with respect to the legitimate purpose of the law receive like treatment.' " (In re Gary W. (1971) 5 Cal.3d 296, 303, 96 Cal.Rptr. 1, 7, 486 P.2d 1201, 1207, quoting Purdy & Fitzpatrick v. State of California (1969), 71 Cal.2d 566, 578, 79 Cal.Rptr. 77, 85). The state does not have the same purpose in sentencing adults to prison that it has in committing minors to the Youth Authority. Adults convicted in the criminal courts are sentenced to prison as punishment while minors adjudged wards of the juvenile courts are committed to the Youth Authority for the purposes of treatment and rehabilitation (In re Aline D. (1975) 14 Cal.3d 557, 567).

This distinction has been significantly sharpened recently. Under the Indeterminate Sentence Law, which was the system under review in *Olivas*, the purposes of imprisonment were deterrence, isolation and rehabilitation. Not the least of these was rehabilitation. "It is generally recognized by the courts and by modern penologists that the purpose of the indeterminate sentence law, like other modern laws in relation to the administration of the criminal law, is to mitigate the punishment which would otherwise be imposed upon the offender. These laws place emphasis upon the reformation of the offender. They seek to make the punishment fit the criminal rather than the crime."

The enactment of the Uniform Determinate Sentencing Act marked a significant change in the penal philosophy of this state regarding adult offenders. "The Legislature finds and declares that the purpose of imprisonment for crime is punishment. This purpose is best served by terms proportionate to the seriousness of the offense with provision for uniformity in the sentences of offenders committing the same offense under similar circumstances. The Legislature further finds and declares that the elimination of disparity and the provision of uniformity of sentences can best be achieved by determinate sentences fixed by statute in proportion to the seriousness of the offense as determined by the Legislature to be imposed by the court with specified discretion." (Pen.Code, § 1170, subd. (a) (1).)

There has been no like revolution in society's attitude toward juvenile offenders. It is still true that "[j]uvenile commitment proceedings are designed for the purposes of rehabilitation and treatment, not punishment." Therefore, Juvenile Court Law continues to provide for indeterminate terms, with provision for parole as soon as appropriate. (Welf. & Inst.Code, § 1176.)

In *Olivas* this court objected that "[t]here has been no showing made that youthful offenders *necessarily* require longer periods of confinement for rehabilitative purposes than older adults." No such objection is appropriate here since under the Determinate Sentencing Act rehabilitation is no longer the standard for term fixing.

. . .

In conclusion, because minors and adults are not "similarly situated" with respect to their interest in liberty, and because minors adjudged wards of the juvenile courts and committed to the Youth Authority and adults convicted in the criminal courts and sentenced to prison are not confined for the same purposes. Welfare and Institutions Code section 726 does not deny minors equal protection of the laws.

. . .

NEWMAN, JUSTICE, dissenting:

I dissent because I agree with views that Justice Wiener articulated as follows when he wrote the opinion for the Court of Appeal in this case. . . .

. . .

"There are those who will undoubtedly say the juvenile has the best of both worlds. He obtains the benefits of the Indeterminate Sentence Law within the juvenile system with the opportunity of being released earlier than the outer limits of his commitment and the benefits of the limitation of a maximum term determined in accordance with the adult penal system. We do not view this as a dramatic result. It is only consistent with the purpose of the juvenile justice system which will still permit the juvenile to be released at any time before the service of the maximum term if deemed rehabilitated or retained for the maximum term if efforts at rehabilitation are unsuccessful. (Welf. & Inst.Code, § 1176.) As a practical matter, we suspect our decision will have little or no impact on the operation of the Youth Authority. There should be a direct correlation between the length of term imposed and successful rehabilitation of youthful offenders, i.e., those who are more likely to be rehabilitated will be given lesser terms; those less likely, longer terms. We anticipate the same class of offenders upon whom are imposed the upper term because of circumstances in aggravation will be identical to the class that would have otherwise remained incarcerated for the upper term.

"We recognize our decision creates an additional facet to the dispositional hearing (Welf. & Inst.Code, § 706) causing additional work for the presently overburdened personnel within the juvenile court system. We cannot allow this administrative consideration, important as it is, to outweigh the guarantees afforded to minors."

. . .

NOTES

(1) The Court in In re Eric J. discusses People v. Olivas, 17 Cal.3d 236, 131 Cal.Rptr. 55, 551 P.2d 375 (1976). In *Olivas*, the court held that equal protection was violated by a statutory scheme that allowed 16- to 21-year-old misdemeanants to be committed to the Youth Authority for a term potentially longer than the maximum jail term that could be imposed on a misdemeanant over 21 years old. The court held that the differential treatment of adults and 16- to 21-year-olds could only be justified by a compelling state interest. The People argued that the disparate treatment was justified by the state's interest in rehabilitating youths. The court rejected this argument. "There has been no showing made that youthful offenders *necessarily* require longer periods of confinement for rehabilitative purposes than older adults." Id. at 255–56 (emphasis in original).

Even though the *Olivas* Court did not directly undercut the importance of the rehabilitative ideal, Id. at 251–52, 257, the decision has been criticized for deprecating the goal of rehabilitation. One commentator has suggested that the result in *Olivas* is a reflection of the court's pragmatic view of the juvenile system: the court has realized that rehabilitation is only an ideal and not a reality. The reality is that a longer "rehabilitative commitment" for youthful offenders is actually greater punishment for the same prohibited behavior. Comment, People v. Olivas: Equalizing the Sentencing of Youthful Offenders With Adult Maximums, 4 Pepperdine L.Rev. 389 (1977).

In contrast to *Olivas*, the District of Columbia Court of Appeal in In re L.M., 432 A.2d 692 (D.C.App.1981), rejected a juvenile's equal protection challenge to her disposition that was considerably more restrictive than could have been imposed on an adult for the same conduct. For smoking on a bus, the trial judge placed her on probation for a year and required her to "obey the law, go to school, remain in the custody of her mother, observe an 8:00 p.m. curfew on weekdays and a 10:00 p. m. curfew on weekends and to stay away from her corespondent." The juvenile challenged her disposition as violative of equal protection in that an adult would only be subject to a maximum of $50 fine for the same violation. The court rejected the juvenile's argument holding that the differential treatment was justified by the government's interest in rehabilitating youthful offenders.

What would have been the result had the case been tried in a jurisdiction that had adopted the Standards on Disposition? What standard of review did the court appear to use in *Olivas*? In In re L.M.? Consider Footnote 4 of United States v. Carolene Products, 304 U.S. 144, 58 S.Ct. 778, 783–84, 82 L.Ed. 1234, 1241–42 (1938): ". . . prejudice against discrete and insular minorities may be a special condition, which tends seriously to curtail the operations of those political processes ordinarily to be relied upon to protect minorities, and which may call for a correspondingly more searching judicial inquiry." Are juveniles a "discrete and insular" minority? Is a "more searching" inquiry necessary when a juvenile is claiming that equal protection is being violated? What access do juveniles have to the political process? For further consideration of such equal protection claims see notes at p. 621 infra.

(2) Although the opinion in *Eric J.* seemed to ignore much of the pertinent statutory language, it has not been overruled.

Consider In re Gregory S., 85 Cal.App.3d 206, 149 Cal.Rptr. 216 (1978), which discussed more clearly the changes in California's statutory language relating to the purposes of the juvenile justice system. Gregory S. was a 13-year-old who was adjudicated a delinquent for kidnapping for the purpose of robbery. The trial court ordered him committed to the Youth Authority and the Court of Appeal affirmed on the basis of protecting the public.

. . . Although only 13 years old, Gregory was very aggressive and violent; pending disposition regarding two violent acts, battery and resisting arrest, he committed other more serious and more violent acts, armed robbery, burglary, and kidnapping for the purpose of robbery with physical assault upon a 15-year-old victim. Even though intelligent, Gregory seldom attended school and made no effort to assist himself. His threats to run away from any type of long-term placement required consideration of the need for a locked facility for his own good. The public was entitled to protection from further criminal acts of Gregory, further necessitating use of a locked facility. Gregory would benefit from the Youth Authority's educational facilities and a commitment to the Youth Authority was in his own best interests.

149 Cal.Rptr. at 220.

The court then held that *Gregory S.* was distinguishable on its facts from earlier cases such as *Aline D.* Moreover, the court reasoned, after *Aline D.*

the Legislature in 1977 (effective Jan. 1, 1978) amended Welfare and Institutions Code section 202 to provide that one of the purposes of the Juvenile Court Law is "to protect the public from criminal conduct by minors." This long overdue objective of juvenile justice was correctly taken into account in deciding upon the commitment.

In Alex T. v. Superior Court, 72 Cal.App.3d 24, 140 Cal.Rptr. 17 (1977), the juvenile sought to have a delinquency petition dismissed because an identical petition had been dismissed earlier when evidence was misplaced. The minor claimed that equal protection was violated by the refiling of the petition in that a petition could not be refiled against an adult. He argued that the amendments to the Juvenile Court Law made the purpose of the juvenile system punitive and therefore rehabilitation could not be used to justify the differential treatment of minors and adults. The court disagreed:

Petitioner places too much of a burden on these amendments. The dominant purpose of the Juvenile Court Law remains the welfare of the minor. At most, the amendments reflect legislative recognition that the welfare of the minor and the protection of the public may sometimes clash and that the latter consideration must be taken "into account . . . ." (§ 202, subd. (b), § 502, subd. (b).)

140 Cal.Rptr. at 23.

See also In re Carrie W., 89 Cal.App.3d 642, 152 Cal.Rptr. 690 (1979) ("the law is designed for the purpose of rehabilitation and treatment, not punishment").

(3) How substantially does the amendment of the California statute differ from the Juvenile Justice Standards? Would you expect different judicial response to a juvenile's equal protection claims under the Standards?

The entire Juvenile Justice Standards Project seems to rely on the concept of more precise legislative standards for the exercise of judicial discretion in the juvenile justice system—especially at disposition in delinquency cases. How does the California experience suggest limits on the viability of the Standards Project's efforts? What other means are available to the legislature to limit the discretion of juvenile judges? Would procedural requirements such as written statements of reasons to justify dispositions, more extensive appealability and periodic review of dispositions be of any more utility than recasted statements of legislative purpose in the effort to curtail judicial excesses?

C. DISPOSITIONAL ALTERNATIVES

1. SOME DIFFERING PERSPECTIVES

The section that follows presents not only traditional alternatives—dismissal, probation, and commitment to an institution—but also other alternatives, including commitment to an adult correctional authority, restitution, public service, and payment of fines. The materials reflect the view of the founders of the juvenile court movement that probation, or some other community-based form of treatment, be the rule and that commitment to an institution be the exception in arriving at an appropriate disposition for a child. In reading the materials that follow, consider how the philosophical change in juvenile justice will affect dispositional alternatives. For instance, will probation be as appropriate an alternative under a system whose goals are to punish the juvenile and to protect society? Additionally, a shift to proportionality should by definition have an impact on the dispositions available to the juvenile judge in a particular case. Within the framework of proportionality, however, the Standards do not suggest limiting the variety of dispositions. For the attorney who represents accused delinquents, often the most critical issue is devising an appropriate disposition. Frequently, the attorney is in the position of representing either someone who has admitted the delinquent behavior or someone who has left such a trail of evidence that the adjudicatory stage is merely pro forma. In this situation, often the most significant aid the attorney can render is to obtain the best possible disposition for his client. In their book Juvenile Law and Procedure, Monrad Paulsen and Charles Whitebread advise:

> The attorney's role at the dispositional hearing is especially important. He can assist the court and his client by attempting to validate the basis upon which a dispositional decision is made. The lawyer has the opportunity to participate actively in formulating a treatment plan.

> An order of disposition ought to be based on accurate facts, on informed judgments about the benefit the child can realistically be expected to receive and on a broad understanding of the treatment resources available to each count.

Mr. Justice Fortas' opinion in *Kent* emphasized that counsel has an obligation to "validate" the basis for disposition. The Court of Appeals had stated in Kent v. United States, 343 F.2d 247, 258 (D.C.Cir. 1965), that the lawyer's role was to present "anything on behalf of the child which might help a court in arriving at a decision; it is not to denigrate the staff's submissions and recommendations." Mr. Justice Fortas disagreed: "[O]n the contrary, if the state's submissions include materials which are susceptible to challenge or impeachment, it is precisely the role of counsel to 'denigrate' such matters." The Justice added that where important decisions are involved, the material which is used by the judge to reach his or her decision should "be subjected, within reasonable limits having regard to the Juvenile Court Act, to examination, criticism and refutation."

The great importance of having a lawyer present at a dispositional hearing is not recognized by everyone. To some the dispositional decision ought to be left to those who, it is supposed, know how to effect beneficial changes in human behavior. For these persons, the choices to be made are clinical or educational. "How can we best serve the needs of this child?" is the classic way of putting the issue. The answer, however, will often turn on an assertion of fact which ought to be tested by the "constant, searching, creative questioning" of the adversary process. Experts, particularly experts who must deal with large numbers of cases, grow weary, make mistakes, take short cuts, bend to frustration, and, in some cases, respond to dislike and prejudice.

Judge Lindsay G. Arthur of Minneapolis has this to say about a lawyer's task of "validating" the work of experts:

> A psychological report is an imposing document, exuding science, overawing the laity. But it can be based on mistakes. A social investigation is magnificent in its detail and completeness. But it is based heavily on hearsay. Hearsay can be unreliable as centuries of experience have demonstrated, and mistakes are unacceptable. A lawyer, familiar with the family, trained to analyze, experienced in cross-examination, can ensure that the disposition will be based on reliable facts and valid conclusions. As a corollary, the lawyer must know the contents of the reports, and most lawyers can be relied on to be discreet in their disclosure of these contents to the family. National Council of Juvenile Court Judges, Counsel for the Child 29 (1964).

Besides, the dispositional decision will be made by a judge, not the expert. A poor expert's advice needs testing; a skilled expert's recommendations deserve support. A family may have a point of view at the time of disposition that they may be unable to articulate. In the great cities of America, the children and their parents need a voice—literally a "mouthpiece." In addition, a good lawyer's intelligence is another resource that can be put to the question, "What are the various dispositional choices?"

There is one final point about the impact of a child's right to counsel at disposition where lawyers examine, criticize, and refute information submitted to the court by the probation staff. The members of the court staff will resist counsel playing such a role. They are likely to see a useful role for lawyers at the fact-finding or adjudicatory stage. If nothing else, television has instructed everyone that counsel has a place at a hearing designed to answer the question, "Did he do it?" In contrast, few in the probation staff will take kindly to the challenges put by lawyers to a probation officer's recommendations regarding the disposition of an adjudicated delinquent. The questions asked by advocates will seem like an attack on the officer's professional qualifications and integrity. The staff is likely to view lawyers as interlopers or as persons who will destroy the possibility of a close relationship between the probation officer and the child, or as misguided amateurs interfering with the delivery of benefits which can be derived from a court acting upon expert information. Yet in the long run both court and staff, it is submitted, will benefit from probing challenges.

M. Paulsen & C. Whitebread, Juvenile Law and Procedure 29–30 (1974).* See also J. Areen, Representing Juveniles in Neglect, PINS and Delinquency Cases in the District of Columbia: A Joint Project, (Washington: Bar Ass'n of the District of Columbia, 1975) and W. Vaughan Stapleton & L. Teitelbaum, In Defense of Youth: A Study of the Role of Counsel in American Juvenile Court (1972).

2. INCARCERATION

The disposition which is best from the juvenile's standpoint, is the one which is the least restrictive of his or her freedom. Objectively, however, the judge may find the best disposition for the juvenile is a rigidly disciplined institution.

Note the comments of the Court in *Gault* on the punitive nature of institutionalization:

> It is of no constitutional consequence—and of limited practical meaning—that the institution to which [a child] is committed is called an Industrial School. The fact of the matter is that, however euphemistic the title, a "receiving home" or an "industrial school" for juveniles is an institution of confinement in which the child is incarcerated for a greater or lesser time.

> His world becomes "a building with whitewashed walls, regimented routine and institutional laws . . ." Instead of mother and father and sisters and brothers and friends and classmates, his world is peopled by guards, custodians, state employees, and "delinquents" . . . . [387 U.S. at 17.]

with research findings suggesting that for certain types of youth measured by experience and maturity levels institutionalization may be more beneficial than release to the community. Warren, The Community Treatment Project, in N. Johnston, L. Savitz & M. Wolfgang, The Sociology of Punishment and Correction 671 (1970). See also Warren, Intervention with Juvenile Delinquents, in Pursuing Justice for the Child 176 (M. Rosenheim ed. 1976).

Read the facts of the following case and try to devise an appropriate dispositional order. First, put yourself in the role of the juvenile's attorney and then take the role of the judge.

* Copyright 1974, National Council of Juvenile Court Judges. Reprinted with permission.

IN RE CARRIE W., 89 Cal.App.3d 642, 152 Cal.Rptr. 690 (1979):

Brown (G. A.), P. J.—Appellant, Carrie W., [also called Carol] a 16-year-old minor, admitted the allegations of a petition filed under Welfare and Institutions Code section 602, charging her with violation of Penal Code section 502.7, subdivision (a)(1) (obtaining telephone services by fraud).

The acts forming the basis of the present petition occurred between July 30, 1977, and November 24, 1977, while Carrie was residing at the Florence Crittenton home for unwed mothers in Los Angeles pursuant to a placement order by the Kern County Juvenile Court. She was then 15 years old. During this period she placed unauthorized long distance telephone calls to her boyfriend (44 times), her mother (11 times), her aunt (4 times), her probation officer (1 time) and friends (51 times), totaling $338.53 in charges. She admitted that she made the calls "on whims" almost every day despite frequent warnings not to and even after her telephone privileges had been suspended. At the insistence of her social worker, appellant paid $50 of the money she earned while at Crittenton to the telephone company.

Her child was born November 19, 1977. On January 13, 1978, she went home to Bakersfield on leave and refused to return to Crittenton. She remained at home with her child, living with her mother and five siblings, and so far as appears on the record she was involved in no delinquent or criminal behavior.

Carrie had been a ward of the juvenile court since July 14, 1975, and spent two short periods in the Kern Youth Facility in 1976 for petty thefts. She was placed in a foster home in January 1977 but after a short period left there without permission to return home. In addition the probation report reflects that before July 14, 1975, she had been detained, admonished and released for two alleged petty thefts and a malicious mischief charge.

Carrie's mother and father were divorced. Her mother is ill and a welfare recipient. She is close to her mother, who feels Carrie should remain at home and take care of her baby. The home is a three-bedroom rented house in the lower socio-economic area of southeast Bakersfield.

During Carrie's stay at Crittenton she showed marked improvement in her school performance, had little difficulty in the parent-child care programs and showed significant improvement in her peer relationships. The flavor of these improvements can be fully appreciated only by quoting from the clinical presentation reports of November 29, 1977, and January 23, 1978 (closing summary).

In the report dated November 29, 1977, it is stated:

"Carol's adjustment to Florence Crittenton has been quite good though she has experienced some difficulty returning from passes on time. Carol's peer relationships are appropriate and she has been able to demonstrate caring feelings and anger and disappointment appropriately. Carol has established some close peer relationships and has also been able to relate well with staff . . . .

" . . . [Carrie's mother] is an ailing woman and is disabled due to a diabetic condition. Carol is very attached to her mother and siblings and has quite an extended family (some of whom reside in the Los Angeles area).

"Carol had a healthy daughter a week and one-half ago and she is doing very well adjusting to her new role. Since her return from the hospital (11–21–77) she has managed to maintain a routine, take care of herself, and consistently care for her child. She is exhibiting appropriate anxiety of a new mother and asks appropriate questions. She was a consistent participant in the prenatal class and is now a participant in the mother's group which occurs weekly.

"Carol's school performance is very good . . . .

"Carol's group performance is very good. She is a consistent participant and is able to exhibit concern and caring feelings. She is somewhat inhibited when it comes to role playing which speaks to her discomfort in acceptance.

"The goal for Carol to return to Bakersfield is a prevalent issue of Carol's. She is continually concerned about the length of time required before returning to her mother's home . . . . The current feeling is that separation of mother and child would be very detrimental to both their well beings, and that every effort should be made to continue them in placement."

The report dated January 23, 1978 (closing summary) states in pertinent part:

"Carol seemed continually homesick and, yet, she would verbalize her desire to complete vocational training at Florence Crittenton as well as her desire that her mother relocate to a larger home. Carol seemed unable to view herself in the future as independent. She feels she will need to care for her mother as her younger brothers grow up. This inability to separate is possibly due to guilt feelings Carol may have because she is away from her mother . . . .

"Carol is an appealing young lady who is able to function with minimal limit setting in an open placement . . . . Carol's self concept has not developed to its fullest and with continued counseling and support this seems possible. She has potential to be a supportive, firm young mother and this should be enhanced by further instruction and supervision. Separation from her infant is not recommended because she is still in the early phase of relationship building and she may learn to rely too heavily on another (possibly her mother) . . . . She refused offers to use an agency phone once-a-week to call home. It seemed that she needed the almost daily contact with those in Bakersfield."

The reports also indicate that Carrie has a poor self-image, is manipulative and somewhat secretive and was suspected of lying about others. She was persistently a day or more late in returning to Crittenton after going home on passes. The report indicates there were reciprocal charges of petty thievery between Carrie and her fellow residents.

The probation officer's report submitted at the time of the dispositional hearing made the following observations:

"The minor is responsible for the care of her six month old daughter and is neither working nor attending school. Carrie has advised this officer that she feels nothing should be done to her as she hopes to 'pay back the money.' She has not attempted to pay back any money nor has she looked for employment in the interim period (January, 1978 to the present). Carrie does not feel that she should be forced to do anything against her wishes. It appears that Kern Youth Facility commitments, foster home and facility placements have not been effective in the rehabilitation of this minor. Carrie is an intelligent young lady but appears to have no desire to benefit by the opportunities presented her. A Youth Authority commitment is felt to be appropriate in this case."

"However, the minor has exhibited an attitude of defiance during the several months of placement and has disregarded reprimands administered by this officer and Lee Pipes, the minor's social worker."

"Carrie's past history appears to be filled with defiance of authority and determination to do her own thing.

"Carrie, being an obstinate and strong-willed young lady, is determined to behave as she pleases irregardless [sic] of orders given by the Court or the rules and regulations given by those who are in authority."

What is an appropriate disposition in Carrie's case? What disposition would Carrie want? What would she need? How would your disposition change if the following facts were changed or added:

(1) Carrie's parents are not divorced.

(2) Carrie is working full time to support herself.

(3) Carrie lives with her family in a wealthy suburb.

(4) Carrie is borderline retarded.

(5) Carrie has no previous record.

(6) Carrie's mother is not ill.

The appellate court, in overturning the juvenile judge's disposition of Carrie to an institution in the California Juvenile Corrections System said in part:

We are, of course, aware that a juvenile court's commitment to the CYA (California Youth Authority) can only be reversed for an abuse of discretion, and in evaluating the evidence and making that determination an appellate court must apply the substantial evidence test. However, whether a commitment in a particular case conforms to the general purposes of the juvenile court law is necessarily included when determining whether a commitment constitutes an abuse of discretion.

For reasons we have set forth, on this record, the conclusion is compelled that appropriate standards for commitment to the CYA were not applied, notwithstanding the court's pro forma finding that the CYA commitment would be of benefit to Carrie. 152 Cal. Rptr. at 690, 695.

Carrie's behavior is relatively tame compared to some other juvenile cases. What disposition would you order in the following case?

———

ANDERSON v. STATE, 381 So.2d 1019 (Miss.1980):

LEE, JUSTICE, for the Court.

There is little contradiction in the evidence. Mrs. Robbie Moore testified for the State that on July 28, 1977, she drove by the home of the victim in Moorehead, Mississippi, and she noticed a young black person [appellant was a black male fifteen (15) years of age] talking to the victim, who was a 16-year-old white girl. Mrs. Monroe continued on her way across town, but, being aware of the victim's mental condition, she returned and observed parts of their lower extremities sticking out from behind an air-conditioning unit located adjacent to the victim's home. She saw appellant get up, run to his bicycle, which was nearby, and ride off. Mrs. Moore found the victim lying nude on the ground and bleeding profusely from her vagina. She called the victim's mother, who was inside the house, and the child was taken to the hospital.

Appellant was apprehended, was identified as the assailant by Mrs. Moore, and he freely and voluntarily admitted the act. Appellant testified at the trial. His testimony did not contradict that of Mrs. Moore or his statement given to the officers, except that he claimed the victim stopped him and asked him to engage in the sexual act. Appellant described the victim to Officer William Staten as being "the one that waves real funny and the one that's kind of off in the head."

Physical examination of the victim by Dr. Walter Rose in the emergency room at the North Sunflower County Hospital reflected that she was bleeding profusely from her vagina, that blood had run down her legs and feet and had dried in those areas, and that she was still bleeding from a tear in her hymen at the time of his examination. She also had a large blood clot on the left side, and at the entrance, of her vagina. Dr. Rose administered a local anesthetic and repaired and sutured the torn areas. He also testified that live sperm was found in the victim's vagina. It was uncontradicted that the victim had been retarded since birth, she could speak only in monosyllables, and had the mind and intellect of a four-year-old child.

Appellant introduced evidence to the effect that he, too, was retarded, that his IQ was only 31, that he was enrolled in special education classes after about the third grade, and that he did not have the intellect to distinguish right from wrong. On the contrary, Dr. Donald Guild and Dr. C. S. Stanley, an eminent psychiatrist and psychologist, respectively, at Mississippi State Hospital, Whitfield, Mississippi, testified that appellant was of normal intelligence, had no evidence of psychosis or major mental disorder, had an IQ within normal range of 91, and was not retarded.

What factors are relevant in determining an appropriate disposition in this case? Did you consider an institutional placement? Would it matter what services were available in the institution? In *Anderson*, the defendant was tried as an adult and sentenced to 15 years in the state penitentiary.

Finally, what is the appropriate standard of review of juvenile court dispositional orders? Did the California court apply the abuse of discretion standard correctly in reviewing and reversing Carrie W.'s disposition? For a more complete discussion of appellate review, see chapter X infra.

STATE EX REL. D. D. H. v. DOSTERT

Supreme Court of Appeals of West Virginia, 1980.
269 S.E.2d 401.

NEELY, CHIEF JUSTICE:

In this case we shall endeavor, with some apprehension, to clarify the proper procedures at the dispositional stage of a juvenile proceeding. . . .

. . .

I

At the outset it is important to recognize that the juvenile law in West Virginia has been in substantial turmoil since this court's decision in State ex rel. Harris v. Calendine, W.Va., 233 S.E.2d 318 (1977) which, among other things, prompted an entire revision of the statutory juvenile law. Historically, protecting society from juvenile delinquency and helping juvenile offenders modify their behavior have been seen as complementary goals of the juvenile law; however, it is now generally recognized that caring for the juvenile and controlling the juvenile are often quite contradictory processes. Much of our juvenile law at the moment is predicated upon a healthy skepticism about the capacity of the State and its agents to help children when they are incarcerated in one of the juvenile detention facilities. Thus, the control of juveniles and the treatment of juveniles (if the expression can be used without conjuring Kafkaesque images) are frequently irreconcilable goals. Furthermore, children can be dangerous, destructive, abusive, and otherwise thoroughly anti-social, which prompts an entirely understandable expectation in society of protection, even if we have matured beyond expecting retribution.

The dispositional stage of a juvenile proceeding is designed to do something which is almost impossible, namely, to reconcile: (1) society's interest in being protected from dangerous and disruptive children; (2) society's interest in nurturing its children in such a way that they will be productive and successful adults; (3) society's interest in providing a deterrent to other children who, but for the specter of the juvenile law, would themselves become disruptive and unamenable to adult control; (4) the citizen's demand that children be responsible for invasion of personal rights; and, (5) the setting of an example of care, love, and forgiveness by the engines of the state in the hope that such qualities will be emulated by the subject children.[8] While

---

8. Many states have been wrestling with some statutory reconciliation of these competing goals. In this regard it is interesting to compare the 1977 amendment to W.Va. Code, 49–1–1(a), the purpose clause for the child welfare chapter, with the 1978 amendment to the same section. The difference is subtle, but it demonstrates a recognition that child welfare cannot be completely "child centered." W.Va. Code, 49–1–1(a) [1977] says:

The purpose of this chapter is to provide a comprehensive system of child welfare throughout the State which will assure to each child such care and guidance, preferably in his own home, as will serve the spiritual, emotional, mental and physical welfare of the child; preserve and strengthen the child's family ties whenever possible with recognition to the fundamental rights of parenthood and with recognition of the state's responsibility to assist the family in providing the necessary education and training and protect the welfare of the general public. In

pursuit of these goals it is the intention of the legislature to provide for removing the child from the custody of parents only when the child's welfare or the safety and protection of the public cannot be adequately safeguarded without removal; and, when the child has to be removed from his own family, to secure for him custody, care and discipline as nearly as possible equivalent to that which should have been given by his parents, consistent with the child's best interests.

W.Va. Code, 49–1–1(a) [1978] says:

The purpose of this chapter is to provide a comprehensive system of child welfare throughout the State which will assure to each child such care and guidance, preferably in his own home, as will serve the spiritual, emotional, mental and physical welfare of the child; preserve and strengthen the child's family ties whenever possible with recognition to the fundamental rights of parenthood and with recognition of the state's responsibility to as-retribution is considered an unhealthy instinct and, conceivably, an immoral instinct in an enlightened society, nonetheless, State imposed retribution has historically been the *quid pro quo* of the State's monopoly of force and its proscription of individual retribution. Retribution is merely another way of saying that children are to be treated as responsible moral agents.

II

It is possible to make the dispositional stage of a juvenile proceeding so burdensome in requiring exhaustive examination of all "less restrictive alternatives," no matter how speculative, that we, in effect, direct lower courts to abandon all hope of confining a child.[9] That is not the clear purport, however, of W.Va. Code, 49–5–13(b) [1978] which says:

> In disposition the court shall not be limited to the relief sought in the petition and shall give precedence to the least restrictive of the following alternatives *consistent with the best interests and welfare of the public and the child . . . .*
>
> [Emphasis supplied by the Court.]

W.Va. Code 49–5–13(b)(5) [1978] says:

> Upon a finding that no less restrictive alternative would accomplish the requisite rehabilitation of the child, and upon an adjudication of delinquency pursuant to subdivision (1), section four [§ 49–1–4], article one of this chapter, commit the child to an industrial home or correctional institution for children. Commitments shall not exceed the maximum term for which an adult could have been sentenced for the same offense, with discretion as to discharge to rest with the director of the institution, who may release the child and return him to the court for further disposition; . . . .

As David Dudley Field, author of the *Field Code*, once pointed out, substantive law can be "gradually secreted in the interstices of procedure." Consequently, it is important to explain exactly what the

---

sist the family in providing the necessary education and training *and to reduce the rate of juvenile delinquency and to provide a system for the rehabilitation or detention of juvenile delinquents and protect the welfare of the general public.* In pursuit of these goals it is the intention of the legislature to provide for removing the child from the custody of parents only when the child's welfare or the safety and protection of the public cannot be adequately safeguarded without removal; and, when the child has to be removed from his own family, to secure for him custody, care and discipline *consistent with the child's best*

interests and other goals herein set out. [Emphasis supplied by the Court]

9. Our Court has recently examined the procedures that must be followed before a juvenile may be properly committed to a juvenile correctional facility in State ex rel. S.J.C. v. Fox, W.Va., 268 S.E.2d 56 (1980). We followed the same procedure established in State ex rel. E.D. v. Aldredge, W.Va., 245 S.E.2d 849 (1978) which required that the court set forth a finding on the record that no less restrictive alternative was available before a transfer to criminal jurisdiction could be effected. . . .

elaborate procedure at the dispositional stage is designed to do. Unless there are clear, understandable standards, procedure becomes confounding at best and disguised legislation at worst.

Chapter 49 of the W.Va. Code covering child welfare is clearly committed to the rehabilitative model. As we noted in State ex rel. Harris v. Calendine, W.Va., 233 S.E.2d 318, 325 (1977),

> The Legislature could choose to punish children guilty of criminal conduct in the same manner as it punishes adults, but as a matter of public policy the Legislature provided instead for a comprehensive system of child welfare. The aim of this system is to protect and rehabilitate children, not to punish them.

The rehabilitative model requires a great deal of information about the child at the dispositional hearing. Much of that information must necessarily focus on the critical issue of whether it is *possible* for the State or other social service agencies to help the child. Although helping the child is the first concern of the juvenile law, it is not the only concern, since at the *operational* rather than *theoretical* level, the rehabilitative approach has dramatic limitations, preeminent among which is that it interferes both with the deterrence of other children and the protection of society. While *Code*, 49–5–13(b) explicitly recognizes this problem, we have not yet refined an approach which intelligently uses procedure to arrive at sufficient information to permit a balancing of the child's liberty interest with society's need for protection and deterrence.

. . .

IV

At the dispositional stage of the juvenile proceeding there are a number of actors whose roles have been established by statute. The first major actor is obviously the judge who, according to W.Va. Code, 49–5–13(a) [1978], is entitled to request the juvenile probation officer or State department worker to make an investigation of the environment of the child and the alternative dispositions possible. The second actor is the probation officer or State department worker who must fulfill this obligation, and the third actor is the counsel for the petitioner who is entitled to review any report made by the probation officer or welfare worker seventy-two hours before the dispositional hearing. In addition there is the child and his parents, guardian, or adult relatives, and the representatives of any social service agencies, including the schools, which have been involved in the case. Since the threshold question at any dispositional hearing is whether the child is delinquent because of his own free will or for environmental reasons which society can attack directly, all of the actors in the dispositional drama should concentrate their attention initially on that one subject. Obviously this is a question which the trial judge has always answered in his own mind. However, the thrust of the formal procedural model which has been evolving is that this question be developed on the record and reasons for determining a particular disposition be articulated for appellate review. We shall now focus on the role of each major actor.

THE ROLE OF COURT APPOINTED COUNSEL:

The dispositional stage of any juvenile proceeding may be the most important stage in the entire process; therefore, it is the obligation of any court appointed or retained counsel to continue active and vigorous representation of the child through that stage. We have already held that counsel has a duty to investigate all resources available to find the least restrictive alternative, State ex rel. C.A.H. v. Strickler, W.Va., 251 S.E.2d 222 (1979), and here we confirm that holding. Court appointed counsel must make an independent investigation of the child's background. Counsel should present to the court any facts which could lead the court to conclude that the child's environment is a major contributing factor to his misbehavior. In this regard counsel should investigate the child's performance in school, his family background, the level of concern and leadership on the part of his parents, the physical conditions under which the child is living, and any health problems. Counsel must also inform himself in detail about the facilities both inside and outside the State of West Virginia which are able to help children.[13]

Armed with adequate information, counsel can then present the court with all reasonable alternative dispositions to incarceration and should have taken the initial steps to secure the tentative acceptance of the child into those facilities. It is not sufficient to suggest upon the record as an abstract proposition that there are alternatives; it is the affirmative obligation of counsel to advise the court of the exact terms, conditions, and costs of such alternatives, whether the Department of Welfare or any other source can pay for such alternative, and under what conditions any alternative facilities would be willing to accept the child.

The faithful discharge of these duties requires substantial industry; however, appointed counsel is entitled to be compensated for his time up to the statutory limit set for the criminal charges fund. Furthermore, energetic advocacy implies that the court must accommodate an adversarial proceeding at the disposition stage. In the case at bar, the court reacted to the legitimate efforts of the appointed attorney to arrange an alternative disposition by finding him in contempt and removing him from his appointment. Such practices are

---

13. The Department of Welfare must prepare a descriptive catalogue of its juvenile programs and services at least once a year and those catalogues are to be readily available under W.Va. Code, 49–5B–7 [1979]. Furthermore, the West Virginia Child Care Association (WVC CA) publishes a Residential Child Care Directory which describes available services. In addition, the WVCCA maintains a Resource Center with a statewide telephone information service designed to assist social workers, agencies, lawyers and others in placing young people in the most appropriate group home or group child care agency. Their office is open Monday–Friday, 8:30 a.m.–5:00 p.m. and their telephone number is (304) 335–6211.

obviously condemned since it is envisaged that the child shall have an advocate who will make a record.[14]

The court undermined the efforts of counsel from the outset of the trial: counsel was given approximately thirty minutes to prepare before the first detention hearing, after which petitioner was placed in the Jefferson County Jail; after counsel obtained release of petitioner she was again placed in the Jefferson County Jail for failing to attend school and counsel received no notice of the second detention hearing; after counsel obtained release of petitioner she was arrested and taken before the court who placed her in the Morgan County Jail again without notice or presence of the child's counsel and with no record save the summary order; after petitioner was adjudicated delinquent, counsel represented the willingness of the Odyssey House in Morgantown to take petitioner for a trial period but the court refused all less restrictive alternatives; and, after placement in the Industrial Home for Girls counsel continued actively to pursue probation for petitioner to which the court reacted by withdrawing the appointment of counsel and requiring his appearance at a contempt hearing. This conduct is so unjustifiable that the State chose not even to address the validity of the contempt citation in its brief.

. . .

THE ROLE OF THE PROBATION OFFICER OR WELFARE WORKER:

The probation officer or welfare worker when requested by the judge is also responsible for discovering whether there are forces which are at work upon the child which either the Department of Welfare or other social service agencies can correct. In the case before us it is obvious that the petitioner had no adult supervision whatsoever and that she was left to fend for herself in the back streets. Obviously, before incarcerating a first offender like the petitioner it would have been incumbent upon the Department of Welfare to find a suitable environment for her. The record amply demonstrates from the history of the petitioner *after* this Court released her from the industrial school, that the petitioner is a somewhat unmanageable and ungovernable child who, at the time, would not remain in a juvenile refuge.[15] Nonetheless, absent at least one predisposition incidence of flight from a reasonable alternative, it was quite improper for the court to place her in the first instance in the industrial school. Upon remand the court must focus on her level of cooperation at the time she is again considered for disposition at the remand.

14. For a cogent analysis of the defense counsel's role in dispositions, *see* IJA/ABA Juvenile Justice Standards Project, Standards Relating to Juvenile Counsel for Private Parties, pp. 168–87 (1977).

15. Petitioner was placed in the Odyssey House, a group home, after her petition for a writ of habeas corpus was granted by this Court and she ran away from that placement. Evidence that is before our Court, but which was not before the circuit court, indicates that petitioner was apprehended in a stolen car on at least two other occasions after her initial disposition.

The record before us also demonstrates that the Department of Welfare did not intervene with this child upon her initial arrest, although any inquiry into her background would have disclosed at the detention hearing that she was in need of help. The appropriate time for the Department of Welfare or the juvenile probation officer to intervene is at the first sign of trouble.

THE ROLE OF THE COURT:

It is the obligation of the court to hear all witnesses who might shed light upon the proper disposition of a child and before incarcerating a child, to find facts *upon the record* which would lead a reasonable appellate court to conclude in the words of the statute, either that "no less restrictive alternative would accomplish the requisite rehabilitation of the child . . . " or "the welfare of the public" requires incarceration. Where the court directs incarceration, he should affirmatively find upon the record either that the child's behavioral problem is not the result of social conditions beyond the child's control, but rather of an intentional failure on the part of the child to conform his actions to the law, or that the child will be dangerous if any other disposition is used, or that the child will not cooperate with any rehabilitative program absent physical restraint. Where the court concludes that simple punishment will be a more effective rehabilitative device than anything else, the conclusion is certainly legitimate and within the discretion of the trial court; nonetheless, the trial court must elaborate on the record his reasons for that conclusion.

If the proceeding is merely the last in a long series involving the same child, the court should set forth any "less restrictive alternatives" which have already been tried and the actions of the child after those alternatives were implemented. Even when the child's behavior results from environmental factors, the court may find the child to pose an imminent danger to society because he will flee from all but secure facilities and, therefore, conclude that incarceration is the only *reasonable* alternative.

The court has a duty to insure that the child's social history is reviewed intelligently so that an individualized treatment plan may be designed when appropriate. This information also insures that the disposition decision is not made simply by reference to the very misbehavior which is the ground for the juvenile proceeding. The effectiveness of treatment is disputed to say the least, and this is particularly true whenever commitment to an institution is involved. Therefore, the judge making the dispositional determination should not place a child who is not dangerous and who can be accommodated elsewhere in an institution under the guise of "treating" the child.

While in the hearing before this Court it appeared that progress has been made in providing basic education and counseling in the State's industrial schools, the fact that these schools have improved does not make them the proper place for "rehabilitation" unless it appears that the child is either dangerous or must be restrained in a secure facility in order to prevent his flight.

. . .

When . . . , there is a consistent pattern of noncooperation which makes alternative rehabilitative programs impossible, the court should set forth the facts upon the record so that this Court will understand why the trial court concludes that there are no alternatives to placement in an institution.[19]

. . .

Commitment to an institution is the most severe disposition that can be imposed upon a juvenile. Generally, institutionalization is considered a last resort to be used only when other alternatives clearly are unacceptable. Note how the concurring opinion in *Gregory S.*, summarizes some of the problems in juvenile institutions.

IN RE GREGORY S.

California Court of Appeal, Third District, 1978.
85 Cal.App.3d 206, 149 Cal.Rptr. 216.

[For the court's opinion by Paras, J. see p. 548, supra.]

REYNOSO, J., concurring in the result only.

. . .

We deal with a youngster who, at the time of the hearing, was 13 years old and weighed 95 pounds.

19. Some states have been more specific in rewriting their purpose clauses to reflect the legislative determination that rehabilitation alone does not exhaust the purposes of the juvenile justice system. For example, California added the [italicized] sections to its purpose clauses:

(a) The purpose of this chapter is to secure for each minor under the jurisdiction of the juvenile court such care and guidance, preferably in his own home, as will serve the spiritual, emotional, mental, and physical welfare of the minor and the best interests of the state; *to protect the public from criminal conduct by minors; to impose on the minor a sense of responsibility for his own acts*; to preserve and strengthen the minor's family ties whenever possible, removing him from the custody of his parents only when necessary for his welfare or for the safety and protection of the public . . . and, when the minor is removed from his own family, to secure for him custody, care, and discipline as nearly as possible equivalent to that which should have been given by his parents. This chapter shall be liberally construed to carry out these purposes.

(b) *The purpose of this chapter also includes the protection of the public from the consequences of criminal activity, and to such purpose probation officers, peace officers, and juvenile courts shall take into account such protection of the public in their determinations under this chapter.* Cal. [Welf. & Inst.] Code, § 202 [1977]. (Emphasis added.)

In Virginia the old purpose clause focused solely on the welfare of the child, Va.Code § 16.1-140 [1956], while the revised statute includes the purpose of "protect[ing] the community against those acts of its citizens which are harmful to others and . . . reduc[ing] the incidence of delinquent behavior." Va. Code § 16.1-227 [1977].

The statute declares that such a youngster cannot be committed to the Youth Authority without a finding on the part of the juvenile court that the incarceration is in the boy's best interest. (Welf. & Inst. Code, § 734.)[2] The trial court has thus ruled that the minor will be benefitted by such incarceration. The statute places the juvenile court in a position of deciding that it is in the best interest of a 13 year old to be incarcerted with older, criminally prone, juveniles in a setting where physical assaults, including sexual attacks, are all too common. How can this be?

The statutory scheme comtemplates a Youth Authority very different from today's reality. The Youth Authority was initially established to benefit youngsters of tender years who would benefit from the educational, rehabilitative, and other helpful efforts. In fact, today's Youth Authority is reserved for "the most severely delinquent youths" (*In re Aline D.*, supra, 14 Cal.3d at p. 564), many of whom reach the Youth Authority through the criminal courts rather than through the juvenile courts. The legislative ideal of rehabilitation has never been a reality, and it is far less so today than yesteryear.

The officials who enforce the law against juveniles have always been far more realistic than the statutes contemplate. Thus, juvenile court judges have traditionally viewed their priorities in dealing with youths as follows: first, rehabilitation; second, deterrence; third, protection of society; and fourth, punishment. When dealing with a crime of violence, even with a boy as young as Gregory, the probation department official tried to balance the interest of the child with the interest of protecting society. That is reality.

Let us examine the sad facts of this case. We deal with a Black youngster who had gotten into the company of some older boys. With them he committed a series of crimes, some of violence. The youngster, according to the probation officer, was used as a mascot by the older boys.

At the dispositional hearing, the juvenile court considered only those matters which were the subject of findings or admissions. The judge had before him for disposition the following:

(1) Petition dated April 18:

    Count I—Battery (Pen. Code. § 242).

(2) Petition dated July 14:

    Count III—Resisting arrest (Pen. Code. § 148).

---

2. Welfare and Institutions Code section 734 reads as follows: "No ward of the juvenile court shall be committed to the Youth Authority unless the judge of the court is fully satisfied that the mental and physical condition and qualifications of the ward are such as to render it probable that he will be benefitted by the reformatory educational discipline or other treatment provided by the Youth Authority."

(3) Petition dated October 18:

  Count I—Kidnapping for purpose of robbery (Pen. Code. § 209).

(4) Petition dated October 21:

  Count I—Robbery (Pen. Code. § 211).

  Count II—Burglary (Pen. Code. § 459).

    . . . While the youth had a propensity for assaultive behavior the probation department rejected the notion of committing him to the Youth Authority for three related reasons. . . .

    The first reason for rejection of Youth Authority by the probation department deals with rehabilitation. Gregory, the probation officer reported, would have a far better opportunity if placed with the Exell James Group Home in Riverside, California. The probation officer had confidence that the home could control Gregory, that a male role model would be afforded, and that he would learn to deal with community standards: This ties to the testimony of the psychologist who found nothing emotionally wrong with Gregory but found that he was conforming to his concepts (rather than community norms) of what a young man growing into adulthood should do. Gregory had been living with his grandmother. What happened to his mother and father does not appear in the record. It does appear that Gregory appears to have had a mother who gave him a good, solid emotional foundation in the first few years of his life.

    The second reason deals with the Youth Authority. Because of Gregory's age and small stature, the probation department felt that he would be subject to assualt, including sexual assault, in the Youth Authority facilities. Were he to avoid that result, he would do so only by aligning himself with some bigger, tougher youngsters with even greater criminal dispositions. That is, Gregory would learn to be a "better" criminal.

    Third, the interest of society would be protected without resort to the Youth Authority. Gregory needed the close supervision at the group home. Perhaps society would be saved the further trauma of another life dedicated to crime. One of the problems with Gregory, all witnesses agreed, was that he lived in an unstructured environment where involvement in violent criminal behavior seemed to have its own rewards.

    The probation office tried to balance the interest of helping the minor and that of protecting society. According to the probation officer, "unless there is such a threat to society that society's welfare takes precedence over the potential treatment versus punishment of the individual," the youngster should not be placed in a "purely punitive setting."

    . . .

    The prosecutor argued at the dispositional hearing that the type of facility that could be most beneficial to Gregory was simply not available. The prosecution argued: "We just don't have anything available other than Youth Authority in that regard, at least in our county, or as far as I'm aware, statewide." Thus, the prosecution's recommendation was that the youth be sent to the Youth Authority "for protection of society." There was no pretense that the youth would be benefitted.

A youngster who violates the law by involving himself in a crime of violence expects to be punished. The record indicates that Gregory expected such punishment. Youngsters, however, have a greater capacity to change than do adults. Further, we as a society have a greater responsibility to attempt to socialize the young than we do with respect to adults. Finally, a youngster is far more subject to peer pressure in becoming involved in criminal behavior (as was Gregory); he can become involved in criminal behavior without yet being a hardened criminal (and Gregory was not a hardened criminal). Thus we cannot give up on the notion of rehabilitation.

The juvenile laws, since they found their way into the California statutes in 1915, support the commonsensical approach of rehabilitation and protection of society. Thus present Welfare and Institutions Code section 202 indicates that the purpose of juvenile law is "to secure for each minor" the care and guidance which will serve the "spiritual, emotional, mental and physical welfare" of that given minor. Deterrence is also mentioned, for another purpose is to protect the "best interest of the state" and to protect the public from "criminal conduct by the minors." Also an aim is the "protection of the public from the consequences of criminal activity" of the minors and "to impose on the minor a sense of responsibility for his own acts." It seems manifest that the best rehabilitative interest of the minor, together with the protection of society, demands punishment when a crime of violence has been committed. Only retributive punishment is proscribed.

Except in the most extreme case the law, in the case of a 13 year old, should not contemplate giving up its rehabilitative aim. The juvenile court seems to have done just that.

The reasons given by the juvenile judge for commitment to the Youth Authority (schooling, discipline and control) could also be met by a placement in a boys' ranch, or to a lesser extent, the home placement. . . .

There is a saving grace. The law contemplates that the Youth Authority may form its own judgment as to whether or not it will accept a youngster. (Welf. & Inst. Code, § 736.) In rare cases, perhaps this one, the Youth Authority will refuse to accept the placement.

———

CREDIT FOR GOOD BEHAVIOR?

Is a juvenile entitled to good behavior credit for time spent in a youth authority facility? In People v. Reynolds, 116 Cal.App.3d 141, 171 Cal.Rptr. 461 (1981), a California Court of Appeal answered this question in the negative in the case of a juvenile who was first sent to the California Youth Authority, then returned to court and sentenced to prison for being incorrigible. Although the youth contended that his prison sentence should be adjusted to reflect good time in the Youth Authority, the court held that the applicable statute did not authorize good time credits for juveniles and that the state's interest in rehabilitating them justified denying them such credits while extending credits to adults. The court further noted that the juvenile's good time claim was logically inconsistent with his removal from the Youth Authority for incorrigibility.

In People v. Austin, 111 Cal.App.3d 148, 168 Cal.Rptr. 511 (1980), however, another Court of Appeal held that equal protection mandated that a juvenile have the opportunity to earn behavior credits while in Youth Authority and presentence custody. Otherwise, the court reasoned, juveniles and their counsel would face a "Hobson's choice". The juvenile who argued he could be rehabilitated might be sent to the Youth Authority but not allowed good time credits. Alternatively, he might profess incorrigibility in the hope of being sent to prison where he could receive good time credits and therefore be released earlier. See also In re Eric J., 25 Cal.3d 522, 159 Cal.Rptr. 317, 601 P.2d 549 (1979); In re Maurice S., 90 Cal.App.3d 190, 153 Cal.Rptr. 317 (1979). In the latter the court held that:

> Youth Authority confinement of juveniles and Adult Authority confinement of adult prisoners share for the purposes of equal protection analysis a common purpose of punishment. No basis has been found for distinguishing between Youth Authority inmates and adult prisoners in regard to credit for time in confinement.

Thus the youth was entitled to good time credit.

Juveniles are not entitled to precommitment credit on precisely the same basis as adults, however. In re Ricky H., 30 Cal.3d 176, 178 Cal.Rptr. 324, 636 P.2d 13 (1981).

The Juvenile Justice Standards Relating to Dispositions provide:

5.3. Reduction for good behavior

The correctional agency with the responsibility for a juvenile may reduce the duration of the juvenile's disposition by an amount not to exceed [5] percent of the original disposition if the juvenile has refrained from major infractions of the dispositional order or of the reasonable regulations governing any facility to which the juvenile is assigned.

COMMUNITY–BASED TREATMENT: THE MASSACHUSETTS EXPERIMENT

In 1970 Massachusetts began a series of reforms in its juvenile corrections system that ultimately led to closing the state training schools in 1972. Through its Department of Youth Services it moved faster and farther toward deinstitutionalization and the establishment of a community-based network of social services than any other state. Many of the new programs were purchased services from the private sector. The experiment provided a broad empirical data base for studying the effectiveness of community-based corrections. In their extensive study of the Massachusetts experiment, Coates, Miller and Ohlin concluded that a community-based system is a workable and indeed preferable alternative to an institutional or training school system. Some of their findings are excerpted below.

R. Coates, A. Miller, & L. Ohlin, Diversity in a Youth Correctional System: Handling Delinquents in Massachusetts 176–78 (1978) *

When we compare responses of a sample of youths from the traditional training-school cottages with a sample from the community-based system, it is evident that youths in the community-based system are more likely to believe that they are exposed to more humane care. These youngsters are more likely to have better relationships with staff and their peers than did youths in the training schools. One does not find the existence of negative peer subcultures to the same extent in the new system as in the old. In addition, youths in the community programs are more favorably disposed toward the reward and punishment measures being employed than youths in the training schools. Observations also support the belief that the use and threat of physical force have diminished during the transition from training schools to community-based programs. While abuses still do remain, and the programs need to be closely monitored to control such abuses, generally the relationships between staff and youths and among youths show sharp improvement.

Linkages between the youths and the community have been greatly expanded in the newly constructed system. In the training-school sample, only 6 percent of the respondents indicated that they had routine contact with the community. In the new system over 50 percent of the youths indicated that they had such contact. However, from the distribution of youths and programs across the institu-tionalization-normalization continuum, it seems clear that most of the youths are in programs that, while more closely linked to local com-munities than the training schools of the past, are still not adequately interacting with the youths' network of family, peers, school officials, and vocational opportunities. This deficiency may be due in part to the community's apathy or its fear of these youths, or it may reflect the private agency's distrust of the community or its need to hold on to youths in order to continue functioning. These issues will be dealt with more fully below.

Short-term outcomes such as improved self-image, improved per-ception of others, and enhanced expectations and aspirations increase in settings that can be described as more normalized within the pro-grams and the community. Again, the data support the notion that the department, in replacing the training-school system with a com-munity-based system, made a move in the right direction.

Long-term gains in self-image, perception of others, and expecta-tions and aspirations were generally not realized. Both pre- and post-program experience in the community tended to affect these out-comes more dramatically than did program experiences. Frequently, short-run gains were diminished as the youths returned to their com-munity networks. Follow-up work with youths in their normal living situations appears to be a badly needed missing link in the delivery of services by the department.

Recidivism, another long-term measure of the youngsters' reinte-gration into the community without further delinquent behavior, proved a complex indicator. Comparisons between a training-school sample and the community-based sample showed an increase in recidi-vism for the latter group. While numerous possible explanations of this difference are plausible, such as the older age of the community-based sample, it seems clear that the new system did not systemati-cally produce the desired decreases in recidivism. Regions that most adequately implemented the reform measures with a diversity of pro-grams did produce decreases in recidivism over time, as did those pro-grams receiving ratings reflecting a higher degree of normalization on the institutionalization-normalization continuum. Regression anal-yses strongly support the notion that for youths who recidivated the department was unable to penetrate the networks to which the youngsters would return. We are left again with the conclusion that while the department has moved in the right direction, the quality of linkages between youths and the networks in the community must be improved to bring about any substantial reduction in recidivism rates.

In economic costs, the community-based system compares quite favorably with the training-school system. The average cost per day (including parole) for the training-school system was $29; for the community-based system the comparable cost was $30. Thus the new model has not placed a substantially higher cost burden on the taxpayer.

As one might expect, the level of costs across program types is quite variable. The breakdown of total costs per day is as follows: nonresidential, $23; foster care, $13; forestry, $40; group care, $31; boarding schools, $28; secure facilities, $57. These figures clearly show that programs that are most community based, such as foster care and nonresidential facilities, were the most economical to operate. Boarding schools, group homes, and forestry programs were more expensive. The most expensive programs were the secure care facilities. Total costs for a system are largely determined by how many youths require group residential and secure care. The more youths who can be adequately supported in nonresidential programs and foster care, the less expensive are the total costs. We have evidence, then, that what seems to be most desirable for a large portion of the treatment population costs the least.

In summary, the findings strongly favor the community-based approach as a viable alternative to the training-school model for facilitating the reintegration of troubled youths into constructive, legitimate roles within their local community settings. Analysis of this experience has yielded numerous suggestions for further sharpening our understanding of community-based service and for forging practical innovations in the delivery of services within community-based settings. . . .

NOTE

To the same effect, see L. Ohlin, et al., Juvenile Correctional Reform in Massachusetts: a preliminary report of the Center for Criminal Justice of the Harvard Law School (1977). See also J. Miller and L. Ohlin, The New Corrections: The Case of Massachusetts, in Pursuing Justice for the Child 154 (M. Rosenheim ed. 1976).

Some commentators have expressed concern that community-based treatment has not lived up to its fiscal or confinement reduction promise. See, for example, the evaluation of deinstitutionalization and diversion projects in California in P. Lerman, Community Treatment and Social Control: A Critical Analysis of Juvenile Correctional Policy (1975). Further study of the Massachusetts deinstitutionalization as implemented in one community has suggested that many of its goals were thwarted by recalcitrant local juvenile authorities not persuaded of the ultimate worth of the program. This illusion of reform due to failure of those within the system to comply with the stated goals of any given program had been anticipated as well in earlier studies of the Massachusetts experiment. See M. Fabricant, Deinstitutionalizing Delinquent Youth (1980). Finally, in Beyond Probation (1979), C. Murray and L. Cox suggest that institutionalization may deter certain groups of delinquents and prove far more affordable than many had believed. See also Lerman, Trends and Issues in the Deinstitutionalization of Youths in Trouble, 26 Crime & Delinq. 281 (1980).

THE RIGHT TO TREATMENT

The poor conditions in many juvenile institutions have given rise to class action suits challenging their administration. Often the confined juveniles assert a right to rehabilitative treatment while institutionalized. Such a right for incarcerated juveniles has been traced back to cases in which courts have held that individuals involuntarily committed to mental institutions have a due process right to psychiatric treatment. See Rouse v. Cameron, 373 F.2d 451 (D.C.Cir. 1966); Wyatt v. Stickney, 325 F.Supp. 781 (M.D.Ala.1971), affirmed sub nom., Wyatt v. Aderholt, 503 F.2d 1305 (5th Cir. 1974). Those cases were called into question by the Supreme Court's decision in O'Connor v. Donaldson, 422 U.S. 563, 95 S.Ct. 2486, 45 L.Ed.2d 396 (1975). The majority of the court did not reach the issue in *O'Connor*, but Chief Justice Burger, in a concurring opinion, rejected the asserted right to treatment:

> In short, the idea that States may not confine the mentally ill except for the purpose of providing them with treatment is of very recent origin, and there is no historical basis for imposing such a limitation on state power. Analysis of the sources of the civil commitment power likewise lends no support to that notion. There can be little doubt that in the exercise of its police power a State may confine individuals solely to protect society from the dangers of significant antisocial acts or communicable disease. Additionally, the States are vested with the historic *parens patriae* power, including the duty to protect "persons under legal disabilities to act for themselves." The classic example of this role is when a State undertakes to act as " 'the general guardian of all infants, idiots, and lunatics.' "

> Of course, an inevitable consequence of exercising the *parens patriae* power is that the ward's personal freedom will be substantially restrained, whether a guardian is appointed to control his property, he is placed in the custody of a private third party, or committed to an institution. Thus, however the power is implemented, due process requires that it not be invoked indiscriminately. . . .

> However, the existence of some due process limitations on the *parens patriae* power does not justify the further conclusion that it may be exercised to confine a mentally ill person only if the purpose of the confinement is treatment. . . .

> . . .

> Alternatively, it has been argued that a Fourteenth Amendment right to treatment for involuntarily confined mental patients derives from the fact that many of the safeguards of the criminal

process are not present in civil commitment. The Court of Appeals described this theory as follows:

"[A] due process right to treatment is based on the principle that when the three central limitations on the government's power to detain—that detention be in retribution for a specific offense; that it be limited to a fixed term; and that it be permitted after a proceeding where the fundamental procedural safeguards are observed—are absent, there must be a *quid pro quo* extended by the government to justify confinement. And the *quid pro quo* most commonly recognized is the provision of rehabilitive treatment." 493 F.2d, at 522.

. . .

The *quid pro quo* theory is a sharp departure from, and cannot coexist with, due process principles. . . . 422 U.S. at 584–86.

Are the Chief Justice's arguments against a right to treatment in the mental health context applicable as well to the juvenile treatment process? Does the answer depend on the purposes of the juvenile justice system?

Under what has been described as the "mutual compact theory" of *parens patriae*, it is asserted that by adopting a juvenile court act a state undertakes to remove the harsh effects and stigma of a criminal proceeding against a child, providing instead some of the basic care and supervision not furnished by the child's parents. In return for this, the child is not afforded certain constitutional protections that would be available to an adult lawbreaker. One of the most influential discussions of this *quid pro quo* theory was written by a distinguished jurist in the juvenile field, Judge Orman Ketcham, in 7 Crime and Delinquency 97, at 100-01 (1961). He points out that "Applying the contractual analogy, it follows that unless the state satisfactorily performs its obligations under the compact, the juvenile and his parents should have the right to consider the agreement broken and to repossess their full constitutional rights."

In light of *Gault* and its progeny, is it an answer to the mutual compact theory of right to treatment that, with the exception of right to jury trial, juveniles now enjoy most of the same rights to which adults are entitled in criminal proceedings?

NELSON v. HEYNE

United States Court of Appeals, Seventh Circuit, 1974.
491 F.2d 352.

KILEY, SENIOR CIRCUIT JUDGE.

The district court in this class civil rights action enjoined defendants from implementing alleged unconstitutional practices and policies in conducting the Indiana Boys School under their administra-

tion; and declared the practices and policies unconstitutional. . . .
We affirm.

The School, located in Plainfield, Indiana, is a medium security
state correctional institution for boys twelve to eighteen years of age,
an estimated one-third of whom are non-criminal offenders. The
boys reside in about sixteen cottages. The School also has academic
and vocational school buildings, a gymnasium and an administrative
building. The average length of a juvenile's stay at the School is
about six and one-half months. Although the School's maximum capacity is less than 300 juveniles, its population is generally maintained at 400. The counselling staff of twenty individuals includes
three psychologists with undergraduate academic degrees, and one
part-time psychiatrist who spends four hours a week at the institution. The medical staff includes one part-time physician, one registered nurse, and one licensed practical nurse.

The complaint alleged that defendants' practices and policies violated the 8th and 14th Amendment rights of the juveniles under their
care. . . .

. . .

I—CRUEL AND UNUSUAL PUNISHMENT

A.

It is not disputed that the juveniles who were returned from escapes or who were accused of assaults on other students or staff
members were beaten routinely by guards under defendants' supervision. There is no proof of formal procedures that governed the beatings which were administered after decision by two or more staff
members. Two staff members were required to observe the beatings.

In beating the juveniles, a "fraternity paddle" between ½" and 2"
thick, 12" long, with a narrow handle, was used. There is testimony
that juveniles weighing about 160 pounds were struck five blows on
the clothed buttocks, often by a staff member weighing 285 pounds.
The beatings caused painful injuries.[3] The district court found that
this disciplinary practice violated the plaintiffs' 8th and 14th Amendment rights, and ordered it stopped immediately.

We recognize that the School is a correctional, as well as an academic, institution. No case precisely in point has been cited or found
which decided whether supervised beatings in a juvenile reformatory
violated the "cruel and unusual" clause of the 8th Amendment.

---

3. The trial record indicates that one
juvenile was struck with such force that
it caused him to sleep on his face for
three days, with black, blue and numb
buttocks. One juvenile testified that he
bled after receiving five blows on his buttocks. Another, Daniel Roberts, testified
that once he pleaded, to no avail, with
staff personnel not to be beaten until after certain blisters on his buttocks ceased
to cause him pain.

However, the test of "cruel and unusual" punishment has been outlined. In his concurring opinion in Furman v. Georgia, 408 U.S. 238, 279, 92 S.Ct. 2720, 2747, 33 L.Ed.2d 346 (1971), Justice Brennan stated that:

> The final principle inherent in the [Cruel and Unusual Punishment] Clause is that a severe punishment must not be excessive. A punishment is excessive under this principle if it is unnecessary: The infliction of a severe punishment by the State cannot comport with human dignity when it is nothing more than the pointless infliction of suffering. If there is a significantly less severe punishment adequate to achieve the purposes for which the punishment is inflicted, the punishment inflicted is unnecessary and therefore excessive.

Expert evidence adduced at the trial unanimously condemned the beatings. The uncontradicted authoritative evidence indicates that the practice does not serve as useful punishment or as treatment, and it actually breeds counter-hostility resulting in greater aggression by a child. For these reasons we find the beatings presently administered are unnecessary and therefore excessive. We think, under the test of *Furman*, that the district court did not err in deciding that the disciplinary beatings shown by this record constituted cruel and unusual punishment.[6]

. . .

There is nothing in the record to show that a less severe punishment would not have accomplished the disciplinary aim. And it is likely that the beatings have aroused animosity toward the School and substantially frustrated its rehabilitative purpose. We find in the record before us, to support our holding, general considerations similar to those the court in Jackson [v. Bishop, 404 F.2d 571 (8th Cir. 1968)] found relevant: (1) corporal punishment is easily subject to abuse in the hands of the sadistic and unscrupulous, and control of the punishment is inadequate; (2) formalized School procedures governing the infliction of the corporal punishment are at a minimum; (3) the infliction of such severe punishment frustrates correctional and rehabilitative goals; and (4) the current sociological trend is toward the elimination of all corporal punishment in all correctional institutions.

. . .

B.

Witnesses for both the School and the juveniles testified at trial that tranquilizing drugs, specifically Sparine and Thorazine, were occasionally administered to the juveniles, not as part of an ongoing psychotherapeutic program, but for the purpose of controlling excited

6. We do not hold that all corporal punishment in juvenile institutions or reformatories is per se cruel and unusual.

behavior.[8] The registered nurse and licensed practical nurse prescribed intramuscular dosages of the drugs upon recommendation of
the custodial staff under standing orders by the physician. Neither
before nor after injections were the juveniles examined by medically
competent staff members to determine their tolerances.

The district court also found this practice to be cruel and unusual
punishment. Accordingly the court ordered the practice stopped immediately, and further ordered that no drug could be administered
intramuscularly unless specifically authorized or directed by a physician in each case, and unless oral medication was first tried, except
where the staff was directed otherwise by a physician in each case.

We agree with defendants that a judge lacking expertise in
medicine should be cautious when considering what are "minimal
medical standards" in particular situations. However, practices and
policies in the field of medicine, among other professional fields, are
within judicial competence when measured against requirements of
the Constitution. We find no error in the competent district court's
determination here that the use of tranquilizing drugs as practiced by
defendants was cruel and unusual punishment.

We are not persuaded by defendants' argument that the use of
tranquilizing drugs is not "punishment." Experts testified that the
tranquilizing drugs administered to the juveniles can cause: the collapse of the cardiovascular system, the closing of a patient's throat
with consequent asphyxiation, a depressant effect on the production
of bone marrow, jaundice from an affected liver, and drowsiness,
hemotological disorders, sore throat and ocular changes.

The interest of the juveniles, the School, and the state must be
considered in determining the validity of the use of the School's tranquilizing drugs policy. The interest of the state appears to be identical more or less with the interest of the maladjusted juveniles committed to the School's care, i.e., reformation so that upon release
from their confinement juveniles may enter free society as well adjusted members. The School's interest is in the attainment and maintenance of reasonable order so that the state's purpose may be pursued in a suitable environment. The School's interest, however, does
not justify exposing its juveniles to the potential dangers noted
above. Nor can Indiana's interest in reforming its delinquent or maladjusted juveniles be so compelling that it can use "cruel and unusual" means to accomplish its benevolent end of reformation.

We hold today only that the use of disciplinary beatings and tranquilizing drugs in the circumstances shown by this record violates

8. Plaintiff Steven Hegg testified that
on one occasion while he was recuper-
ating from a blow to the nose inflicted
upon him by another student, his nose began to bleed profusely and he began to
vomit and "holler for help." The nurse
told him there was nothing seriously
wrong with him; but when Steven continued to request help, she became infuriat-
ed and injected him with a tranquilizing
drug. Eric Nelson testified to the effect
that he was given shots of tranquilizing
drugs on several occasions for the purpose of preventing him from running
away from the School.

plaintiffs' 14th Amendment right protecting them from cruel and unusual punishment. We do not intend that penal and reform institutional physicians cannot prescribe necessary tranquilizing drugs in appropriate cases. Our concern is with actual and potential abuses under policies where juveniles are beaten with an instrument causing serious injuries, and drugs are administered to juveniles intramuscularly by staff, without trying medication short of drugs and without adequate medical guidance and prescription.

II—THE RIGHT TO REHABILITATIVE TREATMENT

The School staff-to-juvenile ratio for purposes of treatment is approximately one to thirty. The sixteen counselors are responsible for developing and implementing individualized treatment programs at the institution, but the counselors need have no specialized training or experience. Administrative tasks ("paper work") occupy more than half of the counselors' time. The duties of the staff psychiatrist are limited to crises. He has no opportunity to develop and manage individual psychotherapy programs. The three staff psychologists do not hold graduate degrees and are not certified by Indiana. They render, principally, diagnostic services, mostly directed toward supervising in-take behavior classifications.

In June, 1971, the School adopted what was described as a differential treatment program, bottomed mainly on the Quay Classification System. Under the Quay System, upon their admission to the School, juveniles are classified with respect to four personality and behavior types on the basis of standardized tests: the inadequate, the neurotic, the aggressive, and the sub-cultural. Each of the sixteen cottages at the School houses twenty to thirty juveniles, with common personality and behavior patterns. Each cottage is served by a staff comprising a house manager, a counselor, an educator, and a consulting psychologist. The cottage staff meets weekly for evaluation of the rehabilitation program of each inmate. Upon admission to a cottage, each juvenile agrees to improve his behavior in four areas of institutional life: "cottage," "recreation," "school," and "treatment." Correspondingly, each has responsibility for physical maintenance of the residential area, social and athletic activities, specified levels of academic or vocational skills, and improved personality goals. With success in each of the four areas, the juvenile earns additional privileges, ultimately culminating in a parole date.

The district court decided that both Indiana law and the federal Constitution secure for juvenile offenders a "right to treatment," and that the School failed to provide minimal rehabilitative treatment. Defendants contend that there exists no right to treatment under the Constitution or Indiana law, and that if there is the right, the Quay Classification System used at the School did not violate the right. We hold, with the district court, that juveniles have a right to rehabilitative treatment.

The right to rehabilitative treatment for juvenile offenders has roots in the general social reform of the late nineteenth century, was nurtured by court decisions throughout the first half of this century, and has been established in state and federal courts in recent years.

. . .

The United States Supreme Court has never definitively decided that a youth confined under the jurisdiction of a juvenile court has a constitutionally guaranteed right to treatment. But the Court has assumed, in passing on the validity of juvenile proceedings, that a state must provide treatment for juveniles. In Kent v. United States, 383 U.S. 541, 86 S.Ct. 1045, 16 L.Ed.2d 84 (1966), the Court reversed the district court's conviction of a sixteen year old after the District of Columbia Juvenile Court had waived its jurisdiction. Justice Fortas there, writing for the Court, commented on the theory and practice of juvenile courts:

> There is evidence, in fact, that there may be grounds for concern that the child receives the worst of both worlds: that he gets neither the protections accorded to adults nor the solicitous care and regenerative treatment postulated for children. 383 U.S. at 556, 86 S.Ct. at 1054.

. . .

. . . [S]everal recent state and federal cases, out of concern— based upon the *parens patriae* doctrine underlying the juvenile justice system—that rehabilitative treatment was not generally accorded in the juvenile reform process, have decided that juvenile inmates have a constitutional right to that treatment. M. v. M., 71 Misc.2d 396, 336 N.Y.S.2d 304 (1972); Inmates of Boys' Training School v. Affleck, 346 F.Supp. 1354 (D.C.R.I.1972); Martarella v. Kelley, 349 F.Supp. 575 (S.D.N.Y.1972).

In *Martarella* the court found a clear constitutional right to treatment for juveniles based on the 8th and 14th Amendments.

> What we have said, although the record would justify more, is sufficient to establish that, however benign the purposes for which members of the plaintiff class are held in custody, and whatever the sad necessities which prompt their detention, they are held in penal condition. Where the State, as *parens patriae*, imposes such detention, it can meet the Constitution's requirement of due process and prohibition of cruel and unusual punishment *if, and only if, it furnishes adequate treatment to the detainee.* 349 F.Supp. at 585. (Emphasis supplied, footnotes omitted.)

. . .

We hold that on the record before us the district court did not err in deciding that the plaintiff juveniles have the right under the 14th Amendment due process clause to rehabilitative treatment.[12]

12. We note that the district court additionally determined that a right to treatment in this case has a statutory basis in view of the "custody, *care,* and discipline" language of the Indiana Juvenile Court Act, Burns Ind.Stat.Ann. § 9–3201,

III—ADEQUACY OF TREATMENT

Experts testified at the trial, and the defendants admit, that the Quay System of behavior classification is not treatment. And case histories of maladjusted juveniles show that use of the System falls far short of its improved personality goals. . . . The record shows very little individual treatment programmed, much less implemented, at the School; and it is unclear exactly how much time is spent in individual counselling. We conclude that the district court could properly infer that the Quay System as used in the School failed to provide adequate rehabilitative treatment.

We leave to the competent district court the decision: what is the minimal treatment required to provide constitutional due process, having in mind that the juvenile process has elements of both the criminal and mental health processes.

In our view the "right to treatment" includes the right to minimum acceptable standards of care and treatment for juveniles and the right to *individualized* care and treatment. Because children differ in their need for rehabilitation, individual need for treatment will differ. When a state assumes the place of a juvenile's parents, it assumes as well the parental duties, and its treatment of its juveniles should, so far as can be reasonably required, be what proper parental care would provide. Without a program of individual treatment the result may be that the juveniles will not be rehabilitated, but warehoused, and that at the termination of detention they will likely be incapable of taking their proper places in free society; their interests and those of the state and the school thereby being defeated.

We therefore affirm the judgment of the district court in each appeal, and remand [to the district court to determine what rehabilitative treatment is required to satisfy due process.]

NOTES

(1) For other cases raising the right to treatment issue see, e.g., Morgan v. Sproat, 432 F.Supp. 1130 (S.D.Miss.1977); Pena v. New York State Division for Youth; 419 F.Supp. 203 (S.D.N.Y.1976); Morales v. Turman, 364 F.Supp. 166 (E.D.Tex.1973); Inmates of Boys' Training School v. Affleck, 346 F.Supp. 1354 (D.R.I.1973).

(2) Recall footnote 12 in Nelson v. Heyne in which the court discussed a statutory right to treatment. Many of the cases recognizing a right to treatment for confined juveniles have emphasized the state statutes creating juvenile systems premised on the rehabilitative ideal. To what extent would the adoption of delinquency sanctions proportional to conduct obviate the right to treatment?

IC 1971, 31–5–7–1. (Emphasis supplied.) We agree with this conclusion. Since we have today determined that the federal Constitution affords juveniles a right to treatment, any interpretation of the Indiana Act which would find no such right to exist would itself be unconstitutional.

(3) On the right to treatment generally, see Gough, The Beyond Control Child and the Right to Treatment: An Exercise in the Synthesis of Paradox, 16 St. Louis U.L.J. 182 (1971); Kittrie, Can the Right to Treatment Remedy the Ills of the Juvenile Process?, 57 Geo.L.J. 848 (1969); Note, A Right to Treatment for Juveniles?, 1973 Wash.U.L.Q. 157.

(4) Generally, after a juvenile is released from an institution, nothing further is done by the juvenile system unless the juvenile becomes a repeat offender. In many cases, however, returning the juvenile to his family and peers negates any rehabilitation that occurred in the institution. Recently commentators and practitioners have urged that the system focus more on the child's reintegration into home and family in order to ensure against reversion to former behavior patterns. Under this approach, a juvenile would leave an institution gradually by a series of progressively longer home visits. After the child is returned home, counseling sessions within the home environment would be utilized to ensure that the behavioral changes that occurred in the institution are not being reversed. See Daum, Aftercare, the Neglected Phase of Adolescent Treatment, 32 Juv. & Fam. Ct. J. 43 (Aug. 1981).

Similarly, sociologists have noted that an effective treatment program for delinquents must take into account that delinquents are often members of a delinquent subculture. Therefore, the child's behavior within a juvenile institution may not be any indication of how the child will readjust in the community. In addition, commitment to a juvenile institution "may actually be more effective in cementing ties to the delinquent system than in destroying them." Empey & Rabow, The Provo Experiment in Delinquency Rehabilitation, 26 Am.Soc.Rev. 679 (1961).

3. PROBATION

The most common disposition for delinquent juveniles, probation, offers many benefits to the juvenile and to the judicial system. It permits a youth to remain in a familiar environment rather than be isolated in an institution. Because it is designed to be a "parental" disposition, the juvenile is more likely to accept its conditions as legitimate rather than view them as constituting outside government interference.

Probation is attractive to juvenile judges because it can be tailored to the particular child. Such individualized treatment often is mandated by statute. The expense of institutionalization also can be avoided while satisfying the legislative direction in many states that a juvenile be kept at home whenever possible.

Despite these perceived advantages, probation is not without critics. A main concern is that success is largely dependent upon the ability or application of the probation officer. All too frequently such officers are inadequately trained, poorly paid and burdened with excessive case loads. The Juvenile Justice Standards are critical of probation because it is imposed too frequently when supervision is neither intended nor necessary.

IN RE WAYNE J.

California Court of Appeal, Second District, Division 1, 1979.
97 Cal.App.3d 776, 159 Cal.Rptr. 106.

LILLIE, ACTING PRESIDING JUSTICE.

Minor appeals from order sustaining petition, declaring him a ward of the court (§ 602, Welf. & Inst. Code) and imposing home probation.

About 7 p.m. the minor and another juvenile were standing on a street corner; minor's companion looked in the direction of officers riding in an unmarked patrol car and turned toward the minor whereupon the minor threw a bag over a hedge and his companion ducked behind a car. The bag, retrieved by one of the officers, contained less than an ounce of marijuana. The minor neither testified nor offered a defense.

. . .

After a dispositional hearing, the court declared the minor a ward of the court under section 602, Welfare and Institutions Code, and the offense to be a misdemeanor, and ordered him placed on home probation on terms and conditions wholly appropriate to a minor. . . . [The minor challenged the disposition as violative of equal protection in that an adult would have been subject only to a $100 fine. The court rejected the minor's equal protection claim.]

Any right of a minor to refuse probation as contended for here because its terms are more onerous than the $100 fine, would be entirely inconsistent with the purpose, nature, reasons for and consequences of probation in juvenile proceedings.

One of the purposes of the Juvenile Court Law is to secure for each minor under the jurisdiction of the juvenile court such care and guidance, preferably in his own home, as will best serve his welfare and "preserve and strengthen the minor's family ties." (§ 202, Welf. & Inst. Code). Thus with this in mind, a comprehensive statutory scheme was devised to best provide for the placement and treatment of juveniles. It is apparent . . . that probation in a juvenile proceeding is not an act of leniency which a minor can refuse but the preferred disposition if warranted by the circumstances. "Unlike adult criminal proceedings . . . the Juvenile Court Law ' "contemplates a progressively restrictive and punitive series of disposition orders in cases such as that now before us—namely, home placement under supervision, foster home placement, placement in a local treatment facility and, as a last resort, Youth Authority placement." ' (In re Aline D., (1975) 14 Cal.3d 557, 564 [121] Cal.Rptr. 816, 536 P.2d 65].)"

. . . The difference in treatment seems justified by the differing characteristics and needs of adult and juvenile offenders.

. . .

The statutory scheme for the processing of applications to cause a petition for wardship under section 602 to be filed in the juvenile court provides for the commencement of such proceedings by the probation officer and contemplates his presence in all court hearings to represent the interests of the minor and furnish all such information and assistance the court may require. For every dispositional hearing the probation officer must prepare a social study of the minor containing such matters as may be relative to a proper disposition of the case and include a recommendation therefor. (§ 280, Welf. & Inst. Code). On the hearing the court shall receive it in evidence and read and consider the same, and so state in its order of disposition. (§ 706, Welf. & Inst. Code). Thus, while an adult may be given summary probation, there is no room in the Juvenile Court Law for such disposition; whatever probation is afforded a juvenile ward under section 602, it was intended by the Legislature to be under the supervision of the probation officer.

Inherent in a section 602 wardship is the continuing jurisdiction over the minor by the court which can place him in the home of his parents under probation supervision. This is exactly what the court did here—it declared the minor a ward under section 602 in that he committed a misdemeanor, ordered him placed in the home of his mother on probation and continued the matter to February 11, 1980. The conditions of probation required the minor to do little more than that appropriate to any minor who resides at home (with the exception of obeying all orders of and reporting to the probation officer). The benefit of probation to the minor under the circumstances is that he is able to remain at home and is given needed guidance and discipline which his parents should, but in many cases cannot or will not give him, and he and his parents are afforded the assistance of a professional counselor in the person of the probation officer. The great advantage of this kind of counseling in such a case as this is the lasting effect it may have on molding the minor's attitudes for the better. Surely the goals of juvenile justice are better served through the use of the trained probation officer familiar with the special problems of juveniles and able to guide them into more responsible attitudes.

. . .

The order is affirmed.

NOTES

(1) While the juvenile disposition may exceed the maximum that would be imposed on an adult (or a juvenile tried as an adult) for the same offense, often the juvenile disposition may be less harsh than the adult sentence for comparable conduct. For example, in People v. Hale, 80 Ill.App.3d 63, 35 Ill. Dec. 509, 399 N.E.2d 343, a 15-year-old and a 17-year-old robbed an elderly blind man in his bedroom. The 15-year-old was sentenced to probation and a weekend in jail by the juvenile court. The 17-year-old was tried as an adult and sentenced to four years in prison. The appellate court held that the four-year sentence was excessive and remanded the case directing the trial

court to consider "(1) a lesser term of imprisonment, (2) periodic imprisonment, or (3) probation conditioned upon a sentence of imprisonment or periodic imprisonment."

(2) Because delinquent children often attend school erratically, juvenile judges frequently condition probation on regular school attendance. Failure to comply can lead to probation violation and concomitant institutionalization. See, e.g., In re Mark M., 109 Cal.App.3d 873, 167 Cal.Rptr. 461 (1980).

(3) May the court impose church attendance as a condition of probation? See Jones v. Commonwealth, 185 Va. 335, 38 S.E.2d 444 (1946), holding that probation conditions of church and Sunday School attendance violated constitutional guarantees of freedom of religion.

(4) Probation offers judges and attorneys a chance to use their imagination in shaping appropriate dispositional orders. Common probation conditions in addition to regular school attendance include obeying all laws, reporting to the probation officer, remaining within the jurisdiction and obeying a curfew. Or a juvenile may be placed on probation with the condition that he perform a certain amount of community service or that he pay for items he damages. (See subsequent sections of this chapter.) Even brief institutionalization can sometimes be imposed as a condition of probation. See In re Ricardo M, 52 Cal.App.3d 744, 125 Cal.Rptr. 291 (1975).

JUVENILE JUSTICE STANDARDS PROJECT, STANDARDS RELATING TO DISPOSITIONS *

3.2 Conditional

The court may sentence the juvenile to comply with one or more conditions, which are specified below, none of which involves removal from the juvenile's home. Such conditions should not interfere with the juvenile's schooling, regular employment, or other activities necessary for normal growth and development.

A. Suspended sentence.

The court may suspend imposition or execution of a more severe, statutorily permissible sentence with the provision that the juvenile meet certain conditions agreed to by him or her and specified in the sentencing order. Such conditions should not exceed, in severity or duration, the maximum sanction permissible for the offense.

B. Financial.

1. Restitution.

a. Restitution should be directly related to the juvenile's offense, the actual harm caused, and the juvenile's ability to pay.

b. The means to carry out a restitution order should be available.

c. Either full or partial restitution may be ordered.

* Reprinted with permission from Standards Relating to Dispositions. Copyright 1980, Ballinger Publishing Company.

d. Repayment may be required in a lump sum or in installments.

e. Consultation with victims may be encouraged but not required. Payments may be made directly to victims, or indirectly, through the court.

f. The juvenile's duty of repayment should be limited in duration; in no event should the time necessary for repayment exceed the maximum term permissible for the offense.

2. Fine.

a. Imposition of a fine is most appropriate in cases where the juvenile has derived monetary gain from the offense.

b. The amount of the fine should be directly related to the seriousness of the juvenile's offense and the juvenile's ability to pay.

c. Payment of a fine may be required in a lump sum or installments.

d. Imposition of a restitution order is preferable to imposition of a fine.

e. The juvenile's duty of payment should be limited in duration; in no event should the time necessary for payment exceed the maximum term permissible for the offense.

3. Community service.

a. In sentencing a juvenile to perform community service, the judge should specify the nature of the work and the number of hours required.

b. The amount of work required should be related to the seriousness of the juvenile's offense.

c. The juvenile's duty to perform community service should be limited in duration; in no event should the duty to work exceed the maximum term permissible for the offense.

C. Supervisory.

1. Community supervision.

The court may sentence the juvenile to a program of community supervision, requiring him or her to report at specified intervals to a probation officer or other designated individual and to comply with any other reasonable conditions that are designed to facilitate supervision and are specified in the sentencing order.

2. Day custody.

The court may sentence the juvenile to a program of day custody, requiring him or her to be present at a specified place for all or part of every day or of certain days. The court also may require the juvenile to comply with any other reasonable conditions that are designed to facilitate supervision and are specified in the sentencing order.

D. Remedial.

1. Remedial programs.

The court may sentence the juvenile to a community program of academic or vocational education or counseling, requiring him or her to attend sessions designed to afford access to opportunities for normal growth and development. The duration of such programs should not exceed the maximum term permissible for the offense.

2. Prohibition of coercive imposition of certain programs.

This standard does not permit the coercive imposition of any program that may have harmful effects. Any such program should comply with the requirements of Standard 4.3 concerning informed consent.

NOTES

(1) The Juvenile Justice Standards authorize three general types of dispositions: nominal (reprimand and release), conditional, and custodial. The conditional disposition is similar to the traditional notion of probation. The commentary to the Standards explains that the term "conditional disposition" was adopted in lieu of "probation" to clear up confusion surrounding the term "probation" and to specify the categories of permissible conditions.

(2) What happens to juveniles who violate their probation? Generally, a probation revocation hearing is required at which the juvenile is entiled to counsel, to present evidence and cross-examine the state's witnesses. See, e.g., Ill.Ann.Stat. ch. 37, § 705–3(3)(c), (4), (5) (1972); Neb.Rev.Stat. § 43–286(4) (Supp.1981); N.C.Gen.Stat. § 7A–656 (1981); Naves v. State, 91 Nev. 106, 531 P.2d 1360 (1975); State ex rel. Gillard v. Cook, 528 S.W.2d 545 (Tenn.1975). If the court revokes probation, it may impose a new sanction (often incarceration). See, e.g., Ill.Ann.Stat. ch. 37, § 705–3(6) (1972).

4. RESTITUTION AND FINES

STATE IN INTEREST OF D. G. W.

Supreme Court of New Jersey, 1976.
70 N.J. 488, 361 A.2d 513.

HUGHES, C. J.

D.G.W., a juvenile, was charged with participating in 1973 and 1974 with three others in four instances of breaking and entering certain residences and school buildings and with theft and destruction of property therein worth thousands of dollars. . . .

[The juvenile pleaded guilty.]

The Juvenile and Domestic Relations Court judge placed the appellant on probation for one year, which he had authority to do under the statute, N.J.S.A. 2A:4 61(c). He determined, over the objection of defense counsel, to apply as a condition to such grant of probation the making of restitution to a victim of the offense.

Having failed to convince the Juvenile and Domestic Relations Court of its lack of jurisdictional authority to order restitution, D.G.W. appealed to the Appellate Division. While his appeal was pending there unheard, we granted certification, 68 N.J. 497, 348 A.2d 538 (1975), primarily to examine the jurisdictional capacity vel non of the court to attach a condition of restitution to a probationary term granted a juvenile offender. . . .

The omission by the Legislature of the sanction of a fine against a juvenile offender seems clearly responsive to the general legislative purpose. Fines are essentially punitive in nature, whereas the statutory policy with respect to juveniles is to correct and rehabilitate rather than punish. Justice Jacobs stated for this Court in State v. Monahan, 15 N.J. 34, 45, 104 A.2d 21, 27 (1954) that:

> Centuries of history indicate that the pathway lies not in unrelenting and vengeful punishment, but in persistently seeking and uprooting the causes of juvenile delinquency and in widening and strengthening the reformative process through socially enlightened movements. . . .

In the same case, JUSTICE HEHER, concurring, wrote:

> Child delinquency is largely due to broken homes and parental irresponsibility and default, and unfavorable environmental and associated factors, involving pressures that are ofttimes beyond the child's control; and the State, as *parens patriae*, undertakes . . . to provide for the wayward victims protective custody, care, discipline, and correctional treatment to fit them, psychologically and physically, for a useful social life. . . . The policy is both preventive and reformative. . . . Wayward children are a community problem; adult behavior ofttimes has its roots in childhood experiences. The redemptive process concerns diagnostic techniques and child therapy, by psychologic, psychiatric and other modes and methods which are not of immediate interest. There are those who would question the wisdom and efficacy of sociological techniques. But, once the legislative field of action is conceded, the legislative policy is not a justiciable issue.

It is against this background that we must determine the threshold question;—whether restitution in its broad sense, including the concept of reparation, may be a valid condition of probation imposed upon a juvenile offender;—or whether it, in essence, [is] discordant with the legislative purpose.

Beyond the validity of the restitution condition itself and the procedural due process necessary for the determination of the extent and terms of restitution to be made, are subsumed other questions raised by appellant. Where several participants are invoked in a joint act of theft or vandalism, and all are required to make restitution, is a pro rata distribution of its burden appropriate? What is the relationship between indigency or ability to make restitution and the enforceability of the remedy of compelling restitution? What is the status of such remedy in the face of actual or potential claim for such damages in a civil action?

I.

As to the disposition of juvenile delinquency cases, the statute provides:

N.J.S.A. 2A:4–61. *Disposition of delinquency cases.*

If a juvenile is adjudged delinquent the juvenile and domestic relations court may order any of the following dispositions:

. . .

c. Place the juvenile on probation to the chief probation officer of the county or to any other suitable person who agrees to accept the duty of probation supervision for a period not to exceed 3 years *upon such written conditions as the court deems will aid rehabilitation of the juvenile*; or

. . .

i. Such other disposition not inconsistent with this act as the court may determine. [emphasis added].

The general statute dealing with the power of courts to suspend sentence and place offenders on probation provides:

N.J.S.A. 2A:168–1. *Power of courts to suspend sentence and place on probation; period of probation.*

. . .

The courts having jurisdiction over juvenile or domestic relations cases, when it shall appear that the best interests of the public as well as of the person adjudged guilty of any offense . . . . before such court will be subserved thereby, shall have power to place the defendant on probation for a period of not less than 1 year nor more than 5 years. Such courts shall also have the power to place on probation under the same conditions children who shall come within the jurisdiction of the court. . . .

The statute authorizing the fixing of conditions of probation provides:

N.J.S.A. 2A:168–2. *Conditions of probation.*

The court shall determine and may, at any time, modify the conditions of probation, and may, among others, include any of the following: That the probationer shall avoid injurious, immoral or vicious habits; shall avoid places or persons of disreputable or harmful character; shall report to the probation officer as directed by the court or probation officer; shall permit the probation officer to visit him at his place of abode or elsewhere; shall answer all reasonable inquiries on the part of the probation officer; shall work faithfully at suitable employment; shall not change his residence without the consent of the court or probation officer; shall pay a fine or the costs of the prosecution, or both, in one or several sums; *shall make reparation or restitution to the ag-*

grieved parties for the damage or loss caused by his offense; shall support his dependents. [emphasis added].

. . .

It is thus apparent that the legislative purpose would accommodate reparation or restitution (for brevity we shall hereafter include both concepts within the term "restitution") as a probation condition.

. . .

We are bound to think, then, that unless restitution has to be considered primarily as punishment and little or nothing else, and thus discordant with the legislative plan, its use as a condition of probation would [be valid].

The dichotomy of punitive and rehabilitative purpose and effect implicit in probation was recognized by Chief Justice Weintraub in In re Buehrer, 50 N.J. 501, 509, 236 A.2d 592, 596 (1967):

> The argument assumes that punishment and rehabilitation are somehow incompatible. Of course they are not. . . . Punishment and rehabilitation are not antagonists.

> Probation assumes the offender can be rehabilitated without serving the suspended jail sentence. But this is not to say that probation is meant to be painless. Probation has an inherent sting, and restrictions upon the freedom of the probationer are realistically punitive in quality. . . . Probation is meant to serve the overall public interest as well as the good of the immediate offender. Thus N.J.S.A. 2A:168–1 authorizes the use of probation "[w]hen it shall appear that the best interests of the public as well as of the defendant will be subserved thereby." [footnote omitted].

. . . Restitution manifestly serves the interest of the public for it is not right that either victim or the public should bear the whole burden, let us say, of loss of extensive juvenile vandalism. . . .

. . .

We hold that a just and fair order as to restitution is a valid and may indeed be a salutary condition of a term of probation. In the case here reviewed the imposition of that condition was proper, but its effectuation, as we shall point out, was procedurally deficient.

[The court then discussed the issue of whether the procedures by which the amount of restitution was arrived at and how it was to be distributed among the four juveniles constituted a denial of due process of law. The court concluded that the manner in which restitution to be paid by the appellant was set, in the absence of a hearing at which he would have had an opportunity to challenge the assessment, constituted a denial of due process of law.]

We remand to the Juvenile and Domestic Relations Court re-establishment of the restitution amount upon which appellant's probation was conditioned, and for the completion of proceedings not inconsistent with this opinion.

NOTES

(1) In accord with the principal case, P.R. v. State, 133 Ga.App. 346, 210 S.E.2d 839 (1974) also authorizes restitution as a condition of probation.

Occasionally, restitution as a condition of probation is explicitly provided for by statute. The following New York provision is typical:

> In cases involving acts of infants over ten and less than sixteen years of age, the court may

> (a) recommend as a condition of placement, or order as a condition of probation or suspended judgment, restitution in an amount representing a fair and reasonable cost to replace the property or repair the damage caused by the infant, not, however, to exceed one thousand dollars. In the case of a placement, the court may recommend that the infant pay out of his or her own funds or earnings the amount of replacement or damage, either in a lump sum or in periodic payments in amounts set by the agency with which he is placed, and in the case of probation or suspended judgment, the court may require that the infant pay out of his or her own funds or earnings the amount of replacement or damage, either in a lump sum or in periodic payments in amounts set by the court;
> . . .

N.Y.Fam.Ct.Act § 758–a(1)(a) (McKinney Supp.1981).

(2) Some jurisdictions provide for restitution by the child not as a condition of probation but rather as an outright disposition. Maryland law, for instance, provides that the court may enter a judgment of restitution against the child or the child's parent. Md.Cts. & Jud.Proc.Code Ann. § 3–829 (Supp. 1981).

(3) Some jurisdictions authorize payment of a fine as an alternate disposition available to the court. Kentucky, for example, provides:

> (2) If a child sixteen (16) years or older is adjudicated delinquent in the commission of any offense the court may in its discretion impose a fine. The imposition of a fine for an offense committed by a child shall be based upon a determination that such disposition is in the best interest of the child and to aid in his rehabilitation. Any such order shall include a finding that the child is financially able to pay such fine.

> (a) Fines shall be levied consistent with the schedule set forth below:

> For a felony, not to exceed $500;

> For a misdemeanor, not to exceed $250;

> For a violation, not to exceed $100.

> (3) When a child is directed by the court to pay a fine, the court may provide for payment to be made within a specified period of time or in specified installments. If such provision is not made a part of the court's disposition, the fine shall be payable immediately. . . .

Ky.Rev.Stat.Ann. § 208E.120(2)–(3) (1980).

Note that the statute limits the amount of the fine and provides that only youths 16 and older can be ordered to pay a fine. Courts in other jurisdictions have prohibited the use of fines holding that they are punitive in nature and thus inconsistent with the basic purposes of the juvenile court's jurisdiction. Recall State in Interest of D.G.W. in which the court noted that fines are "essentially punitive" and inconsistent with the rehabilitative policy with respect to juveniles. See also E.P. v. State, 130 Ga.App. 512, 203 S.E.2d 757 (1973), in which forty juveniles were adjudged delinquent and fined for participating in a "sit-in" at their school. The appellate court upheld the finding of delinquency for engaging in criminal trepass. The court, however, reversed the $50 fine imposed by the juvenile court holding that the juvenile court was without statutory authority to impose a fine.

(4) For a discussion of the varieties of restitution programs in the United States, see Schneider & Schneider, An Overview of Restitution Program Models in the Juvenile Justice System, 31 Juv. & Fam.Ct.J. 3 (Feb. 1980). The authors of the article conclude that where restitution has been utilized, it has become "an integral part" of the rehabilitation of juveniles.

5. COMMUNITY SERVICE

IN RE ERICKSON

Court of Appeals of Washington, 1979.
24 Wn.App. 808, 604 P.2d 513.

SOULE, JUDGE.

Appellant, a 13-year-old girl, pled guilty to taking a motor vehicle without the owner's permission and third-degree theft. The juvenile court sentenced her to 6 months community supervision on the vehicle offense, and 3 months on the theft. Pursuant to RCW 13.40.190, the court ordered her to pay restitution and perform 50 hours of community service. Appellant attacks the constitutionality of the order, alleging that for juvenile offenders compelled community service and restitution constitute involuntary servitude. We reject that allegation and affirm the trial court order.

The thirteenth amendment to the United States Constitution prohibits slavery or involuntary servitude "except as a punishment for crime whereof the party shall have been duly convicted, . . ." Appellant argues, essentially, that since juvenile offenses are not denominated "crimes," and juvenile disposition orders are not considered criminal convictions, they do not fall within the constitutional exception. The Washington Supreme Court recently held in State v. Lawley, 91 Wash.2d 654, 591 P.2d 772 (1979), that the 1977 Juvenile Justice Act did not make juvenile proceedings so similar to adult criminal prosecutions that the accused juvenile had a right to a jury trial. Lawley did, however, recognize the criminal aspect of juvenile proceedings, and that the new law places an emphasis on accountability of juveniles for criminal behavior. The law mandates punishment commensurate with the age, crime, and criminal history of the offender. Although there is no right to a jury trial in juvenile proceedings, the law guarantees basic due process rights to juveniles. The statute specifically describes the performance of community service as "punishment for committing an offense" and defines a juvenile offense as an act which would constitute a crime if it was committed by an adult. Given these similarities with the adult criminal justice system, we hold that the juvenile disposition order did constitute "punishment for crime" sufficient to fall within the constitutional exception to involuntary servitude.

Appellant argues that she cannot pay restitution because she is virtually unemployable at the age of 13, principally due to the Washington Child Labor Law, RCW 26.28.060. The Juvenile Justice Act specifically provides that:

> [t]he court may not require the respondent to pay full or partial restitution if the respondent reasonably satisfies the court that he or she does not have the means to make full or partial restitution and could not reasonably acquire the means to pay such restitution.

RCW 13.40.190(1). Nothing in the record provided indicates that this issue was ever presented to the trial judge, and as such it is deemed waived by the appellant.

The trial court order is affirmed.

NOTES

(1) See M.J.W. v. State, 133 Ga.App. 350, 210 S.E.2d 842 (1974) in which the court rejected the claim that community service work constituted involuntary servitude: The court indicated that a child "may be subjected to restraints that may be necessary for his proper education and discipline that could not be applied to adults."

See also In re Bacon, 240 Cal.App.2d 34, 49 Cal.Rptr. 322 (1966) (juveniles who participated in student protest at university ordered to spend four weekends at probation department's Training Academy cleaning public parks and cemeteries).

(2) The Juvenile Justice Standards Relating to Dispositions * provide that the court may sentence a juvenile to perform community service.

3.2 Conditional

The court may sentence the juvenile to comply with one or more conditions, which are specified below, none of which involves removal from the juvenile's home. Such conditions should not interfere with the juvenile's schooling, regular employment, or other activities necessary for normal growth and development.

. . .

B. Financial

. . .

3. Community service.

a. In sentencing a juvenile to perform community service, the judge should specify the nature of the work and the number of hours required.

---

* Reprinted with permission from Standards Relating to Dispositions, Copyright 1980, Ballinger Publishing Company.

b. The amount of work required should be related to the seriousness of the juvenile's offense.

c. The juvenile's duty to perform community service should be limited in duration; in no event should the duty to work exceed the maximum term possible for the offense.

. . .

Commentary at 54–56:

Although its use as a sanction for offenders has not been widely reported, informal use of a community work as a sentencing alternative is probably more prevalent than it appears from the literature. The classic example is the judge who believes that the best way to teach a lesson to the juvenile found guilty of sounding a false fire alarm is to make him wash fire trucks on weekends.

Some formal programs of community service already exist. In Denver, Colorado, a year-round mountain parks work program for fifteen to seventeen year old boys provides a weekend group living experience in which half of the juvenile's day is spent in school and half the day in work. Denver also has a work program for children who remain in their homes; half the day is spent in school and half working in the city's parks or zoo. It is reported that children remain in this program for an average of thirty days. Joint Commission on Correctional Manpower and Training, "The Future of the Juvenile Court: Implications for Correctional Manpower and Training" 37 (1968).

Young offenders in Multhomah County, Oregon, who agree to participate are given the opportunity to take part in the Alternative Community Service Program, in which they perform specific amounts of work for a nonprofit agency at a time that does not conflict with their regular employment. If the job is done satisfactorily, no further sentence is required. The minimum number of hours of work required is twenty-four; eighty days is the usual upper limit. Work required is for agencies whose services are designed to enhance the social welfare, physical or mental stability, environmental quality, or general well-being of the community.

Programs in California are the best known. In East Palo Alto, youths are referred by the Community Youth Responsibility Program to "work tasks," contractual arrangements in which youths work at some community project selected for its rehabilitative potential, such as supervising recreation programs for young children. See K. R. Geiser, Jr., "Youth Services Field Study: Area 2" (Interim Report prepared for the Juvenile Justice Standards Project, March 4, 1974); Urban and Rural Systems Associates, "Evaluation of the Community Youth Responsibility Program" 17–19 (April 10, 1972). In Ventura County, the probation department uses the Ward Work Training Program as a sentencing alternative. In lieu of fines and further incarceration, a boy may be ordered by the court to put in a specific number of hours working at a county park or other facility. He is supervised by the regular personnel and his work is evaluated to determine if it meets acceptable criteria. Girls, who may be required to work in the county hospital laundry, recently were added to this program.

Judges in Alameda County, California, may offer convicted misdemeanants (adults and juveniles) the option of performing a stipulated number of hours of community service in lieu of paying a fine or serving jail time. Those choosing community work are placed in nonprofit or public agencies. Assignments vary from clerical and maintenance work to staff assistance and child care. It was reported that 69.5 percent of those in the work project between April and June 1973 had successfully completed their service terms; a success rate of 80 percent was projected, and nearly 10 percent of the offenders did more work than was required. Volunteer Bureau of Alameda County, Court Referral Program, "4th Quarterly Report: 4/1/73 to 6/30/73."

. . .

Such work projects are intended to benefit the community, to enable the juvenile to make some form of restitution and to help him or her to develop greater responsibility for his or her actions, appreciate the value of work, and to learn to work with other people. Juveniles sentenced to community service projects need not be financially recompensed for their labor, the work itself is the sanction. Since there is no compensation, the community service required should not interfere with the juvenile's schooling or other employment.

Work assignments should be for the general welfare of the community, within the juvenile's ability and, where possible, related to the nature of the juvenile's offense. Consistent with the principle of determinacy, the type of work and the number of hours required must be specified by the sentencing judge, and the number of hours required must be related to the seriousness of the juvenile's offense. The duration of a community service order should not be longer than would be the duration of the juvenile's duty to fulfill a restitution order or a fine.

(3) Some state statutes authorize courts to order a juvenile to perform community service as an alternative disposition. See, e.g., Conn.Gen.Stat. Ann. § 46b–140(a) (Supp.1982); Ky.Rev.Stat.Ann. § 208E.120(1) (1980); N.Y. Fam.Ct. Act, § 758–a(1)(b), (2)–(3) (McKinney Supp.1981); N.C.Gen.Stat. § 7A–649(4) (1981); S.C.Code Ann. § 20–7–1330(a) (Supp.1981).

X. APPEALS

THE NATURE OF THE RIGHT TO APPEAL

In In re Gault the Supreme Court found it unnecessary to rule on the claim that due process guarantees a right of appeal from a juvenile court order because it decided the case on other grounds. The Court, however, pointed out the difficulties where no provision is made for appeal:

> . . . As the present case illustrates, the consequences of failure to provide an appeal, to record the proceedings, or to make findings or state the grounds for the juvenile court's conclusion may be to throw a burden upon the machinery for habeas corpus, to saddle the reviewing process with the burden of attempting to reconstruct a record, and to impose upon the juvenile judge the unseemly duty of testifying under cross-examination as to the events that transpired in the hearings before him.

387 U.S. at 58.

The Supreme Court has never held that due process affords a right of appeal in criminal proceedings, although it has held that to the extent a state makes an appeal available to criminal defendants generally, equal protection requires that the appeal procedure be available to all such persons, including indigent defendants unable to afford a transcript. Griffin v. Illinois, 351 U.S. 12, 76 S.Ct. 585, 100 L.Ed. 891 (1956). A number of courts accordingly have held that, although there is no constitutional right to appeal from juvenile court orders, any statutory appeal procedure must be administered fairly to all persons to avoid denial of equal protection to a particular class of persons.

Reasoning from *Griffin*, for example, the Third Circuit held unconstitutional a Virgin Islands statute providing for appeals from juvenile court orders only in the discretion of the juvenile court judge. In re Brown, 439 F.2d 47 (3d Cir. 1971). Since the right of appeal was absolute in criminal cases and all other civil cases, the court held that restricting the right in juvenile cases was a violation of equal protection. Similarly, the California Court of Appeals held in In re Arthur N., 36 Cal.App.3d 935, 112 Cal.Rptr. 89 (1974), that equal protection guarantees to juveniles the same right accorded adults by statute to be advised of the rights to appeal and to be represented by counsel on appeal.

Although an appeal procedure is not constitutionally required, almost all states provide by statute for judicial review of orders of juvenile courts. The statutes vary considerably in terms of who may appeal, the court to which an appeal is taken, and the kinds of orders that may be appealed, as well as with respect to procedural matters

594

such as the right to counsel, right to bail, and the effect of an appeal on the operation of the judgment being appealed.[1]

WHO MAY APPEAL?

Most statutes provide that an "aggrieved party" may take an appeal from an order of the juvenile court. See, e.g., Minn.Stat.Ann. § 260.291(1) (Supp.1982). Both the Uniform Juvenile Court Act § 59 (1968) and the Standard Juvenile Court Act § 28 (1959) use similar language. The term "aggrieved party" certainly includes the juvenile, and many statutes expressly include parents. The Missouri statute, for example, provides that a parent may appeal if the order adversely affects him or her. Mo.Ann.Stat. § 211.261 (Vernon 1962). Some statutes also include the state within the meaning of "aggrieved party" or otherwise allow the state a right of appeal. See, e.g., Del.Code Tit. 10, § 962 (1974); N.D.Cent.Code § 27–20–56 (1974).

Allowing the state to appeal under some circumstances would appear to violate the prohibition against double jeopardy.[2] Although it did not decide the case on double jeopardy grounds, the Texas Supreme Court in C.L.B. v. State, 567 S.W.2d 795 (Tex.1978), held that since the applicable statute does not give the state a right of appeal, the state may not appeal from adverse judgments in delinquency proceedings. Louisiana, perhaps out of concern for the protection against double jeopardy, provides that while the state may appeal a judgment of disposition, it may not appeal a judgment declining to adjudicate a child delinquent. La.Code Juv.Proc.Ann. art. 98 (1982); see also Cal.Welf. & Inst.Code § 800 (Supp.1982). An example of a permissible appeal is found in State v. Doe, 95 N.M. 90, 619 P.2d 194 (App.1980), in which the court held that the state could appeal a judgment of disposition committing a status offender to the Boys School for four months because there was no statutory authorization for such a disposition and "[t]he state is aggrieved by a disposition contrary to law . . .."

The Juvenile Justice Standards Project, Standards Relating to Appeals and Collateral Review 2.2 (1980)* provide:

2.2 An appeal may be taken by any of the following parties:

A. the juvenile;

B. his or her parents, custodian, or guardian;

C. the state,

    1. of any final order in other than delinquency cases;

---

1. An excellent if somewhat dated survey of the statutory and decisional law relating to juvenile appeals appears in Bowman, Appeals from Juvenile Courts, 11 Crime & Delinq. 63 (1965); see also M. Paulsen and C. Whitebread, Juvenile Law and Procedure 183–193 (1974).

2. See the discussion of this issue generally in the material on double jeop-ardy following Breed v. Jones in Chapter III at page 252, supra, and in particular the cases dealing with review by the juvenile court of findings of a referee.

2. of only the following orders in delinquency cases:

   a. an order adjudicating a state statute unconstitutional;

   b. any order which by depriving the prosecution of evidence, by upholding the defense of double jeopardy, by holding that a cause of action is not stated under a statute, or by granting a motion to suppress, terminates a delinquency petition;

   c. an order which denies a petition to waive juvenile court jurisdiction in favor of adult criminal prosecution.

WHAT ORDERS MAY BE APPEALED?

Equally as important as who may appeal is the matter of what kinds of orders may be appealed. The Louisiana code provides that appeal may be taken only from a judgment of disposition. La.Code Juv.Proc.Ann. art. 97 (1982). Most states provide that only "final" orders are appealable, which would include an adjudication. See, e.g., Minn.Stat.Ann. § 260.291(1) (Supp.1982). Interlocutory orders or orders interlocutory in nature, e.g., an order waiving jurisdiction and transferring a case for criminal prosecution, often are expressly not appealable.[3]

In In re Doe, III, 87 N.M. 170, 531 P.2d 218 (App.1975), the court held that an order committing a juvenile to the state boys' school for diagnostic purposes was a final, appealable order. The court reasoned that since the order was dispositional in nature it must have been preceded by an implicit finding that the juvenile was delinquent or in need of supervision; therefore, the order was final and appealable. On the other hand, the court in In re Bolden, 37 Ohio App.2d 7, 306 N.E.2d 166 (1973), held that an order for temporary diagnostic commitment following adjudication was not a final, appealable order. The court so held because the legislature had defined "final order" as one that affects a substantial right and that determines the action and prevents a judgment. The order in this case had no such effect, the court concluded.

The Juvenile Justice Standards Project, Standards Relating to Appeals and Collateral Review 2.1 (1980)* provide:

2.1 Upon claim properly filed by any party, review should be had of any final order of the juvenile court. A final order should include:

   A. any order finding absence of jurisdiction;

   B. any order transferring jurisdiction from the juvenile court to another court;

3. This issue is treated in Chapter VII, Transfer Between Courts, at page 399, supra.

* Reprinted with permission from Standards Relating to Appeals and Collateral Review, Copyright 1980, Ballinger Publishing Company.

    C. any order finding a juvenile to be delinquent in which no disposition is made within sixty days or where disposition is to be extensively deferred;

    D. any order of disposition after adjudication;

    E. any order finding a juvenile to be neglected or abused;

    F. any order terminating or modifying custodial rights.[†]

WHERE WILL THE APPEAL BE HEARD?

Statutory provisions vary also with respect to the court to which an appeal is taken. Most states provide that an appeal from a juvenile court order is taken to an appellate court as in the case of an appeal from a criminal conviction. See, e.g., Fla.Stat.Ann. § 39.14(1) (1976); La.Code Juv.Proc.Ann. art. 97 (1982). The Juvenile Justice Standards Project, Standards Relating to Appeals and Collateral Review 1.1(B) (1980) follow this view. In a few states, however, judicial review is not in the form of an appeal but rather a trial de novo in a court of record exercising general jurisdiction. See, e.g., Mass.Gen. Laws Ann. ch. 119, § 56 (Supp.1981); Tenn.Code Ann. § 37–258 (Supp.1981).

In the latter cases some procedural anomalies occasionally occur. For example, in Tennessee, which does not accord juveniles the right to jury trial in juvenile proceedings, when a felony adjudication is taken to the circuit court for trial de novo the juvenile is entitled to a jury trial. Arwood v. State, 62 Tenn.App. 453, 463 S.W.2d 943 (1970). Moreover, jury trial in the circuit court is a matter of right unless waived. State v. Johnson, 574 S.W.2d 739 (Tenn.1978). In Delaware, the Delaware Supreme Court has held that an "appeal" of a juvenile adjudication to the superior court consists of review of the record rather than trial de novo, assuming a record exists. G.D. v. State, 389 A.2d 764 (Del.1978). The court's reasoning was that on trial de novo in superior court the case would be treated the same as a criminal case, i.e., the juvenile could be convicted of a criminal offense and sentenced as an adult. In effect, the appeal would operate the same as a judicial transfer for criminal prosecution. One might contrast the provisions of the Massachusetts statute, supra, which prohibits criminal treatment of a juvenile case on trial de novo.

RIGHT TO A TRANSCRIPT

An appeal can not be taken effectively without a transcript. Most juvenile court codes provide for the proceedings to be recorded in some fashion, although a party may have to request that the proceedings be recorded. The language of the Uniform Juvenile Court Act § 24(c) (1968) is typical: "If requested by a party or ordered by the court the proceedings shall be recorded by stenographic notes or by

---

[†] Other kinds of orders that are appealable or not, depending upon their classification as "final," are covered in M. Paulsen and C. Whitebread, Juvenile Law and Procedure 185–88 (1974).—Ed.

electronic, mechanical, or other appropriate means. If not so recorded full minutes of the proceedings shall be kept by the court."

In Griffin v. Illinois, supra, the Supreme Court held that equal
protection entitles indigent appellants to a free transcript for the purpose of taking an appeal where the state furnishes a right to appeal
generally. In reliance on *Gault* and *Griffin* the Louisiana Court of
Appeals held in In re State ex rel. Aaron, 266 So.2d 726 (La.App.
1972), that due process entitles juveniles to a transcript of the proceedings in juvenile court in order to perfect an appeal.[4] Infrequently, statutes provide a right to a transcript on appeal, including a free
transcript if the juvenile is indigent. See, e.g., Cal.Welf. & Inst.Code
§ 800 (Supp.1982). The latter view is taken in the Juvenile Justice
Standards Project, Standards Relating to Appeals and Collateral Review 3.2, 3.3 (1980).

EFFECT OF THE APPEAL

Virtually all the statutes that address the matter at all provide
that the taking of an appeal does not suspend the operation of a juvenile court's order. Supersedeas is not a matter of right but rather is
granted upon request in the discretion of either the juvenile court or
the reviewing court. See, e.g., Fla.Stat.Ann. § 39.14(3) (Supp.1981);
La.Code Juv.Proc.Ann. art. 103 (1982); Minn.Stat.Ann. § 260.291(1)
(Supp.1982). Since granting a stay of the order pending appeal is discretionary with the court, most appellate courts have held that release of the juvenile pending appeal is discretionary with the court as
well. See e.g., In re Kelly, 236 N.W.2d 50 (Iowa 1975); State ex rel.
Banks, 402 So.2d 690 (La.1981). Contra, In re Hobson, 336 So.2d 763
(Miss.1976) (statute provided for bail pending appeal as a matter of
right). The courts usually list concern for the juvenile or the safety
of the community as the principal reason for leaving to the discretion
of the court the decision whether to grant a stay. See, e.g., In re
Doe, 617 P.2d 826 (Haw.App.1980); In re Kelly, supra.

The Juvenile Justice Standards Project, Standards Relating to Appeals and Collateral Review 5.1–5.6 (1980)* provide:

5.1 The initiation of an appeal should not automatically operate to stay an order of the juvenile court.

5.2 Any party, after the filing of a notice or claim of appeal
or the entry of an order granting leave to appeal, may request the
juvenile court to stay the effect of its order and/or release the
juvenile pending appeal.

---

4. Where statutes are silent, the argument has been forcefully made that
juveniles have a constitutional right to a
transcript on appeal, including one paid
for at public expense if the appellant is
indigent. Comment, Appellate Review
for Juveniles: A "Right" to a Transcript,

4 Colum. Human Rights L.Rev. 485
(1972).

* Reprinted with permission from Standards Relating to Appeals and Collateral
Review, Copyright 1980, Ballinger Publishing Company.

5.3   Upon the filing of an appeal of judgment and disposition, the release of the appellant, with or without conditions, should issue in every case unless the court orders otherwise.   An order of interim detention should be permitted only where the disposition imposed, or most likely to be imposed, by the court includes some form of secure incarceration; and the court finds one or more of the following on the record:

A.   that the juvenile would flee the jurisdiction or not appear before any court for further proceedings during the pendancy of the appeal;

B.   that there is substantial probability that the juvenile would engage in serious violence prior to the resolution of the appeal.

Juveniles should be given credit at disposition for any time spent in a secure facility pending appeal.

5.4   In neglect and abuse cases, the juvenile court may order the juvenile removed to a suitable place pending appeal if the court finds that the juvenile would be in imminent danger if left with or returned to his or her parents, guardian, or other person who is a party to the appeal.

5.5   In those cases in which a stay of judgment or disposition or release pending appeal is denied, the appellate court should afford the appeal the speediest treatment possible.

5.6   In those cases in which a stay of judgment or disposition or release pending appeal is denied by the juvenile court, the appellate court should be empowered to grant the relief requested upon application of a party.

RIGHT TO COUNSEL

Statutes generally make no specific provision for the right to counsel on appeal, although many provide for the right to counsel "at all stages of the proceedings," which presumably would include appeals.   See, e.g., Colo.Rev.Stat.Ann. § 19–1–106(1)(a) (1978); Md.Cts. & Jud.Proc.Ann. § 3–821 (1980); 42 Pa.Cons.Stat.Ann. § 6337 (1981). The Juvenile Justice Standards Project, Standards Relating to Appeals and Collateral Review 3.1 (1980) specifically provide for the right to counsel on appeal, including appointed counsel in the case of an indigent appellant.

Juveniles probably have a due process right to counsel on appeal based on a logical application of the reasoning in *Gault*.   Moreover, equal protection may require counsel for juveniles on appeal if adults are so entitled.   The latter conclusion logically follows from the Supreme Court's decision in Douglas v. California, 372 U.S. 353, 83 S.Ct. 814, 9 L.Ed.2d 811 (1963), in which the Court held that, although no constitutional right to appeal exists, if states afford a statutory appeal procedure fairness dictates that counsel be appointed for persons unable to afford counsel.   As with the requirement of a free transcript for the purpose of taking an appeal, announced in Griffin v.

Illinois, supra, equal protection requires that appellate procedures be administered fairly to all classes of claimants.

Parents, where they are given a statutory right to appeal, may have a right to counsel on appeal under statutes affording "a party" the right to counsel "at all stages of the proceedings." See, e.g., Md.Cts. & Jud.Proc.Ann. § 3–821 (1980); N.D.Cent.Code § 27–20–26 (1974); 42 Pa.Cons.Stat.Ann. § 6337 (1981). The right to counsel would appear to be limited, however, to those cases in which the parent is a party, usually proceedings to terminate parental rights. Some states specifically grant the right to counsel to parents in such cases, although the statutes are not clear on whether the right applies only to the hearing stage or to the appellate stage as well. See, e.g., Conn.Gen.Stat.Ann. § 46b–135(b) (Supp.1981); N.M.Stat.Ann. § 32–1–27(J) (1981) (in contrast, subsec. (H) grants child right to counsel "at all stages of the proceedings"); N.Y.Fam.Ct. Act § 262(a) (i) (McKinney Supp.1981). In the District of Columbia, on the other hand, a parent in a termination proceeding specifically is granted the right to counsel, and the right extends to "all critical stages of the proceedings." D.C.Code § 16–2304(b) (1981).

In In re Jacqueline H., 21 Cal.3d 170, 145 Cal.Rptr. 548, 577 P.2d 683 (1978), the California Supreme Court held that an indigent parent in a termination proceeding has a right to counsel on appeal, although the court based its decision on statutory rather than constitutional grounds. Parents do not have an absolute constitutional right to counsel in juvenile proceedings, even at the adjudicatory hearing; rather, availability of the right is to be decided on a case-by-case basis. Lassiter v. Department of Social Services, 452 U.S. 18, 101 S.Ct. 2153, 68 L.Ed.2d 640 (1981).

COLLATERAL REVIEW

In addition to direct appeal, judgments of a juvenile court are subject to collateral review in various forms. For example, resort may be had to extraordinary writs. See, e.g., In re Richard C., 89 Cal. App.3d 477, 152 Cal.Rptr. 787 (1979) (mandamus); State ex rel. LaFollette v. Circuit Court, 37 Wis.2d 329, 155 N.W.2d 141 (1967) (prohibition); Brumley v. Charles R. Denney Juvenile Center, 77 Wn.2d 702, 466 P.2d 481 (1970) (habeas corpus); State v. Steinhauer, 216 So.2d 214 (Fla.1968) (certiorari). Review has also been authorized pursuant to other common law writs, see, e.g., Marsden v. Commonwealth, 352 Mass. 564, 227 N.E.2d 1 (1967) (writ of error); Sult v. Weber, 210 So. 2d 739 (Fla.App.1968) (coram nobis), as well as under modern postconviction relief statutes, see, e.g., State v. Lueder, 242 N.W.2d 142 (N.D.1976).

In addition, the Juvenile Justice Standards Project, Standards Relating to Appeals and Collateral Review 6.1–6.4 (1980)* provide for other kinds of review:

6.1 Orders of the juvenile court may be modified by that court at any time when it has jurisdiction over the matter after notice and opportunity for hearing to all parties, upon the petition of a party or by the juvenile court sua sponte.

. . .

6.3 Every order committing any juvenile into the custody of the state and every order adjudicating a juvenile to be neglected, regardless of custody, should be reviewed by the juvenile court without the request of any party not less than once in every six months.

6.4 The juvenile, his or her parents, custodian, or guardian may petition the juvenile court to inquire into the adequacy of the treatment being afforded the juvenile.

* Reprinted with permission from Standards Relating to Appeals and Collateral Review, Copyright 1980, Ballinger Publishing Company.

XI. NONCRIMINAL MISBEHAVIOR

A. ORIGINS OF STATUS OFFENSE JURISDICTION

Legal sanctions against noncriminal misbehavior by children pre-
date the juvenile court movement. From colonial days, parents were
given access to courts to enforce discipline. Early Massachusetts
statutes drawn directly on strictures of Biblical texts provided harsh
penalties for children who were disobedient, idle or "congenitally
stubborn". The family was the central building block of Puritan society and the principal agent of social control. Among their remarkable ordinances was the provision that:

> If any Childe or Children above sixteene years old and of suffi-
> cient understanding, shall Curse or smite their natural father or
> mother, hee or they shall bee put to death; unless it can bee suffi-
> ciently testified that the parents have beene very unchristianly
> negligent in the education of such children, or so provoke them by
> extreme, and cruel correction that they have beene forced there-
> unto to preserve themselves from death, maiming.

> If any man have a stubborn or rebelious sonne of sufficient
> yeares and understanding, viz. Sixteene yeares of age, which will
> not obey the voice of his father or the voice of his mother, and
> that when they have chastened he will not harken unto them;
> then may his father and mother, being his natural parents, lay
> hold on him and bring him to the Magistrates assembled in Courte
> and testifie unto them, that theire sonne is stubborn and rebel-
> lious and will not obey their voice and Chastisement, but lives in
> sundry notorious Crimes, such a sonne shall be put to death.[1]

There is no evidence that any children in Puritan Massachusetts
suffered the ultimate Old Testament penalty. The existence of statutes such as the preceding one, along with others punishing truancy,
illustrates how venerable is recourse to law for enforcing parental
decisions about children. These early provisos also reflected the sev-
enteenth century Protestant view that man is essentially wicked and
needs stern molding to social standards in order to produce a godly
society.

By the time the juvenile court movement gained momentum in the
late nineteenth century, many ideas about the nature of childhood
had changed but the fundamental belief that a strong family structure was essential to build an ordered society remained. The "child
savers" of the Progressive Era were concerned especially about
breakdowns in the family caused by industrial capitalism, the flood of

---

1. The General Laws and Liberties of
the Massachusetts Colony (1672) in Juvenile Offenders for a Thousand Years
318–19 (W. Sanders ed. 1970).

immigration and the growth of urban centers of population. Unlike the agrarian model in which the whole family works together to produce the agricultural product, urban industry tended to break up the family into separate producing units, and the extensive use of child and female labor meant that parental supervision of children and their socialization through the family declined dramatically.

Not surprisingly, the jurisdiction of the juvenile courts that were created as a result of the spread of therapeutic impulse to protect children and society from the adverse consequences of family atomization made no distinction between children who committed what would have been criminal conduct for adults and thus offensive to others and those who engaged in non-criminal misbehavior injurious to their own health, welfare or morals. As Judge Mack put it in an early influential essay, juvenile courts were not concerned with the guilt or innocence of the child but with "[w]hat he is, how he has become what he is, and what had best be done in his interest and in the interest of the state to save him from a downward career." [2] The reformers of the nineteenth century made no distinction between criminal and noncriminal conduct but lumped all anti-social behavior under the rubric "delinquency."

Typical of these early catchall statutes is former § 700 of the California Welfare and Institutions Code, 1937 Cal.Stat. ch. 369, p. 1030, § 700, as amended:

> The jurisdiction of the juvenile court extends to any person under the age of 21 years who comes within any of the following descriptions:
>
> (a) Who is found begging, receiving or gathering alms, or who is found in any street, road, or public place for the purpose of so doing, whether actually begging or doing so under the pretext of selling or offering for sale any article, or of singing or playing on any musical instrument, or of giving any public entertainment or accompanying or being used in aid of any person so doing.
>
> (b) Who has no parent or guardian; or who has no parent or guardian willing to exercise or capable of exercising proper parental control; or who has no parent or guardian actually exercising such proper parental control, and who is in need of such control.
>
> (c) Who is destitute, or who is not provided with the necessities of life by his parents, and who has no other means of obtaining such necessities.
>
> (d) Whose home is an unfit place for him, by reason of neglect, cruelty, or depravity of either of his parents, or of his guardian or other person in whose custody or care he is.

2. Mack, The Juvenile Court, 23 Harv. L.Rev. 104, 114 (1907).

(e) Who is found wandering and either has no home, no settled place of abode, no visible means of subsistence or no proper guardianship.

(f) Who is a vagrant or who frequents the company of criminals, vagrants, or prostitutes, or persons so reputed; or who is in any house of prostitution or assignation.

(g) Who habitually visits, without parent or guardian, a public billiard room or public poolroom, or a saloon or a place where any spirituous, vinous, or malt liquors are sold, bartered, exchanged, or given away.

(h) Who habitually uses intoxicating liquors or habitually uses opium, cocaine, morphine, or other similar drug without the direction of a competent physician.

(i) Who persistently or habitually refuses to obey the reasonable and proper orders or directions of his parents, guardian, or custodian; or who is beyond the control of such person.

(j) Who is a habitual truant from school within the meaning of any law of this State or is habitually insubordinate or disorderly while in attendance at school.

(k) Who is leading, or from any cause is in danger of leading, an idle, dissolute, lewd, or immoral life.

(l) Who is insane, feeble-minded, or so far mentally deficient that his parents or guardian are unable to exercise proper parental control over him, or whose mind is so far deranged or impaired as to endanger the health, person, or property of himself or others.

(m) Who violates any law of this State or any ordinance of any town, city, or county, or this State defining crime.

(n) Who is afflicted with syphilis, gonorrhea or chanceroid and is in need of medical and custodial care, or both.

Until recently most states continued to make no distinction between the so-called status offenses—which use noncriminal misbehavior to justify and invoke juvenile court jurisdiction—and juvenile criminal conduct. In the 1960s, California and New York took the lead in reforming their statutes to divide juvenile misbehavior into separate categories: criminal (delinquency) and noncriminal (persons in need of supervision or beyond control). California's Welfare and Institutions Code was amended to provide:

§ 601. Minors habitually refusing to obey parents; habitual truants; minors in danger of leading immoral life

Any person under the age of 18 years who persistently or habitually refuses to obey the reasonable and proper orders or directions of his parents, guardian, custodian or school authorities, or who is beyond the control of such person, or any person who is a habitual truant from school within the meaning of any law of this state, or who from any cause is in danger of leading an idle, dissolute, lewd, or immoral life, is within the jurisdiction of the juvenile court which may adjudge such person to be a ward of the court.

§ 602. Minors violating laws defining crime; minors failing to obey court order

Any person under the age of 18 years who violates any law of this state or of the United States or any ordinance of any city or county of this state defining crime or who, after having been found by the juvenile court to be a person described by Section 601, fails to obey any lawful order of the juvenile court, is within the jurisdiction of the juvenile court, which may adjudge such person to be a ward of the court.

Because any misbehavior sufficient to invoke juvenile court jurisdiction opened up the full range of dispositional alternatives—dismissal, probation or some form of incarceration, merely dividing status offenders into a separate legislative category had little impact on the actual conduct of juvenile courts. With rehabilitation of the child as the goal, disposition is proportional not to the child's conduct but to his perceived rehabilitative needs. For this reason a remarkable number of children were still being incarcerated for noncriminal conduct even in the late 1970s. The actual impact of semantic statutory distinctions was not mirrored by any real differences in treatment. As late as 1974 one major study found that of more than sixty-five thousand incarcerated juveniles, approximately half were status offenders.[3] If anything, the rate of detention appears higher among status offenders (perhaps because of parental refusal to take the child back into the home) than among delinquents. Although status offenses accounted for approximately one quarter of all juvenile court adjudications in the late 1960s and early 1970s, about half of all incarcerations stemmed from such cases.[4] Further, the status offense jurisdiction of the juvenile court is applied far more frequently to females than to males. More than half of the minor girls who appear before juvenile courts do so in response to status offense petitions while only about twenty percent of boys coming to juvenile courts are charged with noncriminal misbehavior.[5]

In response to the extensive incarceration of children on grounds of misbehavior rather than criminality, along with data from the scientific literature suggesting that children have capacity to make rational decisions for themselves, many state legislatures have amended their status offense provisions to remove incarceration as a

3. M. Rector, PINS: An American Scandal, 4 (NCCD, 1974).

4. President's Commission on Law Enforcement and the Administration of Justice, Task Force Report: Juvenile Delinquency 4 (1967); Note, Ungovernabili-ty: The Unjustifiable Jurisdiction, 83 Yale L.J. 1383 (1974).

5. A. Sussman, Sex-Based Discrimination and PINS Jurisdiction, in Teitelbaum and Gough, Beyond Control 179 n.3 (1977).

possible disposition. A typical result of this trend is the 1977 revision of California Welfare and Institutions Code § 207(a–c), infra at p. 632. In addition, the most recent version of Welf. & Inst. Code § 601 reflects the continued effort toward a more precise definition:

§ 601.　Minors habitually disobedient or truant

(a) Any person under the age of 18 years who persistently or habitually refuses to obey the reasonable and proper orders or directions of his parents, guardian, or custodian, or who is beyond the control of such person, or who is under the age of 18 years when he violated any ordinance of any city or county of this state establishing a curfew based solely on age is within the jurisdiction of the juvenile court which may adjudge such person to be a ward of the court.

(b) If a school attendance review board determines that the available public and private services are insufficient or inappropriate to correct the habitual truancy of the minor, or to correct the minor's persistent or habitual refusal to obey the reasonable and proper orders or directions of school authorities, or if the minor fails to respond to directives of a school attendance review board or to services provided, the minor is then within the jurisdiction of the juvenile court which may adjudge such person to be a ward of the court; provided, that it is the intent of the Legislature that no minor who is adjudged a ward of the court pursuant solely to this subdivision shall be removed from the custody of the parent or guardian except during school hours.

B.　CHALLENGES TO JURISDICTION

1.　STATUTORY VAGUENESS

COMMONWEALTH v. BRASHER

Supreme Judicial Court of Massachusetts, 1971.
359 Mass. 550, 270 N.E.2d 389.

QUIRICO, JUSTICE.

On May 3, 1969, a complaint issued from a District Court alleging that the defendant "being between seven and seventeen years of age, is a delinquent child in that during the one month last past before the making of this complaint, at Fall River . . . [she] was a stubborn child and did refuse to submit to the lawful and reasonable commands of . . . Michael T. Walsh whose commands said Dianne Brasher was bound to obey. (Violation of Chapter 272, sec. 53, General Laws)." [1] The defendant was tried in the District Court and was

---

1. General Laws c. 272, § 53, as amended through St.1959, c. 304, § 1, provides: "Stubborn children, runaways, common night walkers, both male and fe-

adjudged a delinquent child. She appealed to the Superior Court where she was again tried and adjudged a delinquent child. On July 2, 1969, the court ordered the defendant committed to the custody of the Youth Service Board (now the Department of Youth Services), suspended execution of the order for three years, and placed her on probation on condition that she be placed in the home of a named individual at Lowell. See G.L. c. 119, §§ 52–59, inclusive, as amended.

The case is before us on two principal issues raised by the defendant's bill of exceptions. The first issue is whether the statutes under which the defendant is being prosecuted are constitutional. The defendant contends that they are not for the reasons that (a) they deal with a subject matter which is beyond the State's police power, and (b) they are unconstitutionally vague and indefinite. . . .

The constitutional issue raised by the defendant is directed at the part of G.L. c. 272, § 53, which provides punishment for stubborn children, and for this reason it will be helpful to review the history and development of this part of the statute. This provision appears to have originated in an act passed by the House of Deputies of the Colony of the Massachusetts Bay in New England on August 22, 1654, stating that "it appears by too much experience that divers children & servants doe behave themselves too disrespectively, disobediently, & disorderly towards their parents, masters, & gouvernors, to the disturbance of families, & discouragement of such parents & gouvernors," and providing "corporall punishment by whiping, or otherwise," for such offenders. Mass. Bay Records, Vol. III (1644–1657) 355. Mass.Col.Laws (1887 ed.) 27.

The next statutory reference to stubborn children is in Prov.St. 1699–1700, c. 8, §§ 2–6, permitting courts to commit various offenders, including stubborn children and other persons now included in G.L. c. 272, § 53, to houses of correction.

When the Constitution of Massachusetts was adopted in 1780, it then provided, and still provides, in Part II, c. 6, art. 6, that "All the laws which have heretofore been adopted, used and approved in the Province, Colony or State of Massachusetts Bay, and usually practised on in the courts of law, shall still remain and be in full force, until altered or repealed by the Legislature; such parts only excepted as are repugnant to the rights and liberties contained in this Constitution." By virtue of this provision, the part of the Province laws relating to the punishment of stubborn children and certain other offenders became a part of the law of this Commonwealth. Over the years

male, common railers and brawlers, persons who with offensive and disorderly act or language accost or annoy persons of the opposite sex, lewd, wanton and lascivious persons in speech or behavior, idle and disorderly persons, prostitutes, disturbers of the peace, keepers of noisy and disorderly houses and persons guilty of indecent exposure may be punished by imprisonment in a jail or house of correction for not more than six months, or by a fine of not more than two hundred dollars, or by both such fine and imprisonment."

the section of the statute which included the punishment of stubborn children was subjected to many amendments and it was included in a number of periodic consolidations and rearrangements of our statutes. Despite this, the provision relating to stubborn children as now contained in G.L. c. 272, § 53, has remained basically the same.

Before discussing this particular case, it is appropriate to note that it is but the latest in a recent series of cases involving attacks, on constitutional grounds, on various provisions of G.L. c. 272, § 53. . . . In Joyner v. Commonwealth, Mass., 260 N.E.2d 664, 666, we held that the words "stubborn children" as used in § 53 did not include "those who have attained their eighteenth birthday," and we therefore were not required to pass on the constitutional attack on the statute. In the case now before us, the person raising the constitutional question is a child born on July 7, 1954. We must therefore now consider and decide the constitutional question which we did not reach in the *Joyner* case. In doing so we shall deal separately with the several grounds on which the defendant's claim of unconstitutionality is based.

(1) The principal ground upon which the defendant relies is that G.L. c. 272, § 53, in so far as it deals with stubborn children, is so vague and indefinite that it "leaves judges and jurors free to decide, without any legally fixed standards, what is prohibited and what is not in each particular case," and therefore violates the due process clause of the Fourteenth Amendment to the Constitution of the United States. . . . Applying . . . constitutional requirements to the part of § 53 which is before us, we think that it is constitutionally adequate.

We note, . . . that § 53 does not purport to create or to define new crimes, but rather it prescribes the penalties for persons committing acts theretofore long recognized by our law as amounting to criminal offences. Therefore, the elements of the crime which is identified by the use of the descriptive words "stubborn children" are not to be determined solely on the basis of the inclusion of those words in § 53. We must start by considering the language of the 1654 Colonial law which said that it was "for the ready prevention" of the evil of children who behave themselves "to disrespectively, disobediently, & disorderly towards their parents, masters & gouvernors." Mass.Bay Records, Vol. III (1644–1657) 355. Mass. Col.Laws (1887 ed.) 27. All later enactments, starting with Prov.St. 1699–1700, c. 8, §§ 2–6, limited themselves to prescribing the punishment for such acts and identified the offenders as "stubborn servants or children," and more recently as "stubborn children."

We also note . . . the permitted forms of complaints and indictments which are set forth in G.L. c. 277, § 79. They were first incorporated into our general statutes by St.1899, c. 409, sometimes referred to as the "act for the simplification of criminal pleading." As to stubborn children the statutory form is: "That A. B., a minor, during the three months next before the making of this complaint, was a stubborn child, and stubbornly refused to submit to the lawful and reasonable commands of C. D., whose commands said A. B. was bound to obey."

The elements of the crime which was established by the Colonial law of 1654 and which is now simply identified by use of the words "stubborn children" in G.L. c. 272, § 53, are ascertainable upon examination and consideration of the entire series of statutes on the subject. The 1654 statute made criminal the disobedience by children and servants toward their parents, masters and governors. After 245 years of experience with that statute and its successor statutes dealing with stubborn children, the Legislature in 1899 enacted a simplified form of complaint for this crime and it has now been in use for about seventy-two years.

The elements which the Commonwealth is required to prove beyond a reasonable doubt in order to constitute the crime commonly identified by use of the words "stubborn children" are the following: (a) that a person having authority to give a child under the age of eighteen lawful and reasonable commands which such child is bound to obey gave such a command to a child; (b) that the child refused to submit to the command, and the refusal was stubborn in the sense that it was wilful, obstinate and persistent for a period of time. The person giving the command is usually one of the child's parents, but it may be another person, as it was in this case. The defendant does not question that such other person, on the particular facts of this case, occupied such a position toward the defendant that he was authorized to give her lawful and reasonable commands which she was bound to obey. Single, infrequent or isolated refusals to obey such commands do not constitute a crime. Neither do manifestations of stubbornness which do not amount to refusals to obey commands. The law clearly does not make mere expressions of disagreement or differences of views or opinions between parent and child a crime on the part of the child. But it does not permit or excuse stubborn refusals by children to obey reasonable and lawful commands of their parents or persons similarly situated on a claim that it is merely the exercise of a right of dissent.

2. The defendant argues further that it is beyond the limits of the police power of the Commonwealth to make laws for the punishment of stubborn children for the reasons (a) that they punish children for disobeying commands having only moral, but not legal sanctions, and (b) that they constitute an impermissible intrusion into the privacy of family life.

The fact that a child is under a moral obligation to obey his parents does not preclude the Legislature, in the exercise of its police power, from making that same obligation a legal one, with criminal penalties for its breach. It has never been contended, nor can it be properly contended, that because it is morally wrong to steal or to do harm to the person of another, or to kill him, the Legislature is without power to make such conduct a crime and to prescribe penalties for the crime.

The argument that a law for the punishment of children who stubbornly disobey their parents is unconstitutional because it is an impermissible intrusion into the privacy of family life is without merit. While "[i]t is cardinal . . . that the custody, care and nurture of the child reside first in the parents, whose primary function and freedom include preparation for obligations . . . [in] the private realm of family life which the state cannot enter," such as religious teaching to children, "the family itself is not beyond regulation in the public interest." Prince v. Massachusetts, 321 U.S. 158, 166. The rights and obligations of members of families in relation to each other have been regulated by laws for centuries. 1 Blackstone, Commentaries (9th ed.) 446–454. In that time the law has always imposed a duty upon parents to support, provide for and protect the children they bring forth. This is an obligation which they owe to their children, but its breach is also a crime against society. In more recent times the law in this regard has been expanded to include the obligation to provide educational guidance. G.L. c. 273, § 1. To enable the parents to discharge that responsibility, the law gives them the custody of and right of control over their children. That carries with it the power to exercise whatever authority is reasonably necessary for the purpose, and to make all reasonable decisions for the control and proper functioning of the family as a harmonious social unit. It permits the parents to give reasonable commands to their children and to require the children to obey those commands. The children in turn owe the parents an obligation to acknowledge and submit to their authority and to obey their reasonable and lawful requests and commands. In short, the governing authority for the proper operation, control and discipline of the family unit is vested in the parents.

While the State defers to the parents with respect to most decisions on family matters, it has an interest in insuring the existence of harmonious relations between family members, and between the family unit and the rest of the public society. To protect this interest, the State may properly require that unemancipated children obey the reasonable and lawful commands of their parents, and it may impose criminal penalties on the children if they persistently disobey such commands. The State is not powerless to prevent or control situations which threaten the proper functioning of a family unit as an important segment of the total society. It may properly extend the protection of its laws in aid of the head of a family unit whose reasonable and lawful commands are being disobeyed by children who are bound to obey them. The making of such laws is within the power of the Legislature "to make, ordain, and establish, all manner of wholesome and reasonable Orders, laws, statutes, and ordinances, directions and instructions, either with penalties or without; . . . as . . . [it] shall judge to be for the good and welfare of this Commonwealth, and for the government and ordering thereof, and of the subjects of the same." Part II, c. 1, § 1, art. 4, of the Constitution of Massachusetts.

A substantial portion of the defendant's brief is devoted to the statement of facts and arguments of a sociological nature criticizing our present statutes governing proceedings against juvenile offenders, criticizing the physical facilities available for the detention of such offenders, and suggesting that many of the children confined in such facilities do not belong there. It also suggests that stubbornness in a child "may be symptomatic of a psychological defect in the child or inadequacy in the parent or both." Arguments of this type are not relevant to the legal issues presented for our decision. They would be more appropriate if addressed to the Legislature which has the power to change the statutes if it is persuaded that such changes are needed. We do not have that power.

. . . .

Exceptions overruled. Hold

DISTRICT OF COLUMBIA v. B.J.R.

District of Columbia Court of Appeals, 1975.
332 A.2d 58.

YEAGLEY, ASSOCIATE JUDGE:

This is an appeal from an order of the Family Division dismissing a petition, as amended, filed under D.C.Code 1973, § 16–2301(8)(A)(iii) and 16–2301(8)(B), on the ground that the definition of "children in need of supervision" in that statute (hereinafter CINS) is "unconstitutionally vague" and cannot be saved by reasonable construction. The amended petition alleged that the appellee was a child "in need of supervision in that she is habitually disobedient of the reasonable and lawful commands of her parent and is ungovernable." Appellee was specifically charged with absconding from home in April and October of 1969, in June and August of 1972, and on February 26, 1973. The last three abscondances were within the nine months preceding the March 6, 1973, filing of the CINS petition in the trial court.

The pertinent portion of § 16–2301 reads as follows:

(8) The term "child in need of supervision" means a child who—

(A) . . .

(iii) is habitually disobedient of the reasonable and lawful commands of his parent, guardian, or other custodian and is ungovernable; and

(B) is in need of care or rehabilitation.

The sole issue on appeal is whether or not this language under attack for vagueness passes constitutional muster. We find that it does.

The Supreme Court in Parker v. Levy, 417 U.S. 733, 752 (1974), recently summarized the due process elements of the "void-for-vagueness" doctrine:

> " 'The doctrine incorporates notions of fair notice or warning. Moreover, it requires legislatures to set reasonably clear guidelines for law enforcement officials and triers of fact in order to prevent "arbitrary and discriminatory enforcement." Where a statute's literal scope, unaided by narrowing state court interpretation, is capable of reaching expression sheltered by the First Amendment, the doctrine demands a greater degree of specificity than in other contexts.'

It is difficult to perceive how our CINS statute could violate these requirements when considered in regard to the conduct of the appellee.

Children of ordinary understanding know that to repeatedly abscond from home in defiance of the lawful commands of one's parent is a rather drastic form of disobedience that may well precipitate some disciplinary or punitive action. The statute here gave the appellee adequate warning that to abscond from home five times in four years, three of those times within the nine months preceding the instant petition, would subject her to the sanctions provided for a child who "is habitually disobedient of the reasonable and lawful commands of [her] parent . . . ." Such conduct establishes the "frequent practice or habit acquired over a period of time" required to satisfy the "habitually" element as that term was authoritatively construed under an earlier version of our juvenile statute . . . .

. . .

While it may be said that the wording of the CINS statute is somewhat broad and general, we must recognize, as did the Supreme Court when it considered the alleged vagueness of the Hatch Act, that

> . . . there are limitations in the English language with respect to being both specific and manageably brief, and it seems to us that although the prohibitions may not satisfy those intent on finding fault at any cost, they are set out in terms that the ordinary person exercising ordinary common sense can sufficiently understand and comply with, without sacrifice to the public interest.

Our juvenile code, particularly the CINS section, is not a criminal statute in the ordinary sense. Further, language limitations are particularly acute for the draftsmen of juvenile laws designed to implement the broad social policy of reinforcing parents in carrying out their responsibility to support and promote the welfare of their children. To enable parents to carry out this legal obligation, the law gives them the authority to control their children through the giving of reasonable and lawful commands. The CINS statute reinforces this authority and may be invoked when children repeatedly refuse to

CHALLENGES TO JURISDICTION

613

recognize their obligation to obey such commands. *See* Common-wealth v. Brasher, 359 Mass. 550, 270 N.E.2d 389 (1971).

The court is also mindful that our present CINS statute, adopted in 1970, is the product of highly competent, contemporaneous legal expertise in the drafting of juvenile court statutes. The definition of "children in need of supervision" is substantially identical to those proposed in the Uniform Juvenile Court Act (U.L.A.) § 2(4) (1973) and the Legislative Guide for Drafting Family and Juvenile Court Acts § 2(p) (Dept. of H.E.W., Children's Bureau Pub. No. 472–1969). The 1970 statute eliminated, *inter alia*, troublesome language from D.C. Code 1967, §§ 11–1551(a)(1)(H) and (I), which gave the juvenile court jurisdiction over children who engaged in "immoral" activities.[3] Neither the lower court nor the appellee has provided us with con-vincing suggestions for further improvement in our present act.

. . .

. . .

The trial court, in finding the CINS statute unconstitutionally vague, limited itself to an examination of the statute's facial validity without consideration of whether its language gave one such as the appellee fair warning that to repeatedly abscond from home would subject her to CINS sanctions. Appellee attempts to continue this line of reasoning on appeal by anticipating potentially abusive appli-cations of the statute in a variety of hypothetical situations, particu-larly emphasizing possible infringements upon First Amendment rights of children. But the Supreme Court in Parker v. Levy, supra, 417 U.S., at 759, 94 S.Ct. at 2563, rejected that approach when it said:

. . . "[e]mbedded in the traditional rules governing constitu-tional adjudication is the principle that a person to whom a statute may constitutionally be applied will not be heard to challenge that statute on the ground that it may conceivably be applied unconsti-tutionally to others, in other situations not before the Court."
. . . "[T]he Court has recognized some limited exceptions to these principles, but only because of the most 'weighty counter-vailing policies.'" One of those exceptions "has been carved out in the area of the First Amendment." . . .

We find no "weighty countervailing policies" in this case to justify allowing an attack on the facial validity of the CINS statute by one whose conduct clearly falls within its parameters.

Concked

. . .

3. Similar language in other statutes had been struck down on "vagueness" grounds in several jurisdictions. See e.g., Gesicki v. Oswald, 336 F.Supp. 371 (S.D.N.Y.1971) (holding unconstitutional N.Y.Code Crim.Proc. § 913–a(5) and (6) which allowed incarceration of children "morally depraved or in danger of be-coming morally depraved"). But see A. v. City of New York, 31 N.Y.2d 83, 286 N.E.2d 432 (1972) (upholding the "per-sons in need of supervision" portion of the same New York juvenile court act which consists of language remarkably similar to our own).

Neither the plainly legitimate sweep of the language of the CINS statute nor the facts of this case suggest a substantial infringement upon the constitutionally protected conduct of children so as to merit facial invalidation. The statute reinforces parents as they attempt to discipline their children in the broad ambit of family life. We conclude that the sort of activity that would establish a child as "habitually disobedient of the reasonable and lawful commands of his parent" would seldom directly and principally involve First Amendment activity such as expressive conduct or pure speech.

We find that the statute gave fair warning to the appellee that the sort of conduct involved here would come within its parameters. While the rule that party may not challenge a statute on the ground that it may be unconstitutionally applied to others has been modified somewhat where there are strong First Amendment considerations such as efforts to control "spoken words", we do not find such considerations in this case.

To the extent that First Amendment activities may be infringed when the CINS statute is applied, we suggest that in balancing such infringement against the right and duty of a parent to teach, control, and discipline a child, we are obliged, if we are to accord some recognition to reality, to grant the parent greater latitude in the First Amendment area than is permitted the state. However, such parental authority would be seriously undermined if not given some official support. It strikes us that in applying the First Amendment the strict enforcement of those rights must be tempered when we consider disciplinary problems involving a parent-child relationship.

. . .

. . . Here we do not find it necessary to impose a limiting construction on the statute to save it from this constitutional attack. The general class of conduct prohibited by the CINS statute is clear and we will not invalidate the statute on the basis of a hypothetical argument that it might conceivably be applied unconstitutionally. For the reasons we have delineated, we hold that it was error for the trial court to dismiss the petition and accordingly it is ordered reinstated.

Reversed and remanded for further proceedings not inconsistent with this opinion.

E.S.G. v. STATE

Court of Civil Appeals of Texas, 1969.
447 S.W.2d 225.

BARROW, CHIEF JUSTICE.

Appellant, a girl fourteen years of age, was adjudged delinquent by the Juvenile Court of Bexar County after a non-jury trial and committed to the custody of the Texas Youth Council for an indefinite term not extending beyond her twenty-first birthday, in accordance with the provisions of the Texas Juvenile Act, Art. 2338–1, Vernon's Ann.Civ.St. She is presently confined in the State Training School for Girls.

The finding of delinquency is based on Sec. 3(f) of said Act, which defines a delinquent child as one who "habitually so deports himself as to injure or endanger the morals or health of himself or others." The question presented here is whether this portion of the statute is unconstitutionally vague. No question is presented as to the fairness of the trial, the adequacy of the evidence, or whether the essentials of due process were observed.

This case was originally drawn by Justice Cadena, and while we find no disagreement with the exhaustive and scholarly presentation of the problem raised by the "void for vagueness" doctrine as set forth in his opinion, we disagree with his conclusion that Sec. 3(f), supra, is unconstitutional. Accordingly, this opinion is filed as the majority opinion of this Court.

The relatively comprehensive word "morals" is one which conveys concrete impressions to the ordinary person. Such word is in constant use in popular parlance, and this word or words of similar import are used in the statutes of most States to define behavior illegal for a child. In thirty-three States a child can be found delinquent if he is guilty of immoral conduct, and the various States' definitions of immoral conduct are all somewhat similar to Sec. 3(f). The obvious reason for granting such broad and general jurisdiction is seen when one makes even a cursory attempt to define all the types and patterns of behavior and conduct injurious to a child. The need to correct habits and patterns of behavior which are injurious to the health or morals of the child goes to the very heart of our Juvenile Act. The judge in this case observed that most girls who came before said court were charged with violation of this section.

It is not questioned that appellant was engaged in a course of conduct injurious to her morals, if not her health. Nor could it be questioned that this fourteen-year-old girl understood that such conduct was injurious to her morals. Even her attorney recognized that her parents had lost control and that the girl desperately needed supervision. She was gone from her home for days at a time and lived with a girl reputed by appellant's mother to be a prostitute. Appellant and this girl hung around the Greyhound Bus Station and other public places. She was brought before the Juvenile Court after her mother had located her in a downtown transient apartment with a young adult male. She had been gone from home for over a week on this occasion, and when apprehended by her mother and a policeman she was only partially dressed. This case history illustrates the need for a provision such as found in Sec. 3(f), supra.

. . .

It is conceded that Sec. 3(f) defines a delinquent child in general terms. However, the petition filed under same must allege the specific acts or conduct which brings the child within the prohibited behavior. This protects the rights of the child in the adjudicatory stage of the proceedings. We do not believe that the section in question is unconstitutionally vague.

. . .

The judgment is affirmed.

CADENA, JUSTICE (dissenting).

The Texas Juvenile Act, is typical of almost every statute on the subject in that, after defining the term "delinquent child" in rather specific language relating to conduct violative of penal statutes and ordinances, it vests broad discretion in the Juvenile Court by extending the definition to include any child who "habitually so deports himself as to injure or endanger the morals or health of himself or others" or who "habitually associates with vicious and immoral persons." In this case, the petition filed by the State alleged that appellant had habitually so conducted herself as to endanger "the morals or health of herself and others," without specifying whether the facts alleged in the petition constituted a threat to appellant's morals or health, or to the morals or health of others.

. . .

The vagueness doctrine requires that a statute be sufficiently clear to give notice of the conduct required or prohibited to those whose activity the statute attempts to regulate. A judgment that a particular statute does not provide the required certainty or definiteness is seldom, if ever, a completely objective conclusion. What is uncertain today may have been certain yesterday and may be certain again tomorrow. What is uncertain to one judge may be certain to another, and what is uncertain to one judge in one area of the law may be certain to the same judge as to another subject matter.

Unfortunately, the decisions which speak of vagueness do so in vague terms which are the source of counter-sounding quotations. Thus, we are told that "a statute which either forbids or requires the doing of an act in terms so vague that men of common intelligence must necessarily guess at its meaning and differ as to its application violates the first essential of due process . . . ." [9] On the other hand, it is a fact, as Mr. Justice Holmes observed, that "the law is full of instances where a man's fate depends on his estimating rightly . . . some matter of degree. If his judgment is wrong, not only may he incur a fine or a short imprisonment . . ., he may incur the penalty of death.[10]

9. Connally v. General Construction Co., 269 U.S. 385, 391, 46 S.Ct. 126, 128, 70 L.Ed. 322 (1926). The statute involved in Connally proscribed the payment to laborers of "less than the current rate of per diem wages in the locality where the work is performed." In holding the statute unconstitutionally vague, the Court seemingly overlooked the fact that it had earlier upheld an almost identical statute. Atkin v. Kansas, 191 U.S. 207, 24 S.Ct. 124, 48 L.Ed. 148.

10. Nash v. United States, 229 U.S. 373, 377, 33 S.Ct. 780, 781, 57 L.Ed. 1232 (1913).

The vagueness doctrine, of course, creates practical difficulties. Although speaking in dissent, Mr. Justice Frankfurter has well articulated the resulting legislative problem:

"In these matters, legislatures are confronted with a dilemma. If a law is framed with narrow particularity, too easy opportunities are afforded to nullify the purpose of the legislation. If the legislation is drafted in terms so vague that no ascertainable line is drawn in advance between innocent and condemned conduct, the purpose of the legislation cannot be enforced because no purpose is defined. . . . The reconciliation of these two contradictories is necessarily an empirical enterprise largely depending on the nature of the particular legislative problem.

"What risks do the innocent run of being caught in a net not designed for them? How important is the policy of the legislation, so that those who really like to pursue innocent conduct are not likely to be caught unaware? How easy is it to be explicitly particular? How necessary is it to leave a somewhat penumbral margin but sufficiently revealed by what is condemned to those who do not want to sail close to the shore of questionable conduct? These and like questions confront legislative draftsmen. Answers to these questions are not to be found in any legislative manual . . . . They are not to be found in the opinions of this Court. . . ."[11]

Appellant here was found guilty of "habitually" engaging in conduct calculated to "injure" or "endanger" the "morals" or "health" of herself or of others. The principal source of uncertainty in the statute probably results from the use of the word "morals," a term involving an appeal to judgment and requiring determination of questions of degree, although, perhaps to a lesser extent, the words "habitually," "injure" and "danger" are also classifiable as ductile terms.[12] The difficulty with terms such as "morals" is that they have no external "object-referent."

. . .

. . . The consistent failure of courts to attempt to define language of the type now before us merely points up the fact that such language has no objective meaning in the sense of contrast with merely individual opinion or preference. If a statute is, in reality, not vague, the result would be that, after the decision in the particular case, the statute is sufficiently clear and precise to enable men of common intelligence and understanding to determine what is prohibited and what is permissible. . . . [T]he opinion in this case [does not] satisfy this test. It is no answer to a vagueness attack to say

11. Winters v. New York, 333 U.S. 507, 525–526, 68 S.Ct. 665, 675, 92 L.Ed. 840 (1948).

12. One writer has distinguished three grades of certainty in statutes: precisely measured terms; abstractions of common certainty; and terms involving an appeal to judgment or questions of degree. Freund, The Use of Indefinite Terms in Statutes, 30 Yale L.J. 437 (1921).

that language is definite and certain while confessing a complete inability to express what the language means.

In any event, cases where judges profess to understand perfectly the meaning of such terms as "morals" are instances where the statutory language is directed to adults. Here, a directive addressed to children is couched in terms which have been the source of controversy among theologians, philosophers and judges for centuries. It is one thing to say that a judge, drawing upon his experience and knowledge of the law and of "meanings" attached to nebulous terms at common law, should understand what is moral and what is not. It is another thing to expect a child of ten or, as in this case, of fourteen, to understand the meaning of words which judges are unable to define while assuring us that the language is "perfectly clear."

. . .

The provision on which the State relies in this case is typically vague and all-encompassing, especially when administered with the informality which is typical of the juvenile court. It establishes the judge or jury as the arbiter of the behavior and morals of every child. The situation is ripe for overreaching, for imposition of the judge's or jury's own code of youthful conduct. Such provisions easily become a means of enforcing conformity. For example, today, most adults seem to associate long hair with immoral conduct, except, perhaps, in the case of their own children, in which instance it is regarded as nothing more than an unsettling and transitory adolescent foible. The provision in question is vague enough to allow almost any child, given compromising circumstances, to be caught up in the jurisdictional net of the juvenile court.

Provisions such as those found in Section 3(f) lack a common meaning; they are not derived from fixed, or even reasonably fixed, criteria; they allow labeling a child as a "delinquent" even where it is clear that his actions are reasonably normal responses to highly provocative or intolerable situations. The statute, lacking reasonable standards, is "susceptible of sweeping and improper application," [17] and it furnishes a convenient tool for use against particular persons or groups who incur official displeasure. Nor is there any overriding need for such vagueness. In the case of appellant, a sufficiently clear warning could have been formulated by the Legislature without calling in the English faculty of a university. All that had to be done was to state that a child who ran away from home was in need of the State's "protection." Such direct statutory language would authorize the commitment of more than a majority of the girls who have been committed to a state training school.

Our Legislature, perhaps, has the power to make the jurisdiction of the juvenile court depend upon unexamined assumptions that cer-

17. N.A.A.C.P. v. Button, 371 U.S. 415, 433, 83 S.Ct. 328, 9 L.Ed.2d 405 (1963).

tain conduct is a precursor to delinquency. I do not accept the explanation that we cannot adequately protect our youth without vesting the courts with power to make their findings of jurisdiction dependent on subjective definitions.

I would reverse the judgment below.

NOTES

(1) Responding to concern (not amounting to constitutional infirmity) that some statutory definitions fail to provide adequate notice to juveniles that their conduct may ground court jurisdiction, California in 1975 amended its Welfare and Institutions Code § 601 to delete from the definition of those beyond control any juvenile "who from any cause is in danger of leading an idle, dissolute, lewd or immoral life" 1975 Cal.Stat. ch. 192, § 1; ch. 1183, § 2.

(2) What if parent and child have different political or religious opinions? Would these decisions permit parents to invoke the aid of the juvenile court to suppress the child's speech or religious practice?

(3) What sorts of sociological, psychological and statistical data do you suppose counsel for Dianne Brasher presented in his brief? Today some courts might find such data more insightful than irrelevant since vagueness as a theoretical concept in constitutional litigation seems so susceptible to circular argument and conclusionary labeling. See for example the data from the New York Family Court presented in Note, Ungovernability: The Unjustifiable Jurisdiction, 83 Yale L.J. 1383 (1974) or Andrews & Cohn, PINS Processing in New York: An Evaluation, in L. Teitelbaum & A. Gough, Beyond Control 45 (1977).

(4) As the dissent in E.S.G. v. State suggests, many vagueness cases refer only to each other in upholding the noncriminal misbehavior statutes. See for example In re Napier, 532 P.2d 423 (Okl.1975). Do you agree with the comment that "[t]his group of juveniles (PINS Children) is brought into the system for the crime of not adjusting well to society's norms, of lacking a caring, supportive home life, or of simply being confused and unaware in their adolescent years. No doubt, most of us could have been classified as children in need of supervision at some point in our early years, but due to our race or economic class or some arbitrary standard were never processed through the juvenile justice system." J. L. King, A Comparative Analysis of Juvenile Codes 26 (U.S. Dept. of Justice, L.E.A.A., Washington, D.C. 1980).

(5) Assuming a continuation of juvenile court jurisdiction over noncriminal misbehavior, can you suggest any more precise definition of the conduct such statutes should cover? Wouldn't a persuasive brief need to contain suggested alternative statutory language that would pass muster under the void-for-vagueness doctrine?

(6) Does rejection of these void-for-vagueness arguments express a judicial preference for legislative reform?

(7) For an argument that the original Massachusetts stubborn child law was "modern", political and typical of other similar colonial legislation about children, see Sutton, Stubborn Children: Law and the Socialization of Deviance in the Puritan Colonies, 15 Fam.L.Q. 31 (1981). The author suggests that by bringing the force of the law to bear on stubborn children, the early

Puritans were engaged in a political as well as religious experiment that called on the whole community to react to deviance. By normalizing and, in that way, socializing deviant behavior, the Puritans presaged later 19th century legal developments such as the creation of special courts for children.

2. EQUAL PROTECTION CHALLENGES

IN RE WALKER

Supreme Court of North Carolina, 1972.
282 N.C. 28, 191 S.E.2d 702.

HUSKINS, JUSTICE:

. . .

Appellant's second contention is that G.S. § 7A–286 violates the Equal Protection Clause of the Fourteenth Amendment in that it subjects an undisciplined child to probation and the concomitant risk of incarceration when the child has committed no criminal offense, while adults are subjected to probation and incarceration only for actual criminal offenses. See G.S. § 15–197.

The Equal Protection Clause "avoids what is done only when it is without any reasonable basis, and therefore is purely arbitrary." Thus, if a classification is "based on differences that are reasonably related to the purposes of the Act in which it is found", then it does not offend the Equal Protection Clause, unless the classification affects "fundamental" interests or is "inherently suspect," in which event it "must be closely scrutinized and carefully confined", and the State must advance a " 'compelling interest' which justifies imposing such heavy burdens" in order for the classification to be constitutional. A showing of mere rationality is insufficient.

The purpose of the Juvenile Court Act "is not for the punishment of offenders but for the salvation of children". Commonwealth v. Fisher, 213 Pa. 48, 62 A. 198 (1905). The Act treats "delinquent children not as criminals, but as wards, and undertakes . . . to give them the control and environment that may lead to their reformation, and enable them to become law-abiding and useful citizens, a support and not a hindrance to the commonwealth." State v. Burnett, 179 N.C. 735, 102 S.E. 711 (1920). The State must exercise its power as "*parens patriae* to protect and provide for the comfort and well-being of such of its citizens as by reason of infancy . . . are unable to take care of themselves." County of McLean v. Humphreys, 104 Ill. 378 (1882). Thus, juveniles are in need of supervision and control due to their inability to protect themselves. In contrast, adults are regarded as self sufficient.

Therefore, the classification here challenged is based on differences between adults and children; and there are so many valid distinctions that the basis for challenge seems shallow. These differences are "reasonably related to the purposes of the Act"—that is, to provide children the needed supervision and control. Consequently, the classification does not offend the Equal Protection Clause . . . and even if it be said that the classification here challenged affects "fundamental interests" or is "inherently suspect," it is our view that the desire of the State to exercise its authority as *parens patriae* and provide for the care and protection of its children supplies a "compellingly rational" justification for the classification.

The conclusion we reach—that G.S. § 7A–278 and related statutes do not violate the Equal Protection Clause by classifying and treating children differently from adults—has also been reached in numerous cases upholding juvenile Acts in other states. . . .

. . .

Affirmed.

[The dissenting opinion of Bobbitt, Chief Justice, is omitted.]

NOTES

(1) As the *Walker* court indicates, the outcome in litigation of equal protection claims usually depends on which party bears the burden of proof. Because of our presumption in favor of legislative judgment in a democracy, usually a litigant who claims a statutory classification denies him or her equal protection bears the burden of persuading the court that the legislative classification has no rational basis. So long as the statute is rationally related to a legitimate legislative purpose, the courts will defer to the legislature's judgment and the challenge will fail. But if the person complaining of unequal treatment can show that the statute or ordinance makes what courts have come to view as a "suspect classification," the litigant is entitled to strict judicial scrutiny of the statutory classification; this effectively shifts to the state the burden of demonstrating a compelling state interest to justify the inequality of treatment. Not surprisingly, the history of the extensive equal protection litigation is a history of the efforts of one social group after another to attain the "suspect classification" status because whoever bears the burden of proof is overwhelmingly likely to lose in most instances. See Bonnie & Whitebread, Forbidden Fruit and the Tree of Knowledge: An Inquiry into the History of American Marihuana Prohibition, 56 Va.L.Rev. 971, 1125–33, 1140–55 (1970).

Race and national origin are suspect classifications and any statute that provides differential treatment based on race is presumptively invalid. Rarely can states show a sufficiently compelling state interest to uphold such legislation. See, however, Ambach v. Norwick, 441 U.S. 68, 99 S.Ct. 1589, 60 L.Ed.2d 49 (1979), in which the United States Supreme Court rejected an equal protection challenge to a New York statute restricting certification of non-citizens as public school teachers. In *Ambach*, two resident aliens who met all state requirements for certification as public school teachers, but who had consistently refused to seek United States citizenship, attempted to enjoin the enforcement of a New York statute forbidding certification as a public school teacher of any person not a citizen of the United States unless that person has manifested an intention to apply for citizenship. The United States District Court for the Southern District of New York, applying the "close judicial scrutiny" standard, held that the statute discriminated against aliens in violation of the equal protection clause of the fourteenth amendment (417 F.Supp 913).

On direct appeal, the United States Supreme Court reversed, holding the statute did not violate equal protection since (1) public school teachers perform one of those governmental functions that are so bound up with the operation of the state as a governmental entity as to permit the exclusion from those functions of all persons who have not become part of the process of self-government (2) the Federal Constitution requires only that a citizenship requirement applicable to public school teaching bear a rational relationship to a legitimate state interest, and (3) the New York statute bore such a rational relationship to the state's interest in furthering its educational goals.

Justice Powell's opinion traces the evolution of strict scrutiny for classifications based on alienage but concludes that certain inherently governmental functions may exclude aliens and that such exclusions are subject only to the rational basis test. Membership in the police force may be denied to aliens, *Foley v. Connelie*, 435 U.S. 291, 98 S.Ct. 1067, 55 L.Ed.2d 287 (1978), because the police function fulfills the "most fundamental obligation of government to its constituency" and because of the substantial discretionary power with which we invest police. Extending *Foley*, Justice Powell in *Ambach* concludes that teachers in public schools perform a task that goes to the heart of representative government—the preparation of individuals for participation as citizens and transmission of democratic social values.

In recent years, other groups such as women and illegitimate children have claimed the special status of suspect classification. Both have failed. The sex discrimination cases have resulted in courts taking a middle ground position in reviewing the constitutionality of legislation that treats the sexes unequally. For application of the intermediate scrutiny concept in sex discrimination cases see the cases on p. 627.

For a discussion of the use of classifications to determine the validity of limitations on inheritance rights for illegitimate children, see p. 117 supra.

(2) Each case in Note 1 involved challenges to statutes treating legitimate and illegitimate children differently. What about the larger claim asserted in *Walker* that children are constitutionally entitled to equality of treatment with adults?

Adults cannot be taken into custody and perhaps ultimately held against their will in a secure facility for a substantial period of time for failing to come home at night, running away or skipping school. When a college or law student elects not to attend class, should school officials, parents or concerned friends be permitted to invoke legal process against the student? Are there enough police to enforce attendance at college or professional school classes given the remarkable incidence of absenteeism?

(3) What legitimate interests of the state persuade you that the historic differences in treatment between adults and juveniles are justified?

Do you agree with the following assessment by Judge Lindsay Arthur of whether children are entitled to equal protection of the law:

> It is abundantly clear that Americans insist that their children have *unequal* protection. Our local, state and federal governments, our churches, United Ways and social groups are all replete with subsidized programs exclusive for children's needs. Children are provided with special pro-

grams for medical and dental care, for reading and writing, for Sunday School, camping, merit badges and Big Brothers. Children have special needs to cope with infancy and adolescence; they need unequal protection.

Youth problems—both criminal and emotional—are more serious than ever before. Society must bring all of its rehabilitative tools to the aid of troubled youth and their parents. Every effort must be made to assure that young lives are not wasted before the child has the maturity and experience to realize the full consequences of his or her actions. The Standards assume that court justification will be necessary to protect society's interests only when a criminal violation has been committed. But society has a crucial interest in the proper socialization of its children. The mores and values transmitted to children are essential to the survival and continuity of America. Although specific mores may be challenged and changed and although diversity must be tolerated and encouraged, this dialectic depends on the overall stability of the social system. The process of socialization or rehabilitation is more effective among susceptible youth, and the dangers of improper socialization are greater. Thus, the legislatures need not and should not restrict juvenile court intervention to the same standard of restraint that is mandated for adults. Youth problems should be corrected before the child commits an antisocial act that is punishable by a criminal statute.

Arthur, Status Offenders Need a Court of Last Resort, 57 B.U.L.Rev. 631, 641–42 (1977).*

(4) For a clear indication the United States Supreme Court still finds persuasive distinctions to justify differential treatment of children and adults, see the discussion in Parham v. J.R., 442 U.S. 584, 99 S.Ct. 2493, 61 L.Ed.2d 101 (1979) supra p. 169, rejecting the argument that children and adults should be entitled to the same procedural protection prior to involuntary civil commitment to a mental hospital.

3. SEX-BASED DISCRIMINATION

LAMB v. BROWN

United States Court of Appeals, Tenth Circuit, 1972.
456 F.2d 18.

BARRETT, CIRCUIT JUDGE.

Danny Ray Lamb, then 17 years of age, was tried as an adult under 10 Okl.St.Ann. § 1101 (Supp.1969) for the crime of burglary of an automobile, a felony proscribed by 21 Okl.St.Ann. § 1435.

Lamb contends that he should have been proceeded against as a juvenile in juvenile court. He argues that 10 Okl.St.Ann. § 1101 (Supp.1969) is unconstitutional in that it allows females the benefits of juvenile court proceedings under the age of 18 years while limiting those same benefits to males under the age of 16 years. The Oklahoma Supreme Court ruled on this issue in Lamb v. State, 475 P.2d 829 (Okl.1970). There the Court said:

> ". . . [A]s we view the section of the statutes, we do not find it to be so repugnant to the Constitution of the United States as the defendants would attempt to lead the Court to believe. As we view the situation, the statute exemplifies the legislative judgment of the Oklahoma State Legislature, *premised upon the demonstrated facts of life;* and we refuse to interfere with that judgment." 475 P.2d at 830. (Emphasis ours).

. . .

Lamb filed a habeas corpus application in the federal district court below alleging that 10 Okl.St.Ann. § 1101 (Supp.1969) is violative of the equal protection clause of the Fourteenth Amendment of the United States Constitution. He appeals from denial of relief.

10 Okl.St.Ann. § 1101(a) provides in pertinent part: "The term 'child' means any male person under the age of sixteen (16) years and any female person under the age of eighteen (18) years." Appellant urges that this distinction between the sexes amounts to an invidious discrimination against males violative of the equal protection clause of the Fourteenth Amendment.

. . .

We are strongly disinclined to hold that the considered judgment of the Oklahoma Legislature in the enactment of 10 Okl.St.Ann. § 1101(a) does not meet the measure of federal constitutional standards. The United States Supreme Court has said this with regard to the equal protection test:

> "The Fourteenth Amendment means 'that no person or class of persons shall be denied the same protection of the laws which is enjoyed by other persons or other classes in the same place and under like circumstances.' (Citation omitted). The general doctrine is that that amendment, in respect of the administration of criminal justice requires that no different degree or higher punishment shall be imposed on one than is imposed on all for like offenses; . . . ."

> "Judicial inquiry under the Equal Protection Clause, therefore, does not end with a showing of equal application among the members of the class defined by the legislation. The courts must reach and determine the question whether the classifications drawn in a statute are reasonable in light of its purpose . . . ." McLaughlin v. Florida, supra, 379 U.S. at 191, 85 S.Ct. at 288.

Lamb v. State, supra, is not helpful in our search for a rational justification for the disparity in treatment between 16–18 year old males and 16–18 year old females under the statute. "Demonstrated facts of life" could mean many things. The "demonstrated facts" which the Court relied upon are not spelled out. They are not obvious or apparent. We therefore cannot weigh them to determine if they "might suffice to characterize the classification as reasonable rather than arbitrary and invidious". McLaughlin v. Florida, supra, 379 U.S. at 191, 85 S.Ct. at 288.

We have not been presented with a logical constitutional justification for the discrimination inherent in 10 Okl.St.Ann. § 1101(a). The State, in its brief and oral argument has simply relied upon the unexplained "demonstrated facts of life". Because the purpose of the disparity in the age classification between 16–18 year old males and 16–18 year old females has not been demonstrated, we hold that 10 Okl.St.Ann. § 1101(a) is violative of the equal protection clause.

Reversed and remanded.

PATRICIA A. v. CITY OF NEW YORK

Court of Appeals of New York, 1972.
31 N.Y.2d 83, 335 N.Y.S.2d 33, 286 N.E.2d 432.

FULD, CHIEF JUDGE.

The appellant Patricia A. has been adjudicated a person in need of supervision (referred to at times as PINS) pursuant to section 712 (subd. [b]) of the Family Court Act. Such a person is there defined as "a male less than sixteen years of age and a female less than eighteen years of age who does not attend school in accord with the provisions of part one of article sixty-five of the education law [relating to truancy or other nonattendance] or who is incorrigible, ungovernable or habitually disobedient and beyond the lawful control of parent or other lawful authority." The appellant, 16 years old at the time of her PINS adjudication, contends, . . . that [the statute] discriminates against the 16 and 17-year-old female in violation of the Equal Protection Clause of the State and Federal Constitutions. . . .

. . .

The object of the PINS statute is to provide rehabilitation and treatment for young persons who engage in the sort of conduct there proscribed. This affords no reasonable ground, however, for differentiating between males and females over 16 and under 18. Girls in that age bracket are no more prone than boys to truancy, disobedience, incorrigible conduct and the like, nor are they more in need of rehabilitation and treatment by reason of such conduct.

The argument that discrimination against females on the basis of age is justified because of the obvious danger of pregnancy in an immature girl and because of out-of-wedlock births which add to the welfare relief burdens of the State and city is without merit. It is enough to say that the contention completely ignores the fact that the statute covers far more than acts of sexual misconduct. But, beyond that, even if we were to assume that the legislation had been prompted by such considerations, there would have been no rational basis for exempting, from the PINS definition, the 16 and 17-year-old boy responsible for the girl's pregnancy or the out-of-wedlock birth. As it is, the conclusion seems inescapable that lurking behind the discrimination is the imputation that females who engage in misconduct, sexual or otherwise, ought more to be censured, and their conduct subject to greater control and regulation, than males.

Somewhat similar moral presumptions have been squarely rejected as a basis or excuse for sexually discriminatory legislation. (See Stanley v. Illinois, 405 U.S. 645, 92 S.Ct. 1208, 31 L.Ed.2d 551, supra; Eisenstadt v. Baird, 405 U.S. 438, 92 S.Ct. 1029, 31 L.Ed.2d 349, supra.) Thus, in the *Stanley* case, the Supreme Court reversed a determination of the Illinois high court upholding a statute which made the children of unwed fathers wards of the State upon the death of the mother. It was a denial of equal protection, the court decided, to refuse a hearing to unmarried fathers as to their fitness to have custody of their children and, in effect, to presume that such fathers, as opposed to unwed mothers and other parents, are unsuitable and neglectful parents (405 U.S., at pp. 654, 655, 92 S.Ct. at pp. 1214, 1215.) If an unwed father may not lose the custody of his children without the hearing to which unmarried mothers and other parents would be entitled, by a parity of reasoning, a girl of 16 or 17 may not be subject to a possible loss of liberty for conduct which would be entirely licit for 16 and 17-year-old boys.

Consequently, since there is no justification for the age-sex distinction, so much of section 712 (subd. [b]) of the Family Court Act as encompasses females between the ages of 16 and 18 must be stricken as unconstitutional.

The order appealed from should be reversed, without costs, and the petition dismissed.

SCILEPPI AND JASEN, JUDGES, dissent and vote to affirm in the following memorandum:

We dissent and vote to affirm on the ground that there is a rational basis for the distinction made between male and female offenders. The additional protection afforded females as provided for in the statute is realistic and reasonable and since the age differential applies to all females alike, there is no denial of equal protection.

NOTES

(1) To the same effect see Ex parte Matthews, 488 S.W.2d 434 (Tex.Cr. App.1973) declaring unconstitutional a similar Texas statute defining females under 18 and males under 17 within juvenile court jurisdiction. As in Lamb v. Brown, the Texas court could find no rational basis for the distinction in treatment between males and females. These and other cases, as well as differential treatment of male and female juveniles in various contexts, are analyzed in Davis and Chaires, Equal Protection for Juveniles: The Present Status of Sex-Based Discrimination in Juvenile Court Laws, 7 Ga.L.Rev. 494 (1973).

(2) Does the dissent in *Patricia A.* make any sense at all? What "reasonable" and "realistic" basis supports the difference in treatment of boys

and girls? What could the dissenters mean when they assert: "since the age differential applies to all females alike, there is no denial of equal protection"? How would you argue against that position?

(3) The state's reliance on concern about female pregnancy to justify the difference in treatment by sex—strongly rejected by Chief Judge Fuld in *Patricia A.*—was persuasive to the United States Supreme Court, which held in Michael M. v. Superior Court, 450 U.S. 464, 101 S.Ct. 1200, 67 L.Ed.2d 437 (1981), that a California statute that makes men alone criminally liable for the act of sexual intercourse with a female under age 18 and not the perpetrator's wife does not violate the equal protection clause of the fourteenth amendment.

In this case, the male defendant approached a 16½ year old female at a bus stop. The defendant and the victim moved away from the bus stop and began to kiss. Both had been drinking. After being hit in the face for resisting defendant's initial advances, the victim submitted to sexual intercourse with the defendant.

Prior to trial, the defendant sought to set aside the case on both state and federal constitutional grounds, claiming that the statute unlawfully discriminated on the basis of gender. Both the trial court and the California Court of Appeal denied the request. The California Supreme Court affirmed this decision. The California Supreme Court held that the law discriminates on the basis of sex because only females may be victims and only males may violate the section. But the court, subjecting the classification to "strict scrutiny," found that the law was justified by a compelling state interest in preventing teenage pregnancies.

In affirming the judgment of the California Supreme Court, the U.S. Supreme Court declined to apply the "strict scrutiny" test. In a plurality opinion, Justice Rehnquist pointed to the decisions in Reed v. Reed, 404 U.S. 71, 92 S.Ct. 251, 30 L.Ed.2d 225 (1971), and Craig v. Boren, 429 U.S. 190, 97 S.Ct. 451, 50 L.Ed.2d 397 (1976) explaining that the classification must only "bear a substantial relationship" to "important governmental objectives." Turning to the California law, the Court ruled that the statute was sufficiently related to the state's objective of preventing illegitimate teenage pregnancies to pass constitutional review. Justice Rehnquist emphasized that "[b]ecause virtually all of the significant harmful and inescapably identifiable consequences of teenage pregnancy fall on the young female, a legislature acts well within its authority when it elects to punish only the participant who, by nature, suffers few of the consequences of his conduct." 450 U.S. at 473. The plurality opinion noted that the risk of pregnancy itself constitutes a deterrence to young females while the criminal sanction imposed solely on males is viewed as an equalizing deterrent. Highlighting the lack of a fourteenth amendment violation, Justice Rehnquist stated:

. . . [B]ecause the Equal Protection Clause does not "demand that a statute necessarily apply equally to all persons" or require " 'things which are different in fact . . . to be treated in law as though they were the same,' " this Court has consistently upheld statutes where the gender classification is not invidious, but rather realistically reflects the fact that the sexes are not similarly situated in certain circumstances.

450 U.S. at 469.

Finally, the plurality opinion rejected defendant's arguments that the statute was overbroad and that a gender-neutral statute would be as effective. With reference to the latter argument, the Court agreed with the state's view that such a scheme would frustrate enforcement efforts. This view stems from the belief that a female would be less likely to report violations of the statute if she were subject to criminal prosecution.

The dissenters principally claimed that the state had not met its burden of proving that the statutory classification was substantially related to achievement of its asserted goal. In addition, they argued that the state had not demonstrated the ineffectiveness of a gender-neutral statute. Justice Brennan, writing for the dissenters, emphasized two flaws in the state's frustration of enforcement position. First, the experience of other jurisdictions that have gender-neutral laws belies the state's frustration argument. Second, even assuming enforcement problems, the state had not shown that such problems would make a gender-neutral statute less effective than the gender-based statute in deterring minor females from engaging in sexual conduct.

(4) Many commentators have attacked the continuation of juvenile court jurisdiction over noncriminal misbehavior in part because females constitute a much higher percentage of status offenders than delinquents. Girls who make up only 25 percent of those subject to juvenile court jurisdiction appear in at least one-half of all status offense proceedings. In one study, 62 percent of status offense petitions in the New York city courts involved girls. Note, Ungovernability: The Unjustifiable Jurisdiction, 83 Yale L.J. 1383, 1387 n. 26 (1974). An earlier New York State study found 11,466 delinquency petitions brought against boys and only 1514 against girls. There were just about an equal number of status offense petitions for each sex—3784 against boys, 3750 against girls. State of New York, *The Judicial Conference, Nineteenth Annual Report* 400–420 (1974). Further, until the recent movement away from institutionalization of status offenders, a substantial percentage of all incarcerated women in this country were those placed in secure facilities as a result of being adjudicated status offenders. See K. Burkhart, Women in Prison (1973).

Professor Alan Sussman suggests three explanations for the use of status offense jurisdiction to enforce a double standard of permissible moral behavior for boys and girls:

Beyond doubt, the vagueness of jurisdictional definitions places children of both sexes at considerable risk. The statutes neither clearly inform the youth of the limits to his or her conduct nor limit the circumstances under which he or she may be charged with wrongdoing. In addition, girls often suffer the further disadvantage of being subject to a stricter code of ethics or a "higher" level of acceptable behavior than boys, and thereby, to greater regulation by parents and courts. This is the case with specific charges of sexual behavior, and it has further been suggested that charges of "ungovernability" or "incorrigibility" also serve as euphemistic vehicles for complaints involving sexual misbehavior or promiscuity. Given the breadth of most PINS provisions—under which nearly every child could be said to be culpable to some degree—and given the fact that most acts of a sexual nature involve partners of both sexes, there seems to be no rational explanation of the high percentage of female PINS respondents other than that the vagueness and broad scope of the statutes facilitate the application of a double standard of permissible behavior for young boys and girls.

This situation results from a variety of factors, including the following: (1) Parents and police are more prone to disapprove of expressions of female than of male sexuality; (2) Judges are generally more "protective" of girls than boys; and (3) Pregnancy is a uniquely female condition.

Sussman, Sex-Based Discrimination and PINS Jurisdiction, in L. Teitelbaum and A. Gough, Beyond Control: Status Offenders in the Juvenile Courts 179, 182 (Ballinger: Cambridge, Mass. 1977).

Traditionally, most juvenile judges were men. Does the growing number of female attorneys and judges mitigate the sexist quality of the status offense jurisdiction?

(5) Others have argued that the weight of status offense jurisdiction falls more heavily on the children of the poor and ethnic and racial minorities. See, e.g., Paulsen, Juvenile Courts, Family Courts and the Poor Man, 54 Calif.L.Rev. 694 (1966).

C. PROCEDURAL RIGHTS OF JUVENILES IN STATUS OFFENSES

Despite the United States Supreme Court's reliance in *Gault* on potential loss of liberty as the dividing line for deciding when juveniles are entitled to due process rights, many states deny to status offenders the constitutionally required procedural rights of those accused of delinquency.

Some jurisdictions, for example, still do not accord status offenders a right to counsel. See e.g., In re Walker, 282 N.C. 28, 191 S.E.2d 702 (1972), reproduced in part at p. 620 supra, in which the Supreme Court of North Carolina concluded that there was no constitutional right to counsel at the hearing on an undisciplined child petition. The court construed North Carolina law to prohibit commitment of an undisciplined child to a facility where her freedom could be curtailed; when the child, without counsel, had been found to be "undisciplined" within the meaning of the statute she was placed on probation. But the case on appeal arose when the state sought incarceration due to the child's failure to comply with the terms of her probation. Thus, even though involuntary loss of liberty could ultimately result from the initial finding that the child was undisciplined, the court found no reason to extend *Gault* to provide a right to counsel at the initial status offense proceeding. To the same effect, see In re K, 26 Or. App. 451, 554 P.2d 180 (1976), holding that because a juvenile was a status offender and not committable to an institution, the full list of *Gault* rights was inapplicable at the adjudicatory hearing. In contrast, the Florida Supreme Court held in In re Hutchins, 345 So.2d 703 (Fla.1977), that a child may not be institutionalized as a delinquent on the basis of that state's statutory provision that a second ungovernability adjudication permits classification of the child as a delinquent when the child did not have counsel at the original ungovernability adjudication.

Some state statutes specifically provide for a right to counsel in cases arising from noncriminal misbehavior. See e.g., Colo.Rev.Stat. Ann. § 19–1–106(1) (1978); D.C.Code § 16–2304(a) (1981); Ga.Code Ann. § 15–11–30(b) (1982); Va.Code § 16.1–266(B) (Supp.1981). And most courts probably would follow the reasoning in In re Spalding, 273 Md. 690, 332 A.2d 246 (1975), in upholding a due process right to counsel anytime a child faces the possibility of commitment to a secure facility based on a status offense adjudication.

Despite the requirement expressed in In re Winship, 397 U.S. 358, 90 S.Ct. 1068, 25 L.Ed.2d 368 (1970) of proof beyond a reasonable doubt to sustain a delinquency petition, only about half the states use the reasonable doubt standard of proof for status offenses. Noncriminal misbehavior can often be proved by a preponderance of the evidence. See e.g., In re Henderson, 199 N.W.2d 111 (Iowa 1972). Moreover, some states permit the use in status cases of hearsay and other evidence generally inadmissible in delinquency matters. Indeed, these differential standards of evidence and proof may explain why some delinquency petitions may be "reduced" to status offense petitions. See e.g., Cal.Welf. & Inst.Code § 701, which applies the civil standard of proof and the civil evidentiary standards to § 601 (Beyond Control) adjudications. See also Office of Children's Services, Judicial Conference of the State of New York, The PINS Child: A Plethora of Problems 17 (1973). In contrast, the Supreme Court of Vermont held hearsay inadmissible to support an adjudication of a juvenile as an "unmanageable child" in striking as improper an adjudication based solely upon the testimony of two social workers as to the contents of a social report based on interviews with third persons rather than their own personal knowledge. In re J.L.M., Juvenile, 139 Vt. 448, 430 A.2d 448 (1981).

D.   DISPOSITIONS—THE ROAD TO REFORM

1. DEINSTITUTIONALIZATION

The 1970s saw a substantial national movement toward deinstitutionalization of status offenders. Concern about the stigma of labeling (see, e.g., F. Allen, The Borderland of Criminal Justice: Essays in Law and Criminology (1964); H. Becker, The Outsiders: Studies in the Sociology of Deviance (1960); K. Erikson, The Wayward Puritans: A Study on the Sociology of Deviance (1966); D. Matza, Delinquency and Drift (1964); A. Platt, The Child Savers: The Invention of Delinquency (1969); E. Schur, Radical Non-Intervention (1973)) combined with evidence that incarcerating children had a negative impact on future development culminated in the passage of the federal Juvenile Justice and Delinquency Prevention Act of 1974, 42 U.S.C.A. §§ 5601–5751 (1977 and Supp.1981). The announced purposes of the Act were to encourage states and localities to conduct effective delinquency prevention programs characterized at least in part by diversions of most juveniles out of the juvenile court (viewed by the Congressional Committee responsible for drafting the Act as the institution of last resort in dealing with the problems of children, [1974] U.S. Code Cong. and Ad. News 5283, 5287–88) and provision of alternatives to traditional juvenile detention and correctional facilities. In order to be eligible for funds under the Act the state juvenile justice system must remove all status offenders from secure institutions:

---

42 U.S.C.A. § 5633(a)(12) (Supp.1981)

§ 5633. State plans

Requirements

(a) In order to receive formula grants under this part, a State shall submit a plan for carrying out its purposes. . . . [S]uch plan must—

. . .

(12)(A) provide within three years after submission of the initial plan that juveniles who are charged with or who have committed offenses that would not be criminal if committed by an adult or offenses which do not constitute violations of valid court orders, or such nonoffenders as dependent or neglected children, shall not be placed in secure detention facilities or secure correctional facilities; and

(B) provide that the State shall submit annual reports to the Administrator containing a review of the progress made by the State to achieve the deinstitutionalization of juveniles described in subparagraph (A) and a review of the progress made by the State to provide that such juveniles, if placed in facilities, are placed in facilities which (i) are the least restrictive alternatives appropriate to the needs of the child and the community; (ii) are in reasonable proximity to the family and the home communities of such juveniles; and (iii) provide the services described in section 5603(1) of this title;

By 1981 about twenty states had enacted legislation prohibiting status offenders from being placed in training schools, jails or other detention facilities as a dispositional alternative. Still other states prohibit pre or post adjudicatory physical confinement in status cases.

Typical of state legislative response is California's approval in 1976 and 1977 of the following addition to the Welfare and Institutions Code:

§ 207.   Place of Detention

. . .

(b) Notwithstanding the provisions of subdivision (a), no minor shall be detained in any jail, lockup, juvenile hall, or other secure facility who is taken into custody solely upon the ground that he is a person described by Section 601 or adjudged to be such or made a ward of the juvenile court solely upon that ground, except as provided in subdivision (c). If any such minor, other than a minor described in subdivision (c), is detained, he shall be detained in a sheltered-care facility or crisis resolution home as provided for in Section 654, or in a nonsecure facility provided for in subdivision (a), (b), (c), or (d) of Section 727.

. . .

A series of problems remains:

(1) Does the prohibition in state statutes apply to pretrial detentions as well as disposition?

(2) May a child be incarcerated as a delinquent for failure to obey an original nonincarcerative court order (probation with conditions, for example) in a status case? See In re Walker discussed at p. 629, supra. The Appellate Court of Illinois in In re R. R., 93 Ill.App.3d 327, 48 Ill.Dec. 835, 417 N.E.2d 237 (1981), held that a juvenile status offender who fails to obey a court order that she attend regular counseling sessions may be sent to a secure facility for contempt of court. Following her adjudication in February, 1980 as a minor in need of supervision, R. R. was placed in a foster home and required to attend certain counseling. In May, 1980 the state required the minor to show cause why she should not be found in contempt of court for being absent without permission overnight from her foster home and for refusing to cooperate with counseling. The court ruled the appropriate punishment for R. R.'s contempt was a sentence of fifteen days in the County Juvenile Detention Center. In affirming the juvenile court's use of the contempt power to enforce its nonincarcerative dispositional orders, the Appellate Court said in part:

> The minor's final argument is that the court did not have the power to sentence the minor to fifteen days detention in a secured facility. The minor argues that she was adjudicated a minor in need of supervision and not a delinquent. Since the Juvenile Act does not permit a minor to be detained in a secured facility unless the minor is a delinquent, she argues that the court could not so order in a contempt hearing. We disagree. A virtually identical issue was dealt with in In re G. B. (1980), 88 Ill.App.3d 64, 43 Ill. Dec. 410, 410 N.E.2d 410. In that case, the minor had violated his supervision order and the trial court found him guilty of contempt and sentenced him to one year probation with sixty days incarceration at a detention facility. On appeal, the court found that the

trial court's inherent power extended to criminal contempt. In dealing with what sentence could be meted out for a finding of criminal contempt, the court stated:

"We recognize the parallel procedures under the Juvenile Court Act and of citation for criminal contempt that were available when the minor violated the supervisory order. When, under those circumstances, the contempt route is selected, a criminal contempt is found to have taken place, and, as here, the court deems the conduct serious enough to require incarceration, we deem the appropriate procedure to ordinarily be for the court to sentence the contemnor to reasonable imprisonment."

In the instant case, the trial court held the criminal contempt to be serious enough to require incarceration and we do not believe this finding to be against the manifest weight of the evidence. Therefore, we believe the trial court had the authority to sentence the minor to fifteen days incarceration.

417 N.E.2d at 239.

(3) Has deinstitutionalization of status offenders led instead to the filing of more delinquency petitions against the same group of juveniles?

(4) What about runaways and others who will not remain in non-secure facilities? In In re Ronald S. 69 Cal.App.3d 866, 138 Cal.Rptr. 387 (1977), the California Court of Appeal noted "it may seem ridiculous to place a runaway in a nonsecure setting." Under pressure from the judiciary and law enforcement officials, the California legislature responded to the problems of runaways by adding to § 207 of the Welfare and Institutions Code that:

(c) A minor taken into custody upon the ground that he is a person described in Section 601, or adjudged to be a ward of the juvenile court solely upon that ground, may be held in a secure facility, other than a facility in which adults are held in secure custody, in any of the following circumstances:

(1) For up to 12 hours after having been taken into custody for the purpose of determining if there are any outstanding wants, warrants, or holds against the minor in cases where the arresting officer or probation officer has cause to believe that such wants, warrants, or holds exist.

(2) For up to 24 hours after having been taken into custody, in order to locate the minor's parent or guardian as soon as possible and to arrange the return of the minor to his parent or guardian.

(3) For up to 24 hours after having been taken into custody, in order to locate the minor's parent or guardian as soon as possible and to arrange the return of the minor to his parent or guardian, whose parent or guardian is a resident outside of the state wherein the minor was taken into custody, except that such period may

be extended to no more than 72 hours when the return of the minor cannot reasonably be accomplished within 24 hours due to the distance of the parents or guardian from the county of custody, difficulty in locating the parents or guardian, or difficulty in locating resources necessary to provide for the return of the minor.

(d) Any minor detained in juvenile hall pursuant to subdivision (c) may not be permitted to come or remain in contact with any person detained on the basis that he has been taken into custody upon the ground that he is a person described in Section 602 or adjudged to be such or made a ward of the juvenile court upon that ground.

(e) Minors detained in juvenile hall pursuant to Sections 601 and 602 may be held in the same facility provided they are not permitted to come or remain in contact within that facility.

(f) Every county shall keep a record of each minor detained under subdivision (c), the place and length of time of such detention, and the reasons why such detention was necessary. Every county shall report, on a monthly basis, this information to the Department of the Youth Authority, on forms to be provided by that agency.

The Youth Authority shall not disclose the name of the detainee, or any personally identifying information contained in reports sent to the Youth Authority under this subdivision.

2. DIVERSION

Despite the apparent retrenchment in California as evidenced by the enactment of § 207(c), some of the most complete data on pretrial diversion and alternative treatments for status offenders comes from the California experience. One study implemented before the change in the statute in 1975 toward deinstitutionalization was the Sacramento 601 Diversion Project in which youths beyond control were diverted out of the juvenile court to a team of probation officers specially trained in crisis intervention and counseling. Four days each week beyond control youths were handled by this method while the remaining three days' referrals were sent through the traditional court procedures. The diverted group participated in voluntary counseling and was referred to a variety of noncoercive community services.

After two years,

54.2 percent of the control group youths had been rebooked for either a 601 offense or for violations of the penal code. The comparable figure for the project group was 46.3 percent. Thus, while the repeat rate for both groups was high, the project cases did noticeably better. Out of 100 youths handled, 7.9 fewer were found to repeat under project handling. The decrease is over 14 percent of the return rate for control cases.

Also extremely important in a practical sense is the fact that these results were accomplished at a lower cost than the cost of service provided prior to the beginning of the project. Based on the twelve-month follow-up data, the average total handling time for project youths was 14.2 hours as compared with 23.7 hours of the control youths. Including detention and placement, costs for the project youth were $274 as compared with $561 for the control group. Thus the cost to the probation department of regular intake care for this kind of case is more than twice as expensive as the cost of diversion.

F. Feeney, The PINS Problem—A "No Fault" Approach, in L. Teitelbaum and A. Gough, Beyond Control: Status Offenders in the Juvenile Courts 249, 254 (Ballinger; Cambridge, Mass. 1977).

A second pilot diversion project in Santa Clara County was based on immediate diversion by law enforcement authorities. The goal of the project was to reduce substantially the number of youths referred to juvenile court or the probation department as 601s (beyond control). The Santa Clara Pre-Delinquent Diversion Program reduced by 67.2 percent the number of 601 referrals. As Professor Aidan Gough summarizes the Santa Clara Project results in his introduction to the Juvenile Justice Standards Relating to Noncriminal Misbehavior 17–19 (Tentative Draft 1977): *

In fact, a reduction of 67.2 percent in the number of beyond-control referrals was achieved; some of the cases that were referred to the court may well have involved runaway minors found some distance from their homes, for whom arrangements to return could not swiftly be made. . . . In the first year of the project 2,951 eligible youth were handled, and in the second year, 3,243; 52.8 percent of the cases handled in the first two years were girls. Each case represents a discrete incident to which the police responded.

Both in terms of the frequency of reinvolvement with the juvenile justice system and in terms of the severity of that reinvolvement, youth handled by this program showed a distinctly better track record than a one year sample of preproject youth. A total of 21 percent of all diverted youth became reinvolved on a new offense, while 48.5 percent of the preproject sample of status offenders handled by the usual processes, tracked for a one year period, committed a new offense. Of the sample, 22 percent had reentered the juvenile justice system for a *third* time within one year.

It was found that 70.8 percent of the youths in a sample of cases handled by the diversion project made contact with the agencies recommended to them by the police, and 62.9 percent actually received services. A sample of parents, on the other hand,

* Reprinted with permission from Standards Relating to Noncriminal Misbehavior (Tentative Draft), Copyright 1977, Ballinger Publishing Company.

followed police recommendations in 51.2 percent of the cases and received help in 44 percent. Roughly 49 percent of the youths and parents indicated that the services were of some help; one-third of the parents, however, felt the services were of little help. Service agency and resource records indicated that the police initiated the contact in more than half the cases, while clients were the initiating party in 35.5 percent of the cases. Twenty percent of a sample of parents felt the handling was too lenient and stated they thought the youth should have been booked into the juvenile hall; 73 percent of those parents said booking "would have impressed upon the child the seriousness of the predelinquent behavior."

Perhaps most impressive, a countywide preprogram survey revealed that the county's law enforcement agencies used a total of fifteen community resources of various kinds, public and private, in attempts to obtain services for unruly children. During the first two years of the program, the number of community resources utilized by police in handling beyond-control cases had grown to 110, about equally divided between public and private resource agencies in frequency of use. It is not known how many of these were in existence before the project began; it seems safe, however, to assume that some of the resources were created or developed because of the demand created by diversion and referral for help on a voluntary basis.

Without the diversion program, to handle the beyond-control referrals in the first two years of the project would have cost the probation department and the juvenile court not less than $1,785,319 and 51,645 work hours in delivering services. With the program in operation, the cost of servicing beyond-control cases during this period was approximately $744,756 and consumed 23,930 work hours, a savings of approximately $1,040,563 and 27,715 work hours. The cost of providing police services during the two-year period was $346,401, with such project expenses as consultation by probation personnel supplies, transportation, and research and evaluation making up the balance.

See American Justice Institute, Research & Education Study of the Santa Clara County, California, Pre-Delinquent Diversion Program (1974) for the detailed data and results of this second California pilot project.

3. SEPARATION FROM DELINQUENTS

STATE EX REL. HARRIS v. CALENDINE

Supreme Court of Appeals of West Virginia, 1977.
___ W. Va. ___, 233 S.E.2d 318.

NEELY, JUSTICE.

This habeas corpus proceeding calls into question the constitutional validity of West Virginia's classification and disposition of juvenile offenders. The Court does not find unconstitutional W. Va. Code, 49–1–4 [1941], which defines a "delinquent child," or W. Va. Code, 49–5–11 [1975], which authorizes certain methods of disposition for children adjudged delinquent; nevertheless, we find that definite guidelines are needed to prevent these statutes from being unconstitutionally applied in violation of W. Va. Const., art. III, § 10, the due process clause, and W. Va. Const., art. III, § 5, the cruel and unusual punishment clause.

The petitioner, Gilbert Harris, is a 16 year old boy now confined in the Davis Center, a forestry camp for boys, pursuant to an order of the Calhoun County Juvenile Court adjudging the petitioner delinquent because he had been absent from school for 50 days.

On April 9, 1976, the Director of Supportive Services for the Calhoun County Board of Education petitioned the juvenile court to find Mr. Harris either neglected or delinquent because of his irregular school attendance. A summons was served on petitioner's mother and stepfather stating that they were required to appear before the Calhoun County Juvenile Court, and after several continuances a hearing was finally held on May 17, 1976 at which the petitioner, his attorney, and petitioner's mother appeared. At the hearing the petitioner did not deny the allegations against him and was adjudicated a delinquent child. The juvenile court committed the petitioner to the care, custody, and control of the Commissioner of Public Institutions for the State of West Virginia for assignment to the Industrial School for Boys at Pruntytown until the petitioner became 16 years old in July 1976. Upon reaching age 16, petitioner was to be reassigned to a Youth Center for the balance of a one year period, after which he was to be remanded to the custody of the Calhoun County Juvenile Court. Petitioner had never been charged with a delinquent act before the bringing of the petition now under review and had never previously appeared before the juvenile court. Furthermore, petitioner was nearly 16 at the time he was adjudged delinquent for truancy, and he was ordered incarcerated for almost a year past the legal age when school attendance is required. W. Va. Code, 18–8–1 [1951].

Petitioner lived in a remote, rural section of Calhoun County and had some difficulty getting to school during the winter months. More importantly, however, it appears that the petitioner was ridiculed and shunned by his classmates because he suffered from a facial disfigurement and was mildly retarded. Petitioner had been enrolled in a special education class during junior high school and high school, but the record does not disclose any details about those classes in the local schools or the programs offered by either the industrial school at Pruntytown or the Forestry Camp at Davis.

. . .

We are . . . concerned with incarceration of children for status offenses. . . . [W]e are concerned with a child who is incorrigible, ungovernable, habitually disobedient and beyond the control of his parents, truant, repeatedly deserts his home or place of abode, engages in an occupation which is in violation of law, or frequents a place the existence of which is in violation of law. The Legislature has vested the juvenile court with jurisdiction over children who commit these status offenses so that the court may enforce order, safety, morality, and family discipline within the community. The intention of the law is laudable; however, the means employed to accomplish these ends are unconstitutional insofar as they result in the commitment of status offenders to secure, prison-like facilities which also house children guilty of criminal conduct, or needlessly subject status offenders to the degradation and physical abuse of incarceration.

. . .

W. Va. Code, 49–5–11 [1975] provides a number of methods of disposition for juvenile offenders, including placing the delinquent child under supervised probation, committing the child to a public or private institution or agency, committing the child to the care and custody of some suitable person, entering any other order which would appear to be in the best interest of the child, and then finally committing the child to an industrial home or correctional institution for minors, i.e., a secure, prison-like facility. It is parsimony which circumscribes our courts' ability to treat status offenders constitutionally, not the absence of statutory authority.

The Equal Protection Standard

We find that with regard to the status offender the procedure for disposition set forth in Code, 49–5–11 [1975] can be applied in a manner repugnant to the basic principles of equal protection because it discriminates invidiously against children based upon social class, sex, and geographic location. It is obvious that a child from a family with financial resources will have an opportunity to use private institutional facilities which are far less restrictive, less dangerous, and less degrading than public correctional institutions. What would have happened to the petitioner in the case before us if he had come from an upper middle-class family in a city such as Charleston or Wheeling? He certainly would have had an opportunity to go to a private school. In the case before us we may reasonably infer that the Calhoun County Juvenile Court committed petitioner to a reform school because of the lack of a reasonable alternative which would have existed if petitioner had been from a different area or belonged to a different socioeconomic class.

Furthermore, the status offender is inherently in a different class from the criminal offender. The Legislature could choose to punish children guilty of criminal conduct in the same manner as it punishes adults, but as a matter of public policy the Legislature provided instead for a comprehensive system of child welfare. The aim of this system is to protect and rehabilitate children, not to punish them. It has always been assumed that the Legislature can at any time withdraw some or all the benefits of this system from children guilty of criminal conduct. There is no such prospect for status offenders, however, since without the child welfare legislation they are guilty of no crimes cognizable and punishable by courts. This explains why status offenders have a special position within the current system, despite the fact that technically they are not distinguished from children guilty of actual criminal conduct. Since the class to which status offenders belong has been created under authority of the State's inherent and sovereign *parens patriae* power, and not under the plenary powers of the State to control criminal activity and punish criminals, status offenders must be treated in a fashion consistent with the *parens patriae* power, namely, they must be helped and not punished, otherwise their classification becomes invidious, and accordingly, unconstitutional.

Finally, it should be noted that status offender legislation discriminates invidiously against females. It is apparent that status offense petitions can easily be used to bring under control young women suspected by their parents or by other authorities of promiscuous behavior. Our society tends to condemn female promiscuity more severely than male promiscuity, and this tendency may explain why females often are unfairly classified and treated as status offenders. This Court offers no explanation for this phenomenon, nor do we make any normative judgments regarding the wisdom of such a distinction; however, we recognize its existence and its discriminatory effect on female status offenders.[6] The control of sexual behavior may be accomplished by other means.

6. A recent study (December 1976) by the Division of Corrections, West Virginia Department of Public Institutions, indicates that female status offenders comprise a much larger percentage of the total number of their sex committed to secure, prison-like facilities than male status offenders comprise of theirs. This study identified 138 status offenders out of the total number of 477 children committed at that time to West Virginia's secure, prison-like facilities. Overall then, 29% of the children committed were status offenders.

There were 404 males in the sample population, of whom 72 were status offenders, or approximately 18%. On the other hand there were 73 females in the sample population, of whom 66 were status offenders, or approximately 90%.

The study provides additional evidence of the uneven treatment of females. Of the 72 males committed for status offenses, 41, or about 57%, had a prior history of criminal conduct. Although this prior history by itself would be insufficient, under the guidelines of this opinion, to justify the commitment of these

The Substantive Due Process Standard

Furthermore the Court finds no rational connection between the legitimate legislative purposes of enforcing family discipline, protecting children, and protecting society from uncontrolled children, and the means by which the State is permitted to accomplish these purposes, namely incarceration of children in secure, prison-like facilities.

It is generally recognized that the greatest colleges for crime are prisons and reform schools.[7] The most egregious punishment inflicted upon a child incarcerated in a West Virginia penal institution is not the deprivation of his liberty but rather his forced association with reprehensible persons. Prisons, by whatsoever name they may be known, are inherently dangerous places. Sexual assaults, physical

male status offenders to secure, prison-like facilities, the figures do suggest that juvenile courts are giving some attention to the severity of male status offenders' behavioral problems before committing them to secure, prison-like facilities. On the other hand, only 12, or about 18% of the 66 females committed for status offenses had a history of prior criminal conduct.

The inequities of the present commitment process are all the more alarming because male and female status offenders are being referred to juvenile courts in approximately equal numbers. According to the West Virginia Department of Welfare statistics, 1974 referrals for status offenses were divided 48% males, 52% females; 1975 referrals for status offenses were divided 47% males, 53% females; and 1976 referrals were 49.7% males, 50.3% females. Therefore, it appears that the present system manifests its sexual bias not in the mere referral of status offenders to the authorities, but rather in the failure to accord even-handed treatment at the stage where a determination is made to commit status offenders to secure, prison-like facilities.

7. Among others, the United States Senate Judiciary Subcommittee to Investigate Juvenile Delinquency has recognized that juvenile penal institutions provide novice criminals a rich education in the ways of crime. The Chairman of the Subcommittee, the Honorable Birch Bayh, noted the particular folly of allowing status offenders to receive an education in crime at public expense: ". . . I have heard testimony from countless juveniles who have been incarcerated for acts which would not have been crimes for adults, and who have emerged from institutions embittered and highly sophisticated in the ways of

crime." Bayh, Juveniles and the Law: An Introduction, 12 Am.Crim.L.Rev. 1 (1974). See also Hearings on Juvenile Detention Before the Subcomm. to Investigate Juvenile Delinquency of the Senate Comm. on the Judiciary, 93 Cong. 1st Sess. (unpublished); Hearings on Juvenile Confinement Institutions and Correctional Systems Before the Subcomm. to Investigate Juvenile Delinquency of the Senate Comm. on the Judiciary, 92 Cong., 1st Sess. (1971); President's Commission on Law Enforcement and Administration of Justice, Task Force Report: Juvenile Delinquency and Youth Crime (1967).

In an effort to remedy the serious problems documented before his subcommittee, Senator Bayh, along with Senator Marlow Cook, introduced in Congress the Juvenile Justice and Delinquency Prevention Act. Passed in 1974 as Public Law 93–415, this act is in part concerned with the exposure of status offenders in juvenile correctional institutions to other juveniles guilty of criminal conduct. In response to this particular problem Congress has by law provided financial incentives to states and localities which are willing to remove status offenders from juvenile detention or correctional facilities and place them in shelter facilities or community based treatment programs. See 42 U.S.C. § 5601 et seq.

For a concurring view of the problem of common custody, see The Report of the California Assembly Interim Committee on Criminal Procedure, Juvenile Justice Processes (1974) at 14 which states that ". . . if any of them [status offenders] were ever on the verge of committing a criminal act, they have been brought to the right place [i.e. joint custody with juvenile delinquents] for a final push."

violence, psychological abuse and total degradation are the likely consequences of incarceration. If one hopes to find rehabilitation in a penal institution, his hopes will be confounded.

. . .

. . . We find with regard to status offenders the same fact we found . . . with regard to the mentally ill, that the State means, namely incarceration in secure, prison-like facilities, except in a limited class of cases, bears no reasonable relationship to legitimate State purposes, namely, rehabilitation, protection of the children, and protection of society.

In view of the foregoing, and in view of the fact that there are numerous alternatives to incarceration for status offenders[9] we hold that the State must exhaust every reasonable alternative to incarceration before committing a status offender to a secure, prison-like facility. Furthermore, for those extreme cases in which commitment of status offenders to a secure, prison-like facility cannot be avoided, the receiving facility must be devoted solely to the custody and rehabilitation of status offenders. In this manner status offenders can be spared contact under degrading and harmful conditions with delinquents who are guilty of criminal conduct and experienced in the ways of crime.

For all of the foregoing reasons, we conclude that the incarceration of status offenders in secure, prison-like facilities along with children guilty of criminal conduct inflicts a constitutionally disproportionate penalty upon status offenders, and as such, violates W. Va. Const., art. III, § 5.

Accordingly, we hold that a status offender may still be adjudged delinquent under W. Va. Code, 49–1–4 [1941]; however, before he may be committed to a penal institution pursuant to the provisions of W. Va. Code, 49–5–11(4) [1975], there must be evidence on the record which clearly supports the conclusion, and the juvenile court must specifically find as a matter of fact, that no other reasonable alternative either is available or could with due diligence and financial commitment on the part of the State be made available to help the child, and that the child is so totally unmanageable, ungovernable, and antisocial that he or she is amenable to no treatment or restraint short of incarceration in a secure, prison-like facility. Furthermore, to reiter-

---

9. Such alternatives include, but are not limited to, supervised probation; specialized foster care arranged through the Department of Welfare; non-secure, adequately supervised residential shelter facilities similar to the Children's Home Society, Wheeling and "Patchwork" in Charleston; a group home program, with structured live-in treatment, and access to counseling and psychiatric care, similar to the Davis-Stuart group homes in Bluefield, Princeton, Beckley and Fayetteville; residential treatment in a hospital setting for status offenders with psychological or emotional problems, similar to Opportunity Hall at Spencer State Hospital; and a residential center for intensive treatment outside the hospital setting, staffed by psychologists and medical professionals. Other satisfactory alternatives to incarceration could also be developed by a society solicitous of the welfare of its children and dedicated to treating the special problems of status offenders.

ate in this context what we said above, no status offender in any event, regardless of incorrigibility, may be incarcerated in a secure, prison-like facility which is not devoted exclusively to the custody and rehabilitation of status offenders. We emphasize here that State parsimony is no defense to an allegation of deprivation of constitutional rights. The State may not punish a person not deserving of punishment merely because such action serves the State's interest in convenience of frugality.

Consequently, the standard which the juvenile court must apply is not a standard of what facilities are *actually* available in the State of West Virginia for the treatment of juvenile status offenders, but rather a standard which looks to what facilities *could reasonably be made* available in an enlightened and humane state solicitous of the welfare of its children but also mindful of other demands upon the State budget for humanitarian purposes. We recognize that problems may arise, as for example, when a court is located in a rural part of West Virginia which lacks child-care facilities, and the court has no place to send a status offender except a correctional facility. Nevertheless, in such cases, if rehabilitation of the status offender could be accomplished by his commitment to a well-run, centralized state residential treatment center, or a local shelter facility where a small number of children live with professionally trained house parents, or by any other reasonable method, then the juvenile judge, as a matter of state constitutional law, must make a disposition under Code 49–5–11 [1975] which does not involve commitment to a secure, prison-like facility, or he must discharge the defendant.

. . . .

Writ awarded.

ELLERY C. v. REDLICH

Court of Appeals of New York, 1973.
32 N.Y.2d 588, 347 N.Y.S.2d 51, 300 N.E.2d 424.

FULD, CHIEF JUDGE.

The appellant, Ellery C., now 16 years old, was adjudged a person in need of supervision (PINS) on the application of his mother in March of 1971. About a year later, the Family Court (Kings County), on recommendation of the Probation Department, sent him to the New York State Training School at Otisville. The Appellate Division, by a closely divided vote, affirmed that disposition (40 A.D.2d 862, 337 N.Y.S.2d 936).

Until 1962, a child who committed acts which now warrant his adjudication as a person in need of supervision was treated as a juvenile delinquent (former Children's Ct. Act, § 2, subd. 2). The new PINS statute (L.1962, ch. 686) "represents enlightened legislative recognition of the difference between youngsters [juvenile delinquents] who commit criminal acts and those who merely misbehave in ways which, frequently, would not be objectionable save for the fact that the actor is a minor (e.g., running away from home, keeping late hours, truancy, etc.)." There is a vital distinction between a finding of delinquency and a determination of a need for supervision. The Family Court Act provides that a "dispositional hearing" in a case involving delinquency is one to determine whether the juvenile requires supervision, treatment or confinement, while such a hearing in a need-for-supervision case is to ascertain whether the youngster requires supervision or treatment. The omission of the word "confinement" is no mere oversight. Children in need of supervision should not be placed in institutions in which juvenile delinquents are confined and, as might be expected, the practice has been severely condemned.[2]

The conclusion is clear. Proper facilities must be made available to provide adequate supervision and treatment for children found to be persons in need of supervision. We thoroughly agree, therefore, with the view, expressed by Justice Shapiro in the course of his dissenting opinion (40 A.D.2d, at p. 864, 337 N.Y.S.2d, at p. 940), that the appellent's confinement in the training school, along with juveniles convicted of committing criminal acts, "can hardly, in any realistic sense, serve as 'supervision' and 'treatment' for him. On the contrary, it may well result in his emerging from his incarceration well tutored in the ways of crime. Such confinement is not consistent with the implied, if not explicit, purposes set forth in section 255 of the Family Court Act, which authorizes the court to seek the co-operation of and use 'the services of all societies or organizations, public or private, having for their object the protection or aid of children or families . . . to the end that the court may be assisted in every reasonable way to give the children . . . within its jurisdiction *such care, protection and assistance as will best enhance their welfare'* (emphasis supplied)."

Nor may the appellant's commitment to the state training school be justified by the respondent's claim that, "while not ideal, [it] is the only facility available which could possibly help this boy become a constructive member of society." In the first place, the record before us does not support that claim and, in the second place, to cull from the dissenting opinion below (40 A.D.2d, at pp. 864–865, 337 N.Y.S.2d, at p. 940), even if it did, it "would hardly justify . . . [appellant's] confinement . . . with adjudicated juvenile delinquents in a prison environment." It follows, therefore, that persons in need of supervision may not validly be placed in a State training school.

. . .

2. It has been well said that the distinction between the two types of children—juvenile delinquents and those in need of supervision—"becomes useless where, as here, the treatment accorded the one must be identical to that accorded the other because no other adequate alternative has been provided." (Matter of Jeanette P., 34 A.D.2d, at p. 661, 310 N.Y.S.2d, at p. 127.)

The order appealed from should be reversed and the proceeding remitted to the Family Court for the purpose of placing the appellant in a suitable environment.

LAVETTE M. v. CORPORATION COUNSEL OF THE CITY OF NEW YORK

Court of Appeals of New York, 1974.
35 N.Y.2d 136, 359 N.Y.S.2d 20, 316 N.E.2d 314.

JASEN, JUDGE.

In each of these cases we are asked to decide whether it is permissible to place a child adjudicated as a person in need of supervision (PINS) in a State training school for PINS children only.

. . .

It is urged that placement of a PINS child in a training school is unlawful per se under our decision in Matter of C., 32 N.Y.2d 588, 347 N.Y.S.2d 51, 300 N.E.2d 424. We disagree. The main thrust of our holding in *C.* was that it is inconsistent with the statutory right to "supervision" and "treatment" to place PINS children in institutions in which juvenile delinquents are confined. (32 N.Y.2d, at p. 591, 347 N.Y.S.2d at p. 53, 300 N.E.2d at p. 425.) We said it is the confinement of PINS children in a prison atmosphere along with juveniles convicted of committing criminal acts that is proscribed, and not the fact alone of placement in a training school. Put another way, it is the adequacy of the supervision and treatment there provided, not the characterization of the facility as a training school, that is determinative.

We are well aware of the current preference for expanded use of community agencies, community residential centers and similar shelters for the treatment of nondelinquent children who are beyond or without parental control. But, absent a clear showing that the treatment provided at a training school is significantly inadequate to the task, the current experiment with training school placement for PINS children, as authorized by statute (Family Ct. Act, § 756), should be permitted. On the total record before us, we cannot assume that the necessary initiatives to establish a fully adequate program of supervision and treatment for PINS children at the training schools, already begun, will not be carried to fruition. A different question will be presented if at a later time it appears that it has not. But for the present, we note that the Division for Youth has made a commendable start toward upgrading the Tryon and Hudson Training Schools and implementing the PINS child's right to necessary care and treatment. Both schools are coeducational and employ the semiautonomous cottage concept, or a variation thereof. Group counseling and therapy are integral aspects of the cottage concept. Regular and remedial educational programs are offered. Each school employs, on a part-time basis at present, a psychiatrist who performs an initial evaluation and follow-up care on an as-needed basis. Each also employs a psychologist who performs diagnostic testing for new residents. Pursuant to a model staffing program presently being implemented by the Division for Youth, the Tryon School has been authorized one additional full time and one part-time psychologist. Additional counselors and social workers, we are told, will be added to each school.

We are frank to acknowledge the practical limitations upon the power of the courts to determine the adequacy and effectiveness of treatment afforded PINS children. By what yardstick shall we measure? Surely the role of formulating criteria to measure the effectiveness of treatment facilities is not and should not be an exclusively judicial function. It should not be our province to determine what is the best possible treatment or to espouse an ideal but perhaps unattainable standard. Rather, our role should be to assure the presence of a bona fide treatment program.

. . .

NOTES

(1). To the same effect as Harris v. Calendine and *Ellery C.*, see dicta in Blondheim v. State, 84 Wn.2d 874, 529 P.2d 1096 (1975).

(2). For criticism of judicially-required separation of delinquents and status offenders on the ground that the two legal categories do not reflect functional differences in the children labelled, see Thomas, Are Status Offenders Really So Different? 22 Crime & Delinq. 438–55 (1976) and Fjeld, Newsom and Fjeld, Delinquents and Status Offenders: The Similarity of Differences, 32 Juv. & Fam. Ct. J. 3 (May, 1981). The Thomas study found: "Knowledge of the type of behavior which brought about an initial court appearance is an exceedingly poor predictor of whether a juvenile would reappear and, if so, the type of misconduct that would prompt the reappearance." 22 Crime & Delinq. at 454. The Fjeld, Newsom and Fjeld research did not support the argument that status offenders were so different from delinquents. The authors concluded that juvenile court jurisdiction should be abandoned in status cases because 43 percent of those studied had both delinquency and status charges, suggesting substantial similarity between the two classifications.

(3). As the court in *Ellery C.* suggests, New York courts have indicated that commitment of persons in need of supervision is not authorized until less restrictive alternatives have been exhausted or previous attempts at rehabilitation have failed. See e.g., In re Jeanette M., 40 A.D.2d 977, 338 N.Y.S.2d 177 (1972).

(4). Most jurisdictions follow in fact what Maryland law expressly prohibits—sending a child in need of supervision to a penal institution. Md. Cts. & Jud. Proc. Code Ann. § 3–823(a) (1980). The Maryland Code also prohibits sending a child in need of supervision to an institution used for confinement of delinquent children. Id. (b).

(5). May the child be excluded entirely from hearing the case against her as a person in need of supervision? What if the child wanders out of the courtroom and returns only to hear the disposition pronounced? See In re Cecelia R., 36 N.Y.2d 317, 367 N.Y.S.2d 770, 327 N.E.2d 812 (1975), holding the child has a right to be present at her dispositional hearing absent extraordinary circumstances.

E. ABOLITION OF JUVENILE COURT JURISDICTION

JUVENILE JUSTICE STANDARDS PROJECT, STANDARDS RELATING TO NONCRIMINAL MISBEHAVIOR
(Tentative Draft 1977) *

1.1 Noncriminal Misbehavior Generally

A juvenile's acts of misbehavior, ungovernability, or unruliness which do not violate the criminal law should not constitute a ground for asserting juvenile court jurisdiction over the juvenile committing them.

———

This bold proposal has proved the most controversial of the standards proposed by the ABA–IJA Juvenile Justice Standards Project. For support for the Standards, see Ketcham, Why Jurisdiction Over Status Offenders Should Be Eliminated From Juvenile Courts, 57 B.U.L.Rev. 645 (1977) (the author attacks existing status jurisdiction as an uneconomic as well as unfair drain on the scarce resources of the juvenile justice system); Note, Ungovernability: The Unjustifiable Jurisdiction, 83 Yale L.J. 1383 (1974) (the authors find that the problems of status offense jurisdiction stem less from lack of effective rehabilitative resources and more from abuses of judicial discretion and serious misassessment of status cases); Skuris, For Troubled Youth—Help, Not Jail, 31 Hastings L.J. 539 (1979) (the author traces the recent California deinstitutionalization experience and suggests a community-based noncoercive youth services model to replace existing status offense jurisdiction of the juvenile court); Sussman, Judicial Control Over Noncriminal Misbehavior, 52 N.Y.U.L. Rev. 1051 (1977) (the author reviews and endorses the proposal of the Standards' Tentative Draft to substitute voluntary social and family services for the coercive intervention of the juvenile or family court.).

One of the most vocal critics of the removal of judicial jurisdiction over status offenders has been Judge Lindsay Arthur of the Hennepin County Juvenile Court. See, e.g., Arthur, Status Offenders Need A Court of Last Resort, 57 B.U.L.Rev. 631 (1977) or Arthur, Should Status Offenders Go to Court?, in L. Teitelbaum and A. Gough, Beyond Control 235–47 (1977). His position reflects that of many juvenile judges when he writes: †

> . . . The reasoning of the Standards follows the line of logic which says that, because some training schools are bad, all are bad; because rehabilitation does not work for all children, it does not work for any; because some status offenders are stigmatized by court process, none should be given court assistance; because some are overlegalized, none should be legally protected. Rather than merely swinging from a child-only focus to a parent-only focus, the Standards could have made a contribution to the advance of juvenile justice by focusing on the <u>rehabilitation of the family</u>—society's basic unit; shifting the focus to the future rather than to the fault; pleading the causing disfunction rather than the caused conduct; and, in general, mobilizing for expertise to rejuvenate the family, not to undercut it even further.

CONCLUSION

<u>Children are *not* small adults</u>. They lack experience; by definition they lack maturity. They cannot choose intelligently between options, because they do not know the options or the consequences of the options. Children should not be emancipated wholesale. If they have the experience to know the immediate and future consequences of various choices, if they have the judgment and self-discipline to select and abide by their selective pace, then emancipation is well indicated. Emancipation should flow with the pace of each child's maturity. But the Standards would emancipate all children of all ages and all conditions. Supportive parental authority would cease. The Standards would undermine the vestiges of the American family.

The Standards are also unrealistic. Communities not only will not, but they cannot, provide restorative services that will be used willingly by such a majority of the troubled juveniles and their families in the community. Moreover, it is unrealistic to expect that even if such services were considered they would be willingly used by all troubled families. Communities can, however, and usually will, provide regionalized services that the troubled families will use voluntarily and most of the rest will use actively if they have to.

Finally, courts *are* able to resolve many family problems that would not be resolved without a court's involuntary intercession. Courts have demonstrated this ability time and again, in juvenile cases, in divorce cases, in guardian cases. <u>Every possible case should be diverted, and every possible resource should be developed to allow maximum diversion; but courts should be, they</u>

† Reprinted with permission from Judge Lindsay Arthur. Copyright 1977 by Lindsay Arthur.

must be, available to require needed help when it is refused or ignored. The focus of this intervention should not be shifted from the culpability of children to the culpability of parents; it should be shifted away from anyone's culpability, so far as the Commission permits. Attention should be directed to causes not symptoms, to needs not conduct, to providing help not jurisdictional niceties, and, when the public's interest and safety require, to providing help when it is resisted.

57 B.U.L.Rev. at 643–44.

The dissenting view of Judge Justine Wise Polier from the Standards' proposal to abolish jurisdiction over noncriminal misbehavior seems to reflect Judge Arthur's concern:

> Unfortunately, the proposed standards, like other statements supporting diversion from courts, places primary emphasis on "dejudicialization of status offenders." This purpose is not matched by positive plans or requirements for creating alternative, accessible, and appropriate services. The standards fail to confront the essential problem of who is to be responsible for the development of alternative services, for their funding, for setting standards, for monitoring, and for protecting the rights of children who are either excluded or denied appropriate services.

> While I concur in the support for increasing alternative services that can be used voluntarily, the premature ending of juvenile court jurisdiction before there is a growth of such services will only lead to losing sight of children and families most in need of services.

JUSTINE WISE POLIER, Dissenting view, Juvenile Justice Standards Relating to Noncriminal Misbehavior 67 (Tent. Draft 1977).

NOTE

Many status offense petitions are brought by parents against their children. Is the legal system appropriate to deal with such conflict? Should parents have recourse to the coercive power of courts to enforce parental decisions? Should we now reverse the course set for us originally in the early history of Massachusetts Colony?

XII. CHILD CUSTODY: SOME NEW PROPOSALS FOR SOLVING OLD PROBLEMS

A. CRITERIA FOR DETERMINATION

Courts may be required to fix or modify child custody when parents separate or divorce, when a child has been entrusted to someone else either with or without judicial approval, or when there has been some major change that dictates reconsideration of the custodial situation in the light of current circumstances. It is common to say that decisions regarding child custody should be based upon what will be in the "best interests of the child". Obviously such a test is likely to be amorphous even in the face of statutory attempts to codify it, and many critics assert that there is virtually no way to avoid having individual values of the decision makers significantly influence the outcome in many, if not most cases where a subjective or individualized appraisal is undertaken. Statutes listing criteria for judicial consideration rarely specify the weight to be applied to each, and such legislation therefore does little to remedy this concern.

For a long time, courts were guided in the largest number of cases by various strong presumptions (or rules) that could have the effect of obviating individualized judicial appraisals. The "tender years rule" provides an illustration. Generally speaking, this creature of either statute or jurisprudence meant that a mother of a young child would be given custodial preference if other factors were equal. Some jurisdictions have abolished the rule as sexually discriminatory. Others that ostensibly retain it nevertheless entertain evidence about whether "other factors are equal", thus considerably increasing the discretion of judges to disregard the presumption.[1]

Since the introduction of "no-fault" or "breakdown" grounds for divorce, the use of separation and settlement agreements by divorcing parties has increased substantially. Spouses who enter such agreements can in many jurisdictions make them judicially nonmodifiable (except in accord with the terms of the contract) as to financial rights and duties between them after their marriage has been legally terminated. However, courts generally continue to have the power

---

1. For a general discussion of the "tender years" presumption and some cases evincing different approaches as to its vitality today, see Roth, The Tender Years Presumption in Child Custody Disputes, 15 J. Fam. L. 423 (1977); Johnson v. Johnson, 564 P.2d 71 (Alaska 1977); People ex rel. Watts v. Watts, 77 Misc.2d 178, 350 N.Y.S.2d 285 (Fam.Ct.N.Y. County 1973); McCreery v. McCreery, 218 Va. 352, 237 S.E.2d 167 (1977). For the results of a study reviewing custody patterns under sex neutral standards, see Pearson, Munson and Thoennes, Legal Change and Child Custody Awards, 3 J. Fam. Issues 5 (1982). An argument that the present call for abandoning the tender years preference in the name of sexual equality is "misconceived and retrograde, however fashionable" is presented in Klaff, The Tender Years Doctrine: A Defense, 70 Calif.L.Rev. 335 (1982).

to modify contractual provisions dealing with child support or custody
regardless of agreements on these matters between parents. This is
illustrated by § 306(f) of the Uniform Marriage and Divorce Act,
which states:

> Except for the terms concerning the support, custody, or visi-
> tation of children, the decree may expressly preclude or limit mod-
> ification of terms set forth in the decree if the separation agree-
> ment so provides.

The materials that follow are designed to illustrate the problems
faced now when courts increasingly find themselves in the dilemma
of determining whether an individualized appraisal should be made to
determine the child's custody and what criteria are most important in
making such appraisals.

UNIFORM MARRIAGE AND DIVORCE ACT
(1970, as amended 1971, 1973)

Section 402. [*Best Interest of Child.*]

The court shall determine custody in accordance with the best interest of the child. The court shall consider all relevant factors including:

(1) the wishes of the child's parent or parents as to his custody;

(2) the wishes of the child as to his custodian;

(3) the interaction and interrelationship of the child with his
parent or parents, his siblings, and any other person who may significantly affect the child's best interest;

(4) the child's adjustment to his home, school, and community;
and

(5) the mental and physical health of all individuals involved.

The court shall not consider conduct of a proposed custodian that
does not affect his relationship to the child.

. . .

Section 404. [*Interviews.*]

(a) The court may interview the child in chambers to ascertain the
child's wishes as to his custodian and as to visitation. The court may
permit counsel to be present at the interview. The court shall cause
a record of the interview to be made and to be part of the record in
the case.

(b) The court may seek the advice of professional personnel,
whether or not employed by the court on a regular basis. The advice
given shall be in writing and made available by the court to counsel
upon request. Counsel may examine as a witness any professional
personnel consulted by the court.

Section 405. [*Investigations and Reports.*]

(a) In contested custody proceedings, and in other custody proceedings if a parent or the child's custodian so requests, the court may order an investigation and report concerning custodial arrangements for the child. The investigation and report may be made by [the court social service agency, the staff of the juvenile court, the local probation or welfare department, or a private agency employed by the court for the purpose].

(b) In preparing his report concerning a child, the investigator may consult any person who may have information about the child and his potential custodial arrangements. Upon order of the court, the investigator may refer the child to professional personnel for diagnosis. The investigator may consult with and obtain information from medical, psychiatric, or other expert persons who have served the child in the past without obtaining the consent of the parent or the child's custodian; but the child's consent must be obtained if he has reached the age of 16, unless the court finds that he lacks mental capacity to consent. If the requirements of subsection (c) are fulfilled, the investigator's report may be received in evidence at the hearing.

(c) The court shall mail the investigator's report to counsel and to any party not represented by counsel at least 10 days prior to the hearing. The investigator shall make available to counsel and to any party not represented by counsel the investigator's file of underlying data, and reports, complete texts of diagnostic reports made to the investigator pursuant to the provisions of subsection (b), and the names and addresses of all persons whom the investigator has consulted. Any party to the proceeding may call the investigator and any person whom he has consulted for cross-examination. A party may not waive his right of cross-examination prior to the hearing.

Section 406. [*Hearings.*]

(a) Custody proceedings shall receive priority in being set for hearing.

(b) The court may tax as costs the payment of necessary travel and other expenses incurred by any person whose presence at the hearing the court deems necessary to determine the best interest of the child.

(c) The court without a jury shall determine questions of law and fact. If it finds that a public hearing may be detrimental to the child's best interest, the court may exclude the public from a custody hearing, but may admit any person who has a direct and legitimate interest in the particular case or a legitimate educational or research interest in the work of the court.

(d) If the court finds it necessary to protect the child's welfare that the record of any interview, report, investigation, or testimony in a custody proceeding be kept secret, the court may make an appropriate order sealing the record.

JACOBSON v. JACOBSON

Supreme Court of North Dakota, 1981.
314 N.W.2d 78.

VANDE WALLE, JUSTICE.

Duane Jacobson appealed from a judgment of divorce entered by the district court of Burleigh County. We affirm in part and reverse in part and remand with directions to enter an order awarding custody of the minor children to Duane.

Sandra and Duane were married in 1966. Two children were born of the union, i.e., T. K., born January 11, 1972, and J. A., born October 12, 1977. Sandra commenced divorce proceedings on or about April 1, 1980, and the couple lived apart from that time. Temporary custody was placed with Sandra, age 33 at time of trial, under an interim order of the trial court. Duane filed an answer containing a general denial and specifically requested custody of the children by way of an amended answer. After trial the trial court issued its findings of fact, conclusions of law, and order for judgment. The trial court determined that irreconcilable differences existed and granted Sandra an absolute decree of divorce from Duane. The trial court further determined that the best interests of the children required that Sandra be given custody. The trial court made additional determinations which are not at issue here. After judgment was entered, Duane appealed. The only issue on appeal is that the trial court erred in awarding custody of the children to Sandra rather than to Duane. Within that issue the parties present several factors in an attempt to sway this court to their respective positions. However, it is clear that the burning issue in this appeal is Sandra's sexual preference. She freely admits to a homosexual relationship with a person named Sue who was 18 years of age at the time of trial. After determining the facts the trial judge indicated there were two areas of concern:

"a. will the children suffer from the 'slings and arrows' of a disapproving society; and

"b. if the custodial parent is homosexual or bisexual is the likelihood increased that the child will become" [*sic*]

The trial judge peremptorily disposed of the first issue, finding that in this particular factual situation "the first question [is] not of great importance as the children will be required to deal with the problem regardless of which parent has custody; . . . ."

With respect to the second concern the trial judge determined that the factor of "role model" is one of natural concern and a proper subject of inquiry. Noting that Sandra's counsel quoted from various sources in her brief the trial judge stated he was disregarding the information as the sources were not available for cross-examination. The trial judge indicated he did extensive research into available case law and determined that the cases appeared to divide themselves into two categories, i.e., "those in which courts, without explaining the reasons for their conclusions, determine that homosexuality is a factor to be considered in awarding custody; those in which, based upon expert testimony, the courts conclude that the subject is irrelevant. The Court therefore finds that the sexual preference issue can only be a factor if the evidence provides some method of weighing that factor with the other factors that cumulatively make up the 'best interests' equation; . . ."

The trial judge then found:

"That the Plaintiff is fit, willing and able to assume the custodial role; the Defendant is likewise fit, willing and able to assume the custodial role. It cannot be determined that the children will clearly be better off with one parent than the other; there would, however, be less disruption if the children were to remain with the Plaintiff, from the standpoint of schooling and from the standpoint of avoiding a change in the parent with whom the children have spent most of their home [life] and have received most of their day to day upbringing."

A review of the district court's memorandum opinion reflects that the trial judge did, indeed, review the several cases which have dealt with this matter. Counsel for both Sandra and Duane, in their briefs on appeal, have also cited for our consideration many cases which are concerned with this issue.

Section 14–09–06.2, N.D.C.C., provides that the best interests and welfare of the child should be considered by the trial court in determining which parent in a divorce proceeding should have custody of the children. Evaluation of all factors affecting the best interests and welfare of the child is to be made, and the statute contains a list of those factors to be considered, when applicable.[1] We have stated

---

1. Section 14–09–06.2, N.D.C.C., provides:

"For the purpose of custody, the best interests and welfare of the child shall be determined by the court's consideration and evaluation of all factors affecting the best interests and welfare of the child. These factors include all of the following when applicable:

"1. The love, affection, and other emotional ties existing between the parents and child.

"2. The capacity and disposition of the parents to give the child love, affection, and guidance and to continue the education of the child.

"3. The disposition of the parents to provide the child with food, clothing, medical care, or other remedial care recognized and permitted under the laws of this state in lieu of medical care, and other material needs.

"4. The length of time the child has lived in a stable, satisfactory environment and the desirability of maintaining continuity.

"5. The permanence, as a family unit, of the existing or proposed custodial home.

"6. The moral fitness of the parents.

"7. The mental and physical health of the parents.

"8. The home, school, and community record of the child.

on many occasions that in reviewing the trial court's determination of child custody in a divorce action, we treat these matters as findings of fact which, on appeal, are subject to the standard of review prescribed by Rule 52(a), N.D.R.Civ.P., i.e., that findings of fact are not to be set aside by this court unless we find them to be clearly erroneous. See, e.g., Miller v. Miller, 305 N.W.2d 666 (N.D.1981). We do not set aside a custody award unless we are left with a definite and firm conviction that a mistake has been made. Gross v. Gross, 287 N.W.2d 457 (N.D.1979). In this instance we are convinced that such a mistake has been made.

The portion of the trial judge's decision quoted above determines that both parents are "fit, willing and able to assume the custodial role." We need not determine whether one or the other parent is fit to have custody of the children; we need only determine that the children's best interests would be served by placing custody in one parent rather than the other parent. Gross v. Gross, supra.[2]

It is not inconceivable that one day our society will accept homosexuality as "normal." Certainly it is more accepted today than it was only a few years ago. We are not prepared to conclude, however, that it is not a significant factor to be considered in determining custody of children, at least in the context of the facts of this particular case. Because the trial court has determined that both parents are "fit, willing and able" to assume custody of the children we believe the homosexuality of Sandra is the overriding factor. Sandra admitted to a sexual relationship with Sue prior to the termination of the marriage. Although that relationship was adulterous as defined by Section 12.1-20-09, N.D.C.C., that fact alone does not influence us. Rather, it is the conceded fact that after the divorce Sandra and Sue would establish a relationship in which they would be living together

"9. The reasonable preference of the child, if the court deems the child to be of sufficient intelligence, understanding, and experience to express a preference.

"10. Any other factors considered by the court to be relevant to a particular child custody dispute.

"In any proceeding under this chapter, the court, at any stage of the proceedings after final judgment, may make orders about what security is to be given for the care, custody, and support of the unmarried minor children of the marriage as from the circumstances of the parties and the nature of the case is equitable."

2. In Bezio v. Patenaude, 381 Mass. 563, 410 N.E.2d 1207 (1980), the Supreme Judicial Court of Massachusetts reversed a judgment denying the natural mother's petition to regain the custody of her children from a guardian and remanded the matter for further proceedings. In *Bezio* the court stated: "In the total absence of evidence suggesting a correlation between the mother's homosexuality and her fitness as a parent, we believe the judge's finding that a lesbian household would adversely affect the children to be without basis in the record." 410 N.E.2d at 1216. We note, however, that the issue in *Bezio* was the unfitness of the mother, i.e., in order to retain custody in a guardian the mother would have to be found unfit. Here, we are not concerned with the unfitness of Sandra, but rather the best interests of the children, accepting as fact that both Sandra and Duane are fit parents.

which gives us concern. In paragraph 9 of its findings the trial court stated:

> "The Plaintiff [Sandra] has admitted a relationship with an adult woman [who] is likewise a strong, intelligent person; they have been discreet about their relationship; it is not outwardly apparent; thus far the children do not appear to be aware of it; the women intend to continue this relationship permanently and live together in the future; the relationship is a positive one; several people are aware of the relationship and it is clear that at some point the children will become aware of it."

Our statutes do not prohibit sexual relations between adult persons who are not married to other persons. Although Section 12.1–20–10, N.D.C.C., makes it a crime for a person to live openly and notoriously with a person of the opposite sex as a married couple without being married to the other person, the statutes contain no such provision with regard to persons of the same sex. The reason is obvious—neither North Dakota nor any other State in this nation, insofar as we can determine, recognizes a legal sexual relationship between two persons of the same sex.[3] Thus, despite the fact that the trial court determined the relationship between Sandra and Sue to be a "positive one," it is a relationship which, under the existing state of the law, never can be a legal relationship. Whether or not it will remain a stable relationship is yet to be determined. Sue is considerably younger than Sandra.

In Jarrett v. Jarrett, 78 Ill.2d 337, 36 Ill.Dec. 1, 400 N.E.2d 421 (1979), cert. denied, 449 U.S. 927, 101 S.Ct. 329, 66 L.Ed.2d 155 (1980), the Illinois Supreme Court affirmed a judgment that the resident presence of the mother's paramour might adversely affect the moral and emotional health of three daughters, ages 12, 10, and 7. In In re Marriage of Olson, 98 Ill.App.3d 316, 53 Ill.Dec. 751, 424 N.E.2d 386 (1981), the Appellate Court of Illinois considered an appeal from a judgment refusing to change the custody of a minor child from the mother to the father because of the mother's sexual relationship with another man. In affirming the trial court's judgment, the Illinois Appellate Court distinguished *Jarrett* because in *Olson* the mother did not cohabit with her lover in the presence of the child. Here, although Sandra was not residing with Sue at the time of the hearing on custody, her intentions to do so in the future were plainly announced to the trial court, as evidenced by its findings, and, at the time of oral argument, we were informed that Sandra and Sue were in fact living together in the same residence in which the children reside. It is this particular fact which we believe to be material in

---

3. See, e.g., In re Adult Anonymous II, Fam. Ct., 443 N.Y.S.2d 1008 (1981), in which that court refused to approve the adoption by one adult male homosexual of another adult homosexual who were "seeking to obtain some legal recognition of the bond that exists between them." In that case the court noted that "a statutory mechanism for conferring status on the relationship, with concomitant rights and obligations, is yet to be devised. . . ."

this instance. Sandra's homosexuality may, indeed, be something which is beyond her control. However, living with another person of the same sex in a sexual relationship is not something beyond her control. It may be argued that to force her to dissolve her living relationship in order to retain custody of her children is too much to ask. However, we need no legal citation to note that concerned parents in many, many instances have made sacrifices of varying degrees for their children.

Furthermore, we cannot lightly dismiss the fact that living in the same house with their mother and her lover may well cause the children to "suffer from the slings and arrows of a disapproving society" to a much greater extent than would an arrangement wherein the children were placed in the custody of their father with visitation rights in the mother. Although we agree with the trial court that the children will be required to deal with the problem regardless of which parent has custody, it is apparent to us that requiring the children to live, day-to-day, in the same residence with the mother and her lover means that the children will have to confront the problem to a significantly greater degree than they would if living with their father. We agree with the trial court that we cannot determine whether or not the fact the custodial parent is homosexual or bisexual will result in an increased likelihood that the children will become homosexual or bisexual. There is insufficient expert testimony to make that determination.[4] However, that issue does not control our conclusion. Rather, we believe that because of the mores of today's society, because Sandra is engaged in a homosexual relationship in the home in which she resides with the children, and because of the lack of legal recognition of the status of a homosexual relationship, the best interests of the children will be better served by placing custody of the children with Duane.

The judgment of the district court is reversed insofar as it awards custody of the minor children to Sandra; in all other matters the judgment is affirmed.

NOTE

Compare Doe v. Doe, 222 Va. 736, 284 S.E.2d 799 (1981), in which the Virginia Supreme Court denied a stepmother permission to adopt a child over the objection of the noncustodial mother who admitted to a lesbian relation-

---

4. A guardian ad litem for the children was appointed by the trial court "for purposes of making whatever investigation, and conducting whatever interviews that are necessary, to enable said Guardian to make a recommendation . . . as to the custodial arrangement that would be in the best interests of the minor children, . . ." Sec. 14–09–06.4, N.D.C.C.; Rule 4.1, N.D. R.O.C. In her report the guardian ad litem, a youth counselor with the office of the Juvenile Supervisor of Burleigh County, stated:

"Sandy's relationship with Sue does seem to play a part of this custody issue. I will be honest and say, I do not know how big a part it plays in 'the best interest of the child.' I know nothing to little on the subject of homosexuality. Because of this, I do not feel I can make a recommendation in this case."

ship. The case is discussed at p. 892 infra. For a discussion of custody disputes involving homosexual parents see L. Weitzman, The Marriage Contract 219–223 (1981).

MNOOKIN, CHILD–CUSTODY ADJUDICATION: JUDICIAL FUNCTIONS IN THE FACE OF INDETERMINACY.

39 Law & Contemp. Probs. 226, 255–262 (1975) *.

. . .

B. The Indeterminacy of Present-Day Standards

Lon Fuller has suggested that when a judge decides about custody under the best-interests principle, he is:[152]

[N]ot applying law or legal rules at all, but is exercising administrative discretion which by its nature cannot be rule-bound. The statutory admonitions to decide the question of custody so as to advance the welfare of the child is as remote from being a rule of law as an instruction to the manager of a state-owned factory that he should follow the principle of maximizing output at the least cost to the state.

Insofar as a court assumes responsibility for seeing how a child is to be raised, it is assuming a managerial role.

When a judge must resolve a custody dispute, he is committed to making a choice among alternatives. The very words of the best-interests-of-the-child principle suggest that the judge should decide by choosing the alternative that "maximizes" what is best for a particular child.[154] Conceived this way, the judge's decision can be framed in a manner consistent with an intellectual tradition that views the decision process as a problem of rational choice. In analyzing the custody decision from this perspective, my purpose is not to describe how judges in fact decide custody disputes nor to propose a method of how they should. Instead, it is to expose the inherent indeterminacy of the best-interests standard.

1. *Rational Choice*

Decision theorists have laid out the logic of rational choice with clarity and mathematical rigor for prototype decision problems. The decision-maker specifies alternative outcomes associated with differ-

152. [L. Fuller, Interaction Between Law and its Social Context (unbound class material for Sociology of Law, Summer 1971, University of California, Berkely] 11.

154. To choose what is least detrimental can be put in exactly the same conceptual framework. It too requires both the specification of alternative outcomes and the assessment of probabilities. The least detrimental alternative is then chosen. Detriment can be regarded as a utility measure that takes into account only harm. Alternatively, detriment may be defined simply as the absence of benefit, in which case it is best interests under a different name. In either event, the specification of a utility function presents the same conceptual difficulties.

ent courses of action and then chooses that alternative that "maximizes" his values, subject to whatever constraints the decision-maker faces. This involves two critical assumptions: first, that the decision-maker can specify alternative outcomes for each course of action; the second, that the decision-maker can assign to each outcome a "utility" measure that integrates his values and allows comparisons among alternative outcomes. Choice does not require certainty about the single outcome that will in fact flow from a particular action. Treating uncertainty as a statistical problem, models have been developed that allow decisions to be made on the basis of "expected" utility. This requires that the decision-maker be able to specify the probability of each possible outcome for a particular course of action. The utility of each possible outcome is then discounted by its probability.

Decision-making under this model also implies certain things about the process. The decision-maker will be receptive and sensitive to informational requirements and will modify his outcome calculations as new information becomes available: [158]

> The quintessential analytic decision-maker is one who strains towards as complete an understanding as possible of the causal forces which determine outcomes. He seeks to predict the flow of events and, where he has leverage, to manipulate them to his advantage. The processing of information on making decisions is all done for the purposes of constructing and improving the blueprint from which the optimal choice emerges.

Unlike adjudication, rational choice does *not* require participation of the affected parties, the use of precedents or rules, or review; today's decision need not be reconciled with similar decisions made earlier.

2. *A Custody Determination Under the Best-Interests-of-the-Child Principle*

Assume that a judge must decide whether a child should live with his mother or his father when the parents are in the process of obtaining a divorce.[159] From the perspective of rational choice, the judge would wish to compare the expected utility for the child of living with his mother with that of living with his father. The judge would need considerable information and predictive ability to do this. The judge would also need some source for the values to measure utility for the child. All three are problematic.

a. The Need for Information: Specifying Possible Outcomes

In the example chosen, the judge would require information about how each parent had behaved in the past, how this behavior had af-

---

158. J. Steinbruner, [The Cybernetic Theory of Decision: New Dimensions of Political Analysis (1974)] at 35–36.

159. The same analysis would apply in a state-initiated neglect proceeding.

See generally Mnookin, [Foster Care—In Whose Best Interests, 43 Harv.Ed.Rev. 599 (1975)].

fected the child, and the child's present condition. Then the judge would need to predict the future behavior and circumstances of each parent if the child were to remain with that parent and to gauge the effects of this behavior and these circumstances on the child. He would also have to consider the behavior of each parent if the child were to live with the other parent and how this might affect the child. If a custody award to one parent would require removing the child from his present circumstances, school, friends, and familiar surrounding, the judge would necessarily wish to predict the effects these changes would have on the child. These predictions would necessarily involve estimates of not only the child's mutual relationships with the custodial parent, but also his future contacts with the other parent and siblings, the probable number of visits by the noncustodial spouse, the probable financial circumstances of each of the spouses, and a myriad of other factors.

One can question how often, if ever, any judge will have the necessary information. In many instances, a judge lacks adequate information about even the most rudimentary aspects of a child's life with his parents and has still less information available about what either parent plans in the future. This is particularly true in many juvenile court proceedings where, at the time of the dispositional hearing, the judge typically has *no* information about where the child will be placed if removal is ordered. The judge usually knows nothing about either the characteristics of the foster family or how long that family will want or be able to keep the child. Indeed, in these custody cases, the court is normally comparing an existing family with an unknown alternative.

b. Predictions Assessing the Probability of Alternative Outcomes

Obviously, more than one outcome is possible for each course of judicial action, so the judge must assess the probability of various outcomes and evaluate the seriousness of possible benefits and harms associated with each. But even where a judge has substantial information about the child's past home life and the present alternatives, present-day knowledge about human behavior provides no basis for the kind of individualized predictions required by the best-interests standard. There are numerous competing theories of human behavior, based on radically different conceptions of the nature of man, and no consensus exists that any one is correct.[161] No theory at all is

---

161. While a book could be written to document this proposition, a comparison of five sample theories with competing implications should suffice for these purposes:

1. *Physiologically-oriented theories* suggest that a child's personality is primarily determined by his physical structure or body type. See, e.g., W. Sheldon, The Varieties of Human Physique: An Introduction to Constitutional Psychology (1940).

2. *Behaviorist theories* view the child as broadly malleable and suggest that his personality development is shaped by environment through a system of reward and punishment. See, e.g., J. Watson, Behaviorism (1920); B. Skinner, Walden II (1948) (affording an extreme perspective on the implications possible in child rearing).

3. *Psychoanalytic theories* suggest that the interaction between parent and child sets into motion various de-

considered widely capable of generating reliable predictions about the psychological and behavioral consequences of alternative dispositions for a particular child.

While psychiatrists and psychoanalysts have at times been enthusiastic in claiming for themselves the largest possible role in custody proceedings, many have conceded that their theories provide no reliable guide for predictions about what is likely to happen to a particular child. Anna Freud, who has devoted her life to the study of the child and who plainly believes that theory can be a useful guide to treatment, has warned: "In spite of . . . advances there remain factors which make clinical foresight, i.e., prediction, difficult and hazardous," not the least of which is that "environmental happenings in a child's life will always remain unpredictable since they are not governed by any known laws. . . ."[163]

The difficulty of making accurate predictions is shown clearly by a study undertaken by Joan Macfarlane and her associates in Berkeley, California.[164] Using various tests and interviews, the Berkeley group, during a thirty-year period, studied a group of 166 infants born in 1929. Their objective was to observe the growth—emotional, mental, and physical—of normal people. As Arlene Skolnick observed, "Over the years this study has generated several significant research findings, but the most surprising of all was the difficulty of predicting what thirty-year-old adults would be like even after the most sophisticated data had been gathered on them as children. . . ."[165]

velopmental and unconscious forces that are the wellsprings of behavior. Freud stresses the importance of the first few years of life, when the child goes through distinct developmental stages. The parents' response to these stages will be the major determinant of the child's later personality. See generally S. Freud, Beyond the Pleasure Principle, in 18 Collected Works 7, 20–21 (J. Strachey ed. & transl. 1955).

4. *Child-development and learning theories* present the child as an active participant in the world around him, basically self-generating and activated by innate tendencies towards involving himself with his environment. See, e.g., J. Piaget, The Origins of Intelligence in Children (1952).

5. *Interpersonal theories* suggest that a child's developing personality is largely determined by the roles and expectations assigned to him by his family. See, e.g., H. Sullivan, The Interpersonal Theory of Psychiatry (1953).

163. A. Freud, Child Observation and Prediction of Development—A Memorial Lecture in Honor of Ernst Kris, in 13 The Psychoanalytic Study of the Child 92,

97–98 (1958). See also Goldstein, Freud, & Solnit [Beyond the Best Interests of the Child (1973)] 51–52; Goldstein, Psychoanalysis and Jurisprudence, 71 Yale L.J. 1053 (1968). The limitations of psychological theory in generating verifiable predictions is suggested by the numerous studies that have attempted to trace effects of various child rearing techniques and parental attitudes on adult personality traits. See, e.g., S. Escalona, The Roots of Individuality: Normal Patterns of Development in Infancy 13 (1968). For an analysis of the difficulties of predicting dangerousness in the civil commitment context, see Diamond, supra note 134.

164. See Macfarlane, Perspectives on Personality Consistency and Change from the Guidance Study, 7 Vita Humana 115 (1964).

165. A. Skolnick, The Intimate Environment, Exploring Marriage and the Family 378 (1973). Skolnick explained the results as follows:

Foremost, the researchers had tended to overestimate the damaging effects of early troubles of various kinds. Most personality theory had been de-

Various studies have attempted to trace personality development to specific antecedent variables to show that these variables have the same effects on different children. This connection is now widely questioned by experimental psychologists such as H. R. Schaffer, who thinks that infants experience external events in individual ways.[166] The implication of this for prediction is described very well by Skolnick: "[I]f the child selectively interprets situations and events, we cannot confidently predict behavior from knowledge of the situation alone."[167]

c. Values to Inform Choice: Assigning Utilities to Various Outcomes

Even if the various outcomes could be specified and their probability estimated, a fundamental problem would remain unsolved. What set of values should a judge use to detemine what is in a child's best interests? If a decision-maker must assign some measure of utility to each possible outcome, how is utility to be determined?

For many decisions in an individualistic society, one asks the person affected what he wants. Applying this notion to custody cases, the child could be asked to specify those values or even to choose. In some cases, especially those involving divorce, the child's preference is sought and given weight. But to make the child responsible for the choice may jeopardize his future relationship with the other parent. And we often lack confidence that the child has the capacity and the maturity appropriately to determine his own utility.

Moreover, whether or not the judge looks to the child for some guidance, there remains the question whether best interests should be viewed from a long-term or a short-term perspective. The conditions that make a person happy at age seven to ten may have adverse consequences at age thirty. Should the judge ask himself what decision will make the child happiest in the next year? Or at thirty? Or at seventy? Should the judge decide by thinking about what decision the child as an adult looking back would have wanted made? In this case, the preference problem is formidable, for how is the judge

rived from observations of troubled people in therapy. The pathology of adult neurotics and psychotics was traced back to disturbances early in childhood—poor parent-child relations, chronic school difficulties, and so forth. Consequently, theories of personality based on clinical observation tended to define adult psychological problems as socialization failures. But the psychiatrist sees only disturbed people; he does not encounter "normal" individuals who may experience childhood difficulties, but who do not grow into troubled adults. The Berkeley method,

however, called for studying such people. Data on the experience of these subjects demonstrated the error of assuming that similar childhood conditions affect every child the same way. Indeed, many instances of what looked like severe pathology to the researchers were put to constructive use by the subjects. . . .

Id. at 379.

166. See H. Schaffer, The Growth of Sociability 16 (1971).

167. A. Skolnick, supra note 165, at 372.

to compare "happiness" at one age with "happiness" at another age?[169]

Deciding what is best for a child poses a question no less ultimate than the purposes and values of life itself. Should the judge be primarily concerned with the child's happiness? Or with the child's spiritual and religious training? Should the judge be concerned with the economic "productivity" of the child when he grows up? Are the primary values of life in warm, interpersonal relationships, or in discipline and self-sacrifice? Is stability and security for a child more desirable than intellectual stimulation? These questions could be elaborated endlessly. And yet, where is the judge to look for the set of values that should inform the choice of what is best for the child? Normally, the custody statutes do not themselves give content or relative weights to the pertinent values. And if the judge looks to society at large, he finds neither a clear consensus as to the best child rearing strategies nor an appropriate hierarchy of ultimate values.

It thus seems clear that a judge in a child-custody case is in a more difficult position than Professor Fuller's factory manager told to maximize his output or profits. While the factory manager's problems of prediction are formidable, he at least has a measure to compare the relative value of possible outcomes. Physical output or money profits, given existing resources, can be maximized. But in a child-custody dispute, what comparable measure does a judge have in a society that lacks a clearly defined and integrated set of values about what is good for particular individuals?

3. *Why Some Custody Cases Are Easy to Decide*

An inquiry about what is best for a child often yields indeterminate results because of the problems of having adequate information, making the necessary predictions, and finding an integrated set of values by which to choose. But some custody cases may still be comparatively easy to decide. While there is no consensus about what is best for a child, there is much consensus about what is very bad (e.g., physical abuse); some short-term predictions about human behavior can be reliably made (e.g., chronic alcoholism or psychosis is difficult quickly to modify). Asking which alternative is in the best interests of a child may have a rather clear-cut answer in situations where one claimant exposes the child to substantial risks of immediate harm and the other claimant already has a substantial personal relationship with the child and poses no such risk. In a private dispute between two parents, for example, if a judge could predict that one parent's conduct would seriously endanger the child's health, it would not be difficult to conclude that the child's expected utility would be higher if he went with the other parent, whose conduct did not, even without the necessity of defining utility carefully. More generally, where one

---

169. Because of the difficulties of making long-term predictions, it has been suggested that only short-run effects be considered. See Goldstein, Freud, & Solnit [Beyond the Best Interests of the Child (1973)] 51–52.

alternative plainly risks irreversible effects on the child that are bad and the other does not, there is no need to make longer-term predictions or more complicated psychological evaluations of what is likely to happen to the child's personality.

But to be easy, a case must involve only one claimant who is well known to the child and whose conduct does not endanger the child. If there are two such claimants or none, difficult choices remain. Most custody disputes pose difficult choices. In child-neglect cases, for example, the existing home may clearly be far from "optimal," but placing the child with a foster family unknown to the child poses serious risks as well. Without knowing the long-term effects of foster care on children, for example, how is the judge to decide in all but the most obvious cases whether a four-year-old child is better off removed from the parental custody of neglectful parents whose conduct does not endanger the child's physical health? And in many private disputes, the court must often choose between parties who each offer advantages and disadvantages, knowing that to deprive the child completely of either relationship will be disruptive. In a divorce custody fight, for example, where the mother is overprotective, possessive, and insecure and the father is demanding, aggressive, and hard-driving, how is the judge to decide where to place a seven-year-old child?

. . . .

PAINTER v. BANNISTER

Supreme Court of Iowa, 1966.
258 Iowa 1390, 140 N.W.2d 152.

STUART, JUSTICE.

We are here setting the course for Mark Wendell Painter's future. Our decision on the custody of this 7 year old boy will have a marked influence on his whole life. The fact that we are called upon many times a year to determine custody matters does not make the exercising of this awesome responsibility any less difficult. Legal training and experience are of little practical help in solving the complex problems of human relations. However, these problems do arise and under our system of government, the burden of rendering a final decision rests upon us. It is frustrating to know we can only resolve, not solve, these unfortunate situations.

The custody dispute before us in this habeas corpus action is between the father, Harold Painter, and the maternal grandparents, Dwight and Margaret Bannister. Mark's mother and younger sister were killed in an automobile accident on December 6, 1962 near Pullman, Washington. The father, after other arrangements for Mark's care had proved unsatisfactory, asked the Bannisters, to take care of Mark. They went to California and brought Mark to their farm home near Ames in July, 1963. Mr. Painter remarried in November, 1964 and about that time indicated he wanted to take Mark back. The Bannisters refused to let him leave and this action was filed in June, 1965. Since July 1965 he has continued to remain in the Bannister home under an order of this court staying execution of the judgment of the trial court awarding custody to the father until the matter could be determined on appeal. For reasons hereinafter stated, we conclude Mark's better interests will be served if he remains with the Bannisters.

Mark's parents came from highly contrasting backgrounds. His mother was born, raised and educated in rural Iowa. Her parents are college graduates. Her father is agricultural information editor for the Iowa State University Extension Service. The Bannister home is in the Gilbert Community and is well kept, roomy and comfortable. The Bannisters are highly respected members of the community. Mr. Bannister has served on the school board and regularly teaches a Sunday school class at the Gilbert Congregational Church. Mark's mother graduated from Grinnell College. She then went to work for a newspaper in Anchorage, Alaska, where she met Harold Painter.

Mark's father was born in California. When he was 2½ years old, his parents were divorced and he was placed in a foster home. Although he has kept in contact with his natural parents, he considers his foster parents, the McNelly's as his family. He flunked out of a high school and a trade school because of a lack of interest in academic subjects, rather than any lack of ability. He joined the navy at 17. He did not like it. After receiving an honorable discharge, he took examinations and obtained his high school diploma. He lived with the McNelly's and went to college for 2½ years under the G.I. bill. He quit college to take a job on a small newspaper in Ephrata, Washington in November 1955. In May 1956, he went to work for the newspaper in Anchorage which employed Jeanne Bannister.

Harold and Jeanne were married in April, 1957. Although there is a conflict in the evidence on the point, we are convinced the marriage, overall, was a happy one with many ups and downs as could be expected in the uniting of two such opposites.

We are not confronted with a situation where one of the contesting parties is not a fit or proper person. There is no criticism of either the Bannisters or their home. There is no suggestion in the record that Mr. Painter is morally unfit. It is obvious the Bannisters did not approve of their daughter's marriage to Harold Painter and do not want their grandchild raised under his guidance. The philosophies of life are entirely different. As stated by the psychiatrist who examined Mr. Painter at the request of Bannisters' attorneys: "It is evident that there exists a large difference in ways of life and value systems between the Bannisters and Mr. Painter, but in this case, there is no evidence that psychiatric instability is involved. Rather, these divergent life patterns seem to represent alternative normal adaptations."

It is not our prerogative to determine custody upon our choice of one of two ways of life within normal and proper limits and we will not do so. However, the philosophies are important as they relate to Mark and his particular needs.

The Bannister home provides Mark with a stable, dependable, conventional, middle-class, middlewest background and an opportunity for a college education and profession, if he desires it. It provides a solid foundation and secure atmosphere. In the Painter home, Mark would have more freedom of conduct and thought with an opportunity to develop his individual talents. It would be more exciting and challenging in many respects, but romantic, impractical and unstable.

. . . .

Our conclusion as to the type of home Mr. Painter would offer is based upon his Bohemian approach to finances and life in general. We feel there is much evidence which supports this conclusion. His main ambition is to be a free lance writer and photographer. He has had some articles and picture stories published, but the income from these efforts has been negligible. At the time of the accident, Jeanne was willingly working to support the family so Harold could devote more time to his writing and photography. In the 10 years since he left college, he has changed jobs seven times. He was asked to leave two of them; two he quit because he didn't like the work; two because he wanted to devote more time to writing and the rest for better pay. He was contemplating a move to Berkeley at the time of trial. His attitude toward his career is typified by his own comments concerning a job offer:

"About the Portland news job, I hope you understand when I say it took guts not to take it; I had to get behind myself and push. It was very, very tempting to accept a good salary and settle down to a steady, easy routine. As I approached Portland, with the intention of taking the job, I began to ask what, in the long run, would be the good of this job: 1, it was not *really* what I wanted; 2, Portland is just another big farm town, with none of the stimulation it takes to get my mind sparking. Anyway, I decided Mark and myself would be better off if I went ahead with what I've started and the hell with the rest, sink, swim or starve."

There is general agreement that Mr. Painter needs help with his finances. Both Jeanne and Marilyn, his present wife, handled most of them. Purchases and sales of books, boats, photographic equipment and houses indicate poor financial judgment and an easy come easy go attitude. He dissipated his wife's estate of about $4300, most of which was a gift from her parents and which she had hoped would be used for the children's education.

The psychiatrist classifies him as "a romantic and somewhat of a dreamer". An apt example are the plans he related for himself and

Mark in February 1963: "My thought now is to settle Mark and myself in Sausilito, near San Francisco; this is a retreat for wealthy artists, writers, and such aspiring artists and writers as can fork up the rent money. My plan is to do expensive portraits ($150 and up), sell prints ($15 and up) to the tourists who flock in from all over the world . . . ."

The house in which Mr. Painter and his present wife live, compared with the well kept Bannister home, exemplifies the contrasting ways of life. In his words "it is a very old and beat up and lovely home . . .". They live in the rear part. The interior is inexpensively but tastefully decorated. The large yard on a hill in the business district of Walnut Creek, California, is of uncut weeds and wild oats. The house "is not painted on the outside because I do not want it painted. I am very fond of the wood on the outside of the house."

The present Mrs. Painter has her master's degree in cinema design and apparently likes and has had considerable contact with children. She is anxious to have Mark in her home. Everything indicates she would provide a leveling influence on Mr. Painter and could ably care for Mark.

Mr. Painter is either an agnostic or atheist and has no concern for formal religious training. He has read a lot of Zen Buddhism and "has been very much influenced by it". Mrs. Painter is Roman Catholic. They plan to send Mark to a Congregational Church near the Catholic Church, on an irregular schedule.

He is a political liberal and got into difficulty in a job at the University of Washington for his support of the activities of the American Civil Liberties Union in the university news bulletin.

There were "two funerals" for his wife. One in the basement of his home in which he alone was present. He conducted the service and wrote her a long letter. The second at a church in Pullman was for the gratification of her friends. He attended in a sport shirt and sweater.

These matters are not related as a criticism of Mr. Painter's conduct, way of life or sense of values. An individual is free to choose his own values, within bounds, which are not exceeded here. They do serve however to support our conclusion as to the kind of life Mark would be exposed to in the Painter household. We believe it would be unstable, unconventional, arty, Bohemian, and probably intellectually stimulating.

Were the question simply which household would be the most suitable in which to raise a child, we would have unhesitatingly chosen the Bannister home. We believe security and stability in the home are more important than intellectual stimulation in the proper development of a child. There are, however, several factors which have made us pause.

First, there is the presumption of parental preference, which though weakened in the past several years, exists by statute. We have a great deal of sympathy for a father, who in the difficult period of adjustment following his wife's death, turns to the maternal grandparents for their help and then finds them unwilling to return the child. There is no merit in the Bannister claim that Mr. Painter permanently relinquished custody. It was intended to be a temporary arrangement. A father should be encouraged to look for help with the children, from those who love them without the risk of thereby losing the custody of the children permanently. This fact must receive consideration in cases of this kind. However, as always the primary consideration is the best interest of the child and if the return of custody to the father is likely to have a seriously disrupting and disturbing effect upon the child's development, this fact must prevail.

Second, Jeanne's will named her husband guardian of her children and if he failed to qualify or ceased to act, named her mother. The parent's wishes are entitled to consideration.

Third, the Bannisters are 60 years old. By the time Mark graduates from high school they will be over 70 years old. Care of young children is a strain on grandparents and Mrs. Bannister's letters indicate as much.

We have considered all of these factors and have concluded that Mark's best interest demands that his custody remain with the Bannisters. Mark was five when he came to their home. The evidence clearly shows he was not well adjusted at that time. He did not distinguish fact from fiction and was inclined to tell "tall tales" emphasizing the big "I". He was very aggressive toward smaller children, cruel to animals, not liked by his classmates and did not seem to know what was acceptable conduct. As stated by one witness: "Mark knew where his freedom was and he didn't know where his boundaries were." In two years he made a great deal of improvement. He now appears to be well disciplined, happy, relatively secure and popular with his classmates, although still subject to more than normal anxiety.

We place a great deal of reliance on the testimony of Dr. Glenn R. Hawks, a child psychologist. The trial court, in effect, disregarded Dr. Hawks' opinions stating: "The court has given full consideration to the good doctor's testimony, but cannot accept it at full face value because of exaggerated statements and the witness' attitude on the stand." We, of course, do not have the advantage of viewing the witness' conduct on the stand, but we have carefully reviewed his testimony and find nothing in the written record to justify such a summary dismissal of the opinions of this eminent child psychologist.

Dr. Hawks is head of the Department of Child Development at Iowa State University. However, there is nothing in the record which suggests that his relationship with the Bannisters is such that his professional opinion would be influenced thereby. Child development is his specialty and he has written many articles and a textbook on the subject. He is recognized nationally, having served on the staff of the 1960 White House Conference on Children and Youth and as consultant on a Ford Foundation program concerning youth in India. . . .

Between June 15th and the time of trial, he spent approximately 25 hours acquiring information about Mark and the Bannisters, including appropriate testing of and "depth interviews" with Mark. Dr. Hawks' testimony covers 70 pages of the record and it is difficult to pinpoint any bit of testimony which precisely summarizes his opinion. He places great emphasis on the "father figure" and discounts the importance of the "biological father". "The father figure is a figure that the child sees as an authority figure, as a helper, he is a nutrient figure, and one who typifies maleness and stands as maleness as far as the child is concerned."

His investigation revealed: ". . . the strength of the father figure before Mark came to the Bannisters is very unclear. Mark is confused about the father figure prior to his contact with Mr. Bannister." Now, "Mark used Mr. Bannister as his father figure. This is very evident. It shows up in the depth interview, and it shows up in the description of Mark's life given by Mark. He has a very warm feeling for Mr. Bannister."

Dr. Hawks concluded that it was not for Mark's best interest to be removed from the Bannister home. He is criticized for reaching this conclusion without investigating the Painter home or finding out more about Mr. Painter's character. He answered:

"I was most concerned about the welfare of the child, not the welfare of Mr. Painter, not about the welfare of the Bannisters. In as much as Mark has already made an adjustment and sees the Bannisters as his parental figures in his psychological makeup, to me this is the most critical factor. Disruption at this point, I think, would be detrimental to the child even though Mr. Painter might well be a paragon of virtue. I think this would be a kind of thing which would not be in the best interest of the child. I think knowing something about where the child is at the present time is vital. I think something about where he might go, in my way of thinking is essentially untenable to me, and relatively unimportant. It isn't even helpful. The thing I was most concerned about was Mark's view of his own reality in which he presently lives. If this is destroyed I think it will have rather bad effects on Mark. I think then if one were to make a determination whether it would be to the parents' household, or the McNelly household, or X-household, then I think the further study would be appropriate."

Dr. Hawks stated: "I am appalled at the tremendous task Mr. Painter would have if Mark were to return to him because he has got to build the relationship from scratch. There is essentially nothing on which to build at the present time. Mark is aware Mr. Painter is his father, but he is not very clear about what this means. In his own mind the father figure is Mr. Bannister. I think it would take a very strong person with everything in his favor in order to build a relationship as Mr. Painter would have to build at this point with Mark."

It was Dr. Hawks' opinion "the chances are very high (Mark) will go wrong if he is returned to his father". This is based on adoption studies which "establish that the majority of adoptions in children who are changed, from ages six to eight, will go bad, if they have had a prior history of instability, some history of prior movement. When I refer to instability I am referring to where there has been no attempt to establish a strong relationship." Although this is not an adoption, the analogy seems appropriate, for Mark who had a history of instability would be removed from the only home in which he has a clearly established "father figure" and placed with his natural father about whom his feelings are unclear.

We know more of Mr. Painter's way of life than Dr. Hawks. We have concluded that it does not offer as great a stability or security as the Bannister home. Throughout his testimony he emphasized Mark's need at this critical time is stability. He has it in the Bannister home.

Other items of Dr. Hawks' testimony which have a bearing on our decision follow. He did not consider the Bannisters' age anyway disqualifying. He was of the opinion that Mark could adjust to a change more easily later on, if one became necessary, when he would have better control over his environment.

He believes the presence of other children in the home would have a detrimental effect upon Mark's adjustment whether this occurred in the Bannister home or the Painter home.

The trial court does not say which of Dr. Hawks' statements he felt were exaggerated. We were most surprised at the inconsequential position to which he relegated the "biological father". He concedes "child psychologists are less concerned about natural parents then probably other professional groups are." We are not inclined to so lightly value the role of the natural father, but find much reason for his evaluation of this particular case.

Mark has established a father-son relationship with Mr. Bannister, which he apparently had never had with his natural father. He is happy, well adjusted and progressing nicely in his development. We do not believe it is for Mark's best interest to take him out of this stable atmosphere in the face of warnings of dire consequences from an eminent child psychologist and send him to an uncertain future in his father's home. Regardless of our appreciation of the father's love for his child and his desire to have him with him, we do not believe we have the moral right to gamble with this child's future. He should be encouraged in every way possible to know his father. We are sure there are many ways in which Mr. Painter can enrich Mark's life.

For the reasons stated, we reverse the trial court and remand the case for judgment in accordance herewith.

NOTES

(1) After visiting with his father in California subsequent to the Iowa court's decision, Mark expressed a desire to stay with him. The grandparents did not oppose the custody change which was effected by a California court in August 1968. See Painter, Mark, I Love You (1969).

For a discussion of *Painter* contrasting its approach with other cases in a work by the Committee on the Family of the Group for the Advancement of Psychiatry, see New Trends in Child Custody Determinations 34 (1980).

(2) A more recent case which received widespread media attention pitted a child's preferences against those of his parents. It drew well-orchestrated international attention because of its political implications. Walter Polovchak and his parents immigrated from the Ukraine in January 1980. In May, Walter's parents decided that they were unhappy in the United States and would return to the Soviet Union. Walter wanted to remain and ran away from the family's apartment. When Walter was picked up by police, instead of being reprimanded and returned to his parents, he was granted political asylum by the United States Immigration and Naturalization Service. Later, at a hearing in Family Court, Walter was declared a ward of the state. Although the case raises a variety of issues, one of the most important is what rights do children have against their parents? At what point are children allowed to decide their futures for themselves? What difference does it make that parents want to raise their children in Russia? What if the Polovchaks wanted to move to the war-torn Middle East? Or if they wished to join guerrillas in a Third World country? Should the political ideology of parents or of a foreign principality ever be considered in determining the best interests of a child? Are juvenile courts competent to make decisions about foreign political systems? Cf. Zschernig v. Miller, 389 U.S. 429 (1968) ("foreign policy attitudes . . . are matters for the Federal Government, not for local probate courts"). Should a juvenile be granted political asylum? Consider the remarks of George Mamedou, a Soviet Embassy official who commented on the Polovchak case: "It should be clear to every educated and unbiased person that a 12-year-old child doesn't understand what political asylum is." Los Angeles Times, Sept. 7, 1981, section 1, page 6, at col. 2.

Interestingly, the American Civil Liberties Union, which has often championed the rights of juveniles in other contexts (free speech, school newspapers, birth control and abortion), decided to represent the parents in this dispute. The ACLU contended that the state should not take custody of children unless their parents are unfit. The fact that parents want to live in a different country or under a different political system does not mean they are unfit. According to the ACLU, the Polovchaks were being punished for political reasons because they wanted to return to the Soviet Union. Furthermore, the ACLU was concerned that the Polovchaks were being denied the fundamentals of due process when Walter's custody hearing was initially held. Apparently, the Polovchaks were at one point represented by counsel but did not have a translator. At another point, they were represented by an attorney from the Ukranian community in Chicago and there was a question whether the parents' statements were being translated accurately.

The parents returned to the Soviet Union without Walter, while the battle for his custody was still being fought in the Illinois courts. See New York Times, Jan. 1, 1982, page 24, col 1.

PROVISIONS FOR A MODEL CHILD PLACEMENT STATUTE

J. Goldstein, A. Freud, and A. Solnit, Beyond the Best Interests
of the Child, at 97–101 (1973).*

SELECTED PROVISIONS FOR THE CHILD PLACEMENT
CODE OF HAMPSTEAD-HAVEN

ARTICLE 10. DEFINITIONS

Para. 10.1 Biological Parents

The biological parents are those who physically produce the child.

Para. 10.2 Wanted Child

A wanted child is one who receives affection and nourishment on a continuing basis from at least one adult and who feels that he or she is and continues to be valued by those who take care of him or her.

Para. 10.3 Psychological Parent

A psychological parent is one who, on a continuing, day-to-day basis, through interaction, companionship, interplay, and mutuality, fulfills the child's psychological needs for a parent, as well as the child's physical needs. The psychological parent may be a biological (Para. 10.1), adoptive, foster, or common-law (Para. 10.4) parent, or any other person. There is no presumption in favor of any of these after the initial assignment at birth (Para. 20).

Para. 10.4 Common-law Parent-child Relationship

A common-law parent-child relationship is a psychological parent (Para. 10.3)—wanted child (Para.10.2) relationship which developed outside of adoption, assignment by custody in separation or divorce proceedings, or the initial assignment at birth of a child to his or her biological parents (Para. 20.1).

Para. 10.5 Child's Sense of Time

A child's sense of time is based on the urgency of his or her instinctual and emotional needs and thus differs from an adult's sense of time, as adults are better able to anticipate the future and thus to manage delay. A child's sense of time changes as he or she develops. Intervals of separation between parent and child that would constitute important breaks in continuity at one age might be of reduced significance at a later age.

Para. 10.6   Least Detrimental Available Alternative

The least detrimental available alternative is that child placement and procedure for child placement which maximizes, in accord with the child's sense of time (Para. 10.5), the child's opportunity for being wanted (Para. 10.2) and for maintaining on a continuous, unconditional, and permanent basis a relationship with at least one adult who is or will become the child's psychological parent (Para. 10.3).

ARTICLE 20.   INITIAL PLACEMENT

Para. 20.   Placement of Child

At birth, a child is placed with his biological parents (Para. 10.1). Unless other adults assume or are assigned the rule, they are presumed to become the child's psychological parents (Para. 10.3).

ARTICLE 30.   INTERVENTION TO ALTER A CHILD'S PLACEMENT

Para. 30.1   State Policy of Minimizing Disruption

It is the policy of this state to minimize disruptions of continuing relationships between a psychological parent (Para. 10.3) and the child. The child's developmental needs are best served by continuing unconditional and permanent relationships. The importance of a relationship's duration and the significance of a disruption's duration vary with the child's developmental stage.

Para. 30.2   Intervenor

An intervenor is any person (including the state, institutions of the state, biological parents, and others) who seeks to disrupt a continuing relationship between psychological parent (Para. 10.3) and child or seeks to establish an opportunity for such a relationship to develop. Upon such interventions the court's decision must secure for the child the least detrimental available alternative (Para. 10.6).

Para. 30.3   Burden on the Intervenor

A child is presumed to be wanted (Para. 10.2) in his or her current placement. If the child's placement is to be altered, the intervenor, except in custody disputes in divorce or separation, must establish *both*:

(i) that the child is unwanted, *and*

(ii) that the child's current placement is not the least detrimental available alternative (Para. 10.6).

In custody disputes in divorce or separation, the intervenor, that is the adult seeking custody, must establish that he or she is the least detrimental available alternative (Para. 10.6).

Para. 30.4 Child's Party Status

Whenever an intervenor seeks to alter a child's placement the child shall be made a party to the dispute. The child shall be represented by independent counsel.

Para. 30.5 Final Unconditional Disposal

All placements shall be unconditional and final, that is, the court shall not retain continuing jurisdiction over a parent-child relationship or establish or enforce such conditions as rights of visitation.

Para. 30.6 Timely Hearing and Appeal

Trials and appeals shall be conducted as rapidly as is consistent with responsible decisionmaking. The court shall establish a timetable for hearing, decision, and review on appeal which, in accord with the specific child's sense of time (Para. 10.5), shall maximize the chances of all interested parties to have their substantive claims heard while still viable, and shall minimize the disruption of parent-child relationships (Para. 30.1).

NOTES

(1) The preceding model appears in a widely acclaimed, sometimes misunderstood, and often controversial work. In place of the "best interests of the child" standard, the authors propose that child placement decisions be based on the "least detrimental available alternative for safeguarding the child's growth and development".

Would the outcome be affected if the Hampstead-Haven model were applied to the cases preceding it in this chapter? How would you explain to a legislative advisory panel considering reform of child custody laws the ways in which the Hampstead-Haven model would effect significant change, aside from those discussed in notes (2) and (3) below?

(2) Visitation rights often are regarded as a source of continuing friction between parents after separation or divorce. Some judges would prefer to limit visitation sharply because of the potential adverse effect on children who may be "caught in the middle". Note the provision of Para. 30.6 of the Hampstead-Haven model in this respect. More typical of state law today is § 407 of the Uniform Marriage and Divorce Act, which provides:

Section 407. [*Visitation.*]

(a) A parent not granted custody of the child is entitled to reasonable visitation rights unless the court finds, after a hearing, that visitation would endanger seriously the child's physical, mental, moral, or emotional health.

(b) The court may modify an order granting or denying visitation rights whenever modification would serve the best interest of the child; but the court shall not restrict a parent's visitation rights unless it finds that the visitation would endanger seriously the child's physical, mental, moral, or emotional health.

(3) Continued attempts at modification of child custody decrees also can lead to exasperation by both courts and participants. Note the provision of Para. 30.5 of the Hampstead-Haven Model in this regard. Significantly, § 409(a) of the Uniform Marriage and Divorce Act also provides that

Section 409. [*Modification.*]

(a) No motion to modify a custody decree may be made earlier than 2 years after its date, unless the court permits it to be made on the basis of affidavits that there is reason to believe the child's present environment may endanger seriously his physical, mental, moral, or emotional health.

Neither provision is typical of existing state law. The remainder of § 409 provides:

(b) If a court of this State has jurisdiction pursuant to the Uniform Child Custody Jurisdiction Act, the court shall not modify a prior custody decree unless it finds, upon the basis of facts that have arisen since the prior decree or that were unknown to the court at the time of entry of the prior decree, that a change has occurred in the circumstances of the child or his custodian, and that the modification is necessary to serve the best interest of the child. In applying these standards the court shall retain the custodian appointed pursuant to the prior decree unless:

(1) the custodian agrees to the modification;

(2) the child has been integrated into the family of the petitioner with consent of the custodian; or

(3) the child's present environment endangers seriously his physical, mental, moral, or emotional health, and the harm likely to be caused by a change of environment is outweighed by its advantages to him.

Attorney fees and costs shall be assessed against a party seeking modification if the court finds that the modification action is vexatious and constitutes harassment.

BENNETT v. JEFFREYS

Court of Appeals of New York, 1976.
40 N.Y.2d 543, 387 N.Y.S.2d 821, 356 N.E.2d 277.

BREITEL, CHIEF JUDGE.

Petitioner is the natural mother of Gina Marie Bennett, now an eight-year-old girl. The mother in this proceeding seeks custody of her daughter from respondent, to whom the child had been entrusted since just after birth. Family Court ruled that, although the mother had not surrendered or abandoned the child and was not unfit, the child should remain with the present custodian, a former schoolmate of the child's grandmother. The Appellate Division reversed, one

Justice dissenting, and awarded custody to the mother. Respondent custodian appeals.[1]

The issue is whether the natural mother, who has not surrendered, abandoned, or persistently neglected her child, may, nevertheless, be deprived of the custody of her child because of a prolonged separation from the child for most of its life.

There should be a reversal and a new hearing before the Family Court. The State may not deprive a parent of the custody of a child absent surrender, abandonment, persisting neglect, unfitness or other like extraordinary circumstances. If any of such extraordinary circumstances are present, the disposition of custody is influenced or controlled by what is in the best interest of the child. In the instant case extraordinary circumstances, namely, the prolonged separation of mother and child for most of the child's life, require inquiry into the best interest of the child. . . .

Some eight years ago, the mother, then 15 years old, unwed, and living with her parents, gave birth to the child. Under pressure from her mother, she reluctantly acquiesced in the transfer of the newborn infant to an older woman, Mrs. Jeffreys, a former classmate of the child's grandmother. The quality and quantity of the mother's later contacts with the child were disputed. The Family Court found, however, that there was no statutory surrender or abandonment. Pointedly, the Family Court found that the mother was not unfit. The Appellate Division agreed with this finding.

There was evidence that Mrs. Jeffreys intended to adopt the child at an early date. She testified, however, that she could not afford to do so and admitted that she never took formal steps to adopt.

The natural mother is now 23 and will soon graduate from college. She still lives with her family, in a private home with quarters available for herself and the child. The attitude of the mother's parents, however, is changed and they are now anxious that their daughter keep her child.

Mrs. Jeffreys, on the other hand, is now separated from her husband, is employed as a domestic and, on occasion, has kept the child in a motel. It is significant that Mrs. Jeffreys once said that she was willing to surrender the child to the parent upon demand when the child reached the age of 12 or 13 years.

At the outset, it is emphasized that not involved is an attempted revocation of a voluntary surrender to an agency or private individual for adoption. Nor is abandonment involved. Nor does the proceeding involve an attempted permanent termination of custody. Nor is there involved the temporary placement into foster care by an authorized agency which is obliged to conduct an investigation and to deter-

1. The child is currently with her mother and will remain there pending final determination of this litigation, a stay of the Appellate Division order having been denied by that court.

mine the qualification of foster parents before placement of a child in need of such care.

Instead, this proceeding was brought by an unwed mother to obtain custody of her daughter from a custodian to whom the child had been voluntarily, although not formally, entrusted by the mother's parents when the mother was only 15 years old. Thus, as an unsupervised private placement, no statute is directly applicable, and the analysis must proceed from common-law principles.

Absent extraordinary circumstances, narrowly categorized, it is not within the power of a court, or, by delegation of the Legislature or court, a social agency, to make significant decisions concerning the custody of children, merely because it could make a better decision or disposition. The State is *parens patriae* and always has been, but it has not displaced the parent in right or responsibility. Indeed, the courts and the law would, under existing constitutional principles, be powerless to supplant parents except for grievous cause or necessity (see Stanley v. Illinois, 405 U.S. 645, 651, 92 S.Ct. 1208, 31 L.Ed.2d 551). Examples of cause or necessity permitting displacement of or intrusion on parental control would be fault or omission by the parent seriously affecting the welfare of a child, the preservation of the child's freedom from serious physical harm, illness or death, or the child's right to an education, and the like.

The parent has a "right" to rear its child, and the child has a "right" to be reared by its parent. However, there are exceptions created by extraordinary circumstances, illustratively, surrender, abandonment, persisting neglect, unfitness, and unfortunate or involuntary disruption of custody over an extended period of time. It is these exceptions which have engendered confusion, sometimes in thought but most often only in language.

The day is long past in this State, if it had ever been, when the right of a parent to the custody of his or her child, where the extraordinary circumstances are present, would be enforced inexorably, contrary to the best interest of the child, on the theory solely of an absolute legal right. Instead, in the extraordinary circumstance, when there is a conflict, the best interest of the child has always been regarded as superior to the right of parental custody. Indeed, analysis of the cases reveals a shifting of emphasis rather than a remaking of substance. This shifting reflects more the modern principle that a child is a person, and not a subperson over whom the parent has an absolute possessory interest. A child has rights too, some of which are of a constitutional magnitude.

Earlier cases . . . emphasized the right of the parent, superior to all others, to the care and custody of the child. This right could be dissolved only by abandonment, surrender, or unfitness. Of course, even in these earlier cases, it was recognized that parental custody is lost or denied not as a moral sanction for parental failure, but because "the child's welfare compels awarding its custody to the nonparent" (People ex rel. Kropp v. Shepsky, 305 N.Y. 465, 469, 113 N.E.2d 801, 804).

Although always recognizing the parent's custodial rights, the concern in the later cases, given the extraordinary circumstances, was consciously with the best interest of the child. . . .

. . . [In] Matter of Spence-Chapin Adoption Serv. v. Polk, 29 N.Y.2d 196, 204, 324 N.Y.S.2d 937, 944, 274 N.E.2d 431, 436, the court rejected any notion of absolute parental rights. The court restated the abiding principle that the child's rights and interests are "paramount" and are not subordinated to the right of parental custody, as important as that right is, p. 204, 324 N.Y.S.2d p. 944, 274 N.E.2d p. 436. Indeed, and this is key, the rights of the parent and the child are ordinarily compatible, for "the generally accepted view [is] that a child's best interest is that it be raised by its parent unless the parent is disqualified by gross misconduct" p. 204, 324 N.Y.S.2d p. 944, 274 N.E.2d 436.

Recently enacted statute law, applicable to related areas of child custody such as adoption and permanent neglect proceedings, has explicitly required the courts to base custody decisions solely upon the best interest of the child. Under these statutes, there is no presumption that the best interest of the child will be promoted by any particular custodial disposition. Only to this limited extent is there a departure from the pre-existing decisional rule, which never gave more than rebuttable presumptive status, however strongly, to the parent's "right."

Such legislative changes conform, of course, to constitutional limitations. Their purpose, because they involve presumptions, or their negation, is only to implement judicial disposition of evidentiary matters in reconciling the "rights of parents" with the "rights of children" in custody dispositions.

But neither decisional rule nor statute can displace a fit parent because someone else could do a "better job" of raising the child in the view of the court (or the Legislature), so long as the parent or parents have not forfeited their "rights" by surrender, abandonment, unfitness, persisting neglect or other extraordinary circumstance. These "rights" are not so much "rights", but responsibilities which reflect the view, noted earlier, that, except when disqualified or displaced by extraordinary circumstances, parents are generally best qualified to care for their own children and therefore entitled to do so (Matter of Spence-Chapin Adoption Serv. v. Polk, 29 N.Y.2d 196, 204, 324 N.Y.S.2d 937, 944, 274 N.E.2d 431, 436, supra).

Indeed, as said earlier, the courts and the law would, under existing constitutional principles, be powerless to supplant parents except for grievous cause or necessity (see Stanley v. Illinois, 405 U.S. 645, 651, 92 S.Ct. 1208, 31 L.Ed.2d 551, in which the principle is plainly stated and stressed as more significant than other essential constitutional rights).

But where there is warrant to consider displacement of the parent, a determination that extraordinary circumstances exist is only the beginning, not the end, of judicial inquiry. Extraordinary circumstances alone do not justify depriving a natural parent of the custody of a child. Instead, once extraordinary circumstances are found, the court must then make the disposition that is in the best interest of the child.

Although the extraordinary circumstances trigger the "best interests of the child" test, this must not mean that parental rights or responsibilities may be relegated to a parity with all the other surrounding circumstances in the analysis of what is best for the child. So for one example only, while it is true that disruption of custody over an extended period of time is the touchstone in many custody cases, where it is voluntary the test is met more easily but where it is involuntary the test is met only with great difficulty, for evident reasons of humanity and policy.

The child's "best interest" is not controlled by whether the natural parent or the nonparent would make a "better" parent, or by whether the parent or the nonparent would afford the child a "better" background or superior creature comforts. Nor is the child's best interest controlled alone by comparing the depth of love and affection between the child and those who vie for its custody. Instead, in ascertaining the child's best interest, the court is guided by principles which reflect "considered social judgments in this society respecting the family and parenthood" (Matter of Spence-Chapin Adoption Serv. v. Polk, 29 N.Y.2d 196, 204, 324 N.Y.S.2d 937, 944, 274 N.E.2d 431, 436). These principles do not, however, dictate that the child's custody be routinely awarded to the natural parent.

To recapitulate: intervention by the State in the right and responsibility of a natural parent to custody of her or his child is warranted if there is first a judicial finding of surrender, abandonment, unfitness, persistent neglect, unfortunate or involuntary extended disruption of custody, or other equivalent but rare extraordinary circumstance which would drastically affect the welfare of the child. It is only on such a premise that the courts may then proceed to inquire into the best interest of the child and to order a custodial disposition on that ground.

In custody matters parties and courts may be very dependent on the auxiliary services of psychiatrists, psychologists, and trained social workers. This is good. But it may be an evil when the dependence is too obsequious or routine or the experts too casual. Particularly important is this caution where one or both parties may not have the means to retain their own experts and where publicly compensated experts or experts compensated by only one side have uncurbed leave to express opinions which may be subjective or are not narrowly controlled by the underlying facts.

The court's determination may be influenced by whether the child is in the present custody of the parent or the nonparent. Changes in conditions which affect the relative desirability of custodians, even when the contest is between two natural parents, are not to be accorded significance unless the advantages of changing custody outweigh the essential principle of continued and stable custody of children.

Moreover, the child may be so long in the custody of the nonparent that, even though there has been no abandonment or persisting neglect by the parent, the psychological trauma of removal is grave enough to threaten destruction of the child. . . .

In this case, there were extraordinary circumstances present, namely, the protracted separation of mother from child, combined with the mother's lack of an established household of her own, her unwed state, and the attachment of the child to the custodian. Thus, application of the principles discussed required an examination by the court into the best interest of the child.

In reaching its conclusion that the child should remain with the nonparent custodian, the Family Court relied primarily upon the seven-year period of custody by the nonparent and evidently on the related testimony of a psychologist. The court did not, however, adequately examine into the nonparent custodian's qualifications and background. Also, the court apparently failed to consider the fact that, absent a finding of abandonment or neglect by the mother, or her consent, the nonparent cannot adopt the child. The Family Court's disposition, if sustained, would therefore have left the child in legal limbo, her status indefinite until the attainment of her majority. For a single example, a question could arise as to whose consent, the parent's or the nonparent custodian's, would be necessary for the child to marry while underage . . . . A similar question could arise with respect to many situations affecting employment and entry into occupations, an adoption, and any other matters requiring the consent of a parent or legal guardian.

On the other hand, the Appellate Division, in awarding custody to the mother, too automatically applied the primary principle that a parent is entitled to the custody of the child. This was not enough if there were extraordinary circumstances, as indeed there were. Other than to agree with Family Court that she was not "unfit", the court did not pursue a further analysis. Most important, no psychological or other background examination of the mother had ever been obtained. There was, therefore, no consideration of whether the mother is an adequate parent, in capacity, motivation, and efficacious planning. Nevertheless, the Appellate Division determination may well be right.

Thus, a new hearing is required because the Family Court did not examine enough into the qualifications and background of the long-time custodian, and the Appellate Division did not require further examination into the qualifications and background of the mother. Each court was excessive in applying abstract principles, a failing, however important those principles are.

. . .

Accordingly, the order of the Appellate Division should be reversed, without costs, and the proceeding remitted to Family Court for a new hearing.

[The concurring opinion of Judge Fuchsberg is omitted.]

————

BENNETT v. MARROW

New York Supreme Court, Appellate Division, 2d Department, 1977.
59 A.D.2d 492, 399 N.Y.S.2d 697.

O'CONNOR, JUSTICE.

There is here presented one of the most difficult and disturbing problems known to the law—the custody of a child. The problem is, of course, compounded when, as here, the conflict rages between the natural mother and a foster mother. The Family Court awarded custody of the child to the foster mother and, after carefully studying this meticulously compiled record, we conclude that the order should be affirmed.

[The court reviews the custody determination principles set forth in Bennett v. Jeffreys, in which the same case was remitted to Family Court for a new hearing.]

The new hearing extended over a four-week period and contains the testimony of some 26 witnesses; that record and the order entered thereon are now before us for review.

We are here concerned with an unsupervised, private placement and, hence, any analysis of the decision of the Family Court must be predicated not upon statute, but upon common law principles.

Fortunately, the hearing was held before the same Judge who had presided at the first hearing some two years before. Predicated upon his observations and findings at the 1975 hearing, the court was in a rather unique position to completely re-examine and re-evaluate the testimony of those witnesses who had testified at both hearings. In the light of his intimate knowledge of the background and history of the case, he was able to conduct a more in-depth examination of the psychiatrists, psychologists, social workers, teachers and other witnesses called by the parties. Most importantly, the court was enabled to clearly and closely observe for a second time the conduct and deportment of the principals, namely the petitioner-appellant (the natural parent), the respondent (the foster parent) and Gina Marie (the infant involved). His comments therefore concerning the changes he found in the personality and demeanor of Gina Marie become all the more significant and persuasive in view of the fact that the child, in the intervening 15 months, had been living in the home of the petitioner, her natural mother.

The trial court, after noting that during the first hearing Gina Marie appeared to be a well-adjusted, happy child, went on to say that "the fact is that notwithstanding a period of some 15 months spent in the home of her mother, Gina Marie has not settled into the household. She does not feel comfortable there, she is not happy there. She continues unswerving in her request to be restored to the custody of Mrs. Marrow."

These surface observations, while bearing some significance, are certainly not controlling; but the court's conclusions concerning the natural mother are perhaps more revealing. The court said: "To the extent that the petitioner has responded to Gina Marie's needs to be housed, to be clothed, to be fed, she could be considered to have performed adequately as a parent. But she has not begun to respond to Gina Marie's emotional needs." At another point the court observed: "I am constrained to consider that Miss Bennett's motivation in seeking custody of Gina Marie stems from a feeling that she is her child and should reside with her. That she has feeling for Gina Marie I am certainly prepared to believe, but in view of the testimony presented during the course of these proceedings, I have serious reservations that she is capable of giving Gina Marie the emotional support so vital to her well-being."

The court then concluded: "This Court was asked to determine whether the mother is an adequate parent. As stated previously, she has provided materially for Gina Marie. That is to say, she has made available to Gina Marie what Welfare has provided in the first instance. But that is virtually all she has given Gina Marie. She had not given significantly of herself. I find that an emotional void exists between mother and daughter that shows no signs of being bridged despite the time they have resided together. This child continues to mourn the loss of her 'mother.'"

Addressing itself then to the relationship between the respondent and Gina Marie, the court gave credence to the testimony of a witness called by the Law Guardian, Dr. Sally Provence, a child psychiatrist from Yale University. Finding her to be "certainly the most impressive expert witness who appeared in this proceeding", the hearing court accepted Dr. Provence's testimony that a psychological parent-child relationship had developed between respondent and the child and the court noted that such bond "appears as strong today as when this case was first heard."

It was Dr. Provence's further testimony, in substance, that to remove the child from such a relationship would endanger the development of the child in many ways and could affect her academic success and her motivation to learn.

This testimony is all the more significant in view of the record, which discloses that in January, 1977 an intelligence test was administered to Gina Marie resulting in a score of 84, in the low-normal range, whereas in April, 1975 she had scored 113. Despite efforts to explain away this rather disturbing pattern, it seems to be, as least to some extent, buttressed by the obvious and drastic decline in the physical, mental and emotional make-up of Gina Marie.

Reflection upon the totality of the testimony and careful consideration of all of the factors involved leads but to one conclusion, the order of the Family Court should be affirmed.

We note in closing that that order properly and fully protects petitioner's rights of visitation but, under the extraordinary circumstances here presented, the best interests of the child require that custody of Gina Marie be awarded to respondent.

Order of the Family Court, Westchester County, dated May 19, 1977, affirmed, without costs or disbursements.

NOTES

(1) How would you describe the legal relationship between Gina Marie and Mrs. Marrow at this point? What would your answer be if you were applying the Hampstead-Haven provisions?

Since Bennett v. Jeffreys was decided, the New York Court of Appeals has been reluctant to extend it further and has in fact seemed to restrict its usage, or at least its application in cases involving allegations of abandonment or termination of parental rights. See, e.g., Dickson v. Lascaris, 53 N.Y.2d 204, 440 N.Y.S.2d 884, 423 N.E.2d 361 (1981); Matter of Sanjivini K., 47 N.Y.2d 374, 418 N.Y.S.2d 339, 391 N.E.2d 1316 (1979); Corey L. v. Martin L., 45 N.Y.2d 383, 408 N.Y.S.2d 439, 380 N.E.2d 266 (1978). For an illustration of judicial willingness in another jurisdiction to allow a child to remain with a long term custodian unrelated by blood, even though a natural parent sought the child's return, see Ross v. Hoffman, 280 Md. 172, 372 A.2d 582 (1977).

(2) An obstacle to increased application of the concept of psychological parenthood in custody determinations is the rigid application in some jurisdictions of the parental preference rule. One of the more extreme interpretations in this regard was rendered by the Supreme Court of Kansas in Sheppard v. Sheppard, 230 Kan. 146, 630 P.2d 1121 (1981). Custody of a minor child had been awarded to the grandparents and the natural mother appealed. At issue was a 1980 statute, Kan.Stat.Ann. 60–1610(b)(2) (Supp. 1980), which provided:

> (2) At any time after custody of any minor child has been awarded pursuant to a divorce, annulment or separate maintenance decree, any person who has had actual physical custody of any such child after such decree was rendered with the consent of the parent having legal custody, where applicable, may request by motion to the court rendering such decree that legal custody of such child or children be awarded to such person. Notwithstanding the parental preference doctrine the court may award custody of any such child to such person if the best interests of such child will be served thereby; and, if the court determines that a parental relationship has been established between such child or children and the moving party. No motion may be made pursuant to this subsec-

tion, unless the movant has had actual physical custody of the child or children within six (6) months from the date of the motion. In determining the best interest of the child, the court shall consider all relevant factors, including but not limited to the following: (A) The length of time that any such child has been under the actual care and control of any person other than a parent and the circumstances relating thereto; (B) the desires of the child's parents as to custody; (C) the desires of the child as to the child's custodian; (D) the interaction and interrelationship of the child with parents, siblings, and any other person who may significantly affect the child's best interests; (E) the child's adjustment to such child's home, school, and community; and (F) the mental and physical health and age of all individuals involved.

In declaring the statute unconstitutional insofar as it permitted favoring a third person over a parent in a custody award without a finding of parental unfitness, the court stated:

It is clear under our decisions and those of the United States Supreme Court that a natural parent's right to the custody of his or her children is a fundamental right which may not be disturbed by the state or by third persons, absent a showing that the natural parent is unfit. As we noted in In re Cooper, 230 Kan. 57, 631 P.2d 632, (1981), a parent's right to the custody, care, and control of his or her child is a fundamental liberty right protected by the Fourteenth Amendment of the Constitution of the United States.

The statute under consideration takes away that right. Fitness of a parent is no longer the criteria. If the trial court determines that the best interests of the child will be served by placing it with third persons, the court may do so. The parent need not consent, and he or she may be perfectly fit, willing, and able to care for and raise the child. No exceptional circumstances need exist.

The exact objective of the legislature is not clear. The act provides an expeditious method of awarding custody, despite the existence of fit parents, to persons who have had temporary custody of the child with the consent of a divorced parent. It reaches only the children of divorced parents, not those of separated or unwed parents. The statute does not appear necessary in order to further the State's interest in the protection of children, for we have the juvenile code provisions to protect neglected children, and provisions in the civil code to provide for changes in custody and support, and for the removal of children from unfit parents.

. . . .

What we hold here is simply this: that a parent who is not found to be unfit, has a fundamental right, protected by the Due Process Clause of the United States Constitution, to the care, custody and control of his or her child, and that the right of such a parent to custody of the child cannot be taken away in favor of a third person, absent a finding of unfitness on the part of the parent. We hold that K.S.A.1980 Supp. 60–1610(*b*) (2), which destroys that fundamental right, is violative of the Due Process Clause and therefore unconstitutional.

MCFARLAND, J., dissenting, expressed a different approach:

I do not view K.S.A.1980 Supp. 60–1610(*b*)(2) as constitutionally impermissible. In the vast majority of factual situations the parental preference doctrine is appropriate and should control. The statute in question merely provides a trial judge a discretionary alternative when certain conditions precedent are found to exist.

. . .

Unlike a juvenile court proceeding, the State is not attempting to take custody of a child. The proceeding authorized by K.S.A.1980 Supp. 60–1610 is, of necessity, only one chapter in an ongoing domestic relations action. By virtue of its specialized conditions, relatively few custody changes could arise from it. However, it is a valuable addition to a trial judge's meager alternatives in child custody disputes.

Nowhere in the majority opinion is there any reference to a child's rights. Does the majority believe that only a parent has any rights? If the parent granted custody of a child sees fit to place that child with another person under such circumstances that a new family unit is created, does the child have no rights at all in the continuance of the new family unit? Does the majority consider the child as only a chattel belonging to the parents, to be lent and returned upon demand?

As a former district court judge I can certainly recall instances where this statute would have been highly desirable. The parent having custody may leave a child with relatives for many years, then suddenly want it back in a fit of guilt or due to changed circumstances. The relatives may well be the only home the child has known and a strong family unit has been created. The trial court should have the discretion to preserve the family unit as it now exists—whether such discretion should be exercised is dependent upon all relevant factors and is subject to judicial review.

. . .

In In re J.P., 648 P.2d 1364 (Utah 1982), the Utah Supreme Court similarly invalidated a provision of the Utah Children's Rights Act which permitted involuntary termination of parental rights on a finding that such a result would be in the child's best interest. The court stated:

. . . [W]e conclude that the right of a parent not to be deprived of parental rights without a showing of unfitness, abandonment or substantial neglect is so fundamental to our society and so basic to our constitutional order . . . that it ranks among those rights referred to in . . . the Utah Constitution and the Ninth Amendment to the United States Constitution as being retained by the people.

This recognition of the due process and retained rights of parents promotes values essential to the preservation of our democratic society. The family is a principal conservator and transmitter of cherished values and traditions. . . . Any invasion of the sanctity of the family, even with the loftiest motives, unavoidably threatens those traditions and values.

For example, family autonomy helps to assure the diversity characteristic of a free society. There is no surer way to preserve pluralism than to allow parents maximum latitude in rearing their own children. Much of the rich variety in American culture has been transmitted from generation to generation by determined parents who were acting against the best interests of their children, as defined by official dogma. Conversely, there is no surer way to threaten pluralism than to terminate the rights of parents who contradict officially approved values imposed by reformers empowered to determine what is in the "best interest" of someone else's child.

How would a holding like *Sheppard* or In re J. P. affect Painter v. Bannister or Bennett v. Marrow?

B. JOINT CUSTODY

Joint custody is an increasingly popular method for dealing with children of divorce today. Even so, the term is not always clearly defined and the legal ramifications of the approach may not be fully understood by those who undertake to utilize it. Basically joint custody provides for equal sharing of decision making between separated or divorced parents; this may be difficult for persons whose problems may have been partly caused or at least exacerbated by disagreements over child raising techniques or policies.

Although some use the terms interchangeably, joint custody is usually distinguished from "divided custody", with the latter designating a plan for shifting physical custody on a regular basis with each parent having control while the child is with him or her.

Although statutes specifically enabling joint custody awards have been enacted in some states, even without them courts are generally considered to have power to give custody jointly to both parents. The popularity of joint custody has not silenced widespread criticism. As pointed out by Justice Felice Shea of the New York Supreme Court in a 1978 opinion:

> Joint custody is an appealing concept. It permits the Court to escape an agonizing choice, to keep from wounding the self-esteem of either parent and to avoid the appearance of discrimination between the sexes. Joint custody allows parents to have an equal voice in making decisions, and it recognizes the advantages of shared responsibility for raising the young. But serious questions remain to be answered. How does joint custody affect children? What are the factors to be considered and weighed? While the Court should not yield to the frivolous objections of one party, it must give thought to whether joint custody is feasible when one party is opposed and court intervention is needed to effectuate it. In the end, as in every child custody decision, it is the welfare of the children which governs and each case will turn on its individual facts and circumstances.

> . . .

> It is well recognized that the children of divorce are subjected to severe strain, and that children often experience loss of security and feelings of rejection as a concomitant of their parents' separation. Experts in the field have expressed opposition to divided custody on the ground that change and discontinuity threaten the child's emotional well-being. It is argued that "joint custody between parents usually requires that 'shuttling back and forth' of

children which must inevitably lead to the lack of stability in home environment which children require." Moreover, joint or divided custody may exacerbate the adults' use of the children to defeat each other in defiance of the children's interest in stability, serenity and continuity. In attempting to maintain positive emotional ties to two hostile adults, children may become prey to severe and crippling loyalty conflicts.

The proponents of joint custody contend that fathers relegated to seeing their children only intermittently experience feelings of deep loss and often react by limiting their involvement with their children. They argue further that there is no scientific data for the *de facto* preference in favor of the mother and that fathers in today's dual career families are equally nurturant and competent to care for their offspring. They contend that a child needs a sustained involvement with both his parents and that the conventional single parent custody arrangement "tends to make ex-parents of fathers, painfully deprived creatures out of the children and overburdened people out of mothers."

These are persuasive arguments. No post-divorce custody arrangement will give to children two loving parents, living together, devoted to each other and to the children's welfare. Joint custody, under the proper circumstances, may be the closest it is possible to come to the shattered ideal. The courts, in dealing with the difficult issues raised by child custody litigation, should consider joint custody as an option, particularly in performing their little noted but frequently exercised role as mediator before trial.

However, when one parent resists joint custody and refuses to be persuaded that it is workable, what will be the result for the children when it is ordered by the Court? There appear to be no social science studies that will answer this question. The most ardent professional proponents of joint custody assume cooperation between parents and agreement about child rearing practices as basic requirements for joint custody. It is hardly surprising that joint custody is generally arrived at by consent.[1]

Other courts have recognized that joint custody should not be imposed on a couple when there is opposition to it by one or both parties[2]; the rationale is that success of such an arrangement hinges on the desire as well as the capacity of both parties to make it work. The Iowa Supreme Court has set forth the following tests for a court

1. Dodd v. Dodd, 93 Misc.2d 641, 645–47, 403 N.Y.S.2d 401, 403–405 (S.Ct. N.Y.County 1978). Braiman v. Braiman, 44 N.Y.2d 584, 407 N.Y.S.2d 449, 378 N.E.2d 1019 (1978).

2. See e.g., In re Marriage of Burham, 283 N.W.2d 269 (Iowa 1979);

to consider in evaluating the feasibility of a joint custody arrangement in any given case:

(1) Is each parent fit and suitable as a custodial parent?

(2) Do the parents agree to joint custody, or is one or both opposed?

(3) Have the parents demonstrated that they are able to communicate and give priority to the child's welfare such that they are capable of reaching shared decisions in the child's best interests?

(4) Is there geographical proximity such that there will be no substantial disruption of the child's schooling, association with friends, religious training, or other routines?

(5) Is there similarity in the environment of each parent's home, or will the child be confronted with vastly different or potentially disruptive environmental changes?

(6) Is there any indication that the psychological and emotional needs and development of the child will suffer due to a particular joint custodial arrangement?

(7) Are the work hours and routines of both parents such that child care will be suitable with either parent?

(8) Is joint custody in accord with the child's wishes and does he or she not have strong opposition to such an arrangement?[3]

The recently adopted California custody law that follows has been the subject of considerable curiosity if not controversy. Is such a statute advisable in the absence of significant experience with and substantial understanding about the impact of joint custody on children who will be subject to it? Is its enactment by the legislature under present circumstances analogous to the courts' past development of presumptions such as the "tender years rule"?

CALIFORNIA CIVIL CODE. CUSTODY OF CHILDREN

§ 4600. Legislative findings and declarations; custody order; preferences; findings; allegations; hearings; exclusion of public

(a) The Legislature finds and declares that it is the public policy of this state to assure minor children of frequent and continuing contact with both parents after the parents have separated or dissolved their marriage, and to encourage parents to share the rights and responsibilities of child rearing in order to effect this policy.

---

3. In re Marriage of Burham, 283 N.W.2d 269, 274 (Iowa 1979).

In any proceeding where there is at issue the custody of a minor child, the court may, during the pendency of the proceeding or at any time thereafter, make such order for the custody of the child during minority as may seem necessary or proper. If a child is of sufficient age and capacity to reason so as to form an intelligent preference as to custody, the court shall consider and give due weight to the wishes of the child in making an award of custody or modification thereof. In determining the person or persons to whom custody shall be awarded under paragraph (2) or (3) of subdivision (b), the court shall consider and give due weight to the nomination of a guardian of the person of the child by a parent under . . . the Probate Code.

(b) Custody should be awarded in the following order of preference according to the best interests of the child:

(1) To both parents jointly pursuant to Section 4600.5 or to either parent. In making an order for custody to either parent, the court shall consider, among other factors, which parent is more likely to allow the child or children frequent and continuing contact with the noncustodial parent, and shall not prefer a parent as custodian because of that parent's sex.

The court, in its discretion, may require the parents to submit to the court a plan for the implementation of the custody order.

(2) If to neither parent, to the person or persons in whose home the child has been living in a wholesome and stable environment.

(3) To any other person or persons deemed by the court to be suitable and able to provide adequate and proper care and guidance for the child.

(c) Before the court makes any order awarding custody to a person or persons other than a parent, without the consent of the parents, it shall make a finding that an award of custody to a parent would be detrimental to the child and the award to a nonparent is required to serve the best interests of the child. Allegations that parental custody would be detrimental to the child, other than a statement of that ultimate fact, shall not appear in the pleadings. The court may, in its discretion, exclude the public from the hearing on this issue.

. . .

§ 4600.5 Joint custody; agreement of parents; presumption; order; reasons for denial; award in other cases; discretion of court; modification or termination; modification of other orders; parental access to records

(a) There shall be a presumption, affecting the burden of proof, that joint custody is in the best interests of a minor child where the parents have agreed to an award of joint custody or so agree in open court at a hearing for the purpose of determining the custody of the minor child or children of the marriage.

If the court declines to enter an order awarding joint custody pursuant to this subdivision, the court shall state in its decision the reasons for denial of an award of joint custody.

(b) Upon the application of either parent, joint custody may be awarded in the discretion of the court in other cases. For the purpose of assisting the court in making a determination whether an award of joint custody is appropriate under this subdivision, the court may direct that an investigation be conducted pursuant to the provisions of Section 4602. If the court declines to enter an order awarding joint custody pursuant to this subdivision, the court shall state in its decision the reasons for denial of an award of joint custody.

(c) For the purposes of this section, "joint custody" means an order awarding custody of the minor child or children to both parents and providing that physical custody shall be shared by the parents in such a way as to assure the child or children of frequent and continuing contact with both parents; provided, however, that such order may award joint legal custody without awarding joint physical custody.

(d) Any order for joint custody may be modified or terminated upon the petition of one or both parents or on the court's own motion if it is shown that the best interests of the child require modification or termination of the order. The court shall state in its decision the reasons for modification or termination of the joint custody order if either parent opposes the modification or termination order.

(e) Any order for the custody of the minor child or children of a marriage entered by a court in this state or any other state may, subject to the jurisdictional requirements set forth in Sections 5152 and 5163, be modified at any time to an order of joint custody in accordance with the provisions of this section.

(f) In counties having a conciliation court, the court or the parties may, at any time, pursuant to local rules of court, consult with the conciliation court for the purpose of assisting the parties to formulate a plan for implementation of the custody order or to resolve any controversy which has arisen in the implementation of a plan for custody.

(g) Notwithstanding any other provision of law, access to records and information pertaining to a minor child, including but not limited to medical, dental, and school records, shall not be denied to a parent because such parent is not the child's custodial parent.

NOTE

Joint custody arrangements can produce special difficulties for interstate enforcement under the Uniform Child Custody Jurisdiction Act (U.C.C.J.A.) if the parties choose to separate geographically. For a discussion of this problem, see Bodenheimer, Progress Under the Uniform Child Custody Jurisdiction Act and Remaining Problems: Punitive Decrees, Joint Custody, and Excessive Modifications, 65 Calif.L.Rev. 978, 1009–12 (1977).

C.   SPECIAL PROBLEMS IN A MOBILE SOCIETY

CARPENTER v. CARPENTER

Supreme Court of Virginia, 1979.
220 Va. 299, 257 S.E.2d 845.

HARMAN, J., delivered the opinion of the Court.

This is an appeal from a decree denying consent for Mary Gladys Richards Carpenter (mother or Mrs. Carpenter) to remove the residence of her two minor children, then ages seven and nine, from the Commonwealth of Virginia and permanently restraining and enjoining such change of residence by the children without prior approval of the court. The sole issue here is whether the trial court abused its discretion in refusing the consent sought by Mrs. Carpenter.

On April 14, 1976, the Chancellor awarded Mrs. Carpenter a divorce from her husband, Brown Hutcheson Carpenter (father or Mr. Carpenter) on the ground of desertion. In this decree the court confirmed, ratified and incorporated a stipulation between the parties under which Mrs. Carpenter, who waived her right to alimony, was awarded custody of the two children born to the union, a son in April, 1968, and a daughter in October, 1969. Under the stipulation the father, who obligated himself to pay $250 monthly for support of his children, was entitled to have the children visit with him on specified birthdays and holidays, every second weekend, every Wednesday afternoon and for three weeks each summer.

In July, 1977, upon learning that his former wife planned to move the children to New York City, Mr. Carpenter filed with the court a sworn petition alleging that such a move would be detrimental to the best interest of his children and praying that their custody be awarded to him. On July 19 the court entered an *ex parte* decree temporarily enjoining Mrs. Carpenter from removing the children from Virginia pending a hearing.

The court convened such a hearing on August 3 and each party appeared with counsel. Inquiry by the court established that neither party questioned the fitness of the other as a parent and that the sole issue for determination was whether the wife's proposed move to New York would serve the best interest of the children.

The father's testimony established the children have lived in the Norfolk-Virginia Beach area since birth. Both were well adjusted and doing well in school. They had many friends and playmates in the neighborhood where their father resided as well as in the neighborhood where they resided with their mother. Mr. Carpenter related that he had been able to maintain a close and affectionate relationship with his children because he had been able to see them often. He had also kept them, with their mother's consent, for periods in addition to those provided by the decree. These periods aggregated several weeks during the preceding year.

Mr. Carpenter viewed his frequent visits with his children and their activities together as beneficial to their education, training and development. He stated that because of the distance and expense involved, he would not be able to see them more than a few times a year if they moved to New York. He also stated that he believed the Tidewater area of Virginia had many cultural and recreational advantages and was a more desirable place to raise his children than New York City.

Mrs. Carpenter's testimony confirmed that a close relationship existed between the father and his children and that she had permitted the children to visit and reside with their father for periods in addition to those provided in the stipulation. She testified that she was a college graduate with a degree in chemistry and had completed some additional courses in business administration. She was unemployed and was receiving unemployment benefits at the time of the hearing. Since her divorce, she related that she had not been able to find employment as a chemist although she had applied to most employers of chemists in the Tidewater area. Because she had been unable to obtain employment as a chemist, she had worked for several employers in lower-paying clerical jobs. Because her own earnings, unemployment benefits and the child support payments provided by her former husband were not sufficient to pay the living expenses of her household, she had been forced to seek and receive financial assistance from her mother.

When asked why she wanted to move to New York, she stated that her employment opportunities would be better there, that her children would have greater cultural and educational advantages there than in Tidewater and that she wanted to live closer to her mother and other relatives who lived in New York.

Cross-examination revealed that Mrs. Carpenter had filed job applications for employment as a chemist with several employers in the New York area but, at the time she testified, had not received an offer from any of them. If permitted to move the children to New York, she proposed to live with her mother and stepfather until she was established and her income permitted her to rent her own residence. She also revealed that on one occasion she had been employed for a short time as a chemist and admitted that she was "fired" from that position. When asked if she had sought employment as a chemist elsewhere in Virginia, Mrs. Carpenter stated that she had not.

Based on the foregoing evidence the court, after commenting that Mrs. Carpenter's proposal was fanciful, entered a decree enjoining Mrs. Carpenter from permanently removing the children from Virginia without prior approval from the court. This decree, by implication, denied the consent sought by Mrs. Carpenter and the change of custody requested by Mr. Carpenter.

The mother argues that the Chancellor erred in not finding that the best interest of the children would be served by permitting her to move them to New York. She points to evidence that she was not able to meet her household expenses in Virginia without assistance from her mother and urges that her increased earnings as a chemist in New York would enable her to provide her children with a "measurably enhanced" life. She says that both children are "gifted" and that New York would provide them with "a more stimulating environment" in which to develop. Another factor making the move to New York desirable, she says, is "the presence of [her] family, including her mother, stepfather, stepbrother[s] and several cousins."

While these were factors to be weighed and considered by the Chancellor, the record also discloses other factors relevant to the issue before him. The evidence showed:

(1) that the children were developing well in the environment where they resided;

(2) that both were happy and well adjusted and were making good grades in school;

(3) that both children had been able to maintain a close and affectionate relationship with both parents;

(4) that both parents continued to play an active role in the care, education and development of their children;

(5) that the number and frequency of the father's visits with his children would be greatly reduced if they were living in New York;

(6) that the mother's expectations of increased income in New York were, at the very least, questionable and speculative; and

(7) that the cultural and educational advantages in New York City were not significantly greater than the cultural, educational and recreational advantages in Tidewater Virginia.

After weighing all factors, the Chancellor concluded that the best interest of the children would not be served by moving them to New York. The decree of the Chancellor determining questions of fact on conflicting evidence *ore tenus* has the weight of a jury verdict, and will be permitted to stand unless plainly wrong or without evidence to support it. Since the Chancellor's ruling is not plainly wrong or without evidence to support it, we find no abuse of discretion and will affirm the decree.

UNIFORM CHILD CUSTODY JURISDICTION ACT (1968)

Commissioners' Prefatory Note

There is growing public concern over the fact that thousands of children are shifted from state to state and from one family to another every year while their parents or other persons battle over their custody in the courts of several states. Children of separated parents may live with their mother, for example, but one day the father snatches them and brings them to another state where he petitions a court to award him custody while the mother starts custody proceedings in her state; or in the case of illness of the mother the children may be cared for by grandparents in a third state, and all three parties may fight over the right to keep the children in several states. These and many similar situations constantly arise in our mobile society where family members often are scattered all over the United States and at times over other countries. A young child may have been moved to another state repeatedly before the case goes to court. When a decree has been rendered awarding custody to one of the parties, this is by no means the end of the child's migrations. It is well known that those who lose a court battle over custody are often unwilling to accept the judgment of the court. They will remove the child in an unguarded moment or fail to return him after a visit and will seek their luck in the court of a distant state where they hope to find—and often do find—a more sympathetic ear for their plea for custody. The party deprived of the child may then resort to similar tactics to recover the child and this "game" may continue for years, with the child thrown back and forth from state to state, never coming to rest in one single home and in one community.

The harm done to children by these experiences can hardly be overestimated. It does not require an expert in the behavioral sciences to know that a child, especially during his early years and the years of growth, needs security and stability of environment and a continuity of affection. A child who has never been given the chance to develop a sense of belonging and whose personal attachments when beginning to form are cruelly disrupted, may well be crippled for life, to his own lasting detriment and the detriment of society.

This unfortunate state of affairs has been aided and facilitated rather than discouraged by the law. There is no statutory law in this area and the judicial law is so unsettled that it seems to offer nothing but a "quicksand foundation" to stand on. There is no certainty as to which state has jurisdiction when persons seeking custody of a child approach the courts of several states simultaneously or successively. There is no certainty as to whether a custody decree rendered in one state is entitled to recognition and enforcement in another; nor as to when one state may alter a custody decree of a sister state.

The judicial trend has been toward permitting custody claimants to sue in the courts of almost any state, no matter how fleeting the contact of the child and family was with the particular state, with little regard to any conflict of law rules. Also, since the United States Supreme Court has never settled the question whether the full faith and credit clause of the Constitution applies to custody decrees, many states have felt free to modify custody decrees of sister states almost at random although the theory usually is that there has been a change of circumstances requiring a custody award to a different person. Compare People ex rel. Halvey v. Halvey, 330 U.S. 610, 67 S.Ct. 903, 91 L.Ed. 1133 (1947); and see Comment, Ford v. Ford: Full Faith and Credit To Child Custody Decrees? 73 Yale L.J. 134 (1963). Generally speaking, there has been a tendency to over-emphasize the need for fluidity and modifiability of custody decrees at the expense of the equal (if not greater) need, from the standpoint of the child, for stability of custody decisions once made.

Under this state of the law the courts of the various states have acted in isolation and at times in competition with each other; often with disastrous consequences. A court of one state may have awarded custody to the mother while another state decreed simultaneously that the child must go to the father. In situations like this the litigants do not know which court to obey. They may face punishment for contempt of court and perhaps criminal charges for child stealing in one state when complying with the decree of the other. Also, a custody decree made in one state one year is often overturned in another jurisdiction the next year or some years later and the child is handed over to another family, to be repeated as long as the feud continues.

In this confused legal situation the person who has possession of the child has an enormous tactical advantage. Physical presence of the child opens the doors of many courts to the petitions and often assures him of a decision in his favor. It is not surprising then that custody claimants tend to take the law into their own hands, that they resort to self-help in the form of child stealing, kidnapping, or various other schemes to gain possession of the child. The irony is that persons who are good, law-abiding citizens are often driven into these tactics against their inclinations; and that lawyers who are reluctant to advise the use of maneuver of doubtful legality may place their clients at a decided disadvantage.

To remedy this intolerable state of affairs where self-help and the rule of "seize-and-run" prevail rather than the orderly processes of the law, uniform legislation has been urged in recent years to bring about a fair measure of interstate stability in custody awards. See Ratner, Child Custody in a Federal System, 62 Mich.L.Rev. 795 (1964); Ratner, Legislative Resolution of the Interstate Child Custody Problem: A Reply to Professor Currie and a Proposed Uniform Act, 38 S.Cal.L.Rev. 183 (1965); and Ehrenzweig, The Interstate Child and Uniform Legislation: A Plea for Extra-Litigious Proceedings, 64

Mich.L.Rev. 1 (1965). In drafting this Act, the National Conference of Commissioners has drawn heavily on the work of these authors and has consulted with other leading authorities. . . .

The Act is designed to bring some semblance of order into the existing chaos. It limits custody jurisdiction to the state where the child has his home or where there are other strong contacts with the child and his family. See Section 3. It provides for the recognition and enforcement of out-of-state custody decrees in many instances. See Sections 13 and 15. Jurisdiction to modify decrees of other states is limited by giving a jurisdictional preference to the prior court under certain conditions. See Section 14. Access to a court may be denied to petitioners who have engaged in child snatching or similar practices. See Section 8. Also, the Act opens up direct lines of communication between courts of different states to prevent jurisdictional conflict and bring about interstate judicial assistance in custody cases.

The Act stresses the importance of the personal appearance before the court of non-residents who claim custody, and of the child himself, and provides for the payment of travel expenses for this purpose. See Section 11. Further provisions insure that the judge receives necessary out-of-state information with the assistance of courts in other states. See Sections 17 through 22.

Underlying the entire Act is the idea that to avoid the jurisdictional conflicts and confusions which have done serious harm to innumerable children, a court in one state must assume major responsibility to determine who is to have custody of a particular child; that this court must reach out for the help of courts in other states in order to arrive at a fully informed judgment which transcends state lines and considers all claimants, residents and nonresidents, on an equal basis and from the standpoint of the welfare of the child. If this can be achieved, it will be less important *which* court exercises jurisdiction but that courts of the several states involved act in partnership to bring about the best possible solution for a child's future.

The Act is not a reciprocal law. It can be put into full operation by each individual state regardless of enactment of other states. But its full benefits will not be reaped until a large number of states have enacted it, and until the courts, perhaps aided by regional or national conferences, have come to develop a new, truly "inter-state" approach to child custody litigation. . . .

NOTE

At least 48 states had adopted the U.C.C.J.A. by 1982. Additionally, the enactment of the Federal Parental Kidnaping Prevention Act of 1980 has extended its potential effects, as will be discussed infra at 710.

The U.C.C.J.A. is designed to have application in cases of disputes across national as well as state boundaries. Section 23 of the Act provides:

> The general policies of this Act extend to the international area. The provisions of this Act relating to the recognition and enforcement of custody decrees of other states apply to custody decrees and decrees involving legal institutions similar in nature to custody institutions rendered by appropriate authorities of other nations if reasonable notice and opportunity to be heard were given to all affected persons.

Prior to adoption of the Act by their state legislatures, state courts often were willing to recognize foreign custody decrees through comity. See, e.g., Oehl v. Oehl, 221 Va. 618, 272 S.E.2d 441 (1980) (the Act was adopted in Virginia while the appeal was pending but the decision was based on comity principles). For an illustration of the application of § 23 in a state court of this country, see Miller v. Superior Court of Los Angeles County, 22 Cal.3d 923, 151 Cal.Rptr. 6, 587 P.2d 723 (1978).

In 1980 the Hague Conference on Private International Law, Fourteenth Session, concluded a Convention on the Civil Aspects of International Child Abduction. There is also a European Convention on Recognition and Enforcement of Decisions Concerning Custody of Children and on Restoration of Custody of Children, drafted by the Council of Europe. For general discussion on this subject, see Westbrook, Law and Treaty Responses to International Child Abduction, 20 Va. J. Int'l. Law 699 (1980).

HOLT v. DISTRICT COURT

Supreme Court of Oklahoma, 1981.
626 P.2d 1336.

LAVENDER, JUSTICE:

This is an application to assume original jurisdiction and petition for writ of prohibition or mandamus in a child custody matter. The facts, as we have gathered them from the pleadings, affidavits, and exhibits, will be set out in some detail.

The petitioner here is Linda Diane Holt. She and her husband, Dean Edwin Holt, were married in 1971 in Ardmore, Oklahoma. They have four children, three sons and a daughter, ages 2 to 7. Apparently they lived in Oklahoma until April 1978. In April 1978 they moved from Oklahoma City to Aurora, Oregon, where they lived together until last summer.

On July 18, 1980, when he returned home from a week of duty with the Oregon Air National Guard, Mr. Holt found his wife moving out of their house, taking the children with her. She left Oregon two days later and went to Borger, Texas, where her grandmother and some other relatives live. Two of the children went with her to Texas. Another child went to stay with Mrs. Holt's mother in Ardmore, Oklahoma, and the other child went to stay with Mrs. Holt's sister in Moore, Oklahoma. Later Mrs. Holt, a registered nurse, found a job paying $900 per month in Memphis, Texas, some 90 miles from Borger. She moved there to begin work on August 4, and the two children who had been in Oklahoma joined her and the other two children on August 18.

On July 29, 1980, Mr. Holt filed for divorce in the Circuit Court of Marion County, Oregon. In his petition and by a separate motion he asked for custody of the children. Mrs. Holt was served with the papers in Texas in August. Since that time the Oregon court has had and has exercised jurisdiction in this matter.

On September 24, 1980, Mrs. Holt filed in the District Court of Hall County, Texas, an "original petition in suit affecting the parent-child relationship." In her petition she alleged that "[n]o court has continuing jurisdiction of this suit or of the children, the subject of this suit." She asked the Texas court to appoint her "temporary managing conservator of the children," to enjoin the father from interfering with her possession of the children or from "taking or attempting to take possession of the children" himself, and to order the father to make child support payments. The pleadings before us do not reveal whether service was obtained on Mr. Holt in the Texas action. Nevertheless, the filing of that action became the foundation for a motion filed by Mrs. Holt on October 3 in the Oregon action, based on the Uniform Child Custody Jurisdiction Act.[1] In her motion she requested the Oregon court to "[decline] to exercise jurisdiction to make a child custody determination for the reasons that this Court is an inconvenient forum and a Court of another state is a more appropriate forum to make a child custody determination under the circumstances of this case."

The Oregon court held a hearing on Mrs. Holt's motion on October 16. On October 28 the judge issued an order denying the motion. He ruled that "[t]he State of Oregon is the home state" of the children and that "[a]s between the State of Oregon and the State of Texas, the State of Oregon is the place where there is optimum access to evidence concerning the present or future care, protection, training and personal relationships of the parties' minor children."

The Oregon court held another hearing on October 22, this one for the purpose of ruling on various other motions that had been filed in the case. Mrs. Holt appeared personally. The judge entered an order on November 3, in which he granted Mrs. Holt temporary custody of the four children, but provided that if she "fails to return said children to the community of Aurora, Oregon and to resume residence in said community within thirty (30) days from the date hereof, temporary custody of the parties' four (4) minor children shall be vested in petitioner [Mr. Holt]." He also ordered that when Mrs. Holt returned Mr. Holt had to move out of the family residence, and he ruled that Mr. Holt "shall not be required to pay for or reimburse respondent

1. Or.Rev.Stat. §§ 109.700–.930. In Oklahoma the Act appears at 10 O.S. Supp.1980 §§ 1601–1627.

[Mrs. Holt] for any costs or expenses incurred by respondent in re-turning herself or the parties' minor children to the State of Oregon."

Mrs. Holt never returned the children to Oregon. On October 23 she moved with the children to Ardmore, Oklahoma, to live with her parents. She had lost her job in Memphis, Texas, (the record does not indicate why), but in Ardmore she found a job paying $1,040 per month.

On December 3, 1980, Mrs. Holt filed a petiton for separate main-tenance and alimony in the District Court of Carter County, Oklaho-ma. She asked for temporary custody of the children, temporary support, and temporary attorney's fees. In her petition, as she did in her pleadings in the actions in Oregon and Texas, Mrs. Holt alleged that she is afraid of her husband, that he has physically abused her, and that he is "guilty of extreme cruelty" toward her and the chil-dren. This Court's attention has not been called to any action in the nature of cruelty.

Mr. Holt was served with the papers in the Carter County action by mail on December 9. On December 11 he filed a motion to stay and a "motion to enforce orders of sister state," moving the court to stay all proceedings in Mrs. Holt's separate maintenance action and to enforce the orders of the Oregon court. To enforce the orders of the Oregon court, Mr. Holt asked the Carter County court for an or-der directing Mrs. Holt to appear personally and deliver actual physi-cal custody of the children to him.

Hearing on Mrs. Holt's motions to stay and to enforce the Oregon court orders was set for December 18, 1980. On December 17 Mrs. Holt filed a motion for a continuance. Her motion alleged that she and her daughter were seeing a "family clinician" at a counseling center called the Guidance Clinic in Ardmore, and informed the court that it would not be until February 1981 that the clinic could "proper-ly evaluate the problems presently existing with [the daughter] and make a recommendation to the Court." The record does not indicate the nature of these problems.

The family clinician testified at the hearing on December 18. Mrs. Holt's motion for a continuance was denied. Mr. Holt's motion to stay was granted. The judge found that Oregon is the home state of the children and that the Oregon court "is exercising jurisdiction sub-stantially in conformity with the Uniform Child Custody Jurisdiction Act." He determined that under the Act, "the Circuit Court of Marion County, State of Oregon, having assumed jurisdiction prior to the filing of the Petition herein, this Court is bound to decline to exer-cise its jurisdiction." Having determined that, he concluded that "ev-idence concerning the best interest of the children with regard to as-suming jurisdiction, establishing a significant connection with this State, and establishing evidence concerning the children's present or future care, protection, training and personal relationships is not nec-essary," and he did not allow Mrs. Holt to put on testimony regarding those things. The judge made no monetary awards, except to order Mr. Holt to continue making payments on the joint indebtedness of the parties. Finally, he ordered Mrs. Holt to deliver custody of the children to Mr. Holt, though he delayed the effectiveness of that part of the order until noon on December 24, Christmas Eve, to enable Mrs. Holt to seek a stay in this court.

[Mrs. Holt] filed this original action on December 23, asking for a stay, a writ of prohibition, and a writ of mandamus. Prohibition is sought to keep the judge in Carter County from enforcing his December 18 order to deliver custody of the children to Mr. Holt. Mandamus is sought to require the judge to hear evidence concerning the best interests of the children, to hear evidence concerning a significant connection between the mother and children and the State of Oklahoma, and to communicate with the judge of the Circuit Court of Marion County, Oregon. We heard argument on December 24, issued a stay until further order of the court, and called for briefs. We now assume original jurisdiction.

I.

This case involves the Uniform Child Custody Jurisdiction Act.[2] That law is a long-awaited and much-needed attempted solution to a number of troubling problems in the area of domestic relations. The main problems it attempts to address are child snatching and multistate jurisdictional squabbles. It goes at these and other problems in several ways, but primarily by limiting the jurisdiction of the courts to act in custody matters. The Act has several purposes, which are set out specifically so that each section of the Act will be read with those purposes in mind. An overriding aim of the Act is to "shift from providing for the child's best interests through ease of modification to an emphasis on continuity of the child's environment."[6] This purpose is expressed in section 1602(4) of the Act, which says that the purpose is to:

> Discourage continuing controversies over child custody in the interest of greater stability of home environment and of secure family relationships for the child.

. . .

This case is a good example of the kind of disrupting moving around the Act is designed to help prevent. All four of the children here have lived in at least three homes since last summer, and three of them have lived in four different homes.[9] The courts of the states

---

2. Hereinafter referred to as the "Act" or the "U.C.C.J.A."

6. Comment, Temporary Custody Under the Uniform Child Custody Jurisdiction Act: Jurisdiction Without Modification, 49 U.Colo.L.Rev. 603, 605 (1977). See also Bodenheimer, Progress Under the Uniform Child Custody Jurisdiction

Act and Remaining Problems: Punitive Decrees, Joint Custody, and Excessive Modifications, 65 Calif.L.Rev. 978, 983 (1977).

9. In fact, we are now informed—though by letter, not by verified pleading or affidavit—that Mrs. Holt has again

involved—Oregon, Texas, and Oklahoma—must now try to act together in the interest of the children to provide them a stable home environment.

II.

In support of her petition for a writ of mandamus, Mrs. Holt asserts that Oklahoma has jurisdiction under section 1605(A)(2) of the U.C.C.J.A., which provides:

> A.   A court of this state which is competent to decide child custody matters has jurisdiction to make a child custody determination by initial or modification decree if:
>
> . . .
>
> 2.   It is in the best interest of the child that a court of this state assume jurisdiction because:
>
> a.   the child and his parents, or the child and at least one contestant, have a significant connection with this state, and
>
> b.   there is available in this state substantial evidence concerning the child's present or future care, protection, training and personal relationships.

She asserts that the Oklahoma court should have taken evidence concerning the best interests of the children, the connection with Oklahoma, and the availability of evidence here regarding the children's care, protection, training, and personal relationships—all with a view toward establishing the existence of jurisdiction.

Mrs. Holt also asserts that the Oklahoma court should have employed the two-step "test" for determining jurisdiction set forth in an Oregon case, Smith v. Smith.[10]   In that opinion, which relied on an earlier Oregon Supreme Court case,[11] the Oregon Court of Appeals held:

> When a petition is filed under the Uniform Child Custody Jurisdiction Act to modify the custody decree of a court of another state two separate and distinct questions are presented which must be resolved in order: (1) Does the Oregon court have jurisdiction under the Act, and (2) if so, *should* the Oregon court exercise its jurisdiction.[12]

Actually, this is not a "test" as such, but rather is an *approach* to determining whether to exercise jurisdiction.   It is a good approach, and we adopt it for the Oklahoma courts in U.C.C.J.A. cases.

Our version of the U.C.C.J.A. contains four prerequisites for jurisdiction, set out in title 10, section 1605(A), subsections (1) through (4).

moved with the children, this time to Lubbock, Texas.

10. 40 Or.App. 257, 594 P.2d 1292 (1979).

11. In re Marriage of Settle (Settle v. Settle), 276 Or. 759, 556 P.2d 962, 965 (1975) (in banc).

12. 594 P.2d at 1294 (emphasis in original).

They are alternative, and if the requirements of any one of the four are met an Oklahoma court has jurisdiction. Even if jurisdiction exists, however, it may not be proper for the court to exercise its jurisdiction. There are three grounds set out in the Act, one mandatory and two discretionary, on which a court must or should decline to exercise jurisdiction. They are: (1) when "at the time of filing the petition a proceeding concerning the custody of the child was pending in a court of another state exercising jurisdiction substantially in conformity with this act,"[14] (2) when Oklahoma is an "inconvenient forum,"[15] and (3) when the petitioner has snatched the child, improperly retained custody after visitation, or "engaged in similar reprehensible conduct."[16] In addition, the jurisdiction of an Oklahoma court to modify a custody decree rendered by a court of another state is substantially curtailed.[17] It can be seen, then, that the approach referred to by Mrs. Holt is actually a multistep process.

Cases may come up in which we, by writ of mandamus, will direct a district court to hear evidence in order to determine whether jurisdiction exists in a child custody matter. The multistep process described above will not always be necessary, however. In some cases it will be as expeditious to assume the existence of jurisdiction and to consider in the first instance whether that jurisdiction should or can be exercised. This will be especially true when title 10, section 1608(A) applies. That section provides:

> A court of this state *shall not* exercise its jurisdiction under this act if at the time of filing the petition a proceeding concerning the custody of the child was pending in a court of another state exercising jurisdiction substantially in conformity with this act, unless the proceeding is stayed by the court of the other state because this state is a more appropriate forum or for other reasons. [Emphasis added.]

This provision can be considered a limitation on jurisdiction or a limitation on the *exercise* of jurisdiction. We need not and do not pass on that question today, for in either event the cases indicate that the proper approach is to go directly to the question of another pending action. If a proceeding concerning custody was pending in another state at the time the Oklahoma action was filed, and the court in that state is exercising jurisdiction substantially in conformity with the U.C.C.J.A. and has not stayed its proceeding, then the statute commands the Oklahoma court not to exercise its jurisdiction.

In this case the Oklahoma court found—and, from the record before us, found correctly—that the Oregon court was exercising jurisdiction substantially in conformity with the Act. He therefore de-

---

14. 10 O.S.Supp.1980 § 1608(A) (mandatory).

15. Id. § 1609 (discretionary).

16. Discretionary when an "initial decree" is petitioned for, id. § 1610(A),

mandatory in certain cases when modification is sought "[u]nless required in the interest of the child." Id. § 1610(B).

17. 10 O.S.Supp.1980 § 1616.

clined to assume jurisdiction, holding that it was unnecessary to hear the evidence that would establish the existence of jurisdiction. Since even if jurisdiction existed the court would be prohibited by section 1608(A) from exercising it, it was proper for him to decline to hear the evidence. We will not issue a writ of mandamus directing him to do so.

III.

In further support of her petition for a writ of mandamus, Mrs. Holt argues that jurisdiction should be assumed under title 10, section 1605(D) of the Act. That section provides:

> The controlling criteria for awarding custody by a court of this state shall always be what is in the best interest of the child, other statutory provisions merely being factors which may be considered.

This provision is not part of the Uniform Act, but was added by the Oklahoma legislature when our version of the U.C.C.J.A. was enacted.

It is necessary to consider the effect of this section. By its language it is not an independent ground for assuming jurisdiction, . . . It merely states that the "criteria for awarding custody" shall be "what is in the best interest of the child," and does not refer to jurisdiction. . . .

The first declared purpose of the U.C.C.J.A. is to "[a]void jurisdictional competition and conflict with courts of other states in matters of child custody." As we have said, the Act goes about accomplishing that and its other purposes primarily by *limiting* the jurisdiction of our courts. . . . For us to hold, as Mrs. Holt urges, that that section provides an independent ground for the assumption of jurisdiction, capable of overriding the other specific grounds for jurisdiction and limitations on a court's exercise thereof, would run contrary to the Act. . . . [I]t appears that the legislature was mandating that once jurisdiction is assumed by a court, the court in *awarding custody* later must do so according to the best interests of the child. The question of whether jurisdiction exists and the question of who should have custody are two entirely different matters. Section 1605(D) applies only to the latter question; it does not provide an independent ground for jurisdiction, . . .

IV.

. . . Mrs. Holt asks for a writ of prohibition to prohibit the district court from enforcing its order requiring her to deliver custody of the children to Mr. Holt. She argues for this writ on several grounds.

First, she argues that the Oregon order, on which the Oklahoma court predicated its order, is punitive and not entitled to enforcement. The Oregon order provided:

> Subject to the conditions stated herein, wife is granted the temporary custody of the parties' minor children, [naming them], during the pendency of this suit. Provided, however, that if respondent [Mrs. Holt] fails to return said children to the community of Aurora, Oregon and to resume residence in said community within thirty (30) days from the date hereof, temporary custody of the parties' four (4) minor children shall be vested in petitioner [Mr. Holt].

For this argument Mrs. Holt relies on an Oregon case, Brooks v. Brooks.[29] In that case the mother, who had custody of the parties' two children, had not allowed the father to visit the children and had moved secretly from Montana to Oregon. The Montana court that had rendered the divorce decree modified the decree, granting custody to the father, who then went to Oregon for a writ of habeas corpus. The writ was denied, and on appeal the denial was affirmed by the Oregon Court of Appeals, which held that the Montana modification was punitive, designed to discipline the mother.[30] The appeals court further held that the circuit court was justified in refusing to enforce the punitive modification and in further modifying the Montana decree to give custody back to the mother.[31]

It is true that under the U.C.C.J.A. punitive orders need not be enforced by sister states.[32] Generally, however, temporary custody orders, because of their temporary nature, should not be deemed punitive.[33] And in this case specifically, we find no intent on the part of the Oregon court to punish Mrs. Holt. At the time of the hearing in question, Mrs. Holt had already left Oregon with the children, moved to one place in Texas, and moved again. Between the time of the hearing and the date the Oregon court issued the order, Mrs. Holt had moved with the children once more, from Texas to Oklahoma. Yet the Oregon court gave temporary custody to Mrs. Holt. The provisions requiring Mrs. Holt to return the children to Oregon appears to be in the interest of the children, to provide them with a stable environment in the home they lived in for the previous two years, not to punish Mrs. Holt. Until facts and circumstances establish otherwise, we must—and do—presume that the Oregon court is acting in the best interest of the children. We therefore hold that the Oregon court order is not punitive.

29. 20 Or.App. 43, 530 P.2d 547 (1979).

30. 530 P.2d at 551.

31. Id. at 552.

32. Id. at 551–52; see Commissioners' Note, Uniform Child Custody Jurisdiction Act § 13, 9 U.L.A. 151, 152 (Master Ed.

1979). See generally Bodenheimer, supra note 6, at 1003–09.

33. Miller v. Superior Court, 22 Cal.3d 923, 587 P.2d 723, 727, 151 Cal.Rptr. 6 (1978). This case applied the U.C.C.J.A. to an international situation. The principle is equally applicable, perhaps more so, to the interstate situation before us.

Second, Mrs. Holt argues that the Oregon order, being punitive, violates her constitutional right to travel. If the order were punitive, a substantial constitutional question would be presented.[35] Having held that it is not punitive, however, we do not find any constitutional violation.

Finally, Mrs. Holt argues that the Oregon order cannot be enforced in Oklahoma because it is not self-executing. . . . Mrs. Holt argues that the order requires further affirmative action by the Oregon court—i.e., a specific order from that court directing her to turn over custody—before the order can be enforced.

It is probably true that Mrs. Holt cannot be held in contempt of the Oregon court until another order specifically directs her to turn over custody. Nevertheless, the Oregon court order can—and we believe under the U.C.C.J.A. must—be enforced in Oklahoma. The enforcement provision of the Act, section 1615, reads:

> The courts of this state *shall* recognize and enforce an initial or modification decree of a court of another state which had assumed jurisdiction under statutory provisions substantially in accordance with this act or which was made under factual circumstances meeting the jurisdictional standards of the act, so long as this decree has not been modified in accordance with jurisdictional standards substantially similar to those of this act. [Emphasis added.]

We have said that each provision of the Act must be read and applied in light of the Act's purposes. Several of those purposes have been discussed. Three others of note here are set out in title 10, section 1602, subsections (6), (7), and (8). They are to:

> 6. Avoid relitigation of custody decisions of other states in this state insofar as feasible;
>
> 7. Facilitate the enforcement of custody decrees of other states; [and]
>
> 8. Promote and expand the exchange of information and other forms of mutual assistance between the courts of this state and those of other states concerned with the same child.

The Act was designed so that its provisions, both the mandatory and the discretionary ones, would coincide with the best interests of the child.[38] Section 1615 mandates enforcement. It is incumbent on our courts to cooperate with courts in other states which are exercising jurisdiction under the U.C.C.J.A. The fact that the order or decree of another state is not self-executing cannot impair the ability of our courts to extend that cooperation. To effect that cooperation, we hold that our courts have the authority under the Act to issue orders which, in effect, execute orders or decrees of other courts that are not self-executing. Given the factual situation before him, and hav-

---

35. See generally Bodenheimer, supra note 6, at 1008–09.

38. See Roberts v. District Court, 596 P.2d 65, 68 (Colo.1979).

ing the power to do so, the Oklahoma court did not err in ordering Mrs. Holt to surrender custody of the children. We decline to issue a writ of prohibition.

V.

We have declined to issue a writ of prohibition, and declined to issue a writ of mandamus for the purpose requested by Mrs. Holt. There is one more matter, however, not argued by the parties but which we raise on our own.

As we have said, in all of her pleadings, Mrs. Holt has alleged that Mr. Holt has abused her and the children. At this point that is just an allegation. If there is substance to it, however, and if the children are still in Oklahoma, it may be proper for the Oklahoma court to take some action. Title 10, section 1605(A)(3) of the Act provides:

A.   A court of this state which is competent to decide child custody matters has jurisdiction to make a child custody determination by initial or modification decree if:

. . .

3.   The child is physically present in this state and:

. . .

b.   it is necessary in an emergency to protect the child because he has been subjected to or threatened with mistreatment or abuse or is otherwise neglected or dependent.

This is referred to as the "emergency jurisdiction" provision. It is "reserved for extraordinary circumstances," [41] and "it must not be misused to defeat the purposes of the act, but [it] nevertheless retains and reaffirms [the state's] *parens patriae* responsibility for children in need of immediate protection." [42] Professor Brigitte Bodenheimer, the Reporter for the Uniform Act, has said this about the provision:

This exceptional jurisdiction exists in very few cases. Naturally, there will be attempts to circumvent the Act by "shouting fire" in every conceivable situation. Emergency jurisdiction must be denied, however, when it is invoked as a pretext in order to reopen a custody controversy. Unless judges and attorneys are constantly alert to the dangers inherent in misuses of emergency jurisdiction to circumvent the Act, the exception could tear so large a hole in the Act that custody decrees made in one state would again be relitigated in other states; and the interstate chaos that the Act was intended to remedy would be revived and perhaps intensified.[43]

41. Commissioners' Note, Uniform Child Custody Jurisdiction Act § 3, 9 U.L.A. 123, 124 (Master Ed. 1979).

42. Priscilla S. v. Albert B., 102 Misc. 2d 650, 424 N.Y.S.2d 613, 617 (Fam.Ct.

1980); see Commissioners' Note, supra note 41.

43. Bodenheimer, supra note 6, at 992–93 (footnotes omitted).

With the caveat, then, that the court should examine very carefully Mrs. Holt's allegations before assuming jurisdiction for this limited purpose, we direct the District Court of Carter County to take evidence on the necessity of making a protective order. . . . If the evidence shows a need for a protective order, the court still may not overrule or modify the Oregon court order. Rather, it should stay its enforcement of the Oregon court order, make such temporary custody order as is needed, and require Mrs. Holt to submit the matter to the Oregon court within a definite time period.[46] Then if there is a problem it can be finally resolved by the Oregon court, which is equally well suited to remedy any potential abuse.

The writ of prohibition is denied. Let a writ of mandamus issue for the limited purpose of requiring the district court to hear any evidence Mrs. Holt cares to present on the question of assuming emergency jurisdiction. Our stay of enforcement of the district court's order requiring Mrs. Holt to deliver custody of the children is hereby continued until the district court has acted on the question of assuming emergency jurisdiction. At that time, or ten days after the date of this opinion if Mrs. Holt has not filed a petition for the court to assume emergency jurisdiction, the District Court of Carter County is authorized to dissolve our stay. Whether or not Mrs. Holt files such a petition, the court is directed to inform the Oregon court of all proceedings held in Oklahoma, including this original action.

NOTE

The U.C.C.J.A. has been criticized because some important nuances—and perhaps even some basic rules—are found in the Comments rather than the text of the Act. The issue of whether punitive decrees must be honored, raised but not controlling in *Holt*, provides one illustration.

Another concern is that in some instances where the answer to a particular problem seems close, if not insoluble, under the Act's basic provisions, the interpreter is then required to seek guidance from the statement of general purposes in § 1 of the Act as in *Holt*. Two states, South Dakota and Virginia, did not enact § 1 in their versions of the U.C.C.J.A. The South Dakota Supreme Court has nevertheless shown its willingness to acknowledge § 1 in interpreting the Act. See Winkleman v. Moses, 279 N.W.2d 897 (S.D.1979).

WEBB v. WEBB

Supreme Court of Georgia, 1980.
245 Ga. 650, 266 S.E.2d 463.

CLARKE, JUSTICE.

This case calls for an interpretation of certain provisions of Georgia's Uniform Child Custody Jurisdiction Act, Code Ann. § 74–501 et seq. The mother appeals an order of the Superior Court of Berrien

---

46. Fry v. Ball, 190 Colo. 128, 544 P.2d 402, 407–08 (1975) (en banc); In re Marriage of Kern (Kern v. Kern), 87 Cal. App.3d 402, 150 Cal.Rptr. 860, 863 (1978).

County modifying a previous final decree of divorce by changing custody from the mother to the father. The court also denied the mother's counterclaim for contempt and her application for a writ of habeas corpus.

The evidence authorized a finding that subsequent to the entrance of a final decree of divorce entered in Berrien County September 22, 1977, giving custody of the minor child to the mother, the mother moved some six times and finally established residency near Gainesville, Florida. On February 17, 1979, the mother left the six-year old child of the parties without adult supervision at her home and flew to Miami for a weekend. Having been contacted by Florida authorities, the father went to Florida, picked up the child and returned to his home in Berrien County, Georgia.

On March 8, 1979, the wife filed an action in Alachua County, Florida, praying for an injunction for the purpose of enforcing the Georgia decree and seeking an order limiting visitation rights of the father. On March 23, 1979, before the issuance of a permanent order in the Florida action, the father filed a complaint in Berrien County, Georgia, asking that the original Georgia decree be modified to change custody of the minor child to him. The mother counterclaimed for contempt and sought a writ of habeas corpus. Subsequent to the filing of the complaint in Georgia by the father, and prior to any hearing in Georgia on the matter, the Florida court entered a final order on April 18, 1979, establishing the Georgia decree as the judgment of the Florida court and modifying the father's visitation rights.

The Superior Court of Berrien County heard evidence on the father's complaint on May 10, 1979, and on June 21, 1979, entered an order changing custody to the father and ruling that the father was not in contempt as alleged by the counterclaim. The mother's counterclaim for habeas corpus was likewise denied. The mother appeals from this order of the Superior Court of Berrien County.

1. The mother contends that Georgia was not an appropriate or convenient forum for determination of the custody of the child because of insufficient contacts between the parties and this State. While it is true that the child was in Florida with the mother under a valid original decree of the Berrien County court giving custody to the mother, we find that the Georgia court was authorized under the evidence to find that the father retrieved the child in the face of an emergency situation created by the mother. The circumstances of the child's retrieval by the father were sufficient to afford Georgia jurisdiction under Code Ann. § 74–504(a)(3).

2. The mother also argues that the pendency of the Florida action preempted Georgia jurisdiction. The action was pending in Florida at the time the father filed his suit, and while the father did not properly inform the Georgia court of this fact, this information was fully supplied to the Georgia court by the mother in her motion to

dismiss. This fact placed a duty upon the trial court to confer with the Florida court with a view toward determining the appropriate forum. Code Ann. § 74–507. This was not done. Correspondingly, the Florida court, having notice in the mother's pleadings that an action might be pending in Georgia, was under a duty to confer with the Georgia court. There is nothing in the record before this court to indicate any effort on the part of the Florida court to fulfill this duty prior to entering its final judgment.

Among the primary purposes of the Uniform Child Custody Jurisdiction Act is to avoid overlapping adjudication and to prevent judgment races. In this case, neither state made a contribution toward that goal. The Georgia court exercised its jurisdiction with knowledge of the case in Florida. The Florida court entered its final order with notice that an action might be pending in Georgia.[1] Neither court consulted the other.

The action required of a court before assuming jurisdiction or conducting a hearing in a custody proceeding is that the court determine whether an action is pending in another state. Code Ann. § 74–507. As subsections (b) and (c) clearly reveal, the crucial determination by the court is whether at the time it assumes jurisdiction another court is presently exercising jurisdiction over the issue of custody of the child. In the present case, at the time of the hearing on May 10, 1979, on the mother's motion to dismiss for lack of jurisdiction and upon the case in chief, the Georgia court had before it the final order of the Florida court entered April 18, 1979, concluding the Florida action. No additional inquiry was necessary, it being apparent that the Florida action had been concluded before the Georgia court exercised jurisdiction, although after the Georgia petition was filed. An investigation at that point would have been futile, and it is clear that the law does not require a useless act. Had the Georgia proceeding been dismissed, there could have been no resolution of the custody dispute by any court unless a new lawsuit were brought. This result would be contrary to principles of judicial economy and orderly administration of justice and would have done nothing to advance the purpose of § 74–507, which is the prevention of jurisdictional conflicts between the states. Consequently, we find that the pendency of the Florida action at the time the Georgia action was filed did not preempt the jurisdiction of the Georgia court.

The mother also assigns error in the court's finding that there had been a material change in circumstances affecting the welfare of the child so that custody should be changed to the father. In making the determination whether there has been a material change in circumstances affecting the child, the trial court is vested with broad discretion which will not be disturbed on appeal unless abused. Wrede v. Beuke, 221 Ga. 778, 147 S.E.2d 324 (1966); Mallette v. Mallette, 220

---

1. The duty of a party to inform the court of any custody proceeding in any other state continues during the entire proceeding. Code Ann. § 74–510(c).

Ga. 401, 139 S.E.2d 322 (1964). We find that the trial court did not abuse its discretion in finding it in the best interest of the child that custody be awarded to the father.

The remaining enumerations of error are without merit.

Judgment affirmed.

HILL, JUSTICE, dissenting.

The mother left her six-year-old son in the care of his 13-year-old step-sister for a weekend. The mother's cousins, who lived next door, were looking after the children. While such conduct may not be proper child care, it does not constitute abandonment or an emergency. The father brought the child back to Georgia on February 18, 1979, and did not file this suit until March 23, over a month later.

The majority find (Division 1, supra) that the Georgia court had jurisdiction under Code Ann. § 74–504(a)(3). That section provides that "A court of this State which is competent to decide child custody matters has jurisdiction to make a child custody determination by initial or modification decree if: . . . (3) The child is physically present in this State and (A) the child has been abandoned or (B) it is necessary in an emergency to protect the child because he has been subjected to or threatened with mistreatment or abuse or is otherwise neglected or dependent." This is § 3(a)(3) of the Uniform Child Custody Jurisdiction Act.

To avoid "child snatching" of allegedly abandoned children, or children found in a situation alleged to be an emergency, I would hold that § 3(a)(3) of the UCCJA, Code Ann. § 74–504(a)(3), supra, gives jurisdiction to a court of that state where the child is physically present when the alleged abandonment or emergency is discovered by his or her parent or person claiming the right to custody. That would be the Florida court in this case. In my view the majority has condoned child snatching contrary to the landmark decision in Matthews v. Matthews, 238 Ga. 201, 232 S.E.2d 76 (1977).

I respectfully dissent to this return to the old ways.

NOTES

(1) The mother's petition for certiorari was dismissed by the Supreme Court for lack of jurisdiction. Webb v. Webb, 451 U.S. 493, 101 S.Ct. 1889, 68 L.Ed.2d 392 (1981). In the opinion of the Court, Justice White explained that the question whether the Florida decree was entitled to full faith and credit in Georgia could not be considered, because it had not been raised in the state proceedings and the Georgia Supreme Court had not ruled on the issue.

Was the U.C.C.J.A. properly applied in the state courts in Webb? Would it have been appropriate for the father to pursue some other course of action than removing the child from Florida? If the purpose of the Act is to avoid or discourage child-snatching, how is the result justified in this situation?

(2) In December of 1980 President Carter signed the Federal Parental Kidnapping Prevention Act of 1980, which had been tacked by rider to a bill dealing with pneumococcal vaccine. The 1980 Act authorizes the Secretary of Health and Human Services to allow states to utilize the Federal Parent Locator Service to find an absent parent for enforcement of a custody decree. It also states the intent of Congress that the Fugitive Felon Act, 18 U.S.C.A. § 1073, shall be applicable "to cases involving parental kidnapping and interstate or international flight to avoid prosecution under applicable State felony statutes." For a table describing various state criminal provisions on kidnapping, custodial interference, or child abduction, see Katz, Legal Remedies for Child Snatching, 15 Fam. L.Q. 103 (1981).

At least of equal importance was the addition of a provision in the 1980 Federal Act dealing with full faith and credit for custody determinations. Under 18 U.S.C.A. § 1738A:

(a) The appropriate authorities of every State shall enforce according to its terms, and shall not modify except as provided in subsection (f) of this section, any child custody determination made consistently with the provisions of this section by a court of another State.

[Subsection (b) includes certain basic definitions]

. . .

(c) A child custody determination made by a court of a State is consistent with the provisions of this section only if—

(1) such court has jurisdiction under the law of such State; and

(2) one of the following conditions is met:

(A) such State (i) is the home State of the child on the date of the commencement of the proceeding, or (ii) had been the child's home State within six months before the date of the commencement of the proceeding and the child is absent from such State because of his removal or retention by a contestant or for other reasons, and a contestant continues to live in such State;

(B)(i) it appears that no other State would have jurisdiction under subparagraph (A), and (ii) it is in the best interest of the child that a court of such State assume jurisdiction because (I) the child and his parents, or the child and at least one contestant, have a significant connection with such State other than mere physical presence in such State, and (II) there is available in such State substantial evidence concerning the child's present or future care, protection, training, and personal relationships;

(C) the child is physically present in such State and (i) the child has been abandoned, or (ii) it is necessary in an emergency to protect the child because he has been subjected to or threatened with mistreatment or abuse;

(D)(i) it appears that no other State would have jurisdiction under subparagraph (A), (B), (C), or (E), or another State has declined to exercise jurisdiction on the ground that the State whose jurisdiction is in issue is the more appropriate forum to determine the custody of the child, and (ii) it is in the best interest of the child that such court assume jurisdiction; or

(E) the court has continuing jurisdiction pursuant to subsection (d) of this section.

(d) The jurisdiction of a court of a State which has made a child custody determination consistently with the provisions of this section continues as long as the requirement of subsection (c)(1) of this section continues to be met and such State remains the residence of the child or of any contestant.

(e) Before a child custody determination is made, reasonable notice and opportunity to be heard shall be given to the contestants, any parent whose parental rights have not been previously terminated and any person who has physical custody of a child.

(f) A court of a State may modify a determination of the custody of the same child made by a court of another State, if—

(1) it has jurisdiction to make such a child custody determination; and

(2) the court of the other State no longer has jurisdiction, or it has declined to exercise such jurisdiction to modify such determination.

(g) A court of a State shall not exercise jurisdiction in any proceeding for a custody determination commenced during the pendency of a proceeding in a court of another State where such court of that other State is exercising jurisdiction consistently with the provisions of this section to make a custody determination.

An important feature of the preceding section is that it will extend to jurisdictions that have not adopted the U.C.C.J.A. Although the jurisdictional criteria in the Federal Act and the U.C.C.J.A. are very similar, they are not identical; in some cases it is probable that § 1738A will control even over the corresponding U.C.C.J.A. provisions. This seems especially likely in the case of continuing jurisdiction, as regulated by subsection (d) of § 1738A. In interpreting § 14 of the U.C.C.J.A., dealing with modification, some courts had "read in" the "home state" provisions of § 3 to hold that after a child and the custodial parent had changed their "home state" the latter might proceed with modifications. This interpretation was criticized by Professor Brigitte Bodenheimer, the Reporter for the U.C.C.J.A., who asserted that § 3 governs only original jurisdiction. See Bodenheimer, Interstate Custody: Initial Jurisdiction and Continuing Jurisdiction under the UCCJA, 14 Fam. L.Q. 203, 219–20 (1981).

In the Comment to U.C.C.J.A. § 14, the drafters refer to a situation in which custody is awarded to a father in state 1 but thereafter a wife keeps the children in state 2 for 6 ½ months (3 ½ beyond her visitation privileges). According to the Comment, state 1 has "preferred jurisdiction" to modify the decree whether the children were kept in state 2 with or without the husband's permission. The illustration then adds that "if the father in the same case continued to live in state 1, but let his wife keep the children for several years without asserting his custody rights and without visits to the children in state 1, modification jurisdiction of state 1 would cease." Would this be the result mandated under 18 U.S.C.A. § 1738A(d) and (f)?

(3) Threat of tort liability may become an increasingly effective deterrent to child snatching. In Fenslage v. Dawkins, 629 F.2d 1107 (5th Cir. 1980), the Fifth Circuit Court of Appeals upheld a jury award of $65,000 in compensatory and another $65,000 in punitive damages to the mother of two minor

children against various relatives of her ex-husband who she had sued for conspiring with him to take and conceal her children from her and intentionally to inflict mental anguish upon her. The court quoted with approval Restatement (2d) of Torts § 700 (1977), which states that:

> One who, with knowledge that the parent does not consent, abducts or otherwise compels or induces a minor child to leave a parent legally entitled to its custody or not to return to the parent after it has been left to him, is subject to liability to the parent.

The court also notes that the comments to § 700 reveal that recovery can be awarded for mental anguish.

(4) For an extensive review and analysis of the relationship between and problems of the various state and federal provisions dealing with child custody across state lines see Coombs, Interstate Child Custody: Jurisdiction, Recognition, and Enforcement, 66 Minn.L.Rev. 711 (1982). For an interesting comparative study of differing approaches to child custody see Blakesley, Child Custody and Parental Authority in France, Louisiana and Other States of the United States: A Comparative Analysis, 4 Boston Coll.Int. & Comp.L.Rev. 257 (1981).

XIII. STATE INTERVENTION TO ENSURE ADEQUATE PARENTING

A. A COMPREHENSIVE PLAN?

BURNETTE v. WAHL

Supreme Court of Oregon, 1978.
284 Or. 705, 588 P.2d 1105.

HOLMAN, JUSTICE.

Three identical cases have been consolidated for appeal. Plaintiffs are five minor children aged two to eight who, through their guardian, are bringing actions against their mothers for emotional and psychological injury caused by failure of defendant-mothers to perform their parental duties to plaintiffs. Plaintiffs appeal from orders of dismissal entered after demurrers were sustained to the complaints. . . .

The complaints allege that plaintiffs are in the custody of the Children's Services Division of the Department of Human Resources of the State of Oregon and are wards of Klamath County Juvenile Court.

The complaints are substantially identical, each one being in three counts. Among these counts are strewn various allegations of parental failure upon which the causes of action rest. They are:

"1. Since [date], defendant intentionally, wilfully, maliciously and with cruel disregard of the consequences failed to provide plaintiff with care, custody, parental nurturance, affection, comfort, companionship, support, regular contact and visitation.

"2. She has failed in violation of ORS 109.010 [1] to maintain plaintiff, who, due to . . . age and indigency, is poor and unable to work to maintain . . . self.

"3. She has abandoned plaintiff by deserting the child with intent to abandon . . . and with intent to abdicate all responsibility for . . . care and raising, in violation of ORS 163.535. [2]

"4. She has neglected the plaintiff by negligently leaving . . . unattended in or at a place for such period of time as

---

1. "ORS 109.010 Duty of Support. Parents are bound to maintain their children who are poor and unable to work to maintain themselves; and children are bound to maintain their parents in like circumstances."

2. "ORS 163.535 Abandonment of a Child. (1) A person commits the crime of abandonment of a child if, being a parent, lawful guardian or other person lawfully charged with the care or custody of a child under 15 years of age, he deserts the child in any place with intent to abandon it.

"(2) Abandonment of a child is a Class C felony."

would have been likely to endanger the health or welfare of the plaintiff, in violation of ORS 163.545.[3]

"5. She has refused or neglected without lawful excuse to provide support for plaintiff, in violation of ORS 163.555.[4]

"6. Defendant has maliciously, intentionally, and with cruel disregard of the consequences, deserted and abandoned her child.

. . .

Preliminary to a more detailed discussion, it should be noted that these claims of parental failure are different from those tort claims usually made upon behalf of children against parents. The adjudicated cases concern physicial or emotional injuries resulting from physical acts inflicted upon children such as beatings and rapes and from automobile accidents. Plaintiffs admit they can cite no cases permitting them to recover from their parents for solely emotional or psychological damage resulting from failure to support, nurture and care for them.

The legislature, recognizing the necessity of parental nurture, support and physical care for children, has enacted a vast array of laws for the purpose of protecting or vindicating those rights. These are much more extensive and all-inclusive than are those statutes alleged to have been violated in plaintiffs' allegations of tortious conduct.[5]

ORS ch. 418 establishes extensive provisions for aid to dependent children, and it is under the provisions of this chapter and as wards of the juvenile court that plaintiffs are presently attempting to have their needs met. Most of the statutes cited in notes 1 through 5 deal

---

3. "ORS 163.545 Child Neglect. (1) A person having custody or control of a child under 10 years of age commits the crime of child neglect if, with criminal negligence, he leaves the child unattended in or at any place for such period of time as may be likely to endanger the health or welfare of such child.

"(2) Child neglect is a Class A misdemeanor."

4. "ORS 163.555 Criminal Nonsupport. (1) A person commits the crime of criminal nonsupport if, being the parent, lawful guardian or other person lawfully charged with the support of a child under 18 years of age, born in or out of wedlock, he refuses or neglects without lawful excuse to provide support for such child.

". . . .

"(3) Criminal nonsupport is a Class C felony."

5. Among these laws are ORS 108.040, providing an action against both parents for family necessities; ORS 108.110 *et seq.*, which allow a petition for the support of children to be brought against a parent by the other parent or a state agency for the support of the children; ORS ch. 110, providing both criminal and civil means for reciprocal enforcement between states of the right of support for children; ORS 411.120(4), providing for assistance to dependent children; ORS ch. 416, establishing the relative responsibility law (specifically see ORS 416.090, 416.100, and 416.220 for the means of enforcement); ORS ch. 418, providing for child welfare services (specifically see ORS 418.135(1) and 418.460, concerning enforcement of parental duties); ORS ch. 419, establishing juvenile courts (specifically see ORS 419.513, 419.515, and 419.517 concerning enforcement of support of children by parents).

with meeting children's physical needs, but plaintiffs' protection is not afforded solely by these laws. ORS 418.015 provides:

"(1) The Children's Services Division may, in its discretion, accept custody of children and may provide care, support and protective services for children who are dependent, neglected, mentally or physically disabled or who for other reasons are in need of public service.

"(2) The Children's Services Division shall accept any child placed in its custody by a court under, but not limited to ORS chapter 419, and shall provide such services for the child as the division finds to be necessary."

"Care," "protective services" and "such services for the child as the division finds to be necessary" are all terms which include emotional nurturing as well as physical care. This reading of the statute is reflected in the Children's Services Division's publication entitled, "Permanent Planning for Children in Substitute Care" (1977).

We recognize that this is not a proceeding to secure parental nurturing, support and physical care for plaintiffs, but rather an action for psychological injury claimed to have been caused by the absence of these services. However, the statutory enactments demonstrate that the legislature has put its mind to the deprivations of which plaintiff children are alleged to be victims and has attempted to remedy such situations by enacting a vast panoply of procedures, both civil and criminal, to insure that children receive proper nurturing, support and physical care. It has never undertaken to establish, however, a cause of action for damages for any emotional injury to the child which may have been caused by a parent's refusal to provide these services. This failure of the legislature to act is significant because this is not a field of recovery which has heretofore been recognized by courts and it would therefore be natural for it to have provided such a remedy if it thought it was wise in view of the social problem it attempts to solve and the statutory provisions it has enacted for that purpose. It has had no difficulty in the past in creating new causes of action for persons aggrieved by conditions which it is attempting to rectify. . . .

The establishment by courts of a civil cause of action based on a criminal or regulatory statute is not premised upon legislative intent to create such an action. It is obvious that had the legislature intended a civil action it would have provided for one, as legislatures many times do.[6] Therefore, the underlying assumption is that it was not

6. See Prosser, The Law of Torts 191, § 36 (4th ed. 1971), in which it is stated:

". . . Where the statute merely declares that conduct is a crime, and makes no mention of any civil remedy, justification becomes more difficult, since the court is then obviously under no compulsion to apply the statute.

Many courts have, however, purported to 'find' in the statute a supposed 'implied', 'constructive', or 'presumed' intent to provide for tort liability. In the ordinary case this is pure fiction concocted for the purpose. The obvious conclusion can only be that when the legislators said nothing about it, they intended that the statute create any civil obligation or afford civil protection against the injuries which it was designed to prevent. When neither the statute nor the common law authorizes an action and the statute does not expressly deny it, the court should recognize that it is being asked to bring into existence a new type of tort liability on the basis of its own appraisal of the policy considerations involved. If a court decides to create a cause of action for the act or omission which violates the statute, the interest which is invaded derives its protection solely from the court although the legislative action in branding the act or omission as culpable is taken into consideration by the court in deciding whether a common law action should be established. If a civil cause of action based upon a statute is established by a court, it is because the court, not the legislature, believes it is necessary and desirable to further vindicate the right or to further enforce the duty created by statute.

Because it is plain to the legislature that it could have created the civil liability and it has not, courts must look carefully not only at the particular statute establishing the right or duty but at all statutes which might bear either directly or indirectly on the legislative purpose. If there is any chance that invasion into the field by the court's establishment of a civil cause of action might interfere with the total legislative scheme, courts should err on the side of non-intrusion because it is always possible for the legislature to establish such a civil cause of action if it desires. Courts have no omnipotence in the field of planning, particularly social planning of the kind involved here. Courts should exercise restraint in fields in which the legislature has attempted fairly comprehensive social regulation.

There is no doubt but that the statutory provisions previously cited show a strong state policy of requiring the kind of parental nurturing, support and physical care of children which the defendants here are alleged to have denied their children. As previously indicated, it does not follow as a matter of course that it would be wise or judicious to vindicate that policy by a tort action for damages by children against their mothers. The state also has other policies within its statutory plan of which such a cause of action might well be destructive, particularly the policy of reuniting abandoned children with their parents, if possible. This policy is demonstrated by ORS 418.485, which states that "it is the policy of the State of Oregon to strengthen family life and to insure the protection of all children either in their own homes or in other appropriate care . . . ." This same policy is even evident in ORS 418.745, in such a serious matter as physical child abuse, which states it to be "facilitating the use of protective social services to prevent further abuse, safeguard and enhance the welfare of abused children, and preserve family life when consistent with the protection of the child by stabilizing the family

either did not have the civil suit in
mind at all, or deliberately omitted to
provide for it."

and improving parental capacity, ..." Also, as part of the Oregon Juvenile Code, we find ORS 419.474(2), which states that the provisions of the Act "shall be liberally construed to the end that a child coming within the jurisdiction of the court may receive such care, guidance and control, preferably in his own home, as will lead to the child's welfare . . .."

It is recognized by the statutory scheme that in some instances the reestablishment of a biological family is impossible and it therefore provides for a proceeding to terminate parental rights in order that a new family unit for the child may be formed. The section providing for parental termination, ORS 419.523, contains the following language in subsection (2) which demonstrates the importance which the legislature puts upon the establishment of the child in the home with its natural parents:

"The rights of the parent or parents may be terminated as provided in subsection (1) of this section if the court finds that the parent or parents are unfit by reason of conduct or condition seriously detrimental to the child *and integration of the child into the home of the parent or parents is improbable in the foreseeable future* due to conduct or conditions not likely to change . . .." (Emphasis added.)

The statute further provides that the court shall, among other things, consider the following in determining whether to terminate the parents' rights:

"(e) Lack of effort of the parent to adjust his circumstances, conduct, or conditions to make the return of the child possible or failure of the parent to effect a lasting adjustment after reasonable efforts by available social agencies for such extended duration of time that it appears reasonable that no lasting adjustment can be effected."

What emerges is a comprehensive plan to furnish children in the position of these plaintiffs with parental nurturing and physical care, preferably in family units with their parents. If this is not possible, it provides for means of divesting parental rights so that a new family unit may be created for the child.

It could be contended that the criminal statutes are inconsistent with such a plan. However, no plan established by the legislature over a period of years can ever have perfect symmetry. Also, the legislature is undoubtedly aware that, for obvious reasons, parents of dependent children are not prosecuted criminally if there is hope of establishing the family unit.

It is significant that plaintiffs' complaints do not allege that proceedings for the termination of the defendants' parental rights have taken place. In such circumstances, it would be exceedingly unwise for this court to step in and to initiate a new and heretofore unrecognized cause of action in a field of social planning to which the legislature has devoted a great deal of time and effort in evolving what appears to be an all-encompassing plan. Those persons designated by statute for aiding the plaintiffs in these cases have not yet taken the step for which the plan provides when there is no longer any hope of reestablishing these children in a family unit with their mothers. Tort actions such as the present ones might well be destructive of any plans the social agencies and the juvenile court might have for these children. It is inappropriate for this court to insert a new cause of action into the picture.

An exhaustive search of the legal literature finds only one article dealing with a right of action by children for emotional damage caused by ineffectual parents: The Rights of Children: A Trust Model, 46 Fordham L.Rev. 669 (1978). It suggests an analogy to the broad equitable principles of trust law as a model for defining the rights and duties existing among the child, his parents and the state. Even such a radical departure from present views does not advocate an action for money damages such as the present one. After a discussion of rights of action against third parties for the benefit of children who have been deprived of the nurturing and physical care of a parent by the acts of such third parties, the authors say:

> ". . . Unlike the remedy of money damages sought as compensation for loss of parental care in actions for alienation of parental affections, remedies more appropriate to the character of the right could be fashioned in emotional nurturing actions, such as psychological care and follow-up to overcome an inadequate capacity for emotional parenting. While the state cannot enforce love, it can reinforce it by providing social services which encourage formation or maintenance of parent-child ties." Id. at 732.

This state has provided appropriate remedies, as suggested by the article. The article further says, at 739, "The possibility of a monetary recovery for lack of nurturing should be limited to adult plaintiffs." While our position does not purport to be one of approval or disapproval of the positions asserted by the authors, the article demonstrates that even those who advocate radical changes in our method of thinking concerning the rights of children do not endorse actions such as those asserted here. Plaintiffs are unable to point to any literature in the field of child care or family planning which advocates an action for money damages to vindicate a right of the kind asserted here.

In addition, there is a limitation to the extent to which use may be made of tort actions for the purpose of accomplishing social aims. If there is ever a field in which juries and general trial courts are ill equipped to do social engineering, it is in the realm of the emotional relationship between mother and child. It is best we leave such matters to other fields of endeavor. There are certain kinds of relationships which are not proper fodder for tort litigation, and we believe this to be one of them. There are probably as many children who have been damaged in some manner by their parents' failure to meet completely their physical, emotional and psychological needs as there are people. A tort action for damages by emotionally deprived persons against their parents is, in our opinion, not going to solve the social problem in the same manner in which the legislature is attempting to solve it.

In addition to the contention that defendants should be liable for civil damages because of their violation of criminal and regulatory statutes, plaintiffs also contend that defendants are responsible because of the infliction of severe emotional distress by intentional acts. Plaintiffs allege that defendants intentionally deserted and abandoned them; however, they do not contend that defendants deserted them for the purpose of inflicting emotional harm upon them. We recognize that this tort usually also encompasses the infliction of emotional harm under circumstances from which a reasonable person would conclude that harm was almost certain to result. We believe this latter rationale is inapplicable as between parents and children. If it were otherwise, the children of divorced parents would almost always have an action for emotional damage against their parents. Divorce has become a way of life with almost certain emotional trauma of a greater or lesser degree to the children from the legal dissolution of the family and the resultant absence of at least one of the parents and sometimes both.

. . .

Plaintiffs generally contend that without respect to previously recognized theories of recovery, we should recognize a new tort of parental desertion. For all the reasons previously given in declining to use recognized theories of recovery, we also decline this invitation.

The judgment of the trial court is affirmed.

. . .

LENT, JUSTICE, concurring in part; dissenting in part.

. . .

The majority seems to take the position that what it finds to be a comprehensive legislative scheme is sufficient unto the evil of the day. I do not agree with that position and the limited condemnation of the defendant's conduct found in that legislative scheme.

The community has still other interests in condemning defendant's conduct and compensating plaintiff's injuries. At present there are over one-third of a million children in the United States who are dependent upon the community for their parental care.[1] . . . The

---

1. This figure is based on a projection of the figures and growth rates given by Subcommittee on Children and Youth, Senate Committee Labor & Public Welfare, 9th Cong., 1st Sess., Foster Care and Adoptions: Some Key Policy Issues, 7 (Committee Print 1975) [hereinafter Senate Committee]. As of 1971, there were 330,373 children in foster care. This figure includes 260,430 in foster families, 5,640 in group homes, and 64,303 in institutions. The growth rate, when adjusted for population increase, is approximately 2.4% per year.

future is bleak for the vast majority of these children, at least those in the position of the plaintiff, whose parents have abandoned them permanently.[3] Only approximately five percent of such children are ever adopted and placed in a permanent parental situation.[4]

The costs—in dollars and cents—of taking care of these children is staggering. . . .

However, the dollars-and-cents picture . . . measures only the direct, monetary loss to the community. Indirect costs are those which result from the *effects* of prolonged foster care—delinquency, economic dependency, crimes and corrections. Possibly the greatest costs are those which cannot be measured by dollars and cents at all—the loss in human potential. . . .

All researchers report the psychological phenomenon known as "separation trauma," the trauma produced by the initial separation from the mother regardless of the circumstances of the case.[13] A second element noted by researchers is the development of ambiguous relationships by the dependent child, with a concomitant loss of self-identity.[14] A third general phenomenon found by the researchers stems from the instability of the foster care system itself, where multiple placements are the norm. This instability in relationships fosters personality disturbance.[15]

The general results of these factors have been summarized in two of the major works in the field. Maas and Engler [16] state:

"These are the children who learn to develop shallow roots in relationships with others, who try to please but cannot trust, or who strike out before they can be let down. These are the children about whom we are most concerned."

3. In a study of foster care and its costs in New York City, Fanshel and Shinn, "Dollars and Sense in the Foster Care of Children," (Child Welfare League, 1971) [hereinafter Dollars and Sense], it was reported that approximately 42% of dependencies resulted from the voluntary act of the mother. These include:

Unwillingness of mother to assume parental duties–9.1%

Abandonment and desertion–12.5%

Neglect and abuse–17.4%

Unwillingness of mother to continue parental duties–2.9%

4. R. Geiser, The Illusion of Caring— Children in Foster Care, 81 (1973). Maas and Engler, in their seminal work, Children in Need of Parents (1959), indicated that a very small percentage of such children are "readily adoptable"—less than

five years old, white, of average or above average intelligence, and with no severe physical or personality problems. Id. at 383.

13. See e.g., Mnookin, Foster Care— In Whose Best Interests?, 43 Harvard Educational Review 599, 623 (1973) and studies cited therein. The risk of harm to the child from separation trauma is "substantial," especially for those separated at ages six months to three years, at approximately six years of age, and at puberty. Id. at 624.

14. Id. at 625.

15. Id. See also H. Maas and R. Engler, Children in Need of Parents 422 (1959) [hereinafter Children in Need].

16. Children in Need, supra n.15 at 356.

And the authors of the influential work Beyond the Best Interests of the Child state:[17]

"Only a child who has at least one person whom he can love, and who also feels loved, valued, and wanted by that person, will develop a healthy self-esteem. He can then become confident of his own chances of achievement in life and convinced of his own human value. Where this positive environmental attitude toward an infant is missing from the start, the consequences become obvious in later childhood and adult life. They take the form of the individual's diminished care for the well-being of his own body, or for his physical appearance and clothing, or for his image presented to his fellow beings. What is damaged is his love and regard for himself, and consequently his capacity to love and care for others, including his own children."

While indirect monetary costs to society are more difficult to document and quantify, they are just as real. Maas reports that forty to fifty percent of the foster children involved in his study exhibited symptoms of maladjustment.[18] Eisenberg reports that the referral rate for psychiatric services for foster children is thirty per one thousand population, about ten times that of the general population.[19] Meier reports a higher than normal incidence of marital breakdown and illegitimate births among former foster children.[20] Finally, McCord reports that "a significantly higher proportion of those who had been placed in foster homes had criminal records in adulthood" when compared to a control group of potentially delinquent boys living at home.[21]

The authors of Beyond the Best Interests of the Child amply summarize the effects of parentless dependency on different age-group children and relate them to the costs to society:

"When *infants and young children* find themselves abandoned by the parent, they not only suffer separation distress and anxiety but also setbacks in the quality of their next attachments, which will be less trustful.[22]

. . .

"Resentment toward the adults who have disappointed them in the past makes [*school age children*] adopt the attitude of not caring for anybody; or of making the new parent the scapegoat for

17. J. Goldstein, A. Freud and A. Solnit, Beyond the Best Interests of the Child 20 (1973) [hereinafter Beyond the Best Interests].

18. Maas, Highlights of the Foster Care Project: Introduction, 38 Child Welfare 5 (1959), cited in Mnookin, supra n. 13 at 623 and n.87.

19. Eisenberg, The Sins of the Fathers: Urban Decay and Social Pathology, 32 American Journal of Orthopsychiatry 14 (1962). See also Mnookin, supra n.13 at 623, n.86.

20. Meier, Current Circumstances of Former Foster Children, 44 Child Welfare 192–206 (1965).

21. McCord, McCord and Thurber, the Effects of Foster-Home Placement in the Prevention of Adult Anti Social Behavior, 34 Social Science Review 415–420 (1960).

22. Beyond the Best Interests, supra n.17 at 33.

the shortcomings of the former one. In any case, multiple placement at these ages puts many children beyond the reach of educational influences, and becomes the direct cause of behavior which
the schools experience as disrupting and the courts label as disso-
cial, delinquent, or even criminal.[23]

"*. . .*

"*Adults* who as children suffered from disruptions of continuity may themselves, in 'identifying' with their many 'parents,' treat
their children as they themselves were treated—continuing a cycle
costly for both a new generation of children as well as for society
itself." [24]

(emphasis added)

The sum of the cost to the community—direct and indirect, monetary and intangible—cannot be computed with complete accuracy;
however, Maas and Engler summarized their findings as follows:[25]

"Adequate care of children is not inexpensive. It is just as
costly to mend a child emotionally crippled by disorganized family
life as it is to cure the crippled leg of a child stricken with polio.
For children in need of parents the community will pay the price
sooner or later. The high incidence of mental disorders, criminality, or at best economic dependency among adults who as children
had lived in the limbo of foster care, is clear evidence of this."

It might be added that experts in the field of abandoned children
have found this emotional damage to be real and important, however
difficult it may be to measure. We heed the words of the authors of
Beyond the Best Interests of the Child, who state:[26]

"While they [legal decision makers] make the interests of a
child paramount over all other claims when his physical well-being
is in jeopardy, they subordinate, often intentionally, his psychological well-being to, for example, an adult's right to assert a biological tie. Yet both well-beings are equally important and any sharp
distinction between them is artificial."

In view of the costs, both tangible and intangible to society of caring for these dependent children who have well been termed the "orphans of the living" and the character of defendant's conduct as admitted by the demurrer, I believe defendant should shoulder so much
of the financial burden as her resources permit. Further, I would
hold that the emotional harm which the demurrer admits plaintiff has
suffered is such as the community should conclude is monetarily com-
pensable. As stated in Justice Linde's dissent plaintiff has alleged a
cause of action.

23. Id. at 34. See also id. at 34, n.2,
which quotes extensively from the case
history given in Carter v. U. S., 102 U.S.
App.D.C. 227, 252 F.2d 608 (1957).

24. Beyond the Best Interests, supra,
n.17 at 34.

25. Children in Need, supra n.15 at
397.

26. J. Goldstein, A. Freud and A.
Solnit, Beyond the Best Interests of the
Child 4 (1973).

LINDE, JUSTICE, dissenting.

. . .

. . . It should be noted at the outset that awarding civil damages for violations of prohibitory laws is not an uncommon or radical theory of recovery. . . .

. . . [O]nly this week we found in a prohibition against discharging an employee for claiming workers' compensation a public policy that supported a civil claim for damages by a worker so discharged. Brown v. Transcon Lines, Or., 588 P.2d 1087 (1978). The American Law Institute's Restatement (Second) of Torts, Tentative Draft No. 23, 1977, lists a number of other illustrations in its discussion of proscriptive or prescriptive statutes as sources of civil liability. Sometimes a common law court will assimilate the statutory duty into an existing principle of liability, . . . but that is not always so. See Restatement (Second) of Torts, Tentative Draft No. 23, 1977, § 874A, Comment *f*.[3]

Of course, the question of civil recovery for breach of a statutory duty can be an issue only when the legislation itself is silent on the point. If the legislature either provides for a civil remedy or clearly indicates that it means other provisions for enforcement to be complete and exclusive, there is nothing for a court to decide. It would help to clarify not only private rights but also the particular public policy if the legislative assembly as a routine step in the drafting of penal legislation faced the question of its civil consequences, or alternatively, if it were to enact a general formula for determining these consequences when a statute is otherwise silent.

Unfortunately legislatures do neither, but nothing can be inferred from that fact, given the existing practice of recognizing such consequences when the nature of the protective statute appears to imply them. The majority overstates the case when it equates legislative silence with an "underlying assumption . . . that it was not intended that the statute create any civil obligation or afford civil protection against the injuries which it was designed to prevent." Nor does it follow, when a court finds that the duty created or defined by the statute does imply a civil cause of action, that the court is engaged in pronouncing common law. The difference between a new common law theory of recovery in tort or otherwise and a civil claim based on a statute is obvious: The latter claim stands and falls with

---

3. As early as 1934, and until 1965, the original Restatement of Torts, § 286, stated:

The violation of a legislative enactment by doing a prohibited act, or by failing to do a required act, makes the actor liable for an invasion of an interest of another if:

(a) the intent of the enactment is exclusively or in part to protect an interest of the other as an individual; and

(b) the interest invaded is one which the enactment is intended to protect; and,

(c) where the enactment is intended to protect an interest from a particular hazard, the invasion of the interests results from that hazard; and,

(d) the violation is a legal cause of the invasion, and the other has not so conducted himself as to disable himself from maintaining an action.

the statute from which it is implied, and it will disappear as soon as the amendment or repeal of the statute indicates a reconsideration of the previous public policy. Thus, while a court is often left at large to divine the implications of a statutory policy, it is equally an over-statement to say that the court simply makes its own judgment whether to "create a cause of action" deriving "solely" from the court's own appraisal whether additional protection for the claimed interest is "necessary and desirable."

The relevance of criminal or regulatory laws to civil liability is more complex than merely being an element "taken into considera-tion by the court in deciding whether a common law action should be established," as the majority puts it. Such laws express distinct kinds of policies. First, the most familiar criminal laws are redefini-tions of common-law crimes against private persons or property. They have equally familiar civil analogues in common-law torts. On-ly "victimless crimes" and crimes deemed to endanger the public as a collectivity, such as bribery, counterfeiting, or tax evasion, are likely to lack a corresponding civil liability. Violations of game laws or en-vironmental protection laws may be other examples. Second, regula-tory laws specify standards of socially responsible conduct for the protection of persons endangered by the conduct. While the tort standard may go further, we have recognized the force of the crimi-nal or regulatory standard in negligence cases even when it was set by agencies or local governments that presumably could not them-selves create civil liability whether or not they had such an intent. Third, governmental sanctions, penal or otherwise, may be enacted to add governmental enforcement to the recognized obligations of a re-lationship existing apart from the legislation. In such a situation the "underlying assumption," to use the majority's phrase, is hardly that the penal sanction makes the civil obligation unnecessary. Rather, the statute shows that the obligation is considered of such importance that it deserves enforcement by public prosecution.

The child protection laws. It can hardly be questioned that a statute like 163.535, which makes it a crime intentionally to desert and abandon a child, is of the third kind. It and the related sections did not enact a novel prohibition against parental neglect for the con-venience of the general public or the protection of taxpayers. They enacted a legislative definition and public enforcement of certain min-imal obligations of an existing relationship. Jurisprudentially it might be said that parents have a duty not to abandon and desert their young children because ORS 163.535 makes it a crime to do so, but a legislator would surely think ORS 163.535 should make it a crime to abandon and desert a child because the parent's existing du-ty—the duty to the child, not to the state—deserved governmental reenforcement. It is the parent's duty thus recognized under Oregon law that plaintiffs invoke in these cases.

The majority does not really deny that ORS 163.535 constitutes such a legislative recognition and reenforcement of the parent's private obligation to the child, not of some socially convenient behavior. Rather, the majority would deny a remedy for the intentional breach of this obligation on the ground that other public policies militate against such a remedy. Upon examination, the majority's statutory citations refer to the single policy of maintaining and preserving the position of the child within a functioning family as long as this is possible. Without in any way questioning that this is indeed the state's public policy, I do not agree that it supports the conclusion that the legislature meant to deny the child a remedy for injuries from a parent's unlawful acts.

First, it must be kept in mind what conduct violates ORS 163.535. The statute makes it a felony to desert one's child with intent to abandon it. Of course, we have no evidence of the actual facts in these cases, but the allegations are that defendants did desert and abandon their children "maliciously, intentionally, and with cruel disregard of the consequences." If that is true, the parents have in fact ended the family unit, so that solicitude about not impairing it by litigation may sacrifice the children's legal rights to a pious hope. Contrary to the majority, I do not believe it is this court's own judgment of the possible effects of litigation on family relations that matters (a question on which counsel was unable to enlighten us and that, if taken seriously, is hardly within judicial notice) but rather what view of these effects may be attributed to the legislature. More important for interpreting the legislative policy, however, the statute means that a district attorney or grand jury on the alleged facts could prosecute the parents for a felony. It is incongruous to hold that the legislature provided for a felony prosecution of parents who egregiously violate a duty toward their children, but that it meant to exclude civil actions on behalf of the maliciously abandoned children for fear of impairing the family unit. To hold that the plaintiffs cannot invoke this duty, one must assume a legislative policy that a deserted and abandoned child (or a guardian on its behalf) should ask a district attorney to seek the criminal punishment of the parent for this desertion, but that the child should have no claim that would be of any benefit to itself. That seems too unlikely a policy to attribute to the legislature without some showing that it was intended.

Moreover, the majority's premise proves too much. For purposes of the issue of law before us on these demurrers, it can be assumed that the plaintiffs have suffered actual, demonstrable injuries of a kind for which the law provides money damages against defendants other than parents, that defendants have assets from which these real injuries of the plaintiffs could be compensated, and that defendants caused these injuries by intentionally breaching a specific duty toward plaintiffs that is recognized in Oregon law. Perhaps the explanation for the majority's unwillingness to follow these assumptions to their conclusion is that the injuries alleged are psychological and emotional rather than physical. But if a civil remedy is denied on the majority's premise that it is precluded by a state policy of preserving family unity, that premise would apply equally to bar recovery of damages by a child crippled by physical abuse.[5]   And despite the majority's reference to statutory proceedings for the termination of parental rights, it is at least questionable that a termination proceeding would create rights to a financial recovery to compensate for such very real and costly harm caused before the termination proceeding.

Although the majority does not say so, its premise is the equivalent of the doctrine of intrafamily tort immunity which Oregon has abandoned at least with respect to intentional torts, though attributed here to a supposed legislative policy subordinating legal claims of children against their parents to reliance on "protective social services."   I perceive no such prescribed reliance on social services when parents who have deliberately mistreated their children in a manner made criminal by statute have the assets to be responsible for the harm caused thereby.   .   .   .

LENT, J., joins in this dissent.

B.   DEPENDENCY AND NEGLECT

MATTER OF B. K.

District of Columbia Court of Appeals, 1981.
429 A.2d 1331.

Before KELLY, FERREN and PRYOR, ASSOCIATE JUDGES.

PER CURIAM:

The District of Columbia has the authority pursuant to D.C.Code 1973, §§ 16–2301, –2320, to protect a "neglected child" by removing that child from the custody of his or her parents.   In this appeal, the father of a child found to be "neglected" challenges both the finding below and the constitutionality of the D.C. Statute.   .   .   .

The young girl, B.K., whose present and future well-being is the central concern of this proceeding, was born on September 19, 1978, at the Georgetown University Hospital.   Both her parents have been diagnosed as suffering from undifferentiated paranoid schizophrenia.

---

5. Defendant presented a "parade of horribles" such as actions for psychological or emotional injury from receiving fewer Christmas gifts than a sibling and the like.   I note this only to point out that the argument misses the point.   The nature of the *breach of duty* in this case is fixed by ORS 163.535 and would not give rise to an expandable common law precedent.   As far as the present issue is concerned, the case would be the same if a child had been deliberately abandoned in an unheated mountain cabin and lost a limb to frostbite or suffered other permanent injuries from lack of food or pneumonia.

Nothing is said here about claims based on other statutes invoked by plaintiffs that deal with general but unintentional neglect or nonsupport of children.   The provision of alternative social services relied on by the majority may militate against implying a civil remedy for these less final and culpable violations of parental duty.

Although appellant argues that the court below incorrectly focused on the parents' mental illness rather than the well-being of the child, it is clear from the record that the parents' condition was considered relevant only insofar as it pertained to their ability to provide proper care for B.K. The evidence showed that they were unable to do so, and that when in their care, B.K.'s physical and emotional health was threatened.

During the period while she was in the hospital delivering her baby, B.K.'s mother exhibited strange behavior which prompted further examination by staff psychiatrists. The mother's condition was diagnosed as a "classic case of schizophrenia" and the prediction was that she would be unable to comprehend her child's emotional and physical needs. Although the Child Protective Services Division of the Department of Human Resources was apprised of the situation by doctors at Georgetown, there was no direct intervention by the Division at that time. On February 16, 1979, the Child Protective Services Division was again contacted about this unfortunate situation when the father of B.K.'s mother informed the Division that his daughter and appellant had been arrested while standing in the middle of the street, apparently under the influence of drugs. The events which finally caused intervention by the Protective Services Division began on March 23, 1979, when pedestrians observed appellant and B.K.'s mother, with B.K. in a stroller, walking downtown at about 11:00 p.m. According to the pedestrians, appellant and B.K.'s mother appeared to be disoriented and intoxicated, and B.K. was screaming. This alarmed the pedestrians who approached the couple. At that point, B.K.'s mother walked away and, after arguing with the pedestrians, appellant also left. The pedestrians, then took B.K., who was clad only in a thin cloth pajama, into the Embassy Row Hotel where they called the police. After police arrived on the scene, B.K.'s mother appeared at the hotel. Since she appeared to be intoxicated, the officers transported her to the detoxification unit of the D.C. General Hospital. Meanwhile, B.K. was taken into custody by the Youth Division of the Metropolitan Police Department.

That night, a police officer and an investigator for the Protective Services Division visited the Kalorama Road house where appellant lived with B.K. and B.K.'s mother. According to their testimony, and the testimony of an inspector for the Housing and Community Development Department who inspected the house on March 27, 1979, the premises were, to put it mildly, not very pleasant. There was plaster falling from holes in the ceiling, cracks in the walls, no adequate kitchen facilities, dirty pampers strewn all over the floor, profuse odors, human and animal feces on the first and second floors, broken windows in the bathroom and, due to a structural defect, water was leaking on exposed wiring. According to the housing inspector, these conditions were dangerous and constituted a health hazard.

When he was visited on the night of March 23, 1979, by the police officer and the housing inspector, appellant agreed to permit the

Child Protective Services Division to provide emergency care for B.K. However, on March 27, 1979, B.K. was released into the custody of her mother, who at that time expressed her willingness to cooperate with Protective Services. Only a few days later, during the evening of April 3, 1979, B.K. was again taken into protective custody. Customers and employees in a restaurant had observed B.K.'s mother, seated at a table, swinging B.K. through the air. With each swing, B.K.'s head came perilously close to colliding with the table top. The acting manager of the restaurant, after talking to B.K.'s mother, became concerned for the safety of the child and called the police. All the while, appellant was seated at the bar, apparently oblivious to the situation. When the police arrived, B.K. and her mother were taken into custody. B.K. was placed in shelter care at St. Ann's Infant Home.

At this point, the Protective Services Division began a more thorough investigation of the circumstances surrounding B.K.'s care and both parents underwent physical and mental examinations. On April 10, 1979, a petition was filed in Superior Court alleging that B.K. was a "neglected child" under D.C.Code 1973, § 16–2301(9)(B) & (C).[1]

A lengthy factfinding hearing was conducted in the Superior Court Family Division beginning on October 15, 1979. Extensive testimony was heard from case workers and psychiatrists regarding B.K. and her parents. Appellant's landlady and a Catholic priest testified on behalf of B.K.'s parents. At the conclusion of the evidence, the court issued its findings of fact and ruled that the government had shown, by a preponderance of the evidence, that B.K. was neglected within the meaning of the statute. A dispositional hearing . . . was held on December 18, 1979, and B.K. was placed in the custody of her maternal grandparents.

We emphasize at the outset that the order below does not terminate parental rights but merely determines custody of the neglected child for a period of two years, at which time further proceedings must be held.

The trial court correctly stated that in a neglect proceeding the government must prove its case by a "preponderance of the evidence." This is clear from the statute itself. Appellant, however, argues that because the ruling below separated him from his child, and thus threatens the sanctity of his family, see Moore v. City of East Cleveland, 431 U.S. 494, 97 S.Ct. 1932, 52 L.Ed.2d 531 (1979), the

---

1. The term "neglected child" means a child—

. . .

(B) who is without proper parental care or control, subsistence, education as required by law, or other care or control necessary for his physical, mental, or emotional health, and the deprivation is not due to the lack of financial means of his parent, guardian, or other custodian;

(C) whose parent, guardian, or other custodian is unable to discharge his responsibilities to and for the child because of incarceration, hospitalization, or other physical or mental incapacity; . . . [D.C.Code 1973, § 16–2301(9) (B) & (C).]

Constitution requires that the standard of proof be "clear and convincing evidence." In In re: J.S.R., D.C.App., 374 A.2d 860 (1977), we stated that the consequences of a finding that parental consent to an adoption was being withheld contrary to the best interests of the child are "far more severe than those of a finding of neglect." Id. at 864. Nonetheless, we held that, although the higher standard of "clear and convincing evidence" was warranted in the adoption case, it was not constitutionally required. Therefore, it follows that in a neglect proceeding the Constitution does not require the "clear and convincing evidence" standard.

Our holding in In re: J.S.R. is not altered by Addington v. Texas, 441 U.S. 418, 99 S.Ct. 1804, 60 L.Ed.2d 323 (1979), in which the Supreme Court held that due process requires the "clear and convincing" standard of proof in a civil proceeding brought to commit an individual involuntarily for an indefinite period of time to a state mental hospital. The individual's liberty interest at stake in *Addington* is greater than appellant's interest in retaining custody of his child, particularly when balanced against the interest of the state in protecting neglected children.

On the basis of the record in this case, we are satisfied the child was shown to be neglected by a preponderance of the evidence. We note also that the trial court stated in its findings that even under the "clear and convincing" standard the government had made its case. That exemplifies both the solicitousness of the trial court for the interests involved and the great weight of the evidence presented by the government.

Appellant also challenges the constitutionality of the neglect statute pursuant to which the petition was brought. We cannot quarrel with appellant's assertion that the state must tread carefully when it intrudes upon the integrity of the family unit. This court recognized that fundamental proposition in In re: J.S.R.:

> The right of a natural parent to raise one's child is a fundamental and essential one which is constitutionally protected. However, it is not an absolute one. The state has both the right and the duty to protect minor children through judicial determinations of their interest. To this end, the state has a substantial range of authority to protect the welfare of a child, and the state's legitimate interest in the child's welfare may be implemented by separating the child from the parent. [Supra at 863 (citations omitted).]

Appellant contends the statutory definition of a "neglected" child is vague, and therefore unconstitutional. In order to withstand a vagueness challenge the statute must state its standard with adequate clarity and make sufficiently distinct boundaries for the law to be fairly administered. Roth v. United States, 354 U.S. 476, 77 S.Ct. 1304, 1 L.Ed.2d 1498 (1957). The Supreme Court has reminded us that in considering vagueness, statutes which do not involve First

Amendment freedoms must be evaluated in light of the facts of the case at hand. United States v. Mazurie, 419 U.S. 544, 95 S.Ct. 710, 42 L.Ed.2d 706 (1975); . . . The statute in question here may be broad in its coverage, but we are not persuaded that it is vague. We point out that "proceedings under this type statute demand and provide a certain amount of elasticity to the court." Matter of C.M.S., 609 P.2d 240, 244 (Mont.1979). The statute requires an investigation into the circumstances of the particular case and provides clear guidelines for determining whether a child is neglected. On the facts of this case, there is no question that such a finding was proper.

Affirmed.

CALIFORNIA WELFARE & INSTITUTIONS CODE, Art. 6, DEPENDENT CHILDREN–JURISDICTION

§ 300. Persons subject to jurisdiction

Any person under the age of 18 years who comes within any of the following descriptions is within the jurisdiction of the juvenile court which may adjudge such person to be a dependent child of the court:

(a) Who is in need of proper and effective parental care or control and has no parent or guardian, or has no parent or guardian willing to exercise or capable of exercising such care or control, or has no parent or guardian actually exercising such care or control. No parent shall be found to be incapable of exercising proper and effective parental care or control solely because of a physical disability, including, but not limited to, a defect in the visual or auditory functions of his or her body, unless the court finds that the disability prevents the parent from exercising such care or control.

(b) Who is destitute, or who is not provided with the necessities of life, or who is not provided with a home or suitable place of abode.

(c) Who is physically dangerous to the public because of a mental or physical deficiency, disorder or abnormality.

(d) Whose home is an unfit place for him by reason of neglect, cruelty, depravity, or physical abuse of either of his parents, or of his guardian or other person in whose custody or care he is.

IN RE JEANNETTE S.

California Court of Appeals, 5th District, 1979.
94 Cal.App.3d 52, 156 Cal.Rptr. 262.

FRANSON, ASSOCIATE JUSTICE.

STATEMENT OF THE CASE

Appellant Margery S. appeals from a judgment of the juvenile court declaring her five-year old daughter Jeannette S. a dependent child of the juvenile court under section 300, subdivisions (a) and (b) of the Welfare and Institutions Code and removing the child from her custody and control under section 361, subdivisions (a) and (b) of that code. (All further statutory references are to the Welfare and Institutions Code unless otherwise specified.)

On January 5, 1978, representatives of the Merced County Department of Human Resources (hereinafter Department) went to appellant's home where Jeannette resided to investigate problems which appellant had mentioned to a Department representative earlier that day. As a result of that investigation, Jeannette was taken into protective custody. On January 6, 1978, Sheila Callan, a Department social worker, filed a petition in the juvenile court alleging that Jeannette was a person described under section 300, subdivisions (a) and (b).

At the detention hearing both appellant and Frank S., the minor's father, were present. The father requested that Jeannette be placed in his custody pending the jurisdictional hearing. The court denied the request, found probable cause to detain Jeannette and ordered her detained. The court appointed separate counsel to represent Jeannette's mother and father at the jurisdictional and dispositional hearings.

At the jurisdictional hearing which commenced on January 25 and was completed after several continued hearings on February 22, 1978, the court found that Jeannette was a person within the provisions of section 300, subdivisions (a) and (b) since she had no parent capable of exercising the necessary care and control or of providing her with a suitable home; she was accordingly declared a dependent child of the court.

The parties agreed to proceed with the dispositional hearing immediately. The judge stated that he had reviewed the dispositional reports and had concluded that the minor should be placed in the custody of the Department for suitable placement. The court found that the allegations of the petition were true; that the award of custody to the parents would be detrimental to the minor; and that the award to the Department would serve the best interests of the child. It was ordered that Jeannette be placed in the custody of the Department for suitable placement. It was further ordered that the matter be continued for a review hearing on January 10, 1979, and that during the interim both parents would have the right to visit Jeannette without supervision.

Appellant filed a timely notice of appeal.

THE EVIDENCE

Jeannette was born to appellant and Frank on July 23, 1972. They were divorced in 1976, and appellant was awarded custody of Jeannette. Jeannette lived with appellant in Merced until she was detained by the Department on January 5. Frank had regularly exercised visitation rights on weekends during the two-year period since the divorce.

Appellant's psychological profile reveals that she is of above average intelligence; that she suffers from chronic anxiety and has a somewhat schizoid personality. Appellant attended a mental health clinic on a daily basis from 9 a. m. to 3 p. m. where she participated in group therapy and other activities. She demonstrates a concern for her child and her relationship with Jeannette is a close and loving one.

Appellant has a limited income and has been active in seeking aid from social agencies. She requested and received visits from a public health nurse who instructed her on child care. She also received assistance from a homemaker assigned by the welfare department for the two weeks preceding January 5, 1978. The homemaker apparently reported to her supervisor that the assignment was "unsuccessful," but the homemaker did not testify at the hearings to explain what the problem was about. Appellant testified that the homemaker merely transported Jeannette to the doctor and to the day-care school while appellant was at the mental health clinic. Other than one time for a five-minute period, the homemaker did not assist appellant in cleaning the house. Appellant acknowledged that it was difficult for her to take criticism but "If it is made in a suggestive way, I can cope with it." Except for the homemaker service for the two weeks preceding January 5, appellant had received no assistance in the care of her home for the past one and a half years. On the afternoon of January 5, appellant went to the Department's office and told one of the supervisors that she had several problems with her home situation and that she needed help, thereby triggering the instant proceedings.

When the Department representatives went to appellant's house on January 5, they found it dirty and cluttered with debris. There were extensive dog feces on the kitchen floor and cat feces in the bathroom. The house smelled of urine and there was spoiled food on the stove. Jeannette had been forced to sleep on the couch in the living room because her bedroom was such a mess.

Appellant kept three dogs and two cats at her residence.

Jeannette was in apparent good health and good spirits on January 5. There was no evidence of trauma or abuse. However, Jeannette's kindergarten teacher testified that the child was frequently dirty when she came to school and her clothing was extremely odoriferous which caused some teasing by the other children. Although Jeannette behaved in a distracted manner at school and had difficulty communicating due to a speech defect, her behavior was not particularly deviant. A psychological evaluation of Jeannette by the school psychologist reveals that she is mildly hyperactive and sometimes has difficulty concentrating in class, but her academic progress is good. She is bright and gets along well with others.

There was some evidence that on occasions appellant did not prepare breakfast or other meals for Jeannette; however, she did not appear undernourished. Frequently appellant was not home when Jeannette returned from school.

Mr. Stutsman, a social worker for the Department, testified at the jurisdictional hearing that he had visited appellant's home on several occasions from January 1976 to August of 1977 because of complaints by school authorities about Jeannette's unclean appearance at school. On one occasion in February 1976, he went into the house and found it to be extremely dirty with animal feces on the floor.

Jeannette's father Frank appeared at both the jurisdictional and dispositional hearings and requested custody of Jeannette. He testified that he loved Jeannette and had a good relationship with her. He had regularly exercised his visitation rights with Jeannette during the two years since his divorce from appellant. Frank lived in a small two-bedroom single-bath house in Merced with Robert and Helen Christiansen (his former brother-in-law and his wife). The Christiansens had moved into Frank's house to provide a home for Jeannette if she should be removed from the custody of her mother. Mr. Christiansen is employed fulltime as a truck driver, and his wife Helen would care for Jeannette at Frank's home. Frank testified that he would give Jeannette his room and would sleep on the couch in the living room.

Sheila Callan, a social worker, investigated Frank's home and filed a supplemental report at the jurisdictional hearing. The report states that because Frank's house has only two bedrooms and one bath that the sleeping arrangements proposed by Frank if he should obtain custody of Jeannette would be unsatisfactory in that he would have to go through Jeannette's bedroom to reach the bathroom. The report states, "This action appears to be antithetical to the well-being of Jeannette because of the crowded living arrangements." The report also noted that Frank has an unstable employment record and receives welfare and unemployment benefits. He also has a serious problem with alcohol and lacks the knowledge and skills required for child rearing.[1] On the basis of her investigation, Ms. Callan opined that Frank was incapable of providing a suitable home for Jeannette due to his alcoholism, financial instability and lack of "parenting skills." She recommended that Jeannette be placed in the custody of the Department for suitable placement.

1. The report also notes that Frank "has an arrest record of contributing to the delinquency of a minor; he molested a six-year old female in December 1965." However, apparently neither the Department nor the juvenile court place any emphasis on the arrest record in making the recommendation and decision not to place Jeannette with Frank. Mrs. Christiansen's presence at Frank's home should have obviated any concern in this regard.

At no time did the Department in its dispositional reports to the court recommend a plan for reuniting Jeannette with her mother or father as required by California Rule of Court 1376, subdivision (b). The dispositional report recommended that the parents' visits with Jeannette be supervised by a social worker "to insure that Jeannette will not be upset by false promises, threats and demands [by the parents]." The court rejected the recommendation.

THERE IS SUFFICIENT EVIDENCE TO SUPPORT THE JURISDICTIONAL FINDING OF DEPENDENCY

The standard of proof required to establish that a minor is a dependent child under section 300 is the "preponderance of the evidence." (§ 355.) If there is any substantial evidence to support the findings of the juvenile court, a reviewing court must uphold the trial court's findings. All reasonable inferences must be drawn in support of the findings and the record must be viewed in the light most favorable to the juvenile court's order.

In the present case, the report prepared by the Department for presentation at the jurisdictional hearing details the condition of Jeannette's inadequate home environment. That report states that Jeannette was sent to school in clothes which were soiled with urine, she was not given breakfast at home, and she frequently returned from school to an empty house. The home was "filthy" and there was no adequate place for Jeannette to sleep because of clutter. The jurisdictional report also stated that appellant had not provided a stable mother role and was unable to place her child's needs above her own. Testimony of witnesses verified the allegations in the report and established that the condition of the home on January 5 was not an isolated occurrence. Thus, there was substantial evidence to support the trial court's order that Jeannette be declared a dependent child of the court.[2]

We have considered and reject the various contentions of appellant that she was deprived of constitutional and statutory procedural due process requirements by lack of notice of the jurisdictional charges under section 300. We also reject her contention regarding the lack of written findings of fact.

___

2. We acknowledge that the dependency order is highly questionable insofar as Frank's ability to provide effective care and control of Jeannette (§ 300, subd. (a)) and to provide Jeannette with the necessities of life and with a suitable place of abode (§ 300, subd. (b)). It is difficult to justify the dependency finding in light of Frank's willingness to accept Jeannette in his home under the care and supervision of Mrs. Christiansen. The crowded living conditions together with Frank's alcoholism and dependence upon welfare services clearly are insufficient, standing alone, to support a finding of dependence. However, Frank has not appealed the dependency order, and we believe that the reversal of the disposition order and a remand for another dispositional hearing will adequately protect Jeannette's interests.

THERE IS INSUFFICIENT EVIDENCE TO SUPPORT THE DIS-
POSITIONAL ORDER REMOVING JEANNETTE FROM
THE CUSTODY OF HER MOTHER AND FATHER
UNDER SECTION 361

It is a cardinal rule of our society that the custody, care and nurture of a child resides first in the parents rather than in a public agency. As stated in In re Carmaleta (1978) 21 Cal.3d 482 at page 489, 146 Cal.Rptr. 623 at page 627, 579 P.2d 514 at page 518:

"Parenting is a fundamental right, and accordingly, is disturbed only in extreme cases of persons acting in a fashion incompatible with parenthood. Thus, . . . '[t]he relationship of . . . natural parent . . . [and] . . . children is a vital human relationship which has far-reaching implications for the growth and development of the child. (See Kay & Phillips, Poverty and the Law of Child Custody (1966) 54 Cal.L.R. 717.) . . . [T]he involuntary termination of that relationship by state action must be viewed as a drastic remedy which should be resorted to only in extreme cases of neglect or abandonment [citations]. . . . '[S]evering the parental relationship [must be] the least detrimental alternative for the child.''

In furtherance of these principles, the courts have imposed a standard of *clear and convincing* proof of parental inability to provide proper care for the child and resulting detriment to the child if it remains with the parent, before custody can be awarded to a nonparent.

The clear and convincing standard was not met in the instant case. First, the juvenile court had two reasonable alternatives available to it short of awarding custody to the Department. It could have returned Jeannette to her mother under stringent conditions of supervision by the welfare department with the warning that if she again let her house get filthy or failed to keep Jeannette in clean clothes and to properly care for her that appellant would lose custody of the child. Moreover, the trial court could have ordered the removal of some or all of the animals at appellant's residence as a condition of returning Jeannette to her mother. It could have ordered homemaker service to assist appellant in keeping her home clean; the fact that she had received some assistance for the two weeks preceding the January 5 incident does not demonstrate a total incapacity to benefit from future homemaking service in light of the fact that she had received no such assistance in the preceding one and half year period. Moreover, the trial court should have ascertained the cause of the difficulty between appellant and the homemaker which triggered appellant's request for help from the Department on January 5. Perhaps, another homemaker would have been successful in getting appellant to clean her house—at least the possibility that this could be accomplished should have been explored. If stringent supervision of appellant's activities with reference to Jeannette did not provide a suitable home environment, then the court could remove Jeannette from the custody of her mother.

Second, assuming the trial court had a reasonable basis for concluding that appellant was incapable of providing a suitable home for Jeannette, it could have placed Jeannette with her father and the Christiansens. Frank offered an alternative home to Jeannette. The fact that the home was small, that Frank was unemployed and that he had a drinking problem does not support a finding that it would be detrimental to Jeannette for her to be with her father and the Christiansens rather than the Department. The presence of Mrs. Christiansen in the home would have alleviated any concern arising from Frank's alcoholism and arrest for child molesting 13 years earlier. Apparently, Frank recognized this when he asked the Christiansens to move in with him. Again, under the trial court's broad powers of supervision over Jeannette and her home environment (§ 362), it could have monitored Jeannette's progress in her father's home to assure her protection.

We observe that none of the social reports filed by the Department at the dispositional hearing included a "recommended plan for reuniting the minor with the family," as required by California Rule of Court rule 1376, subdivision (b). It is readily apparent that the Department had "given up" insofar as appellant and Frank's ability to properly care for Jeannette. While this attitude is understandable, it is contrary to the policy of the law. We deem it appropriate to quote from Judge Homer Thompson's California Juvenile Court Deskbook (2d ed. Cont.Ed.Bar 1978) at page 184:

> "Although placement in the parents' home is utilized at times in all kinds of section 300 cases, it is most frequently used in filthy home cases. These cases are the most responsive to supervision, and are usually referred to the probation department by social workers in the welfare department. Many of these cases involve families on welfare, and a social worker is already working with the family. Frequently the welfare department has a home-services unit or officer who will enter a filthy home and help the mother with the problems that have produced the condition.

> "Filthy home cases are sometimes those in which it is most difficult to remove the children, *and often it could be the most damaging to the children to do so.* Even though the home is a health hazard for the children, the mother is often a good, loving, and attentive mother in other respects. The children have responded to their mother's love and are very close to her. *Removal of such children can be a shattering experience for them.*" (Emphasis added.)

The judgment is reversed as to the dispositional order placing Jeannette in the custody of the Department of Human Resources. The trial court is directed to conduct another dispositional hearing in accordance with the principles expressed herein.

NOTE

A typical neglect or dependency proceeding is instituted through filing a form petition by a child case worker. Allegations forming the basis for two such petitions filed in a California juvenile court under § 300 of the California Welfare and Institutions Code are shown below.

The first petition involved an 11-year old boy:

PARAGRAPH I SUBDIVISION A: Said minor has no parent and/or guardian capable of and actually exercising proper and effective parental care and control and is in need of such care and control, in that: Minor normally resides in the home of his mother and on or about April 6, 1977 minor's home was in an unfit condition and a danger to minor due to the following conditions: The electricity and water being shut off since approximately February 1, 1977, a leaking inoperative gas stove in the kitchen, which filled the home with gas fumes, the family using candles for light; trash, litter, papers, soiled clothing scattered throughout the floors of the home; inoperative toilets filled with fecal matter and animal fecal matter on the floors throughout home, no edible food in home, no clean clothing, the entire home being in a state of disarray having trash and debris scattered throughout; the yard area around home being in a similar condition including having human feces along with soiled toilet paper.

The second petition involved a 6-year-old girl:

PARAGRAPH I SUBDIVISION A: Said minor has no parent and/or guardian capable of and actually exercising proper and effective parental care and control and is in need of such care and control, in that: Minor normally resides in the home of her mother and mother's male companion, and approximately one month ago and on a prior occasion during the past year, minor's mother's male companion performed various sex acts on minor's sister, including sexual intercourse. Further, minor's mother was aware of said sex incidents and failed to and/or was unwilling to protect minor's sister.

C. RESHAPING THE CRITERIA FOR INTERVENTION

JUVENILE JUSTICE STANDARDS PROJECT, STANDARDS RELATING TO ABUSE AND NEGLECT (Tentative Draft 1977)*

2.1 Statutory grounds for intervention.

Courts should be authorized to assume jurisdiction in order to condition continued parental custody upon the parents' accepting supervision or to remove a child from his/her home only when a child is endangered in a manner specified in subsections A.–F.

* Reprinted with permission from Standards Relating to Abuse and Neglect (Tentative Draft), Copyright 1977, Ballinger Publishing Company.

Commentary

This standard specifies that coercive state intervention may occur only if the child is endangered in a manner specified in subsections A.–F. infra.

. . . [F]ew families provide children with "ideal" environments. If intervention is permissible because parents are not sufficiently affectionate, because a home is dirty, because the parents are providing less stimulation than desirable, or because the parents are thought to be "immoral," as defined by judges and social workers, intervention would be pervasive. Yet there is every reason to believe that intervention to protect children from such "harms," especially if removal is the only alternative, would more often result in harms greater to the child than the "harm" from which he/she is being protected. We have neither the resources nor the knowledge to protect children against all harms. Finally, the broader the grounds for intervention, the greater the possibility of arbitrary or discriminatory intervention.

The proposed grounds focus primarily on the child's physical well-being, although intervention is permitted, in very limited circumstances, where a child is suffering from "emotional" damage. The standards specifically omit language authorizing intervention because a child is living in an "immoral" home environment, an "unsuitable" home, a "dirty" home, or with parents who are "inadequate." All of these terms allow overintervention, often on an arbitrary basis, without any evidence of harm to the child. . . .

The proposed grounds for intervention reject the positions of those who advocate limiting intervention solely to cases of physical abuse and those who would support intervention whenever a child is "deprive[d] . . . of equal rights and liberties, and/or [denied] optimal development." See D. Gil, Violence Against Children 202 (1973). Those advocating the narrower definition claim that we lack the knowledge and resources to protect any but the most seriously abused children, i.e., those who are "battered" by their parents. They believe that intervention in nonphysical abuse cases will likely be done in a discriminatory manner and without helping the child. Therefore, according to proponents of this view, coercive intervention should not be permitted unless the parent has severely and willfully injured the child.

Commentators supporting broad definitions tend to minimize the lack of resources and to focus on the well documented fact that many children grow up in quite undesirable conditions. They argue that it is unrealistic to single out physical abuse when children can be equally damaged in other ways. To some degree these commentators recognize that the problem does not always lie with the parents, but they are willing to use neglect laws in lieu of social programs to help all families.

The proposed grounds for intervention attempt to strike a middle ground, isolating a number of harms which are considered most serious, regardless of whether they are physical or emotional, but not including so many harms, or harms so broadly defined, that we cannot hope to intervene usefully in all the cases that will be brought.

. . .

A. [Coercive intervention should be authorized when] a child has suffered, or there is a substantial risk that a child will imminently suffer, a physical harm, inflicted nonaccidentally upon him/her by his/her parents, which causes, or creates a substantial risk of causing disfigurement, impairment of bodily functioning, or other serious physical injury.

Commentary

This standard authorizes intervention when a child has been physically abused by his/her parent, i.e., cases where a parent has nonaccidentally injured the child. Unlike present statutes, which usually do not specify the extent of the injury needed to justify intervention, the standard specifies that the harm must be a serious one, generally evidenced by disfigurement or substantial impairment of bodily functioning. Such injury need not have already occurred to justify intervention, however. If a child has been physically harmed by a parent in a manner that might cause serious harm, but did not do so in the particular instance, intervention would still be permissible.

. . .

The critical part of the standard is the requirement that the child be injured in a way that causes or creates a substantial risk of causing disfigurement, impairment of bodily functioning, or other serious physical injury. The intent of the standard is to prevent injuries such as broken bones, burns, internal injuries, loss of hearing, sight, etc. It is not intended to cover cases of minor bruises or black and blue marks, unless the child was treated in a way that indicates that more serious injury is likely to occur in the future. In making this decision, a course of parental conduct and the psychological state of the parents may be considered, as well as the injury itself.

The standard allows intervention based on the "substantial risk" that parental action may cause or is "likely to imminently" cause such an injury, as well as on the basis of actual injuries. "Substantial risk" denotes real, genuine, and considerable chance or hazard, and "imminently" refers to that which is impending or is threatening to occur in the near future. The fact that in a given instance a child is not killed, disfigured, or substantially impaired should not preclude intervention if it can be shown that the parental actions in the given case create a substantial likelihood of more serious injury in the future. For example, if a parent throws an infant against a wall, but the infant sustains only minor injuries, we should not wait until the child is again injured more seriously before intervening. However, courts should exercise extra caution in intervening when a child has not actually suffered injury, since there is greater possibility of incorrectly predicting the need for intervention.

.   .   .

B.   [Coercive intervention should be authorized when] a child has suffered, or where there is a substantial risk that the child will imminently suffer, physical harm causing disfigurement, impairment of bodily functioning, or other serious physical injury as a result of conditions created by his/her parents or by the failure of the parents to adequately supervise or protect him/her;

Commentary

This standard is an expansion of the grounds provided in Standard 2.1 A. supra. It is designed to cover situations where a child is physically endangered, to the same degree as in Standard 2.1 A. but the danger is created by parental failure to adequately protect or supervise the child, or by home conditions so dangerous that they pose an immediate threat to the child, rather than by intentional infliction of injury by the parent.

At present, "inadequate parental care" constitutes one of the most frequent bases for intervention. Under present statutes, however, there is no requirement that the parental inadequacy or poor home conditions be related to a specific harm to the child. Intervention is often premised on the possibility, not likelihood, of harm. This standard provides a considerably more limited basis for intervention. Intervention would not be justified solely because a home is dirty, because a parent leaves a child unattended for a brief period of time, or because a social agency believes that the parent is providing inadequate care or attention to the child. Instead there would have to be a showing that harm had actually occurred or a finding of specific factors that demonstrate that harm is imminently likely. Moreover, coercive intervention would not be appropriate if the parent is willing and able to correct the situation. In such cases state aid may be necessary to help the parents overcome the problem, but this should be provided without coercive intervention.

.   .   .

.   .   .   [C]oercive intervention generally is not justified, even though a child is seriously endangered, if the danger arises from environmental conditions beyond the parents' control. Unfortunately, there are some children who are endangered because of the poverty of their parents and the consequent inability of their parents to provide them basic protection and necessities. It is wrong for society to take coercive action against these parents and children, especially if this means placing the children in foster care. Coercive intervention should not be a way of remedying societal neglect of the poor. We must face the issue of poverty and its associated negative impact on children directly, not by juvenile court actions.

It must be recognized, however, that at present the only way to provide needed services to the family may be by bringing the child under court jurisdiction. A number of statutes restrict financial help unless the child is under court supervision. Such statutes should be changed; but until they are, a court might still take jurisdiction under this standard in order to provide services. In such cases, removal would be barred.

This exception is only a limited one and should not be seen as generally incorporating "fault" notions into these standards. Except in this situation, intervention is permissible if a child is endangered regardless of parental fault. Thus, intervention would be appropriate if a very young child is repeatedly left unattended because of a parent's mental illness, alcoholism or drug addiction. Intervention might also be based on unexplained serious injuries, especially if there is a history of such injuries. The fact that these are conditions beyond the parents' control should not limit intervention.

This subsection may also be used to assume court jurisdiction in "failure to thrive" cases, i.e., cases where a very young child is evidencing severe malnutrition, extremely low physical growth rate, delayed bone maturation, and significant retardation of motor development. See R. Patton and L. Gardner, Growth Failure in Maternal Deprivation xi, 15, 27–28, 32 (1963). If such a child shows improved growth and eating while under medical care, and the parent refuses continued treatment, intervention would be authorized.

C. [Coercive intervention should be authorized when] a child is suffering serious emotional damage, evidenced by severe anxiety, depression, or withdrawal, or untoward aggressive behavior toward self or others, and the child's parents are not willing to provide treatment for him/her;

Commentary

Standard 2.1 C. authorizes intervention when a child *is suffering* certain types of serious emotional damage which his/her parents are unwilling to have treated. The standard does not require a showing that the parents' behavior is causally connected to the child's emotional problems.

Whether emotional damage should be a basis for intervention is one of the most controversial issues regarding the grounds for intervention. A number of commentators have criticized the failure of most present statutes to explicitly include emotional neglect among the harms justifying intervention. See, e.g., S. Katz, When Parents Fail 62 (1971); Areen, "Intervention Between Parents and Child: A Reappraisal of the State's Role in Child Neglect and Abuse Cases," 63 Geo.L.J. 887, 933–34 (1975). It is contended that children can be at least as badly harmed emotionally as physically, and that the long-term consequences of emotional damage may be even greater than those from physical abuse. Therefore, proponents argue that it is unrealistic and extremely detrimental to children to fail to intervene on this basis.

On the other hand, there are substantial arguments against allowing any intervention for purely emotional harms. The major reasons are: A. because of the great difficulty in developing a workable definition of the term "emotional damage," this ground is subject to widely varied interpretation and opens the way to unwarranted intervention. "Emotional neglect" may be used to bring in cases which the standards attempt to exclude, such as "immoral" homes or "poor parenting" cases. B. Even if we could provide a reasonable definition, we lack the knowledge and resources to intervene successfully in a coercive manner. Treatment will generally require parental involvement or cooperation and this can only be obtained voluntarily.

The difficulty of definition is recognized by supporters of intervention. See Katz, supra at 68; Areen, supra at 933. . . . However, these commentators would rely on the judgment of the court to screen out inappropriate cases.

There is undoubtedly substantial merit to the claims of commentators on both sides of the issue. All commentators recognize the potential harm; they also recognize the substantial possibility of misuse of this ground for intervention. Standard 2.1 C. tries to resolve the problem by defining emotional damage for purposes of authorizing coercive intervention specifically and narrowly, i.e., a child who evidences "severe anxiety, depression, or withdrawal, or untoward aggressive behavior toward self or others," and whose parents are unwilling to provide treatment for him/her, and by requiring that the child *actually* be suffering the harm.

The goal of the definition is to tie intervention to certain specific symptoms, symptoms which have a fairly well defined meaning to mental health professionals. The specific symptoms were selected after a review of the literature on child development and after extensive discussions with pediatricians, psychoanalysts, psychiatrists, psychologists, and social workers. Although other symptoms could undoubtedly be selected in lieu of or in addition to those specified, it is felt that these criteria afford a viable operational definition of emotional damage without providing an open-ended basis for intervention. The application of the standard will entail heavy reliance on mental health professionals. It is hoped that such testimony will take into account developmental and cultural differences in children, as well as the appropriateness of any behavior to the child's environment. For example, a child in an inadequate school or dangerous neighborhood might be quite appropriately anxious, depressed, or even hostile.

. . .

The standard limits intervention to situations where the child is actually evidencing the symptoms. Intervention may not be premised on the prediction of harm. Without actual damage it is extremely difficult both to predict the likely future development of the child and to assess the impact of intervention. Moreover, given the limited resources available to help those children suffering emotional damage whose parents request help, it is extremely unwise to permit intervention where the damage is speculative and the services probably unavailable.

. . .

D. [Coercive intervention should be authorized when] a child has been sexually abused by his/her parent or a member of his/her household (alternative: a child has been sexually abused by his/her parent or a member of his/her household, and is seriously harmed physically or emotionally thereby);

Commentary

Perhaps the most universally condemned behavior of a parent or other family or household member toward a child involves sexual conduct with the child. Thus it may seem apparent that "sexual abuse" clearly ought to be a basis for intervention.

Yet, the available studies come to diverse findings regarding the negative impact of sexual "abuse." See, e.g., Y. Tormes, Child Victims of Incest 7–8 (1968); V. De Francis, Protecting the Child Victim of Sex Crimes Committed by Adults (1969). While some studies find significant harm, see J. Benward and J. Densen-Gerber, Incest as a Causative Factor in Anti-Social Behavior: An Exploratory Study (1975), other commentators concluded that the children studied suffered no significant short or long-term negative effects. See S. Weinberg, Incest Behavior 75, 147–153 (1955); Bender and Blau, "The Reaction of Children to Sexual Relations With Adults," 7 Am.J. Orthopsych. 500 (1937); Yorukoglu and Kemph, "Children Not Severely Damaged by Incest With a Parent," 5 J.Am.Acad.Child Psych. 3 (1966). Moreover, the process of intervention may be more disturbing to the child than the sexual activity. Even the limited public exposure may be traumatic for the child, especially if relatives, friends, or teachers are made aware of the situation. More importantly, the process of proof, requiring repeated interviews of, and possible court testimony by, the child can create great anxiety or other emotional harm. Finally, there is little evidence of the efficacy of treatment programs following intervention which might justify the added trauma. Neither is there evidence that the activity, once discovered, will be continued.

While these factors militate against including sexual abuse among the harms justifying intervention *unless* there is evidence of emotional damage (see alternative), there are several considerations unique to sexual abuse cases that support the broader basis for intervention adopted by these standards. First, according to several studies, sexual abuse is usually only one of several negative factors operative in families where this conduct occurs. The studies report that the father often has physically beaten the children or created an atmosphere of terror in the house. See Y. Tormes, supra at 27–31; S. Weinberg, supra at 55–171. Even though the home situation might not justify intervention if there were no sexual abuse, the added problems caused by the charges of sexual abuse might justify singling out these families for special attention.

Second, while the behavior may have been condoned by both parents and acquiesced in by the child prior to the time it became public knowledge, the fact that the sexual conduct has been reported undoubtedly drastically alters the family situation. The child is now likely to feel guilt or shame. Therefore, it may be essential to intervene in order to assess the impact of the discovery on the child and to insure that the conduct is discontinued.

Finally, sexual abuse cases involve a factor not generally prevalent in neglect situations: the likelihood of a criminal prosecution against the parent. While most criminal child neglect statutes cover conduct other than sexual abuse, the little available evidence indicates that criminal charges are most frequently brought in sexual abuse cases. Criminal proceedings can be extremely harmful to the child. The child must undergo the trauma of interviews and testifying. In many cases additional pressure is created by the parents who encourage the child not to cooperate with the prosecuting authorities.

Moreover, criminal prosecution often results in the father's imprisonment. Splitting up the family and imprisoning the father may add to the child's problems. Meaningful treatment for the child may require treatment of the entire family. In addition, the child may suffer guilt feelings over the parent's imprisonment.

While endangerment proceedings may necessitate questioning the child both in and out of court, the chances are greater that the negative effects can be avoided or minimized in a juvenile court hearing. . . . [T]he juvenile court is concerned solely with the wellbeing of the child and open to a greater range of dispositions than the criminal court. These proceedings will likely be less punitive and more treatment oriented than criminal proceedings.

Therefore, criminal proceedings should be utilized sparingly, if at all. See Part IX infra.* But this requires having available endangerment proceedings through which the child can be protected. For this reason, as well as those previously noted, coercive intervention should be permissible when a parent or other family member or member of the household in which the child lives has "sexually abused" the child.

The standard does not define "sexual abuse." It is intended that intervention be authorized where the subject action would be a violation of the relevant state penal law (or would have been a violation if the laws are repealed). As a factual matter, it may be difficult to distinguish between appropriate displays of affection and fondling or

---

* Standard 9.1 provides:

Criminal prosecution for conduct that is the subject of a petition for court jurisdiction filed pursuant to these standards should be authorized only if the court in which such petition has been filed certifies that such prosecution will not unduly harm the interests of the child named in the petition.—Ed.

other behavior possibly disturbing or damaging to the child. Although relying on penal laws may, in some cases, result in definitional vagueness, it should suffice since only the most severe types of behavior are ordinarily reported.

. . .

[§ 2.1E concerns parental refusal to provide medical care. Also omitted is § 2.1F, which permits intervention when a child is committing delinquent acts as a result of parental encouragement, guidance or approval.]

2.2 Need for intervention in specific case

The fact that a child is endangered in a manner specified in Standard 2.1 A.–F. should be a necessary but not sufficient condition for a court to intervene. In order to assume jurisdiction, a court should also have to find that intervention is necessary to protect the child from being endangered in the future. This decision should be made in accordance with the standards proposed in Part VI.

. . .

PART VI: DISPOSITIONS

6.1 Proceeding to determine disposition of granted petition

If the trier of fact determines that a child is endangered, the court should, as soon as practicable thereafter, convene a hearing to determine the disposition of the petition. If the child is in emergency temporary custody, the court should be required to convene this hearing no later than [two] working days following the finding that the child comes within one of the statutory grounds. However, in such cases the court may grant motions made on behalf of the child, parents, or other persons named in the petition, to conduct such proceedings no later than [six] working days from the granting of the petition. All parties to the proceeding should be able to participate in this hearing, and all matters relevant to the court's determination should be presented in evidence at the hearing.

6.2 Dispositional reports

In deciding the appropriate disposition, the court should have available and should consider a dispositional report, prepared by the investigating agency. The report should contain at a minimum the information elaborated in Standard 5.2 F.

6.3 Available dispositions

A.   A court should have at least the following dispositional alternatives and resources:

1.   dismissal of the case;

2.   wardship with informal supervision;

3.   ordering the parents to accept social work supervision;

4.   ordering the parents and/or the child to accept individual or family therapy or medical treatment;

5.   placement of a homemaker in the home;

6.   placement of the child in a day care program;

7.   placement of the child with a relative, in a foster family or group home, or in a residential treatment center.

B.   A court should have authority to order that the parent accept, and that the state provide, any of the above services.

6.4 Standards for choosing a disposition

A.   General goal.

The goal of all dispositions should be to protect the child from the harm justifying intervention.

B.   Dispositions other than removal of the child.

In ordering a disposition other than removal of the child from his/her home, the court should choose a program designed to alleviate the immediate danger to the child, to mitigate or cure any damage the child has already suffered, and to aid the parents so that the child will not be endangered in the future. In selecting a program, the court should choose those services which least interfere with family autonomy, provided that the services are adequate to protect the child.

[The Standards for Removal are at p. 848 infra.]

NOTE

The Juvenile Justice Standards Relating to Abuse and Neglect were not among the volumes approved by the A.B.A. House of Delegates.* This serves as some indication of the degree of contemporary disagreement over the circumstances in which state intervention should be undertaken to ensure adequate parenting. As the drafters of the initial volume of Standards Relating to Abuse and Neglect made clear, their approach represented a new definition of the grounds for intervention. Indeed the terms "neglect," "abuse," and "dependency" were eliminated and a new term, "endangering," was introduced to replace them.

* A Revised Edition of the Standards Relating to Abuse and Neglect has been published. It carries the designation "Recommended by the IJA–ABA Joint Commission on Juvenile Justice Standards". References in this book are to the original version, known as the 1977 Tentative Draft.

M. WALD, STATE INTERVENTION ON BEHALF OF "NEGLECTED" CHILDREN: A SEARCH FOR REALISTIC STANDARDS

27 Stan.L.Rev. 985, 1021-24 (1975).*

. . .

4. *Inadequate parenting*

While no empirical studies provide a statistical breakdown of the reasons for intervention in neglect cases, probably the largest category of cases involves persons thought to be "inadequate parents." All commentators agree that the great majority of neglect cases involve very poor families who are usually receiving welfare. Most of the parents are not merely poor, however. In addition to the problems directly caused by poverty—poor housing, inadequate medical care, poor nutritional practices—many of these parents can best be described as extremely "marginal" people, that is, they are continually at the borderline of being able to sustain themselves—economically, emotionally, and mentally.

Their plight is reflected in their home situations. Their homes are often dirty and run-down. Feeding arrangements are haphazard. One or both parents may have a drinking or drug problem, suffer from mental illness, or be retarded, which may affect the quality of their child care. If there are two parents, constant bickering and fighting may occur, or the husband may periodically disappear. Often the children's lives are marked by uncertainty and chaos.

Such parents may provide little emotional support for their children. While the children may not be physically abused, left unattended, dangerously malnourished, or overtly rejected, they may receive little love, attention, stimulation, or emotional involvement. The children do not usually evidence emotional damage as serious as that previously discussed. However, they may be relatively listless and may perform poorly in school and in social relations.

It is certainly very tempting to intervene to help such children. Intervention might be justified both to protect the children by providing them with an environment in which they can better reach their potential and to protect the state, since it is claimed that such children will probably end up as delinquents, criminals, or welfare recipients. Without intervention, we may be perpetuating a "culture of poverty." [192]

192. This term became popular in the 1960's, although the nature of the "culture" and the means of its transmission have not been proven. See C. Chilman, Growing Up Poor (1966).

There is some evidence that neglect perpetuates itself. Rein found that 21% of reported neglecting parents had been neglected children known to child-welfare agencies. M. Rein, Child Protective Services in Massachusetts: An Analysis of the Network of Community Agencies 100–01 (1963). . . .

Since neglect and poverty are closely related, it is possible that these figures merely show that many children who

Despite the appeal of these arguments, parental "inadequacy" in and of itself should not be a basis for intervention, other than the offer of services available on a *truly* voluntary basis.[193] The term "inadequate home" or "inadequate parent" is even harder to define than emotional neglect. There is certainly no consensus about what types of "inadequate" behavior would justify intervention. Given the vagueness of the standard, almost unlimited intervention would be possible.

In addition, we cannot predict the consequences for a child of growing up in a home environment that lacks affection or stimulation,[195] or with a parent who suffers from alcoholism, drug addiction, mental illness, or retardation. As White states:

> [G]iven the tenuous evidence showing a causal relationship between home environment and social class on the one hand and retarded child development on the other, it would seem ill-advised

grow up in poverty remain poor as adults and cannot provide adequately for their children. Since poverty itself may often force a family to seek protective services, e.g., when the mother becomes ill and no one can care for the children, it is not clear what these figures prove.

There is evidence, however, that inadequate homes may contribute to poor physical and emotional development of children. See H. Birch & J. Gussow, Disadvantaged Children: Health, Nutrition and School Failure ch. II (1970); . . .

193. These services could be provided by a child-protective service agency. Such agencies not only respond to requests for help but also seek out families who may need help. See G. Penner & H. Welch, The Protective Services Center (1968). An active program to encourage parents of high-risk children, e.g., children whose parents are addicts, alcoholics, retarded, or who have had a history of mental illness, to utilize such services may be appropriate, although the substantial possibility of coercion and the temptation by agencies to overreach requires control. See notes 124–25 supra and accompanying text. Some type of "legalization" of protective services is needed in order to protect parents.

It is also important to recognize that intervention may take place if, as a result of "inadequate parenting," a child comes under one of the categories that would justify intervention. For example, a dirty, rundown house or haphazard feeding arrangements should not ordinarily lead to coercive intervention. However, if the house conditions or feeding arrangements create a substantial threat that the children will suffer serious injury or disease, intervention would be authorized. While I would not encourage judges to expand "physical danger" as a means of avoiding the limitations imposed by the proposed guidelines, it seems to me highly unlikely that a judge would not authorize intervention if she felt the child were seriously endangered. Statutes can place general constraints on judges, but in my experience juvenile court judges often find ways to do what they really want to do, regardless of the statute.

195. This is not to imply that the lack of affection or stimulation is irrelevant. A substantial body of theory and a growing body of data support the idea that both affection and stimulation are very important to normal child development. See, e.g., [J. Goldstein, A. Freud & A. Solnit, Beyond the Best Interests of the Child (1973)] at 6; Ainsworth, Reversible and Irreversible Effects of Maternal Deprivation on Intellectual Development, in Maternal Deprivation 42 (Child Welfare League 1962); Bronfenbrenner, [Is Early Intervention Effective, in 2 A Report on Longitudinal Evaluations of Preschool Programs I (HEW Monograph No. (OHD) 74–25, 1974)] at 1–2.

Yet, even Anna Freud, who has done as much work as anyone to demonstrate the importance of affection and stimulation, warns us to be cautious in making predictions. See Freud, [Child Observation and Prediction of Development, 13 Psychoanalytic Study of the Child 92, 97–98 (1958)].

for public policy to be based on either home environment or social class.[197]

In fact, by focusing solely on parental behavior, child-care workers often ignore the many strengths a given child may be deriving from his environment. As I have stressed, the complexity of the process by which a child relates to any environment defies any attempt to draft laws solely in terms of environmental influences.

Moreover, there is every reason to be extremely pessimistic about the utility of coercive intervention. The services necessary to help these families are generally unavailable. More day-care centers, homemakers, health facilities, and job training programs would all be needed if intervention were to mean anything more than periodic visits by a social worker. Such visits themselves are costly, have not been shown to be effective, and may be resented by the parent who will blame the child for the outside meddling.

Even when "inadequate" parents seek help, agencies often lack the resources or ability to alleviate undesirable home conditions. The chances of success are even lower when the family resists intervention. Few communities have sufficient personnel and programs to permit meaningful intervention, even in cases involving physical abuse or severe emotional damage. It is highly questionable whether limited resources ought to be expended on families with less severe problems, unless the families request services or accept them voluntarily.

Furthermore, when parents do not respond to the "treater," the next step is to remove the children. Yet there is no evidence demonstrating that children from such families are helped through placement.

In an ideal world, children would not be brought up in "inadequate" homes. However, our less than ideal society lacks the ability to provide better alternatives for these children. The best we can do is to expand the social welfare services now offered families on a voluntary basis.

.   .   .

197. 1 S. White, [Federal Programs for Young Children: Review and Recommendations (1973)] at 74.

SUGGESTIONS FOR SOME PROVISIONS OF A CHILD PLACEMENT CODE

J. Goldstein, A. Freud, and A. Solnit, Before the Best Interests
of the Child, at 187–196 (1979).*

ARTICLE 10. DEFINITIONS †

Para. 10.1 Gender

When referring to any person, "he," "his," and "him" may also be
read as "she," "her," and "hers."

Para. 10.2 Child

A Child is a person who, because he is less than 18 years of age
(or some other age established by the legislature), is presumed, in
law, to be dependent and incapable of making decisions for himself.

Para. 10.3 Adult

An Adult is a person who, because he is 18 years or older (or some
other age established by the legislature), is presumed, in law, to be
independent and capable of making decisions for himself.**

Para. 10.4 Parent

Parents are Adults who have the right and responsibility, in law,
to make decisions for their Child. Persons become the Parents of a
Child by

   a. Initial assignment at the birth of their Child; or

   b. Court decree following the request of either or both separating
      Parents; or

   c. Adoption; or

   d. Being designated Foster Parents with Tenure.

Para. 10.5 Longtime caretaker

A Longtime Caretaker is an Adult with whom a Child has been
placed and who has continuously cared for this Child for

   a. A period of 1 or more years if the Child was less than 3 years
      old at the time of placement; *or*

* Reprinted with permission of Macmillan Publishing Co., Inc. from Before the Best Interests of the Child, by Joseph Goldstein, Anna Freud, Albert J. Solnit. Copyright (c) 1979 by The Free Press, a Division of Macmillan Publishing Co., Inc.

† The authors point out that "Words and phrases defined in Article 10 of this code and in the Hampstead-Haven Code [see p. 671, supra] appear in initial capitals throughout these provisions."

** Nonadults who produce a child may become emancipated and treated as Adults in law so long as they remain responsible for the care of their child.

   b. A period of 2 or more years if the Child was 3 years old or older at the time of placement.

Longtime Caretakers are presumed to be Parents.

Para. 10.6 Parental Autonomy

Parental Autonomy is the right of Parents to raise their Children as they think best, in accordance with their own notions of child rearing. The Child's physical and mental development, including the development of mutual attachments between Parent and Child, requires family privacy, free from outside control or coercive intervention by the state.

Para. 10.7 Family Integrity

Family Integrity incorporates the Parents' right to Autonomy, a Child's right to Autonomous Parents, and family privacy.

Para. 10.8 Least Detrimental Available Alternative

The Least Detrimental Available Alternative is that Child Placement and procedure for Child Placement which maximizes, in accord with the Child's Sense of Time, the Child's opportunity for being wanted and for maintaining on a continuous, unconditional, and permanent basis a relationship with at least one Adult who is or will become the Child's Psychological Parent.

Para. 10.9 Temporary Foster Care Placement

A Temporary Foster Care Placement occurs when, with the consent of his Parents, or, in the absence of their consent after a full hearing, a Child is placed under the temporary care of Adults who are not his Parents. The goal of Temporary Foster Care is to maintain the Child's ties to his Parents and to assure their reunion as quickly as possible. Foster Care Placement ceases to be Temporary when the Child's Foster Parents become his Longtime Caretakers.

Para. 10.10 Emergency Placement

An Emergency Placement occurs when, because a Child is reasonably believed to be threatened with imminent risk of death or serious bodily harm, the state is authorized to place him under care and custody pending a hearing to determine whether there is a Ground for Intervention.

Para. 10.11 Permanent Placement

A Permanent Placement is any Placement of a Child that is neither a Temporary Foster Care Placement nor an Emergency Placement. Assignments by birth certificate, by custody decree, by adoption, and by the acquisition of Longtime Caretaker are Permanent Placements. Permanent Placements insulate Adult and Child from intrusion by former Parents or by the state except as authorized by a Ground for Intervention.

Para. 10.12   Foster Care With Tenure

Foster Care with Tenure is the Permanent Placement of a Child with Adults who wish to care for him but who cannot or choose not to adopt him.

Para. 10.13   Ground for Intervention

A Ground for Intervention defines circumstances under which the state is authorized to investigate and/or to modify or terminate the legal relationship between a Child and his Parents.

The goal of intervention is to maintain, reestablish, or establish for the Child a Permanent Placement in a family with Autonomous Parents.

Para. 10.14   Violation of Family Integrity

A Violation of Family Integrity occurs when the state coercively intrudes between Parent and Child except as authorized by a Ground for Intervention.

Para. 10.15   Child Abuse by the State

Child Abuse by the State occurs when there has been a Violation of Family Integrity or when an agent of the state returns a Child to his Parent after an Adjudication that serious bodily injury was inflicted on him by that Parent.

ARTICLE 20.   STAGES OF INTERVENTION

Para. 20.1   Invocation

The Child Placement process may be invoked by

a. The state's investigating a particular Child's circumstances, but only if it has a reasonable basis for believing that a Ground for Intervention might exist.

b. The state's charging a Ground for Intervention if it has probable cause for believing that a Ground for Intervention can be established *and* that a less detrimental alternative can be provided for the Child.

c. A Parent's request for the court to make a Disposition. Such a request eliminates the need for an Adjudication.

Para. 20.2   Adjudication

Following a charge of a Ground for Intervention, the court shall provide Parents with an opportunity to be heard both on their own behalf and as representatives of the Child. The court shall determine whether the state has established a Ground for Intervention. If no Ground for Intervention has been established, the court shall dismiss the action.

Para. 20.3 Disposition

Following an Adjudication that a Ground for Intervention exists, or following a request by a Parent for a Disposition, the court may appoint independent counsel for the Child, and all the parties shall have the opportunity to be heard as to which Disposition they believe to be in the Child's best interest. The court shall order the Least Detrimental Available Placement.

Para. 20.4 Degree of Intervention

The degree of coercive intrusion on Family Integrity at Invocation, Adjudication, and Disposition shall be no greater than necessary. Investigations, hearings, trials and appeals shall be conducted as rapidly as is consistent with responsible decision-making and in accord with the specific Child's Sense of Time.

ARTICLE 30. GROUNDS FOR INTERVENTION

The Grounds for Intervention are:

Para. 30.1 Refusal of Parents to comply with generally applicable immunization, education, and labor laws so far as they apply to their Children.

Para. 30.2 Commission by a Child of an offense which would be criminal if committed by an Adult.

Para. 30.3 The request by either or both separating Parents (whether married to each other or not) for the court to determine custody. The court is authorized to determine the Disposition only of those Children about whose custody their Parents do not agree.

Para. 30.4 The request by a Parent for the court to terminate that Parent's legal relationship to his Child. If only one of two Parents petitions for a termination of rights, the Child's custody shall automatically remain with the other Parent.

Para. 30.5 The death or absence of both Parents or the only Parent, when coupled with their failure to make provision for their Child's custody and care.

Para. 30.6 A Parent's conviction, or acquittal by reason of insanity, of a sexual offense against his Child.

Para. 30.7 Serious bodily injury inflicted by Parents upon their Child, or an attempt to inflict such injury, or the repeated failure of Parents to prevent their Child from suffering such injury.

Para. 30.8 The refusal by Parents to authorize medical care for their Child when

    a. Medical experts agree that treatment is nonexperimental and appropriate for the Child; *and*

    b. Denial of that treatment will result in the Child's death; *and*

    c. The treatment can reasonably be expected to result in a chance for the Child to have normal healthy growth or a life worth living.

Para. 30.9 The request by a Child's Longtime Caretakers to become his Parents, or their refusal to relinquish him to his Parents or to a state agency. If it is established that there are Longtime Caretakers who request to become a Child's Parents or refuse to relinquish him to his Parents or to a state agency, the Longtime Caretakers shall, except as provided below, be designated as adoptive Parents, or, if they are unwilling or unable to adopt, as Foster Parents with Tenure.

Such Dispositions shall be automatic unless qualified absent Parents demand a Disposition hearing. Absent Parents are qualified to demand such a hearing only if

    a. The Child was over 5 years old at the time of Placement with the Longtime Caretakers and had been in the continuous care and control of his Parents for not less than the 3 preceding years; *and*

    b. The child had not been separated from the absent Parents because they inflicted or attempted to inflict serious bodily injury upon him or were convicted, or acquitted by reason of insanity, of a sexual offense against him.

At such a hearing the court shall determine whether the absent Parents are still Psychological Parents of the Child, and whether his return to them would provide the least detrimental alternative. If so, the Child shall be returned to them. If not, the Longtime Caretakers shall be designated as his adoptive Parents or as Foster Parents with Tenure.

Para. 30.10 The establishment of any of the above Grounds for modifying or terminating Parent-Child relationships, or an Emergency Placement pending Adjudication, or a request by Parents who are unable to obtain legal assistance for their Child authorizes court appointment of counsel to represent the Child's interests.*

---

* The authors explain that this provision, coupled with Para. 20.3, is meant to replace Para. 30.4 of the Hampstead-Haven Code, supra at p. 673.

ARTICLE 40. ACCOUNTABILITY

Para. 40.0 Immunity from Liability

Governmental immunity is not a defense to a charge that an agent of the state has violated Family Integrity or has committed Child Abuse.

NOTE

The provisions above are designed as additions or amendments to the Child Placement Code of Hampstead-Haven, published in the earlier work by the same distinguished authors, Beyond the Best Interests of the Child (1973). References to terms such as Psychological Parent (Paras. 10.8, 30.9), and Child's Sense of Time (Para. 20.4) are developed and explained in the prior book. The entire text to which it is published as an Appendix, J. Goldstein, A. Freud, and A. Solnit, Before the Best Interests of the Child (1979) serves as a commentary to the suggested provisions.

The Child Placement Code of Hampstead-Haven appears at p. 671, supra.

M. WALD, THINKING ABOUT PUBLIC POLICY TOWARD ABUSE AND NEGLECT OF CHILDREN: A REVIEW OF BEFORE THE BEST INTERESTS OF THE CHILD

78 Mich.L.Rev. 645, 665–670 (1980).*

. . .

1. *The Validity of the Psychological Premises*

The authors' theories about the psychological needs of children form the core of this book. From these theories, they develop their claims about the harm of intervention and the limited benefit of coercive treatment. The book's central developmental premise is that children need a continuous relationship with an adult who is their "psychological parent" and that the damage to the child in disrupting this relationship, either through removal or the imposition of state supervision of the family, is likely to be greater than any harm a child may suffer other than severe physical injury, criminal sexual acts by the parent, and death.

Thus, to take a few examples of harm from some cases with which I am currently involved, GFS believe that it would be too risky to intervene in the following cases:

(a) Where a child has been physically disciplined by a parent using a paddle in a manner sufficient to leave bruise marks and to cause the child pain in walking, but where it cannot be shown that the parent was attempting to cause more severe injuries.

* Copyright 1980, Michael S. Wald.
Reprinted with permission.

(b) Where a child is locked in a room every day (chained to a bed to make it more gruesome) and not allowed contact with any people, including the parents, but the child is fed and not severely beaten.

(c) Where a parent, due to mental illness, leaves young children unattended, with minimal food or clothing, in a home that has broken glass and exposed wires, but the children have not suffered repeated serious physical injuries.

(d) Where two preteen children are afraid to live at home because their mother believes that they are about to be kidnapped and, in order to prevent the kidnapping, she never allows them to leave the house.

(e) Where a young boy is frequently absent from school, and when he attends school he sits alone in the corner because the parent makes him wear dresses.

(f) Where a mother allows a young child to have sexual relations with the mother's boyfriend.

Admittedly, each of these cases is unique and unusual. Yet each represents a type of harm to children, physical and emotional, that occurs quite frequently and which, I believe, would not be covered by the proposed standards. Additional illustrations could easily be given of harms not covered by the proposed standards. GFS would not permit intervention in these cases, because they believe that the harm of intervention is likely to be greater than the harm being imposed by the parent. To evaluate this proposition, one must carefully analyze the harms they see from intervention.

In essence, their views rest on the assertion that state intervention disrupts the parent-child relationship and that such disruption always harms the child, since it threatens parental autonomy and deprives the child of continuity. The central issue therefore is whether the harm from such disruptions is greater than the harm from inadequate parental care, such as was described in the examples above. In addition, it must be determined whether intervention offers benefits that may outweigh the harms.

Although the whole question of the importance of a child's attachment to a single individual is open to some debate,[49] no expert in child development disputes the importance of some continuous attachment. However, despite the acknowledged importance of continuity, there is no evidence supporting the claim that children need continuity above all else. GFS recognize this, to a degree. They are willing to risk discontinuity if the child is severely beaten, sexually abused or about to die due to lack of medical care. The critical question is whether these are the only harms that justify disrupting parental autonomy or

---

49. GFS often seem to argue that the relationship must be with a single adult, or if to more than one adult, the adults must not be hostile to each other or competing for the child's loyalty. This is part of their reason for recommending that a custodial parent have the right to exclude visits by the noncustodial parent following a divorce. See BEYOND [THE BEST INTERESTS OF THE CHILD] at 38. This view has been challenged by many critics . . . ..

depriving the child of a continuous relationship. GFS assume that they are. This assumption requires careful scrutiny.

In focusing solely on continuity, the authors seem to ignore many other things that developmental psychology teaches us about children's needs. For example, many studies demonstrate a child's need for nurturance, cognitive stimulation, limits, adequate nutrition, and basic medical care. While the exact level of such needs is subject to debate, there is little doubt that if parental care falls below certain minimums in meeting these needs, a child's physical, social, emotional, and intellectual development is jeopardized. If we allow intervention to protect children from emotional abuse, less serious physical abuse and lack of medical care, are we likely to do more harm than good? In order to test the validity of GFS's assumption, it is necessary to distinguish intervention leading to removal of the child from intervention leading to supervision of the family. Although GFS equate these two types of intervention, it seems highly unlikely that supervision of the family carries the same risk as removal.

The strongest case for GFS's assertions is when the child is removed from the home. All of the evidence on the need for continuity comes from studies of children separated from their parents. Separation obviously involves the greatest discontinuity for the child. It also subjects children to the possibility of multiple placements or placement in environments no better than their own homes.

However, in the case of abused and neglected children, the evidence is not clear that children fare worse in foster care than at home. Several years ago in reviewing the literature on foster care, I concluded,

> The evidence [on the harm of foster care] is not all one-sided, however. Several studies have found that children who grew up in foster homes have a similar incidence of criminality, mental illness, and marital success as the general population. Thus any harms from foster placement may not have long-term consequences, at least in these respects. Moreover, one recent study of over 500 neglected children found significant improvement in the children's well-being with respect to their physical health, behavior control, ability to cope in school, and peer relations following foster home placement. In addition, clinical reports provide evidence that some children want to remain in placement rather than return home.

> The critical problem with such studies is that they do not tell us how these children would have fared had they been left in their own homes, especially if their parents were provided social services. On the other hand, we do not know whether some of the negative impact of foster care could be mitigated if children were better prepared for placement, if better foster homes were availa-

ble, and if parents were given a more active role in helping the child adjust to placement.[53]

Although I am aware of no further evidence on this issue, several recent research projects have demonstrated that abuse and neglect not as severe as that required by GFS can severely handicap the physical health and social development of children.

Therefore, it is difficult to determine the costs and benefits of intervention in cases of "lesser" physical abuse or "emotional neglect," *even if the intervention leads to removal.* While the substantial evidence on the negative effects of foster care and the intuitive attractiveness of GFS's psychological theories regarding the child's need for continuity should make one cautious in supporting any policies allowing removal, I do not find that they have made a convincing *psychological* case that removal should be limited as strictly as their proposed standards would require.

Whatever the strength of GFS's psychological premises regarding continuity, I seriously question the validity of their propositions regarding the effects of intervention that does not entail removal. It is a great leap from the theory that a continuous psychological relationship is important to a child to the propositions that such a relationship can be maintained only if the parents are totally autonomous and that the costs from imposing state supervision on parents in order to keep them from acting inadequately are likely to be greater than the benefits of such intrusions.

To bridge this gap, the authors assert, "Children, on their part, react even to temporary infringement of parental autonomy with anxiety, diminishing trust, loosening of emotional ties, or an increasing tendency to be out of control" (p. 25). They state further that "[w]hen family integrity is broken or weakened by state intrusion, [the child's] needs are thwarted and this belief that his parents are omniscient and all-powerful is shaken prematurely. The effect on the child's developmental progress is invariably detrimental" (p. 9).

I am not aware of any data supporting these assertions. Moreover, they seem intuitively incorrect. Although children rely heavily upon their parents and need to trust them, only very young children are likely to see their parents as omnipotent. Older children, who spend hours in school with teachers and peers, and still more hours in front of the television, certainly live in a world where parental values and views are challenged. Children learn that parental authority is limited by the school, by employers and by the state. There is no reason to believe that the impact of this knowledge is "invariably detrimental."

53. Wald II, [State Intervention on Behalf of Neglected Children: Standards for Removal of Children From Their Homes, Monitoring the Status of Children in Foster Care, and Termination of Parental Rights, 28 Stan.L.Rev. 623 (1976)] at 646–47.

Yet on the basis of this claim the authors equate coercive intervention subjecting the family to state supervision with coercive intervention in which the child is removed. In fact, they believe that just an investigation creates the same risk. As a result, they draw extremely narrow standards for intervention to respect the need for autonomy. Although the authors support home supervision or foster care aimed toward quick reunion in some cases, they advocate that in most instances intervention occur only where it will lead to termination of parental rights.

. . .

D. ABUSE: THE BATTERED CHILD PHENOMENON AND SOME INSIDIOUS VARIATIONS

STATE v. WILKERSON

Supreme Court of North Carolina, 1978.
295 N.C. 559, 247 S.E.2d 905.

EXUM, JUSTICE.

The homicide victim in this tragic affair was Kessler Wilkerson, the two-year-old son of defendant and his wife, Nancy. The state's evidence tended to show, and the jury apparently believed, that the child's death was the result of physical abuse inflicted upon him by his father. On his appeal defendant contends the trial court erred in (1) admitting into evidence expert medical opinion having to do with the "battered child" syndrome; (2) permitting cross-examination of defendant's mother as to acts of misconduct earlier committed by defendant; and (3) improperly instructing the jury, principally by failing properly to define the crimes of second degree murder, voluntary manslaughter and involuntary manslaughter. With regard to the first contention, we find no error. We agree with defendant that the cross-examination of his mother was improper; but we also conclude under the circumstances that no prejudice resulted. As to the third contention the error committed was favorable to defendant.

The state's evidence, in summary, is as follows: On 16 October 1976 around 10:30 a. m., neighbors heard loud sounds "like something was being thrown inside the trailer" coming from the Wilkersons' mobile home, the voice of a little boy crying, and defendant shouting at him to shut up. Mrs. Wilkerson appeared at the door of the trailer, said, "Hurry up, Kenny, hurry up," and slammed the door closed. Pursuant to a call an ambulance arrived at the Wilkerson trailer at 12:42 p. m. Defendant delivered the child's limp body to ambulance attendants and told them he had choked on some cereal, swallowed some water, and stopped breathing. Cardiopulmonary resuscitation was applied unsuccessfully en route to the hospital. The child was dead on arrival there. The emergency room physician who examined the child found no fluid in his lungs or other signs of drowning.

Bruises were present on his chest, shoulders, upper arm and forearm. Upon being informed that his son was dead, defendant appeared "quite calm and told his wife something to the effect that it's done, it's over, there's nothing we can do about it now." An autopsy revealed, externally, multiple bruises all over the child's body and, internally, significant bleeding and a deep laceration of the liver. Cause of death was abdominal hemorrhage from a ruptured liver.

Other evidence for the state, consisting of defendant's pre-trial statement made to investigating officers and the testimony of other witnesses who had observed defendant in his relationship with his son, tended to show the kind of disciplinary methods defendant customarily used with the child. According to this evidence defendant frequently kicked the child and on occasion made him stand "spread eagle" against a wall for long periods of time. One such occasion was 14 October 1976, two days before the boy died. Defendant at that time kicked him with such force that his chest hit the wall. One witness testified that defendant had said the little boy had no manners and that he was determined to teach him some manners and bring him up to be a man the way that "his [defendant's] mother has raised him, that his mother put him through hell." When asked why he wanted to repeat his mother's treatment, defendant "said that he didn't really approve of it or like it but it made him a man, and that's the way his son was going to be."

Defendant testified that his relationship with his son had been close. Although admitting disciplining his son and occasionally spanking him with a belt, defendant denied ever hitting or kicking him. He also denied that he was punished excessively as a child or that he ever talked with state's witnesses about his childhood. He said that on the morning of October 16 the child had wet himself on the floor. Defendant spanked him with his wife's belt and then ran some water in a tub and made him get in whereupon the child began "gasping for air and choking." Defendant searched his throat for possible obstructions, patted him on his back, and applied mouth-to-mouth resuscitation, all without any success. On cross-examination defendant admitted spanking his son on 16 October "hard enough to make him cry as long as I beat him."

Several witnesses testified that the relationship between defendant and his son was good and that they had never seen defendant abuse the child in any way. Defendant's mother testified that defendant treated his younger brothers and sisters in a kind manner while growing up in Philadelphia and that she had never beaten defendant severely or seen him abuse any child.

Defendant first assigns as error the testimony of two medical witnesses—Dr. Casey John Jason, a pediatrician who first examined the child at the emergency room of Womack Army Hospital, and Dr. John Edward Grauerholz, who performed the autopsy. Specifically, defendant complains of Dr. Jason's testimony that the bruises he ob-

served on the child were not "the typical bruising pattern that is normally sustained by chidren in [their] normal day-to-day life." Defendant likewise complains of the testimony of Dr. Grauerholz, a
pathologist, who after describing at some length his findings on autopsy testified in part as follows:

"DR. GRAUERHOLZ: All right, I made a diagnosis.

MR. GREGORY: And what was that diagnosis, Doctor?

MR. DOWNING: Object.

COURT: Overruled.

DR. GRAUERHOLZ: Battered child.

MR. DOWNING: Move to strike.

. . .

MR. GREGORY: Dr. Grauerholz, what do you mean by the
term 'battered child'?

DR. GRAUERHOLZ: I mean a child who died as a result of
multiple injuries of a non-accidental nature.

MR. GREGORY: Can you explain what you mean by 'non-accidental nature'?

DR. GRAUERHOLZ: Yes. That these injuries were inflicted
by someone other then the child upon the child.

MR. DOWNING: Move to strike.

COURT: Denied.

. . .

MR. GREGORY: Is the term 'battered child' a relatively new
term in the field of medicine?

MR. DOWNING: Objection.

COURT: Overruled.

DR. GRAUERHOLZ: It's been around for a while. I think
probably in the last ten years or so it has become very well established.

MR. GREGORY: Dr. Grauerholz, without referring to any particular person, can you describe for us about the battered child?

MR. DOWNING: Objection.

COURT: Overruled. You are seeking an explanation of the
term 'battered child'?

MR. GREGORY. Yes sir.

COURT: Overruled. You may give your explanation, Doctor.

DR. GRAUERHOLZ: These are children who suffer multiple
injuries inflicted by others. The injuries are multiple in terms of
distribution on the body and in time of infliction in certain cases.
They are seen in children who have been perhaps over-zealously
disciplined or have in other ways upset or run afoul of their

guardians or their caretakers or usually some adult who is in relation to the child. By 'relation' I mean physical relation.

MR. DOWNING: Move to strike.

COURT: Denied.

. . .

DR. GRAUERHOLZ: They show essentially such things as abdominal injuries or fractures or other damage that is inconsistent with an accidental origin by virtue of the distribution of the injury. There are certain places where children classically do injure themselves when they fall, they run along and they fall, they bang their knees, they fall on their hands and so forth and these children, however, show injuries in noncharacteristic places, across the back, places where they could not spontaneously fall with sufficient force to produce that sort of injury, deep injuries in the abdomen, again which would necessitate a force being directed to the abdomen. One of the classic findings in a lot of these children are multiple fractures of varying ages. The bruising I observed in the chest area of the child were not bruises characteristic of the everyday life of a child, of being a child from day to day and falling. In my opinion an external striking or compressive force of some sort applied to the abdomen would produce the laceration to the liver.

. . .

MR. GREGORY: My question is, without all the paraphrasing, Your Honor, under what circumstances does the battered child syndrome occur?

COURT: Overruled. You may move to strike. The ruling of the Court does not foreclose you opportunity to move to strike. Go ahead, Doctor.

DR. GRAUERHOLZ: The syndrome usually occurs in a disciplinary situation involving the child and some guardian or custodian, a parent, a relative, a babysitter, someone who has physical custody of the child at that time. The injuries are usually inflicted as a disciplinary measure upon the child.

MR. DOWNING: Move to strike.

COURT: Denied.

. . .

MR. GREGORY: Now when you say in disciplining the child, what are you talking about, Dr. Grauerholz?

MR. DOWNING: Objection.

COURT: Overruled.

. . .

DR. GRAUERHOLZ: I am talking about punishment in the sense that one might spank a child for misbehaving. In that sort of situation. A question of corporal punishment. In these cases the punishment is excessive in its result if not necessarily in its intent."

Defendant contends that to permit Dr. Grauerholz to give an opinion that the child was a victim of the battered child syndrome, to explain what this syndrome means, and "to theorize . . . that the child was killed by a parent, a guardian or caretaker who used more force than was called for in a disciplinary situation" was, in effect, to permit the doctor to testify "as to the ultimate fact of the defendant's guilt or innocence" and therefore was improper. Defendant makes no argument in his brief to support his assignment of error with regard to Dr. Jason's testimony. We conclude that all of this testimony was properly admitted.

Defendant relies on the principle that an expert witness should not express an opinion on the very issue to be decided by the jury and thereby invade the jury's province. As this Court has noted before, this principle "is not inflexible, is subject to many exceptions, and is open to criticism." Patrick v. Treadwell, 222 N.C. 1, 4, 21 S.E.2d 818, 821 (1942), . . . "It is frequently relaxed in the admission of evidence as to ultimate facts in regard to matters of science, art or skill." State v. Powell, 238 N.C. 527, 530, 78 S.E.2d 248, 251 (1953). . . .

. . .

Expert medical opinion has been allowed on a wide range of facts, the existence or non-existence of which is ultimately to be determined by the trier of fact. . . .

We conclude, therefore, that in determining whether expert medical opinion is to be admitted into evidence the inquiry should not be whether it invades the province of the jury, but whether the opinion expressed is really one based on the special expertise of the expert, that is, whether the witness because of his expertise is in a better position to have an opinion on the subject than is the trier of fact. The test is as stated in State v. Powell, supra, 238 N.C. at 530, 78 S.E.2d at 250, whether the "opinion required expert skill or knowledge in the medical or pathologic field about which a person of ordinary experience would not be capable of satisfactory conclusions, unaided by expert information from one learned in the medical profession."

The opinions expressed by the physicians in this case fall well within the bounds of permissible medical expert testimony. The basis for Dr. Jason's opinion, that the bruises on the child's chest did not form the typical bruising pattern normally sustained by children in day to day activities, was given in his earlier testimony in which he said:

"In my work in pediatrics I have had the occasion to work with numerous children. At Johns Hopkins I would say somewhere in the neighborhood of five hundred children total. Many times I have had occasion to observe lesions or bruises about children that have occurred in the normal course of events. A child frequently falls on his knees or bangs what we call the tibial surfaces, the area underneath the knee, and, of course, bangs their elbows, and skin their hands and occasionally even fall and hit their heads and in that case get a bruise similar to the one that Kessler had on the front of his head.

MR. GREGORY: Have you had a chance in your work in pediatrics to observe the chests of children?

DR. JASON: Oh, of course, of course."

Likewise, Dr. Grauerholz' opinion that this child was a "battered child" and his explanation of that term were based on his experience as a physician and a pathologist who had at the time of the trial performed over 150 autopsies, and on the fact that the "battered child" syndrome has been a recognized medical diagnosis for over ten years. . . . Dr. Grauerholz' opinion regarding the usual cause of the syndrome, again, was based on his expertise in the area and his knowledge of the subject as contained in the medical literature.

Contrary to what defendant seems to argue, neither physician testified, nor should he have been permitted to do so, that the battered child syndrome from which this victim suffered was in fact caused by any particular person or class of persons engaging in any particular activity or class of activities. Nowhere in the record did either physician express or purport to express an opinion as to defendant's guilt or innocence. On these kinds of factual questions the physicians would have been in no better position to have an opinion than the jury.

Upholding the admission of similar testimony, the California Court of Appeals in People v. Jackson, 18 Cal.App.3d 504, 507, 95 Cal.Rptr. 919, 921 (1971) said:

"A finding, as in this case, of the 'battered child syndrome' is not an opinion by the doctor as to whether any particular person has done anything, but, as this doctor indicated, 'it would take thousands of children to have the severity and number and degree of injuries that this child had over the span of time that we had' by accidental, means. In other words, the 'battered child syndrome' simply indicates that a child found with the type of injuries outlined above has not suffered those injuries by accidental means. This conclusion is based upon an extensive study of the subject by medical science. The additional finding that the injuries were probably occasioned by someone who is ostensibly caring for the child is simply a conclusion based upon logic and reason. Only someone regularly 'caring' for the child has the continuing opportunity to inflict these types of injuries; an isolated contact with a vicious stranger would not result in this pattern of successive injuries stretching through several months."

As far as our research reveals, all courts which have considered the question, including our own Court of Appeals, have concluded that such expert medical testimony concerning the battered child syndrome as was offered in this case is properly admitted into evidence. State v. Periman, 32 N.C.App. 33, 230 S.E.2d 802 (1977); State v. Loss, 295 Minn. 271, 204 N.W.2d 404 (1973); People v. Henson, 33 N.Y.2d 63, 304 N.E.2d 358 (1973); State v. Best, 232 N.W.2d 447 (S.D. 1975).

The cases relied on by defendant are readily distinguishable. In each of these cases the difficulty was that the medical expert was permitted to testify that a certain event had in fact caused the injuries complained of. The court in each case pointed out that it would have been proper to have asked the expert whether the event could or might have caused the injury, but not whether it in fact did cause it. (There may be questions of cause and effect, however, about which an expert should be permitted to give, if he has one, a positive opinion.) . . .

Defendant's first assignment of error is overruled.

. . .

NOTE

The phenomenon of child abuse was first labeled the "battered child syndrome" by Dr. Henry Kempe and his associates in 1962. C.H. Kempe, F.N. Silverman, B.F. Steele, W. Droegemuller, and H.K. Silver, The Battered-Child Syndrome, 181 J.A.M.A. 17 (1962).* They described their use of the term in order "to characterize a clinical condition in young children who have received serious physical abuse, generally from a parent or foster parent," and explained that:

> The clinical manifestations of the battered-child syndrome vary widely from those cases in which the trauma is very mild and is often unsuspected and unrecognized, to those who exhibit the most florid evidence of injury to the soft tissues and skeleton. In the former group, the patients' signs and symptoms may be considered to have resulted from failure to thrive from some other cause or to have been produced by a metabolic disorder, an infectious process, or some other disturbance. In these patients specific findings of trauma such as bruises or characteristic roentgenographic changes as described below may be misinterpreted and their significance not recognized.

> The battered child syndrome may occur at any age, but, in general, the affected children are younger than 3 years. In some instances the clinical manifestations are limited to those resulting from a single episode of trauma, but more often the child's general health is below par, and he shows evidence of neglect including poor skin hygiene, multiple soft tissue injuries, and malnutrition. One often obtains a history of previous episodes suggestive of parental neglect or trauma. A marked discrepan-

cy between clinical findings and historical data as supplied by the parents is a major diagnostic feature of the battered-child syndrome. The fact that no new lesions either of the soft tissue or of the bone, occur while the child is in the hospital or in a protected environment lends added weight to the diagnosis and tends to exclude many diseases of the skeletal or hemopoietic systems in which lesions may occur spontaneously or after minor trauma. Subdural hematoma, with or without fracture of the skull is in our experience, an extremely frequent finding even in the absence of fractures of the long bones. In an occasional case the parent or parent-substitute may also have assaulted the child by administering an overdose of a drug or by exposing the child to natural gas or other toxic substances. The characteristic distribution of these multiple fractures and the observation that the lesions are in different stages of healing are of additional value in making the diagnosis.

The following year Dr. Vincent Fontana and his associates attempted to persuade physicians and others that the designation "battered child syndrome"—with its vivid connotations of physical violence—was underinclusive, and that there were other kinds of abuse inflicted on children with harmful results. They proposed the more inclusive label "maltreatment syndrome." V.J. Fontana, D. Donovan, and R.J. Wong, The "Maltreatment Syndrome" in Children, 269 N.Eng.J.Med. 1389 (1963). They also noted that this pediatric syndrome had often gone unrecognized, and that there was little information on the subject in medical literature. Since that time there has been a flood of literature as professionals have sought to determine the scope of the problem of child abuse and to determine its etiology. Some of the more important works include R.E. Helfer and C.H. Kempe (Eds.), The Battered Child (3d ed. 1980); V. Fontana and D. Besharov, The Maltreated Child (1979); H.P. Martin (Ed.), The Abused Child (1976); V. Fontana, Somewhere a Child Is Crying (1973); C.H. Kempe and R.E. Helfer (Eds.), Helping the Battered Child and His Family (1972); Kerns, Child Abuse and Neglect: The Pediatrician's Role, J. Contin. Educ. Pediat., Vol. 21, No. 7, p. 14 (1979); Kempe, Sexual Abuse, Another Hidden Pediatric Problem, 62 Pediatrics 382 (1978); Fontana The Maltreated Children of Our Times, 23 Vill.L.Rev. 448 (1978); Schmitt and Kempe, The Pediatrician's Role in Child Abuse and Neglect, Current Probs. Pediat., Vol. 5, No. 5, p. 3 (Mar. 1975). An international journal, Child Abuse and Neglect, is published quarterly.

Dr. Kempe and his colleagues were not the first to recognize the phenomenon of child abuse. Other physicians earlier had called attention to the increasing incidence of nonaccidental injuries to children, particularly trauma to the long bones. The developmental history of efforts to diagnose and publicize the problem is chronicled in McCoid, The Battered Child and Other Assaults Upon the Family: Part One, 50 Minn.L.Rev. 1 (1965). For an account of the legislative response to revelations of the seriousness and substantial incidence of child abuse, see Paulsen, Parker, and Adelman, Child Abuse Reporting Laws: Some Legislative History, 34 Geo.Wash.L.Rev. 482 (1966).

The recent tendency has been to broaden the definition of child abuse as a medical phenomenon, which in turn has resulted in a broadening of its definition in reporting statutes, criminal statutes, juvenile court statutes, and for other purposes under the law.

Numerous legal questions are presented by expansion of the definition of abuse. Under what circumstances should the state be authorized to intervene in the lives and relationships of a family? Are there due process limitations on defining abuse, particularly if it extends to acts other than physical abuse or inadequate parenting? What special problems of proof are encountered in attempting to prove that a parent has abused a child?

FLORIDA STATUTES ANNOTATED

827.07 Abuse or Neglect of children

(1) **Legislative intent.—**

The intent of this section is to provide for comprehensive protective services for abused or neglected children found in the state by requiring that reports of each abused or neglected child be made to the Department of Health and Rehabilitative Services in an effort to prevent further harm to the child or any other children living in the home and preserve the family life of the parents and children, to the maximum extent possible, by enhancing the parental capacity for adequate child care.

(2) **Definitions.—**

As used in this section:

(a) "Child" means any person under the age of 18 years.

(b) "Child abuse or neglect" means harm or threatened harm to a child's physical or mental health or welfare by the acts or omissions of the parent or other person responsible for the child's welfare.

(c) "Abused or neglected child" means a child whose physical or mental health or welfare is harmed, or threatened with harm, by the acts or omissions of the parent or other person responsible for the child's welfare.

(d) "Harm" to a child's health or welfare can occur when the parent or other person responsible for the child's welfare:

1. Inflicts, or allows to be inflicted, upon the child physical or mental injury, including injury sustained as a result of excessive corporal punishment;

2. Commits, or allows to be committed, sexual battery, as defined in chapter 794, against the child;

3. Exploits a child, or allows a child to be exploited, for pornographic purposes as provided in §§ 847.014 and 450.151, or for prostitution;

4. Abandons the child;

5. Fails to provide the child with supervision or guardianship by specific acts or omissions of a serious nature requiring the intervention of the department or the court; or

6. Fails to supply the child with adequate food, clothing, shelter, or health care, although financially able to do so or although offered financial or other means to do so; however, a parent or other person

responsible for the child's welfare beliefs, who by legitimately practicing his religious beliefs, who by reason thereof does not provide specified medical treatment for a child shall not be considered abusive or neglectful for that reason alone, but such an exception shall not:

a.   Eliminate the requirement that such a case be reported to the department;

b.   Prevent the department from investigating such a case; or

c.   Preclude a court from ordering, when the health of the child requires it, the provision of medical services by a physician, as defined herein, or treatment by a duly accredited practitioner who relies solely on spiritual means for healing in accordance with the tenets and practices of a well-recognized church or religious organization.

(e)   "Other person responsible for a child's welfare" includes the child's legal guardian, legal custodian, or foster parent; an employee of a public or private child day care center, residential home, institution, or agency; or any other person legally responsible for the child's welfare in a residential setting.

(f)   "Physical injury" means death, permanent or temporary disfigurement, or impairment of any bodily part.

(g)   "Mental injury" means an injury to the intellectual or psychological capacity of a child as evidenced by a discernible and substantial impairment in his ability to function within his normal range of performance and behavior, with due regard to his culture.

.   .   .

WYOMING STATUTES ANNOTATED

§ 14-3-202.   Definitions

(a)   As used in W.S. 14-3-201 through 14-3-215:

(i)   "A person responsible for a child's welfare" includes the child's parent, guardian, custodian, stepparent, foster parent or other person, institution or agency having the physical custody or control of the child;

(ii)   "Abuse" means inflicting or causing physical or mental injury, harm or imminent danger to the physical or mental health or welfare of a child other than by accidental means, including abandonment, excessive or unreasonable corporal punishment, malnutrition or substantial risk thereof by reason of intentional or unintentional neglect, and the commission or allowing the commission of a sexual offense against a child as defined by law:

(A)   "Mental injury" means an injury to the psychological capacity or emotional stability of a child as evidenced by an observable or substantial impairment in his ability to function within a normal range of performance and behavior with due regard to his culture;

(B) "Physical injury" means death or any harm to a child including but not limited to disfigurement, impairment of any bodily organ, skin bruising, bleeding, burns, fracture of any bone, subdural hematoma or substantial malnutrition;

(C) "Substantial risk" means a strong possibility as contrasted with a remote or insignificant possibility;

(D) "Imminent danger" includes threatened harm and means a statement, overt act, condition or status which represents an immediate and substantial risk of sexual abuse or physical or mental injury.

(iii) "Child" means any person under the age of sixteen (16);

. . .

CALIFORNIA PENAL CODE

§ 11165. Definitions

As used in this article:

(a) "Child" means a person under the age of 18 years.

(b) "Sexual assault" means conduct in violation of the following sections of the Penal Code: Sections 261 (rape), 261.5 (unlawful sexual intercourse), 264.1 (rape in concert), 285 (incest), 286 (sodomy), subdivisions (a) and (b) of Section 288 (lewd or lascivious acts upon a child under 14 years of age), and Sections 288a (oral copulation), 289 (penetration of a genital or anal opening by a foreign object), and 647a (child molestation).

(c) "Neglect" means the negligent failure of a person having the care or custody of any child to protect a child from severe malnutrition or medically diagnosed nonorganic failure to thrive. For the purposes of this chapter, a child receiving treatment by spiritual means as provided in Section 16508 of the Welfare and Institutions Code shall not for that reason alone be considered a neglected child.

(d) "Willful cruelty or unjustifiable punishment of a child" means a situation where any person willfully causes or permits any child to suffer, or inflicts thereon, unjustifiable physical pain or mental suffering, or having the care or custody of any child, willfully causes or permits the person or health of such child to be placed in such situation that his or her person or health is endangered.

(e) "Corporal punishment or injury" means a situation where any person willfully inflicts upon any child any cruel or inhuman corporal punishment or injury resulting in a traumatic condition.

(f) "Abuse in out-of-home care" means situations of suspected physical injury on a child which is inflicted by other than accidental means, or of sexual abuse or neglect or the willful cruelty or unjustifiable punishment of a child, as defined in this article, where the person responsible for the child's welfare is a foster parent or the administrator or an employee of a public or private residential home, school, or other institution or agency.

(g) "Child abuse" means a physical injury which is inflicted by other than accidental means on a child by another person. "Child abuse" also means the sexual assault of a child or any act or omission proscribed by Section 273a (willful cruelty or unjustifiable punishment of a child) or 273d (corporal punishment or injury). "Child abuse" also means the neglect of a child or abuse in out-of-home care, as defined in this article.

. . .

NOTES

(1) A number of states include excessive corporal punishment in the definition of abuse or, oddly enough, neglect. Compare the following:

Florida Statutes Annotated § 827.07 (1981).

. . .

(2) Definitions.—

As used in this section:

. . .

(b) "Child abuse or neglect" means harm or threatened harm to a child's physical or mental health or welfare by the acts or omissions of the parent or other person responsible for the child's welfare.

. . .

(d) "Harm" to a child's health or welfare can occur when the parent or other person responsible for the child's welfare:

1. Inflicts, or allows to be inflicted, upon the child physical or mental injury, including injury sustained as a result of excessive corporal punishment; . . .

Illinois Annotated Statutes ch. 23, § 2053 (Supp.1982).

"Abused child" means a child whose parent or immediate family member, or any person responsible for the child's welfare, or any individual residing in the same home as the child, or a paramour of the child's parent:

. . .

(e) inflicts excessive corporal punishment.

. . .

New York Family Court Act § 1012 (McKinney 1975).

When used in this article and unless the specific context indicates otherwise:

. . .

(f) "Neglected child" means a child less than eighteen years of age

(i) whose physical, mental or emotional condition has been impaired or is in imminent danger of becoming impaired as a result of the failure of his parent or other person legally responsible for his care to exercise a minimum degree of care

. . .

(B) in providing the child with proper supervision or guardianship, by unreasonably inflicting or allowing to be inflicted harm, or a substantial risk thereof, including the infliction of excessive corporal punishment.
. . .

. . .

(2) A number of challenges have been leveled against criminal child abuse statutes on the ground of vagueness. In Bowers v. State, 283 Md. 115, 389 A.2d 341 (1978), the defendant appealed from his conviction under a child abuse statute following a disciplinary beating administered to the 15-year-old daughter of the woman with whom he lived. He struck her on her back, neck, arms and legs 15 or 20 times with a belt, which left bruises visible the next day. The statute, which defendant attacked as unconstitutionally vague, defined abuse as any

physical injury or injuries sustained by a child as a result of cruel or inhumane treatment or as a result of malicious act or acts by any parent, adoptive parent or other person who has the permanent or temporary care or custody or responsibility for supervision of a minor child.

In holding the statute valid, the court stated:

Webster's Third New International Dictionary defines the word "cruel" as "disposed to inflict pain [especially] in a wanton, insensate, or vindictive manner: pleased by hurting others: sadistic." The word "inhuman," a variant of "inhumane," is defined by the same authority as "lacking the qualities of mercy, pity, kindness, or tenderness: cruel, barbarous, savage . . . ." Black's Law Dictionary (4th ed. 1968) defines the term "cruelty" as "the intentional and malicious infliction of physical suffering upon living creatures, particularly human beings; . . . applied to the latter, the wanton and unnecessary infliction of pain upon the body." Clearly, then, the standard "cruel or inhumane" has a settled and commonly understood meaning.

. . . Long before the advent of contemporary child abuse legislation, it was a well-recognized precept of Anglo-American jurisprudence that the parent of a minor child or one standing in *loco parentis* was justified in using a reasonable amount of force upon a child for the purpose of safeguarding or promoting the child's welfare. So long as the chastisement was moderate and reasonable, in light of the age, condition and disposition of the child, and other surrounding circumstances, the parent or custodian would not incur criminal liability for assault and battery or a similar offense.

. . .

. . . [T]he terminology employed in Article 27, § 35A(b)(7)(A) appears to be nothing but a codification of the common law principles concerning the limits of permissible parental chastisement. Since the contours of the common law privilege have been subject for centuries to definition and refinement through careful and constant judicial decision-making, terms like "cruel or inhumane" and "malicious" have acquired a relatively widely accepted connotation in the law. The use of such phraseology in the child abuse statute would, therefore, not render the law constitutionally infirm. . . .

283 Md. at 125–27, 389 A.2d at 347–49.

On the other hand, the Supreme Court of Kansas, in State v. Meinert, 225 Kan. 816, 594 P.2d 232 (1979) upheld a constitutional challenge to its state criminal statute against endangering a child because of what it perceived to be the vagueness of the statutory definition of "willfully . . . Causing or permitting a child under the age of eighteen (18) years to suffer unjustifiable physical pain or mental distress. . . ." The words "unjustifiable physical pain" were deemed insufficient to establish a standard of guilt consonant with due process requirements.

(3) Recall that the Standards Relating to Abuse and Neglect, (Tentative Draft), standard 2.1(A) * provide:

A. [Coercive intervention should be authorized when] a child has suffered, or there is a substantial risk that a child will imminently suffer, a physical harm, inflicted nonaccidentally upon him/her by his/her parents, which causes, or creates a substantial risk of causing disfigurement, impairment of bodily functioning, or other serious physical injury.

The Commentary explains:

Intervention to protect a child from physical abuse is currently authorized in all states. Clearly, killing, maiming, or severely beating a human being are not acceptable forms of behavior. There is no greater reason to allow such conduct in a family setting than in society-at-large. Yet there are significant gradations in the types of harms which might result from intentionally striking a child. A recent nationwide survey found that more than half of the reported cases of physical abuse of children involved minor bruises or abrasions that did not require treatment. D. Gil, Violence Against Children 118–119 (1973).

The proposed definition seeks to distinguish between cases of physical discipline which, even if they result in minor bruises, pose no threat of severe or permanent damage, and cases which do pose such a threat. This does not imply acceptance of corporal punishment as a means of discipline. Rather, it reflects the judgment that even in cases of physical injury, unless the actual or potential injury is serious, the detriment from coercive intervention is likely to be greater than the benefit. A family being investigated for physical abuse is subjected to substantial trauma. The child may be removed from the home and subjected to questioning and court appearances. Other children in the family may become frightened and upset.

. . .

The critical part of the standard is the requirement that the child be injured in a way that causes or creates a substantial risk of causing disfigurement, impairment of bodily functioning, or other serious physical injury. The intent of the standard is to prevent injuries such as broken bones, burns, internal injuries, loss of hearing, sight, etc. It is not intended to cover cases of minor bruises or black and blue marks, unless the child was treated in a way that indicates that more serious injury is likely to occur in the future. In making this decision, a course of parental conduct and the psychological state of the parents may be considered, as well as the injury itself.

* Reprinted with permission from Standards Relating to Abuse and Neglect (Tentative Draft), Copyright, 1977, Ballinger Publishing Company.

PEOPLE v. PHILLIPS

California Court of Appeals, 1st District 1981.
122 Cal.App.3d 69, 175 Cal.Rptr. 703.

GRODIN, ASSOCIATE JUSTICE.

Following a lengthy jury trial, appellant was convicted of murdering one of her two adopted children (Pen.Code, § 187), and of willfully endangering the life or health of the other (Pen.Code, § 273a, subd. (1)), by deliberately administering a sodium compound into the food of each of them. As grounds for reversal she asserts juror misconduct, the erroneous admission of certain psychiatric testimony into evidence, and the trial court's failure to instruct the jury *sua sponte* on diminished capacity. We find no reversible error and therefore affirm, for reasons which follow.

SUMMARY OF THE EVIDENCE

By nearly all accounts, Priscilla Phillips was a kind, helpful and loving person, a dutiful wife to her husband and a devoted mother to their two sons, who at the time of trial were nine and six years of age. Highly educated, with a master's degree in social work, she was employed in the Marin County Health and Human Services Department. After the birth of her sons, she turned her attention increasingly to religious and civil volunteer work, and became active in a variety of community organizations. Among the many organizations to which she volunteered time and energy was the Child Protective Services Unit of the Marin County child abuse agency.

After the birth of her second son in 1973, appellant developed physical symptoms which led to a hysterectomy in 1975. Deeply upset that she could not have another child, especially a daughter, appellant and her husband decided to adopt a Korean infant who had been found abandoned on the streets of Seoul. They called her Tia.

Tia arrived at the Phillips' household in November 1975. Appellant promptly took her to Dr. Aimy Taniguchi, a pediatrician at the Kaiser clinic in San Rafael, for examination. Dr. Taniguchi found Tia to be in good health except for a diaper rash and an ear infection, and prescribed treatment for both. By late November the rash and the infection appeared to have been successfully treated.

On January 26, 1976, appellant brought Tia into the clinic and informed Dr. Taniguchi that Tia had a low-grade fever. A urine specimen revealed a urinary tract infection for which Dr. Taniguchi prescribed first a sulfur-based antibiotic, which did not appear to help, and then a different antibiotic, which worked successfully. Tia's ear infection recurred, however, and was twice treated in February.

On February 27, 1976, appellant brought Tia into the clinic and told Dr. Taniguchi that Tia had a fever and had vomited violently in the morning. The source of the fever could not be determined.

On March 2, 1976, appellant brought Tia to the clinic again and reported that she had been vomiting off and on since the last visit. The doctor believed that the ear infection might be persisting, and added another antibiotic. Later that day, appellant brought Tia into the Kaiser Hospital at San Rafael and told the doctor on call that Tia was having brief "staring spells," and Tia was admitted for observation.

Dr. William Leider, a pediatric neurologist from San Francisco Kaiser, was called in to evaluate Tia's condition, and a variety of tests were performed, including blood sugar and blood calcium tests, a urine culture, a lumbar puncture, X-rays, and an intravenous pyleogram, but the tests revealed no abnormalities. Dr. Al Baumann, an ear, nose and throat specialist, examined Tia, found evidence of a low-grade infection, and because of her previous ear infection recommended an operation called a myringotomy, which entails removal of fluid from the ear drums. The operation was performed on March 5. On March 6, Dr. Taniguchi informed appellant that all of the diagnostic tests were complete, that the results were normal, that the ear operation was successful, and that she planned to discharge Tia within 48 hours.

During the evening of March 6, however, while Tia was still in the hospital, she began to cry and was unable to be comforted. The next day she began to vomit and have diarrhea. Her diet was changed from regular baby formula to clear liquid, but she did not improve. By March 9 feeding by mouth was discontinued and Tia was given intravenous fluids. She improved and was given clear fluids by mouth, but on the evening of March 10 the diarrhea attacks recurred. Feeding by mouth was again discontinued, and the diarrhea stopped abruptly.

Tia remained hospitalized, and the pattern continued. Further diagnostic tests revealed no abnormality, and the doctors were baffled. In April 1976 she was transferred to Kaiser Hospital in San Francisco, where a central venous hyperalimentation device was implanted through a catheter to permit introduction of nutritious fluids. She remained in San Francisco until June 8, 1976, and was then returned to Kaiser San Rafael to monitor her progress on anso-gastric feeding. On July 7, 1976, she was taken to Stanford Medical Center for an intestinal biopsy. Although playful and alert when admitted, by the evening of July 8 she had developed cramps, acute diarrhea, and projectile vomiting. The diarrhea stopped abruptly the next morning. On July 10 Tia was transferred to a San Francisco hospital for the performance of a laparotomy to explore for tumors. Two days later, while at that hospital, Tia had another bout of diarrhea. Her doctors found this "inexplicable." On July 14 or 15, while still at the San Francisco hospital, appellant suggested that Tia be given solid foods. The doctors agreed to try her suggestion, and it appeared to work. Tia "really did very well" and had normal body functions. On July 28 she was discharged. The laparotomy was not performed.

On August 6 appellant called Dr. Taniguchi and told her that Tia's illness had recurred, that she was very sick with vomiting and diarrhea. Upon examination at the hospital, Tia was found to be severely dehydrated, lethargic, and unresponsive to stimulation. Tests revealed she was suffering from an extreme level of sodium in her blood. This finding coincided with prior readings, taken during periods when Tia was having attacks of diarrhea and vomiting; these findings also showed abnormally high levels of blood serum sodium, and of bicarbonate. The doctors had no explanation for this phenomenon.

Tia was admitted to the hospital, improved rapidly, and was released on August 9. On August 23, however, she was again hospitalized with the same symptoms. Abdominal X-rays showed no obstruction of the intestinal tract. She was discharged on August 28 but the symptoms reappeared and she was hospitalized twice in September and twice in October. Electrolyte readings continued to fluctuate, but again, all diagnostic tests were normal. In November 1976 a laparotomy was performed at Kaiser Hospital in San Francisco, but it revealed no abnormalities. Tia was discharged on November 26.

On December 3, 1976, Tia was examined by her pediatrician and was found to be doing well. Three days later she was back in the emergency room in shock, vomiting convulsively, and displaying elevated sodium and bicarbonate levels. On December 11, having improved to the point that she could take formula, she was discharged. Less than three hours later she was back with the same symptoms, and was discharged again on December 22. A similar episode occurred in January 1977.

On February 2, 1977, appellant brought Tia to the emergency room for the last time. The child was in critical condition. She was having generalized seizures. She had an extreme level of sodium in her blood. An X-ray showed aspiration of vomit into her right lung. She was unable to eliminate carbon dioxide from her body, and she began to demonstrate abnormal posturings which indicated damage to her central nervous system. She died on February 3.

Several months after Tia's death, appellant and her husband adopted another Korean infant whom they named Mindy. On February 3, 1979—the anniversary of Tia's death—appellant brought Mindy to the hospital. The child had been vomiting, and she had diarrhea. Mindy was admitted to the hospital; her symptoms eventually subsided; and she was discharged on February 10. On February 16 Mindy was hospitalized again with the same symptoms. Her sodium level was elevated. Dr. Taniguchi began to note similarities between Mindy's case and Tia's case: "[T]hinking about it as objectively as possible, I realized that these two girls were not related in any way and . . . it just seemed incredible that they could even possibly have the same type of problem. . . ." At a pediatric staff conference on February 22, all doctors present agreed that "it was important to consider the possibility that this child was being poisoned."

The following day Dr. Arnhold, a pediatrician at Kaiser, gave Dr. Taniguchi a copy of an article from the Journal of the American Medical Association concerning a form of child abuse which had been reported in the British Medical Journal, Lancet, by a physician named Meadow. The article noted Meadow's observations of a case in which one little girl underwent innumerable manipulative, anesthetic, radiologic and surgical procedures during the six years of her life because her parents provided false information about her symptoms, tampered with her urine specimens, and otherwise interfered with observation by physicians and nurses; and of a second case in which a 14-month-old infant died of hypernatremia after repeated hospital admissions for vomiting and drowsiness that were precipitated by ingestion of large quantities of salt given to her surreptitiously by her mother. Both mothers appeared to be loving, cooperative, and appreciative of the care given to their children. Dr. Meadow had denominated the phenomena "Munchausen syndrome by proxy," after the so-called "Munchausen syndrome" in which a patient beguiles a physician into performing unnecessary diagnostic and surgical procedures on the basis of false reports of symptoms.

Dr. Taniguchi proceeded with a series of tests to determine a medical cause for Mindy's symptoms: "Again, I was faced with the puzzling finding of an elevated sodium; and for the first time [I] began to look at it in terms of what was going into the patient and what was coming out of the patient. And, it did not add up. There was much more coming out than was going in." Mindy continued to have diarrhea. Sodium levels were abnormally high.

On February 24, around 2:45 p. m., Leslie McCarcy, a pediatric nurse at the hospital, arrived on duty and received a report from Cathy Place, the outgoing nurse. The question of Mindy's formula came up. Appellant was in Mindy's hospital room at the time. According to Nurse McCarcy, "Mrs. Phillips came out to the desk and Cathy asked her if she had made up the formula and Mrs. Phillips said yes, she had. It was in the refrigerator."

The next morning, February 25, the pediatrician on duty checked Mindy's intake and output charts. "I found that indeed, there was a large amount of unaccountable sodium in Mindy's stool and urine. . . . She was losing about five times the amount of sodium she was receiving." The doctor then went to the nurse on duty and asked her where Mindy's formula was kept. He took a sample of the formula and had it analyzed. The sodium content was 448 milliequivalents per liter. According to the manufacturer's specification, the sodium content should have been only 15 milliequivalents per liter. The doctor had Mindy's formula replaced and transferred her to the intensive care unit.

Appellant was forbidden to feed Mindy, and was forbidden to visit the child except in the presence of a nurse. She was told that sodium appeared to be the cause of Mindy's illness, and that some sort of laxative salt might be a cause of the diarrhea. Appellant said, "I don't know anything about things like that," and asked what the doctor was going to do. When he told her that under the circumstances it was his obligation to call the Child Protective Services, appellant became downcast and said, "Then I'll be a suspect."

Once Mindy was placed in the ICU unit, she recovered quickly. She "seemed fine. . . . She did not have any more diarrhea at all. . . . She ate well, she was happy. . . ."

Dr. Boyd Stephens, Coroner of the City and County of San Francisco, testified on the basis of his observations that the cause of Tia's death was sodium poisoning, and that the amount of the sodium was so high that it had to have been administered into the gastrointestinal tract. Dr. Malcolm Holliday, Professor of Pediatrics at the University of California, concurred, and concluded that since Tia's chloride levels were normal, and her bicarbonate level was high, that the form of the salt was sodium bicarbonate. He testified that two to three teaspoons of sodium bicarbonate, dissolved in liquid, and would have been sufficient to produce the symptoms which Tia and Mindy displayed.

At each of the hospitals to which Tia was admitted, parents were encouraged to participate in the care of their infants and young children; and mothers were permitted to remain overnight and to feed their babies. Throughout Tia's hospitalizations, appellant visited frequently and for prolonged periods of time. Because of her dedication, she won the admiration, sympathy, and respect of hospital staff members. Because of her obvious intelligence, her frequent presence, and her willingness to help, she was allowed to perform "minor nursing chores," including administration of formula through the nasogastric tube. The pediatric facility at each hospital had a small room or kitchen area not visible from the nursing station, which contained an unlocked refrigerator for formulas and other foods. Appellant had access to those areas.

In order to suggest a motive for appellant's alleged conduct, the prosecution, over the objections of defense counsel, presented evidence relating to the so-called "Munchausen's syndrome by proxy" through the testimony of Dr. Martin Blinder, a psychiatrist. Dr. Blinder had not examined appellant, nor had he treated patients who displayed the syndrome which was the subject of his testimony. Rather, his testimony was based upon various reports in professional journals, copies of which were made available to the jury.

In response to a hypothetical question, Dr. Blinder theorized that a mother who repeatedly and surreptitiously administered a cathartic sodium compound to her adopted children, under circumstances identical to those presented by this case, displayed symptoms consistent with Munchausen's syndrome by proxy. He testified that the syndrome "is one in which an individual either directly or through the vehicle of a child feigns, simulates, or actually fabricates a physical illness. . . . Typically, the illness is a dramatic one." "And 'by proxy' simply means instead of the person making themselves ill, they go through the psychodynamic process in another. It's usually the mother. . . . She's outwardly devoted to the child and invariably, the child is very small, less than two years of age. . . . The mothers who perpetrate a child abuse or Munchausen's form of child abuse typically will transfer their own unmet parental needs . . . onto pediatricians, nurses, spouses, maybe even the community and get from these people through their child's illness the attention and sympathy they never got from their own parents."

Describing the syndrome, Dr. Blinder continued: "The mother will flourish on the ward. She seems to almost to blossom in the medical drama of the hospital. . . . The concern, competence and intelligence of these mothers . . . makes it hard for the doctors to suspect them as the possible cause of their child's illness . . . .. When the mother is confronted with evidence that she in fact is responsible for the illness, [she] cannot accept responsibility, even when the evidence is incontrovertible. . . . The literature describes some mothers who are frankly psychotic. . . . But a great number of the mothers who do this to their children are not overtly mentally ill." Asked about appellant herself—as opposed to a hypothetical mother—Dr. Blinder testified, "Without a clinical examination of this defendant herself, I cannot say with the necessary degree of certainty that she indeed is reflecting a Munchausen Syndrome."

Appellant testified in her own behalf. She denied that she had ever given Tia or Mindy sodium bicarbonate or any other sodium compound, and she denied that she had ever done anything to harm either child. She admitted that she had, on "some occasions," prepared Mindy's hospital formula herself. Friends, acquaintances, and hospital nurses testified concerning appellant's reputation for truthfulness and her care and deep concern for Tia and Mindy. Defense psychiatrists testified, based on their examinations of appellant, that her mental condition was "essentially normal" with "none of the distortions in thinking or emotion that have been described in the articles on Munchausen Syndrome by proxy or that one might expect if Mrs. Phillips had committed [the] alleged acts." According to defense experts, appellant was "not suffering from any significant mental disease or illness."

. . .

2. *Admission of Dr. Blinder's testimony was not error*

Appellant argues, "The trial court abused its discretion and committed prejudicial error in permitting expert opinion testimony, in answer to a hypothetical question, on Munchausen syndrome by proxy, where the facts of the question related specifically to appellant and the named victims, where appellant's mental condition was not at issue, and where illness attributed to appellant was not recognized by medical profession." This composite argument contains several components, which we proceed to analyze.

a. *The form of the hypothetical question*

Dr. Blinder first testified as to his qualifications and his familiarity with medicine, psychiatry, family therapy, child abuse, and a group of symptoms called "Munchausen syndrome by proxy." He was then asked for a description of the Munchausen syndrome. The court requested that the prosecution proceed by means of a hypothetical question and then elicit a description of the syndrome. The prosecutor began: "I'll ask . . . that you *assume* the following facts: Number one, that *the defendant, Priscilla E. Phillips,* did repeatedly and surreptitiously administer doses of a cathartic sodium-type compound over a period of approximately 12 months to first one *adopted Korean orphan, Tia Phillips,* . . . and then engaged in similar conduct with a second *adopted Korean orphan, Mindy Phillips,* over a period of approximately one month until this *poisoning* was discovered by hospital officials." (Emphasis added.) At that point, the defense objected: "It's assuming the guilt of the defendant which is totally inadmissible in a criminal proceeding . . . ." The objection was overruled, and the prosecutor continued with his question. The defense then objected that the question was argumentative, complex, and assumed facts not in evidence. The objection was overruled, and the prosecutor continued with his question. The defense then objected to the prosecutor's use of appellant's name. The court thereupon instructed the jury to disregard the prosecutor's mention of appellant: "Strike Mrs. Phillips and just say the defendant involved in this hypothetical case, because it's entirely a hypothetical case presented to the doctor and you're to consider it as such." The prosecutor continued with his question, substituting "the defendant" for "Mrs. Phillips." Further defense objections were overruled, and Dr. Blinder was permitted to testify, "I have an opinion. . . . [Y]our hypothetical person evinces symptoms consistent with . . . Munchausen's Syndrome by proxy."

Dr. Blinder then proceeded to describe the syndrome. He said that he could *not* render an opinion concerning appellant herself, because he had never examined her. Dr. Blinder's testimony continued until the afternoon recess. Immediately following the recess, the court *sua sponte* and without objection read to the jury CALJIC No. 2.82 concerning hypothetical questions. The court read the entire instruction twice, including the following sentence: "It is for you, the jury, to determine from all the evidence whether or not the facts assumed in a hypothetical question have been proved." This instruction was given again at the conclusion of the case, along with CALJIC No. 2.80, concerning expert testimony generally.

Appellant argues that the hypothetical question was phrased improperly in that the names of Mrs. Phillips and the alleged victims were repeatedly used, and that this impropriety was prejudicial because it may have led the jury to believe that Dr. Blinder was expressing an opinion about Mrs. Phillips' mental condition when, in fact, he had never met her much less examined her.

We do not agree. That Dr. Blinder had never met or examined appellant was made clear to the jury repeatedly. Thus, any impropriety in the form of the question could not have misled the jurors. Dr. Blinder was saying, in effect, that the conduct ascribed to appellant was explicable in terms of the syndrome which had been reported in the literature. Whether that testimony was properly admitted is the key question, to which we now turn.

b. *Admissibility of psychiatric evidence by the prosecution where defendant has not made her mental state an issue*

Appellant suggests this may be the "first time in the history of California criminal jurisprudence in which the prosecution was permitted to put into evidence, as part of its case in chief, the mental condition of the defendant without the issue first being raised either by plea or by the introduction of the defendant's state of mind as part of the defense." That may be true, but it is hardly persuasive as to the admissibility of such testimony. The rules of evidence do not preclude innovation.

While a prosecutor ordinarily need not prove motive as an element of a crime, the absence of apparent motive may make proof of the essential elements less persuasive. Clearly that was the principal problem confronting the prosecutor here. In the absence of a motivational hypothesis, and in the light of other information which the jury had concerning her personality and character, the conduct ascribed to appellant was incongruous and apparently inexplicable. As both parties recognize, Dr. Blinder's testimony was designed to fill that gap.

The evidence was thus relevant, and therefore admissible "[e]xcept as otherwise provided by statute" (Evid. Code, § 351). Appellant points to no statutory provision which would preclude the prosecutor from introducing otherwise admissible psychiatric testimony relevant to motivation on the ground that the defendant had not placed his or her mental state in issue.

Appellant relies upon People v. Nicolaus (1967) 65 Cal.2d 866, 880, 56 Cal.Rptr. 635, 423 P.2d 787, as standing for the proposition that such evidence should not be permitted. That case and its predecessor, In re Spencer (1965) 63 Cal.2d 400, 412, 46 Cal.Rptr. 753, 406 P.2d 33, involved the constitutional issues posed when a court-appointed psychiatrist is permitted to testify to incriminating statements made to him by the defendant in the course of the psychiatric interview. Dr. Blinder never interviewed defendant, and consequently no such constitutional issue is implicated here.

c. *Reliability of the evidence*

Evidence Code section 801 describes the boundaries of expert testimony: "If a witness is testifying as an expert, his testimony in the form of an opinion is limited to such an opinion as is: (a) Related to a subject that is sufficiently beyond common experience that the opinion of an expert would assist the trier of fact; and (b) Based on matter (including his special knowledge, skill, experience, training, and education) perceived by or personally known to the witness or made known to him at or before the hearing, whether or not admissible, that is of a type that reasonably may be relied upon by an expert in forming an opinion upon the subject to which his testimony relates, unless an expert is precluded by law from using such matter as a basis for his opinion." Testimony outside these boundaries, i.e., "testimony in the form of an opinion that is based in whole or in significant part on matter that is not a proper basis for such an opinion," is subject to exclusion upon objection. (Evid. Code, § 803).

The existence, nature, validity, and applicability to these facts of the phenomenon characterized as "Munchausen syndrome by proxy" are all matters sufficiently beyond common experience that expert opinion would assist the trier of fact, and appellant does not argue otherwise. Thus, the requirements of subdivision (a) of section 801 are satisfied. It is the provisions of subdivision (b) that form the focus of appellant's attack.

Under the provisions of subdivision (b), the fact that Dr. Blinder's testimony was based in large measure upon reports by others rather than upon his personal observations of the defendant or of other persons displaying that syndrome may affect the weight of his testimony but does not render that testimony inadmissible if those reports meet the standard of reasonable reliability. (See Jefferson, California Evidence Benchbook (1972) § 29.4, 507–509; cf. People v. Brekke (1967) 250 Cal.App.2d 651, 661–662, 58 Cal.Rptr. 854.)

All of the studies cited by Dr. Blinder appeared in professional technical journals and were written by medical specialists on the basis of personal observations.[1] "While a layman may not testify to a

1. Dr. Blinder, in the course of his testimony on direct examination, listed six authorities upon which he relied. Two of these, the report by Dr. Meadow published in Lancet and the summary of that report which appeared in the Journal of the American Medical Association, have previously been described. We here briefly summarize the other four.

In the November 1965 issue of Pediatrics there appeared a report by Dr. Mark S. Dine concerning a mother who fed her 19-month-old son perphenazine, a phenothiazine tranquilizer that had been prescribed for her own use. When confronted with the evidence that she had been poisoning her son, the mother's reaction was one of dismay and denial. Dr. Dine suggested that "the poisoning of children by the deliberate administration of medications or other toxic substances" be regarded as a form of child abuse along

fact which he has learned only by reading a medical book, there is no question that a professional physician may rely upon medical texts as the basis for his testimony. [Citations.]" (Brown v. Colm (1974) 11 Cal.3d 639, 644, 114 Cal.Rptr. 128, 522 P.2d 688.)

Appellant does not question Dr. Blinder's qualifications to appraise the reliability of the studies, nor does she suggest that information contained in them could feasibly have been presented except through the reported data. (Ibid.) Indeed, she does not directly question the trustworthiness of these studies at all, or the accuracy of Dr. Blinder's interpretation of them to the jury. Rather, she rests upon the proposition that Munchausen's syndrome by proxy is an "unrecognized illness . . . not generally accepted by the medical profession," and points to the fact that the syndrome is not listed or discussed as a form of mental illness in the American Psychiatric Association's Diagnostic and Statistical Manual of Mental Disorders.[2]

We are aware of no such requirement. We are not confronted here with the admissibility of evidence developed by some new scien-

with the previously recognized phenomena of the "battered child" syndrome, sexual molestation, and gross neglect; and he cautioned that "physicians who are responsible for the care of children must be alert to the possibility not only of physical trauma inflicted by parents, but also of deliberate drug intoxication as a cause of illness even when the history excludes this factor."

In the British Medical Journal for April 1876 there appeared an article by Rogers, et al., entitled Non-accidental poisoning: an extended syndrome of child abuse. The authors, physicians, psychiatrists and researchers at the Hospital for Sick Children and the poisons unit at Guy's Hospital in London, reported in detail six cases of non-accidental poisoning of children by their parents. One of these involved a trained children's nurse who had administred small doses of salt to her two-month-old infant in her daily feeds. Referring to earlier studies involving such phenomena, the authors cautioned: "This manifestation of child abuse may be commoner than previously supposed."

In the September 1977 issue of the American Journal, Clinical Pediatrics, Drs. Fleisher and Ament from the Departments of Pediatrics and Medicine of the UCLA Center for the Health Sciences reported their findings in three cases of children administered phenolphthalein in the form of laxatives by emotionally disturbed mothers. Based on their studies, they advanced the opinion that the mothers in these cases were using their babies' illnesses to elicit sympathetic in-

terest and involvement when they felt such a need, and to inflict grief or frustration when they felt angry or retaliatory.

The same journal in June of the following year carried an article entitled Intentional Poisoning of Two Siblings by Prescription Drugs: An Unusual Form of Child Abuse. The authors, Drs. Hvizdala and Gellady of the Department of Pediatrics, University of Florida College of Medicine, cited a study in 1975 by Kempe and Schmitt calling attention to intentional poisoning by prescription drugs as a form of child abuse. Their own report involved two instances of deliberate poisoning of children by parents. One of these was a mother who appeared concerned and anxious to help the physicians in determining the cause of her children's problems and who, when first evaluated by the Division of Family Services, was described as "a very responsible and capable parent." The authors noted the similarity to Munchausen's syndrome, and referred to the study by Meadow in Lancet. They concluded that "[t]he scarcity of reports may reflect the difficulty of recognizing this form of deliberate poisoning of children."

2. From the record it appears that the manual is updated and revised from time to time, either by a committee or, as occurred on at least one occasion, regarding the exclusion of homosexuality as a listed mental illness, by majority vote of the member psychiatrists at a meeting. More recent editions of the manual do list Munchausen's syndrome as a category of mental illness.

tific technique such as voiceprint identification, nor with conflict within the scientific community. In People v. Jackson (1971) 18 Cal.App. 3d 504, 507, 95 Cal.Rptr. 919, the court referred to the " 'battered child syndrome' " as an "accepted medical diagnosis" on the basis of medical literature not unlike that presented here. The studies here show intentional poisoning of infants by their mothers to be another form of child abuse. In the absence of some reason to doubt their validity, we find no abuse of discretion in the trial court's decision to allow expert testimony based thereon.

. . . .

The judgment is affirmed.

NOTES

(1) As *Phillips* illustrates, some forms of abuse are all the more dangerous and reprehensible because of their insidiousness. Who are the people who abuse their children and why do they do it? Are there clearly identifiable stereotypes and are we able to identify them with any degree of certainty? In their pioneering article, The Battered Child Syndrome, Dr. Henry Kempe and his colleagues suggested that:

. . . In some . . . published reports the parents, or at least the parent who inflicted the abuse, have been found to be of low intelligence. Often, they are described as psychopathic or sociopathic characters. Alcoholism, sexual promiscuity, unstable marriages, and minor criminal activities are reportedly common amongst them. They are immature, impulsive, self-centered, hypersensitive, and quick to react with poorly controlled aggression. Data in some cases indicate that such attacking parents had themselves been subject to some degree of attack from their parents in their own childhood.

Beating of children, however, is not confined to people with a psychopathic personality or of borderline socioeconomic status. It also occurs among people with good education and stable financial and social background. However, from the scant data that are available, it would appear that in these cases, too, there is a defect in character structure which allows aggressive impulses to be expressed too freely. There is also some suggestion that the attacking parent was subjected to similar abuse in childhood. It would appear that one of the most important factors to be found in families where parental assault occurs is "to do unto others as you have been done by." This is not surprising; it has long been recognized by psychologists and social anthropologists that patterns of child rearing, both good and bad, are passed from one generation to the next in relatively unchanged form. Psychologically, one could describe this phenomenon as an identification with the aggressive parent, this identification occurring despite strong wishes of the person to be different. Not infrequently the beaten infant is a product of an unwanted pregnancy, a pregnancy which began before marriage, too soon after marriage, or at some other time felt to be extremely inconvenient. Sometimes several children in one family have been beaten: at other times one child is singled out for attack while others are treated quite lovingly. We have also seen instances in which the sex of the child who is severely attacked is related to very specific factors in the context of the abusive parent's neurosis.

181 J.A.M.A. 18–19 (1962).*

For other studies dealing with this question see B. F. Steele and C. B. Pollock, A Psychiatric Study of Parents Who Abuse Infants and Small Children, in R. E. Helfer and C. H. Kempe (eds.), The Battered Child at 103 et seq. (1968); L. H. Pelton, The Myth of Classlessness—Child Abuse and Neglect 20 (New Jersey Division of Youth and Family Services 1978).

(2) Given the nature of child abuse and contemporary emphasis on decision making for the best interests of the child, what is a lawyer's role in representing a parent accused of child abuse? In The Battered Child Rebrutalized: Ten Cases of Medical-Legal Confusion, 124 Amer.J.Psychiat. 10 (1968),** Terr and Watson suggest that:

> In the heat of legal contest, lawyers representing the parents may ignore the interests of the child. For example, let us consider Denise, a recently adopted nine-year-old girl who had been subjected to 226 lashes with a belt for failure to bring home her homework papers. Denise's mother, in addition to doing most of the beating, had attempted to breast feed the nine-year-old, check her genitals daily for signs of masturbation, and engage her in games of *Sorry* whenever Denise confessed the impulse to masturbate.

> The parents' lawyer chose to overlook all evidences of severe sexual and hostile provocations to this child. Instead he threatened numerous appeals and delay tactics in the determination of custody in order to protect his clients' rights to Denise. In this case countless delays would guarantee insecurity for this girl throughout most of her childhood despite her desperate need for permanent roots.

> It appears that a lawyer representing battering parents may find himself in a dilemma. If the lawyer *knows* of the child's injury but helps the parents avoid incrimination (or being found at fault), he may help perpetuate a truly dangerous situation for the child. On the other hand, if he decides to tell the juvenile court judge what he knows, he may be breaching, or at least feel he is breaching, his duty to the parents. (We must ask in this regard: If we wish to protect children fully, should not lawyers report child abuse too?) The lawyer's decision will probably depend upon his view of the community's treatment programs versus the community's punitive intentions.

Do you agree with this approach? For an alternate view, see J.L. Isaacs, The Role of the Lawyer in Child Abuse Cases, in Helping the Battered Child and His Family at 225, 233–37 (C.H. Kempe and R.E. Helfer eds. 1972).

What is the role of counsel for the child in a child abuse proceeding? For some differing answers to this question see Redeker, The Right of an Abused Child to Independent Counsel and the Role of the Child Advocate in Child Abuse Cases, 23 Vill.L.Rev. 521, 543–45 (1978); D.N. Duquette, Liberty and Lawyers in Child Protection, in The Battered Child at 316, 319–20 (R.E. Helfer and C.H. Kempe eds. 1980); see also Fraser, Independent Representa-

tion for the Abused and Neglected Child: The Guardian Ad Litem, 13 Cal.
W.L.Rev. 16 (1976); MacDonald, A Case for Independent Counsel to Represent Children in Custody Proceedings, 7 New Eng.L.Rev. 351 (1972).

1. REPORTING ABUSE

JUVENILE JUSTICE STANDARDS PROJECT, STANDARDS
RELATING TO ABUSE AND NEGLECT
(Tentative Draft 1977) *

3.1 Required reports

A. Any physician, nurse, dentist, optometrist, medical examiner, or coroner, or any other medical or mental health professional, Christian Science practitioner, religious healer, schoolteacher
and other pupil personnel, social or public assistance worker, child
care worker in any day care center or child caring institution, police or law enforcement officer who has reasonable cause to suspect that a child, coming before him/her in his/her official or professional capacity, is an abused child as defined by Standard 3.1 B.
should be required to make a report to any report recipient agency
listed for that geographic locality pursuant to Standard 3.2.

B. An "abused child," for purposes of Standard 3.1 A., is a
child who has suffered physical harm, inflicted nonaccidentally upon him/her by his/her parent(s) or person(s) exercising essentially
equivalent custody and control over the child, which injury causes
or creates a substantial risk of causing death, disfigurement, impairment of bodily functioning, or other serious physical injury.

C. Any person making a report or participating in any subsequent proceedings regarding such report pursuant to this Part
should be immune from any civil or criminal liability as a result of
such actions, provided that such person was acting in good faith in
such actions. In any proceeding regarding such liability, good
faith should be presumed.

D. The privileged character of communication between husband and wife and between any professional person and his/her
patient or client, except privilege between attorney and client,
should be abrogated regarding matters subject to this Part, and
should not justify failure to report or the exclusion of evidence in
any proceeding resulting from a report pursuant to this Part.

E. Any person who knowingly fails to make a report required
pursuant to this Part should be guilty of a misdemeanor (and/or
should be liable, regarding any injuries proximately caused by
such failure, for compensatory and/or punitive damages in civil
litigation maintained on behalf of the child or his/her estate).

CALIFORNIA PENAL CODE

§ 11165. Definitions

As used in this article:

. . .

(h) "Child care custodian" means a teacher, administrative officer, supervisor of child welfare and attendance, or certificated pupil personnel employee of any public or private school; an administrator of a public or private day camp; a licensed day care worker; an administrator of a community care facility licensed to care for children; headstart teacher; public assistance worker; employee of a child care institution including, but not limited to, foster parents, group home personnel and personnel of residential care facilities; a social worker or a probation officer.

(i) "Medical practitioner" means a physician and surgeon, psychiatrist, psychologist, dentist, resident, intern, podiatrist, chiropractor, licensed nurse, dental hygienist, or any other person who is currently licensed under Division 2 (commencing with Section 500) of the Business and Professions Code.

(j) "Nonmedical practitioner" means a state or county public health employee who treats a minor for venereal disease or any other condition; a coroner; a paramedic; a marriage, family, or child counselor; or a religious practitioner who diagnoses, examines, or treats children.

(k) "Child protective agency" means a police or sheriff's department, a county probation department, or a county welfare department.

§ 11166. Report; duty; time

(a) Except as provided in subdivision (b), any child care custodian, medical practitioner, nonmedical practitioner, or employee of a child protective agency who has knowledge of or observes a child in his or her professional capacity or within the scope of his or her employment whom he or she reasonably suspects has been the victim of child abuse shall report such suspected instance of child abuse to a child protective agency immediately or as soon as practically possible by telephone and shall prepare and send a written report thereof within 36 hours of receiving the information concerning the incident. For the purposes of this article, "reasonable suspicion" means that it is objectively reasonable for a person to entertain such a suspicion, based upon facts that could cause a reasonable person in a like position, drawing when appropriate on his or her training and experience, to suspect child abuse.

(b) Any child care custodian, medical practitioner, nonmedical practitioner, or employee of a child protective agency who has knowledge of or who reasonably suspects that mental suffering has been inflicted on a child or its emotional well-being is endangered in any other way, may report such suspected instance of child abuse to a child protective agency.

(c) Any other person who had knowledge of or observes a child whom he or she reasonably suspects has been a victim of child abuse may report such suspected instance of child abuse to a child protective agency.

. . .

(f) A county probation or welfare department shall immediately or as soon as practically possible report by telephone every instance of suspected child abuse as defined in Section 11165 reported to it to the law enforcement agency having jurisdiction over the case, and to the agency given responsibility for investigation of cases under Section 300 of the Welfare and Institutions Code, and shall send a written report thereof within 36 hours of receiving the information concerning the incident to that agency.

A law enforcement agency shall immediately or as soon as practically possible report by telephone every instance of suspected child abuse reported to it to county social services and the agency given responsibility for investigation of cases under Section 300 of the Welfare and Institutions Code and shall send a written report thereof within 36 hours of receiving the information concerning the incident to such agency.

§ 11167. Report; contents

(a) A telephone report of suspected child abuse shall include the name of the person making the report, the name of the child, the present location of the child, the nature and extent of the injury, and any other information, including information that led such person to suspect child abuse, requested by the child protective agency.

(b) Information relevant to the incident of child abuse may also be given to an investigator from a child protective agency who is investigating the suspected case of child abuse.

(c) Persons who may report pursuant to subdivision (c) of Section 11166 are not required to include their names. The identity of all persons who report under this article shall be confidential and disclosed only by court order or between child protective agencies or the probation department.

§ 11169. Preliminary reports to department of justice; unfounded reports

A child protective agency shall forward to the Department of Justice a preliminary report in writing of every case of suspected child abuse which it investigates, whether or not any formal action is taken in the case. However, if after investigation the case proves to be unfounded no report shall be retained by the Department of Justice. If a report has previously been filed which has proved unfounded the

Department of Justice shall be notified of that fact. The report shall be in a form approved by the Department of Justice. A child protective agency receiving a written report from another child protective agency shall not send such report to the Department of Justice.

§ 11170. Notice to child protection agency of information maintained; indexed reports

The Department of Justice shall immediately notify a child protective agency which submits a report pursuant to Section 11169 of any information maintained pursuant to Section 11110 which is relevant to the suspected instance of child abuse reported by the agency. The indexed reports retained by the Department of Justice shall be continually updated and shall not contain any unfounded reports. A child protective agency shall make such information available to the reporting medical practitioner, child custodian, or guardian ad litem appointed under Section 318 of the Welfare and Institutions Code, if he or she is treating or investigating a case of suspected child abuse.

When a report is made pursuant to subdivision (a) of Section 11166, the investigating agency shall, upon completion of the investigation or after there has been a final disposition in the matter, inform the person required to report of the results of the investigation and of any action the agency is taking with regard to the child or family.

§ 11171. X-rays of child; exemption from privilege

(a) A physician and surgeon or dentist or their agents and by their direction may take skeletal X-rays of the child without the consent of the child's parent or guardian, but only for purposes of diagnosing the case as one of possible child abuse and determining the extent of such child abuse.

(b) Neither the physician-patient privilege nor the psychotherapist-patient privilege applies to information reported pursuant to this article in any court proceeding or administrative hearing.

§ 11172. Immunity from liability; failure to report; offense

(a) No child care custodian, medical practitioner or nonmedical practitioner reporting a suspected instance of child abuse shall be civilly or criminally liable for any report required or authorized by this article. Any other person reporting a suspected instance of child abuse shall not incur civil or criminal liability as a result of any report authorized by this section unless it can be proved that a false report was made and the person knew or should have known that the report was false. No person required to make a report pursuant to this section, nor any person taking photographs at his or her direction, shall incur any civil or criminal liability for taking photographs of a suspected victim of child abuse, or causing photographs to be taken of a suspected victim of child abuse, without parental consent, or for disseminating such photographs with the reports required by this section. However, the provisions of this section shall not be construed to grant immunity from such liability with respect to any other use of such photographs.

(b) Any person who fails to report as required by this article an instance of child abuse which he or she knows to exist or reasonably should know to exist is guilty of a misdemeanor and is punishable by confinement in the county jail for a term not to exceed six months or by a fine of not more than five hundred dollars ($500) or by both.

NOTE

All 50 states now have child abuse reporting laws. These statutes originally were enacted over a four-year period following revelations about the "battered child syndrome" in the early and mid-60s. Many were based on models proposed in 1963 by the Children's Bureau (The Abused Child—Principles and Suggested Language for Legislation on Reporting of the Physically Abused Child) and the Children's Division of the American Humane Association (Guidelines for Legislation to Protect the Battered Child). Although most statutes share certain basic features, they often differ greatly in language and detail. Definitions of what constitutes abuse vary considerably, as do descriptions of who must report and to whom reports must be made. There is considerable inconsistency about the harshness of sanctions for nonreporting, or even whether there should be sanctions.

Today's typical statute defines the class of persons who must report to include at least health care professionals, teachers and social workers. Most statutes provide for civil immunity for one who reports in good faith, and there is generally a waiver of both the husband-wife and physician-patient privileges. Many statutes specifically authorize physicians to take photographs without parental permission.

An emerging controversy concerns the degree to which there should be central registries on reports that have been made, and the question of who should have access to such information. Some fear that the introduction of such popularized procedures as "hot lines" through which anonymous reports can be made poses a serious threat to civil liberties while offering only marginally incremental effectiveness for the reporting system. In a nation that has shown little favor for informer statutes generally, it seems somewhat surprising that such issues have been slow to draw public dissent.

For further history of the development of child abuse reporting statutes and summaries of their content, see V. DeFrancis and C.L. Lucht, Child Abuse Legislation in the 1970s (Rev. ed. 1974); Paulsen, The Legal Framework for Child Protection, 66 Colum.L.Rev. 679 (1966); Paulsen, Parker and Adelman, Child Abuse Reporting Laws: Some Legislative History, 34 Geo. Wash.L.Rev. 482 (1966).

LANDEROS v. FLOOD

Supreme Court of California, In Bank, 1976.
17 Cal.3d 399, 131 Cal.Rptr. 69, 551 P.2d 389.

MOSK, JUSTICE.

In this medical malpractice action plaintiff Gita Landeros, a minor, appeals from a judgment of dismissal entered upon an order sustaining general demurrers to her amended complaint. . . .

Plaintiff brought the action by her guardian ad litem against A. J. Flood, a physician, and The San Jose Hospitals & Health Center, Inc. (hereinafter called the San Jose Hospital). The amended complaint purports to allege four "causes of action." As we shall explain, the first three of these are actually alternative theories of recovery alleged in support of a single cause of action for compensatory damages for personal injuries caused by defendants' negligence in failing to properly diagnose and treat the condition from which plaintiff was suffering; . . .

[The fourth cause of action, a claim for punitive damages, was abandoned on this appeal.]

The material factual allegations of the amended complaint are as follows. Plaintiff was born on May 14, 1970. On repeated occasions during the first year of her life she was severely beaten by her mother and the latter's common law husband, one Reyes. On April 26, 1971, when plaintiff was 11 months old, her mother took her to the San Jose Hospital for examination, diagnosis, and treatment. The attending physician was defendant Flood, acting on his own behalf and as agent of defendant San Jose Hospital. At the time plaintiff was suffering from a comminuted spiral fracture of the right tibia and fibula, which gave the appearance of having been caused by a twisting force.[2] Plaintiff's mother had no explanation for this injury. Plaintiff also had bruises over her entire back, together with superficial abrasions on other parts of her body. In addition, she had a nondepressed linear fracture of the skull, which was then in the process of healing.[3] Plaintiff demonstrated fear and apprehension when approached. Inasmuch as all plaintiff's injuries gave the appearance of having been intentionally inflicted by other persons, she exhibited the medical condition known as the battered child syndrome.

It is alleged that proper diagnosis of plaintiff's condition would have included taking X-rays of her entire skeletal structure, and that such procedure would have revealed the fracture of her skull. Defendants negligently failed to take such X-rays, and thereby negligently failed to diagnose her true condition. It is further alleged that

2. A comminuted fracture is "a fracture in which the bone is splintered or crushed into numerous pieces." (Webster's New Inter-Nat.Dict. (3d ed. 1961) p. 457.)

3. A nondepressed linear skull fracture is ordinarily detectable only by X-ray examination.

proper medical treatment of plaintiff's battered child syndrome would have included reporting her injuries to local law enforcement authorities or juvenile probation department. Such a report would have resulted in an investigation by the concerned agencies, followed by a placement of plaintiff in protective custody until her safety was assured. Defendants negligently failed to make such report.

The complaint avers that as a proximate result of the foregoing negligence plaintiff was released from the San Jose Hospital without proper diagnosis and treatment of her battered child syndrome, and was returned to the custody of her mother and Reyes who resumed physically abusing her until she sustained traumatic blows to her right eye and back, puncture wounds over her left lower leg and across her back, severe bites on her face, and second and third degree burns of her left hand.

On July 1, 1971, plaintiff was again brought in for medical care, but to a different doctor and hospital. Her battered child syndrome was immediately diagnosed and reported to local police and juvenile probation authorities, and she was taken into protective custody. Following hospitalization and surgery she was placed with foster parents, and the latter subsequently undertook proceedings to adopt her. Plaintiff's mother and Reyes fled the state, but were apprehended, returned for trial, and convicted of the crime of child abuse. (Pen. Code, 273a.)

With respect to damages the complaint alleges that as a proximate result of defendants' negligence plaintiff suffered painful permanent physical injuries and great mental distress, including the probable loss of use or amputation of her left hand.

The second and third "causes of action" are predicated on defendants' failure to comply with three related sections of the Penal Code. Section 11160 provides in relevant part that every hospital to which any person is brought who is suffering from any injuries inflicted "in violation of any penal law of this State" [4] must report that fact immediately, by telephone and in writing, to the local law enforcement authorities. Section 11161 imposes the identical duty on every physician who has under his care any person suffering from any such injuries. Section 11161.5 deals specifically with child abuse, and declares in pertinent part that in any case in which a minor is under a physician's care or is brought to him for diagnosis, examination or treatment, and "it appears to the physician" from observation of the minor that the latter has any physical injuries "which appear to have been inflicted upon him by other than accidental means by any person," he must report that fact by telephone and in writing to the local law enforcement authorities and the juvenile probation department.[5]

4. Among such laws, of course, are the statutes penalizing child abuse. (Pen.Code, §§ 273a, 273d.)

5. The statute imposes the same duty on certain other health care professionals, school officials and teachers, child care supervisors, and social workers.

All three sections require the report to state the name of the victim, if known, together with his whereabouts and the character and extent of his injuries; and a violation of any of the sections is a misdemeanor (§ 11162).

By means of allegations phrased largely in the statutory language plaintiff undertakes to charge defendants with a duty to comply with section 11161.5 (second "cause of action") and sections 11160 and 11161 (third "cause of action"), and avers that they failed to make the reports thus required by law. Her allegations of proximate cause and damages on these counts are essentially identical to those of the first count.

. . .

The standard of care in malpractice cases is also well known. With unimportant variations in phrasing, we have consistently held that a physician is required to possess and exercise, in both diagnosis and treatment, that reasonable degree of knowledge and skill which is ordinarily possessed and exercised by other members of his profession in similar circumstances. . . .

The first question presented, accordingly, is whether the foregoing standard of care includes a requirement that the physician know how to diagnose and treat the battered child syndrome.

It appears from the literature that the battered child syndrome was first tentatively identified and reported to the medical profession in the early 1950s. Further surveys and analyses of the syndrome followed, culminating in a landmark article published in 1962 in the Journal of the American Medical Association. (Kempe et al., The Battered-Child Syndrome (1962) 181 A.M.A.J. 17.) Since that date numerous additional studies of the condition have been undertaken, and their results and recommendations publicized in the medical journals.

California courts have not been oblivious to this development. In a prosecution for child abuse reviewed in 1971—the same year as the events here in issue—the Court of Appeal held admissible the testimony of a physician identifying the typical elements of the battered child syndrome. (People v. Jackson (1971) 18 Cal.App.3d 504, 506, 95 Cal.Rptr. 919.) The court explained that a physician's diagnosis of battered child syndrome essentially means that the victim's injuries were not inflicted by accidental means, and "This conclusion is based upon an extensive study of the subject by medical science." (Id. at p. 507, 95 Cal.Rptr. at p. 921.) Citing portions of the literature referred to hereinabove, the court concluded (*ibid.*) that "the diagnosis of the 'battered child syndrome' has become *an accepted medical diagnosis.*" (Italics added.) Indeed, the Court of Appeal added that "Trial courts have long recognized the 'battered child syndrome' and it has been accepted as a legally qualified diagnosis on the trial court level for some time . . . ." (Id. at pp. 507–508, 95 Cal.Rptr. at p. 921; . . .)

While helpful, the foregoing general history of the battered child syndrome is not conclusive on the precise question in the case at bar. The question is whether a reasonably prudent physician examining this plaintiff in 1971 would have been led to suspect she was a victim of the battered child syndrome from the particular injuries and circumstances presented to him, would have confirmed that diagnosis by ordering X-rays of her entire skeleton, and would have promptly reported his findings to appropriate authorities to prevent a recurrence of the injuries. There are numerous recommendations to follow each of these diagnostic and treatment procedures in the medical literature cited above.[7]

Despite these published admonitions to the profession, however, neither this nor any other court possesses the specialized knowledge necessary to resolve the issue as a matter of law. We simply do not know whether the views espoused in the literature had been generally adopted in the medical profession by the year 1971, and whether the ordinarily prudent physician was conducting his practice in accordance therewith. The question remains one of fact, to be decided on the basis of expert testimony: "The standard of care against which the acts of a physician are to be measured is a matter peculiarly within the knowledge of experts; it presents the basic issue in a malpractice action and can only be proved by their testimony [citations], unless the conduct required by the particular circumstances is within the common knowledge of the layman." (Sinz v. Owens (1949) 33 Cal.2d 749, 753, 205 P.2d 3, 5; . . .)

Inasmuch as the "common knowledge" exception to the foregoing rule does not apply on the facts here alleged, the trial court could not properly conclude as a matter of law that defendants' standard of professional care did not include the diagnostic and treatment procedures outlined in the complaint. Plaintiff is therefore entitled to the opportunity to prove by way of expert testimony that in the circum-

---

7. For example, the leading article by Kempe et al., op. cit. supra, 181 A.M.A.J. 17, states that "A physician needs to have a high initial level of suspicion of the diagnosis of the battered-child syndrome in instances of subdural hematoma, multiple unexplained fractures at different stages of healing, failure to thrive, when soft tissue swelling or skin bruising are present, or in any other situation where the degree and type of injury is at variance with the history given regarding its occurrence . . . ." (Id. at p. 20.) Of the different types of fractures exhibited, an arm or leg fracture caused by a twisting force is particularly significant because "The extremities are the 'handles' for rough handling" of the child by adults. (Id. at p. 22.) The article also contains numerous recommendations to conduct a "radiologic examination of the entire skeleton" for the purpose of confirming the diagnosis, explaining that "To the informed physician, the bones tell a story the child is too young or too frightened to tell." (Id. at p. 18.) Finally, on the subject of management of the case it is repeatedly emphasized that the physician "should report possible willful trauma to the police department or any special children's protective service that operates in his community" (id. at p. 23) in order to forestall further injury to the child: "All too often, despite the apparent cooperativeness of the parents and their apparent desire to have the child with them, the child returns to his home only to be assaulted again and suffer permanent brain damage or death." (Id. at p. 24.)

stances of this case a reasonably prudent physician would have followed those procedures.[8]

The second principal question in the case is proximate cause. Under the allegations of the complaint it is evident that the continued beating inflicted on plaintiff by her mother and Reyes after she was released from the San Jose Hospital and returned to their custody constituted an "intervening act" that was the immediate cause in fact of the injuries for which she seeks to recover. (Rest.2d Torts, § 441.) It is well settled in this state, however, that an intervening act does not amount to a "superseding cause" relieving the negligent defendant of liability (id., § 440) if it was reasonably foreseeable: "[A]n actor may be liable if his negligence is a substantial factor in causing an injury, and he is not relieved of liability because of the intervening act of a third person if such act was reasonably foreseeable at the time of his negligent conduct." (Vesely v. Sager (1971) 5 Cal.3d 153, 163, 95 Cal.Rptr. 623, 630, 486 P.2d 151, 158, and cases cited.) Moreover, under section 449 of the Restatement Second of Torts that foreseeability may arise directly from the risk created by the original act of negligence: "If the likelihood that a third person may act in a particular manner is the hazard or one of the hazards which makes the actor negligent, such an act whether innocent, negligent, intentionally tortious, *or criminal* does not prevent the actor from being liable for harm caused thereby." (Italics added.)

. . . .

We cannot say categorically that an ordinarily prudent physician who had correctly diagnosed that plaintiff was a victim of the bat-

---

8. Whether the physician would have followed the procedure of reporting plaintiff's injuries to the authorities, however, is not solely a question of good medical practice. The above-cited reporting statutes (Pen.Code, §§ 11160–11161.5) were in force in 1971. They evidence a determination by the Legislature that in the event a physician does diagnose a battered child syndrome, due care includes a duty to report that fact to the authorities. In other words, since the enactment of these statutes a physician who diagnoses a battered child syndrome will not be heard to say that other members of his profession would not have made such a report. The same is true of each of the persons and entities covered by this legislation. Accordingly, although expert testimony on the issue of a duty to report is admissible, it is not mandatory.

The statute also lays to rest defendant Flood's concern that if he were required to report his findings to the authorities he might be held liable for violation of the physician-patient privilege. (Evid. Code, § 992.) Section 11161.5 specifical-

ly exempts the physician from any civil or criminal liability for making a report pursuant to its terms.

Defendants complain that the first "cause of action" is nevertheless fatally defective because it assertedly fails to allege certain specific facts, i.e., that Dr. Flood negligently treated plaintiff's leg fracture, that proper treatment of that fracture or the bruises on plaintiff's back included taking an X-ray of her skull, and that Dr. Flood negligently failed to ask plaintiff's mother for an explanation of the cause of the fracture. None of these allegations is necessary, however, because they are irrelevant to the gist of the complaint. Plaintiff's theory is that in the circumstances of this case the fracture, the bruises, and the lack of an explanation offered by her mother are themselves indicia of the underlying battered child syndrome of which plaintiff was the victim, and it was that condition which defendants negligently failed to diagnose and treat. For the reasons stated, the complaint adequately alleges the facts necessary to support such a theory.

tered child syndrome would not have foreseen the likelihood of further serious injuries to her if she were returned directly to the custody of her caretakers. On the contrary, it appears from the professional literature that one of the distinguishing characteristics of the battered child syndrome is that the assault on the victim is not an isolated, atypical event but part of an environmental mosaic of repeated beatings and abuse that will not only continue but will become more severe unless there is appropriate medicolegal intervention.[9] If the risk of a resumption of physical abuse is thus a principal reason why a doctor's failure to diagnose and treat the battered child syndrome constitutes negligence, under section 449 of the Restatement the fact that the risk eventuates does not relieve him of responsibility.

Accordingly, the trial court in the case at bar could not properly rule as a matter of law that the defendants' negligence was not the proximate cause of plaintiff's injuries. Plaintiff is entitled to prove by expert testimony that defendants should reasonably have foreseen that her caretakers were likely to resume their physical abuse and inflict further injuries on her if she were returned directly to their custody.

There remain for consideration plaintiff's allegations that defendants violated Penal Code sections 11160, 11161, and 11161.5, summarized hereinabove, requiring doctors and hospitals to report certain injuries to the authorities. As noted at the outset, the complaint separately sets forth these violations as the second and third "causes of action." In fact, plaintiff has only one cause of action because only one of her primary rights has been invaded—her right to be free from bodily harm. . . . The charged statutory violations constitute simply an alternative legal theory in support of plaintiff's cause of action for personal injuries. . . .

Pursuant to our duty to liberally construe pleadings with a view to achieving substantial justice (Code Civ.Proc., § 452), we therefore treat the second and third "causes of action" as alternative counts setting forth plaintiff's theory of statutory liability. The purpose of that theory is manifestly to raise a presumption that by omitting to report plaintiff's injuries to the authorities as required by law, de-

9. See, e.g., Kempe et al., The Battered-Child Syndrome (1962) 181 A.M.A.J. 17, 24, quoted in footnote 7, ante; Boardman, A Project to Rescue Children from Inflicted Injuries (1962) 7 Soc.Work 43, 49 ("Experiences with the repetitive nature of injuries indicate that an adult who has once injured a child is likely to repeat. . . . [T]he child must be considered to be in grave danger unless his environment can be proved to be safe"); Fontana et al., The "Maltreatment Syndrome" in Children (1963) 269 New England J.Med. 1389, 1393 ("over 50 per cent of these children are liable to secondary injuries or death if appropriate steps are not taken to remove them from their environment"); Friedman, The Need for Intensive Follow-Up of Abused Children, in Helping the Battered Child and his Family (Kempe & Helfer eds. 1972) ch. 6, p. 79 ("it would appear from our investigations that the severe permanent damage associated with the 'battered child syndrome' usually does not occur with the initial incident. [Fns. omitted.] Identification of abuse at this time thus offers an opportunity for intervention with the goal of preventing subsequent trauma and irreversible injury to the child").

fendants failed to exercise due care—a presumption now codified in Evidence Code section 669.[11] Defendant Flood correctly concedes that the complaint alleges facts showing compliance with the first, third and fourth of the conditions specified in subdivision (a) of section 669; he reiterates his contention that the allegations of proximate cause are defective, but for the reasons stated above the point is not well taken. It follows that plaintiff is entitled to prove compliance and each of the four statutory conditions for invoking the presumption of lack of due care, shifting to defendants the burden of rebutting that presumption.[12]

Finally, defendants raise two questions of statutory interpretation. They contend that even if plaintiff may rely on Penal Code section 11161.5 in this case, she cannot invoke sections 11160 and 11161 because the latter are "general" statutes which have assertedly been superseded by the former as a "special" statute on the same topic. But such supersession occurs only when the provisions are "inconsistent" (Code Civ.Proc., § 1859), which is not here the case. Sections 11160 and 11161.5 are directed to different classes of persons, and hence are not inconsistent but complimentary. Sections 11161 and 11161.5 on the other hand, are duplicative of each other to the extent that the former deals with physical injuries unlawfully inflicted on minors and the latter deals with the observation of such injuries by a physician. But inasmuch as the same penalty is provided for a violation of each section, they do not present an irreconcilable conflict requiring one to give way to the other. There is nothing to prevent the Legislature from imposing a reporting requirement on physicians in two separate statutes, even if their coverage apparently overlaps.

Defendants next contend that plaintiff can rely on section 11161.5 only if she can prove that Dr. Flood *in fact* observed her various inju-

---

11. Insofar as relevant here, section 669 provides:

"(a) The failure of a person to exercise due care is presumed if:

"(1) He violated a statute, ordinance, or regulation of a public entity;

"(2) The violation proximately caused death or injury to person or property;

"(3) The death or injury resulted from an occurrence of the nature which the statute, ordinance, or regulation was designed to prevent; and

"(4) The person suffering the death or the injury to his person or property was one of the class of persons for whose protection the statute, ordinance, or regulation was adopted.

"(b) This presumption may be rebutted by proof that:

"(1) The person violating the statute, ordinance, or regulation did what might reasonably be expected of a person of ordinary prudence, acting under similar circumstances, who desired to comply with the law; . . ."

12. A number of recent commentators support this theory of liability. (See, e.g., Isaacson, Child Abuse Reporting Statutes: The Case for Holding Physicians Civilly Liable for Failing to Report (1975) 12 San Diego L.Rev. 743, 756–762; Ramsey & Lawler, The Battered Child Syndrome (1974) 1 Pepperdine L.Rev. 372; Fraser, A Pragmatic Alternative to Current Legislative Approaches to Child Abuse (1974) 12 Am.Crim.L.Rev. 103, 115 & fn. 51; Paulsen, Child Abuse Reporting Laws: The Shape of the Legislation (1967) 67 Colum.L.Rev. 1, 34–36; for a published recommendation to the same effect by one of plaintiff's counsel in the case at bar, see Kohlman, Malpractice Liability for Failing to Report Child Abuse (1974) 49 State Bar J. 118.)

ries and *in fact* formed the opinion they were caused by other than accidental means and by another person—in other words, that his failure to comply with the reporting requirement of the statute was intentional rather than negligent. We first note that the complaint in effect so alleges, thereby mooting the issue at this pleading stage. For the guidance of the court at the trial, however, we briefly address the point of proof.

The provision of section 11161.5 is ambiguous with respect to the required state of mind of the physician. It has been suggested that for the purposes of a criminal prosecution "the more reasonable interpretation of the statutory language is that no physician can be convicted unless it is shown that it *actually* appeared to him that the injuries were inflicted upon the child." (Italics added.) (Note, The California Legislative Approach to Problems of Willful Child Abuse (1966) 54 Cal.L.Rev. 1805, 1814.) We adopt that construction, as it resolves the ambiguity in favor of the offender. It is also applicable in the present civil action, because the presumption of lack of due care is predicated inter alia upon proof that the defendant "violated a statute" (Evid.Code, § 669, subd. (a)(1)), here section 11161.5. If plaintiff wishes to satisfy that requirement, it will therefore be necessary for her to persuade the trier of fact that defendant Flood actually observed her injuries and formed the opinion they were intentionally inflicted on her.[13]

The judgment is reversed.

NOTES

(1) If the abuse in the principal case had been in the nature of emotional abuse or sexual abuse, would the physician have had a statutory duty to report? Under current California law (see the reporting statute, supra p. 786), reporting of suspected infliction of mental suffering or emotional abuse is not mandatory for physicians or anyone else. Standard 3.1 of the Juvenile Justice Standards Relating to Abuse and Neglect only mandates reporting of physical abuse "inflicted nonaccidentally upon him/her by his/her parent(s) or person(s) exercising essentially equivalent custody and control over the child, which injury causes or creates a substantial risk of causing death, dis-

---

13. By parity of reasoning, the same rule will apply if plaintiff elects to rely at trial on sections 11160 and 11161 as well.

This does not mean, of course, that plaintiff can meet her burden only by extracting damaging admissions from defendant Flood. "The knowledge a person may have when material to an issue in a judicial proceeding is a fact to be proven as any other fact. It differs from physical objects and phenomena in that it is a state of mind like belief or consciousness and cannot be seen, heard or otherwise directly observed by other persons. It may be evidenced by the affirmative statement or admission of the possessor

of it. If he is silent or says he did not have such knowledge, it may be evidenced in other ways," i.e., by circumstantial evidence and the inferences which the trier of fact may draw therefrom. (Oil Workers Intl. Union v. Superior Court (1951) 103 Cal.App.2d 512, 532–533, 230 P.2d 71.) Plaintiff will therefore be entitled to introduce proof of facts alleged in her complaint as circumstantial evidence that defendant Flood possessed the requisite state of mind, and any conflict between such evidence and direct testimony of defendant Flood will be for the trier of fact to resolve.

figurement, impairment of bodily functioning, or other serious physical injury."

(2) Many statutes, e.g., the current California provision, supra p. 786, provide for a criminal penalty for failure to report a suspected case of child abuse, at least where the person failing to report is one required to report under the statute. Is the criminal sanction, which usually makes such failure to report a misdemeanor, likely to provide an effective incentive to report? Is the threat of civil liability for failure to report, as in Landeros v. Flood, a greater incentive? Standard 3.1(E) of the Juvenile Justice Standards on Abuse and Neglect provides for both a criminal penalty and civil liability for any injuries proximately caused by failure to report, supra p. 785. The Commentary expresses some misgivings whether either sanction is likely to furnish an effective incentive to report:

> The reporting statutes of twenty-nine states and the Virgin Islands provide misdemeanor penalties for failure to report. See also the proposed provision in A. Sussman, Reporting Child Abuse and Neglect: Guidelines for Legislation 33–34 (1975). This criminal penalty has, however, rarely been enforced in any state. It may be that the threat of civil liability, to reimburse the child or his/her estate, for harm coming from failure to report would be a more effective spur toward reporting. Initiative for such litigation would, however, rest with private parties and thus there is no great likelihood of its frequent or aggressive invocation. The question of choice between civil or criminal liability, or conjoining both, thus appears quite close, and the proposed standard reflects that conclusion.

Juvenile Justice Standards Project, Standards Relating to Abuse and Neglect, Standard 3.1(E), Commentary 69 (1980).

(3) Why would anyone, particularly a professional such as a physician, be reluctant to report a suspected case of child abuse, or fail to recognize a case of child abuse? Before the advent of child abuse reporting laws, this failure was perhaps easier to explain:

> The voluntary reporting of suspected cases to community authorities has been inhibited by many factors. . . . Neighbors and friends hesitate to make accusations. An abusive father or mother, facile with explanations, often escapes discovery because of the common assumption: "Certainly these respectable people couldn't do such a terrible thing to their children."
>
> Over the years, many physicians have failed to alert the community's resources for child protection to suspected cases of abuse. For a number of special reasons, they have kept their suspicions to themselves, treated the child for his injuries, and sent him home despite the possiblity of repeated abuse. Some physicians have not reported such cases because of their fear of civil or criminal liability; others have been reluctant to play the role of the "officious intermeddler," particularly when they will have to face irate parents. Some physicians have regarded reporting as a breach of the special confidential relationship between physician and patient, and still others have failed to report either because they did not know to whom to report, or because they had no reason to believe that reporting would result in benefit to the child.

Paulsen, The Legal Framework for Child Protection, 66 Colum.L.Rev. 679, 710 (1966).*

While the reluctance of friends, neighbors, and other nonprofessionals to report might still be explainable in part by incredulity, most of the objections that physicians and other professionals might have had in the past have been overcome by the waiver of privilege and immunity from civil liability found in most modern reporting statutes. What might explain any further resistance to reporting?

NATIONAL INSTITUTE FOR JUVENILE JUSTICE AND DELINQUENCY PREVENTION, A PRELIMINARY NATIONAL ASSESSMENT OF CHILD ABUSE AND NEGLECT AND THE JUVENILE JUSTICE SYSTEM: THE SHADOWS OF DISTRESS (April 1980) †

Incidence of Child Abuse and Neglect

Abuse

Efforts to determine the prevalence of child abuse in the U.S. during a specified period of time have been generally unsuccessful for a number of reasons. Due to the great variance in reporting laws, legal definitions of child abuse and neglect, and wide variation in data collection methods, statistical measures of the incidence of child abuse and neglect are presently unreliable. Increased public and professional awareness of the problem, as well as enforcement of reporting mandates, does not permit reliable trend analysis. In addition to problems with data collection, the difficulty in detecting or proving acts of abuse and neglect tends to confound efforts to develop a reliable method for determining the national incidence of child abuse. Therefore, to date, incidence data on child abuse and neglect must be considered as estimates rather than reliable indicators of the occurrence of the behavior. Table 1 clearly indicates the wide range of abuse and neglect estimates and the diverse sources of these estimates. The degree of specificity of the measurement criteria can be seen as an important factor influencing the reported incidence.

. . .

The most recent data on abuse is from a national study of official neglect and abuse reporting conducted by the American Humane Association.[1] This study used statistical information on officially reported cases from 28 participating States and three U.S. Territories for the year 1976. Prevalence data was collected on validated and non-validated reported cases of abuse, neglect, and the aggregate abuse and neglect.

* Copyright 1966, Columbia Law Review. Reprinted with permission.

† Copyright 1980, the American Justice Institute. Reprinted with permission.

1. The American Humane Association, National Analysis of Official Child Neglect and Abuse Reporting (1978).

Table 1

Comparison of National Estimates of the Extent of Abuse, 1962–1975

Measurement Criteria	Estimate of Incidence	Origin of data	Reference
Abuse, not further specified	662	Newspaper accounts, 1962 data	De Francis, V. (1963)
Abuse, not further specified	302	71 Hospitals, 1962 data	Kempe, et al. (1962)
Abuse, not further specified	447	77 district attorneys, 1962 data	Kempe, et al. (1962)
Abuse that resulted in some degree of injury	2,500,000–4,070,000 *	National survey, 1965 data	Gil (1970)
Serious injury by non-accidental means	10,000–15,000	1966 data, no source given	Helfer & Pollack (1968)
Abuse that resulted in some degree of injury	6,617	Central registries, nationwide, 1968 data	Gil (1970)
Reported abuse	60,000	Additive estimate, based on cases reported in Denver and New York City, 1972 data	Kempe & Helfer (1972)
Reported abuse	41,104	Official reporting systems from 10 largest states, 1973 data	Cohen & Sussman (1975)
Reported abuse	167,000	Agency survey, 1972–1973 data	Nagi (1975)
Abuse, not reported	91,000	Difference between projections from rate of reports in Florida and rate from agency survey, 1972–1973 data	Nagi (1975)
Parent-to-child violence	1,400,000–1,900,000	Household survey, 1975 data	Gelles (1977)

Source: *1977 Analysis of Child Abuse and Neglect Research*, Table 2, p. 9. (U. S. Department of Health, Education, and Welfare, National Center on Child Abuse and Neglect, January 1978).

* The report explains the disparity of these figures when compared to the others:

Gil's data has generally been regarded as an overestimate of the problem, since respondents probably used an imprecise definition of abuse and many of these incidents were never officially reported. Light [Abused and Neglected Children in America: A Study of Alternative Policies, 43 Harv.Educ.Rev. 556 (1973)] reanalyzed Gil's data and derived a lower estimate of 124,000 abusive families. Considering that these families may abuse more than one child, it is estimated that between 200,000 and 500,000 children are probably abused each year. Further, the same child may be abused more than once each year.

A total of 99,579 cases of abuse and neglect were reported by the participating States; however, 53 percent of these cases were not validated. This percentage indicates the significance of the issue of validating national data on child abuse and neglect. The definition of a "validated" case varies nationally; in some instances it means the case had been adjudicated; in others it means the social worker has determined that a case file has been created for the family; still in others it means that the reported incident did actually take place.

Neglect

Although national data on neglect is no better than data on abuse, and suffers from the same definitional and methodological deficiencies, it is generally agreed that neglect occurs more often. Cohen and Sussman [2] cite a ratio of 6:1 neglect to abuse; however, Polansky, Borgman, and De Saix,[3] analyzing data from the first 18 months of Florida's new reporting system, revealed more than a 3:1 ratio. Burt and Blair [4] cited a 9:1 ratio using neglect and dependency petitions for Nashville and Davidson County, Tennessee.

Nagi [5] estimated 432,000 cases of neglect reported in 1972–73 in the U.S. and 234,000 cases as not reported. Light [6] estimated a national figure of 465,000 cases of neglect and other maltreated incidents, excluding abuse.

Problems with Abuse and Neglect Estimates

Therefore, national estimates of the incidence of child abuse and neglect are confusing and often contradictory. According to the 1977 Analysis of Child Abuse and Neglect Research, the wide discrepancy in estimates may be attributed to a number of causes, most of which are related to the types of data sources used for activity incidence rates and the variation in definitions and awareness of the child abuse and neglect problem. Table 2 summarizes the problems with developing national estimates of child abuse and neglect.[7]

2. Cohen and Sussman, The Incidence of Child Abuse in the U.S., 54 Child Welfare 432 (1975).

3. N. Polansky, R. Borgman, and C. De Saix, Roots of Futility (1972).

4. Cited in K. Webb et al., Report and Plan on Recommended Approach(es) and Methods for Determination of National Incidence of Child Abuse and Neglect (1975).

5. S. Nagi, The Structure and Performance of Programs on Child Abuse and Neglect (1975).

6. Light, Abused and Neglected Children in America: A Study of Alternative Policies, 43 Harv.Educ.Rev. 556 (1973).

7. National Center on Child Abuse and Neglect, 1977 Analysis of Child Abuse and Neglect and Research (1978).

Table 2
Factors Affecting Discrepancies in Determining A
National Rate of Abuse and Neglect Incidents

FACTOR	DESCRIPTION
Accuracy of detection	Reluctance of persons to report child abuse and neglect to authorities. Lack of central reporting which permits hospital "hopping" by the parents.
Public and professional awareness	Awareness of the problem is increasing; however, more training and education of public and professionals is needed.
Degree of enforcement	States inadequately enforce reporting statutes. Also, there is great variation in reporting laws themselves.
Reporting bias	There is socioeconomic bias in reporting—middle-class cases are less likely than lower-class to be reported—because private doctors are reluctant to report, agencies are less likely to intervene with affluent families, therefore affluent families can maintain privacy and seclusion, and child welfare becomes viewed as a "poor people's service."
Comparability of statutes	States vary as to definitions of child abuse and neglect. Often child abuse and neglect statutes are difficult to interpret and apply.
Availability of resources	A community's resources influence what is reported. It appears that where there is a high level of need but little resources, fewer cases are reported and generally those reported are the more serious.
Sampling techniques	There is variation in sampling methods and reluctance of respondents to admit behavior that is socially undesirable and illegal.

Source: Table developed by National Juvenile Justice System Assessment Center, 1978

In summary, because of the many problems in obtaining accurate and reliable data on the national incidence of child abuse and neglect and the wide discrepancies in available estimates, it is difficult to have much confidence in even the most recent rates which vary from 40,000 abused children in 1973 to approximately 2 million children "vulnerable to injury" in 1975.[8]

NOTE ON THE INCIDENCE OF CHILD ABUSE AND NEGLECT: AN UPDATE

Since the foregoing analysis was published, two further significant studies have been published. The first, issued in 1979 and revised in November 1981, is the National Analysis of Official Child Neglect and Abuse Reporting for 1979, the latest in a series of annual reports conducted since 1976 by the American Humane Association for the National Center on Child Abuse and Neglect. This report is a summary and analysis of abuse actually reported by the states. The second, also prepared for and published by the National Center on Child Abuse and Neglect, is a report of the findings of the National Study of the Incidence and Severity of Child Abuse and Neglect, issued in September 1981. Unlike the first study, the second study was based on data collection resulting from sampling and a program definition of child maltreatment. It sought to avoid the inaccuracies inherent in using actual reported figures and attempted to develop a program design and methodology that would produce more realistic estimates of the incidence of child abuse and neglect.

In the first report, covering cases actually reported by the official state agencies, all 50 states, the District of Columbia, and three U.S. territories (Guam, Puerto Rico, and the Virgin Islands) submitted total numbers of cases of reported abuse and neglect, although only 30 states plus the three territories submitted individual case data giving more detailed information differentiating between abuse and neglect and between types of maltreatment. The total figure for *reported* abuse *and* neglect from all 50 states, the District of Columbia, and the three territories, without any further available information, was 711,142.

Perhaps more revealing, however, are the figures from the 30 states and three territories submitting individual case data. This group reported a total of 296,321 cases of combined neglect and abuse. Of this figure 62,014 were reported as cases of abuse, and 43,577 were reported as involving both neglect and abuse. Cases involving only neglect numbered 116,484, and the remaining 74,244 cases were reported as "Other" (which included "missing", "unspecified", and "other").

8. R. Gelles, "Violence Towards Children in the United States," paper presented to the American Association for the Advancement of Science, Denver, Colorado, February 1977.

Again, one must keep in mind the hazards of developing accurate figures for the incidence of abuse. The authors of the report note:

The total of 296,321 reports in the National Study data base in 1979 represents an increase of 55 percent over the total for 1978. This increase can be attributed primarily to two factors. First, while the total number of states that submitted case data remained 33, there was some change in the specific states submitting data. Part of the increase is due to the fact that some of the "new" states have larger populations—and therefore more reports—than was characteristic of those states that did not continue to provide data for 1979. Another factor is that state reporting systems themselves continue to develop in technical sophistication, which enables them to receive and process more reports and subsequently, to submit them to the National Study.

Among the group of states and territories reporting fully, using a data base of 225,514 reported cases, the figures were further broken down by type of maltreatment:

Major Physical Injury	4.38%
Minor Physical Injury	15.39%
Physical Injury (Unspec.)	2.46%
Sexual Maltreatment	5.76%
Deprivation of Necessities	63.08%
Emotional Maltreatment	14.86%
Other Maltreatment	8.87% *

* More than one type of injury may have been reported for a single child; therefore, the total for the figures shown is greater than 100 percent.

In the second report, one basic premise was that cases actually reported to child protective services (CPS) agencies and recognized as abuse and neglect represent only a small part of the larger problem; there are other cases not known to CPS but known to other investigatory agencies (police, public health departments, courts, etc.), and to professionals in schools, hospitals, and social service and mental health agencies, and to individuals such as the child, the abuser, friends, or neighbors. There are also cases of abuse that are not known or recognized by anyone, i.e., the abusing parent may not recognize his or her behavior as abusive, nor may the child or anyone else. These latter cases cannot be accurately measured.

On the basis of this program design and methodology the study arrived at a figure of 651,900 cases of abuse and neglect (or "maltreatment") over the one-year study period. This total was derived as follows. Of 1,101,500 cases reported to CPS agencies, 470,500 were children substantiated as victims of maltreatment by the CPS agencies, but only 212,400 of the latter number fit the study requirements (e.g., the definition of "maltreatment"). To these 212,400 cases, however, were added another 439,500 cases that came from non-CPS sources (i.e., law enforcement, courts, professionals in schools and hospitals, friends, neighbors, and all other sources mentioned above). The combined figures give a total of 651,900 cases. The report conservatively estimates, however, that over 1,000,000, and perhaps substantially more children are maltreated each year.

2. EVIDENTIARY PROBLEMS

Because child abuse occurs in the privacy of the family home and often involves persons with testimonial privilege, evidence in such cases is unusually susceptible to admissibility challenges. As one commentator has pointed out:

> The evidence that is available from eyewitnesses is for the most part useless. Even if the child is alive and mature enough to testify, he may have changed his account of the incident to match the abuser's version. The victim of child abuse is far more susceptible to the influence of the alleged abuser than are most victims of other crimes. While other siblings often are present when the child is abused, they also are easily influenced and intimidated. Further, the husband-wife privilege may prevent the other parent from testifying. The defendant, who alone may know how the injury occurred, usually will maintain that the child was hurt accidentally.
>
> . . .
>
> Most of the available evidence in child abuse cases is circumstantial. The jury must weigh not only the credibility of the witnesses but also the probabilities of the inferences that the prosecution desires the jury to draw. Therefore, the sufficiency of the evidence frequently becomes an important question.

Comment, L.L. Plaine, Evidentiary Problems in Criminal Child Abuse Prosecutions, 63 Geo.L.J. 257, 263–64 (1974).*

Testimony by one parent as to the other's abusive conduct has at times presented problems. At common law neither spouse was competent to testify for or against the other. Later on, spouses were allowed to testify for each other as the disqualification for interest was abrogated in favor of a rule that allowed interest to go to the issue of credibility. The rule that prevented spouses from testifying against each other remained, however, in the form of a testimonial "privilege" belonging to the spouse against whom the testimony was offered. Today, many of these testimonial privilege rules have been altered to permit a willing spouse to testify against the other spouse; the privilege thus belongs to the witness spouse. McCormick on Evidence § 66 (E. Cleary ed. 2d ed. 1972); see also Trammel v. United States, 445 U.S. 40, 100 S.Ct. 906, 63 L.Ed.2d 186 (1980).

Even where the testimonial privilege remains, it often is limited in application to criminal cases and even then an exception is made in a

* Reprinted with the permission of the Publisher, c. 1974 the Georgetown Law Journal Association.

case in which one spouse is charged with abusing a child of either spouse; the effect is that in either a civil or criminal case alleging parental abuse the other spouse would be free to give adverse testimony. See, e.g., Tex.Code Crim.Proc. art. 38.11 (1979). In states in which the privilege applies to both civil and criminal cases, the exception allowing spousal testimony in child abuse cases sometimes applies to civil and criminal cases alike. See, e.g., Calif.Evid.Code § 972 (1981). Sometimes, however, where the privilege applies to both civil and criminal cases, the exception is allowed only in criminal cases alleging child abuse. See, e.g., Minn.Stat.Ann. § 595.02 (Supp.1982). In addition, the exception itself sometimes is drawn so narrowly, e.g., to apply only where one spouse is charged with abusing the other, that spousal testimony is effectively precluded in child abuse cases. See, e.g., State v. McGonigal, 89 Idaho 177, 403 P.2d 745 (1965); State v. Riley, 83 Idaho 346, 362 P.2d 1075 (1961) (statutes were later amended to allow exception to privilege in child abuse cases, see Idaho Code §§ 9–203(1), 19–3002 (Supp.1980)). The problem may well be alleviated in any event if the child abuse reporting statute is one that provides for waiver of any privilege that otherwise would be applicable.

The marital communications privilege is quite different from the testimonial privilege. It is not a rule that disqualifies one spouse from testifying against the other but rather is a rule that seeks to protect the confidentiality of communications between spouses. Thus, one spouse would be competent to testify against the other spouse but could not testify as to any confidential communications between them. Nevertheless, an exception to the privilege is sometimes allowed as a part of the statute creating the privilege itself, to permit testimony even as to confidential matters in child abuse cases. See, e.g., Fla.Stat.Ann. § 90.504(3)(b) (1979). In addition, any waiver provision contained in the child abuse reporting statute would operate as a waiver of the marital communications privilege.

A number of jurisdictions have specifically eliminated the physician-patient privilege as well as the husband-wife privilege where child abuse is alleged. For example, Virginia's reporting statute, Va. Code § 63.1–248.11 provides:

> In any legal proceeding resulting from the filing of any report or complaint pursuant to this chapter, the physician-patient and husband-wife privileges shall not apply.

Similarly, Oregon's child abuse reporting statute includes a provision, Or.Rev.Stat. § 418.775, that:

> (1) In the case of abuse of a child, as defined in ORS 418.740, the physician-patient privilege, the husband-wife privilege, and the privilege extended to staff members of schools and to nurses under ORS 44.040 shall not be a ground for excluding evidence regarding a child's abuse, or the cause thereof, in any judicial proceeding resulting from a report made pursuant to ORS 418.750.

(2) In any judicial proceedings resulting from a report made pursuant to ORS 418.750, either spouse shall be a competent and compellable witness against the other.

In State v. Suttles, 287 Or. 15, 597 P.2d 786 (1979), the Supreme Court of Oregon reversed a holding by the Court of Appeals that a letter from a defendant convicted of sodomy on his 9-year-old stepson, written to his wife, was inadmissible as a "confidential communication". The Supreme Court held that the exception in the reporting statute was applicable in criminal trials despite the defendant's argument to the contrary.

NOTE

Meeting the burden of proof in either a dependency or neglect proceeding or a criminal prosecution may be difficult when the evidence has been largely circumstantial. Some have urged that a doctrine such as *res ipsa loquitur* should be applied in child injury cases where all the medical indications would seem to point to abuse and the parents can give no satisfactory explanation for the injuries. In Higgins v. Dallas County Child Welfare Unit, 544 S.W.2d 745 (Tex.Civ.App.1976), the court declined to apply the *res ipsa loquitur* doctrine in the strict tort law sense, but further explained its views on the matter of proof:

The application of *res ipsa loquitur* to child abuse and child neglect cases is a question of first impression in Texas. In some jurisdictions this doctrine has been adopted by statute. Some courts have applied it without express statutory authority. In re S, 46 Misc.2d 161, 259 N.Y.S.2d 164, 165 (Fam.Ct.1965); see also Brown, Medical and Legal Aspects of the Battered Child Syndrome, 50 Chi-Kent L.Rev. 45, 70 (1973). Learned commentators have pointed out that in many such cases the only proof available is circumstantial evidence since abusive actions usually occur within the privacy of the home, the child is either intimidated or too young to testify, and the parents tend to protect each other. . . .

Without necessarily adopting the doctrine of *res ipsa loquitur* with all of its implications in the law of torts, we agree that circumstantial evidence may be sufficient to establish child abuse or child neglect within § 15.02. Accordingly, we hold that a fact finding that parents either abused a child or knowingly allowed it to remain in dangerous conditions may be supported by evidence of (1) multiple injuries or other serious impairment of health that ordinarily would not occur in the absence of abuse or gross neglect, and (2) the parents' control over the child during the period when the abuse or neglect is alleged to have occurred. Lack of any reasonable explanation by the parents of the child's condition is an additional circumstance that may be considered in support of such a finding. The elements of proof above enumerated are not to be considered to be exclusive proof of other facts and circumstances to raise the issue of child abuse or neglect.

STATE v. WILKERSON

Supreme Court of North Carolina, 1978.
295 N.C. 559, 247 S.E.2d 905.

(For the opinion in this case, see page 759, supra).

NOTE

On the admissibility of expert testimony about the battered child syndrome generally see Annot., 98 A.L.R.3d 306 (1980); see also Note, 42 Fordham L.Rev. 935 (1974).

3. COMPETENCE OF CHILDREN TO TESTIFY

STATE v. SKIPPER

Supreme Court of Louisiana, 1980.
387 So.2d 592.

BLANCHE, JUSTICE.

The defendant, Timothy Skipper, was charged by bill of information with two counts of cruelty to a juvenile in violation of La.R.S. 14:93. Subsequent to defendant's waiver of trial by jury, the trial judge found defendant guilty as charged and sentenced defendant to five years at hard labor and fined him $1,000 plus court costs. The defense now appeals on the basis of six assignments of error.

On January 20, 1979, Virginia Skipper brought her five year old son, Barry Pontiff, to the emergency room of East Jefferson Hospital. Young Barry had second and third degree burns on both feet and on the lower part of both legs (the left leg had a sock type burn which extended from the middle of the calf downward) and had bruises all over his body. He was also so withdrawn that he showed no signs of pain and would not talk.

At trial, both Barry and Larry Pontiff, Barry's seven year old brother, testified that Barry's feet were burned when their stepfather, the defendant, put Barry into a tub of hot water. They also testified that defendant had whipped Barry on various occasions with a belt and with a stick. Officer Charles Lee testified concerning a statement given by defendant to the police. Defendant claimed that Barry's legs were burned when Barry, while unsupervised, ran the hot water into the bathtub and got into the tub on his own, and that the bruises occurred when Barry fell off a skateboard. He did admit that in the past, he had whipped Barry with a belt.

Dr. Herbert Rothschild, an expert on the battered child syndrome, testified that in his opinion, both the burns and the bruises could only be the result of child abuse. He stated that the injuries were not consistent with defendant's explanation as to how Barry had received them. As to the burns, he rendered the opinion that it was impossible for a child to get into a tub of hot water on his own and to burn both feet at the same time because no person steps into a bathtub except by putting one foot first. Also, as to the bruises, he believed their haphazard and linear nature indicated they were caused by something striking the child and were not all inflicted on the same occasion. He also opined that a skateboard fall ought not cause bruises over the entire body. Based on this evidence, the trial judge found defendant guilty as charged.

. . .

Assignments of Error Numbers 3 and 4

Defense counsel contends the trial judged erred in ruling that both Larry Pontiff, age 7, and Barry Pontiff age 5, were competent to testify. Defense counsel complained, both at the time of the rulings and in a motion for a new trial, that the two children lacked sufficient understanding to be witnesses.

La.R.S. 15:469 provides:

"Understanding, and not age, must determine whether any person tendered as a witness shall be sworn; but no child less than twelve years of age shall, over the objection either of the district attorney or of the defendant, be sworn as a witness, until the court is satisfied, after examination that such child has sufficient understanding to be a witness."

A trial judge's ruling as to the competency of a child witness is entitled to great weight upon appeal because he has had the opportunity to see and hear the child. State v. Thompson, 364 So.2d 908 (La. 1978); State v. Noble, 342 So.2d 170 (La.1977); State v. Francis, 337 So.2d 487 (La.1976).

The trial judge examined both Larry and Barry to determine their understanding. As to Larry, this 7 year old answered in the affirmative when asked if he understood the difference between telling the truth and not telling the truth, and also when asked if he understood why he was in court. He testified that his brother was burned when Timothy (the defendant) put him in hot water. He also said Timothy had whipped his brother with a stick and a belt. He was able to handle the defense attorney's questions concerning who had brought him to court, whether anyone had told him what to say, and whether what he told the judge was what he actually saw. Nothing in his testimony leads us to believe the trial judge abused his discretion in ruling that Larry was competent to testify.

Five year old Barry, the victim, also answered in the affirmative when asked if he understood why he was in court and if he knew he had to be truthful (although he did not know what a "fib" was). He understood the judge wanted him to tell his story about what happened to him. He testified that Timothy had whipped him. When questioned about the burns on his legs, he answered as follows:

"Q. How with [were] your legs burned?

"A. In hot water.

"Q. How were they put [in] this hot water?

"A. He put me in it.

"Q. Who is he?

"A. Timothy."

As with Larry, we do not believe the trial judge abused his discretion in deciding that Barry had sufficient understanding to testify. It was the trial judge who had the advantage of observing the manner of both Barry and Larry, a factor of great importance in determining their understanding.

Accordingly, these assignments are without merit.

. . .

Affirmed.

NOTE

In The Rights of Child Witnesses: Is the Court a Protector or a Perpetrator?, 17 New Eng.L.Rev. 643 (1982), Professor Jacqueline Parker proposes model legislation that would reduce the trauma to a child required to testify in court while also protecting the rights of the accused. For a discussion of possible approaches to this problem in the context of sexual abuse, see G. Melton, Procedural Reforms to Protect Child/Victim Witnesses in Sex Offense Proceedings, in Sexual Abuse and the Law (a Report of the American Bar Association National Legal Resource Center for Child Advocacy and Protection (1981) at 184 (J. Bulkley ed. 1981). For a more general discussion of problems of evidence in child abuse cases see Plaine, Evidentiary Problems in Criminal Child Abuse Prosecutions, 63 Geo.L.J. 257 (1974).

4. USE OF THE "BATTERING PARENT" PROFILE

STATE v. LOEBACH

Supreme Court of Minnesota, 1981.
310 N.W.2d 58.

YETKA, JUSTICE.

On July 31, 1978, appellant was charged with third-degree murder (Minn.Stat. § 609.195 (1980)) and first-degree manslaughter (Minn. Stat. § 609.20 (1980)) in connection with the June 1, 1978, death of his three-month-old son Michael. The case was tried to a jury in November 1978, in Wabasha County District Court, resulting in a verdict of guilty of third-degree murder. On March 9, 1979, appellant was sentenced to a maximum term of 15 years. This appeal followed. We affirm.

. . .

The victim, Michael Loebach, was born February 13, 1978. His mother, Anna, who had been serving in the U. S. Army in Georgia, was pregnant with Michael when she met appellant, who was also serving in the U. S. Army. She and appellant were married a month before the baby was born. Anna was discharged in December because of her pregnancy. Appellant received a general discharge in early March. In late March of 1978, they began living in an apartment building in Millville, Minnesota, where Anna's half-sister lived.

Both appellant and Anna looked for jobs, but only Anna was successful. She began work as a waitress in Rochester in mid-April. Because appellant remained unemployed, he acted as the babysitter whenever Anna worked. With one exception, the baby was in the custody and presence of either or both Anna and appellant during his entire short life. The one exception was in April, when appellant and Anna took a weekend trip and left the baby with Anna's half-sister. It was undisputed that the baby was not injured in any way on that occasion. The evidence was clear that the baby had no "accidents" and showed no bruises before Anna began leaving him in appellant's care while she worked.

Anna's half-sister, Laurel Hermanson, testified that late in April she saw a serious bruise on the baby's chin which followed the jawbone all the way to the end of the jawline. She testified, as did Anna, that appellant's explanation was that he had accidentally dropped the baby when he was bathing it and that the baby's chin had hit the tub.

Mrs. Hermanson testified that on another occasion, in early May, Anna brought the baby over to her and asked her, "Do babies get like this?" She testified that the baby had a bruised face, marks on his head, and looked terrible. She told Anna that babies don't get like that and she confronted appellant, asking him if he had hurt the baby. When appellant denied having done anything to hurt the baby, she told him they should take the baby to the clinic and that they should be prepared to answer questions because the doctor would certainly want an explanation. The baby was never taken to the clinic.

There was also testimony that the baby had numerous facial scratches, head bumps and black eyes during this period, but the explanation by both Anna and appellant was that the baby scratched himself a lot, bumped his head on the crib, and poked his eye until it was black and blue. Anna also admitted that she saw appellant "spank" the baby once.

In addition to the testimony of Mrs. Hermanson, who did not see Anna or the baby after May 15, and the reluctant testimony of Anna, the jury also heard the testimony of one of the neighbors in the apartment building. The neighbor testified that when Anna was gone and appellant was caring for the baby, he heard the baby crying, heard a slapping sound, and then heard appellant saying, "Now you stop that!"

The baby died sometime on the evening of June 1, 1978, when Anna was at work and appellant was in charge. The testimony of a number of appellant's neighbors who visited with appellant in the hall that evening was that appellant was drinking and was unusually sociable. One of these neighbors, Mrs. Lori Stock, went in to look at the baby around 8:00 or 8:30 p. m. that evening while appellant and Mr. Stock were talking. She testified that she put her hand on the baby, who was lying on his abdomen with his head facing the wall, but did not notice anything unusual. Mrs. Stock testified that she did not touch the baby for more than a moment because appellant came in and asked her to leave because he didn't want her to wake the baby. Sometime around 11:00 p. m., Anna arrived home but could not get into the apartment. Her loud pounding on the door failed to wake appellant. With the help of neighbors, Anna was able to get into the apartment through a window. Anna testified that when she got in, she found appellant asleep on the bathroom floor. She apparently checked the baby when she first arrived but did not notice anything wrong. When she checked the baby again at midnight, she noticed how cold he was and immediately knew that he was dead. She then ran out to the neighbors for help. The baby was in the same position it had been in when Mrs. Stock saw it at 8:00 or 8:30 that evening. There is strong medical evidence that the baby was dead by 9:00 p. m., possibly even when Mrs. Stock touched him sometime before that hour.

There is a conflict in the testimony of people who observed appellant and Anna shortly after the baby's death was discovered. Some testified that appellant was shook up and upset; others testified that his behavior was strange and inappropriate—for example, that he was cool, did not seem remorseful, expressed unusual concern about an ashtray, and turned on the stereo when the undertaker arrived.

A sheriff's deputy testified that appellant, who was obviously intoxicated, told him when he arrived that the baby had not been acting right, had not taken milk, and had died of crib death. Concerning bruises on the baby, appellant said he must have squeezed Michael too hard and that when he was giving the baby a bath, the baby must have slipped out.

The coroner, a licensed physician, testified that he immediately noticed an unusual bruise high on the baby's cheek near the temple and some 2- or 3-day-old bruises on the baby's back. Further, he testified that as he examined the baby, appellant interjected, in explanation of the bruises, that he had tossed the baby in the air playfully and that when he caught it, his fingernails had caused the back bruises. Both appellant and Anna objected when the doctor stated that he was ordering an autopsy. One witness testified that appellant was enraged by this.

The autopsy revealed back bruises, several bruises above one ear, one bruise on the jaw, and one between the nipples. The internal examination revealed 2- or 3-week-old rib fractures close to the spine. It also revealed that although there was no skull fracture, there was extensive brain hemorrhaging, some of which was caused by injuries occurring within the previous 24 hours and some by injuries 3 or more weeks old. It was determined that the hemorrhaging caused the death and that the injuries which caused the hemorrhaging were caused by some blunt force.

Appellant, in an interview by an investigator, repeated his version of the cause of the back bruises, claiming this incident occurred 2 to 3 days before the baby's death. Appellant also claimed that the baby often picked at his eye and even hit himself on the head. He admitted shouting at the baby if it cried, admitted spanking the baby, and admitted slapping it once in Georgia. The investigator testified that Anna said she occasionally noticed spots on the baby's head and that appellant's explanation was that the baby poked himself. The investigator also testified that Anna admitted asking appellant on two or three occasions if he had abused the baby and that Anna said his reply, which she believed, was that he had not.

Dr. Robert ten Bensel, an expert on child abuse, testified concerning the so-called "battered child syndrome." He concluded that it fit this case almost perfectly. The baby had not thrived and there were no organic reasons for this disclosed by the autopsy. The baby was in the 95th percentile by weight when born, but in only the 10th percentile at death; it was in the 95th percentile by height when born, but in only the 50th at death. At death, the baby had multiple bruises and injuries of different parts of the body, including the head. These injuries were both old and new. Dr. ten Bensel testified that he had never before seen rib fractures like those revealed by the autopsy. He testified that the fractures were so close to the spine that it would require almost total compression of the ribs and total squeezing of the body to cause these injuries. He also testified that throwing the baby in the air and catching it could not have caused such fractures. As for the hemorrhaging, some were 1 to 3 weeks old and some had occurred within 24 hours of death. The fresh bleeding was the result of multiple blows. The multiple injuries were clearly not caused by accidents of the kind the defendant stated and were not self-inflicted. Dr. ten Bensel was firmly convinced that the baby's death was the final result of nonaccidental physical abuse of the baby over a period of time.

Dr. ten Bensel also was permitted to testify, over a general objection by defense counsel, that battering parents tend to have similar personality traits and personal histories.

Defense counsel objected generally to the state's calling of two witnesses from appellant's past in an attempt to prove appellant fit the pattern of a "battering parent." Judith Carpenter is a former case worker who was assigned to appellant when he was a juvenile in Illinois. She testified that appellant's mother, who raised appellant alone, had abused him until he was old enough to fight back, that his mother expected too much of him, and that appellant was not good at controlling his anger. Charles Nelson, an employee of a school for disturbed adolescent boys which appellant attended for 3 years until he reached age 18, testified that appellant often withdrew from others, had a low frustration level, and was adolescent in behavior. Testimony from other witnesses also aided in showing that appellant fit the "battering parent" profile. There was testimony that appellant and Anna were isolated and did not have contact with many people and that in April 1978, appellant had slapped her and broken her nose. Defense counsel did not object to the testimony concerning the broken nose.

The defense strategy for countering this testimony was partly to show that the "battering parent" profile also fit Anna and that it did not necessarily fit appellant. In cross-examining Anna's sister, defense counsel elicited testimony that appellant was proud, confident and not lacking in self-esteem, whereas Anna was hypertense, unable to cope, unable to handle liquor, and was herself a victim of child abuse. Appellant's direct testimony, however, tended to corroborate the state's evidence that he fit the profile. He testified that his mother called him the man of the family and that he developed a bad temper.

Appellant denied abusing the baby. He testified that he did not see anyone else abuse the baby and that he had no explanation for the injuries the doctor found in the autopsy, although he thought he might have broken the baby's ribs when he accidentaly dropped the baby one day. He also testified that for a period of time, until warned by Mrs. Hermanson that it was dangerous, he had playfully thrown the baby high in the air and caught it. He testified that he stopped doing this 1 to 2 months before the baby died. He also testified that while he admitted slapping the baby once, the slap was more like a love pat.

1. Appellant contends that the state's use of evidence of his character constitutes prejudicial error and warrants reversal. The specific testimony objected to concerns that given by the state's expert, Dr. ten Bensel, and the two prosecution witnesses who knew appellant as an adolescent.

On direct examination, Dr. ten Bensel was asked to state the characteristics of a "battering parent." According to Dr. ten Bensel, the "battering parent" syndrome is an "inner [sic] generational phenomena" in that adults who abuse their children were often abused themselves. The doctor testified that abusing parents frequently experience role reversal and often expect their children to care for them. He also stated that battering parents often exhibit similar characteristics such as low empathy, a short fuse, low temper, short temper, low boiling point, high blood pressure, strict authoritarianism, uncommunicativeness, low self-esteem, isolation and lack of trust. Dr. ten Bensel did not testify that appellant possessed any of these characteristics, but the state's witnesses, Judith Carpenter and Charles Nelson, suggested that he did.

The obvious purpose for the introduction of the Carpenter and Nelson testimony and other character evidence was to demonstrate that appellant fit within the "battering parent" profile. The general rule as to the admission of such character evidence is contained in Minn.R.Evid. 404(a) which provides in relevant part as follows:

(a) *Character evidence generally.* Evidence of a person's character or a trait of his character is not admissible for the purpose of proving that he acted in conformity therewith on a particular occasion, except:

(1) *Character of accused.* Evidence of a pertinent trait of his character offered by an accused, or by the prosecution to rebut the same;

. . .

Appellant did not put his character in evidence in this case so the cited exception to the rule's general prohibition does not apply.

Even prior to the adoption of the Minnesota Rules of Evidence by this court, the general prohibition against the use of character evidence was well established in Minnesota. In City of St. Paul v. Harris, 150 Minn. 170, 184 N.W. 840 (1921), the long history of the rule was recognized by the court when it noted, "No rule of criminal law is more thoroughly established than the rule that the character of the defendant cannot be attacked until he himself puts it in issue by offering evidence of his good character." Id. at 171, 184 N.W. at 840; see State v. McCorvey, 262 Minn. 361, 114 N.W.2d 703 (1962); State v. Nelson, 148 Minn. 285, 181 N.W. 850 (1921).

There are three basic reasons for the exclusion of character evidence used to prove a criminal defendant acted in conformity with such character. First, there is the possibility that the jury will convict a defendant in order to penalize him for his past misdeeds or simply because he is an undesirable person. Second, there is the danger that a jury will overvalue the character evidence in assessing the guilt for the crime charged. Finally, it is unfair to require an accused to be prepared not only to defend against immediate charges, but also to disprove or explain his personality or prior actions. Justice Jackson, in Michelson v. United States, 335 U.S. 469, 69 S.Ct. 213, 93 L.Ed. 168 (1948), recognized the nature and extent of the potential prejudice to a defendant generated by character evidence. In a widely cited opinion he stated the reasons for exclusion of character evidence as follows:

> Courts that follow the common-law tradition almost unanimously have come to disallow resort by the prosecution to any kind of evidence of a defendant's evil character to establish a probability of his guilt. Not that the law invests the defendant with a presumption of good character, . . . but it simply closes the whole matter of character, disposition and reputation on the prosecution's case-in-chief. The state may not show defendant's prior trouble with the law, specific criminal acts, or ill name among his neighbors, even though such facts might logically be persuasive that he is by propensity a probable perpetrator of the crime. The inquiry is not rejected because character is irrelevant; on the contrary, it is said to weigh too much with the jury and to so overpersuade them as to prejudge one with a bad general record and deny him a fair opportunity to defend against a particular charge. The overriding policy of excluding such evidence, despite its admitted probative value, is the practical experience that its disallowance tends to prevent confusion of issues, unfair surprise and undue prejudice.

Id. at 475–76, 69 S.Ct. at 218–19 (citation and footnotes omitted).

The state argues that the potential for prejudice to defendants that justifies the rule excluding character evidence is outweighed by the public interest in assuring conviction of persons who batter children. The state's position is that the difficulties involved in prosecuting those who abuse children warrant an exception to the general rule. The victim, as the state's expert testified, is usually an infant and therefore particularly defenseless. Children who are abused are also almost wholly dependent on those who inflict the abuse. The victims' age and dependence act to prevent them from testifying against abusing caretakers. Finally, abuse almost always occurs when the child is in the exclusive care of a battering caretaker. These features of abuse cases make it very difficult to establish a defendant's guilt by means of direct evidence. The state contends, therefore, that an exception to the general rule is necessary to offset these obstacles to the prosecution of battering individuals.

In State v. Loss, 295 Minn. 271, 204 N.W.2d 404 (1973), the court was not directly confronted with the issue of the propriety of "battering parent" evidence, but rather with a sufficiency of the evidence question. What might be construed as approving that doctrine was simply dictum. In State v. Goblirsch, 309 Minn. 401, 246 N.W.2d 12 (1976), the court determined that "battering parent" evidence was not an indispensable element of the state's case in a prosecution arising from child abuse, but held it was not reversible error to receive it into evidence.

We now hold that in future cases the prosecution will not be permitted to introduce evidence of "battering parent" syndrome or to establish the character of the defendant as a "battering parent" unless the defendant first raises that issue. We feel this finding is required until further evidence of the scientific accuracy and reliability of syndrome or profile diagnoses can be established.

Our determination that the "battering parent" evidence should not have been admitted does not affect the result of this case in the court below. A defendant claiming error in the trial court's reception of evidence has the burden of showing both the error and the prejudice resulting from the error. A reversal is warranted only when the error substantially influences the jury to convict.

The record in this case indicates that the "battering parent" testimony consisted of only a small percentage of the evidence. The record also reveals that there was overwhelming evidence of appellant's guilt even without the "battering parent" testimony.

Various bruises and other injuries were observed on the baby prior to its death. The baby was in the exclusive care of appellant for a considerable amount of time. Appellant's statements as to how the baby was injured were inconsistent with the physical evidence and his earlier versions of what occurred. Appellant's wife did observe him spanking the victim, a 3-month-old baby, on one occasion. Testimony from a neighbor suggested that on another occasion appellant slapped and yelled at the baby. Appellant admitted that he slapped and spanked the baby at different times.

The physical evidence of abuse was substantial. There were bruises of different ages, head injuries, rib fractures of different ages, and brain hemorrhaging of different ages. The baby's weight and growth were not consistent with normal development. The state's expert testified that the baby's injuries could not have been sustained in the manner appellant claimed. It was the opinion of the state's expert that the child died as a result of battered child syndrome.

In light of this substantial evidence to support appellant's conviction, the error in admitting "battering parent" testimony was not prejudicial.

. . .

The conviction is affirmed.

NOTE

Courts are divided on the question of admissibility of character evidence in the form of evidence of prior acts of abuse. Representative of cases holding such evidence inadmissible is Harvey v. State, 604 P.2d 586 (Alaska 1979). An example of cases favoring admissibility under the exception allowing evidence of prior bad acts to show motive, identity, intent, and the like, is Grabill v. State, 621 P.2d 802 (Wyo.1980) (evidence of prior abusive conduct admissible to prove identity and intent or reckless disregard of consequences). The latter decision was criticized in Note, 16 Land & Water L.Rev. 769 (1981).

E. FOSTER CARE: AN INTERIM DIS-
POSITION WITH PROBLEMS

Since the virtual disappearance of orphanages some time ago, the United States has had no significant institution in which children can be placed when removed from their homes for neglect, abuse or dependency. Instead we have placed great reliance on foster placement. Foster parents who care for such children are approved, paid, and often licensed by the state. However the exact nature of the relationship between the foster parent and the child in his or her care has been the subject of increased controversy in recent years, as the cases that follow indicate.

While at one time foster care was considered only temporary, in fact this often is not the case. The term "permanent foster care" is now being used regularly in some contexts. Because of the concern that some children may never be returned to their natural parents after entering foster care, and that others may simply become lost in the system, there is considerable sentiment today for assuring that initial removal of a child from the home for foster placement is a step that should be taken only with the utmost care. For an analysis of the present standards for removal applied by the courts and a persuasive argument that removal should be a last resort, see Mnookin, Foster Care—In Whose Best Interests?, 43 Harv.Ed.Rev. 599 (1973).

In formulating any policy that would attempt to impose limitations on the removal of children from their homes for placement in foster care, it is important to understand that many placements that technically are labelled "voluntary" on the part of the parents actually result from the threat of proceeding under a neglect or dependency petition. The Juvenile Justice Standards on Abuse and Neglect (Tentative Draft 1977) * recognize the potential impact of a voluntary placement and urge that:

10.2 Need for statutory regulation

All states should adopt a statutory structure regulating voluntary placements.

10.3 Preplacement inquiries

Prior to accepting a child for voluntary placement, the agency worker should:

A. Explore fully with the parents the need for placement and the alternatives to placement of the child.

B. Prepare a social study on the need for placement; the study should explore alternatives to placement and elaborate the reasons why placement is necessary. However, a child may be

---

* Reprinted with permission from Standards Relating to Abuse and Neglect (Tentative Draft), Copyright 1977, Ballinger Publishing Company.

placed prior to completion of the social study if the child would be endangered if left at home or the parents cannot care for the child at home even if provided with services.

C.   Review with an agency supervisor the decision to place the child.

D.   Determine that an adequate placement is in fact available for the child.

10.4   Placement agreements

When a child is accepted for placement, the agency should enter into a formal agreement with the parents specifying the rights and obligations of each party.   The agreement should contain at least the following provisions:

A.   a statement by the parents that the placement is completely voluntary on their part and not made under any threats or pressure from an agency;

B.   a statement by the parents that they have discussed the need for placement, and alternatives to placement, with the agency worker and have concluded that they cannot care for their child at home;

C.   notice that the parents may resume custody of their child within forty-eight hours of notifying the agency of their desire to do so;

D.   a statement by the parents that they will maintain contact with the child while he/she is in placement;

E.   a statement by the agency that it will provide the parents with services to enable them to resume custody of their child;

F.   notification to the parents of the specific worker in charge of helping them resume custody and an agreement that the agency will inform the parents immediately if there is a change in workers assigned to them;

G.   a statement that if the child remains in placement longer than six months, the case will automatically be reviewed by the juvenile court, and that termination of parental rights might occur if the child remains in placement for one year.

10.5   Parental involvement in placement

The agency should involve the parents, and the child, in the placement process to the maximum extent possible, including consulting with the parents, and the child if he/she is of sufficient maturity, in the choice of an appropriate placement and should request the parents to participate in bringing the child to the new home or facility.

10.6   Written plans

Within two weeks of accepting a child for placement, the agency and parents should develop a written plan describing the steps that will be taken by each to facilitate the quickest possible return of the child and to maximize parent-child contact during placement. The plan should contain at least the following elements:

A.   provisions for maximum possible visitation;

B.   a description of the specific services that will be provided by the agency to aid the parents;

C.   a description of the specific changes in parental condition or home environment that are necessary in order for the parents to resume custody; and

D.   provisions for helping the parents participate in the care of the child while he/she is in placement.

10.7   Juvenile court supervision

No child should remain in placement longer than six months unless the child is made a ward of the juvenile court, and the court, at a hearing in which both the parents and child are represented by counsel, finds that continued placement is necessary.

J.M.A. v. STATE

Supreme Court of Alaska, 1975.
542 P.2d 170.

BOOCHEVER, JUSTICE.

[A foster parent, licensed by the State of Alaska and receiving a monthly allowance of $233 per child from the State, became concerned that visits to her home by children who were strangers might be related to trafficking in drugs. The foster parent, Mrs. Blankenship, searched the room of her foster child, J.M.A., and listened on an extension telephone to one of his calls without the child's permission. She found a bag of marijuana in one of his pockets and consulted the social worker assigned to J.M.A. for advice on how to deal with the problem. The social worker called the police. A police officer went to the Blankenship home, confronted J.M.A. and questioned him about the marijuana without giving any *Miranda* warnings. At trial, J.M.A.'s counsel moved to suppress the evidence obtained by the foster parent. The motion was denied and J.M.A. was adjudicated a delinquent child and committed to the Department of Social Services to be placed in a correctional or detention facility for an indeterminate period not to extend past his 19th birthday. J.M.A. appeals from the delinquency adjudication and the ruling on the motion to suppress.]

. . . [W]e must determine whether the state and federal constitutional prohibitions [4] against unreasonable searches and seizures apply to a foster parent, licensed and paid by the state, and if so, whether the exclusionary rule, whereby evidence obtained in violation of the constitution is held inadmissible, should apply. Our analysis must initially focus on the question of whether the foster parent stands in such a relationship to the state as to be subject to the constitutional prohibitions against unreasonable searches and seizures. J.M.A. contends that the evidence gathered by Mrs. Blankenship should be suppressed since these warrantless searches were executed while Mrs. Blankenship was acting as an agent of the state, and thus did not comport with constitutional requirements concerning such actions. The state, to the contrary, argues that Mrs. Blankenship, as a foster parent, is not an agent of the state for purposes of the fourth amendment.

. . .

Although the constitutional prohibitions against unreasonable searches and seizures have not been specifically limited to state action, there is little doubt but that was the original intent. . . .

There is a further limitation on the scope of the fourth amendment in that it does not apply to searches engaged in by governmental officials when such officials act for a private purpose or outside the scope of duties related to law enforcement. Such a limitation involves a question of the capacity in which the state agent acts during the course of the search. . . .

. . .

. . . [I]t is apparent that, in some respects, Mrs. Blankenship is an agent of the state. Her home is licensed and regulated by the state, and she is paid by the state for caring for foster children. But she also acts in a private capacity in managing the home for her family and herself. In all likelihood, her search of J.M.A.'s room and her listening to his telephone conversation involved both her state duties and her private functions. In both capacities, she had a need to supervise the young people placed under her control, and, solely as a private person, she had a legitimate concern about the illegal activities taking place in her home.

The mere fact that Mrs. Blankenship may have been acting in part as an agent of the state, however, does not necessarily mean that fourth amendment prohibitions apply. . . .

. . .

A foster parent is required both to assume temporarily the role of a natural parent to the child committed to his custody and to aid in the discharge of the government's obligation to care for and super-

4. The fourth amendment of the United States Constitution provides in part:

The right of the people to be secure in their persons, houses, papers and effects, against unreasonable searches and seizures, shall not be violated

. . . .

. . .

vise those juveniles who have become the responsibility of the state. In substituting for a natural parent, the foster parent is no more an agent of the police than would be any natural parent. The actions of Mrs. Blankenship were in no manner instigated by the police. She testified that she did not want her children to get into trouble with the police and that she sought to work out such problems without police involvement. In fact, even after discovering the marijuana, she contacted J.M.A.'s social worker rather than the police. There is no reason for regarding Mrs. Blankenship's actions undertaken while fulfilling this parental role, which did not involve collaboration with the police, as being any different from the actions of a private parent, and, therefore, not subject to fourth amendment constitutional restraints.

The second function undertaken by foster parents, that of caring for and supervising foster children on behalf of the state, quite obviously involves the foster parent in a relationship with the state which may be characterized as an agency relationship. At least insofar as the supervision of J.M.A. is concerned, even as an agent of the state, we suggest without deciding that Mrs. Blankenship had the right to search J.M.A.'s room. He had previously been declared a delinquent and was placed in the Blankenship home as an alternative to placement in a correctional institution. Had he been placed in a correctional institution, his room would have been legally subject to searches. "In prison, official surveillance has traditionally been the order of the day."

Thus, if Mrs. Blankenship's relationship with J.M.A. is analogized to that of parent and child, the search did not violate the fourth amendment, and if the relationship were to be construed as similar to that involved had J.M.A. been placed in a correctional institution, again there would be no violation. In this instance, the operator of a foster home is in the extremely difficult position of endeavoring to fulfill the role of parent, and, at the same time, perform the task of supervising the activities of a minor found to be a delinquent. Under the circumstances of such a relationship, a search of the room can hardly be regarded as the type of unreasonable activity constitutionally prohibited. Nevertheless, we believe that the privacy of both natural and foster children should be respected to the fullest extent consistent with parental responsibilities.

Quite obviously, the duties of foster parents do not encompass responsibilities of a law enforcement officer . . . . Foster parents are not charged with the enforcement of penal statutes or regulations, nor are they entrusted with ensuring the physical security of the public. . . . They merely supervise on behalf of the state those children committed to their care. . . . [A]ccordingly, we hold that foster parents are not agents of the state for purposes of the fourth amendment.

Our conclusion that the trial court did not err in denying the motion to suppress is bolstered by application of the policies underlying the exclusionary rule to the facts of this case. . . . .

. . .

. . . [T]he purpose of the rule is not to give shelter to those who have violated criminal laws but to insure that the constitutional rights of all citizens will be maintained. Police, knowing that illegally-obtained evidence cannot be used, are encouraged to comply with constitutional provisions. In the instant case, a principal motivating factor of Mrs. Blankenship's actions must have been a desire to aid her foster child as well as to have her home free of illegal drugs and criminal activity. Excluding the evidence seized herein would do nothing to deter similar future conduct by the Blankenships and other foster parents as that interest is entirely separate from a desire to have a person convicted of a crime or adjudged a delinquent. Put another way, the incentive to make a search under the circumstances here involved would not be lessened because of the likelihood that the evidence would be suppressed. In short, the primary purpose to be served by the exclusionary rule would not be served by its application in this case or ones similar to it.

. . .

NOTE

In Carroll v. Washington Township Zoning Commission, 63 Ohio St.2d 249, 408 N.E.2d 191 (1980), a married couple who served as foster parents to five or six children under contract with the Ohio Youth Commission sought a declaratory judgment that they were in compliance with township zoning regulations limiting their house to use as a one family residential dwelling unit. The Supreme Court of Ohio upheld a finding that the foster home violated the ordinance, which was a reasonable enactment of the township governing body. The Court found that "the children are in effect transients, staying varying periods from six months to a year. . . ."

Brown, J., dissenting, pointed out that "The factors relied upon by the majority to indicate that the Carroll family was not integrated could be used to conclude that any foster family, even a family with only one foster child", would not be permitted to live in a single family residential district. He added that "the policy considerations associated with foster homes . . weigh in favor of permitting such homes whenever possible in residential neighborhoods."

For a view contrary to that of the Ohio Supreme Court, see Group House of Port Washington v. Board of Zoning, 45 N.Y.2d 266, 408 N.Y.S.2d 377, 380 N.E.2d 207 (1978), in which the New York Court of Appeals stated:

Any foster care program . . . is in a very real way "temporary," since foster care by its very nature is simply a method of caring for children until they can either be returned to their natural parents or until an adoptive home can be found for them. Thus, the argument that petitioner's "group home" is not a family simply because petitioner hopes to eventually return the children to their natural families is unconvincing.

If this rationale were accepted, it could as readily be applied to allow the exclusion of a family with more than two foster children under this town ordinance. Such a result would, of course, be absurd. The flaw in respondent's position is that it would have us simply take the word "temporary," give it some talismanic significance, and apply it to exclude any "group home" regardless of the underlying realities.

Petitioner's very purpose is to create a stable, family type environment for children whose natural families unfortunately cannot provide such a home. As such, petitioner's "group home" would in no way detract from the family and youth values which one-family zoning is intended to protect. In fact, petitioner's "group home" might actually support and further those values even more effectively than certain natural families. If petitioner's "group home" is to be a success, it would most appropriately be placed in just such a quiet, residential neighborhood, for that is the very type of atmosphere which it seeks to emulate.

The surrogate family which petitioner hopes to create is in fact a permanent family structure, and not a temporary residence for transients. Although some of the resident children will be replaced by others as time passes, the family unit itself will continue.

Group homes also have been opposed on the basis of private subdivision covenants restricting use to single family residences. The subject is carefully analyzed in Brussack, Group Homes, Families, and Meaning in the Law of Subdivision Covenants, 16 Ga.L.Rev. 33 (1981).

SMITH v. ORGANIZATION OF FOSTER FAMILIES FOR EQUALITY AND REFORM

Supreme Court of the United States, 1977.
431 U.S. 816, 97 S.Ct. 2094, 53 L.Ed.2d 14.

MR. JUSTICE BRENNAN delivered the opinion of the Court.

Appellees, individual foster parents [1] and an organization of foster parents, brought this civil rights class action pursuant to 42 U.S.C.

1. Appellee Madeleine Smith is the foster parent with whom Eric and Danielle Gandy have been placed since 1970. The Gandy children, who are now 12 and 9 years old respectively, were voluntarily placed in foster care by their natural mother in 1968, and have had no contact with her at least since being placed with Mrs. Smith. The foster-care agency has sought to remove the children from Mrs. Smith's care because her arthritis, in the agency's judgment makes it difficult for her to continue to provide adequate care.

. . . .

Appellees Ralph and Christiane Goldberg were the foster parents of Rafael Serrano, now 14. His parents placed him in foster care voluntarily in 1969 after an abuse complaint was filed against them. It is alleged that the agency supervising the placement had informally indicated to Mr. and Mrs. Goldberg that

it intended to transfer Rafael to the home of his aunt in contemplation of permanent placement. This effort has apparently failed. A petition for foster-care review under Soc.Serv. Law § 392 filed by the agency alleges that the Goldbergs are now separated, Mrs. Goldberg having moved out of the house, taking her own child but leaving Rafael. The child is now in a residential treatment center, where Mr. Goldberg continues to visit him.

Appellees Walter and Dorothy Lhotan were foster parents of the four Wallace sisters, who were voluntarily placed in foster care by their mother in 1970. The two older girls were placed with the Lhotans in that year, their two younger sisters in 1972. In June 1974, the Lhotans were informed that the agency had decided to return the two younger girls to their mother and transfer the two

§ 1983 in the United States District Court for the Southern District of New York, on their own behalf and on behalf of children for whom they have provided homes for a year or more. They sought declaratory and injunctive relief against New York State and New York City officials, alleging that the procedures governing the removal of foster children from foster homes provided in N.Y.Soc.Serv. Law §§ 383(2) and 400 (McKinney 1976), and in 18 N.Y.C.R.R. § 450.14 (1974) violated the Due Process and Equal Protection Clauses of the Fourteenth Amendment.[3] The District Court appointed independent

older girls to another foster home. The agency apparently felt that the Lhotans were too emotionally involved with the girls and were damaging the agency's efforts to prepare them to return to their mother. The state courts have ordered that all the Wallace children be returned to their mother. We are told that the children have been returned and are adjusting successfully.

3. New York Soc.Serv. Law § 383(2) (McKinney 1976) provides:

"The custody of a child placed out or boarded out and not legally adopted or for whom legal guardianship has not been granted shall be vested during his minority, or until discharged by such authorized agency from its care and supervision, in the authorized agency placing out or boarding out such child and any such authorized agency may in its discretion remove such child from the home where placed or boarded."

New York Soc.Serv. Law § 400 (McKinney 1976) provides:

"Removal of children

"1. When any child shall have been placed in an institution or in a family home by a commissioner of public welfare or a city public welfare officer, the commissioner or city public welfare officer may remove such child from such institution or family home and make such disposition of such child as is provided by law.

"2. Any person aggrieved by such decision of the commissioner of public welfare or city welfare officer may appeal to the department, which upon receipt of the appeal shall review the case, shall give the person making the appeal an opportunity for a fair hearing thereon and within thirty days render its decision. The department may also, on its own motions, review any such decision made by the public welfare official. The department may make such additional investigation as it may deem necessary. All decisions of

the department shall be binding upon the public welfare district involved and shall be complied with by the public welfare officials thereof."

Title 18 N.Y.C.R.R. § 450.14, which was renumbered § 450.10 as of September 18, 1974, provides:

"Removal from foster family care. (a) Whenever a social services official of another authorized agency acting on his behalf proposes to remove a child in foster family care from the foster family home, he or such other authorized agency, as may be appropriate, shall notify the foster family parents, in writing of the intention to remove such child at least 10 days prior to the proposed effective date of such removal, except where the health or safety of the child requires that he be removed immediately from the foster family home. Such notification shall further advise the foster family parents that they may request a conference with the social services official or a designated employee of his social services department at which time they may appear, with or without a representative to have the proposed action reviewed, be advised of the reasons therefore and be afforded an opportunity to submit reasons why the child should not be removed. Each social services official shall instruct and require any authorized agency acting on his behalf to furnish notice in accordance with the provisions of this section. Foster parents who do not object to the removal of the child from their home may waive in writing their right to the 10 day notice, provided, however, that such waiver shall not be executed prior to the social services official's determination to remove the child from the foster home and notifying the foster parents thereof.

"(b) Upon the receipt of a request for such conference, the social services official shall set a time and place for such conference to be held within 10

counsel for the foster children to forestall any possibility of conflict between their interests and the interests asserted by the foster parents. A group of natural mothers of children in foster care[5] were granted leave to intervene on behalf of themselves and others similarly situated.

A divided three-judge District Court concluded that "the pre-removal procedures presently employed by the State are constitutionally defective," holding that "before a foster child can be peremptorily transferred from the foster home in which he has been living, be it to another foster home or to the natural parents who initially placed him in foster care, he is entitled to a hearing at which all concerned parties may present any relevant information to the administrative decisionmaker charged with determining the future placement of the child," Organization of Foster Families v. Dumpson, 418 F.Supp. 277, 282 (1976). . . . We reverse.

. . .

The expressed central policy of the New York system is that "it is generally desirable for the child to remain with or be returned to the natural parent because the child's need for a normal family life will usually best be met in the natural home, and . . . parents are entitled to bring up their own children unless the best interests of the child would be thereby endangered," Soc.Serv. Law § 384–b(1)(a)(ii) (McKinney Supp.1976–1977). But the State has opted for foster care as one response to those situations where the natural parents are unable to provide the "positive, nurturing family relationships" and

days of receipt of such request and shall send written notice of such conference to the foster family parents and their representative, if any, and to the authorized agency, if any, at least five days prior to the date of such conference.

"(c) The social services official shall render and issue his decision as expeditiously as possible but not later than five days after the conference and shall send a written notice of his decision to the foster family parents and their representative, if any, and to the authorized agency, if any. Such decision shall advise the foster family parents of their right to appeal to the department and request a fair hearing in accordance with section 400 of the Social Services Law.

"(d) In the event there is a request for a conference, the child shall not be removed from the foster family home until at least three days after the notice of decision is sent, or prior to the proposed effective date of removal, whichever occurs later.

"(e) In any agreement for foster care between a social services official or another authorized agency acting on his behalf and foster parents, there shall be contained therein a statement of a foster parent's rights provided under this section."

5. Intervenor Naomi Rodriguez, who is blind, placed her newborn son Edwin in foster care in 1973 because of marital difficulties. When Mrs. Rodriguez separated from her husband three months later, she sought return of her child. Her efforts over the next nine months to obtain return of the child were resisted by the agency, apparently because it felt her handicap prevented her from providing adequate care. Eventually, she sought return of her child in the state courts, and finally prevailed, three years after she first sought return of the child. Rodriguez v. Dumpson, 52 A.D.2d 299, 383 N.Y.S.2d 883 (1976). The other named intervenors describe similar instances of voluntary placements during family emergencies followed by lengthy and frustrating attempts to get their children back.

"normal family life in a permanent home" that offer "the best opportunity for children to develop and thrive." §§ 384–b(1)(b), (1)(a)(i).

Foster care has been defined as "[a] child welfare service which provides substitute family care for a planned period for a child when his own family cannot care for him for a temporary or extended period, and when adoption is neither desirable nor possible." Child Welfare League of America, Standards for Foster Family Care Service, 5 (1959).[8] Thus, the distinctive features of foster care are, first, "that it is care in a *family*, it is noninstitutional substitute care," and, second, "that it is for a *planned* period—either temporary or extended. This is unlike adoptive placement, which implies a *permanent* substitution of one home for another." Kadushin 355.

Under the New York scheme children may be placed in foster care either by voluntary placement or by court order. Most foster care placements are voluntary.[9] They occur when physical or mental illness, economic problems, or other family crises make it impossible for natural parents, particularly single parents, to provide a stable home life for their children for some limited period.[10] Resort to such placements is almost compelled when it is not possible in such circumstance to place the child with a relative or friend, or to pay for the services of a homemaker or boarding school.

Voluntary placement requires the signing of a written agreement by the natural parent or guardian, transferring the care and custody of the child to an authorized child welfare agency.[11] N.Y.Soc.Serv.

8. The term "foster care" is often used more generally to apply to any type of care that substitutes others for the natural parent in the parental role, including group homes, adoptive homes, and institutions, as well as foster family homes. A. Kadushin, Child Welfare Services 355 (1967) (hereafter Kadushin). Cf. Mnookin, Foster Care—In Whose Best Interests?, 43 Harv.Educ.Rev. 599, 600 (1973) (hereafter Mnookin I). Since this case is only concerned with children in foster family homes, the term will generally be used here in the more restricted sense defined in the text.

9. The record indicates that as many as 80% of the children in foster care in New York City are voluntarily placed. Deposition of Prof. David Fanshel, App. 178a. But cf. Child Welfare Information Services, Characteristics of Children in Foster Care, New York City Reports, Table No. 11 (Dec. 31, 1976). Other studies from New York and elsewhere variously estimate the percentage of voluntary placements between 50% and 90%.

10. Experienced commentators have suggested that typical parents in this situation might be "[a] divorced parent in a financial bind, an unwed adolescent

mother still too immature to rear a child, or a welfare mother confronted with hospitalization and therefore temporarily incapable of caring for her child." Weiss & Chase, The Case for Repeal of Section 383 of the New York Social Services Law, 4 Colum. Human Rights L.Rev. 325, 326 (1972). A leading text on child-care services suggests that "[f]amily disruption, marginal economic circumstances, and poor health" are principal factors leading to placement of children in foster care. Kadushin 366. Other studies suggest, however, that neglect, abuse, abandonment and exploitation of children, which presumably account for most of the children who enter foster care by court order, are also involved in many cases of voluntary placement.

11. "Authorized agency" is defined in N.Y.Soc.Serv. Law § 371(10) (McKinney 1976) and "includes any local public welfare children's bureau, such as the defendants New York City Bureau of Child Welfare and Nassau County Children's Bureau, and any voluntary child-care agency under the supervision of the New York State Board of Social Welfare, such as the defendant Catholic Guardian Socie-

Law § 384–a(1). Although by statute the terms of such agreements are open to negotiation, § 384–a(2)(a), it is contended that agencies require execution of standardized forms. The agreement may provide for return of the child to the natural parent at a specified date or upon occurrence of a particular event, and if it does not, the child must be returned by the agency, in the absence of a court order, within 20 days of notice from the parent. § 384–a(2)(a).

The agency may maintain the child in an institutional setting, but more commonly acts under its authority to "place out and board out" children in foster homes. § 374(1).[13] Foster parents, who are licensed by the State or an authorized foster-care agency, §§ 376, 377, provide care under a contractual arrangement with the agency, and are compensated for their services. The typical contract expressly reserves the right of the agency to remove the child on request. Conversely, the foster parent may cancel the agreement at will.[15]

The New York system divides parental functions among agency, foster parents, and natural parents, and the definitions of the respective roles are often complex and often unclear.[16] The law transfers "care and custody" to the agency, but day-to-day supervision of the child and his activities, and most of the functions ordinarily associated with legal custody, are the responsibility of the foster parent. Nevertheless, agency supervision of the performance of the foster parents takes forms indicating that the foster parent does not have the full authority of a legal custodian.[18] Moreover, the natural par-

ty of New York." 418 F.Supp., at 278 n. 5.

An *amicus curiae* brief states that in New York City, 85% of the children in foster care are placed with voluntary child-care agencies licensed by the State, while most children in foster care outside New York City are placed directly with the local Department of Social Services. Brief for Legal Aid Society of City of New York, Juvenile Rights Division, as *Amicus Curiae* 14 n. 22.

13. The record indicates that at the end of 1973, of 48,812 children in foster care under the supervision of the New York State Board of Social Welfare and the New York State Department of Social Services, 35,287 (about 72%) were placed in foster family homes, and the rest in institutions or other facilities. App. 117a.

15. . . . Evidence in the record indicates that as many as one-third of all transfers within the foster-care system are at the request of the foster parents.

16. The resulting confusion not only produces anomalous legal relationships but also affects the child's emotional status. The foster child's loyalties, emotional involvements, and responsibilities are often divided among three adult authority figures—the natural parent, the foster parent, and the social worker representing the foster-care agency. See, e.g., Kadushin 387–389; see also Mnookin I 624; Wald, State Intervention on Behalf of "Neglected" Children: Standards for Removal of Children from Their Homes, Monitoring the Status of Children in Foster Care, and Termination of Parental Rights, 28 Stan.L.Rev. 623, 645 (1976) (hereafter Wald); E. Weinstein, The Self-Image of the Foster Child 15 (1960).

18. "The agency sets limits and advances directives as to how the foster parents are to behave toward the child— a situation not normally encountered by natural parents. The shared control and responsibility for the child is clearly set forth in the instruction pamphlets issued to foster parents." Id., at 394. Agencies frequently prohibit corporal punishment; require that children over a certain age be given an allowance; forbid changes in the child's sleeping arrangements or vacations out of State without agency approval; require the foster parent to discuss the child's behavioral problems with the agency. Id., at 394–395. Furthermore, since the cost of supporting the child is borne by the agency, the

ent's placement of the child with the agency does not surrender legal guardianship; [19] the parent retains authority to act with respect to the child in certain circumstances.[20] The natural parent has not only the right but the obligation to visit the foster child and plan for his future; failure of a parent with capacity to fulfill the obligation for more than a year can result in a court order terminating the parent's rights on the ground of neglect.

Children may also enter foster care by court order. The Family Court may order that a child be placed in the custody of an authorized child-care agency after a full adversary judicial hearing under Art. 10 of the New York Family Court Act, if it is found that the child has been abused or neglected by his natural parents. In addition, a minor adjudicated a juvenile delinquent, or "person in need of supervision" may be placed by the court with an agency. The consequences of foster-care placement by court order do not differ substantially from those for children voluntarily placed, except that the parent is not entitled to return of the child on demand pursuant to Soc.Serv. Law § 384–a(2)(a); termination of foster care must then be consented to by the court.[22]

The provisions of the scheme specifically at issue in this litigation come into play when the agency having legal custody determines to remove the foster child from the foster home, either because it has determined that it would be in the child's best interests to transfer him to some other foster home, or to return the child to his natural parents in accordance with the statute or placement agreement. Most children are removed in order to be transferred to another foster home.[23] The procedures by which foster parents may challenge a removal made for that purpose differ somewhat from those where the removal is made to return the child to his natural parent.

responsibility, as well as the authority, of the foster parent is shared with the agency. Ibid.

19. Voluntary placement in foster care is entirely distinct from the "surrender" of both "the guardianship of the person and the custody" of a child under Soc.Serv. Law § 384, which frees the child for adoption. § 384(2). "Adoption is the legal proceeding whereby a person takes another person into the legal relation of child and thereby acquires the rights and incurs the responsibilities of parent in respect of such other person." N.Y.Dom.Rel. Law § 110 (McKinney 1964). A child may also be free for adoption by abandonment or consent. § 111 (McKinney Supp.1976-1977); Soc.Serv. Law § 384–b.

20. "[A]lthough the agency usually obtains legal custody in foster family care, the child still legally 'belongs' to the parent and the parent retains guardianship. This means that, for some crucial aspects to the child's life, the agency has no authority to act. Only the parent can consent to surgery for the child, or consent to his marriage, or permit his enlistment in the armed forces, or represent him at law." Kadushin 355. But see Soc.Serv. Law § 383–b.

22. The Family Court is also empowered permanently to sever the ties of parent and child if the parent fails to maintain contact with the child while in foster care.

23. The record shows that in 1973–1974 approximately 80% of the children removed from foster homes in New York State after living in the foster home for one year or more were transferred to another foster placement. Thirteen percent were returned to the biological parents, and 7% were adopted.

Section 383(2), n. 3, supra, provides that the "authorized agency placing out or boarding [a foster] child . . . may in its discretion remove such child from the home where placed or boarded." Administrative regulations implement this provision. The agency is required, except in emergencies, to notify the foster parents in writing 10 days in advance of any removal. 18 N.Y.C.R.R. § 450.10(a) (1976). The notice advises the foster parents that if they object to the child's removal they may request a "conference" with the Social Services Department. Ibid. The department schedules requested conferences within 10 days of the receipt of the request. § 450.10(b). The foster parent may appear with counsel at the conference, where he will "be advised of the reasons [for the removal of the child], and be afforded an opportunity to submit reasons why the child should not be removed." § 450.10(a). The official must render a decision in writing within five days after the close of the conference, and send notice of his decision to the foster parents and the agency. § 450.10(c). The proposed removal is stayed pending the outcome of the conference. § 450.10(d).

removal conference [margin annotation]

If the child is removed after the conference, the foster parent may appeal to the Department of Social Services for a "fair hearing," that is, a full adversary administrative hearing, under Soc.Serv.Law § 400, the determination of which is subject to judicial review under N.Y.Civ.Prac.Law § 7801 et seq. (McKinney 1963); Art. 78; however, the removal is not automatically stayed pending the hearing and judicial review.

hearing [margin annotation]

This statutory and regulatory scheme applies statewide. In addition, regulations promulgated by the New York City Human Resources Administration, Department of Social Services—Special Services for Children (SSC) provide even greater procedural safeguards there. Under SSC Procedure No. 5 (Aug. 5, 1974), in place of or in addition to the conference provided by the state regulations, the foster parents may request a full trial-type hearing *before* the child is removed from their home. This procedure applies, however, only if the child is being transferred to another foster home, and not if the child is being returned to his natural parents.

One further preremoval procedural safeguard is available. Under Soc.Serv. Law § 392, the Family Court has jurisdiction to review, on petition of the foster parent or the agency, the status of any child who has been in foster care for 18 months or longer.[30] The foster parents, the natural parents, and all interested agencies are made parties to the proceeding. . . .

sofegal [margin annotation]

. . .

30. The agency is required to initiate such a review when a child has remained in foster care for 18 months, § 392(2)(a), and if the child remains in foster care, the court "shall rehear the matter whenever it deems necessary or desirable, or upon petition by any party entitled to notice in proceedings under this section, but at least every twenty-four months." § 392(10).

Foster care of children is a sensitive and emotion-laden subject, and foster-care programs consequently stir strong controversy. The New York regulatory scheme is no exception. New York would have us view the scheme as described in its brief:

"Today New York premises its foster care system on the accepted principle that the placement of a child into foster care is solely a temporary, transitional action intended to lead to the future reunion of the child with his natural parent or parents, or if such a reunion is not possible, to legal adoption and the establishment of a new permanent home for the child."

Some of the parties and *amici* argue that this is a misleadingly idealized picture.

. . .

From the standpont of natural parents, such as the appellant intervenors here, foster care has been condemned as a class-based intrusion into the family life of the poor. See, e.g., Jenkins, Child Welfare as a Class System, in Children and Decent People 3 (A. Schorr ed. 1974). It is certainly true that the poor resort to foster care more often than other citizens. For example, over 50% of all children in foster care in New York City are from female-headed families receiving Aid to Families with Dependent Children. Minority families are also more likely to turn to foster care; 52.3% of the children in foster care in New York City are black and 25.5% are Puerto Rican. This disproportionate resort to foster care by the poor and victims of discrimination doubtless reflects in part the greater likelihood of disruption of poverty-stricken families. Commentators have also noted, however, that middle- and upper-income families who need temporary care services for their children have the resources to purchase private care. . . .

The extent to which supposedly "voluntary" placements are in fact voluntary has been questioned on other grounds as well. For example, it has been said that many "voluntary" placements are in fact coerced by threat of neglect proceedings . . . Studies also suggest that social workers of middle-class backgrounds, perhaps unconsciously, incline to favor continued placement in foster care with a generally higher-status family rather than return the child to his natural family, thus reflecting a bias that treats the natural parents' poverty and lifestyle as prejudicial to the best interests of the child. This accounts,[35] it has been said, for the hostility of agencies to the efforts of natural parents to obtain the return of their children.

Appellee foster parents as well as natural parents question the accuracy of the idealized picture portrayed by New York. They note

---

35. Other factors alleged to bias agencies in favor of retention in foster care are the lack of sufficient staff to provide social work services needed by the natural parent to resolve their problems and prepare for return of the child; policies of many agencies to discourage involvement of the natural parent in the care of the child while in foster care; and systems of foster-care funding that encourage agencies to keep the child in foster care.

that children often stay in "temporary" foster care for much longer than contemplated by the theory of the system. The District Court found as a fact that the median time spent in foster care in New York was over four years. Indeed, many children apparently remain in this "limbo" indefinitely. The District Court also found that the longer a child remains in foster care, the more likely it is that he will never leave: "[T]he probability of a foster child being returned to his biological parents declined markedly after the first year in foster care." 418 F.Supp., at 279 n. 6. It is not surprising then that many children, particularly those that enter foster care at a very early age and have little or no contact with their natural parents during extended stays in foster care, often develop deep emotional ties with their foster parents.[40]

Yet such ties do not seem to be regarded as obstacles to transfer of the child from one foster placement to another. The record in this case indicates that nearly 60% of the children in foster care in New York City have experienced more than one placement, and about 28% have experienced three or more. . . . [E]ven when it is clear that a foster child will not be returned to his natural parents, it is rare that he achieves a stable home life through final termination of parental ties and adoption into a new permanent family. Fanshel, Status Changes of Children in Foster Care: Final Results of the Columbia University Longitudinal Study, 55 Child Welfare 143, 145, 157 (1976); . . .

. . . [W]e present this summary in the view that some understanding of those criticisms is necessary for a full appreciation of the complex and controversial system with which this lawsuit is concerned.[41] But the issue presented by the case is a narrow one.

---

40. The development of such ties points up an intrinsic ambiguity of foster care that is central to this case. The warmer and more homelike environment of foster care is intended to be its main advantage over institutional child care, yet because in theory foster care is intended to be only temporary, foster parents are urged not to become too attached to the children in their care. Mnookin I 613. Indeed, the New York courts have upheld removal from a foster home for the very reason that the foster parents had become too emotionally involved with the child. In re Jewish Child Care Assn. (Sanders), 5 N.Y.2d 222, 183 N.Y.S.2d 65, 156 N.E.2d 700 (1959). See also the case of the Lhotans, named appellees in this case, n. 1, supra.

On the other hand, too warm a relation between foster parent and foster child is not the only possible problem in foster care. Qualified foster parents are hard to find, and very little training is provided to equip them to handle the often complicated demands of their role; it is thus sometimes possible that foster homes may provide inadequate care. . . .

41. It must be noted, however, that both appellee foster parents and intervening natural parents present incomplete pictures of the foster-care system. Although seeking relief applicable to all removal situations, the foster parents focus on intra-foster-care transfers, portraying a foster-care system in which children neglected by their parents and condemned to a permanent limbo of foster care are arbitrarily shunted about by social workers whenever they become attached to a foster home. The natural parents, who focus on foster children being returned to their parent, portray a system under which poor and minority parents, deprived of their children under hard necessity and bureaucratic pressures, are obstructed in their efforts to maintain relationships with their children and ultimately to regain custody, by hostile agencies and meddling foster par-

. . . The relief sought in this case is entirely procedural. Our task is only to determine whether the District Court correctly held that the present procedures preceding the removal from a foster home of children resident there a year or more are constitutionally inadequate.
. . .

ISSUE

Our first inquiry is whether appellees have asserted interests within the Fourteenth Amendment's protection of "liberty" and "property." Board of Regents v. Roth, 408 U.S. 564, 571, 92 S.Ct. 2701, 2706, 33 L.Ed.2d 548 (1972).

1

The appellees have not renewed in this Court their contention, rejected by the District Court, that the realities of the foster-care system in New York gave them a justified expectation amounting to a "property" interest that their status as foster parents would be continued. Our inquiry is therefore narrowed to the question whether their asserted interests are within the "liberty" protected by the Fourteenth Amendment.

The appellees' basic contention is that when a child has lived in a foster home for a year or more, a psychological tie is created between the child and the foster parents which constitutes the foster family the true "psychological family" of the child. See J. Goldstein, A. Freud, & A. Solnit, Beyond the Best Interests of the Child (1973). That family, they argue, has a "liberty interest" in its survival as a family protected by the Fourteenth Amendment. Upon this premise they conclude that the foster child cannot be removed without a prior hearing satisfying due process. Appointed counsel for the children, appellants in No. 76–5200, however, disagrees, and has consistently argued that the foster parents have no such liberty interest independent of the interests of the foster children, and that the best interests of the children would not be served by procedural protections beyond those already provided by New York law. The intervening natural parents of children in foster care, appellants in No. 76–5193, also oppose the foster parents, arguing that recognition of the procedural right claimed would undercut both the substantive family law of New York, which favors the return of children to their natural parents as expeditiously as possible, and their constitutionally protected right of family privacy, by forcing them to submit to a hearing and defend their rights to their children before the children could be returned to them.

f'p arg

np arg

. . .

We . . . turn to appellees' assertion that they have a constitutionally protected liberty interest—in the words of the District Court, a "right to familial privacy," 418 F.Supp., at 279—in the integrity of their family unit. . . .

ents. As the experiences of the named parties to this suit, and the critical studies of foster care cited demonstrate, there are elements of truth in both pictures. But neither represents the whole truth about the system.

834 ADEQUATE PARENTING

It is, of course, true that "freedom of personal choice in matters of . . . family life is one of the liberties protected by the Due Process Clause of the Fourteenth Amendment." Cleveland Board of Education v. LaFleur, 414 U.S. 632, 639–640, 94 S.Ct. 791, 796, 39 L.Ed.2d 52 (1974). There does exist a "private realm of family life which the state cannot enter," Prince v. Massachusetts, 321 U.S. 158, 166, 64 S.Ct. 438, 442, 88 L.Ed. 645 (1944), that has been afforded both substantive and procedural [47] protection. But is the relation of foster parent to foster child sufficiently akin to the concept of "family" recognized in our precedents to merit similar protection? [48] Although considerable difficulty has attended the task of defining "family" for purposes of the Due Process Clause, we are not without guides to some of the elements that define the concept of "family" and contribute to its place in our society.

First the usual understanding of "family" implies biological relationships, and most decisions treating the relation between parent and child have stressed this element. Stanley v. Illinois, 405 U.S. 645, 651, 92 S.Ct. 1208, 1212, 31 L.Ed.2d 551 (1972), for example, spoke of "[t]he rights to conceive and to raise one's children" as essential rights, citing Meyer v. Nebraska, 262 U.S. 390, 43 S.Ct. 625, 67 L.Ed. 1042 (1923), and Skinner v. Oklahoma, ex rel. Williamson, 316 U.S. 535, 62 S.Ct. 1110, 86 L.Ed. 1655 (1942). And Prince v. Massachusetts, stated:

"It is cardinal with us that the custody, care and nurture of the child reside first in the parents, whose primary function and freedom include preparation for obligations the state can neither supply nor hinder." 321 U.S., at 166, 64 S.Ct., at 442.[49]

A biological relationship is not present in the case of the usual foster family. But biological relationships are not exclusive determination of the existence of a family. The basic foundation of the family in our society, the marriage relationship, is of course not a matter of blood relation. Yet its importance has been strongly emphasized in our cases:

"We deal with a right of privacy older than the Bill of Rights— older than our political parties, older than our school system. Marriage is a coming together for better or for worse, hopefully enduring, and intimate to the degree of being sacred. It is an association that promotes a way of life, not causes; a harmony in living, not political faiths; a bilateral loyalty, not commercial or social projects. Yet it is an association for as noble a purpose as

47. See, e.g., Stanley v. Illinois, 405 U.S. 645, 651, 92 S.Ct. 1208, 1212, 31 L.Ed.2d 551 (1972); . . .

48. Of course, recognition of a liberty interest in foster families for purposes of the procedural protections of the Due Process Clause would not necessarily require that foster families be treated as fully equivalent to biological families for

purposes of substantive due process review. Cf. Moore v. City of East Cleveland, supra, 431 U.S., at 546–547, 97 S.Ct., at 1960 (White, J., dissenting).

49. The scope of these rights extends beyond natural parents. The "parent" in Prince itself, for example, was the child's aunt and legal custodian.

any involved in our prior decisions." Griswold v. Connecticut, 381 U.S. 479, 486, 85 S.Ct. 1678, 1682, 14 L.Ed.2d 510 (1965).

See also Loving v. Virginia, 388 U.S. 1, 12, 87 S.Ct. 1817, 1823, 18 L.Ed.2d 1010 (1967).

Thus the importance of the familial relationship, to the individuals involved and to the society, stems from the emotional attachments *Reason* that derive from the intimacy of daily association, and from the role it plays in "promot[ing] a way of life" through the instruction of children, Wisconsin v. Yoder, 406 U.S. 205, 231–233, 92 S.Ct. 1526, 1541–1542, 32 L.Ed.2d 15 (1972), as well as from the fact of blood relationship. No one would seriously dispute that a deeply loving and interdependent relationship between an adult and a child in his or her care may exist even in the absence of blood relationship.[51] At least where a child has been placed in foster care as an infant, has never known his natural parents, and has remained continuously for several years in the care of the same foster parents, it is natural that the foster family should hold the same place in the emotional life of the foster child, and fulfill the same socializing functions, as a natural family.[52] For this reason, we cannot dismiss the foster family as a mere collection of unrelated individuals.

But there are also important distinctions between the foster fami- *+ v n* ly and the natural family. (First) unlike the earlier cases recognizing a right to family privacy, the State here seeks to interfere, not with a relationship having its origins entirely apart from the power of the State, but rather with a foster family which has its source in state law and contractual arrangements. The individual's freedom to marry and reproduce is "older than the Bill of Rights," Griswold v. Connecticut, 381 U.S., at 486, 85 S.Ct., at 1682. Accordingly, unlike the property interests that are also protected by the Fourteenth Amendment cf. Board of Regents v. Roth, 408 U.S., at 577, 92 S.Ct., at 2709, the liberty interest in family privacy has its source, and its contours are ordinarily to be sought, not in state law,[53] but in intrinsic human rights, . . . Here, however, whatever emotional ties may develop between foster parent and foster child have their origins in an arrangement in which the State has been a partner from the outset. . . . In this case, the limited recognition accorded to the foster

51. Adoption, for example, is recognized as the legal equivalent of biological parenthood. See, e.g., N.Y.Dom.Rel.Law § 110, supra, n. 19.

52. The briefs dispute at some length the validity of the "psychological parent" theory propounded in J. Goldstein, A. Freud, & A. Solnit, Beyond the Best Interests of the Child (1973). That book, on which appellee foster parents relied to some extent in the District Court, is indeed controversial. But this case turns, not on the disputed validity of any particular psychological theory, but on the le-

gal consequences of the undisputed fact that the emotional ties between foster parent and foster child are in many cases quite close, and undoubtedly in some as close as those existing in biological families.

53. The legal status of families has never been regarded as controlling: "Nor has the [Constitution] refused to recognize those family relationships unlegitimized by a marriage ceremony." Stanley v. Illinois, 405 U.S., at 651, 92 S.Ct., at 1213.

family by the New York statutes and the contracts executed by the foster parents argue against any but the most limited constitutional "liberty" in the foster family.

A second consideration related to this is that ordinarily procedural protection may be afforded to a liberty interest of one person without derogating from the substantive liberty of another. Here, however, such a tension is virtually unavoidable. Under New York law, the natural parent of a foster child in voluntary placement has an absolute right to the return of his child in the absence of a court order obtainable only upon compliance with rigorous substantive and procedural standards, which reflect the constitutional protection accorded the natural family. Moreover, the natural parent initially gave up his child to the State only on the express understanding that the child would be returned in those circumstances. These rights are difficult to reconcile with the liberty interest in the foster family relationship claimed by appellees. It is one thing to say that individuals may acquire a liberty interest against arbitrary governmental interference in the family-like associations into which they have freely entered, even in the absence of biological connection or state-law recognition of the relationship. It is quite another to say that one may acquire such an interest in the face of another's constitutionally recognized liberty interest that derives from blood relationship, state-law sanction, and basic human right—an interest the foster parent has recognized by contract from the outset.[54] Whatever liberty interest might otherwise exist in the foster family as an institution, that interest must be substantially attenuated where the proposed removal from the foster family is to return the child to his natural parents.

As this discussion suggests, appellees' claim to a constitutionally protected liberty interest raises complex and novel questions. It is unnecessary for us to resolve those questions definitively in this case, however, for like the District Court, we conclude that "narrower grounds exist to support" our reversal. We are persuaded that, even on the assumption that appellees have a protected "liberty interest," the District Court erred in holding that the preremoval procedures presently employed by the State are constitutionally defective.

Where procedural due process must be afforded because a "liberty" or "property" interest is within the Fourteenth Amendment's protection, there must be determined "what process is due" in the particular context. . . .

It is true that "[b]efore a person is deprived of a protected interest, he must be afforded opportunity for some kind of a hearing, 'except for extraordinary situations where some valid governmental interest is at stake that justifies postponing the hearing until after the

---

54. The New York Court of Appeals has as a matter of state law "[p]articularly rejected . . . the notion . . . that third-party custodians may acquire some sort of squatter's rights in another's child." Bennett v. Jeffreys, 40 N.Y.2d 543, 552 n. 2, 387 N.Y.S.2d 821, 829 n. 2, 356 N.E.2d 277, 285 n. 2 (1976).

event.' " Board of Regents v. Roth, 408 U.S., at 570 n. 7. . . . But the hearing required is only one "appropriate to the nature of the case." Mullane v. Central Hanover Bank & Trust Co., 339 U.S. 306, 313, . . . Only last Term, the Court held that "identification of the specific dictates of due process generally requires consideration of three distinct factors: First, the private interest that will be affected by the official action; second, the risk of an erroneous deprivation of such interest through the procedures used, and the probable value, if any, of additional or substitute procedural safeguards; and finally, the Government's interest, including the function involved and the fiscal and administrative burdens that the additional or substitute procedural requirement would entail." Mathews v. Eldridge, 424 U.S. 319, 335, 96 S.Ct. 893, 903, 47 L.Ed.2d 18 (1976). Consideration of the procedures employed by the State and New York City in light of these three factors requires the conclusion that those procedures satisfy constitutional standards.

DP

Turning first to the procedure applicable in New York City, SSC Procedure No. 5 provides that before a child is removed from a foster home for transfer to another foster home, the foster parents may request an "independent review." . . . Such a procedure would appear to give a more elaborate trial-type hearing to foster families than this Court has found required in other contexts of administrative determinations. Cf. Goldberg v. Kelly, supra, 397 U.S., at 266–271, 90 S.Ct., at 1019–1022. [The District Court had held below that the review procedure was insufficient because it was available only at the request of foster parents. The Court reasoned that because the child is not able to request review the child's interest would not be protected. The Supreme Court responded: ". . . [i]t is difficult to see what right . . . of the foster child is protected by holding a hearing to determine whether removal would impair his emotional attachments to a foster parent who does not care enough about the child to contest the removal."]

. . . [T]he District Court faulted the city procedure on the ground that participation is limited to the foster parents and the agency and the natural parent and the child are not made parties to the hearing. This is not fatal in light of the nature of the alleged constitutional interests at stake. When the child's transfer from one foster home to another is pending, the interest arguably requiring protection is that of the foster family, not that of the natural parents. Moreover, the natural parent can generally add little to the accuracy of factfinding concerning the wisdom of such a transfer, since the foster parents and the agency, through its caseworkers, will usually be most knowledgeable about conditions in the foster home. Of course, in those cases where the natural parent does have a special interest in the proposed transfer or particular information that would assist the factfinder, nothing in the city's procedure prevents any party from securing his testimony.

DG

Reason

. . . . [Another] defect in the city procedure found by the District Court must also be rejected. [It] is that the procedure does not extend to the removal of a child from foster care to be returned to his natural parent. But as we have already held, whatever liberty interest may be argued to exist in the foster family is significantly weaker in the case of removals preceding return to the natural parent, and the balance of due process interests must accordingly be different. If the city procedure is adequate where it is applicable, it is no criticism of the procedure that it does not apply in other situations where different interests are at stake. . . .

Outside New York City, where only the statewide procedures apply, foster parents are provided not only with the procedures of a preremoval conference and postremoval hearing provided by 18 N.Y. C.R.R. § 450.10 (1976) and Soc.Serv. Law § 400, but also with the preremoval *judicial* hearing available on request to foster parents who have in their care children who have been in foster care for 18 months or more, Soc.Serv. Law § 392. . . . [A] foster parent in such case may obtain an order that the child remain in his care.

The District Court found three defects in this full judicial process. First, a § 392 proceeding is available only to those foster children who have been in foster care for 18 months or more. The class certified by the court was broader, including children who had been in the care of the same foster parents for more than one year. Thus, not all class members had access to the § 392 remedy. We do not think that the 18-month limitation on § 392 actions renders the New York scheme constitutionally inadequate. The assumed liberty interest to be protected in this case is one rooted in the emotional attachments that develop over time between a child and the adults who care for him. But there is no reason to assume that those attachments ripen at less than 18 months or indeed at any precise point. Indeed, testimony in the record, see App. 177a, 204a, as well as material in published psychological tests, see e.g., J. Goldstein, A. Freud, & A. Solnit, Beyond the Best Interests of the Child 40–42, 49 (1973), suggests that the amount of time necessary for the development of the sort of tie appellees seek to protect varies considerably depending on the age and previous attachments of the child. In a matter of such imprecision and delicacy, we see no justification for the District Court's substitution of its view of the appropriate cutoff date for that chosen by the New York Legislature, given that any line is likely to be somewhat arbitrary and fail to protect some families where relationships have developed quickly while protecting others where no such bonds have formed. If New York sees 18 months rather than 12 as the time at which temporary foster care begins to turn into a more permanent and family-like setting requiring procedural protection and/or judicial inquiry into the propriety of continuing foster care, it would take far more than this record provides to justify a finding of constitutional infirmity in New York's choice.

. . . .

. . . [T]he § 392 hearing is available to foster parents, both in and outside New York City, even where the removal sought is for the purpose of returning the child to his natural parents. Since this remedy provides a sufficient constitutional preremoval hearing to protect whatever liberty interest might exist in the continued existence of the foster family when the State seeks to transfer the child to another foster home, *a fortiori* the procedure is adequate to protect the lesser interest of the foster family in remaining together at the expense of the disruption of the natural family.

. . . Since we hold that the procedures provided by New York State in § 392 and by New York City's SSC Procedure No. 5 are adequate to protect whatever liberty interest appellees may have, the judgment of the District Court is

Reversed.

MR. JUSTICE STEWART, with whom THE CHIEF JUSTICE and MR. JUSTICE REHNQUIST join, concurring in the judgment.

. . .

Clearly, New York has deprived nobody of his life in these cases. It seems to me just as clear that the State has deprived nobody of his liberty or property. Putting to one side the District Court's erroneous "grievous loss" analysis, the appellees are left with very little ground on which to stand. Their argument seems to be that New York, by providing foster children with the opportunity to live in a foster home and to form a close relationship with foster parents, has created "liberty" or "property" that it may not withdraw without complying with the procedural safeguards that the Due Process Clause confers. . . .

. . . New York confers no right on foster families to remain intact, defeasible only upon proof of specific acts or circumstances. . . .

. . . New York law provides no basis for a justifiable expectation on the part of foster families that their relationship will continue indefinitely. The District Court in this litigation recognized as much, noting that the typical foster-care contract gives the agency the right to recall the child "upon request," and commenting that the discretionary authority vested in the agency "is on its face incompatible with plaintiffs' claim of legal entitlement." 418 F.Supp., at 281. To be sure, the New York system has not operated perfectly. As the state legislature found, foster care has in many cases been unnecessarily protracted, no doubt sometimes resulting in the expectation on the part of some foster families that their relationship will continue indefinitely. But, . . . the New York Court of Appeals has unequivocally rejected the notion that under New York law prolonged third-party custody of children creates some sort of "squatter's rights." . . .

. . . [T]he protection that foster children have is simply the requirement of state law that decisions about their placement be determined in the light of their best interests. See, e.g., Bennett v. Jeffreys, 40 N.Y.2d 543, 387 N.Y.S.2d 821, 356 N.E.2d 277; . . . This requirement is not "liberty or property" protected by the Due Process Clause, and it confers no right or expectancy of any kind in the continuity of the relationship between foster parents and children. See e.g., Bennett, supra, 40 N.Y.2d, at 552 n. 2, 387 N.Y.S.2d, at 829 n. 2, 356 N.E.2d, at 285 n. 2: "Third-party custodians acquire 'rights' . . . only derivatively by virtue of the child's best interests being considered . . . ."

What remains of the appellees' argument is the theory that the relation of the foster parent to the foster child may generate emotional attachments similar to those found in natural families. The Court surmises that foster families who share these attachments might enjoy the same constitutional interest in "family privacy" as natural families.

. . .

But under New York's foster-care laws, any case where the foster parents had assumed the emotional role of the child's natural parents would represent not a triumph of the system, to be constitutionally safe-guarded from state intrusion, but a failure. The goal of foster care, at least in New York, is not to provide a permanent substitute for the natural or adoptive home, but to prepare the child for his return to his real parents or placement in a permanent adoptive home by giving him temporary shelter in a family setting. Thus, the New York Court of Appeals has recognized that the development of close emotional ties between foster parents and a child may hinder the child's ultimate adjustment in a permanent home, and provide a basis for the *termination* of the foster family relationship. Perhaps it is to be expected that children who spend unduly long stays in what should have been temporary foster care will develop strong emotional ties with their foster parents. But this does not mean, and I cannot believe, that such breakdowns of the New York system must be protected or forever frozen in their existence by the Due Process Clause of the Fourteenth Amendment.

One of the liberties protected by the Due Process Clause, the Court has held, is the freedom to "establish a home and bring up children." Meyer v. Nebraska, supra, 262 U.S., at 399, 43 S.Ct., at 626. If a State were to attempt to force the breakup of a natural family, over the objections of the parents and their children, without some showing of unfitness and for the sole reason that to do so was thought to be in the children's best interest, I should have little doubt that the State would have intruded impermissibly on "the private realm of family life which the state cannot enter." Prince v. Massachusetts, 321 U.S. 158, 166, 64 S.Ct. 438, 88 L.Ed. 645. But this constitutional concept is simply not in point when we deal with foster families as New York law has defined them. The family life upon which the State "intrudes" is simply a temporary status which the State itself has created. It is a "family life" defined and controlled by the law of New York, for which New York pays, and the goals of which New York is entitled to and does set for itself.

NOTES

(1) Although the Supreme Court did not resolve the question whether children in foster care and their foster parents have a protectible "liberty interest" in their relationship, such an argument has been specifically rejected by two U. S. circuit courts. See Kyees v. County Department of Public Welfare, 600 F.2d 693 (7th Cir. 1979); Drummond v. Fulton County Department of Family & Children's Services, 563 F.2d 1200 (5th Cir. 1977). For a discussion of these decisions, see Musewicz, The Failure of Foster Care: Federal Statutory Reform and the Child's Right to Permanence, 54 So.Cal.L. Rev. 633, 666 et seq. (1981).

(2) Persons who serve as foster parents, like almost everyone else who practices a profession or engages in business these days, are typically subject to state licensing requirements. The authority administering the licensure provisions will maintain or be provided with certain standards with which an applicant or an existing licensee must comply. Often a provisional license may be issued for one who is temporarily in noncompliance with such standards who nevertheless submits a plan for overcoming any deficiencies within the time limit of the provisional licensing period.

In Sherrard v. Owens, 484 F.Supp. 728 (W.D.Mich.1980), foster parents whose two foster children had been removed from their home when their provisional license expired and was not renewed by the agency sought injunctive and declaratory relief to prevent further action with respect to the children and to secure their return. The court denied any such relief, finding that the plaintiffs had no reasonable expectation of continued licensure as a foster home after expiration of their provisional license and that no liberty right had developed. The Michigan provisions for revocation of foster home licenses also were held to be constitutionally adequate.

(3) Some courts have considered the preference of the children in deciding whether they should be returned from foster homes to their natural parents. In In Interest of Ross, 29 Ill.App.3d 157, 329 N.E.2d 333 (1975), two girls, 12 and 14 years old, appealed from a custody decision determining that they should be returned to their natural parents after having lived with foster parents more than 6½ years. In reversing the decision and remanding the cause for taking further evidence and redetermining what would be in the best interests of the children at the present time, the appellate court stated:

> "Irrespective of the basis for such feelings, the adamant expression of the girls over the years not to return to their natural parents should be given considerable weight in the court's determination since these children are now 14 and 12 years old and are of average to above-average intelligence."

MATTER OF SANJIVINI K.

Court of Appeals of New York, 1979.
47 N.Y.2d 374, 418 N.Y.S.2d 339, 391 N.E.2d 1316.

WACHTLER, JUDGE.

In this case a mother who temporarily placed her infant daughter with the Rockland County Department of Social Services for foster care seeks to regain custody of the child. The department has repeatedly denied her requests and for several years has sought to offer the child for adoption by attempting to prove, in successive proceedings and on a variety of grounds, that the mother is unfit. Despite financial and legal obstacles the mother has maintained ties with her daughter and in the various proceedings it has been held, by the Family Court or on appeal, that she has not abandoned or neglected the child and is not otherwise unfit. Now the department claims, and the Appellate Division has held, that it would be in the child's "best interests" that she be freed for adoption by the foster parents with whom she has resided throughout the prolonged litigation.

On this appeal the mother argues that statutory and constitutional limitations prohibit the State from purporting to act in the child's "best interests" by offering her for adoption by foster parents when the child has not been permanently surrendered, abandoned or neglected by her mother who has sought, for many years, to resume custody and support.

The appellant, Usha K, was born in India. She is an only child whose father died when she was 12. She and her mother then moved to Bombay. When she was 14 years old she began working full time and attending secretarial school at night so that she might eventually earn enough money to come to this country for a college education. She arrived in the United States in 1962 and began to study agriculture and nutrition. Two years later she obtained an associate degree from the State University system. That same year her mother died in India.

While in New York the appellant met an Indian student who apparently agreed to marry her; but when she later became pregnant, in 1965, he deserted her. She dropped out of school and in May of 1966 her daughter, Sanjivini, was born in Rockland County. Unwed and temporarily unable to support the child she agreed to place her in the custody of the Department of Social Services. She refused, however, to surrender the child for adoption and would only consent to temporary foster care.

After the birth of the child the appellant did not return to school. Instead she obtained a job in order to reimburse the department for medical expenses and also to contribute to the support of her daughter. In May of 1967 the immigration authorities commenced deportation proceedings claiming that her student visa had expired. These proceedings were suspended when the Department of Social Services, concerned that the child might be removed to India, filed a neglect petition in the Family Court and obtained a temporary order of placement. Later, after a hearing, the Family Court issued a dispositional order which, although continuing the placement for 12 months, expressly states that "the Court has no finding concerning any acts of the mother that might have constituted a neglect."

In the latter part of 1967 the appellant returned to school after reimbursing the department $800 for her medical expenses. With the aid of a scholarship and part-time employment she attended a university in Maryland and then in North Carolina, which apparently were the only schools within her means which offered the necessary courses. She still continued to visit her child when able, generally once every two or three months. When her education was completed she returned to New York. In the interim her daughter had resided in two foster homes. In 1968 she had been transferred to the foster parents with whom she still resides.

In November, 1970 the appellant asked the Department of Social Services to return the child and also requested that they assist her in obtaining employment in Rockland County. At that time the child was four years old and had resided with the foster parents for only two years. But the agency refused to return her and did little or nothing to help the mother make possible the child's return. Apparently the agency worker assigned to the case merely furnished appellant with the names and addresses of two potential employers, selected from the telephone book, and did nothing more even though the appellant informed her that she had already been denied employment at those locations.

Thereafter the appellant was unable to find a job in Rockland County largely, the Appellate Division has noted, because of her immigrant status (53 A.D.2d 863, 385 N.Y.S.2d 354). Finally she obtained clerical employment in New York City. She contributes monthly to the child's support and once every other week she travels from New York City to Rockland County to visit the girl. Over the years the department has repeatedly refused to return the child and instead has sought in various proceedings to free the child for adoption by the foster parents by attempting to show that the mother is unfit.

In 1973 the department filed a permanent neglect petition. But, after a hearing, the Family Court concluded in 1974, that the mother had not neglected the child. The mother then filed a petition to terminate custody. While that application was pending she asked the department to permit her to take her daughter to her apartment in New York City, during visitations, in order to ease the transition from foster care. The department however, repeatedly refused to allow visitation on these terms and the mother's visits lapsed. However she resumed visitation in Rockland County when the Family Court denied her application to terminate custody.*

The department then claimed, during a proceeding to periodically review the foster care placement (Social Services Law, § 392), that the mother had abandoned the child in 1974 by refusing to visit her on the terms fixed by the department. At the conclusion of that hearing the Family Court found that it was in the best interests of the child that her permanent status be ascertained as soon as possible. The court directed the department or the foster parents to file a petition to free the child for adoption and further ordered that if such a proceeding is not commenced within 30 days foster care would terminate and the child would be returned to her mother.

The Appellate Division reversed and directed that the child be immediately returned to her mother's custody. The court noted that the mother is employed and financially able to support the child, that the department had found her apartment "nicely furnished with moderate accommodations but adequate" and that she had made arrangements for schooling and after-school day care for the child. The court also noted that the record indicates that there is a significant possibility that her immigration status "will ultimately be stabilized and validated". With respect to the charge of abandonment the Appellate Division stated "In our opinion the evidence clearly establishes that the six-month gap in visitation in 1974 was caused by misunderstandings generated by Usha's strong desire to re-establish a full and normal relationship with the child. The record certainly does not establish that Usha abandoned her child or is an unfit mother" (53 A.D.2d 863, 385 N.Y.S.2d 350).

On appeal to our court it was noted that the department had already filed the petition directed by the Family Court and in that related proceeding the court had held that the child had been permanently neglected. Noting also that that determination was then on appeal to the Appellate Division we concluded (40 N.Y.2d 1025, 1026, 391 N.Y.S.2d 535, 536, 359 N.E.2d 1330, 1331) that the record then before us was incomplete and that "the present foster care review proceeding is not the appropriate judicial vehicle in which to determine the permanent status of the child". Accordingly we reversed, and without expressing any view as to "whether the child should remain with her foster parents or be returned to her mother", reinstated the Family Court order which directed the filing of the petition.

Now we have the record of that related proceeding before us. It shows that the Family Court conducted a hearing on the department's petition and found that the mother had "permanently neglected" the child by failing to plan for her future although financially able to do so and despite diligent efforts by the department to

* The mother's appeal from this order was dismissed by the Appellate Division when the attorneys assigned to represent her failed to perfect the appeal (53 A.D.2d 863, 385 N.Y.S.2d 354).

encourage her relationship with the child (see Family Ct. Act, § 614; Social Services Law, § 384–b, subd. 7). The court conceded that the appellant's educational plan had been successfully completed but found that this plan had been for the mother's benefit and not for the benefit of the child. In support of this conclusion the court found that while the mother was completing her education "visitations . . . were most infrequent" and thus the child, instead of benefiting from the mother's plan, was actually a "victim of the mother's own ambitions, however laudable." The court failed to note, however, that in the permanent neglect proceeding concluded in 1974 it was found that the mother had not neglected the child during this period. After a further dispositional hearing the court ordered that the child be freed for adoption by the foster parents.

The Appellate Division affirmed on a different ground. It rejected, implicitly, the Family Court's factual finding that the mother had failed to plan for the child's future and the holding that she was guilty of permanent neglect as statutorily defined. Instead, relying on Matter of Bennett v. Jeffreys, 40 N.Y.2d 543, 387 N.Y.S.2d 821, 356 N.E.2d 277, the court held that there were " 'extraordinary circumstances' requiring affirmance". Noting the appellant's inability to obtain employment in Rockland County, her unsettled immigration status and the extended foster care, the court concluded that it would be in the child's "best interest" that she be offered for adoption by the foster parents. "Viewed from the standpoint of the impact on the child", the court said, "a *de facto* permanent neglect must be deemed to have been established."

On this record there is no legal basis for offering the child for adoption against her mother's wishes. The prolonged separation of mother and daughter is, of course, regrettable. But that was due to litigation initiated or necessitated by the department's actions and was not the result of any parental neglect. Indeed despite the financial and subsequent legal inability of the mother to provide full custody and care, she has, through uncommon effort, preserved parental ties throughout the child's life. Thus, in this and the earlier proceedings the department has repeatedly failed, either in the Family Court or on appeal, to prove the mother guilty of statutory abandonment or permanent neglect or to show that she is unfit. Absent such a finding the courts may not permanently sever all parental ties (Social Services Law, § 384–b, subd. 4).

If we were only concerned with deciding custody the prolonged separation might be entitled to greater weight. In Matter of Bennett v. Jeffreys (supra) we held that a mother who permitted her child to remain with a family friend for an extended period might be denied the right to regain custody, without regard to fault, if disruption of the existing custody would not be in the child's best interest. That case involved an informal arrangement and, we noted (at p. 545, 387 N.Y.S.2d at p. 824, 356 N.E.2d at p. 281) "as an unsupervised private placement, no statute is directly applicable, and the analysis must proceed from common-law principles". But even if that rule were applicable to an agency placement governed by statute, it is doubtful whether it could be found to be in the child's best interests to deny her mother's persistent demands for custody simply because it took so long for her to obtain it legally. In any event a court may not terminate all parental rights by offering a child for adoption when there has been no parental consent, abandonment, neglect or proven unfitness, even though some might find adoption to be in the child's best interests (Matter of Corey L. v. Martin L., 45 N.Y.2d 383, 408 N.Y.S.2d 439, 380 N.E.2d 266).

These are not merely technical rules involving statutory authority, nor are they based on the assumption that a parent's rights and interests are superior to the child's. A child, of course, is not a parent's property, but neither is the child the property of the State (Pierce v. Society of Sisters, 268 U.S. 510, 535, 45 S.Ct. 571, 69 L.Ed. 1070; Stanley v. Illinois, 405 U.S. 645, 92 S.Ct. 1208, 31 L.Ed.2d 551). In many cases the State may, and under some legal systems undoubtedly does, find "better" parents for a child even though the natural parents may be willing and able to provide proper care. But it is fundamental to our legal and social system, that it is in the best interest of a child to be raised by his parents, unless the parents are unfit (see, e.g., Matter of Spence-Chapin Adoption Serv. v. Polk, 29 N.Y.2d 196, 204, 324 N.Y.S.2d 937, 944, 274 N.E.2d 431, 436; . . . Stanley v. Illinois, supra).

Finally, we note again that it has already been determined on the last appeal that it is in the child's best interests that her permanent status be resolved, by either permitting her mother to regain custody, or permitting the foster parents to adopt. Thus, in view of our conclusion that the petition to free the child for adoption should be dismissed, the child should be returned to her mother's custody.

Accordingly, the order of the Appellate Division should be reversed and the petition dismissed, with costs.

FUCHSBERG, JUDGE (concurring).

I agree that permanent neglect by the mother has not been established and that the proceeding to free the child for adoption therefore must be dismissed.

But on the matter of custody, as distinguished from parenthood, I concur in result only. On the particular circumstances in this case, I agree that the permanent neglect proceeding having been dismissed, the child should be returned to the custody of the biological mother.

These circumstances include the fact that the mother and Sanjivini have for some years been visiting regularly so that the existence of a dual relationship—of parent and child and foster parents and child— is not strange to her life. Above all, it preserved the parental ties. Furthermore, now over 13, past puberty and into adolescence and early adulthood, the child is likely to be able to handle the transition in stride. Also I am impressed by the fact that the custody in the foster parents was known to all—mother, child, foster parents—to have been intended to be only temporary; the mother's ties with her daughter, both by support and personal contact, despite the immense obstacles placed in her path by the social and legal vicissitudes the majority has detailed, have left no possibility of any misunderstanding on that score. In addition, the unfortunate prolongation of the litigation, for which there is no indication that the mother is blameworthy, has made for periodic examination and re-examination of the developing relationships involved. Add to this the favorable report on the mother's living and schooling accommodations. On balance, then, as indicated, I agree that in this case, despite the long separation, custody of the child should be returned to the mother.

So voting, however, I wish to make it clear that, in my view, absent these circumstances, where there has been an unusually long separation and fostering of new ties, I do not believe, simply because the placement was statutory and the permanent neglect proceeding was decided in favor of the mother, that custody would have to be returned to the mother. Once the foster relationship has, willy-nilly, shifted from a "temporary" to a "permanent" one, best interest factors in another case could contraindicate disruption of that relationship and instead dictate an opposite result . . . .

FOSTER PARENTS AND ADOPTION

The ambivalence over just what sort of relationship foster parents should develop with the children committed to their care has surfaced frequently in recent years in contests over the right to adopt. Some children are placed in foster care with the understanding that they will be relinquished to the placing agency when the child becomes legally available for adoption as a result of termination of parental rights or relinquishment. Although the foster parents may have executed a contract specifically agreeing to relinquish the child on demand, some of them have sought to assert a preference to be considered for adoption. From the agency's standpoint the question may be viewed as one of determining whether the foster parents would be the best available—or even appropriate—adopters. Factors such as advanced age might make them seem satisfactory for temporary placement but not for adoption, which creates a permanent, long term parent-child relationship.

In In Adoption of Runyon, 268 Cal.App.2d 918, 74 Cal.Rptr. 514 (1969), foster parents were advised three weeks after a placement that their foster child had a serious heart problem; they were given the option of returning the child or continuing the placement. They chose the latter course and saw the child through successful heart surgery, after which he was placed with another couple for adoption. The former foster parents also petitioned to adopt the child but the court construed the language of California's adoption statute to mean that "where a parent or parents place a child with an agency only the prospective parents selected by the agency may adopt the child."

Legislatures in some states have adopted statutes designed to assure foster parents some preference, or at least standing to be heard, in adoptions which take place after a significant period of foster care. N.Y. Social Services Law § 383, for example, provides:

> 3. Any adult husband and his adult wife and any adult unmarried person, who, as foster parent or parents, have cared for a child continuously for a period of eighteen months or more, may apply to such authorized agency for the placement of said child with them for the purpose of adoption, and if said child is eligible for adoption, the agency shall give preference and first consideration to their application over all other applications for adoption placements. However, final determination of the propriety of said adoption of such foster child shall be within the sole discretion of the court, as otherwise provided herein.

> Foster parents having had continuous care of a child, for more than eighteen months, through an authorized agency, shall be permitted as a matter of right, as an interested party to intervene in any proceeding involving the custody of the child. Such intervention may be made anonymously or in the true name of said foster parents.

If the goal in foster care truly is to effect the return of the child to the natural parents as soon as feasible, are there dangers in providing a special advantage for foster parents to adopt? Should this preference operate only against other potential adopters?

JUVENILE JUSTICE STANDARDS PROJECT, STANDARDS RELATING TO ABUSE AND NEGLECT (Tentative Draft) *

6.4 Standards for choosing a disposition

. . .

C. Removal.

A child should not be removed from his/her home unless the court finds that:

1. the child has been physically abused as defined in Standard 2.1 A., and there is a preponderance of evidence that the child cannot be protected from further physical abuse without being removed from his/her home; or

2. the child has been endangered in one of the other ways specified by statute and there is clear and convincing evidence that the child cannot be protected from further harm of the type justifying intervention unless removed from his/her home.

* Reprinted with permission from Standards Relating to Abuse and Neglect (Tentative Draft), copyright 1977, Ballinger Publishing Company.

3. Even if a court finds subsections 1. or 2. applicable, before any child is removed from his/her home, the court must find that there is a placement in fact available in which the child will not be endangered.

4. Even if a court finds subsections 1. or 2. applicable, the court should not be authorized to remove a child when the child is endangered solely due to environmental conditions beyond the control of the parents, which the parents would be willing to remedy if they were able to do so.

5. Those advocating removal should bear the burden of proof on all these issues.

6.5 Initial plans

(A.) Children left in their own home.

Whenever a child is left in his/her own home, the agency should develop with the parent a specific plan detailing any changes in parental behavior or home conditions that must be made in order for the child not to be endangered. The plan should also specify the services that will be provided to the parent and/or the child to insure that the child will not be endangered. This plan, which will be a more detailed version of the agency dispositional report . . . , should be developed by the time of the dispositional hearing or within two weeks thereafter. A copy of the plan should be submitted to the court if the plan is not presented at the dispositional hearing. If there is a dispute regarding any aspect of the plan, final resolution should be by the court.

(B.) Children removed from their homes.

Before a child is ordered removed from his/her home, the agency charged with his/her care should provide the court with a specific plan as to where the child will be placed, what steps will be taken to return the child home, and what actions the agency will take to maintain parent-child ties. Whenever possible, this plan should be developed in consultation with the parent, who should be encouraged to help in the placement. If there is a dispute regarding any aspect of the plan, final resolution should be by the court.

1. The plan should specify what services the parents will receive in order to enable them to resume custody and what actions the parents must take in order for them to resume custody.

2. The plan should provide for the maximum parent-child contact possible, unless the court finds that visitation rights should be limited because it will be seriously detrimental to the child.

3. A child generally should be placed as close to home as possible, preferably in his/her own neighborhood, unless the court finds that placement at a greater distance is necessary to promote the child's wellbeing.

6.6 Rights of parents and children following removal

A. Unless . . . parental rights are terminated at the disposi-tional hearing, all placements are for a temporary period. Every ef-fort should be made to facilitate the return of the child as quickly as possible.

B. When a child is removed from his/her home, his/her parents should retain the right to consent to major medical decisions, to the child's marriage, or to the child's joining the armed services, unless parental consent is not generally required for any of these decisions or the court finds that the parents' refusal to consent would be seri-ously detrimental to the child.

C. Depending on the child's age and maturity, the agency should also solicit and consider the child's participation in decisions regard-ing his/her care while in placement.

NOTE

In addition to the fear that some children will be removed from their nat-ural parents unnecessarily, one of the concerns about placing children in fos-ter care is that they will be "lost" or forgotten in the system. One means for dealing with this is a requirement that foster care plans must be pre-pared and submitted at the time of initial placement or soon thereafter. Va. Code § 16.1–281, for example, requires the filing of such a plan with the juvenile and domestic relations court within 60 days (subject to a possible 60 day extension for good cause shown). A foster care review then follows for all children "who have not been returned to their prior family or placed in an adoptive home or permanent foster care placement" within twelve months of the filing of a foster care plan. Id. § 16.1–282.

Calif.Welfare & Inst.Code § 600.5 requires the Department of Social Ser-vices to prepare and issue an annual report on foster care in the state:

The report shall be based on a sample of foster children drawn from counties which collectively include at least 65 percent of all the foster children in this state. The report shall include an analysis, evaluation or estimate, as appropriate, of the following, on a statewide basis:

(1) The number of foster children;

(2) The amount of funds expended by federal, state and local govern-ment for maintenance payments to foster parents, group homes and insti-tutions;

(3) The amount of funds expended by federal, state and local govern-ment on services to foster children and their natural parents or guardi-ans;

(4) The types of services being offered to parents and their children in order to keep the family together;

(5) The number of foster children who are of adoptable age, the num-ber of such children adopted, and the number of foster children deter-mined not to be adoptable and the reasons therefor;

(6) The number of foster children placed in permanent foster care or guardianship;

(7) The size of caseloads of probation officers and social workers, the effect such caseloads have on the services offered to parents or their children, and the effectiveness of such services;

(8) The movement of foster children within the program from placement to placement and the shifting responsibility for such children within the county probation department or welfare department;

(9) The foster care-related qualifications, education, and in-service training of social workers and probation officers who handle such cases;

(10) Any other matters relating to foster children which the department deems appropriate to be included in such report. The report shall be submitted to the Governor and Legislature no later than January of each year.

For an analysis of problems and proposals concerning foster care review, along with an evaluation and discussion of the federal government's attempts to reduce the number of children in foster care through the Adoption Assistance and Child Welfare Act of 1980, see Musewicz, The Failure of Foster Care: Federal Statutory Reform and the Child's Right to Permanence, 54 So.Cal.L.Rev. 633 (1981).

F.   TERMINATING THE LEGAL RELATIONSHIP BETWEEN PARENT AND CHILD

SANTOSKY v. KRAMER

Supreme Court of the United States, 1982.
___ U.S. ___, 102 S.Ct. 1388, 71 L.Ed.2d 599.

JUSTICE BLACKMUN delivered the opinion of the Court.

Under New York law, the State may terminate, over parental objection, the rights of parents in their natural child upon a finding that the child is "permanently neglected." N.Y.Soc.Serv.Law §§ 384–b.4.(d), 384–b.7.(a) (McKinney Supp.1981–1982) (Soc.Serv.Law). The New York Family Court Act § 622 (McKinney 1975 & Supp. 1981–1982) (Fam.Ct.Act) requires that only a "fair preponderance of the evidence" support that finding. Thus, in New York, the factual certainty required to extinguish the parent-child relationship is no greater than that necessary to award money damages in an ordinary civil action.

Today we hold that the Due Process Clause of the Fourteenth Amendment demands more than this. Before a State may sever completely and irrevocably the rights of parents in their natural child, due process requires that the State support its allegations by at least clear and convincing evidence.

I

A

New York authorizes its officials to remove a child temporarily from his or her home if the child appears "neglected," within the meaning of Art. 10 of the Family Court Act. See §§ 1012(f), 1021–1029. Once removed, a child under the age of 18 customarily is placed "in the care of an authorized agency," Soc.Serv.Law § 384–b.7.(a), usually a state institution or a foster home. At that point, "the state's first obligation is to help the family with services to . . . reunite it. . . ." § 384–b.1.(a)(iii). But if convinced that "positive, nurturing parent-child relationships no longer exist," § 384–b.-1.(b), the State may initiate "permanent neglect" proceedings to free the child for adoption.

The State bifurcates its permanent neglect proceeding into "factfinding" and "dispositional" hearings. Fam.Ct.Act §§ 622, 623. At the factfinding stage, the State must prove that the child has been "permanently neglected," as defined by Fam.Ct.Act §§ 614.1.(a)–(d) and Soc.Serv.Law § 384–b.7.(a). See Fam.Ct.Act § 622. The Family Court judge then determines at a subsequent dispositional hearing what placement would serve the child's best interests. §§ 623, 631.

At the factfinding hearing, the State must establish, among other things, that for more than a year after the child entered state custody, the agency "made diligent efforts to encourage and strengthen the parental relationship." Fam.Ct.Act §§ 614.1.(c), 611. The State must further prove that during that same period, the child's natural parents failed "substantially and continuously or repeatedly to maintain contact with or plan for the future of the child although physically and financially able to do so." § 614.1.(d). Should the State support its allegations by "a fair preponderance of the evidence," § 622, the child may be declared permanently neglected. § 611. That declaration empowers the Family Court judge to terminate permanently the natural parents' rights in the child. §§ 631(c), 634. Termination denies the natural parents physical custody, as well as the rights ever to visit, communicate with, or regain custody of the child.

New York's permanent neglect statute provides natural parents with certain procedural protections.[2] But New York permits its officials to establish "permanent neglect" with less proof than most States require. Thirty-three States, the District of Columbia, and the Virgin Islands currently specify a higher standard of proof, in parental rights termination proceedings, than a "fair preponderance of the evidence." . . . The question here is whether New York's "fair

---

2. Most notably, natural parents have a statutory right to the assistance of counsel and of court-appointed counsel if they are indigent. Fam.Ct.Act § 262(a) (iii).

preponderance of the evidence" standard is constitutionally sufficient.

B

Petitioners John Santosky II and Annie Santosky are the natural
parents of Tina and John III. In November 1973, after incidents reflecting parental neglect, respondent Kramer, Commissioner of the
Ulster County Department of Social Services, initiated a neglect proceeding under Fam.Ct.Act § 1022 and removed Tina from her natural
home. About 10 months later, he removed John III and placed him
with foster parents. On the day John was taken, Annie Santosky
gave birth to a third child, Jed. When Jed was only three days old,
respondent transferred him to a foster home on the ground that immediate removal was necessary to avoid imminent danger to his life
or health.

In October 1978, respondent petitioned the Ulster County Family
Court to terminate petitioners' parental rights in the three children.
Petitioners challenged the constitutionality of the "fair preponderance of the evidence" standard specified in Fam.Ct.Act § 622. The
Family Court judge rejected this constitutional challenge, and
weighed the evidence under the statutory standard. While acknowledging that the Santoskys had maintained contact with their children,
the judge found those visits "at best superficial and devoid of any
real emotional content." After deciding that the agency had made
" 'diligent efforts' to encourage and strengthen the parental relationship," he concluded that the Santoskys were incapable, even with
public assistance, of planning for the future of their children. The
judge later held a dispositional hearing and ruled that the best interests of the three children required permanent termination of the
Santoskys' custody.[5]

Petitioners appealed, again contesting the constitutionality of
§ 622's standard of proof. The New York Supreme Court, Appellate
Division, affirmed, holding application of the preponderance of the evidence standard "proper and constitutional." In re John AA, 75 App.
Div.2d 910, 427 N.Y.S.2d 319, 320 (1980). That standard, the court
reasoned, "recognizes and seeks to balance rights possessed by the
child . . . with those of the natural parents. . . . " Ibid.

The New York Court of Appeals then dismissed petitioners' appeal to that court "upon the ground that no substantial constitutional
question is directly involved." We granted certiorari to consider petitioners' constitutional claim. 450 U.S. 993, 101 S.Ct. 1694, 68 L.Ed.2d
192 (1981).

---

5. Since respondent took custody of
Tina, John III, and Jed, the Santoskys
have had two other children, James and
Jeremy. The State has taken no action
to remove these younger children. At
oral argument, counsel for respondent replied affirmatively when asked whether
he was asserting that petitioners were
"unfit to handle the three older ones but
not unfit to handle the two younger
ones."

II

Last Term, in Lassiter v. Department of Social Services, 452 U.S. 18, 101 S.Ct. 2153, 68 L.Ed.2d 640 (1981), this Court, by a 5–4 vote, held that the Fourteenth Amendment's Due Process Clause does not require the appointment of counsel for indigent parents in every parental status termination proceeding. The case casts light, however, on the two central questions here—whether process is constitutionally due a natural parent at a State's parental rights termination proceeding, and, if so, what process is due.

In *Lassiter*, it was "not disputed that state intervention to terminate the relationship between [a parent] and [the] child must be accomplished by procedures meeting the requisites of the Due Process Clause." 452 U.S., at 37, 101 S.Ct., at 2165 (dissenting opinion); see id., at 24–32, 101 S.Ct., at 2158–2162 (opinion for the Court); id., at 59–60, 101 S.Ct., at 2176 (Stevens, J., dissenting). See also Little v. Streater, 452 U.S. 1, 13, 101 S.Ct. 2202, 2209, 68 L.Ed.2d 627 (1981). The absence of dispute reflected this Court's historical recognition that freedom of personal choice in matters of family life is a fundamental liberty interest protected by the Fourteenth Amendment.

The fundamental liberty interest of natural parents in the care, custody, and management of their child does not evaporate simply because they have not been model parents or have lost temporary custody of their child to the State. Even when blood relationships are strained, parents retain a vital interest in preventing the irretrievable destruction of their family life. If anything, persons faced with forced dissolution of their parental rights have a more critical need for procedural protections than do those resisting state intervention into ongoing family affairs. When the State moves to destroy weakened familial bonds, it must provide the parents with fundamentally fair procedures.

In *Lassiter*, the Court and three dissenters agreed that the nature of the process due in parental rights termination proceedings turns on a balancing of the "three distinct factors" specified in Mathews v. Eldridge, 424 U.S. 319, 335, 96 S.Ct. 893, 903, 47 L.Ed.2d 18 (1976): the private interests affected by the proceeding; the risk of error created by the State's chosen procedure; and the countervailing governmental interest supporting use of the challenged procedure. . . .

In *Lassiter*, to be sure, the Court held that fundamental fairness may be maintained in parental rights termination proceedings even when some procedures are mandated only on a case-by-case basis, rather than through rules of general application. 452 U.S., at 31–32, 101 S.Ct., at 2161, (natural parent's right to court-appointed counsel should be determined by the trial court, subject to appellate review). But this Court never has approved case-by-case determination of the proper *standard of proof* for a given proceeding. Standards of proof, like other "procedural due process rules[,] are shaped by the risk of error inherent in the truth-finding process as applied to the *generality of cases,* not the rare exceptions." Mathews v. Eldridge, 424 U.S., at 344, 96 S.Ct., at 907 (emphasis added). Since the litigants and the factfinder must know at the outset of a given proceeding how the risk of error will be allocated, the standard of proof necessarily must be calibrated in advance. Retrospective case-by-case review cannot preserve fundamental fairness when a class of proceedings is governed by a constitutionally defective evidentiary standard.

III

In parental rights termination proceedings, the private interest affected is commanding; the risk of error from using a preponderance standard is substantial; and the courtervailing governmental interest favoring that standard is comparatively slight. Evaluation of the three *Eldridge* factors compels the conclusion that use of a "fair preponderance of the evidence" standard in such proceedings is inconsistent with due process.

A

"The extent to which procedural due process must be afforded the recipient is influenced by the extent to which he may be 'condemned to suffer grievous loss.'" Goldberg v. Kelly, 397 U.S. 254, 262–263, 90 S.Ct. 1011, 1017–18, 25 L.Ed.2d 287 (1970), quoting Joint Anti-Fascist Refugee Committee v. McGrath, 341 U.S. 123, 168, 71 S.Ct. 624, 646, 95 L.Ed. 817 (1951) (Frankfurter, J., concurring). Whether the loss threatened by a particular type of proceeding is sufficiently grave to warrant more than average certainty on the part of the factfinder turns on both the nature of the private interest threatened and the permanency of the threatened loss.

Lassiter declared it "plain beyond the need for multiple citation" that a natural parent's "desire for and right to 'the companionship, care, custody, and management of his or her children' " is an interest far more precious than any property right. 452 U.S., at 27, 101 S.Ct., at 2160, quoting Stanley v. Illinois, 405 U.S., at 651, 92 S.Ct., at 1212. When the State initiates a parental rights termination proceeding, it seeks not merely to infringe that fundamental liberty interest, but to end it. "If the State prevails, it will have worked a unique kind of deprivation. . . . A parent's interest in the accuracy and justice of the decision to terminate his or her parental status is, therefore, a commanding one." 452 U.S., at 27, 101 S.Ct., at 2160.

In government-initiated proceedings to determine juvenile delinquency, this Court has identified losses of individual liberty sufficiently serious to warrant imposition of an elevated burden of proof. Yet juvenile delinquency adjudications, civil commitment, deportation, and denaturalization, at least to a degree, are all *reversible* official actions. Once affirmed on appeal, a New York decision terminating

parental rights is *final* and irrevocable.   Few forms of state action
are both so severe and so irreversible.

Thus, the first *Eldridge* factor—the private interest affected—
weighs heavily against use of the preponderance standard at a State-
initiated permanent neglect proceeding.   We do not deny that the
child and his foster parents are also deeply interested in the outcome
of that contest.   But at the factfinding stage of the New York proceeding, the focus emphatically is not on them.

The factfinding does not purport—and is not intended—to balance
the child's interest in a normal family home against the parents' interest in raising the child.   Nor does it purport to determine whether
the natural parents or the foster parents would provide the better
home.   Rather, the factfinding hearing pits the State directly against
the parents.   The State alleges that the natural parents are at fault.
Fam.Ct.Act § 614.1.(d).   The questions disputed and decided are what
the State did—"made diligent efforts," § 614.1.(c)—and what the natural parents did not do—"maintain contact with or plan for the future
of the child." § 614.1.(d).   The State marshals an array of public resources to prove its case and disprove the parents' case.   Victory by
the State not only makes termination of parental rights possible; it
entails a judicial determination that the parents are unfit to raise
their own children.[10]

At the factfinding, the State cannot presume that a child and his
parents are adversaries.   After the State has established parental unfitness at that initial proceeding, the court may assume at the *dispositional* stage that the interests of the child and the natural parents
do diverge.   But until the State proves parental unfitness, the child
and his parents share a vital interest in preventing erroneous termination of their natural relationship.[11]   Thus, at the factfinding, the
interests of the child and his natural parents coincide to favor use of
error-reducing procedures.

10. The Family Court judge in the
present case expressly refused to terminate petitioners' parental rights on a
"non-statutory, no-fault basis."   Nor is it
clear that the State constitutionally could
terminate a parent's rights *without*
showing parental unfitness.   See Quilloin
v. Walcott, 434 U.S. 246, 255, 98 S.Ct.
549, 554, 54 L.Ed.2d 511 (1978) ("We
have little doubt that the Due Process
Clause would be offended '[i]f a State
were to attempt to force the breakup of a
natural family, over the objections of the
parents and their children, without some
showing of unfitness and for the sole
reason that to do so was thought to be in
the children's best interest,'" quoting
Smith v. Organization of Foster Families,
431 U.S. 816, 862–863, 97 S.Ct. 2094,
2119, 53 L.Ed.2d 14 (1977) (Stewart, J.,
concurring in the judgment)).

11. For a child, the consequences of
termination of his natural parents' rights
may well be far-reaching.   In Colorado,
for example, it has been noted: "The
child loses the right of support and maintenance, for which he may thereafter be
dependent upon society; the right to inherit; and all other rights inherent in the
legal parent-child relationship, not just
for [a limited] period . . . ., but forever." In re K. S., 33 Colo.App. 72, 76, 515
P.2d 130, 133 (1973).

Some losses cannot be measured.   In
this case, for example, Jed Santosky was
removed from his natural parents' custody when he was only three days old; the
judge's finding of permanent neglect effectively foreclosed the possibility that
Jed would ever know his natural parents.

However substantial the foster parents' interests may be, cf. Smith v. Organization of Foster Families, 431 U.S., at 845–847, 97 S.Ct., at 2110–2111, they are not implicated directly in the factfinding stage of a State-initiated permanent neglect proceeding against the natural parents. If authorized, the foster parents may pit their interests directly against those of the natural parents by initiating their own permanent neglect proceeding. Fam.Ct.Act §§ 615, 1055(d); Soc.Serv.Law § 392.7.(c). Alternatively, the foster parents can make their case for custody at the dispositional stage of a State-initiated proceeding, where the judge already has decided the issue of permanent neglect and is focusing on the placement that would serve the child's best interests. Fam.Ct.Act §§ 623, 631. For the foster parents, the State's failure to prove permanent neglect may prolong the delay and uncertainty until their foster child is freed for adoption. But for the natural parents, a finding of permanent neglect can cut off forever their rights in their child. Given this disparity of consequence, we have no difficulty finding that the balance of private interests strongly favors heightened procedural protections.

B

Under Mathews v. Eldridge, we next must consider both the risk of erroneous deprivation of private interests resulting from use of a "fair preponderance" standard and the likelihood that a higher evidentiary standard would reduce that risk. See 424 U.S., at 335, 96 S.Ct., at 903. Since the factfinding phase of a permanent neglect proceeding is an adversary contest between the State and the natural parents, the relevant question is whether a preponderance standard fairly allocates the risk of an erroneous factfinding between these two parties.

In New York, the factfinding stage of a State-initiated permanent neglect proceeding bears many of the indicia of a criminal trial. The Commissioner of Social Services charges the parents with permanent neglect. They are served by summons. The factfinding hearing is conducted pursuant to formal rules of evidence. The State, the parents, and the child are all represented by counsel. The State seeks to establish a series of historical facts about the intensity of its agency's efforts to reunite the family, the infrequency and insubstantiality of the parents' contacts with their child, and the parents' inability or unwillingness to formulate a plan for the child's future. The attorneys submit documentary evidence, and call witnesses who are subject to cross-examination. Based on all the evidence, the judge then determines whether the State has proved the statutory elements of permanent neglect by a fair preponderance of the evidence.

At such a proceeding, numerous factors combine to magnify the risk of erroneous factfinding. Permanent neglect proceedings employ imprecise substantive standards that leave determinations unusually open to the subjective values of the judge. See Smith v. Organization of Foster Families, 431 U.S., at 835, n. 36, 97 S.Ct., at 2105, n. 36. In appraising the nature and quality of a complex series of encounters among the agency, the parents, and the child, the court possesses unusual discretion to underweigh probative facts that might favor the parent.[12] Because parents subject to termination proceedings are often poor, uneducated, or members of minority groups, such proceedings are often vulnerable to judgments based on cultural or class bias.

The State's ability to assemble its case almost inevitably dwarfs the parents' ability to mount a defense. No predetermined limits restrict the sums an agency may spend in prosecuting a given termination proceeding. The State's attorney usually will be expert on the issues contested and the procedures employed at the factfinding hearing, and enjoys full access to all public records concerning the family. The State may call on experts in family relations, psychology, and medicine to bolster its case. Furthermore, the primary witnesses at the hearing will be the agency's own professional caseworkers whom the State has empowered both to investigate the family situation and to testify against the parents. Indeed, because the child is already in agency custody, the State even has the power to shape the historical events that form the basis for termination.[13]

The disparity between the adversaries' litigation resources is matched by a striking asymmetry in their litigation options. Unlike criminal defendants, natural parents have no "double jeopardy" defense against repeated state termination efforts. If the State initially fails to win termination, as New York did here, it always can try once again to cut off the parents' rights after gathering more or better evidence. Yet even when the parents have attained the level of

12. For example, a New York court appraising an agency's "diligent efforts" to provide the parents with social services can excuse efforts *not* made on the grounds that they would have been "detrimental to the moral and temporal welfare of the child." Fam.Ct.Act § 614.1.(c). In determining whether the parent "substantially and continuously or repeatedly" failed to "maintain contact with . . . the child." § 614.1.(d), the judge can discount actual visits or communications on the grounds that they were insubstantial or "overtly demonstrat[ed] a lack of affectionate and concerned parenthood." Soc.Serv.Law § 384–b.7.(b). When determining whether the parent planned for the child's future, the judge can reject as unrealistic plans based on overly optimistic estimates of physical or financial ability. § 384.b.7.(c). . . .

13. In this case, for example, the parents claim that the State sought court or-

ders denying them the right to visit their children, which would have prevented them from maintaining the contact required by Fam.Ct.Act § 614.1.(d). The parents further claim that the State cited their rejection of social services they found offensive or superfluous as proof of the agency's "diligent efforts" and their own "failure to plan" for the children's future.

We need not accept these statements as true to recognize that the State's unusual ability to structure the evidence increases the risk of an erroneous factfinding. Of course, the disparity between the litigants' resources will be vastly greater in States where there is no statutory right to court-appointed counsel. See Lassiter v. Department of Social Services, 452 U.S., at 34, 101 S.Ct., at 2163 (only 33 States and the District of Columbia provide that right by statute).

fitness required by the State, they have no similar means by which they can forestall future termination efforts.

Coupled with a "preponderance of the evidence" standard, these factors create a significant prospect of erroneous termination. A standard of proof that by its very terms demands consideration of the quantity, rather than the quality, of the evidence may misdirect the factfinder in the marginal case. Given the weight of the private interests at stake, the social cost of even occasional error is sizable.

. . .

The Appellate Division approved New York's preponderance standard on the ground that it properly "balanced rights possessed by the child . . . with those of the natural parents. . . ." 75 App. Div.2d, at 910, 427 N.Y.S.2d, at 320. By so saying, the court suggested that a preponderance standard properly allocates the risk of error *between* the parents and the child. That view is fundamentally mistaken.

The court's theory assumes that termination of the natural parents' rights invariably will benefit the child.[15] Yet we have noted above that the parents and the child share an interest in avoiding erroneous termination. Even accepting the court's assumption, we cannot agree with its conclusion that a preponderance standard fairly distributes the risk of error between parent and child. Use of that standard reflects the judgment that society is nearly neutral between erroneous termination of parental rights and erroneous failure to terminate those rights. Cf. In re Winship, 397 U.S., at 371, 90 S.Ct., at 1076 (Harlan, J., concurring). For the child, the likely consequence of an erroneous failure to terminate is preservation of an uneasy status quo.[16] For the natural parents, however, the consequence of an erro-

---

15. This is a hazardous assumption at best. Even when a child's natural home is imperfect, permanent removal from that home will not necessarily improve his welfare. See, e.g., Wald, State Intervention on Behalf of "Neglected" Children: A Search for Realistic Standards, 27 Stan.L.Rev. 985, 993 (1975) ("In fact, under current practice, coercive intervention frequently results in placing a child in a more detrimental situation than he would be in without intervention.").

Nor does termination of parental rights necessarily ensure adoption. See Brief for Community Action for Legal Services, Inc., et al., as *Amicus Curiae* 22–23 (in 1979; only 12% of the adoptable children in foster care in New York City were actually adopted, although some had been waiting for years, citing Redirecting Foster Care, A Report to the Mayor of the City of New York 69, 43 (1980)). Even when a child eventually finds an adoptive family, he may spend years moving between state institutions

and "temporary" foster placements after his ties to his natural parents have been severed. See Smith v. Organization of Foster Families, 431 U.S., at 833–838, 97 S.Ct., at 2103–06 (describing the "limbo" of the New York foster care system).

16. When the termination proceeding occurs, the child is not living at his natural home. A child cannot be adjudicated "permanently neglected" until, "for a period of more than a year," he has been in "the care of an authorized agency." Soc. Serv.Law § 384–b.7.(a); Fam.Ct.Act § 614.1.(d). See also dissenting opinion, at 20–21.

Under New York law, a judge has ample discretion to ensure that, once removed from his natural parents on grounds of neglect, a child will not return to a hostile environment. In this case, when the State's initial termination effort failed for lack of proof, see n. 4, supra, the court simply issued orders under Fam.Ct.Act § 1055(b) extending the

heous termination is the unnecessary destruction of their natural family. A standard that allocates the risk of error nearly equally between those two outcomes does not reflect properly their relative severity.

C

Two state interests are at stake in parental rights termination proceedings—a *parens patriae* interest in preserving and promoting the welfare of the child and a fiscal and administrative interest in reducing the cost and burden of such proceedings. A standard of proof more strict than preponderance of the evidence is consistent with both interests.

"Since the State has an urgent interest in the welfare of the child, it shares the parent's interest in an accurate and just decision" at the *factfinding* proceeding. As *parens patriae*, the State's goal is to provide the child with a permanent home. Yet while there is still reason to believe that positive, nurturing parent-child relationships exist, the *parens patriae* interest favors preservation, not severance, of natural familial bonds.[17] § 384–b.1.(a)(ii). "[T]he State registers no gain towards its declared goals when it separates children from the custody of fit parents." Stanley v. Illinois, 405 U.S., at 652, 92 S.Ct., at 1213.

The State's interest in finding the child an alternative permanent home arises only "when it is *clear* that the natural parent cannot or will not provide a normal family home for the child." Soc.Serv.Law § 384–b.1.(a)(iv) (emphasis added). At the factfinding, that goal is served by procedures that promote an accurate determination of whether the natural parents can and will provide a normal home.

Unlike a constitutional requirement of hearings, or court-appointed counsel, a stricter standard of proof would reduce factual error without imposing substantial fiscal burdens upon the State.
. . .

Nor would an elevated standard of proof create any real administrative burdens for the State's factfinders. New York Family Court judges already are familiar with a higher evidentiary standard in other parental rights termination proceedings not involving permanent neglect. . . . New York also demands at least clear and convincing evidence in proceedings of far less moment than parental rights termination proceedings. . . .
. . .

period of the child's foster home placement. See App. 19–20. See also Fam.Ct. Act § 632(b) (when State's permanent neglect petition is dismissed for insufficient evidence, judge retains jurisdiction to reconsider underlying orders of placement); § 633 (judge may suspend judgment at dispositional hearing for an additional year).

17. Any *parens patriae* interest in terminating the natural parents' rights arises only at the dispositional phase, *after* the parents have been found unfit.

We . . . , express no view on the merits of petitioners' claims. At a hearing conducted under a constitutionally proper standard, they may or may not prevail. Without deciding the outcome under any of the standards we have approved, we vacate the judgment of the Appellate Division and remand the case for further proceedings not inconsistent with this opinion.

JUSTICE REHNQUIST, with whom THE CHIEF JUSTICE, JUSTICE WHITE, and JUSTICE O'CONNOR join, dissenting.

. . . New York has created an exhaustive program to assist parents in regaining the custody of their children and to protect parents from the unfair deprivation of their parental rights. And yet the majority's myopic scrutiny of the standard of proof blinds it to the very considerations and procedures which make the New York scheme "fundamentally fair."

[The opinion reviews the procedures of the New York statute both with regard to temporary removal of children from the home and termination of parental rights.]

The three children to which this case relates were removed from petitioners' custody in 1973 and 1974, before petitioners' other two children were born. The removals were made pursuant to the procedures detailed above and in response to what can only be described as shockingly abusive treatment.[10] At the temporary removal hearing held before the Family Court on September 30, 1974, petitioners were represented by counsel, and allowed the Ulster County Department of Social Services ("Department") to take custody of the three children.

Temporary removal of the children was continued at an evidentiary hearing held before the Family Court in December 1975, after which the court issued a written opinion concluding that petitioners were unable to resume their parental responsibilities due to personality disorders. Unsatisfied with the progress petitioners were making, the court also directed the Department to reduce to writing the plan which it had designed to solve the problems at petitioners' home and reunite the family.

A plan for providing petitioners with extensive counseling and training services was submitted to the court and approved in Februa-

10. Tina Apel, the oldest of petitioners' five children, was removed from their custody by court order in November 1973 when she was two years old. Removal proceedings were commenced in response to complaints by neighbors and reports from a local hospital that Tina had suffered injuries in petitioners' home including a fractured left femur, treated with a homemade splint; bruises on the upper arms, forehead, flank, and spine; and abrasions of the upper leg. The following summer John Santosky III, peti-tioners' second oldest child, was also removed from petitioners' custody. John, who was less than one year old at the time, was admitted to the hospital suffering malnutrition, bruises on the eye and forehead, cuts on the foot, blisters on the hand, and multiple pin pricks on the back. Jed Santosky, the third oldest of petitioners' children, was removed from his parents' custody when only three days old as a result of the abusive treatment of the two older children.

ry 1976. Under the plan, petitioners received training by a mother's aide, a nutritional aide, and a public health nurse, and counseling at a family planning clinic. In addition, the plan provided psychiatric treatment and vocational training for the father, and counseling at a family service center for the mother. Respondent's Brief 1–7. Between early 1976 and the final termination decision in April 1979, the State spent more than $15,000 in these efforts to rehabilitate petitioners as parents. App. 34.

Petitioners' response to the State's effort was marginal at best. They wholly disregarded some of the available services and participated only sporadically in the others. As a result, and out of growing concern over the length of the childrens' stay in foster care, the Department petitioned in September 1976 for permanent termination of petitioners' parental rights so that the children could be adopted by other families. Although the Family Court recognized that petitioners' reaction to the State's efforts was generally "non-responsive, even resentful," the fact that they were "at least superficially cooperative" led it to conclude that there was yet hope of further improvement and an eventual reuniting of the family. Exhibit to Respondent's Brief 618. Accordingly, the petition for permanent termination was dismissed.

Whatever progress petitioners were making prior to the 1976 termination hearing, they made little or no progress thereafter. In October 1978, the Department again filed a termination petition alleging that petitioners had completely failed to plan for the childrens' future despite the considerable efforts rendered in their behalf. This time, the Family Court agreed. The court found that petitioners had "failed in any meaningful way to take advantage of the many social and rehabilitative services that have not only been made available to them but have been diligently urged upon them." In addition, the court found that the "infrequent" visits "between the parents and their children were at best superficial and devoid of any real emotional content." The court thus found "nothing in the situation which holds out any hope that [petitioners] may ever become financially self sufficient or emotionally mature enough to be independent of the services of social agencies. More than a reasonable amount of time has passed and still, in the words of the case workers, there has been no discernible forward movement. At some point in time, it must be said, 'enough is enough.' "

In accordance with the statutory requirements set forth above, the court found that petitioners' failure to plan for the future of their children, who were then seven, five, and four years old and had been out of petitioners' custody for at least four years, rose to the level of permanent neglect. At a subsequent dispositional hearing, the court terminated petitioners' parental rights, thereby freeing the three children for adoption.

As this account demonstrates, the State's extraordinary four-year effort to reunite petitioners' family was not just unsuccessful, it was altogether rebuffed by parents unwilling to improve their circumstances sufficiently to permit a return of their children. At every step of this protracted process petitioners were accorded those procedures and protections which traditionally have been required by due process of law. Moreover, from the beginning to the end of this sad story all judicial determinations were made by one family court judge. After four and one-half years of involvement with petitioners, more than seven complete hearings, and additional periodic supervision of the State's rehabilitative efforts, the judge no doubt was intimately familiar with this case and the prospects for petitioners' rehabilitation.

It is inconceivable to me that these procedures were "fundamentally unfair" to petitioners. Only by its obsessive focus on the standard of proof and its almost complete disregard of the facts of this case does the majority find otherwise.[11] As the discussion above indicates, however, such a focus does not comport with the flexible stan-

---

11. The majority finds, without any reference to the facts of this case, that "numerous factors [in New York termination proceedings] combine to magnify the risk of erroneous factfinding." Among the factors identified by the majority are the "unusual discretion" of the family court judge "to underweigh probative facts that might favor the parent"; the often uneducated, minority status of the parents and their consequent "vulnerab[ility] to judgments based on cultural or class bias"; the "State's ability to assemble its case," which "dwarfs the parents' ability to mount a defense" by including an unlimited budget, expert attorneys, and "full access to all public records concerning the family"; and the fact that "natural parents have no 'double jeopardy' defense against repeated state" efforts, "with more or better evidence," to terminate parental rights "even when the parents have attained the level of fitness required by the State." In short, the majority characterizes the State as a wealthy and powerful bully bent on taking children away from defenseless parents. Such characterization finds no support in the record.

The intent of New York has been stated with eminent clarity: "the [S]tate's *first obligation* is to *help* the family with services to *prevent* its break-up or to *reunite* it if the child has already left home." SSL § 384–b(1)(a)(iii) (emphasis added). There is simply no basis in fact for believing, as the majority does, that the State does not mean what it says; in-

deed, the facts of this case demonstrate that New York has gone the extra mile in seeking to effectuate its declared purpose. More importantly, there should be no room in the jurisprudence of this Court for decisions based on unsupported, inaccurate assumptions.

A brief examination of the "factors" relied upon by the majority demonstrates its error. The "unusual" discretion of the family court judge to consider the "affectio[n] and concer[n]" displayed by parents during visits with their children, is nothing more than discretion to consider reality; there is not one shred of evidence in this case suggesting that the determination of the family court was "based on cultural or class bias"; if parents lack the "ability to mount a defense," the State provides them with the full services of an attorney, FCA § 262, and they, like the State, have "full access to all *public* records concerning the family" (emphasis added); and the absence of "double jeopardy" protection simply recognizes the fact that family problems are often ongoing and may in the future warrant action that currently is unnecessary. In this case the family court dismissed the first termination petition because it desired to give petitioners "the benefit of the doubt," and a second opportunity to raise themselves to "an acceptable minimal level of competency as parents." It was their complete failure to do so that prompted the second, successful termination petition.

dard of fundamental fairness embodied in the Due Process Clause of the Fourteenth Amendment.

B

In addition to the basic fairness of the process afforded petitioners, the standard of proof chosen by New York clearly reflects a constitutionally permissible balance of the interests at stake in this case. The standard of proof "represents an attempt to instruct the factfinder concerning the degree of confidence our society thinks he should have in the correctness of factual conclusions for a particular type of adjudication." In re Winship, 397 U.S. 358, 370, 90 S.Ct. 1068, 1076, 25 L.Ed.2d 368 (1970) (Harlan, J. concurring); Addington v. Texas, 441 U.S. 418, 423, 99 S.Ct. 1804, 1807, 60 L.Ed.2d 323 (1979). In this respect, the standard of proof is a crucial component of legal process, the primary function of which is "to minimize the risk of erroneous decisions." [12]

In determining the propriety of a particular standard of proof in a given case, however, it is not enough simply to say that we are trying to minimize the risk of error. Because errors in factfinding affect more than one interest, we try to minimize error as to those interests which we consider to be most important. As Justice Harlan explained in his well-known concurrence to In re Winship:

> "In a lawsuit between two parties, a factual error can make a difference in one of two ways. First, it can result in a judgment in favor of the plaintiff when the true facts warrant a judgment for the defendant. The analogue in a criminal case would be the conviction of an innocent man. On the other hand, an erroneous factual determination can result in a judgment for the defendant

12. It is worth noting that the significance of the standard of proof in New York parental termination proceedings differs from the significance of the standard in other forms of litigation. In the usual adjudicatory setting, the factfinder has had little or no prior exposure to the facts of the case. His only knowledge of those facts comes from the evidence adduced at trial, and he renders his findings solely upon the basis of that evidence. Thus, normally, the standard of proof is a crucial factor in the final outcome of the case, for it is the scale upon which the factfinder weighs his knowledge and makes his decision.

Although the standard serves the same function in New York parental termination proceedings, additional assurances of accuracy are present in its application. As was adduced at oral argument, the practice in New York is to assign one judge to supervise a case from the initial temporary removal of the child to the final termination of parental rights. Therefore, as discussed above, the factfinder is intimately familiar with the case before the termination proceedings ever begin. Indeed, as in this case, he often will have been closely involved in protracted efforts to rehabilitate the parents. Even if a change in judges occurs, the Family Court retains jurisdiction of the case and the newly assigned judge may take judicial notice of all prior proceedings. Given this familiarity with the case, and the necessarily lengthy efforts which must precede a termination action in New York, decisions in termination cases are made by judges steeped in the background of the case and peculiarly able to judge the accuracy of evidence placed before them. This does not mean that the standard of proof in these cases can escape due process scrutiny, only that additional assurances of accuracy attend the application of the standard in New York termination proceedings.

when the true facts justify a judgment in plaintiff's favor. The criminal analogue would be the acquittal of a guilty man.

The standard of proof influences the relative frequency of these two types of erroneous outcomes. If, for example, the standard of proof for a criminal trial were a preponderance of the evidence rather than proof beyond a reasonable doubt, there would be a smaller risk of factual errors that result in freeing guilty persons, but a far greater risk of factual errors that result in convicting the innocent. Because the standard of proof affects the comparative frequency of these two types of erroneous outcomes, the choice of the standard to be applied in a particular kind of litigation should, in a rational world, reflect an assessment of the comparative social disutility of each." 397 U.S., at 370–372, 90 S.Ct., at 1076.

When the standard of proof is understood as reflecting such an assessment, an examination of the interests at stake in a particular case becomes essential to determining the propriety of the specified standard of proof. Because proof by a preponderance of the evidence requires that "[t]he litigants . . . share the risk of error in a roughly equal fashion," Addington v. Texas, supra, 441 U.S., at 423, 99 S.Ct. at 1808, it rationally should be applied only when the interests at stake are of roughly equal societal importance. The interests at stake in this case demonstrate that New York has selected a constitutionally permissible standard of proof.

On one side is the interest of parents in a continuation of the family unit and the raising of their own children. The importance of this interest cannot easily be overstated. Few consequences of judicial action are so grave as the severance of natural family ties. Even the convict committed to prison and thereby deprived of his physical liberty often retains the love and support of family members. "This Court's decisions have by now made plain beyond the need for multiple citation that a parent's desire for and right to 'the companionship, care, custody and management of his or her children' is an important interest that 'undeniably warrants deference and, absent a powerful countervailing interest, protection.' Stanley v. Illinois, 405 U.S. 645, 651 [92 S.Ct. 1208, 1212, 31 L.Ed.2d 551]." Lassiter v. Department of Social Services, 452 U.S. 18, 27, 101 S.Ct. 2153, 2161, 68 L.Ed.2d 640 (1981). In creating the scheme at issue in this case, the New York legislature was expressly aware of this right of parents "to bring up their own children." SSL § 384–b(1)(a)(ii).

On the other side of the termination proceeding are the often countervailing interests of the child.[13] A stable, loving homelife is

13. The majority dismisses the child's interest in the accuracy of determinations made at the factfinding hearing because "[t]he factfinding does not purport . . . to balance the child's interest in a normal family life against the parents' interest in raising the child," but instead "pits the State directly against the parents." Only "[a]fter the State has established parental unfitness," the majority reasons, may the court "assume . . .

essential to a child's physical, emotional, and spiritual well-being. It requires no citation of authority to assert that children who are abused in their youth generally face extraordinary problems developing into responsible, productive citizens. The same can be said of children who, though not physically or emotionally abused, are passed from one foster home to another with no constancy of love, trust, or discipline. If the Family Court makes an incorrect factual determination resulting in a failure to terminate a parent-child relationship which rightfully should be ended, the child involved must return either to an abusive home or to the often unstable world of foster care. The reality of these risks is magnified by the fact that the only families faced with termination actions are those which have voluntarily surrendered custody of their child to the State, or, as in this case, those from which the child has been removed by judicial action because of threatened irreparable injury through abuse or neglect. Permanent neglect findings also occur only in families where the child has been in foster care for at least one year.

In addition to the child's interest in a normal homelife, "the State has an urgent interest in the welfare of the child." Lassiter v. Department of Social Services, supra, at 27, 101 S.Ct., at 2160.[16] Few could doubt that the most valuable resource of a self-governing society is its population of children who will one day become adults and themselves assume the responsibility of self-governance. "A demo-

that the interests of the child and the natural parents do diverge."

This reasoning misses the mark. The child has an interest in the outcome of the factfinding hearing independent of that of the parent. To be sure, "the child and his parents share a vital interest in preventing *erroneous* termination of their natural relationship." (emphasis added). But the child's interest in a continuation of the family unit exists only to the extent that such a continuation would not be harmful to him. An error *in the factfinding hearing* that results in a failure to terminate a parent-child relationship which rightfully should be terminated may well detrimentally affect the child.

The preponderance of the evidence standard, which allocates the risk of error more or less evenly, is employed when the social disutility of error in *either direction* is roughly equal—that is, when an incorrect finding of fault would produce consequences as undesirable as the consequences that would be produced by an incorrect findng of *no* fault. Only when the disutility of error in one direction discernibly outweighs the disutility of error in the other direction do we choose, by means of the standard of proof, to reduce the likelihood of the

more onerous outcome. See In re Winship, 397 U.S. 358, 370–372, 90 S.Ct. 1068, 1075–1077, 25 L.Ed.2d 368 (1970) (Harlan, J., concurring).

New York's adoption of the preponderance of the evidence standard reflects its conclusion that the undesirable consequence of an erroneous finding of parental unfitness—the unwarranted termination of the family relationship—is roughly equal to the undesirable consequence of an erroneous finding of parental fitness—the risk of permanent injury to the child either by return of the child to an abusive home or by the child's continued lack of a permanent home. Such a conclusion is well within the province of state legislatures. It cannot be said that the New York procedures are unconstitutional simply because a majority of the members of this Court disagree with the New York legislature's weighing of the interests of the parents and the child in an error-free factfinding hearing.

16. The majority's conclusion that a state interest in the child's well-being arises only after a determination of parental unfitness suffers from the same error as its assertion that the child has no interest, separate from that of its parents, in the accuracy of the factfinding hearing.

cratic society rests, for its continuance, upon the healthy, well-rounded growth of young people into full maturity as citizens, with all that implies." Prince v. Massachusetts, 321 U.S. 158, 168, 64 S.Ct. 438, 443, 88 L.Ed. 645 (1944). Thus, "the whole community" has an interest "that children be both safeguarded from abuses and given opportunities for growth into free and independent well-developed . . . citizens." Id., at 165. See also Ginsberg v. New York, 390 U.S. 629, 640–641, 88 S.Ct. 1274, 1281–82, 20 L.Ed.2d 195 (1968).

When, in the context of a permanent neglect termination proceeding, the interests of the child and the State in a stable, nurturing homelife are balanced against the interests of the parents in the rearing of their child, it cannot be said that either set of interests is so clearly paramount as to require that the risk of error be allocated to one side or the other. Accordingly, a State constitutionally may conclude that the risk of error should be borne in roughly equal fashion by use of the preponderance of the evidence standard of proof. . . .

III

For the reasons heretofore stated, I believe that the Court today errs in concluding that the New York standard of proof in parental-rights termination proceedings violates due process of law. The decision disregards New York's earnest efforts to *aid* parents in regaining the custody of their children and a host of procedural protections placed around parental rights and interests. The Court finds a constitutional violation only by a tunnel-vision application of due process principles that altogether loses sight of the unmistakable fairness of the New York procedure.

Even more worrisome, today's decision cavalierly rejects the considered judgment of the New York legislature in an area traditionally entrusted to state care. The Court thereby begins, I fear, a trend of federal intervention in state family law matters which surely will stifle creative responses to vexing problems. Accordingly, I dissent.

NOTE

In Lassiter v. Department of Social Services, discussed in both the majority and dissenting opinions in *Santosky*, the petitioner was a mother whose infant son had been adjudicated a neglected child and placed in custody of a state agency in 1975. A year later the mother was convicted of second-degree murder and she began serving a 25–40 year prison term. In 1978 a termination proceeding was instituted. Petitioner was brought from prison to the hearing. Finding that she had been given ample time to obtain counsel and that her failure to do so was without just cause, the court did not postpone the proceeding. Because petitioner did not aver that she was indigent, counsel was not appointed for her. During the hearing petitioner and her mother responded to questions by the court, and petitioner cross-examined a social worker. The court terminated petitioner's parental rights, finding that she had "willfully failed to maintain concern or responsibility for the welfare of the minor." The issue on appeal was whether petitioner had been denied due process because of the court's failure to appoint counsel for her.

Explaining how to determine whether counsel need be appointed in a particular case, the opinion of the Court stated:

The case of Mathews v. Eldridge, 424 U.S. 319, 335, 96 S.Ct. 893, 903, 47 L.Ed.2d 18, propounds three elements to be evaluated in deciding what due process requires, viz., the private interests at stake, the government's interest, and the risk that the procedures used will lead to erroneous decisions. We must balance these elements against each other, and then set their net weight in the scales against the presumption that there is a right to appointed counsel only where the indigent, if he is unsuccessful, may lose his personal freedom.

This Court's decisions have by now made plain beyond the need for multiple citation that a parent's desire for and right to "the companionship, care, custody and management of his or her children" is an important interest that "undeniably warrants deference and, absent a powerful countervailing interest, protection." Stanley v. Illinois, 405 U.S. 645, 651, 92 S.Ct. 1208, 1212, 31 L.Ed. 551. Here the State has sought not simply to infringe upon that interest but to end it. If the State prevails, it will have worked a unique kind of deprivation. Cf. May v. Anderson, 345 U.S. 528, 533, 73 S.Ct. 840, 843, 97 L.Ed. 1221; Armstrong v. Manzo, 380 U.S. 545, 85 S.Ct. 1187, 14 L.Ed.2d 62. A parent's interest in the accuracy and justice of the decision to terminate his or her parental status is, therefore a commanding one.[3]

Since the State has an urgent interest in the welfare of the child, it shares the parent's interest in an accurate and just decision. For this reason, the State may share the indigent parent's interest in the availability of appointed counsel. If, as our adversary system presupposes, accurate and just results are most likely to be obtained through the equal contest of opposed interests, the State's interest in the child's welfare may perhaps best be served by a hearing in which both the parent and the State acting for the child are represented by counsel, without whom the contest of interests may become unwholesomely unequal. North Carolina itself acknowledges as much by providing that where a parent files a written answer to a termination petition, the State must supply a lawyer to represent the child. N.C.G.S. § 7A–289.29.

The State's interests, however, clearly diverge from the parent's insofar as the State wishes the termination decision to be made as economically as possible and thus wants to avoid both the expense of appointed counsel and the cost of the lengthened proceedings his presence may cause. But though the State's pecuniary interest is legitimate, it is hardly significant enough to overcome private interests as important as those here, particularly in light of the concession in the respondent's brief that the "potential costs of appointed counsel in termination proceedings

3. Some parents will have an additional interest to protect. Petitions to terminate parental rights are not uncommonly based on alleged criminal activity. Parents so accused may need legal counsel to guide them in understanding the problems such petitions may create.

. . . is [*sic*] admittedly *de minimis* compared to the costs in all criminal actions."

Finally, consideration must be given to the risk that a parent will be erroneously deprived of his or her child because the parent is not represented by counsel.

[The Court details the safeguards prescribed by contemporary N.C. termination procedure.]

. . .

The respondent argues that the subject of a termination hearing—the parent's relationship with her child—far from being abstruse, technical, or unfamiliar, is one as to which the parent must be uniquely well informed and to which the parent must have given prolonged thought. The respondent also contends that a termination hearing is not likely to produce difficult points of evidentiary law, or even of substantive law, since the evidentiary problems peculiar to criminal trials are not present and since the standards for termination are not complicated. In fact, the respondent reports, the North Carolina Departments of Social Services are themselves sometimes represented at termination hearings by social workers instead of by lawyers.

Yet the ultimate issues with which a termination hearing deals are not always simple, however commonplace they may be. Expert medical and psychiatric testimony, which few parents are equipped to understand and fewer still to confute, is sometimes presented. The parents are likely to be people with little education, who have had uncommon difficulty in dealing with life, and who are, at the hearing, thrust into a distressing and disorienting situation. That these factors may combine to overwhelm an uncounselled parent is evident from the findings some courts have made. Thus, courts have generally held that the State must appoint counsel for indigent parents at termination proceedings. The respondent is able to point to no presently authoritative case, except for the North Carolina judgment now before us, holding that an indigent parent has no due process right to appointed counsel in termination proceedings.

The dispositive question . . . is whether the three *Eldridge* factors, when weighed against the presumption that there is no right to appointed counsel in the absence of at least a potential deprivation of physical liberty, suffice to rebut that presumption and thus to lead to the conclusion that the Due Process Clause requires the appointment of counsel when a State seeks to terminate an indigent's parental status. To summarize the above discussion of the *Eldridge* factors: the parent's interest is an extremely important one (and may be supplemented by the dangers of criminal liability inherent in some termination proceedings); the State shares with the parent an interest in a correct decision, has a relatively weak pecuniary interest, and, in some but not all cases, has a possibly stronger interest in informal procedures; and the complexity of the proceeding and the incapacity of the uncounselled parent could be, but would not always be, great enough to make the risk of an erroneous deprivation of the parent's rights insupportably high.

If, in a given case, the parent's interests were at their strongest, the State's interests were at their weakest, and the risks of error were at their peak, it could not be said that the *Eldridge* factors did not overcome the presumption against the right to appointed counsel, and that due process did not therefore require the appointment of counsel. But since the *Eldridge* factors will not always be so distributed, and since "due process is not so rigid as to require that the significant interests in informality, flexibility and economy must always be sacrificed," Gagnon v. Scarpelli, supra, 411 U.S., at 788, 93 S.Ct., at 1762, neither can we say that the Constitution requires the appointment of counsel in every parental termination proceeding. We therefore adopt the standard found appropriate in Gagnon v. Scarpelli, and leave the decision whether due process calls for the appointment of counsel for indigent parents in termination proceedings to be answered in the first instance by the trial court, subject, of course, to appellate review.

. . .

In its Fourteenth Amendment, our Constitution imposes on the States the standards necessary to ensure that judicial proceedings are fundamentally fair. A wise public policy, however, may require that higher standards be adopted than those minimally tolerable under the Constitution. Informed opinion has clearly come to hold that an indigent parent is entitled to the assistance of appointed counsel not only in parental termination proceedings, but in dependency and neglect proceedings as well. Most significantly, 33 States and the District of Columbia provide statutorily for the appointment of counsel in termination cases. The Court's opinion today in no way implies that the standards increasingly urged by informed public opinion and now widely followed by the States are other than enlightened and wise.

In Besharov, Terminating Parental Rights: The Indigent Parent's Right to Counsel after Lassiter v. North Carolina, 15 Fam.L.Q. 205, 216 (1981) * we find this analysis of the possible meanings of *Lassiter* by a commentator long involved in the children's field:

The *Lassiter* decision can be interpreted in two diametrically opposed ways. First, it can be viewed as a rejection of the indigent parent's right to counsel in termination proceedings. On the day after the decision was announced, for example, the *front page* headline in the *Washington Post* read: "Courts Can Take Child Away From Parents Without Providing Lawyer, Justices Say."

On the other hand, *Lassiter* can also be viewed as a cautious, but nevertheless striking, expansion of due process doctrine to include the right to counsel in "civil" proceedings. Focusing on the fate of Abby Lassiter's appeal obscures the historical potential of the Court's decision. *Lassiter* may be the first evolutionary step in an ultimately revolutionary recognition of the due process right of indigents to appointed counsel in "civil" proceedings. In three opinions, eight out of nine Justices opened the door to the future provision of counsel in some, if not all, termination proceedings. Only the Chief Justice seemed willing to foreclose the possibility. The four dissenting Justices, of course, would have held that there is an automatic right to counsel in all termination proceedings. That four Justices unambiguously adopted this position was, in itself, a major step toward a holding in favor of the right to counsel. But perhaps more importantly, four other Justices, speaking through Justice

Stewart, all but said that there is a right to counsel under certain circumstances. The key passage in Stewart's opinion reads:

> If, in a given case, the parent's interests were at their strongest, the State's interests were at their weakest, and the risks of error were at their peak, it could not be said that the *Eldridge* factors did not overcome the presumption against the right to appointed counsel, and that due process did not therefore require the appointment of counsel.

Moreover, the factors that the Justices seemed to consider crucial suggest that they would find a right to counsel in many, if not most, termination proceedings. Basically, the grounds for most involuntary terminations divide into three broad categories: (1) severe abuse or neglect; (2) severe, and apparently long term, parental inability to care properly for the child; and (3) constructive abandonment. Cases in the first category, because of the possibility of criminal prosecution, seem to fall within the Court's guidelines for the appointment of counsel. So would cases in the second category, because they usually require expert testimony about the parent's prognosis for improvement. Only cases in the third category seem to fall outside of the Court's holding. These cases involve parents who, for no good cause, fail to maintain contact with a child over a sufficient period of time, or otherwise demonstrate a clear lack of concern about the child's care and welfare. Given the realities of current practice in such cases, the appointment of counsel is unlikely to have more than a marginal effect on the outcome of the proceeding.

Many observers will warn against taking the majority too seriously; they will accuse Justice Stewart's decision of being a tortured escape from the logic of past precedents—which will be distinguished or otherwise watered down in subsequent cases. But beyond basic respect for the Court, there are other good reasons for taking the Justices who joined in Stewart's opinion at their collective word.

First, if they did not share his views, the other Justices could have joined in the Chief Justice's opinion, or written one of their own. Second, if one believes, as they said they did, that the existence of the right to counsel depends on the circumstances, then there were sufficient reasons for rejecting Ms. Lassiter's appeal. . . . Since her son was first taken away from her in 1975, Ms. Lassiter had apparently made no attempt to see him. In their opinions, both Stewart and Burger were critical of Ms. Lassiter's apparent lack of concern for her son. Justice Stewart claimed that "the weight of the evidence" was that Ms. Lassiter had "few sparks" of "interest in her son." He pointed to her:

> plain demonstration that she was not interested in attending a [prior] hearing . . . . Ms. Lassiter had not even bothered to speak to her retained lawyer after being notified of the termination hearing, and the court specifically found that Ms. Lassiter's failure to make an effort to contest the termination proceeding was without cause.

Similarly, Chief Justice Burger said that Ms. Lassiter "showed little interest in her child." Perhaps the case-by-case approach will eventually prove to be impractically cumbersome, but this was hardly the kind of fact situation upon which to expect a major departure from past Constitutional doctrine.

Unfortunately, there is no way of knowing whether the nascent doctrine enunciated in *Lassiter* will form the basis of a full blown right to counsel, in much the same way that Betts v. Brady eventually lead to Gideon v. Wainwright, or whether it was merely an awkward retreat from past liberalism. Only time and the future membership of the Court will decide. We will have to wait and see how the Court applies, in subsequent cases, the guidelines that it seems to have established in *Lassiter*. We will have to see what the Court does in cases where there is the possibility of a criminal prosecution, where the issues are complicated or require the use of expert witnesses, where the parent has demonstrated at least a minimal interest in the welfare of the child, or where the weight of the evidence is not clearly in favor of termination.

Some states specifically provide for appointing counsel for children in parental rights termination cases. For a discussion of this in the context of the California law, see Bellah, Appointing Counsel for the Child in Actions to Terminate Parental Rights, 70 Calif.L.Rev. 481 (1982). It would seem that several obvious duties of such counsel would be to investigate the facts fully and to examine the possible alternatives available under the circumstances. What other functions do you believe that counsel should serve? How much should counsel be an advocate for the child's own choice rather than a neutral evaluator for the court?

KNOX v. LYNCHBURG DIVISION OF SOCIAL SERVICES

Supreme Court of Virginia, 1982.
223 Va. 213, 288 S.E.2d 399.

CARRICO, CHIEF JUSTICE.

In this case, the trial court terminated the residual parental rights of the mother of three minor children. The principal question presented stems from our 1975 decision in Rocka v. Roanoke Co. Dep't of Welfare, 215 Va. 515, 211 S.E.2d 76, and the General Assembly's 1977 enactment of Code § 16.1–283.[1] Specifically, the question is

---

1. § 16.1–283. Termination of residual parental rights.—A. The residual parental rights of a parent or parents may be terminated by the court as hereinafter provided in a separate proceeding if the petition specifically requests such relief. No petition seeking termination of residual parental rights shall be accepted by the court prior to the filing of a foster care plan, pursuant to § 16.1–281, which documents termination of residual parental rights as being in the best interests of the child. The court may terminate the residual parental rights of one parent without affecting the rights of the other parent. Any order terminating residual parental rights shall be accompanied by an order continuing or granting custody to a local board of public welfare or social services, to a licensed child-placing agency or the granting of custody or guardianship to a relative or other interested individual. An order continuing or granting custody to a local board of public welfare or social services or to a licensed child-placing agency shall indicate whether that board or agency shall have the authority to place the child for adoption and consent thereto. The summons shall be served upon the parent or parents and the other parties specified in § 16.1–263. Written notice of the hearing shall also be provided to the foster parents of the child if they have had physical custody of the child for more than twelve months informing them that they may appear as witnesses at the hearing to give testimony and, within the discretion of the court, otherwise participate in the proceeding. The summons or notice of hearing shall clearly state the consequences of a termination of residual parental rights. Service shall be made pursuant to § 16.1–264.

B. The residual parental rights of a parent or parents of a child found by the court to be neglected or abused and placed in foster care as a result of (i) court commitment, (ii) an entrustment

whether § 16.1–283 modifies the *Rocka* rule that, in a contest be-

agreement entered into by the parent or parents or (iii) other voluntary relinquishment by the parent or parents may be terminated if the court finds, based upon clear and convincing evidence, that it is in the best interests of the child and that:

1. The neglect or abuse suffered by such child presented a serious and substantial threat to his or her life, health or development; and

2. It is not reasonably likely that the conditions which resulted in such neglect or abuse can be substantially corrected or eliminated so as to allow the child's safe return to his or her parent or parents within a reasonable period of time.

Proof of any of the following shall constitute prima facie evidence of the conditions set forth in subparagraph B 2 hereof:

a. The parent or parents are suffering from a mental or emotional illness or mental deficiency of such severity that there is no reasonable expectation that such parent will be able to undertake responsibility for the care needed by the child in accordance with his or her age and stage of development;

b. The parent or parents have habitually abused or are addicted to intoxicating liquors, narcotics or other dangerous drugs to the extent that proper parental ability has been seriously impaired and the parent, without good cause, has not responded to or followed through with recommended and available treatment which could have improved the capacity for adequate parental functioning; or

c. The parent or parents, without good cause, have not responded to or followed through with appropriate, available and reasonable rehabilitative efforts on the part of social, medical, mental health or other rehabilitative agencies designed to reduce, eliminate or prevent the neglect or abuse of the child.

C. The residual parental rights of a parent or parents of a child placed in foster care as a result of court commitment, an entrustment agreement entered into by the parent or parents or other voluntary relinquishment by the parent or parents may be terminated if the court finds, based upon clear and convincing evidence, that it is in the best interests of the child and that:

1. The parent or parents have, without good cause, failed to maintain contact with and to provide or substantially plan for the future of the child for a period of twelve months after the child's placement in foster care notwithstanding the reasonable and appropriate efforts of social, medical, mental health or other rehabilitative agencies to communicate with the parent or parents and to strengthen the parent-child relationship; or

2. The parent or parents, without good cause, have been unwilling or unable within a reasonable period to remedy substantially the conditions which led to the child's foster care placement, notwithstanding the reasonable and appropriate efforts of social, medical, mental health or other rehabilitative agencies to such end.

Proof of any of the following shall constitute prima facie evidence of the conditions set forth in subparagraphs C 1 or 2 hereof:

a. The parent or parents have failed, without good cause, to communicate on a continuing or planned basis with the child for a period of twelve months; or

b. The parent or parents, without good cause, have failed or have been unable to make reasonable progress towards the elimination of the conditions which led to the child's foster care placement in accordance with their obligations under and within the time limits or goals set forth in a foster care plan filed with the court or any other plan jointly designed and agreed to by the parent or parents and a social, medical, mental health or other rehabilitative agency.

D. The residual parental rights of a parent or parents of a child found by the court to be neglected or abused upon the ground of abandonment may be terminated if the court finds, based upon clear and convincing evidence, that it is in the best interests of the child and that:

1. The child was abandoned under such circumstances that the identity of the parent or parents cannot be determined; and

2. The child's parent or parents, guardian or relatives have not come forward to identify such child and claim a relationship to the child within six months following the issuance of an order by the court placing the child in foster care; and

3. Diligent efforts have been made to locate the child's parent or parents without avail.

tween a parent and a social service agency, the court may not terminate the rights of the parent absent an express finding of parental unfitness.[2]

The present case involves a girl, born April 14, 1973, and twin boys, born August 24, 1974. Their parents, Dorothy Tweedy Knox and Robert P. Knox, were married in May, 1972.

On January 2, 1975, the father was arrested, and the mother placed the children with Christine Beasley, a family friend who operated a foster care home. At the time, the twins were in "very bad" physical condition. On January 24, the father and mother signed agreements entrusting the children temporarily to the Lynchburg Division of Social Services.

The Beasley home was not an approved foster care facility. However, the Division gave it special approval so the children could remain there, near their parents' residence.

In February, 1975, the father was sentenced to serve five years in the Virginia penitentiary. During the next year, the mother changed jobs and residences often. Her contacts with the Division were "sporadic" until May, 1977, when they became frequent. In the meantime, the Division was awarded temporary custody of the three children.

In September, 1977, the father was released from prison. He and the mother acquired a place to live, visited the children in the Beasley home, and made plans for the children's return. In December, however, the parents separated. Thereafter, they appeared in court for "fighting" and were "ordered to stay away from each other."

In the early months of 1978, based in part on the mother's complaints, the Division became concerned about conditions in the Beasley home. In an effort to prepare for the children's return to the mother, the Division had her sign an agreement dated June 2, 1978, which required her to maintain regular contact with her social worker, to visit the children every two weeks, to obtain suitable housing, and to establish financial stability. The agreement stated further that a social worker would counsel the mother regarding sources of employment and housing, provide transportation in seeking work and living quarters, and arrange visits with the children.

At the end of June, 1978, the Division removed the mother's social worker and did not designate a new worker until August. When the new worker was assigned, she arranged to transfer the children from the Beasley home to a foster home in Bedford County, "over twenty miles away." The change upset the mother because she lacked "ready transportation" to visit the children.

E. Notwithstanding any other provisions of this section, residual parental rights shall not be terminated if it is established that the child, if he or she be fourteen years of age or older or otherwise of an age of discretion as determined by the court, objects to such termination.

2. We reaffirmed the *Rocka* rule in Berrien v. Greene County, 216 Va. 241, 217 S.E.2d 854 (1975).

From September until the end of December, 1978, the Division experienced "significant differences and difficulties" with the mother concerning "visits, finances, living quarters and related matters." In January, 1979, both the mother and the father discussed with the social worker the children's situation. The father indicated his desire to "give up" the children, but said he was willing for the mother to assume their responsibility. The mother stated she wanted "to get the children back," but she refused to sign a revised agreement covering "financial and other arrangements" the Division considered necessary for the mother to regain custody.

The conflict between the mother and the Division continued, accentuated by the mother's failure to return the children to their foster home following an Easter visit. In addition, the mother lost her job at a nursing home and was unable to find full-time employment.

The Knox's divorce became final in April, 1979. On May 10, 1979, the father executed an agreement entrusting the children to the Division permanently and authorizing their placement for adoption. When the Division requested the mother to sign a similar agreement, she refused. Later, the Division filed petitions in juvenile and domestic relations district court, seeking termination of parental rights and permission for adoption placement. The petitions were granted, and the mother appealed to the circuit court.

After a hearing on December 13, 1979, the circuit court continued the matter to give the mother an opportunity, with the assistance of a new social worker, to "show progress in her financial and living arrangements." When the case returned to court on April 7, 1980, it was continued again to permit the mother to pursue the employment plan worked out by her social worker and "to see if further progress in her overall situation could be made." At a hearing on July 7, 1980, it appeared that the mother "had not pursued the plan" and that her overall situation had not improved.

The circuit court entered orders reciting that termination of parental rights was in the children's best interests and that the mother "without good cause, [had] been unwilling and unable, within a period in excess of five (5) years, to remedy substantially the conditions which led to [the children's] foster care placement, notwithstanding reasonable and appropriate efforts of social, employment, mental health and other rehabilitative agencies to such end." The orders terminated the mother's rights and authorized the Division to place the children for adoption.

As indicated earlier, the principal question for decision is whether the 1977 enactment of Code § 16.1–283 modified the *Rocka-Berrien* rule that, in a contest between a parent and a social service agency, the rights of the parent may not be terminated absent a specific finding of unfitness. The mother contends that a specific finding of unfitness is still required and that, because the trial court made no such finding, it erred in terminating her parental rights.

We disagree with the mother. *Rocka* and *Berrien* were decided under Code § 16.1–178, which permitted severance of parental rights if it was "for the child's best interest and that of the State that such child be separated permanently from its parent, parents or guardian." In *Rocka*, we held that a trial court's finding that an award of permanent custody to a social service agency would promote the child's best interests was not equivalent to a finding of parental unfitness. *Berrien* reaffirmed that holding. In both cases, we said that before a court could terminate parental rights, it must find not only that the child's best interests would be served but also that the parent was unfit.

In apparent response to the *Rocka* and *Berrien* decisions, the General Assembly repealed § 16.1–178 and replaced it with § 16.1–283. Now, by statute, the court is required to find both that the termination of parental rights will promote the best interests of the child and that certain factors listed in the statute are present. Once the court finds these factors are present, it need not make a further finding of parental unfitness. In our opinion, a finding that the factors exist is tantamount to a finding of parental unfitness.

The mother contends next that the trial court's decision "is not supported by sufficient evidence of facts required by Code § 16.1–283(C)(2) in order to terminate [her] parental rights and place her children for adoption." Subsection (C)(2) permits termination of parental rights if the "parent or parents, without good cause, have been unwilling or unable within a reasonable period to remedy substantially the conditions which led to the child's foster care placement, notwithstanding the reasonable and appropriate efforts of social, medical, mental health or other rehabilitative agencies to such end."

The mother concedes that when the Division assumed responsibility for her children in January, 1975, her "situation was grim"; she had meager financial resources and her husband faced a possible prison term. Nevertheless, the mother says, she persisted in her efforts to provide for her children despite the hardships she faced; she sought employment, she placed the children in the Beasley home, she visited them regularly, and she agreed to the Division's terms for the return of the children to her custody.

The mother claims that the Division thwarted her efforts to establish her ability to resume care of the children. The "first thing that happened," she asserts, was the removal of her social worker in June, 1978, and the failure of the Division to appoint a replacement for two months. The record shows, however, that "the social worker supervisor" handled the mother's case during the two-month period and was available for the mother's consultation.

The "next significant development," the mother says, was the transfer of the children from the Beasley home to a foster home in Bedford County, "over twenty miles away." The mother insists that the transfer and an unsympathetic social worker made it difficult to arrange visits with the children. But the Bedford location was chosen because it was "the nearest approved and available foster home." Furthermore, the Division was willing to provide the mother with transportation to visit the children at the Bedford home, and it never refused a request by the mother for visitation; indeed, the Division tried to schedule visits for the mother, but the effort was unsuccessful because she failed to give the Division any "concrete dates."

Then, the mother states, there began a deterioration of her relationship with the Division that culminated in the filing of the petitions to terminate parental rights. The mother charges that "[d]eception and recrimination characterized the Division's actions in working out the permanent separation of the children from [the mother]." We find nothing in the record, however, to support this charge, and we dismiss it as wholly lacking in merit.

Finally, the mother alleges that the Division made "little or no efforts" to provide the range of services and assistance required by Code § 16.1–283(C)(2). Only after the case reached circuit court, the mother asserts, were any services furnished her, and then only at the direction of the court. She responded to the court's action in "limited fashion," the mother says, by persisting in her search for work and suitable living quarters, but her endeavors apparently were "too little [and] too late."

We do not believe, however, that the record supports these allegations. We think the record shows clearly that the Division met often with the mother and counseled her concerning her needs and problems, advised her of the social and rehabilitative services available to assist her, and offered to provide her with transportation to obtain those services. Of particular significance is the evidence concerning the seven-month period from December 13, 1979, to July 7, 1980, during which the trial court held the case in abeyance for the Division to work with the mother to improve her situation. In this period, the mother was offered vocational rehabilitation and job training programs, assistance in job placement, training in a "sheltered workshop" program, testing, evaluation, and counseling in a mental health clinic, and classes in parenthood training. For these purposes, the Division scheduled appointments for the mother, reminded her of the appointments, and offered to provide her with transportation. Yet, the mother refused to accept many of the services offered her, failed to keep a number of the appointments, and rejected the Division's offer of transportation. More important, the mother exhibited little ability or willingness to improve the situation that existed when the Division first assumed responsibility for the children.

The mother contends, however, that the trial court erred in taking into account the events occurring in this seven-month period. The court should have confined its consideration of the evidence, the mother maintains, to the time preceding the filing of the petitions in juvenile court. She was already in "poisoned waters" as a result of the filing of the petitions, the mother complains, and, in any event, seven months is "too short a time to expect rehabilitation."

We do not agree that it was improper for the trial court to consider the events occurring in the seven-month period. Rather, we believe it was within that court's sound discretion to continue the case to allow further services by the Division and to evaluate the mother's progress during this period in determining whether to terminate her parental rights.

We are of opinion that the trial court's decision to terminate the mother's residual parental rights is supported by clear and convincing evidence showing both that the termination is in the best interests of the children and that the factors required by Code § 16.1–283(C)(2) are present. This brings us to the mother's final contention, *viz.*, that, even though the decision may be "in accord" with § 16.1–283, the statute itself is unconstitutional because it permits termination of parental rights in violation of the Fifth and Fourteenth Amendments to the Constitution of the United States and Article I, §§ 1 and 11 of the Virginia Constitution.

The mother argues that her rights to her children are fundamental and can be altered only for compelling cause. The mother asserts that § 16.1–283 violates this principle and is invalid because (1) it denies substantive due process by permitting termination in the absence of a compelling state interest, (2) it is unconstitutionally vague, and (3) it permits termination of parental rights on proof by a mere preponderance of evidence.

We do not agree with the mother. Clearly, the protection of children from harm, whether moral, emotional, mental, or physical, is a valid and compelling state interest. Stanley v. Illinois, 405 U.S. 645, 652, 92 S.Ct. 1208, 1213, 31 L.Ed.2d 551 (1972). Section 16.1–283 plainly is designed to implement that interest. And the section contemplates the use, where possible, of alternatives less drastic than termination of parental rights. For example, subsection (C)(2), with which we are concerned here, applies only where a child previously has been placed in foster care and the parent, without good cause and after receiving the assistance of social and rehabilitative agencies, has been unable or unwilling to correct the conditions that led to foster care in the first place.

Further, we believe that § 16.1–283 contains clear and specific guidelines for its application in particular cases. And, finally, a finding that the § 16.1–283 factors exist, which, as we have seen, is tantamount to a finding of parental unfitness, must be supported by clear and convincing evidence. Hence, § 16.1–283 survives the mother's constitutional attack.

For the reasons assigned, we will affirm the judgments of the trial court terminating the residual parental rights of the mother to the three children involved in this proceeding.

NOTE

Footnote 10 of the Supreme Court's opinion in *Santosky*, supra at p. 851, states:

Nor is it clear that the State constitutionally could terminate a parent's rights without showing parental unfitness.

Did the Virginia Supreme Court find "unfitness" on the part of the parent in *Knox*? Does the Virginia statute require a showing of unfitness, i.e. are the circumstances prescribed as sufficient for terminating parental rights tantamount to a finding of unfitness? If so, what are the limitations on legislatures in shaping such definitions?

Use of the term "unfitness" to define the circumstance under which termination of parental rights can be effected has led to constitutional attack for vagueness in recent years. In In re Brooks, 228 Kan. 541, 618 P.2d 814 (1980) the Supreme Court of Kansas rejected such a challenge, finding that the Kansas courts had repeatedly construed the term "unfit" in their statute. They distinguished an earlier federal court decision, Alsager v. District Court of Polk County, Iowa, 406 F.Supp. 10 (S.D.Iowa 1975), affirmed 545 F.2d 1137 (8th Cir. 1976), stating:

The *Alsager* conclusions relative to vagueness are intermingled with other concerns, such as notice of the proceedings, adequacy of the termination proceedings, and standard of proof. A careful reading of the case reflects that the court essentially applied the criminal statute test for vagueness. Further, the court was concerned that the Iowa statute permitted termination without a showing of "high and substantial degree of harm to the children."

They also pointed out that:

The Iowa statute involved in *Alsager* is distinguishable. In Iowa the action was brought to sever the parental rights. In making such a determination the court could sever parental rights if the parents had committed any of the specified acts *or* were unfit. Under the Kansas statute the court must find the children to be deprived before the issue of termination is reached. The termination of parental rights is rather dispositional in nature.

Although the Kansas court rejected a test which would require a court to explore and specifically eliminate alternative remedies before severing parental rights, it did conclude that:

The court should carefully consider any particular alternative remedy proposed by an interested party in the case, and if rejected the court should state its reasons for such rejection. The drastic remedy of termination of parental rights should not be utilized unless the court is satisfied there is no realistic alternative and so finds.

**JUVENILE JUSTICE STANDARDS PROJECT, STANDARDS
RELATING TO ABUSE AND NEGLECT
(Tentative Draft 1977) ***

8.1 Proceedings to review need for termination

The issue of termination of parental rights may be considered at
the time of the dispositional hearing following a finding of endangerment and should be considered at every review hearing thereafter.
Both parents should be notified of the possibility of termination
where it is in issue, and the standard for determining termination.
The parents should be afforded the opportunity to present evidence
on the relevant issues, which are specified in Standards 8.2–8.4.
These hearings should be the only forum for considering termination
when a child is under court supervision.

8.2 Termination at the dispositional hearing

A. Except as provided in Standard 8.2 B. 1.–3., termination
should not be permissible at the dispositional hearing following a
finding that the child is endangered.

B. A court should be authorized, although not required, to order
termination at the dispositional hearing following a finding of endangerment only if:

1. The child has been abandoned: a child has been abandoned
when he/she has not been cared for or contacted by his/her parents, although the parents are physically able to do so, for [sixty]
days prior to the adjudicatory hearing, and despite adequate efforts to notify the parents, they do not appear at the adjudicatory
or dispositional hearing.

2. The child has been removed from the parents previously
under the test established in Standard 6.4 C., has been returned to
his/her parents, and after return the child must be removed again.

3. Court jurisdiction in the present case is based on a finding
that the child comes within Standard 2.1 A., the child or another
child in the family has been previously found endangered under
2.1 A., and the parents have received therapy after the first instance of abuse. The party requesting termination should be required to prove that therapy was provided or offered to the parents previously.

C. Regardless of the provisions of Standard 8.2 B. 1.–3., a court
should not be authorized to order termination if any of the exceptions
in Standard 8.4 are applicable.

8.3 Standard for termination when child is in placement

A.   For children who were under three at the time of placement, a court should order termination after the child has been in placement for six months, if the child cannot be returned home at that time, unless the court finds by clear and convincing evidence that an exception specified in Standard 8.4 applies.

B.   For a child who was over three at the time of placement, the court should order termination after the child has been in placement for one year if the child cannot be returned home at that time, unless the court finds by clear and convincing evidence that an exception specified in Standard 8.4 applies. However, if at the six-month review hearing the court finds that the parents have failed to maintain contact with the child during the previous six months and to reasonably plan for resumption of care of the child, the court may terminate parental rights at that time unless one of the exceptions specified in Standard 8.4 applies.

C.   Whenever parental rights have not been terminated under subsections A. and B. because the child falls within one of the exceptions, the case should be reviewed every six months to determine whether the exceptions continue to be applicable. If not, termination should be ordered.

8.4 Situations in which termination should not be ordered

Even if a child comes within the provisions of Standard 8.2 or 8.3, a court should not order termination if it finds by clear and convincing evidence that any of the following are applicable:

A.   because of the closeness of the parent-child relationship, it would be detrimental to the child to terminate parental rights;

B.   the child is placed with a relative who does not wish to adopt the child;

C.   because of the nature of the child's problems, the child is placed in a residential treatment facility, and continuation of parental rights will not prevent finding the child a permanent family placement if the parents cannot resume custody when residential care is no longer needed;

D.   the child cannot be placed permanently in a family environment and failure to terminate will not impair the child's opportunity for a permanent placement in a family setting;

E.   a child over age ten objects to termination.

8.5 Actions following termination

A.   When parental rights are terminated, a court should order the child placed for adoption, placed with legal guardians, or left in long-term foster care. Where possible, adoption is preferable. However, a child should not be removed from a foster home if the foster parents are unwilling or unable to adopt the child, but are willing to provide, and are capable of providing, the child with a permanent home, and the removal of the child from the physical custody of the foster parents would be detrimental to his/her emotional wellbeing because the child has substantial psychological ties to the foster parents.

B.   When an adoption or guardianship has been perfected, the court should terminate its jurisdiction over the child. If some other long-term placement for the child has been made, the court should continue the hearing to a specific future date not more than one year after the date of the order of continued jurisdiction.

NATIONAL COUNCIL OF JUVENILE COURT JUDGES, MODEL STATUTE FOR TERMINATION OF PARENTAL RIGHTS

[The first part of the statute deals with Permanent Custody and with procedural matters.]

. . .

Sec. 12   Termination of Parental Rights

(1) The Court may terminate parental rights when the Court finds the parent unfit or that the conduct or condition of the parent is such as to render him/her unable to properly care for the child and that such conduct or condition is unlikely to change in the foreseeable future. In determining unfitness, conduct or condition the Court shall consider, but is not limited to the following:

(a) Emotional illness, mental illness or mental deficiency of the parent, of such duration or nature as to render the parent unlikely to care for the ongoing physical, mental and emotional needs of the child.

(b) Conduct towards a child of a physically, emotionally or sexually cruel or abusive nature.

(c) Excessive use of intoxicating liquors or narcotic or dangerous drugs.

(d) Physical, mental or emotional neglect of the child.

(e) Conviction of a felony and imprisonment.

(f) Unexplained injury or death of a sibling.

(g) Reasonable efforts by appropriate public or private child caring agencies have been unable to rehabilitate the family.

(2) Where a child is not in the physical custody of the parent, the Court, in proceedings concerning the termination of parental rights, in addition to the foregoing, shall also consider, but is not limited to the following:

(a) Failure to provide care, or pay a reasonable portion of substitute physical care and maintenance where custody is lodged with others.

(b) Failure to maintain regular visitation or other contact with the child as designed in a plan to reunite the child with the parent.

(c) Failure to maintain reasonably consistent contact and/or communication with child.

(d) Lack of effort on the part of the parent to adjust his circumstances, conduct or conditions to meet the needs of the child.

(3) Where a child has been placed in foster care by a Court order or has been otherwise placed by parents or others into the physical custody of such family, the Court shall in proceedings concerning the termination of parental rights and responsibilities consider whether said child has become integrated into the foster family to the extent that his familial identity is with that family, and said family or person is able and willing to permanently so integrate the child. In such considerations, the Court shall note, but is not limited to the following:

(a) The love, affection and other emotional ties existing between the child and the parents, and his ties with the integrating family.

(b) The capacity and disposition of the parents from whom he was removed as compared with that of the integrating family to give the child love, affection and guidance and continuing the education of the child.

(c) The capacity and disposition of the parents from whom the child was removed and the integrating family to provide the child with food, clothing, medical care and other physical, mental and emotional needs.

(d) The length of time the child has lived in a stable, satisfactory environment and the desirability of maintaining such continuity.

(e) The permanence as a family unit of the integrating family or person.

(f) The moral fitness, physical and mental health of the parents from whom the child was removed and that of the integrating family or person.

(g) The home, school and community record of the child, both when with the parents from whom he was removed and when with the integrating family.

(h) The reasonable preference of the child, if the Court deems the child of sufficient capacity to express a preference.

(i) Any other factor considered by the Court to be relevant to a particular placement of the child.

(4) The rights of the parents may be terminated as provided herein if the Court finds that the parents have abandoned the child or the child was left under such circumstances that the identity of the parents is unknown and cannot be ascertained, despite diligent searching, and the parents have not come forward to claim the child within three months following the finding of the child.

(5) In considering any of the above basis for terminating the rights of a parent, the Court shall give primary consideration to the physical, mental or emotional condition and needs of the child.

NOTE

For another illustration of a legislative proposal in this area, see Katz, A Model Act to Free Children, 12 Fam.L.Q. 203 (1978). A discussion of these two models and various others can be found in Hardin & Tazzara, A Comparison of Model Acts on Parental Rights Termination, 7 Fam.L.Rep. 4025 (July 14, 1981).

STANLEY v. ILLINOIS

Supreme Court of the United States, 1972.
405 U.S. 645, 92 S.Ct. 1208, 31 L.Ed.2d 551.

(See p. 122, supra, for the opinions in this case.)

QUILLOIN v. WALCOTT

Supreme Court of the United States, 1978.
434 U.S. 246, 98 S.Ct. 549, 54 L.Ed.2d 511.

MR. JUSTICE MARSHALL delivered the opinion of the Court.

The issue in this case is the constitutionality of Georgia's adoption laws as applied to deny an unwed father authority to prevent adoption of his illegitimate child. The child was born in December 1964 and has been in the custody and control of his mother, appellee Ardell Williams Walcott, for his entire life. The mother and the child's natural father, appellant Leon Webster Quilloin, never married each other or established a home together, and in September 1967 the mother married appellee Randall Walcott.[1] In March 1976, she consented to adoption of the child by her husband, who immediately filed a petition for adoption. Appellant attempted to block the adoption and to secure visitation rights, but he did not seek custody or object to the child's continuing to live with appellees. Although appellant was not found to be an unfit parent, the adoption was granted over his objection.

In Stanley v. Illinois, 405 U.S. 645, 92 S.Ct. 1208, 31 L.Ed.2d 551 (1972), this Court held that the State of Illinois was barred, as a matter of both due process and equal protection, from taking custody of the children of an unwed father, absent a hearing and a particularized finding that the father was an unfit parent. The Court concluded, on the one hand, that a father's interest in the "companionship, care, custody, and management" of his children is "cognizable and substantial," id., at 651–652, 92 S.Ct., at 1212–13, and, on the other hand, that the State's interest in caring for the children is "*de*

---

1. The child lived with his maternal grandmother for the initial period of the marriage, but moved in with appellees in 1969 and lived with them thereafter.

minimis" if the father is in fact a fit parent, id., at 657–658, 92 S.Ct., at 1215–1216. *Stanley* left unresolved the degree of protection a State must afford to the rights of an unwed father in a situation, such as that presented here, in which the countervailing interests are more substantial.

I

Generally speaking, under Georgia law a child born in wedlock cannot be adopted without the consent of each living parent who has not voluntarily surrendered rights in the child or been adjudicated an unfair parent.[2] Even where the child's parents are divorced or separated at the time of the adoption proceedings, either parent may veto the adoption. In contrast, only the consent of the mother is required for adoption of an illegitimate child. Ga.Code § 74–403(3) (1975).[3] To acquire the same veto authority possessed by other parents, the father of a child born out of wedlock must legitimate his offspring, either by marrying the mother and acknowledging the child as his own, § 74–101, or by obtaining a court order declaring the child legitimate and capable of inheriting from the father, § 74–103.[4] But unless and until the child is legitimated, the mother is the only recognized parent and is given exclusive authority to exercise all parental prerogatives, § 74–203,[5] including the power to veto adoption of the child.

2. See Ga.Code §§ 74–403(1), (2) (1975). Section 74–403(1) sets forth the general rule that "no adoption shall be permitted except with the written consent of the living parents of a child." Section 74–403(2) provides that consent is not required from a parent who (1) has surrendered rights in the child to a child-placing agency or to the adoption court; (2) is found by the adoption court to have abandoned the child, or to have willfully failed for a year or longer to comply with a court-imposed support order with respect to the child; (3) has had his or her parental rights terminated by court order, see Ga.Code § 24A–3201; (4) is insane or otherwise incapacitated from giving consent; or (5) cannot be found after a diligent search has been made.

3. Section 74–403(3), which operates as an exception to the rule stated in § 74–403(1), see n. 2, supra, provides:

"Illegitimate children.—If the child be illegitimate, the consent of the mother alone shall suffice. Such consent, however, shall not be required if the mother has surrenderd all of her rights to said child to a licensed child-placing agency, or to the State Department of Family and Children Services."

Sections of Ga.Code (1975) will hereinafter be referred to merely by their numbers.

4. Section 74–103 provides in full:

"A father of an illegitimate child may render the same legitimate by petitioning the superior court of the county of his residence, setting forth the name, age, and sex of such child, and also the name of the mother; and if he desires the name changed, stating the new name, and praying the legitimation of such child. Of this application the mother, if alive, shall have notice. Upon such application, presented and filed, the court may pass an order declaring said child to be legitimate, and capable of inheriting from the father in the same manner as if born in lawful wedlock, and the name by which he or she shall be known."

5. Section 74–203 states:

"The mother of an illegitimate child shall be entitled to the possession of the child, unless the father shall legitimate him as before provided. Being the only recognized parent, she may exercise all the paternal power."

In its opinion in this case, the Georgia Supreme Court indicated that the word "pa-

Appellant did not petition for legitimation of his child at any time during the 11 years between the child's birth and the filing of Randall Walcott's adoption petition.[6] However, in response to Walcott's petition, appellant filed an application for a writ of habeas corpus seeking visitation rights, a petition for legitimation, and an objection to the adoption.[7] Shortly thereafter, appellant amended his pleadings by adding the claim that §§ 74–203 and 74–403(3) were unconstitutional as applied to his case, insofar as they denied him the rights granted to married parents, and presumed unwed fathers to be unfit as a matter of law.

The petitions for adoption, legitimation and writ of habeas corpus were consolidated for trial in the Superior Court of Fulton County, Ga. The court expressly stated that these matters were being tried on the basis of a consolidated record to allow "the biological father . . . a right to be heard with respect to any issue or other thing upon which he desire[s] to be heard, including his fitness as a parent . . . ."[8] After receiving extensive testimony from the parties and other witnesses, the trial court found that, although the child had never been abandoned or deprived, appellant had provided support only on an irregular basis.[9] Moreover, while the child previously had visited with appellant on "many occasions," and had been given toys and gifts by appellant "from time to time," the mother had recently concluded that these contacts were having a disruptive effect on the child and on appellees' entire family.[10] The child himself expressed a

ternal" in the second sentence of this provision is the result of a misprint, and was instead intended to read "parental." See 238 Ga. 230, 231, 232 S.E.2d 246, 247 (1977).

6. It does appear that appellant consented to entry of his name on the child's birth certificate. See § 88–1709(d)(2). The adoption petition gave the name of the child as "Darrell Webster Quilloin," and appellant alleges in his brief that the child has always been known by that name, . . .

7. Appellant had been notified by the State's Department of Human Resources that an adoption petition had been filed.

8. In re: Application of Randall Walcott for Adoption of Child, Adoption Case No. 8466 (Ga.Super.Ct., July 12, 1976), App. 70.

Sections 74–103, 74–203, and 74–403(3) are silent as to the appropriate procedure in the event that a petition for legitimation is filed after an adoption proceeding has already been initiated. Prior to this Court's decision in Stanley v. Illinois, 405 U.S. 645, 92 S.Ct. 1208, 31 L.Ed.2d 551 (1972), and without consideration of potential constitutional problems, the Georgia Supreme Court had concluded that an

unwed father could not petition for legitimation after the mother had consented to an adoption. Smith v. Smith, 224 Ga. 442, 445–446, 162 S.E.2d 379, 383–384 (1968). But cf. Clark v. Buttry, 226 Ga. 687, 177 S.E.2d 89 (1970), aff'g, 121 Ga. App. 492, 174 S.E.2d 356. However, the Georgia Supreme Court had not had occasion to reconsider this conclusion in light of *Stanley,* and, in the face of appellant's constitutional challenge to §§ 74–203, 74–403(3), the trial court evidently concluded that concurrent consideration of the legitimation and adoption petitions was consistent with the statutory provisions. See n. 12, infra.

9. Under § 74–202, appellant had a duty to support his child, but for reasons not appearing in the record the mother never brought an action to enforce this duty. Since no court ever ordered appellant to support his child, denial of veto authority over the adoption could not have been justified on the ground of willful failure to comply with a support order. See n. 2, supra.

10. In addition to Darrell, appellees' family included a son born several years after appellees were married. The mother testified that Darrell's visits with ap-

desire to be adopted by Randall Walcott and to take on Walcott's name,[11] and the court found Walcott to be a fit and proper person to adopt the child.

On the basis of these findings, as well as findings relating to appellees' marriage and the mother's custody of the child for all of the child's life, the trial court determined that the proposed adoption was in the "best interests of [the] child." The court concluded, further, that granting either the legitimation or the visitation rights requested by appellant would not be in the "best interests of the child," and that both should consequently be denied. The court then applied §§ 74–203 and 74–403(3) to the situation at hand, and, since appellant had failed to obtain a court order granting legitimation, he was found to lack standing to object to the adoption. Ruling that appellant's constitutional claims were without merit, the court granted the adoption petition and denied the legitimation and visitation petitions.

Appellant took an appeal to the Supreme Court of Georgia, claiming that §§ 74–203 and 74–403(3), as applied by the trial court to his case, violated the Equal Protection and Due Process Clauses of the Fourteenth Amendment. In particular, appellant contended that he was entitled to the same power to veto an adoption as is provided under Georgia law to married or divorced parents and to unwed mothers, and, since the trial court did not make a finding of abandonment or other unfitness on the part of appellant, see n. 2, supra, the adoption of his child should not have been allowed.

Over a dissent which urged that § 74–403(3) was invalid under Stanley v. Illinois, the Georgia Supreme Court affirmed the decision of the trial court. 238 Ga. 230, 232 S.E.2d 246 (1977).[12] The majority relied generally on the strong state policy of rearing children in a family setting, a policy which in the court's view might be thwarted if unwed fathers were required to consent to adoptions. The court also emphasized the special force of this policy under the facts of this case, pointing out that the adoption was sought by the child's stepfather, who was part of the family unit in which the child was in fact

pellant were having unhealthy effects on both children.

11. The child also expressed a desire to continue to visit with appellant on occasion after the adoption. The child's desire to be adopted, however, could not be given effect under Georgia law without divesting appellant of any parental rights he might otherwise have or acquire, including visitation rights. See § 74–414.

12. The Supreme Court addressed itself only to the constitutionality of the statutes as applied by the trial court and thus, at least for purposes of this case, accepted the trial court's construction of §§ 74–203 and 74–403(3), as allowing concurrent consideration of the adoption and legitimation petitions. See n. 8, supra.

Subsequent to the Supreme Court's decision in this case, the Georgia Legislature enacted a comprehensive revision of the State's adoption laws, which became effective January 1, 1978. 1977 Ga.Laws 201. The new law expressly gives an unwed father the right to petition for legitimation subsequent to the filing of an adoption petition concerning his child. See Ga.Code § 74–406 (1977 Supp.). The revision also leaves intact §§ 74–103 and 74–203, and carries forward the substance of § 74–403(3), and thus appellant would not have received any greater protection under the new law than he was actually afforded by the trial court.

living, and that the child's natural father had not taken steps to support or legitimate the child over a period of more than 11 years. The court noted in addition that, unlike the father in *Stanley*, appellant had never been a *de facto* member of the child's family unit.

Appellant brought this appeal pursuant to 28 U.S.C. § 1257(2), continuing to challenge the constitutionality of §§ 74–203 and 74–403(3) as applied to his case, and claiming that he was entitled as a matter of due process and equal protection to an absolute veto over adoption of his child, absent a finding of his unfitness as a parent. In contrast to appellant's somewhat broader statement of the issue in the Georgia Supreme Court, on this appeal he focused his equal protection claim solely on the disparate statutory treatment of his case and that of a married father. . . . [W]e now affirm.

II

At the outset, we observe that appellant does not challenge the sufficiency of the notice he received with respect to the adoption proceeding, nor can he claim that he was deprived of a right to a hearing on his individualized interests in his child, prior to entry of the order of adoption. Although the trial court's ultimate conclusion was that appellant lacked standing to object to the adoption, this conclusion was reached only after appellant had been afforded a full hearing on his legitimation petition, at which he was given the opportunity to offer evidence on any matter he thought relevant, including his fitness as a parent. Had the trial court granted legitimation, appellant would have acquired the veto authority he is now seeking.

The fact that appellant was provided with a hearing on his legitimation petition is not, however, a complete answer to his attack on the constitutionality of §§ 74–203 and 74–403(3). The trial court denied appellant's petition, and thereby precluded him from gaining veto authority, on the ground that legitimation was not in the "best interests of the child"; appellant contends that he was entitled to recognition and preservation of his parental rights absent a showing of his "unfitness." Thus, the underlying issue is whether, in the circumstances of this case and in light of the authority granted by Georgia law to married fathers, appellant's interests were adequately protected by a "best interests of the child" standard. We examine this issue first under the Due Process Clause and then under the Equal Protection Clause.

A

Appellees suggest that due process was not violated, regardless of the standard applied by the trial court, since any constitutionally protected interest appellant might have had was lost by his failure to petition for legitimation during the 11 years prior to filing of Randall Walcott's adoption petition. We would hesitate to rest decision on this ground, in light of the evidence in the record that appellant was not aware of the legitimation procedure until after the adoption petition was filed.[14]   But in any event we need not go that far, since under the circumstances of this case appellant's substantive rights were not violated by application of a "best interests of the child" standard.

We have recognized on numerous occasions that the relationship between parent and child is constitutionally protected. See, e.g., Wisconsin v. Yoder, 406 U.S. 205, 231–233, 92 S.Ct. 1526, 1541–42, 32 L.Ed.2d 15 (1972); Stanley v. Illinois, supra; Meyer v. Nebraska, 262 U.S. 390, 399–401, 43 S.Ct. 625, 626–27, 67 L.Ed. 1042 (1923).   "It is cardinal with us that the custody, care and nurture of the child reside first in the parents, whose primary function and freedom include preparation for obligations the state can neither supply nor hinder." Prince v. Massachusetts, 321 U.S. 158, 166, 64 S.Ct. 438, 442, 88 L.Ed. 645 (1944).   And it is now firmly established that "freedom of personal choice in matters of . . . family life is one of the liberties protected by the Due Process Clause of the Fourteenth Amendment." Cleveland Board of Education v. LaFleur, 414 U.S. 632, 639–640, 94 S.Ct. 791, 796, 39 L.Ed.2d 52 (1974).

We have little doubt that the Due Process Clause would be offended "[i]f a State were to attempt to force the breakup of a natural family, over the objections of the parents and their children, without some showing of unfitness and for the sole reason that to do so was thought to be in the children's best interest."   Smith v. Organization of Foster Families, 431 U.S. 816, 862–863, 97 S.Ct. 2094, 2119, 53 L.Ed.2d 14 (1977) (Stewart, J., concurring in judgment).   But this is not a case in which the unwed father at any time had, or sought, actual or legal custody of his child.   Nor is this a case in which the proposed adoption would place the child with a new set of parents with whom the child had never before lived.   Rather, the result of the adoption in this case is to give full recognition to a family unit already in existence, a result desired by all concerned, except appellant. Whatever might be required in other situations, we cannot say that the State was required in this situation to find anything more than that the adoption, and denial of legitimation, were in the "best interests of the child."

B

Appellant contends that even if he is not entitled to prevail as a matter of due process, principles of equal protection require that his authority to veto an adoption be measured by the same standard that

14. At the hearing in the trial court, the following colloquy took place between appellees' counsel and appellant:

"Q Had you made any effort prior to this time [prior to the instant pro-

ceedings], during the eleven years of Darrell's life to legitimate him?

"A . . .   I didn't know that was process even you went through [sic]."

would have been applied to a married father. In particular, appellant asserts that his interests are indistinguishable from those of a married father who is separated or divorced from the mother and is no longer living with his child, and therefore the State acted impermissibly in treating his case differently. We think appellant's interests are readily distinguishable from those of a separated or divorced father, and accordingly believe that the State could permissibly give appellant less veto authority than it provides to a married father.

Although appellant was subject, for the years prior to these proceedings, to essentially the same child-support obligation as a married father would have had, compare § 74–202 with § 74–105 and § 30–301, he has never exercised actual or legal custody over his child, and thus has never shouldered any significant responsibility with respect to the daily supervision, education, protection, or care of the child. Appellant does not complain of his exemption from these responsibilities and, indeed, he does not even now seek custody of his child. In contrast, legal custody of children is, of course, a central aspect of the marital relationship, and even a father whose marriage has broken apart will have borne full responsibility for the rearing of his children during the period of the marriage. Under any standard of review, the State was not foreclosed from recognizing this difference in the extent of commitment to the welfare of the child.

For these reasons, we conclude that §§ 74–203 and 74–403(3), as applied in this case, did not deprive appellant of his asserted rights under the Due Process and Equal Protection Clauses. The judgment of the Supreme Court of Georgia is accordingly,

Affirmed.

NOTES

(1) One must recognize that adoption also provides a means for extinguishing parental rights. It differs from the separate action to terminate parental rights in that a new parent-child relationship is legally created by the adoption proceeding. At least in cases of placement for adoption by a state or a state-licensed agency, it is generally considered appropriate that a formal termination of parental rights take place beforehand. Failure to do so can spawn the sort of competition between foster parents who care for a child prior to parental rights termination and the agency seeking return of the child for adoptive placement or even the potential adoptive parents, as discussed at p. 847, supra.

Should the criteria for permitting adoption without consent from the natural parents be any less stringent than those applicable in a separate action for termination of parental rights?

(2) Many would argue that Stanley v. Illinois, discussed in more detail at p. 122, supra, was as much a case on sex discrimination as on childrens' rights. In any event, it has led to considerable confusion about criteria for termination of parental rights through the adoption process. As Justice Marshall points out in his opinion for the Court in *Quilloin*, situations calling for a more difficult balancing of the countervailing interests between

parent and child of an unwed father were left unresolved by *Stanley*. How far does *Quilloin* go in answering such questions? Does it formulate a workable rule for "closer" cases?

In Caban v. Mohammed, 441 U.S. 380, 99 S.Ct. 1760, 60 L.Ed.2d 297 (1979), the Supreme Court was called on to review N.Y.Dom.Rel.Law § 111 which provides that:

> consent to adoption shall be required as follows: . . . (b) Of the parents or surviving parent, whether adult or infant, of a child born in wedlock; [and] (c) Of the mother, whether adult or infant, of a child born out of wedlock. . . ."

Appellant Caban was living with appellee Maria at the time she gave birth to two children in 1969 and 1971; he was identified as the father on their birth certificates. Appellee later married Kazim Mohammed in 1974. The children resided with them until they went to Puerto Rico with Maria Mohammed's mother at the Mohammeds' request; appellees planned to join the children there when they had saved enough money to start a business. Appellant went to Puerto Rico and was permitted by the grandmother to have the children visit with him for several days with the understanding that he would then return them. Instead appellant took the children back to New York with him. Appellees instituted a custody proceeding in New York and the Family Court awarded temporary custody to the Mohammeds with visiting rights to appellant and his new wife. Thereafter appellees filed a petition to adopt the children, and appellant filed a similar cross-petition. (N.Y. Dom.Rel.Law § 110 provides that a husband and wife "together may adopt a child of either of them born out of wedlock and [a husband or wife] may adopt such a child of the other spouse.") The New York courts permitted the adoption by appellees, thus cutting off appellant Caban's parental rights. He appealed, arguing that the New York law drew an impermissible distinction between adoption rights of an unwed father and those of other parents, and that Quilloin v. Walcott "recognized the due process right of natural fathers to maintain a parental relationship with their children absent a finding that they are unfit as parents."

The United States Supreme Court reversed the decision allowing appellees to adopt, finding § 111 of the N.Y.Dom.Rel.Law to be an overbroad generalization of a gender-based classification. However, the Court's opinion explained that it was not passing on whether the "special difficulties attendant upon locating and identifying unwed fathers at birth would justify a legislative distinction between mothers and fathers of newborns", noting that such a case was not before them and that "these difficulties need not persist past infancy."

(3) Stepparents may attempt to adopt children without the consent of the noncustodial natural parent through utilization of statutes granting courts discretion to waive an otherwise necessary consent that is withheld contrary to a child's best interests. A literal reading of such statutes would indicate that the legislatures intended to invest considerable authority in the judiciary to permit such adoptions. The courts, however, often have appeared reluctant to exercise such power. An illustration is seen in the interpretation (some might say "rewriting") of Va.Code § 63.1–225(4), which provides:

> If after hearing evidence the court finds that the consent of any person or agency whose consent is hereinabove required is withheld contrary

to the best interests of the child, . . . the court may [after giving notice as provided by statute] grant the petition without such consent.

In Malpass v. Morgan, 213 Va. 393, 192 S.E.2d 794 (1972), the Supreme Court of Virginia refused to permit a stepfather to adopt his wife's child without the consent of the noncustodial father, who had been awarded custody rights on divorce. The court in effect formulated a new rule, stating that:

> Where, as here, there is no question of the fitness of the non-consenting parent and he has not by conduct or previous legal action lost his rights to the child, it must be shown that continuance of the relationship between the two would be detrimental to the child's welfare.

See also, In re Adoption of Children by D., 61 N.J., 89, 293 A.2d 171 (1972); Cunningham v. Gray, 221 Va. 792, 273 S.E.2d 562 (1981); Simpson, The Unfit Parent: Conditions Under Which a Child May Be Adopted Without the Consent of His Parent, 39 U.Det.L.Rev. 347, 377 (1962).

In Petition of J. O. L., 409 A.2d 1073 (D.C.App.1979), a stepfather's petition to adopt was granted over the objection of the child's natural father. D.C.Code § 16–304(e), applied by the court, provides:

> The court may grant a petition for adoption without any [consent from natural parent(s)] . . . when the court finds, after a hearing, that the consent or consents are withheld contrary to the best interests of the child.

The court noted that for one period of five years, commencing about two years after the natural father and mother were divorced, the father had ceased visiting the children at all, first stopping as a result of continuing dispute between the parties regarding visitation. This factor, coupled with the children's view of the stepparent as their "real father", seemed to weigh heavily in the court's decision. The court also rejected the natural father's assertion that the D.C. statute was substantively and procedurally unconstitutional.

(4) A possible concern about using a "best interests of the child" test to permit adoption over the objection of a noncustodial natural parent is that it might allow judges to place too much emphasis on their own personal values regarding lifestyles or their own views about conformity in childrearing.

In Doe v. Doe, 222 Va. 736, 284 S.E.2d 799 (1981), for example, the Virginia Supreme Court reversed a trial judge's decision to permit a stepmother to adopt her husband's child despite refusal of consent by the natural mother, who acknowledged that she was living in what the court described as a lesbian relationship. The court explained:

> If Jane Doe is an unfit parent, it is solely her lesbian relationship which renders her unfit, and this must be to such an extent as to make the continuance of the parent-child relationship heretofore existing between her and her son detrimental to the child's welfare. The petitioners introduced no evidence, scientific or otherwise, to establish this fact. Regardless of how offensive we may find Jane's life-style, its effect on her son's welfare is not a matter of which we can take judicial notice. We take judicial notice of generally known or easily ascertainable facts.
>
> . . . .
>
> We decline to hold that every lesbian mother or homosexual father is *per se* an unfit parent. However, this is not to be construed as approv-

ing, condoning, or sanctioning such unorthodox conduct, even in the slightest degree. Jane's unnatural life-style was a proper factor to have been considered in determining her fitness as a mother and what was in the best interest of the child. It is not determinative in the case under review because, standing alone as it does, proof of Jane's unorthodox life-style did not outweigh the clear and convincing evidence that she is a devoted mother and, in every other respect, a fit parent. Further, in determining her fitness as a mother and the future welfare of her son, we are not unmindful of her testimony that should it become necessary, for her son's sake, she would sever the relationship with the woman with whom she now lives. There may come a time when the welfare and best interest of her son require that she honor this commitment.

G.   MEDICAL CARE: THE CONTINUING DEBATE OVER WHO SHOULD DECIDE

Although much of the material on medical care for children might appropriately have been subsumed in the coverage of abuse, neglect, and dependency found earlier in this chapter, a number of highly significant problems regarding children's autonomy and the role of state intervention in the going family make this subject desirable for treatment in a separate part that provides an epilogue to the book.

The notion that children are merely chattels of their parents ostensibly was discarded from our law long ago. However, today's family might be characterized as a governmental unit in which the minor child has certain basic rights although the powers of governance are vested largely with the custodial parent or parents during the child's infancy. Parental rule is in turn subject to state supervision, under which an incompetent or harmful parent can be stripped of all or part of these governing powers. Such action is considered drastic because our society continues to place great value on supporting and maintaining traditional family relationships. But the extent of contemporary recognition that parental rule can be dangerous or even malevolent in a significant number of instances is reflected in the legislative enactments mandating reports of child abuse and expanding the circumstances under which parental rights can be terminated. Such legislation follows a long period under which courts exercised a general "hands off" policy in cases not involving bad faith or extreme incompetence and, as already pointed out, the debate continues on what criteria should be applied to justify state intervention that requires a step such as removal of a child from the home.

Even in so sensitive an area as ensuring provision of medical care for children, courts and legislatures long followed a "hands off" policy except in the most extreme cases. Parental decisions about what (if any) course of treatment might be appropriate thus were insulated from official advice or scrutiny. Society seemed to take as its premise that parents should be the principal, if not sole, decision makers for their unemancipated children in medical matters; judges and legislators appeared to share the conviction that they lacked either the moral authority or the expertise to second-guess them.

This traditional approach has eroded considerably in recent years. After developing a "life threatening" criterion for justifying intervention to overrule parental decisions with regard to medical treatment, courts have been subjected to continuing requests for expansion even to include determination that certain treatment should be afforded in order to assure that a particular child is afforded a certain quality of life. At the same time, pressures for greater autonomy in decision making for children on matters vitally important to them (which certainly should embrace medical care) have presented new questions. The appropriate allocation of power to make medical decisions for children as among the parents, the child and the state, is made far more sensitive and difficult because so many of the cases involve fundamental constitutional rights such as religious freedom and personal privacy. The following material about medical care is an apt conclusion to consideration of children in the legal system. Nowhere is recourse to law to overrule or enforce parental decisions more poignant, or the limits of law and legal institutions more telling.

PEOPLE EX REL. WALLACE v. LABRENZ

Supreme Court of Illinois, 1952.
411 Ill. 618, 104 N.E.2d 769.

SCHAEFER, JUSTICE.

After a hearing upon a petition filed in the circuit court of Cook County, an order was entered finding that Cheryl Linn Labrenz, an infant then eight days old, was a dependent child whose life was endangered by the refusal of her parents to consent to a necessary blood transfusion. The court appointed a guardian for the child and authorized the guardian to consent to a blood transfusion. The propriety of that action is challenged here upon a writ of error raising constitutional issues.

The petition was filed on April 17, 1951. It alleged that Cheryl Linn Labrenz was born on April 11, 1951, that she was then in a hospital in Chicago, and that her parents, Darrell and Rhoda Labrenz, were wholly unwilling to care for and protect her, so that she had become a dependent child. The petition prayed that the child be taken from its parents and placed under the guardianship of a suitable person to be appointed by the court.

At the hearing which was had on this petition on April 18, 1951, the evidence showed that the child suffered from erythrobastosis fetalis (commonly called the RH blood condition,) a disease in which the red blood cells are destroyed by antibodies, or poisons. Hospital records and medical testimony established that the child's blood count had been dropping steadily since her birth; that the normal blood count of a child of her age was about 5,000,000, whereas her blood count was 1,950,000; that antibodies in the baby's blood stream were gradually destroying all of the red blood cells; that her blood-supplying system was unable to furnish a supply of its own blood adequate to overcome the condition, and that a blood transfusion was necessary.

Three doctors testified. Two were certain that the child would die unless a transfusion was administered. The third doctor testified that the child had a slim chance to live without a transfusion, but that even if she did live, without a transfusion her brain would probably be so injured that she would be mentally impaired for life. The medical testimony also dealt with the degree of risk involved in a blood transfusion. One doctor testified that there would be no more hazard in a transfusion than in taking an aspirin. While all three doctors testified that there would be risks involved if diseased or mistyped blood was used in the transfusion, all of them agreed that such risk as existed was due to the impossibility of eliminating completely the chance of human error, and that, properly conducted, a transfusion would not involve any serious hazard.

The parents of the child testified that their refusal to consent to a transfusion was based upon religious grounds. Darrell Labrenz, the child's father, testified: "it is my belief that the commandment given us in Genesis, Chapter 9, Verse 4, and subsequent commandment of Leviticus, Chapter 17, Verse 14, and also in the testimony after Christ's time and recorded in Acts, 15th Chapter, it is my opinion that any use of the blood is prohibited whether it be for food or whether it be for, as modern medical science puts it, for injections into the blood stream and as such I object to it. The life is in the blood and the life belongs to our father, Jehovah, and it is only his to give or take; it isn't ours, and as such I object to the using of the blood in connection with this case."

Rhoda Labrenz, the mother, testified that "we believe it would be breaking God's commandment to take away blood which he told us to eat of the flesh but should not take of the blood into our systems. The life is in the blood and blood should not be drained out. We feel that we would be breaking God's commandment, also destroying the baby's life for the future, not only this life, in case the baby should die and breaks the commandment, not only destroys our chances but also the baby's chances for future life. We feel it is more important than this life."

At the conclusion of the evidence offered on behalf of the State, and again at the conclusion of all the evidence, a motion to dismiss the petition was overruled. The court appointed its chief probation officer to be guardian of the person of Cheryl Linn Labrenz, directed him to consent to a blood transfusion, and retained jurisdiction for the purpose of making further orders for the welfare of the child. On May 4, 1951, the guardian reported to the court that a transfusion had been administered on April 18, 1951, and that the child's health had greatly improved. The court then ordered that the child be released from the hospital and returned to the custody of her parents but refused to discharge the guardian because it found that further periodic medical examinations would be necessary to determine the need for additional transfusions. On June 15, 1951, the court discharged the guardian, released the child to her parents, and ordered that the proceeding be dismissed.

Before we reach the merits, we meet the State's contention that the case is now moot and should be dismissed because the blood transfusion has been administered, the guardian discharged, and the proceeding dismissed. Because the function of courts is to decide controverted issues in adversary proceedings, moot cases which do not present live issues are not ordinarily entertained. . . .

But when the issue presented is of substantial public interest, a well-recognized exception exists to the general rule that a case which has become moot will be dismissed upon appeal. Among the criteria considered in determining the existence of the requisite degree of public interest are the public or private nature of the question presented, the desirability of an authoritative determination for the future guidance of public officers, and the likelihood of future recurrence of the question.

Applying these criteria, we find that the present case falls within that highly sensitive area in which governmental action comes into contact with the religious beliefs of individual citizens. Both the construction of the statute under which the trial court acted and its validity are challenged. In situations like this one, public authorities must act promptly if their action is to be effective, and although the precise limits of authorized conduct cannot be fixed in advance, no greater uncertainty should exist than the nature of the problems makes inevitable. In addition, the very urgency which presses for prompt action by public officials makes it probable that any similar case arising in the future will likewise become moot by ordinary standards before it can be determined by this court. For these reasons the case should not be dismissed as moot.

As an additional reason for retaining the case for decision, plaintiffs in error suggest that the determination below, even though standing unreviewed, would nevertheless bar a subsequent action to recover damages for a violation of the rights of the parents or of the child. So far as we have been able to ascertain, the effect, as *res judicata*, of a judgment which could not be reviewed because intervening circumstances made the case moot, has not been settled in this State. Such authority as exists elsewhere is not in agreement. Because we hold that the public interest requires that the case be retained for decision, we do not decide this issue.

Turning now to the merits of the case, plaintiffs in error first argue that the court below lacked jurisdiction because the child was not a "neglected" or "dependent" child within the meaning of the statute.

The jurisdiction which was exercised in this case stems from the responsibility of government, in its character as *parens patriae*, to care for infants within its jurisdiction and to protect them from neglect, abuse and fraud. Historically exercised by courts of chancery, it is "of ancient origin." Cowles v. Cowles, 3 Gilman 435. That ancient equitable jurisdiction was codified in our Juvenile Court Act, which expressly authorizes the court, if circumstances warrant, to remove the child from the custody of its parents and award its custody to an appointed guardian. Ill.Rev.Stat.1949, chap. 23, pars. 190–220.

So far as here pertinent, the statute defines a dependent or neglected child as one which "has not proper parental care." (Ill.Rev. Stat.1949, chap. 23, par. 190). The record contains no suggestion of any improper conduct on the part of the parents except in their refusal to consent to a blood transfusion. And it is argued that this refusal on the part of the parents does not show neglect, or a lack of parental care. Neglect, however, is the failure to exercise the care that the circumstances justly demand. It embraces wilful as well as unintentional disregard of duty. It is not a term of fixed and measured meaning. It takes its content always from specific circumstances, and its meaning varies as the context of surrounding circumstances changes. The question here is whether a child whose parents refuse to permit a blood transfusion, when lack of a transfusion means that the child will almost certainly die or at best will be mentally impaired for life, is a neglected child. In answering that question it is of no consequence that the parents have not failed in their duty in other respects. We entertain no doubt that this child, whose parents were deliberately depriving it of life or subjecting it to permanent mental impairment, was a neglected child within the meaning of the statute. The circuit court did not lack jurisdiction.

Plaintiffs in error argue that they merely exercised their right to avoid the risk of a proposed hazardous operation—the transfusion—and that such a choice does not indicate a lack of proper parental care. The short answer is that the facts here disclose no such perilous undertaking, but, on the contrary, an urgently needed transfusion—virtually certain of success if given in time—with only such attendant risk as is inescapable in all of the affairs of life. The argument, based upon such cases as In re Hudson, 13 Wash.2d 673, 126 P.2d 765, and In re Tuttendario, 21 Pa.Dist.R. 561, which deal with operations involving substantial risk of life, is obviously not in point.

It is next contended that if the Juvenile Court Act is held to be applicable, it deprives the parents of freedom of religion, and of their rights as parents, in violation of the fourteenth amendment to the constitution of the United States and of section 3 of article II of the constitution of Illinois, S.H.A. This contention is based upon the parents' objection to the transfusion because of their belief that blood transfusions are forbidden by the Scriptures. Because the governing principles are well settled, this argument requires no extensive discussion. Concededly, freedom of religion and the right of parents to the care and training of their children are to be accorded the highest possible respect in our basic scheme. West Virginia State Board of Education v. Barnette, 319 U.S. 624, 63 S.Ct. 1178, 87 L.Ed. 1628; Meyer v. Nebraska, 262 U.S. 390, 43 S.Ct. 625, 67 L.Ed. 1042; Pierce v. Society of Sisters, 268 U.S. 510, 45 S.Ct. 571, 69 L.Ed. 1070. But "neither rights of religion or rights of parenthood are beyond limitation." Prince v. Massachusetts, 321 U.S. 158, 167, 64 S.Ct. 438, 88 L.Ed. 645; . . . .

. . .

. . . [T]he court observed in reaching its conclusion in the Prince case, 321 U.S. at pages 166, 170, 64 S.Ct. at pages 442, 444: "The right to practice religion freely does not include liberty to expose the community or child to communicable disease or the latter to ill health or death. . . . Parents may be free to become martyrs themselves. But it does not follow they are free, in identical circumstances, to make martyrs of their children before they have reached the age of full and legal discretion when they can make that choice for themselves."

We hold, therefore, that neither the statute nor the action of the court pursuant to the statute violated the constitutional rights of plaintiffs in error.

. . .

Judgment affirmed.

NOTE

It was through the emergency blood transfusion cases that the so-called "life-threatening" exception to the rule (or at least presumption) against interference in parental decision making about medical care for children was developed. Because minors are legally incompetent to make such decisions for themselves, parental consent would be necessary to avoid the possibility of a battery action against the person invading the child's protected bodily interest. The *Labrenz* holding was widely followed in other states. See, e.g., State v. Perricone, 37 N.J. 463, 181 A.2d 751 (1962).

In Raleigh Fitkin-Paul Morgan Memorial Hospital v. Anderson, 42 N.J. 421, 201 A.2d 537 (1964), a hospital sought authority to administer blood transfusions to a pregnant mother against her wishes necessary to save her life and the life of the unborn child. The trial court held that the judiciary could not intervene. Although the New Jersey Supreme Court was advised at the time of the appellate argument that the mother had left the hospital against medical advice, they proceeded to determine the issues since it seemed likely to them that the matter would arise again. The court found no difficulty in holding that the state could intervene with respect to the infant child. Because the child's and the mother's welfare were "so intertwined and inseparable", they further ordered that the special guardian to be appointed would have authority to consent to such blood transfusions as might be necessary to save the life of the mother or the child.

APPLICATION OF CICERO

Supreme Court, Special Term, Bronx County, Part I, 1979.
101 Misc.2d 699, 421 N.Y.S.2d 965.

MARTIN B. STECHER, JUSTICE.

By order to show cause dated August 28, 1979, the petitioner, chief executive officer of Misericordia Hospital, petitioned to be appointed guardian of the infant girl born to Lena Vataj on August 20, 1979, for "the sole purpose of consenting to repair of Meningomyelocele," a spinal disorder with which the infant was born.

According to the Nelson Textbook of Pediatrics [10th Ed., W. B. Saunders Company, Philadelphia 1975, pp. 1412 et seq.] spina bifida with meningomyelocele "is a midline defect of skin, vertebral arches and neural tube, usually in the lumbosacral region . . . (It) is evident at birth as a skin defect over the back, bordered laterally by bony prominences of the unfused neural arches of the vertebrae. The defect is usually covered by a transparent membrane which may have neural tissue attached to its inner surface." Cerebrospinal fluid may accumulate under the membrane causing it to bulge. This is the condition with which the Vataj infant was born.

Failure to repair the opening presents a danger of perforation, highly probable infection, such as spinal meningitis, and death. The likelihood of survival beyond the age of six months is poor, absent treatment. Treatment is recommended within 48 hours of birth. The membrane covering this child's lesion shows signs of progressive erosion making immediate surgery necessary.

The parents have refused treatment and insist on taking the child home. Their attitude, as expressed by the child's father, is "let God decide" if the child is to live or die.* Their rejection of treatment does not appear to stem from the kind of religious conviction with which judges are often faced [cf. Application of President and Directors of Georgetown College, Inc., 118 U.S.App.D.C. 80, 331 F.2d 1000, rehearing den., 118 U.S.App.D.C. 90, 331 F.2d 1010, cert. den. 377 U.S. 978, 84 S.Ct. 1883, 12 L.Ed.2d 746].

Initially, the father consented to surgery but appears to have withdrawn that consent only when the potential enormity of this disorder was fully explained to him by the physicians.

The degree of neural disfunction in a spina bifida case is related to the location of the lesion in the spine. The higher it occurs, the greater the number of organs removed from voluntary control. A cervical or thoracic lesion, for instance, presents a high probability of

---

* There has been some expression of fear on the parents' part that this disorder is so rare that the petitioner and associated physicians regard the child as an object of experimentation. Unfortunately, spina bifida is not that rare. It has been estimated that its incidence varies between 0.5 and 4 per thousand and that in this area the incidence is about 3 per thousand. It would thus appear that of 106,000 births recorded in this city in 1978, approximately 300 cases of this disorder could have been expected to appear in New York City alone.

an invalid life, paralyzed and impaired in most functions. The lower the lesion, the better the opportunity for a useful life providing many of its satisfactions. The Vataj baby has a relatively low lesion. Treated, her extremity deficits will, hopefully, be only at the leg level below the ankles. Additionally, she will lack sphincter control of the bladder and anus; but modern medicine and surgery can ameliorate these conditions too. She should be able to walk with short leg braces and hopefully have a "normal" intellectual development.

Children suffering from this disorder usually run a high risk of hydrocephalus, a disorder in which fluid fails to drain from the cranial areas. Untreated, hydrocephalus results in grossly distorted skull growth and mental retardation. Where a child shows evidence of hydrocephalus at birth, prognosis is poor. Later developing hydrocephalus is treatable by a "shunt" operation, providing a drain for the excess fluid; and, if successfully treated, the distortion may be avoided and the chances of retardation substantially reduced.

The Vataj child shows no present sign of hydrocephalus.

This is not a case where the court is asked to preserve an existence which cannot be a life. What is asked is that a child born with handicaps be given a reasonable opportunity to live, to grow and hopefully to surmount those handicaps. If the power to make that choice is vested in the court, there can be no doubt as to what the choice must be.

The Supreme Court, under its general equity jurisdiction, may act as *parens patriae* to protect an infant unable to protect her own interests [Matter of Weberlist, 79 Misc.2d 753, 755–756, 360 N.Y.S.2d 783, 786]. Additionally, there is statutory authority. The statutory authority for this proceeding is to be found in Article 10 of the Family Court Act which defines a neglected child [F.C.A. Sec. 1012(f)(i)(A)] as one, among others, whose "physical . . . condition . . . is in imminent danger of becoming impaired as a result of the failure of his parent . . . to exercise a minimum degree of care . . . in supplying the child with adequate . . . surgical care, though financially able to do so or offered financial or other reasonable means to do so."

From the evidence adduced—and there was no contrary or conflicting evidence—and after hearing held on August 30, and September 4, 1979, I find that this infant's physical condition is in imminent danger of becoming impaired unless the recommended surgery is performed; that irrespective of the parents' financial means, thus far undisclosed, the opportunity to have the surgery performed by a competent surgeon is available and that the parents of the child, without justification, refuse to consent to that surgery.

The argument is made that by granting the petition the parental right to choose the treatment, upbringing and welfare of the child is infringed upon by the court.

Parental rights, however, are not absolute. Children are not property whose disposition is left to parental discretion without hindrance. Where the child's welfare demands judicial intervention, this court is empowered to intervene. Certainly, every physician who prefers a course of treatment rejected by a parent is not privileged to have the court decide upon the treatment under its *parens patriae* powers [cf. Matter of Seiferth, 309 N.Y. 80, 127 N.E.2d 820; Matter of Hofbauer, 65 A.D.2d 108, 411 N.Y.S.2d 416; In re Phillip B., 92 Cal.App.3d 796, 156 Cal.Rptr. 48].

But where, as here, a child has a reasonable chance to live a useful, fulfilled life, the court will not permit parental inaction to deny that chance.

There is a hint in this proceeding of a philosophy that newborn, "hopeless" lives should be permitted to expire without an effort to save those lives. Fortunately, the medical evidence here is such that we do not confront a "hopeless" life. As Justice Asch has pointed out [Matter of Weberlist, 79 Misc.2d 753, 757, 360 N.Y.S.2d 783, 787], "(t)here is a strident cry in America to terminate the lives of *other* people—deemed physically or mentally defective." (Emphasis in original.) This court was not constituted to heed that cry. Rather, to paraphrase Justice Asch, supra, it is our function to secure to each his opportunity for "[l]ife, liberty and the pursuit of happiness."

The petition is granted to the extent of designating Simon Rosenzweig, Esq., of 122 East 42nd Street, New York City, guardian of "Baby Girl" Vataj for the purpose of consenting to the surgery for the repair of the meningomyelocele, the shunt operation for treatment of hydrocephalus, the selection of a hospital in which such surgery shall be performed and the selection of such physician or physicians as shall be required to render such treatment to the child.

This constitutes the decision and judgment of the court. The execution of the judgment is stayed until 11 a. m. September 7, 1979.

NOTES

(1) Reports of cases affirming the decision not to treat deformed infants are difficult to find because such decisions are usually made in private. In April 1982, however, there were newspaper reports of "Infant Doe", a child born in an Indiana hospital with Down's syndrome and tracheoesophageal fistula, a respiratory complication that increases the likelihood of accompanying heart problems. The parents evidently received medical advice that although there was perhaps an even chance of success in remedying the respiratory problem through major surgery, the child's retardation could not be treated. The parents elected not to proceed with treatment. A lower court decision not to interfere with the parents' decision was allowed to stand when the Indiana Supreme Court declined review. According to a newspaper account, the child died while Indiana authorities were seeking intervention by the United States Supreme Court. Washington Post, Apr. 17, 1982, at A1, col. 4.

902 ADEQUATE PARENTING

Following publicity about the Indiana case, Health and Human Services Secretary Richard S. Schweiker sent letters to 6,800 hospitals receiving federal financial aid from sources such as Medicaid or Medicare that withholding medical or surgical assistance from handicapped infants could violate Section 504 of the Rehabilitation Act of 1973, 29 U.S.C.A. 794, which states that "no otherwise qualified handicapped individual . . . shall, solely by reason of his handicap, be excluded from the participation in, be denied the benefits of, or be subjected to discrimination under any program activity receiving Federal financial assistance. . . ." The letters warned that violators could lose federal funding. The Secretary stated that "President [Reagan] has instructed me to make absolutely clear to health care providers in this nation that federal law does not allow medical discrimination against handicapped infants." H.H.S. News, May 18, 1982.

(2) In a world now intensely concerned with protecting young children, as evidenced most prominently by statutes such as those mandating reporting of child abuse, supra at p. 786, the physician's alternatives in cases such as Application of Cicero and Infant Doe may be difficult to define and unpalatable for some to follow. Fear of civil or even criminal actions may make hospitals and doctors err on the side of seeking legal approval even when parental instructions are in accordance with the physician's view. Statutes on homicide and manslaughter contain no specific exceptions for active or passive euthanasia. Although the potential for criminal prosecution based on withholding treatment from severely deformed or retarded neonates was long thought to be low, the threat probably is perceived as real by many today. Further, child abuse reporting statutes often cover a wide group of health care personnel within their mandate, and an even broader group of persons is covered by the immunity from civil damages for good faith reporting. In such an atmosphere, it may be difficult for the decision to withhold treatment to escape question by unrelated parties who seek judicial intervention to protect the child by invoking the panoply of sanctions and remedies discussed in the context of dependency, abuse, and neglect.

For a discussion of the attitudes of staff in special-care facilities about decisions not to treat severely defective infants, see Duff and Campbell, Moral and Ethical Dilemmas in the Special-Care Nursery, 289 New Eng.J.Med. 890 (1973), in which the authors urge that parents, with the help of their doctors, should be free to decide on the extent of medical treatment without intervention by others. Support for such a position also is found in Goldstein, Medical Care for the Child at Risk: On State Supervention of Parental Autonomy, 86 Yale L.J. 645 (1975). In the Goldstein, Freud and Solnit Suggestions for Some Provisions of a Child Placement Code, in Before the Best Interests of the Child, supra at p. 750, Para. 30.8 lists as a Ground for Intervention:

The refusal by Parents to authorize medical care for their Child when

a. Medical experts agree that treatment is nonexperimental and appropriate for the Child; and

b. Denial of the treatment will result in the Child's death; and

c. The treatment can reasonably be expected to result in a chance for the Child to have normal healthy growth or a life worth living.*

* Reprinted with permission of Macmillan Publishing Co., Inc. from Before the Best Interests of the Child, by Joseph Goldstein, Anna Freud, Albert J. Solnit. Copyright © 1979 by The Free Press, a

For a careful review of the potential liability of parents and physicians under current criminal laws, neglect provisions, and abuse reporting statutes, see Robertson, Involuntary Euthanasia of Defective Newborns: A Legal Analysis, 27 Stan.L.Rev. 213 (1975). After reviewing existing laws, Professor Robertson states: [†]

It is reasonably clear that parents who withhold ordinary care from a defective infant, as well as physicians, nurses, and hospital officials who acquiesce in this decision, risk liability for crimes ranging from homicide to neglect and violation of the child-abuse reporting laws. The chance of prosecution at the present time, however, is small.

One may ask whether either full or partial enforcement of the law is a desirable mode of regulation, or whether some alternative legal arrangement would better resolve the conflicting values in the defective-infant situation. Duff and Campbell, for instance, argue that "[i]f working out these dilemmas in ways such as [we] suggest is in violation of the law, . . . the law should be changed," an opinion apparently shared by many other physicians. Other persons consider withholding care from the newborn as morally unjustifiable, and presumably prefer to see the law fully enforced. Still others suggest that new laws be enacted to handle the situation. Possible modifications include amending the homicide and neglect statutes and creating a separate offense of withholding treatment from defective newborns; subjecting to further review the decision not to treat an infant; or designating a decisionmaker wholly independent of parents and physicians to make these decisions.

The appropriate legal response to the defective-infant situation depends on our expectations of what law can and should accomplish. A minimum requirement should guarantee certainty of rule and rule enforcement, thereby informing people of the limits of their discretion and enhancing freedom by permitting them to take legal rules into account. In addition to certainty, however, the law should create a system of expectations that resolves conflicting interests consistent with prevailing morality and our sense of what is just and right. An arrangement exacting too heavy a cost in the values of life; personal, parental and professional autonomy; scarce resources; or other strongly held values will be unacceptable.

What legal rule best comports with dominant values, while doing minimal violence to conflicting interests and providing certainty of application? This question can be answered only by considering two other questions that are at the core of the defective-infant dilemma. The first is whether there is a definable class of beings, such as defective newborns, from whom, under prevailing moral standards, ordinary medical care may be withheld without their consent. If withholding care can never be justified, the sole policy question then is whether existing legal categories best implement that goal or whether a new offense and penalty structure should be created. The second question arises if we conclude that withholding care in some instances is morally justified or socially desirable and asks who among parents, physicians, or other decisionmakers is best equipped to decide when care is to be withheld. Legal rules in this re-

Division of Macmillan Publishing Co., Inc.

gard must focus on criteria, procedures, and decisionmaking processes for implementing a social policy of involuntary passive euthanasia. Until we thoroughly canvass these questions, decisions about legal policy cannot reasonably be made.

Id. at 244–46.

In his conclusion, the author finds:

The pervasive practice of withholding ordinary medical care from defective newborns demonstrates that we have embarked on a widespread program of involuntary euthanasia. This practice has not resulted from a careful consideration of public policy alternatives, nor has it been arrived at by a public or collective decision. Formal public policy, in fact, condemns the practice, and until recently, the medical profession rarely acknowledged its existence. But now, as a result of new-found technological skills and perhaps changing attitudes toward social-utility assessments of human life, the practice has come to be accepted in the interstices of medical and legal practice. Given this situation, the crucial question is whether nontreatment of defective neonates is the opening wedge in expanding involuntary euthanasia, or whether its scope and impact can be limited. How we practice involuntary euthanasia thus becomes as important as the practice itself.

The problem of treating defective newborns may usefully be viewed as a problem of the proper limits of discretion, and is therefore amenable to traditional legal controls on discretion—rules, procedures, and review. Nonenforcement of existing criminal laws grants parents and physicians effective discretion to decide the fate of infants born with a range of defects. Their decisions inevitably reflect their perception of the child's, the family's, and perhaps society's interests. In short, they implicitly or explicitly constitute judgments as to when social costs outweigh the benefits of treatment. But these criteria are rarely articulated, and their judgments do not undergo the close scrutiny that decisions of such magnitude warrant. In nearly all cases in which the attending physician concurs in the parental decision to withhold care, neither parents nor physicians are required to justify their choice, nor is the decision reviewed by a disinterested party. The absence of due process for the infant is all the more striking given the emotional circumstances of the parental decision and the lack of publicly certified guidelines or criteria for withholding care. We thus have a situation in which interests other than the infants can dominate, and in which arbitrary and unjustified killings can and have occurred.

It is highly unlikely that full enforcement of present laws can correct the imbalances of the present situation. Some prosecutors might begin to enforce the law as the practice is more widely publicized. Yet if such enforcement occurs at all, it is likely to be scattered or sporadic. Although the law clothes the defective infant with a right to life, and a corresponding duty of care from those in certain relations with him, many people think that that right ends when it conflicts with the interests of parents, the medical profession, and the infant's own potential for full development. The law in action is likely to reflect this view, and, if the law in theory differs, this difference probably will be ignored.

If the nontreatment of defective newborns has become deeply engrained in medical practice, one can only hope that it will be confined to those cases in which the clearest and most indisputable grounds for with-holding care exist. The attending physician is a partial check on parents who would unjustifiably deny treatment, even if the criminal law is not. But the peculiarities of his role, the risk of conflicting interests, and the lack of special ethical skill or training, make the physician an unreliable protector of the infant. In fact, granting the physician this authority may only foster present tendencies of the medical profession to assume decisionmaking authority over issues that are not theirs by law, training, or expertise to make. Unless physicians are to be final arbiters of all social policy and ethical issues with a medical component, they should not have such authority here.

By requiring that certain procedures be followed in deciding whether parents' nontreatment decision is to be final, the exercise of discretion can be structured to maximize the possibility of providing a disinterested decisionmaker who is equipped with relevant information and is sensitive to all interests. However, enforcing these procedures may present major problems, and even if administratively feasible, undoubtedly will require a relatively unfocused judgment as to whether care can be justifiably withheld.

Thus, in addition to procedures, the decisionmaking should be confined or limited by specific criteria, identifying the cases in which treatment can be justifiably withheld. Drafting criteria creates problems and diffi-cult ethical choices, but these are no more significant than those that faced the Harvard Medical School committee that produced a definition of brain death. Rather, the problem will be in deciding whether rules such as "no anencephalics need be treated" or "no hydrocephalic can be denied treatment for this defect alone" provide justifiable differentiations in de-ciding the need for treatment.

The use of criteria thus confronts us with the question of whether there are classes of infants who may justifiably be allowed to die when parents so choose, and whether we can openly acknowledge the criteria which inform our decisionmaking. For while we may save lives and limit discretion by formalizing decisionmaking, we risk establishing a prece-dent that once loosed, is not easily cabined. Given the current acceptance of involuntary euthanasia of defective newborns, further danger from formalizing the precedent appears small. Indeed, subjecting the non-treatment decision to rules and procedures may demonstrate the solemn nature of a difficult situation. Since the power to cause the death of a defective newborn is an awesome one, it is essential that such decisions be carefully confined by law.

Id. at 268–69.

(3) In Dilemmas of "Informed Consent" in Children, 289 New Eng.J.Med. 885 (1973), a distinguished pediatric surgeon, Dr. Anthony Shaw, presents a series of case reports followed by comments discussing the moral and ethical dilemmas that may arise in obtaining parental consent when its denial means death. Several of these reports and the comments to them follow.* How would you assess the legal problems in each instance?

* Excerpted by permission of The New England Journal of Medicine (volume 289, pp. 885–87 (1973)).

Case Reports

A. Baby A was referred to me at 22 hours of age with a diagnosis of esophageal atresia and tracheoesophageal fistula. The infant, the first-born of a professional couple in their early thirties, had obvious signs of mongolism, about which they were fully informed by the referring physician. After explaining the nature of the surgery to the distraught father, I offered him the operative consent. His pen hesitated briefly above the form and then as he signed, he muttered, "I have no choice, do I?" He didn't seem to expect an answer, and I gave him none. The esophageal anomaly was corrected in routine fashion, and the infant was discharged to a state institution for the retarded without ever being seen again by either parent.

Comment

In my opinion, this case was mishandled from the point of view of Baby A's family, in that consent was not truly informed. The answer to Mr. A's question should have been, "You *do* have a choice. You might want to consider not signing the operative consent at all." Although some of my surgical colleagues believe that there is no alternative to attempting to save the life of every infant, no matter what his potential, in my opinion, the doctrine of informed consent should, under some circumstances, include the right to withhold consent. If the parents do have the right to withhold consent for surgery in a case such as Baby A, who should take the responsibility for pointing that fact out to them—the obstetrician, the pediatrician or the surgeon?

Another question raised by this case lies in the parents' responsibility toward their baby, who has been saved by their own decision to allow surgery. Should they be obligated to provide a home for the infant? If their intention is to place the baby after operation in a state-funded institution, should the initial decision regarding medical or surgical treatment for their infant be theirs alone?

B. Baby B was referred at the age of 36 hours with duodenal obstruction and signs of Down's syndrome. His young parents had a 10-year-old daughter, and he was the son they had been trying to have for 10 years; yet, when they were approached with the operative consent, they hesitated. They wanted to know beyond any doubt whether the baby had Down's syndrome. If so, they wanted time to consider whether or not to permit the surgery to be done. Within 8 hours a geneticist was able to identify cells containing 47 chromosomes in a bone-marrow sample. Over the next 3 days the infant's gastrointestinal tract was decompressed with a nasogastric tube, and he was supported with intravenous fluids while the parents consulted with their ministers, with family physicians in their home community and with our geneticists. At the end of that time the B's decided not to permit surgery. The infant died 3 days later after withdrawal of supportive therapy.

Comment

Unlike the parents of Baby A, Mr. and Mrs. B realized that they did have a choice—to consent or not to consent to the intestinal surgery. They were afforded access to a wide range of resources to help them make an informed decision. The infant's deterioration was temporarily prevented by adequate intestinal decompression and intravenous fluids.

Again, some of the same questions are raised here as with Baby A. Do the parents have the right to make the decision to allow their baby to die without surgery?

Can the parents make a reasonable decision within hours or days after the birth of a retarded or brain-damaged infant? During that time they are overwhelmed by feelings of shock, fear, guilt, horror and shame. What is the proper role of the medical staff and the hospital administration? Can parents make an intelligent decision under these circumstances, or are they simply reacting to a combination of their own instincts and fears as well as to the opinions and biases of medical staff? Rickham has described the interaction of physician and parents in such situations as follows:

> Every conscientious doctor will, of course, give as correct a prognosis and as impartial an opinion about the possible future of the child as he can, but he will not be able to be wholly impartial, and, whether he wants it or not, his opinion will influence the parents. At the end it is usually the doctor who has to decide the issue. It is not only cruel to ask the parents whether they want their child to live or die, it is dishonest, because in the vast majority of cases, the parents are consciously or unconsciously influenced by the doctor's opinion.

I believe that parents often *can* make an informed decision if, like the B's, they are afforded access to a range of resources beyond the expertise and bias of a single doctor and afforded sufficient time for contemplation of the alternatives. Once the parents have made a decision, should members of the medical staff support them in their decision regardless of their own feelings? (This support may be important to assuage recurrent feelings of guilt for months or even years after the parents' decision.)

When nutritional and fluid support was withdrawn, intestinal intubation and pain medication were provided to prevent suffering. To what extent should palliative treatment be given in a case in which definitive treatment is withheld? The lingering death of a newborn infant whose parents have denied consent for surgery can have a disastrous effect on hospital personnel, as illustrated last year by the well publicized Johns Hopkins Hospital case, which raised a national storm of controversy. In this case, involving an infant with mongoloidism and duodenal atresia, several of the infant's physicians violently disagreed with the parents' decision not to allow surgery. The baby's lingering death (15 days) severely demoralized the nursing and house staffs. In addition, it prolonged the agony for the parents, who called daily to find out if the baby was still alive. Colleagues of mine who have continued to keep such infants on gastrointestinal decompression and intravenous fluids for weeks after the parents have decided against surgery have told me of several cases in which the parents have finally changed their minds and give the surgeon a green light! Does such a change of heart represent a more deliberative decision on the part of the parents or merely their capitulation on the basis of emotional fatigue?

After the sensationalized case in Baltimore, Johns Hopkins Hospital established a committee to work with physicians and parents who are confronted by similar problems. Do such medical-ethics committees serve as a useful resource for physicians and families, or do they, in fact, further complicate the decision-making process by multiplying the number of opinions?

Finally, should a decision to withhold surgery on an infant with Down's syndrome or other genetically determined mental-retardation states be allowed on clinical grounds only, without clear-cut chromosomal evidence?

C. I was called to the Newborn Nursery to see Baby C, whose father was a busy surgeon with 3 teen-age children. The diagnoses of imperforate anus and microcephalus were obvious. Doctor C called me after being informed of the situation by the pediatrician. "I'm not going to sign that op permit," he said. When I didn't reply, he said, "What would you do, doctor, if he were your baby?" "I wouldn't let him be operated on either," I replied. Palliative support only was provided, and the infant died 48 hours later.

Comment

Doctor C asked me bluntly what I would do were it my baby, and I gave him my answer. Was my response appropriate? In this case I simply reinforced his own decision. Suppose he has asked me for my opinion before expressing his own inclination? Should my answer in any case have been simply been, "It's not my baby"—with a refusal to discuss the subject further? Should I have insisted that he take more time to think about it and discuss it further with his family and clergy, like the parents of Baby B? Is there a moral difference between withholding surgery on a baby with microcephalus and withholding surgery on a baby with Down's syndrome?

Some who think that all children with mongolism should be salvaged since many of them are trainable, would not dispute a decision to allow a baby with less potential such as microcephalic Baby C to die. Should, then, decisions about life and death be made on the basis of IQ? In a recent article, Professor Joseph Fletcher outlined criteria for what he calls "humanhood"—minimal standards by which we could judge whether a living organism is or is not a human being. These criteria (further defined in Dr. Fletcher's article) include minimal intelligence, self-awareness, self-control, a sense of time, a sense of futurity, a sense of the past, the capability to relate to others, concern for others, communication, control of existence, curiosity, change and changeability, balance of rationality and feeling, idiosyncrasy and neocortical function. Dr. Fletcher also offers a shorter list of what a human being is not. By trying to arrive at a definition of what we call "human," Doctor Fletcher has, of course, stirred up a hornet's nest. But in so doing, he is not laying down a set of rigid standards but is issuing a challenge that should be a particularly attractive one to the medical profession. Is it possible that physicians and philosophers can agree on a "profile of man" that might afford more rational grounds for approaching problems in biomedical ethics?

D. In 1972 I wrote in a piece published by the New York Times, "Parents of mongoloids have the legal (and, I believe, the moral) responsibility of determining if their child with a potentially deadly but surgically correctable defect should live or die." After reading this article, Mr. D called me for advice concerning his 2-week-old grandson. This infant had been born in a New York hospital with Down's syndrome and with bilateral hydroureteronephrosis secondary to urethral valves, for the correction of which the family had refused surgery. Since the infant was becoming increasingly uremic, the family was being strongly pressured by the medical staff to consent to surgery. After an absolute refusal to sign, the family was ordered to take the infant home immediately despite the wish for the baby to die in the hospital. At my last conversation with the infant's grandfather, the family and the hospital had reached an impasse about discharge and the infant was dying slowly of uremia.

Comment

In threatening to discharge the dying infant, the medical staff was trying to coerce the family into signing consent for surgery. Aside from the issue of coercion here, is providing facilities for dying patients a proper role for a hospital? The parents refused to take the infant home because of the devastating emotional impact that the dying baby would have on the entire family. The hospital wanted to discharge the infant partly because of the devastating emotional impact that the dying infant was having on the hospital staff. Can we prepare hospital, medical and paramedical personnel to accept the death of infants under these circumstances without the destruction of morale? Can we realistically expect hospital staff to be able to make such an emotional accommodation no matter how they view the situation from an intellectual standpoint? Finally, if the decision is not to operate, where does one draw the line between palliation of the infant's suffering and active shortening of the infant's life? This, of course, is one of the areas where the question of euthanasia has been raised. To my knowledge, the question of whether Baby D died at home or in the hospital finally became a legal matter to be resolved between the hospital's legal counsel and the family's attorney.

If the medical staff felt strongly that allowing Baby D to die for lack of simple surgery was immoral, why did they not obtain a court order permitting them to operate?

. . .

(4) In Custody of a Minor, 385 Mass. 697, 434 N.E.2d 601 (1982) the Supreme Judicial Court of Massachusetts upheld the judgment of a juvenile judge who had permitted a hospital administrator to enter a "no code" order for a newborn child with serious cardiac problems. The child, abandoned at birth by his mother, had been declared to be "in need of care and protection" and placed in the temporary custody of the Department of Social Services. The Department, as a matter of policy, would not consent to the order that would direct the hospital staff "not to apply extraordinary intrusive resuscitative measures in the event of cardiac or respiratory failure." A guardian ad litem also declined to consent. The appeals court found that the juvenile court had jurisdiction, that the hospital had standing to bring a care and protection proceeding for a child who was abandoned, abused or neglected, and that the juvenile court was not in error in applying the substituted judgment rule as to the "no code" order.

MATTER OF HOFBAUER

Court of Appeals of New York, 1979.
47 N.Y.2d 648, 419 N.Y.S.2d 936, 393 N.E.2d 1009.

JASEN, JUDGE.

This appeal involves the issue whether a child suffering from Hodgkin's disease whose parents failed to follow the recommendation of an attending physician to have their child treated by radiation and chemotherapy, but, rather, placed their child under the care of physicians advocating a nutritional or metabolic therapy, including injections of laetrile, is a "neglected child" within the meaning of section 1012 of the Family Court Act. This case does not involve the legality of the use of laetrile per se in this State inasmuch as neither party contends that a duly licensed New York physician may not administer laetrile to his or her own patients. Nor is this an action brought against a physician to test the validity of his determination to treat Hodgkin's disease by prescribing metabolic therapy and injections of laetrile. Rather, the issue presented for our determination is whether the parents of a child afflicted with Hodgkin's disease have failed to exercise a minimum degree of care in supplying their child with adequate medical care by entrusting the child's physical well-being to a duly licensed physician who advocates a treatment not widely embraced by the medical community.

The relevant facts are as follows: In October, 1977, Joseph Hofbauer, then a seven-year-old child, was diagnosed as suffering from Hodgkin's disease,[1] a disease which is almost always fatal if left untreated. The then attending physician, Dr. Arthur Cohn, recommended that Joseph be seen by an oncologist or hematologist for further treatment which would have included radiation treatments and possibly chemotherapy, the conventional modes of treatment. Joseph's parents, however, after making numerous inquiries, rejected Dr. Cohn's advice and elected to take Joseph to Fairfield Medical Clinic in Jamaica where a course of nutritional or metabolic therapy, including injections of laetrile, was initiated.

Upon Joseph's return home to Saratoga County in November, 1977, the instant neglect proceeding was commenced, pursuant to article 10 of the Family Court Act, upon the filing of a petition in Family Court by the Saratoga County Commissioner of Social Services. The petition alleged, in substance, that Joseph's parents neglected their son by their failure to follow the advice of Dr. Cohn with respect to treatment and, instead, chose a course of treatment for Joseph in the form of nutritional therapy and laetrile. A preliminary hearing was held and the court, finding "that there exists the probability of neglect of [Joseph] by his parents," ordered that Joseph be temporarily removed from the custody of his parents and placed in St. Peter's Hospital in Albany.

Thereafter, Joseph's parents made an application to have Joseph returned to their custody. A hearing was duly commenced in December, 1977, but the proceeding was suspended for six months when a stipulation was entered into by the parties returning Joseph to the custody and care of his parents, and authorizing Joseph to come under the care of Dr. Michael Schachter, a physician duly licensed in New York who is a proponent of metabolic therapy. The stipulation

---

1. Hodgkin's disease is a "disease marked by chronic inflammatory enlargement of the lymph nodes, first the cervical and then the axillary, inguinal, mediastinal, mesenteric, etc., together with enlargement of the spleen, and often of the liver and kidneys, with lymphoid infiltration along the blood vessels; there is no pronounced leukocytosis." (Stedman's Medical Dictionary [19th ed.].)

further provided that at least one other physician would be consulted regularly, with medical reports to be submitted to the court periodically.[2]

At the direction of the Appellate Division, a fact-finding hearing on the merits of this case was conducted by Family Court in June, 1978. A review of the testimony adduced at the hearing reveals a sharp conflict in medical opinion as to the effectiveness of the treatment being administered to Joseph. The physicians produced by appellants testified, in substance, that radiation and chemotherapy were the accepted methods of treating Hodgkin's disease and that nutritional therapy was an inadequate and ineffective mode of treatment. In addition, two physicians, who by stipulation examined Joseph during the hearing, testified, in essence, that there had been a progression of the disease and denounced the treatment being rendered to Joseph as ineffective.

Two physicians produced by respondents, however, testified that they prescribed nutritional therapy for cancer patients and considered such therapy as a beneficial and effective mode of treatment, although they did not preclude the use of conventional therapy—radiation treatments and chemotherapy—in some cases. In addition, a biologist testified as to a study which had been conducted which demonstrated significant regression in cancerous tumors in mice which had been treated with amygdalin (laetrile), vitamin A, and proteolytic enzymes. Dr. Schachter, the attending physician, then testified that in his opinion Joseph was responding well to the nutritional therapy and that both his appetite and energy levels were good. Dr. Schachter further stated that he had consulted with numerous other physicians concerning Joseph's treatment, and that he never ruled out the possibility of conventional treatment if the boy's condition appeared to be deteriorating beyond control. Significantly, Joseph's father also testified that he would allow his son to be treated by conventional means if Dr. Schachter so advised. Both appellants' and respondents' witnesses testified as to the potentially dangerous side effects of radiation treatments and chemotherapy which could include, among other things, fibrosis of the body organs, swelling of the heart, impairment of the growth centers and leukemia.

Family Court, finding that Joseph's mother and father are concerned and loving parents who have employed conscientious efforts to secure for their child a viable alternative of medical treatment ad-

2. In February, 1978, the New York Commissioners of Health and Social Services moved to intervene in the neglect proceeding. Although such motion was denied by Family Court, the Appellate Division reversed, and granted the motion to intervene. (61 A.D.2d 1102, 403 N.Y.S.2d 714.) Thereafter, the intervenors applied to vacate the stipulation and requested that a plenary hearing pursuant to article 10 of the Family Court Act be held immediately. The Family Court denied the requested relief and the Appellate Division affirmed such order (62 A.D.2d 508, 405 N.Y.S.2d 799). The Appellate Division, however, did direct Family Court, immediately upon expiration of the stipulation, to proceed with the requisite "fact-finding" and dispositional hearing on the merits.

ministered by a duly licensed physician, found that Joseph was not a neglected child within the meaning of section 1012 of the Family Court Act and dismissed the petitions. On appeal, a unanimous Appellate Division affirmed. Leave to appeal to this court was granted by the Appellate Division. There should be an affirmance.

. . . [O]ur scope of review is narrow in a case, such as this, coming to us with affirmed findings of fact. This is so because this court is without power to review the findings of fact if such findings are supported by evidence in the record. Thus, our review is confined solely to the legal issues raised by the parties.

Our threshold task in this case is, by necessity, the identification of the standard of neglect against which the facts of this case may be measured. So far as is material for the issue under consideration, a neglected child is defined, by statute, to "[mean] a child less than eighteen years of age whose physical . . . condition has been impaired or is in imminent danger of becoming impaired as a result of the failure of his parent . . . to exercise a minimum degree of care in supplying the child with adequate . . . medical . . . care, though financially able to do so." [3] (Family Ct.Act, § 1012 subd. [f], par. [i], cl. [A].)

A reading of this statutory provision makes it clear that the Legislature has imposed upon the parents of a child the non-delegable affirmative duty to provide their child with adequate medical care. What constitutes adequate medical care, however, cannot be judged in a vacuum free from external influences, but, rather, each case must be decided on its own particular facts. In this regard, we deem certain factors significant in determining whether Joseph was afforded adequate medical care.

It is readily apparent that the phrase "adequate medical care" does not require a parent to beckon the assistance of a physician for every trifling affliction which a child may suffer for everyday experience teaches us that many of a child's ills may be overcome by simple household nursing. We believe, however, that the statute does require a parent to entrust the child's care to that of a physician when such course would be undertaken by an ordinarily prudent and loving parent, "solicitous for the welfare of his child and anxious to promote [the child's] recovery." (See People v. Pierson, 176 N.Y. 201, 206, 68 N.E. 243, 244.) This obligation, however, is not without qualification.

It surely cannot be disputed that every parent has a fundamental right to rear its child. While this right is not absolute inasmuch as the State, as *parens patriae*, may intervene to ensure that a child's health or welfare is not being seriously jeopardized by a parent's fault or omission, great deference must be accorded a parent's choice

---

3. It was stipulated by the parties that Joseph's parents are financially able to provide medical care.

as to the mode of medical treatment to be undertaken and the physician selected to administer the same. . . .

In this regard, it is important to stress that a parent, in making the sensitive decision as how the child should be treated, may rely upon the recommendations and competency of the attending physician if he or she is duly licensed to practice medicine in this State, for "[i]f a physician is licensed by the State, he is recognized by the State as capable of exercising acceptable clinical judgment." (Doe v. Bolton, 410 U.S. 179, 199, 93 S.Ct. 739, 751, 35 L.Ed.2d 201, 217, ...) Obviously, for all practical purposes, the average parent must rely upon the recommendations and competency of the attending physician since the physician is both trained and in the best position to evaluate the medical needs of the child.

Ultimately, however, the most significant factor in determining whether a child is being deprived of adequate medical care, and, thus, a neglected child within the meaning of the statute, is whether the parents have provided an acceptable course of medical treatment for their child in light of all the surrounding circumstances. This inquiry cannot be posed in terms of whether the parent has made a "right" or a "wrong" decision, for the present state of the practice of medicine, despite its vast advances, very seldom permits such definitive conclusions. Nor can a court assume the role of a surrogate parent and establish as the objective criteria with which to evaluate a parent's decision its own judgment as to the exact method or degree of medical treatment which should be provided, for such standard is fraught with subjectivity. Rather, in our view, the court's inquiry should be whether the parents, once having sought accredited medical assistance and having been made aware of the seriousness of their child's affliction and the possibility of cure if a certain mode of treatment is undertaken, have provided for their child a treatment which is recommended by their physician and which has not been totally rejected by all responsible medical authority.

With these considerations in mind and cognizant that the State has the burden of demonstrating neglect, we now examine the facts of this case. It is abundantly clear that this is not a case where the parents, for religious reasons, refused necessary medical procedures for their child (e.g., Matter of Sampson, 37 A.D.2d 668, 323 N.E.2d 253, affd. 29 N.Y.2d 900, 326 N.Y.S.2d 398; . . .), nor is this a case where the parents have made an irreversible decision to deprive their child of a certain mode of treatment (Custody of a Minor, 379 N.E.2d 1053 [Mass.]). Indeed, this is not a case where the child is receiving no medical treatment, for the record discloses that Joseph's mother and father were concerned and loving parents who sought qualified medical assistance for their child.[4]

---

4. We would note that it appears that no appropriate State agency has taken any disciplinary action against Dr. Schachter for his treatment of Joseph.

Rather, appellants predicate their charge of neglect upon the basis that Joseph's parents have selected for their child a mode of treatment which is inadequate and ineffective. Both courts below found, however—and we conclude that these findings are supported by the record—that numerous qualified doctors have been consulted by Dr. Schachter and have contributed to the child's care; that the parents have both serious and justifiable concerns about the deleterious effects of radiation treatments and chemotherapy; that there is medical proof that the nutritional treatment being administered Joseph was controlling his condition and that such treatment is not as toxic as is the conventional treatment; and that conventional treatments will be administered to the child if his condition so warrants. In light of these affirmed findings of fact, we are unable to conclude, as a matter of law, that Joseph's parents have not undertaken reasonable efforts to ensure that acceptable medical treatment is being provided their child.

By our decision today, we are by no means advocating the use of nutritional or metabolic therapy, including injections of laetrile, as a means to cure or control cancer, since this is not, in the context of this case, an issue for our resolution. . . .

. . . [T]he order of the Appellate Division should be affirmed.
. . .

NOTES

(1) Joey Hofbauer died during 1980 at age 10. According to a story in the New York Times after his death, his father stated in an interview that the boy had been "a pioneer whose purpose was to establish the right of parents to make these decisions for their children and to keep [New York] Governor Carey and his faceless bureaucrats out of the family." N.Y. Times, July 18, 1980, at D13, col. 5.

(2) In a celebrated Massachusetts case involving infant Chad Green, the Supreme Judicial Court was called upon to deal with the problems of a very young boy with acute lymphocytic leukemia. His doctors had prescribed a course of chemotherapy which they thought would give him a substantial chance of a cure or long term remission of the disease. The parents wished to augment or to replace this treatment with a regimen centering around the use of laetrile. A trial judge found the minor to be in need of care and protection and issued an order requiring the parents to allow the child to undergo chemotherapy under a board certified hematologist of their choice in the state; legal custody of the child was vested in the Department of Public Welfare for the limited purpose of assuring that the medical treatment was administered. This order was affirmed on appeal, the court stating that

> Essentially, the judge's findings, which we affirm here, are that there is a substantial chance for a cure and a normal life for the child if he undergoes chemotherapy treatment. The uncontradicted medical testimony supports those conclusions, and no evidence of any alternative treatment consistent with good medical practice was offered.

Custody of a Minor, 375 Mass. 733, 379 N.E.2d 1053, 1056 (1978).

The boy's parents later petitioned for a review and redetermination of the need for care and protection. The trial judge continued in effect the prior order requiring chemotherapy and further ordered that the parents cease administering laetrile, enzyme enemas, and certain other treatments to the child. When the appeal from that decision reached the Massachusetts Supreme Judicial Court in 1979, the boy was three years old. The court was informed at oral argument that the parents had taken the child from the state in violation of the trial judge's orders, but it nevertheless passed the issue of standing because it had not been argued before them and "particularly since a small child is concerned". Custody of a Minor, 378 Mass. 732, 393 N.E.2d 836 (1979). The court began by restating the relevant principles:

> The principles governing this case are set out fully in our prior opinion concerning this child. Custody of a Minor, 379 N.E.2d 1053 (1978). . . . Basically they place three sets of interests in competition: the natural rights of the parents, the responsibilities of the State, and the best interests of the child.

> While recognizing that there exists a private realm of family life which the State cannot enter, Prince v. Massachusetts, 321 U.S. 158, 166 (1944), we think that family autonomy is not absolute, and may be limited where, as here, it appears that parental decisions will jeopardize the health or safety of a child. Custody of a Minor, 389 N.E.2d 68 (1979). Wisconsin v. Yoder, 406 U.S. 205, 234 (1972).

> It is well settled that parents are the "natural guardians of their children . . . [with] the legal as well as the moral obligation to support . . . educate" and care for their children's development and well-being. Richards v. Forrest, 278 Mass. 547, 553, 180 N.E. 508, 511 (1932). See Purinton v. Jamrock, 195 Mass. 187, 199, 80 N.E. 802 (1907). As such, it is they who have the primary right to raise their children according to the dictates of their own consciences. See Quilloin v. Walcott, 434 U.S. 246, 255, 98 S.Ct. 549 (1978), quoting from Prince v. Massachusetts, 321 U.S. 158, 166 (1944). Pierce v. Society of Sisters, 268 U.S. 510, 535 (1925). Meyer v. Nebraska, 262 U.S. 390, 399 (1923). Indeed, these "natural rights" of parents have been recognized as encompassing an entire private realm of family life which must be afforded protection from unwarranted State interference. Quilloin v. Walcott, supra. Smith v. Organization of Foster Families for Equality & Reform, 431 U.S. 816, 842 (1977). In light of these principles, this court and others have sought to treat the exercise of parental prerogative with great deference.

> It is also well established, however, that the parental rights described above do not clothe parents with life and death authority over their children. This court has stated that the parental right to control a child's nurture is grounded not in any absolute property right which can be enforced to the detriment of the child, but rather is akin to a trust, subject to a correlative duty to care for and protect the child, and terminable by the parents' failure to discharge their obligations. Richards v. Forrest, supra, 278 Mass. at 553, 180 N.E. 508. Purinton v. Jamrock, supra, 195 Mass. at 201, 80 N.E. 802. Donnelly v. Donnelly, 4 Mass.App. 162, 164, 344 N.E.2d 195 (1976). Thus we have stated that where a child's well-being is placed in issue, it is not the rights of parents that are chiefly to be considered. The first and paramount duty is to consult the welfare of the child.

The standard to be applied in such circumstances is articulated in G.L. c. 119, § 24. Pursuant to this provision, a child may be taken from the custody of his parents on a showing that the child is without necessary and proper physical care and that the parents are unwilling to provide such care. The essential inquiry involves application of the "substituted judgment" or "best interests of the child" principles, . . . On a proper showing that parental conduct threatens a child's well-being, the interests of the State and of the individual child may mandate intervention.

Because we are dealing with a child, we find little relevance in arguments which posit the existence of a fundamental right in competent adults to make personal health care decisions and to choose or reject medical treatment, whether orthodox or unorthodox, rational or foolish. We appreciate that the law presently appears to impose certain limitations on such rights in competent adults, and express no opinion as to whether there is such unfettered freedom of choice arising from the constitutional right of privacy and the right of bodily integrity, or whether such freedom of choice might be deemed a logical extension of the right to refuse life-prolonging and life-saving medical care in appropriate circumstances. Cf. Superintendent of Belchertown State School v. Saikewicz, 373 Mass. 728, 370 N.E.2d 417 (1977); Lane v. Candura, 376 N.E.2d 1232 (1978).

Even were we to assume that competent adults have the right to use controversial treatments without limitation, we are dealing here with a three year old child. The parents do not—and indeed cannot—assert on their own behalf the privacy rights of their child. Custody of a Minor, 379 N.E.2d 1053 (1978). On the other hand, the child's own rights of privacy and bodily integrity are fully recognized in principles set out in this opinion. "[T]he State must recognize the dignity and worth of [an incompetent] person and afford to that person the same panoply of rights and choices it recognizes in competent persons." *Saikewicz*, supra, 370 N.E. 2d at 428. Such respect is manifested by use of the "substituted judgment" doctrine, according to which a court must seek to identify and effectuate the actual values and preferences of the incompetent individual. Id. at 370 N.E.2d 417. In the case of a child, however, the substituted judgment doctrine and the "best interests of the child" test are essentially coextensive, involving examination of the same criteria and application of the same basic reasoning. Custody of a Minor, supra, 379 N.E.2d 1053.

Applying these principles to the case before it, the court affirmed the trial judge's decision as "clearly warranted, and probably required, on the evidence before him." The trial court had found that none of the metabolic therapy components the parents wished to use were shown to have any curative or ameliorative effect in the treatment of acute lymphocytic anemia and that some posed the threat of damage. In concluding, the appellate court stated:

It is with sadness that we review the entire history of this case. The child's disease under chemotherapy treatment has been in constant remission except for a period of months when the parents, without knowledge of the attending physician, discontinued the medication. Only after the first Superior Court hearing was completed, and was on appeal, did the parents make any mention of laetrile.

Now the parents concede that chemotherapy must be continued, but they persist in their support of metabolic therapy, including laetrile, despite the proof that this regimen is not only useless but dangerous for their child.

This is not a case where, in either of the two hearings, conflicting testimony was weighed as to the merits of contesting theories or opinions. The evidence in the first hearing supportive of chemotherapy as the sole hope for amelioration or cure of the disease was undisputed. Likewise, in the second hearing, the evidence was essentially uncontested that metabolic therapy for this child is useless and dangerous. The decisions entered after both hearings were supported by convincing, even overwhelming, evidence.

The judgment of the parents has been consistently poor, from the child's standpoint, and his well-being seriously threatened as a result. Their persistence in pursuing for their child a course against all credible medical advice cannot be explained in terms of despair of a cure, or by the suffering of serious side effects of chemotherapy. The chance for cure with chemotherapy is good; the side effects of chemotherapy in this case have been minor and readily controllable. The parents' actions must be viewed with compassion, but beyond doubt their poor judgment has added immeasurably and unnecessarily to their difficulties, and to those of the child.

This case well illustrates that parents do not and must not have absolute authority over the life and death of their children. Under our free and constitutional government, it is only under serious provocation that we permit interference by the State with parental rights. That provocation is clear here. It is beyond argument that a drug or course of treatment is unsafe if its potential for inflicting death or physical injury is not offset by the possibility of therapeutic benefit. The position of the parents in this case, however well intentioned, is indefensible against the overwhelming weight of medical evidence.

Judgment affirmed.

As the Massachusetts court noted, Chad Green's parents had removed him from the state by the time the case was last heard on appeal. The boy died in October 1979 at age 3 in Mexico, where he had been receiving treatments using laetrile. Afterward the press continued coverage of this widely celebrated case, focusing on the issue of whether the parents would be held in criminal contempt for violating the Massachusetts judicial order. According to one newspaper report, California's Governor Jerry Brown said he would not approve any request for extradition of the Greens, criticizing the Massachusetts action as the medical establishment's attempt "to dictate a family choice." San Francisco Chronicle, Oct. 19, 1979, at 1, col. 1. The following year, after the Greens had returned to Massachusetts, a Superior Court Judge there did hold them in contempt but declined to impose either a fine or a jail sentence on them under the rationale that they had suffered enough. N.Y. Times, Dec. 9, 1980, sec. 2, at 21, col. 1.

IN RE PHILLIP B.

California Court of Appeal, 1st District, 1979.
92 Cal.App.3d 796, 156 Cal.Rptr. 48.

CALDECOTT, PRESIDING JUSTICE.

A petition was filed by the juvenile probation department in the juvenile court, alleging that Phillip B., a minor, came within the provision of Welfare and Institutions Code section 300, subdivision (b),[1] because he was not provided with the "necessities of life."

The petition requested that Phillip be declared a dependent child of the court for the special purpose of ensuring that he receive cardiac surgery for a congenital heart defect. Phillip's parents had refused to consent to the surgery. The juvenile court dismissed the petition. The appeal is from the order.

Phillip is a 12-year-old boy suffering from Down's Syndrome.[2] At birth his parents decided he should live in a residential care facility. Phillip suffers from a congenital heart defect—a ventricular septal defect[3] that results in elevated pulmonary blood pressure. Due to the defect, Phillip's heart must work three times harder than normal to supply blood to his body. When he overexerts, unoxygenated blood travels the wrong way through the septal hole reaching his circulation, rather than the lungs.

If the congenital heart defect is not corrected, damage to the lungs will increase to the point where his lungs will be unable to carry and oxygenate any blood. As a result, death follows. During the deterioration of the lungs, Phillip will suffer from a progressive loss of energy and vitality until he is forced to lead a bed-to-chair existence.

Phillip's heart condition has been known since 1973. At that time Dr. Gathman, a pediatric cardiologist, examined Phillip and recommended cardiac catheterization to further define the anatomy and dynamics of Phillip's condition. Phillip's parents refused.

In 1977, Dr. Gathman again recommended catheterization and this time Phillip's parents consented. The catheterization revealed the extensive nature of Phillip's septal defect, thus it was Dr. Gathman's recommendation that surgery be performed.

Dr. Gathman referred Phillip to a second pediatric cardiologist, Dr. William French of Stanford Medical Center. Dr. French estimates the surgical mortality rate to be five to ten percent, and notes that Down's Syndrome children face a higher than average risk of

1. All statutory references are to the Welfare and Institutions Code, unless otherwise stated.

2. "Down's syndrome or mongolism is a chromosomal disorder producing mental retardation caused by the presence of 47 rather than 46 chromosomes in a patient's cells, and marked by a distinctively shaped head, neck, trunk, and abdomen." (Robertson, Involuntary Euthanasia of Defective Newborns: A Legal Analysis, 27 StanL.Rev. 213, fn. 5.)

3. In other words, a hole between his right and left ventricles.

postoperative complications. Dr. French found that Phillip's pulmonary vessels have already undergone some change from high pulmonary artery pressure. Without the operation, Phillip will begin to function less physically until he will be severely incapacitated. Dr. French agrees with Dr. Gathman that Phillip will enjoy a significant expansion of his life span if his defect is surgically corrected. Without the surgery, Phillip may live at the outset 20 more years. Dr. French's opinion on the advisability of surgery was not asked.

I

It is fundamental that parental autonomy is constitutionally protected. The United States Supreme Court has articulated the concept of personal liberty found in the Fourteenth Amendment as a right of privacy which extends to certain aspects of a family relationship. . . . "It is cardinal with us that the custody, care and nurture of the child reside first in the parents, whose primary function and freedom include preparation for obligations the state can neither supply nor hinder." (Prince v. Massachusetts (1944) 321 U.S. 158, 166, 64 S.Ct. 438, 442, 88 L.Ed. 645.)

Inherent in the preference for parental autonomy is a commitment to diverse lifestyles, including the right of parents to raise their children as they think best. Legal judgments regarding the value of childrearing patterns should be kept to a minimum so long as the child is afforded the best available opportunity to fulfill his potential in society.

Parental autonomy, however, is not absolute. The state is the guardian of society's basic values. Under the doctrine of *parens patriae*, the state has a right, indeed, a duty, to protect children. See, e.g., Prince v. Massachusetts, 321 U.S. 158 [1944]. State officials may interfere in family matters to safeguard the child's health, educational development and emotional well-being.

One of the most basic values protected by the state is the sanctity of human life. (U.S.Const., 14th Amend., § 1.) Where parents fail to provide their children with adequate medical care, the state is justified to intervene. However, since the state should usually defer to the wishes of the parents, it has a serious burden of justification before abridging parental autonomy by substituting its judgment for that of the parents.

Several relevant factors must be taken into consideration before a state insists upon medical treatment rejected by the parents. The state should examine the seriousness of the harm the child is suffering or the substantial likelihood that he will suffer serious harm; the evaluation for the treatment by the medical profession; the risks involved in medically treating the child; and the expressed preferences of the child. Of course, the underlying consideration is the child's welfare and whether his best interests will be served by the medical treatment.

Section 300, subdivision (b), permits a court to adjudge a child under the age of 18 years a dependent of the court if the child is not provided with the "necessities of life."

The trial judge dismissed the petition on the ground that there was "no clear and convincing evidence to sustain this petition."

The rule is clear that the power of the appellate court begins and ends with a determination as to whether there is any substantial evidence, contradicted or uncontradicted, which will support the conclusion reached by the trier of fact. The "clear and convincing evidence" standard of proof applies only to the trial court, and is not the standard for appellate review.

Turning to the facts of this case, one expert witness testified that Phillip's case was more risky than the average for two reasons. One, he has pulmonary vascular changes and statistically this would make the operation more risky in that he would be subject to more complications than if he did not have these changes. Two, children with Down's Syndrome have more problems in the postoperative period. This witness put the mortality rate at five to ten percent, and the morbidity would be somewhat higher. When asked if he knew of a case in which this type of operation had been performed on a Down's Syndrome child, the witness replied that he did, but could not remember a case involving a child who had the degree of pulmonary vascular change that Phillip had. Another expert witness testified that one of the risks of surgery to correct a ventricular septal defect was damage to the nerve that controls the heart beat as the nerve is in the same area as the defect. When this occurs a pacemaker would be required.

The trial judge, in announcing his decision, cited the inconclusiveness of the evidence to support the petition.

On reading the record we can see the trial court's attempt to balance the possible benefits to be gained from the operation against the risks involved. The court had before it a child suffering not only from a ventricular septal defect but also from Down's Syndrome, with its higher than average morbidity, and the presence of pulmonary vascular changes. In light of these facts, we cannot say as a matter of law that there was no substantial evidence to support the decision of the trial court.

II

In denying the petition the trial court ruled that there was no clear and convincing evidence to sustain the petition. The state contends the proper standard of proof is by a preponderance of the evidence and not by the clear and convincing test. The state asserts that only when a permanent severance of the parent-child relationship is ordered by the court must the clear and convincing standard of proof be applied. Since the petition did not seek permanent severance but only authorization for corrective heart surgery, the state contends the lower standard of proof should have been applied.

In the case of In re Robert P. (1976) 61 Cal.App.3d 310, 318, 132 Cal.Rptr. 5, the court pointed out that a dependency hearing . . . need not result in a permanent severance of the parent-child relationship. Section 366 . . . requires subsequent hearings at periods not exceeding one year until such time as the court's jurisdiction over such minor is terminated. In re Robert P. held that even though the severance need not be permanent the standard of proof was "clear and convincing" and not a "preponderance of the evidence." The statement in In re Christopher B. (1978) 82 Cal.App.3d 608, 147 Cal. Rptr. 390, cited by appellant, that clear and convincing proof is required only when the final result is to sever the parent-child relationship and award custody to a nonparent is dicta. The *Christopher* court did not remove the child from the parents' custody but simply retained jurisdiction to supervise proper maintenance of the child's environment. The "clear and convincing standard" was proper in this case.

. . .

The order dismissing the petition is affirmed.

NOTE

In the next chapter of the judicial history of Phillip B. a trial court followed an 11-day hearing with the appointment of Herbert and Patsy Heath as guardians of the child's person and estate. While it was ordered that they not have surgery performed on Phillip without the court's permission, they were authorized to have a heart catheterization performed to determine the desirability and feasibility of surgical repair. Phillip was to remain at the same facility, "subject to reasonable visitation and overnight visitation with the Heaths." See Guardianship of Phillip Becker, Memorandum of Decision (unreported), Superior Court of Santa Clara County, Calif., No. 101981, Aug. 7, 1981. See 7 Fam.L.Rep. (BNA) 2647 (1981). The Heaths, who were volunteer workers, had formed a close relationship with Phillip at the facility for handicapped children where he had spent most of his life. The trial court found them to be the "psychological parents" of Phillip, acknowledging the lack of any precedent "which has determined that overnight home visiting and weekly visiting of a child in a board and care facility by adults such as the Heaths have done with Phillip constitutes psychological parenting."

The court pointed out that while California provides no method for a mentally retarded child's statement of preference, courts of other states have used the "substituted judgment doctrine" to determine a child's preferences and this "is held to be consistent with the 'best interests of the child' doctrine." Judge Fernandez then proposed that:

In our case the use of the substituted judgment method to arrive at Phillip's preference may best be stated in the form of a platonic dialogue

with the court posing the choices to Phillip and Phillip's preference being
ascertained from the more logical choice. The dialogue begins:

> The Court: "Phillip I am convinced by the evidence that you have ar-
> rived at a crossroad in your life. Whatever path you choose you must
> follow and will be bound to for the rest of your life. Your first choice
> will lead you to a room in an institution where you will live. You will
> be fed, housed, and clothed but you will not receive any life prolong-
> ing medical care. If you do receive medical care, it will be basic care
> only. You will not be given an opportunity to add to your basic skills
> or to your motor skills and in fact will be treated as if you are a per-
> manently mentally retarded person incapable of learning and not fit to
> enter into society. You will not be allowed to become attached to any
> person, in fact efforts will be made to prevent any such attachments.
> Your biological parents will visit you occasionally, but their love and
> caring for you will at best be ambivalent. In fact they believe that
> you will be happy so long as your physical needs are taken care of,
> and that this kind of care may come from other people, your institu-
> tional caretakers."

> Your second choice Phillip will lead you to a private home where you
> will be bathed in the love and affection of your psychological parents.
> You will be given all of the benefits of a home environment. You will
> be given private tutoring and one on one training. The purpose of
> this education and training will be to improve your motor skills and
> your basic skills in order that some day you may enter into society and
> be a productive member or our community. Your psychological par-
> ents believe that you are educable and will do all in their power to help
> you receive the education you may need to care for yourself and to
> secure work when you are an adult. You will have a chance for life
> prolonging surgery as well as receiving all the medical care that you
> need. Even if life prolonging surgery cannot be performed, your psy-
> chological parents will always be there to comfort you and care for
> you in the dark times of your final illness. Best of all, your psycho-
> logical parents will do all in their power to involve your biological par-
> ents in your habilitation and to unite both families together in ensur-
> ing for you a life that is worth living

In my view, the dialogue would end with Phillip choosing to live with
the Heaths.

Sad to say the foregoing legal analysis has no precedent in California
law. There is no way under our present law for a mentally retarded child
like Phillip to say: I want habilitation. I want life prolonging surgery.
Those choices belong to his parents or guardians. Phillip's case may
pave the way the way for recognition of a developmentally disabled
child's right to choose his fate or destiny by the substituted judgment
approach, or by the type of legal proceedings we are presently engaged
in.

Phillip's parents sought a writ of supersedeas, pending their appeal, to
stay the trial court's ruling awarding guardianship to the Heaths and authorizing the catheterization procedure. This was denied by the Court of Appeal,
which noted:

> In evaluating this difficult issue, we are aided considerably by the
> views of the guardian ad litem who, as a matter of law, is charged with

representing Phillip's interests independently of the interests of either the Heaths or the Beckers. His opposition to the Beckers' petition for supersedeas observes that while medical testimony indicated that the risks to Phillip presented by a heart catheterization were within an acceptable range as of May 1, 1981, it is possible that the medical situation may have changed since then, and that it is therefore "important that new information be gathered and be evaluated by a competent decision-maker." In that regard, he urges that "[t]he overwhelming weight of the evidence introduced in the Court below established that Phillip's psychological parents, Herbert and Patsy Heath, are competent decision-makers regarding his care and treatment," and that "Phillip's natural parents, the Beckers, have repeatedly demonstrated that they do not have the capacity to act as competent decision-makers on behalf of Phillip, especially when the issue is heart surgery." He observes, further, that according to medical evidence "Phillip's heart is changing fairly rapidly and . . . further delays could increase the risk of a heart catheterization or surgery." His opposition appends a deposition of a physician who observed substantial change in Phillip's condition in the relatively short time of one year and two months.

In view of the substantial record in the court below, and the inability of the parties to stipulate to a record on appeal, it appears likely that even if the appeal is expedited it will take several months or longer before a final decision can be rendered. It was impliedly the view of the trial court, which denied a stay pending appeal, that the risks entailed in such a delay were too great. On the basis of what is before us, we are unable to disagree. It may be, as the guardian ad litem suggest, that upon further inquiry the Heaths will decide that catheterization is not warranted; or, if catheterization is conducted, there remains the possibility that surgery will not be indicated. In any event, as the trial court's opinion and order made quite clear, the Heaths would have to return to the court for permission to consent to surgery if they decide that surgery is warranted. And, if the trial court were to grant that permission, its action in doing so would, of course, be subject to review.[2]

Guardianship of Phillip Becker, Calif.Ct.App. (1st App. Dist.), 1 Civil 53419 (unpublished opinion), Oct. 19, 1981. See also 8 Fam.L.Rep. (BNA) 1005 (1981).

For a critical appraisal of the ongoing judicial struggle over deciding how to deal with Phillip Becker's problems see Annas, 'A Wonderful Case and an Irrational Tragedy': The Phillip Becker Case Continues, 12 Hastings Center Report 25 (1982). The title is based on a description of the case in the trial court opinion of Judge Fernandez, who viewed it as "wonderful because so many people have come forward to try to make a little boy's life better" and "tragic, because God and nature may already have determined Phillip's future life course. He may very well be entering the dark time of his existence."

2. If these events transpire, the trial court would be well advised to consider granting at least a temporary stay of any order authorizing surgery, so as to permit time for evaluation of any writ application.

IN RE GREEN

Supreme Court of Pennsylvania, 1972.
448 Pa. 338, 292 A.2d 387.

JONES, CHIEF JUSTICE

[Ricky Green, age fifteen, was the subject of a neglect petition brought by the Director of the State Hospital for Crippled Children, who sought appointment of a guardian to consent to corrective surgery. The Court of Common Pleas dismissed the petition. The Superior Court reversed that decision.]

. . . [Ricky] lives with his mother as his parents are separated and the father pays support pursuant to a court order. Ricky has had two attacks of poliomyelitis which have generated problems of obesity and, in addition, Ricky now suffers from paralytic scoliosis (94% curvature of the spine).

Due to this curvature of the spine, Ricky is presently a "sitter," unable to stand or ambulate due to the collapse of his spine; if nothing is done, Ricky could become a bed patient. Doctors have recommended a "spinal fusion" to relieve Ricky's bent position, which would involved moving bone from Ricky's pelvis to his spine. Although an orthopedic specialist testified, "there is no question that there is danger in this type of operation," the mother did consent conditionally to the surgery. The condition is that, since the mother is a Jehovah's Witness who believes that the Bible proscribes any blood transfusions which would be necessary for this surgery, she would not consent to any blood transfusions. Initially, we must recognize that, while the operation would be beneficial, there is no evidence that Ricky's life is in danger or that the operation must be performed immediately. Accordingly, we are faced with the situation of a parent who will not consent to a dangerous operation on her minor son requiring blood transfusions solely because of her religious beliefs.

. . .

Almost a century ago, the United States Supreme Court enunciated the twofold concept of the Free Exercise clause: "Laws are made for the government of actions, and while they cannot interfere with mere religious belief and opinions, they may with practices." Reynolds v. United States, 98 U.S. 145, 166, 25 L.Ed. 244 (1878). Thus, it was stated in Prince v. Massachusetts, 321 U.S. 158, 166–67, 64 S.Ct. 438, 442, 88 L.Ed. 645 (1944):

"But the family itself is not beyond regulation in the public interest, as against a claim of religious liberty. Reynolds v. United States, 98 U.S. 145, 25 L.Ed. 244; Davis v. Beason, 133 U.S. 333, 10 S.Ct. 299, 33 L.Ed. 637. And neither rights of religion nor rights of parenthood are beyond limitation. Acting to guard the general interest in youth's well being, the state as *parens patriae* may restrict the parent's control by requiring school attendance [footnote omitted], regulating or prohibiting the child's labor [footnote omitted] and in many other ways [footnote omitted]. Its authority is not nullified merely because the parent grounds his claim to control the child's course of conduct on religion or conscience. Thus, he cannot claim freedom from compulsory vaccination for the child more than for himself on religious grounds [footnote omitted]. The right to practice religion freely does not include liberty to expose the community or the child to communicable disease or the latter to ill health or death. People v. Pierson, 176 N.Y. 201, 68 N.E. 243 [footnote omitted]. The catalogue need not be lengthened. It is sufficient to show what indeed appellant hardly disputes, that the state has a wide range of power for limiting parental freedom and authority in things affecting the child's welfare; and that this includes, to some extent, matters of conscience and religious conviction."

On the other hand, the United States Supreme Court recently stated, "to agree that religiously grounded conduct must often be subject to the broad police power of the State is not to deny that there are areas of conduct protected by the Free Exercise Clause of the First Amendment and thus beyond the power of the State to control, even under regulations of general applicability." Wisconsin v. Yoder, 406 U.S. 205, 92 S.Ct. 1526, 32 L.Ed.2d 15 (1972). "The conduct or actions so regulated have invariably posed some substantial threat to public safety, peace or order." Sherbert v. Verner, 374 U.S. 398, 403, 83 S.Ct. 1790, 1793, 10 L.Ed.2d 965 (1963). Without appearing callous, Ricky's unfortunate condition, unlike polygamy, vaccination, child labor and the like, does not pose a substantial threat to society; in this fashion, *Pierce* and its progeny are readily distinguishable.

. . .

. . . [W]here an adult refuses to consent to blood transfusions necessary to save the life of his infant son or daughter, other jurisdictions have uniformly held that the state can order such blood transfusions over the parents' religious objections. . . .

In a somewhat different posture, the United States District Court for the Western District of Washington entertained a class action brought on behalf of all Jehovah's Witnesses in the State against certain physicians and hospitals in that State. The relief requested was a declaration that a "dependent child" statute similar to our own was unconstitutionally applied to sustain blood transfusions for children of Jehovah's Witnesses where the blood transfusion "was or would be vital to save the life of the patient." Jehovah's Witnesses in State of Washington v. King County Hospital, 278 F.Supp. 488, 503 n. 10 (W.D.Wash.1967). Relying on Prince v. Massachusetts, 321 U.S. 158, 64 S.Ct. 438, 88 L.Ed. 645 (1944), that court held that the statute in question was constitutionally valid. On appeal, the United States Supreme Court, citing the *Prince* opinion, affirmed per curiam, 390 U.S. 598, 88 S.Ct. 1260, 20 L.Ed.2d 158 (1968). Because the Washington case directly contested the constitutional application of the state statute in the situation *where the children's lives were in imminent danger*, we do not consider this Court to be bound by the Supreme Court's per curiam affirmance under the factual posture in the case at bar.

In our view, the penultimate question presented by this appeal is whether the state may interfere with a parent's control over his or her child in order to enhance the child's physical well-being when the child's life is in no immediate danger and when the state's intrusion conflicts with the parent's religious beliefs. Stated differently, does the State have an interest of sufficient magnitude to warrant the abridgment of a parent's right to freely practice his or her religion when those beliefs preclude medical treatment of a son or daughter whose life is not in immediate danger? We are not confronted with a life or death situation as in the cases cited earlier in this opinion. Nor is there any question in the case at bar of a parent's omission or neglect for non-religious reasons

. . .

Our research disclosed only two opinions on point: both are from the New York Court of Appeals but the results differ. In Matter of Seiferth, 309 N.Y. 80, 127 N.E.2d 820 (1955), the State of New York sought the appointment of a guardian for a "neglected child," a fourteen-year-old boy with a cleft palate and harelip. The father's purely personal philosophy, "not classified as religion," precluded any and all surgery as he believed in mental healing; moreover, the father had "inculcated a distrust and dread of surgery in the boy since childhood." 309 N.Y. at 84, 127 N.E.2d at 822. The boy was medically advised and the Children's Court judge interviewed both the boy and his father in chambers. The trial judge concluded that the operation should not be performed until the boy agreed. After reversal by the Appellate Division, Fourth Department, the Court of Appeals, by a four-to-three vote, reinstated the order of the Children's Court. The primary thrust of the opinion was the child's antagonism to the operation and the need for the boy's cooperation for treatment; since the Children's Court judge saw and heard the parties involved and was aware of this aspect, the Court of Appeals decided that the discretion of the Children's Court judge should be affirmed.

On facts virtually identical to this appeal, the Family Court of Ulster County ordered a blood transfusion in In re Sampson, 65 Misc. 2d 658, 317 N.Y.S.2d 641 (1970). Kevin Sampson, fifteen years old, suffered from Von Recklinghausen's disease which caused a massive disfigurement of the right side of his face and neck. While the incurable disease posed no immediate threat to his life, the dangerous surgery requiring blood transfusions would improve "not only the function but the appearance" of his face and neck. It should also be noted that all physicians involved counselled delay until the boy was old enough to decide since the surgical risk would increase as the boy grew older. The Family Court judge ruled in an extensive opinion that the State's interest in the child's health was paramount to the mother's religious beliefs. That court further decided not to place this difficult decision on the boy and to order an immediate operation, thereby preventing psychological problems. On appeal, the Appellate Division, Third Department, unanimously affirmed the order in a memorandum decision. In re Sampson, 37 A.D.2d 668, 323 N.Y.S.2d 253 (1971). That court rejected the argument that "State intervention is permitted only where the life of the child is in danger by a failure to act . . . [as] a much too restricted approach." 37 A.D.2d at 669, 323 N.Y.S.2d at 255. When the matter reached the Court of Appeals, In re Sampson, 29 N.Y.2d 900, 328 N.Y.S.2d 686, 278 N.E.2d 918 (1972), that Court affirmed per curiam the opinion of the Family Court but added two observations: (1) the *Seiferth* opinion turned upon the question of a court's discretion and not the existence of its power to order surgery in a non-fatal case, and (2) religious objections to blood transfusions do not "present a bar at least where the transfusion is necessary to the success of the required surgery," 29 N.Y.2d at 901, 328 N.Y.S.2d at 687, 278 N.E.2d at 919.

With all deference to the New York Court of Appeals, we disagree with the second observation in a non-fatal situation and express no view of the propriety of that statement in a life or death situation. If we were to describe this surgery as "required," like the Court of Appeals, our decision would conflict with the mother's religious beliefs. Aside from religious considerations, one can also question the use of that adjective on medical grounds since an orthopedic specialist testified that the operation itself was dangerous. Indeed, one can question who, other than the Creator, has the right to term certain surgery as "required." This fatal/non-fatal distinction also steers the courts of this Commonwealth away from a medical and philosophical morass: if spinal surgery can be ordered, what about a hernia or gall bladder operation or a hysterectomy? The problems created by *Sampson* are endless. We are of the opinion that as between a parent and the state, the state does not have an interest of sufficient magnitude outweighing a parent's religious beliefs when the child's life is *not immediately imperiled* by his physical condition.

Unlike *Yoder* and *Sampson*, our inquiry does not end at this point since we believe the wishes of this sixteen-year old boy should be ascertained; the ultimate question, in our view, is whether a parent's religious beliefs are paramount to the possibly adverse decision of the child. In *Yoder*, Mr. Justice Douglas, dissenting in part, wanted to remand the matter in order to determine whether the Amish children wished to continue their education in spite of their parents' beliefs: "if an Amish child desires to attend high school, and is mature enough to have that desire respected, the State may well be able to override the parents' religiously motivated objections," 406 U.S. at 242, 92 S.Ct. at 1546. The majority opinion as well as the concurring opinion of Mr. Justice Stewart did not think it wise to reach this point for two principal reasons: (1) it was the parents, not the children, who were criminally prosecuted for their religious beliefs; and (2) the record did not indicate a parent-child conflict as the testimony of the lone child witness coincided with her parents' religious beliefs. While the record before us gives no indication of Ricky's thinking, it is the child rather than the parent in this appeal who is directly involved which thereby distinguishes *Yoder's* decision not to discuss the beliefs of the parents vis-a-vis the children. In *Sampson*, the Family Court judge decided not to "evade the responsibility for a decision now by the simple expedient of foisting upon this boy the responsibility for making a decision at some later day. . . ." 65 Misc.2d 658, 317 N.Y.S.2d at 655. While we are cognizant of the realistic problems of this approach enunciated by Judge (now Chief Judge) Fuld in his *Seiferth* dissent, we believe that Ricky should be heard.

It would be most anomalous to ignore Ricky in this situation when we consider the preference of an intelligent child of sufficient maturity in determining custody. Moreover, we have held that a child of the same age can waive constitutional rights and receive a life sentence. Indeed, minors can now bring a personal injury action in Pennsylvania against their parents. We need not extend this litany of the rights of children any further to support the proposition that Ricky should be heard. The record before us does not even note whether Ricky is a Jehovah's Witness or plans to become one. We shall, therefore, reserve any decision regarding a possible parent-child conflict and remand the matter for an evidentiary hearing similar to the one conducted in *Seiferth* in order to determine Ricky's wishes.

The order of the Superior Court is reversed and the matter remanded . . . for proceedings consistent with the views expressed in this opinion. In the meantime, awaiting the evidentiary hearing and result thereof, we will retain our jurisdiction in this matter.

EAGEN, JUSTICE (dissenting).

With all due deference to the majority of this Court, I am compelled to dissent. I would affirm the order of the Superior Court.

The Court's analysis presumes there are two primary interests at stake, that of the state to protect its citizens, and that of the mother to follow her religious convictions. The difficulty, and what I believe to be the fatal flaw in this reasoning, is that too little consideration and attention is given to the interests of the health and well-being of this young boy. Although the mother's religious beliefs must be given the fullest protection and respect, I do not believe the mother's religious convictions should be our primary consideration. As Mr. Justice Rutledge aptly stated:

"Parents may be free to become martyrs themselves. But it does not follow they are free, in identical circumstances, to make martyrs of their children before they have reached the age of full and legal discretion when they can make that choice for themselves."

Prince v. Commonwealth, 321 U.S. 158, 170, 64 S.Ct. 438, 444, 88 L.Ed. 645 (1944).

. . .

. . . With the approach of the Superior Court and the *Sampson* court, I wholeheartedly agree.

The majority takes the approach that the broad holding of Yoder v. Wisconsin, 406 U.S. 205, 92 S.Ct. 1526, 32 L.Ed.2d 15 (1972), supports the position of the mother. However, I do not read *Yoder* as having any bearing on this case, and if it has any, it would support the position the boy should have the operation. The Court used the following language which I believe indicates *Yoder* is not involved:

> "This case, of course, is not one in which *any harm to the physical or mental health of the child* or to the public safety, peace, order, or welfare has been demonstrated or may be properly inferred. The record is to the contrary, and any reliance on that theory [Prince] would find no support in the evidence." [Emphasis supplied.] Id. at 230, 92 S.Ct. at 1540–1541.

Moreover, the following language supports the position that the boy should have the operation:

> "To be sure, the power of the parent, even when linked to a free exercise, may be subject to limitation under *Prince* if it appears *that the parental decisions will jeopardize the health* or safety of the child, or have a potential for significant social burdens." [Emphasis supplied.] Id. at 233–234, 92 S.Ct. 1542.

Furthermore, I believe one of the prime considerations in *Yoder* was the effect of compulsory education on the religious beliefs of the children,[1] this is absent in the present case. Our sole consideration with respect to the child should be his health, a consideration not present in *Yoder*.

I also do not agree with the emphasis the majority places on the fact this is not a life or death situation. The statute with which we are dealing (Juvenile Court Law, Act of June 2, 1933, P.L. 1433 § 1, as amended, 11 P.S. § 243 et seq.) does not contain any such language, nor do I find support for this position in the case law (note the use of the word health in the *Yoder* and *Prince* opinions). The statute in pertinent part states:

> "A child whose parent . . . neglects or refuses to provide *proper or necessary* subsistence, education, *medical or surgical*

---

1. The *Yoder* Court stated:

"Indeed it seems clear that if the State is empowered, as *parens patriae*, to 'save' a child from himself or his Amish parents by requiring an additional two years of compulsory formal high school education, the State will in large measure influence, if not determine, the religious future of the child. Even more markedly than in *Prince*, therefore, this case involves the fundamental interest of parents, as contrasted with that of the State, to guide the religious future and education of the children." 406 U.S. 232, 92 S.Ct. at 1541.

care, or other care necessary for his or her health . . .." [Emphasis supplied.] 11 P.S. § 243(5)(c)

The statute only speaks in terms of "health", not life or death. If there is a substantial threat to health, then I believe the courts can and should intervene to protect Ricky. By the decision of this Court today, this boy may never enjoy any semblance of a normal life which the vast majority of our society has come to enjoy and cherish.

Lastly, I must take issue with the manner in which the majority finally disposes of the case. I do not believe that sending the case back to allow Ricky to be heard is an adequate solution. We are herein dealing with a young boy who has been crippled most of his life, consequently, he has been under the direct control and guidance of his parents for that time. To now presume that he could make an independent decision as to what is best for his welfare and health is not reasonable. See In Matter of Seiferth, 309 N.Y. 80, 85, 127 N.E. 820, 823 (1955) (dissenting opinion, Fuld, J.). Moreover, the mandate of the Court presents this youth with a most painful choice between the wishes of his parents and their religious convictions on the one hand, and his chance for a normal, healthy life on the other hand. We should not confront him with this dilemma.

On the basis of the foregoing, I would affirm the Order of the Superior Court.

NOTE

At the subsequent hearing to determine Ricky's wishes, he indicated that he did not wish to submit to surgery. His decision was not based solely on religious beliefs. He stated that he had been in the hospital a long time and no one had said "it is going to come out right." In re Green, 452 Pa. 373, 307 A.2d 279 (1973).

INTERVENTION FOR CONDITIONS POSING NO THREAT TO LIFE

When life itself is at issue for a child other than a defective neonate, courts stand ready to override parental choices regardless of the motivation behind them. Perhaps it was the imminence of a threat to life and the near certainty of successful outcome if medical treatment were ordered that gave judges special confidence in their own authority and expertise to decide cases such as those involving emergency blood transfusions, which established the rule. If the courts viewed life as an absolute value, any action reasonably designed to avert immediate death could not be error. In any event, willingness to intervene only in life-threatening circumstances became the hallmark of self-restraint.

Even so, courts have historically been asked to review parental decisions about medical care where no serious threat to life was involved. In 1911 a Pennsylvania court confronted the case of Tony Tuttendario, a 7-year-old boy afflicted with rickets. The damage wrought by the disease was progressive and would leave him permanently crippled if left uncorrected. Doctors recommended a fairly well-established surgical procedure to be performed while Tony was still young, but his mother refused. Neither expense nor religion was a factor in her decision; she had lost other children and she refused to permit the operation because of an exaggerated fear that it might prove fatal.

An agent of the Society for the Prevention of Cruelty to Children sought judicial commitment of Tony to that organization so that appropriate medical treatment could be authorized. Reviewing the history of state encroachment on parental governance of children, the court concluded that "the natural right of parents to the care and custody of their children has been abridged only in cases where they have been guilty of inflicting physical or moral injury upon their children with malicious intent." The court eloquently voiced its reaction to the prospect of increased intervention:

> We have not yet adopted as public policy the Spartan rule that children belong, not to their parents, but to the state. As the law stands, the parents forfeit their natural right of guardianship only in cases where they have shown their unfitness by reason of moral depravity.

The court then noted that medical progress in 1911 still left much to be desired and there was a "residuum of the unknown . . . which scientists, by a necessary law for the development of science, disregard, but which parents, in their natural love for their children, regard with apprehension and terror." The parental decision was upheld.[1]

Later cases followed that lead. In re Hudson [2] involved a 12-year-old girl whose arm had grown to abnormal size and length, straining her heart and skeletal system. Her mother regarded amputation as too dangerous. Deferring to the natural rights of parents, the Supreme Court of Washington reversed the trial judge's order requiring surgery. In Matter of Seiferth,[3] the New York Court of Appeals refused to compel surgical correction of the cleft palate and split lip of a 14-year-old boy. The child suffered substantial speech impairment, but his father insisted that the son would be healed by "letting the forces of the universe work on the body." The court allowed his decision to stand. Neither *Hudson* nor *Seiferth* involved an immediate threat to a child's life. In both cases, courts allowed parents to have the last word and left children with no escape from parental decisions that some would regard as grievously wrong.

1. In re Tuttendario, 21 Pa.Dist. 561 (Q.S.Phila.1912).

2. 13 Wn.2d 673. 126 P.2d 765 (1972).

3. 309 N.Y. 80, 127 N.E.2d 820 (1955).

In 1970 the first major, reported decision crossed the line that had seemingly barred intervention absent life-threatening circumstances. Kevin Sampson, 15-years-old when his case came before a family court in New York, had suffered since early childhood from neurofibromatosis. A large, bag-like growth enveloped one side of his face. It caused one ear, cheek, and eyelid to droop and one side of his face to be roughly twice as large as the other. Because of his deformity, he had not attended school for several years. A lengthy and dangerous operation, followed by prolonged treatment, might alleviate his condition cosmetically but would not effect a cure. The surgery required transfusions of whole blood, but because of her beliefs as a Jehovah's Witness, Kevin's mother would allow only the use of plasma. In a proceeding instituted by the County Health Commissioner, the Family Court declared Kevin a "neglected" child and ordered his mother to permit such surgery as the Commissioner deemed necessary.[4] The Appellate Division upheld the order, carefully pointing out that Kevin was "neglected" only in a technical sense, for his mother was not shown to have failed her son except in this one decision.[5] The Court of Appeals affirmed per curiam.[6] Not one judge dissented as the case passed through the state's entire judicial process.

The *Sampson* facts did not present a general pattern of abuse or culpable neglect but only a single, controversial parental decision. Both the Family Court and the Appellate Division explicitly recognized that inaction did not mean probable death and that the operation would remove only some of the unsightly growth. Plastic surgery and several years of continuing treatment would be necessary. One surgeon described the initial operation as "a risky surgical procedure" of six to eight hours duration and occasioning great loss of blood. And far from demanding immediate action, according to the witness, the operation would be less hazardous if postponed until the boy reached maturity. Then the potential blood loss would be less in relation to his body's total supply. In short, it was not the mother's refusal to consent but the operation itself that was life-threatening.

Under these circumstances, how did the court justify overriding objections lodged both by the child's mother and his law guardian? The answer lies in a humane desire to salvage some semblance of a normal life for Kevin Sampson:

> I am persuaded that if this court is to meet its responsibilities to this boy it can neither shift the responsibility onto his shoulders nor can it permit his mother's religious beliefs to stand in the way of obtaining through corrective surgery whatever chance he may

4. In re Sampson, 65 Misc.2d 658, 317 N.Y.S.2d 641 (Fam.Ct. Ulster Cty.1970).

5. In re Sampson, 37 A.D.2d 668, 323 N.Y.S.2d 253 (1971).

6. In re Sampson, 29 N.Y.2d 900, 328 N.Y.S.2d 686, 278 N.E.2d 918 (1972).

have for a normal, happy existence, which . . . is difficult of attainment under the most propitious circumstances, but will unquestionably be impossible if the disfigurement is not corrected.[7]

The three judicial decisions in *Sampson* illustrate the degree to which the courts that rendered them regarded intervention as a question of whether to exercise discretion rather than whether they had the power to do so. The Family Court's extensive opinion deals initially with the first amendment problems of court-ordered blood transfusions and comes down squarely in accord with the cases permitting intervention even in the face of parental objection based on religious belief. The judge acknowledged the possible inconsistency of intervention for Sampson but not for Seiferth, but he distinguished the latter decisions as reflecting outdated views of children's rights and family independence from state action. The Court of Appeals, in a brief per curiam affirmance, rewrote the rules of the game somewhat by shifting the governing principle from abstention to discretion, asserting judicial power "to direct surgery even in the absence of risk to the physical health or life of the subject or to the public." The upshot of *Sampson*, as expressed in the Family Court's opinion, might be considered a complete rout of the prior rule against state intervention in cases not posing a threat to life:

> [T]his Court's authority to deal with the abused, neglected or physically handicapped child is not limited to 'drastic situations' or to those which constitute a 'present emergency,' . . . the Court has a 'wide discretion' to order medical or surgical care and treatment for an infant even over parental objection, if in the Court's judgment the child's health, safety or welfare requires it.[8]

By what criteria should a judge determine whether to intervene in family decision-making in a particular instance? Of course, in a very real sense intervention is accomplished by a full review of parental conduct, regardless of the ultimate outcome of the case. Perhaps this observation is no more than a semantic quibble, but it does highlight an important change in the judicial role after *Sampson*. Under the old view, a court first inquired into the presence or absence of life-threatening circumstances. If the judge discerned no immediate danger of death, she did not need to proceed further. And if she did find that the child would die absent judicial action, all other aspects of the inquiry faded into near-irrelevance. The choice was clean and comparatively straight-forward, at least unless the parent interposed a specifically religious claim. Under the *Sampson* approach, almost any question of medical decision-making may occasion a full and wide-ranging inquiry into the host of factors arguably relevant to a determination of that elusive concept known as the "child's best interest." It was doubtless this expanded scope of review that prompted

7. 317 N.Y.S.2d at 657.   8. Id. at 654.

the Supreme Court of Pennsylvania to comment on the "endless" problems raised by the *Sampson* decision.

In *Sampson* the trial judge engaged in an admittedly ad hoc balancing of values, which he styled "The Potential Good vs. The Risk to Life." In many cases, of course, the contemplated medical procedure will involve no discernible risk to the child's life, and the balancing of values would be accomplished under the more general rubric of weighing the potential benefit against the potential detriment. Any such formula mandates a free-wheeling approach in which a court must attempt to balance all relevant factors. Usually, the judge would evaluate the probability of successful treatment, its potential benefit (both physiological and psychological), the risk to the child, and the importance of immediate action. To these factors should be added some general value of non-intervention because whatever the demands of a particular case, courts should not lightly abrogate the parental function in the name of child welfare. We would not willingly tolerate a judge overruling parents' decisions every time their choice failed to mirror her own preferences.

Another alternative to a completely unstructured balancing approach would be a "mere rationality" test, analogous to the business judgment rule applied to the directors of corporations. Under this test a court would not interfere with a parental decision regarding elective surgery unless it were patently arbitrary and nonrational. Such a formula would reserve final authority to the parents in the vast majority of cases but would retain the opportunity for judicial intervention in truly outrageous circumstances. Unfortunately, this test at once structures and distorts the inquiry. In many cases a court cannot and should not attempt to evaluate a parental decision in terms of rationality. Where, for example, the parents withhold their consent because of religious scruples, the question of rationality is entirely inapposite. The judge cannot decide whether a particular religious belief is reasonable, but neither can she simply ignore that belief and look solely to the medical evidence. A patient's emotional attitude toward a proposed medical procedure may well affect the prognosis for success, and the judge must also consider the potential deterioration of family relationships that might result if, for example, a child is forced by a court to undergo treatment that contravenes a parent's deeply held religious conviction. In other instances, a parental decision may be patently nonrational but simply not important enough to warrant judicial intervention.

Some might look for a statutory solution. In all probability, however, medical neglect legislation confirming judicial power to intervene and announcing a public policy in favor of limited review of parental decisions would do no more than counter remaining judicial allegiance to the old hands-off policy. Legislatures might provide a "laundry list" of factors to be considered in medical neglect cases, but such a statute could scarcely provide a dependable restraint on judicial inclination. It may be, therefore, that no useful standard can

be devised within the traditional legal framework of statutes, doctrines, and presumptions. The courts must either abide by the time-
honored limitation of relief to life-threatening circumstances or engage in a series of wholly ad hoc responses to differing factual situations.

IN RE KARWATH

Supreme Court of Iowa, 1972.
199 N.W.2d 147.

McCormick, Justice.

In this appeal the natural father of three children in legal custody
of the Scott County Department of Social Services seeks reversal of a
juvenile court order for surgical removal of the children's tonsils and
adenoids. We affirm. . . .

The children involved are Bryan, ten, Colleen, eight, and Neil, six.
The parents Raymond and Nellie Karwath asked to be relieved of
their care and custody in January 1970. The father was unemployed
and indigent and the mother emotionally ill.

On July 7, 1971, juvenile court hearing was held upon the department's application for authorization for surgical removal of the children's tonsils and adenoids. The father resisted. All medical evidence supported the application.

Bryan started getting sore throats in March 1971. They brought
sneezing, coughing and difficulty in breathing through his nose. The
combined discomfort caused him to miss school several times. During about his fourth sore throat he was seen by Dr. E. L. Manning, a
specialist, who noted markedly enlarged and inflamed tonsils and prescribed medication. Although some relief followed, the condition persisted and tonsilloadenoidectomy was scheduled for June 8, 1971, but
has not yet been done because of this controversy.

Neil had sore throats from the time he was first placed in foster
care. Dr. Manning found his tonsils enlarged and inflamed in June
1971, and he had middle ear infection in both ears. He was also
scheduled for June 8, 1971, surgery.

Dr. Manning believed both boys needed their tonsils and adenoids
out to prevent further middle ear infections and tonsillitis. Hearing
loss and rheumatic fever are possible results of continuing recurrence. Present emergency did not exist, but the surgery was needed
within a matter of weeks.

. . .

When asked to state his objection to his children's surgery, Mr.
Karwath said:

"My convictions are that unless it is absolutely necessary, beyond
the shadow of a doubt, that this should not be done. That all oth-

er courses of remedy should be taken first and given a sufficient well formulated trial period, enough to really prove whether it is going to do any good or not."

He based his convictions on "religious faith" not further explained. He did not oppose medication or surgery but asked six months' delay to see if surgery was still advised. He wanted chiropractic, medication and the surgery resorted to in that order. He claimed Colleen's problem had been helped in the past by three or four months' chiropractic treatments. Even at the end of six months he would not agree to surgery without taking the children to several doctors himself to get "a fresh opinion without all the history dug up."

This court stayed the surgery to permit appeal. The sole issue is whether the evidence supports the order for surgery against the father's wishes.

These children were adjudged dependent because their parents desired to be relieved of their care and custody. § 232.2(14)(c), The Code. Legal custody was placed in the county department of social services pursuant to Code § 232.33(3)(b). Legal custody imposes a duty to provide "food, clothing, housing, education, and necessary medical care, all subject to residual parental rights and responsibilities . . . ." § 232.2(9), The Code. When a child is removed from parental control the court "shall secure for him care as nearly as possible equivalent to that which he should have been given." § 232.1, The Code. The objective is the child's best interest and welfare. . . .

Here we have a conflict between legal custodian and holder of residual parental rights as to what medical care is in these children's best interests, and the juvenile court sided with the legal custodian. Appellant claims a showing of medical crisis demonstrating an immediate threat to life and limb is essential before that result is justified. We do not agree.

The State has a duty to see children receive proper care and treatment. In re Loeffelholz, 162 N.W.2d 415 (Iowa 1968). This means parents have no right to deprive their children of proper medical care. The legal custodian's statutory duty to provide ordinary medical care presupposes a right to do so in appropriate circumstances over parental objection even in absence of immediate risk to life or limb.

In this case the children are admittedly dependent upon the State for medical care. The evidence shows they need it. The State has duty and power to provide it. Appellant protests the nature rather than necessity of treatment. His view is without support in the record apart from this subjective speculation. Our paramount concern for the best interest and welfare of the children overrides the father's contention that absolute medical certitude of necessity and success should precede surgery. Nor is it required that a medical crisis be shown constituting an immediate threat to life and limb.

Where the best interests and welfare of children in care and custody of the State reasonably require medical treatment opposed by a parent, residual parental rights cannot be invoked to prevent it. The evidence clearly shows removal of tonsils and adenoids is necessary with reasonable medical certainty to restore and preserve the health of these wards of the State. . . .

NOTE

In In re Commissioner of Social Services, 72 Misc.2d 428, 339 N.Y.S.2d 89 (Fam.Ct., Kings County 1972), the Commissioner instituted a proceeding to have a child declared neglected because of parental abandonment and also to obtain court authorization for corrective surgery to deal with the child's undescended testicle. Although the child allegedly had been abandoned more than ten years earlier by his mother, whose whereabouts were unknown at the time the petition was filed, no proceeding had been instituted during that period to terminate parental custody. For three years immediately preceding the suit, the child had been a resident at Children's Village, where a pediatrician discovered the condition for which permission to administer remedial treatment was sought. The law guardian designated to represent the child moved to dismiss the petition on the ground that the court lacked jurisdiction and that petitioner already had the power to consent to the surgery without court intervention. The court first found that the legislature had conferred on the court the power to make the decision in question. As to whether the Commissioner of Social Services had authority to proceed without judicial approval, the court stated:

The contention of the law guardian raises a host of intriguing questions which appear never to have been judicially considered. Is the consent to surgery by a parent or other person standing *in loco parentis* to the child necessary only because the child, by virtue of his infancy lacks the capacity to consent or is consent necessary because the parent has a property interest in the body of his child? If consent is necessary solely because of the child's incapacity, then does the Commissioner of Social Services or any other duly authorized association, agency, society or institution charged with the responsibility for care or custody of a child have the power to consent? If consent is necessary because the right of the parent in the body of his child is akin to a property right or because there are residual parental rights which remain after the transfer of custody of the child, what are those residual rights? See Kleinfeld, The Balance of Power Among Infants, their Parents and the State, 4 Family Law Quarterly 320, 410 (1970) and 5 Family Law Quarterly 64 (1971). What is the nature of the legal relationship created between the child and a person or duly authorized association, agency, society or institution with whom he is placed pursuant to Family Court Act Sections 756 or 1055? In such case what are the rights and responsibilities, if any, remaining in the parent *vis-a-vis* the person or agency with whom the child is placed? Is there a difference regarding those relationships when the child is remanded pending final disposition rather than placed? Is the person or duly authorized facility liable for failing to provide necessary medical or surgical care? Are there valid policy reasons for insisting that court authorization be obtained for surgery upon a child and not leaving that decision solely to the public or private agency or official? The desirability, indeed, the necessity, for addressing those questions with intensive scholarship and care is or should be manifest.

The court then concluded:

> For purposes of this proceeding, it is not necessary to come to grips with those questions. Assuming without deciding that the petitioner does have the power to consent to surgery upon a child within his care or custody, the law guardian does not contend nor is there any statutory or judicial basis for the contention that such authority is exclusive and precludes this court from making an appropriate order under Family Court Act § 232(b). The motion of the law guardian is, therefore, denied.

> Sufficient basis having been shown, authorization is hereby given for the necessary operation relating to the undescended right testicle of the child named herein. In accordance with the testimony of the expert witness, the authorization is conditioned upon the surgery being performed by a duly qualified urological surgeon. . . .

HART v. BROWN

Superior Court of Connecticut, Fairfield County, 1972.
29 Conn.Sup. 368, 289 A.2d 386.

TESTO, JUDGE.

This matter is before this court by way of an action for a declaratory judgment.

The plaintiffs are Peter Hart and Eleanor Hart, the parents and natural guardians of Katheleen A. Hart and Margaret H. Hart, minors, identical twins, age seven years and ten months. The minor twins appear herein by court-appointed guardians ad litem: Attorney Thomas Dolan for the minor Margaret, and Mrs. Sylvia Chandler for the minor Katheleen. The defendants are practicing physicians licensed in this state and the Yale-New Haven Hospital, Inc., a duly organized Connecticut corporation located in the city and county of New Haven.

The plaintiff minor Katheleen A. Hart is presently a patient in the Yale-New Haven Hospital awaiting a kidney transplant. It is reasonably probable that if such procedure does not occur soon she will die. The defendant physicians have in the past performed successful kidney transplantation operations, and they are of the opinion that a successful transplantation operation can be performed on the plaintiff minors, Katheleen A. Hart as donee and Margaret H. Hart as donor.

The plaintiffs Peter Hart and Eleanor Hart, each of whom had originally offered a kidney, have requested as parents and natural guardians of the identical twins the transplantation operation of the kidney, but the defendant physicians are unwilling to perform this operation and the defendant hospital refuses the use of its facilities unless this court declares that the parents and/or guardians ad litem of the minors have the right to give their consent to the operation upon the minor twins.

The equity powers of a court must be cautiously and sparingly exercised and only in rare instances should they be exercised. The need must be urgent, the probabilities of success should be most favorable, and the duty must be clear. If it were otherwise, a court of equity, in a case such as this, might assume omnipotent powers; to do so is not the function of the court and must be avoided.

The inherent power of a court of equity to grant the relief sought herein has been decided previously in our American courts. In earlier decisions, the English courts took a broader view of this power, with respect to incompetents. Ex parte Whitbread, 2 Mer. 99, 35 Eng.Rep. 878 (Ch.1816). That case held that a court of equity has the power to make provisions for a needy brother from the estate of an incompetent. This inherent rule was followed in this country in New York; Re Willoughby, 11 Paige 257 (N.Y.Ch.1844); where the court stated that a chancellor has the power to deal with the estate of an incompetent in the same manner as the incompetent if he had his faculties. This rule has been extended to cover not only property matters but also the personal affairs of an incompetent. 27 Am.Jur.2d 592, Equity, § 69. "[A] court of equity has full and complete jurisdiction over the persons of those who labor under any legal disability . . . . The court's action . . . is not limited by any narrow bounds, but it is empowered to stretch forth its arm in whatever direction its aid . . . may be needed. While this indeed is a special exercise of equity jurisdiction, it is beyond question that by virtue thereof the court may pass upon purely personal rights." Ibid. The right to act for an incompetent has been recognized as the "doctrine of substituted judgment" and is broad enough to cover all matters touching on the well-being of legally incapacitated persons. The doctrine has been recognized in American courts since 1844.

This court is not being asked to act where a person is legally incompetent. The matter, however, does involve two minors who do not have the legal capacity to consent. This situation was dealt with in three earlier unreported cases decided in our sister state of Massachusetts. The commonwealth of Massachusetts ruled that a court of equity does have the power to permit the natural parents of minor twins to give their consent to a procedure such as is being contemplated by this court. Masden v. Harrison, No. 68651, Eq.Mass.Sup. Jud.Ct. (June 12, 1957); Hushey v. Harrison, No. 68666, Eq.Mass.Sup. Jud.Ct. (Aug. 30, 1957); Foster v. Harrison, No. 68674, Eq.Mass.Sup. Jud.Ct. (Nov. 20, 1957). Those cases involved minors of the ages of nineteen, fourteen and fourteen. In a similar case, Strunk v. Strunk, 445 S.W.2d 145 (Ky.1969), a court of equity was confronted with whether or not it had the power to permit the natural parent of a twenty-seven-year-old mental incompetent with a mentality of a six-year-old to give her consent to a kidney transplantation operation. The Kentucky case dealt with a transplant from the mental incompetent to his twenty-eight-year-old brother. The court held that a court of equity does have such power, applying also the "doctrine of substituted judgment."

Therefore, this court is of the opinion that it has the power to act in this matter.

The facts of the case as testified to by competent medical witnesses are as follows: Katheleen Hart is a minor of the age of seven years and ten months and is suffering from a hemolytic uremic syndrome. This is a disorder of the kidneys with clots within the small blood vessels. This disease has no known etiology and is prevalent primarily in young children. The diagnosis was confirmed on November 29, 1971, after a kidney biopsy was performed. Hemodialysis treatments were commenced on December 8, 1971, along with other treatment to correct this disorder. On February 1, 1972, her kidney was biopsied for the second time because of the onsent of a malignant type of blood pressure elevation, and this biopsy disclosed a new and more disastrous lesion—malignant hypertension—which could prove fatal. On February 17, 1972, a bilateral nephrectomy was performed with removal of both kidneys to control the situation. As of that date, Katheleen became a patient with fixed uremia with no potential kidney function and required dialysis treatments twice weekly. The prospect of survival is, because of her age, at best questionable. It was medically advised that she not continue this dialysis therapy but rather that a kidney transplantation take place.

The types of kidney transplantations discussed in this matter were a parental homograft—transfer of tissue from one human being to another—and an isograft, that is, a one-egg twin graft from one to another. The parental homograft always presents a serious problem of rejection by the donee. Because the human body rejects any foreign organs, the donee must be placed upon a program of immunosuppressive drugs to combat such rejection. An isograft transplantation, on the other hand, is not presented with the problem of rejection. A one-egg twin carries the same genetic material, and, because of this, rejection is not a factor in the success rate of the graft.

The chance of Katheleen's surviving dialysis therapy for a period of five years was estimated at fifty-fifty, with the possibility of many other complications setting in. The ultimate purpose of dialysis treatment in a child this age is to keep the patient alive until a kidney transplant is found. Because of the many complications involved in a transplantation procedure other than with the minor identical twin as donor, it has been medically advised that an isograft transplantation be recommended.

Since 1966, it is reported in the Ninth Report of the Human Renal Transplant Registry, twelve twin grafts have been performed. All twelve have been successful, as reported by the Registry, at one- and two-year follow-ups. In the identical-twin donations since 1966, grafts are functioning at 100 percent. Before 1966, because of technical matters, the survival rate was about 90 percent. Of all isografts followed since 1966, all are successful. In this type of a graft there is substantially a 100 percent chance that the twins will live out a normal life span—emotionally and physically.

If a parent donates the kidney, the statistics show less success. The average percent of success in that type of transplant has been 70 percent at one year and 65 percent or so over a two-year period. The falloff thereafter runs another 5 to 10 or more percent per year. The long-range survival of a parent transplant runs around 50 to 55 percent over a period of five years and appears to fall off to about 37 percent over a period of seven years.

The side effects of the immunosuppressive drugs in a parental homograft are numerous and include the possibility of bone marrow toxicity, liver damage, and a syndrome called Cushing syndrome—a roundish face, a "buffalo hump" on the back of the neck, and growth retardation. Some less common side effects are a demineralization of the bone mass which will result in the collapsing of bones of the spine; aseptic necrosis of the femoral head of the hip, making a person unable to walk; peptic ulcer disease with bleeding; hairiness; sexual immaturity; and cataracts of the eyes. It has also been reported that two suicides have occurred because of the psychological effect upon young girls resulting from immunosuppressive drugs. An overall percentage of around 70 to 77 percent would be expected to survive two years from a parental graft. It is also possible that 40 to 50 percent of the patients might still be surviving at near ten years with a parental graft.

Of 3000 recorded kidney operations of live donors, there is reported only one death of a donor, and even this death may have been from causes unrelated to the procedure. The short-range risk to a donor is negligible. The operating surgeon testified that the surgical risk is no more than the risk of the anesthesia. The operative procedure would last about two and one-half hours. There would be some minor postoperative pain but no more than in any other surgical procedure. The donor would be hospitalized for about eight days and would be able to resume normal activities in thirty days. Assuming an uneventful recovery, the donor would thereafter be restricted only from violent contact sports. She would be able to engage in all of the normal life activities of an active young girl. Medical testimony indicated that the risk to the donor is such that life insurance actuaries do not rate such individuals higher than those with two kidneys. The only real risk would be trauma to the one remaining kidney, but testimony indicated that such trauma is extremely rare in civilian life.

The tests to be performed on the donor are an intravenous pyelogram and an aortagram. The former would permit the examiner to visualize the structure and anatomy of the kidneys, while the latter would outline the blood vessels that supply the blood to the kidneys. Both tests involve a single needle puncture—one into a vein and one into an artery. There might be a skin graft test performed if necessary to confirm the fact that donor and donee are identical twins. The operation would not be performed if the medical team was not fully satisfied that the donor and the donee are identical twins.

A psychiatrist who examined the donor gave testimony that the donor has a strong identification with her twin sister. He also testified that if the expected successful results are achieved they would be of immense benefit to the donor in that the donor would be better off in a family that was happy than in a family that was distressed and in that it would be a very great loss to the donor if the donee were to die from her illness.

The donor has been informed of the operation and insofar as she may be capable of understanding she desires to donate her kidney so that her sister may return to her. A clergyman was also a witness and his testimony was that the decision by the parents of the donor and donee was morally and ethically sound. The court-appointed guardian ad litem for the donor gave testimony that he conferred with the parents, the physicians, the donor, and other men in the religious profession, and he has consented to the performance of the operation.

The medical testimony given at this hearing clearly indicates that scientifically this type of procedure is a "perfect" transplant.

The court has weighed the testimony of the clergyman who stated that the natural parents are making a morally sound decision. Also, the testimony of the court-appointed guardians ad litem was that they are giving their consent to the procedure. The psychiatric testimony is of limited value only because of the ages of the minors. The testimony of the natural parents was reviewed by this court, and it is apparent that they came to their decision only after many hours of agonizing consideration.

One of the legal problems in this matter presents a balancing of the rights of the natural parents and the rights of minor children— more directly, the rights of the donor child. Because of the unusual circumstances of this case and the fact of great medical progress in this field, it would appear that the natural parents would be able to substitute their consent for that of their minor children after a close, independent and objective investigation of their motivation and reasoning. This has been accomplished in this matter by the participation of a clergyman, the defendant physicians, an attorney guardian ad litem for the donor, the guardian ad litem for the donee, and, indeed, this court itself.

A further question before this court is whether it should abandon the donee to a brief medically complicated life and eventual death or permit the natural parents to take some action based on reason and medical probability in order to keep both children alive. The court will choose the latter course, being of the opinion that the kidney transplant procedure contemplated herein—an isograft—has progressed at this time to the point of being a medically proven fact of life. Testimony was offered that this type of procedure is not clinical experimentation but rather medically accepted therapy.

There is authority in our American jurisdiction that nontherapeutic operations can be legally permitted on a minor as long as the parents or other guardians consent to the procedure. Bonner v. Moran, 75 U.S.App.D.C. 156, 126 F.2d 121 (1941). That case involved skin grafting from a fifteen-year-old boy to his cousin, who was severely burned. The year of the case was 1941, when such skin homografting—transferring tissue from one human being to another—was relatively novel. "[H]ere we have a case of a surgical operation not for the benefit of the person operated on but for another, and also so involved in its technique as to require a mature mind to understand precisely what the donor was offering to give." Id., 123. The court held that the consent of the parent was necessary.

In Strunk v. Strunk, 445 S.W.2d 145 (Ky.1969), the adult donor was a legal incompetent. The court in the commonwealth of Kentucky authorized the parent to give her consent. The incompetent had the mental capacity of a six-year-old. The court further held that the saving of the life of the incompetent's brother would be of benefit to the donor. In the instant case, it has been stated that the donor would enjoy a better future life if her ailing twin sister were kept alive. The difference between the cases is subtle. The donor here is almost eight years old. In the *Strunk* case, the donor was an adult with the mentality of a six-year-old. The risks to the donee in the *Strunk* case were more than what are presented here, the procedure there being a related homograft as compared to an isograft in this case, as discussed earlier in this opinion. The accomplished results in that matter and in this matter are identical.

Thus, also, in the Massachusetts cases discussed above, where the doctrine of "grave emotional impact" to the donors was first used, the courts of that state permitted the procedures.

This court is confronted with a combination of the *Strunk* case and the Massachusetts cases in that the procedures in the latter involved minor identical twins and in the former a legally incompetent adult with the mental capacity of an infant. In the case at bar we have an identical twin donor almost eight years old. Justice was accomplished in all of the aforementioned cases. Justice will be accomplished in this case.

This court can and will make a determination of this matter, using the doctrines of law as stated in the *Strunk* case, in the *Bonner* case, and in the Massachusetts cases.

The court understands that the operation on the donee is a necessity for her continued life; that there are negligible risks involved to both donor and donee; that to subject the donee to a parental homograft may be cruel and inhuman because of the possible side effects of the immunosuppressive drugs; that the prognosis for good health and long life to both children is excellent; that there is no known opposition to having the operations performed; that it will be most beneficial to the donee; and that it will be of some benefit to the donor. To prohibit the natural parents and the guardians ad litem of the minor children the right to give their consent under these circumstances, where there is supervision by this court and other persons in examining their judgment, would be most unjust, inequitable and injudicious. Therefore, natural parents of a minor should have the right to give their consent to an isograft kidney transplantation procedure when their motivation and reasoning are favorably reviewed by a community representation which includes a court of equity.

It is the judgment of this court that Eleanor Hart and Peter Hart have the right, under the particular facts and circumstances of this matter, to give their consent to the operations on both minor children and to give their consent to the defendant physicians to conduct the further medical tests that the defendants deem necessary prior to the performing of the operations, provided the defendant physicians medically establish the children to be identical twins and a report of their findings is filed with this court.

Judgment accordingly.

NOTE

A Louisiana court reached a different conclusion on a similar set of facts in In re Richardson, 284 So.2d 185 (La.App.1973). Parents wanted the court to authorize a kidney transplant from their retarded son to their normal daughter, who needed either a new kidney or renal dialysis to stay alive. Medical indications at the time favored use of the sibling's kidney to reduce the risk of rejection by the daughter's body. The court held that neither the parents nor the court could authorize the kidney donation under such circumstances, noting that the transplant from the brother was not immediately necessary to save his sister's life. Some reliance was placed on a Louisiana law prohibiting donation of a minor's property unless it is in the minor's best interest. The court rejected as speculative the argument that because the sister could provide future care for her retarded brother the donation would be in his best interest. In contrast, a Kentucky court in Strunk v. Strunk, 445 S.W.2d 145 (Ky.1969), authorized a kidney transplant from a retarded adult to his brother who was dying of a fatal kidney disease, finding that the donor's well-being "would be jeopardized more severely by the loss of his brother than by removal of a kidney." Id. at 446.

Does the holding in Hart v. Brown require judicial approval in any similar case which might arise in Connecticut in the future? Does it require parents who want to donate tissue from one of their children to another to comply with the same sort of "town meeting" procedure in order to determine what is acceptable to the community?

STUMP v. SPARKMAN

Supreme Court of the United States, 1978.
435 U.S. 349, 98 S.Ct. 1099, 55 L.Ed.2d 331.

MR. JUSTICE WHITE delivered the opinion of the Court.

. . . .

On July 9, 1971, Ora Spitler McFarlin, the mother of respondent Linda Kay Spitler Sparkman, presented to Judge Harold D. Stump of the Circuit Court of DeKalb County, Ind., a document captioned "Petition To Have Tubal Ligation Performed On Minor and Indemnity Agreement." The document had been drafted by her attorney, a petitioner here. In this petition Mrs. McFarlin stated under oath that her daughter was 15 years of age and was "somewhat retarded," although she attended public school and had been promoted each year with her class. The petition further stated that Linda had been associating with "older youth or young men" and had stayed out overnight with them on several occasions. As a result of this behavior and Linda's mental capabilities, it was stated that it would be in the daughter's best interest if she underwent a tubal ligation in order "to prevent unfortunate circumstances . . . ." In the same document Mrs. McFarlin also undertook to indemnify and hold harmless Dr. John Hines, who was to perform the operation, and the DeKalb Memorial Hospital, where the operation was to take place, against all causes of action that might arise as a result of the performance of the tubal ligation.

The petition was approved by Judge Stump on the same day. He affixed his signature as "Judge, DeKalb Circuit Court," to the statement that he did "hereby approve the above Petition by affidavit form on behalf of Ora Spitler McFarlin, to have Tubal Ligation performed upon her minor daughter, Linda Spitler, subject to said Ora Spitler McFarlin covenanting and agreeing to indemnify and keep indemnified Dr. John Hines and the DeKalb Memorial Hospital from any matters or causes of action arising therefrom."

On July 15, 1971, Linda Spitler entered the DeKalb Memorial Hospital, having been told that she was to have her appendix removed. The following day a tubal ligation was performed upon her. She was released several days later, unaware of the true nature of her surgery.

Approximately two years after the operation, Linda Spitler was married to respondent Leo Sparkman. Her inability to become pregnant led her to discover that she had been sterilized during the 1971 operation. As a result of this revelation, the Sparkmans filed suit in the United States District Court for the Northern District of Indiana against Mrs. McFarlin, her attorney, Judge Stump, the doctors who had performed and assisted in the tubal ligation, and the DeKalb Memorial Hospital. Respondents sought damages for the alleged violation of Linda Sparkman's constitutional rights; also asserted were pendent state claims for assault and battery, medical malpractice, and loss of potential fatherhood.

Ruling upon the defendants' various motions to dismiss the complaint, the District Court concluded that each of the constitutional claims asserted by respondents required a showing of state action and that the only state action alleged in the complaint was the approval by Judge Stump, acting as Circuit Court Judge, of the petition presented to him by Mrs. McFarlin. The Sparkmans sought to hold the private defendants liable on a theory that they had conspired with Judge Stump to bring about the allegedly unconstitutional acts. The District Court, however, held that no federal action would lie against any of the defendants because Judge Stump, the only state agent, was absolutely immune from suit under the doctrine of judicial immunity. . . .

. . .

II

The governing principle of law is well established and is not questioned by the parties. As early as 1872, the Court recognized that it was "a general principle of the highest importance to the proper administration of justice that a judicial officer, in exercising the authority vested in him, [should] be free to act upon his own convictions, without apprehension of personal consequences to himself." *Bradley v. Fisher* [13 Wall. 335, 347 (1872)]. For that reason the Court held that "judges of courts of superior or general jurisdiction are not liable to civil actions for their judicial acts, even when such acts are in excess of their jurisdiction, and are alleged to have been done maliciously or corruptly." 13 Wall., at 351. Later we held that this doctrine of judicial immunity was applicable in suits under § 1 of the Civil Rights Act of 1871, 42 U.S.C. § 1983, for the legislative record gave no indication that Congress intended to abolish this long-established principle. *Pierson v. Ray*, 386 U.S. 547, 87 S.Ct. 1213, 18 L.Ed. 2d 288 (1967).

The Court of Appeals correctly recognized that the necessary inquiry in determining whether a defendant judge is immune from suit is whether at the time he took the challenged action he had jurisdiction over the subject matter before him. Because "some of the most difficult and embarrassing questions which a judicial officer is called upon to consider and determine relate to his jurisdiction . . . ," *Bradley*, supra, at 352, the scope of the judge's jurisdiction must be construed broadly where the issue is the immunity of the judge. A judge will not be deprived of immunity because the action he took was in error, was done maliciously, or was in excess of his authority; rather, he will be subject to liability only when he has acted in the "clear absence of all jurisdiction." [7] 13 Wall., at 351.

7. In *Bradley*, the Court illustrated the distinction between lack of jurisdiction and excess of jurisdiction with the following examples: if a probate judge,

We cannot agree that there was a "clear absence of all jurisdiction" in the DeKalb County Circuit Court to consider the petition presented by Mrs. McFarlin. As an Indiana Circuit Court Judge, Judge Stump had "original exclusive jurisdiction in all cases at law and in equity whatsoever . . .," jurisdiction over the settlement of estates and over guardianships, appellate jurisdiction as conferred by law, and jurisdiction over "all other causes, matters and proceedings where exclusive jurisdiction thereof is not conferred by law upon some other court, board or officer." Ind.Code § 33–4–4–3 (1975). This is indeed a broad jurisdictional grant; yet the Court of Appeals concluded that Judge Stump did not have jurisdiction over the petition authorizing Linda Sparkman's sterilization.

In so doing, the Court of Appeals noted that the Indiana statutes provided for the sterilization of institutionalized persons under certain circumstances, see Ind.Code §§ 16–13–13–1 through 16–13–13–4 (1973), but otherwise contained no express authority for judicial approval of tubal ligations. It is true that the statutory grant of general jurisdiction to the Indiana circuit courts does not itemize types of cases those courts may hear and hence does not expressly mention sterilization petitions presented by the parents of a minor. But in our view, it is more significant that there was no Indiana statute and no case law in 1971 prohibiting a circuit court, a court of general jurisdiction, from considering a petition of the type presented to Judge Stump. The statutory authority for the sterilization of institutionalized persons in the custody of the State does not warrant the inference that a court of general jurisdiction has no power to act on a petition for sterilization of a minor in the custody of her parents, particularly where the parents have authority under the Indiana statutes to "consent to and contract for medical or hospital care or treatment of [the minor] including surgery." Ind.Code § 16–8–4–2 (1973). The District Court concluded that Judge Stump had jurisdiction under § 33–4–4–3 to entertain and act upon Mrs. McFarlin's petition. We agree with the District Court, it appearing that neither by statute nor by case law has the broad jurisdiction granted to the circuit courts of Indiana been circumscribed to foreclose consideration of a petition for authorization of a minor's sterilization.

The Court of Appeals also concluded that support for Judge Stump's actions could not be found in the common law of Indiana, relying in particular on the Indiana Court of Appeals' intervening decision in A. L. v. G. R. H., 163 Ind.App. 636, 325 N.E.2d 501 (1975). In that case the Indiana court held that a parent does not have a common-law right to have a minor child sterilized, even though the parent might "sincerely believe the child's adulthood would benefit

with jurisdiction over only wills and estates, should try a criminal case, he would be acting in the clear absence of jurisdiction and would not be immune from liability for his action; on the other hand, if a judge of a criminal court should convict a defendant of a nonexistent crime, he would merely be acting in excess of his jurisdiction and would be immune. Id., at 352.

therefrom." Id., at 638, 325 N.E.2d, at 502. The opinion, however, speaks only of the rights of the parents to consent to the sterilization of their child and does not question the *jurisdiction* of a circuit judge who is presented with such a petition from a parent. Although under that case a circuit judge would err as a matter of law if he were to approve a parent's petition seeking the sterilization of a child, the opinion in A. L. v. G. R. H. does not indicate that a circuit judge is without jurisdiction to entertain the petition. Indeed, the clear implication of the opinion is that, when presented with such a petition, the circuit judge should deny it on its merits rather than dismiss it for lack of jurisdiction.

Perhaps realizing the broad scope of Judge Stump's jurisdiction, the Court of Appeals stated that, even if the action taken by him was not foreclosed under the Indiana statutory scheme, it would still be "an illegitimate exercise of his common law power because of his failure to comply with elementary principles of procedural due process." This misconceives the doctrine of judicial immunity. A judge is absolutely immune from liability for his judicial acts even if his exercise of authority is flawed by the commission of grave procedural errors.

. . .

. . . Because the court over which Judge Stump presides is one of general jurisdiction, neither the procedural errors he may have committed nor the lack of a specific statute authorizing his approval of the petition in question rendered him liable in damages for the consequences of his actions.

The respondents argue that even if Judge Stump had jurisdiction to consider the petition presented to him by Mrs. McFarlin, he is still not entitled to judicial immunity because his approval of the petition did not constitute a "judicial" act. It is only for acts performed in his "judicial" capacity that a judge is absolutely immune, they say. We do not disagree with this statement of the law, but we cannot characterize the approval of the petition as a nonjudicial act.

. . . [Respondents] argue that Judge Stump's approval of the petition was not a judicial act because the petition was not given a docket number, was not placed on file with the clerk's office, and was approved in an *ex parte* proceeding without notice to the minor, without a hearing, and without the appointment of a guardian *ad litem*.

. . .

The relevant cases demonstrate that the factors determining whether an act by a judge is a "judicial" one relate to the nature of the act itself, i.e., whether it is a function normally performed by a judge, and to the expectations of the parties, i.e., whether they dealt with the judge in his judicial capacity. Here, both factors indicate that Judge Stump's approval of the sterilization petition was a judicial act. State judges with general jurisdiction not infrequently are called upon in their official capacity to approve petitions relating to the affairs of minors, as for example, a petition to settle a minor's claim. Furthermore, as even respondents have admitted, at the time he approved the petition presented to him by Mrs. McFarlin, Judge Stump was "acting as a county circuit court judge." See supra, at 1106. We may infer from the record that it was only because Judge Stump served in that position that Mrs. McFarlin, on the advice of counsel, submitted the petition to him for his approval. Because Judge Stump performed the type of act normally performed only by judges and because he did so in his capacity as a Circuit Court Judge, we find no merit to respondents' argument that the informality with which he proceeded rendered his action nonjudicial and deprived him of his absolute immunity.

Both the Court of Appeals and the respondents seem to suggest that, because of the tragic consequences of Judge Stump's actions, he should not be immune. For example, the Court of Appeals noted that "[t]here are actions of purported judicial character that a judge, even when exercising general jurisdiction, is not empowered to take," 552 F.2d, at 176, and respondents argue that Judge Stump's action was "so unfair" and "so totally devoid of judicial concern for the interests and well-being of the young girl involved" as to disqualify it as a judicial act. Disagreement with the action taken by the judge, however, does not justify depriving that judge of his immunity. Despite the unfairness to litigants that sometimes results, the doctrine of judicial immunity is thought to be in the best interests of "the proper administration of justice . . . [, for it allows] a judicial officer, in exercising the authority vested in him [to] be free to act upon his own convictions, without apprehension of personal consequences to himself." Bradley v. Fisher, 13 Wall., at 347. The fact that the issue before the judge is a controversial one is all the more reason that he should be able to act without fear of suit. . . .

The Indiana law vested in Judge Stump the power to entertain and act upon the petition for sterilization. He is, therefore, under the controlling cases, immune from damages liability even if his approval of the petition was in error. Accordingly, the judgment of the Court of Appeals is reversed, and the case is remanded for further proceedings consistent with this opinion.[13]

It is so ordered.

MR. JUSTICE BRENNAN took no part in the consideration or decision of this case.

[The dissenting opinion of MR. JUSTICE STEWART, with whom MR. JUSTICE MARSHALL and MR. JUSTICE POWELL join, is omitted.]

---

13. The issue is not presented and we do not decide whether the District Court correctly concluded that the federal claims against the other defendants were required to be dismissed if Judge Stump, the only state agent, was found to be absolutely immune. Compare Kermit Constr. Corp. v. Banco Credito y Ahorro Ponceno, 547 F.2d 1 (CA1 1976), with Guedry v. Ford, 431 F.2d 660 (CA5 1970).

NOTE

In In re A.W., ___ Colo. ___, 637 P.2d 366 (1981), the Supreme Court of Colorado dealt with the question whether to permit sterilization of a mentally retarded minor female on the petition of her parents. The court concluded that the state's statutes concerning sterilization of mentally retarded persons did not address the particular issue of sterilization of minors. They added that allowing parents to substitute their decision and consent for the incompetent was not an adequate solution, noting the history of abuse "which indicates that parents, at least in this limited context, cannot be presumed to have an identity of interest with their children." Id. at 370. Deciding that it is within the inherent authority of a district court to entertain a petition for sterilization, the court determined in the absence of any legislative pronouncement to promulgate standards for determining when such a procedure should be authorized:

Procedural protection requires a court order for sterilization of mentally retarded minors. See Wyatt v. Aderholt, 368 F.Supp. 1382 (D.C.Ala. 1974). Neither the individual mentally retarded person nor that person's parent, guardian or custodian may consent to sterilization unless ordered by the court. Upon petition to the court, the court shall appoint a guardian ad litem who will represent the interests of the mentally retarded person at a full judicial hearing. To ensure that adequate evidence will be presented at the hearing, the court shall appoint one or more experts in the field of mental retardation to examine the mentally retarded person and to testify at the hearing about the person's mental and physical condition and any other relevant factors.

As to the substance of the matters to be decided, the district court shall make the following preliminary determinations. First, while the mentally retarded person need not testify or be present at the proceedings if the person's presence would serve no useful purpose, the trial judge should talk with the person and observe the person's physical and mental condition. The wishes of the person, although not conclusive, are relevant, and a strong indication that the person does not wish to be sterilized must weigh heavily against authorizing the procedure. Second, the district court must determine that the person's capacity to make a decision about sterilization is unlikely to improve in the future. Special care must be taken to allow for possible further development of mental capacity. We agree with the Supreme Court of Washington that the youth of a minor retarded person "may make it difficult or impossible to prove by clear, cogent and convincing evidence that he or she will *never* be capable of making an informed judgment about sterilization or of caring for a child." Matter of Guardianship of Hayes, 608 P.2d at 641. Third, the person for whom sterilization is requested must be proven capable of reproduction.

Once the district court determines preliminary matters, it must find by clear and convincing evidence that the sterilization is medically essential. A sterilization is medically essential if clearly necessary, in the opinion of experts, to preserve the life or physical or mental health of the mentally retarded person. The term "medically essential" is reasonably precise and provides protection from abuses prevalent in this area in the past. The term also avoids confusion as to whose interests are to be considered.

It is not the welfare of society, or the convenience or peace of mind of parents or guardians that these standards are intended to protect. The purpose of the standards is to protect the health of the minor retarded person, and to prevent that person's fundamental procreative rights from being abridged. In some circumstances, the possibility of pregnancy, if supported by sufficient evidence that it would threaten the physical or mental health of the person and that no less intrusive means of birth control would prove safe and effective, could justify granting a petition for sterilization as medically essential.

. . . [W]e note that the record before us contains no evidence at all on a number of crucial issues, including the degree of A.W.'s retardation and her capacity to mature and progress intellectually. On remand, testimony must be developed on these and all other relevant issues before a clear and convincing case for sterilization can be established.

For other recent cases deciding that courts have jurisdiction to permit sterilization of incompetents, even in the absence of specific statutory authority, see In re C.D.M., 627 P.2d 607 (Alaska 1981); In re Grady, 85 N.J. 235, 426 A.2d 467 (1981); In re Guardianship of Hayes, 93 Wn.2d 228, 608 P.2d 635 (1980); In re Guardianship of Eberhardy, 102 Wis.2d 539, 307 N.W.2d 881 (1981). For a contrary view, see Guardianship of Tulley, 83 Cal. App.3d 698, 146 Cal.Rptr. 266 (1978), cert. denied 440 U.S. 967.

H. L. v. MATHESON

Supreme Court of the United States, 1981.
450 U.S. 398, 101 S.Ct. 1164, 67 L.Ed.2d 388.

(For the text of the opinion, see p. 183, supra.)

WADLINGTON, MINORS AND HEALTH CARE: THE AGE OF MEDICAL CONSENT

11 Osgoode Hall L.J. 115, 117–120 (1973).*

. . .

The "Mature Minor" Rule: A Creature of Necessity If Not Emergency

Judicial response to the harshness of a requirement of parental consent for all medical care to minors has come largely through development of what is widely labeled the "mature minor" rule. The effect of this rule is to allow a subjective appraisal of at least some cases in which physicians proceed with non-emergency medical care for minors with only the patient's consent. Two recent cases and two older ones provide good illustrations of the circumstances under which judges have been willing to invoke it.

In Johnston v. Wellesley Hospital,[11] no parental consent had been obtained by a dermatologist for non-emergency treatment of a 20 year old male to remove facial marks caused by acne. The claimant

---

* Copyright 1973, Osgoode Hall Law Journal. Reprinted with permission.   11. (1970), 17 D.L.R. (3d) 139.

asserted both negligence and invasion of his body without appropriate consent. As to the latter claim, Addy, J., of the Ontario High Court, pointed out that:

> Although the common law imposes very strict limitations on the capacity of persons under 21 years of age to hold, or rather to divest themselves of, property, or to enter into contracts concerning matters other than necessities, it would be ridiculous in this day and age, where the voting age is being reduced generally to 18 years, to state that a person of 20 years of age, who is obviously intelligent and as fully capable of understanding the possible consequences of a medical or surgical procedure as an adult, would, at law, be incapable of consenting thereto.[12]

In short, the court was willing to look at the capacity of the particular "infant" under the given circumstances, here an elective operation performed on one only months away from majority.

In Younts v. St. Francis Hospital and School of Nursing, Inc.,[13] the Supreme Court of Kansas was asked to hold that taking a skin graft from the forearm of a 17-year-old girl to repair her injured finger was a battery because the surgeon had not first secured parental consent. The girl's injury had occurred when her hand was caught accidentally in the door of the hospital room in which her mother had been placed following major surgery. The mother, still semi-conscious from a general anesthetic, was in no condition to consent. The girl's father, from whom the mother was divorced, lived in another city 200 miles away and his address was unknown and not immediately available. The daughter was taken to the hospital's emergency room where a repair operation and skin graft was effected.

Despite what apparently was a successful operation from a medical standpoint, the daughter later sued the hospital alleging that taking a pinch graft from her forearm was tortious because no parental consent had been obtained.[14] To some it might seem that the court could have denied recovery under the "emergency" exception. In any event, they elected not to do so, but held that given the particular circumstances this 17 year old "was mature enough to understand the nature and consequences and to knowingly consent to the beneficial surgical procedure made necessary by the accident." The court clearly took into consideration both the non-availability of either parent and the fact that before the skin graft was effected the treating surgeon had discussed the proposed procedure with the girl's regular family physician and had obtained his approval (even though he had no more legal authority to consent for the child than did the surgeon himself).

12. Id., at 144.

13. Younts v. St. Francis Hospital & School of Nursing, Inc., supra, note 3.

14. The daughter also alleged that a nurse employed by the hospital had negligently closed the door on her finger, causing the injury in the first place. This, of course, had nothing to do with the question of consent.

In dismissing the plaintiff's allegation of battery in the *Younts* case, the Kansas court cited with approval an earlier Ohio decision in which an 18-year-old girl had responded to a telephone directory advertisement which urged readers to reshape their noses through plastic surgery. At an initial interview with an agent of the defendant doctor the plaintiff stated that she had no money, but she was assured that a loan could be obtained for her to finance the cosmetic procedure. A date for the operation then was set and she returned to the doctor's office. The girl's testimony, which made the operation sound somewhat like an encounter with a mad acupuncturist, was met with the doctor's own statement that she had told him that she was 21 years of age and that following the operation she had called at his office on several occasions for follow-up treatment. An intermediate court reversed the judgment of a trial court which had awarded damages for assault and battery. The reversal was upheld on appeal to the Ohio Supreme Court, which affirmed *Per Curiam* but prepared an official syllabus.[15] Two concurring opinions also were written and variously joined in by members of the court, evidencing a split in views on the issue of the age of consent; an opinion joined in by four of the seven members, however, stressed that the trial court had erred "in charging that a minor of 18 could not consent to what the jury from the evidence might have determined was only a *simple operation*."[16] This view also was translated into the officially prepared syllabus.

A somewhat different problem was presented to the United States Court of Appeals for the District of Columbia in Bonner v. Moran,[17] the second of our "older" cases. The plaintiff male, at age fifteen, had been hospitalized for some two months and was permanently disfigured through serving as a tissue donor for a severely burned cousin.

The request for the boy's participation as a donor had come from an aunt of both children. At the time of the request, the boy's mother was ill and she was not advised of the proposed medical procedure. After the boy appeared at the hospital for a blood typing procedure he was admitted for the first of a series of operations in which "a tube of flesh was cut and formed from his arm pit to his waist line"[18] and one end of the tube was attached to his cousin. Unfortunately, the procedure turned out to be a failure. The boy brought suit to recover for his disfigurement but the trial court refused to instruct the jury that consent of both the boy and his mother was necessary, instead telling them that "if they believed that [the plaintiff] himself was capable of appreciating and did appreciate the nature and consequences of the operation and actually consented, or by his conduct

15. Lacey v. Laird (1956), 166 Ohio St. 12, 139 N.E.2d 25 (Sup.Ct.). The plaintiff had also alleged malpractice (negligence) but lost on this count in a directed verdict.

16. (1956), 166 Ohio St. 12 at 26, 139 N.E.2d 25 at 34. [emphasis by the court].

17. (1941), 126 F.2d 121 (D.C.Cir.).

18. Id.

implicitly consented, their verdict must be for the defendant."[19] The appellate court held this charge to be incorrect and reversed and remanded the case with the opinion that consent of the parent should have been considered necessary. The appeals court specifically noted its concern over the fact that the boy underwent the surgical operation for the benefit of another rather than for his own health needs.[20]

The preceding decisions, along with some half a dozen others, allow us to draw certain inferences about the type of situation in which courts which recognize the "mature minor" rule will be likely to apply it and dispense with the requirement of parental consent. The cases in which the rule has been applied generally have had the following factors in common:

(1) The treatment was undertaken for the benefit of the minor rather than a third party.

(2) The particular minor was near majority (or at least in the range of 15 years of age upward), and was considered to have sufficient mental capacity to understand fully the nature and importance of the medical steps proposed.

(3) The medical procedures could be characterized by the courts as something less than "major" or "serious" in nature.

In a good number of the cases, it also seemed that the situation at least bordered on one in which the emergency doctrine could have been invoked, and it may be of some significance that the allegation of a battery frequently accompanied a specific charge of negligence. As to the latter point, one may question whether suit would have been brought in the first place simply for the "technical" trespass unless a negligence action also were being filed.

WHEN SHOULD THE CHILD'S CONSENT BE SUFFICIENT?

Judicial development of the mature minor rule may be attributed largely to concern about imposing liability in instances where most persons would consider it unrealistic, if not unconscionable. But the mature minor doctrine does not abrogate the requirement that consent to medical treatment must be obtained from someone competent to give it. Consent for treatment of children generally must be obtained from their parents. Should children be able to consent to medical care at some point before reaching majority? Legislatures in a great many states have answered this question affirmatively by adopting statutes giving minors authority to consent to all treatment after a certain age, or in specifically enumerated instances at any age or at some designated point before reaching majority. From a policy

19. Id., at 122.

20. Id., at 123. Although they acknowledged that the question was not before them, the court pointed out that it was possible that the mother could have ratified the treatment by her conduct after learning of it.

standpoint, some deem the latter statutes troublesome because they single out specific concerns such as birth control, pregnancy, or substance abuse as the areas where children can give consent. This is no doubt a response to expediency more than anything else. The thought is that if children cannot secure contraceptives or talk to a professional about drug or alcohol problems without first discussing the matter with their parents, then they may not secure any assistance. Yet these can be matters of particular sensitivity in our troubled family life these days.

Such concerns have been voiced recently at the federal level, at least with regard to family planning. The Department of Health and Human Services, for example, has proposed rules that would require federally supported family planning projects to notify parents of unemancipated minors who seek family planning services and are provided with prescription drugs or devices. See 47 Fed.Reg. 7699 (1982) (to be codified at 42 C.F.R. § 59.5).

The statutes that follow, along with the Juvenile Justice Standards, illustrate the many problems associated with legislation expanding the authority of minors to consent. Of particular concern is the question of privacy. Is it realistic to allow minors to consent and yet require physicians to reveal the medical information to parents? Should children be able to block any information going to parents and, if so, should the parents be responsible for the financial obligations associated with such treatment? Physicians often regard themselves as caught in the middle of this struggle to define the borders of children's autonomy and parental rights.

Another problem too seldom recognized is that merely lowering the age of consent for medical treatment does not necessarily solve the problem of obtaining informed consent. Under this tort doctrine the consent obtained by a physician for any invasive procedure must be "informed"—that is, the patient must be told enough about the procedure and the alternatives to make a reasoned choice. Failure to comply with such a duty of disclosure can lead to a negligence action if it can be determined that a properly informed patient would not have consented. Should the standard for disclosure vary with the age and capacity of a child?

What limits would you impose in a consent statute for minors with regard to age, parental disclosure, or limitation as to specific illnesses, conditions, or treatments?

Recall the discussion of waiver of constitutional rights by juveniles in delinquency proceedings in Chapter Four. Should the same legal standards apply to informed consent by minors in the medical context as govern juvenile waivers of constitutional rights in the *Miranda* setting, for example? Whatever your answer to that question, how should both informed consent and waiver of rights by minors be squared with the traditional legal disabilities presented in Chapter One?

NOTE

Should a minor child of any age be permitted to refuse treatment if death will result from implementing such a decision? Schowalter, Fernholt and Mann, in The Adolescent Patient's Decision to Die, 51 Pediatrics 97 (1973), relate the case of a 16-year-old girl who was permitted to withdraw from a program of hemodialysis necessary to keep her alive after rejection of a kidney transplant.

For additional discussion of the problems of determining the appropriate decision makers for children's medical care, see Bennett, Allocation of Child Medical Care Decisionmaking Authority: A Suggested Interest Analysis, 62 Va.L.Rev. 285 (1976); A. R. Holder, Legal Issues in Adolescent and Pediatric Medicine (1977).

MASS. GEN. LAWS ANN., ch. 112

§ 12E. Drug dependent minors; consent to medical care; liability for payment; records

A minor twelve years of age or older who is found to be drug dependent by two or more physicians may give his consent to the furnishing of hospital and medical care related to the diagnosis or treatment of such drug dependency. Such consent shall not be subject to disaffirmance because of minority. The consent of the parent or legal guardian of such minor shall not be necessary to authorize hospital and medical care related to such drug dependency and, notwithstanding any provision of section fifty-four of chapter one hundred and twenty-three to the contrary, such parent or legal guardian shall not be liable for the payment of any care rendered pursuant to this section. Records shall be kept of such care. The provisions of this section shall not apply to methadone maintenance therapy.

§ 12F. Emergency treatment of minors; absence of consent; immunity of physicians, dentists, clinics, and hospitals; confidential records

No physician, dentist or hospital shall be held liable for damages for failure to obtain consent of a parent, legal guardian, or other person having custody or control of a minor child, or of the spouse of a patient, to emergency examination and treatment, including blood transfusions, when delay in treatment will endanger the life, limb, or mental well-being of the patient.

Any minor may give consent to his medical or dental care at the time such care is sought if (*i*) he is married, widowed, divorced; or (*ii*) he is the parent of a child, in which case he may also give consent to medical or dental care of the child; or (*iii*) he is a member of any of the armed forces; or (*iv*) she is pregnant or believes herself to be pregnant; or (*v*) he is living separate and apart from his parent or legal guardian, and is managing his own financial affairs; or (*vi*) he reasonably believes himself to be suffering from or to have come in contact with any disease defined as dangerous to the public health pursuant to section six of chapter one hundred and eleven; provided, however, that such minor may only consent to care which relates to the diagnosis or treatment of such disease.

Consent shall not be granted under subparagraphs (*ii*) through (*vi*), inclusive, for abortion or sterilization.

Consent given under this section shall not be subject to later disaffirmance because of minority. The consent of the parent or legal guardian shall not be required to authorize such care and, notwithstanding any other provisions of law, such parent or legal guardian shall not be liable for the payment for any care rendered pursuant to this section unless such parent or legal guardian has expressly agreed to pay for such care.

No physician or dentist, nor any hospital, clinic or infirmary shall be liable, civilly and criminally, for not obtaining the consent of the parent or legal guardian to render medical or dental care to a minor, if, at the time such care was rendered, such person or facility: (*i*) relied in good faith upon the representations of such minor that he is legally able to consent to such treatment under this section; or (*ii*) relied in good faith upon the representations of such minor that he is over eighteen years of age.

All information and records kept in connection with the medical or dental care of a minor who consents thereto in accordance with this section shall be confidential between the minor and the physician or dentist, and shall not be released except upon the written consent of the minor or a proper judicial order. When the physician or dentist attending a minor reasonably believes the condition of said minor to be so serious that his life or limb is endangered, the physician or dentist shall notify the parents, legal guardian or foster parents of said condition and shall inform the minor of said notification.

NEW YORK PUBLIC HEALTH LAW

§ 2504. Enabling certain persons to consent for certain medical, dental, health and hospital services

1. Any person who is eighteen years of age or older, or is the parent of a child or has married, may give effective consent for medical, dental, health and hospital services for himself or herself, and the consent of no other person shall be necessary.

2. Any person who has been married or who has borne a child may give effective consent for medical, dental, health and hospital services for his or her child.

3. Medical, dental, health and hospital services may be rendered to persons of any age without the consent of a parent or legal guardian when, in the physician's judgment an emergency exists and the

person is in immediate need of medical attention and an attempt to secure consent would result in delay of treatment which would increase the risk to the person's life or health.

4.   Anyone who acts in good faith based on the representation by a person that he is eligible to consent pursuant to the terms of this section shall be deemed to have received effective consent.

JUVENILE JUSTICE STANDARDS PROJECT, STANDARDS RELATING TO RIGHTS OF MINORS*

PART IV: MEDICAL CARE

4.1   Prior parental consent

A.   No medical procedures, services, or treatment should be provided to a minor without prior parental consent, except as specified in Standards 4.4–4.9.

B.   Circumstances where parents refuse to consent to treatment are governed by the *Abuse and Neglect* volume.

4.2   Notification of treatment

A.   Where prior parental consent is not required to provide medical services or treatment to a minor, the provider should promptly notify the parent or responsible custodian of such treatment and obtain his or her consent to further treatment, except as hereinafter specified.

B.   Where the medical services provided are for the treatment of chemical dependency, Standard 4.7, or venereal disease, contraception, and pregnancy, Standard 4.8, the physician should first seek and obtain the minor's permission to notify the parent of such treatments.

1.   If the minor-patient objects to notification of the parent, the physician should not notify the parent that treatment was or is being provided unless he or she concludes that failing to inform the parent could seriously jeopardize the health of the minor, taking into consideration:

a.   the impact that such notification could have on the course of treatment;

b.   the medical considerations which require such notification;

c.   the nature, basis, and strength of the minor's objections;

d.   the extent to which parental involvement in the course of treatment is required or desirable.

2.   A physician who concludes that notification of the parent is medically required should:

a.   indicate the medical justifications in the minor-patient's file; and

b.   inform the parent only after making all reasonable efforts to persuade the minor to consent to notification of the parent.

C.   Where the medical services provided are for the treatment of a mental or emotional disorder pursuant to Standard 4.9, after three sessions the provider should notify the parent of such treatment and obtain his or her consent to further treatment.

.   .   .

4.4   Emancipated minor

A.   An emancipated minor who is living separate and apart from his or her parent and who is managing his or her own financial affairs may consent to medical treatment on the same terms and conditions as an adult.   Accordingly, parental consent should not be required, nor should there be subsequent notification of the parent, or financial liability.

1.   If a physician treats a minor who is not actually emancipated, it should be a defense to a suit basing liability on lack of parental consent, that he or she relied in good faith on the minor's representations of emancipation.

4.5   Emergency treatment

A.   Under emergency circumstances, a minor may receive medical services or treatment without prior parental consent.

1.   Emergency circumstances exist when delaying treatment to first secure parental consent would endanger the life or health of the minor.

2.   It should be a defense to an action basing liability on lack of parental consent, that the medical services were provided under emergency circumstances.

B.   Where medical services or treatment are provided under emergency circumstances, the parent should be notified as promptly as possible, and his or her consent should be obtained for further treatment.

C.   A parent should be financially liable to persons providing emergency medical treatment.

D.   Where the emergency medical services are for treatment of chemical dependency (Standard 4.7); venereal disease, contraception, or pregnancy (Standard 4.8); or mental or emotional disorder (Standard 4.9), questions of notification of the parent and financial liability are governed by those provisions and Standards 4.2 B., 4.2 C., and 4.3.

4.6 Mature minor

A.   A minor of [sixteen] or older who has sufficient capacity to understand the nature and consequences of a proposed medical treatment for his or her benefit may consent to that treatment on the same terms and conditions as an adult.

B.   The treating physician should notify the minor's parent of any medical treatment provided under this standard, subject to the provisions of Standard 4.2 B.

4.7 Chemical dependency

A.   A minor of any age may consent to medical services, treatment, or therapy for problems or conditions related to alcohol or drug abuse or addiction.

B.   If the minor objects to notification of the parent, the person or agency providing treatment under this standard should notify the parent of such treatment only if he or she concludes that failing to inform the parent would seriously jeopardize the health of the minor, and complies with the provisions of Standard 4.2.

4.8 Venereal disease, contraception, and pregnancy

A.   A minor of any age may consent to medical services, therapy, or counseling for:

    1.   treatment of venereal disease;

    2.   family planning, contraception, or birth control other than a procedure which results in sterilization; or

    3.   treatment related to pregnancy, including abortion.

B.   If the minor objects to notification of the parent, the person or agency providing treatment under this standard should notify the parent of such treatment only if he or she concludes that failing to inform the parent would seriously jeopardize the health of the minor, and complies with the provisions of Standard 4.2.

4.9 Mental or emotional disorder

A.   A minor of fourteen or older who has or professes to suffer from a mental or emotional disorder may consent to three sessions with a psychotherapist or counselor for diagnosis and consultation.

B.   Following three sessions for crisis intervention and/or diagnosis, the provider should notify the parent of such sessions and obtain his or her consent to further treatment.

IN RE TANNER

Supreme Court of Utah, 1976.
549 P.2d 703.

CROCKETT, JUSTICE:

The State Division of Family Services (herein called Family Services) appeals from an order of the juvenile court that it pay for corrective orthodontic treatment of Michael Gene Tanner, a minor. It contends: (1) that the juvenile court had no authority to enter the order, and (2) even if it did, Michael is ineligible to receive services.

Michael Tanner is a 16-year-old boy (born August 18, 1959) whose mother is dead and whose father has long since vanished from the scene. After it was determined that his parents had abandoned him, he was placed in the guardianship of Family Services by order of the juvenile court on June 26, 1967. On July 31, 1971, upon the Division's motion, guardianship was placed with Mr. and Mrs. Melvin Edwards, in whose home Michael had been under foster care for a long time. Two years later, in July 1973, that guardianship was terminated and again given to Family Services; but Michael was still placed with the Edwards for foster care.

There is no dispute about the fact that Michael Tanner has a problem with his teeth which should be treated. It is described as: "severe protrusion of his upper incisors," i.e., what is sometimes referred to as "buck teeth." This causes no immediate hazard to his health. But there is the pyschological problem which may affect his personality and adjustment in society; and also there is risk of the early loss of his teeth because of non-occlusion with his lower teeth. The proposed corrective treatment would take three to four years and cost between $800 and $1,500.

The matter of the failure of Family Services to accord him treatment for this condition was presented to the juvenile court by Attorney David Dolowitz, who had been appointed by the court to safeguard Michael's interest. Pursuant to a hearing on an order to show cause on June 2, 1975, the court ordered Family Services to provide the needed orthodontic services.

Family Services' argument that the juvenile court was without authority to make this order is based on the following restriction which the 1975 Appropriation Act places on its funds:

. . . funds appropriated to the Division of Family Services may not be expended for the purpose of support or other expense for a child placed in any institution, facility, home, school, or other setting or program, which is not licensed, regulated, or otherwise approved by the Division of Family Services pursuant to its regulations and policies.

The answer on behalf of the minor is that the authority of the juvenile court to make the order derives from the general grant of power under Section 55–10–77, U.C.A.1953, over dependent and neglected children without any limitation thereon. There is no doubt that Section 55–10–77(2)(a) gives the juvenile court jurisdiction over Michael who had been determined to be a neglected child.[2] This jurisdiction continued even after the Division was given guardianship, for a juvenile court retains jurisdiction over a neglected or dependent child until he reaches his majority; and its power to inquire into and safeguard a child's welfare continues, regardless of the fact that a third party may be providing care. This is consistent with the concept inherent in our law respecting children: that in a civilized society all children, even those without parents or a home, should be provided not only food, clothing and shelter, but other basic needs, including necessary medical and dental care.

When a child is without a home or parents this responsibility is imposed upon the Division of Family Services by Section 55–10–110, U.C.A.1953:

> (1) When legal custody of a child is vested by the court in an individual or agency other than his parents . . . the court may . . . inquire into the ability of the parents, a parent, or any other person who may be obligated, to support the child and to pay any other expenses of the child, including the expense of any medical, psychiatric, or psychological examination or treatment *provided under order of the court.*
>
>   . . .
>
> (3) If the court finds that the parents are unable to pay for full or partial support, and other expenses of the child and that no other provision for the payment of such support and expenses has been made, . . . *the division of family services shall be responsible for the payment* of such support and other expenses for the neglected, dependent, or delinquent child . . . . [Emphasis added.]

Because of the duty thus imposed upon Family Services and also because, as his guardian, it stands in loco parentis to this minor it has the responsibility of providing him with his necessities; and when there is a serious failure therein, the remedy is to resort to the court as was done here. In that regard, we are duly appreciative of the fact that the juvenile court, the same as any other court, should be reluctant to intrude into the affairs of or interfere with the actions of an administrative agency. Nevertheless, when there is some such serious neglect relating to basic necessities as to put the health and welfare of a minor in hazard, there must be some remedy; and as will

2. This minor is both a neglected and dependent child. Sec. 55–10–64, U.C.A.1953, subsection (17), defines a neglected child as one ". . . whose parent . . . has abandoned him . . ."; and subsection (18) defines a dependent child to include ". . . a child who is homeless . . . ." See the statement of policy in Sec. 55–10–63, U.C.A.1953: "It is the purpose of this act to secure for each child coming before the juvenile court such care . . . as will serve his welfare and . . . assist him to develop in a responsible citizen . . . ."

be seen from the statutes referred to above, this is the special responsibility of the juvenile court. Moreover, when the juvenile court has made its determination through proper procedure, this court will accord its findings and judgment the traditional presumptions of verity; and will not disturb them unless the appellant has sustained its burden of showing that they are in error.

[The court rejected the argument that the minor had not exhausted his administrative remedies. Because of its conclusion as to the controlling issue in the case, the court also found it unnecessary to discuss the question of which provisions of the Federal Social Security Act might be applicable in the particular situation.]

Affirmed. No costs awarded.

NOTE

The question of who must pay for elaborate medical care for a child sometimes has been skirted in decisions involving the question whether a state could or should intervene to overrule a parental decision. In some instances this may have been a matter of strategy; if it was assured that treatment, if authorized, would be effected without cost to parent or child, the constitutional problems would be uncluttered. It seems clear, however, that many statutes defining parental support duties or neglect, include medical care within their ambit and thus a parent would seem to bear the financial obligation if the care is deemed necessary and the parent has the financial ability to pay. Virginia Code § 63.1–248.2 (Supp.1981), for example, defines an "abused or neglected child" as one less than age eighteen whose parent or other person responsible for his care "[n]eglects or refuses to provide care necessary for his health; . . . " Code § 16.1–275 (Supp.1981) specifically empowers a juvenile court to order the parent or other supervisory person to provide "nursing, medical or surgical care" and "pay the expenses thereof."

Some states have enacted statutes making clear that minors cannot disaffirm contracts for medical services that are deemed necessaries or for which they have been given legal capacity to consent. Section 4.3 of the Juvenile Justice Standards on Rights of Minors * provides a model:

4.3 Financial liability

A. A parent should be financially liable to persons providing medical treatment to his or her minor child if the parent consents to such services, or if the services are provided under emergency circumstances pursuant to Standard 4.5.

B. A minor who consents to his or her own medical treatment under Standards 4.6–4.9 should be financially liable for payment for such services, and should not disaffirm the financial obligation on account of minority.

C. A public or private health insurance policy or plan under which a minor is a beneficiary should allow a minor who consents to medical services or treatment to file claims and receive benefits, regardless of whether the parent has consented to the treatment.

D.   A public or private health insurer should not inform a parent or policy holder that a minor has filed a claim or received a benefit under a health insurance policy or plan of which the minor is a beneficiary, unless the physician has previously notified the parent of the treatment for which the claim is submitted.

Difficult money problems can arise for special treatment of a child in custodial or institutional care or when parents cannot afford treatment.   Medicaid and other assistance programs may provide the answer when parents are unable to pay but may raise questions as to what services are covered. See, e.g., Alice v. State Department of Social Welfare, 55 Cal.App.3d 1039, 128 Cal.Rptr. 374 (1976) (medical aid ordered for unmarried pregnant minors who alleged that they were emancipated); Brooks v. Smith, 356 A.2d 723 (Me.1976) (state's refusal to provide orthodontic care under Medicaid program upheld).   Budgetary concerns can produce conflicts between state agencies, courts and parents over special program costs, also.   See, e.g., In re L., 24 Or.App. 257, 546 P.2d 153 (1976) (court exceeded authority to the extent that it ordered treatment irrespective of budget limitations imposed by legislature on Children's Services Division); In re Doe, ___ R.I. ___, 390 A.2d 390 (1978).   Courts often determine what portion of a child's medical bills a parent must pay (usually based on financial capacity) and what part must be borne by a state agency with legal custody.   See, e.g., In re Welfare of Feldman, 94 Wn.2d 244, 615 P.2d 1290 (1980).

CELESTE: A PROBLEM FOR DISCUSSION

Celeste, an introspective twelve-year-old child, has a severe problem with her tooth and jaw structure.   Doctors familiar with her condition say that it can be improved considerably through a lengthy course of orthodontia; they believe that without such treatment she will become increasingly less attractive and lose most of her teeth at an early age.   In view of her already manifest social insecurity, they fear that she also faces substantial psychological problems if nothing is done now to remedy her physical condition.

School health authorities have sent Celeste's parents a series of detailed reports about the child's situation and have strongly urged that treatment be instituted without delay.   Her mother and father have elected to ignore the problem.   Shy and somewhat afraid of her parents, Celeste rarely discusses her situation with anyone.   At school she is described as the kid who can "eat peas from a jug" and she is the regular target of unkind jokes about her appearance.   After such incidents she frequently feigns illness in order to remain home and enjoy temporary respite from callous and insensitive remarks.

You have been consulted by health officials and a local social agency about Celeste's case, which has come to their attention through school authorities. How would you answer the following questions:

1. Is a child abuse report mandated under any of the reporting statutes or the Juvenile Justice Standards at p. —— et seq.? Is there potential liability for anyone who does not report?

2. Can a dentist safely undertake the orthodontia without approval from her parents if Celeste requests it and agrees to it?

3. What legal action, if any, can be taken to require Celeste's parents to obtain treatment for her? Can they be forced to pay for treatment to which they did not consent?

4. If Celeste's parents refuse to cooperate with treatment authorized by a court, what steps can be taken to compel their compliance?

5. If you were a judge presented with this situation what would you do?

*

INDEX

967

†